Green Building Costs with RSMeans data

Wafaa Hamitou, Senior Editor

GORDIAN®

2018
8th annual edition

Chief Data Officer
Noam Reininger

Engineering Director
Bob Mewis, CCP

Contributing Editors
Christopher Babbitt
Sam Babbitt
Michelle Curran
Matthew Doheny (8)
Cheryl Elsmore
Linval Gentles
John Gomes (13, 41)
Derrick Hale, PE (2, 31, 32, 33, 34, 35, 44, 46)
Wafaa Hamitou (11, 12)
Joseph Kelble (14, 21, 22, 23, 25, 26, 27, 28, 48)
Charles Kibbee (1, 4)
Gerard Lafond, PE
Thomas Lane (6, 7)
Genevieve Medeiros
Elisa Mello
Ken Monty
Marilyn Phelan, AIA (9, 10)
Stephen C. Plotner (3, 5)
Callum Riley
Stephen Rosenberg
Jeff Sessions
Gabe Sirota
Matthew Sorrentino
Kevin Souza
Keegan Spraker
Tim Tonello
Jen Walsh
David Yazbek

Product Manager
Andrea Sillah

Production Manager
Debbie Panarelli

Production
Jonathan Forgit
Mary Lou Geary

Sharon Larsen
Sheryl Rose

Technical Support
Judy Abbruzzese
Gary L. Hoitt

Cover Design
Blaire Collins

Data Analytics
Tim Duggan
Todd Glowac
Matthew Kelliher-Gibson

*Numbers in italics are the divisional responsibilities for each editor. Please contact the designated editor directly with any questions.

Gordian RSMeans data
Construction Publishers & Consultants
1099 Hingham Street, Suite 201
Rockland, MA 02370
United States of America
1-800-448-8182
www.RSMeans.com

Copyright 2017 by The Gordian Group Inc.
All rights reserved.
Cover photo © iStock.com/golero

Printed in the United States of America
ISSN 2161-5810
ISBN 978-1-946872-08-1

Gordian's authors, editors, and engineers apply diligence and judgment in locating and using reliable sources for the information published. However, Gordian makes no express or implied warranty or guarantee in connection with the content of the information contained herein, including the accuracy, correctness, value, sufficiency, or completeness of the data, methods, and other information contained herein. Gordian makes no express or implied warranty of merchantability or fitness for a particular purpose. Gordian shall have no liability to any customer or third party for any loss, expense, or damage, including consequential, incidental, special, or punitive damage, including lost profits or lost revenue, caused directly or indirectly by any error or omission, or arising out of, or in connection with, the information contained herein. For the purposes of this paragraph, "Gordian" shall include The Gordian Group, Inc., and its divisions, subsidiaries, successors, parent companies, and their employees, partners, principals, agents and representatives, and any third-party providers or sources of information or data. Gordian grants the purchaser of this publication limited license to use the cost data contained herein for purchaser's internal business purposes in connection with construction estimating and related work. The publication, and all cost data contained herein, may not be reproduced, integrated into any software or computer program, developed into a database or other electronic compilation, stored in an information storage or retrieval system, or transmitted or distributed to anyone in any form or by any means, electronic or mechanical, including photocopying or scanning, without prior written permission of Gordian. This publication is subject to protection under copyright law, trade secret law and other intellectual property laws of the United States, Canada and other jurisdictions. Gordian and its affiliates exclusively own and retain all rights, title and interest in and to this publication and the cost data contained herein including, without limitation, all copyright, patent, trademark and trade secret rights. Except for the limited license contained herein, your purchase of this publication does not grant you any intellectual property rights in the publication or the cost data.

0558 $266.99 per copy (in United States)
Price is subject to change without prior notice.

Related Data and Services

2018 Green Building Costs with RSMeans data has been tirelessly researched and carefully compiled to provide construction cost data for commercial and industrial projects or large multi-family housing projects costing $3,500,000 and up.

Our engineers recommend the following products and services to complement *Green Building Costs with RSMeans data:*

Annual Cost Data Books
2018 Assemblies Costs with RSMeans data
2018 Square Foot Costs with RSMeans data

Reference Books
Estimating Building Costs
RSMeans Estimating Handbook
Green Building: Project Planning & Estimating
How to Estimate with RSMeans data
Plan Reading & Material Takeoff
Project Scheduling & Management for Construction
Universal Design for Style, Comfort & Safety

Seminars and In-House Training
Unit Price Estimating
Training for our online estimating solution
Practical Project Management for Construction Professionals
Scheduling with MSProject for Construction Professionals
Mechanical & Electrical Estimating

RSMeans data Online
For access to the latest cost data, an intuitive search, and an easy-to-use estimate builder, take advantage of the time savings available from our online application. To learn more visit: www.RSMeans.com/2018online.

Enterprise Solutions
Building owners, facility managers, building product manufacturers, and attorneys across the public and private sectors engage with RSMeans data Enterprise to solve unique challenges where trusted construction cost data is critical. To learn more visit: www.RSMeans.com/Enterprise.

Custom Built Data Sets
Building and Space Models: Quickly plan construction costs across multiple locations based on geography, project size, building system component, product options, and other variables for precise budgeting and cost control.

Predictive Analytics: Accurately plan future builds with custom graphical interactive dashboards, negotiate future costs of tenant build-outs, and identify and compare national account pricing.

Consulting
Building Product Manufacturing Analytics: Validate your claims and assist with new product launches.

Third-Party Legal Resources: Used in cases of construction cost or estimate disputes, construction product failure vs. installation failure, eminent domain, class action construction product liability, and more.

API
For resellers or internal application integration, RSMeans data is offered via API. Deliver Unit, Assembly, and Square Foot Model data within your interface. To learn more about how you can provide your customers with the latest in localized construction cost data visit: www.RSMeans.com/API.

GORDIAN

Table of Contents

Foreword	iv
MasterFormat® Comparison Table	v
How the Cost Data Is Built: An Overview	vii
Estimating with RSMeans data: Unit Prices	ix
How to Use the Cost Data: The Details	xi
Unit Price Section	1
RSMeans data: Unit Prices—How They Work	4
Assemblies Section	305
RSMeans data: Assemblies—How They Work	306
Green Commercial/Industrial/Institutional Section	347
Reference Section	407
Construction Equipment Rental Costs	409
Crew Listings	421
Historical Cost Indexes	458
City Cost Indexes	459
Location Factors	502
Reference Tables	508
Change Orders	548
Project Costs	551
Abbreviations	556
Index	560
Other Data and Services	573
Labor Trade Rates including Overhead & Profit	Inside Back Cover

Foreword

The Value of RSMeans data from Gordian
Since 1942, RSMeans data has been the industry-standard materials, labor, and equipment cost information database for contractors, facility owners and managers, architects, engineers, and anyone else that requires the latest localized construction cost information. Over 75 years later, the objective remains the same: to provide facility and construction professionals with the most current and comprehensive construction cost database possible.

With the constant influx of new construction methods and materials, in addition to ever-changing labor and material costs, last year's cost data is not reliable for today's designs, estimates, or budgets. The RSMeans data engineers invest over 22,000 hours in cost research annually and apply real-world construction experience to identify and quantify new building products and methodologies, adjust productivity rates, and adjust costs to local market conditions across the nation. This unparalleled construction cost expertise is why so many facility and construction professionals rely on RSMeans data year over year.

About Gordian
Gordian originated in the spirit of innovation and a strong commitment to helping clients reach and exceed their construction goals. In 1982, Gordian's Chairman and Founder, Harry H. Mellon, created Job Order Contracting while serving as Chief Engineer at the Supreme Headquarters Allied Powers Europe. Job Order Contracting is a unique indefinite delivery/indefinite quantity (IDIQ) process, which enables facility owners to complete a substantial number of repair, maintenance, and construction projects with a single, competitively awarded contract. Realizing facility and infrastructure owners across various industries could greatly benefit from the time and cost saving advantages of this innovative construction procurement solution, he established Gordian in 1990.

Continuing the commitment to providing the most relevant and accurate facility and construction data, software, and expertise in the industry, Gordian enhanced the fortitude of its data with the acquisition of RSMeans in 2014. And in an effort to expand its facility management capabilities, Gordian acquired Sightlines, the leading provider of facilities benchmarking data and analysis, in 2015.

Our Offerings
Gordian is the leader in facility and construction cost data, software, and expertise for all phases of the building life cycle. From planning to design, procurement, construction, and operations, Gordian's solutions help clients maximize efficiency, optimize cost savings, and increase building quality with its highly specialized data engineers, software, and unique proprietary data sets.

Our Commitment
At Gordian, we do more than talk about the quality of our data and the usefulness of its application. We stand behind all of our RSMeans data—from historical cost indexes to construction materials and techniques—to craft current costs and predict future trends. If you have any questions about our products or services, please call us toll-free at 800-448-8182 or visit our website at www.gordian.com.

MasterFormat® 2014/ MasterFormat® 2016 Comparison Table

This table compares the 2014 edition of the Construction Specifications Institute's MasterFormat® to the expanded 2016 edition. For your convenience, all revised 2014 numbers and titles are listed along with the corresponding 2016 numbers and titles. In some cases, a designation of RSMeans is used to identify sections of data numbered exclusively in RSMeans products.

CSI 2014 MF ID	CSI 2014 MF Description	2014 Designation	CSI 2016 MF ID	CSI 2016 MF Description	2016 Designation
35 20 23.23	Hydraulic Dredging	CSI	35 24 13.13	Cutter Suction Dredging	RSMeans
35 20 23.13	Mechanical Dredging	CSI	35 24 23.13	Mechanical Dredging	CSI
35 20 23	Dredging	CSI	35 24 23	Clamshell Dredging	RSMeans
35 20 16.73	Slide Gates	RSMeans	35 22 73.16	Slide Gates	CSI
35 20 16.69	Knife Gates	RSMeans	35 22 69.16	Knife Gates	RSMeans
35 20 16.66	Flap Gates	RSMeans	35 22 66.16	Flap Gates	RSMeans
35 20 16.63	Canal Gates	RSMeans	35 22 63.16	Canal Gates	RSMeans
35 20 16.26	Hydraulic Sluice Gates	CSI	35 22 26.16	Hydraulic Sluice Gates	RSMeans
35 20 16	Hydraulic Gates	CSI	35 22 26	Sluice Gates	RSMeans
35 20	Waterway and Marine Construction and Equipment	CSI	35 22	Hydraulic Gates	RSMeans
33 72 33.46	Substation Converter Stations	CSI	33 78 33.46	Substation Converter Stations	RSMeans
33 72 33.36	Cable Trays For Utility Substations	CSI	26 05 36.36	Cable Trays For Utility Substations	CSI
33 72 33.33	Raceway/Boxes For Utility Substations	CSI	26 05 33.33	Raceway/Boxes For Utility Substations	CSI
33 52 43.13	Aviation Fuel Piping	CSI	33 52 13.43	Aviation Fuel Piping	RSMeans
33 52 16.13	Gasoline Piping	CSI	33 52 13.16	Gasoline Piping	RSMeans
33 52 13.14	Petroleum Products	RSMeans	33 52 13.19	Petroleum Products	RSMeans
33 51 33.10	Piping, Valves & Meters, Gas Distribution	RSMeans	33 59 33.10	Piping, Valves & Meters, Gas Distribution	CSI
33 51 33	Natural-Gas Metering	CSI	33 59 33	Natural-Gas Metering	CSI
33 51 13.30	Piping, Gas Service & Distribution, Steel	RSMeans	33 52 16.16	Piping, Gas Service & Distribution, Steel	RSMeans
33 51 13.20	Piping, Gas Service & Distribution, Steel	RSMeans	33 52 16.13	Steel Natural Gas Piping	RSMeans
33 51 13.10	Piping, Gas Service and Distribution, Polyethylene	RSMeans	33 52 16.20	Piping, Gas Service And Distribution, Polyethylene	CSI
33 49 23	Storm Drainage Water Retention Structures	CSI	33 46 23	Modular Buried Stormwater Storage Units	CSI
33 49 13	Storm Drainage Manholes, Frames, and Covers	CSI	33 05 61	Concrete Manholes	RSMeans
33 47 19	Water Ponds and Reservoirs	CSI	33 46 11	Stormwater Ponds	CSI
33 47 13.54	Garden Ponds	RSMeans	13 12 13.54	Garden Ponds	CSI
33 47 13.53	Reservoir Liners HDPE	CSI	31 05 19.53	Reservoir Liners HDPE	RSMeans
33 47 13	Pond and Reservoir Liners	CSI	31 05 19	Geosynthetics for Earthwork	RSMeans
33 46 26.10	Geotextiles For Subsurface Drainage	RSMeans	33 41 23.19	Geosynthetic Drainage Layers	RSMeans
33 46 26	Geotextile Subsurface Drainage Filtration	CSI	33 41 23	Drainage Layers	CSI
33 46 16	Subdrainage Piping	CSI	33 41 16	Subdrainage Piping	CSI
33 46	Subdrainage	CSI	33 41	Subdrainage	CSI
33 44 16	Utility Trench Drains	CSI	33 42 36	Stormwater Trench Drains	CSI
33 44 13	Utility Area Drains	CSI	33 42 33	Stormwater Curbside Drains and Inlets	RSMeans
33 42 16.15	Oval Arch Culverts	RSMeans	33 42 13.15	Oval Arch Culverts	RSMeans
33 42 16.13	Culverts & Box Trench Sections	CSI	33 42 13.14	Culverts & Box Trench Sections	RSMeans
33 41 13	Public Storm Utility Drainage Piping	CSI	33 42 11	Stormwater Gravity Piping	CSI
33 41	Storm Utility Drainage Piping	CSI	33 42	Stormwater Conveyance	CSI
33 36 50	Drainage Field Systems	RSMeans	33 34 51	Drainage Field System	CSI
33 36 33.13	Utility Septic Tank Tile Drainage Field	CSI	33 34 51.13	Utility Septic Tank Tile Drainage Field	RSMeans
33 36 19	Utility Septic Tank Effluent Filter	CSI	33 34 16	Septic Tank Effluent Filters	CSI
33 36 13.19	Polyethylene Utility Septic Tank	CSI	33 34 13.33	Polyethylene Septic Tanks	CSI
33 36 13.13	Concrete Utility Septic Tank	CSI	33 34 13.13	Concrete Septic Tanks	RSMeans
33 36 13	Utility Septic Tank and Effluent Wet Wells	CSI	33 34 13	Septic Tanks	CSI
33 36	Utility Septic Tanks	CSI	33 34	Onsite Wastewater Disposal	CSI
33 31 13	Public Sanitary Utility Sewerage Piping	CSI	33 31 11	Public Sanitary Sewerage Gravity Piping	CSI
33 21 13	Public Water Supply Wells	CSI	33 11 13	Potable Water Supply Wells	RSMeans
33 21	Water Supply Wells	CSI	33 11	Groundwater Sources	CSI
33 16 19.50	Elevated Water Storage Tanks	RSMeans	33 16 11.50	Elevated Water Storage Tanks	CSI
33 16 19	Elevated Water Utility Storage Tanks	CSI	33 16 11	Elevated Composite Water Storage Tanks	CSI
33 16 13.29	Wood Water Storage Tanks	RSMeans	33 16 59.29	Wood Water Storage Tanks	CSI
33 16 13.23	Plastic-Coated Fabric Pillow Water Tanks	RSMeans	33 16 56.23	Plastic-Coated Fabric Pillow Water Tanks	CSI
33 16 13.19	Horizontal Plastic Water Tanks	CSI	33 16 56.19	Horizontal Plastic Water Tanks	CSI
33 16 13.16	Prestressed Conc. Water Storage Tanks	CSI	33 16 36.16	Prestressed Conc. Water Storage Tanks	RSMeans
33 16 13.13	Steel Water Storage Tanks	CSI	33 16 23.13	Steel Water Storage Tanks	RSMeans
33 16 13	Aboveground Water Utility Storage Tanks	CSI	33 16 23	Ground-Level Steel Water Storage Tanks	CSI
33 12 19.10	Fire Hydrants	RSMeans	33 14 19.30	Fire Hydrants	CSI
33 12 16.20	Valves	RSMeans	33 14 19.20	Valves	CSI

33 12 16.10	Valves	RSMeans		33 14 19.10	Valves	CSI
33 12 16	Water Utility Distribution Valves	CSI		33 14 19	Valves and Hydrants for Water Utility Service	CSI
33 12 13.15	Tapping, Crosses and Sleeves	RSMeans		33 14 17.15	Tapping, Crosses and Sleeves	CSI
33 12 13	Water Service Connections	CSI		33 14 17	Site Water Utility Service Laterals	RSMeans
33 11 13	Public Water Utility Distribution Piping	CSI		33 14 13	Public Water Utility Distribution Piping	RSMeans
33 11	Water Utility Distribution Piping	CSI		33 14	Water Utility Transmission and Distribution	CSI
33 05 26	Utility Identification	CSI		33 05 97	Identification and Signage for Utilities	RSMeans
33 05 23.22	Directional Drilling	RSMeans		33 05 07.13	Utility Directional Drilling	RSMeans
33 05 23.20	Horizontal Boring	RSMeans		33 05 07.23	Utility Boring and Jacking	CSI
33 05 23.19	Microtunneling	CSI		33 05 07.36	Microtunneling	CSI
33 05 23	Trenchless Utility Installation	CSI		33 05 07	Trenchless Installation of Utility Piping	RSMeans
33 05 16	Utility Structures	CSI		33 05 63	Concrete Vaults and Chambers	RSMeans
33 01 30.71	Rehabilitation of Sewer Utilities	CSI		33 01 30.23	Pipe Bursting	RSMeans
33 01 30.16	TV Inspection of Sewer Pipelines	CSI		33 01 30.11	Television Inspection of Sewers	CSI
32 31 13.30	Fence, Chain Link, Gates & Posts	RSMeans		32 31 11.10	Gate Operators	CSI
31 71 21.10	Cut and Cover Tunnels	RSMeans		31 71 23.10	Cut and Cover Tunnels	CSI
31 71 21	Tunnel Excavation by Cut and Cover	RSMeans		31 71 23	Tunneling by Cut and Cover	CSI
28 46 13	Hard-Wired Detention Monitoring & Control Systems	CSI		28 52 11	Detention Monitoring and Control Systems	CSI
28 46	Electronic Detention Monitoring & Control Systems	CSI		28 52	Detention Security Systems	CSI
28 41 13	Building Systems	RSMeans		28 33 11	Electronic Structural Monitoring Systems	RSMeans
28 39 10	Notification Systems	RSMeans		28 47 12	Notification Systems	CSI
28 39	Mass Notification Systems	CSI		28 47	Mass Notification	RSMeans
28 33 33	Gas Detection Sensors	CSI		28 42 15	Gas Detection Sensors	CSI
28 33	Gas Detection and Alarm	CSI		28 42	Gas Detection and Alarm	RSMeans
28 32 33	Radiation Detection Sensors	CSI		28 41 15	Radiation Detection Sensors	CSI
28 31 49.50	Carbon-Monoxide Detectors	RSMeans		28 46 11.21	Carbon-Monoxide Detection Sensors	CSI
28 31 46.50	Smoke Detectors	RSMeans		28 46 11.27	Other Sensors	CSI
28 31 43	Fire Detection Sensors	CSI		28 46 11	Fire Sensors and Detectors	CSI
28 31 23	Fire Det. & Alarm Annunciation Panels & Fire Station	CSI		28 46 21	Fire Alarm	CSI
28 23 19.10	Digital Video Recorder (DVR)	RSMeans		28 05 19.11	Digital Video Recorders	RSMeans
28 23 19	Digital Video Recorders & Analog Recording Devices	CSI		28 05 19	Storage Appliances for Electronic Safety & Security	RSMeans
28 16 16	Intrusion Detection Systems Infrastructure	CSI		28 31 16	Intrusion Detection Systems Infrastructure	RSMeans
28 13 53.39	Security Access Full Body Imaging Machine	RSMeans		28 18 15.39	Security Access Full Body Imaging Machine	CSI
28 13 53.36	Security Access Debugging Kit	RSMeans		28 18 53.36	Security Access Debugging Kit	CSI
28 13 53.33	Security Access Counterfeit Money Detector	RSMeans		28 18 53.33	Security Access Counterfeit Money Detector	CSI
28 13 53.23	Security Access Explosive Detection Equipment	CSI		28 18 15.23	Security Access Explosive Detection Equipment	CSI
28 13 53.16	Security Access X-Ray Equipment	CSI		28 18 13.16	Security Access X-Ray Equipment	CSI
28 13 53.13	Security Access Metal Detectors	CSI		28 18 11.13	Security Access Metal Detectors	RSMeans
28 13 53	Security Access Detection	CSI		28 18 11	Security Access Metal Detectors	CSI
28 13 23.50	Vehicle Barriers	RSMeans		28 19 15.50	Vehicle Barriers	CSI
28 13 23	Access Control Remote Devices	RSMeans		28 19 15	Perimeter Vehicle Access Management Systems	RSMeans
28 13	Access Control	CSI		28 19	Access Control Vehicle Identification Systems	CSI
28 05 13.23	Fire Alarm Communications Conductors and Cables	CSI		27 15 01.19	Fire Alarm Communications Conductors and Cables	RSMeans
28 05 13.10	Alarm & Communications Cable	RSMeans		27 15 01.11	Conductors & Cables For Electronic Safety & Security	CSI
28 01 30.51	Maint. and Admin. of Elec. Detection and Alarm	CSI		28 01 80.51	Maint. & Administration of Fire Detection & Alarm	RSMeans
28 01 30	Operation and Maint. of Elec. Detection and Alarm	CSI		28 01 80	Operation and Maint. of Fire Detection and Alarm	RSMeans
26 56 19.20	Roadway Luminaire	RSMeans		26 56 21.20	Roadway Luminaire	RSMeans
26 56 19.10	Roadway Lighting Fixtures	RSMeans		26 56 21.10	LED Exterior Lighting	RSMeans
26 56 16.55	Parking LED Lighting	RSMeans		26 56 19.60	Parking LED Lighting	RSMeans
26 53 13.10	Exit Lighting Fixtures	RSMeans		26 52 13.16	Exit Signs	CSI
26 26 13.10	Power Distribution Unit	RSMeans		26 27 33.20	Power Distribution Unit	RSMeans
13 34 23.35	Geodesic Domes	RSMeans		13 33 13.35	Geodesic Domes	CSI
13 34 23.15	Domes	RSMeans		13 34 56.15	Domes	CSI
11 14 13.13	Portable Posts and Railings	CSI		11 14 19.13	Portable Posts and Railings	CSI
10 21 13.20	Plastic Toilet Compartment Components	RSMeans		10 21 14.19	Plastic Toilet Compartment Components	CSI
10 21 13.17	Plastic-Laminate Clad Toilet Compartment Components	RSMeans		10 21 14.16	Plastic-Laminate Clad Toilet Compartment Components	CSI
10 21 13.14	Metal Toilet Compartment Components	RSMeans		10 21 14.13	Metal Toilet Compartment Components	CSI
08 74 23.50	Security Access Control Accessories	RSMeans		28 15 11.19	Security Access Control Accessories	CSI
08 74 19.50	Biometric Identity Access	RSMeans		28 15 11.15	Biometric Identity Devices	RSMeans
08 74 16.50	Keypad Access	RSMeans		28 15 11.13	Keypads	RSMeans
08 74 13	Card Key Access Control Hardware	CSI		28 15 11	Integrated Credential Readers & Field Entry Mgmt	RSMeans
08 74	Access Control Hardware	CSI		28 15	Access Control Hardware Devices	CSI
08 56 63	Detention Windows	CSI		11 98 21	Detention Windows	RSMeans
08 34 63	Detention Doors and Frames	CSI		11 98 12	Detention Doors and Frames	RSMeans
07 72 73.10	Pitch Pockets, Variable Sizes	RSMeans		07 71 16.20	Pitch Pockets, Variable Sizes	CSI
05 53 13.70	Expanded Steel Grating, at Ground	RSMeans		05 53 19.20	Expanded Grating, Steel	CSI
02 85 33	Removal and Disposal of Materials with Mold	CSI		02 87 13.33	Removal and Disposal of Materials with Mold	RSMeans
02 85 16	Mold Remediation Preparation and Containment	CSI		02 87 13	Mold Remediation	RSMeans
02 85	Mold Remediation	CSI		02 87	Biohazard Remediation	CSI

For additional tools that help with the utilization of the Construction Specifications Institute's 2016 edition of MasterFormat® please visit the following website: http://www.masterformat.com/revisions/

How the Cost Data Is Built: An Overview

Unit Prices*
All cost data have been divided into 50 divisions according to the MasterFormat® system of classification and numbering.

Assemblies*
The cost data in this section have been organized in an "Assemblies" format. These assemblies are the functional elements of a building and are arranged according to the 7 elements of the UNIFORMAT II classification system. For a complete explanation of a typical "Assembly", see "RSMeans data: Assemblies—How They Work."

Residential Models*
Model buildings for four classes of construction—economy, average, custom, and luxury—are developed and shown with complete costs per square foot.

Commercial/Industrial/Institutional Models*
This section contains complete costs for 77 typical model buildings expressed as costs per square foot.

Green Commercial/Industrial/Institutional Models*
This section contains complete costs for 25 green model buildings expressed as costs per square foot.

References*
This section includes information on Equipment Rental Costs, Crew Listings, Historical Cost Indexes, City Cost Indexes, Location Factors, Reference Tables, and Change Orders, as well as a listing of abbreviations.

- **Equipment Rental Costs:** Included are the average costs to rent and operate hundreds of pieces of construction equipment.
- **Crew Listings:** This section lists all the crews referenced in the cost data. A crew is composed of more than one trade classification and/or the addition of power equipment to any trade classification. Power equipment is included in the cost of the crew. Costs are shown both with bare labor rates and with the installing contractor's overhead and profit added. For each, the total crew cost per eight-hour day and the composite cost per labor-hour are listed.
- **Historical Cost Indexes:** These indexes provide you with data to adjust construction costs over time.
- **City Cost Indexes:** All costs in this data set are U.S. national averages. Costs vary by region. You can adjust for this by CSI Division to over 730 cities in 900+ 3-digit zip codes throughout the U.S. and Canada by using this data.
- **Location Factors:** You can adjust total project costs to over 730 cities in 900+ 3-digit zip codes throughout the U.S. and Canada by using the weighted number, which applies across all divisions.
- **Reference Tables:** At the beginning of selected major classifications in the Unit Prices are reference numbers indicators. These numbers refer you to related information in the Reference Section. In this section, you'll find reference tables, explanations, and estimating information that support how we develop the unit price data, technical data, and estimating procedures.
- **Change Orders:** This section includes information on the factors that influence the pricing of change orders.
- **Abbreviations:** A listing of abbreviations used throughout this information, along with the terms they represent, is included.

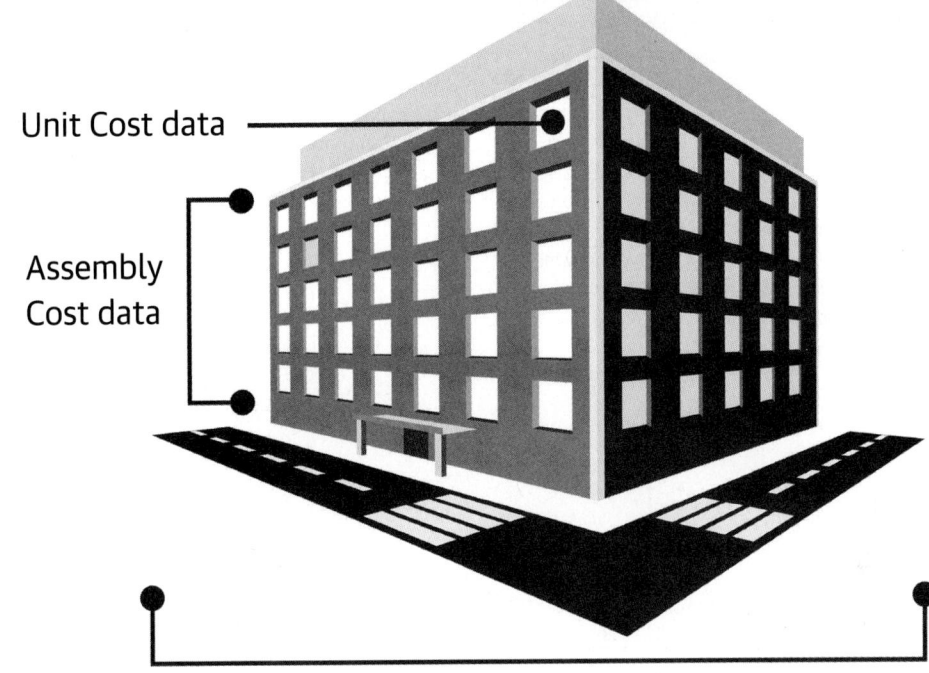

Index (printed versions only)
A comprehensive listing of all terms and subjects will help you quickly find what you need when you are not sure where it occurs in MasterFormat®.

Conclusion
This information is designed to be as comprehensive and easy to use as possible.

The Construction Specifications Institute (CSI) and Construction Specifications Canada (CSC) have produced the 2016 edition of MasterFormat®, a system of titles and numbers used extensively to organize construction information.

All unit prices in the RSMeans cost data are now arranged in the 50-division MasterFormat® 2016 system.

---

* Not all information is available in all data sets

Note: The material prices in RSMeans cost data are "contractor's prices." They are the prices that contractors can expect to pay at the lumberyards, suppliers'/distributors' warehouses, etc. Small orders of specialty items would be higher than the costs shown, while very large orders, such as truckload lots, would be less. The variation would depend on the size, timing, and negotiating power of the contractor. The labor costs are primarily for new construction or major renovation rather than repairs or minor alterations. With reasonable exercise of judgment, the figures can be used for any building work.

Estimating with RSMeans data: Unit Prices

Following these steps will allow you to complete an accurate estimate using RSMeans data Unit Prices.

1. Scope Out the Project
- Think through the project and identify the CSI divisions needed in your estimate.
- Identify the individual work tasks that will need to be covered in your estimate.
- The Unit Price data have been divided into 50 divisions according to CSI MasterFormat® 2016.
- In printed versions, the Unit Price Section Table of Contents on page 1 may also be helpful when scoping out your project.
- Experienced estimators find it helpful to begin with Division 2 and continue through completion. Division 1 can be estimated after the full project scope is known.

2. Quantify
- Determine the number of units required for each work task that you identified.
- Experienced estimators include an allowance for waste in their quantities. (Waste is not included in our Unit Price line items unless otherwise stated.)

3. Price the Quantities
- Use the search tools available to locate individual Unit Price line items for your estimate.
- Reference Numbers indicated within a Unit Price section refer to additional information that you may find useful.
- The crew indicates who is performing the work for that task. Crew codes are expanded in the Crew Listings in the Reference Section to include all trades and equipment that comprise the crew.
- The Daily Output is the amount of work the crew is expected to complete in one day.
- The Labor-Hours value is the amount of time it will take for the crew to install one unit of work.
- The abbreviated Unit designation indicates the unit of measure upon which the crew, productivity, and prices are based.
- Bare Costs are shown for materials, labor, and equipment needed to complete the Unit Price line item. Bare costs do not include waste, project overhead, payroll insurance, payroll taxes, main office overhead, or profit.
- The Total Incl O&P cost is the billing rate or invoice amount of the installing contractor or subcontractor who performs the work for the Unit Price line item.

4. Multiply
- Multiply the total number of units needed for your project by the Total Incl O&P cost for each Unit Price line item.
- Be careful that your take off unit of measure matches the unit of measure in the Unit column.
- The price you calculate is an estimate for a completed item of work.
- Keep scoping individual tasks, determining the number of units required for those tasks, matching each task with individual Unit Price line items, and multiplying quantities by Total Incl O&P costs.
- An estimate completed in this manner is priced as if a subcontractor, or set of subcontractors, is performing the work. The estimate does not yet include Project Overhead or Estimate Summary components such as general contractor markups on subcontracted work, general contractor office overhead and profit, contingency, and location factors.

5. Project Overhead
- Include project overhead items from Division 1-General Requirements.
- These items are needed to make the job run. They are typically, but not always, provided by the general contractor. Items include, but are not limited to, field personnel, insurance, performance bond, permits, testing, temporary utilities, field office and storage facilities, temporary scaffolding and platforms, equipment mobilization and demobilization, temporary roads and sidewalks, winter protection, temporary barricades and fencing, temporary security, temporary signs, field engineering and layout, final cleaning, and commissioning.
- Each item should be quantified and matched to individual Unit Price line items in Division 1, then priced and added to your estimate.
- An alternate method of estimating project overhead costs is to apply a percentage of the total project cost, usually 5% to 15% with an average of 10% (see General Conditions).
- Include other project related expenses in your estimate such as:
  - Rented equipment not itemized in the Crew Listings
  - Rubbish handling throughout the project (see section 02 41 19.19)

6. Estimate Summary
- Include sales tax as required by laws of your state or county.
- Include the general contractor's markup on self-performed work, usually 5% to 15% with an average of 10%.
- Include the general contractor's markup on subcontracted work, usually 5% to 15% with an average of 10%.
- Include the general contractor's main office overhead and profit:
  - RSMeans data provides general guidelines on the general contractor's main office overhead (see section 01 31 13.60 and Reference Number R013113-50).
  - Markups will depend on the size of the general contractor's operations, projected annual revenue, the level of risk, and the level of competition in the local area and for this project in particular.
- Include a contingency, usually 3% to 5%, if appropriate.
- Adjust your estimate to the project's location by using the City Cost Indexes or the Location Factors in the Reference Section:
  - Look at the rules in "How to Use the City Cost Indexes" to see how to apply the Indexes for your location.
  - When the proper Index or Factor has been identified for the project's location, convert it to a multiplier by dividing it by 100, then multiply that multiplier by your estimated total cost. The original estimated total cost will now be adjusted up or down from the national average to a total that is appropriate for your location.

*Editors' Note:
We urge you to spend time reading and understanding the supporting material. An accurate estimate requires experience, knowledge, and careful calculation. The more you know about how we at RSMeans developed the data, the more accurate your estimate will be. In addition, it is important to take into consideration the reference material such as Equipment Listings, Crew Listings, City Cost Indexes, Location Factors, and Reference Tables.*

How to Use the Cost Data: The Details

What's Behind the Numbers? The Development of Cost data

RSMeans data engineers continually monitor developments in the construction industry in order to ensure reliable, thorough, and up-to-date cost information. While overall construction costs may vary relative to general economic conditions, price fluctuations within the industry are dependent upon many factors. Individual price variations may, in fact, be opposite to overall economic trends. Therefore, costs are constantly tracked, and complete updates are performed yearly. Also, new items are frequently added in response to changes in materials and methods.

Costs in U.S. Dollars

All costs represent U.S. national averages and are given in U.S. dollars. The City Cost Index (CCI) with RSMeans data can be used to adjust costs to a particular location. The CCI for Canada can be used to adjust U.S. national averages to local costs in Canadian dollars. No exchange rate conversion is necessary because it has already been factored in.

G The processes or products identified by the green symbol in our publications have been determined to be environmentally responsible and/or resource-efficient solely by RSMeans data engineering staff. The inclusion of the green symbol does not represent compliance with any specific industry association or standard.

Material Costs

RSMeans data engineers contact manufacturers, dealers, distributors, and contractors all across the U.S. and Canada to determine national average material costs. If you have access to current material costs for your specific location, you may wish to make adjustments to reflect differences from the national average. Included within material costs are fasteners for a normal installation. RSMeans data engineers use manufacturers' recommendations, written specifications, and/or standard construction practices for the sizing and spacing of fasteners. Adjustments to material costs may be required for your specific application or location. The manufacturer's warranty is assumed. Extended warranties are not included in the material costs.
Material costs do not include sales tax.

Labor Costs

Labor costs are based upon a mathematical average of trade-specific wages in 30 major U.S. cities. The type of wage (union, open shop, or residential) is identified on the inside back cover of printed publications or is selected by the estimator when using the electronic products. Markups for the wages can also be found on the inside back cover of printed publications and/or under the labor references found in the electronic products.

- If wage rates in your area vary from those used, or if rate increases are expected within a given year, labor costs should be adjusted accordingly.

Labor costs reflect productivity based on actual working conditions. In addition to actual installation, these figures include time spent during a normal weekday on tasks, such as material receiving and handling, mobilization at site, site movement, breaks, and cleanup.

Productivity data is developed over an extended period so as not to be influenced by abnormal variations and reflects a typical average.

Equipment Costs

Equipment costs include not only rental but also operating costs for equipment under normal use. The operating costs include parts and labor for routine servicing, such as the repair and replacement of pumps, filters, and worn lines. Normal operating expendables, such as fuel, lubricants, tires, and electricity (where applicable), are also included. Extraordinary operating expendables with highly variable wear patterns, such as diamond bits and blades, are excluded. These costs are included under materials. Equipment rental rates are obtained from industry sources throughout North America—contractors, suppliers, dealers, manufacturers, and distributors.

Rental rates can also be treated as reimbursement costs for contractor-owned equipment. Owned equipment costs include depreciation, loan payments, interest, taxes, insurance, storage, and major repairs.

Equipment costs do not include operators' wages.

Equipment Cost/Day—The cost of equipment required for each crew is included in the Crew Listings in the Reference Section (small tools that are considered essential everyday tools are not listed out separately). The Crew Listings itemize specialized tools and heavy equipment along with labor trades. The daily cost of itemized equipment included in a crew is based on dividing the weekly bare rental rate by 5 (number of working days per week), then adding the hourly operating cost times 8 (the number of hours per day). This Equipment Cost/Day is shown in the last column of the Equipment Rental Costs in the Reference Section.

Mobilization, Demobilization—The cost to move construction equipment from an equipment yard or rental company to the job site and back again is not included in equipment costs. Mobilization (to the site) and demobilization (from the site) costs can be found in the Unit Price Section. If a piece of equipment is already at the job site, it is not appropriate to utilize mobilization or demobilization costs again in an estimate.

Overhead and Profit

Total Cost including O&P for the installing contractor is shown in the last column of the Unit Price and/or Assemblies. This figure is the sum of the bare material cost plus 10% for profit, the bare labor cost plus total overhead and profit, and the bare equipment cost plus 10% for profit. Details for the calculation of overhead and profit on labor are shown on the inside back cover of the printed product and in the Reference Section of the electronic product.

General Conditions

Cost data in this data set are presented in two ways: Bare Costs and Total Cost including O&P (Overhead and Profit). General Conditions, or General Requirements, of the contract should also be added to the Total Cost including O&P when applicable. Costs for General Conditions are listed in Division 1 of the Unit Price Section and in the Reference Section.

General Conditions for the installing contractor may range from 0% to 10% of the Total Cost including O&P. For the general or prime contractor, costs for General Conditions may range from 5% to 15% of the Total Cost including O&P, with a figure of 10% as the most typical allowance. If applicable, the Assemblies and Models sections use costs that include the installing contractor's overhead and profit (O&P).

Factors Affecting Costs

Costs can vary depending upon a number of variables. Here's a listing of some factors that affect costs and points to consider.

Quality—The prices for materials and the workmanship upon which productivity is based represent sound construction work. They are also in line with industry standard and manufacturer specifications and are frequently used by federal, state, and local governments.

Overtime—We have made no allowance for overtime. If you anticipate premium time or work beyond normal working hours, be sure to make an appropriate adjustment to your labor costs.

Productivity—The productivity, daily output, and labor-hour figures for each line item are based on an eight-hour work day in daylight hours in moderate temperatures, and up to a 14' working height unless otherwise indicated. For work that extends beyond normal work hours or is performed under adverse conditions, productivity may decrease.

Size of Project—The size, scope of work, and type of construction project will have a significant impact on cost. Economies of scale can reduce costs for large projects. Unit costs can often run higher for small projects.

Location—Material prices are for metropolitan areas. However, in dense urban areas, traffic and site storage limitations may increase costs. Beyond a 20-mile radius of metropolitan areas, extra trucking or transportation charges may also increase the material costs slightly. On the other hand, lower wage rates may be in effect. Be sure to consider both of these factors when preparing an estimate, particularly if the job site is located in a central city or remote rural location. In addition, highly specialized subcontract items may require travel and per-diem expenses for mechanics.

Other Factors—
- season of year
- contractor management
- weather conditions
- local union restrictions
- building code requirements
- availability of:
  - adequate energy
  - skilled labor
  - building materials
- owner's special requirements/restrictions
- safety requirements
- environmental considerations
- access

Unpredictable Factors—General business conditions influence "in-place" costs of all items. Substitute materials and construction methods may have to be employed. These may affect the installed cost and/or life cycle costs. Such factors may be difficult to evaluate and cannot necessarily be predicted on the basis of the job's location in a particular section of the country. Thus, where these factors apply, you may find significant but unavoidable cost variations for which you will have to apply a measure of judgment to your estimate.

Rounding of Costs

In printed publications only, all unit prices in excess of $5.00 have been rounded to make them easier to use and still maintain adequate precision of the results.

How Subcontracted Items Affect Costs

A considerable portion of all large construction jobs is usually subcontracted. In fact, the percentage done by subcontractors is constantly increasing and may run over 90%. Since the workers employed by these companies do nothing else but install their particular product, they soon become experts in that line. The result is, installation by these firms is accomplished so efficiently that the total in-place cost, even with the general contractor's overhead and profit, is no more, and often less, than if the principal contractor had handled the installation. Companies that deal with construction specialties are anxious to have their product perform well and, consequently, the installation will be the best possible.

Contingencies

The allowance for contingencies generally provides for unforeseen construction difficulties. On alterations or repair jobs, 20% is not too much. If drawings are final and only field contingencies are being considered, 2% or 3% is probably sufficient, and often nothing needs to be added. Contractually, changes in plans will be covered by extras. The contractor should consider inflationary price trends and possible material shortages during the course of the job. These escalation factors are dependent upon both economic conditions and the anticipated time between the estimate and actual construction. If drawings are not complete or approved, or a budget cost is wanted, it is wise to add 5% to 10%. Contingencies, then, are a matter of judgment.

Important Estimating Considerations

The productivity, or daily output, of each craftsman or crew assumes a well-managed job where tradesmen with the proper tools and equipment, along with the appropriate construction materials, are present. Included are daily set-up and cleanup time, break time, and plan layout time. Unless otherwise indicated, time for material movement on site (for items that can be transported by hand) of up to 200' into the building and to the first or second floor is also included. If material has to be transported by other means, over greater distances, or to higher floors, an additional allowance should be considered by the estimator.

While horizontal movement is typically a sole function of distances, vertical transport introduces other variables that can significantly impact productivity. In an occupied building, the use of elevators (assuming access, size, and required protective measures are acceptable) must be understood at the time of the estimate. For new construction, hoist wait and cycle times can easily be 15 minutes and may result in scheduled access extending beyond the normal work day. Finally, all vertical transport will impose strict weight limits likely to preclude the use of any motorized material handling.

The productivity, or daily output, also assumes installation that meets manufacturer/designer/standard specifications. A time allowance for quality control checks, minor adjustments, and any task required to ensure the proper function or operation is also included. For items that require connections to services, time is included for positioning, leveling, securing the unit, and for making all the necessary connections (and start up where applicable), ensuring a complete installation. Estimating of the services themselves (electrical, plumbing, water, steam, hydraulics, dust collection, etc.) is separate.

In some cases, the estimator must consider the use of a crane and an appropriate crew for the installation of large or heavy items. For those situations where a crane is not included in the assigned crew and as part of the line item cost, then equipment rental costs, mobilization and demobilization costs, and operator and support personnel costs must be considered.

Labor-Hours

The labor-hours expressed in this publication are derived by dividing the total daily labor-hours for the crew by the daily output. Based on average installation time and the assumptions listed above, the labor-hours include: direct labor, indirect labor, and nonproductive time. A typical day for a craftsman might include, but is not limited to:

- Direct Work
  - Measuring and layout
  - Preparing materials
  - Actual installation
  - Quality assurance/quality control
- Indirect Work
  - Reading plans or specifications
  - Preparing space
  - Receiving materials
  - Material movement
  - Giving or receiving instruction
  - Miscellaneous
- Non-Work
  - Chatting
  - Personal issues
  - Breaks
  - Interruptions (i.e., sickness, weather, material or equipment shortages, etc.)

If any of the items for a typical day do not apply to the particular work or project situation, the estimator should make any necessary adjustments.

Final Checklist

Estimating can be a straightforward process provided you remember the basics. Here's a checklist of some of the steps you should remember to complete before finalizing your estimate.

Did you remember to:

- factor in the City Cost Index for your locale?
- take into consideration which items have been marked up and by how much?
- mark up the entire estimate sufficiently for your purposes?
- read the background information on techniques and technical matters that could impact your project time span and cost?
- include all components of your project in the final estimate?
- double check your figures for accuracy?
- call RSMeans data engineers if you have any questions about your estimate or the data you've used? Remember, Gordian stands behind all of our products, including our extensive RSMeans data solutions. If you have any questions about your estimate, about the costs you've used from our data, or even about the technical aspects of the job that may affect your estimate, feel free to call the Gordian RSMeans editors at 1-800-448-8182.

Access Quarterly Data Updates

rsmeans.com/2018books

Unit Price Section

Table of Contents

Sect. No.		Page
	General Requirements	
01 11	Summary of Work	10
01 21	Allowances	11
01 31	Project Management and Coordination	11
01 45	Quality Control	12
01 54	Construction Aids	13
01 56	Temporary Barriers and Enclosures	14
01 66	Product Storage and Handling Requirements	15
01 71	Examination and Preparation	15
01 91	Commissioning	15
01 93	Facility Maintenance	15
	Existing Conditions	
02 41	Demolition	18
02 42	Removal and Salvage of Construction Materials	19
02 43	Structure Moving	21
02 65	Underground Storage Tank Rmvl.	22
02 81	Transportation and Disposal of Hazardous Materials	23
02 82	Asbestos Remediation	23
02 83	Lead Remediation	23
	Concrete	
03 05	Common Work Results for Concrete	26
03 11	Concrete Forming	26
03 15	Concrete Accessories	30
03 21	Reinforcement Bars	39
03 22	Fabric and Grid Reinforcing	43
03 23	Stressed Tendon Reinforcing	44
03 24	Fibrous Reinforcing	44
03 30	Cast-In-Place Concrete	45
03 31	Structural Concrete	46
03 35	Concrete Finishing	47
03 39	Concrete Curing	48
03 45	Precast Architectural Concrete	48
03 48	Precast Concrete Specialties	48
03 51	Cast Roof Decks	49
03 52	Lightweight Concrete Roof Insulation	49
03 81	Concrete Cutting	49
	Masonry	
04 05	Common Work Results for Masonry	52
04 22	Concrete Unit Masonry	53
04 24	Adobe Unit Masonry	54
04 41	Dry-Placed Stone	55
04 43	Stone Masonry	55
04 71	Manufactured Brick Masonry	55
04 72	Cast Stone Masonry	55
04 73	Manufactured Stone Masonry	56
	Metals	
05 05	Common Work Results for Metals	58
05 12	Structural Steel Framing	63
05 14	Structural Aluminum Framing	72
05 15	Wire Rope Assemblies	72
05 21	Steel Joist Framing	74
05 31	Steel Decking	78
05 35	Raceway Decking Assemblies	79
05 41	Structural Metal Stud Framing	80
05 42	Cold-Formed Metal Joist Framing	83
05 44	Cold-Formed Metal Trusses	89
05 51	Metal Stairs	90
05 52	Metal Railings	92
05 53	Metal Gratings	93
05 54	Metal Floor Plates	95
05 55	Metal Stair Treads and Nosings	96
05 56	Metal Castings	98
05 58	Formed Metal Fabrications	98

Sect. No.		Page
05 71	Decorative Metal Stairs	99
05 73	Decorative Metal Railings	99
05 75	Decorative Formed Metal	100
	Wood, Plastics & Composites	
06 05	Common Work Results for Wood, Plastics, and Composites	102
06 11	Wood Framing	102
06 12	Structural Panels	107
06 16	Sheathing	108
06 18	Glued-Laminated Construction	110
06 25	Prefinished Paneling	111
06 51	Structural Plastic Shapes and Plates	113
	Thermal & Moisture Protection	
07 01	Operation and Maint. of Thermal and Moisture Protection	116
07 21	Thermal Insulation	116
07 22	Roof and Deck Insulation	120
07 24	Exterior Insulation and Finish Systems	122
07 26	Vapor Retarders	122
07 27	Air Barriers	123
07 31	Shingles and Shakes	123
07 32	Roof Tiles	125
07 33	Natural Roof Coverings	127
07 41	Roof Panels	127
07 44	Faced Panels	129
07 46	Siding	129
07 51	Built-Up Bituminous Roofing	131
07 53	Elastomeric Membrane Roofing	132
07 54	Thermoplastic Membrane Roofing	133
07 61	Sheet Metal Roofing	134
07 95	Expansion Control	134
	Openings	
08 01	Operation and Maintenance of Openings	136
08 05	Common Work Results for Openings	137
08 12	Metal Frames	137
08 13	Metal Doors	138
08 14	Wood Doors	140
08 16	Composite Doors	146
08 32	Sliding Glass Doors	146
08 34	Special Function Doors	147
08 45	Translucent Wall and Roof Assemblies	148
08 52	Wood Windows	148
08 53	Plastic Windows	156
08 54	Composite Windows	158
08 62	Unit Skylights	159
08 81	Glass Glazing	160
08 83	Mirrors	160
08 84	Plastic Glazing	160
08 87	Glazing Surface Films	161
	Finishes	
09 05	Common Work Results for Finishes	164
09 25	Other Plastering	165
09 29	Gypsum Board	166
09 31	Thin-Set Tiling	168
09 51	Acoustical Ceilings	168
09 53	Acoustical Ceiling Suspension Assemblies	168
09 62	Specialty Flooring	168
09 63	Masonry Flooring	169
09 64	Wood Flooring	170
09 65	Resilient Flooring	171
09 68	Carpeting	171
09 72	Wall Coverings	172
09 81	Acoustic Insulation	172
09 91	Painting	172

Sect. No.		Page
	Specialties	
10 21	Compartments and Cubicles	178
10 35	Stoves	178
10 51	Lockers	178
10 56	Storage Assemblies	178
10 71	Exterior Protection	179
	Equipment	
11 13	Loading Dock Equipment	182
11 30	Residential Equipment	182
11 41	Foodservice Storage Equipment	183
11 44	Food Cooking Equipment	183
11 48	Foodservice Cleaning and Disposal Equipment	183
11 68	Play Field Equipment and Structures	184
	Furnishings	
12 24	Window Shades	186
12 36	Countertops	186
12 46	Furnishing Accessories	186
12 48	Rugs and Mats	186
12 92	Interior Planters and Artificial Plants	187
12 93	Interior Public Space Furnishings	189
	Special Construction	
13 05	Common Work Results for Special Construction	192
13 12	Fountains	192
13 31	Fabric Structures	193
13 33	Geodesic Structures	194
13 34	Fabricated Engineered Structures	194
13 48	Sound, Vibration, and Seismic Control	195
	Plumbing	
22 07	Plumbing Insulation	198
22 11	Facility Water Distribution	216
22 12	Facility Potable-Water Storage Tanks	217
22 13	Facility Sanitary Sewerage	217
22 14	Facility Storm Drainage	218
22 32	Domestic Water Filtration Equipment	219
22 34	Fuel-Fired Domestic Water Heaters	220
22 35	Domestic Water Heat Exchangers	220
22 41	Residential Plumbing Fixtures	220
22 42	Commercial Plumbing Fixtures	221
	Heating Ventilation Air Conditioning	
23 07	HVAC Insulation	224
23 09	Instrumentation and Control for HVAC	225
23 21	Hydronic Piping and Pumps	230
23 33	Air Duct Accessories	230
23 34	HVAC Fans	233
23 41	Particulate Air Filtration	233
23 42	Gas-Phase Air Filtration	235
23 43	Electronic Air Cleaners	235
23 52	Heating Boilers	235
23 54	Furnaces	237
23 55	Fuel-Fired Heaters	238
23 56	Solar Energy Heating Equipment	239
23 72	Air-to-Air Energy Recovery Equipment	242
23 74	Packaged Outdoor HVAC Equipment	242
23 76	Evaporative Air-Cooling Equipment	243
23 81	Decentralized Unitary HVAC Equipment	243
23 82	Convection Heating and Cooling Units	245
23 83	Radiant Heating Units	246
23 84	Humidity Control Equipment	248

Table of Contents (cont.)

Sect. No.		Page
	Electrical	
26 05	Common Work Results for Electrical	252
26 09	Instrumentation and Control for Electrical Systems	252
26 27	Low-Voltage Distribution Equipment	253
26 29	Low-Voltage Controllers	253
26 31	Photovoltaic Collectors	254
26 33	Battery Equipment	255
26 51	Interior Lighting	255
26 52	Safety Lighting	260
26 54	Classified Location Lighting	261
26 55	Special Purpose Lighting	261
26 56	Exterior Lighting	262
26 61	Lighting Systems and Accessories	266
	Electronic Safety & Security	
28 42	Gas Detection and Alarm	270
28 46	Fire Detection and Alarm	270
	Earthwork	
31 05	Common Work Results for Earthwork	272
31 23	Excavation and Fill	272
31 25	Erosion and Sedimentation Controls	272

Sect. No.		Page
31 31	Soil Treatment	273
31 32	Soil Stabilization	273
31 62	Driven Piles	273
	Exterior Improvements	
32 01	Operation and Maintenance of Exterior Improvements	280
32 11	Base Courses	280
32 12	Flexible Paving	281
32 14	Unit Paving	282
32 17	Paving Specialties	282
32 31	Fences and Gates	282
32 32	Retaining Walls	283
32 33	Site Furnishings	283
32 84	Planting Irrigation	284
32 91	Planting Preparation	284
32 93	Plants	285
32 94	Planting Accessories	289
	Utilities	
33 01	Operation and Maintenance of Utilities	292
33 11	Groundwater Sources	292
33 41	Subdrainage	292
33 46	Stormwater Management	293

Sect. No.		Page
	Water and Wastewater Equipment	
46 07	Packaged Water and Wastewater Treatment Equipment	296
46 23	Grit Removal and Handling Equipment	296
46 25	Oil and Grease Separation and Removal Equipment	296
46 51	Air and Gas Diffusion Equipment	297
46 53	Biological Treatment Systems	300
	Electrical Power Generation	
48 15	Wind Energy Electrical Power Generation Equipment	304
48 18	Fuel Cell Electrical Power Generation Equipment	304

RSMeans data: Unit Prices— How They Work

All RSMeans data: Unit Prices are organized in the same way.

03 30 Cast-In-Place Concrete

03 30 53 – Miscellaneous Cast-In-Place Concrete

03 30 53.40 Concrete In Place ❶

			Crew ❺	Daily Output ❻	Labor-Hours ❼	Unit ❽	Material	2018 Bare Costs Labor	Equipment ❾	Total ❿	Total Incl O&P ⓫
0010	**CONCRETE IN PLACE**	R033105-10 ❹									
0020	Including forms (4 uses), Grade 60 rebar, concrete (Portland cement										
0050	Type I), placement and finishing unless otherwise indicated										
0500	Chimney foundations (5000 psi), over 5 C.Y.		C-14C	32.22	3.476	C.Y.	171	167	.80	338.80	445
0510	(3500 psi), under 5 C.Y. ❸	R033105-70	"	23.71	4.724	"	198	227	1.09	426.09	565
3540	Equipment pad (3000 psi), 3' x 3' x 6" thick		C-14H	45	1.067	Ea.	44.50	52.50	.57	97.57	130
❷ 3550	4' x 4' x 6" thick			30	1.600		69	79	.85	148.85	197
3560	5' x 5' x 8" thick			18	2.667		126	132	1.41	259.41	340
3570	6' x 6' x 8" thick			14	3.429		173	169	1.82	343.82	450
3580	8' x 8' x 10" thick			8	6		370	296	3.18	669.18	860
3590	10' x 10' x 12" thick			5	9.600		645	475	5.10	1,125.10	1,425
3800	Footings (3000 psi), spread under 1 C.Y.		C-14C	28	4	C.Y.	185	192	.92	377.92	495
3825	1 C.Y. to 5 C.Y.			43	2.605		219	125	.60	344.60	430
3850	Over 5 C.Y.	R033105-80		75	1.493		203	72	.34	275.34	330

It is important to understand the structure of RSMeans data: Unit Prices, so that you can find information easily and use it correctly.

❶ Line Numbers
Line Numbers consist of 12 characters, which identify a unique location in the database for each task. The first 6 or 8 digits conform to the Construction Specifications Institute MasterFormat® 2016. The remainder of the digits are a further breakdown in order to arrange items in understandable groups of similar tasks. Line numbers are consistent across all of our publications, so a line number in any of our products will always refer to the same item of work.

❷ Descriptions
Descriptions are shown in a hierarchical structure to make them readable. In order to read a complete description, read up through the indents to the top of the section. Include everything that is above and to the left that is not contradicted by information below. For instance, the complete description for line 03 30 53.40 3550 is "Concrete in place, including forms (4 uses), Grade 60 rebar, concrete (Portland cement Type 1), placement and finishing unless otherwise indicated; Equipment pad (3000 psi), 4' × 4' × 6" thick."

❸ RSMeans data
When using **RSMeans data**, it is important to read through an entire section to ensure that you use the data that most closely matches your work. Note that sometimes there is additional information shown in the section that may improve your price. There are frequently lines that further describe, add to, or adjust data for specific situations.

❹ Reference Information
Gordian's RSMeans engineers have created **reference** information to assist you in your estimate. **If** there is information that applies to a section, it will be indicated at the start of the section. The Reference Section is located in the back of the data set.

❺ Crews
Crews include labor and/or equipment necessary to accomplish each task. In this case, Crew C-14H is used. Gordian's RSMeans staff selects a crew to represent the workers and equipment that are

4

typically used for that task. In this case, Crew C-14H consists of one carpenter foreman (outside), two carpenters, one rodman, one laborer, one cement finisher, and one gas engine vibrator. Details of all crews can be found in the Reference Section.

Crews - Standard

Crew No.	Bare Costs		Incl. Subs O&P		Cost Per Labor-Hour	
Crew C-14H	Hr.	Daily	Hr.	Daily	Bare Costs	Incl. O&P
1 Carpenter Foreman (outside)	$52.70	$421.60	$80.25	$642.00	$49.36	$74.88
2 Carpenters	50.70	811.20	77.20	1235.20		
1 Rodman (reinf.)	54.65	437.20	83.45	667.60		
1 Laborer	39.85	318.80	60.70	485.60		
1 Cement Finisher	47.55	380.40	70.45	563.60		
1 Gas Engine Vibrator		25.60		28.16	.53	.59
48 L.H., Daily Totals		$2394.80		$3622.16	$49.89	$75.46

6 Daily Output

The **Daily Output** is the amount of work that the crew can do in a normal 8-hour workday, including mobilization, layout, movement of materials, and cleanup. In this case, crew C-14H can install thirty 4' × 4' × 6" thick concrete pads in a day. Daily output is variable and based on many factors, including the size of the job, location, and environmental conditions. RSMeans data represents work done in daylight (or adequate lighting) and temperate conditions.

7 Labor-Hours

The figure in the **Labor-Hours** column is the amount of labor required to perform one unit of work—in this case the amount of labor required to construct one 4' × 4' equipment pad. This figure is calculated by dividing the number of hours of labor in the crew by the daily output (48 labor-hours divided by 30 pads = 1.6 hours of labor per pad). Multiply 1.6 times 60 to see the value in minutes: 60 × 1.6 = 96 minutes. Note: the labor-hour figure is not dependent on the crew size. A change in crew size will result in a corresponding change in daily output, but the labor-hours per unit of work will not change.

8 Unit of Measure

All RSMeans data: Unit Prices include the typical **Unit of Measure** used for estimating that item. For concrete-in-place the typical unit is cubic yards (C.Y.) or each (Ea.). For installing broadloom carpet it is square yard, and for gypsum board it is square foot. The estimator needs to take special care that the unit in the data matches the unit in the take-off. Unit conversions may be found in the Reference Section.

9 Bare Costs

Bare Costs are the costs of materials, labor, and equipment that the installing contractor pays. They represent the cost, in U.S. dollars, for one unit of work. They do not include any markups for profit or labor burden.

10 Bare Total

The **Total column** represents the total bare cost for the installing contractor in U.S. dollars. In this case, the sum of $69 for material + $79 for labor + $.85 for equipment is $148.85.

11 Total Incl O&P

The **Total Incl O&P column** is the total cost, including overhead and profit, that the installing contractor will charge the customer. This represents the cost of materials plus 10% profit, the cost of labor plus labor burden and 10% profit, and the cost of equipment plus 10% profit. It does not include the general contractor's overhead and profit. Note: See the inside back cover of the printed product or the Reference Section of the electronic product for details of how the labor burden is calculated.

National Average

*The RSMeans data in our print publications represents a "national average" cost. This data should be modified to the project location using the **City Cost Indexes** or **Location Factors** tables found in the Reference Section. Use the Location Factors to adjust estimate totals if the project covers multiple trades. Use the City Cost Indexes (CCI) for single trade projects or projects where a more detailed analysis is required. All figures in the two tables are derived from the same research. The last row of data in the CCI—the weighted average—is the same as the numbers reported for each location in the location factor table.*

RSMeans data: Unit Prices— How They Work (Continued)

Project Name: Pre-Engineered Steel Building
Architect: As Shown
Location: Anywhere, USA
Date: 01/01/18 **STD**

Line Number	Description	Qty	Unit	Material	Labor	Equipment	SubContract	Estimate Total
03 30 53.40 3940	Strip footing, 12" x 24", reinforced	34	C.Y.	$5,406.00	$3,808.00	$18.36	$0.00	
03 30 53.40 3950	Strip footing, 12" x 36", reinforced	15	C.Y.	$2,295.00	$1,350.00	$6.45	$0.00	
03 11 13.65 3000	Concrete slab edge forms	500	L.F.	$145.00	$1,280.00	$0.00	$0.00	
03 22 11.10 0200	Welded wire fabric reinforcing	150	C.S.F.	$2,940.00	$4,200.00	$0.00	$0.00	
03 31 13.35 0300	Ready mix concrete, 4000 psi for slab on grade	278	C.Y.	$35,584.00	$0.00	$0.00	$0.00	
03 31 13.70 4300	Place, strike off & consolidate concrete slab	278	C.Y.	$0.00	$5,031.80	$130.66	$0.00	
03 35 13.30 0250	Machine float & trowel concrete slab	15,000	S.F.	$0.00	$9,450.00	$300.00	$0.00	
03 15 16.20 0140	Cut control joints in concrete slab	950	L.F.	$47.50	$399.00	$57.00	$0.00	
03 39 23.13 0300	Sprayed concrete curing membrane	150	C.S.F.	$1,815.00	$1,005.00	$0.00	$0.00	
Division 03	**Subtotal**			**$48,232.50**	**$26,523.80**	**$512.47**	**$0.00**	**$75,268.77**
08 36 13.10 2650	Manual 10' x 10' steel sectional overhead door	8	Ea.	$10,400.00	$3,600.00	$0.00	$0.00	
08 36 13.10 2860	Insulation and steel back panel for OH door	800	S.F.	$4,000.00	$0.00	$0.00	$0.00	
Division 08	**Subtotal**			**$14,400.00**	**$3,600.00**	**$0.00**	**$0.00**	**$18,000.00**
13 34 19.50 1100	Pre-Engineered Steel Building, 100' x 150' x 24'	15,000	SF Flr.	$0.00	$0.00	$0.00	$367,500.00	
13 34 19.50 6050	Framing for PESB door opening, 3' x 7'	4	Opng.	$0.00	$0.00	$0.00	$2,240.00	
13 34 19.50 6100	Framing for PESB door opening, 10' x 10'	8	Opng.	$0.00	$0.00	$0.00	$9,200.00	
13 34 19.50 6200	Framing for PESB window opening, 4' x 3'	6	Opng.	$0.00	$0.00	$0.00	$3,330.00	
13 34 19.50 5750	PESB door, 3' x 7', single leaf	4	Opng.	$2,620.00	$700.00	$0.00	$0.00	
13 34 19.50 7750	PESB sliding window, 4' x 3' with screen	6	Opng.	$2,550.00	$600.00	$45.30	$0.00	
13 34 19.50 6550	PESB gutter, eave type, 26 ga., painted	300	L.F.	$2,220.00	$819.00	$0.00	$0.00	
13 34 19.50 8650	PESB roof vent, 12" wide x 10' long	15	Ea.	$555.00	$3,285.00	$0.00	$0.00	
13 34 19.50 6900	PESB insulation, vinyl faced, 4" thick	27,400	S.F.	$13,152.00	$9,590.00	$0.00	$0.00	
Division 13	**Subtotal**			**$21,097.00**	**$14,994.00**	**$45.30**	**$382,270.00**	**$418,406.30**
	Subtotal			$83,729.50	$45,117.80	$557.77	$382,270.00	$511,675.07
Division 01	General Requirements @ 7%			5,861.07	3,158.25	39.04	26,758.90	
	Estimate Subtotal			$89,590.57	$48,276.05	$596.81	$409,028.90	$511,675.07
	Sales Tax @ 5%			4,479.53		29.84	10,225.72	
	Subtotal A			94,070.09	48,276.05	626.65	419,254.62	
	GC O & P			9,407.01	25,634.58	62.67	41,925.46	
	Subtotal B			103,477.10	73,910.63	689.32	461,180.08	$639,257.13
	Contingency @ 5%							31,962.86
	Subtotal C							$671,219.99
	Bond @ $12/1000 +10% O&P							8,860.10
	Subtotal D							$680,080.09
	Location Adjustment Factor				102.30			15,641.84
	Grand Total							**$695,721.94**

This estimate is based on an interactive spreadsheet. You are free to download it and adjust it to your methodology. A copy of this spreadsheet is available at www.RSMeans.com/2018books.

Sample Estimate

This sample demonstrates the elements of an estimate, including a tally of the RSMeans data lines and a summary of the markups on a contractor's work to arrive at a total cost to the owner. The Location Factor with RSMeans data is added at the bottom of the estimate to adjust the cost of the work to a specific location.

❶ Work Performed

The body of the estimate shows the RSMeans data selected, including the line number, a brief description of each item, its take-off unit and quantity, and the bare costs of materials, labor, and equipment. This estimate also includes a column titled "SubContract." This data is taken from the column "Total Incl O&P" and represents the total that a subcontractor would charge a general contractor for the work, including the sub's markup for overhead and profit.

❷ Division 1, General Requirements

This is the first division numerically but the last division estimated. Division 1 includes project-wide needs provided by the general contractor. These requirements vary by project but may include temporary facilities and utilities, security, testing, project cleanup, etc. For small projects a percentage can be used—typically between 5% and 15% of project cost. For large projects the costs may be itemized and priced individually.

❸ Sales Tax

If the work is subject to state or local sales taxes, the amount must be added to the estimate. Sales tax may be added to material costs, equipment costs, and subcontracted work. In this case, sales tax was added in all three categories. It was assumed that approximately half the subcontracted work would be material cost, so the tax was applied to 50% of the subcontract total.

❹ GC O&P

This entry represents the general contractor's markup on material, labor, equipment, and subcontractor costs. Our standard markup on materials, equipment, and subcontracted work is 10%. In this estimate, the markup on the labor performed by the GC's workers uses "Skilled Workers Average" shown in Column F on the table "Installing Contractor's Overhead & Profit," which can be found on the inside back cover of the printed product or in the Reference Section of the electronic product.

❺ Contingency

A factor for contingency may be added to any estimate to represent the cost of unknowns that may occur between the time that the estimate is performed and the time the project is constructed. The amount of the allowance will depend on the stage of design at which the estimate is done and the contractor's assessment of the risk involved. Refer to section 01 21 16.50 for contingency allowances.

❻ Bonds

Bond costs should be added to the estimate. The figures here represent a typical performance bond, ensuring the owner that if the general contractor does not complete the obligations in the construction contract the bonding company will pay the cost for completion of the work.

❼ Location Adjustment

Published prices are based on national average costs. If necessary, adjust the total cost of the project using a location factor from the "Location Factor" table or the "City Cost Index" table. Use location factors if the work is general, covering multiple trades. If the work is by a single trade (e.g., masonry) use the more specific data found in the "City Cost Indexes."

Estimating Tips
01 20 00 Price and Payment Procedures
- Allowances that should be added to estimates to cover contingencies and job conditions that are not included in the national average material and labor costs are shown in Section 01 21.
- When estimating historic preservation projects (depending on the condition of the existing structure and the owner's requirements), a 15%–20% contingency or allowance is recommended, regardless of the stage of the drawings.

01 30 00 Administrative Requirements
- Before determining a final cost estimate, it is a good practice to review all the items listed in Subdivisions 01 31 and 01 32 to make final adjustments for items that may need customizing to specific job conditions.
- Requirements for initial and periodic submittals can represent a significant cost to the General Requirements of a job. Thoroughly check the submittal specifications when estimating a project to determine any costs that should be included.

01 40 00 Quality Requirements
- All projects will require some degree of quality control. This cost is not included in the unit cost of construction listed in each division. Depending upon the terms of the contract, the various costs of inspection and testing can be the responsibility of either the owner or the contractor. Be sure to include the required costs in your estimate.

01 50 00 Temporary Facilities and Controls
- Barricades, access roads, safety nets, scaffolding, security, and many more requirements for the execution of a safe project are elements of direct cost. These costs can easily be overlooked when preparing an estimate. When looking through the major classifications of this subdivision, determine which items apply to each division in your estimate.
- Construction equipment rental costs can be found in the Reference Section in Section 01 54 33. Operators' wages are not included in equipment rental costs.
- Equipment mobilization and demobilization costs are not included in equipment rental costs and must be considered separately.
- The cost of small tools provided by the installing contractor for his workers is covered in the "Overhead" column on the "Installing Contractor's Overhead and Profit" table that lists labor trades, base rates, and markups and, therefore, is included in the "Total Incl. O&P" cost of any unit price line item.

01 70 00 Execution and Closeout Requirements
- When preparing an estimate, thoroughly read the specifications to determine the requirements for Contract Closeout. Final cleaning, record documentation, operation and maintenance data, warranties and bonds, and spare parts and maintenance materials can all be elements of cost for the completion of a contract. Do not overlook these in your estimate.

Reference Numbers
Reference numbers are shown at the beginning of some major classifications. These numbers refer to related items in the Reference Section. The reference information may be an estimating procedure, an alternate pricing method, or technical information.

Note: Not all subdivisions listed here necessarily appear. ■

Did you know?

RSMeans data is available through our online application with 24/7 access:
- Search for unit prices by keyword
- Leverage the most up-to-date data
- Build and export estimates

Try it free for 30 days!
www.rsmeans.com/2018freetrial

No part of this cost data may be reproduced, stored in a retrieval system, or transmitted in any form or by any means without prior written permission of Gordian.

01 11 Summary of Work

01 11 31 – Professional Consultants

01 11 31.10 Architectural Fees

		Crew	Daily Output	Labor-Hours	Unit	Material	2018 Bare Costs Labor	Equipment	Total	Total Incl O&P
0010	**ARCHITECTURAL FEES** R011110-10									
0020	For new construction									
0060	Minimum				Project				4.90%	4.90%
0090	Maximum								16%	16%
0100	For alteration work, to $500,000, add to new construction fee								50%	50%
0150	Over $500,000, add to new construction fee								25%	25%
2000	For "Greening" of building [G]								3%	3%

01 11 31.30 Engineering Fees

0010	**ENGINEERING FEES** R011110-30									
0020	Educational planning consultant, minimum				Project				.50%	.50%
0100	Maximum				"				2.50%	2.50%
0200	Electrical, minimum				Contrct				4.10%	4.10%
0300	Maximum								10.10%	10.10%
0400	Elevator & conveying systems, minimum								2.50%	2.50%
0500	Maximum								5%	5%
0600	Food service & kitchen equipment, minimum								8%	8%
0700	Maximum								12%	12%
0800	Landscaping & site development, minimum								2.50%	2.50%
0900	Maximum								6%	6%
1000	Mechanical (plumbing & HVAC), minimum								4.10%	4.10%
1100	Maximum								10.10%	10.10%
1200	Structural, minimum				Project				1%	1%
1300	Maximum				"				2.50%	2.50%

01 11 31.40 Energy Modeling Fees

0010	**ENERGY MODELING FEES**									
0100	Academic buildings to 10,000 S.F.				Ea.				9,000	9,000
0120	Greater than 10,000 S.F., add				S.F.				.20	.20
0200	Offices buildings to 10,000 S.F.				Ea.				11,000	11,000
0220	Greater than 10,000 S.F., add				S.F.				.04	.04
0300	Medical buildings to 50,000 S.F. to 200,000 S.F.				Ea.				30,000	30,000
0400	Multifamily residential 30,000 S.F. to 50,000 S.F.				"				15,000	15,000

01 11 31.80 Green Building Certification

0010	**GREEN BUILDING CERTIFICATION**									
0020	USGBC Registration, Construction & Design Fees									
0100	Fees for Commercial, Schools, Core & Shell Construction									
0200	Project Registration Fees				Project				900	900
0300	Certification Fees-New Construction									
0310	Design and Construction Review									
0320	Less than 50,000 S.F.				Project				2,250	2,250
0330	50,000 S.F. to 500,000 S.F.				S.F.				.05	.05
0340	Greater than 50,000 S.F.				Project				22,500	22,500
0400	Certification Fees-Existing Buildings (O&M)									
0410	Design and Construction Review (O&M)									
0420	Less than 50,000 S.F.				Project				1,500	1,500
0430	50,000 S.F. to 500,000 S.F.				S.F.				.03	.03
0440	Greater than 50,000 S.F.				Project				15,000	15,000
1000	Green Globes Fees for Commercial, Schools, Core & Shell Construction									
1010	Third Party Assessment/Certification-New Construction R011110-80									
1020	Software Subscription-New Building				Ea.				500	500
1030	Third Party Complete based on Enclosed Space									
1050	Less than 10,000 S.F.				Project				7,000	7,000
1080	300,000 S.F. to less than 400,000 S.F.								13,500	13,500

01 11 Summary of Work

01 11 31 – Professional Consultants

01 11 31.80 Green Building Certification

		Crew	Daily Output	Labor-Hours	Unit	Material	2018 Bare Costs Labor	Equipment	Total	Total Incl O&P
1090	400,000 S.F. to less than 500,000 S.F.				Project				18,000	18,000
1100	More than 500,000 S.F.				↓				22,500	22,500
1110	Additional Fees									
1120	Travel Expenses Flat Fee				Project				1,500	1,500
1140	Multiple Space Types/Complexity Min, add								1,500	1,500
1150	Multiple Space Types/Complexity Max, add				↓				3,500	3,500
1160	Third Party Assessment/Certification-Existing Building	R011110-90								
1170	Software Subscription-Existing Building (CEIB)				Ea.				1,000	1,000
1180	Third Party Assessment/Certification based on Encl Space (CEIB)									
1190	Less than 100,000 S.F.				Project				4,000	4,000
1200	100,000 S.F. to less than 200,000 S.F.								5,000	5,000
1230	400,000 S.F. to less than 500,000 S.F.								12,000	12,000
1240	More than 500,000 S.F.				↓				15,000	15,000
1250	Third Party Recertification every 3 years based on Encl Space (CEIB)									
1260	Less than 100,000 S.F.				Project				3,000	3,000
1270	100,000 S.F. to less than 200,000 S.F.								4,000	4,000
1280	200,000 S.F. to less than 300,000 S.F.								4,500	4,500
1290	300,000 S.F. to less than 400,000 S.F.								6,000	6,000
1300	400,000 S.F. to less than 500,000 S.F.								8,000	8,000
1310	More than 500,000 S.F.				↓				10,000	10,000
1320	Additional Fees									
1330	Travel Expenses Flat Fee				Project				1,500	1,500
1340	Travel Expenses Actual Expense plus Overhead				%				20%	20%
1350	Multiple Space Types/Complexity Min, add				Project				1,000	1,000
1360	Multiple Space Types/Complexity Max, add				"				3,500	3,500

01 21 Allowances

01 21 16 – Contingency Allowances

01 21 16.50 Contingencies

		Crew	Daily Output	Labor-Hours	Unit	Material	Labor	Equipment	Total	Total Incl O&P
0010	**CONTINGENCIES**, Add to estimate									
0020	Conceptual stage				Project				20%	20%
0050	Schematic stage								15%	15%
0100	Preliminary working drawing stage (Design Dev.)								10%	10%
0150	Final working drawing stage				↓				3%	3%

01 31 Project Management and Coordination

01 31 13 – Project Coordination

01 31 13.40 Main Office Expense

		Crew	Daily Output	Labor-Hours	Unit	Material	Labor	Equipment	Total	Total Incl O&P
0010	**MAIN OFFICE EXPENSE** Average for General Contractors									
0020	As a percentage of their annual volume									
0030	Annual volume to $300,000, minimum				% Vol.				20%	
0040	Maximum								30%	
0060	To $500,000, minimum								17%	
0070	Maximum								22%	
0080	To $1,000,000, minimum								16%	
0090	Maximum								19%	
0110	To $3,000,000, minimum								14%	
0120	Maximum								16%	
0125	Annual volume under $1,000,000				↓				17.50%	

01 31 Project Management and Coordination

01 31 13 – Project Coordination

01 31 13.40 Main Office Expense		Crew	Daily Output	Labor-Hours	Unit	Material	2018 Bare Costs Labor	Equipment	Total	Total Incl O&P
0130	To $5,000,000, minimum				% Vol.				8%	
0140	Maximum				↓				10%	

01 45 Quality Control

01 45 23 – Testing and Inspecting Services

01 45 23.50 Testing

		Crew	Daily Output	Labor-Hours	Unit	Material	Labor	Equipment	Total	Total Incl O&P
0010	**TESTING** and Inspecting Services									
0015	For concrete building costing $1,000,000, minimum				Project				4,725	5,200
0020	Maximum								38,000	41,800
0050	Steel building, minimum								4,725	5,200
0070	Maximum								14,800	16,300
0100	For building costing $10,000,000, minimum								30,100	33,100
0150	Maximum				↓				48,200	53,000
0600	Concrete testing, aggregates, abrasion, ASTM C 131				Ea.				136	150
0650	Absorption, ASTM C 127								42	46
1800	Compressive test, cylinder, delivered to lab, ASTM C 39								12	13
1900	Picked up by lab, minimum								14	15
1950	Average								18	20
2000	Maximum								27	30
2200	Compressive strength, cores (not incl. drilling), ASTM C 42				↓				36	40
2250	Core drilling, 4" diameter (plus technician)				Inch				23	25
2260	Technician for core drilling				Hr.				45	50
2300	Patching core holes				Ea.				22	24
4730	Soil testing									
4735	Soil density, nuclear method, ASTM D 2922				Ea.				35	38.50
4740	Sand cone method, ASTM D 1556								27	30
4750	Moisture content, ASTM D 2216								9	10
4780	Permeability test, double ring infiltrometer								500	550
4800	Permeability, var. or constant head, undist., ASTM D 2434								227	250
4850	Recompacted								250	275
4900	Proctor compaction, 4" standard mold, ASTM D 698								123	135
4950	6" modified mold								68	75
5100	Shear tests, triaxial, minimum								410	450
5150	Maximum								545	600
5300	Direct shear, minimum, ASTM D 3080								320	350
5350	Maximum								410	450
5550	Technician for inspection, per day, earthwork								320	350
5650	Bolting								400	440
5750	Roofing								480	530
5790	Welding				↓				480	530
5820	Non-destructive metal testing, dye penetrant				Day				310	340
5840	Magnetic particle								310	340
5860	Radiography								450	495
5880	Ultrasonic				↓				310	340
6000	Welding certification, minimum				Ea.				91	100
6100	Maximum				"				250	275
7000	Underground storage tank									
7500	Volumetric tightness test, <=12,000 gal.				Ea.				435	480
7510	<=30,000 gal.				"				615	675
7600	Vadose zone (soil gas) sampling, 10-40 samples, min.				Day				1,375	1,500
7610	Maximum				"				2,275	2,500

01 45 Quality Control

01 45 23 – Testing and Inspecting Services

01 45 23.50 Testing

		Crew	Daily Output	Labor-Hours	Unit	Material	2018 Bare Costs Labor	Equipment	Total	Total Incl O&P
7700	Ground water monitoring incl. drilling 3 wells, min.				Total				4,550	5,000
7710	Maximum				"				6,375	7,000
8000	X-ray concrete slabs				Ea.				182	200
9000	Thermographic testing, for bldg envelope heat loss, average 2,000 S.F. [G]				"				500	500

01 54 Construction Aids

01 54 09 – Protection Equipment

01 54 09.50 Personnel Protective Equipment

		Crew	Daily Output	Labor-Hours	Unit	Material	2018 Bare Costs Labor	Equipment	Total	Total Incl O&P
0010	**PERSONNEL PROTECTIVE EQUIPMENT**									
0015	Hazardous waste protection									
0020	Respirator mask only, full face, silicone				Ea.	287			287	315
0030	Half face, silicone					49.50			49.50	54.50
0040	Respirator cartridges, 2 req'd/mask, dust or asbestos					4.76			4.76	5.25
0050	Chemical vapor					4.28			4.28	4.71
0060	Combination vapor and dust					11.70			11.70	12.90
0100	Emergency escape breathing apparatus, 5 minutes					705			705	780
0110	10 minutes					870			870	955
0150	Self contained breathing apparatus with full face piece, 30 minutes					2,275			2,275	2,525
0160	60 minutes					3,000			3,000	3,300
0200	Encapsulating suits, limited use, level A					1,775			1,775	1,975
0210	Level B					405			405	445
0300	Over boots, latex				Pr.	8.05			8.05	8.85
0310	PVC					33			33	36.50
0320	Neoprene					31			31	34.50
0400	Gloves, nitrile/PVC					85.50			85.50	94
0410	Neoprene coated					41.50			41.50	46

01 54 09.60 Safety Nets

		Crew	Daily Output	Labor-Hours	Unit	Material	2018 Bare Costs Labor	Equipment	Total	Total Incl O&P
0010	**SAFETY NETS**									
0020	No supports, stock sizes, nylon, 3-1/2" mesh				S.F.	3.11			3.11	3.42
0100	Polypropylene, 6" mesh					1.63			1.63	1.79
0200	Small mesh debris nets, 1/4" mesh, stock sizes					.54			.54	.59
0220	Combined 3-1/2" mesh and 1/4" mesh, stock sizes					4.85			4.85	5.35
0300	Rental, 4" mesh, stock sizes, 3 months					.73			.73	.80
0320	6 month rental					1.03			1.03	1.13
0340	12 months					1.41			1.41	1.55

01 54 19 – Temporary Cranes

01 54 19.50 Daily Crane Crews

		Crew	Daily Output	Labor-Hours	Unit	Material	2018 Bare Costs Labor	Equipment	Total	Total Incl O&P
0010	**DAILY CRANE CREWS** for small jobs, portal to portal									
0100	12-ton truck-mounted hydraulic crane	A-3H	1	8	Day		450	630	1,080	1,375
0200	25-ton	A-3I	1	8			450	760	1,210	1,500
0300	40-ton	A-3J	1	8			450	1,325	1,775	2,125
0400	55-ton	A-3K	1	16			840	1,500	2,340	2,925
0500	80-ton	A-3L	1	16			840	2,250	3,090	3,750
0900	If crane is needed on a Saturday, Sunday or Holiday									
0910	At time-and-a-half, add				Day		50%			
0920	At double time, add				"		100%			

01 54 Construction Aids

01 54 36 – Equipment Mobilization

01 54 36.50 Mobilization

		Crew	Daily Output	Labor-Hours	Unit	Material	2018 Bare Costs Labor	Equipment	Total	Total Incl O&P
0010	**MOBILIZATION** (Use line item again for demobilization)									
0015	Up to 25 mi. haul dist. (50 mi. RT for mob/demob crew)									
1200	Small equipment, placed in rear of, or towed by pickup truck	A-3A	4	2	Ea.		103	31.50	134.50	190
1300	Equipment hauled on 3-ton capacity towed trailer	A-3Q	2.67	3			154	57	211	295
1400	20-ton capacity	B-34U	2	8			390	212	602	820
1500	40-ton capacity	B-34N	2	8			400	330	730	960
1600	50-ton capacity	B-34V	1	24			1,225	910	2,135	2,850
1700	Crane, truck-mounted, up to 75 ton (driver only)	1 Eqhv	4	2			112		112	169
1800	Over 75 ton (with chase vehicle)	A-3E	2.50	6.400			325	50.50	375.50	545
2400	Crane, large lattice boom, requiring assembly	B-34W	.50	144			7,025	6,725	13,750	18,000
2500	For each additional 5 miles haul distance, add						10%	10%		

01 56 Temporary Barriers and Enclosures

01 56 16 – Temporary Dust Barriers

01 56 16.10 Dust Barriers, Temporary

		Crew	Daily Output	Labor-Hours	Unit	Material	Labor	Equipment	Total	Total Incl O&P
0010	**DUST BARRIERS, TEMPORARY**									
0020	Spring loaded telescoping pole & head, to 12', erect and dismantle	1 Clab	240	.033	Ea.		1.33		1.33	2.02
0025	Cost per day (based upon 250 days)				Day	.29			.29	.31
0030	To 21', erect and dismantle	1 Clab	240	.033	Ea.		1.33		1.33	2.02
0035	Cost per day (based upon 250 days)				Day	.58			.58	.63
0040	Accessories, caution tape reel, erect and dismantle	1 Clab	480	.017	Ea.		.66		.66	1.01
0045	Cost per day (based upon 250 days)				Day	.34			.34	.37
0060	Foam rail and connector, erect and dismantle	1 Clab	240	.033	Ea.		1.33		1.33	2.02
0065	Cost per day (based upon 250 days)				Day	.12			.12	.13
0070	Caution tape	1 Clab	384	.021	C.L.F.	3.13	.83		3.96	4.71
0080	Zipper, standard duty		60	.133	Ea.	7.30	5.30		12.60	16.10
0090	Heavy duty		48	.167	"	9.75	6.65		16.40	21
0100	Polyethylene sheet, 4 mil		37	.216	Sq.	2.58	8.60		11.18	15.95
0110	6 mil		37	.216	"	3.73	8.60		12.33	17.20
1000	Dust partition, 6 mil polyethylene, 1" x 3" frame	2 Carp	2000	.008	S.F.	.32	.41		.73	.97
1080	2" x 4" frame	"	2000	.008	"	.35	.41		.76	1

01 56 26 – Temporary Fencing

01 56 26.50 Temporary Fencing

		Crew	Daily Output	Labor-Hours	Unit	Material	Labor	Equipment	Total	Total Incl O&P
0010	**TEMPORARY FENCING**									
0020	Chain link, 11 ga., 4' high	2 Clab	400	.040	L.F.	1.63	1.59		3.22	4.22
0100	6' high		300	.053		4.55	2.13		6.68	8.25
0200	Rented chain link, 6' high, to 1000' (up to 12 mo.)		400	.040		2.99	1.59		4.58	5.70
0250	Over 1000' (up to 12 mo.)		300	.053		3.19	2.13		5.32	6.75
0350	Plywood, painted, 2" x 4" frame, 4' high	A-4	135	.178		6.35	8.55		14.90	19.90
0400	4" x 4" frame, 8' high	"	110	.218		12.10	10.45		22.55	29
0500	Wire mesh on 4" x 4" posts, 4' high	2 Carp	100	.160		10.35	8.10		18.45	24
0550	8' high	"	80	.200		15.60	10.15		25.75	32.50

01 66 Product Storage and Handling Requirements

01 66 19 – Material Handling

01 66 19.10 Material Handling		Crew	Daily Output	Labor-Hours	Unit	Material	2018 Bare Costs Labor	Equipment	Total	Total Incl O&P
0010	**MATERIAL HANDLING**									
0020	Above 2nd story, via stairs, per C.Y. of material per floor	2 Clab	145	.110	C.Y.		4.40		4.40	6.70
0030	Via elevator, per C.Y. of material		240	.067			2.66		2.66	4.05
0050	Distances greater than 200', per C.Y. of material per each addl 200'		300	.053			2.13		2.13	3.24

01 71 Examination and Preparation

01 71 23 – Field Engineering

01 71 23.13 Construction Layout

		Crew	Daily Output	Labor-Hours	Unit	Material	Labor	Equipment	Total	Total Incl O&P
0010	**CONSTRUCTION LAYOUT**									
1100	Crew for layout of building, trenching or pipe laying, 2 person crew	A-6	1	16	Day		805	50.50	855.50	1,275
1200	3 person crew	A-7	1	24			1,325	50.50	1,375.50	2,050
1400	Crew for roadway layout, 4 person crew	A-8	1	32			1,700	50.50	1,750.50	2,650

01 91 Commissioning

01 91 13 – General Commissioning Requirements

01 91 13.50 Building Commissioning

		Crew	Daily Output	Labor-Hours	Unit	Material	Labor	Equipment	Total	Total Incl O&P
0010	**BUILDING COMMISSIONING**									
0100	Systems operation and verification during turnover				%				.25%	.25%
0150	Including all systems subcontractors								.50%	.50%
0200	Systems design assistance, operation, verification and training								.50%	.50%
0250	Including all systems subcontractors								1%	1%

01 93 Facility Maintenance

01 93 13 – Facility Maintenance Procedures

01 93 13.15 Mechanical Facilities Maintenance

			Crew	Daily Output	Labor-Hours	Unit	Material	Labor	Equipment	Total	Total Incl O&P
0010	**MECHANICAL FACILITIES MAINTENANCE**										
0100	Air conditioning system maintenance										
0800	Ductwork, clean										
0810	Rectangular										
0820	6"	G	1 Shee	187.50	.043	L.F.		2.55		2.55	3.89
0830	8"	G		140.63	.057			3.40		3.40	5.20
0840	10"	G		112.50	.071			4.25		4.25	6.50
0850	12"	G		93.75	.085			5.10		5.10	7.80
0860	14"	G		80.36	.100			5.95		5.95	9.10
0870	16"	G		70.31	.114			6.80		6.80	10.40
0900	Round										
0910	4"	G	1 Shee	358.10	.022	L.F.		1.34		1.34	2.04
0920	6"	G		238.73	.034			2		2	3.06
0930	8"	G		179.05	.045			2.67		2.67	4.08
0940	10"	G		143.24	.056			3.34		3.34	5.10
0950	12"	G		119.37	.067			4.01		4.01	6.10
0960	16"	G		89.52	.089			5.35		5.35	8.15

Division Notes

		CREW	DAILY OUTPUT	LABOR-HOURS	UNIT	MAT.	LABOR	EQUIP.	TOTAL	TOTAL INCL O&P
							BARE COSTS			

Estimating Tips
02 30 00 Subsurface Investigation
In preparing estimates on structures involving earthwork or foundations, all information concerning soil characteristics should be obtained. Look particularly for hazardous waste, evidence of prior dumping of debris, and previous stream beds.

02 40 00 Demolition and Structure Moving
The costs shown for selective demolition do not include rubbish handling or disposal. These items should be estimated separately using RSMeans data or other sources.
- Historic preservation often requires that the contractor remove materials from the existing structure, rehab them, and replace them. The estimator must be aware of any related measures and precautions that must be taken when doing selective demolition and cutting and patching. Requirements may include special handling and storage, as well as security.
- In addition to Subdivision 02 41 00, you can find selective demolition items in each division. Example: Roofing demolition is in Division 7.
- Absent of any other specific reference, an approximate demolish-in-place cost can be obtained by halving the new-install labor cost. To remove for reuse, allow the entire new-install labor figure.

02 40 00 Building Deconstruction
This section provides costs for the careful dismantling and recycling of most low-rise building materials.

02 50 00 Containment of Hazardous Waste
This section addresses on-site hazardous waste disposal costs.

02 80 00 Hazardous Material Disposal/Remediation
This subdivision includes information on hazardous waste handling, asbestos remediation, lead remediation, and mold remediation. See reference numbers R028213-20 and R028319-60 for further guidance in using these unit price lines.

02 90 00 Monitoring Chemical Sampling, Testing Analysis
This section provides costs for on-site sampling and testing hazardous waste.

Reference Numbers
Reference numbers are shown at the beginning of some major classifications. These numbers refer to related items in the Reference Section. The reference information may be an estimating procedure, an alternate pricing method, or technical information.

Note: Not all subdivisions listed here necessarily appear. ∎

Did you know?

RSMeans data is available through our online application with 24/7 access:
- Search for unit prices by keyword
- Leverage the most up-to-date data
- Build and export estimates

Try it free for 30 days!
www.rsmeans.com/2018freetrial

No part of this cost data may be reproduced, stored in a retrieval system, or transmitted in any form or by any means without prior written permission of Gordian.

02 41 Demolition

02 41 16 – Structure Demolition

02 41 16.19 Minor Building Deconstruction

		Crew	Daily Output	Labor-Hours	Unit	Material	2018 Bare Costs Labor	Equipment	Total	Total Incl O&P
0010	**MINOR BUILDING DECONSTRUCTION** R024119-10									
0011	For salvage, avg house									
0225	2 story, pre 1970 house, 1400 S.F., labor for all salv mat, min	G	6 Clab	25	1.920	SF Flr.		76.50		76.50	117
0230	Maximum	G	"	15	3.200	"		128		128	194
0235	Salvage of carpet, tackless	G	2 Clab	2400	.007	S.F.		.27		.27	.40
0240	Wood floors, incl denailing and packaging	G	3 Clab	270	.089	"		3.54		3.54	5.40
0260	Wood doors and trim, standard	G	1 Clab	16	.500	Ea.		19.95		19.95	30.50
0280	Base or cove mouldings, incl denailing and packaging	G		500	.016	L.F.		.64		.64	.97
0320	Closet shelving and trim, incl denailing and packaging	G		18	.444	Set		17.70		17.70	27
0340	Kitchen cabinets, uppers and lowers, prefab type	G	2 Clab	24	.667	L.F.		26.50		26.50	40.50
0360	Kitchen cabinets, uppers and lowers, built-in	G		12	1.333	"		53		53	81
0370	Bath fixt, incl toilet, tub, vanity, and med cabinet	G		3	5.333	Set		213		213	325

02 41 19 – Selective Demolition

02 41 19.19 Selective Demolition

		Crew	Daily Output	Labor-Hours	Unit	Material	Labor	Equipment	Total	Total Incl O&P
0010	**SELECTIVE DEMOLITION**, Rubbish Handling									
0020	The following are to be added to the demolition prices									
0600	Dumpster, weekly rental, 1 dump/week, 6 C.Y. capacity (2 tons)					Week	415			415	455
0700	10 C.Y. capacity (3 tons)						480			480	530
0725	20 C.Y. capacity (5 tons)						565			565	625
0800	30 C.Y. capacity (7 tons)						730			730	800
0840	40 C.Y. capacity (10 tons)						775			775	850
2000	Load, haul, dump and return, 0'-50' haul, hand carried		2 Clab	24	.667	C.Y.		26.50		26.50	40.50
2005	Wheeled			37	.432			17.25		17.25	26.50
2040	0'-100' haul, hand carried			16.50	.970			38.50		38.50	59
2045	Wheeled			25	.640			25.50		25.50	39
2050	Forklift		A-3R	25	.320			16.40	5.95	22.35	31.50
2080	Haul and return, add per each extra 100' haul, hand carried		2 Clab	35.50	.451			17.95		17.95	27.50
2085	Wheeled			54	.296			11.80		11.80	18
2120	For travel in elevators, up to 10 floors, add			140	.114			4.55		4.55	6.95
2130	0'-50' haul, incl. up to 5 riser stairs, hand carried			23	.696			27.50		27.50	42
2135	Wheeled			35	.457			18.20		18.20	28
2140	6-10 riser stairs, hand carried			22	.727			29		29	44
2145	Wheeled			34	.471			18.75		18.75	28.50
2150	11-20 riser stairs, hand carried			20	.800			32		32	48.50
2155	Wheeled			31	.516			20.50		20.50	31.50
2160	21-40 riser stairs, hand carried			16	1			40		40	60.50
2165	Wheeled			24	.667			26.50		26.50	40.50
2170	0-100' haul, incl. 5 riser stairs, hand carried			15	1.067			42.50		42.50	65
2175	Wheeled			23	.696			27.50		27.50	42
2180	6-10 riser stairs, hand carried			14	1.143			45.50		45.50	69.50
2185	Wheeled			21	.762			30.50		30.50	46.50
2190	11-20 riser stairs, hand carried			12	1.333			53		53	81
2195	Wheeled			18	.889			35.50		35.50	54
2200	21-40 riser stairs, hand carried			8	2			79.50		79.50	121
2205	Wheeled			12	1.333			53		53	81

For customer support on your Green Building Costs with RSMeans data, call 800.448.8182.

02 42 Removal and Salvage of Construction Materials

02 42 10 – Building Deconstruction

02 42 10.10 Estimated Salvage Value or Savings

			Crew	Daily Output	Labor-Hours	Unit	Material	2018 Bare Costs Labor	Equipment	Total	Total Incl O&P
0010	**ESTIMATED SALVAGE VALUE OR SAVINGS**										
0015	Excludes material handling, packaging, container costs and										
0020	transportation for salvage or disposal										
0050	All items in Section 02 42 10.10 are credit deducts and not costs										
0100	Copper wire salvage value	G				Lb.				1.60	1.60
0110	Disposal savings	G								.04	.04
0200	Copper pipe salvage value	G								2.50	2.50
0210	Disposal savings	G								.05	.05
0300	Steel pipe salvage value	G								.06	.06
0310	Disposal savings	G								.03	.03
0400	Cast iron pipe salvage value	G								.03	.03
0410	Disposal savings	G								.01	.01
0500	Steel doors or windows salvage value	G								.06	.06
0510	Aluminum	G								.55	.55
0520	Disposal savings	G								.03	.03
0600	Aluminum siding salvage value	G								.49	.49
0630	Disposal savings	G				↓				.03	.03
0640	Wood siding (no lead or asbestos)	G				C.Y.				12	12
0800	Clean concrete disposal savings	G				Ton				62	62
0850	Asphalt shingles disposal savings	G				"				60	60
1000	Wood wall framing clean salvage value	G				M.B.F.				55	55
1010	Painted	G								44	44
1020	Floor framing	G								55	55
1030	Painted	G								44	44
1050	Roof framing	G								55	55
1060	Painted	G								44	44
1100	Wood beams salvage value	G				↓				55	55
1200	Wood framing and beams disposal savings	G				Ton				66	66
1220	Wood sheathing and sub-base flooring	G								72.50	72.50
1230	Wood wall paneling (1/4" thick)	G				↓				66	66
1300	Wood panel 3/4"-1" thick low salvage value	G				S.F.				.55	.55
1350	High salvage value	G				"				2.20	2.20
1400	Disposal savings	G				Ton				66	66
1500	Flooring tongue and groove 25/32" thick low salvage value	G				S.F.				.55	.55
1530	High salvage value	G				"				1.10	1.10
1560	Disposal savings	G				Ton				66	66
1600	Drywall or sheet rock salvage value	G								22	22
1650	Disposal savings	G				↓				66	66

02 42 10.20 Deconstruction of Building Components

			Crew	Daily Output	Labor-Hours	Unit	Material	Labor	Equipment	Total	Total Incl O&P
0010	**DECONSTRUCTION OF BUILDING COMPONENTS**										
0012	Buildings one or two stories only										
0015	Excludes material handling, packaging, container costs and										
0020	transportation for salvage or disposal										
0050	Deconstruction of plumbing fixtures										
0100	Wall hung or countertop lavatory	G	2 Clab	16	1	Ea.		40		40	60.50
0110	Single or double compartment kitchen sink	G		14	1.143			45.50		45.50	69.50
0120	Wall hung urinal	G		14	1.143			45.50		45.50	69.50
0130	Floor mounted	G		8	2			79.50		79.50	121
0140	Floor mounted water closet	G		16	1			40		40	60.50
0150	Wall hung	G		14	1.143			45.50		45.50	69.50
0160	Water fountain, free standing	G		16	1			40		40	60.50
0170	Wall hung or deck mounted	G	↓	12	1.333	↓		53		53	81

For customer support on your Green Building Costs with RSMeans data, call 800.448.8182.

02 42 Removal and Salvage of Construction Materials

02 42 10 – Building Deconstruction

02 42 10.20 Deconstruction of Building Components		Crew	Daily Output	Labor-Hours	Unit	Material	2018 Bare Costs Labor	Equipment	Total	Total Incl O&P
0180	Bathtub, steel or fiberglass	2 Clab	10	1.600	Ea.		64		64	97
0190	Cast iron	G	8	2			79.50		79.50	121
0200	Shower, single	G	6	2.667			106		106	162
0210	Group	G	7	2.286			91		91	139
0300	Deconstruction of electrical fixtures									
0310	Surface mounted incandescent fixtures	G 2 Clab	48	.333	Ea.		13.30		13.30	20
0320	Fluorescent, 2 lamp	G	32	.500			19.95		19.95	30.50
0330	4 lamp	G	24	.667			26.50		26.50	40.50
0340	Strip fluorescent, 1 lamp	G	40	.400			15.95		15.95	24.50
0350	2 lamp	G	32	.500			19.95		19.95	30.50
0400	Recessed drop-in fluorescent fixture, 2 lamp	G	27	.593			23.50		23.50	36
0410	4 lamp	G	18	.889			35.50		35.50	54
0500	Deconstruction of appliances									
0510	Cooking stoves	G 2 Clab	26	.615	Ea.		24.50		24.50	37.50
0520	Dishwashers	G "	26	.615	"		24.50		24.50	37.50
0600	Deconstruction of millwork and trim									
0610	Cabinets, wood	G 2 Carp	40	.400	L.F.		20.50		20.50	31
0620	Countertops	G	100	.160	"		8.10		8.10	12.35
0630	Wall paneling, 1" thick	G	500	.032	S.F.		1.62		1.62	2.47
0640	Ceiling trim	G	500	.032	L.F.		1.62		1.62	2.47
0650	Wainscoting	G	500	.032	S.F.		1.62		1.62	2.47
0660	Base, 3/4"-1" thick	G	600	.027	L.F.		1.35		1.35	2.06
0700	Deconstruction of doors and windows									
0710	Doors, wrap, interior, wood, single, no closers	G 2 Carp	21	.762	Ea.	4.75	38.50		43.25	64.50
0720	Double	G	13	1.231		9.50	62.50		72	105
0730	Solid core, single, exterior or interior	G	10	1.600		4.75	81		85.75	129
0740	Double	G	8	2		9.50	101		110.50	164
0810	Windows, wrap, wood, single									
0812	with no casement or cladding	G 2 Carp	21	.762	Ea.	4.75	38.50		43.25	64.50
0820	with casement and/or cladding	G "	18	.889	"	4.75	45		49.75	74
0900	Deconstruction of interior finishes									
0910	Drywall for recycling	G 2 Clab	1775	.009	S.F.		.36		.36	.55
0920	Plaster wall, first floor	G	1775	.009			.36		.36	.55
0930	Second floor	G	1330	.012			.48		.48	.73
1000	Deconstruction of roofing and accessories									
1010	Built-up roofs	G 2 Clab	570	.028	S.F.		1.12		1.12	1.70
1020	Gutters, fascia and rakes	G "	1140	.014	L.F.		.56		.56	.85
2000	Deconstruction of wood components									
2010	Roof sheeting	G 2 Clab	570	.028	S.F.		1.12		1.12	1.70
2020	Main roof framing	G	760	.021	L.F.		.84		.84	1.28
2030	Porch roof framing	G	445	.036			1.43		1.43	2.18
2040	Beams 4" x 8"	G B-1	375	.064			2.59		2.59	3.95
2050	4" x 10"	G	300	.080			3.24		3.24	4.94
2055	4" x 12"	G	250	.096			3.89		3.89	5.95
2060	6" x 8"	G	250	.096			3.89		3.89	5.95
2065	6" x 10"	G	200	.120			4.86		4.86	7.40
2070	6" x 12"	G	170	.141			5.70		5.70	8.70
2075	8" x 12"	G	126	.190			7.70		7.70	11.75
2080	10" x 12"	G	100	.240			9.70		9.70	14.80
2100	Ceiling joists	G 2 Clab	800	.020			.80		.80	1.21
2150	Wall framing, interior	G	1230	.013			.52		.52	.79
2160	Sub-floor	G	2000	.008	S.F.		.32		.32	.49
2170	Floor joists	G	2000	.008	L.F.		.32		.32	.49

02 42 Removal and Salvage of Construction Materials

02 42 10 – Building Deconstruction

02 42 10.20 Deconstruction of Building Components

			Crew	Daily Output	Labor-Hours	Unit	Material	2018 Bare Costs Labor	Equipment	Total	Total Incl O&P
2200	Wood siding (no lead or asbestos)	G	2 Clab	1300	.012	S.F.		.49		.49	.75
2300	Wall framing, exterior	G		1600	.010	L.F.		.40		.40	.61
2400	Stair risers	G		53	.302	Ea.		12.05		12.05	18.30
2500	Posts	G		800	.020	L.F.		.80		.80	1.21
3000	Deconstruction of exterior brick walls										
3010	Exterior brick walls, first floor	G	2 Clab	200	.080	S.F.		3.19		3.19	4.86
3020	Second floor	G		64	.250	"		9.95		9.95	15.20
3030	Brick chimney	G		100	.160	C.F.		6.40		6.40	9.70
4000	Deconstruction of concrete										
4010	Slab on grade, 4" thick, plain concrete	G	B-9	500	.080	S.F.		3.22	.47	3.69	5.40
4020	Wire mesh reinforced	G		470	.085			3.43	.50	3.93	5.75
4030	Rod reinforced	G		400	.100			4.03	.59	4.62	6.80
4110	Foundation wall, 6" thick, plain concrete	G		160	.250			10.05	1.46	11.51	16.95
4120	8" thick	G		140	.286			11.50	1.67	13.17	19.35
4130	10" thick	G		120	.333			13.40	1.95	15.35	22.50
9000	Deconstruction process, support equipment as needed										
9010	Daily use, portal to portal, 12-ton truck-mounted hydraulic crane crew	G	A-3H	1	8	Day		450	630	1,080	1,375
9020	Daily use, skid steer and operator	G	A-3C	1	8			410	365	775	1,025
9030	Daily use, backhoe 48 HP, operator and labor	G	"	1	8			410	365	775	1,025

02 42 10.30 Deconstruction Material Handling

			Crew	Daily Output	Labor-Hours	Unit	Material	Labor	Equipment	Total	Total Incl O&P
0010	**DECONSTRUCTION MATERIAL HANDLING**										
0012	Buildings one or two stories only										
0100	Clean and stack brick on pallet	G	2 Clab	1200	.013	Ea.		.53		.53	.81
0200	Haul 50' and load rough lumber up to 2" x 8" size	G		2000	.008	"		.32		.32	.49
0210	Lumber larger than 2" x 8"	G		3200	.005	B.F.		.20		.20	.30
0300	Finish wood for recycling stack and wrap per pallet	G		8	2	Ea.	38	79.50		117.50	163
0350	Light fixtures			6	2.667		68.50	106		174.50	237
0375	Windows			6	2.667		64.50	106		170.50	233
0400	Miscellaneous materials			8	2		19	79.50		98.50	142

02 43 Structure Moving

02 43 13 – Structure Relocation

02 43 13.13 Building Relocation

			Crew	Daily Output	Labor-Hours	Unit	Material	Labor	Equipment	Total	Total Incl O&P
0010	**BUILDING RELOCATION**										
0011	One day move, up to 24' wide										
0020	Reset on existing foundation					Total				11,500	11,500
0040	Wood or steel frame bldg., based on ground floor area	G	B-4	185	.259	S.F.		10.70	2.54	13.24	19.05
0060	Masonry bldg., based on ground floor area	G	"	137	.350			14.45	3.43	17.88	26
0200	For 24'-42' wide, add									15%	15%

02 65 Underground Storage Tank Removal

02 65 10 – Underground Tank and Contaminated Soil Removal

02 65 10.30 Removal of Underground Storage Tanks		Crew	Daily Output	Labor-Hours	Unit	Material	2018 Bare Costs Labor	Equipment	Total	Total Incl O&P
0010	**REMOVAL OF UNDERGROUND STORAGE TANKS**	R026510-20								
0011	Petroleum storage tanks, non-leaking									
0100	Excavate & load onto trailer									
0110	3,000 gal. to 5,000 gal. tank	G	B-14	4	12	Ea.		505	78	583	855
0120	6,000 gal. to 8,000 gal. tank	G	B-3A	3	13.333			570	298	868	1,200
0130	9,000 gal. to 12,000 gal. tank	G	"	2	20			855	445	1,300	1,800
0190	Known leaking tank, add					%				100%	100%
0200	Remove sludge, water and remaining product from bottom										
0201	of tank with vacuum truck										
0300	3,000 gal. to 5,000 gal. tank	G	A-13	5	1.600	Ea.		82	144	226	282
0310	6,000 gal. to 8,000 gal. tank	G		4	2			103	180	283	355
0320	9,000 gal. to 12,000 gal. tank	G		3	2.667			137	240	377	470
0390	Dispose of sludge off-site, average					Gal.				6.25	6.80
0400	Insert inert solid CO_2 "dry ice" into tank										
0401	For cleaning/transporting tanks (1.5 lb./100 gal. cap)	G	1 Clab	500	.016	Lb.	1.19	.64		1.83	2.28
0403	Insert solid carbon dioxide, 1.5 lb./100 gal.	G	"	400	.020	"	1.19	.80		1.99	2.52
0503	Disconnect and remove piping	G	1 Plum	160	.050	L.F.		3.11		3.11	4.68
0603	Transfer liquids, 10% of volume	G	"	1600	.005	Gal.		.31		.31	.47
0703	Cut accessway into underground storage tank	G	1 Clab	5.33	1.501	Ea.		60		60	91
0813	Remove sludge, wash and wipe tank, 500 gal.	G	1 Plum	8	1			62		62	93.50
0823	3,000 gal.	G		6.67	1.199			74.50		74.50	112
0833	5,000 gal.	G		6.15	1.301			81		81	122
0843	8,000 gal.	G		5.33	1.501			93.50		93.50	140
0853	10,000 gal.	G		4.57	1.751			109		109	164
0863	12,000 gal.	G		4.21	1.900			118		118	178
1020	Haul tank to certified salvage dump, 100 miles round trip										
1023	3,000 gal. to 5,000 gal. tank					Ea.				760	830
1026	6,000 gal. to 8,000 gal. tank									880	960
1029	9,000 gal. to 12,000 gal. tank									1,050	1,150
1100	Disposal of contaminated soil to landfill										
1110	Minimum					C.Y.				145	160
1111	Maximum					"				400	440
1120	Disposal of contaminated soil to										
1121	bituminous concrete batch plant										
1130	Minimum					C.Y.				80	88
1131	Maximum					"				115	125
1203	Excavate, pull, & load tank, backfill hole, 8,000 gal. +	G	B-12C	.50	32	Ea.		1,525	2,100	3,625	4,650
1213	Haul tank to certified dump, 100 miles rt, 8,000 gal. +	G	B-34K	1	8			370	835	1,205	1,475
1223	Excavate, pull, & load tank, backfill hole, 500 gal.	G	B-11C	1	16			750	310	1,060	1,475
1233	Excavate, pull, & load tank, backfill hole, 3,000-5,000 gal.	G	B-11M	.50	32			1,500	770	2,270	3,125
1243	Haul tank to certified dump, 100 miles rt, 500 gal.	G	B-34L	1	8			410	188	598	825
1253	Haul tank to certified dump, 100 miles rt, 3,000-5,000 gal.	G	B-34M	1	8			410	238	648	880
2010	Decontamination of soil on site incl poly tarp on top/bottom										
2011	Soil containment berm and chemical treatment										
2020	Minimum	G	B-11C	100	.160	C.Y.	7.45	7.50	3.12	18.07	23
2021	Maximum	G	"	100	.160		9.65	7.50	3.12	20.27	25.50
2050	Disposal of decontaminated soil, minimum									135	150
2055	Maximum									400	440

02 81 Transportation and Disposal of Hazardous Materials

02 81 20 – Hazardous Waste Handling

02 81 20.10 Hazardous Waste Cleanup/Pickup/Disposal

		Crew	Daily Output	Labor-Hours	Unit	Material	2018 Bare Costs Labor	Equipment	Total	Total Incl O&P
0010	**HAZARDOUS WASTE CLEANUP/PICKUP/DISPOSAL**									
0100	For contractor rental equipment, i.e., dozer,									
0110	Front end loader, dump truck, etc., see 01 54 33 Reference Section									
1000	Solid pickup									
1100	55 gal. drums				Ea.				240	265
1120	Bulk material, minimum				Ton				190	210
1130	Maximum				"				595	655
1200	Transportation to disposal site									
1220	Truckload = 80 drums or 25 C.Y. or 18 tons									
1260	Minimum				Mile				3.95	4.45
1270	Maximum				"				7.25	7.35
3000	Liquid pickup, vacuum truck, stainless steel tank									
3100	Minimum charge, 4 hours									
3110	1 compartment, 2200 gallon				Hr.				140	155
3120	2 compartment, 5000 gallon				"				200	225
3400	Transportation in 6900 gallon bulk truck				Mile				7.95	8.75
3410	In teflon lined truck				"				10.20	11.25
5000	Heavy sludge or dry vacuumable material				Hr.				140	160
6000	Dumpsite disposal charge, minimum				Ton				140	155
6020	Maximum				"				415	455

02 82 Asbestos Remediation

02 82 13 – Asbestos Abatement

02 82 13.39 Asbestos Remediation Plans and Methods

0010	**ASBESTOS REMEDIATION PLANS AND METHODS**									
0100	Building Survey-Commercial Building				Ea.				2,200	2,400
0200	Asbestos Abatement Remediation Plan				"				1,350	1,475

02 83 Lead Remediation

02 83 19 – Lead-Based Paint Remediation

02 83 19.21 Lead Paint Remediation Plans and Methods

0010	**LEAD PAINT REMEDIATION PLANS AND METHODS**									
0100	Building Survey-Commercial Building				Ea.				2,050	2,250
0200	Lead Abatement Remediation Plan									1,225	1,350
0300	Lead Paint Testing, AAS Analysis									51	56
0400	Lead Paint Testing, X-Ray Fluorescence				▼				51	56

Division Notes

	CREW	DAILY OUTPUT	LABOR-HOURS	UNIT	BARE COSTS MAT.	LABOR	EQUIP.	TOTAL	TOTAL INCL O&P

Estimating Tips
General
- Carefully check all the plans and specifications. Concrete often appears on drawings other than structural drawings, including mechanical and electrical drawings for equipment pads. The cost of cutting and patching is often difficult to estimate. See Subdivision 03 81 for Concrete Cutting, Subdivision 02 41 19.16 for Cutout Demolition, Subdivision 03 05 05.10 for Concrete Demolition, and Subdivision 02 41 19.19 for Rubbish Handling (handling, loading, and hauling of debris).
- Always obtain concrete prices from suppliers near the job site. A volume discount can often be negotiated, depending upon competition in the area. Remember to add for waste, particularly for slabs and footings on grade.

03 10 00 Concrete Forming and Accessories
- A primary cost for concrete construction is forming. Most jobs today are constructed with prefabricated forms. The selection of the forms best suited for the job and the total square feet of forms required for efficient concrete forming and placing are key elements in estimating concrete construction. Enough forms must be available for erection to make efficient use of the concrete placing equipment and crew.
- Concrete accessories for forming and placing depend upon the systems used. Study the plans and specifications to ensure that all special accessory requirements have been included in the cost estimate, such as anchor bolts, inserts, and hangers.
- Included within costs for forms-in-place are all necessary bracing and shoring.

03 20 00 Concrete Reinforcing
- Ascertain that the reinforcing steel supplier has included all accessories, cutting, bending, and an allowance for lapping, splicing, and waste. A good rule of thumb is 10% for lapping, splicing, and waste. Also, 10% waste should be allowed for welded wire fabric.
- The unit price items in the subdivisions for Reinforcing In Place, Glass Fiber Reinforcing, and Welded Wire Fabric include the labor to install accessories such as beam and slab bolsters, high chairs, and bar ties and tie wire. The material cost for these accessories is not included; they may be obtained from the Accessories Subdivisions.

03 30 00 Cast-In-Place Concrete
- When estimating structural concrete, pay particular attention to requirements for concrete additives, curing methods, and surface treatments. Special consideration for climate, hot or cold, must be included in your estimate. Be sure to include requirements for concrete placing equipment and concrete finishing.
- For accurate concrete estimating, the estimator must consider each of the following major components individually: forms, reinforcing steel, ready-mix concrete, placement of the concrete, and finishing of the top surface. For faster estimating, Subdivision 03 30 53.40 for Concrete-In-Place can be used; here, various items of concrete work are presented that include the costs of all five major components (unless specifically stated otherwise).

03 40 00 Precast Concrete
03 50 00 Cast Decks and Underlayment
- The cost of hauling precast concrete structural members is often an important factor. For this reason, it is important to get a quote from the nearest supplier. It may become economically feasible to set up precasting beds on the site if the hauling costs are prohibitive.

Reference Numbers
Reference numbers are shown at the beginning of some major classifications. These numbers refer to related items in the Reference Section. The reference information may be an estimating procedure, an alternate pricing method, or technical information.

Note: Not all subdivisions listed here necessarily appear. ■

Did you know?

RSMeans data is available through our online application with 24/7 access:
- Search for unit prices by keyword
- Leverage the most up-to-date data
- Build and export estimates

Try it free for 30 days!
www.rsmeans.com/2018freetrial

03 05 Common Work Results for Concrete

03 05 05 – Selective Demolition for Concrete

03 05 05.10 Selective Demolition, Concrete

		Crew	Daily Output	Labor-Hours	Unit	Material	2018 Bare Costs Labor	Equipment	Total	Total Incl O&P
0010	**SELECTIVE DEMOLITION, CONCRETE** R024119-10									
0012	Excludes saw cutting, torch cutting, loading or hauling									
0050	Break into small pieces, reinf. less than 1% of cross-sectional area	B-9	24	1.667	C.Y.		67	9.75	76.75	113
0060	Reinforcing 1% to 2% of cross-sectional area		16	2.500			101	14.65	115.65	169
0070	Reinforcing more than 2% of cross-sectional area		8	5			201	29.50	230.50	335
0150	Remove whole pieces, up to 2 tons per piece	E-18	36	1.111	Ea.		61	30	91	131
0160	2-5 tons per piece		30	1.333			73	36	109	158
0170	5-10 tons per piece		24	1.667			91.50	45	136.50	197
0180	10-15 tons per piece		18	2.222			122	60	182	262
0250	Precast unit embedded in masonry, up to 1 C.F.	D-1	16	1			45		45	68.50
0260	1-2 C.F.		12	1.333			59.50		59.50	91.50
0270	2-5 C.F.		10	1.600			71.50		71.50	110
0280	5-10 C.F.		8	2			89.50		89.50	137

03 05 13 – Basic Concrete Materials

03 05 13.20 Concrete Admixtures and Surface Treatments

					Unit	Material			Total	Total Incl O&P
0010	**CONCRETE ADMIXTURES AND SURFACE TREATMENTS**									
0200	Air entraining agent, .7 to 1.5 oz. per bag, 55 gallon drum				Gal.	21			21	23
0220	5 gallon pail					29			29	32
0920	Dustproofing compound, 250 S.F./gal., 5 gallon pail					7.10			7.10	7.80
1590	Concrete release agent for forms, 100% biodegradable, zero VOC, 5 gal. pail G					21.50			21.50	23.50
1595	55 gallon drum G					18.15			18.15	19.95
1650	Sealer, water based, 350 S.F., 55 gallon drum					21.50			21.50	23.50
1660	5 gallon pail					24			24	26.50
6000	Concrete ready mix additives, recycled coal fly ash, mixed at plant G				Ton	63			63	69
6010	Recycled blast furnace slag, mixed at plant G				"	90.50			90.50	99.50

03 05 13.25 Aggregate

					Unit	Material			Total	Total Incl O&P
0010	**AGGREGATE** R033105-20									
0100	Lightweight vermiculite or perlite, 4 C.F. bag, C.L. lots G				Bag	22.50			22.50	24.50
0150	L.C.L. lots G				"	25			25	27.50

03 11 Concrete Forming

03 11 13 – Structural Cast-In-Place Concrete Forming

03 11 13.05 Forms, Buy or Rent

					Unit	Material			Total	Total Incl O&P
0010	**FORMS, BUY OR RENT**									
0015	Aluminum, smooth face, 3' x 8', buy G				SFCA	12.95			12.95	14.25
0020	2' x 8' G					16.80			16.80	18.50
0050	12" x 8' G					21			21	23
0100	6" x 8' G					28.50			28.50	31
0150	3' x 4' G					15.75			15.75	17.35
0200	2' x 4' G					19.15			19.15	21
0250	12" x 4' G					24.50			24.50	27
0300	6" x 4' G					34			34	37
0500	Textured brick face, 3' x 8', buy G					15.65			15.65	17.25
0550	2' x 8' G					22			22	24.50
0600	12" x 8' G					31.50			31.50	34.50
0650	6" x 8' G					49			49	54
0700	3' x 4' G					19.45			19.45	21.50
0750	2' x 4' G					26.50			26.50	29.50
0800	12" x 4' G					38			38	41.50
0850	6" x 4' G					59			59	65

03 11 Concrete Forming

03 11 13 – Structural Cast-In-Place Concrete Forming

03 11 13.05 Forms, Buy or Rent

		Crew	Daily Output	Labor-Hours	Unit	Material	2018 Bare Costs Labor	Equipment	Total	Total Incl O&P
1000	Average cost incl. accessories but not incl. ties, buy	G			SFCA	22.50			22.50	25
1100	Rent per month	G					1.13		1.13	1.25

03 11 13.20 Forms In Place, Beams and Girders

			Crew	Daily Output	Labor-Hours	Unit	Material	Labor	Equipment	Total	Total Incl O&P
0010	**FORMS IN PLACE, BEAMS AND GIRDERS**	R031113-40									
0500	Exterior spandrel, job-built plywood, 12" wide, 1 use	R031113-60	C-2	225	.213	SFCA	3.05	10.50		13.55	19.35
0550	2 use			275	.175		1.60	8.60		10.20	14.85
0600	3 use			295	.163		1.22	8		9.22	13.55
0650	4 use			310	.155		.99	7.60		8.59	12.70
2000	Interior beam, job-built plywood, 12" wide, 1 use			300	.160		3.71	7.90		11.61	16.10
2050	2 use			340	.141		1.79	6.95		8.74	12.55
2100	3 use			364	.132		1.48	6.50		7.98	11.55
2150	4 use			377	.127		1.21	6.25		7.46	10.90

03 11 13.25 Forms In Place, Columns

				Crew	Daily Output	Labor-Hours	Unit	Material	Labor	Equipment	Total	Total Incl O&P
0010	**FORMS IN PLACE, COLUMNS**	R031113-40										
1500	Round fiber tube, recycled paper, 1 use, 8" diameter		G	C-1	155	.206	L.F.	2.88	9.90		12.78	18.25
1550	10" diameter		G		155	.206		3.61	9.90		13.51	19.05
1600	12" diameter		G		150	.213		4.05	10.25		14.30	20
1650	14" diameter		G		145	.221		4.29	10.60		14.89	21
1700	16" diameter		G		140	.229		5.30	10.95		16.25	22.50
1720	18" diameter		G		140	.229		6.20	10.95		17.15	23.50
1750	20" diameter		G		135	.237		7.75	11.40		19.15	26
1800	24" diameter		G		130	.246		9.65	11.80		21.45	28.50
1850	30" diameter		G		125	.256		14.50	12.30		26.80	34.50
1900	36" diameter		G		115	.278		19.60	13.35		32.95	42
1950	42" diameter		G		100	.320		43.50	15.35		58.85	71.50
2000	48" diameter		G		85	.376		54.50	18.05		72.55	87.50
2200	For seamless type, add							15%				
3000	Round, steel, 4 use per mo., rent, regular duty, 14" diameter		G	C-1	145	.221	L.F.	18.10	10.60		28.70	36
3050	16" diameter		G		125	.256		18.45	12.30		30.75	39
3100	Heavy duty, 20" diameter		G		105	.305		20	14.65		34.65	44.50
3150	24" diameter		G		85	.376		22	18.05		40.05	51.50
3200	30" diameter		G		70	.457		25	22		47	61
3250	36" diameter		G		60	.533		27	25.50		52.50	68.50
3300	48" diameter		G		50	.640		40	30.50		70.50	91
3350	60" diameter		G		45	.711		49.50	34		83.50	107
4500	For second and succeeding months, deduct							50%				
5000	Job-built plywood, 8" x 8" columns, 1 use			C-1	165	.194	SFCA	2.66	9.30		11.96	17.10
5050	2 use				195	.164		1.52	7.90		9.42	13.70
5100	3 use				210	.152		1.06	7.30		8.36	12.30
5150	4 use				215	.149		.88	7.15		8.03	11.85
5500	12" x 12" columns, 1 use				180	.178		2.58	8.55		11.13	15.85
5550	2 use				210	.152		1.42	7.30		8.72	12.70
5600	3 use				220	.145		1.03	7		8.03	11.80
5650	4 use				225	.142		.84	6.85		7.69	11.30
7400	Steel framed plywood, based on 50 uses of purchased											
7420	forms, and 4 uses of bracing lumber											
7500	8" x 8" column			C-1	340	.094	SFCA	2.18	4.52		6.70	9.30
7550	10" x 10"				350	.091		1.89	4.39		6.28	8.80
7600	12" x 12"				370	.086		1.61	4.15		5.76	8.05

03 11 Concrete Forming

03 11 13 – Structural Cast-In-Place Concrete Forming

03 11 13.35 Forms In Place, Elevated Slabs

			Crew	Daily Output	Labor-Hours	Unit	Material	2018 Bare Costs Labor	Equipment	Total	Total Incl O&P
0010	**FORMS IN PLACE, ELEVATED SLABS**	R031113-40									
1000	Flat plate, job-built plywood, to 15' high, 1 use	R031113-60	C-2	470	.102	S.F.	3.87	5.05		8.92	11.90
1050	2 use			520	.092		2.13	4.54		6.67	9.25
1100	3 use			545	.088		1.55	4.34		5.89	8.30
1150	4 use			560	.086		1.26	4.22		5.48	7.80
2000	Flat slab, drop panels, job-built plywood, to 15' high, 1 use			449	.107		4.45	5.25		9.70	12.90
2050	2 use			509	.094		2.45	4.64		7.09	9.75
2100	3 use			532	.090		1.78	4.44		6.22	8.70
2150	4 use			544	.088		1.45	4.34		5.79	8.20
6200	Slab bulkhead form, 4-1/2" high, exp metal, w/keyway & stakes G		C-1	1200	.027	L.F.	.91	1.28		2.19	2.95
6210	5-1/2" high G			1100	.029		1.14	1.40		2.54	3.38
6215	7-1/2" high G			960	.033		1.37	1.60		2.97	3.95
6220	9-1/2" high G			840	.038		1.49	1.83		3.32	4.42
8500	Void forms, round plastic, 8" high x 3" diameter G			450	.071	Ea.	2.02	3.41		5.43	7.40
8550	4" diameter G			425	.075		2.29	3.61		5.90	8
8600	6" diameter G			400	.080		4.09	3.84		7.93	10.35
8650	8" diameter G			375	.085		6.75	4.10		10.85	13.70

03 11 13.45 Forms In Place, Footings

			Crew	Daily Output	Labor-Hours	Unit	Material	Labor	Equipment	Total	Total Incl O&P
0010	**FORMS IN PLACE, FOOTINGS**										
0020	Continuous wall, plywood, 1 use		C-1	375	.085	SFCA	6.60	4.10		10.70	13.50
0050	2 use	R031113-60		440	.073		3.62	3.49		7.11	9.30
0100	3 use			470	.068		2.63	3.27		5.90	7.90
0150	4 use			485	.066		2.15	3.17		5.32	7.20
5000	Spread footings, job-built lumber, 1 use			305	.105		2.10	5.05		7.15	9.95
5050	2 use			371	.086		1.17	4.14		5.31	7.60
5100	3 use			401	.080		.84	3.83		4.67	6.75
5150	4 use			414	.077		.68	3.71		4.39	6.40

03 11 13.47 Forms In Place, Gas Station Forms

			Crew	Daily Output	Labor-Hours	Unit	Material	Labor	Equipment	Total	Total Incl O&P
0010	**FORMS IN PLACE, GAS STATION FORMS**										
0050	Curb fascia, with template, 12 ga. steel, left in place, 9" high G		1 Carp	50	.160	L.F.	14.10	8.10		22.20	28
1000	Sign or light bases, 18" diameter, 9" high G			9	.889	Ea.	89	45		134	166
1050	30" diameter, 13" high G			8	1		141	50.50		191.50	232
2000	Island forms, 10' long, 9" high, 3'-6" wide G		C-1	10	3.200		395	154		549	670
2050	4' wide G			9	3.556		405	171		576	710
2500	20' long, 9" high, 4' wide G			6	5.333		655	256		911	1,100
2550	5' wide G			5	6.400		680	305		985	1,225

03 11 13.50 Forms In Place, Grade Beam

			Crew	Daily Output	Labor-Hours	Unit	Material	Labor	Equipment	Total	Total Incl O&P
0010	**FORMS IN PLACE, GRADE BEAM**	R031113-40									
0020	Job-built plywood, 1 use		C-2	530	.091	SFCA	2.97	4.46		7.43	10.05
0050	2 use	R031113-60		580	.083		1.63	4.07		5.70	8
0100	3 use			600	.080		1.19	3.94		5.13	7.30
0150	4 use			605	.079		.96	3.91		4.87	7

03 11 13.55 Forms In Place, Mat Foundation

			Crew	Daily Output	Labor-Hours	Unit	Material	Labor	Equipment	Total	Total Incl O&P
0010	**FORMS IN PLACE, MAT FOUNDATION**	R031113-40									
0020	Job-built plywood, 1 use		C-2	290	.166	SFCA	2.93	8.15		11.08	15.60
0050	2 use	R031113-60		310	.155		1.15	7.60		8.75	12.85
0100	3 use			330	.145		.74	7.15		7.89	11.70
0120	4 use			350	.137		.68	6.75		7.43	11.05

03 11 Concrete Forming

03 11 13 – Structural Cast-In-Place Concrete Forming

03 11 13.65 Forms In Place, Slab On Grade

		Crew	Daily Output	Labor-Hours	Unit	Material	2018 Bare Costs Labor	Equipment	Total	Total Incl O&P
0010	**FORMS IN PLACE, SLAB ON GRADE**									
1000	Bulkhead forms w/keyway, wood, 6" high, 1 use	C-1	510	.063	L.F.	1.05	3.01		4.06	5.75
1050	2 uses		400	.080		.58	3.84		4.42	6.50
1100	4 uses		350	.091		.34	4.39		4.73	7.10
1400	Bulkhead form for slab, 4-1/2" high, exp metal, incl keyway & stakes		1200	.027		.91	1.28		2.19	2.95
1410	5-1/2" high		1100	.029		1.14	1.40		2.54	3.38
1420	7-1/2" high		960	.033		1.37	1.60		2.97	3.95
1430	9-1/2" high		840	.038		1.49	1.83		3.32	4.42
3000	Edge forms, wood, 4 use, on grade, to 6" high		600	.053		.29	2.56		2.85	4.22
3050	7" to 12" high		435	.074	SFCA	.69	3.53		4.22	6.15
3060	Over 12"		350	.091	"	.93	4.39		5.32	7.70
8760	Void form, corrugated fiberboard, 4" x 12", 4' long		3000	.011	S.F.	3.43	.51		3.94	4.55
8770	6" x 12", 4' long		3000	.011		4.10	.51		4.61	5.30
8780	1/4" thick hardboard protective cover for void form	2 Carp	1500	.011		.68	.54		1.22	1.57

03 11 13.85 Forms In Place, Walls

		Crew	Daily Output	Labor-Hours	Unit	Material	Labor	Equipment	Total	Total Incl O&P
0010	**FORMS IN PLACE, WALLS**									
0600	Bulkhead forms with keyway, 1 piece expanded metal, 8" wall	C-1	1000	.032	L.F.	1.37	1.54		2.91	3.85
0610	10" wall		800	.040		1.49	1.92		3.41	4.56
0620	12" wall		525	.061		1.79	2.93		4.72	6.40
2000	Wall, job-built plywood, to 8' high, 1 use	C-2	370	.130	SFCA	2.76	6.40		9.16	12.75
2050	2 use		435	.110		1.75	5.45		7.20	10.20
2100	3 use		495	.097		1.28	4.77		6.05	8.65
2150	4 use		505	.095		1.04	4.68		5.72	8.25
2400	Over 8' to 16' high, 1 use		280	.171		3.05	8.45		11.50	16.20
7800	Modular prefabricated plywood, based on 20 uses of purchased									
7820	forms, and 4 uses of bracing lumber									
7860	To 8' high	C-2	800	.060	SFCA	1.09	2.95		4.04	5.70
8060	Over 8' to 16' high	"	600	.080	"	1.15	3.94		5.09	7.25
9010	Steel framed plywood, based on 50 uses of purchased									
9020	forms, and 4 uses of bracing lumber									
9060	To 8' high	C-2	600	.080	SFCA	.73	3.94		4.67	6.80
9260	Over 8' to 16' high		450	.107		.73	5.25		5.98	8.80
9460	Over 16' to 20' high		400	.120		.73	5.90		6.63	9.80

03 11 19 – Insulating Concrete Forming

03 11 19.10 Insulating Forms, Left In Place

		Crew	Daily Output	Labor-Hours	Unit	Material	Labor	Equipment	Total	Total Incl O&P
0010	**INSULATING FORMS, LEFT IN PLACE**									
0020	S.F. is for exterior face, but includes forms for both faces (total R22)									
2000	4" wall, straight block, 16" x 48" (5.33 S.F.)	2 Carp	90	.178	Ea.	21	9		30	37
2010	90 corner block, exterior 16" x 38" x 22" (6.67 S.F.)		75	.213		25.50	10.80		36.30	44.50
2020	45 corner block, exterior 16" x 34" x 18" (5.78 S.F.)		75	.213		25	10.80		35.80	44
2100	6" wall, straight block, 16" x 48" (5.33 S.F.)		90	.178		22	9		31	37.50
2110	90 corner block, exterior 16" x 32" x 24" (6.22 S.F.)		75	.213		25	10.80		35.80	44
2120	45 corner block, exterior 16" x 26" x 18" (4.89 S.F.)		75	.213		24.50	10.80		35.30	43.50
2130	Brick ledge block, 16" x 48" (5.33 S.F.)		80	.200		27	10.15		37.15	45.50
2140	Taper top block, 16" x 48" (5.33 S.F.)		80	.200		25.50	10.15		35.65	43.50
2200	8" wall, straight block, 16" x 48" (5.33 S.F.)		90	.178		23	9		32	39
2210	90 corner block, exterior 16" x 34" x 26" (6.67 S.F.)		75	.213		31	10.80		41.80	50.50
2220	45 corner block, exterior 16" x 28" x 20" (5.33 S.F.)		75	.213		25.50	10.80		36.30	44.50
2230	Brick ledge block, 16" x 48" (5.33 S.F.)		80	.200		28	10.15		38.15	46.50
2240	Taper top block, 16" x 48" (5.33 S.F.)		80	.200		26.50	10.15		36.65	44.50

For customer support on your Green Building Costs with RSMeans data, call 800.448.8182.

03 11 Concrete Forming

03 11 19 – Insulating Concrete Forming

03 11 19.60 Roof Deck Form Boards

03 11 19.60 Roof Deck Form Boards		Crew	Daily Output	Labor-Hours	Unit	Material	2018 Bare Costs Labor	Equipment	Total	Total Incl O&P
0010	ROOF DECK FORM BOARDS R051223-50									
0050	Includes bulb tee sub-purlins @ 32-5/8" OC									
0070	Non-asbestos fiber cement, 5/16" thick	C-13	2950	.008	S.F.	2.97	.43	.03	3.43	3.99
0100	Fiberglass, 1" thick		2700	.009		3.65	.47	.04	4.16	4.81
0500	Wood fiber, 1" thick [G]		2700	.009		2.29	.47	.04	2.80	3.31

03 11 23 – Permanent Stair Forming

03 11 23.75 Forms In Place, Stairs

		Crew	Daily Output	Labor-Hours	Unit	Material	Labor	Equipment	Total	Total Incl O&P
0010	FORMS IN PLACE, STAIRS R031113-40									
0015	(Slant length x width), 1 use	C-2	165	.291	S.F.	5.75	14.30		20.05	28.50
0050	2 use R031113-60		170	.282		3.26	13.90		17.16	24.50
0100	3 use R031113-60		180	.267		2.44	13.15		15.59	22.50
0150	4 use R031113-60		190	.253		2.03	12.45		14.48	21

03 15 Concrete Accessories

03 15 05 – Concrete Forming Accessories

03 15 05.15 Column Form Accessories

					Unit	Material	Labor	Equipment	Total	Total Incl O&P
0010	COLUMN FORM ACCESSORIES									
1000	Column clamps, adjustable to 24" x 24", buy [G]				Set	172			172	189
1100	Rent per month [G]					12.25			12.25	13.50
1300	For sizes to 30" x 30", buy [G]					201			201	221
1400	Rent per month [G]					14.05			14.05	15.50
1600	For sizes to 36" x 36", buy [G]					248			248	273
1700	Rent per month [G]					17.20			17.20	18.95
2000	Bar type with wedges, 36" x 36", buy [G]					160			160	176
2100	Rent per month [G]					11.20			11.20	12.30
2300	48" x 48", buy [G]					220			220	242
2400	Rent per month [G]					15.40			15.40	16.95
3000	Scissor type with wedges, 36" x 36", buy [G]					138			138	151
3100	Rent per month [G]					13.75			13.75	15.15
3300	60" x 60", buy [G]					192			192	211
3400	Rent per month [G]					19.25			19.25	21
4000	Friction collars 2'-6" diam., buy [G]					2,700			2,700	2,975
4100	Rent per month [G]					189			189	208
4300	4'-0" diam., buy [G]					3,300			3,300	3,625
4400	Rent per month [G]					231			231	254

03 15 05.30 Hangers

					Unit	Material	Labor	Equipment	Total	Total Incl O&P
0010	HANGERS									
0020	Slab and beam form									
0500	Banding iron									
0550	3/4" x 22 ga., 14 L.F./lb. or 1/2" x 14 ga., 7 L.F./lb. [G]				Lb.	1.37			1.37	1.51
1000	Fascia ties, coil type, to 24" long [G]				C	465			465	515
1500	Frame ties to 8-1/8" [G]					545			545	600
1550	8-1/8" to 10-1/8" [G]					575			575	635
1600	10-1/8" to 12-1/8" [G]					590			590	650
1650	12-1/8" to 14-1/8" [G]					610			610	670
1700	14-1/8" to 16-1/8" [G]					630			630	695
2000	Half hanger [G]					800			800	880
2500	Haunch hanger, for 1" haunch									
2600	Flange to 8-1/8" [G]				C	595			595	655
2650	8-1/8" to 10-1/8" [G]					630			630	695

03 15 Concrete Accessories

03 15 05 – Concrete Forming Accessories

03 15 05.30 Hangers

			Crew	Daily Output	Labor-Hours	Unit	Material	2018 Bare Costs Labor	Equipment	Total	Total Incl O&P
2700	10-1/8" to 12-1/8"	G				C	660			660	730
2750	12-1/8" to 14-1/8"	G					685			685	750
2800	14-1/8" to 16-1/8"	G					720			720	795
3000	Haunch half hanger, for 1" haunch	G					420			420	465
5000	Snap tie hanger, to 30" overall length, 3000#	G					465			465	515
5050	To 36" overall length	G					525			525	580
5100	To 48" overall length	G					645			645	710
5500	Steel beam hanger										
5600	Flange to 8-1/8"	G				C	545			545	600
5650	8-1/8" to 10-1/8"	G					575			575	635
5700	10-1/8" to 12-1/8"	G					590			590	650
5750	12-1/8" to 14-1/8"	G					610			610	670
5800	14-1/8" to 16-1/8"	G					630			630	695
5900	Coil threaded rods, continuous, 1/2" diameter	G				L.F.	1.41			1.41	1.55
6000	Tie hangers to 30" overall length, 4000#	G				C	530			530	580
6100	To 36" overall length	G					590			590	645
6150	To 48" overall length	G					710			710	780
6500	Tie back hanger, up to 12-1/8" flange	G					1,475			1,475	1,625
8000	Wire beam saddles, to 18" overall length										
8100	1-1/2" joist, 7 gauge	G				C	595			595	655
8200	4 gauge	G				"	625			625	690
8500	Wire, black annealed, 15 gauge	G				Cwt.	154			154	169
8600	16 gauge	G				"	170			170	187

03 15 05.70 Shores

			Crew	Daily Output	Labor-Hours	Unit	Material	Labor	Equipment	Total	Total Incl O&P
0010	**SHORES**										
0020	Erect and strip, by hand, horizontal members										
0500	Aluminum joists and stringers	G	2 Carp	60	.267	Ea.		13.50		13.50	20.50
0600	Steel, adjustable beams	G		45	.356			18.05		18.05	27.50
0700	Wood joists			50	.320			16.20		16.20	24.50
0800	Wood stringers			30	.533			27		27	41
1000	Vertical members to 10' high	G		55	.291			14.75		14.75	22.50
1050	To 13' high	G		50	.320			16.20		16.20	24.50
1100	To 16' high	G		45	.356			18.05		18.05	27.50
1500	Reshoring	G		1400	.011	S.F.	.61	.58		1.19	1.55
1600	Flying truss system	G	C-17D	9600	.009	SFCA		.46	.08	.54	.80
1760	Horizontal, aluminum joists, 6-1/4" high x 5' to 21' span, buy	G				L.F.	16.25			16.25	17.85
1770	Beams, 7-1/4" high x 4' to 30' span	G				"	19			19	21
1810	Horizontal, steel beam, W8x10, 7' span, buy	G				Ea.	61			61	67.50
1830	10' span	G					71			71	78
1920	15' span	G					122			122	135
1940	20' span	G					172			172	189
1970	Steel stringer, W8x10, 4' to 16' span, buy	G				L.F.	7.10			7.10	7.85
3000	Rent for job duration, aluminum joist @ 2' OC, per mo.	G				SF Flr.	.41			.41	.45
3050	Steel W8x10	G					.18			.18	.20
3060	Steel adjustable	G					.18			.18	.20
3500	#1 post shore, steel, 5'-7" to 9'-6" high, 10,000# cap., buy	G				Ea.	155			155	171
3550	#2 post shore, 7'-3" to 12'-10" high, 7800# capacity	G					180			180	198
3600	#3 post shore, 8'-10" to 16'-1" high, 3800# capacity	G					196			196	216
5010	Frame shoring systems, steel, 12,000#/leg, buy										
5040	Frame, 2' wide x 6' high	G				Ea.	115			115	127
5250	X-brace	G					20			20	22
5550	Base plate	G					17.70			17.70	19.45

03 15 Concrete Accessories

03 15 05 – Concrete Forming Accessories

03 15 05.70 Shores

		Crew	Daily Output	Labor-Hours	Unit	Material	2018 Bare Costs Labor	Equipment	Total	Total Incl O&P
5600	Screw jack [G]				Ea.	39			39	42.50
5650	U-head, 8" x 8" [G]					22			22	24

03 15 05.75 Sleeves and Chases

		Crew	Daily Output	Labor-Hours	Unit	Material	Labor	Equipment	Total	Total Incl O&P
0010	**SLEEVES AND CHASES**									
0100	Plastic, 1 use, 12" long, 2" diameter	1 Carp	100	.080	Ea.	1.89	4.06		5.95	8.30
0150	4" diameter		90	.089		5.30	4.51		9.81	12.70
0200	6" diameter		75	.107		9.30	5.40		14.70	18.50
0250	12" diameter		60	.133		27.50	6.75		34.25	41
5000	Sheet metal, 2" diameter [G]		100	.080		1.49	4.06		5.55	7.85
5100	4" diameter [G]		90	.089		1.86	4.51		6.37	8.90
5150	6" diameter [G]		75	.107		1.86	5.40		7.26	10.30
5200	12" diameter [G]		60	.133		3.72	6.75		10.47	14.40
6000	Steel pipe, 2" diameter [G]		100	.080		2.98	4.06		7.04	9.50
6100	4" diameter [G]		90	.089		10.85	4.51		15.36	18.80
6150	6" diameter [G]		75	.107		35	5.40		40.40	47
6200	12" diameter [G]		60	.133		83.50	6.75		90.25	102

03 15 05.80 Snap Ties

		Crew	Daily Output	Labor-Hours	Unit	Material	Labor	Equipment	Total	Total Incl O&P
0010	**SNAP TIES**, 8-1/4" L&W (Lumber and wedge)									
0100	2250 lb., w/flat washer, 8" wall [G]				C	93			93	102
0150	10" wall [G]					135			135	149
0200	12" wall [G]					140			140	154
0250	16" wall [G]					155			155	171
0300	18" wall [G]					161			161	177
0500	With plastic cone, 8" wall [G]					82			82	90
0550	10" wall [G]					85			85	93.50
0600	12" wall [G]					92			92	101
0650	16" wall [G]					101			101	111
0700	18" wall [G]					104			104	114
1000	3350 lb., w/flat washer, 8" wall [G]					168			168	185
1100	10" wall [G]					184			184	202
1150	12" wall [G]					188			188	207
1200	16" wall [G]					216			216	238
1250	18" wall [G]					225			225	248
1500	With plastic cone, 8" wall [G]					136			136	150
1550	10" wall [G]					149			149	164
1600	12" wall [G]					153			153	168
1650	16" wall [G]					175			175	193
1700	18" wall [G]					181			181	199

03 15 05.85 Stair Tread Inserts

		Crew	Daily Output	Labor-Hours	Unit	Material	Labor	Equipment	Total	Total Incl O&P
0010	**STAIR TREAD INSERTS**									
0105	Cast nosing insert, abrasive surface, pre-drilled, includes screws									
0110	Aluminum, 3" wide x 3' long	1 Cefi	32	.250	Ea.	52	11.90		63.90	75
0120	4' long		31	.258		69.50	12.25		81.75	94.50
0130	5' long		30	.267		86.50	12.70		99.20	114
0135	Extruded nosing insert, black abrasive strips, continuous anchor									
0140	Aluminum, 3" wide x 3' long	1 Cefi	64	.125	Ea.	33.50	5.95		39.45	46
0150	4' long		60	.133		45	6.35		51.35	59
0160	5' long		56	.143		56	6.80		62.80	71.50
0165	Extruded nosing insert, black abrasive strips, pre-drilled, incl. screws									
0170	Aluminum, 3" wide x 3' long	1 Cefi	32	.250	Ea.	42	11.90		53.90	63.50
0180	4' long		31	.258		56	12.25		68.25	79.50
0190	5' long		30	.267		70	12.70		82.70	96

03 15 Concrete Accessories

03 15 05 – Concrete Forming Accessories

03 15 05.95 Wall and Foundation Form Accessories

			Crew	Daily Output	Labor-Hours	Unit	Material	2018 Bare Costs Labor	Equipment	Total	Total Incl O&P
0010	**WALL AND FOUNDATION FORM ACCESSORIES**										
0020	Coil tie system										
0050	Coil ties 1/2", 6000 lb., to 8"	G				C	255			255	281
0100	10" to 12"	G					305			305	340
0120	18"	G					360			360	400
0150	24"	G					430			430	475
0200	36"	G					555			555	610
0220	48"	G					680			680	750
0300	3/4", 12,000 lb., to 8"	G					490			490	540
0320	10" to 12"	G					550			550	605
0350	18"	G					645			645	710
0400	24"	G					730			730	805
0420	36"	G					1,000			1,000	1,100
0450	48"	G					1,275			1,275	1,425
0500	1", 24,000 lb., to 8"	G					865			865	950
0520	10" to 12"	G					1,025			1,025	1,125
0550	18"	G					1,175			1,175	1,275
0600	24"	G					1,475			1,475	1,625
0620	36"	G					1,925			1,925	2,125
0650	48"	G					2,375			2,375	2,600
0700	1-1/4", 36,000 lb., to 8"	G					1,275			1,275	1,400
0720	10" to 12"	G					1,550			1,550	1,700
0750	18"	G					1,975			1,975	2,175
0800	24"	G					2,425			2,425	2,650
0820	36"	G					3,300			3,300	3,625
0850	48"	G					4,175			4,175	4,575
0900	Coil bolts, 1/2" diameter x 3" long	G					144			144	158
0920	6" long	G					234			234	257
0940	12" long	G					410			410	455
0960	18" long	G					540			540	595
1000	3/4" diameter x 3" long	G					315			315	345
1020	6" long	G					580			580	640
1040	12" long	G					865			865	950
1060	18" long	G					1,125			1,125	1,250
1100	1" diameter x 3" long	G					1,350			1,350	1,475
1120	6" long	G					1,400			1,400	1,525
1140	12" long	G					2,125			2,125	2,325
1160	18" long	G					2,875			2,875	3,150
1200	1-1/4" diameter x 3" long	G					2,150			2,150	2,350
1220	6" long	G					2,175			2,175	2,400
1240	12" long	G					3,375			3,375	3,700
1260	18" long	G					4,325			4,325	4,750
1300	Adjustable coil tie, 3/4" diameter, 20" long	G					1,200			1,200	1,325
1350	3/4" diameter, 36" long	G					1,475			1,475	1,625
1400	Tie cones, plastic, 1" setback length, 1/2" bolt diameter						87			87	95.50
1420	3/4" bolt diameter						171			171	188
1440	2" setback length, 1" bolt diameter						465			465	515
1460	1-1/4" bolt diameter						560			560	620
1500	Welding coil tie, 1/2" diameter x 4" long	G					235			235	259
1550	3/4" diameter x 6" long	G					315			315	345
1600	1" diameter x 8" long	G					490			490	540
1700	Waler holders, 1/2" diameter	G					242			242	266

For customer support on your Green Building Costs with RSMeans data, call 800.448.8182.

03 15 Concrete Accessories

03 15 05 – Concrete Forming Accessories

03 15 05.95 Wall and Foundation Form Accessories

		Crew	Daily Output	Labor-Hours	Unit	Material	2018 Bare Costs Labor	Equipment	Total	Total Incl O&P
1750	3/4" diameter G				C	270			270	297
1900	Flat washers, 4" x 5" x 1/4" for 3/4" diameter G					990			990	1,075
1950	5" x 5" x 7/16" for 1" diameter G				↓	1,325			1,325	1,450
2000	Footings, turnbuckle form aligner G				Ea.	16.65			16.65	18.30
2050	Spreaders for footer, adjustable G				"	25			25	27.50
2100	Lagstud, threaded, 1/2" diameter G				C.L.F.	141			141	155
2150	3/4" diameter G					300			300	330
2200	1" diameter G					515			515	570
2250	1-1/4" diameter G				↓	1,250			1,250	1,375
2300	Lagnuts, 1/2" diameter G				C	34			34	37.50
2350	3/4" diameter G					82			82	90
2400	1" diameter G					237			237	261
2450	1-1/4" diameter G					400			400	440
2600	Lagnuts with handle, 1/2" diameter G					310			310	340
2650	3/4" diameter G					470			470	520
2700	1" diameter G					870			870	960
2750	Plastic set back plugs for 3/4" diameter					99			99	109
2800	Rock anchors, 1/2" diameter G					1,175			1,175	1,300
2850	3/4" diameter G					1,575			1,575	1,725
2900	1" diameter G					1,675			1,675	1,850
2950	Batter washer, 1/2" diameter G				↓	665			665	730
4000	Nail stakes, 3/4" diameter, 18" long G				Ea.	1.98			1.98	2.18
4050	24" long G					2.50			2.50	2.75
4200	30" long G					3.16			3.16	3.48
4250	36" long G				↓	3.99			3.99	4.39
5000	Pencil rods, 1/4" diameter G				C.L.F.	49			49	54
5200	Clamps for 1/4" pencil rods G				Ea.	6			6	6.60
5300	Clamping jacks for 1/4" pencil rod clamp G				"	78.50			78.50	86
6000	She-bolts, 7/8" x 20" G				C	4,600			4,600	5,050
6150	1-1/4" x 20" G					6,125			6,125	6,750
6200	1-1/2" x 20" G					8,175			8,175	8,975
6300	Inside rods, threaded, 1/2" diameter x 6" G					190			190	209
6350	1/2" diameter x 12" G					276			276	305
6400	5/8" diameter x 6" G					370			370	405
6450	5/8" diameter x 12" G					540			540	590
6500	3/4" diameter x 6" G					410			410	450
6550	3/4" diameter x 12" G				↓	570			570	630
6700	For wing nuts, see taper ties									
7000	Taper tie system									
7100	Taper ties, 3/4" to 1/2" diameter x 30" G				Ea.	56.50			56.50	62
7150	1" to 3/4" diameter x 30" G					64.50			64.50	71
7200	1-1/4" to 1" diameter x 30" G				↓	75			75	82.50
7300	Wing nuts, 1/2" diameter G				C	695			695	765
7350	3/4" diameter G					745			745	820
7400	7/8" diameter G					815			815	900
7450	1" diameter G					815			815	900
7500	1-1/8" diameter G					940			940	1,025
7550	1-1/4" diameter G					1,050			1,050	1,150
7600	1-1/2" diameter G					1,225			1,225	1,350
7700	Flat washers, 1/4" x 3" x 4", for 1/2" diam. bolt G					282			282	310
7750	1/4" x 4" x 5", for 3/4" diam. bolt G					990			990	1,075
7800	7/16" x 5" x 5", for 1" diam. bolt G					1,325			1,325	1,450
7850	7/16" x 5" x 5", for 1-1/4" diam. bolt G				↓	1,500			1,500	1,625

For customer support on your Green Building Costs with RSMeans data, call 800.448.8182.

03 15 Concrete Accessories

03 15 05 – Concrete Forming Accessories

03 15 05.95 Wall and Foundation Form Accessories		Crew	Daily Output	Labor-Hours	Unit	Material	2018 Bare Costs Labor	Equipment	Total	Total Incl O&P
9000	Wood form accessories									
9100	Tie plate	G			C	625			625	690
9200	Corner washer	G				1,250			1,250	1,375
9300	Panel bolt	G				930			930	1,025
9400	Panel wedge	G				164			164	180
9500	Stud clamp	G				700			700	770

03 15 16 – Concrete Construction Joints

03 15 16.30 Expansion Joints

0010	**EXPANSION JOINTS**									
0020	Keyed, cold, 24 ga., incl. stakes, 3-1/2" high	G	1 Carp	200	.040	L.F.	.85	2.03		2.88	4.03
0050	4-1/2" high	G		200	.040		.91	2.03		2.94	4.09
0100	5-1/2" high	G		195	.041		1.14	2.08		3.22	4.42
0150	7-1/2" high	G		190	.042		1.37	2.14		3.51	4.76
0160	9-1/2" high	G		185	.043		1.49	2.19		3.68	4.98
2140	Concrete expansion joint, recycled paper and fiber, 1/2" x 6"	G		390	.021		.42	1.04		1.46	2.04
2150	1/2" x 12"	G		360	.022		.84	1.13		1.97	2.65

03 15 19 – Cast-In Concrete Anchors

03 15 19.05 Anchor Bolt Accessories

0010	**ANCHOR BOLT ACCESSORIES**										
8800	Templates, steel, 8" bolt spacing	G	2 Carp	16	1	Ea.	10.95	50.50		61.45	89
8850	12" bolt spacing	G		15	1.067		11.45	54		65.45	95
8900	16" bolt spacing	G		14	1.143		13.70	58		71.70	103
8950	24" bolt spacing	G		12	1.333		18.30	67.50		85.80	123

03 15 19.10 Anchor Bolts

0010	**ANCHOR BOLTS**										
0015	Made from recycled materials										
0025	Single bolts installed in fresh concrete, no templates										
0030	Hooked w/nut and washer, 1/2" diameter, 8" long	G	1 Carp	132	.061	Ea.	1.42	3.07		4.49	6.25
0040	12" long	G		131	.061		1.58	3.10		4.68	6.45
0050	5/8" diameter, 8" long	G		129	.062		3.80	3.14		6.94	8.95
0060	12" long	G		127	.063		4.67	3.19		7.86	10
0070	3/4" diameter, 8" long	G		127	.063		4.67	3.19		7.86	10
0080	12" long	G		125	.064		5.85	3.24		9.09	11.35
0090	2-bolt pattern, including job-built 2-hole template, per set										
0100	J-type, incl. hex nut & washer, 1/2" diameter x 6" long	G	1 Carp	21	.381	Set	5.15	19.30		24.45	35
0110	12" long	G		21	.381		5.75	19.30		25.05	36
0120	18" long	G		21	.381		6.70	19.30		26	37
0130	3/4" diameter x 8" long	G		20	.400		11.95	20.50		32.45	44
0140	12" long	G		20	.400		14.30	20.50		34.80	46.50
0150	18" long	G		20	.400		17.80	20.50		38.30	50.50
0160	1" diameter x 12" long	G		19	.421		22.50	21.50		44	57.50
0170	18" long	G		19	.421		27	21.50		48.50	62
0180	24" long	G		19	.421		32	21.50		53.50	68
0190	36" long	G		18	.444		43	22.50		65.50	82
0200	1-1/2" diameter x 18" long	G		17	.471		41.50	24		65.50	82
0210	24" long	G		16	.500		48.50	25.50		74	92
0300	L-type, incl. hex nut & washer, 3/4" diameter x 12" long	G		20	.400		14.10	20.50		34.60	46.50
0310	18" long	G		20	.400		17.35	20.50		37.85	50
0320	24" long	G		20	.400		20.50	20.50		41	53.50
0330	30" long	G		20	.400		25.50	20.50		46	59
0340	36" long	G		20	.400		28.50	20.50		49	62.50

03 15 Concrete Accessories

03 15 19 – Cast-In Concrete Anchors

03 15 19.10 Anchor Bolts		Crew	Daily Output	Labor-Hours	Unit	Material	2018 Bare Costs Labor	Equipment	Total	Total Incl O&P
0350	1" diameter x 12" long	G 1 Carp	19	.421	Set	22	21.50		43.50	56.50
0360	18" long	G	19	.421		26.50	21.50		48	61.50
0370	24" long	G	19	.421		32	21.50		53.50	68
0380	30" long	G	19	.421		37.50	21.50		59	73.50
0390	36" long	G	18	.444		42.50	22.50		65	81
0400	42" long	G	18	.444		51	22.50		73.50	90.50
0410	48" long	G	18	.444		57	22.50		79.50	97
0420	1-1/4" diameter x 18" long	G	18	.444		33.50	22.50		56	71.50
0430	24" long	G	18	.444		39	22.50		61.50	77.50
0440	30" long	G	17	.471		45	24		69	86
0450	36" long	G	17	.471		50.50	24		74.50	92.50
0460	42" long	G 2 Carp	32	.500		57	25.50		82.50	101
0470	48" long	G	32	.500		64.50	25.50		90	110
0480	54" long	G	31	.516		76	26		102	124
0490	60" long	G	31	.516		83	26		109	132
0500	1-1/2" diameter x 18" long	G	33	.485		49.50	24.50		74	92
0510	24" long	G	32	.500		57	25.50		82.50	102
0520	30" long	G	31	.516		64.50	26		90.50	111
0530	36" long	G	30	.533		73.50	27		100.50	122
0540	42" long	G	30	.533		83.50	27		110.50	133
0550	48" long	G	29	.552		93.50	28		121.50	146
0560	54" long	G	28	.571		113	29		142	168
0570	60" long	G	28	.571		124	29		153	180
0580	1-3/4" diameter x 18" long	G	31	.516		64	26		90	111
0590	24" long	G	30	.533		74.50	27		101.50	123
0600	30" long	G	29	.552		86.50	28		114.50	138
0610	36" long	G	28	.571		98	29		127	152
0620	42" long	G	27	.593		110	30		140	167
0630	48" long	G	26	.615		120	31		151	181
0640	54" long	G	26	.615		149	31		180	212
0650	60" long	G	25	.640		161	32.50		193.50	227
0660	2" diameter x 24" long	G	27	.593		121	30		151	179
0670	30" long	G	27	.593		136	30		166	196
0680	36" long	G	26	.615		149	31		180	212
0690	42" long	G	25	.640		166	32.50		198.50	233
0700	48" long	G	24	.667		190	34		224	261
0710	54" long	G	23	.696		226	35.50		261.50	305
0720	60" long	G	23	.696		243	35.50		278.50	320
0730	66" long	G	22	.727		260	37		297	340
0740	72" long	G	21	.762		284	38.50		322.50	375
1000	4-bolt pattern, including job-built 4-hole template, per set									
1100	J-type, incl. hex nut & washer, 1/2" diameter x 6" long	G 1 Carp	19	.421	Set	7.65	21.50		29.15	41
1110	12" long	G	19	.421		8.95	21.50		30.45	42.50
1120	18" long	G	18	.444		10.85	22.50		33.35	46.50
1130	3/4" diameter x 8" long	G	17	.471		21.50	24		45.50	60
1140	12" long	G	17	.471		26	24		50	65
1150	18" long	G	17	.471		33	24		57	73
1160	1" diameter x 12" long	G	16	.500		42.50	25.50		68	85.50
1170	18" long	G	15	.533		51	27		78	97
1180	24" long	G	15	.533		61.50	27		88.50	109
1190	36" long	G	15	.533		83.50	27		110.50	133
1200	1-1/2" diameter x 18" long	G	13	.615		80	31		111	136
1210	24" long	G	12	.667		94.50	34		128.50	156

03 15 Concrete Accessories

03 15 19 – Cast-In Concrete Anchors

03 15 19.10 Anchor Bolts

			Crew	Daily Output	Labor-Hours	Unit	Material	2018 Bare Costs Labor	Equipment	Total	Total Incl O&P
1300	L-type, incl. hex nut & washer, 3/4" diameter x 12" long	G	1 Carp	17	.471	Set	25.50	24		49.50	64.50
1310	18" long	G		17	.471		32	24		56	72
1320	24" long	G		17	.471		38.50	24		62.50	79
1330	30" long	G		16	.500		48	25.50		73.50	91.50
1340	36" long	G		16	.500		54.50	25.50		80	98.50
1350	1" diameter x 12" long	G		16	.500		41	25.50		66.50	83.50
1360	18" long	G		15	.533		50.50	27		77.50	96.50
1370	24" long	G		15	.533		61.50	27		88.50	109
1380	30" long	G		15	.533		72	27		99	121
1390	36" long	G		15	.533		82	27		109	132
1400	42" long	G		14	.571		99.50	29		128.50	153
1410	48" long	G		14	.571		111	29		140	166
1420	1-1/4" diameter x 18" long	G		14	.571		64	29		93	115
1430	24" long	G		14	.571		76	29		105	128
1440	30" long	G		13	.615		87.50	31		118.50	144
1450	36" long	G		13	.615		99	31		130	157
1460	42" long	G	2 Carp	25	.640		111	32.50		143.50	173
1470	48" long	G		24	.667		127	34		161	191
1480	54" long	G		23	.696		149	35.50		184.50	218
1490	60" long	G		23	.696		163	35.50		198.50	234
1500	1-1/2" diameter x 18" long	G		25	.640		96	32.50		128.50	156
1510	24" long	G		24	.667		112	34		146	175
1520	30" long	G		23	.696		126	35.50		161.50	193
1530	36" long	G		22	.727		144	37		181	215
1540	42" long	G		22	.727		164	37		201	237
1550	48" long	G		21	.762		184	38.50		222.50	261
1560	54" long	G		20	.800		224	40.50		264.50	310
1570	60" long	G		20	.800		245	40.50		285.50	330
1580	1-3/4" diameter x 18" long	G		22	.727		125	37		162	194
1590	24" long	G		21	.762		146	38.50		184.50	220
1600	30" long	G		21	.762		170	38.50		208.50	246
1610	36" long	G		20	.800		194	40.50		234.50	275
1620	42" long	G		19	.842		217	42.50		259.50	305
1630	48" long	G		18	.889		238	45		283	330
1640	54" long	G		18	.889		295	45		340	395
1650	60" long	G		17	.941		320	47.50		367.50	425
1660	2" diameter x 24" long	G		19	.842		239	42.50		281.50	330
1670	30" long	G		18	.889		269	45		314	365
1680	36" long	G		18	.889		295	45		340	395
1690	42" long	G		17	.941		330	47.50		377.50	435
1700	48" long	G		16	1		380	50.50		430.50	490
1710	54" long	G		15	1.067		450	54		504	580
1720	60" long	G		15	1.067		485	54		539	615
1730	66" long	G		14	1.143		515	58		573	660
1740	72" long	G		14	1.143		565	58		623	710

03 15 19.20 Dovetail Anchor System

			Crew	Daily Output	Labor-Hours	Unit	Material	Labor	Equipment	Total	Total Incl O&P
0010	**DOVETAIL ANCHOR SYSTEM**										
0500	Dovetail anchor slot, galvanized, foam-filled, 26 ga.	G	1 Carp	425	.019	L.F.	1.17	.95		2.12	2.74
0600	24 ga.	G		400	.020		1.61	1.01		2.62	3.31
0625	22 ga.	G		400	.020		1.75	1.01		2.76	3.47
0900	Stainless steel, foam-filled, 26 ga.	G		375	.021		1.87	1.08		2.95	3.71
1200	Dovetail brick anchor, corrugated, galvanized, 3-1/2" long, 16 ga.	G	1 Bric	10.50	.762	C	40.50	38.50		79	103

For customer support on your Green Building Costs with RSMeans data, call 800.448.8182.

03 15 Concrete Accessories

03 15 19 – Cast-In Concrete Anchors

03 15 19.20 Dovetail Anchor System

			Crew	Daily Output	Labor-Hours	Unit	Material	2018 Bare Costs Labor	Equipment	Total	Total Incl O&P
1300	12 ga.	G	1 Bric	10.50	.762	C	60	38.50		98.50	125
1500	Seismic, galvanized, 3-1/2" long, 16 ga.	G		10.50	.762		71	38.50		109.50	137
1600	12 ga.	G		10.50	.762		84	38.50		122.50	151
2000	Dovetail cavity wall, corrugated, galvanized, 5-1/2" long, 16 ga.	G		10.50	.762		40	38.50		78.50	103
2100	12 ga.	G		10.50	.762		57	38.50		95.50	121
3000	Dovetail furring anchors, corrugated, galvanized, 1-1/2" long, 16 ga.	G		10.50	.762		24	38.50		62.50	85
3100	12 ga.	G		10.50	.762		31	38.50		69.50	92.50
6000	Dovetail stone panel anchors, galvanized, 1/8" x 1" wide, 3-1/2" long	G		10.50	.762		97	38.50		135.50	166
6100	1/4" x 1" wide	G		10.50	.762		164	38.50		202.50	239

03 15 19.30 Inserts

			Crew	Daily Output	Labor-Hours	Unit	Material	Labor	Equipment	Total	Incl O&P
0010	**INSERTS**										
1000	Inserts, slotted nut type for 3/4" bolts, 4" long	G	1 Carp	84	.095	Ea.	20	4.83		24.83	30
2100	6" long	G		84	.095		23	4.83		27.83	32.50
2150	8" long	G		84	.095		30.50	4.83		35.33	41
2200	Slotted, strap type, 4" long	G		84	.095		22	4.83		26.83	31.50
2250	6" long	G		84	.095		24.50	4.83		29.33	34.50
2300	8" long	G		84	.095		32.50	4.83		37.33	43.50
2350	Strap for slotted insert, 4" long	G		84	.095		11.90	4.83		16.73	20.50
4100	6" long	G		84	.095		12.95	4.83		17.78	21.50
4150	8" long	G		84	.095		16.15	4.83		20.98	25
4200	10" long	G		84	.095		19.60	4.83		24.43	29
6000	Thin slab, ferrule type										
6100	1/2" diameter bolt	G	1 Carp	60	.133	Ea.	4.22	6.75		10.97	14.95
6150	5/8" diameter bolt	G		60	.133		5.20	6.75		11.95	16
6200	3/4" diameter bolt	G		60	.133		6.05	6.75		12.80	16.95
6250	1" diameter bolt	G		60	.133		9.75	6.75		16.50	21
7000	Loop ferrule type										
7100	1/4" diameter bolt	G	1 Carp	84	.095	Ea.	2.32	4.83		7.15	9.90
7150	3/8" diameter bolt	G		84	.095		2.32	4.83		7.15	9.90
7200	1/2" diameter bolt	G		84	.095		2.78	4.83		7.61	10.40
7250	5/8" diameter bolt	G		84	.095		3.72	4.83		8.55	11.45
7300	3/4" diameter bolt	G		84	.095		4.18	4.83		9.01	11.95
7350	7/8" diameter bolt	G		84	.095		10.80	4.83		15.63	19.20
7400	1" diameter bolt	G		84	.095		10.80	4.83		15.63	19.20
7500	Threaded coil type with filler plug										
7600	3/4" diameter bolt	G	1 Carp	60	.133	Ea.	4.96	6.75		11.71	15.75
7650	1" diameter bolt	G		60	.133		9.35	6.75		16.10	20.50
7700	1-1/4" diameter bolt	G		60	.133		17.65	6.75		24.40	30
7750	1-1/2" diameter bolt	G		60	.133		28.50	6.75		35.25	41.50
9000	Wedge type										
9100	For 3/4" diameter bolt	G	1 Carp	60	.133	Ea.	9.70	6.75		16.45	21
9200	Askew head bolts, black										
9400	3/4" diameter, 1-1/2" long	G				Ea.	4.57			4.57	5.05
9450	2" long	G					5			5	5.50
9500	3" long	G					9.10			9.10	10
9600	Nuts, black										
9700	3/4" bolt	G				Ea.	1.90			1.90	2.09
9800	Cut washers, black										
9900	3/4" bolt	G				Ea.	1.21			1.21	1.33
9950	For galvanized inserts, add						30%				

03 15 Concrete Accessories

03 15 19 – Cast-In Concrete Anchors

03 15 19.45 Machinery Anchors

		Crew	Daily Output	Labor-Hours	Unit	Material	2018 Bare Costs Labor	Equipment	Total	Total Incl O&P
0010	**MACHINERY ANCHORS**, heavy duty, incl. sleeve, floating base nut,									
0020	lower stud & coupling nut, fiber plug, connecting stud, washer & nut.									
0030	For flush mounted embedment in poured concrete heavy equip. pads.									
0200	Stud & bolt, 1/2" diameter G	E-16	40	.400	Ea.	52.50	22.50	2.46	77.46	97
0300	5/8" diameter G		35	.457		61	25.50	2.81	89.31	112
0500	3/4" diameter G		30	.533		72.50	29.50	3.28	105.28	132
0600	7/8" diameter G		25	.640		82.50	35.50	3.94	121.94	153
0800	1" diameter G		20	.800		88.50	44.50	4.92	137.92	176
0900	1-1/4" diameter G		15	1.067		118	59.50	6.55	184.05	234

03 21 Reinforcement Bars

03 21 05 – Reinforcing Steel Accessories

03 21 05.10 Rebar Accessories

						Unit	Material			Total	Total Incl O&P
0010	**REBAR ACCESSORIES** R032110-80										
0030	Steel & plastic made from recycled materials										
0100	Beam bolsters (BB), lower, 1-1/2" high, plain steel G					C.L.F.	35			35	38.50
0102	Galvanized G						42			42	46
0104	Stainless tipped legs G						460			460	505
0106	Plastic tipped legs G						51			51	56
0108	Epoxy dipped G						88			88	97
0110	2" high, plain G						44			44	48.50
0120	Galvanized G						53			53	58
0140	Stainless tipped legs G						470			470	515
0160	Plastic tipped legs G						60			60	66
0162	Epoxy dipped G						100			100	110
0200	Upper (BBU), 1-1/2" high, plain steel G						85			85	93.50
0210	3" high G						96			96	106
0500	Slab bolsters, continuous (SB), 1" high, plain steel G						30			30	33
0502	Galvanized G						36			36	39.50
0504	Stainless tipped legs G						455			455	500
0506	Plastic tipped legs G						44			44	48.50
0510	2" high, plain steel G						38			38	42
0515	Galvanized G						45.50			45.50	50
0520	Stainless tipped legs G						465			465	510
0525	Plastic tipped legs G						51			51	56
0530	For bolsters with wire runners (SBR), add G						41			41	45
0540	For bolsters with plates (SBP), add G						97			97	107
0700	Bag ties, 16 ga., plain, 4" long G					C	4			4	4.40
0710	5" long G						5			5	5.50
0720	6" long G						4			4	4.40
0730	7" long G						5			5	5.50
1200	High chairs, individual (HC), 3" high, plain steel G						62			62	68
1202	Galvanized G						74.50			74.50	82
1204	Stainless tipped legs G						485			485	535
1206	Plastic tipped legs G						67			67	73.50
1210	5" high, plain G						90			90	99
1212	Galvanized G						108			108	119
1214	Stainless tipped legs G						515			515	565
1216	Plastic tipped legs G						99			99	109
1220	8" high, plain G						132			132	145

For customer support on your Green Building Costs with RSMeans data, call 800.448.8182.

03 21 Reinforcement Bars

03 21 05 – Reinforcing Steel Accessories

03 21 05.10 Rebar Accessories

			Crew	Daily Output	Labor-Hours	Unit	Material	2018 Bare Costs Labor	Equipment	Total	Total Incl O&P
1222	Galvanized	G				C	158			158	174
1224	Stainless tipped legs	G					555			555	615
1226	Plastic tipped legs	G					146			146	161
1230	12" high, plain	G					315			315	345
1232	Galvanized	G					380			380	415
1234	Stainless tipped legs	G					740			740	815
1236	Plastic tipped legs	G					345			345	380
1400	Individual high chairs, with plate (HCP), 5" high	G					188			188	207
1410	8" high	G					260			260	286
1500	Bar chair (BC), 1-1/2" high, plain steel	G					40			40	44
1520	Galvanized	G					45			45	49.50
1530	Stainless tipped legs	G					465			465	510
1540	Plastic tipped legs	G					43			43	47.50
1700	Continuous high chairs (CHC), legs 8" OC, 4" high, plain steel	G				C.L.F.	54			54	59.50
1705	Galvanized	G					65			65	71.50
1710	Stainless tipped legs	G					480			480	525
1715	Plastic tipped legs	G					72			72	79
1718	Epoxy dipped	G					93			93	102
1720	6" high, plain	G					74			74	81.50
1725	Galvanized	G					89			89	97.50
1730	Stainless tipped legs	G					500			500	550
1735	Plastic tipped legs	G					99			99	109
1738	Epoxy dipped	G					127			127	140
1740	8" high, plain	G					105			105	116
1745	Galvanized	G					126			126	139
1750	Stainless tipped legs	G					530			530	585
1755	Plastic tipped legs	G					125			125	137
1758	Epoxy dipped	G					161			161	177
1900	For continuous bottom wire runners, add	G					29			29	32
1940	For continuous bottom plate, add	G					199			199	219
2200	Screed chair base, 1/2" coil thread diam., 2-1/2" high, plain steel	G				C	335			335	370
2210	Galvanized	G					405			405	445
2220	5-1/2" high, plain	G					405			405	445
2250	Galvanized	G					485			485	535
2300	3/4" coil thread diam., 2-1/2" high, plain steel	G					420			420	465
2310	Galvanized	G					505			505	555
2320	5-1/2" high, plain steel	G					520			520	570
2350	Galvanized	G					625			625	685
2400	Screed holder, 1/2" coil thread diam. for pipe screed, plain steel, 6" long	G					405			405	445
2420	12" long	G					625			625	685
2500	3/4" coil thread diam. for pipe screed, plain steel, 6" long	G					585			585	640
2520	12" long	G					935			935	1,025
2700	Screw anchor for bolts, plain steel, 3/4" diameter x 4" long	G					565			565	620
2720	1" diameter x 6" long	G					930			930	1,025
2740	1-1/2" diameter x 8" long	G					1,175			1,175	1,300
2800	Screw anchor eye bolts, 3/4" x 3" long	G					2,950			2,950	3,250
2820	1" x 3-1/2" long	G					3,950			3,950	4,350
2840	1-1/2" x 6" long	G					12,100			12,100	13,300
2900	Screw anchor bolts, 3/4" x 9" long	G					1,700			1,700	1,850
2920	1" x 12" long	G					3,250			3,250	3,575
3001	Slab lifting inserts, single pickup, galv, 3/4" diam., 5" high	G					1,825			1,825	2,000
3010	6" high	G					1,850			1,850	2,025
3030	7" high	G					1,875			1,875	2,075

03 21 Reinforcement Bars

03 21 05 – Reinforcing Steel Accessories

03 21 05.10 Rebar Accessories

		Crew	Daily Output	Labor-Hours	Unit	Material	2018 Bare Costs Labor	Equipment	Total	Total Incl O&P
3100	1" diameter, 5-1/2" high	G			C	1,925			1,925	2,125
3120	7" high	G				1,975			1,975	2,175
3200	Double pickup lifting inserts, 1" diameter, 5-1/2" high	G				3,700			3,700	4,075
3220	7" high	G				4,100			4,100	4,525
3330	1-1/2" diameter, 8" high	G				5,175			5,175	5,675
3800	Subgrade chairs, #4 bar head, 3-1/2" high	G				40			40	44
3850	12" high	G				47			47	51.50
3900	#6 bar head, 3-1/2" high	G				40			40	44
3950	12" high	G				47			47	51.50
4200	Subgrade stakes, no nail holes, 3/4" diameter, 12" long	G				145			145	160
4250	24" long	G				240			240	264
4300	7/8" diameter, 12" long	G				390			390	430
4350	24" long	G				660			660	725
4500	Tie wire, 16 ga. annealed steel	G			Cwt.	170			170	187

03 21 05.75 Splicing Reinforcing Bars

		Crew	Daily Output	Labor-Hours	Unit	Material	Labor	Equipment	Total	Total Incl O&P
0010	**SPLICING REINFORCING BARS**									
0020	Including holding bars in place while splicing									
0100	Standard, self-aligning type, taper threaded, #4 bars	G	C-25	190	.168	Ea.	7.25	7.35		14.60	19.70
0105	#5 bars	G		170	.188		9.05	8.25		17.30	23
0110	#6 bars	G		150	.213		10.20	9.35		19.55	26
0120	#7 bars	G		130	.246		11.80	10.75		22.55	30
0300	#8 bars	G		115	.278		19.55	12.15		31.70	41
0305	#9 bars	G	C-5	105	.533		23	29	5.65	57.65	75
0310	#10 bars	G		95	.589		25.50	32	6.20	63.70	83.50
0320	#11 bars	G		85	.659		27	36	6.95	69.95	91.50
0330	#14 bars	G		65	.862		35	47	9.10	91.10	120
0340	#18 bars	G		45	1.244		53.50	67.50	13.15	134.15	176
0500	Transition self-aligning, taper threaded, #18-14	G		45	1.244		71	67.50	13.15	151.65	195
0510	#18-11	G		45	1.244		72	67.50	13.15	152.65	197
0520	#14-11	G		65	.862		47.50	47	9.10	103.60	134
0540	#11-10	G		85	.659		33	36	6.95	75.95	98.50
0550	#10-9	G		95	.589		31.50	32	6.20	69.70	90
0560	#9-8	G	C-25	105	.305		28.50	13.35		41.85	52.50
0580	#8-7	G		115	.278		26.50	12.15		38.65	48.50
0590	#7-6	G		130	.246		18.30	10.75		29.05	37
0600	Position coupler for curved bars, taper threaded, #4 bars	G		160	.200		34.50	8.75		43.25	52
0610	#5 bars	G		145	.221		36.50	9.65		46.15	55.50
0620	#6 bars	G		130	.246		44	10.75		54.75	65
0630	#7 bars	G		110	.291		46.50	12.75		59.25	71.50
0640	#8 bars	G		100	.320		48.50	14		62.50	75
0650	#9 bars	G	C-5	90	.622		53	34	6.55	93.55	117
0660	#10 bars	G		80	.700		57	38	7.40	102.40	129
0670	#11 bars	G		70	.800		59.50	43.50	8.45	111.45	140
0680	#14 bars	G		55	1.018		74	55.50	10.75	140.25	177
0690	#18 bars	G		40	1.400		91.50	76	14.75	182.25	233
0700	Transition position coupler for curved bars, taper threaded, #18-14	G		40	1.400		121	76	14.75	211.75	265
0710	#18-11	G		40	1.400		122	76	14.75	212.75	267
0720	#14-11	G		55	1.018		85	55.50	10.75	151.25	189
0730	#11-10	G		70	.800		69	43.50	8.45	120.95	151
0740	#10-9	G		80	.700		66	38	7.40	111.40	139
0750	#9-8	G	C-25	90	.356		61.50	15.55		77.05	92.50
0760	#8-7	G		100	.320		56.50	14		70.50	84

For customer support on your Green Building Costs with RSMeans data, call 800.448.8182.

03 21 Reinforcement Bars

03 21 05 – Reinforcing Steel Accessories

03 21 05.75 Splicing Reinforcing Bars

			Crew	Daily Output	Labor-Hours	Unit	Material	2018 Bare Costs Labor	Equipment	Total	Total Incl O&P
0770	#7-6	G	C-25	110	.291	Ea.	55	12.75		67.75	80.50
0800	Sleeve type w/grout filler, for precast concrete, #6 bars	G		72	.444		29	19.45		48.45	62.50
0802	#7 bars	G		64	.500		34.50	22		56.50	72
0805	#8 bars	G		56	.571		41	25		66	84.50
0807	#9 bars	G		48	.667		47	29		76	98.50
0810	#10 bars	G	C-5	40	1.400		57.50	76	14.75	148.25	195
0900	#11 bars	G		32	1.750		63.50	95	18.45	176.95	236
0920	#14 bars	G		24	2.333		98.50	127	24.50	250	330
1000	Sleeve type w/ferrous filler, for critical structures, #6 bars	G	C-25	72	.444		91	19.45		110.45	131
1210	#7 bars	G		64	.500		92.50	22		114.50	137
1220	#8 bars	G		56	.571		97	25		122	147
1230	#9 bars	G	C-5	48	1.167		101	63.50	12.30	176.80	221
1240	#10 bars	G		40	1.400		106	76	14.75	196.75	249
1250	#11 bars	G		32	1.750		129	95	18.45	242.45	305
1260	#14 bars	G		24	2.333		161	127	24.50	312.50	395
1270	#18 bars	G		16	3.500		233	190	37	460	585
2000	Weldable half coupler, taper threaded, #4 bars	G	E-16	120	.133		11.35	7.40	.82	19.57	25.50
2100	#5 bars	G		112	.143		13.35	7.95	.88	22.18	28.50
2200	#6 bars	G		104	.154		21	8.55	.95	30.50	38.50
2300	#7 bars	G		96	.167		24.50	9.30	1.03	34.83	43.50
2400	#8 bars	G		88	.182		25.50	10.10	1.12	36.72	46.50
2500	#9 bars	G		80	.200		28.50	11.15	1.23	40.88	50.50
2600	#10 bars	G		72	.222		29	12.35	1.37	42.72	53.50
2700	#11 bars	G		64	.250		31	13.90	1.54	46.44	58.50
2800	#14 bars	G		56	.286		35.50	15.90	1.76	53.16	67.50
2900	#18 bars	G		48	.333		58	18.55	2.05	78.60	97

03 21 11 – Plain Steel Reinforcement Bars

03 21 11.50 Reinforcing Steel, Mill Base Plus Extras

						Unit	Material	Labor	Equipment	Total	Total Incl O&P
0010	**REINFORCING STEEL, MILL BASE PLUS EXTRAS**										
0150	Reinforcing, A615 grade 40, mill base	G				Ton	670			670	740
0200	Detailed, cut, bent, and delivered	G					960			960	1,050
0650	Reinforcing steel, A615 grade 60, mill base	G					670			670	740
0700	Detailed, cut, bent, and delivered	G					960			960	1,050

03 21 11.60 Reinforcing In Place

			Crew	Daily Output	Labor-Hours	Unit	Material	Labor	Equipment	Total	Total Incl O&P
0010	**REINFORCING IN PLACE**, 50-60 ton lots, A615 Grade 60 R032110-10										
0020	Includes labor, but not material cost, to install accessories										
0030	Made from recycled materials										
0100	Beams & Girders, #3 to #7	G	4 Rodm	1.60	20	Ton	960	1,100		2,060	2,725
0150	#8 to #18	G		2.70	11.852		960	650		1,610	2,050
0200	Columns, #3 to #7	G		1.50	21.333		960	1,175		2,135	2,825
0210	#3 to #7, alternate method	G		3000	.011	Lb.	.50	.58		1.08	1.44
0250	#8 to #18	G		2.30	13.913	Ton	960	760		1,720	2,200
0260	#8 to #18, alternate method	G		4600	.007	Lb.	.50	.38		.88	1.13
0300	Spirals, hot rolled, 8" to 15" diameter	G		2.20	14.545	Ton	1,575	795		2,370	2,950
0320	15" to 24" diameter R032110-50	G		2.20	14.545		1,500	795		2,295	2,875
0330	24" to 36" diameter	G		2.30	13.913		1,425	760		2,185	2,725
0340	36" to 48" diameter R032110-70	G		2.40	13.333		1,350	730		2,080	2,625
0360	48" to 64" diameter	G		2.50	12.800		1,500	700		2,200	2,725
0380	64" to 84" diameter	G		2.60	12.308		1,575	675		2,250	2,750
0390	84" to 96" diameter	G		2.70	11.852		1,650	650		2,300	2,800
0400	Elevated slabs, #4 to #7 R032110-80	G		2.90	11.034		960	605		1,565	1,975
0500	Footings, #4 to #7	G		2.10	15.238		960	835		1,795	2,325

03 21 Reinforcement Bars

03 21 11 – Plain Steel Reinforcement Bars

03 21 11.60 Reinforcing In Place

			Crew	Daily Output	Labor-Hours	Unit	Material	2018 Bare Costs Labor	Equipment	Total	Total Incl O&P
0550	#8 to #18	R032110-20 G	4 Rodm	3.60	8.889	Ton	960	485		1,445	1,800
0600	Slab on grade, #3 to #7	G		2.30	13.913		960	760		1,720	2,200
0700	Walls, #3 to #7	G		3	10.667		960	585		1,545	1,950
0750	#8 to #18	G		4	8		960	435		1,395	1,725
0900	For other than 50-60 ton lots										
1000	Under 10 ton job, #3 to #7, add						25%	10%			
1010	#8 to #18, add						20%	10%			
1050	10-50 ton job, #3 to #7, add						10%				
1060	#8 to #18, add						5%				
1100	60-100 ton job, #3 to #7, deduct	R032110-80					5%				
1110	#8 to #18, deduct						10%				
1150	Over 100 ton job, #3 to #7, deduct						10%				
1160	#8 to #18, deduct						15%				
1200	Reinforcing in place, A615 Grade 75, add	G				Ton	91.50			91.50	101
2000	Unloading & sorting, add to above		C-5	100	.560			30.50	5.90	36.40	53
2200	Crane cost for handling, 90 picks/day, up to 1.5 tons/bundle, add to above			135	.415			22.50	4.38	26.88	39.50
2210	1.0 ton/bundle			92	.609			33	6.40	39.40	57.50
2220	0.5 ton/bundle			35	1.600			87	16.90	103.90	151
2400	Dowels, 2 feet long, deformed, #3	G	2 Rodm	520	.031	Ea.	.40	1.68		2.08	3.01
2410	#4	G		480	.033		.70	1.82		2.52	3.55
2420	#5	G		435	.037		1.10	2.01		3.11	4.28
2430	#6	G		360	.044		1.58	2.43		4.01	5.45
2450	Longer and heavier dowels, add	G		725	.022	Lb.	.53	1.21		1.74	2.42
2500	Smooth dowels, 12" long, 1/4" or 3/8" diameter	G		140	.114	Ea.	.73	6.25		6.98	10.35
2520	5/8" diameter	G		125	.128		1.28	7		8.28	12.10
2530	3/4" diameter	G		110	.145		1.58	7.95		9.53	13.90

03 21 19 – Stainless Steel Reinforcement Bars

03 21 19.10 Stainless Steel Reinforcing

0010	**STAINLESS STEEL REINFORCING**										
0100	Add to plain steel rebar pricing for stainless steel rebar						300%				

03 22 Fabric and Grid Reinforcing

03 22 11 – Plain Welded Wire Fabric Reinforcing

03 22 11.10 Plain Welded Wire Fabric

			Crew	Daily Output	Labor-Hours	Unit	Material	Labor	Equipment	Total	Total Incl O&P
0010	**PLAIN WELDED WIRE FABRIC** ASTM A185										
0020	Includes labor, but not material cost, to install accessories										
0030	Made from recycled materials										
0050	Sheets										
0100	6 x 6 - W1.4 x W1.4 (10 x 10) 21 lb./C.S.F.	G	2 Rodm	35	.457	C.S.F.	15.10	25		40.10	54.50
0200	6 x 6 - W2.1 x W2.1 (8 x 8) 30 lb./C.S.F.	G		31	.516		19.60	28		47.60	64.50
0300	6 x 6 - W2.9 x W2.9 (6 x 6) 42 lb./C.S.F.	G		29	.552		25.50	30		55.50	74
0400	6 x 6 - W4 x W4 (4 x 4) 58 lb./C.S.F.	G		27	.593		35	32.50		67.50	88
0500	4 x 4 - W1.4 x W1.4 (10 x 10) 31 lb./C.S.F.	G		31	.516		22.50	28		50.50	68
0600	4 x 4 - W2.1 x W2.1 (8 x 8) 44 lb./C.S.F.	G		29	.552		28	30		58	77
0650	4 x 4 - W2.9 x W2.9 (6 x 6) 61 lb./C.S.F.	G		27	.593		45	32.50		77.50	99
0700	4 x 4 - W4 x W4 (4 x 4) 85 lb./C.S.F.	G		25	.640		56.50	35		91.50	116
0750	Rolls										
0800	2 x 2 - #14 galv., 21 lb./C.S.F., beam & column wrap	G	2 Rodm	6.50	2.462	C.S.F.	46.50	135		181.50	256
0900	2 x 2 - #12 galv. for gunite reinforcing	G	"	6.50	2.462	"	70	135		205	282

03 22 Fabric and Grid Reinforcing

03 22 13 – Galvanized Welded Wire Fabric Reinforcing

03 22 13.10 Galvanized Welded Wire Fabric		Crew	Daily Output	Labor-Hours	Unit	Material	2018 Bare Costs Labor	Equipment	Total	Total Incl O&P
0010	**GALVANIZED WELDED WIRE FABRIC**									
0100	Add to plain welded wire pricing for galvanized welded wire				Lb.	.23			.23	.25

03 22 16 – Epoxy-Coated Welded Wire Fabric Reinforcing

03 22 16.10 Epoxy-Coated Welded Wire Fabric

		Crew	Daily Output	Labor-Hours	Unit	Material	Labor	Equipment	Total	Total Incl O&P
0010	**EPOXY-COATED WELDED WIRE FABRIC**									
0100	Add to plain welded wire pricing for epoxy-coated welded wire				Lb.	.39			.39	.43

03 23 Stressed Tendon Reinforcing

03 23 05 – Prestressing Tendons

03 23 05.50 Prestressing Steel

			Crew	Daily Output	Labor-Hours	Unit	Material	Labor	Equipment	Total	Total Incl O&P
0010	**PRESTRESSING STEEL**	R034136-90									
0100	Grouted strand, in beams, post-tensioned in field, 50' span, 100 kip	G	C-3	1200	.053	Lb.	2.85	2.71	.09	5.65	7.35
0150	300 kip	G		2700	.024		1.18	1.20	.04	2.42	3.18
0300	100' span, 100 kip	G		1700	.038		2.85	1.91	.07	4.83	6.10
0350	300 kip	G		3200	.020		2.44	1.02	.03	3.49	4.28
0500	200' span, 100 kip	G		2700	.024		2.85	1.20	.04	4.09	5
0550	300 kip	G		3500	.018		2.44	.93	.03	3.40	4.13
0800	Grouted bars, in beams, 50' span, 42 kip	G		2600	.025		1.10	1.25	.04	2.39	3.17
0850	143 kip	G		3200	.020		1.05	1.02	.03	2.10	2.75
1000	75' span, 42 kip	G		3200	.020		1.12	1.02	.03	2.17	2.82
1050	143 kip	G		4200	.015		.93	.77	.03	1.73	2.23
1200	Ungrouted strand, in beams, 50' span, 100 kip	G	C-4	1275	.025		.62	1.38	.02	2.02	2.82
1250	300 kip	G		1475	.022		.62	1.20	.02	1.84	2.53
1400	100' span, 100 kip	G		1500	.021		.62	1.18	.02	1.82	2.50
1450	300 kip	G		1650	.019		.62	1.07	.02	1.71	2.33
1600	200' span, 100 kip	G		1500	.021		.62	1.18	.02	1.82	2.50
1650	300 kip	G		1700	.019		.62	1.04	.02	1.68	2.28
1800	Ungrouted bars, in beams, 50' span, 42 kip	G		1400	.023		.48	1.26	.02	1.76	2.48
1850	143 kip	G		1700	.019		.48	1.04	.02	1.54	2.13
2000	75' span, 42 kip	G		1800	.018		.48	.98	.02	1.48	2.05
2050	143 kip	G		2200	.015		.48	.80	.01	1.29	1.78
2220	Ungrouted single strand, 100' elevated slab, 25 kip	G		1200	.027		.62	1.47	.03	2.12	2.96
2250	35 kip	G		1475	.022		.62	1.20	.02	1.84	2.53

03 24 Fibrous Reinforcing

03 24 05 – Reinforcing Fibers

03 24 05.70 Steel Fibers

			Crew	Daily Output	Labor-Hours	Unit	Material	Labor	Equipment	Total	Total Incl O&P
0010	**STEEL FIBERS**										
0140	ASTM A850, Type V, continuously deformed, 1-1/2" long x 0.045" diam.										
0150	Add to price of ready mix concrete	G				Lb.	1.22			1.22	1.34
0205	Alternate pricing, dosing at 5 lb./C.Y., add to price of RMC	G				C.Y.	6.10			6.10	6.70
0210	10 lb./C.Y.						12.20			12.20	13.40
0215	15 lb./C.Y.	G					18.30			18.30	20
0220	20 lb./C.Y.	G					24.50			24.50	27
0225	25 lb./C.Y.	G					30.50			30.50	33.50
0230	30 lb./C.Y.	G					36.50			36.50	40.50
0235	35 lb./C.Y.	G					42.50			42.50	47
0240	40 lb./C.Y.	G					49			49	53.50

For customer support on your Green Building Costs with RSMeans data, call 800.448.8182.

03 24 Fibrous Reinforcing

03 24 05 – Reinforcing Fibers

03 24 05.70 Steel Fibers

		Crew	Daily Output	Labor-Hours	Unit	Material	2018 Bare Costs Labor	Equipment	Total	Total Incl O&P
0250	50 lb./C.Y.	G			C.Y.	61			61	67
0275	75 lb./C.Y.	G				91.50			91.50	101
0300	100 lb./C.Y.	G				122			122	134

03 30 Cast-In-Place Concrete

03 30 53 – Miscellaneous Cast-In-Place Concrete

03 30 53.40 Concrete In Place

			Crew	Daily Output	Labor-Hours	Unit	Material	Labor	Equipment	Total	Total Incl O&P
0010	**CONCRETE IN PLACE**	R033105-10									
0020	Including forms (4 uses), Grade 60 rebar, concrete (Portland cement										
0050	Type I), placement and finishing unless otherwise indicated										
0500	Chimney foundations (5000 psi), over 5 C.Y.		C-14C	32.22	3.476	C.Y.	171	167	.80	338.80	445
0510	(3500 psi), under 5 C.Y.	R033105-70	"	23.71	4.724	"	198	227	1.09	426.09	565
3540	Equipment pad (3000 psi), 3' x 3' x 6" thick		C-14H	45	1.067	Ea.	44.50	52.50	.57	97.57	130
3550	4' x 4' x 6" thick			30	1.600		69	79	.85	148.85	197
3560	5' x 5' x 8" thick			18	2.667		126	132	1.41	259.41	340
3570	6' x 6' x 8" thick			14	3.429		173	169	1.82	343.82	450
3580	8' x 8' x 10" thick			8	6		370	296	3.18	669.18	860
3590	10' x 10' x 12" thick			5	9.600		645	475	5.10	1,125.10	1,425
3800	Footings (3000 psi), spread under 1 C.Y.		C-14C	28	4	C.Y.	185	192	.92	377.92	495
3825	1 C.Y. to 5 C.Y.			43	2.605		219	125	.60	344.60	430
3850	Over 5 C.Y.	R033105-80		75	1.493		203	72	.34	275.34	330
3900	Footings, strip (3000 psi), 18" x 9", unreinforced		C-14L	40	2.400		146	113	.65	259.65	335
3920	18" x 9", reinforced	R033105-85	C-14C	35	3.200		169	154	.74	323.74	420
3925	20" x 10", unreinforced		C-14L	45	2.133		142	100	.58	242.58	310
3930	20" x 10", reinforced		C-14C	40	2.800		161	135	.64	296.64	385
3935	24" x 12", unreinforced		C-14L	55	1.745		140	82	.47	222.47	280
3940	24" x 12", reinforced		C-14C	48	2.333		159	112	.54	271.54	345
3945	36" x 12", unreinforced		C-14L	70	1.371		136	64.50	.37	200.87	248
3950	36" x 12", reinforced		C-14C	60	1.867		153	90	.43	243.43	305
4000	Foundation mat (3000 psi), under 10 C.Y.			38.67	2.896		221	139	.67	360.67	455
4050	Over 20 C.Y.			56.40	1.986		196	95.50	.46	291.96	360
4520	Handicap access ramp (4000 psi), railing both sides, 3' wide		C-14H	14.58	3.292	L.F.	360	163	1.74	524.74	645
4525	5' wide			12.22	3.928		370	194	2.08	566.08	705
4530	With 6" curb and rails both sides, 3' wide			8.55	5.614		370	277	2.98	649.98	835
4535	5' wide			7.31	6.566		375	325	3.48	703.48	910
4751	Slab on grade (3500 psi), incl. troweled finish, not incl. forms										
4760	or reinforcing, over 10,000 S.F., 4" thick		C-14F	3425	.021	S.F.	1.61	.95	.01	2.57	3.21
4820	6" thick		"	3350	.021	"	2.36	.97	.01	3.34	4.06
5000	Slab on grade (3000 psi), incl. broom finish, not incl. forms										
5001	or reinforcing, 4" thick		C-14G	2873	.019	S.F.	1.57	.87	.01	2.45	3.04
5010	6" thick			2590	.022		2.46	.96	.01	3.43	4.15
5020	8" thick			2320	.024		3.20	1.08	.01	4.29	5.15
6800	Stairs (3500 psi), not including safety treads, free standing, 3'-6" wide		C-14H	83	.578	LF Nose	6.05	28.50	.31	34.86	50.50
6850	Cast on ground			125	.384	"	5.15	18.95	.20	24.30	35
7000	Stair landings, free standing			200	.240	S.F.	4.83	11.85	.13	16.81	23.50
7050	Cast on ground			475	.101	"	3.93	4.99	.05	8.97	11.95

For customer support on your Green Building Costs with RSMeans data, call 800.448.8182.

45

03 31 Structural Concrete

03 31 13 – Heavyweight Structural Concrete

03 31 13.35 Heavyweight Concrete, Ready Mix

			Crew	Daily Output	Labor-Hours	Unit	Material	2018 Bare Costs Labor	Equipment	Total	Total Incl O&P
0010	**HEAVYWEIGHT CONCRETE, READY MIX**, delivered	R033105-10									
0012	Includes local aggregate, sand, Portland cement (Type I) and water	R033105-40									
0015	Excludes all additives and treatments										
0020	2000 psi					C.Y.	115			115	127
0100	2500 psi						119			119	130
0150	3000 psi						121			121	133
0200	3500 psi	R033105-40					124			124	137
0300	4000 psi						128			128	140
0350	4500 psi	R033105-50					131			131	144
0400	5000 psi						134			134	148
1300	For winter concrete (hot water), add						5.35			5.35	5.90
1410	For mid-range water reducer, add						3.59			3.59	3.95
1420	For high-range water reducer/superplasticizer, add						6.30			6.30	6.90
1430	For retarder, add						3.23			3.23	3.55
1440	For non-Chloride accelerator, add						6.40			6.40	7.05
1450	For Chloride accelerator, per 1%, add						3.86			3.86	4.25
1460	For fiber reinforcing, synthetic (1 lb./C.Y.), add						8			8	8.80
1500	For Saturday delivery, add						8.50			8.50	9.35
1510	For truck holding/waiting time past 1st hour per load, add					Hr.	105			105	116
1520	For short load (less than 4 C.Y.), add per load					Ea.	86			86	94.50
4000	Flowable fill: ash, cement, aggregate, water										
4100	40 – 80 psi					C.Y.	80.50			80.50	89
4150	Structural: ash, cement, aggregate, water & sand										
4200	50 psi					C.Y.	80.50			80.50	89
4250	140 psi						81.50			81.50	89.50
4300	500 psi						84			84	92.50
4350	1000 psi						87			87	96

03 31 13.70 Placing Concrete

			Crew	Daily Output	Labor-Hours	Unit	Material	Labor	Equipment	Total	Total Incl O&P
0010	**PLACING CONCRETE**	R033105-70									
0020	Includes labor and equipment to place, level (strike off) and consolidate										
0050	Beams, elevated, small beams, pumped		C-20	60	1.067	C.Y.		45.50	15.55	61.05	86
0100	With crane and bucket		C-7	45	1.600			69.50	24	93.50	131
0400	Columns, square or round, 12" thick, pumped		C-20	60	1.067			45.50	15.55	61.05	86
0450	With crane and bucket		C-7	40	1.800			78	27	105	148
0600	18" thick, pumped		C-20	90	.711			30.50	10.35	40.85	57.50
0650	With crane and bucket		C-7	55	1.309			57	19.45	76.45	108
0800	24" thick, pumped		C-20	92	.696			30	10.15	40.15	56
0850	With crane and bucket		C-7	70	1.029			44.50	15.30	59.80	84.50
1400	Elevated slabs, less than 6" thick, pumped		C-20	140	.457			19.55	6.65	26.20	37
1450	With crane and bucket		C-7	95	.758			33	11.25	44.25	62.50
1500	6" to 10" thick, pumped		C-20	160	.400			17.10	5.85	22.95	32.50
1550	With crane and bucket		C-7	110	.655			28.50	9.75	38.25	53.50
1900	Footings, continuous, shallow, direct chute		C-6	120	.400			16.60	.43	17.03	25.50
1950	Pumped		C-20	150	.427			18.25	6.20	24.45	34.50
2000	With crane and bucket		C-7	90	.800			35	11.90	46.90	65.50
2400	Footings, spread, under 1 C.Y., direct chute		C-6	55	.873			36	.93	36.93	56
2450	Pumped		C-20	65	.985			42	14.35	56.35	80
2500	With crane and bucket		C-7	45	1.600			69.50	24	93.50	131
4300	Slab on grade, up to 6" thick, direct chute		C-6	110	.436			18.10	.47	18.57	28
4350	Pumped		C-20	130	.492			21	7.20	28.20	40
4400	With crane and bucket		C-7	110	.655			28.50	9.75	38.25	53.50
4600	Over 6" thick, direct chute		C-6	165	.291			12.05	.31	12.36	18.65

03 31 Structural Concrete

03 31 13 – Heavyweight Structural Concrete

03 31 13.70 Placing Concrete

		Crew	Daily Output	Labor-Hours	Unit	Material	2018 Bare Costs Labor	Equipment	Total	Total Incl O&P
4650	Pumped	C-20	185	.346	C.Y.		14.80	5.05	19.85	28
4700	With crane and bucket	C-7	145	.497			21.50	7.40	28.90	40.50
4900	Walls, 8" thick, direct chute	C-6	90	.533			22	.57	22.57	34
4950	Pumped	C-20	100	.640			27.50	9.35	36.85	52
5000	With crane and bucket	C-7	80	.900			39	13.35	52.35	73.50
5050	12" thick, direct chute	C-6	100	.480			19.90	.51	20.41	30.50
5100	Pumped	C-20	110	.582			25	8.50	33.50	47
5200	With crane and bucket	C-7	90	.800			35	11.90	46.90	65.50

03 31 16 – Lightweight Structural Concrete

03 31 16.10 Lightweight Concrete, Ready Mix

		Crew	Daily Output	Labor-Hours	Unit	Material	Labor	Equipment	Total	Total Incl O&P
0010	**LIGHTWEIGHT CONCRETE, READY MIX**									
0700	Lightweight, 110#/C.F.									
0740	2500 psi				C.Y.	116			116	127
0760	3000 psi					127			127	139
0780	3500 psi					128			128	141
0820	4000 psi					133			133	146
0840	4500 psi					140			140	153
0860	5000 psi					137			137	151

03 35 Concrete Finishing

03 35 13 – High-Tolerance Concrete Floor Finishing

03 35 13.30 Finishing Floors, High Tolerance

		Crew	Daily Output	Labor-Hours	Unit	Material	Labor	Equipment	Total	Total Incl O&P
0010	**FINISHING FLOORS, HIGH TOLERANCE**									
0100	Bull float only	C-10	4000	.006	S.F.		.27		.27	.40
0125	Bull float & manual float		2000	.012			.54		.54	.81
0150	Bull float, manual float & broom finish, w/edging & joints		1850	.013			.58		.58	.87
0200	Bull float, manual float & manual steel trowel		1265	.019			.85		.85	1.27
0250	Bull float, machine float & machine trowel (walk-behind)	C-10C	1715	.014			.63	.02	.65	.97
0300	Power screed, bull float, machine float & trowel (walk-behind)	C-10D	2400	.010			.45	.05	.50	.72
0350	Power screed, bull float, machine float & trowel (ride-on)	C-10E	4000	.006			.27	.06	.33	.47

03 35 43 – Polished Concrete Finishing

03 35 43.10 Polished Concrete Floors

		Crew	Daily Output	Labor-Hours	Unit	Material	Labor	Equipment	Total	Total Incl O&P
0010	**POLISHED CONCRETE FLOORS**									
0015	Processing of cured concrete to include grinding, honing,									
0020	and polishing of interior floors with 22" segmented diamond									
0025	planetary floor grinder (2 passes in different directions per grit)									
0100	Removal of pre-existing coatings, dry, with carbide discs using									
0105	dry vacuum pick-up system, final hand sweeping									
0110	Glue, adhesive or tar	J-4	1.60	15	M.S.F.	21	675	152	848	1,200
0120	Paint, epoxy, 1 coat		3.60	6.667		21	300	67.50	388.50	550
0130	2 coats		1.80	13.333		21	600	135	756	1,075
0200	Grinding and edging, wet, including wet vac pick-up and auto									
0205	scrubbing between grit changes									
0210	40-grit diamond/metal matrix	J-4A	1.60	20	M.S.F.	41.50	875	310	1,226.50	1,675
0220	80-grit diamond/metal matrix		2	16		41.50	700	249	990.50	1,375
0230	120-grit diamond/metal matrix		2.40	13.333		41.50	585	207	833.50	1,150
0240	200-grit diamond/metal matrix		2.80	11.429		41.50	500	178	719.50	990
0300	Spray on dye or stain (1 coat)	1 Cefi	16	.500		222	24		246	279
0400	Spray on densifier/hardener (2 coats)	"	8	1		365	47.50		412.50	470
0410	Auto scrubbing after 2nd coat, when dry	J-4B	16	.500			19.95	15.90	35.85	48

03 35 Concrete Finishing

03 35 43 – Polished Concrete Finishing

03 35 43.10 Polished Concrete Floors

		Crew	Daily Output	Labor-Hours	Unit	Material	2018 Bare Costs Labor	Equipment	Total	Total Incl O&P
0500	Honing and edging, wet, including wet vac pick-up and auto									
0505	scrubbing between grit changes									
0510	100-grit diamond/resin matrix	J-4A	2.80	11.429	M.S.F.	41.50	500	178	719.50	990
0520	200-grit diamond/resin matrix	"	2.80	11.429	"	41.50	500	178	719.50	990
0530	Dry, including dry vacuum pick-up system, final hand sweeping									
0540	400-grit diamond/resin matrix	J-4A	2.80	11.429	M.S.F.	41.50	500	178	719.50	990
0600	Polishing and edging, dry, including dry vac pick-up and hand									
0605	sweeping between grit changes									
0610	800-grit diamond/resin matrix	J-4A	2.80	11.429	M.S.F.	41.50	500	178	719.50	990
0620	1500-grit diamond/resin matrix		2.80	11.429		41.50	500	178	719.50	990
0630	3000-grit diamond/resin matrix		2.80	11.429		41.50	500	178	719.50	990
0700	Auto scrubbing after final polishing step	J-4B	16	.500			19.95	15.90	35.85	48

03 39 Concrete Curing

03 39 23 – Membrane Concrete Curing

03 39 23.13 Chemical Compound Membrane Concrete Curing

		Crew	Daily Output	Labor-Hours	Unit	Material	Labor	Equipment	Total	Total Incl O&P
0010	**CHEMICAL COMPOUND MEMBRANE CONCRETE CURING**									
0800	Curing compound, water based, 250 S.F./gal., 55 gallon lots				Gal.	21.50			21.50	23.50
0820	5 gallon lots				"	24			24	26.50

03 45 Precast Architectural Concrete

03 45 13 – Faced Architectural Precast Concrete

03 45 13.50 Precast Wall Panels

		Crew	Daily Output	Labor-Hours	Unit	Material	Labor	Equipment	Total	Total Incl O&P
0010	**PRECAST WALL PANELS** R034513-10									
0050	Uninsulated, smooth gray									
0150	Low rise, 4' x 8' x 4" thick	C-11	320	.225	S.F.	27.50	12.25	6.30	46.05	56.50
0210	8' x 8', 4" thick		576	.125		27	6.80	3.50	37.30	45
0250	8' x 16' x 4" thick		1024	.070		27	3.82	1.97	32.79	38
0600	High rise, 4' x 8' x 4" thick		288	.250		27.50	13.60	7	48.10	59.50
0650	8' x 8' x 4" thick		512	.141		27	7.65	3.94	38.59	46.50
0700	8' x 16' x 4" thick		768	.094		27	5.10	2.63	34.73	40.50
0750	10' x 20', 6" thick		1400	.051		46	2.80	1.44	50.24	56.50
0800	Insulated panel, 2" polystyrene, add					1.14			1.14	1.25
0850	2" urethane, add					.90			.90	.99

03 48 Precast Concrete Specialties

03 48 43 – Precast Concrete Trim

03 48 43.40 Precast Lintels

		Crew	Daily Output	Labor-Hours	Unit	Material	Labor	Equipment	Total	Total Incl O&P
0010	**PRECAST LINTELS**, smooth gray, prestressed, stock units only									
0800	4" wide, 8" high, x 4' long	D-10	28	1.143	Ea.	32.50	56.50	13	102	136
1000	6" wide, 8" high, x 4' long		26	1.231		48	61	14	123	161
1200	8" wide, 8" high, x 4' long		24	1.333		56.50	66	15.15	137.65	180

03 48 43.90 Precast Window Sills

		Crew	Daily Output	Labor-Hours	Unit	Material	Labor	Equipment	Total	Total Incl O&P
0010	**PRECAST WINDOW SILLS**									
0600	Precast concrete, 4" tapers to 3", 9" wide	D-1	70	.229	L.F.	19	10.25		29.25	36.50
0650	11" wide	"	60	.267	"	31	11.95		42.95	52.50

03 51 Cast Roof Decks

03 51 13 – Cementitious Wood Fiber Decks

03 51 13.50 Cementitious/Wood Fiber Planks

			Crew	Daily Output	Labor-Hours	Unit	Material	2018 Bare Costs Labor	Equipment	Total	Total Incl O&P
0010	**CEMENTITIOUS/WOOD FIBER PLANKS**	R051223-50									
0050	Plank, beveled edge, 1" thick		2 Carp	1000	.016	S.F.	3.41	.81		4.22	4.99
0100	1-1/2" thick			975	.016		4.42	.83		5.25	6.15
0150	T&G, 2" thick			950	.017		3.75	.85		4.60	5.45
0200	2-1/2" thick			925	.017		4.09	.88		4.97	5.85
0250	3" thick			900	.018		4.63	.90		5.53	6.45
1000	Bulb tee, sub-purlin and grout, 6' span, add		E-1	5000	.005		2.16	.26	.02	2.44	2.81
1100	8' span		"	4200	.006		2.16	.31	.02	2.49	2.90

03 52 Lightweight Concrete Roof Insulation

03 52 16 – Lightweight Insulating Concrete

03 52 16.13 Lightweight Cellular Insulating Concrete

				Crew	Daily Output	Labor-Hours	Unit	Material	Labor	Equipment	Total	Total Incl O&P
0010	**LIGHTWEIGHT CELLULAR INSULATING CONCRETE**		R035216-10									
0020	Portland cement and foaming agent	G		C-8	50	1.120	C.Y.	128	49.50	17.65	195.15	234

03 52 16.16 Lightweight Aggregate Insulating Concrete

			Crew	Daily Output	Labor-Hours	Unit	Material	Labor	Equipment	Total	Total Incl O&P
0010	**LIGHTWEIGHT AGGREGATE INSULATING CONCRETE**										
0100	Poured vermiculite or perlite, field mix,										
0110	1:6 field mix	G	C-8	50	1.120	C.Y.	255	49.50	17.65	322.15	375
0200	Ready mix, 1:6 mix, roof fill, 2" thick	G		10000	.006	S.F.	1.42	.25	.09	1.76	2.03
0250	3" thick	G		7700	.007		2.13	.32	.11	2.56	2.96
0400	Expanded volcanic glass rock, 1" thick	G	2 Carp	1500	.011		.62	.54		1.16	1.50
0450	3" thick	G	"	1200	.013		1.87	.68		2.55	3.08
1020	Lightweight insulating fill										
1040	1000 psi	G				C.Y.	113			113	124
1200	1:6 mix perlite					"	115			115	127

03 81 Concrete Cutting

03 81 13 – Flat Concrete Sawing

03 81 13.50 Concrete Floor/Slab Cutting

		Crew	Daily Output	Labor-Hours	Unit	Material	Labor	Equipment	Total	Total Incl O&P
0010	**CONCRETE FLOOR/SLAB CUTTING**									
0050	Includes blade cost, layout and set-up time									
0300	Saw cut concrete slabs, plain, up to 3" deep	B-89	1060	.015	L.F.	.12	.72	.40	1.24	1.67
0320	Each additional inch of depth		3180	.005		.04	.24	.13	.41	.56
0400	Mesh reinforced, up to 3" deep		980	.016		.14	.78	.43	1.35	1.80
0420	Each additional inch of depth		2940	.005		.05	.26	.14	.45	.60
0500	Rod reinforced, up to 3" deep		800	.020		.17	.96	.53	1.66	2.21
0520	Each additional inch of depth		2400	.007		.06	.32	.18	.56	.73

03 81 13.75 Concrete Saw Blades

		Unit	Material			Total	Total Incl O&P
0010	**CONCRETE SAW BLADES**						
3000	Blades for saw cutting, included in cutting line items						
3040	18" diameter	Ea.	415			415	460
3080	24" diameter		695			695	765
3120	30" diameter		980			980	1,075
3160	36" diameter		1,300			1,300	1,425
3200	42" diameter		2,550			2,550	2,800

03 81 Concrete Cutting

03 81 16 – Track Mounted Concrete Wall Sawing

03 81 16.50 Concrete Wall Cutting		Crew	Daily Output	Labor-Hours	Unit	Material	2018 Bare Costs Labor	Equipment	Total	Total Incl O&P
0010	**CONCRETE WALL CUTTING**									
0750	Includes blade cost, layout and set-up time									
0800	Concrete walls, hydraulic saw, plain, per inch of depth	B-89B	250	.064	L.F.	.04	3.07	2.69	5.80	7.65
0820	Rod reinforcing, per inch of depth	"	150	.107	"	.06	5.10	4.48	9.64	12.70

Division 4 — Masonry

Estimating Tips
04 05 00 Common Work Results for Masonry

- The terms mortar and grout are often used interchangeably—and incorrectly. Mortar is used to bed masonry units, seal the entry of air and moisture, provide architectural appearance, and allow for size variations in the units. Grout is used primarily in reinforced masonry construction and to bond the masonry to the reinforcing steel. Common mortar types are M (2500 psi), S (1800 psi), N (750 psi), and O (350 psi), and they conform to ASTM C270. Grout is either fine or coarse and conforms to ASTM C476, and in-place strengths generally exceed 2500 psi. Mortar and grout are different components of masonry construction and are placed by entirely different methods. An estimator should be aware of their unique uses and costs.
- Mortar is included in all assembled masonry line items. The mortar cost, part of the assembled masonry material cost, includes all ingredients, all labor, and all equipment required. Please see reference number R040513-10.
- Waste, specifically the loss/droppings of mortar and the breakage of brick and block, is included in all unit cost lines that include mortar and masonry units in this division. A factor of 25% is added for mortar and 3% for brick and concrete masonry units.
- Scaffolding or staging is not included in any of the Division 4 costs. Refer to Subdivision 01 54 23 for scaffolding and staging costs.

04 20 00 Unit Masonry

- The most common types of unit masonry are brick and concrete masonry. The major classifications of brick are building brick (ASTM C62), facing brick (ASTM C216), glazed brick, fire brick, and pavers. Many varieties of texture and appearance can exist within these classifications, and the estimator would be wise to check local custom and availability within the project area. For repair and remodeling jobs, matching the existing brick may be the most important criteria.
- Brick and concrete block are priced by the piece and then converted into a price per square foot of wall. Openings less than two square feet are generally ignored by the estimator because any savings in units used are offset by the cutting and trimming required.
- It is often difficult and expensive to find and purchase small lots of historic brick. Costs can vary widely. Many design issues affect costs, selection of mortar mix, and repairs or replacement of masonry materials. Cleaning techniques must be reflected in the estimate.
- All masonry walls, whether interior or exterior, require bracing. The cost of bracing walls during construction should be included by the estimator, and this bracing must remain in place until permanent bracing is complete. Permanent bracing of masonry walls is accomplished by masonry itself, in the form of pilasters or abutting wall corners, or by anchoring the walls to the structural frame. Accessories in the form of anchors, anchor slots, and ties are used, but their supply and installation can be by different trades. For instance, anchor slots on spandrel beams and columns are supplied and welded in place by the steel fabricator, but the ties from the slots into the masonry are installed by the bricklayer. Regardless of the installation method, the estimator must be certain that these accessories are accounted for in pricing.

Reference Numbers

Reference numbers are shown at the beginning of some major classifications. These numbers refer to related items in the Reference Section. The reference information may be an estimating procedure, an alternate pricing method, or technical information.

Note: Not all subdivisions listed here necessarily appear. ■

Did you know?

RSMeans data is available through our online application with 24/7 access:

- Search for unit prices by keyword
- Leverage the most up-to-date data
- Build and export estimates

Try it free for 30 days!
www.rsmeans.com/2018freetrial

No part of this cost data may be reproduced, stored in a retrieval system, or transmitted in any form or by any means without prior written permission of Gordian.

04 05 Common Work Results for Masonry

04 05 05 – Selective Demolition for Masonry

04 05 05.10 Selective Demolition		Crew	Daily Output	Labor-Hours	Unit	Material	2018 Bare Costs Labor	Equipment	Total	Total Incl O&P
0010	**SELECTIVE DEMOLITION** R024119-10									
0200	Bond beams, 8" block with #4 bar	2 Clab	32	.500	L.F.		19.95		19.95	30.50
0300	Concrete block walls, unreinforced, 2" thick		1200	.013	S.F.		.53		.53	.81
0310	4" thick		1150	.014			.55		.55	.84
0320	6" thick		1100	.015			.58		.58	.88
0330	8" thick		1050	.015			.61		.61	.93
0340	10" thick		1000	.016			.64		.64	.97
0360	12" thick		950	.017			.67		.67	1.02
0380	Reinforced alternate courses, 2" thick		1130	.014			.56		.56	.86
0390	4" thick		1080	.015			.59		.59	.90
0400	6" thick		1035	.015			.62		.62	.94
0410	8" thick		990	.016			.64		.64	.98
0420	10" thick		940	.017			.68		.68	1.03
0430	12" thick		890	.018			.72		.72	1.09
0440	Reinforced alternate courses & vertically 48" OC, 4" thick		900	.018			.71		.71	1.08
0450	6" thick		850	.019			.75		.75	1.14
0460	8" thick		800	.020			.80		.80	1.21
0480	10" thick		750	.021			.85		.85	1.29
0490	12" thick		700	.023			.91		.91	1.39
1000	Chimney, 16" x 16", soft old mortar	1 Clab	55	.145	C.F.		5.80		5.80	8.85
1020	Hard mortar		40	.200			7.95		7.95	12.15
1030	16" x 20", soft old mortar		55	.145			5.80		5.80	8.85
1040	Hard mortar		40	.200			7.95		7.95	12.15
1050	16" x 24", soft old mortar		55	.145			5.80		5.80	8.85
1060	Hard mortar		40	.200			7.95		7.95	12.15
1080	20" x 20", soft old mortar		55	.145			5.80		5.80	8.85
1100	Hard mortar		40	.200			7.95		7.95	12.15
1110	20" x 24", soft old mortar		55	.145			5.80		5.80	8.85
1120	Hard mortar		40	.200			7.95		7.95	12.15
1140	20" x 32", soft old mortar		55	.145			5.80		5.80	8.85
1160	Hard mortar		40	.200			7.95		7.95	12.15
1200	48" x 48", soft old mortar		55	.145			5.80		5.80	8.85
1220	Hard mortar		40	.200			7.95		7.95	12.15
1250	Metal, high temp steel jacket, 24" diameter	E-2	130	.431	V.L.F.		23.50	13	36.50	52
1260	60" diameter	"	60	.933			50.50	28	78.50	112
1280	Flue lining, up to 12" x 12"	1 Clab	200	.040			1.59		1.59	2.43
1282	Up to 24" x 24"		150	.053			2.13		2.13	3.24
2000	Columns, 8" x 8", soft old mortar		48	.167			6.65		6.65	10.10
2020	Hard mortar		40	.200			7.95		7.95	12.15
2060	16" x 16", soft old mortar		16	.500			19.95		19.95	30.50
2100	Hard mortar		14	.571			23		23	34.50
2140	24" x 24", soft old mortar		8	1			40		40	60.50
2160	Hard mortar		6	1.333			53		53	81
2200	36" x 36", soft old mortar		4	2			79.50		79.50	121
2220	Hard mortar		3	2.667			106		106	162
2230	Alternate pricing method, soft old mortar		30	.267	C.F.		10.65		10.65	16.20
2240	Hard mortar		23	.348	"		13.85		13.85	21
3000	Copings, precast or masonry, to 8" wide									
3020	Soft old mortar	1 Clab	180	.044	L.F.		1.77		1.77	2.70
3040	Hard mortar	"	160	.050	"		1.99		1.99	3.04
3100	To 12" wide									
3120	Soft old mortar	1 Clab	160	.050	L.F.		1.99		1.99	3.04
3140	Hard mortar	"	140	.057	"		2.28		2.28	3.47

04 05 Common Work Results for Masonry

04 05 05 – Selective Demolition for Masonry

04 05 05.10 Selective Demolition

		Crew	Daily Output	Labor-Hours	Unit	Material	2018 Bare Costs Labor	Equipment	Total	Total Incl O&P
4000	Fireplace, brick, 30" x 24" opening									
4020	Soft old mortar	1 Clab	2	4	Ea.		159		159	243
4040	Hard mortar		1.25	6.400			255		255	390
4100	Stone, soft old mortar		1.50	5.333			213		213	325
4120	Hard mortar		1	8			320		320	485
4150	Up to 48" fireplace, 15' chimney and foundation		.28	28.571			1,150		1,150	1,725
4400	Premanufactured, up to 48"	2 Clab	14	1.143			45.50		45.50	69.50
5000	Veneers, brick, soft old mortar	1 Clab	140	.057	S.F.		2.28		2.28	3.47
5020	Hard mortar		125	.064			2.55		2.55	3.88
5050	Glass block, up to 4" thick		500	.016			.64		.64	.97
5100	Granite and marble, 2" thick		180	.044			1.77		1.77	2.70
5120	4" thick		170	.047			1.88		1.88	2.86
5140	Stone, 4" thick		180	.044			1.77		1.77	2.70
5160	8" thick		175	.046			1.82		1.82	2.77
5400	Alternate pricing method, stone, 4" thick		60	.133	C.F.		5.30		5.30	8.10
5420	8" thick		85	.094			3.75		3.75	5.70
5450	Solid masonry		130	.062			2.45		2.45	3.74
5460	Stone or precast sills, treads, copings		130	.062			2.45		2.45	3.74
5470	Solid stone or precast		110	.073			2.90		2.90	4.41
5500	Remove and reset steel lintel	1 Bric	40	.200	L.F.		10.05		10.05	15.40
5600	Vent box removal	1 Clab	50	.160	S.F.		6.40		6.40	9.70
5700	Remove block pilaster for fence, 6' high		2.33	3.433	Ea.		137		137	208
5800	Remove 12" x 12" step flashing from mortar joints		240	.033	C.F.		1.33		1.33	2.02

04 22 Concrete Unit Masonry

04 22 10 – Concrete Masonry Units

04 22 10.10 Concrete Block

0010	**CONCRETE BLOCK** Material Only R042210-20									
0020	2" x 8" x 16" solid, normal-weight, 2,000 psi				Ea.	1.12			1.12	1.23
0050	3,500 psi					1.24			1.24	1.36
0100	5,000 psi					1.41			1.41	1.55
0150	Lightweight, std.					1.35			1.35	1.49
0300	3" x 8" x 16" solid, normal-weight, 2,000 psi					.98			.98	1.08
0350	3,500 psi					1.35			1.35	1.49
0400	5,000 psi					1.53			1.53	1.68
0450	Lightweight, std.					1.33			1.33	1.46
0600	4" x 8" x 16" hollow, normal-weight, 2,000 psi					1.29			1.29	1.42
0650	3,500 psi					1.43			1.43	1.57
0700	5,000 psi					1.71			1.71	1.88
0750	Lightweight, std.					1.40			1.40	1.54
1300	Solid, normal-weight, 2,000 psi					1.52			1.52	1.67
1350	3,500 psi					1.74			1.74	1.91
1400	5,000 psi					1.43			1.43	1.57
1450	Lightweight, std.					1.20			1.20	1.32
1600	6" x 8" x 16" hollow, normal-weight, 2,000 psi					1.68			1.68	1.85
1650	3,500 psi					1.91			1.91	2.10
1700	5,000 psi					2.11			2.11	2.32
1750	Lightweight, std.					1.99			1.99	2.19
2300	Solid, normal-weight, 2,000 psi					1.74			1.74	1.91
2350	3,500 psi					1.60			1.60	1.76
2400	5,000 psi					2.13			2.13	2.34

04 22 Concrete Unit Masonry

04 22 10 – Concrete Masonry Units

04 22 10.10 Concrete Block

		Crew	Daily Output	Labor-Hours	Unit	Material	2018 Bare Costs Labor	Equipment	Total	Total Incl O&P
2450	Lightweight, std.				Ea.	2.44			2.44	2.68
2600	8" x 8" x 16" hollow, normal-weight, 2,000 psi					1.70			1.70	1.87
2650	3,500 psi					1.82			1.82	2
2700	5,000 psi					2.56			2.56	2.82
2750	Lightweight, std.					2.40			2.40	2.64
3060	Conc. block, C145, 8" x 8" x 16", 1.125 per S.F.				S.F.	2.99			2.99	3.29
3200	Solid, normal-weight, 2,000 psi				Ea.	2.69			2.69	2.96
3250	3,500 psi					2.65			2.65	2.92
3300	5,000 psi					3.13			3.13	3.44
3350	Lightweight, std.					2.68			2.68	2.95
3400	10" x 8" x 16" hollow, normal-weight, 2,000 psi					1.70			1.70	1.87
3410	3,500 psi					1.82			1.82	2
3420	5,000 psi					2.56			2.56	2.82
3430	Lightweight, std.					2.40			2.40	2.64
3480	Solid, normal-weight, 2,000 psi					2.69			2.69	2.96
3490	3,500 psi					2.65			2.65	2.92
3500	5,000 psi					3.13			3.13	3.44
3510	Lightweight, std.					2.68			2.68	2.95
3600	12" x 8" x 16" hollow, normal-weight, 2,000 psi					2.96			2.96	3.26
3650	3,500 psi					2.99			2.99	3.29
3700	5,000 psi					3.43			3.43	3.77
3750	Lightweight, std.					2.97			2.97	3.27
4300	Solid, normal-weight, 2,000 psi					4.14			4.14	4.55
4350	3,500 psi					3.57			3.57	3.93
4400	5,000 psi					3.46			3.46	3.81
4500	Lightweight, std.					2.89			2.89	3.18

04 22 10.11 Autoclave Aerated Concrete Block

				Crew	Daily Output	Labor-Hours	Unit	Material	Labor	Equipment	Total	Incl O&P
0010	**AUTOCLAVE AERATED CONCRETE BLOCK**, excl. scaffolding, grout & reinforcing											
0050	Solid, 4" x 8" x 24", incl. mortar		G	D-8	600	.067	S.F.	1.50	3.06		4.56	6.35
0060	6" x 8" x 24"	R042110-50			600	.067		2.25	3.06		5.31	7.15
0070	8" x 8" x 24"		G		575	.070		3	3.19		6.19	8.20
0080	10" x 8" x 24"		G		575	.070		3.66	3.19		6.85	8.90
0090	12" x 8" x 24"		G		550	.073		4.50	3.34		7.84	10.05

04 24 Adobe Unit Masonry

04 24 16 – Manufactured Adobe Unit Masonry

04 24 16.06 Adobe Brick

			Crew	Daily Output	Labor-Hours	Unit	Material	Labor	Equipment	Total	Incl O&P
0010	**ADOBE BRICK**, Semi-stabilized, with cement mortar										
0060	Brick, 10" x 4" x 14", 2.6/S.F.	G	D-8	560	.071	S.F.	4.78	3.28		8.06	10.25
0080	12" x 4" x 16", 2.3/S.F.	G		580	.069		7	3.17		10.17	12.55
0100	10" x 4" x 16", 2.3/S.F.	G		590	.068		6.55	3.11		9.66	11.95
0120	8" x 4" x 16", 2.3/S.F.	G		560	.071		4.99	3.28		8.27	10.50
0140	4" x 4" x 16", 2.3/S.F.	G		540	.074		4.88	3.40		8.28	10.55
0160	6" x 4" x 16", 2.3/S.F.	G		540	.074		4.53	3.40		7.93	10.20
0180	4" x 4" x 12", 3.0/S.F.	G		520	.077		5.25	3.53		8.78	11.20
0200	8" x 4" x 12", 3.0/S.F.	G		520	.077		4.34	3.53		7.87	10.20

04 41 Dry-Placed Stone

04 41 10 – Dry Placed Stone

04 41 10.10 Rough Stone Wall

		Crew	Daily Output	Labor-Hours	Unit	Material	2018 Bare Costs Labor	Equipment	Total	Total Incl O&P
0011	**ROUGH STONE WALL**, Dry									
0012	Dry laid (no mortar), under 18" thick	G	D-1	60	.267	C.F.	13.50	11.95		25.45	33
0100	Random fieldstone, under 18" thick	G	D-12	60	.533		13.50	24		37.50	52
0150	Over 18" thick	G	"	63	.508		16.20	23		39.20	53
0500	Field stone veneer	G	D-8	120	.333	S.F.	12.65	15.30		27.95	37.50
0510	Valley stone veneer	G		120	.333		12.65	15.30		27.95	37.50
0520	River stone veneer	G		120	.333		12.65	15.30		27.95	37.50
0600	Rubble stone walls, in mortar bed, up to 18" thick	G	D-11	75	.320	C.F.	16.30	15.15		31.45	41

04 43 Stone Masonry

04 43 10 – Masonry with Natural and Processed Stone

04 43 10.50 Lightweight Natural Stone

		Crew	Daily Output	Labor-Hours	Unit	Material	Labor	Equipment	Total	Total Incl O&P
0011	**LIGHTWEIGHT NATURAL STONE** Lava type									
0100	Veneer, rubble face, sawed back, irregular shapes	G	D-10	130	.246	S.F.	8.95	12.20	2.80	23.95	31.50
0200	Sawed face and back, irregular shapes	G		130	.246	"	8.95	12.20	2.80	23.95	31.50
1000	Reclaimed or antique, barn or foundation stone			1	32	Ton	395	1,575	365	2,335	3,250

04 71 Manufactured Brick Masonry

04 71 10 – Simulated or Manufactured Brick

04 71 10.10 Simulated Brick

		Crew	Daily Output	Labor-Hours	Unit	Material	Labor	Equipment	Total	Total Incl O&P
0010	**SIMULATED BRICK**									
0020	Aluminum, baked on colors	1 Carp	200	.040	S.F.	4.50	2.03		6.53	8.05
0050	Fiberglass panels		200	.040		10	2.03		12.03	14.10
0100	Urethane pieces cemented in mastic		150	.053		8.60	2.70		11.30	13.55
0150	Vinyl siding panels		200	.040		10.90	2.03		12.93	15.10
0160	Cement base, brick, incl. mastic	D-1	100	.160		9.75	7.15		16.90	21.50
0170	Corner		50	.320	V.L.F.	21.50	14.35		35.85	45.50
0180	Stone face, incl. mastic		100	.160	S.F.	10.40	7.15		17.55	22.50
0190	Corner		50	.320	V.L.F.	24.50	14.35		38.85	49

04 72 Cast Stone Masonry

04 72 20 – Cultured Stone Veneer

04 72 20.10 Cultured Stone Veneer Components

		Crew	Daily Output	Labor-Hours	Unit	Material	Labor	Equipment	Total	Total Incl O&P
0010	**CULTURED STONE VENEER COMPONENTS**									
0110	On wood frame and sheathing substrate, random sized cobbles, corner stones	D-8	70	.571	V.L.F.	10.40	26		36.40	51.50
0120	Field stones		140	.286	S.F.	7.55	13.10		20.65	28.50
0130	Random sized flats, corner stones		70	.571	V.L.F.	10.70	26		36.70	52
0140	Field stones		140	.286	S.F.	8.90	13.10		22	30
0150	Horizontal lined ledgestones, corner stones		75	.533	V.L.F.	10.40	24.50		34.90	49
0160	Field stones		150	.267	S.F.	7.55	12.25		19.80	27
0170	Random shaped flats, corner stones		65	.615	V.L.F.	10.40	28.50		38.90	54.50
0180	Field stones		150	.267	S.F.	7.55	12.25		19.80	27
0190	Random shaped/textured face, corner stones		65	.615	V.L.F.	10.40	28.50		38.90	54.50
0200	Field stones		130	.308	S.F.	7.55	14.10		21.65	30
0210	Random shaped river rock, corner stones		65	.615	V.L.F.	10.40	28.50		38.90	54.50
0220	Field stones		130	.308	S.F.	7.55	14.10		21.65	30
0240	On concrete or CMU substrate, random sized cobbles, corner stones		70	.571	V.L.F.	9.70	26		35.70	50.50

04 72 Cast Stone Masonry

04 72 20 – Cultured Stone Veneer

04 72 20.10 Cultured Stone Veneer Components

		Crew	Daily Output	Labor-Hours	Unit	Material	2018 Bare Costs Labor	Equipment	Total	Total Incl O&P
0250	Field stones	D-8	140	.286	S.F.	7.20	13.10		20.30	28
0260	Random sized flats, corner stones		70	.571	V.L.F.	10	26		36	51
0270	Field stones		140	.286	S.F.	8.55	13.10		21.65	29.50
0280	Horizontal lined ledgestones, corner stones		75	.533	V.L.F.	9.70	24.50		34.20	48
0290	Field stones		150	.267	S.F.	7.20	12.25		19.45	26.50
0300	Random shaped flats, corner stones		70	.571	V.L.F.	9.70	26		35.70	50.50
0310	Field stones		140	.286	S.F.	7.20	13.10		20.30	28
0320	Random shaped/textured face, corner stones		65	.615	V.L.F.	9.70	28.50		38.20	53.50
0330	Field stones		130	.308	S.F.	7.20	14.10		21.30	29.50
0340	Random shaped river rock, corner stones		65	.615	V.L.F.	9.70	28.50		38.20	53.50
0350	Field stones		130	.308	S.F.	7.20	14.10		21.30	29.50
0360	Cultured stone veneer, #15 felt weather resistant barrier	1 Clab	3700	.002	Sq.	5.35	.09		5.44	6.05
0370	Expanded metal lath, diamond, 2.5 lb./S.Y., galvanized	1 Lath	85	.094	S.Y.	3.10	4.63		7.73	10.25
0390	Water table or window sill, 18" long	1 Bric	80	.100	Ea.	10	5.05		15.05	18.70

04 73 Manufactured Stone Masonry

04 73 20 – Simulated or Manufactured Stone

04 73 20.10 Simulated Stone

		Crew	Daily Output	Labor-Hours	Unit	Material	Labor	Equipment	Total	Total Incl O&P
0010	**SIMULATED STONE**									
0100	Insulated fiberglass panels, 5/8" ply backer	L-4	200	.120	S.F.	10	5.70		15.70	19.75

56   For customer support on your Green Building Costs with RSMeans data, call 800.448.8182.

Estimating Tips

05 05 00 Common Work Results for Metals

- Nuts, bolts, washers, connection angles, and plates can add a significant amount to both the tonnage of a structural steel job and the estimated cost. As a rule of thumb, add 10% to the total weight to account for these accessories.
- Type 2 steel construction, commonly referred to as "simple construction," consists generally of field-bolted connections with lateral bracing supplied by other elements of the building, such as masonry walls or x-bracing. The estimator should be aware, however, that shop connections may be accomplished by welding or bolting. The method may be particular to the fabrication shop and may have an impact on the estimated cost.

05 10 00 Structural Steel

- Steel items can be obtained from two sources: a fabrication shop or a metals service center. Fabrication shops can fabricate items under more controlled conditions than crews in the field can. They are also more efficient and can produce items more economically. Metal service centers serve as a source of long mill shapes to both fabrication shops and contractors.
- Most line items in this structural steel subdivision, and most items in 05 50 00 Metal Fabrications, are indicated as being shop fabricated. The bare material cost for these shop fabricated items is the "Invoice Cost" from the shop and includes the mill base price of steel plus mill extras, transportation to the shop, shop drawings and detailing where warranted, shop fabrication and handling, sandblasting and a shop coat of primer paint, all necessary structural bolts, and delivery to the job site. The bare labor cost and bare equipment cost for these shop fabricated items are for field installation or erection.
- Line items in Subdivision 05 12 23.40 Lightweight Framing, and other items scattered in Division 5, are indicated as being field fabricated. The bare material cost for these field fabricated items is the "Invoice Cost" from the metals service center and includes the mill base price of steel plus mill extras, transportation to the metals service center, material handling, and delivery of long lengths of mill shapes to the job site. Material costs for structural bolts and welding rods should be added to the estimate. The bare labor cost and bare equipment cost for these items are for both field fabrication and field installation or erection, and include time for cutting, welding, and drilling in the fabricated metal items. Drilling into concrete and fasteners to fasten field fabricated items to other work are not included and should be added to the estimate.

05 20 00 Steel Joist Framing

- In any given project the total weight of open web steel joists is determined by the loads to be supported and the design. However, economies can be realized in minimizing the amount of labor used to place the joists. This is done by maximizing the joist spacing, and therefore minimizing the number of joists required to be installed on the job. Certain spacings and locations may be required by the design, but in other cases maximizing the spacing and keeping it as uniform as possible will keep the costs down.

05 30 00 Steel Decking

- The takeoff and estimating of a metal deck involves more than the area of the floor or roof and the type of deck specified or shown on the drawings. Many different sizes and types of openings may exist. Small openings for individual pipes or conduits may be drilled after the floor/roof is installed, but larger openings may require special deck lengths as well as reinforcing or structural support. The estimator should determine who will be supplying this reinforcing. Additionally, some deck terminations are part of the deck package, such as screed angles and pour stops, and others will be part of the steel contract, such as angles attached to structural members and cast-in-place angles and plates. The estimator must ensure that all pieces are accounted for in the complete estimate.

05 50 00 Metal Fabrications

- The most economical steel stairs are those that use common materials, standard details, and most importantly, a uniform and relatively simple method of field assembly. Commonly available A36/A992 channels and plates are very good choices for the main stringers of the stairs, as are angles and tees for the carrier members. Risers and treads are usually made by specialty shops, and it is most economical to use a typical detail in as many places as possible. The stairs should be pre-assembled and shipped directly to the site. The field connections should be simple and straightforward enough to be accomplished efficiently, and with minimum equipment and labor.

Reference Numbers

Reference numbers are shown at the beginning of some major classifications. These numbers refer to related items in the Reference Section. The reference information may be an estimating procedure, an alternate pricing method, or technical information.

Note: Not all subdivisions listed here necessarily appear. ■

No part of this cost data may be reproduced, stored in a retrieval system, or transmitted in any form or by any means without prior written permission of Gordian.

Did you know?

RSMeans data is available through our online application with 24/7 access:
- Search for unit prices by keyword
- Leverage the most up-to-date data
- Build and export estimates

Try it free for 30 days!
www.rsmeans.com/2018freetrial

05 05 Common Work Results for Metals

05 05 05 – Selective Demolition for Metals

05 05 05.10 Selective Demolition, Metals

		Crew	Daily Output	Labor-Hours	Unit	Material	2018 Bare Costs Labor	Equipment	Total	Total Incl O&P
0010	**SELECTIVE DEMOLITION, METALS**	R024119-10								
0015	Excludes shores, bracing, cutting, loading, hauling, dumping									
0020	Remove nuts only up to 3/4" diameter	1 Sswk	480	.017	Ea.		.91		.91	1.49
0030	7/8" to 1-1/4" diameter		240	.033			1.82		1.82	2.98
0040	1-3/8" to 2" diameter		160	.050			2.73		2.73	4.47
0060	Unbolt and remove structural bolts up to 3/4" diameter		240	.033			1.82		1.82	2.98
0070	7/8" to 2" diameter		160	.050			2.73		2.73	4.47
0140	Light weight framing members, remove whole or cut up, up to 20 lb.		240	.033			1.82		1.82	2.98
0150	21-40 lb.	2 Sswk	210	.076			4.16		4.16	6.80
0160	41-80 lb.	3 Sswk	180	.133			7.30		7.30	11.90
0170	81-120 lb.	4 Sswk	150	.213			11.65		11.65	19.05
0230	Structural members, remove whole or cut up, up to 500 lb.	E-19	48	.500			27	22.50	49.50	68
0240	1/4-2 tons	E-18	36	1.111			61	30	91	131
0250	2-5 tons	E-24	30	1.067			58	19.70	77.70	115
0260	5-10 tons	E-20	24	2.667			145	55	200	293
0270	10-15 tons	E-2	18	3.111			169	93.50	262.50	375
0340	Fabricated item, remove whole or cut up, up to 20 lb.	1 Sswk	96	.083			4.55		4.55	7.45
0350	21-40 lb.	2 Sswk	84	.190			10.40		10.40	17
0360	41-80 lb.	3 Sswk	72	.333			18.20		18.20	30
0370	81-120 lb.	4 Sswk	60	.533			29		29	47.50
0380	121-500 lb.	E-19	48	.500			27	22.50	49.50	68
0390	501-1000 lb.	"	36	.667			36	30	66	90.50
0500	Steel roof decking, uncovered, bare	B-2	5000	.008	S.F.		.32		.32	.49

05 05 19 – Post-Installed Concrete Anchors

05 05 19.20 Expansion Anchors

			Crew	Daily Output	Labor-Hours	Unit	Material	Labor	Equipment	Total	Total Incl O&P
0010	**EXPANSION ANCHORS**										
0100	Anchors for concrete, brick or stone, no layout and drilling										
0200	Expansion shields, zinc, 1/4" diameter, 1-5/16" long, single	G	1 Carp	90	.089	Ea.	.45	4.51		4.96	7.35
0300	1-3/8" long, double	G		85	.094		.58	4.77		5.35	7.90
0400	3/8" diameter, 1-1/2" long, single	G		85	.094		.69	4.77		5.46	8
0500	2" long, double	G		80	.100		1.15	5.05		6.20	8.95
0600	1/2" diameter, 2-1/16" long, single	G		80	.100		1.26	5.05		6.31	9.10
0700	2-1/2" long, double	G		75	.107		2.13	5.40		7.53	10.60
0800	5/8" diameter, 2-5/8" long, single	G		75	.107		2.18	5.40		7.58	10.65
0900	2-3/4" long, double	G		70	.114		2.92	5.80		8.72	12
1000	3/4" diameter, 2-3/4" long, single	G		70	.114		3.29	5.80		9.09	12.40
1100	3-15/16" long, double	G		65	.123		5.45	6.25		11.70	15.50
2100	Hollow wall anchors for gypsum wall board, plaster or tile										
2300	1/8" diameter, short	G	1 Carp	160	.050	Ea.	.33	2.54		2.87	4.22
2400	Long	G		150	.053		.32	2.70		3.02	4.47
2500	3/16" diameter, short	G		150	.053		.51	2.70		3.21	4.68
2600	Long	G		140	.057		.67	2.90		3.57	5.15
2700	1/4" diameter, short	G		140	.057		.73	2.90		3.63	5.20
2800	Long	G		130	.062		.80	3.12		3.92	5.65
3000	Toggle bolts, bright steel, 1/8" diameter, 2" long	G		85	.094		.25	4.77		5.02	7.55
3100	4" long	G		80	.100		.29	5.05		5.34	8
3200	3/16" diameter, 3" long	G		80	.100		.33	5.05		5.38	8.05
3300	6" long	G		75	.107		.45	5.40		5.85	8.75
3400	1/4" diameter, 3" long	G		75	.107		.41	5.40		5.81	8.70
3500	6" long	G		70	.114		.59	5.80		6.39	9.45
3600	3/8" diameter, 3" long	G		70	.114		.86	5.80		6.66	9.75
3700	6" long	G		60	.133		1.50	6.75		8.25	11.95

05 05 Common Work Results for Metals

05 05 19 – Post-Installed Concrete Anchors

05 05 19.20 Expansion Anchors		Crew	Daily Output	Labor-Hours	Unit	Material	2018 Bare Costs Labor	Equipment	Total	Total Incl O&P
3800	1/2" diameter, 4" long	G 1 Carp	60	.133	Ea.	1.65	6.75		8.40	12.10
3900	6" long	G	50	.160		2.08	8.10		10.18	14.65
4000	Nailing anchors									
4100	Nylon nailing anchor, 1/4" diameter, 1" long	1 Carp	3.20	2.500	C	23	127		150	218
4200	1-1/2" long		2.80	2.857		25.50	145		170.50	250
4300	2" long		2.40	3.333		27.50	169		196.50	287
4400	Metal nailing anchor, 1/4" diameter, 1" long	G	3.20	2.500		22.50	127		149.50	218
4500	1-1/2" long	G	2.80	2.857		29	145		174	253
4600	2" long	G	2.40	3.333		35.50	169		204.50	296
5000	Screw anchors for concrete, masonry,									
5100	stone & tile, no layout or drilling included									
5700	Lag screw shields, 1/4" diameter, short	G 1 Carp	90	.089	Ea.	.47	4.51		4.98	7.35
5800	Long	G	85	.094		.54	4.77		5.31	7.85
5900	3/8" diameter, short		85	.094		.72	4.77		5.49	8.05
6000	Long		80	.100		.92	5.05		5.97	8.70
6100	1/2" diameter, short		80	.100		1.03	5.05		6.08	8.85
6200	Long		75	.107		1.37	5.40		6.77	9.75
6300	5/8" diameter, short		70	.114		1.42	5.80		7.22	10.35
6400	Long		65	.123		1.96	6.25		8.21	11.65
6600	Lead, #6 & #8, 3/4" long	G	260	.031		.19	1.56		1.75	2.59
6700	#10 - #14, 1-1/2" long	G	200	.040		.38	2.03		2.41	3.51
6800	#16 & #18, 1-1/2" long	G	160	.050		.41	2.54		2.95	4.31
6900	Plastic, #6 & #8, 3/4" long		260	.031		.05	1.56		1.61	2.44
7000	#8 & #10, 7/8" long		240	.033		.06	1.69		1.75	2.64
7100	#10 & #12, 1" long		220	.036		.07	1.84		1.91	2.89
7200	#14 & #16, 1-1/2" long		160	.050		.07	2.54		2.61	3.94
8000	Wedge anchors, not including layout or drilling									
8050	Carbon steel, 1/4" diameter, 1-3/4" long	G 1 Carp	150	.053	Ea.	.51	2.70		3.21	4.68
8100	3-1/4" long	G	140	.057		.67	2.90		3.57	5.15
8150	3/8" diameter, 2-1/4" long	G	145	.055		.54	2.80		3.34	4.86
8200	5" long	G	140	.057		.95	2.90		3.85	5.45
8250	1/2" diameter, 2-3/4" long	G	140	.057		1.07	2.90		3.97	5.60
8300	7" long	G	125	.064		1.82	3.24		5.06	6.95
8350	5/8" diameter, 3-1/2" long	G	130	.062		1.81	3.12		4.93	6.75
8400	8-1/2" long	G	115	.070		3.86	3.53		7.39	9.60
8450	3/4" diameter, 4-1/4" long	G	115	.070		2.75	3.53		6.28	8.35
8500	10" long	G	95	.084		6.25	4.27		10.52	13.35
8550	1" diameter, 6" long	G	100	.080		8.70	4.06		12.76	15.80
8575	9" long	G	85	.094		11.35	4.77		16.12	19.70
8600	12" long	G	75	.107		12.25	5.40		17.65	21.50
8650	1-1/4" diameter, 9" long	G	70	.114		22	5.80		27.80	33
8700	12" long	G	60	.133		28	6.75		34.75	41
8800	For type 316 stainless steel, add					450%				
8950	Self-drilling concrete screw, hex washer head, 3/16" diam. x 1-3/4" long	G 1 Carp	300	.027	Ea.	.19	1.35		1.54	2.27
8960	2-1/4" long	G	250	.032		.21	1.62		1.83	2.70
8970	Phillips flat head, 3/16" diam. x 1-3/4" long		300	.027		.19	1.35		1.54	2.27
8980	2-1/4" long		250	.032		.21	1.62		1.83	2.70

For customer support on your Green Building Costs with RSMeans data, call 800.448.8182.

05 05 Common Work Results for Metals

05 05 21 – Fastening Methods for Metal

05 05 21.10 Cutting Steel

		Crew	Daily Output	Labor-Hours	Unit	Material	2018 Bare Costs Labor	Equipment	Total	Total Incl O&P
0010	**CUTTING STEEL**									
0020	Hand burning, incl. preparation, torch cutting & grinding, no staging									
0050	Steel to 1/4" thick	E-25	400	.020	L.F.	.20	1.13	.03	1.36	2.10
0100	1/2" thick		320	.025		.37	1.42	.04	1.83	2.77
0150	3/4" thick		260	.031		.61	1.74	.05	2.40	3.57
0200	1" thick		200	.040		.87	2.27	.06	3.20	4.73

05 05 21.90 Welding Steel

			Crew	Daily Output	Labor-Hours	Unit	Material	Labor	Equipment	Total	Total Incl O&P
0010	**WELDING STEEL**, Structural	R050521-20									
0020	Field welding, 1/8" E6011, cost per welder, no operating engineer		E-14	8	1	Hr.	4.71	56.50	12.30	73.51	111
0200	With 1/2 operating engineer		E-13	8	1.500		4.71	82.50	12.30	99.51	150
0300	With 1 operating engineer		E-12	8	2		4.71	108	12.30	125.01	189
0500	With no operating engineer, 2# weld rod per ton		E-14	8	1	Ton	4.71	56.50	12.30	73.51	111
0600	8# E6011 per ton		"	2	4		18.85	227	49	294.85	445
0800	With one operating engineer per welder, 2# E6011 per ton		E-12	8	2		4.71	108	12.30	125.01	189
0900	8# E6011 per ton		"	2	8		18.85	430	49	497.85	755
1200	Continuous fillet, down welding										
1300	Single pass, 1/8" thick, 0.1#/L.F.		E-14	150	.053	L.F.	.24	3.02	.66	3.92	5.90
1400	3/16" thick, 0.2#/L.F.			75	.107		.47	6.05	1.31	7.83	11.85
1500	1/4" thick, 0.3#/L.F.			50	.160		.71	9.05	1.97	11.73	17.75
1610	5/16" thick, 0.4#/L.F.			38	.211		.94	11.95	2.59	15.48	23.50

05 05 23 – Metal Fastenings

05 05 23.10 Bolts and Hex Nuts

			Crew	Daily Output	Labor-Hours	Unit	Material	Labor	Equipment	Total	Total Incl O&P
0010	**BOLTS & HEX NUTS**, Steel, A307										
0100	1/4" diameter, 1/2" long	G	1 Sswk	140	.057	Ea.	.06	3.12		3.18	5.15
0200	1" long	G		140	.057		.07	3.12		3.19	5.20
0300	2" long	G		130	.062		.10	3.36		3.46	5.60
0400	3" long	G		130	.062		.15	3.36		3.51	5.65
0500	4" long	G		120	.067		.17	3.64		3.81	6.15
0600	3/8" diameter, 1" long	G		130	.062		.14	3.36		3.50	5.65
0700	2" long	G		130	.062		.18	3.36		3.54	5.70
0800	3" long	G		120	.067		.24	3.64		3.88	6.20
0900	4" long	G		120	.067		.30	3.64		3.94	6.30
1000	5" long	G		115	.070		.38	3.80		4.18	6.60
1100	1/2" diameter, 1-1/2" long	G		120	.067		.40	3.64		4.04	6.40
1200	2" long	G		120	.067		.46	3.64		4.10	6.45
1300	4" long	G		115	.070		.75	3.80		4.55	7.05
1400	6" long	G		110	.073		1.05	3.97		5.02	7.65
1500	8" long	G		105	.076		1.38	4.16		5.54	8.30
1600	5/8" diameter, 1-1/2" long	G		120	.067		.85	3.64		4.49	6.90
1700	2" long	G		120	.067		.94	3.64		4.58	7
1800	4" long	G		115	.070		1.34	3.80		5.14	7.70
1900	6" long	G		110	.073		1.72	3.97		5.69	8.40
2000	8" long	G		105	.076		2.55	4.16		6.71	9.60
2100	10" long	G		100	.080		3.20	4.37		7.57	10.65
2200	3/4" diameter, 2" long	G		120	.067		1.15	3.64		4.79	7.20
2300	4" long	G		110	.073		1.65	3.97		5.62	8.30
2400	6" long	G		105	.076		2.12	4.16		6.28	9.15
2500	8" long	G		95	.084		3.20	4.60		7.80	11
2600	10" long	G		85	.094		4.20	5.15		9.35	13
2700	12" long	G		80	.100		4.92	5.45		10.37	14.35
2800	1" diameter, 3" long	G		105	.076		2.89	4.16		7.05	9.95

05 05 Common Work Results for Metals

05 05 23 – Metal Fastenings

05 05 23.10 Bolts and Hex Nuts

		Crew	Daily Output	Labor-Hours	Unit	Material	2018 Bare Costs Labor	Equipment	Total	Total Incl O&P
2900	6" long	1 Sswk [G]	90	.089	Ea.	4.20	4.86		9.06	12.55
3000	12" long	[G]	75	.107		7.50	5.85		13.35	17.80
3100	For galvanized, add					75%				
3200	For stainless, add					350%				

05 05 23.25 High Strength Bolts

		Crew	Daily Output	Labor-Hours	Unit	Material	Labor	Equipment	Total	Total Incl O&P
0010	**HIGH STRENGTH BOLTS**									
0020	A325 Type 1, structural steel, bolt-nut-washer set									
0100	1/2" diameter x 1-1/2" long	1 Sswk [G]	130	.062	Ea.	.94	3.36		4.30	6.55
0120	2" long	[G]	125	.064		1.02	3.50		4.52	6.80
0150	3" long	[G]	120	.067		1.42	3.64		5.06	7.50
0170	5/8" diameter x 1-1/2" long	[G]	125	.064		1.78	3.50		5.28	7.65
0180	2" long	[G]	120	.067		1.92	3.64		5.56	8.05
0190	3" long	[G]	115	.070		2.38	3.80		6.18	8.80
0200	3/4" diameter x 2" long	[G]	120	.067		3	3.64		6.64	9.25
0220	3" long	[G]	115	.070		3.61	3.80		7.41	10.15
0250	4" long	[G]	110	.073		4.44	3.97		8.41	11.40
0300	6" long	[G]	105	.076		5.80	4.16		9.96	13.15
0350	8" long	[G]	95	.084		11.55	4.60		16.15	20
0360	7/8" diameter x 2" long	[G]	115	.070		4.01	3.80		7.81	10.60
0365	3" long	[G]	110	.073		4.75	3.97		8.72	11.75
0370	4" long	[G]	105	.076		5.75	4.16		9.91	13.10
0380	6" long	[G]	100	.080		7.30	4.37		11.67	15.20
0390	8" long	[G]	90	.089		11.65	4.86		16.51	21
0400	1" diameter x 2" long	[G]	105	.076		3.92	4.16		8.08	11.10
0420	3" long	[G]	100	.080		4.39	4.37		8.76	12
0450	4" long	[G]	95	.084		4.95	4.60		9.55	12.95
0500	6" long	[G]	90	.089		6.50	4.86		11.36	15.10
0550	8" long	[G]	85	.094		11.10	5.15		16.25	20.50
0600	1-1/4" diameter x 3" long	[G]	85	.094		10.90	5.15		16.05	20.50
0650	4" long	[G]	80	.100		11.90	5.45		17.35	22
0700	6" long	[G]	75	.107		15.50	5.85		21.35	26.50
0750	8" long	[G]	70	.114		19.80	6.25		26.05	32
1020	A490, bolt-nut-washer set									
1170	5/8" diameter x 1-1/2" long	1 Sswk [G]	125	.064	Ea.	4.49	3.50		7.99	10.65
1180	2" long	[G]	120	.067		5.35	3.64		8.99	11.85
1190	3" long	[G]	115	.070		6.55	3.80		10.35	13.40
1200	3/4" diameter x 2" long	[G]	120	.067		4.11	3.64		7.75	10.45
1220	3" long	[G]	115	.070		4.87	3.80		8.67	11.55
1250	4" long	[G]	110	.073		5.65	3.97		9.62	12.75
1300	6" long	[G]	105	.076		8.35	4.16		12.51	16
1350	8" long	[G]	95	.084		14.20	4.60		18.80	23
1360	7/8" diameter x 2" long	[G]	115	.070		6.20	3.80		10	13
1365	3" long	[G]	110	.073		7.30	3.97		11.27	14.55
1370	4" long	[G]	105	.076		9.05	4.16		13.21	16.80
1380	6" long	[G]	100	.080		12.80	4.37		17.17	21
1390	8" long	[G]	90	.089		18.60	4.86		23.46	28.50
1400	1" diameter x 2" long	[G]	105	.076		8.15	4.16		12.31	15.80
1420	3" long	[G]	100	.080		9.90	4.37		14.27	18.05
1450	4" long	[G]	95	.084		11.45	4.60		16.05	20
1500	6" long	[G]	90	.089		15.35	4.86		20.21	25
1550	8" long	[G]	85	.094		24.50	5.15		29.65	35.50
1600	1-1/4" diameter x 3" long	[G]	85	.094		45	5.15		50.15	58

For customer support on your Green Building Costs with RSMeans data, call 800.448.8182.

05 05 Common Work Results for Metals

05 05 23 – Metal Fastenings

05 05 23.25 High Strength Bolts

			Crew	Daily Output	Labor-Hours	Unit	Material	2018 Bare Costs Labor	Equipment	Total	Total Incl O&P
1650	4" long	G	1 Sswk	80	.100	Ea.	52.50	5.45		57.95	66.50
1700	6" long	G		75	.107		73	5.85		78.85	90
1750	8" long	G		70	.114		96	6.25		102.25	116

05 05 23.30 Lag Screws

0010	**LAG SCREWS**										
0020	Steel, 1/4" diameter, 2" long	G	1 Carp	200	.040	Ea.	.10	2.03		2.13	3.20
0100	3/8" diameter, 3" long	G		150	.053		.28	2.70		2.98	4.43
0200	1/2" diameter, 3" long	G		130	.062		.66	3.12		3.78	5.50
0300	5/8" diameter, 3" long	G		120	.067		1.29	3.38		4.67	6.55

05 05 23.35 Machine Screws

0010	**MACHINE SCREWS**										
0020	Steel, round head, #8 x 1" long	G	1 Carp	4.80	1.667	C	4.06	84.50		88.56	133
0110	#8 x 2" long	G		2.40	3.333		8.10	169		177.10	266
0200	#10 x 1" long	G		4	2		5.05	101		106.05	160
0300	#10 x 2" long	G		2	4		8.75	203		211.75	320

05 05 23.50 Powder Actuated Tools and Fasteners

0010	**POWDER ACTUATED TOOLS & FASTENERS**										
0020	Stud driver, .22 caliber, single shot					Ea.	152			152	167
0100	.27 caliber, semi automatic, strip					"	460			460	505
0300	Powder load, single shot, .22 cal, power level 2, brown					C	5.65			5.65	6.25
0400	Strip, .27 cal, power level 4, red						8.15			8.15	9
0600	Drive pin, .300 x 3/4" long	G	1 Carp	4.80	1.667		4.39	84.50		88.89	134
0700	.300 x 3" long with washer	G	"	4	2		13.40	101		114.40	169

05 05 23.55 Rivets

0010	**RIVETS**										
0100	Aluminum rivet & mandrel, 1/2" grip length x 1/8" diameter	G	1 Carp	4.80	1.667	C	7.70	84.50		92.20	137
0200	3/16" diameter	G		4	2		10.80	101		111.80	166
0300	Aluminum rivet, steel mandrel, 1/8" diameter	G		4.80	1.667		10.40	84.50		94.90	140
0400	3/16" diameter	G		4	2		16.65	101		117.65	172
0500	Copper rivet, steel mandrel, 1/8" diameter	G		4.80	1.667		9.95	84.50		94.45	140
0800	Stainless rivet & mandrel, 1/8" diameter	G		4.80	1.667		23	84.50		107.50	154
0900	3/16" diameter	G		4	2		37.50	101		138.50	196
1000	Stainless rivet, steel mandrel, 1/8" diameter	G		4.80	1.667		15.95	84.50		100.45	147
1100	3/16" diameter	G		4	2		26	101		127	183
1200	Steel rivet and mandrel, 1/8" diameter	G		4.80	1.667		7.55	84.50		92.05	137
1300	3/16" diameter	G		4	2		10.95	101		111.95	166
1400	Hand riveting tool, standard					Ea.	70			70	77
1500	Deluxe						395			395	435
1600	Power riveting tool, standard						540			540	595
1700	Deluxe						1,650			1,650	1,825

05 05 23.70 Structural Blind Bolts

0010	**STRUCTURAL BLIND BOLTS**										
0100	1/4" diameter x 1/4" grip	G	1 Sswk	240	.033	Ea.	1.73	1.82		3.55	4.88
0150	1/2" grip	G		216	.037		1.86	2.02		3.88	5.35
0200	3/8" diameter x 1/2" grip	G		232	.034		3.12	1.88		5	6.50
0250	3/4" grip	G		208	.038		3.27	2.10		5.37	7.05
0300	1/2" diameter x 1/2" grip	G		224	.036		6.05	1.95		8	9.85
0350	3/4" grip	G		200	.040		8.20	2.19		10.39	12.55
0400	5/8" diameter x 3/4" grip	G		216	.037		10.90	2.02		12.92	15.30
0450	1" grip	G		192	.042		14.80	2.28		17.08	19.95

05 05 Common Work Results for Metals

05 05 23 – Metal Fastenings

05 05 23.85 Weld Shear Connectors

		Crew	Daily Output	Labor-Hours	Unit	Material	2018 Bare Costs Labor	Equipment	Total	Total Incl O&P
0010	**WELD SHEAR CONNECTORS**									
0020	3/4" diameter, 3-3/16" long G	E-10	960	.017	Ea.	.55	.93	.35	1.83	2.51
0030	3-3/8" long G		950	.017		.57	.94	.35	1.86	2.55
0200	3-7/8" long G		945	.017		.61	.94	.36	1.91	2.61
0300	4-3/16" long G		935	.017		.64	.95	.36	1.95	2.67
0500	4-7/8" long G		930	.017		.72	.96	.36	2.04	2.75
0600	5-3/16" long G		920	.017		.75	.97	.37	2.09	2.80
0800	5-3/8" long G		910	.018		.76	.98	.37	2.11	2.84
0900	6-3/16" long G		905	.018		.83	.98	.37	2.18	2.93
1000	7-3/16" long G		895	.018		1.03	1	.38	2.41	3.17
1100	8-3/16" long G		890	.018		1.13	1	.38	2.51	3.30
1500	7/8" diameter, 3-11/16" long G		920	.017		.89	.97	.37	2.23	2.96
1600	4-3/16" long G		910	.018		.95	.98	.37	2.30	3.06
1700	5-3/16" long G		905	.018		1.08	.98	.37	2.43	3.21
1800	6-3/16" long G		895	.018		1.21	1	.38	2.59	3.37
1900	7-3/16" long G		890	.018		1.34	1	.38	2.72	3.54
2000	8-3/16" long G		880	.018		1.47	1.01	.38	2.86	3.68

05 05 23.87 Weld Studs

		Crew	Daily Output	Labor-Hours	Unit	Material	Labor	Equipment	Total	Total Incl O&P
0010	**WELD STUDS**									
0020	1/4" diameter, 2-11/16" long G	E-10	1120	.014	Ea.	.37	.80	.30	1.47	2.04
0100	4-1/8" long G		1080	.015		.35	.82	.31	1.48	2.08
0200	3/8" diameter, 4-1/8" long G		1080	.015		.40	.82	.31	1.53	2.13
0300	6-1/8" long G		1040	.015		.52	.86	.32	1.70	2.33
0400	1/2" diameter, 2-1/8" long G		1040	.015		.37	.86	.32	1.55	2.16
0500	3-1/8" long G		1025	.016		.44	.87	.33	1.64	2.27
0600	4-1/8" long G		1010	.016		.52	.88	.33	1.73	2.38
0700	5-5/16" long G		990	.016		.64	.90	.34	1.88	2.54
0800	6-1/8" long G		975	.016		.69	.91	.35	1.95	2.63
0900	8-1/8" long G		960	.017		.98	.93	.35	2.26	2.98
1000	5/8" diameter, 2-11/16" long G		1000	.016		.63	.89	.34	1.86	2.53
1010	4-3/16" long G		990	.016		.78	.90	.34	2.02	2.70
1100	6-9/16" long G		975	.016		1.02	.91	.35	2.28	2.99
1200	8-3/16" long G		960	.017		1.37	.93	.35	2.65	3.41

05 12 Structural Steel Framing

05 12 23 – Structural Steel for Buildings

05 12 23.05 Canopy Framing

		Crew	Daily Output	Labor-Hours	Unit	Material	Labor	Equipment	Total	Total Incl O&P
0010	**CANOPY FRAMING**									
0020	6" and 8" members, shop fabricated G	E-4	3000	.011	Lb.	1.62	.59	.03	2.24	2.78

05 12 23.10 Ceiling Supports

		Crew	Daily Output	Labor-Hours	Unit	Material	Labor	Equipment	Total	Total Incl O&P
0010	**CEILING SUPPORTS**									
1000	Entrance door/folding partition supports, shop fabricated G	E-4	60	.533	L.F.	27	29.50	1.64	58.14	79.50
1100	Linear accelerator door supports G		14	2.286		123	126	7.05	256.05	350
1200	Lintels or shelf angles, hung, exterior hot dipped galv. G		267	.120		18.40	6.60	.37	25.37	31
1250	Two coats primer paint instead of galv. G		267	.120		15.95	6.60	.37	22.92	28.50
1400	Monitor support, ceiling hung, expansion bolted G		4	8	Ea.	425	440	24.50	889.50	1,225
1450	Hung from pre-set inserts G		6	5.333		460	294	16.45	770.45	1,000
1600	Motor supports for overhead doors G		4	8		217	440	24.50	681.50	985
1700	Partition support for heavy folding partitions, without pocket G		24	1.333	L.F.	61.50	73.50	4.11	139.11	192
1750	Supports at pocket only G		12	2.667		123	147	8.20	278.20	385

For customer support on your Green Building Costs with RSMeans data, call 800.448.8182.

05 12 Structural Steel Framing

05 12 23 – Structural Steel for Buildings

05 12 23.10 Ceiling Supports

			Crew	Daily Output	Labor-Hours	Unit	Material	2018 Bare Costs Labor	Equipment	Total	Total Incl O&P
2000	Rolling grilles & fire door supports	G	E-4	34	.941	L.F.	52.50	52	2.90	107.40	146
2100	Spider-leg light supports, expansion bolted to ceiling slab	G		8	4	Ea.	175	221	12.30	408.30	565
2150	Hung from pre-set inserts	G		12	2.667	"	188	147	8.20	343.20	455
2400	Toilet partition support	G		36	.889	L.F.	61.50	49	2.74	113.24	151
2500	X-ray travel gantry support	G		12	2.667	"	210	147	8.20	365.20	480

05 12 23.15 Columns, Lightweight

			Crew	Daily Output	Labor-Hours	Unit	Material	Labor	Equipment	Total	Incl O&P
0010	**COLUMNS, LIGHTWEIGHT**										
1000	Lightweight units (lally), 3-1/2" diameter		E-2	780	.072	L.F.	5.70	3.90	2.16	11.76	14.95
1050	4" diameter		"	900	.062	"	7.60	3.38	1.87	12.85	15.85
5800	Adjustable jack post, 8' maximum height, 2-3/4" diameter	G				Ea.	52.50			52.50	57.50
5850	4" diameter	G				"	84			84	92

05 12 23.17 Columns, Structural

			Crew	Daily Output	Labor-Hours	Unit	Material	Labor	Equipment	Total	Incl O&P
0010	**COLUMNS, STRUCTURAL** R051223-10										
0015	Made from recycled materials										
0020	Shop fab'd for 100-ton, 1-2 story project, bolted connections										
0800	Steel, concrete filled, extra strong pipe, 3-1/2" diameter		E-2	660	.085	L.F.	44.50	4.61	2.56	51.67	59
0830	4" diameter			780	.072		49.50	3.90	2.16	55.56	63
0890	5" diameter			1020	.055		59	2.98	1.65	63.63	71.50
0930	6" diameter			1200	.047		78	2.53	1.41	81.94	91.50
0940	8" diameter			1100	.051		78	2.76	1.53	82.29	92
1100	For galvanizing, add					Lb.	.25			.25	.28
1300	For web ties, angles, etc., add per added lb.		1 Sswk	945	.008		1.35	.46		1.81	2.24
1500	Steel pipe, extra strong, no concrete, 3" to 5" diameter	G	E-2	16000	.004		1.35	.19	.11	1.65	1.90
1600	6" to 12" diameter	G		14000	.004		1.35	.22	.12	1.69	1.96
1700	Steel pipe, extra strong, no concrete, 3" diameter x 12'-0"	G		60	.933	Ea.	166	50.50	28	244.50	294
1750	4" diameter x 12'-0"	G		58	.966		242	52.50	29	323.50	380
1800	6" diameter x 12'-0"	G		54	1.037		460	56.50	31.50	548	635
1850	8" diameter x 14'-0"	G		50	1.120		820	61	34	915	1,025
1900	10" diameter x 16'-0"	G		48	1.167		1,175	63.50	35	1,273.50	1,450
1950	12" diameter x 18'-0"	G		45	1.244		1,575	67.50	37.50	1,680	1,900
3300	Structural tubing, square, A500GrB, 4" to 6" square, light section	G		11270	.005	Lb.	1.35	.27	.15	1.77	2.07
3600	Heavy section	G		32000	.002	"	1.35	.10	.05	1.50	1.69
4000	Concrete filled, add					L.F.	4.78			4.78	5.25
4500	Structural tubing, square, 4" x 4" x 1/4" x 12'-0"	G	E-2	58	.966	Ea.	222	52.50	29	303.50	360
4550	6" x 6" x 1/4" x 12'-0"	G		54	1.037		365	56.50	31.50	453	525
4600	8" x 8" x 3/8" x 14'-0"	G		50	1.120		790	61	34	885	1,000
4650	10" x 10" x 1/2" x 16'-0"	G		48	1.167		1,450	63.50	35	1,548.50	1,750
5100	Structural tubing, rect., 5" to 6" wide, light section	G		8000	.007	Lb.	1.35	.38	.21	1.94	2.32
5200	Heavy section	G		12000	.005		1.35	.25	.14	1.74	2.04
5300	7" to 10" wide, light section	G		15000	.004		1.35	.20	.11	1.66	1.92
5400	Heavy section	G		18000	.003		1.35	.17	.09	1.61	1.85
5500	Structural tubing, rect., 5" x 3" x 1/4" x 12'-0"	G		58	.966	Ea.	215	52.50	29	296.50	355
5550	6" x 4" x 5/16" x 12'-0"	G		54	1.037		335	56.50	31.50	423	495
5600	8" x 4" x 3/8" x 12'-0"	G		54	1.037		490	56.50	31.50	578	665
5650	10" x 6" x 3/8" x 14'-0"	G		50	1.120		790	61	34	885	1,000
5700	12" x 8" x 1/2" x 16'-0"	G		48	1.167		1,450	63.50	35	1,548.50	1,750
6800	W Shape, A992 steel, 2 tier, W8 x 24	G		1080	.052	L.F.	35.50	2.81	1.56	39.87	45
6850	W8 x 31	G		1080	.052		46	2.81	1.56	50.37	56.50
6900	W8 x 48	G		1032	.054		71	2.95	1.63	75.58	84.50
6950	W8 x 67	G		984	.057		99	3.09	1.71	103.80	116
7000	W10 x 45	G		1032	.054		66.50	2.95	1.63	71.08	80
7050	W10 x 68	G		984	.057		101	3.09	1.71	105.80	118

05 12 Structural Steel Framing

05 12 23 – Structural Steel for Buildings

05 12 23.17 Columns, Structural

		Crew	Daily Output	Labor-Hours	Unit	Material	2018 Bare Costs Labor	Equipment	Total	Total Incl O&P
7100	W10 x 112 [G]	E-2	960	.058	L.F.	166	3.17	1.76	170.93	189
7150	W12 x 50 [G]		1032	.054		74	2.95	1.63	78.58	88
7200	W12 x 87 [G]		984	.057		129	3.09	1.71	133.80	149
7250	W12 x 120 [G]		960	.058		178	3.17	1.76	182.93	202
7300	W12 x 190 [G]		912	.061		281	3.33	1.85	286.18	315
7350	W14 x 74 [G]		984	.057		110	3.09	1.71	114.80	128
7400	W14 x 120 [G]		960	.058		178	3.17	1.76	182.93	202
7450	W14 x 176 [G]		912	.061		261	3.33	1.85	266.18	294
8090	For projects 75 to 99 tons, add				%	10%				
8092	50 to 74 tons, add					20%				
8094	25 to 49 tons, add					30%	10%			
8096	10 to 24 tons, add					50%	25%			
8098	2 to 9 tons, add					75%	50%			
8099	Less than 2 tons, add					100%	100%			

05 12 23.20 Curb Edging

		Crew	Daily Output	Labor-Hours	Unit	Material	Labor	Equipment	Total	Total Incl O&P
0010	**CURB EDGING**									
0020	Steel angle w/anchors, shop fabricated, on forms, 1" x 1", 0.8#/L.F. [G]	E-4	350	.091	L.F.	1.67	5.05	.28	7	10.40
0100	2" x 2" angles, 3.92#/L.F. [G]		330	.097		6.70	5.35	.30	12.35	16.50
0200	3" x 3" angles, 6.1#/L.F. [G]		300	.107		10.85	5.90	.33	17.08	22
0300	4" x 4" angles, 8.2#/L.F. [G]		275	.116		14.25	6.40	.36	21.01	26.50
1000	6" x 4" angles, 12.3#/L.F. [G]		250	.128		21	7.05	.39	28.44	35
1050	Steel channels with anchors, on forms, 3" channel, 5#/L.F. [G]		290	.110		8.45	6.10	.34	14.89	19.60
1100	4" channel, 5.4#/L.F. [G]		270	.119		9.10	6.55	.37	16.02	21
1200	6" channel, 8.2#/L.F. [G]		255	.125		14.25	6.90	.39	21.54	27.50
1300	8" channel, 11.5#/L.F. [G]		225	.142		19.60	7.85	.44	27.89	35
1400	10" channel, 15.3#/L.F. [G]		180	.178		25.50	9.80	.55	35.85	45
1500	12" channel, 20.7#/L.F. [G]		140	.229		34.50	12.60	.70	47.80	59.50
2000	For curved edging, add					35%	10%			

05 12 23.40 Lightweight Framing

		Crew	Daily Output	Labor-Hours	Unit	Material	Labor	Equipment	Total	Total Incl O&P
0010	**LIGHTWEIGHT FRAMING** R051223-35									
0015	Made from recycled materials									
0200	For load-bearing steel studs see Section 05 41 13.30									
0400	Angle framing, field fabricated, 4" and larger R051223-45 [G]	E-3	440	.055	Lb.	.78	3.02	.22	4.02	6.05
0450	Less than 4" angles [G]		265	.091	"	.81	5	.37	6.18	9.50
0460	1/2" x 1/2" x 1/8" [G]		200	.120	L.F.	.16	6.65	.49	7.30	11.55
0462	3/4" x 3/4" x 1/8" [G]		160	.150		.45	8.30	.62	9.37	14.75
0464	1" x 1" x 1/8" [G]		135	.178		.65	9.85	.73	11.23	17.60
0466	1-1/4" x 1-1/4" x 3/16" [G]		115	.209		1.20	11.55	.86	13.61	21
0468	1-1/2" x 1-1/2" x 3/16" [G]		100	.240		1.45	13.30	.98	15.73	24
0470	2" x 2" x 1/4" [G]		90	.267		2.58	14.75	1.09	18.42	28
0472	2-1/2" x 2-1/2" x 1/4" [G]		72	.333		3.31	18.45	1.37	23.13	35
0474	3" x 2" x 3/8" [G]		65	.369		4.77	20.50	1.51	26.78	40.50
0476	3" x 3" x 3/8" [G]		57	.421		5.80	23.50	1.73	31.03	46.50
0600	Channel framing, field fabricated, 8" and larger [G]		500	.048	Lb.	.81	2.66	.20	3.67	5.45
0650	Less than 8" channels [G]		335	.072	"	.81	3.96	.29	5.06	7.70
0660	C2 x 1.78 [G]		115	.209	L.F.	1.44	11.55	.86	13.85	21.50
0662	C3 x 4.1 [G]		80	.300		3.31	16.60	1.23	21.14	32
0664	C4 x 5.4 [G]		66	.364		4.36	20	1.49	25.85	39.50
0666	C5 x 6.7 [G]		57	.421		5.40	23.50	1.73	30.63	46
0668	C6 x 8.2 [G]		55	.436		6.40	24	1.79	32.19	48.50
0670	C7 x 9.8 [G]		40	.600		7.90	33	2.46	43.36	66
0672	C8 x 11.5 [G]		36	.667		9.30	37	2.73	49.03	73.50

05 12 Structural Steel Framing

05 12 23 – Structural Steel for Buildings

05 12 23.40 Lightweight Framing

			Crew	Daily Output	Labor-Hours	Unit	Material	2018 Bare Costs Labor	Equipment	Total	Total Incl O&P
0710	Structural bar tee, field fabricated, 3/4" x 3/4" x 1/8"	G	E-3	160	.150	L.F.	.45	8.30	.62	9.37	14.75
0712	1" x 1" x 1/8"	G		135	.178		.65	9.85	.73	11.23	17.60
0714	1-1/2" x 1-1/2" x 1/4"	G		114	.211		1.89	11.65	.86	14.40	22
0716	2" x 2" x 1/4"	G		89	.270		2.58	14.90	1.11	18.59	28.50
0718	2-1/2" x 2-1/2" x 3/8"	G		72	.333		4.77	18.45	1.37	24.59	37
0720	3" x 3" x 3/8"	G		57	.421		5.80	23.50	1.73	31.03	46.50
0730	Structural zee, field fabricated, 1-1/4" x 1-3/4" x 1-3/4"	G		114	.211		.61	11.65	.86	13.12	20.50
0732	2-11/16" x 3" x 2-11/16"	G		114	.211		1.44	11.65	.86	13.95	21.50
0734	3-1/16" x 4" x 3-1/16"	G		133	.180		2.17	10	.74	12.91	19.50
0736	3-1/4" x 5" x 3-1/4"	G		133	.180		2.96	10	.74	13.70	20.50
0738	3-1/2" x 6" x 3-1/2"	G		160	.150		4.47	8.30	.62	13.39	19.15
0740	Junior beam, field fabricated, 3"	G		80	.300		4.60	16.60	1.23	22.43	33.50
0742	4"	G		72	.333		6.20	18.45	1.37	26.02	38.50
0744	5"	G		67	.358		8.10	19.80	1.47	29.37	43
0746	6"	G		62	.387		10.10	21.50	1.59	33.19	48
0748	7"	G		57	.421		12.35	23.50	1.73	37.58	53.50
0750	8"	G		53	.453		14.85	25	1.86	41.71	59.50
1000	Continuous slotted channel framing system, shop fab, simple framing	G	2 Sswk	2400	.007	Lb.	4.17	.36		4.53	5.20
1200	Complex framing	G	"	1600	.010		4.71	.55		5.26	6.10
1250	Plate & bar stock for reinforcing beams and trusses	G					1.48			1.48	1.63
1300	Cross bracing, rods, shop fabricated, 3/4" diameter	G	E-3	700	.034		1.62	1.90	.14	3.66	5.05
1310	7/8" diameter	G		850	.028		1.62	1.56	.12	3.30	4.46
1320	1" diameter	G		1000	.024		1.62	1.33	.10	3.05	4.06
1330	Angle, 5" x 5" x 3/8"	G		2800	.009		1.62	.47	.04	2.13	2.60
1350	Hanging lintels, shop fabricated	G		850	.028		1.62	1.56	.12	3.30	4.46
1380	Roof frames, shop fabricated, 3'-0" square, 5' span	G	E-2	4200	.013		1.62	.72	.40	2.74	3.38
1400	Tie rod, not upset, 1-1/2" to 4" diameter, with turnbuckle	G	2 Sswk	800	.020		1.75	1.09		2.84	3.72
1420	No turnbuckle	G		700	.023		1.68	1.25		2.93	3.89
1500	Upset, 1-3/4" to 4" diameter, with turnbuckle	G		800	.020		1.75	1.09		2.84	3.72
1520	No turnbuckle	G		700	.023		1.68	1.25		2.93	3.89

05 12 23.45 Lintels

			Crew	Daily Output	Labor-Hours	Unit	Material	Labor	Equipment	Total	Total Incl O&P
0010	**LINTELS**										
0015	Made from recycled materials										
0020	Plain steel angles, shop fabricated, under 500 lb.	G	1 Bric	550	.015	Lb.	1.04	.73		1.77	2.26
0100	500 to 1,000 lb.	G		640	.013		1.01	.63		1.64	2.07
0200	1,000 to 2,000 lb.	G		640	.013		.98	.63		1.61	2.04
0300	2,000 to 4,000 lb.	G		640	.013		.96	.63		1.59	2.01
0500	For built-up angles and plates, add to above						1.35			1.35	1.48
0700	For engineering, add to above						.13			.13	.15
0900	For galvanizing, add to above, under 500 lb.						.30			.30	.33
0950	500 to 2,000 lb.						.27			.27	.30
1000	Over 2,000 lb.						.25			.25	.28
2000	Steel angles, 3-1/2" x 3", 1/4" thick, 2'-6" long	G	1 Bric	47	.170	Ea.	14.55	8.55		23.10	29
2100	4'-6" long	G		26	.308		26	15.50		41.50	52.50
2500	3-1/2" x 3-1/2" x 5/16", 5'-0" long	G		18	.444		39	22.50		61.50	76.50
2600	4" x 3-1/2", 1/4" thick, 5'-0" long	G		21	.381		33.50	19.15		52.65	66
2700	9'-0" long	G		12	.667		60	33.50		93.50	118
2800	4" x 3-1/2" x 5/16", 7'-0" long	G		12	.667		58	33.50		91.50	116
2900	5" x 3-1/2" x 5/16", 10'-0" long	G		8	1		93.50	50.50		144	180

05 12 Structural Steel Framing

05 12 23 – Structural Steel for Buildings

05 12 23.60 Pipe Support Framing

		Crew	Daily Output	Labor-Hours	Unit	Material	2018 Bare Costs Labor	Equipment	Total	Total Incl O&P
0010	**PIPE SUPPORT FRAMING**									
0020	Under 10#/L.F., shop fabricated	G E-4	3900	.008	Lb.	1.80	.45	.03	2.28	2.75
0200	10.1 to 15#/L.F.	G	4300	.007		1.78	.41	.02	2.21	2.65
0400	15.1 to 20#/L.F.	G	4800	.007		1.75	.37	.02	2.14	2.55
0600	Over 20#/L.F.	G	5400	.006		1.72	.33	.02	2.07	2.45

05 12 23.65 Plates

		Crew	Daily Output	Labor-Hours	Unit	Material	Labor	Equipment	Total	Total Incl O&P
0010	**PLATES** R051223-80									
0015	Made from recycled materials									
0020	For connections & stiffener plates, shop fabricated									
0050	1/8" thick (5.1 lb./S.F.)	G			S.F.	6.85			6.85	7.55
0100	1/4" thick (10.2 lb./S.F.)	G				13.75			13.75	15.10
0300	3/8" thick (15.3 lb./S.F.)	G				20.50			20.50	22.50
0400	1/2" thick (20.4 lb./S.F.)	G				27.50			27.50	30
0450	3/4" thick (30.6 lb./S.F.)	G				41			41	45.50
0500	1" thick (40.8 lb./S.F.)	G				55			55	60.50
2000	Steel plate, warehouse prices, no shop fabrication									
2100	1/4" thick (10.2 lb./S.F.)	G			S.F.	7.30			7.30	8

05 12 23.70 Stressed Skin Steel Roof and Ceiling System

		Crew	Daily Output	Labor-Hours	Unit	Material	Labor	Equipment	Total	Total Incl O&P
0010	**STRESSED SKIN STEEL ROOF & CEILING SYSTEM**									
0020	Double panel flat roof, spans to 100'	G E-2	1150	.049	S.F.	10.75	2.64	1.47	14.86	17.70
0100	Double panel convex roof, spans to 200'	G	960	.058		17.50	3.17	1.76	22.43	26
0200	Double panel arched roof, spans to 300'	G	760	.074		27	4	2.22	33.22	38.50

05 12 23.75 Structural Steel Members

		Crew	Daily Output	Labor-Hours	Unit	Material	Labor	Equipment	Total	Total Incl O&P
0010	**STRUCTURAL STEEL MEMBERS** R051223-10									
0015	Made from recycled materials									
0020	Shop fab'd for 100-ton, 1-2 story project, bolted connections									
0100	Beam or girder, W 6 x 9	G E-2	600	.093	L.F.	13.35	5.05	2.81	21.21	26
0120	x 15	G	600	.093		22	5.05	2.81	29.86	35.50
0140	x 20	G	600	.093		29.50	5.05	2.81	37.36	43.50
0300	W 8 x 10	G	600	.093		14.80	5.05	2.81	22.66	27.50
0320	x 15	G	600	.093		22	5.05	2.81	29.86	35.50
0350	x 21	G	600	.093		31	5.05	2.81	38.86	45
0360	x 24	G	550	.102		35.50	5.55	3.07	44.12	51
0370	x 28	G	550	.102		41.50	5.55	3.07	50.12	57.50
0500	x 31	G	550	.102		46	5.55	3.07	54.62	62.50
0520	x 35	G	550	.102		52	5.55	3.07	60.62	69
0540	x 48	G	550	.102		71	5.55	3.07	79.62	90
0600	W 10 x 12	G	600	.093		17.75	5.05	2.81	25.61	30.50
0620	x 15	G	600	.093		22	5.05	2.81	29.86	35.50
0700	x 22	G	600	.093		32.50	5.05	2.81	40.36	47
0720	x 26	G	600	.093		38.50	5.05	2.81	46.36	53.50
0740	x 33	G	550	.102		49	5.55	3.07	57.62	66
0900	x 49	G	550	.102		72.50	5.55	3.07	81.12	92
1100	W 12 x 16	G	880	.064		23.50	3.45	1.92	28.87	33.50
1300	x 22	G	880	.064		32.50	3.45	1.92	37.87	43.50
1500	x 26	G	880	.064		38.50	3.45	1.92	43.87	50
1520	x 35	G	810	.069		52	3.75	2.08	57.83	65.50
1560	x 50	G	750	.075		74	4.05	2.25	80.30	90.50
1580	x 58	G	750	.075		86	4.05	2.25	92.30	103
1700	x 72	G	640	.088		107	4.75	2.64	114.39	128
1740	x 87	G	640	.088		129	4.75	2.64	136.39	153

For customer support on your Green Building Costs with RSMeans data, call 800.448.8182.

05 12 Structural Steel Framing

05 12 23 – Structural Steel for Buildings

05 12 23.75 Structural Steel Members

			Crew	Daily Output	Labor-Hours	Unit	Material	2018 Bare Costs Labor	Equipment	Total	Total Incl O&P
1900	W 14 x 26	G	E-2	990	.057	L.F.	38.50	3.07	1.70	43.27	49.50
2100	x 30	G		900	.062		44.50	3.38	1.87	49.75	56.50
2300	x 34	G		810	.069		50.50	3.75	2.08	56.33	64
2320	x 43	G		810	.069		63.50	3.75	2.08	69.33	78.50
2340	x 53	G		800	.070		78.50	3.80	2.11	84.41	95
2360	x 74	G		760	.074		110	4	2.22	116.22	130
2380	x 90	G		740	.076		133	4.11	2.28	139.39	156
2500	x 120	G		720	.078		178	4.22	2.34	184.56	204
2700	W 16 x 26	G		1000	.056		38.50	3.04	1.69	43.23	49
2900	x 31	G		900	.062		46	3.38	1.87	51.25	58
3100	x 40	G		800	.070		59	3.80	2.11	64.91	73.50
3120	x 50	G		800	.070		74	3.80	2.11	79.91	90
3140	x 67	G		760	.074		99	4	2.22	105.22	118
3300	W 18 x 35	G	E-5	960	.083		52	4.55	1.86	58.41	66.50
3500	x 40	G		960	.083		59	4.55	1.86	65.41	74.50
3520	x 46	G		960	.083		68	4.55	1.86	74.41	84.50
3700	x 50	G		912	.088		74	4.79	1.96	80.75	91.50
3900	x 55	G		912	.088		81.50	4.79	1.96	88.25	99.50
3920	x 65	G		900	.089		96.50	4.85	1.98	103.33	116
3940	x 76	G		900	.089		113	4.85	1.98	119.83	134
3960	x 86	G		900	.089		127	4.85	1.98	133.83	150
3980	x 106	G		900	.089		157	4.85	1.98	163.83	183
4100	W 21 x 44	G		1064	.075		65	4.10	1.68	70.78	80
4300	x 50	G		1064	.075		74	4.10	1.68	79.78	90
4500	x 62	G		1036	.077		92	4.22	1.72	97.94	110
4700	x 68	G		1036	.077		101	4.22	1.72	106.94	120
4720	x 83	G		1000	.080		123	4.37	1.79	129.16	144
4740	x 93	G		1000	.080		138	4.37	1.79	144.16	160
4760	x 101	G		1000	.080		150	4.37	1.79	156.16	174
4780	x 122	G		1000	.080		181	4.37	1.79	187.16	208
4900	W 24 x 55	G		1110	.072		81.50	3.93	1.61	87.04	97.50
5100	x 62	G		1110	.072		92	3.93	1.61	97.54	109
5300	x 68	G		1110	.072		101	3.93	1.61	106.54	119
5500	x 76	G		1110	.072		113	3.93	1.61	118.54	132
5700	x 84	G		1080	.074		124	4.04	1.65	129.69	145
5720	x 94	G		1080	.074		139	4.04	1.65	144.69	161
5740	x 104	G		1050	.076		154	4.16	1.70	159.86	178
5760	x 117	G		1050	.076		173	4.16	1.70	178.86	200
5780	x 146	G		1050	.076		216	4.16	1.70	221.86	247
5800	W 27 x 84	G		1190	.067		124	3.67	1.50	129.17	145
5900	x 94	G		1190	.067		139	3.67	1.50	144.17	161
5920	x 114	G		1150	.070		169	3.80	1.55	174.35	194
5940	x 146	G		1150	.070		216	3.80	1.55	221.35	246
5960	x 161	G		1150	.070		238	3.80	1.55	243.35	270
6100	W 30 x 99	G		1200	.067		147	3.64	1.49	152.13	168
6300	x 108	G		1200	.067		160	3.64	1.49	165.13	183
6500	x 116	G		1160	.069		172	3.77	1.54	177.31	197
6520	x 132	G		1160	.069		195	3.77	1.54	200.31	223
6540	x 148	G		1160	.069		219	3.77	1.54	224.31	249
6560	x 173	G		1120	.071		256	3.90	1.59	261.49	290
6580	x 191	G		1120	.071		283	3.90	1.59	288.49	320
6700	W 33 x 118	G		1176	.068		175	3.71	1.52	180.23	200
6900	x 130	G		1134	.071		193	3.85	1.57	198.42	220

For customer support on your Green Building Costs with RSMeans data, call 800.448.8182.

05 12 Structural Steel Framing

05 12 23 – Structural Steel for Buildings

05 12 23.75 Structural Steel Members

		Crew	Daily Output	Labor-Hours	Unit	Material	2018 Bare Costs Labor	Equipment	Total	Total Incl O&P
7100	x 141	E-5	1134	.071	L.F.	209	3.85	1.57	214.42	238
7120	x 169		1100	.073		250	3.97	1.62	255.59	283
7140	x 201		1100	.073		298	3.97	1.62	303.59	335
7300	W 36 x 135		1170	.068		200	3.73	1.53	205.26	228
7500	x 150		1170	.068		222	3.73	1.53	227.26	252
7600	x 170		1150	.070		252	3.80	1.55	257.35	285
7700	x 194		1125	.071		287	3.88	1.59	292.47	325
7900	x 231		1125	.071		340	3.88	1.59	345.47	385
7920	x 262		1035	.077		390	4.22	1.73	395.95	435
8100	x 302		1035	.077		445	4.22	1.73	450.95	500
8490	For projects 75 to 99 tons, add					10%				
8492	50 to 74 tons, add					20%				
8494	25 to 49 tons, add					30%	10%			
8496	10 to 24 tons, add					50%	25%			
8498	2 to 9 tons, add					75%	50%			
8499	Less than 2 tons, add					100%	100%			

05 12 23.77 Structural Steel Projects

		Crew	Daily Output	Labor-Hours	Unit	Material	Labor	Equipment	Total	Total Incl O&P
0010	**STRUCTURAL STEEL PROJECTS**									
0015	Made from recycled materials									
0020	Shop fab'd for 100-ton, 1-2 story project, bolted connections									
0200	Apartments, nursing homes, etc., 1 to 2 stories R050523-10	E-5	10.30	7.767	Ton	2,700	425	173	3,298	3,825
0300	3 to 6 stories	"	10.10	7.921		2,750	430	177	3,357	3,925
0400	7 to 15 stories R051223-10	E-6	14.20	9.014		2,800	490	137	3,427	4,025
0500	Over 15 stories	"	13.90	9.209		2,900	500	140	3,540	4,175
0700	Offices, hospitals, etc., steel bearing, 1 to 2 stories R051223-20	E-5	10.30	7.767		2,700	425	173	3,298	3,825
0800	3 to 6 stories	E-6	14.40	8.889		2,750	485	135	3,370	3,950
0900	7 to 15 stories		14.20	9.014		2,800	490	137	3,427	4,025
1000	Over 15 stories		13.90	9.209		2,900	500	140	3,540	4,175
1100	For multi-story masonry wall bearing construction, add R051223-30						30%			
1300	Industrial bldgs., 1 story, beams & girders, steel bearing R050521-20	E-5	12.90	6.202		2,700	340	138	3,178	3,650
1400	Masonry bearing	"	10	8		2,700	435	179	3,314	3,850
1500	Industrial bldgs., 1 story, under 10 tons,									
1510	steel from warehouse, trucked	E-2	7.50	7.467	Ton	3,225	405	225	3,855	4,450
1600	1 story with roof trusses, steel bearing	E-5	10.60	7.547		3,175	410	168	3,753	4,350
1700	Masonry bearing	"	8.30	9.639		3,175	525	215	3,915	4,575
1900	Monumental structures, banks, stores, etc., simple connections	E-6	13	9.846		2,700	535	149	3,384	3,975
2000	Moment/composite connections	"	9	14.222		4,475	775	215	5,465	6,400
2200	Churches, simple connections	E-5	11.60	6.897		2,500	375	154	3,029	3,525
2300	Moment/composite connections	"	5.20	15.385		3,350	840	345	4,535	5,400
2800	Power stations, fossil fuels, simple connections	E-6	11	11.636		2,700	635	176	3,511	4,175
2900	Moment/composite connections		5.70	22.456		4,050	1,225	340	5,615	6,800
2950	Nuclear fuels, non-safety steel, simple connections		7	18.286		2,700	995	277	3,972	4,850
3000	Moment/composite connections		5.50	23.273		4,050	1,275	355	5,680	6,900
3040	Safety steel, simple connections		2.50	51.200		3,925	2,800	775	7,500	9,675
3070	Moment/composite connections		1.50	85.333		5,175	4,650	1,300	11,125	14,600
3100	Roof trusses, simple connections	E-5	13	6.154		3,775	335	137	4,247	4,850
3200	Moment/composite connections		8.30	9.639		4,575	525	215	5,315	6,100
3210	Schools, simple connections		14.50	5.517		2,700	300	123	3,123	3,575
3220	Moment/composite connections		8.30	9.639		3,925	525	215	4,665	5,400
3400	Welded construction, simple commercial bldgs., 1 to 2 stories	E-7	7.60	10.526		2,750	575	248	3,573	4,225
3500	7 to 15 stories	E-9	8.30	15.422		3,175	840	262	4,277	5,150
3700	Welded rigid frame, 1 story, simple connections	E-7	15.80	5.063		2,800	276	119	3,195	3,650

05 12 Structural Steel Framing

05 12 23 – Structural Steel for Buildings

05 12 23.77 Structural Steel Projects

		Crew	Daily Output	Labor-Hours	Unit	Material	2018 Bare Costs Labor	Equipment	Total	Total Incl O&P
3800	Moment/composite connections	G E-7	5.50	14.545	Ton	3,625	795	345	4,765	5,650
3810	Fabrication shop costs (incl in project bare material cost, above)									
3820	Mini mill base price, Grade A992	G			Ton	730			730	800
3830	Mill extras plus delivery to warehouse					280			280	310
3835	Delivery from warehouse to fabrication shop					108			108	118
3840	Shop extra for shop drawings and detailing					325			325	355
3850	Shop fabricating and handling					965			965	1,050
3860	Shop sandblasting and primer coat of paint					148			148	163
3870	Shop delivery to the job site					139			139	153
3880	Total material cost, shop fabricated, primed, delivered					2,700			2,700	2,950
3900	High strength steel mill spec extras:									
3950	A529, A572 (50 ksi) and A36: same as A992 steel (no extra)									
4000	Add to A992 price for A572 (60, 65 ksi)	G			Ton	82			82	90.50
4100	A242 and A588 Weathering	G			"	82			82	90.50
4200	Mill size extras for W-Shapes: 0 to 30 plf: no extra charge									
4210	Member sizes 31 to 65 plf, add	G			Ton	5.10			5.10	5.65
4220	Member sizes 66 to 100 plf, add	G				61.50			61.50	68
4230	Member sizes 101 to 387 plf, add	G				149			149	164
4300	Column base plates, light, up to 150 lb.	G	2 Sswk	2000	.008	Lb.	1.48	.44		1.92	2.34
4400	Heavy, over 150 lb.	G	E-2	7500	.007	"	1.55	.41	.23	2.19	2.60
4600	Castellated beams, light sections, to 50#/L.F., simple connections	G		10.70	5.234	Ton	2,825	284	158	3,267	3,725
4700	Moment/composite connections	G		7	8		3,100	435	241	3,776	4,350
4900	Heavy sections, over 50 plf, simple connections	G		11.70	4.786		2,950	260	144	3,354	3,825
5000	Moment/composite connections	G		7.80	7.179		3,225	390	216	3,831	4,425
5390	For projects 75 to 99 tons, add						10%				
5392	50 to 74 tons, add						20%				
5394	25 to 49 tons, add						30%	10%			
5396	10 to 24 tons, add						50%	25%			
5398	2 to 9 tons, add						75%	50%			
5399	Less than 2 tons, add						100%	100%			

05 12 23.78 Structural Steel Secondary Members

		Crew	Daily Output	Labor-Hours	Unit	Material	Labor	Equipment	Total	Total Incl O&P
0010	**STRUCTURAL STEEL SECONDARY MEMBERS**									
0015	Made from recycled materials									
0020	Shop fabricated for 20-ton girt/purlin framing package, materials only									
0100	Girts/purlins, C/Z-shapes, includes clips and bolts									
0110	6" x 2-1/2" x 2-1/2", 16 ga., 3.0 lb./L.F.				L.F.	3.63			3.63	4
0115	14 ga., 3.5 lb./L.F.					4.24			4.24	4.66
0120	8" x 2-3/4" x 2-3/4", 16 ga., 3.4 lb./L.F.					4.12			4.12	4.53
0125	14 ga., 4.1 lb./L.F.					4.97			4.97	5.45
0130	12 ga., 5.6 lb./L.F.					6.80			6.80	7.45
0135	10" x 3-1/2" x 3-1/2", 14 ga., 4.7 lb./L.F.					5.70			5.70	6.25
0140	12 ga., 6.7 lb./L.F.					8.10			8.10	8.95
0145	12" x 3-1/2" x 3-1/2", 14 ga., 5.3 lb./L.F.					6.40			6.40	7.05
0150	12 ga., 7.4 lb./L.F.					8.95			8.95	9.85
0200	Eave struts, C-shape, includes clips and bolts									
0210	6" x 4" x 3", 16 ga., 3.1 lb./L.F.				L.F.	3.76			3.76	4.13
0215	14 ga., 3.9 lb./L.F.					4.73			4.73	5.20
0220	8" x 4" x 3", 16 ga., 3.5 lb./L.F.					4.24			4.24	4.66
0225	14 ga., 4.4 lb./L.F.					5.35			5.35	5.85
0230	12 ga., 6.2 lb./L.F.					7.50			7.50	8.25
0235	10" x 5" x 3", 14 ga., 5.2 lb./L.F.					6.30			6.30	6.95
0240	12 ga., 7.3 lb./L.F.					8.85			8.85	9.75

05 12 Structural Steel Framing

05 12 23 – Structural Steel for Buildings

05 12 23.78 Structural Steel Secondary Members

		Crew	Daily Output	Labor-Hours	Unit	Material	2018 Bare Costs Labor	Equipment	Total	Total Incl O&P
0245	12" x 5" x 4", 14 ga., 6.0 lb./L.F.				L.F.	7.25			7.25	8
0250	12 ga., 8.4 lb./L.F.					10.20			10.20	11.20
0300	Rake/base angle, excludes concrete drilling and expansion anchors									
0310	2" x 2", 14 ga., 1.0 lb./L.F.	2 Sswk	640	.025	L.F.	1.21	1.37		2.58	3.56
0315	3" x 2", 14 ga., 1.3 lb./L.F.		535	.030		1.58	1.63		3.21	4.40
0320	3" x 3", 14 ga., 1.6 lb./L.F.		500	.032		1.94	1.75		3.69	4.99
0325	4" x 3", 14 ga., 1.8 lb./L.F.		480	.033		2.18	1.82		4	5.40
0600	Installation of secondary members, erection only									
0610	Girts, purlins, eave struts, 16 ga., 6" deep	E-18	100	.400	Ea.		22	10.85	32.85	47.50
0615	8" deep		80	.500			27.50	13.55	41.05	59
0620	14 ga., 6" deep		80	.500			27.50	13.55	41.05	59
0625	8" deep		65	.615			34	16.65	50.65	73
0630	10" deep		55	.727			40	19.70	59.70	86
0635	12" deep		50	.800			44	21.50	65.50	94.50
0640	12 ga., 8" deep		50	.800			44	21.50	65.50	94.50
0645	10" deep		45	.889			49	24	73	105
0650	12" deep		40	1			55	27	82	119
0900	For less than 20-ton job lots									
0905	For 15 to 19 tons, add				%	10%				
0910	For 10 to 14 tons, add					25%				
0915	For 5 to 9 tons, add					50%	50%	50%		
0920	For 1 to 4 tons, add					75%	75%	75%		
0925	For less than 1 ton, add					100%	100%	100%		

05 12 23.79 Structural Steel

		Crew	Daily Output	Labor-Hours	Unit	Material	Labor	Equipment	Total	Total Incl O&P
0010	**STRUCTURAL STEEL**									
0020	Shop fab'd for 100-ton, 1-2 story project, bolted conn's.									
0050	Beams, W 6 x 9 [G]	E-2	720	.078	L.F.	14.55	4.22	2.34	21.11	25.50
0100	W 8 x 10 [G]		720	.078		16.15	4.22	2.34	22.71	27
0200	Columns, W 6 x 15 [G]		540	.104		26.50	5.65	3.12	35.27	41.50
0250	W 8 x 31 [G]		540	.104		54.50	5.65	3.12	63.27	72
7990	For projects 75 to 99 tons, add				All	10%				
7992	50 to 75 tons, add					20%				
7994	25 to 49 tons, add					30%	10%			
7996	10 to 24 tons, add					50%	25%			
7998	2 to 9 tons, add					75%	50%			
7999	Less than 2 tons, add					100%	100%			

05 12 23.80 Subpurlins

		Crew	Daily Output	Labor-Hours	Unit	Material	Labor	Equipment	Total	Total Incl O&P
0010	**SUBPURLINS** R051223-50									
0015	Made from recycled materials									
0020	Bulb tees, shop fabricated, painted, 32-5/8" OC, 40 psf L.L.									
0200	Type 218, max 10'-2" span, 3.19 plf, 2-1/8" high x 2-1/8" wide [G]	E-1	3100	.008	S.F.	1.73	.42	.03	2.18	2.60
1420	For 24-5/8" spacing, add					33%	33%			
1430	For 48-5/8" spacing, deduct					33%	33%			

05 14 Structural Aluminum Framing

05 14 23 – Non-Exposed Structural Aluminum Framing

05 14 23.05 Aluminum Shapes

			Crew	Daily Output	Labor-Hours	Unit	Material	2018 Bare Costs Labor	Equipment	Total	Total Incl O&P
0010	**ALUMINUM SHAPES**										
0015	Made from recycled materials										
0020	Structural shapes, 1" to 10" members, under 1 ton	G	E-2	4000	.014	Lb.	3.71	.76	.42	4.89	5.75
0050	1 to 5 tons	G		4300	.013		3.40	.71	.39	4.50	5.30
0100	Over 5 tons	G		4600	.012		3.24	.66	.37	4.27	5
0300	Extrusions, over 5 tons, stock shapes	G		1330	.042		3.41	2.29	1.27	6.97	8.80
0400	Custom shapes	G		1330	.042		4.52	2.29	1.27	8.08	10.05

05 15 Wire Rope Assemblies

05 15 16 – Steel Wire Rope Assemblies

05 15 16.05 Accessories for Steel Wire Rope

			Crew	Daily Output	Labor-Hours	Unit	Material	2018 Bare Costs Labor	Equipment	Total	Total Incl O&P
0010	**ACCESSORIES FOR STEEL WIRE ROPE**										
0015	Made from recycled materials										
1500	Thimbles, heavy duty, 1/4"	G	E-17	160	.100	Ea.	.37	5.55		5.92	9.50
1510	1/2"	G		160	.100		1.63	5.55		7.18	10.90
1520	3/4"	G		105	.152		3.72	8.50		12.22	17.95
1530	1"	G		52	.308		7.45	17.10		24.55	36
1540	1-1/4"	G		38	.421		11.45	23.50		34.95	51
1550	1-1/2"	G		13	1.231		32	68.50		100.50	148
1560	1-3/4"	G		8	2		66.50	111		177.50	255
1570	2"	G		6	2.667		96.50	148		244.50	350
1580	2-1/4"	G		4	4		131	223		354	510
1600	Clips, 1/4" diameter	G		160	.100		1.98	5.55		7.53	11.30
1610	3/8" diameter	G		160	.100		2.17	5.55		7.72	11.50
1620	1/2" diameter	G		160	.100		3.49	5.55		9.04	12.95
1630	3/4" diameter	G		102	.157		5.65	8.75		14.40	20.50
1640	1" diameter	G		64	.250		9.45	13.90		23.35	33.50
1650	1-1/4" diameter	G		35	.457		15.45	25.50		40.95	58.50
1670	1-1/2" diameter	G		26	.615		21	34.50		55.50	79
1680	1-3/4" diameter	G		16	1		48.50	55.50		104	145
1690	2" diameter	G		12	1.333		54	74		128	181
1700	2-1/4" diameter	G		10	1.600		79.50	89		168.50	234
1800	Sockets, open swage, 1/4" diameter	G		160	.100		26	5.55		31.55	37.50
1810	1/2" diameter	G		77	.208		37.50	11.55		49.05	60
1820	3/4" diameter	G		19	.842		58	47		105	141
1830	1" diameter	G		9	1.778		104	99		203	276
1840	1-1/4" diameter	G		5	3.200		144	178		322	450
1850	1-1/2" diameter	G		3	5.333		315	297		612	835
1860	1-3/4" diameter	G		3	5.333		560	297		857	1,100
1870	2" diameter	G		1.50	10.667		850	595		1,445	1,900
1900	Closed swage, 1/4" diameter	G		160	.100		15.60	5.55		21.15	26.50
1910	1/2" diameter	G		104	.154		27	8.55		35.55	43.50
1920	3/4" diameter	G		32	.500		40.50	28		68.50	90
1930	1" diameter	G		15	1.067		71	59.50		130.50	175
1940	1-1/4" diameter	G		7	2.286		106	127		233	325
1950	1-1/2" diameter	G		4	4		193	223		416	575
1960	1-3/4" diameter	G		3	5.333		284	297		581	800
1970	2" diameter	G		2	8		555	445		1,000	1,350
2000	Open spelter, galv., 1/4" diameter	G		160	.100		35	5.55		40.55	47.50
2010	1/2" diameter	G		70	.229		36.50	12.70		49.20	61
2020	3/4" diameter	G		26	.615		55	34.50		89.50	117

05 15 Wire Rope Assemblies

05 15 16 – Steel Wire Rope Assemblies

05 15 16.05 Accessories for Steel Wire Rope

			Crew	Daily Output	Labor-Hours	Unit	Material	2018 Bare Costs Labor	Equipment	Total	Total Incl O&P
2030	1" diameter	G	E-17	10	1.600	Ea.	152	89		241	315
2040	1-1/4" diameter	G		5	3.200		218	178		396	530
2050	1-1/2" diameter	G		4	4		460	223		683	870
2060	1-3/4" diameter	G		2	8		805	445		1,250	1,625
2070	2" diameter	G		1.20	13.333		925	740		1,665	2,250
2080	2-1/2" diameter	G		1	16		1,700	890		2,590	3,325
2100	Closed spelter, galv., 1/4" diameter	G		160	.100		29	5.55		34.55	41
2110	1/2" diameter	G		88	.182		31	10.10		41.10	51
2120	3/4" diameter	G		30	.533		47	29.50		76.50	101
2130	1" diameter	G		13	1.231		101	68.50		169.50	223
2140	1-1/4" diameter	G		7	2.286		161	127		288	385
2150	1-1/2" diameter	G		6	2.667		345	148		493	625
2160	1-3/4" diameter	G		2.80	5.714		460	320		780	1,025
2170	2" diameter	G		2	8		570	445		1,015	1,350
2200	Jaw & jaw turnbuckles, 1/4" x 4"	G		160	.100		12	5.55		17.55	22.50
2250	1/2" x 6"	G		96	.167		15.15	9.30		24.45	32
2260	1/2" x 9"	G		77	.208		20	11.55		31.55	41
2270	1/2" x 12"	G		66	.242		22.50	13.50		36	47
2300	3/4" x 6"	G		38	.421		29.50	23.50		53	71
2310	3/4" x 9"	G		30	.533		33	29.50		62.50	84.50
2320	3/4" x 12"	G		28	.571		42.50	32		74.50	98.50
2330	3/4" x 18"	G		23	.696		50.50	38.50		89	119
2350	1" x 6"	G		17	.941		57.50	52.50		110	149
2360	1" x 12"	G		13	1.231		63	68.50		131.50	182
2370	1" x 18"	G		10	1.600		94.50	89		183.50	250
2380	1" x 24"	G		9	1.778		104	99		203	276
2400	1-1/4" x 12"	G		7	2.286		106	127		233	325
2410	1-1/4" x 18"	G		6.50	2.462		131	137		268	370
2420	1-1/4" x 24"	G		5.60	2.857		177	159		336	455
2450	1-1/2" x 12"	G		5.20	3.077		232	171		403	535
2460	1-1/2" x 18"	G		4	4		248	223		471	640
2470	1-1/2" x 24"	G		3.20	5		335	278		613	820
2500	1-3/4" x 18"	G		3.20	5		505	278		783	1,000
2510	1-3/4" x 24"	G		2.80	5.714		575	320		895	1,150
2550	2" x 24"	G		1.60	10		775	555		1,330	1,750

05 15 16.50 Steel Wire Rope

			Crew	Daily Output	Labor-Hours	Unit	Material	Labor	Equipment	Total	Total Incl O&P
0010	**STEEL WIRE ROPE**										
0015	Made from recycled materials										
0020	6 x 19, bright, fiber core, 5000' rolls, 1/2" diameter	G				L.F.	.86			.86	.94
0050	Steel core	G					1.13			1.13	1.24
0100	Fiber core, 1" diameter	G					2.89			2.89	3.18
0150	Steel core	G					3.30			3.30	3.63
0300	6 x 19, galvanized, fiber core, 1/2" diameter	G					1.27			1.27	1.39
0350	Steel core	G					1.45			1.45	1.59
0400	Fiber core, 1" diameter	G					3.71			3.71	4.08
0450	Steel core	G					3.89			3.89	4.28
0500	6 x 7, bright, IPS, fiber core, <500 L.F. w/acc., 1/4" diameter	G	E-17	6400	.003		1.11	.14		1.25	1.45
0510	1/2" diameter	G		2100	.008		2.70	.42		3.12	3.66
0520	3/4" diameter	G		960	.017		4.89	.93		5.82	6.90
0550	6 x 19, bright, IPS, IWRC, <500 L.F. w/acc., 1/4" diameter	G		5760	.003		.95	.15		1.10	1.29
0560	1/2" diameter	G		1730	.009		1.54	.51		2.05	2.53
0570	3/4" diameter	G		770	.021		2.67	1.16		3.83	4.82

For customer support on your Green Building Costs with RSMeans data, call 800.448.8182.

05 15 Wire Rope Assemblies

05 15 16 – Steel Wire Rope Assemblies

05 15 16.50 Steel Wire Rope

			Crew	Daily Output	Labor-Hours	Unit	Material	2018 Bare Costs Labor	Equipment	Total	Total Incl O&P
0580	1" diameter	G	E-17	420	.038	L.F.	4.52	2.12		6.64	8.45
0590	1-1/4" diameter	G		290	.055		7.50	3.07		10.57	13.25
0600	1-1/2" diameter	G		192	.083		9.20	4.64		13.84	17.75
0610	1-3/4" diameter	G	E-18	240	.167		14.70	9.15	4.51	28.36	36
0620	2" diameter	G		160	.250		18.85	13.70	6.75	39.30	50
0630	2-1/4" diameter	G		160	.250		25	13.70	6.75	45.45	57
0650	6 x 37, bright, IPS, IWRC, <500 L.F. w/acc., 1/4" diameter	G	E-17	6400	.003		1.11	.14		1.25	1.45
0660	1/2" diameter	G		1730	.009		1.88	.51		2.39	2.90
0670	3/4" diameter	G		770	.021		3.03	1.16		4.19	5.20
0680	1" diameter	G		430	.037		4.81	2.07		6.88	8.70
0690	1-1/4" diameter	G		290	.055		7.25	3.07		10.32	13
0700	1-1/2" diameter	G		190	.084		10.40	4.69		15.09	19.10
0710	1-3/4" diameter	G	E-18	260	.154		16.50	8.45	4.17	29.12	36.50
0720	2" diameter	G		200	.200		21.50	10.95	5.40	37.85	47
0730	2-1/4" diameter	G		160	.250		28.50	13.70	6.75	48.95	60.50
0800	6 x 19 & 6 x 37, swaged, 1/2" diameter	G	E-17	1220	.013		2.53	.73		3.26	3.97
0810	9/16" diameter	G		1120	.014		2.94	.80		3.74	4.54
0820	5/8" diameter	G		930	.017		3.49	.96		4.45	5.40
0830	3/4" diameter	G		640	.025		4.45	1.39		5.84	7.15
0840	7/8" diameter	G		480	.033		5.60	1.85		7.45	9.20
0850	1" diameter	G		350	.046		6.85	2.54		9.39	11.65
0860	1-1/8" diameter	G		288	.056		8.40	3.09		11.49	14.30
0870	1-1/4" diameter	G		230	.070		10.20	3.87		14.07	17.55
0880	1-3/8" diameter	G		192	.083		11.75	4.64		16.39	20.50
0890	1-1/2" diameter	G	E-18	300	.133		14.30	7.30	3.61	25.21	31.50

05 15 16.60 Galvanized Steel Wire Rope and Accessories

			Crew	Daily Output	Labor-Hours	Unit	Material	Labor	Equipment	Total	Total Incl O&P
0010	**GALVANIZED STEEL WIRE ROPE & ACCESSORIES**										
0015	Made from recycled materials										
3000	Aircraft cable, galvanized, 7 x 7 x 1/8"	G	E-17	5000	.003	L.F.	.20	.18		.38	.51
3100	Clamps, 1/8"	G	"	125	.128	Ea.	1.41	7.10		8.51	13.20

05 15 16.70 Temporary Cable Safety Railing

			Crew	Daily Output	Labor-Hours	Unit	Material	Labor	Equipment	Total	Total Incl O&P
0010	**TEMPORARY CABLE SAFETY RAILING**, Each 100' strand incl.										
0020	2 eyebolts, 1 turnbuckle, 100' cable, 2 thimbles, 6 clips										
0025	Made from recycled materials										
0100	One strand using 1/4" cable & accessories	G	2 Sswk	4	4	C.L.F.	153	219		372	525
0200	1/2" cable & accessories	G	"	2	8	"	325	435		760	1,075

05 21 Steel Joist Framing

05 21 13 – Deep Longspan Steel Joist Framing

05 21 13.50 Deep Longspan Joists

			Crew	Daily Output	Labor-Hours	Unit	Material	Labor	Equipment	Total	Total Incl O&P
0010	**DEEP LONGSPAN JOISTS**										
3010	DLH series, 40-ton job lots, bolted cross bridging, shop primer										
3015	Made from recycled materials										
3040	Spans to 144' (shipped in 2 pieces)	G	E-7	13	6.154	Ton	2,125	335	145	2,605	3,025
3200	52DLH11, 26 lb./L.F.	G		2000	.040	L.F.	26.50	2.18	.94	29.62	33.50
3220	52DLH16, 45 lb./L.F.	G		2000	.040		48	2.18	.94	51.12	57
3240	56DLH11, 26 lb./L.F.	G		2000	.040		27.50	2.18	.94	30.62	35
3260	56DLH16, 46 lb./L.F.	G		2000	.040		49	2.18	.94	52.12	58.50
3280	60DLH12, 29 lb./L.F.	G		2000	.040		31	2.18	.94	34.12	38.50
3300	60DLH17, 52 lb./L.F.	G		2000	.040		55	2.18	.94	58.12	65.50

05 21 Steel Joist Framing

05 21 13 – Deep Longspan Steel Joist Framing

05 21 13.50 Deep Longspan Joists

		Crew	Daily Output	Labor-Hours	Unit	Material	2018 Bare Costs Labor	Equipment	Total	Total Incl O&P
3320	64DLH12, 31 lb./L.F. G	E-7	2200	.036	L.F.	33	1.98	.86	35.84	40
3340	64DLH17, 52 lb./L.F. G		2200	.036		55	1.98	.86	57.84	65
3360	68DLH13, 37 lb./L.F. G		2200	.036		39.50	1.98	.86	42.34	47
3380	68DLH18, 61 lb./L.F. G		2200	.036		65	1.98	.86	67.84	75.50
3400	72DLH14, 41 lb./L.F. G		2200	.036		43.50	1.98	.86	46.34	52
3420	72DLH19, 70 lb./L.F. G		2200	.036		74.50	1.98	.86	77.34	86
3500	For less than 40-ton job lots									
3502	For 30 to 39 tons, add				%	10%				
3504	20 to 29 tons, add					20%				
3506	10 to 19 tons, add					30%				
3507	5 to 9 tons, add					50%	25%			
3508	1 to 4 tons, add					75%	50%			
3509	Less than 1 ton, add					100%	100%			
4010	SLH series, 40-ton job lots, bolted cross bridging, shop primer									
4040	Spans to 200′ (shipped in 3 pieces) G	E-7	13	6.154	Ton	2,200	335	145	2,680	3,125
4200	80SLH15, 40 lb./L.F. G		1500	.053	L.F.	44	2.91	1.26	48.17	54.50
4220	80SLH20, 75 lb./L.F. G		1500	.053		82.50	2.91	1.26	86.67	96.50
4240	88SLH16, 46 lb./L.F. G		1500	.053		50.50	2.91	1.26	54.67	61.50
4260	88SLH21, 89 lb./L.F. G		1500	.053		97.50	2.91	1.26	101.67	113
4280	96SLH17, 52 lb./L.F. G		1500	.053		57	2.91	1.26	61.17	69
4300	96SLH22, 102 lb./L.F. G		1500	.053		112	2.91	1.26	116.17	129
4320	104SLH18, 59 lb./L.F. G		1800	.044		65	2.43	1.05	68.48	76
4340	104SLH23, 109 lb./L.F. G		1800	.044		120	2.43	1.05	123.48	137
4360	112SLH19, 67 lb./L.F. G		1800	.044		73.50	2.43	1.05	76.98	86
4380	112SLH24, 131 lb./L.F. G		1800	.044		144	2.43	1.05	147.48	163
4400	120SLH20, 77 lb./L.F. G		1800	.044		84.50	2.43	1.05	87.98	98
4420	120SLH25, 152 lb./L.F. G		1800	.044		167	2.43	1.05	170.48	189
6100	For less than 40-ton job lots									
6102	For 30 to 39 tons, add				%	10%				
6104	20 to 29 tons, add					20%				
6106	10 to 19 tons, add					30%				
6107	5 to 9 tons, add					50%	25%			
6108	1 to 4 tons, add					75%	50%			
6109	Less than 1 ton, add					100%	100%			

05 21 16 – Longspan Steel Joist Framing

05 21 16.50 Longspan Joists

		Crew	Daily Output	Labor-Hours	Unit	Material	Labor	Equipment	Total	Total Incl O&P
0010	**LONGSPAN JOISTS**									
2000	LH series, 40-ton job lots, bolted cross bridging, shop primer									
2015	Made from recycled materials									
2040	Longspan joists, LH series, up to 96′ G	E-7	13	6.154	Ton	2,025	335	145	2,505	2,950
2200	18LH04, 12 lb./L.F. G		1400	.057	L.F.	12.20	3.12	1.35	16.67	19.95
2220	18LH08, 19 lb./L.F. G		1400	.057		19.35	3.12	1.35	23.82	28
2240	20LH04, 12 lb./L.F. G		1400	.057		12.20	3.12	1.35	16.67	19.95
2260	20LH08, 19 lb./L.F. G		1400	.057		19.35	3.12	1.35	23.82	28
2280	24LH05, 13 lb./L.F. G		1400	.057		13.25	3.12	1.35	17.72	21
2300	24LH10, 23 lb./L.F. G		1400	.057		23.50	3.12	1.35	27.97	32.50
2320	28LH06, 16 lb./L.F. G		1800	.044		16.30	2.43	1.05	19.78	23
2340	28LH11, 25 lb./L.F. G		1800	.044		25.50	2.43	1.05	28.98	33
2360	32LH08, 17 lb./L.F. G		1800	.044		17.30	2.43	1.05	20.78	24
2380	32LH13, 30 lb./L.F. G		1800	.044		30.50	2.43	1.05	33.98	38.50
2400	36LH09, 21 lb./L.F. G		1800	.044		21.50	2.43	1.05	24.98	28.50
2420	36LH14, 36 lb./L.F. G		1800	.044		36.50	2.43	1.05	39.98	45.50

For customer support on your Green Building Costs with RSMeans data, call 800.448.8182.

05 21 Steel Joist Framing

05 21 16 – Longspan Steel Joist Framing

05 21 16.50 Longspan Joists

		Crew	Daily Output	Labor-Hours	Unit	Material	2018 Bare Costs Labor	Equipment	Total	Total Incl O&P
2440	40LH10, 21 lb./L.F. G	E-7	2200	.036	L.F.	21.50	1.98	.86	24.34	27.50
2460	40LH15, 36 lb./L.F. G		2200	.036		36.50	1.98	.86	39.34	44.50
2480	44LH11, 22 lb./L.F. G		2200	.036		22.50	1.98	.86	25.34	28.50
2500	44LH16, 42 lb./L.F. G		2200	.036		43	1.98	.86	45.84	51
2520	48LH11, 22 lb./L.F. G		2200	.036		22.50	1.98	.86	25.34	28.50
2540	48LH16, 42 lb./L.F. G		2200	.036		43	1.98	.86	45.84	51
2600	For less than 40-ton job lots									
2602	For 30 to 39 tons, add				%	10%				
2604	20 to 29 tons, add					20%				
2606	10 to 19 tons, add					30%				
2607	5 to 9 tons, add					50%	25%			
2608	1 to 4 tons, add					75%	50%			
2609	Less than 1 ton, add					100%	100%			
6000	For welded cross bridging, add						30%			

05 21 19 – Open Web Steel Joist Framing

05 21 19.10 Open Web Joists

		Crew	Daily Output	Labor-Hours	Unit	Material	Labor	Equipment	Total	Total Incl O&P
0010	**OPEN WEB JOISTS**									
0015	Made from recycled materials									
0050	K series, 40-ton lots, horiz. bridging, spans to 30', shop primer G	E-7	12	6.667	Ton	1,800	365	157	2,322	2,725
0130	8K1, 5.1 lb./L.F. G		1200	.067	L.F.	4.60	3.64	1.57	9.81	12.65
0140	10K1, 5.0 lb./L.F. G		1200	.067		4.51	3.64	1.57	9.72	12.55
0160	12K3, 5.7 lb./L.F. G		1500	.053		5.15	2.91	1.26	9.32	11.70
0180	14K3, 6.0 lb./L.F. G		1500	.053		5.40	2.91	1.26	9.57	12
0200	16K3, 6.3 lb./L.F. G		1800	.044		5.70	2.43	1.05	9.18	11.30
0220	16K6, 8.1 lb./L.F. G		1800	.044		7.30	2.43	1.05	10.78	13.10
0240	18K5, 7.7 lb./L.F. G		2000	.040		6.95	2.18	.94	10.07	12.20
0260	18K9, 10.2 lb./L.F. G		2000	.040		9.20	2.18	.94	12.32	14.70
0440	K series, 30' to 50' spans G		17	4.706	Ton	1,775	257	111	2,143	2,475
0500	20K5, 8.2 lb./L.F. G		2000	.040	L.F.	7.25	2.18	.94	10.37	12.55
0520	20K9, 10.8 lb./L.F. G		2000	.040		9.55	2.18	.94	12.67	15.05
0540	22K5, 8.8 lb./L.F. G		2000	.040		7.80	2.18	.94	10.92	13.10
0560	22K9, 11.3 lb./L.F. G		2000	.040		10	2.18	.94	13.12	15.55
0580	24K6, 9.7 lb./L.F. G		2200	.036		8.60	1.98	.86	11.44	13.60
0600	24K10, 13.1 lb./L.F. G		2200	.036		11.60	1.98	.86	14.44	16.90
0620	26K6, 10.6 lb./L.F. G		2200	.036		9.40	1.98	.86	12.24	14.45
0640	26K10, 13.8 lb./L.F. G		2200	.036		12.20	1.98	.86	15.04	17.60
0660	28K8, 12.7 lb./L.F. G		2400	.033		11.25	1.82	.78	13.85	16.15
0680	28K12, 17.1 lb./L.F. G		2400	.033		15.15	1.82	.78	17.75	20.50
0700	30K8, 13.2 lb./L.F. G		2400	.033		11.70	1.82	.78	14.30	16.65
0720	30K12, 17.6 lb./L.F. G		2400	.033		15.60	1.82	.78	18.20	21
0800	For less than 40-ton job lots									
0802	For 30 to 39 tons, add				%	10%				
0804	20 to 29 tons, add					20%				
0806	10 to 19 tons, add					30%				
0807	5 to 9 tons, add					50%	25%			
0808	1 to 4 tons, add					75%	50%			
0809	Less than 1 ton, add					100%	100%			
1010	CS series, 40-ton job lots, horizontal bridging, shop primer									
1040	Spans to 30' G	E-7	12	6.667	Ton	1,850	365	157	2,372	2,800
1100	10CS2, 7.5 lb./L.F. G		1200	.067	L.F.	6.95	3.64	1.57	12.16	15.25
1120	12CS2, 8.0 lb./L.F. G		1500	.053		7.45	2.91	1.26	11.62	14.25
1140	14CS2, 8.0 lb./L.F. G		1500	.053		7.45	2.91	1.26	11.62	14.25

05 21 Steel Joist Framing

05 21 19 – Open Web Steel Joist Framing

05 21 19.10 Open Web Joists

			Crew	Daily Output	Labor-Hours	Unit	Material	2018 Bare Costs Labor	Equipment	Total	Total Incl O&P
1160	16CS2, 8.5 lb./L.F.	G	E-7	1800	.044	L.F.	7.90	2.43	1.05	11.38	13.75
1180	16CS4, 14.5 lb./L.F.	G		1800	.044		13.50	2.43	1.05	16.98	19.85
1200	18CS2, 9.0 lb./L.F.	G		2000	.040		8.35	2.18	.94	11.47	13.75
1220	18CS4, 15.0 lb./L.F.	G		2000	.040		13.95	2.18	.94	17.07	19.90
1240	20CS2, 9.5 lb./L.F.	G		2000	.040		8.85	2.18	.94	11.97	14.25
1260	20CS4, 16.5 lb./L.F.	G		2000	.040		15.35	2.18	.94	18.47	21.50
1280	22CS2, 10.0 lb./L.F.	G		2000	.040		9.30	2.18	.94	12.42	14.75
1300	22CS4, 16.5 lb./L.F.	G		2000	.040		15.35	2.18	.94	18.47	21.50
1320	24CS2, 10.0 lb./L.F.	G		2200	.036		9.30	1.98	.86	12.14	14.35
1340	24CS4, 16.5 lb./L.F.	G		2200	.036		15.35	1.98	.86	18.19	21
1360	26CS2, 10.0 lb./L.F.	G		2200	.036		9.30	1.98	.86	12.14	14.35
1380	26CS4, 16.5 lb./L.F.	G		2200	.036		15.35	1.98	.86	18.19	21
1400	28CS2, 10.5 lb./L.F.	G		2400	.033		9.75	1.82	.78	12.35	14.55
1420	28CS4, 16.5 lb./L.F.	G		2400	.033		15.35	1.82	.78	17.95	20.50
1440	30CS2, 11.0 lb./L.F.	G		2400	.033		10.20	1.82	.78	12.80	15.05
1460	30CS4, 16.5 lb./L.F.	G		2400	.033		15.35	1.82	.78	17.95	20.50
1500	For less than 40-ton job lots										
1502	For 30 to 39 tons, add					%	10%				
1504	20 to 29 tons, add						20%				
1506	10 to 19 tons, add						30%				
1507	5 to 9 tons, add						50%	25%			
1508	1 to 4 tons, add						75%	50%			
1509	Less than 1 ton, add						100%	100%			
6200	For shop prime paint other than mfrs. standard, add						20%				
6300	For bottom chord extensions, add per chord	G				Ea.	40			40	44
6400	Individual steel bearing plate, 6" x 6" x 1/4" with J-hook	G	1 Bric	160	.050	"	8.10	2.52		10.62	12.75

05 21 23 – Steel Joist Girder Framing

05 21 23.50 Joist Girders

0010	**JOIST GIRDERS**										
0015	Made from recycled materials										
7020	Joist girders, 40-ton job lots, shop primer	G	E-5	13	6.154	Ton	1,800	335	137	2,272	2,675
7100	For less than 40-ton job lots										
7102	For 30 to 39 tons, add					Ton	10%				
7104	20 to 29 tons, add						20%				
7106	10 to 19 tons, add						30%				
7107	5 to 9 tons, add						50%	25%			
7108	1 to 4 tons, add						75%	50%			
7109	Less than 1 ton, add						100%	100%			
8000	Trusses, 40-ton job lots, shop fabricated WT chords, shop primer	G	E-5	11	7.273		5,925	395	162	6,482	7,350
8100	For less than 40-ton job lots										
8102	For 30 to 39 tons, add					Ton	10%				
8104	20 to 29 tons, add						20%				
8106	10 to 19 tons, add						30%				
8107	5 to 9 tons, add						50%	25%			
8108	1 to 4 tons, add						75%	50%			
8109	Less than 1 ton, add						100%	100%			

05 31 Steel Decking

05 31 13 – Steel Floor Decking

05 31 13.50 Floor Decking

		Crew	Daily Output	Labor-Hours	Unit	Material	2018 Bare Costs Labor	Equipment	Total	Total Incl O&P
0010	**FLOOR DECKING** R053100-10									
0015	Made from recycled materials									
5100	Non-cellular composite decking, galvanized, 1-1/2" deep, 16 ga. G	E-4	3500	.009	S.F.	4.01	.50	.03	4.54	5.25
5120	18 ga. G		3650	.009		3.24	.48	.03	3.75	4.38
5140	20 ga. G		3800	.008		2.58	.46	.03	3.07	3.63
5200	2" deep, 22 ga. G		3860	.008		2.22	.46	.03	2.71	3.22
5300	20 ga. G		3600	.009		2.48	.49	.03	3	3.56
5400	18 ga. G		3380	.009		3.17	.52	.03	3.72	4.36
5500	16 ga. G		3200	.010		3.96	.55	.03	4.54	5.30
5700	3" deep, 22 ga. G		3200	.010		2.42	.55	.03	3	3.59
5800	20 ga. G		3000	.011		2.73	.59	.03	3.35	4
5900	18 ga. G		2850	.011		3.37	.62	.03	4.02	4.76
6000	16 ga. G		2700	.012		4.50	.65	.04	5.19	6.05

05 31 23 – Steel Roof Decking

05 31 23.50 Roof Decking

		Crew	Daily Output	Labor-Hours	Unit	Material	Labor	Equipment	Total	Total Incl O&P
0010	**ROOF DECKING**									
0015	Made from recycled materials									
2100	Open type, 1-1/2" deep, Type B, wide rib, galv., 22 ga., under 50 sq. G	E-4	4500	.007	S.F.	2.38	.39	.02	2.79	3.28
2200	50-500 squares G		4900	.007		1.85	.36	.02	2.23	2.65
2400	Over 500 squares G		5100	.006		1.71	.35	.02	2.08	2.48
2600	20 ga., under 50 squares G		3865	.008		2.78	.46	.03	3.27	3.84
2650	50-500 squares G		4170	.008		2.22	.42	.02	2.66	3.17
2700	Over 500 squares G		4300	.007		2	.41	.02	2.43	2.90
2900	18 ga., under 50 squares G		3800	.008		3.58	.46	.03	4.07	4.73
2950	50-500 squares G		4100	.008		2.86	.43	.02	3.31	3.88
3000	Over 500 squares G		4300	.007		2.58	.41	.02	3.01	3.53
3050	16 ga., under 50 squares G		3700	.009		4.84	.48	.03	5.35	6.15
3060	50-500 squares G		4000	.008		3.87	.44	.02	4.33	5
3100	Over 500 squares G		4200	.008		3.49	.42	.02	3.93	4.55
3200	3" deep, Type N, 22 ga., under 50 squares G		3600	.009		3.50	.49	.03	4.02	4.68
3250	50-500 squares G		3800	.008		2.80	.46	.03	3.29	3.87
3260	over 500 squares G		4000	.008		2.52	.44	.02	2.98	3.52
3300	20 ga., under 50 squares G		3400	.009		3.76	.52	.03	4.31	5
3350	50-500 squares G		3600	.009		3.01	.49	.03	3.53	4.14
3360	over 500 squares G		3800	.008		2.71	.46	.03	3.20	3.77
3400	18 ga., under 50 squares G		3200	.010		4.88	.55	.03	5.46	6.30
3450	50-500 squares G		3400	.009		3.90	.52	.03	4.45	5.15
3460	over 500 squares G		3600	.009		3.51	.49	.03	4.03	4.69
3500	16 ga., under 50 squares G		3000	.011		6.45	.59	.03	7.07	8.10
3550	50-500 squares G		3200	.010		5.15	.55	.03	5.73	6.65
3560	over 500 squares G		3400	.009		4.64	.52	.03	5.19	6
3700	4-1/2" deep, Type J, 20 ga., over 50 squares G		2700	.012		4.24	.65	.04	4.93	5.75
3800	18 ga. G		2460	.013		5.55	.72	.04	6.31	7.35
3900	16 ga. G		2350	.014		7.25	.75	.04	8.04	9.30
4100	6" deep, Type H, 18 ga., over 50 squares G		2000	.016		6.70	.88	.05	7.63	8.85
4200	16 ga. G		1930	.017		8.35	.91	.05	9.31	10.75
4300	14 ga. G		1860	.017		10.75	.95	.05	11.75	13.40
4500	7-1/2" deep, Type H, 18 ga., over 50 squares G		1690	.019		7.95	1.04	.06	9.05	10.50
4600	16 ga. G		1590	.020		9.90	1.11	.06	11.07	12.80
4700	14 ga. G		1490	.021		12.30	1.18	.07	13.55	15.55
4800	For painted instead of galvanized, deduct					5%				
5000	For acoustical perforated with fiberglass insulation, add				S.F.	25%				

05 31 Steel Decking

05 31 23 – Steel Roof Decking

05 31 23.50 Roof Decking

		Crew	Daily Output	Labor-Hours	Unit	Material	Labor	Equipment	Total	Total Incl O&P
5100	For type F intermediate rib instead of type B wide rib, add	G			S.F.	25%				
5150	For type A narrow rib instead of type B wide rib, add	G				25%				

05 31 33 – Steel Form Decking

05 31 33.50 Form Decking

		Crew	Daily Output	Labor-Hours	Unit	Material	Labor	Equipment	Total	Total Incl O&P
0010	**FORM DECKING**									
0015	Made from recycled materials									
6100	Slab form, steel, 28 ga., 9/16" deep, Type UFS, uncoated	G	E-4	4000	.008	S.F.	1.80	.44	.02	2.26	2.73
6200	Galvanized	G		4000	.008		1.59	.44	.02	2.05	2.50
6220	24 ga., 1" deep, Type UF1X, uncoated	G		3900	.008		1.72	.45	.03	2.20	2.66
6240	Galvanized	G		3900	.008		2.02	.45	.03	2.50	2.99
6300	24 ga., 1-5/16" deep, Type UFX, uncoated	G		3800	.008		1.83	.46	.03	2.32	2.80
6400	Galvanized	G		3800	.008		2.15	.46	.03	2.64	3.16
6500	22 ga., 1-5/16" deep, uncoated	G		3700	.009		2.32	.48	.03	2.83	3.36
6600	Galvanized	G		3700	.009		2.37	.48	.03	2.88	3.42
6700	22 ga., 2" deep, uncoated	G		3600	.009		3.02	.49	.03	3.54	4.15
6800	Galvanized	G		3600	.009		2.96	.49	.03	3.48	4.09
7000	Sheet metal edge closure form, 12" wide with 2 bends, galvanized										
7100	18 ga.	G	E-14	360	.022	L.F.	4.88	1.26	.27	6.41	7.70
7200	16 ga.	G	"	360	.022	"	6.60	1.26	.27	8.13	9.60

05 35 Raceway Decking Assemblies

05 35 13 – Steel Cellular Decking

05 35 13.50 Cellular Decking

		Crew	Daily Output	Labor-Hours	Unit	Material	Labor	Equipment	Total	Total Incl O&P
0010	**CELLULAR DECKING**									
0015	Made from recycled materials									
0200	Cellular units, galv, 1-1/2" deep, Type BC, 20-20 ga., over 15 squares	G	E-4	1460	.022	S.F.	10.10	1.21	.07	11.38	13.15
0250	18-20 ga.	G		1420	.023		11.45	1.24	.07	12.76	14.70
0300	18-18 ga.	G		1390	.023		11.75	1.27	.07	13.09	15.05
0320	16-18 ga.	G		1360	.024		14	1.30	.07	15.37	17.60
0340	16-16 ga.	G		1330	.024		15.60	1.33	.07	17	19.40
0400	3" deep, Type NC, galvanized, 20-20 ga.	G		1375	.023		11.10	1.28	.07	12.45	14.40
0500	18-20 ga.	G		1350	.024		13.40	1.31	.07	14.78	16.95
0600	18-18 ga.	G		1290	.025		13.35	1.37	.08	14.80	17
0700	16-18 ga.	G		1230	.026		15.05	1.44	.08	16.57	19
0800	16-16 ga.	G		1150	.028		16.40	1.53	.09	18.02	20.50
1000	4-1/2" deep, Type JC, galvanized, 18-20 ga.	G		1100	.029		15.45	1.60	.09	17.14	19.70
1100	18-18 ga.	G		1040	.031		15.35	1.70	.09	17.14	19.75
1200	16-18 ga.	G		980	.033		17.30	1.80	.10	19.20	22
1300	16-16 ga.	G		935	.034		18.85	1.89	.11	20.85	24
1500	For acoustical deck, add						15%				
1700	For cells used for ventilation, add						15%				
1900	For multi-story or congested site, add							50%			
8000	Metal deck and trench, 2" thick, 20 ga., combination										
8010	60% cellular, 40% non-cellular, inserts and trench	G	R-4	1100	.036	S.F.	20	2.03	.09	22.12	25.50

05 41 Structural Metal Stud Framing

05 41 13 – Load-Bearing Metal Stud Framing

05 41 13.05 Bracing

			Crew	Daily Output	Labor-Hours	Unit	Material	2018 Bare Costs Labor	Equipment	Total	Total Incl O&P
0010	**BRACING**, shear wall X-bracing, per 10' x 10' bay, one face										
0015	Made of recycled materials										
0120	Metal strap, 20 ga. x 4" wide	G	2 Carp	18	.889	Ea.	18.90	45		63.90	89.50
0130	6" wide	G		18	.889		31.50	45		76.50	103
0160	18 ga. x 4" wide	G		16	1		33	50.50		83.50	113
0170	6" wide	G		16	1		48.50	50.50		99	131
0410	Continuous strap bracing, per horizontal row on both faces										
0420	Metal strap, 20 ga. x 2" wide, studs 12" OC	G	1 Carp	7	1.143	C.L.F.	57	58		115	151
0430	16" OC	G		8	1		57	50.50		107.50	140
0440	24" OC	G		10	.800		57	40.50		97.50	125
0450	18 ga. x 2" wide, studs 12" OC	G		6	1.333		79	67.50		146.50	190
0460	16" OC	G		7	1.143		79	58		137	175
0470	24" OC	G		8	1		79	50.50		129.50	164

05 41 13.10 Bridging

			Crew	Daily Output	Labor-Hours	Unit	Material	2018 Bare Costs Labor	Equipment	Total	Total Incl O&P
0010	**BRIDGING**, solid between studs w/1-1/4" leg track, per stud bay										
0015	Made from recycled materials										
0200	Studs 12" OC, 18 ga. x 2-1/2" wide	G	1 Carp	125	.064	Ea.	.95	3.24		4.19	6
0210	3-5/8" wide	G		120	.067		1.16	3.38		4.54	6.40
0220	4" wide	G		120	.067		1.22	3.38		4.60	6.50
0230	6" wide	G		115	.070		1.60	3.53		5.13	7.10
0240	8" wide	G		110	.073		1.97	3.69		5.66	7.75
0300	16 ga. x 2-1/2" wide	G		115	.070		1.21	3.53		4.74	6.70
0310	3-5/8" wide	G		110	.073		1.47	3.69		5.16	7.20
0320	4" wide	G		110	.073		1.57	3.69		5.26	7.35
0330	6" wide	G		105	.076		2.01	3.86		5.87	8.10
0340	8" wide	G		100	.080		2.51	4.06		6.57	8.95
1200	Studs 16" OC, 18 ga. x 2-1/2" wide	G		125	.064		1.22	3.24		4.46	6.30
1210	3-5/8" wide	G		120	.067		1.49	3.38		4.87	6.80
1220	4" wide	G		120	.067		1.57	3.38		4.95	6.85
1230	6" wide	G		115	.070		2.05	3.53		5.58	7.60
1240	8" wide	G		110	.073		2.52	3.69		6.21	8.40
1300	16 ga. x 2-1/2" wide	G		115	.070		1.55	3.53		5.08	7.05
1310	3-5/8" wide	G		110	.073		1.88	3.69		5.57	7.65
1320	4" wide	G		110	.073		2.01	3.69		5.70	7.80
1330	6" wide	G		105	.076		2.57	3.86		6.43	8.75
1340	8" wide	G		100	.080		3.22	4.06		7.28	9.75
2200	Studs 24" OC, 18 ga. x 2-1/2" wide	G		125	.064		1.77	3.24		5.01	6.90
2210	3-5/8" wide	G		120	.067		2.15	3.38		5.53	7.50
2220	4" wide	G		120	.067		2.27	3.38		5.65	7.65
2230	6" wide	G		115	.070		2.96	3.53		6.49	8.60
2240	8" wide	G		110	.073		3.65	3.69		7.34	9.60
2300	16 ga. x 2-1/2" wide	G		115	.070		2.24	3.53		5.77	7.80
2310	3-5/8" wide	G		110	.073		2.72	3.69		6.41	8.60
2320	4" wide	G		110	.073		2.91	3.69		6.60	8.80
2330	6" wide	G		105	.076		3.72	3.86		7.58	10
2340	8" wide	G		100	.080		4.65	4.06		8.71	11.30
3000	Continuous bridging, per row										
3100	16 ga. x 1-1/2" channel thru studs 12" OC	G	1 Carp	6	1.333	C.L.F.	51.50	67.50		119	160
3110	16" OC	G		7	1.143		51.50	58		109.50	145
3120	24" OC	G		8.80	.909		51.50	46		97.50	127
4100	2" x 2" angle x 18 ga., studs 12" OC	G		7	1.143		80.50	58		138.50	177
4110	16" OC	G		9	.889		80.50	45		125.50	157

For customer support on your Green Building Costs with RSMeans data, call 800.448.8182.

05 41 Structural Metal Stud Framing

05 41 13 – Load-Bearing Metal Stud Framing

05 41 13.10 Bridging

		Crew	Daily Output	Labor-Hours	Unit	Material	2018 Bare Costs Labor	Equipment	Total	Total Incl O&P
4120	24" OC	1 Carp G	12	.667	C.L.F.	80.50	34		114.50	140
4200	16 ga., studs 12" OC	G	5	1.600		101	81		182	235
4210	16" OC	G	7	1.143		101	58		159	199
4220	24" OC	G	10	.800		101	40.50		141.50	173

05 41 13.25 Framing, Boxed Headers/Beams

		Crew	Daily Output	Labor-Hours	Unit	Material	Labor	Equipment	Total	Total Incl O&P
0010	**FRAMING, BOXED HEADERS/BEAMS**									
0015	Made from recycled materials									
0200	Double, 18 ga. x 6" deep	2 Carp G	220	.073	L.F.	5.50	3.69		9.19	11.65
0210	8" deep	G	210	.076		6.05	3.86		9.91	12.55
0220	10" deep	G	200	.080		7.40	4.06		11.46	14.35
0230	12" deep	G	190	.084		8.05	4.27		12.32	15.35
0300	16 ga. x 8" deep	G	180	.089		7	4.51		11.51	14.55
0310	10" deep	G	170	.094		8.45	4.77		13.22	16.50
0320	12" deep	G	160	.100		9.15	5.05		14.20	17.80
0400	14 ga. x 10" deep	G	140	.114		9.75	5.80		15.55	19.50
0410	12" deep	G	130	.123		10.65	6.25		16.90	21.50
1210	Triple, 18 ga. x 8" deep	G	170	.094		8.75	4.77		13.52	16.90
1220	10" deep	G	165	.097		10.60	4.92		15.52	19.15
1230	12" deep	G	160	.100		11.60	5.05		16.65	20.50
1300	16 ga. x 8" deep	G	145	.110		10.15	5.60		15.75	19.65
1310	10" deep	G	140	.114		12.15	5.80		17.95	22
1320	12" deep	G	135	.119		13.25	6		19.25	24
1400	14 ga. x 10" deep	G	115	.139		13.25	7.05		20.30	25.50
1410	12" deep	G	110	.145		14.65	7.35		22	27.50

05 41 13.30 Framing, Stud Walls

		Crew	Daily Output	Labor-Hours	Unit	Material	Labor	Equipment	Total	Total Incl O&P
0010	**FRAMING, STUD WALLS** w/top & bottom track, no openings,									
0020	Headers, beams, bridging or bracing									
0025	Made from recycled materials									
4100	8' high walls, 18 ga. x 2-1/2" wide, studs 12" OC	2 Carp G	54	.296	L.F.	9.15	15		24.15	33
4110	16" OC	G	77	.208		7.35	10.55		17.90	24
4120	24" OC	G	107	.150		5.50	7.60		13.10	17.60
4130	3-5/8" wide, studs 12" OC	G	53	.302		10.85	15.30		26.15	35.50
4140	16" OC	G	76	.211		8.70	10.65		19.35	26
4150	24" OC	G	105	.152		6.55	7.75		14.30	18.95
4160	4" wide, studs 12" OC	G	52	.308		11.30	15.60		26.90	36.50
4170	16" OC	G	74	.216		9.05	10.95		20	26.50
4180	24" OC	G	103	.155		6.80	7.90		14.70	19.50
4190	6" wide, studs 12" OC	G	51	.314		14.40	15.90		30.30	40
4200	16" OC	G	73	.219		11.55	11.10		22.65	29.50
4210	24" OC	G	101	.158		8.70	8.05		16.75	22
4220	8" wide, studs 12" OC	G	50	.320		17.45	16.20		33.65	43.50
4230	16" OC	G	72	.222		14	11.25		25.25	32.50
4240	24" OC	G	100	.160		10.60	8.10		18.70	24
4300	16 ga. x 2-1/2" wide, studs 12" OC	G	47	.340		10.85	17.25		28.10	38.50
4310	16" OC	G	68	.235		8.60	11.95		20.55	27.50
4320	24" OC	G	94	.170		6.35	8.65		15	20
4330	3-5/8" wide, studs 12" OC	G	46	.348		12.95	17.65		30.60	41
4340	16" OC	G	66	.242		10.25	12.30		22.55	30
4350	24" OC	G	92	.174		7.55	8.80		16.35	22
4360	4" wide, studs 12" OC	G	45	.356		13.55	18.05		31.60	42.50
4370	16" OC	G	65	.246		10.75	12.50		23.25	31
4380	24" OC	G	90	.178		7.95	9		16.95	22.50

For customer support on your Green Building Costs with RSMeans data, call 800.448.8182.

05 41 Structural Metal Stud Framing

05 41 13 – Load-Bearing Metal Stud Framing

05 41 13.30 Framing, Stud Walls		Crew	Daily Output	Labor-Hours	Unit	Material	2018 Bare Costs Labor	Equipment	Total	Total Incl O&P
4390	6" wide, studs 12" OC	G	2 Carp	44	.364	L.F.	17.05	18.45		35.50	47
4400	16" OC	G		64	.250		13.55	12.70		26.25	34
4410	24" OC	G		88	.182		10.05	9.20		19.25	25
4420	8" wide, studs 12" OC	G		43	.372		21	18.85		39.85	51.50
4430	16" OC	G		63	.254		16.60	12.90		29.50	38
4440	24" OC	G		86	.186		12.30	9.45		21.75	28
5100	10' high walls, 18 ga. x 2-1/2" wide, studs 12" OC	G		54	.296		11	15		26	35
5110	16" OC	G		77	.208		8.70	10.55		19.25	25.50
5120	24" OC	G		107	.150		6.40	7.60		14	18.60
5130	3-5/8" wide, studs 12" OC	G		53	.302		13	15.30		28.30	38
5140	16" OC	G		76	.211		10.30	10.65		20.95	27.50
5150	24" OC	G		105	.152		7.60	7.75		15.35	20
5160	4" wide, studs 12" OC	G		52	.308		13.55	15.60		29.15	39
5170	16" OC	G		74	.216		10.75	10.95		21.70	28.50
5180	24" OC	G		103	.155		7.95	7.90		15.85	20.50
5190	6" wide, studs 12" OC	G		51	.314		17.25	15.90		33.15	43
5200	16" OC	G		73	.219		13.70	11.10		24.80	32
5210	24" OC	G		101	.158		10.15	8.05		18.20	23.50
5220	8" wide, studs 12" OC	G		50	.320		21	16.20		37.20	47.50
5230	16" OC	G		72	.222		16.55	11.25		27.80	35.50
5240	24" OC	G		100	.160		12.30	8.10		20.40	26
5300	16 ga. x 2-1/2" wide, studs 12" OC	G		47	.340		13.10	17.25		30.35	41
5310	16" OC	G		68	.235		10.30	11.95		22.25	29.50
5320	24" OC	G		94	.170		7.45	8.65		16.10	21.50
5330	3-5/8" wide, studs 12" OC	G		46	.348		15.60	17.65		33.25	44
5340	16" OC	G		66	.242		12.25	12.30		24.55	32
5350	24" OC	G		92	.174		8.90	8.80		17.70	23.50
5360	4" wide, studs 12" OC	G		45	.356		16.35	18.05		34.40	45.50
5370	16" OC	G		65	.246		12.85	12.50		25.35	33
5380	24" OC	G		90	.178		9.35	9		18.35	24
5390	6" wide, studs 12" OC	G		44	.364		20.50	18.45		38.95	50.50
5400	16" OC	G		64	.250		16.15	12.70		28.85	37
5410	24" OC	G		88	.182		11.80	9.20		21	27
5420	8" wide, studs 12" OC	G		43	.372		25	18.85		43.85	56
5430	16" OC	G		63	.254		19.80	12.90		32.70	41.50
5440	24" OC	G		86	.186		14.45	9.45		23.90	30.50
6190	12' high walls, 18 ga. x 6" wide, studs 12" OC	G		41	.390		20	19.80		39.80	52
6200	16" OC	G		58	.276		15.80	14		29.80	39
6210	24" OC	G		81	.198		11.55	10		21.55	28
6220	8" wide, studs 12" OC	G		40	.400		24.50	20.50		45	57.50
6230	16" OC	G		57	.281		19.15	14.25		33.40	42.50
6240	24" OC	G		80	.200		14	10.15		24.15	31
6390	16 ga. x 6" wide, studs 12" OC	G		35	.457		24	23		47	62
6400	16" OC	G		51	.314		18.80	15.90		34.70	44.50
6410	24" OC	G		70	.229		13.55	11.60		25.15	32.50
6420	8" wide, studs 12" OC	G		34	.471		29.50	24		53.50	69
6430	16" OC	G		50	.320		23	16.20		39.20	50
6440	24" OC	G		69	.232		16.60	11.75		28.35	36
6530	14 ga. x 3-5/8" wide, studs 12" OC	G		34	.471		22.50	24		46.50	61.50
6540	16" OC	G		48	.333		17.75	16.90		34.65	45
6550	24" OC	G		65	.246		12.75	12.50		25.25	33
6560	4" wide, studs 12" OC	G		33	.485		24	24.50		48.50	64
6570	16" OC	G		47	.340		18.75	17.25		36	47

For customer support on your Green Building Costs with RSMeans data, call 800.448.8182.

05 41 Structural Metal Stud Framing

05 41 13 – Load-Bearing Metal Stud Framing

05 41 13.30 Framing, Stud Walls

		Crew	Daily Output	Labor-Hours	Unit	Material	2018 Bare Costs Labor	Equipment	Total	Total Incl O&P
6580	24" OC	2 Carp	64	.250	L.F.	13.50	12.70		26.20	34
6730	12 ga. x 3-5/8" wide, studs 12" OC		31	.516		31.50	26		57.50	74.50
6740	16" OC		43	.372		24.50	18.85		43.35	55
6750	24" OC		59	.271		17.15	13.75		30.90	40
6760	4" wide, studs 12" OC		30	.533		33.50	27		60.50	78
6770	16" OC		42	.381		26	19.30		45.30	58
6780	24" OC		58	.276		18.30	14		32.30	41.50
7390	16' high walls, 16 ga. x 6" wide, studs 12" OC		33	.485		31	24.50		55.50	71.50
7400	16" OC		48	.333		24	16.90		40.90	52
7410	24" OC		67	.239		17.05	12.10		29.15	37
7420	8" wide, studs 12" OC		32	.500		38	25.50		63.50	80.50
7430	16" OC		47	.340		29.50	17.25		46.75	59
7440	24" OC		66	.242		21	12.30		33.30	41.50
7560	14 ga. x 4" wide, studs 12" OC		31	.516		31	26		57	74
7570	16" OC		45	.356		24	18.05		42.05	54
7580	24" OC		61	.262		17	13.30		30.30	39
7590	6" wide, studs 12" OC		30	.533		39	27		66	84
7600	16" OC		44	.364		30	18.45		48.45	61
7610	24" OC		60	.267		21.50	13.50		35	44
7760	12 ga. x 4" wide, studs 12" OC		29	.552		44	28		72	90.50
7770	16" OC		40	.400		33.50	20.50		54	68
7780	24" OC		55	.291		23.50	14.75		38.25	48
7790	6" wide, studs 12" OC		28	.571		55.50	29		84.50	105
7800	16" OC		39	.410		42.50	21		63.50	78
7810	24" OC		54	.296		29.50	15		44.50	55.50
8590	20' high walls, 14 ga. x 6" wide, studs 12" OC		29	.552		48	28		76	95
8600	16" OC		42	.381		37	19.30		56.30	70
8610	24" OC		57	.281		26	14.25		40.25	50
8620	8" wide, studs 12" OC		28	.571		52	29		81	101
8630	16" OC		41	.390		40	19.80		59.80	74
8640	24" OC		56	.286		28.50	14.50		43	53
8790	12 ga. x 6" wide, studs 12" OC		27	.593		68	30		98	121
8800	16" OC		37	.432		52	22		74	91
8810	24" OC		51	.314		36	15.90		51.90	63.50
8820	8" wide, studs 12" OC		26	.615		82.50	31		113.50	139
8830	16" OC		36	.444		63	22.50		85.50	104
8840	24" OC		50	.320		43.50	16.20		59.70	72.50

05 42 Cold-Formed Metal Joist Framing

05 42 13 – Cold-Formed Metal Floor Joist Framing

05 42 13.05 Bracing

		Crew	Daily Output	Labor-Hours	Unit	Material	Labor	Equipment	Total	Total Incl O&P
0010	**BRACING**, continuous, per row, top & bottom									
0015	Made from recycled materials									
0120	Flat strap, 20 ga. x 2" wide, joists at 12" OC	1 Carp	4.67	1.713	C.L.F.	60	87		147	198
0130	16" OC		5.33	1.501		57.50	76		133.50	180
0140	24" OC		6.66	1.201		55.50	61		116.50	154
0150	18 ga. x 2" wide, joists at 12" OC		4	2		78.50	101		179.50	241
0160	16" OC		4.67	1.713		77	87		164	217
0170	24" OC		5.33	1.501		75.50	76		151.50	199

83

05 42 Cold-Formed Metal Joist Framing

05 42 13 – Cold-Formed Metal Floor Joist Framing

05 42 13.10 Bridging

			Crew	Daily Output	Labor-Hours	Unit	Material	2018 Bare Costs Labor	Equipment	Total	Total Incl O&P
0010	**BRIDGING**, solid between joists w/1-1/4" leg track, per joist bay										
0015	Made from recycled materials										
0230	Joists 12" OC, 18 ga. track x 6" wide	G	1 Carp	80	.100	Ea.	1.60	5.05		6.65	9.45
0240	8" wide	G		75	.107		1.97	5.40		7.37	10.40
0250	10" wide	G		70	.114		2.46	5.80		8.26	11.50
0260	12" wide	G		65	.123		2.78	6.25		9.03	12.55
0330	16 ga. track x 6" wide	G		70	.114		2.01	5.80		7.81	11
0340	8" wide	G		65	.123		2.51	6.25		8.76	12.25
0350	10" wide	G		60	.133		3.10	6.75		9.85	13.70
0360	12" wide	G		55	.145		3.58	7.35		10.93	15.20
0440	14 ga. track x 8" wide	G		60	.133		3.13	6.75		9.88	13.75
0450	10" wide	G		55	.145		3.89	7.35		11.24	15.55
0460	12" wide	G		50	.160		4.49	8.10		12.59	17.30
0550	12 ga. track x 10" wide	G		45	.178		5.70	9		14.70	19.95
0560	12" wide	G		40	.200		5.80	10.15		15.95	22
1230	16" OC, 18 ga. track x 6" wide	G		80	.100		2.05	5.05		7.10	9.95
1240	8" wide	G		75	.107		2.52	5.40		7.92	11.05
1250	10" wide	G		70	.114		3.15	5.80		8.95	12.25
1260	12" wide	G		65	.123		3.56	6.25		9.81	13.40
1330	16 ga. track x 6" wide	G		70	.114		2.57	5.80		8.37	11.65
1340	8" wide	G		65	.123		3.22	6.25		9.47	13.05
1350	10" wide	G		60	.133		3.98	6.75		10.73	14.65
1360	12" wide	G		55	.145		4.59	7.35		11.94	16.30
1440	14 ga. track x 8" wide	G		60	.133		4.01	6.75		10.76	14.70
1450	10" wide	G		55	.145		4.98	7.35		12.33	16.75
1460	12" wide	G		50	.160		5.75	8.10		13.85	18.70
1550	12 ga. track x 10" wide	G		45	.178		7.30	9		16.30	21.50
1560	12" wide	G		40	.200		7.45	10.15		17.60	23.50
2230	24" OC, 18 ga. track x 6" wide	G		80	.100		2.96	5.05		8.01	10.95
2240	8" wide	G		75	.107		3.65	5.40		9.05	12.25
2250	10" wide	G		70	.114		4.56	5.80		10.36	13.80
2260	12" wide	G		65	.123		5.15	6.25		11.40	15.15
2330	16 ga. track x 6" wide	G		70	.114		3.72	5.80		9.52	12.90
2340	8" wide	G		65	.123		4.65	6.25		10.90	14.60
2350	10" wide	G		60	.133		5.75	6.75		12.50	16.65
2360	12" wide	G		55	.145		6.65	7.35		14	18.55
2440	14 ga. track x 8" wide	G		60	.133		5.80	6.75		12.55	16.70
2450	10" wide	G		55	.145		7.20	7.35		14.55	19.20
2460	12" wide	G		50	.160		8.35	8.10		16.45	21.50
2550	12 ga. track x 10" wide	G		45	.178		10.55	9		19.55	25.50
2560	12" wide	G		40	.200		10.80	10.15		20.95	27.50

05 42 13.25 Framing, Band Joist

			Crew	Daily Output	Labor-Hours	Unit	Material	Labor	Equipment	Total	Total Incl O&P
0010	**FRAMING, BAND JOIST** (track) fastened to bearing wall										
0015	Made from recycled materials										
0220	18 ga. track x 6" deep	G	2 Carp	1000	.016	L.F.	1.30	.81		2.11	2.67
0230	8" deep	G		920	.017		1.61	.88		2.49	3.11
0240	10" deep	G		860	.019		2.01	.94		2.95	3.65
0320	16 ga. track x 6" deep	G		900	.018		1.64	.90		2.54	3.17
0330	8" deep	G		840	.019		2.05	.97		3.02	3.72
0340	10" deep	G		780	.021		2.53	1.04		3.57	4.36
0350	12" deep	G		740	.022		2.92	1.10		4.02	4.88
0430	14 ga. track x 8" deep	G		750	.021		2.55	1.08		3.63	4.46

05 42 Cold-Formed Metal Joist Framing

05 42 13 – Cold-Formed Metal Floor Joist Framing

05 42 13.25 Framing, Band Joist

		Crew	Daily Output	Labor-Hours	Unit	Material	2018 Bare Costs Labor	Equipment	Total	Total Incl O&P
0440	10" deep	G 2 Carp	720	.022	L.F.	3.17	1.13		4.30	5.20
0450	12" deep	G	700	.023		3.66	1.16		4.82	5.80
0540	12 ga. track x 10" deep	G	670	.024		4.64	1.21		5.85	6.95
0550	12" deep	G	650	.025		4.75	1.25		6	7.10

05 42 13.30 Framing, Boxed Headers/Beams

		Crew	Daily Output	Labor-Hours	Unit	Material	Labor	Equipment	Total	Total Incl O&P
0010	**FRAMING, BOXED HEADERS/BEAMS**									
0015	Made from recycled materials									
0200	Double, 18 ga. x 6" deep	G 2 Carp	220	.073	L.F.	5.50	3.69		9.19	11.65
0210	8" deep	G	210	.076		6.05	3.86		9.91	12.55
0220	10" deep	G	200	.080		7.40	4.06		11.46	14.35
0230	12" deep	G	190	.084		8.05	4.27		12.32	15.35
0300	16 ga. x 8" deep	G	180	.089		7	4.51		11.51	14.55
0310	10" deep	G	170	.094		8.45	4.77		13.22	16.50
0320	12" deep	G	160	.100		9.15	5.05		14.20	17.80
0400	14 ga. x 10" deep	G	140	.114		9.75	5.80		15.55	19.50
0410	12" deep	G	130	.123		10.65	6.25		16.90	21.50
0500	12 ga. x 10" deep	G	110	.145		12.85	7.35		20.20	25.50
0510	12" deep	G	100	.160		14.15	8.10		22.25	28
1210	Triple, 18 ga. x 8" deep	G	170	.094		8.75	4.77		13.52	16.90
1220	10" deep	G	165	.097		10.60	4.92		15.52	19.15
1230	12" deep	G	160	.100		11.60	5.05		16.65	20.50
1300	16 ga. x 8" deep	G	145	.110		10.15	5.60		15.75	19.65
1310	10" deep	G	140	.114		12.15	5.80		17.95	22
1320	12" deep	G	135	.119		13.25	6		19.25	24
1400	14 ga. x 10" deep	G	115	.139		14.10	7.05		21.15	26.50
1410	12" deep	G	110	.145		15.50	7.35		22.85	28.50
1500	12 ga. x 10" deep	G	90	.178		18.75	9		27.75	34
1510	12" deep	G	85	.188		21	9.55		30.55	37.50

05 42 13.40 Framing, Joists

		Crew	Daily Output	Labor-Hours	Unit	Material	Labor	Equipment	Total	Total Incl O&P
0010	**FRAMING, JOISTS**, no band joists (track), web stiffeners, headers,									
0020	Beams, bridging or bracing									
0025	Made from recycled materials									
0030	Joists (2" flange) and fasteners, materials only									
0220	18 ga. x 6" deep	G			L.F.	1.69			1.69	1.86
0230	8" deep	G				1.98			1.98	2.18
0240	10" deep	G				2.34			2.34	2.58
0320	16 ga. x 6" deep	G				2.07			2.07	2.28
0330	8" deep	G				2.47			2.47	2.71
0340	10" deep	G				2.89			2.89	3.18
0350	12" deep	G				3.28			3.28	3.60
0430	14 ga. x 8" deep	G				3.10			3.10	3.41
0440	10" deep	G				3.57			3.57	3.93
0450	12" deep	G				4.06			4.06	4.47
0540	12 ga. x 10" deep	G				5.20			5.20	5.70
0550	12" deep	G				5.90			5.90	6.50
1010	Installation of joists to band joists, beams & headers, labor only									
1220	18 ga. x 6" deep	2 Carp	110	.145	Ea.		7.35		7.35	11.25
1230	8" deep		90	.178			9		9	13.70
1240	10" deep		80	.200			10.15		10.15	15.45
1320	16 ga. x 6" deep		95	.168			8.55		8.55	13
1330	8" deep		70	.229			11.60		11.60	17.65
1340	10" deep		60	.267			13.50		13.50	20.50

For customer support on your Green Building Costs with RSMeans data, call 800.448.8182.

05 42 Cold-Formed Metal Joist Framing

05 42 13 – Cold-Formed Metal Floor Joist Framing

05 42 13.40 Framing, Joists

		Crew	Daily Output	Labor-Hours	Unit	Material	Labor	Equipment	Total	Total Incl O&P
1350	12" deep	2 Carp	55	.291	Ea.		14.75		14.75	22.50
1430	14 ga. x 8" deep		65	.246			12.50		12.50	19
1440	10" deep		45	.356			18.05		18.05	27.50
1450	12" deep		35	.457			23		23	35.50
1540	12 ga. x 10" deep		40	.400			20.50		20.50	31
1550	12" deep		30	.533			27		27	41

05 42 13.45 Framing, Web Stiffeners

			Crew	Daily Output	Labor-Hours	Unit	Material	Labor	Equipment	Total	Total Incl O&P
0010	**FRAMING, WEB STIFFENERS** at joist bearing, fabricated from										
0020	Stud piece (1-5/8" flange) to stiffen joist (2" flange)										
0025	Made from recycled materials										
2120	For 6" deep joist, with 18 ga. x 2-1/2" stud	G	1 Carp	120	.067	Ea.	.92	3.38		4.30	6.15
2130	3-5/8" stud	G		110	.073		1.08	3.69		4.77	6.80
2140	4" stud	G		105	.076		1.12	3.86		4.98	7.15
2150	6" stud	G		100	.080		1.42	4.06		5.48	7.75
2160	8" stud	G		95	.084		1.71	4.27		5.98	8.40
2220	8" deep joist, with 2-1/2" stud	G		120	.067		1.23	3.38		4.61	6.50
2230	3-5/8" stud	G		110	.073		1.45	3.69		5.14	7.20
2240	4" stud	G		105	.076		1.50	3.86		5.36	7.55
2250	6" stud	G		100	.080		1.90	4.06		5.96	8.30
2260	8" stud	G		95	.084		2.29	4.27		6.56	9
2320	10" deep joist, with 2-1/2" stud	G		110	.073		1.53	3.69		5.22	7.30
2330	3-5/8" stud	G		100	.080		1.79	4.06		5.85	8.15
2340	4" stud	G		95	.084		1.86	4.27		6.13	8.55
2350	6" stud	G		90	.089		2.36	4.51		6.87	9.45
2360	8" stud	G		85	.094		2.84	4.77		7.61	10.35
2420	12" deep joist, with 2-1/2" stud	G		110	.073		1.84	3.69		5.53	7.60
2430	3-5/8" stud	G		100	.080		2.16	4.06		6.22	8.60
2440	4" stud	G		95	.084		2.24	4.27		6.51	8.95
2450	6" stud	G		90	.089		2.84	4.51		7.35	9.95
2460	8" stud	G		85	.094		3.42	4.77		8.19	11
3130	For 6" deep joist, with 16 ga. x 3-5/8" stud	G		100	.080		1.34	4.06		5.40	7.65
3140	4" stud	G		95	.084		1.40	4.27		5.67	8.05
3150	6" stud	G		90	.089		1.75	4.51		6.26	8.80
3160	8" stud	G		85	.094		2.14	4.77		6.91	9.60
3230	8" deep joist, with 3-5/8" stud	G		100	.080		1.80	4.06		5.86	8.20
3240	4" stud	G		95	.084		1.88	4.27		6.15	8.55
3250	6" stud	G		90	.089		2.35	4.51		6.86	9.45
3260	8" stud	G		85	.094		2.87	4.77		7.64	10.40
3330	10" deep joist, with 3-5/8" stud	G		85	.094		2.22	4.77		6.99	9.70
3340	4" stud	G		80	.100		2.32	5.05		7.37	10.25
3350	6" stud	G		75	.107		2.91	5.40		8.31	11.45
3360	8" stud	G		70	.114		3.55	5.80		9.35	12.70
3430	12" deep joist, with 3-5/8" stud	G		85	.094		2.68	4.77		7.45	10.20
3440	4" stud	G		80	.100		2.80	5.05		7.85	10.80
3450	6" stud	G		75	.107		3.50	5.40		8.90	12.10
3460	8" stud	G		70	.114		4.28	5.80		10.08	13.50
4230	For 8" deep joist, with 14 ga. x 3-5/8" stud	G		90	.089		2.22	4.51		6.73	9.30
4240	4" stud	G		85	.094		2.35	4.77		7.12	9.85
4250	6" stud	G		80	.100		2.95	5.05		8	10.95
4260	8" stud	G		75	.107		3.15	5.40		8.55	11.70
4330	10" deep joist, with 3-5/8" stud	G		75	.107		2.76	5.40		8.16	11.30
4340	4" stud	G		70	.114		2.91	5.80		8.71	12

05 42 Cold-Formed Metal Joist Framing

05 42 13 – Cold-Formed Metal Floor Joist Framing

05 42 13.45 Framing, Web Stiffeners

			Crew	Daily Output	Labor-Hours	Unit	Material	2018 Bare Costs Labor	Equipment	Total	Total Incl O&P
4350	6" stud	G	1 Carp	65	.123	Ea.	3.65	6.25		9.90	13.50
4360	8" stud	G		60	.133		3.90	6.75		10.65	14.60
4430	12" deep joist, with 3-5/8" stud	G		75	.107		3.32	5.40		8.72	11.90
4440	4" stud	G		70	.114		3.50	5.80		9.30	12.65
4450	6" stud	G		65	.123		4.40	6.25		10.65	14.35
4460	8" stud	G		60	.133		4.70	6.75		11.45	15.45
5330	For 10" deep joist, with 12 ga. x 3-5/8" stud	G		65	.123		3.97	6.25		10.22	13.85
5340	4" stud	G		60	.133		4.23	6.75		10.98	14.95
5350	6" stud	G		55	.145		5.35	7.35		12.70	17.15
5360	8" stud	G		50	.160		6.45	8.10		14.55	19.45
5430	12" deep joist, with 3-5/8" stud	G		65	.123		4.78	6.25		11.03	14.75
5440	4" stud	G		60	.133		5.10	6.75		11.85	15.90
5450	6" stud	G		55	.145		6.45	7.35		13.80	18.35
5460	8" stud	G		50	.160		7.80	8.10		15.90	21

05 42 23 – Cold-Formed Metal Roof Joist Framing

05 42 23.05 Framing, Bracing

			Crew	Daily Output	Labor-Hours	Unit	Material	Labor	Equipment	Total	Total Incl O&P
0010	**FRAMING, BRACING**										
0015	Made from recycled materials										
0020	Continuous bracing, per row										
0100	16 ga. x 1-1/2" channel thru rafters/trusses @ 16" OC	G	1 Carp	4.50	1.778	C.L.F.	51.50	90		141.50	194
0120	24" OC	G		6	1.333		51.50	67.50		119	160
0300	2" x 2" angle x 18 ga., rafters/trusses @ 16" OC	G		6	1.333		80.50	67.50		148	192
0320	24" OC	G		8	1		80.50	50.50		131	166
0400	16 ga., rafters/trusses @ 16" OC	G		4.50	1.778		101	90		191	248
0420	24" OC	G		6.50	1.231		101	62.50		163.50	206

05 42 23.10 Framing, Bridging

			Crew	Daily Output	Labor-Hours	Unit	Material	Labor	Equipment	Total	Total Incl O&P
0010	**FRAMING, BRIDGING**										
0015	Made from recycled materials										
0020	Solid, between rafters w/1-1/4" leg track, per rafter bay										
1200	Rafters 16" OC, 18 ga. x 4" deep	G	1 Carp	60	.133	Ea.	1.57	6.75		8.32	12
1210	6" deep	G		57	.140		2.05	7.10		9.15	13.10
1220	8" deep	G		55	.145		2.52	7.35		9.87	14.05
1230	10" deep	G		52	.154		3.15	7.80		10.95	15.35
1240	12" deep	G		50	.160		3.56	8.10		11.66	16.25
2200	24" OC, 18 ga. x 4" deep	G		60	.133		2.27	6.75		9.02	12.80
2210	6" deep	G		57	.140		2.96	7.10		10.06	14.10
2220	8" deep	G		55	.145		3.65	7.35		11	15.25
2230	10" deep	G		52	.154		4.56	7.80		12.36	16.90
2240	12" deep	G		50	.160		5.15	8.10		13.25	18

05 42 23.50 Framing, Parapets

			Crew	Daily Output	Labor-Hours	Unit	Material	Labor	Equipment	Total	Total Incl O&P
0010	**FRAMING, PARAPETS**										
0015	Made from recycled materials										
0100	3' high installed on 1st story, 18 ga. x 4" wide studs, 12" OC	G	2 Carp	100	.160	L.F.	5.70	8.10		13.80	18.60
0110	16" OC	G		150	.107		4.85	5.40		10.25	13.60
0120	24" OC	G		200	.080		4.01	4.06		8.07	10.60
0200	6" wide studs, 12" OC	G		100	.160		7.30	8.10		15.40	20.50
0210	16" OC	G		150	.107		6.25	5.40		11.65	15.10
0220	24" OC	G		200	.080		5.15	4.06		9.21	11.90
1100	Installed on 2nd story, 18 ga. x 4" wide studs, 12" OC	G		95	.168		5.70	8.55		14.25	19.25
1110	16" OC	G		145	.110		4.85	5.60		10.45	13.85
1120	24" OC	G		190	.084		4.01	4.27		8.28	10.90
1200	6" wide studs, 12" OC	G		95	.168		7.30	8.55		15.85	21

For customer support on your Green Building Costs with RSMeans data, call 800.448.8182.

05 42 Cold-Formed Metal Joist Framing

05 42 23 – Cold-Formed Metal Roof Joist Framing

05 42 23.50 Framing, Parapets

			Crew	Daily Output	Labor-Hours	Unit	Material	2018 Bare Costs Labor	Equipment	Total	Total Incl O&P
1210	16" OC	G	2 Carp	145	.110	L.F.	6.25	5.60		11.85	15.35
1220	24" OC	G		190	.084		5.15	4.27		9.42	12.20
2100	Installed on gable, 18 ga. x 4" wide studs, 12" OC	G		85	.188		5.70	9.55		15.25	21
2110	16" OC	G		130	.123		4.85	6.25		11.10	14.85
2120	24" OC	G		170	.094		4.01	4.77		8.78	11.65
2200	6" wide studs, 12" OC	G		85	.188		7.30	9.55		16.85	22.50
2210	16" OC	G		130	.123		6.25	6.25		12.50	16.35
2220	24" OC	G		170	.094		5.15	4.77		9.92	12.95

05 42 23.60 Framing, Roof Rafters

			Crew	Daily Output	Labor-Hours	Unit	Material	Labor	Equipment	Total	Total Incl O&P
0010	**FRAMING, ROOF RAFTERS**										
0015	Made from recycled materials										
0100	Boxed ridge beam, double, 18 ga. x 6" deep	G	2 Carp	160	.100	L.F.	5.50	5.05		10.55	13.75
0110	8" deep	G		150	.107		6.05	5.40		11.45	14.90
0120	10" deep	G		140	.114		7.40	5.80		13.20	16.95
0130	12" deep	G		130	.123		8.05	6.25		14.30	18.35
0200	16 ga. x 6" deep	G		150	.107		6.20	5.40		11.60	15.10
0210	8" deep	G		140	.114		7	5.80		12.80	16.50
0220	10" deep	G		130	.123		8.45	6.25		14.70	18.75
0230	12" deep	G		120	.133		9.15	6.75		15.90	20.50
1100	Rafters, 2" flange, material only, 18 ga. x 6" deep	G					1.69			1.69	1.86
1110	8" deep	G					1.98			1.98	2.18
1120	10" deep	G					2.34			2.34	2.58
1130	12" deep	G					2.70			2.70	2.97
1200	16 ga. x 6" deep	G					2.07			2.07	2.28
1210	8" deep	G					2.47			2.47	2.71
1220	10" deep	G					2.89			2.89	3.18
1230	12" deep	G					3.28			3.28	3.60
2100	Installation only, ordinary rafter to 4:12 pitch, 18 ga. x 6" deep		2 Carp	35	.457	Ea.		23		23	35.50
2110	8" deep			30	.533			27		27	41
2120	10" deep			25	.640			32.50		32.50	49.50
2130	12" deep			20	.800			40.50		40.50	62
2200	16 ga. x 6" deep			30	.533			27		27	41
2210	8" deep			25	.640			32.50		32.50	49.50
2220	10" deep			20	.800			40.50		40.50	62
2230	12" deep			15	1.067			54		54	82.50
8100	Add to labor, ordinary rafters on steep roofs							25%			
8110	Dormers & complex roofs							50%			
8200	Hip & valley rafters to 4:12 pitch							25%			
8210	Steep roofs							50%			
8220	Dormers & complex roofs							75%			
8300	Hip & valley jack rafters to 4:12 pitch							50%			
8310	Steep roofs							75%			
8320	Dormers & complex roofs							100%			

05 42 23.70 Framing, Soffits and Canopies

			Crew	Daily Output	Labor-Hours	Unit	Material	Labor	Equipment	Total	Total Incl O&P
0010	**FRAMING, SOFFITS & CANOPIES**										
0015	Made from recycled materials										
0130	Continuous ledger track @ wall, studs @ 16" OC, 18 ga. x 4" wide	G	2 Carp	535	.030	L.F.	1.05	1.52		2.57	3.46
0140	6" wide	G		500	.032		1.36	1.62		2.98	3.97
0150	8" wide	G		465	.034		1.68	1.74		3.42	4.51
0160	10" wide	G		430	.037		2.10	1.89		3.99	5.20
0230	Studs @ 24" OC, 18 ga. x 4" wide	G		800	.020		1	1.01		2.01	2.64
0240	6" wide	G		750	.021		1.30	1.08		2.38	3.08

05 42 Cold-Formed Metal Joist Framing

05 42 23 – Cold-Formed Metal Roof Joist Framing

05 42 23.70 Framing, Soffits and Canopies

		Crew	Daily Output	Labor-Hours	Unit	Material	2018 Bare Costs Labor	Equipment	Total	Total Incl O&P
0250	8" wide	G 2 Carp	700	.023	L.F.	1.61	1.16		2.77	3.53
0260	10" wide	G	650	.025		2.01	1.25		3.26	4.11
1000	Horizontal soffit and canopy members, material only									
1030	1-5/8" flange studs, 18 ga. x 4" deep	G			L.F.	1.34			1.34	1.48
1040	6" deep	G				1.70			1.70	1.87
1050	8" deep	G				2.05			2.05	2.26
1140	2" flange joists, 18 ga. x 6" deep	G				1.93			1.93	2.13
1150	8" deep	G				2.27			2.27	2.49
1160	10" deep	G				2.68			2.68	2.94
4030	Installation only, 18 ga., 1-5/8" flange x 4" deep	2 Carp	130	.123	Ea.		6.25		6.25	9.50
4040	6" deep		110	.145			7.35		7.35	11.25
4050	8" deep		90	.178			9		9	13.70
4140	2" flange, 18 ga. x 6" deep		110	.145			7.35		7.35	11.25
4150	8" deep		90	.178			9		9	13.70
4160	10" deep		80	.200			10.15		10.15	15.45
6010	Clips to attach fascia to rafter tails, 2" x 2" x 18 ga. angle	G 1 Carp	120	.067		.95	3.38		4.33	6.20
6020	16 ga. angle	G "	100	.080		1.20	4.06		5.26	7.50

05 44 Cold-Formed Metal Trusses

05 44 13 – Cold-Formed Metal Roof Trusses

05 44 13.60 Framing, Roof Trusses

		Crew	Daily Output	Labor-Hours	Unit	Material	2018 Bare Costs Labor	Equipment	Total	Total Incl O&P
0010	**FRAMING, ROOF TRUSSES**									
0015	Made from recycled materials									
0020	Fabrication of trusses on ground, Fink (W) or King Post, to 4:12 pitch									
0120	18 ga. x 4" chords, 16' span	G 2 Carp	12	1.333	Ea.	62.50	67.50		130	172
0130	20' span	G	11	1.455		78.50	74		152.50	198
0140	24' span	G	11	1.455		94	74		168	215
0150	28' span	G	10	1.600		110	81		191	245
0160	32' span	G	10	1.600		125	81		206	262
0250	6" chords, 28' span	G	9	1.778		139	90		229	290
0260	32' span	G	9	1.778		159	90		249	310
0270	36' span	G	8	2		179	101		280	350
0280	40' span	G	8	2		199	101		300	375
1120	5:12 to 8:12 pitch, 18 ga. x 4" chords, 16' span	G	10	1.600		71.50	81		152.50	203
1130	20' span	G	9	1.778		89.50	90		179.50	236
1140	24' span	G	9	1.778		108	90		198	255
1150	28' span	G	8	2		125	101		226	292
1160	32' span	G	8	2		143	101		244	310
1250	6" chords, 28' span	G	7	2.286		159	116		275	350
1260	32' span	G	7	2.286		182	116		298	375
1270	36' span	G	6	2.667		204	135		339	430
1280	40' span	G	6	2.667		227	135		362	455
2120	9:12 to 12:12 pitch, 18 ga. x 4" chords, 16' span	G	8	2		89.50	101		190.50	253
2130	20' span	G	7	2.286		112	116		228	299
2140	24' span	G	7	2.286		134	116		250	325
2150	28' span	G	6	2.667		157	135		292	380
2160	32' span	G	6	2.667		179	135		314	405
2250	6" chords, 28' span	G	5	3.200		199	162		361	465
2260	32' span	G	5	3.200		227	162		389	495
2270	36' span	G	4	4		256	203		459	590
2280	40' span	G	4	4		284	203		487	620

For customer support on your Green Building Costs with RSMeans data, call 800.448.8182.

05 44 Cold-Formed Metal Trusses

05 44 13 – Cold-Formed Metal Roof Trusses

05 44 13.60 Framing, Roof Trusses

		Crew	Daily Output	Labor-Hours	Unit	Material	2018 Bare Costs Labor	Equipment	Total	Total Incl O&P
5120	Erection only of roof trusses, to 4:12 pitch, 16' span	F-6	48	.833	Ea.		39.50	10.35	49.85	71.50
5130	20' span		46	.870			41.50	10.80	52.30	74.50
5140	24' span		44	.909			43	11.25	54.25	78
5150	28' span		42	.952			45	11.80	56.80	81.50
5160	32' span		40	1			47.50	12.40	59.90	85.50
5170	36' span		38	1.053			50	13.05	63.05	90.50
5180	40' span		36	1.111			52.50	13.80	66.30	95
5220	5:12 to 8:12 pitch, 16' span		42	.952			45	11.80	56.80	81.50
5230	20' span		40	1			47.50	12.40	59.90	85.50
5240	24' span		38	1.053			50	13.05	63.05	90.50
5250	28' span		36	1.111			52.50	13.80	66.30	95
5260	32' span		34	1.176			56	14.60	70.60	101
5270	36' span		32	1.250			59.50	15.50	75	107
5280	40' span		30	1.333			63.50	16.55	80.05	114
5320	9:12 to 12:12 pitch, 16' span		36	1.111			52.50	13.80	66.30	95
5330	20' span		34	1.176			56	14.60	70.60	101
5340	24' span		32	1.250			59.50	15.50	75	107
5350	28' span		30	1.333			63.50	16.55	80.05	114
5360	32' span		28	1.429			68	17.70	85.70	123
5370	36' span		26	1.538			73	19.10	92.10	132
5380	40' span		24	1.667			79	20.50	99.50	143

05 51 Metal Stairs

05 51 13 – Metal Pan Stairs

05 51 13.50 Pan Stairs

			Crew	Daily Output	Labor-Hours	Unit	Material	Labor	Equipment	Total	Total Incl O&P
0010	**PAN STAIRS**, shop fabricated, steel stringers										
0015	Made from recycled materials										
0200	Metal pan tread for concrete in-fill, picket rail, 3'-6" wide	G	E-4	35	.914	Riser	560	50.50	2.82	613.32	700
0300	4'-0" wide	G		30	1.067		625	59	3.29	687.29	785
0350	Wall rail, both sides, 3'-6" wide	G		53	.604		425	33.50	1.86	460.36	525
1500	Landing, steel pan, conventional	G		160	.200	S.F.	74.50	11.05	.62	86.17	101
1600	Pre-erected	G		255	.125	"	132	6.90	.39	139.29	157
1700	Pre-erected, steel pan tread, 3'-6" wide, 2 line pipe rail	G	E-2	87	.644	Riser	555	35	19.40	609.40	690
1800	With flat bar picket rail	G	"	87	.644	"	615	35	19.40	669.40	760

05 51 16 – Metal Floor Plate Stairs

05 51 16.50 Floor Plate Stairs

			Crew	Daily Output	Labor-Hours	Unit	Material	Labor	Equipment	Total	Total Incl O&P
0010	**FLOOR PLATE STAIRS**, shop fabricated, steel stringers										
0015	Made from recycled materials										
0400	Cast iron tread and pipe rail, 3'-6" wide	G	E-4	35	.914	Riser	600	50.50	2.82	653.32	745
0450	4'-0" wide	G		30	1.067		630	59	3.29	692.29	790
0475	5'-0" wide	G		28	1.143		695	63	3.52	761.52	865
0500	Checkered plate tread, industrial, 3'-6" wide	G		28	1.143		365	63	3.52	431.52	505
0550	Circular, for tanks, 3'-0" wide	G		33	.970		415	53.50	2.99	471.49	550
0600	For isolated stairs, add							100%			
0800	Custom steel stairs, 3'-6" wide, economy	G	E-4	35	.914		560	50.50	2.82	613.32	700
0810	Medium priced	G		30	1.067		740	59	3.29	802.29	915
0900	Deluxe	G		20	1.600		920	88	4.93	1,012.93	1,175
1100	For 4' wide stairs, add						5%	5%			
1300	For 5' wide stairs, add						10%	10%			

05 51 Metal Stairs

05 51 19 – Metal Grating Stairs

05 51 19.50 Grating Stairs

		Crew	Daily Output	Labor-Hours	Unit	Material	2018 Bare Costs Labor	Equipment	Total	Total Incl O&P
0010	**GRATING STAIRS**, shop fabricated, steel stringers, safety nosing on treads									
0015	Made from recycled materials									
0020	Grating tread and pipe railing, 3'-6" wide	G E-4	35	.914	Riser	365	50.50	2.82	418.32	485
0100	4'-0" wide	G "	30	1.067	"	420	59	3.29	482.29	565

05 51 23 – Metal Fire Escapes

05 51 23.25 Fire Escapes

		Crew	Daily Output	Labor-Hours	Unit	Material	Labor	Equipment	Total	Incl O&P
0010	**FIRE ESCAPES**, shop fabricated									
0200	2' wide balcony, 1" x 1/4" bars 1-1/2" OC, with railing	G 2 Sswk	10	1.600	L.F.	60	87.50		147.50	209
0400	1st story cantilevered stair, standard, with railing	G	.50	32	Ea.	2,500	1,750		4,250	5,600
0500	Cable counterweighted, with railing	G	.40	40	"	2,325	2,175		4,500	6,125
0700	36" x 40" platform & fixed stair, with railing	G	.40	40	Flight	1,100	2,175		3,275	4,800
0900	For 3'-6" wide escapes, add to above					100%	150%			

05 51 23.50 Fire Escape Stairs

		Crew	Daily Output	Labor-Hours	Unit	Material	Labor	Equipment	Total	Incl O&P
0010	**FIRE ESCAPE STAIRS**, portable									
0100	Portable ladder				Ea.	128			128	141

05 51 33 – Metal Ladders

05 51 33.13 Vertical Metal Ladders

		Crew	Daily Output	Labor-Hours	Unit	Material	Labor	Equipment	Total	Incl O&P
0010	**VERTICAL METAL LADDERS**, shop fabricated									
0015	Made from recycled materials									
0020	Steel, 20" wide, bolted to concrete, with cage	G E-4	50	.640	V.L.F.	67	35.50	1.97	104.47	133
0100	Without cage	G	85	.376		36.50	21	1.16	58.66	75.50
0300	Aluminum, bolted to concrete, with cage	G	50	.640		133	35.50	1.97	170.47	206
0400	Without cage	G	85	.376		52	21	1.16	74.16	92.50

05 51 33.16 Inclined Metal Ladders

		Crew	Daily Output	Labor-Hours	Unit	Material	Labor	Equipment	Total	Incl O&P
0010	**INCLINED METAL LADDERS**, shop fabricated									
0015	Made from recycled materials									
3900	Industrial ships ladder, steel, 24" W, grating treads, 2 line pipe rail	G E-4	30	1.067	Riser	214	59	3.29	276.29	335
4000	Aluminum	G "	30	1.067	"	299	59	3.29	361.29	430

05 51 33.23 Alternating Tread Ladders

		Crew	Daily Output	Labor-Hours	Unit	Material	Labor	Equipment	Total	Incl O&P
0010	**ALTERNATING TREAD LADDERS**, shop fabricated									
0015	Made from recycled materials									
0800	Alternating tread ladders, 68-degree angle of incline									
0810	8' vertical rise, steel, 149 lb., standard paint color	B-68G	3	5.333	Ea.	2,400	291	93	2,784	3,225
0820	Non-standard paint color		3	5.333		2,850	291	93	3,234	3,700
0830	Galvanized		3	5.333		2,825	291	93	3,209	3,675
0840	Stainless		3	5.333		4,075	291	93	4,459	5,075
0850	Aluminum, 87 lb.		3	5.333		2,975	291	93	3,359	3,850
1010	10' vertical rise, steel, 181 lb., standard paint color		2.75	5.818		2,925	320	101	3,346	3,825
1020	Non-standard paint color		2.75	5.818		3,400	320	101	3,821	4,350
1030	Galvanized		2.75	5.818		3,400	320	101	3,821	4,375
1040	Stainless		2.75	5.818		4,925	320	101	5,346	6,025
1050	Aluminum, 103 lb.		2.75	5.818		3,600	320	101	4,021	4,575
1210	12' vertical rise, steel, 245 lb., standard paint color		2.50	6.400		3,425	350	112	3,887	4,475
1220	Non-standard paint color		2.50	6.400		3,925	350	112	4,387	5,025
1230	Galvanized		2.50	6.400		4,000	350	112	4,462	5,100
1240	Stainless		2.50	6.400		5,750	350	112	6,212	7,025
1250	Aluminum, 103 lb.		2.50	6.400		4,200	350	112	4,662	5,325
1410	14' vertical rise, steel, 281 lb., standard paint color		2.25	7.111		3,925	390	124	4,439	5,100
1420	Non-standard paint color		2.25	7.111		4,475	390	124	4,989	5,700
1430	Galvanized		2.25	7.111		4,600	390	124	5,114	5,825

05 51 Metal Stairs

05 51 33 – Metal Ladders

05 51 33.23 Alternating Tread Ladders

		Crew	Daily Output	Labor-Hours	Unit	Material	2018 Bare Costs Labor	Equipment	Total	Total Incl O&P
1440	Stainless	B-68G	2.25	7.111	Ea.	6,575	390	124	7,089	8,025
1450	Aluminum, 136 lb.		2.25	7.111		4,825	390	124	5,339	6,075
1610	16' vertical rise, steel, 317 lb., standard paint color		2	8		4,450	435	140	5,025	5,750
1620	Non-standard paint color		2	8		5,025	435	140	5,600	6,400
1630	Galvanized		2	8		5,175	435	140	5,750	6,575
1640	Stainless		2	8		7,425	435	140	8,000	9,025
1650	Aluminum, 153 lb.		2	8		5,425	435	140	6,000	6,850

05 52 Metal Railings

05 52 13 – Pipe and Tube Railings

05 52 13.50 Railings, Pipe

			Crew	Daily Output	Labor-Hours	Unit	Material	Labor	Equipment	Total	Total Incl O&P
0010	**RAILINGS, PIPE**, shop fab'd, 3'-6" high, posts @ 5' OC										
0015	Made from recycled materials										
0020	Aluminum, 2 rail, satin finish, 1-1/4" diameter	G	E-4	160	.200	L.F.	52.50	11.05	.62	64.17	76.50
0030	Clear anodized	G		160	.200		64.50	11.05	.62	76.17	89.50
0040	Dark anodized	G		160	.200		71.50	11.05	.62	83.17	97
0080	1-1/2" diameter, satin finish	G		160	.200		61.50	11.05	.62	73.17	86.50
0090	Clear anodized	G		160	.200		69.50	11.05	.62	81.17	94.50
0100	Dark anodized	G		160	.200		76.50	11.05	.62	88.17	103
0140	Aluminum, 3 rail, 1-1/4" diam., satin finish	G		137	.234		68	12.90	.72	81.62	96.50
0150	Clear anodized	G		137	.234		84.50	12.90	.72	98.12	115
0160	Dark anodized	G		137	.234		93	12.90	.72	106.62	124
0200	1-1/2" diameter, satin finish	G		137	.234		80.50	12.90	.72	94.12	110
0210	Clear anodized	G		137	.234		91.50	12.90	.72	105.12	123
0220	Dark anodized	G		137	.234		101	12.90	.72	114.62	133
0500	Steel, 2 rail, on stairs, primed, 1-1/4" diameter	G		160	.200		29	11.05	.62	40.67	50.50
0520	1-1/2" diameter	G		160	.200		31.50	11.05	.62	43.17	53
0540	Galvanized, 1-1/4" diameter	G		160	.200		39	11.05	.62	50.67	61.50
0560	1-1/2" diameter	G		160	.200		44	11.05	.62	55.67	67
0580	Steel, 3 rail, primed, 1-1/4" diameter	G		137	.234		43	12.90	.72	56.62	69.50
0600	1-1/2" diameter	G		137	.234		45.50	12.90	.72	59.12	72
0620	Galvanized, 1-1/4" diameter	G		137	.234		60.50	12.90	.72	74.12	88.50
0640	1-1/2" diameter	G		137	.234		70	12.90	.72	83.62	99
0700	Stainless steel, 2 rail, 1-1/4" diam., #4 finish	G		137	.234		128	12.90	.72	141.62	162
0720	High polish	G		137	.234		206	12.90	.72	219.62	249
0740	Mirror polish	G		137	.234		258	12.90	.72	271.62	305
0760	Stainless steel, 3 rail, 1-1/2" diam., #4 finish	G		120	.267		192	14.70	.82	207.52	236
0770	High polish	G		120	.267		320	14.70	.82	335.52	375
0780	Mirror finish	G		120	.267		390	14.70	.82	405.52	450
0900	Wall rail, alum. pipe, 1-1/4" diam., satin finish	G		213	.150		25	8.30	.46	33.76	41.50
0905	Clear anodized	G		213	.150		31.50	8.30	.46	40.26	48.50
0910	Dark anodized	G		213	.150		37	8.30	.46	45.76	55
0915	1-1/2" diameter, satin finish	G		213	.150		28	8.30	.46	36.76	45
0920	Clear anodized	G		213	.150		35	8.30	.46	43.76	52.50
0925	Dark anodized	G		213	.150		44	8.30	.46	52.76	62.50
0930	Steel pipe, 1-1/4" diameter, primed	G		213	.150		17.35	8.30	.46	26.11	33
0935	Galvanized	G		213	.150		25	8.30	.46	33.76	41.50
0940	1-1/2" diameter	G		176	.182		17.90	10.05	.56	28.51	36.50
0945	Galvanized	G		213	.150		25	8.30	.46	33.76	41.50
0955	Stainless steel pipe, 1-1/2" diam., #4 finish	G		107	.299		102	16.50	.92	119.42	140
0960	High polish	G		107	.299		207	16.50	.92	224.42	256

For customer support on your Green Building Costs with RSMeans data, call 800.448.8182.

05 52 Metal Railings

05 52 13 – Pipe and Tube Railings

05 52 13.50 Railings, Pipe

		Crew	Daily Output	Labor-Hours	Unit	Material	2018 Bare Costs Labor	Equipment	Total	Total Incl O&P
0965	Mirror polish	G E-4	107	.299	L.F.	245	16.50	.92	262.42	298
2000	2-line pipe rail (1-1/2" T&B) with 1/2" pickets @ 4-1/2" OC,									
2005	attached handrail on brackets									
2010	42" high aluminum, satin finish, straight & level	G E-4	120	.267	L.F.	268	14.70	.82	283.52	320
2050	42" high steel, primed, straight & level	G "	120	.267	"	147	14.70	.82	162.52	186

05 52 16 – Industrial Railings

05 52 16.50 Railings, Industrial

		Crew	Daily Output	Labor-Hours	Unit	Material	Labor	Equipment	Total	Total Incl O&P
0010	**RAILINGS, INDUSTRIAL**, shop fab'd, 3'-6" high, posts @ 5' OC									
0020	2 rail, 3'-6" high, 1-1/2" pipe	G E-4	255	.125	L.F.	41.50	6.90	.39	48.79	57
0100	2" angle rail	G "	255	.125		37.50	6.90	.39	44.79	52.50
0200	For 4" high kick plate, 10 ga., add	G				5.90			5.90	6.45
0300	1/4" thick, add	G				7.70			7.70	8.45
0500	For curved level rails, add					10%	10%			
0550	For sloped rails for stairs, add					30%	30%			

05 53 Metal Gratings

05 53 13 – Bar Gratings

05 53 13.10 Floor Grating, Aluminum

		Crew	Daily Output	Labor-Hours	Unit	Material	Labor	Equipment	Total	Total Incl O&P
0010	**FLOOR GRATING, ALUMINUM**, field fabricated from panels									
0015	Made from recycled materials									
0110	Bearing bars @ 1-3/16" OC, cross bars @ 4" OC,									
0111	Up to 300 S.F., 1" x 1/8" bar	G E-4	900	.036	S.F.	17.40	1.96	.11	19.47	22.50
0112	Over 300 S.F.	G	850	.038		15.80	2.08	.12	18	21
0113	1-1/4" x 1/8" bar, up to 300 S.F.	G	800	.040		17.65	2.21	.12	19.98	23
0114	Over 300 S.F.	G	1000	.032		16.05	1.76	.10	17.91	20.50
0122	1-1/4" x 3/16" bar, up to 300 S.F.	G	750	.043		28	2.35	.13	30.48	34.50
0124	Over 300 S.F.	G	1000	.032		25.50	1.76	.10	27.36	31
0132	1-1/2" x 3/16" bar, up to 300 S.F.	G	700	.046		31.50	2.52	.14	34.16	39.50
0134	Over 300 S.F.	G	1000	.032		29	1.76	.10	30.86	34.50
0136	1-3/4" x 3/16" bar, up to 300 S.F.	G	500	.064		34.50	3.53	.20	38.23	44
0138	Over 300 S.F.	G	1000	.032		31.50	1.76	.10	33.36	37.50
0146	2-1/4" x 3/16" bar, up to 300 S.F.	G	600	.053		44	2.94	.16	47.10	53.50
0148	Over 300 S.F.	G	1000	.032		40	1.76	.10	41.86	47
0162	Cross bars @ 2" OC, 1" x 1/8", up to 300 S.F.	G	600	.053		31	2.94	.16	34.10	39.50
0164	Over 300 S.F.	G	1000	.032		28.50	1.76	.10	30.36	34
0172	1-1/4" x 3/16" bar, up to 300 S.F.	G	600	.053		50	2.94	.16	53.10	60
0174	Over 300 S.F.	G	1000	.032		45.50	1.76	.10	47.36	53
0182	1-1/2" x 3/16" bar, up to 300 S.F.	G	600	.053		60	2.94	.16	63.10	71
0184	Over 300 S.F.	G	1000	.032		54.50	1.76	.10	56.36	63
0186	1-3/4" x 3/16" bar, up to 300 S.F.	G	600	.053		63	2.94	.16	66.10	74.50
0188	Over 300 S.F.	G	1000	.032		57.50	1.76	.10	59.36	66
0200	For straight cuts, add				L.F.	4.40			4.40	4.84
0212	Bearing bars @ 15/16" OC, 1" x 1/8", up to 300 S.F.	G E-4	520	.062	S.F.	31.50	3.39	.19	35.08	41
0214	Over 300 S.F.	G	920	.035		29	1.92	.11	31.03	35
0222	1-1/4" x 3/16", up to 300 S.F.	G	520	.062		50.50	3.39	.19	54.08	61.50
0224	Over 300 S.F.	G	920	.035		46	1.92	.11	48.03	54
0232	1-1/2" x 3/16", up to 300 S.F.	G	520	.062		57	3.39	.19	60.58	69
0234	Over 300 S.F.	G	920	.035		52	1.92	.11	54.03	60.50
0300	For curved cuts, add				L.F.	5.40			5.40	5.95
0400	For straight banding, add	G				5.60			5.60	6.20

For customer support on your Green Building Costs with RSMeans data, call 800.448.8182.

05 53 Metal Gratings

05 53 13 – Bar Gratings

05 53 13.10 Floor Grating, Aluminum

		Crew	Daily Output	Labor-Hours	Unit	Material	2018 Bare Costs Labor	Equipment	Total	Total Incl O&P
0500	For curved banding, add	G			L.F.	6.75			6.75	7.45
0600	For aluminum checkered plate nosings, add	G				7.30			7.30	8.05
0700	For straight toe plate, add	G				11.05			11.05	12.15
0800	For curved toe plate, add	G				12.90			12.90	14.15
1000	For cast aluminum abrasive nosings, add	G				10.75			10.75	11.80
1600	Heavy duty, all extruded plank, 3/4" deep, 1.8 #/S.F.	G	E-4	1100	.029	S.F.	26.50	1.60	.09	28.19	31.50
1700	1-1/4" deep, 2.9 #/S.F.	G		1000	.032		31	1.76	.10	32.86	37
1800	1-3/4" deep, 4.2 #/S.F.	G		925	.035		43.50	1.91	.11	45.52	51
1900	2-1/4" deep, 5.0 #/S.F.	G		875	.037		64.50	2.02	.11	66.63	74.50

05 53 13.70 Floor Grating, Steel

		Crew	Daily Output	Labor-Hours	Unit	Material	Labor	Equipment	Total	Total Incl O&P
0010	**FLOOR GRATING, STEEL**, field fabricated from panels									
0015	Made from recycled materials									
0300	Platforms, to 12' high, rectangular	G	E-4	3150	.010	Lb.	3.21	.56	.03	3.80	4.48
0400	Circular	G	"	2300	.014	"	4.01	.77	.04	4.82	5.70
0410	Painted bearing bars @ 1-3/16"										
0412	Cross bars @ 4" OC, 3/4" x 1/8" bar, up to 300 S.F.	G	E-2	500	.112	S.F.	7.80	6.10	3.37	17.27	22
0414	Over 300 S.F.	G		750	.075		7.10	4.05	2.25	13.40	16.75
0422	1-1/4" x 3/16", up to 300 S.F.	G		400	.140		12.10	7.60	4.22	23.92	30
0424	Over 300 S.F.	G		600	.093		11	5.05	2.81	18.86	23.50
0432	1-1/2" x 3/16", up to 300 S.F.	G		400	.140		14.05	7.60	4.22	25.87	32.50
0434	Over 300 S.F.	G		600	.093		12.80	5.05	2.81	20.66	25
0436	1-3/4" x 3/16", up to 300 S.F.	G		400	.140		17.70	7.60	4.22	29.52	36
0438	Over 300 S.F.	G		600	.093		16.10	5.05	2.81	23.96	29
0452	2-1/4" x 3/16", up to 300 S.F.	G		300	.187		21	10.15	5.60	36.75	45.50
0454	Over 300 S.F.	G		450	.124		19.10	6.75	3.75	29.60	36
0462	Cross bars @ 2" OC, 3/4" x 1/8", up to 300 S.F.	G		500	.112		15.15	6.10	3.37	24.62	30
0464	Over 300 S.F.	G		750	.075		12.60	4.05	2.25	18.90	23
0472	1-1/4" x 3/16", up to 300 S.F.	G		400	.140		19.80	7.60	4.22	31.62	39
0474	Over 300 S.F.	G		600	.093		16.50	5.05	2.81	24.36	29.50
0482	1-1/2" x 3/16", up to 300 S.F.	G		400	.140		22.50	7.60	4.22	34.32	41.50
0484	Over 300 S.F.	G		600	.093		18.55	5.05	2.81	26.41	31.50
0486	1-3/4" x 3/16", up to 300 S.F.	G		400	.140		33.50	7.60	4.22	45.32	54
0488	Over 300 S.F.	G		600	.093		28	5.05	2.81	35.86	42
0502	2-1/4" x 3/16", up to 300 S.F.	G		300	.187		33	10.15	5.60	48.75	58.50
0504	Over 300 S.F.	G		450	.124		27.50	6.75	3.75	38	45
0612	Up to 300 S.F., 3/4" x 3/16" bars	G	E-4	850	.038		12.20	2.08	.12	14.40	16.90
0622	1-1/4" x 3/16" bars	G		600	.053		15.45	2.94	.16	18.55	22
0632	1-1/2" x 3/16" bars	G		550	.058		19.35	3.21	.18	22.74	27
0636	1-3/4" x 3/16" bars	G		450	.071		24.50	3.92	.22	28.64	33.50
0652	2-1/4" x 3/16" bars	G	E-2	300	.187		25.50	10.15	5.60	41.25	50.50
0662	Cross bars @ 2" OC, up to 300 S.F., 3/4" x 3/16"	G		500	.112		15.80	6.10	3.37	25.27	31
0672	1-1/4" x 3/16" bars	G		400	.140		20	7.60	4.22	31.82	39
0682	1-1/2" x 3/16" bars	G		400	.140		23	7.60	4.22	34.82	42
0686	1-3/4" x 3/16" bars	G		300	.187		29	10.15	5.60	44.75	54
0690	For galvanized grating, add						25%				
0800	For straight cuts, add					L.F.	6.30			6.30	6.90
0900	For curved cuts, add						8			8	8.80
1000	For straight banding, add	G					6.75			6.75	7.45
1100	For curved banding, add	G					8.90			8.90	9.80
1200	For checkered plate nosings, add	G					7.85			7.85	8.60
1300	For straight toe or kick plate, add	G					14			14	15.40
1400	For curved toe or kick plate, add	G					15.85			15.85	17.45

05 53 Metal Gratings

05 53 13 – Bar Gratings

05 53 13.70 Floor Grating, Steel

		Crew	Daily Output	Labor-Hours	Unit	Material	2018 Bare Costs Labor	Equipment	Total	Total Incl O&P
1500	For abrasive nosings, add	G			L.F.	10.40			10.40	11.40
2000	Stainless steel gratings, close spaced, 1" x 1/8" bars, up to 300 S.F.	G	E-4	450	.071	S.F.	76.50	3.92	.22	80.64	90.50
2100	Standard spacing, 3/4" x 1/8" bars	G		500	.064		84	3.53	.20	87.73	98
2200	1-1/4" x 3/16" bars	G		400	.080		82	4.41	.25	86.66	98

05 53 16 – Plank Gratings

05 53 16.50 Grating Planks

		Crew	Daily Output	Labor-Hours	Unit	Material	Labor	Equipment	Total	Total Incl O&P
0010	**GRATING PLANKS**, field fabricated from planks										
0020	Aluminum, 9-1/2" wide, 14 ga., 2" rib	G	E-4	950	.034	L.F.	32	1.86	.10	33.96	38
0200	Galvanized steel, 9-1/2" wide, 14 ga., 2-1/2" rib	G		950	.034		16.55	1.86	.10	18.51	21.50
0300	4" rib	G		950	.034		18.10	1.86	.10	20.06	23
0500	12 ga., 2-1/2" rib	G		950	.034		16.75	1.86	.10	18.71	21.50
0600	3" rib	G		950	.034		21.50	1.86	.10	23.46	27
0800	Stainless steel, type 304, 16 ga., 2" rib	G		950	.034		41	1.86	.10	42.96	48
0900	Type 316	G		950	.034		56.50	1.86	.10	58.46	65

05 53 19 – Expanded Metal Gratings

05 53 19.10 Expanded Grating, Aluminum

		Crew	Daily Output	Labor-Hours	Unit	Material	Labor	Equipment	Total	Total Incl O&P
0010	**EXPANDED GRATING, ALUMINUM**										
1200	Expanded aluminum, .65 #/S.F.	G	E-4	1050	.030	S.F.	21.50	1.68	.09	23.27	26.50

05 53 19.20 Expanded Grating, Steel

		Crew	Daily Output	Labor-Hours	Unit	Material	Labor	Equipment	Total	Total Incl O&P
0010	**EXPANDED GRATING, STEEL**										
2400	Expanded steel grating, at ground, 3.0 #/S.F.	G	E-4	900	.036	S.F.	8.05	1.96	.11	10.12	12.25
2500	3.14 #/S.F.	G		900	.036		7.05	1.96	.11	9.12	11.10
2600	4.0 #/S.F.	G		850	.038		8.35	2.08	.12	10.55	12.65
2650	4.27 #/S.F.	G		850	.038		9.50	2.08	.12	11.70	13.95
2700	5.0 #/S.F.	G		800	.040		13.80	2.21	.12	16.13	18.90
2800	6.25 #/S.F.	G		750	.043		17.80	2.35	.13	20.28	23.50
2900	7.0 #/S.F.	G		700	.046		19.65	2.52	.14	22.31	26

05 53 19.30 Grating Frame

		Crew	Daily Output	Labor-Hours	Unit	Material	Labor	Equipment	Total	Total Incl O&P
0010	**GRATING FRAME**, field fabricated										
0020	Aluminum, for gratings 1" to 1-1/2" deep	G	1 Sswk	70	.114	L.F.	3.83	6.25		10.08	14.40
0100	For each corner, add	G				Ea.	5.75			5.75	6.30

05 54 Metal Floor Plates

05 54 13 – Floor Plates

05 54 13.20 Checkered Plates

		Crew	Daily Output	Labor-Hours	Unit	Material	Labor	Equipment	Total	Total Incl O&P
0010	**CHECKERED PLATES**, steel, field fabricated										
0015	Made from recycled materials										
0020	1/4" & 3/8", 2000 to 5000 S.F., bolted	G	E-4	2900	.011	Lb.	.74	.61	.03	1.38	1.84
0100	Welded	G		4400	.007	"	.70	.40	.02	1.12	1.45
0300	Pit or trench cover and frame, 1/4" plate, 2' to 3' wide	G		100	.320	S.F.	9.35	17.65	.99	27.99	40.50
0400	For galvanizing, add	G				Lb.	.28			.28	.31
0500	Platforms, 1/4" plate, no handrails included, rectangular	G	E-4	4200	.008		3.52	.42	.02	3.96	4.59
0600	Circular	G	"	2500	.013		4.40	.71	.04	5.15	6.05

05 54 13.70 Trench Covers

		Crew	Daily Output	Labor-Hours	Unit	Material	Labor	Equipment	Total	Total Incl O&P
0010	**TRENCH COVERS**, field fabricated										
0020	Cast iron grating with bar stops and angle frame, to 18" wide	G	1 Sswk	20	.400	L.F.	213	22		235	270
0100	Frame only (both sides of trench), 1" grating	G		45	.178		1.30	9.70		11	17.35
0150	2" grating	G		35	.229		2.86	12.50		15.36	23.50
0200	Aluminum, stock units, including frames and										

05 54 Metal Floor Plates

05 54 13 – Floor Plates

05 54 13.70 Trench Covers

			Crew	Daily Output	Labor-Hours	Unit	Material	2018 Bare Costs Labor	Equipment	Total	Total Incl O&P
0210	3/8" plain cover plate, 4" opening	G	E-4	205	.156	L.F.	17.80	8.60	.48	26.88	34
0300	6" opening	G		185	.173		22.50	9.55	.53	32.58	41
0400	10" opening	G		170	.188		32	10.40	.58	42.98	53
0500	16" opening	G	↓	155	.206		46.50	11.40	.64	58.54	70.50
0700	Add per inch for additional widths to 24"	G					1.98			1.98	2.18
0900	For custom fabrication, add						50%				
1100	For 1/4" plain cover plate, deduct						12%				
1500	For cover recessed for tile, 1/4" thick, deduct						12%				
1600	3/8" thick, add						5%				
1800	For checkered plate cover, 1/4" thick, deduct						12%				
1900	3/8" thick, add						2%				
2100	For slotted or round holes in cover, 1/4" thick, add						3%				
2200	3/8" thick, add						4%				
2300	For abrasive cover, add				↓		12%				

05 55 Metal Stair Treads and Nosings

05 55 13 – Metal Stair Treads

05 55 13.50 Stair Treads

			Crew	Daily Output	Labor-Hours	Unit	Material	Labor	Equipment	Total	Total Incl O&P
0010	**STAIR TREADS**, stringers and bolts not included										
3000	Diamond plate treads, steel, 1/8" thick										
3005	Open riser, black enamel										
3010	9" deep x 36" long	G	2 Sswk	48	.333	Ea.	91.50	18.20		109.70	130
3020	42" long	G		48	.333		96.50	18.20		114.70	136
3030	48" long	G		48	.333		101	18.20		119.20	141
3040	11" deep x 36" long	G		44	.364		96.50	19.85		116.35	139
3050	42" long	G		44	.364		102	19.85		121.85	145
3060	48" long	G		44	.364		108	19.85		127.85	152
3110	Galvanized, 9" deep x 36" long	G		48	.333		144	18.20		162.20	189
3120	42" long	G		48	.333		153	18.20		171.20	199
3130	48" long	G		48	.333		163	18.20		181.20	209
3140	11" deep x 36" long	G		44	.364		149	19.85		168.85	197
3150	42" long	G		44	.364		163	19.85		182.85	212
3160	48" long	G	↓	44	.364	↓	169	19.85		188.85	219
3200	Closed riser, black enamel										
3210	12" deep x 36" long	G	2 Sswk	40	.400	Ea.	110	22		132	157
3220	42" long	G		40	.400		119	22		141	167
3230	48" long	G		40	.400		126	22		148	174
3240	Galvanized, 12" deep x 36" long	G		40	.400		173	22		195	227
3250	42" long	G		40	.400		189	22		211	244
3260	48" long	G	↓	40	.400	↓	198	22		220	254
4000	Bar grating treads										
4005	Steel, 1-1/4" x 3/16" bars, anti-skid nosing, black enamel										
4010	8-5/8" deep x 30" long	G	2 Sswk	48	.333	Ea.	54	18.20		72.20	89.50
4020	36" long	G		48	.333		63.50	18.20		81.70	99.50
4030	48" long	G		48	.333		97.50	18.20		115.70	137
4040	10-15/16" deep x 36" long	G		44	.364		70	19.85		89.85	110
4050	48" long	G		44	.364		100	19.85		119.85	143
4060	Galvanized, 8-5/8" deep x 30" long	G		48	.333		62	18.20		80.20	98.50
4070	36" long	G		48	.333		73.50	18.20		91.70	111
4080	48" long	G		48	.333		108	18.20		126.20	149
4090	10-15/16" deep x 36" long	G		44	.364		86.50	19.85		106.35	128

05 55 Metal Stair Treads and Nosings

05 55 13 – Metal Stair Treads

05 55 13.50 Stair Treads

		Crew	Daily Output	Labor-Hours	Unit	Material	2018 Bare Costs Labor	Equipment	Total	Total Incl O&P
4100	48" long	2 Sswk	44	.364	Ea.	112	19.85		131.85	156
4200	Aluminum, 1-1/4" x 3/16" bars, serrated, with nosing									
4210	7-5/8" deep x 18" long	2 Sswk	52	.308	Ea.	50	16.80		66.80	82.50
4220	24" long		52	.308		59	16.80		75.80	92.50
4230	30" long		52	.308		68.50	16.80		85.30	103
4240	36" long		52	.308		177	16.80		193.80	223
4250	8-13/16" deep x 18" long		48	.333		67	18.20		85.20	104
4260	24" long		48	.333		99.50	18.20		117.70	139
4270	30" long		48	.333		115	18.20		133.20	156
4280	36" long		48	.333		194	18.20		212.20	244
4290	10" deep x 18" long		44	.364		130	19.85		149.85	176
4300	30" long		44	.364		173	19.85		192.85	223
4310	36" long		44	.364		210	19.85		229.85	264
5000	Channel grating treads									
5005	Steel, 14 ga., 2-1/2" thick, galvanized									
5010	9" deep x 36" long	2 Sswk	48	.333	Ea.	103	18.20		121.20	143
5020	48" long	"	48	.333	"	139	18.20		157.20	182

05 55 19 – Metal Stair Tread Covers

05 55 19.50 Stair Tread Covers for Renovation

		Crew	Daily Output	Labor-Hours	Unit	Material	Labor	Equipment	Total	Total Incl O&P
0010	**STAIR TREAD COVERS FOR RENOVATION**									
0205	Extruded tread cover with nosing, pre-drilled, includes screws									
0210	Aluminum with black abrasive strips, 9" wide x 3' long	1 Carp	24	.333	Ea.	104	16.90		120.90	141
0220	4' long		22	.364		139	18.45		157.45	181
0230	5' long		20	.400		179	20.50		199.50	228
0240	11" wide x 3' long		24	.333		135	16.90		151.90	174
0250	4' long		22	.364		180	18.45		198.45	226
0260	5' long		20	.400		221	20.50		241.50	274
0305	Black abrasive strips with yellow front strips									
0310	Aluminum, 9" wide x 3' long	1 Carp	24	.333	Ea.	117	16.90		133.90	155
0320	4' long		22	.364		156	18.45		174.45	200
0330	5' long		20	.400		195	20.50		215.50	246
0340	11" wide x 3' long		24	.333		141	16.90		157.90	181
0350	4' long		22	.364		186	18.45		204.45	232
0360	5' long		20	.400		236	20.50		256.50	290
0405	Black abrasive strips with photoluminescent front strips									
0410	Aluminum, 9" wide x 3' long	1 Carp	24	.333	Ea.	150	16.90		166.90	191
0420	4' long		22	.364		183	18.45		201.45	230
0430	5' long		20	.400		229	20.50		249.50	283
0440	11" wide x 3' long		24	.333		163	16.90		179.90	205
0450	4' long		22	.364		218	18.45		236.45	267
0460	5' long		20	.400		272	20.50		292.50	330

05 56 Metal Castings

05 56 13 – Metal Construction Castings

05 56 13.50 Construction Castings

		Crew	Daily Output	Labor-Hours	Unit	Material	2018 Bare Costs Labor	Equipment	Total	Total Incl O&P
0010	**CONSTRUCTION CASTINGS**									
0100	Column bases, cast iron, 16" x 16", approx. 65 lb.	G E-4	46	.696	Ea.	142	38.50	2.14	182.64	221
0200	32" x 32", approx. 256 lb.	G "	23	1.391		520	76.50	4.29	600.79	705
0400	Cast aluminum for wood columns, 8" x 8"	G 1 Carp	32	.250		46	12.70		58.70	70
0500	12" x 12"	G "	32	.250	↓	70	12.70		82.70	97
0600	Miscellaneous C.I. castings, light sections, less than 150 lb.	G E-4	3200	.010	Lb.	8.95	.55	.03	9.53	10.80
1100	Heavy sections, more than 150 lb.	G	4200	.008		5.15	.42	.02	5.59	6.40
1300	Special low volume items	G ↓	3200	.010		11.25	.55	.03	11.83	13.30
1500	For ductile iron, add				↓	100%				

05 58 Formed Metal Fabrications

05 58 21 – Formed Chain

05 58 21.05 Alloy Steel Chain

		Crew	Daily Output	Labor-Hours	Unit	Material	Labor	Equipment	Total	Total Incl O&P
0010	**ALLOY STEEL CHAIN**, Grade 80, for lifting									
0015	Self-colored, cut lengths, 1/4"	G E-17	4	4	C.L.F.	900	223		1,123	1,350
0020	3/8"	G	2	8		1,125	445		1,570	1,950
0030	1/2"	G	1.20	13.333		1,750	740		2,490	3,150
0040	5/8"	G ↓	.72	22.222		2,850	1,225		4,075	5,150
0050	3/4"	G E-18	.48	83.333		3,675	4,575	2,250	10,500	13,900
0060	7/8"	G	.40	100		6,675	5,475	2,700	14,850	19,200
0070	1"	G	.35	114		8,550	6,275	3,100	17,925	22,900
0080	1-1/4"	G	.24	167	↓	13,100	9,150	4,525	26,775	34,200
0110	Hook, Grade 80, Clevis slip, 1/4"	G			Ea.	28.50			28.50	31.50
0120	3/8"	G				42.50			42.50	47
0130	1/2"	G				67			67	73.50
0140	5/8"	G				102			102	112
0150	3/4"	G				129			129	142
0160	Hook, Grade 80, eye/sling w/hammerlock coupling, 15 ton	G				395			395	435
0170	22 ton	G				965			965	1,075
0180	37 ton	G			↓	3,125			3,125	3,450

05 58 23 – Formed Metal Guards

05 58 23.90 Window Guards

		Crew	Daily Output	Labor-Hours	Unit	Material	Labor	Equipment	Total	Total Incl O&P
0010	**WINDOW GUARDS**, shop fabricated									
0015	Expanded metal, steel angle frame, permanent	G E-4	350	.091	S.F.	23.50	5.05	.28	28.83	34
0025	Steel bars, 1/2" x 1/2", spaced 5" OC	G "	290	.110	"	16.25	6.10	.34	22.69	28
0030	Hinge mounted, add	G			Opng.	47			47	52
0040	Removable type, add	G			"	29.50			29.50	32.50
0050	For galvanized guards, add	G			S.F.	35%				
0070	For pivoted or projected type, add	G				105%	40%			
0100	Mild steel, stock units, economy	G E-4	405	.079		6.40	4.36	.24	11	14.35
0200	Deluxe	G	405	.079	↓	12.95	4.36	.24	17.55	21.50
0400	Woven wire, stock units, 3/8" channel frame, 3' x 5' opening	G	40	.800	Opng.	172	44	2.46	218.46	265
0500	4' x 6' opening	G ↓	38	.842		276	46.50	2.59	325.09	385
0800	Basket guards for above, add	G				238			238	262
1000	Swinging guards for above, add	G			↓	81			81	89

05 58 25 – Formed Lamp Posts

05 58 25.40 Lamp Posts

		Crew	Daily Output	Labor-Hours	Unit	Material	Labor	Equipment	Total	Total Incl O&P
0010	**LAMP POSTS**									
0020	Aluminum, 7' high, stock units, post only	G 1 Carp	16	.500	Ea.	85.50	25.50		111	133
0100	Mild steel, plain	G "	16	.500	"	63.50	25.50		89	108

For customer support on your Green Building Costs with RSMeans data, call 800.448.8182.

05 71 Decorative Metal Stairs

05 71 13 – Fabricated Metal Spiral Stairs

05 71 13.50 Spiral Stairs

		Crew	Daily Output	Labor-Hours	Unit	Material	2018 Bare Costs Labor	Equipment	Total	Total Incl O&P
0010	**SPIRAL STAIRS**									
1810	Aluminum, 5'-0" diameter, plain units	G E-4	45	.711	Riser	580	39	2.19	621.19	700
1820	Fancy units	G	45	.711		1,000	39	2.19	1,041.19	1,175
1900	Cast iron, 4'-0" diameter, plain units	G	45	.711		745	39	2.19	786.19	885
1920	Fancy units	G	25	1.280		1,300	70.50	3.94	1,374.44	1,550
2000	Steel, industrial checkered plate, 4' diameter	G	45	.711		490	39	2.19	531.19	605
2200	6' diameter	G	40	.800		695	44	2.46	741.46	835
3110	Steel, flat metal treads, primed, 3'-6" diameter	G 2 Carp	1.60	10	Flight	1,350	505		1,855	2,250
3120	4'-0" diameter	G	1.45	11.034		1,525	560		2,085	2,525
3130	4'-6" diameter	G	1.35	11.852		1,700	600		2,300	2,775
3140	5'-0" diameter	G	1.25	12.800		1,850	650		2,500	3,050
3210	Galvanized, 3'-6" diameter	G	1.60	10		1,850	505		2,355	2,825
3220	4'-0" diameter	G	1.45	11.034		2,200	560		2,760	3,275
3230	4'-6" diameter	G	1.35	11.852		2,425	600		3,025	3,600
3240	5'-0" diameter	G	1.25	12.800		2,650	650		3,300	3,925
3310	Checkered plate tread, primed, 3'-6" diameter	G	1.45	11.034		1,600	560		2,160	2,600
3320	4'-0" diameter	G	1.35	11.852		1,800	600		2,400	2,900
3330	4'-6" diameter	G	1.25	12.800		1,975	650		2,625	3,150
3340	5'-0" diameter	G	1.15	13.913		2,150	705		2,855	3,450
3410	Galvanized, 3'-6" diameter	G	1.45	11.034		2,200	560		2,760	3,250
3420	4'-0" diameter	G	1.35	11.852		2,525	600		3,125	3,700
3430	4'-6" diameter	G	1.25	12.800		2,775	650		3,425	4,050
3440	5'-0" diameter	G	1.15	13.913		3,000	705		3,705	4,375
3510	Red oak covers on flat metal treads, 3'-6" diameter		1.35	11.852		2,450	600		3,050	3,600
3520	4'-0" diameter		1.25	12.800		2,925	650		3,575	4,200
3530	4'-6" diameter		1.15	13.913		3,150	705		3,855	4,550
3540	5'-0" diameter		1.05	15.238		3,400	775		4,175	4,900

05 73 Decorative Metal Railings

05 73 16 – Wire Rope Decorative Metal Railings

05 73 16.10 Cable Railings

		Crew	Daily Output	Labor-Hours	Unit	Material	Labor	Equipment	Total	Total Incl O&P
0010	**CABLE RAILINGS**, with 316 stainless steel 1 x 19 cable, 3/16" diameter									
0015	Made from recycled materials									
0100	1-3/4" diameter stainless steel posts x 42" high, cables 4" OC	G 2 Sswk	25	.640	L.F.	45.50	35		80.50	107

05 73 23 – Ornamental Railings

05 73 23.50 Railings, Ornamental

		Crew	Daily Output	Labor-Hours	Unit	Material	Labor	Equipment	Total	Total Incl O&P
0010	**RAILINGS, ORNAMENTAL**, 3'-6" high, posts @ 6' OC									
0020	Bronze or stainless, hand forged, plain	G 2 Sswk	24	.667	L.F.	260	36.50		296.50	345
0100	Fancy	G	18	.889		520	48.50		568.50	650
0200	Aluminum, panelized, plain	G	24	.667		12.20	36.50		48.70	73
0300	Fancy	G	18	.889		25.50	48.50		74	108
0400	Wrought iron, hand forged, plain	G	24	.667		94	36.50		130.50	164
0500	Fancy	G	18	.889		231	48.50		279.50	335
0550	Steel, panelized, plain	G	24	.667		20.50	36.50		57	82
0560	Fancy	G	18	.889		30	48.50		78.50	113
0600	Composite metal/wood/glass, plain		18	.889		142	48.50		190.50	236
0700	Fancy		12	1.333		284	73		357	435

For customer support on your Green Building Costs with RSMeans data, call 800.448.8182.

05 75 Decorative Formed Metal

05 75 13 – Columns

05 75 13.10 Aluminum Columns

		Crew	Daily Output	Labor-Hours	Unit	Material	2018 Bare Costs Labor	Equipment	Total	Total Incl O&P
0010	**ALUMINUM COLUMNS**									
0015	Made from recycled materials									
0020	Aluminum, extruded, stock units, no cap or base, 6" diameter	G	E-4	240	.133	L.F.	12.85	7.35	.41	20.61	26.50
0100	8" diameter	G		170	.188		16.75	10.40	.58	27.73	36
0200	10" diameter	G		150	.213		22	11.75	.66	34.41	44.50
0300	12" diameter	G		140	.229		35.50	12.60	.70	48.80	61
0400	15" diameter	G	↓	120	.267	↓	49	14.70	.82	64.52	79
0410	Caps and bases, plain, 6" diameter	G				Set	25			25	27.50
0420	8" diameter	G					31			31	34.50
0430	10" diameter	G					47			47	51.50
0440	12" diameter	G					77			77	84.50
0450	15" diameter	G					138			138	152
0460	Caps, ornamental, plain	G					310			310	340
0470	Fancy	G				↓	1,550			1,550	1,725
0500	For square columns, add to column prices above					L.F.	50%				
0700	Residential, flat, 8' high, plain	G	E-4	20	1.600	Ea.	101	88	4.93	193.93	260
0720	Fancy	G		20	1.600		196	88	4.93	288.93	365
0740	Corner type, plain	G		20	1.600		174	88	4.93	266.93	340
0760	Fancy	G	↓	20	1.600	↓	345	88	4.93	437.93	530

05 75 13.20 Columns, Ornamental

			Crew	Daily Output	Labor-Hours	Unit	Material	Labor	Equipment	Total	Total Incl O&P
0010	**COLUMNS, ORNAMENTAL**, shop fabricated	R051223-10									
6400	Mild steel, flat, 9" wide, stock units, painted, plain	G	E-4	160	.200	V.L.F.	9.45	11.05	.62	21.12	29
6450	Fancy	G		160	.200		18.40	11.05	.62	30.07	39
6500	Corner columns, painted, plain	G		160	.200		16.35	11.05	.62	28.02	36.50
6550	Fancy	G	↓	160	.200	↓	32.50	11.05	.62	44.17	54

Estimating Tips
06 05 00 Common Work Results for Wood, Plastics, and Composites

- Common to any wood-framed structure are the accessory connector items such as screws, nails, adhesives, hangers, connector plates, straps, angles, and hold-downs. For typical wood-framed buildings, such as residential projects, the aggregate total for these items can be significant, especially in areas where seismic loading is a concern. For floor and wall framing, the material cost is based on 10 to 25 lbs. of accessory connectors per MBF. Hold-downs, hangers, and other connectors should be taken off by the piece.

  Included with material costs are fasteners for a normal installation. Gordian's RSMeans engineers use manufacturers' recommendations, written specifications, and/or standard construction practice for the sizing and spacing of fasteners. Prices for various fasteners are shown for informational purposes only. Adjustments should be made if unusual fastening conditions exist.

06 10 00 Carpentry

- Lumber is a traded commodity and therefore sensitive to supply and demand in the marketplace. Even with "budgetary" estimating of wood-framed projects, it is advisable to call local suppliers for the latest market pricing.

- The common quantity unit for wood-framed projects is "thousand board feet" (MBF). A board foot is a volume of wood—1" x 1' x 1' or 144 cubic inches. Board-foot quantities are generally calculated using nominal material dimensions— dressed sizes are ignored. Board foot per lineal foot of any stick of lumber can be calculated by dividing the nominal cross-sectional area by 12. As an example, 2,000 lineal feet of 2 x 12 equates to 4 MBF by dividing the nominal area, 2 x 12, by 12, which equals 2, and multiplying by 2,000 to give 4,000 board feet. This simple rule applies to all nominal dimensioned lumber.

- Waste is an issue of concern at the quantity takeoff for any area of construction. Framing lumber is sold in even foot lengths, i.e., 8', 10', 12', 14', 16' and depending on spans, wall heights, and the grade of lumber, waste is inevitable. A rule of thumb for lumber waste is 5%–10% depending on material quality and the complexity of the framing.

- Wood in various forms and shapes is used in many projects, even where the main structural framing is steel, concrete, or masonry. Plywood as a back-up partition material and 2x boards used as blocking and cant strips around roof edges are two common examples. The estimator should ensure that the costs of all wood materials are included in the final estimate.

06 20 00 Finish Carpentry

- It is necessary to consider the grade of workmanship when estimating labor costs for erecting millwork and an interior finish. In practice, there are three grades: premium, custom, and economy. The RSMeans daily output for base and case moldings is in the range of 200 to 250 L.F. per carpenter per day. This is appropriate for most average custom-grade projects. For premium projects, an adjustment to productivity of 25%–50% should be made, depending on the complexity of the job.

Reference Numbers

Reference numbers are shown at the beginning of some major classifications. These numbers refer to related items in the Reference Section. The reference information may be an estimating procedure, an alternate pricing method, or technical information.

Note: Not all subdivisions listed here necessarily appear. ■

Did you know?

RSMeans data is available through our online application with 24/7 access:

- Search for unit prices by keyword
- Leverage the most up-to-date data
- Build and export estimates

Try it free for 30 days!
www.rsmeans.com/2018freetrial

No part of this cost data may be reproduced, stored in a retrieval system, or transmitted in any form or by any means without prior written permission of Gordian.

06 05 Common Work Results for Wood, Plastics, and Composites

06 05 23 – Wood, Plastic, and Composite Fastenings

06 05 23.30 Recycled Steel Nails

			Crew	Daily Output	Labor-Hours	Unit	Material	2018 Bare Costs Labor	Equipment	Total	Total Incl O&P
0010	**RECYCLED STEEL NAILS**										
2000	Recycled steel, dbl. hot-dipped galv., box nail, 3-20D	G				Lb.	2.20			2.20	2.42
2010	Common, 3-20D	G					2.16			2.16	2.38
2020	Annular/spiral thread, 3-20D	G					2.20			2.20	2.42
2030	Drywall nails	G					2.49			2.49	2.74
2040	Finish nails, 4-10D	G					2.54			2.54	2.79
2050	Flooring nails, 4-10D	G					2.84			2.84	3.12
2060	Masonry nails, plain shank	G					3.92			3.92	4.31
2070	Roofing nails, plain shank	G					2.21			2.21	2.43
2080	Roofing nails, spiral shank	G					2.48			2.48	2.73
2090	Siding nails, plain shank	G					2.57			2.57	2.83
2100	Siding nails, spiral shank	G					2.99			2.99	3.29
2110	For air nailers, carton of 2500, 6D	G				Ea.	63.50			63.50	69.50
2120	For air nailers, carton of 2500, 8D	G					63.50			63.50	69.50
2130	For air nailers, carton of 2500, 10D	G					92.50			92.50	102
2140	For air nailers, carton of 2500, 16D	G					126			126	138

06 05 23.90 Recycled Plastic Shims

			Crew	Daily Output	Labor-Hours	Unit	Material	Labor	Equipment	Total	Total Incl O&P
0010	**RECYCLED PLASTIC SHIMS**										
5000	Made from recycled plastic, 8"L x 1-1/4"W	G				Ea.	.17			.17	.18
5010	Case of 360	G				"	60			60	66

06 11 Wood Framing

06 11 10 – Framing with Dimensional, Engineered or Composite Lumber

06 11 10.01 Forest Stewardship Council Certification

			Crew	Daily Output	Labor-Hours	Unit	Material	Labor	Equipment	Total	Total Incl O&P
0010	**FOREST STEWARDSHIP COUNCIL CERTIFICATION**										
0020	For Forest Stewardship Council (FSC) cert dimension lumber, add	G					65%				

06 11 10.10 Beam and Girder Framing

			Crew	Daily Output	Labor-Hours	Unit	Material	Labor	Equipment	Total	Total Incl O&P
0010	**BEAM AND GIRDER FRAMING**	R061110-30									
1000	Single, 2" x 6"		2 Carp	700	.023	L.F.	.64	1.16		1.80	2.47
1005	Pneumatic nailed			812	.020		.65	1		1.65	2.24
1020	2" x 8"			650	.025		.89	1.25		2.14	2.88
1025	Pneumatic nailed			754	.021		.90	1.08		1.98	2.63
1040	2" x 10"			600	.027		1.41	1.35		2.76	3.61
1045	Pneumatic nailed			696	.023		1.42	1.17		2.59	3.33
1060	2" x 12"			550	.029		1.79	1.47		3.26	4.22
1065	Pneumatic nailed			638	.025		1.81	1.27		3.08	3.93
1080	2" x 14"			500	.032		2.27	1.62		3.89	4.96
1085	Pneumatic nailed			580	.028		2.28	1.40		3.68	4.64
1100	3" x 8"			550	.029		2.87	1.47		4.34	5.40
1120	3" x 10"			500	.032		3.62	1.62		5.24	6.45
1140	3" x 12"			450	.036		4.34	1.80		6.14	7.55
1160	3" x 14"			400	.040		5.05	2.03		7.08	8.65
1170	4" x 6"		F-3	1100	.036		3.06	1.88	.45	5.39	6.75
1180	4" x 8"			1000	.040		4.15	2.07	.50	6.72	8.25
1200	4" x 10"			950	.042		4.96	2.18	.52	7.66	9.35
1220	4" x 12"			900	.044		5.50	2.30	.55	8.35	10.15
1240	4" x 14"			850	.047		6.40	2.44	.58	9.42	11.40
1250	6" x 8"			525	.076		7.90	3.95	.94	12.79	15.75
1260	6" x 10"			500	.080		6.90	4.14	.99	12.03	15
1290	8" x 12"			300	.133		16.55	6.90	1.65	25.10	30.50

06 11 Wood Framing

06 11 10 – Framing with Dimensional, Engineered or Composite Lumber

06 11 10.10 Beam and Girder Framing

		Crew	Daily Output	Labor-Hours	Unit	Material	2018 Bare Costs Labor	Equipment	Total	Total Incl O&P
1300	Treated, single, 2" x 4"	2 Carp	700	.023	L.F.	.59	1.16		1.75	2.41
1320	2" x 6"		700	.023		.74	1.16		1.90	2.58
1340	2" x 8"		650	.025		1.13	1.25		2.38	3.14
1360	2" x 10"		600	.027		1.42	1.35		2.77	3.62
1380	2" x 12"		550	.029		2.04	1.47		3.51	4.50
1400	2" x 14"		500	.032		2.79	1.62		4.41	5.55
1420	3" x 8"		550	.029		3.37	1.47		4.84	5.95
1440	3" x 10"		500	.032		4.70	1.62		6.32	7.60
1460	3" x 12"		450	.036		.11	1.80		1.91	2.88
1480	3" x 14"		400	.040		6.10	2.03		8.13	9.85
1500	4" x 8"	F-3	1000	.040		3.92	2.07	.50	6.49	8
1520	4" x 10"		950	.042		5.65	2.18	.52	8.35	10.10
1540	4" x 12"		900	.044		6.75	2.30	.55	9.60	11.55
1560	4" x 14"		850	.047		10.40	2.44	.58	13.42	15.80
2000	Double, 2" x 6"	2 Carp	625	.026		1.29	1.30		2.59	3.40
2005	Pneumatic nailed		725	.022		1.30	1.12		2.42	3.13
2020	2" x 8"		575	.028		1.79	1.41		3.20	4.12
2025	Pneumatic nailed		667	.024		1.81	1.22		3.03	3.84
2040	2" x 10"		550	.029		2.82	1.47		4.29	5.35
2045	Pneumatic nailed		638	.025		2.85	1.27		4.12	5.05
2060	2" x 12"		525	.030		3.59	1.55		5.14	6.30
2065	Pneumatic nailed		610	.026		3.62	1.33		4.95	6
2080	2" x 14"		475	.034		4.53	1.71		6.24	7.60
2085	Pneumatic nailed		551	.029		4.56	1.47		6.03	7.25
2200	Treated, double, 2" x 6"		625	.026		.76	1.30		2.06	2.82
2220	2" x 8"		575	.028		1.15	1.41		2.56	3.42
2240	2" x 10"		550	.029		1.45	1.47		2.92	3.84
2260	2" x 12"		525	.030		2.08	1.55		3.63	4.64
2280	2" x 14"		475	.034		2.83	1.71		4.54	5.70
3000	Triple, 2" x 6"		550	.029		1.93	1.47		3.40	4.37
3005	Pneumatic nailed		638	.025		1.95	1.27		3.22	4.09
3020	2" x 8"		525	.030		2.68	1.55		4.23	5.30
3025	Pneumatic nailed		609	.026		2.71	1.33		4.04	5
3040	2" x 10"		500	.032		4.23	1.62		5.85	7.10
3045	Pneumatic nailed		580	.028		4.27	1.40		5.67	6.80
3060	2" x 12"		475	.034		5.40	1.71		7.11	8.50
3065	Pneumatic nailed		551	.029		5.45	1.47		6.92	8.20
3080	2" x 14"		450	.036		7.40	1.80		9.20	10.85
3085	Pneumatic nailed		522	.031		6.85	1.55		8.40	9.90

06 11 10.28 Porch or Deck Framing

			Crew	Daily Output	Labor-Hours	Unit	Material	Labor	Equipment	Total	Total Incl O&P
0010	**PORCH OR DECK FRAMING**										
1420	Alternative decking, wood/plastic composite, 5/4" x 6"	G	2 Carp	640	.025	L.F.	3.27	1.27		4.54	5.55
1465	Framing, porch or deck, alt deck fastening, screws, add		1 Carp	240	.033	S.F.		1.69		1.69	2.57

06 11 10.40 Wall Framing

			Crew	Daily Output	Labor-Hours	Unit	Material	Labor	Equipment	Total	Total Incl O&P
0010	**WALL FRAMING**	R061110-30									
0100	Door buck, studs, header, access, 8' high, 2" x 4" wall, 3' wide		1 Carp	32	.250	Ea.	17.55	12.70		30.25	38.50
0110	4' wide			32	.250		18.85	12.70		31.55	40
0120	5' wide			32	.250		22.50	12.70		35.20	44.50
0130	6' wide			32	.250		24.50	12.70		37.20	46.50
0140	8' wide			30	.267		36.50	13.50		50	60.50
0150	10' wide			30	.267		50	13.50		63.50	75.50
0160	12' wide			30	.267		68.50	13.50		82	96

For customer support on your Green Building Costs with RSMeans data, call 800.448.8182.

103

06 11 Wood Framing

06 11 10 – Framing with Dimensional, Engineered or Composite Lumber

06 11 10.40 Wall Framing

		Crew	Daily Output	Labor-Hours	Unit	Material	2018 Bare Costs Labor	Equipment	Total	Total Incl O&P
0170	2" x 6" wall, 3' wide	1 Carp	32	.250	Ea.	25	12.70		37.70	46.50
0180	4' wide		32	.250		26	12.70		38.70	48
0190	5' wide		32	.250		30	12.70		42.70	52.50
0200	6' wide		32	.250		31.50	12.70		44.20	54.50
0210	8' wide		30	.267		43.50	13.50		57	68.50
0220	10' wide		30	.267		57	13.50		70.50	83.50
0230	12' wide		30	.267		76	13.50		89.50	104
0240	Window buck, studs, header & access, 8' high 2" x 4" wall, 2' wide		24	.333		18.60	16.90		35.50	46
0250	3' wide		24	.333		21.50	16.90		38.40	49.50
0260	4' wide		24	.333		24	16.90		40.90	51.50
0270	5' wide		24	.333		27.50	16.90		44.40	56
0280	6' wide		24	.333		31	16.90		47.90	59.50
0290	7' wide		24	.333		41	16.90		57.90	70.50
0300	8' wide		22	.364		45.50	18.45		63.95	78
0310	10' wide		22	.364		60	18.45		78.45	94
0320	12' wide		22	.364		81	18.45		99.45	117
0330	2" x 6" wall, 2' wide		24	.333		27.50	16.90		44.40	56
0340	3' wide		24	.333		31	16.90		47.90	59.50
0350	4' wide		24	.333		33.50	16.90		50.40	62.50
0360	5' wide		24	.333		37.50	16.90		54.40	67
0370	6' wide		24	.333		41.50	16.90		58.40	71
0380	7' wide		24	.333		52.50	16.90		69.40	83
0390	8' wide		22	.364		57	18.45		75.45	91
0400	10' wide		22	.364		72.50	18.45		90.95	108
0410	12' wide		22	.364		95	18.45		113.45	133
2000	Headers over openings, 2" x 6"	2 Carp	360	.044	L.F.	.64	2.25		2.89	4.14
2005	2" x 6", pneumatic nailed		432	.037		.65	1.88		2.53	3.58
2050	2" x 8"		340	.047		.89	2.39		3.28	4.61
2055	2" x 8", pneumatic nailed		408	.039		.90	1.99		2.89	4.02
2100	2" x 10"		320	.050		1.41	2.54		3.95	5.40
2105	2" x 10", pneumatic nailed		384	.042		1.42	2.11		3.53	4.78
2150	2" x 12"		300	.053		1.79	2.70		4.49	6.10
2155	2" x 12", pneumatic nailed		360	.044		1.81	2.25		4.06	5.40
2190	4" x 10"		240	.067		4.96	3.38		8.34	10.60
2195	4" x 10", pneumatic nailed		288	.056		4.99	2.82		7.81	9.80
2200	4" x 12"		190	.084		5.50	4.27		9.77	12.55
2205	4" x 12", pneumatic nailed		228	.070		5.50	3.56		9.06	11.45
2210	4" x 14"		160	.100		6.40	5.05		11.45	14.75
2215	4" x 14", pneumatic nailed		192	.083		6.45	4.22		10.67	13.55
2230	6" x 8"	1 Carp	180	.044		7.90	2.25		10.15	12.15
2240	6" x 10"	2 Carp	165	.097		6.90	4.92		11.82	15.10
2245	6" x 10", pneumatic nailed		198	.081		6.95	4.10		11.05	13.90
2250	6" x 12"		140	.114		8.70	5.80		14.50	18.35
2255	6" x 12", pneumatic nailed		168	.095		8.75	4.83		13.58	16.95
2500	Treated, 2" x 4"		380	.042		.59	2.14		2.73	3.90
2520	2" x 6"		360	.044		.74	2.25		2.99	4.24
2540	2" x 8"		340	.047		1.12	2.39		3.51	4.86
2560	2" x 10"		320	.050		1.40	2.54		3.94	5.40
2580	2" x 12"		300	.053		2.03	2.70		4.73	6.35
2600	2" x 14"		280	.057		2.77	2.90		5.67	7.45
2700	4" x 4"		280	.057		1.17	2.90		4.07	5.70
2720	4" x 6"		230	.070		1.90	3.53		5.43	7.45
2740	4" x 8"		170	.094		3.90	4.77		8.67	11.55

06 11 Wood Framing

06 11 10 – Framing with Dimensional, Engineered or Composite Lumber

06 11 10.40 Wall Framing		Crew	Daily Output	Labor-Hours	Unit	Material	2018 Bare Costs Labor	Equipment	Total	Total Incl O&P
2760	4" x 10"	2 Carp	100	.160	L.F.	5.60	8.10		13.70	18.50
2780	4" x 12"		90	.178		5.60	9		14.60	19.85
5000	Plates, untreated, 2" x 3"		850	.019		.42	.95		1.37	1.92
5005	2" x 3", pneumatic nailed		1020	.016		.43	.80		1.23	1.68
5020	2" x 4"		800	.020		.42	1.01		1.43	2
5025	2" x 4", pneumatic nailed		960	.017		.42	.85		1.27	1.76
5040	2" x 6"		750	.021		.64	1.08		1.72	2.36
5042	2" x 8"		725	.022		.89	1.12		2.01	2.68
5044	2" x 10"		700	.023		1.41	1.16		2.57	3.31
5045	2" x 6", pneumatic nailed		900	.018		.65	.90		1.55	2.09
5047	2" x 8", pneumatic nailed		870	.018		.90	.93		1.83	2.41
5049	2" x 10", pneumatic nailed		840	.019		1.42	.97		2.39	3.03
5050	2" x 12"		670	.024		1.79	1.21		3	3.81
5055	2" x 12", pneumatic nailed		804	.020		1.81	1.01		2.82	3.53
5060	Treated, 2" x 3"		850	.019		.52	.95		1.47	2.02
5065	2" x 3", treated, pneumatic nailed		1020	.016		.52	.80		1.32	1.78
5080	2" x 4"		800	.020		.59	1.01		1.60	2.19
5085	2" x 4", treated, pneumatic nailed		960	.017		.59	.85		1.44	1.94
5100	2" x 6"		750	.021		.74	1.08		1.82	2.46
5102	2 x 8		725	.022		1.12	1.12		2.24	2.93
5103	2" x 6", treated, pneumatic nailed		900	.018		.74	.90		1.64	2.19
5104	2 x 10		700	.023		1.40	1.16		2.56	3.30
5105	2" x 12"		670	.024		2.03	1.21		3.24	4.07
5107	2" x 8", pneumatic nailed		870	.018		1.13	.93		2.06	2.66
5108	2" x 10", pneumatic nailed		840	.019		1.41	.97		2.38	3.03
5109	2" x 12", pneumatic nailed		804	.020		2.04	1.01		3.05	3.78
5110	Plates, double, untreated, 2" x 6"		400	.040		1.29	2.03		3.32	4.51
5112	2" x 8"		370	.043		1.79	2.19		3.98	5.30
5114	2" x 10"		350	.046		2.82	2.32		5.14	6.65
5115	2" x 6", pneumatic nailed		480	.033		1.28	1.69		2.97	3.98
5117	2" x 8", pneumatic nailed		444	.036		1.79	1.83		3.62	4.74
5119	2" x 10", pneumatic nailed		420	.038		2.82	1.93		4.75	6.05
5120	Studs, 8' high wall, 2" x 3"		1200	.013		.42	.68		1.10	1.50
5125	2" x 3", pneumatic nailed		1440	.011		.43	.56		.99	1.33
5140	2" x 4"		1100	.015		.42	.74		1.16	1.58
5146	2" x 4", pneumatic nailed		1320	.012		.42	.61		1.03	1.41
5160	2" x 6"		1000	.016		.64	.81		1.45	1.95
5166	2" x 6", pneumatic nailed		1200	.013		.65	.68		1.33	1.75
5171	2" x 8"		900	.018		.89	.90		1.79	2.35
5172	2" x 8", pneumatic nailed		1080	.015		.90	.75		1.65	2.13
5175	2" x 10"		900	.018		1.41	.90		2.31	2.92
5176	2" x 10", pneumatic nailed		1080	.015		1.42	.75		2.17	2.70
5178	2" x 12"		850	.019		1.79	.95		2.74	3.42
5179	2" x 12", pneumatic nailed		1020	.016		1.81	.80		2.61	3.20
5180	3" x 4"		800	.020		1.20	1.01		2.21	2.86
5185	3" x 4", pneumatic nailed		960	.017		1.21	.85		2.06	2.62
5200	Installed on second story, 2" x 3"		1170	.014		.42	.69		1.11	1.53
5205	2" x 3", pneumatic nailed		1404	.011		.43	.58		1.01	1.35
5220	2" x 4"		1015	.016		.42	.80		1.22	1.68
5225	2" x 4", pneumatic nailed		1218	.013		.42	.67		1.09	1.48
5240	2" x 6"		890	.018		.64	.91		1.55	2.10
5245	2" x 6", pneumatic nailed		1080	.015		.65	.75		1.40	1.86
5260	3" x 4"		800	.020		1.20	1.01		2.21	2.86

For customer support on your Green Building Costs with RSMeans data, call 800.448.8182.

06 11 Wood Framing

06 11 10 – Framing with Dimensional, Engineered or Composite Lumber

06 11 10.40 Wall Framing		Crew	Daily Output	Labor-Hours	Unit	Material	2018 Bare Costs Labor	Equipment	Total	Total Incl O&P
5265	3" x 4", pneumatic nailed	2 Carp	960	.017	L.F.	1.21	.85		2.06	2.62
5280	Installed on dormer or gable, 2" x 3"		1045	.015		.42	.78		1.20	1.65
5285	2" x 3", pneumatic nailed		1254	.013		.43	.65		1.08	1.46
5300	2" x 4"		905	.018		.42	.90		1.32	1.82
5305	2" x 4", pneumatic nailed		1086	.015		.42	.75		1.17	1.61
5320	2" x 6"		800	.020		.64	1.01		1.65	2.25
5325	2" x 6", pneumatic nailed		960	.017		.65	.85		1.50	2.01
5340	3" x 4"		700	.023		1.20	1.16		2.36	3.08
5345	3" x 4", pneumatic nailed		840	.019		1.21	.97		2.18	2.80
5360	6' high wall, 2" x 3"		970	.016		.42	.84		1.26	1.74
5365	2" x 3", pneumatic nailed		1164	.014		.43	.70		1.13	1.53
5380	2" x 4"		850	.019		.42	.95		1.37	1.91
5385	2" x 4", pneumatic nailed		1020	.016		.42	.80		1.22	1.68
5400	2" x 6"		740	.022		.64	1.10		1.74	2.38
5405	2" x 6", pneumatic nailed		888	.018		.65	.91		1.56	2.11
5420	3" x 4"		600	.027		1.20	1.35		2.55	3.38
5425	3" x 4", pneumatic nailed		720	.022		1.21	1.13		2.34	3.05
5440	Installed on second story, 2" x 3"		950	.017		.42	.85		1.27	1.77
5445	2" x 3", pneumatic nailed		1140	.014		.43	.71		1.14	1.55
5460	2" x 4"		810	.020		.42	1		1.42	1.98
5465	2" x 4", pneumatic nailed		972	.016		.42	.83		1.25	1.74
5480	2" x 6"		700	.023		.64	1.16		1.80	2.47
5485	2" x 6", pneumatic nailed		840	.019		.65	.97		1.62	2.19
5500	3" x 4"		550	.029		1.20	1.47		2.67	3.57
5505	3" x 4", pneumatic nailed		660	.024		1.21	1.23		2.44	3.20
5520	Installed on dormer or gable, 2" x 3"		850	.019		.42	.95		1.37	1.92
5525	2" x 3", pneumatic nailed		1020	.016		.43	.80		1.23	1.68
5540	2" x 4"		720	.022		.42	1.13		1.55	2.18
5545	2" x 4", pneumatic nailed		864	.019		.42	.94		1.36	1.90
5560	2" x 6"		620	.026		.64	1.31		1.95	2.70
5565	2" x 6", pneumatic nailed		744	.022		.65	1.09		1.74	2.38
5580	3" x 4"		480	.033		1.20	1.69		2.89	3.89
5585	3" x 4", pneumatic nailed		576	.028		1.21	1.41		2.62	3.47
5600	3' high wall, 2" x 3"		740	.022		.42	1.10		1.52	2.14
5605	2" x 3", pneumatic nailed		888	.018		.43	.91		1.34	1.86
5620	2" x 4"		640	.025		.42	1.27		1.69	2.39
5625	2" x 4", pneumatic nailed		768	.021		.42	1.06		1.48	2.08
5640	2" x 6"		550	.029		.64	1.47		2.11	2.96
5645	2" x 6", pneumatic nailed		660	.024		.65	1.23		1.88	2.59
5660	3" x 4"		440	.036		1.20	1.84		3.04	4.13
5665	3" x 4", pneumatic nailed		528	.030		1.21	1.54		2.75	3.67
5680	Installed on second story, 2" x 3"		700	.023		.42	1.16		1.58	2.23
5685	2" x 3", pneumatic nailed		840	.019		.43	.97		1.40	1.94
5700	2" x 4"		610	.026		.42	1.33		1.75	2.49
5705	2" x 4", pneumatic nailed		732	.022		.42	1.11		1.53	2.16
5720	2" x 6"		520	.031		.64	1.56		2.20	3.09
5725	2" x 6", pneumatic nailed		624	.026		.65	1.30		1.95	2.70
5740	3" x 4"		430	.037		1.20	1.89		3.09	4.19
5745	3" x 4", pneumatic nailed		516	.031		1.21	1.57		2.78	3.72
5760	Installed on dormer or gable, 2" x 3"		625	.026		.42	1.30		1.72	2.45
5765	2" x 3", pneumatic nailed		750	.021		.43	1.08		1.51	2.12
5780	2" x 4"		545	.029		.42	1.49		1.91	2.73
5785	2" x 4", pneumatic nailed		654	.024		.42	1.24		1.66	2.36

06 11 Wood Framing

06 11 10 – Framing with Dimensional, Engineered or Composite Lumber

06 11 10.40 Wall Framing

		Crew	Daily Output	Labor-Hours	Unit	Material	2018 Bare Costs Labor	Equipment	Total	Total Incl O&P
5800	2" x 6"	2 Carp	465	.034	L.F.	.64	1.74		2.38	3.37
5805	2" x 6", pneumatic nailed		558	.029		.65	1.45		2.10	2.93
5820	3" x 4"		380	.042		1.20	2.14		3.34	4.57
5825	3" x 4", pneumatic nailed		456	.035		1.21	1.78		2.99	4.04
5830	Studs, 10' high wall, 2" x 4"		1407	.011		.42	.58		1	1.34
5832	2" x 4", pneumatic nailed		1688	.009		.42	.48		.90	1.20
5834	2" x 6"		1025	.016		.64	.79		1.43	1.92
5836	2" x 6", pneumatic nailed		1230	.013		.65	.66		1.31	1.72
5838	12' high wall, 2" x 4"		1447	.011		.42	.56		.98	1.31
5840	2" x 4", pneumatic nailed		1736	.009		.42	.47		.89	1.18
5842	2" x 6"		1050	.015		.64	.77		1.41	1.89
5844	2" x 6", pneumatic nailed		1260	.013		.65	.64		1.29	1.70
5846	9' high wall, 2" x 4"		1253	.013		.42	.65		1.07	1.45
5848	2" x 4", pneumatic nailed		1504	.011		.42	.54		.96	1.29
5850	2" x 6"		1012	.016		.64	.80		1.44	1.93
5852	2" x 6", pneumatic nailed		1230	.013		.65	.66		1.31	1.72

06 12 Structural Panels

06 12 10 – Structural Insulated Panels

06 12 10.10 OSB Faced Panels

			Crew	Daily Output	Labor-Hours	Unit	Material	Labor	Equipment	Total	Total Incl O&P
0010	**OSB FACED PANELS**										
0100	Structural insul. panels, 7/16" OSB both faces, EPS insul., 3-5/8" T	G	F-3	2075	.019	S.F.	3.65	1	.24	4.89	5.80
0110	5-5/8" thick	G		1725	.023		4.10	1.20	.29	5.59	6.65
0120	7-3/8" thick	G		1425	.028		4.45	1.45	.35	6.25	7.50
0130	9-3/8" thick	G		1125	.036		4.75	1.84	.44	7.03	8.55
0140	7/16" OSB one face, EPS insul., 3-5/8" thick	G		2175	.018		3.75	.95	.23	4.93	5.85
0150	5-5/8" thick	G		1825	.022		4.35	1.14	.27	5.76	6.80
0160	7-3/8" thick	G		1525	.026		4.85	1.36	.33	6.54	7.75
0170	9-3/8" thick	G		1225	.033		5.35	1.69	.40	7.44	8.90
0190	7/16" OSB - 1/2" GWB faces, EPS insul., 3-5/8" T	G		2075	.019		3.45	1	.24	4.69	5.60
0200	5-5/8" thick	G		1725	.023		4.10	1.20	.29	5.59	6.65
0210	7-3/8" thick	G		1425	.028		4.65	1.45	.35	6.45	7.70
0220	9-3/8" thick	G		1125	.036		5.25	1.84	.44	7.53	9.10
0240	7/16" OSB - 1/2" MRGWB faces, EPS insul., 3-5/8" T	G		2075	.019		3.55	1	.24	4.79	5.70
0250	5-5/8" thick	G		1725	.023		4.25	1.20	.29	5.74	6.80
0260	7-3/8" thick	G		1425	.028		4.65	1.45	.35	6.45	7.70
0270	9-3/8" thick	G		1125	.036		5.35	1.84	.44	7.63	9.20
0300	For 1/2" GWB added to OSB skin, add	G					1.40			1.40	1.54
0310	For 1/2" MRGWB added to OSB skin, add	G					1.40			1.40	1.54
0320	For one T1-11 skin, add to OSB-OSB	G					1.95			1.95	2.15
0330	For one 19/32" CDX skin, add to OSB-OSB	G					1.50			1.50	1.65
0500	Structural insulated panel, 7/16" OSB both sides, straw core										
0510	4-3/8" T, walls (w/sill, splines, plates)	G	F-6	2400	.017	S.F.	7.55	.79	.21	8.55	9.75
0520	Floors (w/splines)	G		2400	.017		7.55	.79	.21	8.55	9.75
0530	Roof (w/splines)	G		2400	.017		7.55	.79	.21	8.55	9.75
0550	7-7/8" T, walls (w/sill, splines, plates)	G		2400	.017		11.40	.79	.21	12.40	14
0560	Floors (w/splines)	G		2400	.017		11.40	.79	.21	12.40	14
0570	Roof (w/splines)	G		2400	.017		11.40	.79	.21	12.40	14

06 16 Sheathing

06 16 13 – Insulating Sheathing

06 16 13.10 Insulating Sheathing

		Crew	Daily Output	Labor-Hours	Unit	Material	2018 Bare Costs Labor	Equipment	Total	Total Incl O&P
0010	**INSULATING SHEATHING**									
0020	Expanded polystyrene, 1#/C.F. density, 3/4" thick, R2.89 G	2 Carp	1400	.011	S.F.	.36	.58		.94	1.28
0030	1" thick, R3.85 G		1300	.012		.43	.62		1.05	1.42
0040	2" thick, R7.69 G		1200	.013		.70	.68		1.38	1.80
0050	Extruded polystyrene, 15 psi compressive strength, 1" thick, R5 G		1300	.012		.71	.62		1.33	1.73
0060	2" thick, R10 G		1200	.013		.87	.68		1.55	1.99
0070	Polyisocyanurate, 2#/C.F. density, 3/4" thick G		1400	.011		.58	.58		1.16	1.52
0080	1" thick G		1300	.012		.59	.62		1.21	1.60
0090	1-1/2" thick G		1250	.013		.74	.65		1.39	1.80
0100	2" thick G		1200	.013		.90	.68		1.58	2.02

06 16 26 – Underlayment

06 16 26.10 Wood Product Underlayment

		Crew	Daily Output	Labor-Hours	Unit	Material	Labor	Equipment	Total	Total Incl O&P
0010	**WOOD PRODUCT UNDERLAYMENT** R061636-20									
0015	Plywood, underlayment grade, 1/4" thick	2 Carp	1500	.011	S.F.	.94	.54		1.48	1.85
0018	Pneumatic nailed		1860	.009		.94	.44		1.38	1.69
0100	1/2" thick		1450	.011		1.23	.56		1.79	2.20
0105	Pneumatic nailed		1798	.009		1.23	.45		1.68	2.04
0200	5/8" thick		1400	.011		1.36	.58		1.94	2.38
0205	Pneumatic nailed		1736	.009		1.36	.47		1.83	2.21
0300	3/4" thick		1300	.012		1.47	.62		2.09	2.57
0305	Pneumatic nailed		1612	.010		1.47	.50		1.97	2.39
0500	Particle board, 3/8" thick G		1500	.011		.41	.54		.95	1.27
0505	Pneumatic nailed G		1860	.009		.41	.44		.85	1.11
0600	1/2" thick G		1450	.011		.43	.56		.99	1.32
0605	Pneumatic nailed G		1798	.009		.43	.45		.88	1.16
0800	5/8" thick G		1400	.011		.55	.58		1.13	1.49
0805	Pneumatic nailed G		1736	.009		.55	.47		1.02	1.32
0900	3/4" thick G		1300	.012		.67	.62		1.29	1.69
0905	Pneumatic nailed G		1612	.010		.67	.50		1.17	1.51
0955	Particleboard, 100% recycled straw/wheat, 4' x 8' x 1/4" G		1450	.011		.32	.56		.88	1.20
0960	4' x 8' x 3/8" G		1450	.011		.52	.56		1.08	1.42
0965	4' x 8' x 1/2" G		1350	.012		.64	.60		1.24	1.61
0970	4' x 8' x 5/8" G		1300	.012		.79	.62		1.41	1.82
0975	4' x 8' x 3/4" G		1250	.013		.87	.65		1.52	1.95
0980	4' x 8' x 1" G		1150	.014		1.18	.71		1.89	2.37
0985	4' x 8' x 1-1/4" G		1100	.015		1.31	.74		2.05	2.56
1100	Hardboard, underlayment grade, 4' x 4', .215" thick G		1500	.011		.68	.54		1.22	1.57
1200	1/4" thick G		1500	.011		.76	.54		1.30	1.66

06 16 33 – Wood Board Sheathing

06 16 33.10 Board Sheathing

		Crew	Daily Output	Labor-Hours	Unit	Material	Labor	Equipment	Total	Total Incl O&P
0009	**BOARD SHEATHING**									
0010	Roof, 1" x 6" boards, laid horizontal	2 Carp	725	.022	S.F.	1.70	1.12		2.82	3.56
0020	On steep roof		520	.031		1.70	1.56		3.26	4.24
0040	On dormers, hips, & valleys		480	.033		1.70	1.69		3.39	4.43
0050	Laid diagonal		650	.025		1.70	1.25		2.95	3.76
0070	1" x 8" boards, laid horizontal		875	.018		2.07	.93		3	3.69
0080	On steep roof		635	.025		2.07	1.28		3.35	4.23
0090	On dormers, hips, & valleys		580	.028		2.12	1.40		3.52	4.46
0100	Laid diagonal		725	.022		2.07	1.12		3.19	3.98
0110	Skip sheathing, 1" x 4", 7" OC	1 Carp	1200	.007		.63	.34		.97	1.21
0120	1" x 6", 9" OC		1450	.006		.78	.28		1.06	1.29
0180	T&G sheathing/decking, 1" x 6"		1000	.008		1.80	.41		2.21	2.60

06 16 Sheathing

06 16 33 – Wood Board Sheathing

06 16 33.10 Board Sheathing

		Crew	Daily Output	Labor-Hours	Unit	Material	2018 Bare Costs Labor	Equipment	Total	Total Incl O&P
0190	2" x 6"	1 Carp	1000	.008	S.F.	3.86	.41		4.27	4.87
0200	Walls, 1" x 6" boards, laid regular	2 Carp	650	.025		1.70	1.25		2.95	3.76
0210	Laid diagonal		585	.027		1.70	1.39		3.09	3.97
0220	1" x 8" boards, laid regular		765	.021		2.07	1.06		3.13	3.90
0230	Laid diagonal		650	.025		2.07	1.25		3.32	4.18

06 16 36 – Wood Panel Product Sheathing

06 16 36.10 Sheathing

		Crew	Daily Output	Labor-Hours	Unit	Material	Labor	Equipment	Total	Total Incl O&P
0010	SHEATHING R061636-20									
0012	Plywood on roofs, CDX									
0030	5/16" thick	2 Carp	1600	.010	S.F.	.59	.51		1.10	1.41
0035	Pneumatic nailed		1952	.008		.59	.42		1.01	1.27
0050	3/8" thick		1525	.010		.60	.53		1.13	1.47
0055	Pneumatic nailed		1860	.009		.60	.44		1.04	1.32
0100	1/2" thick		1400	.011		.62	.58		1.20	1.56
0105	Pneumatic nailed		1708	.009		.62	.48		1.10	1.40
0120	On steep roofs		1040	.015		.62	.78		1.40	1.87
0125	On steep roofs, pneumatic nailed		1270	.013		.62	.64		1.26	1.65
0140	On dormers, hips, & valleys		970	.016		.62	.84		1.46	1.95
0145	On dormers, hips, & valleys, pneumatic nailed		1270	.013		.62	.64		1.26	1.65
0200	5/8" thick		1300	.012		.77	.62		1.39	1.79
0205	Pneumatic nailed		1586	.010		.77	.51		1.28	1.62
0300	3/4" thick		1200	.013		.92	.68		1.60	2.05
0305	Pneumatic nailed		1464	.011		.92	.55		1.47	1.86
0400	Structural use APA exposure 1, 3/8" thick		1525	.010		.73	.53		1.26	1.61
0450	1/2" thick		1400	.011		.83	.58		1.41	1.80
0500	Plywood on walls, with exterior CDX, 3/8" thick		1200	.013		.60	.68		1.28	1.69
0505	Pneumatic nailed		1488	.011		.60	.55		1.15	1.49
0600	1/2" thick		1125	.014		.62	.72		1.34	1.78
0605	Pneumatic nailed		1395	.011		.62	.58		1.20	1.57
0700	5/8" thick		1050	.015		.77	.77		1.54	2.02
0705	Pneumatic nailed		1302	.012		.77	.62		1.39	1.79
0800	3/4" thick		975	.016		.92	.83		1.75	2.29
0805	Pneumatic nailed		1209	.013		.92	.67		1.59	2.04
0900	For exterior C-C grade plywood, add					15%				
0920	For application to metal studs, joists, rafters, add						20%			
1000	For shear wall construction, add						20%			
1200	For structural 1 exterior plywood, add				S.F.	10%				
3000	Wood fiber, regular, no vapor barrier, 1/2" thick	2 Carp	1200	.013		.64	.68		1.32	1.73
3100	5/8" thick		1200	.013		.70	.68		1.38	1.80
3300	No vapor barrier, in colors, 1/2" thick		1200	.013		.81	.68		1.49	1.92
3400	5/8" thick		1200	.013		.85	.68		1.53	1.97
3600	With vapor barrier one side, white, 1/2" thick		1200	.013		.63	.68		1.31	1.72
3700	Vapor barrier 2 sides, 1/2" thick		1200	.013		.84	.68		1.52	1.95
3800	Asphalt impregnated, 25/32" thick		1200	.013		.32	.68		1	1.38
3850	Intermediate, 1/2" thick		1200	.013		.32	.68		1	1.38
4500	Oriented strand board, on roof, 7/16" thick [G]		1460	.011		.48	.56		1.04	1.38
4505	Pneumatic nailed [G]		1780	.009		.48	.46		.94	1.22
4550	1/2" thick [G]		1400	.011		.48	.58		1.06	1.41
4555	Pneumatic nailed [G]		1736	.009		.48	.47		.95	1.24
4600	5/8" thick [G]		1300	.012		.54	.62		1.16	1.54
4605	Pneumatic nailed [G]		1586	.010		.54	.51		1.05	1.37
4610	On walls, 7/16" thick [G]		1200	.013		.48	.68		1.16	1.56

For customer support on your Green Building Costs with RSMeans data, call 800.448.8182.

06 16 Sheathing

06 16 36 – Wood Panel Product Sheathing

06 16 36.10 Sheathing

		Crew	Daily Output	Labor-Hours	Unit	Material	2018 Bare Costs Labor	Equipment	Total	Total Incl O&P
4615	Pneumatic nailed	G 2 Carp	1488	.011	S.F.	.48	.55		1.03	1.36
4620	1/2" thick	G	1195	.013		.48	.68		1.16	1.56
4625	Pneumatic nailed	G	1325	.012		.48	.61		1.09	1.46
4630	5/8" thick	G	1050	.015		.54	.77		1.31	1.77
4635	Pneumatic nailed	G	1302	.012		.54	.62		1.16	1.54
4700	Oriented strand board, factory laminated W.R. barrier, on roof, 1/2" thick	G	1400	.011		.75	.58		1.33	1.71
4705	Pneumatic nailed	G	1736	.009		.75	.47		1.22	1.54
4720	5/8" thick	G	1300	.012		.91	.62		1.53	1.95
4725	Pneumatic nailed	G	1586	.010		.91	.51		1.42	1.78
4730	5/8" thick, T&G	G	1150	.014		1.09	.71		1.80	2.27
4735	Pneumatic nailed, T&G	G	1400	.011		1.09	.58		1.67	2.08
4740	On walls, 7/16" thick	G	1200	.013		.69	.68		1.37	1.79
4745	Pneumatic nailed	G	1488	.011		.69	.55		1.24	1.59
4750	1/2" thick	G	1195	.013		.75	.68		1.43	1.86
4755	Pneumatic nailed	G	1325	.012		.75	.61		1.36	1.76
4800	Joint sealant tape, 3-1/2"		7600	.002	L.F.	.28	.11		.39	.47
4810	Joint sealant tape, 6"		7600	.002	"	.41	.11		.52	.61

06 16 43 – Gypsum Sheathing

06 16 43.10 Gypsum Sheathing

		Crew	Daily Output	Labor-Hours	Unit	Material	Labor	Equipment	Total	Total Incl O&P
0010	**GYPSUM SHEATHING**									
0020	Gypsum, weatherproof, 1/2" thick	2 Carp	1125	.014	S.F.	.46	.72		1.18	1.61
0040	With embedded glass mats	"	1100	.015	"	.71	.74		1.45	1.90

06 18 Glued-Laminated Construction

06 18 13 – Glued-Laminated Beams

06 18 13.20 Laminated Framing

		Crew	Daily Output	Labor-Hours	Unit	Material	Labor	Equipment	Total	Total Incl O&P
0010	**LAMINATED FRAMING**									
0200	Straight roof beams, 20' clear span, beams 8' OC	F-3	2560	.016	SF Flr.	2.26	.81	.19	3.26	3.93
0300	Beams 16' OC		3200	.013		1.65	.65	.16	2.46	2.97
0500	40' clear span, beams 8' OC		3200	.013		4.29	.65	.16	5.10	5.85
0600	Beams 16' OC		3840	.010		3.54	.54	.13	4.21	4.85
0800	60' clear span, beams 8' OC	F-4	2880	.017		7.35	.85	.35	8.55	9.80
0900	Beams 16' OC	"	3840	.013		5.50	.64	.26	6.40	7.30
1100	Tudor arches, 30' to 40' clear span, frames 8' OC	F-3	1680	.024		9.60	1.23	.30	11.13	12.75
1200	Frames 16' OC	"	2240	.018		7.50	.92	.22	8.64	9.90
1400	50' to 60' clear span, frames 8' OC	F-4	2200	.022		10.30	1.12	.45	11.87	13.55
1500	Frames 16' OC		2640	.018		8.80	.93	.38	10.11	11.50
1700	Radial arches, 60' clear span, frames 8' OC		1920	.025		9.65	1.28	.52	11.45	13.15
1800	Frames 16' OC		2880	.017		7.65	.85	.35	8.85	10.10
2000	100' clear span, frames 8' OC		1600	.030		9.95	1.54	.62	12.11	13.95
2100	Frames 16' OC		2400	.020		8.80	1.03	.41	10.24	11.65
2300	120' clear span, frames 8' OC		1440	.033		13.25	1.71	.69	15.65	17.90
2400	Frames 16' OC		1920	.025		12.10	1.28	.52	13.90	15.80
2600	Bowstring trusses, 20' OC, 40' clear span	F-3	2400	.017		6	.86	.21	7.07	8.15
2700	60' clear span	F-4	3600	.013		5.40	.68	.28	6.36	7.30
2800	100' clear span		4000	.012		7.65	.62	.25	8.52	9.60
2900	120' clear span		3600	.013		8.10	.68	.28	9.06	10.25
3000	For less than 1000 B.F., add					20%				
3050	For over 5000 B.F., deduct					10%				
3100	For premium appearance, add to S.F. prices					5%				

06 18 Glued-Laminated Construction

06 18 13 – Glued-Laminated Beams

06 18 13.20 Laminated Framing

		Crew	Daily Output	Labor-Hours	Unit	Material	2018 Bare Costs Labor	Equipment	Total	Total Incl O&P
3300	For industrial type, deduct				SF Flr.	15%				
3500	For stain and varnish, add					5%				
3900	For 3/4" laminations, add to straight					25%				
4100	Add to curved					15%				
4300	Alternate pricing method: (use nominal footage of									
4310	components). Straight beams, camber less than 6"	F-3	3.50	11.429	M.B.F.	3,175	590	142	3,907	4,550
4400	Columns, including hardware		2	20		3,425	1,025	248	4,698	5,600
4600	Curved members, radius over 32'		2.50	16		3,500	830	198	4,528	5,325
4700	Radius 10' to 32'		3	13.333		3,475	690	165	4,330	5,025
4900	For complicated shapes, add maximum					100%				
5100	For pressure treating, add to straight					35%				
5200	Add to curved					45%				
6000	Laminated veneer members, southern pine or western species									
6050	1-3/4" wide x 5-1/2" deep	2 Carp	480	.033	L.F.	3.47	1.69		5.16	6.40
6100	9-1/2" deep		480	.033		4.25	1.69		5.94	7.25
6150	14" deep		450	.036		7.35	1.80		9.15	10.85
6200	18" deep		450	.036		10.30	1.80		12.10	14.05
6300	Parallel strand members, southern pine or western species									
6350	1-3/4" wide x 9-1/4" deep	2 Carp	480	.033	L.F.	4.77	1.69		6.46	7.80
6400	11-1/4" deep		450	.036		4.94	1.80		6.74	8.20
6450	14" deep		400	.040		7.60	2.03		9.63	11.45
6500	3-1/2" wide x 9-1/4" deep		480	.033		16.10	1.69		17.79	20.50
6550	11-1/4" deep		450	.036		19.90	1.80		21.70	25
6600	14" deep		400	.040		22.50	2.03		24.53	27.50
6650	7" wide x 9-1/4" deep		450	.036		33.50	1.80		35.30	40
6700	11-1/4" deep		420	.038		42	1.93		43.93	49.50
6750	14" deep		400	.040		50	2.03		52.03	58

06 25 Prefinished Paneling

06 25 13 – Prefinished Hardboard Paneling

06 25 13.10 Paneling, Hardboard

			Crew	Daily Output	Labor-Hours	Unit	Material	Labor	Equipment	Total	Total Incl O&P
0010	**PANELING, HARDBOARD**										
0050	Not incl. furring or trim, hardboard, tempered, 1/8" thick	G	2 Carp	500	.032	S.F.	.45	1.62		2.07	2.97
0100	1/4" thick	G		500	.032		.64	1.62		2.26	3.17
0200	Plastic faced, 1/4" thick	G		500	.032		.83	1.62		2.45	3.38
0300	Tempered pegboard, 1/8" thick	G		500	.032		.44	1.62		2.06	2.95
0400	1/4" thick	G		500	.032		.70	1.62		2.32	3.24
0500	Plastic faced, 1/4" thick	G		500	.032		.90	1.62		2.52	3.46
0600	Untempered hardboard, natural finish, 1/8" thick	G		500	.032		.44	1.62		2.06	2.95
0700	1/4" thick	G		500	.032		.53	1.62		2.15	3.05
0800	Plastic faced, 1/4" thick	G		500	.032		.70	1.62		2.32	3.24
0900	Untempered pegboard, 1/8" thick	G		500	.032		.48	1.62		2.10	3
1000	1/4" thick	G		500	.032		.48	1.62		2.10	3
1100	Plastic faced, 1/4" thick	G		500	.032		.95	1.62		2.57	3.52
1200	Plastic faced hardboard, 1/8" thick	G		500	.032		.62	1.62		2.24	3.15
1300	1/4" thick	G		500	.032		.84	1.62		2.46	3.39
1500	Plastic faced pegboard, 1/8" thick	G		500	.032		.62	1.62		2.24	3.15
1600	1/4" thick	G		500	.032		.80	1.62		2.42	3.35
1800	Wood grained, plain or grooved, 1/8" thick	G		500	.032		.65	1.62		2.27	3.19
1900	1/4" thick	G		425	.038		1.42	1.91		3.33	4.47
2100	Moldings, wood grained MDF			500	.032	L.F.	.41	1.62		2.03	2.92

For customer support on your Green Building Costs with RSMeans data, call 800.448.8182.

06 25 Prefinished Paneling

06 25 13 – Prefinished Hardboard Paneling

06 25 13.10 Paneling, Hardboard

		Crew	Daily Output	Labor-Hours	Unit	Material	2018 Bare Costs Labor	Equipment	Total	Total Incl O&P
2200	Pine	2 Carp	425	.038	L.F.	1.41	1.91		3.32	4.46
2210	Plastic	1 Carp	400	.020	↓	.79	1.01		1.80	2.41
2300	For ceiling installation, add						30%			
2310	For installation on metal studs or furring, add						11%			
2320	For glue down installation, add					5%	5%			
2330	For 10' or 12' long panels, add					60%				

06 25 16 – Prefinished Plywood Paneling

06 25 16.10 Paneling, Plywood

		Crew	Daily Output	Labor-Hours	Unit	Material	Labor	Equipment	Total	Total Incl O&P
0010	**PANELING, PLYWOOD** R061636-20									
0100	Unfinished, 1/4" thick, with trim, birch, natural	2 Carp	445	.036	S.F.	1.39	1.82		3.21	4.31
0120	Select		445	.036		1.35	1.82		3.17	4.27
0200	Cedar, standard grade		355	.045		1.57	2.29		3.86	5.20
0220	Particle board		355	.045		.95	2.29		3.24	4.53
0300	Knotty pine, grade AA		400	.040		2.02	2.03		4.05	5.30
0320	Grade AD	↓	400	.040	↓	1.63	2.03		3.66	4.88
0800	For waterproof glue, add					7%				
0810	For ceiling installation, add						30%			
0820	For installation on metal studs or furring, add						11%			
0830	For glue down installation, add					5%	5%			
0840	For lumber core, add					11%				
0850	For 10' or 12' long panels, add					60%				
0860	For 1/8" thick paneling, deduct					25%	7%			
0870	For 1/2" thick paneling, add					34%	12%			
0880	For 5/8" thick paneling, add					45%	12%			
0890	For 3/4" thick paneling, add					50%	12%			
1000	Unfinished, plywood, 1/4" thick, lauan	2 Carp	500	.032	S.F.	.62	1.62		2.24	3.16
1020	Birch		500	.032		1.32	1.62		2.94	3.92
1040	Ash		500	.032		1.63	1.62		3.25	4.26
1060	Oak		500	.032		1.31	1.62		2.93	3.91
1500	Prefinished, plywood, 1/8" thick		450	.036		.41	1.80		2.21	3.20
1520	Photo print		450	.036		.81	1.80		2.61	3.64
1540	Wood veneer		450	.036		1.19	1.80		2.99	4.06
1560	Plywood back	↓	450	.036		1.19	1.80		2.99	4.06
1600	Hardboard, smooth, solid color	1 Carp	400	.020		.41	1.01		1.42	1.99
1620	Patterned color		400	.020		.69	1.01		1.70	2.30
1640	Textured, solid color		400	.020		.93	1.01		1.94	2.57
1660	Patterned color	↓	400	.020	↓	1.25	1.01		2.26	2.91
2400	Plywood, prefinished, 1/4" thick, 4' x 8' sheets									
2410	with vertical grooves. Birch faced, economy	2 Carp	500	.032	S.F.	1.47	1.62		3.09	4.09
2415	Wall paneling, 1/4" plywood-backed					1.20			1.20	1.32
2420	Average	2 Carp	420	.038	↓	1.20	1.93		3.13	4.26
2421	Average		13.13	1.219	Ea.	38.50	62		100.50	136
2425	Average, per sheet		13.13	1.219	"	38.50	62		100.50	136
2430	Custom		350	.046	S.F.	1.10	2.32		3.42	4.74
2600	Mahogany, African		400	.040		2.45	2.03		4.48	5.80
2700	Philippine (Lauan)		500	.032		.65	1.62		2.27	3.19
2900	Oak		500	.032		1.34	1.62		2.96	3.94
3000	Cherry		400	.040		2	2.03		4.03	5.30
3200	Rosewood		320	.050		3.10	2.54		5.64	7.25
3400	Teak		400	.040		3.12	2.03		5.15	6.50
3600	Chestnut		375	.043		5.30	2.16		7.46	9.10
3800	Pecan		400	.040	↓	2.50	2.03		4.53	5.85

06 25 Prefinished Paneling

06 25 16 – Prefinished Plywood Paneling

06 25 16.10 Paneling, Plywood		Crew	Daily Output	Labor-Hours	Unit	Material	2018 Bare Costs Labor	Equipment	Total	Total Incl O&P
3900	Walnut, average	2 Carp	500	.032	S.F.	2.47	1.62		4.09	5.20
3950	Custom		400	.040		2.46	2.03		4.49	5.80
3960	Install paneling capping	1 Carp	175	.046	L.F.	.53	2.32		2.85	4.11
4000	Plywood, prefinished, 3/4" thick, stock grades, economy	2 Carp	320	.050	S.F.	1.44	2.54		3.98	5.45
4100	Average		224	.071		4.93	3.62		8.55	10.90
4300	Architectural grade, custom		224	.071		5.40	3.62		9.02	11.40
4400	Luxury		160	.100		5.30	5.05		10.35	13.50
4600	Plywood, "A" face, birch, VC, 1/2" thick, natural		450	.036		1.38	1.80		3.18	4.27
4700	Select		450	.036		1.95	1.80		3.75	4.90
4900	Veneer core, 3/4" thick, natural		320	.050		2.25	2.54		4.79	6.35
4910	Wall paneling, 3/4" plywood-backed					2.25			2.25	2.48
5000	Select	2 Carp	320	.050		2.53	2.54		5.07	6.65
5200	Lumber core, 3/4" thick, natural		320	.050		3.14	2.54		5.68	7.30
5300	Select		320	.050		3.11	2.54		5.65	7.30
5500	Plywood, knotty pine, 1/4" thick, A2 grade		450	.036		1.53	1.80		3.33	4.43
5600	A3 grade		450	.036		2.09	1.80		3.89	5.05
5800	3/4" thick, veneer core, A2 grade		320	.050		2.31	2.54		4.85	6.40
5900	A3 grade		320	.050		2.39	2.54		4.93	6.50
6100	Aromatic cedar, 1/4" thick, plywood		400	.040		2.25	2.03		4.28	5.55
6200	1/4" thick, particle board		400	.040		1.15	2.03		3.18	4.36
6400	Bamboo, unfinished, 4' x 8' x 3/4" T G		320	.050		8.95	2.54		11.49	13.70
6410	1' W x 6' L x 3/4" T G		250	.064		6.25	3.24		9.49	11.85
6420	Finished, 1' W x 6' L x 3/4" T G		250	.064		7.50	3.24		10.74	13.20
8000	Construction adhesive for, 99% VOC free, 10.5 oz. tube				Ea.	3.77			3.77	4.15

06 51 Structural Plastic Shapes and Plates

06 51 13 – Plastic Lumber

06 51 13.10 Recycled Plastic Lumber

			Crew	Daily Output	Labor-Hours	Unit	Material	Labor	Equipment	Total	Total Incl O&P
0010	**RECYCLED PLASTIC LUMBER**										
4000	Sheeting, recycled plastic, black or white, 4' x 8' x 1/8"	G	2 Carp	1100	.015	S.F.	1.09	.74		1.83	2.32
4010	4' x 8' x 3/16"	G		1100	.015		1.51	.74		2.25	2.78
4020	4' x 8' x 1/4"	G		950	.017		1.81	.85		2.66	3.29
4030	4' x 8' x 3/8"	G		950	.017		3.02	.85		3.87	4.62
4040	4' x 8' x 1/2"	G		900	.018		4.03	.90		4.93	5.80
4050	4' x 8' x 5/8"	G		900	.018		6	.90		6.90	7.95
4060	4' x 8' x 3/4"	G		850	.019		7.50	.95		8.45	9.70
4070	Add for colors	G				Ea.	5%				
8500	100% recycled plastic, var colors, NLB, 2" x 2"	G				L.F.	1.90			1.90	2.09
8510	2" x 4"	G					3.90			3.90	4.29
8520	2" x 6"	G					6.10			6.10	6.75
8530	2" x 8"	G					8.60			8.60	9.50
8540	2" x 10"	G					12.25			12.25	13.50
8550	5/4" x 4"	G					4.58			4.58	5.05
8560	5/4" x 6"	G					5.70			5.70	6.25
8570	1" x 6"	G					2.83			2.83	3.11
8580	1/2" x 8"	G					3.32			3.32	3.65
8590	2" x 10" T&G	G					12.65			12.65	13.90
8600	3" x 10" T&G	G					18.95			18.95	21
8610	Add for premium colors	G					20%				

For customer support on your Green Building Costs with RSMeans data, call 800.448.8182.

113

06 51 Structural Plastic Shapes and Plates

06 51 13 – Plastic Lumber

06 51 13.12 Structural Plastic Lumber		Crew	Daily Output	Labor-Hours	Unit	Material	2018 Bare Costs Labor	Equipment	Total	Total Incl O&P
0010	**STRUCTURAL PLASTIC LUMBER**									
1320	Plastic lumber, posts or columns, 4" x 4"	2 Carp	390	.041	L.F.	11.10	2.08		13.18	15.40
1325	4" x 6"		275	.058		13.30	2.95		16.25	19.15
1330	4" x 8"		220	.073		19.55	3.69		23.24	27
1340	Girder, single, 4" x 4"		675	.024		11.10	1.20		12.30	14.10
1345	4" x 6"		600	.027		13.30	1.35		14.65	16.70
1350	4" x 8"		525	.030		19.55	1.55		21.10	24
1352	Double, 2" x 4"		625	.026		7.95	1.30		9.25	10.75
1354	2" x 6"		600	.027		9.65	1.35		11	12.65
1356	2" x 8"		575	.028		16.85	1.41		18.26	20.50
1358	2" x 10"		550	.029		23.50	1.47		24.97	28.50
1360	2" x 12"		525	.030		25	1.55		26.55	30
1362	Triple, 2" x 4"		575	.028		11.90	1.41		13.31	15.25
1364	2" x 6"		550	.029		14.45	1.47		15.92	18.15
1366	2" x 8"		525	.030		25	1.55		26.55	30.50
1368	2" x 10"		500	.032		35.50	1.62		37.12	41.50
1370	2" x 12"		475	.034		37.50	1.71		39.21	43.50
1372	Ledger, bolted 4' OC, 2" x 4"		400	.040		4.12	2.03		6.15	7.60
1374	2" x 6"		550	.029		4.89	1.47		6.36	7.65
1376	2" x 8"		390	.041		8.55	2.08		10.63	12.55
1378	2" x 10"		385	.042		11.90	2.11		14.01	16.30
1380	2" x 12"		380	.042		12.60	2.14		14.74	17.10
1382	Joists, 2" x 4"		1250	.013		3.97	.65		4.62	5.35
1384	2" x 6"		1250	.013		4.83	.65		5.48	6.30
1386	2" x 8"		1100	.015		8.40	.74		9.14	10.35
1388	2" x 10"		500	.032		11.90	1.62		13.52	15.55
1390	2" x 12"		875	.018		12.50	.93		13.43	15.15
1392	Railings and trim, 5/4" x 4"	1 Carp	300	.027		4.35	1.35		5.70	6.85
1394	2" x 2"		300	.027		1.91	1.35		3.26	4.16
1396	2" x 4"		300	.027		3.95	1.35		5.30	6.40
1398	2" x 6"		300	.027		4.79	1.35		6.14	7.30

Division 7 — Thermal & Moisture Protection

Estimating Tips
07 10 00 Dampproofing and Waterproofing
- Be sure of the job specifications before pricing this subdivision. The difference in cost between waterproofing and dampproofing can be great. Waterproofing will hold back standing water. Dampproofing prevents the transmission of water vapor. Also included in this section are vapor retarding membranes.

07 20 00 Thermal Protection
- Insulation and fireproofing products are measured by area, thickness, volume or R-value. Specifications may give only what the specific R-value should be in a certain situation. The estimator may need to choose the type of insulation to meet that R-value.

07 30 00 Steep Slope Roofing
07 40 00 Roofing and Siding Panels
- Many roofing and siding products are bought and sold by the square. One square is equal to an area that measures 100 square feet.

  This simple change in unit of measure could create a large error if the estimator is not observant. Accessories necessary for a complete installation must be figured into any calculations for both material and labor.

07 50 00 Membrane Roofing
07 60 00 Flashing and Sheet Metal
07 70 00 Roofing and Wall Specialties and Accessories
- The items in these subdivisions compose a roofing system. No one component completes the installation, and all must be estimated. Built-up or single-ply membrane roofing systems are made up of many products and installation trades. Wood blocking at roof perimeters or penetrations, parapet coverings, reglets, roof drains, gutters, downspouts, sheet metal flashing, skylights, smoke vents, and roof hatches all need to be considered along with the roofing material. Several different installation trades will need to work together on the roofing system. Inherent difficulties in the scheduling and coordination of various trades must be accounted for when estimating labor costs.

07 90 00 Joint Protection
- To complete the weather-tight shell, the sealants and caulkings must be estimated. Where different materials meet—at expansion joints, at flashing penetrations, and at hundreds of other locations throughout a construction project—caulking and sealants provide another line of defense against water penetration. Often, an entire system is based on the proper location and placement of caulking or sealants. The detailed drawings that are included as part of a set of architectural plans show typical locations for these materials. When caulking or sealants are shown at typical locations, this means the estimator must include them for all the locations where this detail is applicable. Be careful to keep different types of sealants separate, and remember to consider backer rods and primers if necessary.

Reference Numbers
Reference numbers are shown at the beginning of some major classifications. These numbers refer to related items in the Reference Section. The reference information may be an estimating procedure, an alternate pricing method, or technical information.

Note: Not all subdivisions listed here necessarily appear. ■

Did you know?
RSMeans data is available through our online application with 24/7 access:
- Search for unit prices by keyword
- Leverage the most up-to-date data
- Build and export estimates

Try it free for 30 days!
www.rsmeans.com/2018freetrial

No part of this cost data may be reproduced, stored in a retrieval system, or transmitted in any form or by any means without prior written permission of Gordian.

07 01 Operation and Maint. of Thermal and Moisture Protection

07 01 50 – Maintenance of Membrane Roofing

07 01 50.10 Roof Coatings

		Crew	Daily Output	Labor-Hours	Unit	Material	2018 Bare Costs Labor	Equipment	Total	Total Incl O&P
0010	**ROOF COATINGS**									
0012	Asphalt, brush grade, material only				Gal.	8.85			8.85	9.75
0200	Asphalt base, fibered aluminum coating	G				8.40			8.40	9.25
0300	Asphalt primer, 5 gal.					7.50			7.50	8.25
0600	Coal tar pitch, 200 lb. barrels				Ton	1,250			1,250	1,375
0700	Tar roof cement, 5 gal. lots				Gal.	14.25			14.25	15.65
0800	Glass fibered roof & patching cement, 5 gal.				"	8.40			8.40	9.25
0900	Reinforcing glass membrane, 450 S.F./roll				Ea.	59.50			59.50	65.50
1000	Neoprene roof coating, 5 gal., 2 gal./sq.				Gal.	30.50			30.50	33.50
1100	Roof patch & flashing cement, 5 gal.					8.90			8.90	9.80
1200	Roof resaturant, glass fibered, 3 gal./sq.					9.65			9.65	10.60
1600	Reflective roof coating, white, elastomeric, approx. 50 S.F./gal.	G				17.20			17.20	18.90

07 21 Thermal Insulation

07 21 13 – Board Insulation

07 21 13.10 Rigid Insulation

			Crew	Daily Output	Labor-Hours	Unit	Material	Labor	Equipment	Total	Total Incl O&P
0010	**RIGID INSULATION**, for walls										
0020	Fiberboard, 3/4" thick, R2.08	G	1 Carp	1100	.007	S.F.	.42	.37		.79	1.02
0025	1" thick, R2.78	G		800	.010		.56	.51		1.07	1.39
0030	2" thick, R5.26	G		730	.011		1.08	.56		1.64	2.04
0040	Fiberglass, 1.5#/C.F., unfaced, 1" thick, R4.1	G		1000	.008		.34	.41		.75	.99
0060	1-1/2" thick, R6.2	G		1000	.008		.40	.41		.81	1.06
0080	2" thick, R8.3	G		1000	.008		.50	.41		.91	1.17
0120	3" thick, R12.4	G		800	.010		.60	.51		1.11	1.43
0370	3#/C.F., unfaced, 1" thick, R4.3	G		1000	.008		.54	.41		.95	1.21
0390	1-1/2" thick, R6.5	G		1000	.008		.79	.41		1.20	1.49
0400	2" thick, R8.7	G		890	.009		1.07	.46		1.53	1.87
0420	2-1/2" thick, R10.9	G		800	.010		1.11	.51		1.62	1.99
0440	3" thick, R13	G		800	.010		1.62	.51		2.13	2.55
0520	Foil faced, 1" thick, R4.3	G		1000	.008		.84	.41		1.25	1.54
0540	1-1/2" thick, R6.5	G		1000	.008		1.25	.41		1.66	2
0560	2" thick, R8.7	G		890	.009		1.58	.46		2.04	2.43
0580	2-1/2" thick, R10.9	G		800	.010		1.86	.51		2.37	2.82
0600	3" thick, R13	G		800	.010		2.09	.51		2.60	3.07
1600	Isocyanurate, 4' x 8' sheet, foil faced, both sides										
1610	1/2" thick	G	1 Carp	800	.010	S.F.	.31	.51		.82	1.11
1620	5/8" thick	G		800	.010		.48	.51		.99	1.30
1630	3/4" thick	G		800	.010		.45	.51		.96	1.27
1640	1" thick	G		800	.010		.61	.51		1.12	1.44
1650	1-1/2" thick	G		730	.011		.67	.56		1.23	1.59
1660	2" thick	G		730	.011		.90	.56		1.46	1.84
1670	3" thick	G		730	.011		2.76	.56		3.32	3.89
1680	4" thick	G		730	.011		2.52	.56		3.08	3.62
1700	Perlite, 1" thick, R2.77	G		800	.010		.47	.51		.98	1.29
1750	2" thick, R5.55	G		730	.011		.78	.56		1.34	1.71
1900	Extruded polystyrene, 25 psi compressive strength, 1" thick, R5	G		800	.010		.57	.51		1.08	1.40
1940	2" thick, R10	G		730	.011		1.14	.56		1.70	2.10
1960	3" thick, R15	G		730	.011		1.59	.56		2.15	2.60
2100	Expanded polystyrene, 1" thick, R3.85	G		800	.010		.27	.51		.78	1.07
2120	2" thick, R7.69	G		730	.011		.54	.56		1.10	1.44
2140	3" thick, R11.49	G		730	.011		.81	.56		1.37	1.74

07 21 Thermal Insulation

07 21 13 – Board Insulation

07 21 13.10 Rigid Insulation

		Crew	Daily Output	Labor-Hours	Unit	Material	2018 Bare Costs Labor	Equipment	Total	Total Incl O&P
2360	Fiberboard, low density, 1/2" thick, R1.39	G 1 Carp	750	.011	S.F.	.35	.54		.89	1.21
2400	Wood fiber, 1" thick, R3.85	G	1000	.008		.56	.41		.97	1.24
2410	2" thick, R7.7	G	1000	.008		1.08	.41		1.49	1.81
2680	Mineral fiberboard, rigid, 1" thick, R4.2	G	800	.010		.56	.51		1.07	1.39
2700	2" thick, R8.4	G	730	.011		1.08	.56		1.64	2.04

07 21 13.13 Foam Board Insulation

0010	**FOAM BOARD INSULATION**									
0600	Polystyrene, expanded, 1" thick, R4	G 1 Carp	680	.012	S.F.	.27	.60		.87	1.21
0700	2" thick, R8	G "	675	.012	"	.54	.60		1.14	1.50

07 21 16 – Blanket Insulation

07 21 16.10 Blanket Insulation for Floors/Ceilings

0010	**BLANKET INSULATION FOR FLOORS/CEILINGS**									
0020	Including spring type wire fasteners									
2000	Fiberglass, blankets or batts, paper or foil backing									
2100	3-1/2" thick, R13	G 1 Carp	700	.011	S.F.	.41	.58		.99	1.33
2150	6-1/4" thick, R19	G	600	.013		.51	.68		1.19	1.59
2210	9-1/2" thick, R30	G	500	.016		.73	.81		1.54	2.04
2220	12" thick, R38	G	475	.017		1.05	.85		1.90	2.46
3000	Unfaced, 3-1/2" thick, R13	G	600	.013		.33	.68		1.01	1.39
3010	6-1/4" thick, R19	G	500	.016		.39	.81		1.20	1.67
3020	9-1/2" thick, R30	G	450	.018		.60	.90		1.50	2.03
3030	12" thick, R38	G	425	.019		.75	.95		1.70	2.28

07 21 16.20 Blanket Insulation for Walls

0010	**BLANKET INSULATION FOR WALLS**									
0020	Kraft faced fiberglass, 3-1/2" thick, R11, 15" wide	G 1 Carp	1350	.006	S.F.	.32	.30		.62	.81
0030	23" wide	G	1600	.005		.32	.25		.57	.74
0060	R13, 11" wide	G	1150	.007		.34	.35		.69	.91
0080	15" wide	G	1350	.006		.34	.30		.64	.83
0100	23" wide	G	1600	.005		.34	.25		.59	.76
0110	R15, 11" wide	G	1150	.007		.49	.35		.84	1.08
0120	15" wide	G	1350	.006		.49	.30		.79	1
0130	23" wide	G	1600	.005		.49	.25		.74	.93
0140	6" thick, R19, 11" wide	G	1150	.007		.44	.35		.79	1.02
0160	15" wide	G	1350	.006		.44	.30		.74	.94
0180	23" wide	G	1600	.005		.44	.25		.69	.87
0182	R21, 11" wide	G	1150	.007		.66	.35		1.01	1.27
0184	15" wide	G	1350	.006		.66	.30		.96	1.19
0186	23" wide	G	1600	.005		.66	.25		.91	1.12
0188	9" thick, R30, 11" wide	G	985	.008		.73	.41		1.14	1.43
0200	15" wide	G	1150	.007		.73	.35		1.08	1.34
0220	23" wide	G	1350	.006		.73	.30		1.03	1.26
0230	12" thick, R38, 11" wide	G	985	.008		1.05	.41		1.46	1.79
0240	15" wide	G	1150	.007		1.05	.35		1.40	1.70
0260	23" wide	G	1350	.006		1.05	.30		1.35	1.62
0410	Foil faced fiberglass, 3-1/2" thick, R13, 11" wide	G	1150	.007		.47	.35		.82	1.06
0420	15" wide	G	1350	.006		.47	.30		.77	.98
0440	23" wide	G	1600	.005		.47	.25		.72	.91
0442	R15, 11" wide	G	1150	.007		.48	.35		.83	1.07
0444	15" wide	G	1350	.006		.48	.30		.78	.99
0446	23" wide	G	1600	.005		.48	.25		.73	.92
0448	6" thick, R19, 11" wide	G	1150	.007		.62	.35		.97	1.22
0460	15" wide	G	1350	.006		.62	.30		.92	1.14

For customer support on your Green Building Costs with RSMeans data, call 800.448.8182.

07 21 Thermal Insulation

07 21 16 – Blanket Insulation

07 21 16.20 Blanket Insulation for Walls

			Crew	Daily Output	Labor-Hours	Unit	Material	2018 Bare Costs Labor	Equipment	Total	Total Incl O&P
0480	23" wide	G	1 Carp	1600	.005	S.F.	.62	.25		.87	1.07
0482	R21, 11" wide	G		1150	.007		.64	.35		.99	1.24
0484	15" wide	G		1350	.006		.64	.30		.94	1.16
0486	23" wide	G		1600	.005		.64	.25		.89	1.09
0488	9" thick, R30, 11" wide	G		985	.008		.94	.41		1.35	1.66
0500	15" wide	G		1150	.007		.94	.35		1.29	1.57
0550	23" wide	G		1350	.006		.94	.30		1.24	1.49
0560	12" thick, R38, 11" wide	G		985	.008		1.15	.41		1.56	1.90
0570	15" wide	G		1150	.007		1.15	.35		1.50	1.81
0580	23" wide	G		1350	.006		1.15	.30		1.45	1.73
0620	Unfaced fiberglass, 3-1/2" thick, R13, 11" wide	G		1150	.007		.33	.35		.68	.90
0820	15" wide	G		1350	.006		.33	.30		.63	.82
0830	23" wide	G		1600	.005		.33	.25		.58	.75
0832	R15, 11" wide	G		1150	.007		.46	.35		.81	1.05
0834	15" wide	G		1350	.006		.46	.30		.76	.97
0836	23" wide	G		1600	.005		.46	.25		.71	.90
0838	6" thick, R19, 11" wide	G		1150	.007		.39	.35		.74	.97
0860	15" wide	G		1150	.007		.39	.35		.74	.97
0880	23" wide	G		1350	.006		.39	.30		.69	.89
0882	R21, 11" wide	G		1150	.007		.69	.35		1.04	1.30
0886	15" wide	G		1350	.006		.69	.30		.99	1.22
0888	23" wide	G		1600	.005		.69	.25		.94	1.15
0890	9" thick, R30, 11" wide	G		985	.008		.60	.41		1.01	1.29
0900	15" wide	G		1150	.007		.60	.35		.95	1.20
0920	23" wide	G		1350	.006		.60	.30		.90	1.12
0930	12" thick, R38, 11" wide	G		985	.008		.75	.41		1.16	1.46
0940	15" wide	G		1000	.008		.75	.41		1.16	1.45
0960	23" wide	G		1150	.007		.75	.35		1.10	1.37
1300	Wall or ceiling insulation, mineral wool batts										
1320	3-1/2" thick, R15	G	1 Carp	1600	.005	S.F.	.77	.25		1.02	1.24
1340	5-1/2" thick, R23	G		1600	.005		1.21	.25		1.46	1.72
1380	7-1/4" thick, R30	G		1350	.006		1.60	.30		1.90	2.21
1700	Non-rigid insul., recycled blue cotton fiber, unfaced batts, R13, 16" wide	G		1600	.005		.99	.25		1.24	1.48
1710	R19, 16" wide	G		1600	.005		1.35	.25		1.60	1.88

07 21 19 – Foamed In Place Insulation

07 21 19.10 Masonry Foamed In Place Insulation

			Crew	Daily Output	Labor-Hours	Unit	Material	Labor	Equipment	Total	Total Incl O&P
0010	**MASONRY FOAMED IN PLACE INSULATION**										
0100	Amino-plast foam, injected into block core, 6" block	G	G-2A	6000	.004	Ea.	.17	.16	.10	.43	.55
0110	8" block	G		5000	.005		.20	.19	.12	.51	.66
0120	10" block			4000	.006		.25	.23	.15	.63	.83
0130	12" block	G		3000	.008		.34	.31	.20	.85	1.12
0140	Injected into cavity wall	G		13000	.002	B.F.	.06	.07	.05	.18	.24
0150	Preparation, drill holes into mortar joint every 4 V.L.F., 5/8" diameter		1 Clab	960	.008	Ea.		.33		.33	.51
0160	7/8" diameter			680	.012			.47		.47	.71
0170	Patch drilled holes, 5/8" diameter			1800	.004		.04	.18		.22	.31
0180	7/8" diameter			1200	.007		.05	.27		.32	.46

07 21 23 – Loose-Fill Insulation

07 21 23.10 Poured Loose-Fill Insulation

			Crew	Daily Output	Labor-Hours	Unit	Material	Labor	Equipment	Total	Total Incl O&P
0010	**POURED LOOSE-FILL INSULATION**										
0020	Cellulose fiber, R3.8 per inch	G	1 Carp	200	.040	C.F.	.69	2.03		2.72	3.85
0021	4" thick	G		1000	.008	S.F.	.17	.41		.58	.80
0022	6" thick	G		800	.010	"	.28	.51		.79	1.08

07 21 Thermal Insulation

07 21 23 – Loose-Fill Insulation

07 21 23.10 Poured Loose-Fill Insulation

		Crew	Daily Output	Labor-Hours	Unit	Material	2018 Bare Costs Labor	Equipment	Total	Total Incl O&P
0080	Fiberglass wool, R4 per inch	G 1 Carp	200	.040	C.F.	.62	2.03		2.65	3.77
0081	4" thick	G	600	.013	S.F.	.21	.68		.89	1.26
0082	6" thick	G	400	.020	"	.30	1.01		1.31	1.87
0100	Mineral wool, R3 per inch	G	200	.040	C.F.	.49	2.03		2.52	3.63
0101	4" thick	G	600	.013	S.F.	.16	.68		.84	1.21
0102	6" thick	G	400	.020	"	.25	1.01		1.26	1.81
0300	Polystyrene, R4 per inch	G	200	.040	C.F.	1.42	2.03		3.45	4.65
0301	4" thick	G	600	.013	S.F.	.47	.68		1.15	1.55
0302	6" thick	G	400	.020	"	.71	1.01		1.72	2.32
0400	Perlite, R2.78 per inch	G	200	.040	C.F.	5.30	2.03		7.33	8.90
0401	4" thick	G	1000	.008	S.F.	1.76	.41		2.17	2.56
0402	6" thick	G	800	.010	"	2.65	.51		3.16	3.68
0410	Poured insulation, perlite, R2.7 per inch, water repellent	G D-1	250	.064	C.F.	5.30	2.87		8.17	10.20
1000	For each floor above 4 floors, add						33%			

07 21 23.20 Masonry Loose-Fill Insulation

		Crew	Daily Output	Labor-Hours	Unit	Material	Labor	Equipment	Total	Total Incl O&P
0010	**MASONRY LOOSE-FILL INSULATION**, vermiculite or perlite									
0100	In cores of concrete block, 4" thick wall, .115 C.F./S.F.	G D-1	4800	.003	S.F.	.61	.15		.76	.90
0200	6" thick wall, .175 C.F./S.F.	G	3000	.005		.93	.24		1.17	1.39
0300	8" thick wall, .258 C.F./S.F.	G	2400	.007		1.36	.30		1.66	1.96
0400	10" thick wall, .340 C.F./S.F.	G	1850	.009		1.80	.39		2.19	2.57
0500	12" thick wall, .422 C.F./S.F.	G	1200	.013		2.23	.60		2.83	3.37
0600	Poured cavity wall, vermiculite or perlite, water repellent	G	250	.064	C.F.	5.30	2.87		8.17	10.20
0700	Foamed in place, urethane in 2-5/8" cavity	G G-2A	1035	.023	S.F.	1.35	.90	.59	2.84	3.60
0800	For each 1" added thickness, add	G "	2372	.010	"	.51	.39	.26	1.16	1.49

07 21 26 – Blown Insulation

07 21 26.10 Blown Insulation

		Crew	Daily Output	Labor-Hours	Unit	Material	Labor	Equipment	Total	Total Incl O&P
0010	**BLOWN INSULATION** Ceilings, with open access									
0020	Cellulose, 3-1/2" thick, R13	G G-4	5000	.005	S.F.	.24	.19	.06	.49	.63
0030	5-3/16" thick, R19	G	3800	.006		.35	.26	.08	.69	.87
0050	6-1/2" thick, R22	G	3000	.008		.45	.32	.10	.87	1.10
0100	8-11/16" thick, R30	G	2600	.009		.61	.37	.12	1.10	1.37
0120	10-7/8" thick, R38	G	1800	.013		.78	.54	.17	1.49	1.86
1000	Fiberglass, 5.5" thick, R11	G	3800	.006		.21	.26	.08	.55	.71
1050	6" thick, R12	G	3000	.008		.30	.32	.10	.72	.93
1100	8.8" thick, R19	G	2200	.011		.37	.44	.14	.95	1.23
1200	10" thick, R22	G	1800	.013		.43	.54	.17	1.14	1.49
1300	11.5" thick, R26	G	1500	.016		.52	.65	.20	1.37	1.78
1350	13" thick, R30	G	1400	.017		.60	.69	.22	1.51	1.96
1400	15" thick, R34	G	1220	.020		.67	.80	.25	1.72	2.23
1450	16" thick, R38	G	1145	.021		.77	.85	.27	1.89	2.42
1500	20" thick, R49	G	920	.026		1.01	1.06	.33	2.40	3.09
3000	Fiberglass, 5" thick, R11, in wall w/wood siding	G	690	.035		.28	1.41	.44	2.13	2.95
3100	8-1/2" thick, R19	G	600	.040		.44	1.62	.51	2.57	3.52

07 21 27 – Reflective Insulation

07 21 27.10 Reflective Insulation Options

		Crew	Daily Output	Labor-Hours	Unit	Material	Labor	Equipment	Total	Total Incl O&P
0010	**REFLECTIVE INSULATION OPTIONS**									
0020	Aluminum foil on reinforced scrim	G 1 Carp	19	.421	C.S.F.	15	21.50		36.50	49
0100	Reinforced with woven polyolefin	G	19	.421		22	21.50		43.50	57
0500	With single bubble air space, R8.8	G	15	.533		26	27		53	70
0600	With double bubble air space, R9.8	G	15	.533		31.50	27		58.50	75.50

For customer support on your Green Building Costs with RSMeans data, call 800.448.8182.

07 21 Thermal Insulation

07 21 29 – Sprayed Insulation

07 21 29.10 Sprayed-On Insulation

		Crew	Daily Output	Labor-Hours	Unit	Material	2018 Bare Costs Labor	Equipment	Total	Total Incl O&P
0010	**SPRAYED-ON INSULATION**									
0020	Fibrous/cementitious, finished wall, 1" thick, R3.7	G	G-2	2050	.012	S.F.	.36	.49	.06	.91	1.21
0100	Attic, 5.2" thick, R19	G		1550	.015	"	.42	.65	.08	1.15	1.53
0200	Fiberglass, R4 per inch, vertical	G		1600	.015	B.F.	.19	.63	.08	.90	1.25
0210	Horizontal	G		1200	.020	"	.19	.84	.11	1.14	1.60
0300	Closed cell, spray polyurethane foam, 2 lb./C.F. density										
0310	1" thick	G	G-2A	6000	.004	S.F.	.51	.16	.10	.77	.92
0320	2" thick	G		3000	.008		1.03	.31	.20	1.54	1.87
0330	3" thick	G		2000	.012		1.54	.47	.31	2.32	2.79
0335	3-1/2" thick	G		1715	.014		1.80	.54	.36	2.70	3.26
0340	4" thick	G		1500	.016		2.05	.62	.41	3.08	3.72
0350	5" thick	G		1200	.020		2.57	.78	.51	3.86	4.65
0355	5-1/2" thick	G		1090	.022		2.82	.86	.56	4.24	5.10
0360	6" thick	G		1000	.024		3.08	.93	.61	4.62	5.60

07 22 Roof and Deck Insulation

07 22 16 – Roof Board Insulation

07 22 16.10 Roof Deck Insulation

			Crew	Daily Output	Labor-Hours	Unit	Material	Labor	Equipment	Total	Total Incl O&P
0010	**ROOF DECK INSULATION**, fastening excluded										
0016	Asphaltic cover board, fiberglass lined, 1/8" thick		1 Rofc	1400	.006	S.F.	.48	.25		.73	.95
0018	1/4" thick			1400	.006		.96	.25		1.21	1.48
0020	Fiberboard low density, 1/2" thick, R1.39	G		1300	.006		.35	.27		.62	.84
0030	1" thick, R2.78	G		1040	.008		.58	.34		.92	1.21
0080	1-1/2" thick, R4.17	G		1040	.008		.89	.34		1.23	1.55
0100	2" thick, R5.56	G		1040	.008		1.15	.34		1.49	1.84
0110	Fiberboard high density, 1/2" thick, R1.3	G		1300	.006		.27	.27		.54	.75
0120	1" thick, R2.5	G		1040	.008		.56	.34		.90	1.19
0130	1-1/2" thick, R3.8	G		1040	.008		.83	.34		1.17	1.48
0200	Fiberglass, 3/4" thick, R2.78	G		1300	.006		.62	.27		.89	1.13
0400	15/16" thick, R3.70	G		1300	.006		.82	.27		1.09	1.35
0460	1-1/16" thick, R4.17	G		1300	.006		1.07	.27		1.34	1.63
0600	1-5/16" thick, R5.26	G		1300	.006		1.42	.27		1.69	2.01
0650	2-1/16" thick, R8.33	G		1040	.008		1.52	.34		1.86	2.24
0700	2-7/16" thick, R10	G		1040	.008		1.72	.34		2.06	2.46
0800	Gypsum cover board, fiberglass mat facer, 1/4" thick			1400	.006		.48	.25		.73	.95
0810	1/2" thick			1300	.006		.59	.27		.86	1.10
0820	5/8" thick			1200	.007		.62	.29		.91	1.17
0830	Primed fiberglass mat facer, 1/4" thick			1400	.006		.50	.25		.75	.97
0840	1/2" thick			1300	.006		.58	.27		.85	1.09
0850	5/8" thick			1200	.007		.61	.29		.90	1.16
1650	Perlite, 1/2" thick, R1.32	G		1365	.006		.27	.26		.53	.73
1655	3/4" thick, R2.08	G		1040	.008		.38	.34		.72	.99
1660	1" thick, R2.78	G		1040	.008		.54	.34		.88	1.16
1670	1-1/2" thick, R4.17	G		1040	.008		.80	.34		1.14	1.45
1680	2" thick, R5.56	G		910	.009		1.08	.39		1.47	1.84
1685	2-1/2" thick, R6.67	G		910	.009		1.45	.39		1.84	2.25
1690	Tapered for drainage	G		1040	.008	B.F.	1.05	.34		1.39	1.73
1700	Polyisocyanurate, 2#/C.F. density, 3/4" thick	G		1950	.004	S.F.	.42	.18		.60	.76
1705	1" thick	G		1820	.004		.43	.19		.62	.80
1715	1-1/2" thick	G		1625	.005		.58	.22		.80	1

07 22 Roof and Deck Insulation

07 22 16 – Roof Board Insulation

	07 22 16.10 Roof Deck Insulation		Crew	Daily Output	Labor-Hours	Unit	Material	2018 Bare Costs Labor	Equipment	Total	Total Incl O&P
1725	2" thick	G	1 Rofc	1430	.006	S.F.	.74	.25		.99	1.22
1735	2-1/2" thick	G		1365	.006		.99	.26		1.25	1.52
1745	3" thick	G		1300	.006		1.10	.27		1.37	1.66
1755	3-1/2" thick	G		1300	.006		1.71	.27		1.98	2.33
1765	Tapered for drainage	G		1820	.004	B.F.	.52	.19		.71	.90
1900	Extruded polystyrene										
1910	15 psi compressive strength, 1" thick, R5	G	1 Rofc	1950	.004	S.F.	.55	.18		.73	.91
1920	2" thick, R10	G		1625	.005		.72	.22		.94	1.15
1930	3" thick, R15	G		1300	.006		1.43	.27		1.70	2.02
1932	4" thick, R20	G		1300	.006		1.93	.27		2.20	2.57
1934	Tapered for drainage	G		1950	.004	B.F.	.51	.18		.69	.86
1940	25 psi compressive strength, 1" thick, R5	G		1950	.004	S.F.	1.11	.18		1.29	1.52
1942	2" thick, R10	G		1625	.005		2.11	.22		2.33	2.68
1944	3" thick, R15	G		1300	.006		3.22	.27		3.49	3.99
1946	4" thick, R20	G		1300	.006		4.44	.27		4.71	5.35
1948	Tapered for drainage	G		1950	.004	B.F.	.56	.18		.74	.92
1950	40 psi compressive strength, 1" thick, R5	G		1950	.004	S.F.	.87	.18		1.05	1.26
1952	2" thick, R10	G		1625	.005		1.65	.22		1.87	2.18
1954	3" thick, R15	G		1300	.006		2.39	.27		2.66	3.08
1956	4" thick, R20	G		1300	.006		3.13	.27		3.40	3.90
1958	Tapered for drainage	G		1820	.004	B.F.	.87	.19		1.06	1.29
1960	60 psi compressive strength, 1" thick, R5	G		1885	.004	S.F.	1.05	.19		1.24	1.47
1962	2" thick, R10	G		1560	.005		2	.23		2.23	2.57
1964	3" thick, R15	G		1270	.006		3.26	.28		3.54	4.05
1966	4" thick, R20	G		1235	.006		4.04	.28		4.32	4.93
1968	Tapered for drainage	G		1820	.004	B.F.	1	.19		1.19	1.43
2010	Expanded polystyrene, 1#/C.F. density, 3/4" thick, R2.89	G		1950	.004	S.F.	.20	.18		.38	.52
2020	1" thick, R3.85	G		1950	.004		.27	.18		.45	.60
2100	2" thick, R7.69	G		1625	.005		.54	.22		.76	.95
2110	3" thick, R11.49	G		1625	.005		.81	.22		1.03	1.25
2120	4" thick, R15.38	G		1625	.005		1.08	.22		1.30	1.55
2130	5" thick, R19.23	G		1495	.005		1.35	.24		1.59	1.89
2140	6" thick, R23.26	G		1495	.005		1.62	.24		1.86	2.18
2150	Tapered for drainage	G		1950	.004	B.F.	.53	.18		.71	.88
2400	Composites with 2" EPS										
2410	1" fiberboard	G	1 Rofc	1325	.006	S.F.	1.45	.27		1.72	2.05
2420	7/16" oriented strand board	G		1040	.008		1.15	.34		1.49	1.84
2430	1/2" plywood	G		1040	.008		1.44	.34		1.78	2.15
2440	1" perlite	G		1040	.008		1.17	.34		1.51	1.86
2450	Composites with 1-1/2" polyisocyanurate										
2460	1" fiberboard	G	1 Rofc	1040	.008	S.F.	1.07	.34		1.41	1.75
2470	1" perlite	G		1105	.007		.96	.32		1.28	1.60
2480	7/16" oriented strand board	G		1040	.008		.84	.34		1.18	1.49
3000	Fastening alternatives, coated screws, 2" long			3744	.002	Ea.	.06	.09		.15	.23
3010	4" long			3120	.003		.11	.11		.22	.31
3020	6" long			2675	.003		.19	.13		.32	.43
3030	8" long			2340	.003		.28	.15		.43	.56
3040	10" long			1872	.004		.47	.19		.66	.84
3050	Pre-drill and drive wedge spike, 2-1/2"			1248	.006		.40	.28		.68	.91
3060	3-1/2"			1101	.007		.58	.32		.90	1.18
3070	4-1/2"			936	.009		.65	.38		1.03	1.35
3075	3" galvanized deck plates			7488	.001		.08	.05		.13	.17
3080	Spot mop asphalt		G-1	295	.190	Sq.	5.80	7.80	1.74	15.34	21.50

For customer support on your Green Building Costs with RSMeans data, call 800.448.8182.

07 22 Roof and Deck Insulation

07 22 16 – Roof Board Insulation

07 22 16.10 Roof Deck Insulation

		Crew	Daily Output	Labor-Hours	Unit	Material	2018 Bare Costs Labor	Equipment	Total	Total Incl O&P
3090	Full mop asphalt	G-1	192	.292	Sq.	11.60	12	2.68	26.28	35.50
3110	Low-rise polyurethane adhesive, from 5 gallon kit, 12" OC beads	1 Rofc	45	.178		33	7.80		40.80	49.50
3120	6" OC beads		32	.250		66	11		77	91
3130	4" OC beads		30	.267		99	11.70		110.70	129

07 24 Exterior Insulation and Finish Systems

07 24 13 – Polymer-Based Exterior Insulation and Finish System

07 24 13.10 Exterior Insulation and Finish Systems

			Crew	Daily Output	Labor-Hours	Unit	Material	Labor	Equipment	Total	Total Incl O&P
0010	**EXTERIOR INSULATION AND FINISH SYSTEMS**										
0095	Field applied, 1" EPS insulation	G	J-1	390	.103	S.F.	1.80	4.49	.34	6.63	9.10
0100	With 1/2" cement board sheathing	G		268	.149		2.59	6.55	.50	9.64	13.20
0105	2" EPS insulation	G		390	.103		2.07	4.49	.34	6.90	9.40
0110	With 1/2" cement board sheathing	G		268	.149		2.86	6.55	.50	9.91	13.50
0115	3" EPS insulation	G		390	.103		2.34	4.49	.34	7.17	9.70
0120	With 1/2" cement board sheathing	G		268	.149		3.13	6.55	.50	10.18	13.80
0125	4" EPS insulation	G		390	.103		2.61	4.49	.34	7.44	10
0130	With 1/2" cement board sheathing	G		268	.149		4.18	6.55	.50	11.23	14.95
0140	Premium finish add			1265	.032		.36	1.38	.11	1.85	2.60
0150	Heavy duty reinforcement add			914	.044		.60	1.92	.15	2.67	3.69
0160	2.5#/S.Y. metal lath substrate add		1 Lath	75	.107	S.Y.	3.10	5.25		8.35	11.15
0170	3.4#/S.Y. metal lath substrate add		"	75	.107	"	4.44	5.25		9.69	12.65
0180	Color or texture change		J-1	1265	.032	S.F.	.82	1.38	.11	2.31	3.10
0190	With substrate leveling base coat		1 Plas	530	.015		.83	.70		1.53	1.96
0210	With substrate sealing base coat		1 Pord	1224	.007		.12	.28		.40	.55
0370	V groove shape in panel face					L.F.	.68			.68	.75
0380	U groove shape in panel face					"	.85			.85	.94
0440	For higher than one story, add							25%			

07 26 Vapor Retarders

07 26 10 – Above-Grade Vapor Retarders

07 26 10.10 Vapor Retarders

			Crew	Daily Output	Labor-Hours	Unit	Material	Labor	Equipment	Total	Total Incl O&P
0010	**VAPOR RETARDERS**										
0020	Aluminum and kraft laminated, foil 1 side	G	1 Carp	37	.216	Sq.	13.65	10.95		24.60	31.50
0100	Foil 2 sides	G		37	.216		14.15	10.95		25.10	32.50
0600	Polyethylene vapor barrier, standard, 2 mil	G		37	.216		1.50	10.95		12.45	18.35
0700	4 mil	G		37	.216		2.58	10.95		13.53	19.55
0880	Vapor retarder, recycled plastic, clear, 4 mil, 10' x 100' roll	G		36	.222		6.05	11.25		17.30	24
0890	6 mil, 10' x 100' roll	G		36	.222		7.15	11.25		18.40	25
0900	6 mil	G		37	.216		3.73	10.95		14.68	21
1200	10 mil	G		37	.216		8.75	10.95		19.70	26.50
1300	Clear reinforced, fire retardant, 8 mil	G		37	.216		26.50	10.95		37.45	45.50
1350	Cross laminated type, 3 mil	G		37	.216		12.35	10.95		23.30	30.50
1400	4 mil	G		37	.216		13.10	10.95		24.05	31
1800	Reinf. waterproof, 2 mil polyethylene backing, 1 side			37	.216		9.95	10.95		20.90	27.50
1900	2 sides			37	.216		12.90	10.95		23.85	31
2400	Waterproofed kraft with sisal or fiberglass fibers			37	.216		21	10.95		31.95	39.50

07 27 Air Barriers

07 27 13 – Modified Bituminous Sheet Air Barriers

07 27 13.10 Modified Bituminous Sheet Air Barrier

		Crew	Daily Output	Labor-Hours	Unit	Material	2018 Bare Costs Labor	Equipment	Total	Total Incl O&P
0010	**MODIFIED BITUMINOUS SHEET AIR BARRIER**									
0100	SBS modified sheet laminated to polyethylene sheet, 40 mils, 4" wide	1 Carp	1200	.007	L.F.	.33	.34		.67	.87
0120	6" wide		1100	.007		.45	.37		.82	1.05
0140	9" wide		1000	.008		.62	.41		1.03	1.31
0160	12" wide		900	.009		.80	.45		1.25	1.57
0180	18" wide	2 Carp	1700	.009	S.F.	.75	.48		1.23	1.55
0200	36" wide	"	1800	.009		.73	.45		1.18	1.49
0220	Adhesive for above	1 Carp	1400	.006		.31	.29		.60	.79

07 27 16 – Sheet Metal Membrane Air Barriers

07 27 16.10 Sheet Metal Membrane Air Barrier

			Crew	Daily Output	Labor-Hours	Unit	Material	Labor	Equipment	Total	Total Incl O&P
0010	**SHEET METAL MEMBRANE AIR BARRIER**										
2000	Radiant barrier, double sided aluminum over bubble-wrap core, 16" wide	G	1 Carp	1500	.005	S.F.	.43	.27		.70	.88
2010	24" wide	G		1500	.005		.49	.27		.76	.95
2020	48" wide	G		1500	.005		.41	.27		.68	.86

07 27 26 – Fluid-Applied Membrane Air Barriers

07 27 26.10 Fluid Applied Membrane Air Barrier

		Crew	Daily Output	Labor-Hours	Unit	Material	Labor	Equipment	Total	Total Incl O&P
0010	**FLUID APPLIED MEMBRANE AIR BARRIER**									
0100	Spray applied vapor barrier, 25 S.F./gallon	1 Pord	1375	.006	S.F.	.01	.25		.26	.39

07 31 Shingles and Shakes

07 31 13 – Asphalt Shingles

07 31 13.10 Asphalt Roof Shingles

		Crew	Daily Output	Labor-Hours	Unit	Material	Labor	Equipment	Total	Total Incl O&P
0010	**ASPHALT ROOF SHINGLES**									
0100	Standard strip shingles									
0150	Inorganic, class A, 25 year	1 Rofc	5.50	1.455	Sq.	75	64		139	191
0155	Pneumatic nailed		7	1.143		75	50		125	167
0200	30 year		5	1.600		95.50	70.50		166	223
0205	Pneumatic nailed		6.25	1.280		95.50	56.50		152	200
0250	Standard laminated multi-layered shingles									
0300	Class A, 240-260 lb./square	1 Rofc	4.50	1.778	Sq.	110	78		188	252
0305	Pneumatic nailed		5.63	1.422		110	62.50		172.50	226
0350	Class A, 250-270 lb./square		4	2		110	88		198	269
0355	Pneumatic nailed		5	1.600		110	70.50		180.50	239
0400	Premium, laminated multi-layered shingles									
0450	Class A, 260-300 lb./square	1 Rofc	3.50	2.286	Sq.	144	100		244	325
0455	Pneumatic nailed		4.37	1.831		144	80.50		224.50	293
0460	40 year architectural shingle		3	2.667		144	117		261	355
0500	Class A, 300-385 lb./square		3	2.667		260	117		377	485
0505	Pneumatic nailed		3.75	2.133		260	94		354	445
0800	#15 felt underlayment		64	.125		5.35	5.50		10.85	15.15
0825	#30 felt underlayment		58	.138		10.30	6.05		16.35	21.50
0850	Self adhering polyethylene and rubberized asphalt underlayment		22	.364		78	16		94	113
0900	Ridge shingles		330	.024	L.F.	2.27	1.07		3.34	4.29
0905	Pneumatic nailed		412.50	.019	"	2.27	.85		3.12	3.93
1000	For steep roofs (7 to 12 pitch or greater), add						50%			

07 31 Shingles and Shakes

07 31 26 – Slate Shingles

07 31 26.10 Slate Roof Shingles

		Crew	Daily Output	Labor-Hours	Unit	Material	2018 Bare Costs Labor	Equipment	Total	Total Incl O&P
0010	**SLATE ROOF SHINGLES** R073126-20									
0100	Buckingham Virginia black, 3/16" - 1/4" thick G	1 Rots	1.75	4.571	Sq.	555	202		757	950
0200	1/4" thick G		1.75	4.571		555	202		757	950
0900	Pennsylvania black, Bangor, #1 clear G		1.75	4.571		495	202		697	885
1200	Vermont, unfading, green, mottled green G		1.75	4.571		505	202		707	895
1300	Semi-weathering green & gray G		1.75	4.571		360	202		562	735
1400	Purple G		1.75	4.571		435	202		637	820
1500	Black or gray G		1.75	4.571		485	202		687	875
1600	Red G		1.75	4.571		1,175	202		1,377	1,625
1800	Roofing tiles, imitation slate, recycled plastic, grey or black G		1.75	4.571		520	202		722	910
1810	Green G		1.75	4.571		565	202		767	960
1820	Mulberry G		1.75	4.571		580	202		782	980
1850	Roofing tiles, recycled composite of slate, clay and binders G		1.75	4.571		305	202		507	680
1880	Roofing tiles, slate, salvaged, greens/greys/mottled colors G		1.75	4.571		285	202		487	655
1890	Reds G		1.75	4.571		450	202		652	835
2500	Slate roof repair, extensive replacement		1	8		600	355		955	1,250
2600	Repair individual pieces, scattered		19	.421	Ea.	7.05	18.60		25.65	39.50
2700	Ridge shingles, slate		200	.040	L.F.	10.10	1.77		11.87	14.05

07 31 29 – Wood Shingles and Shakes

07 31 29.13 Wood Shingles

		Crew	Daily Output	Labor-Hours	Unit	Material	2018 Bare Costs Labor	Equipment	Total	Total Incl O&P
0010	**WOOD SHINGLES** R061110-30									
0012	16" No. 1 red cedar shingles, 5" exposure, on roof	1 Carp	2.50	3.200	Sq.	295	162		457	570
0015	Pneumatic nailed		3.25	2.462		295	125		420	515
0200	7-1/2" exposure, on walls		2.05	3.902		196	198		394	515
0201	With fire retardant shingles		2.05	3.902		233	198		431	555
0205	Pneumatic nailed		2.67	2.996		196	152		348	445
0210	16" No. 2 red cedar, on roof		2.50	3.200		160	162		322	425
0300	18" No. 1 red cedar perfections, 5-1/2" exposure, on roof		2.75	2.909		253	147		400	505
0301	5-1/2" exposure, 18", #1 red cedar fire proof		2.75	2.909		310	147		457	565
0305	Pneumatic nailed		3.57	2.241		253	114		367	450
0500	7-1/2" exposure, on walls		2.25	3.556		186	180		366	480
0505	Pneumatic nailed		2.92	2.740		186	139		325	415
0550	18" No. 2 red cedar perfections, 5-1/2" exposure on roof		2	4		190	203		393	520
0600	Resquared and rebutted, 5-1/2" exposure, on roof		3	2.667		290	135		425	525
0601	5-1/2" exposure, 18", fire retardant resquared		3	2.667		345	135		480	585
0605	Pneumatic nailed		3.90	2.051		290	104		394	480
0900	7-1/2" exposure, on walls		2.45	3.265		214	166		380	485
0901	With fire retardant shingles		2.45	3.265		254	166		420	530
0905	Pneumatic nailed		3.18	2.516		214	128		342	430
1000	Add to above for fire retardant shingles					55			55	60.50
2000	White cedar shingles, 16" long, extras, 5" exposure, on roof	1 Carp	2.40	3.333		197	169		366	475
2005	Pneumatic nailed		3.12	2.564		197	130		327	415
2050	5" exposure on walls		2	4		197	203		400	525
2055	Pneumatic nailed		2.60	3.077		197	156		353	455
2100	7-1/2" exposure, on walls		2	4		141	203		344	465
2105	Pneumatic nailed		2.60	3.077		141	156		297	395
2150	"B" grade, 5" exposure on walls		2	4		172	203		375	500
2155	Pneumatic nailed		2.60	3.077		172	156		328	425
2200	Shingles, custom scalloped white cedar, 7-1/2" exposure on walls		1.50	5.333		285	270		555	725
2300	For #15 organic felt underlayment on roof, 1 layer, add		64	.125		5.35	6.35		11.70	15.55
2400	2 layers, add		32	.250		10.75	12.70		23.45	31
2600	For steep roofs (7/12 pitch or greater), add to above						50%			

07 31 Shingles and Shakes

07 31 29 – Wood Shingles and Shakes

07 31 29.13 Wood Shingles

		Crew	Daily Output	Labor-Hours	Unit	Material	2018 Bare Costs Labor	Equipment	Total	Total Incl O&P
2700	Panelized systems, No.1 cedar shingles on 5/16" CDX plywood									
2800	On walls, 8' strips, 7" or 14" exposure	2 Carp	700	.023	S.F.	6.40	1.16		7.56	8.80
3000	Ridge shakes or shingle, wood	1 Carp	280	.029	L.F.	4.75	1.45		6.20	7.45
3500	On roofs, 8' strips, 7" or 14" exposure		3	2.667	Sq.	665	135		800	935
3505	Pneumatic nailed		4	2	"	665	101		766	885
8000	Replace shingle on roof		40	.200	Ea.	73	10.15		83.15	95.50
8900	Roof shingles, imitation wood shakes, from recycled plastic [G]		1.75	4.571	Sq.	375	232		607	770
8910	Ridge cap for [G]		170	.047	L.F.	6.35	2.39		8.74	10.65
8920	Roof shingles, imitation wood shakes, from recycled aluminum, installed [G]				Sq.	305			305	335
8930	Roof shingles, imitation wood shingles, from recycled steel, installed [G]				"	305			305	335

07 31 29.16 Wood Shakes

		Crew	Daily Output	Labor-Hours	Unit	Material	Labor	Equipment	Total	Total Incl O&P
0010	**WOOD SHAKES**									
1100	Hand-split red cedar shakes, 1/2" thick x 24" long, 10" exp. on roof	1 Carp	2.50	3.200	Sq.	300	162		462	575
1101	With fire retardant shakes		2.50	3.200		355	162		517	635
1105	Pneumatic nailed		3.25	2.462		300	125		425	520
1110	3/4" thick x 24" long, 10" exp. on roof		2.25	3.556		300	180		480	605
1115	Pneumatic nailed		2.92	2.740		300	139		439	540
1200	1/2" thick, 18" long, 8-1/2" exp. on roof		2	4		275	203		478	610
1201	With fire retardant shakes		2	4		330	203		533	675
1205	Pneumatic nailed		2.60	3.077		275	156		431	540
1210	3/4" thick x 18" long, 8-1/2" exp. on roof		1.80	4.444		275	225		500	645
1215	Pneumatic nailed		2.34	3.419		275	173		448	565
1255	10" exposure on walls		2	4		265	203		468	600
1260	10" exposure on walls, pneumatic nailed		2.60	3.077		265	156		421	530
1300	Cedar shake, tapersplit, 24"		2.20	3.636		272	184		456	580
1310	Straight split, 18"		2.20	3.636		295	184		479	605
1320	24"		2.20	3.636		315	184		499	625
1700	Add to above for fire retardant shakes, 24" long					55			55	60.50
1800	18" long					55			55	60.50
1810	Ridge shakes	1 Carp	350	.023	L.F.	5.75	1.16		6.91	8.10
1930	3/4" x 24" red cedar shakes, with 30# felt, 10" exp. on walls	"	2	4	Sq.	305	203		508	645

07 32 Roof Tiles

07 32 13 – Clay Roof Tiles

07 32 13.10 Clay Tiles

		Crew	Daily Output	Labor-Hours	Unit	Material	Labor	Equipment	Total	Total Incl O&P
0010	**CLAY TILES**, including accessories									
0300	Flat shingle, interlocking, 15", 166 pcs./sq., fireflashed blend	3 Rots	6	4	Sq.	470	177		647	810
0500	Terra cotta red		6	4		520	177		697	865
0600	Roman pan and top, 18", 102 pcs./sq., fireflashed blend		5.50	4.364		505	193		698	880
0640	Terra cotta red	1 Rots	2.40	3.333		570	147		717	875
1100	Barrel mission tile, 18", 166 pcs./sq., fireflashed blend	3 Rots	5.50	4.364		415	193		608	780
1140	Terra cotta red		5.50	4.364		420	193		613	785
1700	Scalloped edge flat shingle, 14", 145 pcs./sq., fireflashed blend		6	4		1,150	177		1,327	1,575
1800	Terra cotta red		6	4		1,050	177		1,227	1,450
3010	#15 felt underlayment	1 Rofc	64	.125		5.35	5.50		10.85	15.15
3020	#30 felt underlayment		58	.138		10.30	6.05		16.35	21.50
3040	Polyethylene and rubberized asph. underlayment		22	.364		78	16		94	113
8910	Maintenance, rebed and repoint tile roof mortar, up to 1930 S.F.	1 Rots	150	.053	S.F.	.35	2.35		2.70	4.35
8950	Install cap		200	.040	L.F.	4.93	1.77		6.70	8.40
8955	Rebed and repoint cap		200	.040		.35	1.77		2.12	3.36
8960	Install ridge, hip or verge		200	.040		4.93	1.77		6.70	8.40

For customer support on your Green Building Costs with RSMeans data, call 800.448.8182.

07 32 Roof Tiles

07 32 16 – Concrete Roof Tiles

07 32 16.10 Concrete Tiles

		Crew	Daily Output	Labor-Hours	Unit	Material	2018 Bare Costs Labor	Equipment	Total	Total Incl O&P
0010	**CONCRETE TILES**									
0020	Corrugated, 13" x 16-1/2", 90 per sq., 950 lb./sq.									
0050	Earthtone colors, nailed to wood deck	1 Rots	1.35	5.926	Sq.	105	262		367	555
0150	Blues		1.35	5.926		105	262		367	555
0200	Greens		1.35	5.926		106	262		368	555
0250	Premium colors		1.35	5.926		106	262		368	555
0300	Gray		1.35	5.926		105	262		367	555
0310	Red/brown		1.35	5.926		105	262		367	555
0320	Bright red		1.35	5.926		106	262		368	555
0330	Green		1.35	5.926		106	262		368	555
0340	Blue		1.35	5.926		106	262		368	555
0350	Black		1.35	5.926		106	262		368	555
0400	Flat, natural gray		1.35	5.926		125	262		387	580
0410	Red/brown		1.35	5.926		125	262		387	580
0420	Bright red		1.35	5.926		125	262		387	580
0430	Green		1.35	5.926		125	262		387	580
0440	Blue		1.35	5.926		125	262		387	580
0450	Black		1.35	5.926		125	262		387	580
0500	Shakes, 13" x 16-1/2", 90 per sq., 950 lb./sq.									
0600	All colors, nailed to wood deck	1 Rots	1.50	5.333	Sq.	126	235		361	535
1000	Lightweight concrete roof tiles		220	.036	S.F.	.82	1.61		2.43	3.60
1500	Accessory pieces, ridge & hip, 10" x 16-1/2", 8 lb. each		120	.067	Ea.	3.80	2.94		6.74	9.15
1700	Rake, 6-1/2" x 16-3/4", 9 lb. each					3.80			3.80	4.18
1800	Mansard hip, 10" x 16-1/2", 9.2 lb. each					3.80			3.80	4.18
1900	Hip starter, 10" x 16-1/2", 10.5 lb. each					10.50			10.50	11.55
2000	3 or 4 way apex, 10" each side, 11.5 lb. each					12			12	13.20
3000	Concrete tile, #15 felt underlayment	1 Rofc	64	.125	Sq.	5.35	5.50		10.85	15.15
3020	Concrete tile, #30 felt underlayment		58	.138		10.30	6.05		16.35	21.50
3040	Concrete tile, polyethylene and rubberized asph. underlayment		22	.364		78	16		94	113

07 32 19 – Metal Roof Tiles

07 32 19.10 Metal Roof Tiles

			Crew	Daily Output	Labor-Hours	Unit	Material	Labor	Equipment	Total	Total Incl O&P
0010	**METAL ROOF TILES**										
4000	Roof tiles, 100% recycled copper, 9" x 15"	G	1 Carp	2.50	3.200	Sq.	830	162		992	1,150
4010	Starter strip for, 8'	G		50	.160	Ea.	24.50	8.10		32.60	39.50
4020	Gable end strip for, 8'	G		38	.211		24.50	10.65		35.15	43.50
4030	Sidewall or end strip for, 8'	G		38	.211		50.50	10.65		61.15	72
4040	Pipe flashing tile w/rubber boot, for 1-1/2" pipe	G		16	.500		40.50	25.50		66	83
4050	For 2-1/2" pipe	G		16	.500		40.50	25.50		66	83
4060	For 3-1/2" pipe	G		16	.500		44	25.50		69.50	87
4070	For 4-1/2" pipe	G		16	.500		44	25.50		69.50	87
4080	Continuous valley strip for, 10'	G		24	.333		66.50	16.90		83.40	98.50
4090	16" x 50' copper roll, material only	G					440			440	485
4100	Roof tiles, 100% recycled aluminum, 9" x 15"	G	1 Carp	2.50	3.200	Sq.	190	162		352	455
4110	Starter strip for, 8'	G		50	.160	Ea.	11.50	8.10		19.60	25
4120	Gable end strip for, 8'	G		38	.211		11.50	10.65		22.15	29
4130	End or sidewall strip for, 8'	G		38	.211		14.50	10.65		25.15	32
4140	Flashing tile w/rubber boot, for 1-1/2" pipe	G		16	.500		13.90	25.50		39.40	54
4150	For 2-1/2" pipe	G		16	.500		14.80	25.50		40.30	55
4160	For 3-1/2" pipe	G		16	.500		17	25.50		42.50	57
4170	For 4-1/2" pipe	G		16	.500		17.60	25.50		43.10	58
4180	Continuous valley strip for, 10'	G		24	.333		23.50	16.90		40.40	51.50
4190	16" x 50' roll, material only	G					95			95	105

For customer support on your Green Building Costs with RSMeans data, call 800.448.8182.

07 33 Natural Roof Coverings

07 33 63 – Vegetated Roofing

07 33 63.10 Green Roof Systems

		Crew	Daily Output	Labor-Hours	Unit	Material	2018 Bare Costs Labor	Equipment	Total	Total Incl O&P
0010	**GREEN ROOF SYSTEMS**									
0020	Soil mixture for green roof 30% sand, 55% gravel, 15% soil									
0100	Hoist and spread soil mixture 4" depth up to 5 stories tall roof	G B-13B	4000	.014	S.F.	.23	.61	.25	1.09	1.45
0150	6" depth	G	2667	.021		.35	.92	.37	1.64	2.18
0200	8" depth	G	2000	.028		.46	1.22	.50	2.18	2.92
0250	10" depth	G	1600	.035		.58	1.53	.62	2.73	3.63
0300	12" depth	G	1335	.042		.69	1.83	.74	3.26	4.36
0310	Alt. man-made soil mix, hoist & spread, 4" deep up to 5 stories tall roof	G	4000	.014		1.92	.61	.25	2.78	3.31
0350	Mobilization 55 ton crane to site	G 1 Eqhv	3.60	2.222	Ea.		125		125	188
0355	Hoisting cost to 5 stories per day (Avg. 28 picks per day)	G B-13B	1	56	Day		2,450	995	3,445	4,825
0360	Mobilization or demobilization, 100 ton crane to site driver & escort	G A-3E	2.50	6.400	Ea.		325	50.50	375.50	545
0365	Hoisting cost 6-10 stories per day (Avg. 21 picks per day)	G B-13C	1	56	Day		2,450	1,875	4,325	5,775
0370	Hoist and spread soil mixture 4" depth 6-10 stories tall roof	G	4000	.014	S.F.	.23	.61	.47	1.31	1.69
0375	6" depth	G	2667	.021		.35	.92	.70	1.97	2.54
0380	8" depth	G	2000	.028		.46	1.22	.94	2.62	3.40
0385	10" depth	G	1600	.035		.58	1.53	1.17	3.28	4.24
0390	12" depth	G	1335	.042		.69	1.83	1.40	3.92	5.10
0400	Green roof edging treated lumber 4" x 4", no hoisting included	G 2 Carp	400	.040	L.F.	1.20	2.03		3.23	4.41
0410	4" x 6"	G	400	.040		1.94	2.03		3.97	5.25
0420	4" x 8"	G	360	.044		3.96	2.25		6.21	7.80
0430	4" x 6" double stacked	G	300	.053		3.89	2.70		6.59	8.40
0500	Green roof edging redwood lumber 4" x 4", no hoisting included	G	400	.040		6.45	2.03		8.48	10.20
0510	4" x 6"	G	400	.040		12.60	2.03		14.63	16.95
0520	4" x 8"	G	360	.044		23.50	2.25		25.75	29.50
0530	4" x 6" double stacked	G	300	.053		25	2.70		27.70	31.50
0550	Components, not including membrane or insulation:									
0560	Fluid applied rubber membrane, reinforced, 215 mil thick	G G-5	350	.114	S.F.	.30	4.56	.52	5.38	8.60
0570	Root barrier	G 2 Rofc	775	.021		.70	.91		1.61	2.30
0580	Moisture retention barrier and reservoir	G "	900	.018		2.66	.78		3.44	4.24
0600	Planting sedum, light soil, potted, 2-1/4" diameter, 2 per S.F.	G 1 Clab	420	.019		6.10	.76		6.86	7.85
0610	1 per S.F.	G "	840	.010		3.05	.38		3.43	3.94
0630	Planting sedum mat per S.F. including shipping (4000 S.F. min)	G 4 Clab	4000	.008		7.30	.32		7.62	8.55
0640	Installation sedum mat system (no soil required) per S.F. (4000 S.F. min)	G "	4000	.008		10.20	.32		10.52	11.70
0645	Note: pricing of sedum mats shipped in full truck loads (4000-5000 S.F.)									

07 41 Roof Panels

07 41 13 – Metal Roof Panels

07 41 13.10 Aluminum Roof Panels

		Crew	Daily Output	Labor-Hours	Unit	Material	Labor	Equipment	Total	Total Incl O&P
0010	**ALUMINUM ROOF PANELS**									
0020	Corrugated or ribbed, .0155" thick, natural	G-3	1200	.027	S.F.	1	1.33		2.33	3.13
0300	Painted		1200	.027		1.45	1.33		2.78	3.63
0400	Corrugated, .018" thick, on steel frame, natural finish		1200	.027		1.24	1.33		2.57	3.39
0600	Painted		1200	.027		1.55	1.33		2.88	3.74
0700	Corrugated, on steel frame, natural, .024" thick		1200	.027		1.80	1.33		3.13	4.01
0800	Painted		1200	.027		2.20	1.33		3.53	4.45
0900	.032" thick, natural		1200	.027		3.04	1.33		4.37	5.35
1200	Painted		1200	.027		3.28	1.33		4.61	5.65
1300	V-Beam, on steel frame construction, .032" thick, natural		1200	.027		2.62	1.33		3.95	4.91
1500	Painted		1200	.027		3.91	1.33		5.24	6.35
1600	.040" thick, natural		1200	.027		3.82	1.33		5.15	6.25
1800	Painted		1200	.027		4.61	1.33		5.94	7.10

07 41 Roof Panels

07 41 13 – Metal Roof Panels

07 41 13.10 Aluminum Roof Panels

		Crew	Daily Output	Labor-Hours	Unit	Material	2018 Bare Costs Labor	Equipment	Total	Total Incl O&P
1900	.050" thick, natural	G-3	1200	.027	S.F.	3.95	1.33		5.28	6.40
2100	Painted		1200	.027		4.75	1.33		6.08	7.30
2160	Corrugated or ribbed, galvanized, on steel frame, .015 mils		1000	.032		1.38	1.59		2.97	3.95
2200	For roofing on wood frame, deduct		4600	.007		.08	.35		.43	.62
2400	Ridge cap, .032" thick, natural		800	.040	L.F.	3.18	1.99		5.17	6.55
2410	Ridge roll, 10" wide		800	.040		2.69	1.99		4.68	6
2420	20" wide		800	.040		4.43	1.99		6.42	7.90

07 41 13.20 Steel Roofing Panels

		Crew	Daily Output	Labor-Hours	Unit	Material	Labor	Equipment	Total	Total Incl O&P
0010	**STEEL ROOFING PANELS**									
0012	Corrugated or ribbed, on steel framing, 30 ga. galv	G-3	1100	.029	S.F.	1.67	1.45		3.12	4.05
0100	28 ga.		1050	.030		1.44	1.52		2.96	3.90
0300	26 ga.		1000	.032		2.02	1.59		3.61	4.65
0400	24 ga.		950	.034		3	1.68		4.68	5.85
0510	Painted, including fasteners, 18 ga. G		850	.038		4.11	1.88		5.99	7.40
0520	20 ga. G		875	.037		3.18	1.82		5	6.30
0530	22 ga. G		900	.036		4.40	1.77		6.17	7.55
0600	Colored, 28 ga.		1050	.030		1.81	1.52		3.33	4.31
0700	26 ga.		1000	.032		2.12	1.59		3.71	4.76
0710	Flat profile, 1-3/4" standing seams, 10" wide, standard finish, 26 ga.		1000	.032		3.93	1.59		5.52	6.75
0715	24 ga.		950	.034		4.60	1.68		6.28	7.60
0720	22 ga.		900	.036		5.70	1.77		7.47	8.95
0725	Zinc aluminum alloy finish, 26 ga.		1000	.032		3.20	1.59		4.79	5.95
0730	24 ga.		950	.034		3.72	1.68		5.40	6.65
0735	22 ga.		900	.036		4.24	1.77		6.01	7.35
0740	12" wide, standard finish, 26 ga.		1000	.032		3.98	1.59		5.57	6.80
0745	24 ga.		950	.034		5.15	1.68		6.83	8.20
0750	Zinc aluminum alloy finish, 26 ga.		1000	.032		4.44	1.59		6.03	7.30
0755	24 ga.		950	.034		3.72	1.68		5.40	6.65
0840	Flat profile, 1" x 3/8" batten, 12" wide, standard finish, 26 ga.		1000	.032		3.46	1.59		5.05	6.25
0845	24 ga.		950	.034		4.08	1.68		5.76	7.05
0850	22 ga.		900	.036		4.91	1.77		6.68	8.10
0855	Zinc aluminum alloy finish, 26 ga.		1000	.032		3.36	1.59		4.95	6.15
0860	24 ga.		950	.034		3.82	1.68		5.50	6.75
0865	22 ga.		900	.036		4.34	1.77		6.11	7.45
0870	16-1/2" wide, standard finish, 24 ga.		950	.034		4.03	1.68		5.71	7
0875	22 ga.		900	.036		4.55	1.77		6.32	7.70
0880	Zinc aluminum alloy finish, 24 ga.		950	.034		3.51	1.68		5.19	6.40
0885	22 ga.		900	.036		3.98	1.77		5.75	7.10
0890	Flat profile, 2" x 2" batten, 12" wide, standard finish, 26 ga.		1000	.032		4.03	1.59		5.62	6.85
0895	24 ga.		950	.034		4.86	1.68		6.54	7.90
0900	22 ga.		900	.036		5.90	1.77		7.67	9.20
0905	Zinc aluminum alloy finish, 26 ga.		1000	.032		3.82	1.59		5.41	6.65
0910	24 ga.		950	.034		4.29	1.68		5.97	7.30
0915	22 ga.		900	.036		4.96	1.77		6.73	8.15
0920	16-1/2" wide, standard finish, 24 ga.		950	.034		4.44	1.68		6.12	7.45
0925	22 ga.		900	.036		5.10	1.77		6.87	8.35
0930	Zinc aluminum alloy finish, 24 ga.		950	.034		3.98	1.68		5.66	6.95
0935	22 ga.		900	.036		4.55	1.77		6.32	7.70
0950	Box rib roof panels, painted, including fasteners, 18 ga. G		850	.038		3.77	1.88		5.65	7
0960	20 ga. G		875	.037		3.29	1.82		5.11	6.40
0970	22 ga. G		900	.036		4.16	1.77		5.93	7.30
1000	4" rib panel, painted, including fasteners, 22 ga. G		900	.036		3.14	1.77		4.91	6.15

07 41 Roof Panels

07 41 13 – Metal Roof Panels

07 41 13.20 Steel Roofing Panels

		Crew	Daily Output	Labor-Hours	Unit	Material	2018 Bare Costs Labor	Equipment	Total	Total Incl O&P
1010	20 ga.	G-3 [G]	875	.037	S.F.	3.24	1.82		5.06	6.35
1020	18 ga.	[G]	850	.038		6.45	1.88		8.33	9.90
1050	On substrate, 2" standing seam panel, painted, 22 ga.	[G]	900	.036		5.80	1.77		7.57	9.05
1060	24 ga.	[G]	950	.034		5.35	1.68		7.03	8.45
1070	26 ga.	[G]	1000	.032		2.72	1.59		4.31	5.40
1200	Ridge, galvanized, 10" wide		800	.040	L.F.	3.23	1.99		5.22	6.60
1203	14" wide	[G]	2 Shee 316	.051		3.88	3.03		6.91	8.90
1205	18" wide	"	308	.052		4.52	3.11		7.63	9.70
1210	20" wide	G-3	750	.043		4.25	2.13		6.38	7.90

07 41 33 – Plastic Roof Panels

07 41 33.10 Fiberglass Panels

		Crew	Daily Output	Labor-Hours	Unit	Material	Labor	Equipment	Total	Total Incl O&P
0010	**FIBERGLASS PANELS**									
0012	Corrugated panels, roofing, 8 oz./S.F.	G-3	1000	.032	S.F.	2.47	1.59		4.06	5.15
0100	12 oz./S.F.	"	1000	.032	"	4.52	1.59		6.11	7.40

07 44 Faced Panels

07 44 73 – Metal Faced Panels

07 44 73.10 Metal Faced Panels and Accessories

		Crew	Daily Output	Labor-Hours	Unit	Material	Labor	Equipment	Total	Total Incl O&P
0010	**METAL FACED PANELS AND ACCESSORIES**									
0400	Textured aluminum, 4' x 8' x 5/16" plywood backing, single face	2 Shee	375	.043	S.F.	4.13	2.55		6.68	8.45
0600	Double face		375	.043		5.40	2.55		7.95	9.85
0700	4' x 10' x 5/16" plywood backing, single face		375	.043		4.40	2.55		6.95	8.75
0900	Double face		375	.043		5.90	2.55		8.45	10.40
1000	4' x 12' x 5/16" plywood backing, single face		375	.043		4.40	2.55		6.95	8.75
1010	Paneling, textured alum, 5/16" plywood-backed					4.13			4.13	4.54
1300	Smooth aluminum, 1/4" plywood panel, fluoropolymer finish, double face	2 Shee	375	.043		6.15	2.55		8.70	10.65
1350	Clear anodized finish, double face		375	.043		10.20	2.55		12.75	15.10
1400	Double face textured aluminum, structural panel, 1" EPS insulation		375	.043		5.80	2.55		8.35	10.30
1500	Accessories, outside corner	1 Shee	175	.046	L.F.	1.92	2.73		4.65	6.30
1600	Inside corner		175	.046		1.38	2.73		4.11	5.70
1800	Batten mounting clip		200	.040		.50	2.39		2.89	4.20
1900	Low profile batten		480	.017		.62	1		1.62	2.20
2100	High profile batten		480	.017		1.43	1		2.43	3.09
2200	Water table		200	.040		2.16	2.39		4.55	6.05
2400	Horizontal joint connector		200	.040		1.70	2.39		4.09	5.50
2500	Corner cap		200	.040		1.88	2.39		4.27	5.70
2700	H - moulding		480	.017		1.27	1		2.27	2.92

07 46 Siding

07 46 23 – Wood Siding

07 46 23.10 Wood Board Siding

		Crew	Daily Output	Labor-Hours	Unit	Material	Labor	Equipment	Total	Total Incl O&P
0010	**WOOD BOARD SIDING**									
4510	1" x 6", cedar	1 Carp	295	.027	S.F.	3.39	1.38		4.77	5.80
4520	1" x 8", cedar		330	.024		3.39	1.23		4.62	5.60
4550	T&G, 1" x 6", cypress		295	.027		3.14	1.38		4.52	5.55
4560	1" x 8", cypress		330	.024		3.14	1.23		4.37	5.30

For customer support on your Green Building Costs with RSMeans data, call 800.448.8182.

07 46 Siding

07 46 33 – Plastic Siding

07 46 33.10 Vinyl Siding

		Crew	Daily Output	Labor-Hours	Unit	Material	2018 Bare Costs Labor	Equipment	Total	Total Incl O&P
0010	**VINYL SIDING**									
3995	Clapboard profile, woodgrain texture, .048 thick, double 4	2 Carp	495	.032	S.F.	1.07	1.64		2.71	3.68
4000	Double 5		550	.029		1.07	1.47		2.54	3.43
4005	Single 8		495	.032		1.37	1.64		3.01	4.01
4010	Single 10		550	.029		1.65	1.47		3.12	4.06
4015	.044 thick, double 4		495	.032		1.05	1.64		2.69	3.66
4020	Double 5		550	.029		1.07	1.47		2.54	3.43
4025	.042 thick, double 4		495	.032		1.07	1.64		2.71	3.68
4030	Double 5		550	.029		1.07	1.47		2.54	3.43
4035	Cross sawn texture, .040 thick, double 4		495	.032		.73	1.64		2.37	3.31
4040	Double 5		550	.029		.67	1.47		2.14	2.99
4045	Smooth texture, .042 thick, double 4		495	.032		.80	1.64		2.44	3.38
4050	Double 5		550	.029		.80	1.47		2.27	3.13
4055	Single 8		495	.032		.80	1.64		2.44	3.38
4060	Cedar texture, .044 thick, double 4		495	.032		1.14	1.64		2.78	3.76
4065	Double 6		600	.027		1.15	1.35		2.50	3.33
4070	Dutch lap profile, woodgrain texture, .048 thick, double 5		550	.029		1.09	1.47		2.56	3.45
4075	.044 thick, double 4.5		525	.030		1.09	1.55		2.64	3.55
4080	.042 thick, double 4.5		525	.030		.92	1.55		2.47	3.37
4085	.040 thick, double 4.5		525	.030		.73	1.55		2.28	3.16
4100	Shake profile, 10" wide		400	.040		3.71	2.03		5.74	7.20
4105	Vertical pattern, .046 thick, double 5		550	.029		1.56	1.47		3.03	3.97
4110	.044 thick, triple 3		550	.029		1.78	1.47		3.25	4.21
4115	.040 thick, triple 4		550	.029		1.68	1.47		3.15	4.10
4120	.040 thick, triple 2.66		550	.029		1.78	1.47		3.25	4.21
4125	Insulation, fan folded extruded polystyrene, 1/4"		2000	.008		.29	.41		.70	.94
4130	3/8"		2000	.008		.32	.41		.73	.97
4135	Accessories, J channel, 5/8" pocket		700	.023	L.F.	.51	1.16		1.67	2.32
4140	3/4" pocket		695	.023		.56	1.17		1.73	2.39
4145	1-1/4" pocket		680	.024		.86	1.19		2.05	2.76
4150	Flexible, 3/4" pocket		600	.027		2.39	1.35		3.74	4.69
4155	Under sill finish trim		500	.032		.56	1.62		2.18	3.08
4160	Vinyl starter strip		700	.023		.66	1.16		1.82	2.48
4165	Aluminum starter strip		700	.023		.29	1.16		1.45	2.08
4170	Window casing, 2-1/2" wide, 3/4" pocket		510	.031		1.71	1.59		3.30	4.30
4175	Outside corner, woodgrain finish, 4" face, 3/4" pocket		700	.023		2.15	1.16		3.31	4.13
4180	5/8" pocket		700	.023		2.13	1.16		3.29	4.11
4185	Smooth finish, 4" face, 3/4" pocket		700	.023		2.13	1.16		3.29	4.11
4190	7/8" pocket		690	.023		2.03	1.18		3.21	4.03
4195	1-1/4" pocket		700	.023		1.42	1.16		2.58	3.33
4200	Soffit and fascia, 1' overhang, solid		120	.133		4.72	6.75		11.47	15.50
4205	Vented		120	.133		4.72	6.75		11.47	15.50
4207	18" overhang, solid		110	.145		5.50	7.35		12.85	17.30
4208	Vented		110	.145		5.50	7.35		12.85	17.30
4210	2' overhang, solid		100	.160		6.30	8.10		14.40	19.25
4215	Vented		100	.160		6.30	8.10		14.40	19.25
4217	3' overhang, solid		100	.160		7.85	8.10		15.95	21
4218	Vented		100	.160		7.85	8.10		15.95	21
4220	Colors for siding and soffits, add				S.F.	.15			.15	.17
4225	Colors for accessories and trim, add				L.F.	.31			.31	.34

For customer support on your Green Building Costs with RSMeans data, call 800.448.8182.

07 46 Siding

07 46 33 – Plastic Siding

07 46 33.20 Polypropylene Siding

		Crew	Daily Output	Labor-Hours	Unit	Material	2018 Bare Costs Labor	Equipment	Total	Total Incl O&P
0010	**POLYPROPYLENE SIDING**									
4090	Shingle profile, random grooves, double 7	2 Carp	400	.040	S.F.	3.24	2.03		5.27	6.65
4092	Cornerpost for above	1 Carp	365	.022	L.F.	13.10	1.11		14.21	16.10
4095	Triple 5	2 Carp	400	.040	S.F.	3.24	2.03		5.27	6.65
4097	Cornerpost for above	1 Carp	365	.022	L.F.	12.30	1.11		13.41	15.25
5000	Staggered butt, double 7"	2 Carp	400	.040	S.F.	3.70	2.03		5.73	7.15
5002	Cornerpost for above	1 Carp	365	.022	L.F.	13.10	1.11		14.21	16.10
5010	Half round, double 6-1/4"	2 Carp	360	.044	S.F.	3.70	2.25		5.95	7.50
5020	Shake profile, staggered butt, double 9"	"	510	.031	"	3.70	1.59		5.29	6.50
5022	Cornerpost for above	1 Carp	365	.022	L.F.	9.80	1.11		10.91	12.45
5030	Straight butt, double 7"	2 Carp	400	.040	S.F.	3.70	2.03		5.73	7.15
5032	Cornerpost for above	1 Carp	365	.022	L.F.	13	1.11		14.11	16
6000	Accessories, J channel, 5/8" pocket	2 Carp	700	.023		.51	1.16		1.67	2.32
6010	3/4" pocket		695	.023		.56	1.17		1.73	2.39
6020	1-1/4" pocket		680	.024		.86	1.19		2.05	2.76
6030	Aluminum starter strip		700	.023		.29	1.16		1.45	2.08

07 51 Built-Up Bituminous Roofing

07 51 13 – Built-Up Asphalt Roofing

07 51 13.20 Built-Up Roofing Systems

		Crew	Daily Output	Labor-Hours	Unit	Material	Labor	Equipment	Total	Total Incl O&P
0010	**BUILT-UP ROOFING SYSTEMS** R075113-20									
0120	Asphalt flood coat with gravel/slag surfacing, not including									
0140	Insulation, flashing or wood nailers									
0160	3-ply asphalt, no flood coat	G-1	24	2.333	Sq.	75	96	21.50	192.50	267
0200	Asphalt base sheet, 3 plies #15 asphalt felt, mopped		22	2.545		104	105	23.50	232.50	315
0350	On nailable decks		21	2.667		107	109	24.50	240.50	330
0500	4 plies #15 asphalt felt, mopped		20	2.800		142	115	25.50	282.50	380
0550	On nailable decks		19	2.947		126	121	27	274	370
0700	Coated glass base sheet, 2 plies glass (type IV), mopped		22	2.545		111	105	23.50	239.50	325
0850	3 plies glass, mopped		20	2.800		134	115	25.50	274.50	370
0950	On nailable decks		19	2.947		126	121	27	274	370
1100	4 plies glass fiber felt (type IV), mopped		20	2.800		165	115	25.50	305.50	405
1150	On nailable decks		19	2.947		149	121	27	297	400
1200	Coated & saturated base sheet, 3 plies #15 asph. felt, mopped		20	2.800		116	115	25.50	256.50	350
1250	On nailable decks		19	2.947		108	121	27	256	355
1300	4 plies #15 asphalt felt, mopped		22	2.545		135	105	23.50	263.50	350
2000	Asphalt flood coat, smooth surface									
2200	Asphalt base sheet & 3 plies #15 asphalt felt, mopped	G-1	24	2.333	Sq.	110	96	21.50	227.50	305
2400	On nailable decks		23	2.435		102	100	22.50	224.50	305
2600	4 plies #15 asphalt felt, mopped		24	2.333		129	96	21.50	246.50	325
2700	On nailable decks		23	2.435		121	100	22.50	243.50	325
2900	Coated glass fiber base sheet, mopped, and 2 plies of									
2910	glass fiber felt (type IV)	G-1	25	2.240	Sq.	106	92	20.50	218.50	295
3100	On nailable decks		24	2.333		100	96	21.50	217.50	295
3200	3 plies, mopped		23	2.435		129	100	22.50	251.50	335
3300	On nailable decks		22	2.545		121	105	23.50	249.50	335
3800	4 plies glass fiber felt (type IV), mopped		23	2.435		152	100	22.50	274.50	360
3900	On nailable decks		22	2.545		144	105	23.50	272.50	360
4000	Coated & saturated base sheet, 3 plies #15 asph. felt, mopped		24	2.333		111	96	21.50	228.50	305
4200	On nailable decks		23	2.435		103	100	22.50	225.50	305

For customer support on your Green Building Costs with RSMeans data, call 800.448.8182.

07 51 Built-Up Bituminous Roofing

07 51 13 – Built-Up Asphalt Roofing

07 51 13.20 Built-Up Roofing Systems

		Crew	Daily Output	Labor-Hours	Unit	Material	2018 Bare Costs Labor	Equipment	Total	Total Incl O&P
4300	4 plies #15 organic felt, mopped	G-1	22	2.545	Sq.	130	105	23.50	258.50	345
4425	Inverted roof membrane sys., 3 ply BUR, 2" EPS insul., gravel ballast		20	2.800	C.S.F.	169	115	25.50	309.50	410
4440	To repl gravel w/12" x 12" x 1-1/2" concrete pavers, add					40%	18%			
4500	Coal tar pitch with gravel/slag surfacing									
4600	4 plies #15 tarred felt, mopped	G-1	21	2.667	Sq.	199	109	24.50	332.50	430
4800	3 plies glass fiber felt (type IV), mopped	"	19	2.947	"	164	121	27	312	415
5000	Coated glass fiber base sheet, and 2 plies of									
5010	glass fiber felt (type IV), mopped	G-1	19	2.947	Sq.	170	121	27	318	420
5300	On nailable decks		18	3.111		148	128	28.50	304.50	410
5600	4 plies glass fiber felt (type IV), mopped		21	2.667		228	109	24.50	361.50	460
5800	On nailable decks		20	2.800		207	115	25.50	347.50	450
6000	Flood coat	2 Rofc	13	1.231		29	54		83	123
6050	Gravel coat	"	24	.667		5.10	29.50		34.60	55
6100	Aluminum UV coating	G	G-5	8	5		31.50	200	22.50	254	395
6110	With fiber	G	2 Rofc	13	1.231		23.50	54		77.50	117
6120	Fire rated		13	1.231		21.50	54		75.50	115
6400	Remove/replace gravel with flood coat		4	4		34	176		210	335
6510	Walkway, asphalt impregnated, 1/2" thick		475	.034	S.F.	2.12	1.48		3.60	4.82
6520	3/4" thick		450	.036		2.62	1.56		4.18	5.50
6530	1" thick		375	.043		2.93	1.88		4.81	6.40
8000	Emergency repairs	G-1	1.40	40	Ea.	204	1,650	365	2,219	3,400

07 51 13.50 Walkways for Built-Up Roofs

		Crew	Daily Output	Labor-Hours	Unit	Material	Labor	Equipment	Total	Incl O&P
0010	**WALKWAYS FOR BUILT-UP ROOFS**									
0600	100% recycled rubber, 3' x 4' x 3/8"	G	1 Rofc	400	.020	L.F.	6.50	.88		7.38	8.65
0610	3' x 4' x 1/2"	G		400	.020		6.85	.88		7.73	9.05
0620	3' x 4' x 3/4"	G		400	.020		8.50	.88		9.38	10.85

07 53 Elastomeric Membrane Roofing

07 53 16 – Chlorosulfonate-Polyethylene Roofing

07 53 16.10 Chlorosulfonated Polyethylene Roofing

		Crew	Daily Output	Labor-Hours	Unit	Material	Labor	Equipment	Total	Incl O&P
0010	**CHLOROSULFONATED POLYETHYLENE ROOFING**									
0800	Chlorosulfonated polyethylene (CSPE)									
0900	45 mils, heat welded seams, plate attachment	G-5	35	1.143	Sq.	241	45.50	5.20	291.70	350
1100	Heat welded seams, plate attachment and ballasted		26	1.538		252	61.50	6.95	320.45	390
1200	60 mils, heat welded seams, plate attachment		35	1.143		310	45.50	5.20	360.70	430
1300	Heat welded seams, plate attachment and ballasted		26	1.538		320	61.50	6.95	388.45	465

07 53 23 – Ethylene-Propylene-Diene-Monomer Roofing

07 53 23.20 Ethylene-Propylene-Diene-Monomer Roofing

		Crew	Daily Output	Labor-Hours	Unit	Material	Labor	Equipment	Total	Incl O&P
0010	**ETHYLENE-PROPYLENE-DIENE-MONOMER ROOFING (EPDM)**									
0100	Butyl, 1/16" thick	G-5	7	5.714	Sq.	395	228	26	649	850
0110	1/32"	"	7	5.714	"	260	228	26	514	700
3500	Ethylene-propylene-diene-monomer (EPDM), 45 mils, 0.28 psf									
3600	Loose-laid & ballasted with stone (10 psf)	G-5	51	.784	Sq.	85	31.50	3.55	120.05	150
3700	Mechanically attached		35	1.143		79	45.50	5.20	129.70	170
3800	Fully adhered with adhesive		26	1.538		112	61.50	6.95	180.45	235
4500	60 mils, 0.40 psf									
4600	Loose-laid & ballasted with stone (10 psf)	G-5	51	.784	Sq.	101	31.50	3.55	136.05	167
4700	Mechanically attached		35	1.143		94	45.50	5.20	144.70	186
4800	Fully adhered with adhesive		26	1.538		127	61.50	6.95	195.45	251
4810	45 mil, 0.28 psf, membrane only					49			49	54

07 53 Elastomeric Membrane Roofing

07 53 23 – Ethylene-Propylene-Diene-Monomer Roofing

07 53 23.20 Ethylene-Propylene-Diene-Monomer Roofing

		Crew	Daily Output	Labor-Hours	Unit	Material	2018 Bare Costs Labor	Equipment	Total	Total Incl O&P
4820	60 mil, 0.40 psf, membrane only				Sq.	62.50			62.50	68.50
4850	Seam tape for membrane, 3" x 100' roll				Ea.	44.50			44.50	49
4900	Batten strips, 10' sections					3.94			3.94	4.33
4910	Cover tape for batten strips, 6" x 100' roll					187			187	206
4930	Plate anchors				M	81			81	89
4970	Adhesive for fully adhered systems, 60 S.F./gal.				Gal.	20.50			20.50	22.50

07 53 29 – Polyisobutylene Roofing

07 53 29.10 Polyisobutylene Roofing

		Crew	Daily Output	Labor-Hours	Unit	Material	Labor	Equipment	Total	Total Incl O&P
0010	**POLYISOBUTYLENE ROOFING**									
7500	Polyisobutylene (PIB), 100 mils, 0.57 psf									
7600	Loose-laid & ballasted with stone/gravel (10 psf)	G-5	51	.784	Sq.	211	31.50	3.55	246.05	288
7700	Partially adhered with adhesive		35	1.143		251	45.50	5.20	301.70	360
7800	Hot asphalt attachment		35	1.143		241	45.50	5.20	291.70	350
7900	Fully adhered with contact cement		26	1.538		262	61.50	6.95	330.45	400

07 54 Thermoplastic Membrane Roofing

07 54 23 – Thermoplastic-Polyolefin Roofing

07 54 23.10 Thermoplastic Polyolefin Roofing (T.P.O.)

		Crew	Daily Output	Labor-Hours	Unit	Material	Labor	Equipment	Total	Total Incl O&P
0010	**THERMOPLASTIC POLYOLEFIN ROOFING (T.P.O.)**									
0100	45 mil, loose laid & ballasted with stone (1/2 ton/sq.)	G-5	51	.784	Sq.	88	31.50	3.55	123.05	153
0120	Fully adhered		25	1.600		78.50	64	7.25	149.75	201
0140	Mechanically attached		34	1.176		78	47	5.35	130.35	170
0160	Self adhered		35	1.143		78.50	45.50	5.20	129.20	169
0180	60 mil membrane, heat welded seams, ballasted		50	.800		100	32	3.62	135.62	167
0200	Fully adhered		25	1.600		90	64	7.25	161.25	214
0220	Mechanically attached		34	1.176		94	47	5.35	146.35	189
0240	Self adhered		35	1.143		106	45.50	5.20	156.70	200

07 54 30 – Ketone Ethylene Ester Roofing

07 54 30.10 Ketone Ethylene Ester Roofing

		Crew	Daily Output	Labor-Hours	Unit	Material	Labor	Equipment	Total	Total Incl O&P
0010	**KETONE ETHYLENE ESTER ROOFING**									
0100	Ketone ethylene ester roofing, 50 mil, fully adhered	G-5	26	1.538	Sq.	202	61.50	6.95	270.45	335
0120	Mechanically attached		35	1.143		131	45.50	5.20	181.70	227
0140	Ballasted with stone		51	.784		138	31.50	3.55	173.05	208
0160	50 mil, fleece backed, adhered w/hot asphalt	G-1	26	2.154		162	88.50	19.75	270.25	350
0180	Accessories, pipe boot	1 Rofc	32	.250	Ea.	25.50	11		36.50	47
0200	Pre-formed corners		32	.250	"	8.90	11		19.90	28.50
0220	Ketone clad metal, including up to 4 bends		330	.024	S.F.	4.12	1.07		5.19	6.30
0240	Walkway pad	2 Rofc	800	.020	"	4.33	.88		5.21	6.25
0260	Stripping material	1 Rofc	310	.026	L.F.	1	1.13		2.13	3.01

07 61 Sheet Metal Roofing

07 61 13 – Standing Seam Sheet Metal Roofing

07 61 13.10 Standing Seam Sheet Metal Roofing, Field Fab.

		Crew	Daily Output	Labor-Hours	Unit	Material	2018 Bare Costs Labor	Equipment	Total	Total Incl O&P
0010	**STANDING SEAM SHEET METAL ROOFING, FIELD FABRICATED**									
1350	Bay window roof kit, 100% recycled copper, 8' wide opening [G]	1 Carp	3	2.667	Ea.	750	135		885	1,025

07 95 Expansion Control

07 95 13 – Expansion Joint Cover Assemblies

07 95 13.50 Expansion Joint Assemblies

		Crew	Daily Output	Labor-Hours	Unit	Material	Labor	Equipment	Total	Total Incl O&P
0010	**EXPANSION JOINT ASSEMBLIES**									
0015	Made from recycled materials									
0200	Floor cover assemblies, 1" space, aluminum	1 Sswk	38	.211	L.F.	19	11.50		30.50	40
0300	Bronze		38	.211		60.50	11.50		72	85.50
0500	2" space, aluminum		38	.211		18.50	11.50		30	39.50
0600	Bronze		38	.211		60.50	11.50		72	85.50
0800	Wall and ceiling assemblies, 1" space, aluminum		38	.211		16.75	11.50		28.25	37.50
0900	Bronze		38	.211		53.50	11.50		65	78
1100	2" space, aluminum		38	.211		17.10	11.50		28.60	37.50
1200	Bronze		38	.211		52.50	11.50		64	76.50
1400	Floor to wall assemblies, 1" space, aluminum		38	.211		19.50	11.50		31	40.50
1500	Bronze or stainless		38	.211		64.50	11.50		76	90
1700	Gym floor angle covers, aluminum, 3" x 3" angle		46	.174		19.50	9.50		29	37
1800	3" x 4" angle		46	.174		23	9.50		32.50	41
2000	Roof closures, aluminum, flat roof, low profile, 1" space		57	.140		24	7.65		31.65	39
2100	High profile		57	.140		26	7.65		33.65	41
2300	Roof to wall, low profile, 1" space		57	.140		23.50	7.65		31.15	38
2400	High profile		57	.140		26	7.65		33.65	41

Division 8 Openings

Estimating Tips
08 10 00 Doors and Frames
All exterior doors should be addressed for their energy conservation (insulation and seals).
- Most metal doors and frames look alike, but there may be significant differences among them. When estimating these items, be sure to choose the line item that most closely compares to the specification or door schedule requirements regarding:
  - ☐ type of metal
  - ☐ metal gauge
  - ☐ door core material
  - ☐ fire rating
  - ☐ finish
- Wood and plastic doors vary considerably in price. The primary determinant is the veneer material. Lauan, birch, and oak are the most common veneers. Other variables include the following:
  - ☐ hollow or solid core
  - ☐ fire rating
  - ☐ flush or raised panel
  - ☐ finish
- Door pricing includes bore for cylindrical locksets and mortise for hinges.

08 30 00 Specialty Doors and Frames
- There are many varieties of special doors, and they are usually priced per each. Add frames, hardware, or operators required for a complete installation.

08 40 00 Entrances, Storefronts, and Curtain Walls
- Glazed curtain walls consist of the metal tube framing and the glazing material. The cost data in this subdivision is presented for the metal tube framing alone or the composite wall. If your estimate requires a detailed takeoff of the framing, be sure to add the glazing cost and any tints.

08 50 00 Windows
- Steel windows are unglazed and aluminum can be glazed or unglazed. Some metal windows are priced without glass. Refer to 08 80 00 Glazing for glass pricing. The grade C indicates commercial grade windows, usually ASTM C-35.
- All wood windows and vinyl are priced preglazed. The glazing is insulating glass. Add the cost of screens and grills if required and not already included.

08 70 00 Hardware
- Hardware costs add considerably to the cost of a door. The most efficient method to determine the hardware requirements for a project is to review the door and hardware schedule together. One type of door may have different hardware, depending on the door usage.
- Door hinges are priced by the pair, with most doors requiring 1-1/2 pairs per door. The hinge prices do not include installation labor, because it is included in door installation. Hinges are classified according to the frequency of use, base material, and finish.

08 80 00 Glazing
- Different openings require different types of glass. The most common types are:
  - ☐ float
  - ☐ tempered
  - ☐ insulating
  - ☐ impact-resistant
  - ☐ ballistic-resistant
- Most exterior windows are glazed with insulating glass. Entrance doors and window walls, where the glass is less than 18" from the floor, are generally glazed with tempered glass. Interior windows and some residential windows are glazed with float glass.
- Coastal communities require the use of impact-resistant glass, dependent on wind speed.
- The insulation or 'u' value is a strong consideration, along with solar heat gain, to determine total energy efficiency.

Reference Numbers
Reference numbers are shown at the beginning of some major classifications. These numbers refer to related items in the Reference Section. The reference information may be an estimating procedure, an alternate pricing method, or technical information.

Note: Not all subdivisions listed here necessarily appear. ■

No part of this cost data may be reproduced, stored in a retrieval system, or transmitted in any form or by any means without prior written permission of Gordian.

Did you know?
RSMeans data is available through our online application with 24/7 access:
- Search for unit prices by keyword
- Leverage the most up-to-date data
- Build and export estimates

Try it free for 30 days!
www.rsmeans.com/2018freetrial

08 01 Operation and Maintenance of Openings

08 01 53 – Operation and Maintenance of Plastic Windows

08 01 53.81 Solid Vinyl Replacement Windows		Crew	Daily Output	Labor-Hours	Unit	Material	2018 Bare Costs Labor	Equipment	Total	Total Incl O&P
0010	**SOLID VINYL REPLACEMENT WINDOWS** R085313-20									
0020	Double-hung, insulated glass, up to 83 united inches G	2 Carp	8	2	Ea.	173	101		274	345
0040	84 to 93 G		8	2		199	101		300	375
0060	94 to 101 G		6	2.667		199	135		334	425
0080	102 to 111 G		6	2.667		208	135		343	435
0100	112 to 120 G		6	2.667		222	135		357	450
0120	For each united inch over 120, add G		800	.020	Inch	2.79	1.01		3.80	4.61
0140	Casement windows, one operating sash, 42 to 60 united inches G		8	2	Ea.	228	101		329	405
0160	61 to 70 G		8	2		259	101		360	440
0180	71 to 80 G		8	2		283	101		384	465
0200	81 to 96 G		8	2		298	101		399	485
0220	Two operating sash, 58 to 78 united inches G		8	2		455	101		556	655
0240	79 to 88 G		8	2		490	101		591	690
0260	89 to 98 G		8	2		525	101		626	735
0280	99 to 108 G		6	2.667		555	135		690	815
0300	109 to 121 G		6	2.667		595	135		730	860
0320	Two operating, one fixed sash, 73 to 108 united inches G		8	2		715	101		816	945
0340	109 to 118 G		8	2		755	101		856	985
0360	119 to 128 G		6	2.667		775	135		910	1,050
0380	129 to 138 G		6	2.667		820	135		955	1,100
0400	139 to 156 G		6	2.667		860	135		995	1,150
0420	Four operating sash, 98 to 118 united inches G		8	2		1,025	101		1,126	1,275
0440	119 to 128 G		8	2		1,100	101		1,201	1,350
0460	129 to 138 G		6	2.667		1,175	135		1,310	1,475
0480	139 to 148 G		6	2.667		1,225	135		1,360	1,550
0500	149 to 168 G		6	2.667		1,300	135		1,435	1,650
0520	169 to 178 G		6	2.667		1,425	135		1,560	1,750
0560	Fixed picture window, up to 63 united inches G		8	2		170	101		271	340
0580	64 to 83 G		8	2		200	101		301	375
0600	84 to 101 G		8	2		240	101		341	420
0620	For each united inch over 101, add G		900	.018	Inch	2.85	.90		3.75	4.51
0800	Cellulose fiber insulation, poured into sash balance cavity G	1 Carp	36	.222	C.F.	.69	11.25		11.94	17.90
0820	Silicone caulking at perimeter G	"	800	.010	L.F.	.17	.51		.68	.96
2000	Impact resistant replacement windows									
2005	Laminated glass, 120 MPH rating, measure in united inches									
2010	Installation labor does not cover any rework of the window opening									
2020	Double-hung, insulated glass, up to 101 united inches	2 Carp	8	2	Ea.	520	101		621	725
2025	For each united inch over 101, add		80	.200	Inch	3.30	10.15		13.45	19.10
2100	Casement windows, impact resistant, up to 60 united inches		8	2	Ea.	480	101		581	680
2120	61 to 70		8	2		505	101		606	710
2130	71 to 80		8	2		535	101		636	740
2140	81 to 100		8	2		550	101		651	755
2150	For each united inch over 100, add		80	.200	Inch	4.65	10.15		14.80	20.50
2200	Awning windows, impact resistant, up to 60 united inches		8	2	Ea.	490	101		591	695
2220	61 to 70		8	2		515	101		616	720
2230	71 to 80		8	2		525	101		626	730
2240	For each united inch over 80, add		80	.200	Inch	4.65	10.15		14.80	20.50
2300	Picture windows, impact resistant, up to 63 united inches		8	2	Ea.	355	101		456	545
2320	63 to 83		8	2		385	101		486	575
2330	84 to 101		8	2		420	101		521	615
2340	For each united inch over 101, add		80	.200	Inch	3.30	10.15		13.45	19.10

08 05 Common Work Results for Openings

08 05 05 – Selective Demolition for Openings

08 05 05.20 Selective Demolition of Windows

		Crew	Daily Output	Labor-Hours	Unit	Material	2018 Bare Costs Labor	Equipment	Total	Total Incl O&P
0010	**SELECTIVE DEMOLITION OF WINDOWS** R024119-10									
4410	Remove skylight, plstc domes, flush/curb mtd	2 Carp	395	.041	S.F.		2.05		2.05	3.13
4420	Remove skylight, plstc/glass up to 2' x 3'	1 Carp	15	.533	Ea.		27		27	41
4440	Remove skylight, plstc/glass up to 4' x 6'	2 Carp	10	1.600			81		81	124
4480	Remove roof window up to 3' x 4'	1 Carp	8	1			50.50		50.50	77
4500	Remove roof window up to 4' x 6'	2 Carp	6	2.667	↓		135		135	206

08 12 Metal Frames

08 12 13 – Hollow Metal Frames

08 12 13.13 Standard Hollow Metal Frames

			Crew	Daily Output	Labor-Hours	Unit	Material	Labor	Equipment	Total	Total Incl O&P
0010	**STANDARD HOLLOW METAL FRAMES**										
0020	16 ga., up to 5-3/4" jamb depth										
0025	3'-0" x 6'-8" single	G	2 Carp	16	1	Ea.	121	50.50		171.50	210
0028	3'-6" wide, single	G		16	1		232	50.50		282.50	330
0030	4'-0" wide, single	G		16	1		268	50.50		318.50	370
0040	6'-0" wide, double	G		14	1.143		227	58		285	340
0045	8'-0" wide, double	G		14	1.143		227	58		285	340
0100	3'-0" x 7'-0" single	G		16	1		192	50.50		242.50	288
0110	3'-6" wide, single	G		16	1		194	50.50		244.50	290
0112	4'-0" wide, single	G		16	1		227	50.50		277.50	325
0140	6'-0" wide, double	G		14	1.143		227	58		285	340
0145	8'-0" wide, double	G		14	1.143		237	58		295	350
1000	16 ga., up to 4-7/8" deep, 3'-0" x 7'-0" single	G		16	1		181	50.50		231.50	276
1140	6'-0" wide, double	G		14	1.143		204	58		262	315
1200	16 ga., 8-3/4" deep, 3'-0" x 7'-0" single	G		16	1		192	50.50		242.50	288
1240	6'-0" wide, double	G		14	1.143		256	58		314	370
2800	14 ga., up to 3-7/8" deep, 3'-0" x 7'-0" single	G		16	1		247	50.50		297.50	350
2840	6'-0" wide, double	G		14	1.143		278	58		336	395
2900	14 ga., 4-3/4" deep, 2'-0" x 7'-0" high, single	G		15	1.067		182	54		236	283
2910	2'-4" wide	G		15	1.067		219	54		273	325
2920	2'-6" wide	G		15	1.067		219	54		273	325
2930	2'-8" wide	G		15	1.067		219	54		273	325
2940	3'-0" wide	G		15	1.067		219	54		273	325
2950	3'-4" wide	G		15	1.067		227	54		281	335
2960	6'-0" wide, double	G		12	1.333		253	67.50		320.50	380
3000	14 ga., up to 5-3/4" deep, 3'-0" x 6'-8" single	G		16	1		154	50.50		204.50	246
3002	3'-6" wide, single	G		16	1		239	50.50		289.50	340
3005	4'-0" wide, single	G		16	1		155	50.50		205.50	248
3600	up to 5-3/4" jamb depth, 4'-0" x 7'-0" single	G		15	1.067		237	54		291	345
3620	6'-0" wide, double	G		12	1.333		177	67.50		244.50	297
3640	8'-0" wide, double	G		12	1.333		282	67.50		349.50	415
3700	8'-0" high, 4'-0" wide, single	G		15	1.067		270	54		324	380
3740	8'-0" wide, double	G		12	1.333		320	67.50		387.50	455
4000	6-3/4" deep, 4'-0" x 7'-0" single	G		15	1.067		266	54		320	375
4020	6'-0" wide, double	G		12	1.333		300	67.50		367.50	435
4040	8'-0" wide, double	G		12	1.333		224	67.50		291.50	350
4100	8'-0" high, 4'-0" wide, single	G		15	1.067		176	54		230	276
4140	8'-0" wide, double	G		12	1.333		415	67.50		482.50	560
4400	8-3/4" deep, 4'-0" x 7'-0", single	G		15	1.067		385	54		439	505
4440	8'-0" wide, double	G		12	1.333		405	67.50		472.50	555
4500	4'-0" x 8'-0", single	G		15	1.067		440	54		494	570

For customer support on your Green Building Costs with RSMeans data, call 800.448.8182.

08 12 Metal Frames

08 12 13 – Hollow Metal Frames

08 12 13.13 Standard Hollow Metal Frames

		Crew	Daily Output	Labor-Hours	Unit	Material	2018 Bare Costs Labor	Equipment	Total	Total Incl O&P
4540	8'-0" wide, double	2 Carp	12	1.333	Ea.	450	67.50		517.50	600
4900	For welded frames, add					51			51	56
5400	14 ga., "B" label, up to 5-3/4" deep, 4'-0" x 7'-0" single	2 Carp	15	1.067		167	54		221	267
5440	8'-0" wide, double		12	1.333		219	67.50		286.50	345
5800	6-3/4" deep, 7'-0" high, 4'-0" wide, single		15	1.067		173	54		227	274
5840	8'-0" wide, double		12	1.333		305	67.50		372.50	445
6200	8-3/4" deep, 4'-0" x 7'-0" single		15	1.067		247	54		301	355
6240	8'-0" wide, double		12	1.333		380	67.50		447.50	525
6300	For "A" label use same price as "B" label									
6400	For baked enamel finish, add					30%	15%			
6500	For galvanizing, add					20%				
6600	For hospital stop, add				Ea.	235			235	259
6620	For hospital stop, stainless steel, add				"	109			109	120
7900	Transom lite frames, fixed, add	2 Carp	155	.103	S.F.	43	5.25		48.25	55.50
8000	Movable, add	"	130	.123	"	55	6.25		61.25	70

08 12 13.25 Channel Metal Frames

		Crew	Daily Output	Labor-Hours	Unit	Material	Labor	Equipment	Total	Total Incl O&P
0010	**CHANNEL METAL FRAMES**									
0020	Steel channels with anchors and bar stops									
0100	6" channel @ 8.2#/L.F., 3' x 7' door, weighs 150#	E-4	13	2.462	Ea.	242	136	7.60	385.60	495
0103	Metal door frame		10	3.200		242	176	9.85	427.85	565
0200	8" channel @ 11.5#/L.F., 6' x 8' door, weighs 275#		9	3.556		445	196	10.95	651.95	820
0203	Sliding door frame		6.92	4.622		445	255	14.25	714.25	920
0300	8' x 12' door, weighs 400#		6.50	4.923		645	272	15.15	932.15	1,175
0400	10" channel @ 15.3#/L.F., 10' x 10' door, weighs 500#		6	5.333		810	294	16.45	1,120.45	1,400
0500	12' x 12' door, weighs 600#		5.50	5.818		970	320	17.90	1,307.90	1,625
0600	12" channel @ 20.7#/L.F., 12' x 12' door, weighs 825#		4.50	7.111		1,325	390	22	1,737	2,150
0700	12' x 16' door, weighs 1000#		4	8		1,625	440	24.50	2,089.50	2,525
0800	For frames without bar stops, light sections, deduct					15%				
0900	Heavy sections, deduct					10%				

08 13 Metal Doors

08 13 13 – Hollow Metal Doors

08 13 13.13 Standard Hollow Metal Doors

		Crew	Daily Output	Labor-Hours	Unit	Material	Labor	Equipment	Total	Total Incl O&P
0010	**STANDARD HOLLOW METAL DOORS** R081313-20									
0015	Flush, full panel, hollow core									
0017	When noted doors are prepared but do not include glass or louvers									
0020	1-3/8" thick, 20 ga., 2'-0" x 6'-8"	2 Carp	20	.800	Ea.	340	40.50		380.50	435
0040	2'-8" x 6'-8"		18	.889		350	45		395	455
0060	3'-0" x 6'-8"		17	.941		355	47.50		402.50	465
0100	3'-0" x 7'-0"		17	.941		365	47.50		412.50	480
0120	For vision lite, add					108			108	119
0140	For narrow lite, add					116			116	128
0320	Half glass, 20 ga., 2'-0" x 6'-8"	2 Carp	20	.800		600	40.50		640.50	720
0340	2'-8" x 6'-8"		18	.889		600	45		645	730
0360	3'-0" x 6'-8"		17	.941		600	47.50		647.50	735
0400	3'-0" x 7'-0"		17	.941		400	47.50		447.50	515
0410	1-3/8" thick, 18 ga., 2'-0" x 6'-8"		20	.800		405	40.50		445.50	505
0420	3'-0" x 6'-8"		17	.941		410	47.50		457.50	525
0425	3'-0" x 7'-0"		17	.941		430	47.50		477.50	550
0450	For vision lite, add					108			108	119
0452	For narrow lite, add					116			116	128

08 13 Metal Doors

08 13 13 – Hollow Metal Doors

08 13 13.13 Standard Hollow Metal Doors

			Crew	Daily Output	Labor-Hours	Unit	Material	2018 Bare Costs Labor	Equipment	Total	Total Incl O&P
0460	Half glass, 18 ga., 2'-0" x 6'-8"	G	2 Carp	20	.800	Ea.	560	40.50		600.50	680
0465	2'-8" x 6'-8"	G		18	.889		580	45		625	710
0470	3'-0" x 6'-8"	G		17	.941		570	47.50		617.50	700
0475	3'-0" x 7'-0"	G		17	.941		585	47.50		632.50	720
0500	Hollow core, 1-3/4" thick, full panel, 20 ga., 2'-8" x 6'-8"	G		18	.889		435	45		480	550
0520	3'-0" x 6'-8"	G		17	.941		435	47.50		482.50	555
0640	3'-0" x 7'-0"	G		17	.941		465	47.50		512.50	585
0680	4'-0" x 7'-0"	G		15	1.067		635	54		689	780
0700	4'-0" x 8'-0"	G		13	1.231		750	62.50		812.50	915
1000	18 ga., 2'-8" x 6'-8"	G		17	.941		485	47.50		532.50	605
1020	3'-0" x 6'-8"	G		16	1		485	50.50		535.50	605
1120	3'-0" x 7'-0"	G		17	.941		495	47.50		542.50	620
1180	4'-0" x 7'-0"	G		14	1.143		695	58		753	855
1200	4'-0" x 8'-0"	G		17	.941		850	47.50		897.50	1,000
1212	For vision lite, add						108			108	119
1214	For narrow lite, add						116			116	128
1230	Half glass, 20 ga., 2'-8" x 6'-8"	G	2 Carp	20	.800		580	40.50		620.50	700
1240	3'-0" x 6'-8"	G		18	.889		580	45		625	705
1260	3'-0" x 7'-0"	G		18	.889		595	45		640	725
1280	Embossed panel, 1-3/4" thick, poly core, 20 ga., 3'-0" x 7'-0"	G		18	.889		420	45		465	530
1290	Half glass, 1-3/4" thick, poly core, 20 ga., 3'-0" x 7'-0"	G		18	.889		615	45		660	745
1320	18 ga., 2'-8" x 6'-8"	G		18	.889		640	45		685	775
1340	3'-0" x 6'-8"	G		17	.941		635	47.50		682.50	770
1360	3'-0" x 7'-0"	G		17	.941		645	47.50		692.50	785
1380	4'-0" x 7'-0"	G		15	1.067		795	54		849	960
1400	4'-0" x 8'-0"	G		14	1.143		895	58		953	1,075
1500	Flush full panel, 16 ga., steel hollow core										
1520	2'-0" x 6'-8"	G	2 Carp	20	.800	Ea.	570	40.50		610.50	685
1530	2'-8" x 6'-8"	G		20	.800		570	40.50		610.50	685
1540	3'-0" x 6'-8"	G		20	.800		555	40.50		595.50	670
1560	2'-8" x 7'-0"	G		18	.889		580	45		625	710
1570	3'-0" x 7'-0"	G		18	.889		560	45		605	690
1580	3'-6" x 7'-0"	G		18	.889		665	45		710	805
1590	4'-0" x 7'-0"	G		18	.889		730	45		775	875
1600	2'-8" x 8'-0"	G		18	.889		715	45		760	855
1620	3'-0" x 8'-0"	G		18	.889		730	45		775	870
1630	3'-6" x 8'-0"	G		18	.889		810	45		855	960
1640	4'-0" x 8'-0"	G		18	.889		850	45		895	1,000
1720	Insulated, 1-3/4" thick, full panel, 18 ga., 3'-0" x 6'-8"	G		15	1.067		485	54		539	620
1740	2'-8" x 7'-0"	G		16	1		505	50.50		555.50	630
1760	3'-0" x 7'-0"	G		15	1.067		505	54		559	640
1800	4'-0" x 8'-0"	G		13	1.231		780	62.50		842.50	955
1820	Half glass, 18 ga., 3'-0" x 6'-8"	G		16	1		635	50.50		685.50	770
1840	2'-8" x 7'-0"	G		17	.941		665	47.50		712.50	805
1860	3'-0" x 7'-0"	G		16	1		690	50.50		740.50	835
1900	4'-0" x 8'-0"	G		14	1.143		555	58		613	700
2000	For vision lite, add						108			108	119
2010	For narrow lite, add						116			116	128
8100	For bottom louver, add						224			224	246
8110	For baked enamel finish, add						30%	15%			
8120	For galvanizing, add						20%				

For customer support on your Green Building Costs with RSMeans data, call 800.448.8182.

08 13 Metal Doors

08 13 13 – Hollow Metal Doors

08 13 13.20 Residential Steel Doors

			Crew	Daily Output	Labor-Hours	Unit	Material	2018 Bare Costs Labor	Equipment	Total	Total Incl O&P
0010	**RESIDENTIAL STEEL DOORS**										
0020	Prehung, insulated, exterior										
0030	Embossed, full panel, 2'-8" x 6'-8"	G	2 Carp	17	.941	Ea.	405	47.50		452.50	525
0040	3'-0" x 6'-8"	G		15	1.067		290	54		344	405
0060	3'-0" x 7'-0"	G		15	1.067		350	54		404	470
0070	5'-4" x 6'-8", double	G		8	2		575	101		676	790

08 14 Wood Doors

08 14 16 – Flush Wood Doors

08 14 16.09 Smooth Wood Doors

		Crew	Daily Output	Labor-Hours	Unit	Material	2018 Bare Costs Labor	Equipment	Total	Total Incl O&P
0010	**SMOOTH WOOD DOORS**									
0015	Flush, interior, hollow core									
0025	Lauan face, 1-3/8", 3'-0" x 6'-8"	2 Carp	17	.941	Ea.	55	47.50		102.50	133
0030	4'-0" x 6'-8"		16	1		126	50.50		176.50	216
0080	1-3/4", 2'-0" x 6'-8"		17	.941		55	47.50		102.50	133
0106	2'-8" x 7'-0"		16	1		118	50.50		168.50	207
0108	3'-0" x 7'-0"		16	1		206	50.50		256.50	305
0110	3'-4" x 7'-0"		15	1.067		238	54		292	345
0112	Pair of 3'-0" x 7'-0"		9	1.778	Pr.	132	90		222	282
0140	Birch face, 1-3/8", 2'-6" x 6'-8"		17	.941	Ea.	113	47.50		160.50	198
0180	3'-0" x 6'-8"		17	.941		97	47.50		144.50	180
0200	4'-0" x 6'-8"		16	1		158	50.50		208.50	251
0202	1-3/4", 2'-0" x 6'-8"		17	.941		57.50	47.50		105	136
0204	2'-4" x 7'-0"		16	1		120	50.50		170.50	209
0206	2'-6" x 7'-0"		16	1		124	50.50		174.50	213
0208	2'-8" x 7'-0"		16	1		139	50.50		189.50	230
0210	3'-0" x 7'-0"		16	1		158	50.50		208.50	250
0212	3'-4" x 7'-0"		15	1.067		220	54		274	325
0214	Pair of 3'-0" x 7'-0"		9	1.778	Pr.	259	90		349	420
0220	Oak face, 1-3/8", 2'-0" x 6'-8"		17	.941	Ea.	110	47.50		157.50	194
0241	2'-8" x 6'-8"		17	.941		125	47.50		172.50	210
0280	3'-0" x 6'-8"		17	.941		115	47.50		162.50	199
0300	4'-0" x 6'-8"		16	1		141	50.50		191.50	232
0305	1-3/4", 2'-6" x 6'-8"		17	.941		125	47.50		172.50	210
0310	3'-0" x 7'-0"		16	1		250	50.50		300.50	350
0410	Hardboard face, 2'-4" x 7'-0"		16	1		105	50.50		155.50	192
0412	2'-6" x 7'-0"		16	1		109	50.50		159.50	197
0414	2'-8" x 7'-0"		16	1		117	50.50		167.50	206
0416	3'-0" x 7'-0"		16	1		145	50.50		195.50	236
0418	3'-4" x 7'-0"		15	1.067		183	54		237	285
0420	Pair of 3'-0" x 7'-0"		9	1.778	Pr.	245	90		335	405
0430	For 7'-0" high, add				Ea.	27			27	30
0440	For 8'-0" high, add					39.50			39.50	43.50
0480	For prefinishing, clear, add					48.50			48.50	53
0500	For prefinishing, stain, add					60.50			60.50	66.50
0620	For dutch door with shelf, add					140%				
1320	M.D. overlay on hardboard, 1-3/8", 2'-0" x 6'-8"	2 Carp	17	.941	Ea.	123	47.50		170.50	208
1340	2'-6" x 6'-8"		17	.941		124	47.50		171.50	209
1380	3'-0" x 6'-8"		17	.941		130	47.50		177.50	216
1400	4'-0" x 6'-8"		16	1		185	50.50		235.50	281

08 14 Wood Doors

08 14 16 – Flush Wood Doors

08 14 16.09 Smooth Wood Doors

		Crew	Daily Output	Labor-Hours	Unit	Material	2018 Bare Costs Labor	Equipment	Total	Total Incl O&P
1420	For 7'-0" high, add				Ea.	17.90			17.90	19.65
1440	For 8'-0" high, add					35.50			35.50	39
1720	H.P. plastic laminate, 1-3/8", 2'-0" x 6'-8"	2 Carp	16	1		275	50.50		325.50	380
1740	2'-6" x 6'-8"		16	1		270	50.50		320.50	375
1780	3'-0" x 6'-8"		15	1.067		299	54		353	415
1800	4'-0" x 6'-8"		14	1.143		395	58		453	525
1820	For 7'-0" high, add					17.90			17.90	19.70
1840	For 8'-0" high, add					35			35	39
2020	Particle core, lauan face, 1-3/8", 2'-6" x 6'-8"	2 Carp	15	1.067		97	54		151	190
2040	3'-0" x 6'-8"		14	1.143		101	58		159	199
2080	3'-0" x 7'-0"		13	1.231		120	62.50		182.50	227
2085	4'-0" x 7'-0"		12	1.333		129	67.50		196.50	245
2110	1-3/4", 3'-0" x 7'-0"		13	1.231		206	62.50		268.50	320
2120	Birch face, 1-3/8", 2'-6" x 6'-8"		15	1.067		110	54		164	204
2140	3'-0" x 6'-8"		14	1.143		121	58		179	221
2180	3'-0" x 7'-0"		13	1.231		132	62.50		194.50	240
2200	4'-0" x 7'-0"		12	1.333		148	67.50		215.50	266
2205	1-3/4", 3'-0" x 7'-0"		13	1.231		195	62.50		257.50	310
2220	Oak face, 1-3/8", 2'-6" x 6'-8"		15	1.067		122	54		176	217
2240	3'-0" x 6'-8"		14	1.143		134	58		192	235
2280	3'-0" x 7'-0"		13	1.231		140	62.50		202.50	249
2300	4'-0" x 7'-0"		12	1.333		166	67.50		233.50	286
2305	1-3/4", 3'-0" x 7'-0"		13	1.231		236	62.50		298.50	355
2440	For 8'-0" high, add					44.50			44.50	49
2460	For 8'-0" high walnut, add					40.50			40.50	44.50
2720	For prefinishing, clear, add					39.50			39.50	43.50
2740	For prefinishing, stain, add					57			57	62.50
3320	M.D. overlay on hardboard, 1-3/8", 2'-6" x 6'-8"	2 Carp	14	1.143		178	58		236	284
3340	3'-0" x 6'-8"		13	1.231		193	62.50		255.50	305
3380	3'-0" x 7'-0"		12	1.333		196	67.50		263.50	320
3400	4'-0" x 7'-0"		10	1.600		265	81		346	415
3440	For 8'-0" height, add					39.50			39.50	43.50
3460	For solid wood core, add					70.50			70.50	77.50
3720	H.P. plastic laminate, 1-3/8", 2'-6" x 6'-8"	2 Carp	13	1.231		160	62.50		222.50	271
3740	3'-0" x 6'-8"		12	1.333		188	67.50		255.50	310
3780	3'-0" x 7'-0"		11	1.455		193	74		267	325
3800	4'-0" x 7'-0"		8	2		380	101		481	570
3840	For 8'-0" height, add					39.50			39.50	43.50
3860	For solid wood core, add					43			43	47.50
4000	Exterior, flush, solid core, birch, 1-3/4" x 2'-6" x 7'-0"	2 Carp	15	1.067		166	54		220	266
4020	2'-8" wide		15	1.067		247	54		301	355
4040	3'-0" wide		14	1.143		217	58		275	325
4100	Oak faced 1-3/4" x 2'-6" x 7'-0"		15	1.067		222	54		276	325
4120	2'-8" wide		15	1.067		227	54		281	335
4140	3'-0" wide		14	1.143		215	58		273	325
4300	For 6'-8" high door, deduct from 7'-0" door					18.05			18.05	19.90
5000	Wood doors, for vision lite, add					108			108	119
5010	Wood doors, for narrow lite, add					116			116	128
5015	Wood doors, for bottom (or top) louver, add					224			224	246
7280	3'-0" x 9'-0"	1 Carp	7	1.143		550	58		608	695

For customer support on your Green Building Costs with RSMeans data, call 800.448.8182.

141

08 14 Wood Doors

08 14 33 – Stile and Rail Wood Doors

08 14 33.10 Wood Doors Paneled

		Crew	Daily Output	Labor-Hours	Unit	Material	2018 Bare Costs Labor	Equipment	Total	Total Incl O&P
0010	**WOOD DOORS PANELED**									
0020	Interior, six panel, hollow core, 1-3/8" thick									
0040	Molded hardboard, 2'-0" x 6'-8"	2 Carp	17	.941	Ea.	62	47.50		109.50	141
0060	2'-6" x 6'-8"		17	.941		64	47.50		111.50	143
0070	2'-8" x 6'-8"		17	.941		67	47.50		114.50	146
0080	3'-0" x 6'-8"		17	.941		73.50	47.50		121	154
0140	Embossed print, molded hardboard, 2'-0" x 6'-8"		17	.941		64	47.50		111.50	143
0160	2'-6" x 6'-8"		17	.941		64	47.50		111.50	143
0180	3'-0" x 6'-8"		17	.941		73.50	47.50		121	154
0540	Six panel, solid, 1-3/8" thick, pine, 2'-0" x 6'-8"		15	1.067		155	54		209	254
0560	2'-6" x 6'-8"		14	1.143		154	58		212	258
0580	3'-0" x 6'-8"		13	1.231		148	62.50		210.50	258
1040	2'-0" x 6'-8"		15	1.067		320	54		374	440
1060	2'-6" x 6'-8"		14	1.143		365	58		423	490
1340	Two panel, solid, 1-3/8" thick, fir, 2'-0" x 6'-8"		15	1.067		160	54		214	259
1360	2'-6" x 6'-8"		14	1.143		215	58		273	325
1380	3'-0" x 6'-8"		13	1.231		375	62.50		437.50	510
1740	Five panel, solid, 1-3/8" thick, fir, 2'-0" x 6'-8"		15	1.067		286	54		340	400
1760	2'-6" x 6'-8"		14	1.143		380	58		438	510
1780	3'-0" x 6'-8"		13	1.231		380	62.50		442.50	515

08 14 33.20 Wood Doors Residential

		Crew	Daily Output	Labor-Hours	Unit	Material	Labor	Equipment	Total	Total Incl O&P
0010	**WOOD DOORS RESIDENTIAL**									
0200	Exterior, combination storm & screen, pine									
0220	Cross buck, 6'-9" x 2'-6" wide	2 Carp	11	1.455	Ea.	340	74		414	480
0260	2'-8" wide		10	1.600		310	81		391	470
0280	3'-0" wide		9	1.778		325	90		415	495
0300	7'-1" x 3'-0" wide		9	1.778		355	90		445	525
0400	Full lite, 6'-9" x 2'-6" wide		11	1.455		325	74		399	470
0420	2'-8" wide		10	1.600		330	81		411	490
0440	3'-0" wide		9	1.778		335	90		425	500
0500	7'-1" x 3'-0" wide		9	1.778		365	90		455	535
0604	Door, screen, plain full		12	1.333		292	67.50		359.50	425
0614	Divided		12	1.333		420	67.50		487.50	565
0634	Decor full		12	1.333		505	67.50		572.50	660
0700	Dutch door, pine, 1-3/4" x 2'-8" x 6'-8", 6 panel		12	1.333		695	67.50		762.50	870
0720	Half glass		10	1.600		985	81		1,066	1,200
0800	3'-0" wide, 6 panel		12	1.333		590	67.50		657.50	755
0820	Half glass		10	1.600		1,050	81		1,131	1,275
1000	Entrance door, colonial, 1-3/4" x 6'-8" x 2'-8" wide		16	1		570	50.50		620.50	700
1020	6 panel pine, 3'-0" wide		15	1.067		560	54		614	700
1100	8 panel pine, 2'-8" wide		16	1		685	50.50		735.50	825
1120	3'-0" wide		15	1.067		635	54		689	785
1200	For tempered safety glass lites (min. of 2), add					85.50			85.50	94
1300	Flush, birch, solid core, 1-3/4" x 6'-8" x 2'-8" wide	2 Carp	16	1		142	50.50		192.50	234
1320	3'-0" wide		15	1.067		152	54		206	250
1335	7'-0" x 2'-4" wide		16	1		134	50.50		184.50	224
1340	2'-6" wide		16	1		164	50.50		214.50	258
1350	7'-0" x 2'-8" wide		16	1		133	50.50		183.50	224
1360	3'-0" wide		15	1.067		155	54		209	254
1370	3'-4" wide		15	1.067		335	54		389	455
1375	Pair of 3'-0" wide		9	1.778	Pr.	310	90		400	475
1380	For tempered safety glass lites, add				Ea.	114			114	126

08 14 Wood Doors

08 14 33 – Stile and Rail Wood Doors

08 14 33.20 Wood Doors Residential

		Crew	Daily Output	Labor-Hours	Unit	Material	2018 Bare Costs Labor	Equipment	Total	Total Incl O&P
1400	Ext. door, 1/2 glass low E w/grille, 1-3/4" x 6'-8" x 2'-8" wide, pine	2 Carp	16	1	Ea.	740	50.50		790.50	890
1420	6'-8" x 3'-0" wide, fir		16	1		505	50.50		555.50	635
1480	6'-8" x 3'-0" wide, pine		15	1.067		675	54		729	830
1800	Lauan, solid core, 1-3/4" x 7'-0" x 2'-4" wide		16	1		137	50.50		187.50	228
1810	2'-6" wide		15	1.067		144	54		198	241
1820	2'-8" wide		9	1.778		149	90		239	300
1830	3'-0" wide		16	1		164	50.50		214.50	257
1840	3'-4" wide		16	1		254	50.50		304.50	355
1850	Pair of 3'-0" wide		15	1.067	Pr.	330	54		384	445
1860	Hardboard, solid core, 1-3/4" x 7'-0" x 2'-4" wide		16	1	Ea.	139	50.50		189.50	230
1870	2'-8" wide		16	1		156	50.50		206.50	249
1880	3'-0" wide		16	1		160	50.50		210.50	253
1890	3'-4" wide		15	1.067		178	54		232	279
1900	Pair of 3'-0" wide		9	1.778	Pr.	320	90		410	485
2700	Interior, closet, bi-fold, w/hardware, no frame or trim incl.									
2710	Birch, unfinished, 7'-0" x 4'-0" wide	2 Carp	12	1.333	Ea.	123	67.50		190.50	238
2715	6'-0" wide		10	1.600		143	81		224	281
2720	Flush, birch, 2'-6" x 6'-8"		13	1.231		73	62.50		135.50	175
2740	3'-0" wide		13	1.231		74.50	62.50		137	177
2760	4'-0" wide		12	1.333		115	67.50		182.50	230
2780	5'-0" wide		11	1.455		114	74		188	238
2800	6'-0" wide		10	1.600		135	81		216	272
2804	Flush lauan 2'-0" x 6'-8"		14	1.143		50	58		108	143
2810	8'-0" wide		9	1.778		203	90		293	360
2820	Flush, hardboard, primed, 6'-8" x 2'-6" wide		13	1.231		73.50	62.50		136	176
2840	3'-0" wide		13	1.231		85	62.50		147.50	189
2860	4'-0" wide		12	1.333		148	67.50		215.50	266
2880	5'-0" wide		11	1.455		177	74		251	305
2900	6'-0" wide		10	1.600		179	81		260	320
2920	Hardboard, primed 7'-0" x 4'-0" wide		12	1.333		193	67.50		260.50	315
2930	6'-0" wide		10	1.600		187	81		268	330
3000	Raised panel pine, 6'-6" or 6'-8" x 2'-6" wide		13	1.231		179	62.50		241.50	292
3020	3'-0" wide		13	1.231		289	62.50		351.50	415
3025	Door, interior paneled bi-fold, pine, 3/0 x 6/8					289			289	320
3040	4'-0" wide	2 Carp	12	1.333		315	67.50		382.50	450
3060	5'-0" wide		11	1.455		405	74		479	555
3080	6'-0" wide		10	1.600		445	81		526	615
3100	7'-0" x 3'-0" wide		12	1.333		300	67.50		367.50	435
3120	6'-0" wide		10	1.600		430	81		511	600
3140	For oak or ash, add					125%				
3180	Louvered, pine, 6'-6" or 6'-8" x 1'-6" wide	2 Carp	13	1.231	Ea.	196	62.50		258.50	310
3190	2'-0" wide		14	1.143		175	58		233	281
3200	Louvered, pine, 6'-6" or 6'-8" x 2'-6" wide		13	1.231		154	62.50		216.50	264
3220	3'-0" wide		13	1.231		239	62.50		301.50	360
3240	4'-0" wide		12	1.333		251	67.50		318.50	380
3260	5'-0" wide		11	1.455		278	74		352	415
3280	6'-0" wide		10	1.600		310	81		391	465
3290	8'-0" wide		10	1.600		470	81		551	645
3300	7'-0" x 3'-0" wide		12	1.333		281	67.50		348.50	415
3320	6'-0" wide		10	1.600		340	81		421	500
4400	Bi-passing closet, incl. hardware and frame, no trim incl.									
4420	Flush, lauan, 6'-8" x 4'-0" wide	2 Carp	12	1.333	Opng.	167	67.50		234.50	287
4440	5'-0" wide		11	1.455		183	74		257	315

For customer support on your Green Building Costs with RSMeans data, call 800.448.8182.

143

08 14 Wood Doors

08 14 33 – Stile and Rail Wood Doors

08 14 33.20 Wood Doors Residential		Crew	Daily Output	Labor-Hours	Unit	Material	2018 Bare Costs Labor	Equipment	Total	Total Incl O&P
4460	6'-0" wide	2 Carp	10	1.600	Opng.	169	81		250	310
4480	8'-0" wide	1 Carp	10	.800		335	40.50		375.50	425
4600	Flush, birch, 6'-8" x 4'-0" wide	2 Carp	12	1.333		254	67.50		321.50	385
4620	5'-0" wide		11	1.455		223	74		297	355
4640	6'-0" wide		10	1.600		335	81		416	495
4700	Birch, primed, 6'-8" x 4'-0" wide		12	1.333		224	67.50		291.50	350
4720	6'-0" wide		10	1.600		279	81		360	430
4800	Louvered, pine, 6'-8" x 4'-0" wide		12	1.333		485	67.50		552.50	635
4820	5'-0" wide		11	1.455		610	74		684	780
4840	6'-0" wide		10	1.600		720	81		801	915
4900	Mirrored, 6'-8" x 4'-0" wide		12	1.333	Ea.	320	67.50		387.50	455
5000	Paneled, pine, 6'-8" x 4'-0" wide		12	1.333	Opng.	490	67.50		557.50	645
5020	5'-0" wide		11	1.455		630	74		704	800
5040	6'-0" wide		10	1.600		840	81		921	1,050
5042	8'-0" wide		12	1.333		980	67.50		1,047.50	1,175
5061	Hardboard, 6'-8" x 4'-0" wide		10	1.600		206	81		287	350
5062	5'-0" wide		10	1.600		207	81		288	350
5063	6'-0" wide		10	1.600		230	81		311	375
5064	7'-0" wide		9	1.778		261	90		351	425
5065	8'-0" wide		9	1.778		284	90		374	445
5500	Closet door, hollow core, lauan, 2'-0" x 6'-8"		16	1	Ea.	48.50	50.50		99	131
6100	Folding accordion, closet, including track and frame									
6120	Vinyl, 2 layer, stock	2 Carp	10	1.600	Ea.	68	81		149	199
6121	Vinyl, 2 layer, stock		400	.040	S.F.	3.41	2.03		5.44	6.85
6140	Woven mahogany and vinyl, stock		10	1.600	Ea.	58.50	81		139.50	188
6160	Wood slats with vinyl overlay, stock		10	1.600		159	81		240	299
6180	Economy vinyl, stock		10	1.600		39	81		120	167
6200	Rigid PVC		10	1.600		108	81		189	243
7310	Passage doors, flush, no frame included									
7320	Hardboard, hollow core, 1-3/8" x 6'-8" x 1'-6" wide	2 Carp	18	.889	Ea.	41.50	45		86.50	115
7330	2'-0" wide		18	.889		45	45		90	118
7340	2'-6" wide		18	.889		52.50	45		97.50	126
7350	2'-8" wide		18	.889		53	45		98	127
7360	3'-0" wide		17	.941		55	47.50		102.50	133
7370	7'-0" x 2'-4" wide		16	1		92	50.50		142.50	178
7375	2'-6" wide		16	1		92	50.50		142.50	178
7380	2'-8" wide		16	1		97	50.50		147.50	184
7385	3'-0" wide		16	1		142	50.50		192.50	233
7395	Pair of 3'-0" wide		9	1.778	Pr.	202	90		292	360
7420	Lauan, hollow core, 1-3/8" x 6'-8" x 1'-6" wide		18	.889	Ea.	53	45		98	127
7440	2'-0" wide		18	.889		60	45		105	135
7450	2'-4" wide		18	.889		68	45		113	144
7460	2'-6" wide		18	.889		68	45		113	144
7480	2'-8" wide		18	.889		70	45		115	146
7500	3'-0" wide		17	.941		75	47.50		122.50	155
7540	2'-6" wide		16	1		83	50.50		133.50	169
7560	2'-8" wide		16	1		86	50.50		136.50	172
7580	3'-0" wide		16	1		90	50.50		140.50	176
7595	Pair of 3'-0" wide		9	1.778	Pr.	180	90		270	335
7700	Birch, hollow core, 1-3/8" x 6'-8" x 1'-6" wide		18	.889	Ea.	62	45		107	137
7720	2'-0" wide		18	.889		69	45		114	145
7740	2'-6" wide		18	.889		79	45		124	156
7760	2'-8" wide		18	.889		82	45		127	159

08 14 Wood Doors

08 14 33 – Stile and Rail Wood Doors

08 14 33.20 Wood Doors Residential

		Crew	Daily Output	Labor-Hours	Unit	Material	2018 Bare Costs Labor	Equipment	Total	Total Incl O&P
7780	3'-0" wide	2 Carp	17	.941	Ea.	88	47.50		135.50	170
7790	2'-6" ash/oak door with hinges		18	.889		92	45		137	170
7910	2'-8" wide		16	1		78.50	50.50		129	164
7920	3'-0" wide		16	1		189	50.50		239.50	285
7940	Pair of 3'-0" wide		9	1.778	Pr.	380	90		470	550
8000	Pine louvered, 1-3/8" x 6'-8" x 1'-6" wide		19	.842	Ea.	148	42.50		190.50	228
8020	2'-0" wide		18	.889		164	45		209	249
8040	2'-6" wide		18	.889		199	45		244	288
8060	2'-8" wide		18	.889		209	45		254	299
8080	3'-0" wide		17	.941		219	47.50		266.50	315
8300	Pine paneled, 1-3/8" x 6'-8" x 1'-6" wide		19	.842		191	42.50		233.50	275
8320	2'-0" wide		18	.889		223	45		268	315
8330	2'-4" wide		18	.889		241	45		286	335
8340	2'-6" wide		18	.889		250	45		295	345
8360	2'-8" wide		18	.889		258	45		303	355
8380	3'-0" wide		17	.941		271	47.50		318.50	370
8450	French door, pine, 15 lites, 1-3/8" x 6'-8" x 2'-6" wide		18	.889		247	45		292	340
8470	2'-8" wide		18	.889		256	45		301	350
8490	3'-0" wide		17	.941		264	47.50		311.50	365
8804	Pocket door, 6 panel pine, 2'-6" x 6'-8" with frame		10.50	1.524		370	77.50		447.50	525
8814	2'-8" x 6'-8"		10.50	1.524		375	77.50		452.50	530
8824	3'-0" x 6'-8"		10.50	1.524		385	77.50		462.50	540
9000	Passage doors, flush, no frame, birch, solid core, 1-3/8" x 2'-4" x 7'-0"		16	1		125	50.50		175.50	215
9020	2'-8" wide		16	1		133	50.50		183.50	223
9040	3'-0" wide		16	1		146	50.50		196.50	238
9060	3'-4" wide		15	1.067		271	54		325	380
9080	Pair of 3'-0" wide		9	1.778	Pr.	291	90		381	455
9100	Lauan, solid core, 1-3/8" x 7'-0" x 2'-4" wide		16	1	Ea.	163	50.50		213.50	256
9120	2'-8" wide		16	1		147	50.50		197.50	239
9140	3'-0" wide		16	1		192	50.50		242.50	288
9160	3'-4" wide		15	1.067		206	54		260	310
9180	Pair of 3'-0" wide		9	1.778	Pr.	385	90		475	555
9200	Hardboard, solid core, 1-3/8" x 7'-0" x 2'-4" wide		16	1	Ea.	167	50.50		217.50	260
9220	2'-8" wide		16	1		174	50.50		224.50	268
9240	3'-0" wide		16	1		179	50.50		229.50	274
9260	3'-4" wide		15	1.067		340	54		394	460
9280	Pair of 3'-0" wide		9	1.778	Pr.	370	90		460	545
9300	For additional 12" of height, add					30%				
9320	For dutch door with shelf, add					140%				

08 14 35 – Torrified Doors

08 14 35.10 Torrified Exterior Doors

		Crew	Daily Output	Labor-Hours	Unit	Material	2018 Bare Costs Labor	Equipment	Total	Total Incl O&P
0010	**TORRIFIED EXTERIOR DOORS**									
0020	Wood doors made from torrified wood, exterior									
0030	All doors require a finish be applied, all glass is insulated									
0040	All doors require pilot holes for all fasteners									
0100	6 panel, paint grade poplar, 1-3/4" x 3'-0" x 6'-8"	2 Carp	12	1.333	Ea.	1,325	67.50		1,392.50	1,550
0120	Half glass 3'-0" x 6'-8"	"	12	1.333		1,425	67.50		1,492.50	1,650
0200	Side lite, full glass, 1-3/4" x 1'-2" x 6'-8"					930			930	1,025
0220	Side lite, half glass, 1-3/4" x 1'-2" x 6'-8"					910			910	1,000
0300	Raised face, 2 panel, paint grade poplar, 1-3/4" x 3'-0" x 7'-0"	2 Carp	12	1.333		1,325	67.50		1,392.50	1,550
0320	Side lite, raised face, half glass, 1-3/4" x 1'-2" x 7'-0"					1,050			1,050	1,175
0500	6 panel, Fir, 1-3/4" x 3'-0" x 6'-8"	2 Carp	12	1.333		1,875	67.50		1,942.50	2,150

08 14 Wood Doors

08 14 35 – Torrified Doors

08 14 35.10 Torrified Exterior Doors

		Crew	Daily Output	Labor-Hours	Unit	Material	2018 Bare Costs Labor	Equipment	Total	Total Incl O&P
0520	Half glass 3'-0" x 6'-8"	2 Carp	12	1.333	Ea.	1,850	67.50		1,917.50	2,150
0600	Side lite, full glass, 1-3/4" x 1'-2" x 6'-8"					940			940	1,025
0620	Side lite, half glass, 1-3/4" x 1'-2" x 6'-8"					970			970	1,075
0700	6 panel, Mahogany, 1-3/4" x 3'-0" x 6'-8"	2 Carp	12	1.333		1,975	67.50		2,042.50	2,275
0800	Side lite, full glass, 1-3/4" x 1'-2" x 6'-8"					1,050			1,050	1,150
0820	Side lite, half glass, 1-3/4" x 1'-2" x 6'-8"					1,050			1,050	1,150

08 16 Composite Doors

08 16 13 – Fiberglass Doors

08 16 13.10 Entrance Doors, Fibrous Glass

			Crew	Daily Output	Labor-Hours	Unit	Material	Labor	Equipment	Total	Total Incl O&P
0010	**ENTRANCE DOORS, FIBROUS GLASS**										
0020	Exterior, fiberglass, door, 2'-8" wide x 6'-8" high	G	2 Carp	15	1.067	Ea.	281	54		335	395
0040	3'-0" wide x 6'-8" high	G		15	1.067		274	54		328	385
0060	3'-0" wide x 7'-0" high	G		15	1.067		490	54		544	620
0080	3'-0" wide x 6'-8" high, with two lites	G		15	1.067		340	54		394	460
0100	3'-0" wide x 8'-0" high, with two lites	G		15	1.067		525	54		579	665
0110	Half glass, 3'-0" wide x 6'-8" high	G		15	1.067		450	54		504	580
0120	3'-0" wide x 6'-8" high, low E	G		15	1.067		490	54		544	620
0130	3'-0" wide x 8'-0" high	G		15	1.067		585	54		639	730
0140	3'-0" wide x 8'-0" high, low E	G		15	1.067		675	54		729	830
0150	Side lights, 1'-0" wide x 6'-8" high	G					281			281	310
0160	1'-0" wide x 6'-8" high, low E	G					289			289	320
0180	1'-0" wide x 6'-8" high, full glass	G					340			340	370
0190	1'-0" wide x 6'-8" high, low E	G					360			360	395

08 16 14 – French Doors

08 16 14.10 Exterior Doors With Glass Lites

		Crew	Daily Output	Labor-Hours	Unit	Material	Labor	Equipment	Total	Total Incl O&P
0010	**EXTERIOR DOORS WITH GLASS LITES**									
0020	French, Fir, 1-3/4", 3'-0" wide x 6'-8" high	2 Carp	12	1.333	Ea.	620	67.50		687.50	785
0025	Double		12	1.333		1,250	67.50		1,317.50	1,450
0030	Maple, 1-3/4", 3'-0" wide x 6'-8" high		12	1.333		695	67.50		762.50	870
0035	Double		12	1.333		1,400	67.50		1,467.50	1,625
0040	Cherry, 1-3/4", 3'-0" wide x 6'-8" high		12	1.333		810	67.50		877.50	995
0045	Double		12	1.333		1,625	67.50		1,692.50	1,875
0110	Fir, 1-3/4", 3'-0" wide x 8'-0" high		10	1.600		1,225	81		1,306	1,475
0115	Double		10	1.600		2,475	81		2,556	2,850
0120	Oak, 1-3/4", 3'-0" wide x 8'-0" high		10	1.600		1,875	81		1,956	2,200
0125	Double		10	1.600		3,750	81		3,831	4,250

08 32 Sliding Glass Doors

08 32 13 – Sliding Aluminum-Framed Glass Doors

08 32 13.10 Sliding Aluminum Doors

		Crew	Daily Output	Labor-Hours	Unit	Material	Labor	Equipment	Total	Total Incl O&P
0010	**SLIDING ALUMINUM DOORS**									
0350	Aluminum, 5/8" tempered insulated glass, 6' wide									
0400	Premium	2 Carp	4	4	Ea.	1,550	203		1,753	2,000
0450	Economy		4	4		820	203		1,023	1,225
0500	8' wide, premium		3	5.333		1,700	270		1,970	2,275
0550	Economy		3	5.333		1,475	270		1,745	2,025
0600	12' wide, premium		2.50	6.400		3,000	325		3,325	3,800
0650	Economy		2.50	6.400		1,575	325		1,900	2,225

For customer support on your Green Building Costs with RSMeans data, call 800.448.8182.

08 32 Sliding Glass Doors

08 32 13 – Sliding Aluminum-Framed Glass Doors

08 32 13.10 Sliding Aluminum Doors

		Crew	Daily Output	Labor-Hours	Unit	Material	2018 Bare Costs Labor	Equipment	Total	Total Incl O&P
4000	Aluminum, baked on enamel, temp glass, 6'-8" x 10'-0" wide	2 Carp	4	4	Ea.	1,100	203		1,303	1,500
4020	Insulating glass, 6'-8" x 6'-0" wide		4	4		955	203		1,158	1,350
4040	8'-0" wide		3	5.333		1,125	270		1,395	1,625
4060	10'-0" wide		2	8		1,400	405		1,805	2,175
4080	Anodized, temp glass, 6'-8" x 6'-0" wide		4	4		455	203		658	810
4100	8'-0" wide		3	5.333		575	270		845	1,050
4120	10'-0" wide		2	8		660	405		1,065	1,350
5000	Aluminum sliding glass door system									
5010	Sliding door 4' wide opening single side	2 Carp	2	8	Ea.	6,000	405		6,405	7,225
5015	8' wide opening single side		2	8		9,000	405		9,405	10,500
5020	Telescoping glass door system, 4' wide opening biparting		2	8		5,100	405		5,505	6,225
5025	8' wide opening biparting		2	8		6,000	405		6,405	7,225
5030	Folding glass door, 4' wide opening biparting		2	8		8,000	405		8,405	9,425
5035	8' wide opening biparting		2	8		10,000	405		10,405	11,600
5040	ICU-CCU sliding telescoping glass door, 4' x 7', single side opening		2	8		3,050	405		3,455	3,975
5045	8' x 7', single side opening		2	8		4,625	405		5,030	5,725

08 32 19 – Sliding Wood-Framed Glass Doors

08 32 19.15 Sliding Glass Vinyl-Clad Wood Doors

			Crew	Daily Output	Labor-Hours	Unit	Material	Labor	Equipment	Total	Total Incl O&P
0010	**SLIDING GLASS VINYL-CLAD WOOD DOORS**										
0020	Glass, sliding vinyl-clad, insul. glass, 6'-0" x 6'-8"	G	2 Carp	4	4	Opng.	1,525	203		1,728	1,975
0025	6'-0" x 6'-10" high	G		4	4		1,700	203		1,903	2,150
0030	6'-0" x 8'-0" high	G		4	4		2,050	203		2,253	2,550
0050	5'-0" x 6'-8" high	G		4	4		1,575	203		1,778	2,050
0100	8'-0" x 6'-10" high	G		4	4		2,025	203		2,228	2,525
0104	8'-0" x 6'-8" high	G		4	4		2,025	203		2,228	2,525
0150	8'-0" x 8'-0" high	G		4	4		2,350	203		2,553	2,900
0500	4 leaf, 9'-0" x 6'-10" high	G		3	5.333		3,350	270		3,620	4,100
0550	9'-0" x 8'-0" high	G		3	5.333		3,925	270		4,195	4,700
0600	12'-0" x 6'-10" high	G		3	5.333		4,025	270		4,295	4,825
0650	12'-0" x 8'-0" high	G		3	5.333		4,025	270		4,295	4,825

08 34 Special Function Doors

08 34 56 – Security Gates

08 34 56.10 Gates

		Crew	Daily Output	Labor-Hours	Unit	Material	Labor	Equipment	Total	Total Incl O&P
0010	**GATES**									
0015	Driveway gates include mounting hardware									
0500	Wood, security gate, driveway, dual, 10' wide	H-4	.80	25	Opng.	3,775	1,175		4,950	5,950
0505	12' wide		.80	25		3,650	1,175		4,825	5,800
0510	15' wide		.80	25		4,325	1,175		5,500	6,575
0600	Steel, security gate, driveway, single, 10' wide		.80	25		1,700	1,175		2,875	3,675
0605	12' wide		.80	25		1,900	1,175		3,075	3,900
0620	Steel, security gate, driveway, dual, 12' wide		.80	25		2,050	1,175		3,225	4,075
0625	14' wide		.80	25		2,250	1,175		3,425	4,275
0630	16' wide		.80	25		2,450	1,175		3,625	4,500
0700	Aluminum, security gate, driveway, dual, 10' wide		.80	25		3,200	1,175		4,375	5,325
0705	12' wide		.80	25		3,850	1,175		5,025	6,025
0710	16' wide		.80	25		4,375	1,175		5,550	6,625
1000	Security gate, driveway, opener 12 VDC				Ea.	830			830	910
1010	Wireless					1,900			1,900	2,075
1020	Security gate, driveway, opener 24 VDC					1,425			1,425	1,550

For customer support on your Green Building Costs with RSMeans data, call 800.448.8182.

08 34 Special Function Doors

08 34 56 – Security Gates

08 34 56.10 Gates

		Crew	Daily Output	Labor-Hours	Unit	Material	2018 Bare Costs Labor	Equipment	Total	Total Incl O&P
1030	Wireless				Ea.	1,575			1,575	1,750
1040	Security gate, driveway, opener 12 VDC, solar panel 10 watt	1 Elec	2	4		445	233		678	840
1050	20 watt	"	2	4		585	233		818	995

08 45 Translucent Wall and Roof Assemblies

08 45 10 – Translucent Roof Assemblies

08 45 10.10 Skyroofs

		Crew	Daily Output	Labor-Hours	Unit	Material	Labor	Equipment	Total	Total Incl O&P
0010	**SKYROOFS**									
1200	Skylights, circular, clear, double glazed acrylic									
1230	30" diameter	2 Carp	3	5.333	Ea.	3,000	270		3,270	3,700
1250	60" diameter		3	5.333		4,000	270		4,270	4,800
1290	96" diameter		2	8		5,000	405		5,405	6,125
1300	Skylight Barrel Vault, clear, double glazed, acrylic									
1330	3'-0" x 12'-0"	G-3	3	10.667	Ea.	5,000	530		5,530	6,300
1350	4'-0" x 12'-0"		3	10.667		5,500	530		6,030	6,850
1390	5'-0" x 12'-0"		2	16		6,000	795		6,795	7,825
1400	Skylight Pyramid, aluminum frame, clear low E laminated glass									
1410	The glass is installed in the frame except where noted									
1430	Square, 3' x 3'	G-3	3	10.667	Ea.	6,000	530		6,530	7,400
1440	4' x 4'		3	10.667		7,000	530		7,530	8,500
1450	5' x 5', glass must be field installed		3	10.667		8,000	530		8,530	9,600
1460	6' x 6', glass must be field installed		2	16		10,000	795		10,795	12,200
1550	Install pre-cut laminated glass in aluminum frame on a flat roof	2 Glaz	55	.291	SF Surf		14.10		14.10	21.50
1560	Install pre-cut laminated glass in aluminum frame on a sloped roof	"	40	.400	"		19.40		19.40	29.50

08 52 Wood Windows

08 52 10 – Plain Wood Windows

08 52 10.20 Awning Window

		Crew	Daily Output	Labor-Hours	Unit	Material	Labor	Equipment	Total	Total Incl O&P
0010	**AWNING WINDOW**, Including frame, screens and grilles									
0100	34" x 22", insulated glass	1 Carp	10	.800	Ea.	276	40.50		316.50	365
0200	Low E glass		10	.800		298	40.50		338.50	390
0300	40" x 28", insulated glass		9	.889		315	45		360	415
0400	Low E glass		9	.889		345	45		390	450
0500	48" x 36", insulated glass		8	1		470	50.50		520.50	590
0600	Low E glass		8	1		495	50.50		545.50	620

08 52 10.40 Casement Window

			Crew	Daily Output	Labor-Hours	Unit	Material	Labor	Equipment	Total	Total Incl O&P
0010	**CASEMENT WINDOW**, including frame, screen and grilles	R085216-10									
0100	2'-0" x 3'-0" H, double insulated glass	G	1 Carp	10	.800	Ea.	282	40.50		322.50	370
0150	Low E glass	G		10	.800		275	40.50		315.50	360
0200	2'-0" x 4'-6" high, double insulated glass	G		9	.889		385	45		430	495
0250	Low E glass	G		9	.889		385	45		430	495
0260	Casement 4'-2" x 4'-2" double insulated glass	G		11	.727		920	37		957	1,050
0270	4'-0" x 4'-0" Low E glass	G		11	.727		550	37		587	655
0290	6'-4" x 5'-7" Low E glass	G		9	.889		1,175	45		1,220	1,375
0300	2'-4" x 6'-0" high, double insulated glass	G		8	1		445	50.50		495.50	565
0350	Low E glass	G		8	1		440	50.50		490.50	560
0400	Vinyl-clad, premium, double insulated glass, 1'-4" x 4'-0"	G	2 Carp	20	.800		350	40.50		390.50	445
0406	Budget	G		20	.800		281	40.50		321.50	370
0407	Custom	G		20	.800		420	40.50		460.50	525

08 52 Wood Windows

08 52 10 – Plain Wood Windows

08 52 10.40 Casement Window

		Crew	Daily Output	Labor-Hours	Unit	Material	2018 Bare Costs Labor	Equipment	Total	Total Incl O&P
0450	1'-6" x 4'-0" G	2 Carp	20	.800	Ea.	350	40.50		390.50	445
0456	Budget G		20	.800		281	40.50		321.50	370
0457	Custom G		20	.800		420	40.50		460.50	525
0460	Wood, insul. glazed, 1 leaf, 1'-10" x 3'-2" high	1 Carp	10	.800		330	40.50		370.50	425
0465	2 leaf, 4'-2" x 4'-5" high G	"	8	1		820	50.50		870.50	980
0466	For each removable mullion, add					30			30	33
0470	3 leaf, 5'-11" x 5'-2" high G	2 Carp	15	1.067		1,100	54		1,154	1,275
0471	For each removable mullion, add					24.50			24.50	27
0500	1'-6" x 5'-0" G	1 Carp	8	1		350	50.50		400.50	460
0506	Budget G		8	1		281	50.50		331.50	385
0507	Custom G		8	1		420	50.50		470.50	540
0510	1'-6" x 6'-0" G		8	1		415	50.50		465.50	530
0511	1'-8" x 3'-0" G		9	.889		268	45		313	365
0512	1'-8" x 5'-0" G		8	1		370	50.50		420.50	485
0513	1'-8" x 4'-0" G		9	.889		320	45		365	420
0514	1'-8" x 6'-0" G		8	1		415	50.50		465.50	530
0515	2'-0" x 2'-0" G		12	.667		240	34		274	315
0516	Budget G		8	1		330	50.50		380.50	440
0517	Custom G		8	1		495	50.50		545.50	620
0518	Budget G		9	.889		215	45		260	305
0519	Custom G		9	.889		320	45		365	425
0520	1'-6" x 6'-8" G	2 Carp	18	.889		410	45		455	520
0522	Vinyl-clad, premium, double insulated glass, 2'-0" x 3'-0" G	1 Carp	10	.800		285	40.50		325.50	375
0524	2'-0" x 4'-0" G		9	.889		330	45		375	435
0525	2'-0" x 5'-0" G		8	1		380	50.50		430.50	495
0526	Budget G	2 Carp	18	.889		325	45		370	430
0527	Custom G	"	18	.889		490	45		535	610
0528	2'-0" x 6'-0" G	1 Carp	8	1		400	50.50		450.50	520
0550	2'-4" x 4'-0" G		8	1		380	50.50		430.50	495
0556	Budget G		8	1		305	50.50		355.50	410
0557	Custom G		8	1		455	50.50		505.50	575
0560	2'-6" x 5'-0" G	2 Carp	17	.941		495	47.50		542.50	620
0566	Budget G		17	.941		395	47.50		442.50	510
0567	Custom G		17	.941		595	47.50		642.50	730
0600	3'-0" x 5'-0" G	1 Carp	8	1		700	50.50		750.50	840
0700	4'-0" x 3'-0" G		8	1		765	50.50		815.50	915
0710	4'-0" x 4'-0" G		8	1		655	50.50		705.50	795
0716	Budget G		8	1		525	50.50		575.50	655
0717	Custom G		8	1		790	50.50		840.50	940
0720	4'-8" x 4'-0" G		8	1		720	50.50		770.50	870
0730	4'-8" x 5'-0" G		6	1.333		825	67.50		892.50	1,000
0740	4'-8" x 6'-0" G		6	1.333		930	67.50		997.50	1,125
0750	6'-0" x 4'-0" G		6	1.333		845	67.50		912.50	1,025
0800	6'-0" x 5'-0" G		6	1.333		930	67.50		997.50	1,125
0900	5'-6" x 5'-6" G	2 Carp	15	1.067		1,475	54		1,529	1,700
0906	Budget G		15	1.067		1,200	54		1,254	1,375
0907	Custom G		15	1.067		1,775	54		1,829	2,025
3020	Vinyl-clad, premium, double insulated glass, multiple leaf units									
3080	Single unit, 1'-6" x 5'-0" G	2 Carp	20	.800	Ea.	330	40.50		370.50	420
3086	Budget G		20	.800		263	40.50		303.50	350
3087	Custom G		20	.800		395	40.50		435.50	495
3100	2'-0" x 2'-0" G		20	.800		225	40.50		265.50	310
3106	Budget G		20	.800		180	40.50		220.50	260

For customer support on your Green Building Costs with RSMeans data, call 800.448.8182.

08 52 Wood Windows

08 52 10 – Plain Wood Windows

08 52 10.40	Casement Window		Crew	Daily Output	Labor-Hours	Unit	Material	2018 Bare Costs Labor	Equipment	Total	Total Incl O&P
3107	Custom	G	2 Carp	20	.800	Ea.	270	40.50		310.50	360
3140	2'-0" x 2'-6"	G		20	.800		285	40.50		325.50	375
3146	Budget	G		20	.800		228	40.50		268.50	315
3147	Custom	G		20	.800		340	40.50		380.50	435
3220	2'-0" x 3'-6"	G		20	.800		290	40.50		330.50	380
3226	Budget	G		20	.800		232	40.50		272.50	315
3227	Custom	G		20	.800		350	40.50		390.50	445
3260	2'-0" x 4'-0"	G		19	.842		330	42.50		372.50	430
3266	Budget	G		19	.842		264	42.50		306.50	355
3267	Custom	G		19	.842		395	42.50		437.50	500
3300	2'-0" x 4'-6"	G		19	.842		335	42.50		377.50	435
3306	Budget	G		19	.842		269	42.50		311.50	360
3307	Custom	G		19	.842		405	42.50		447.50	510
3340	2'-0" x 5'-0"	G		18	.889		380	45		425	490
3346	Budget	G		18	.889		305	45		350	405
3347	Custom	G		18	.889		455	45		500	570
3460	2'-4" x 3'-0"	G		20	.800		290	40.50		330.50	380
3466	Budget	G		20	.800		232	40.50		272.50	315
3467	Custom	G		20	.800		350	40.50		390.50	445
3500	2'-4" x 4'-0"	G		19	.842		360	42.50		402.50	460
3506	Budget	G		19	.842		288	42.50		330.50	380
3507	Custom	G		19	.842		430	42.50		472.50	540
3540	2'-4" x 5'-0"	G		18	.889		425	45		470	540
3546	Budget	G		18	.889		340	45		385	445
3547	Custom	G		18	.889		510	45		555	630
3700	Double unit, 2'-8" x 5'-0"	G		18	.889		600	45		645	730
3706	Budget	G		18	.889		480	45		525	600
3707	Custom	G		18	.889		720	45		765	860
3740	2'-8" x 6'-0"	G		17	.941		695	47.50		742.50	840
3746	Budget	G		17	.941		555	47.50		602.50	690
3747	Custom	G		17	.941		835	47.50		882.50	995
3840	3'-0" x 4'-6"	G		18	.889		540	45		585	665
3846	Budget	G		18	.889		435	45		480	545
3847	Custom	G		18	.889		650	45		695	785
3860	3'-0" x 5'-0"	G		17	.941		700	47.50		747.50	840
3866	Budget	G		17	.941		560	47.50		607.50	690
3867	Custom	G		17	.941		835	47.50		882.50	995
3880	3'-0" x 6'-0"	G		17	.941		755	47.50		802.50	905
3886	Budget	G		17	.941		605	47.50		652.50	740
3887	Custom	G		17	.941		905	47.50		952.50	1,075
3980	3'-4" x 2'-6"	G		19	.842		460	42.50		502.50	570
3986	Budget	G		19	.842		370	42.50		412.50	470
3987	Custom	G		19	.842		555	42.50		597.50	675
4000	3'-4" x 3'-0"	G		12	1.333		465	67.50		532.50	615
4006	Budget	G		12	1.333		370	67.50		437.50	515
4007	Custom	G		12	1.333		555	67.50		622.50	720
4030	3'-4" x 4'-0"	G		18	.889		560	45		605	685
4036	Budget	G		18	.889		450	45		495	565
4037	Custom	G		18	.889		675	45		720	810
4050	3'-4" x 5'-0"	G		12	1.333		700	67.50		767.50	875
4056	Budget	G		12	1.333		560	67.50		627.50	720
4057	Custom	G		12	1.333		840	67.50		907.50	1,025
4100	3'-4" x 6'-0"	G		11	1.455		755	74		829	940

For customer support on your Green Building Costs with RSMeans data, call 800.448.8182.

08 52 Wood Windows

08 52 10 – Plain Wood Windows

08 52 10.40 Casement Window

		Crew	Daily Output	Labor-Hours	Unit	Material	2018 Bare Costs Labor	Equipment	Total	Total Incl O&P
4106	Budget G	2 Carp	11	1.455	Ea.	605	74		679	775
4107	Custom G		11	1.455		905	74		979	1,100
4200	3'-6" x 3'-0" G		18	.889		540	45		585	665
4206	Budget G		18	.889		435	45		480	545
4207	Custom G		18	.889		650	45		695	785
4340	4'-0" x 3'-0" G		18	.889		520	45		565	645
4346	Budget G		18	.889		420	45		465	530
4347	Custom G		18	.889		625	45		670	760
4380	4'-0" x 3'-6" G		17	.941		560	47.50		607.50	690
4386	Budget G		17	.941		450	47.50		497.50	570
4387	Custom G		17	.941		675	47.50		722.50	815
4420	4'-0" x 4'-0" G		16	1		655	50.50		705.50	795
4426	Budget G		16	1		525	50.50		575.50	655
4427	Custom G		16	1		790	50.50		840.50	940
4460	4'-0" x 4'-4" G		16	1		660	50.50		710.50	800
4466	Budget G		16	1		525	50.50		575.50	655
4467	Custom G		16	1		790	50.50		840.50	945
4540	4'-0" x 5'-0" G		16	1		715	50.50		765.50	860
4546	Budget G		16	1		575	50.50		625.50	705
4547	Custom G		16	1		860	50.50		910.50	1,025
4580	4'-0" x 6'-0" G		15	1.067		815	54		869	980
4586	Budget G		15	1.067		650	54		704	800
4587	Custom G		15	1.067		975	54		1,029	1,150
4740	4'-8" x 3'-0" G		18	.889		580	45		625	710
4746	Budget G		18	.889		465	45		510	580
4747	Custom G		18	.889		695	45		740	835
4780	4'-8" x 3'-6" G		17	.941		620	47.50		667.50	755
4786	Budget G		17	.941		495	47.50		542.50	620
4787	Custom G		17	.941		745	47.50		792.50	890
4820	4'-8" x 4'-0" G		16	1		720	50.50		770.50	870
4826	Budget G		16	1		580	50.50		630.50	710
4827	Custom G		16	1		865	50.50		915.50	1,025
4860	4'-8" x 5'-0" G		15	1.067		825	54		879	990
4866	Budget G		15	1.067		660	54		714	810
4867	Custom G		15	1.067		990	54		1,044	1,175
4900	4'-8" x 6'-0" G		15	1.067		930	54		984	1,100
4906	Budget G		15	1.067		745	54		799	900
4907	Custom G		15	1.067		1,125	54		1,179	1,300
5026	Budget G		15	1.067		650	54		704	800
5027	Custom G		15	1.067		975	54		1,029	1,150
5060	5'-0" x 5'-0" G		15	1.067		1,075	54		1,129	1,275
5066	Budget G		15	1.067		865	54		919	1,050
5067	Custom G		15	1.067		1,300	54		1,354	1,500
5100	Triple unit, 5'-6" x 3'-0" G		17	.941		735	47.50		782.50	885
5106	Budget G		17	.941		590	47.50		637.50	720
5107	Custom G		17	.941		880	47.50		927.50	1,050
5140	5'-6" x 3'-6" G		16	1		825	50.50		875.50	985
5146	Budget G		16	1		660	50.50		710.50	800
5147	Custom G		16	1		990	50.50		1,040.50	1,175
5180	5'-6" x 4'-6" G		15	1.067		890	54		944	1,075
5186	Budget G		15	1.067		710	54		764	870
5187	Custom G		15	1.067		1,075	54		1,129	1,250
5220	5'-6" x 5'-6" G		15	1.067		1,150	54		1,204	1,350

For customer support on your Green Building Costs with RSMeans data, call 800.448.8182.

08 52 Wood Windows

08 52 10 – Plain Wood Windows

08 52 10.40 Casement Window		Crew	Daily Output	Labor-Hours	Unit	Material	2018 Bare Costs Labor	Equipment	Total	Total Incl O&P
5226	Budget	G	2 Carp	15	1.067	Ea.	930	54		984	1,100
5227	Custom	G		15	1.067		1,400	54		1,454	1,600
5300	6'-0" x 4'-6"	G		15	1.067		900	54		954	1,075
5306	Budget	G		15	1.067		720	54		774	875
5307	Custom	G		15	1.067		1,075	54		1,129	1,275
5850	5'-0" x 3'-0"	G		12	1.333		620	67.50		687.50	785
5856	Budget	G		12	1.333		495	67.50		562.50	650
5857	Custom	G		12	1.333		745	67.50		812.50	920
5900	5'-0" x 4'-0"	G		11	1.455		960	74		1,034	1,150
5906	Budget	G		11	1.455		510	74		584	675
5907	Custom	G		11	1.455		770	74		844	955
6006	Budget	G		10	1.600		890	81		971	1,100
6007	Custom	G		10	1.600		1,325	81		1,406	1,600
6100	5'-0" x 5'-6"	G		10	1.600		1,100	81		1,181	1,350
6106	Budget	G		10	1.600		880	81		961	1,100
6107	Custom	G		10	1.600		1,325	81		1,406	1,575
6150	5'-0" x 6'-0"	G		10	1.600		1,250	81		1,331	1,475
6156	Budget	G		10	1.600		990	81		1,071	1,225
6157	Custom	G		10	1.600		1,475	81		1,556	1,750
6200	6'-0" x 3'-0"	G		12	1.333		1,200	67.50		1,267.50	1,425
6206	Budget	G		12	1.333		960	67.50		1,027.50	1,150
6207	Custom	G		12	1.333		1,450	67.50		1,517.50	1,675
6250	6'-0" x 3'-4"	G		12	1.333		675	67.50		742.50	850
6256	Budget	G		12	1.333		675	67.50		742.50	850
6257	Custom	G		12	1.333		675	67.50		742.50	850
6300	6'-0" x 4'-0"	G		11	1.455		860	74		934	1,050
6306	Budget	G		11	1.455		685	74		759	865
6307	Custom	G		11	1.455		1,025	74		1,099	1,225
6350	6'-0" x 5'-0"	G		10	1.600		950	81		1,031	1,175
6356	Budget	G		10	1.600		760	81		841	960
6357	Custom	G		10	1.600		1,150	81		1,231	1,375
6400	6'-0" x 6'-0"	G		10	1.600		1,200	81		1,281	1,450
6500	Quadruple unit, 7'-0" x 4'-0"	G		9	1.778		1,150	90		1,240	1,375
6506	Budget	G		9	1.778		910	90		1,000	1,125
6507	Custom	G		9	1.778		1,375	90		1,465	1,625
6700	8'-0" x 4'-6"	G		9	1.778		1,425	90		1,515	1,700
6706	Budget	G		9	1.778		1,150	90		1,240	1,375
6707	Custom	G		9	1.778		1,700	90		1,790	2,000
6950	6'-8" x 4'-0"	G		10	1.600		1,125	81		1,206	1,350
6956	Budget	G		10	1.600		900	81		981	1,125
6957	Custom	G		10	1.600		1,350	81		1,431	1,600
7000	6'-8" x 6'-0"	G		10	1.600		1,500	81		1,581	1,775
7006	Budget	G		10	1.600		1,200	81		1,281	1,450
7007	Custom	G		10	1.600		1,800	81		1,881	2,125
8190	For installation, add per leaf							15%			
8200	For multiple leaf units, deduct for stationary sash										
8220	2' high					Ea.	24			24	26.50
8240	4'-6" high						27			27	30
8260	6' high						36.50			36.50	40

08 52 Wood Windows

08 52 10 – Plain Wood Windows

08 52 10.50 Double-Hung

		Crew	Daily Output	Labor-Hours	Unit	Material	2018 Bare Costs Labor	Equipment	Total	Total Incl O&P
0010	DOUBLE-HUNG, Including frame, screens and grilles R085216-10									
0100	2'-0" x 3'-0" high, low E insul. glass G	1 Carp	10	.800	Ea.	193	40.50		233.50	274
0200	3'-0" x 4'-0" high, double insulated glass G	"	9	.889		288	45		333	385
0206	Wood window, dbl. hung, low E insulated glass, 3' x 4' G					288			288	315
0300	4'-0" x 4'-6" high, low E insulated glass G	1 Carp	8	1	↓	335	50.50		385.50	445
3000	Window replacement channel guide, aluminum	"	160	.050	L.F.	5.30	2.54		7.84	9.70

08 52 10.70 Sliding Windows

		Crew	Daily Output	Labor-Hours	Unit	Material	Labor	Equipment	Total	Incl O&P
0010	SLIDING WINDOWS									
0100	3'-0" x 3'-0" high, double insulated G	1 Carp	10	.800	Ea.	293	40.50		333.50	380
0120	Low E glass G		10	.800		320	40.50		360.50	410
0200	4'-0" x 3'-6" high, double insulated G		9	.889		380	45		425	490
0220	Low E glass G		9	.889		385	45		430	490
0300	6'-0" x 5'-0" high, double insulated G		8	1		505	50.50		555.50	630
0320	Low E glass G	↓	8	1	↓	550	50.50		600.50	680

08 52 13 – Metal-Clad Wood Windows

08 52 13.10 Awning Windows, Metal-Clad

		Crew	Daily Output	Labor-Hours	Unit	Material	Labor	Equipment	Total	Incl O&P
0010	AWNING WINDOWS, METAL-CLAD									
2000	Metal-clad, awning deluxe, double insulated glass, 34" x 22"	1 Carp	9	.889	Ea.	255	45		300	350
2050	36" x 25"		9	.889		276	45		321	375
2100	40" x 22"		9	.889		295	45		340	395
2150	40" x 30"		9	.889		340	45		385	445
2200	48" x 28"		8	1		350	50.50		400.50	460
2250	60" x 36"	↓	8	1	↓	375	50.50		425.50	485

08 52 13.20 Casement Windows, Metal-Clad

		Crew	Daily Output	Labor-Hours	Unit	Material	Labor	Equipment	Total	Incl O&P
0010	CASEMENT WINDOWS, METAL-CLAD									
0100	Metal-clad, deluxe, dbl. insul. glass, 2'-0" x 3'-0" high G	1 Carp	10	.800	Ea.	294	40.50		334.50	385
0120	2'-0" x 4'-0" high G		9	.889		320	45		365	420
0130	2'-0" x 5'-0" high G		8	1		340	50.50		390.50	450
0140	2'-0" x 6'-0" high G		8	1		380	50.50		430.50	495
0150	Casement window, metal-clad, double insul. glass, 3'-6" x 3'-6" G	↓	8.90	.899	↓	505	45.50		550.50	625

08 52 13.30 Double-Hung Windows, Metal-Clad

		Crew	Daily Output	Labor-Hours	Unit	Material	Labor	Equipment	Total	Incl O&P
0010	DOUBLE-HUNG WINDOWS, METAL-CLAD									
0100	Metal-clad, deluxe, dbl. insul. glass, 2'-6" x 3'-0" high G	1 Carp	10	.800	Ea.	285	40.50		325.50	375
0120	3'-0" x 3'-6" high G		10	.800		325	40.50		365.50	420
0140	3'-0" x 4'-0" high G		9	.889		340	45		385	445
0160	3'-0" x 4'-6" high G		9	.889		355	45		400	460
0180	3'-0" x 5'-0" high G		8	1		385	50.50		435.50	500
0200	3'-6" x 6'-0" high G	↓	8	1	↓	465	50.50		515.50	585

08 52 13.35 Picture and Sliding Windows Metal-Clad

		Crew	Daily Output	Labor-Hours	Unit	Material	Labor	Equipment	Total	Incl O&P
0010	PICTURE AND SLIDING WINDOWS METAL-CLAD									
2400	Metal-clad, dlx sliding, dbl. insul. glass, 3'-0" x 3'-0" high G	1 Carp	10	.800	Ea.	330	40.50		370.50	420
2420	4'-0" x 3'-6" high G		9	.889		400	45		445	510
2440	5'-0" x 4'-0" high G		9	.889		480	45		525	595
2460	6'-0" x 5'-0" high G	↓	8	1	↓	745	50.50		795.50	895

08 52 16 – Plastic-Clad Wood Windows

08 52 16.15 Awning Window Vinyl-Clad

		Crew	Daily Output	Labor-Hours	Unit	Material	Labor	Equipment	Total	Incl O&P
0010	AWNING WINDOW VINYL-CLAD including frames, screens, and grilles									
0240	Vinyl-clad, 34" x 22"	1 Carp	10	.800	Ea.	267	40.50		307.50	355
0280	36" x 28"		9	.889		305	45		350	410
0300	36" x 36"	↓	9	.889	↓	350	45		395	455

For customer support on your Green Building Costs with RSMeans data, call 800.448.8182.

153

08 52 Wood Windows

08 52 16 – Plastic-Clad Wood Windows

08 52 16.15 Awning Window Vinyl-Clad

		Crew	Daily Output	Labor-Hours	Unit	Material	2018 Bare Costs Labor	Equipment	Total	Total Incl O&P
0340	40" x 22"	1 Carp	10	.800	Ea.	295	40.50		335.50	385
0360	48" x 28"		8	1		370	50.50		420.50	485
0380	60" x 36"		8	1		520	50.50		570.50	645

08 52 16.35 Double-Hung Window

			Crew	Daily Output	Labor-Hours	Unit	Material	Labor	Equipment	Total	Incl O&P
0010	**DOUBLE-HUNG WINDOW** including frames, screens, and grilles										
0140	Vinyl-clad, premium, double insulated glass, 1'-8" x 4'-0"	G	1 Carp	11	.727	Ea.	345	37		382	430
0146	Budget	G		11	.727		275	37		312	355
0147	Custom	G		11	.727		410	37		447	510
0160	1'-8" x 5'-0"	G		11	.727		375	37		412	470
0166	Budget	G		11	.727		300	37		337	385
0167	Custom	G		11	.727		450	37		487	550
0180	1'-8" x 6'-0"	G		11	.727		415	37		452	510
0187	Custom	G		11	.727		495	37		532	600
0200	2'-0" x 4'-0"	G		11	.727		375	37		412	470
0201	Budget	G		11	.727		300	37		337	385
0202	Custom	G		11	.727		450	37		487	550
0203	2'-0" x 4'-8"	G		11	.727		400	37		437	495
0206	Budget	G		11	.727		320	37		357	405
0207	Custom	G		11	.727		480	37		517	585
0210	2'-0" x 5'-0"	G		11	.727		420	37		457	515
0211	2'-0" x 5'-0", 2 units	G		6	1.333		840	67.50		907.50	1,025
0215	2'-0" x 6'-0"	G		10	.800		450	40.50		490.50	555
0216	Budget	G		10	.800		360	40.50		400.50	455
0217	Custom	G		10	.800		540	40.50		580.50	655
0220	2'-4" x 3'-4"	G		11	.727		340	37		377	425
0226	Budget	G		11	.727		270	37		307	355
0227	Custom	G		11	.727		405	37		442	500
0230	2'-4" x 4'-0"	G		10	.800		395	40.50		435.50	495
0231	Budget	G		10	.800		315	40.50		355.50	405
0232	Custom	G		10	.800		475	40.50		515.50	580
0235	2'-4" x 4'-0", 2 units	G		6	1.333		765	67.50		832.50	945
0236	Budget	G		6	1.333		610	67.50		677.50	775
0237	Custom	G		6	1.333		915	67.50		982.50	1,100
0240	2'-4" x 4'-8"	G		10	.800		375	40.50		415.50	475
0246	Budget	G		10	.800		300	40.50		340.50	390
0247	Custom	G		10	.800		450	40.50		490.50	555
0260	2'-4" x 4'-8", 2 units	G	2 Carp	11	1.455		750	74		824	935
0266	Budget	G		11	1.455		750	74		824	935
0267	Custom	G		11	1.455		750	74		824	935
0280	2'-4" x 4'-8", 3 units	G	1 Carp	8	1		1,125	50.50		1,175.50	1,325
0286	Budget	G		8	1		1,325	50.50		1,375.50	1,525
0287	Custom	G		8	1		1,325	50.50		1,375.50	1,525
0290	2'-4" x 5'-6"	G		10	.800		420	40.50		460.50	520
0291	Budget	G		10	.800		335	40.50		375.50	430
0292	Custom	G		10	.800		505	40.50		545.50	615
0295	2'-4" x 6'-0"	G		10	.800		420	40.50		460.50	520
0296	Budget	G		10	.800		335	40.50		375.50	430
0297	Custom	G		10	.800		505	40.50		545.50	615
0300	Vinyl-clad, premium, double insulated glass, 2'-6" x 3'-0"	G		10	.800		340	40.50		380.50	430
0305	2'-6" x 4'-0"	G		10	.800		375	40.50		415.50	475
0306	Budget	G		10	.800		300	40.50		340.50	390
0307	Custom	G		10	.800		450	40.50		490.50	555

For customer support on your Green Building Costs with RSMeans data, call 800.448.8182.

08 52 Wood Windows

08 52 16 – Plastic-Clad Wood Windows

08 52 16.35 Double-Hung Window

		Crew	Daily Output	Labor-Hours	Unit	Material	2018 Bare Costs Labor	Equipment	Total	Total Incl O&P
0315	2'-8" x 4'-0"	G 1 Carp	6	1.333	Ea.	570	67.50		637.50	735
0316	Budget	G	6	1.333		460	67.50		527.50	610
0317	Custom	G	6	1.333		685	67.50		752.50	860
0320	2'-8" x 4'-8"	G	9	.889		420	45		465	530
0326	Budget	G	9	.889		335	45		380	440
0327	Custom	G	9	.889		505	45		550	625
0340	2'-8" x 5'-0"	G	8	1		450	50.50		500.50	570
0346	Budget	G	8	1		360	50.50		410.50	470
0347	Custom	G	8	1		540	50.50		590.50	670
0360	2'-8" x 6'-0"	G	8	1		440	50.50		490.50	560
0361	Budget	G	8	1		355	50.50		405.50	465
0362	Custom	G	8	1		530	50.50		580.50	660
0400	3'-0" x 3'-6"	G	10	.800		345	40.50		385.50	435
0405	Budget	G	10	.800		275	40.50		315.50	360
0407	Custom	G	10	.800		410	40.50		450.50	515
0500	3'-0" x 4'-0"	G	9	.889		400	45		445	510
0505	Vinyl-clad wood window, dbl. hung, double insulated glass, 3' x 4'	G				400			400	440
0506	Budget	G 1 Carp	9	.889		320	45		365	425
0507	Custom	G	9	.889		480	45		525	600
0600	3'-0" x 4'-6"	G	9	.889		425	45		470	540
0620	3'-0" x 4'-8"	G	9	.889		445	45		490	560
0621	Budget	G	9	.889		360	45		405	465
0622	Custom	G	9	.889		535	45		580	660
0700	3'-0" x 5'-0"	G	8	1		460	50.50		510.50	580
0706	Budget	G	8	1		365	50.50		415.50	480
0707	Custom	G	8	1		550	50.50		600.50	680
0760	3'-0" x 6'-0"	G	8	1		400	50.50		450.50	515
0766	Budget	G	8	1		320	50.50		370.50	425
0767	Custom	G	8	1		480	50.50		530.50	605
0785	3'-4" x 4'-0"	G	8	1		440	50.50		490.50	555
0790	3'-4" x 5'-0"	G	8	1		450	50.50		500.50	570
0794	3'-4" x 6'-0"	G	8	1		475	50.50		525.50	600
0798	3'-6" x 5'-6"	G	8	1		490	50.50		540.50	610
0800	3'-6" x 6'-0"	G	8	1		515	50.50		565.50	640
0820	4'-0" x 5'-0"	G	7	1.143		570	58		628	720
0826	Budget	G	7	1.143		460	58		518	595
0827	Custom	G	7	1.143		685	58		743	845
0830	4'-0" x 6'-0"	G	7	1.143		725	58		783	885
0836	Budget	G	7	1.143		580	58		638	730
0837	Custom	G	7	1.143		870	58		928	1,050

08 52 16.70 Vinyl-Clad, Premium, DBL. Insul. Glass

		Crew	Daily Output	Labor-Hours	Unit	Material	Labor	Equipment	Total	Total Incl O&P
0010	**VINYL-CLAD, PREMIUM, DBL. INSUL. GLASS**									
1000	Sliding, 3'-0" x 3'-0"	G 1 Carp	10	.800	Ea.	625	40.50		665.50	745
1020	4'-0" x 1'-11"	G	11	.727		600	37		637	715
1026	Budget	G	11	.727		480	37		517	585
1027	Custom	G	11	.727		720	37		757	845
1040	4'-0" x 3'-0"	G	10	.800		750	40.50		790.50	885
1046	Budget	G	10	.800		600	40.50		640.50	720
1047	Custom	G	10	.800		900	40.50		940.50	1,050
1050	4'-0" x 3'-6"	G	9	.889		690	45		735	830
1056	Budget	G	9	.889		550	45		595	675
1057	Custom	G	9	.889		825	45		870	980

For customer support on your Green Building Costs with RSMeans data, call 800.448.8182.

08 52 Wood Windows

08 52 16 – Plastic-Clad Wood Windows

08 52 16.70 Vinyl-Clad, Premium, DBL. Insul. Glass

			Crew	Daily Output	Labor-Hours	Unit	Material	2018 Bare Costs Labor	Equipment	Total	Total Incl O&P
1080	4'-0" x 4'-0"	G	1 Carp	9	.889	Ea.	825	45		870	980
1090	4'-0" x 5'-0"	G		9	.889		940	45		985	1,100
1096	Budget	G		9	.889		750	45		795	895
1097	Custom	G		9	.889		1,125	45		1,170	1,325
1100	5'-0" x 4'-0"	G		9	.889		920	45		965	1,075
1106	Budget	G		9	.889		735	45		780	880
1107	Custom	G		9	.889		1,100	45		1,145	1,300
1120	5'-0" x 5'-0"	G		8	1		1,075	50.50		1,125.50	1,275
1126	Budget	G		8	1		865	50.50		915.50	1,025
1127	Custom	G		8	1		1,300	50.50		1,350.50	1,500
1140	6'-0" x 4'-0"	G		8	1		1,125	50.50		1,175.50	1,300
1146	Budget	G		8	1		890	50.50		940.50	1,050
1147	Custom	G		8	1		1,325	50.50		1,375.50	1,550
1150	6'-0" x 5'-0"	G		8	1		1,175	50.50		1,225.50	1,350
1300	8'-0" x 5'-0"	G		6	1.333		1,875	67.50		1,942.50	2,175
1306	Budget	G		6	1.333		1,500	67.50		1,567.50	1,750
1307	Custom	G		6	1.333		2,250	67.50		2,317.50	2,575

08 52 69 – Wood Storm Windows

08 52 69.10 Storm Windows

			Crew	Daily Output	Labor-Hours	Unit	Material	Labor	Equipment	Total	Total Incl O&P
0010	**STORM WINDOWS**, aluminum residential										
0300	Basement, mill finish, incl. fiberglass screen										
0320	1'-10" x 1'-0" high	G	2 Carp	30	.533	Ea.	36	27		63	80.50
0340	2'-9" x 1'-6" high	G		30	.533		39	27		66	84
0360	3'-4" x 2'-0" high	G		30	.533		46	27		73	91.50
1600	Double-hung, combination, storm & screen										
2000	Clear anodic coating, 2'-0" x 3'-5" high	G	2 Carp	30	.533	Ea.	97	27		124	148
2020	2'-6" x 5'-0" high	G		28	.571		124	29		153	180
2040	4'-0" x 6'-0" high	G		25	.640		135	32.50		167.50	199
2400	White painted, 2'-0" x 3'-5" high	G		30	.533		95	27		122	146
2420	2'-6" x 5'-0" high	G		28	.571		100	29		129	154
2440	4'-0" x 6'-0" high	G		25	.640		115	32.50		147.50	177
2600	Mill finish, 2'-0" x 3'-5" high	G		30	.533		90	27		117	140
2620	2'-6" x 5'-0" high	G		28	.571		95	29		124	149
2640	4'-0" x 6'-8" high	G		25	.640		115	32.50		147.50	177

08 53 Plastic Windows

08 53 13 – Vinyl Windows

08 53 13.20 Vinyl Single-Hung Windows

			Crew	Daily Output	Labor-Hours	Unit	Material	Labor	Equipment	Total	Total Incl O&P
0010	**VINYL SINGLE-HUNG WINDOWS**, insulated glass										
0020	Grids, low E, J fin, extension jambs										
0130	25" x 41"	G	2 Carp	20	.800	Ea.	210	40.50		250.50	293
0140	25" x 49"	G		18	.889		220	45		265	310
0150	25" x 57"	G		17	.941		230	47.50		277.50	325
0160	25" x 65"	G		16	1		250	50.50		300.50	350
0170	29" x 41"	G		18	.889		210	45		255	300
0180	29" x 53"	G		18	.889		230	45		275	320
0190	29" x 57"	G		17	.941		240	47.50		287.50	335
0200	29" x 65"	G		16	1		250	50.50		300.50	350
0210	33" x 41"	G		20	.800		225	40.50		265.50	310
0220	33" x 53"	G		18	.889		245	45		290	340

08 53 Plastic Windows

08 53 13 – Vinyl Windows

08 53 13.20 Vinyl Single-Hung Windows

			Crew	Daily Output	Labor-Hours	Unit	Material	2018 Bare Costs Labor	Equipment	Total	Total Incl O&P
0230	33" x 57"	G	2 Carp	17	.941	Ea.	250	47.50		297.50	350
0240	33" x 65"	G		16	1		260	50.50		310.50	365
0250	37" x 41"	G		20	.800		250	40.50		290.50	335
0260	37" x 53"	G		18	.889		275	45		320	375
0270	37" x 57"	G		17	.941		285	47.50		332.50	390
0280	37" x 65"	G		16	1		300	50.50		350.50	405

08 53 13.30 Vinyl Double-Hung Windows

			Crew	Daily Output	Labor-Hours	Unit	Material	Labor	Equipment	Total	Total Incl O&P
0010	**VINYL DOUBLE-HUNG WINDOWS**, insulated glass										
0100	Grids, low E, J fin, ext. jambs, 21" x 53"	G	2 Carp	18	.889	Ea.	220	45		265	310
0102	21" x 37"	G		18	.889		230	45		275	320
0104	21" x 41"	G		18	.889		240	45		285	335
0106	21" x 49"	G		18	.889		250	45		295	345
0110	21" x 57"	G		17	.941		270	47.50		317.50	370
0120	21" x 65"	G		16	1		285	50.50		335.50	390
0128	25" x 37"	G		20	.800		240	40.50		280.50	325
0130	25" x 41"	G		20	.800		250	40.50		290.50	335
0140	25" x 49"	G		18	.889		260	45		305	355
0145	25" x 53"	G		18	.889		275	45		320	375
0150	25" x 57"	G		17	.941		280	47.50		327.50	385
0160	25" x 65"	G		16	1		295	50.50		345.50	400
0162	25" x 69"	G		16	1		300	50.50		350.50	405
0164	25" x 77"	G		16	1		325	50.50		375.50	435
0168	29" x 37"	G		18	.889		250	45		295	345
0170	29" x 41"	G		18	.889		260	45		305	355
0172	29" x 49"	G		18	.889		270	45		315	365
0180	29" x 53"	G		18	.889		280	45		325	380
0190	29" x 57"	G		17	.941		290	47.50		337.50	395
0200	29" x 65"	G		16	1		310	50.50		360.50	415
0202	29" x 69"	G		16	1		315	50.50		365.50	420
0205	29" x 77"	G		16	1		340	50.50		390.50	450
0208	33" x 37"	G		20	.800		265	40.50		305.50	355
0210	33" x 41"	G		20	.800		270	40.50		310.50	360
0215	33" x 49"	G		20	.800		285	40.50		325.50	375
0220	33" x 53"	G		18	.889		290	45		335	390
0230	33" x 57"	G		17	.941		300	47.50		347.50	405
0240	33" x 65"	G		16	1		320	50.50		370.50	425
0242	33" x 69"	G		16	1		330	50.50		380.50	440
0246	33" x 77"	G		16	1		350	50.50		400.50	460
0250	37" x 41"	G		20	.800		295	40.50		335.50	385
0255	37" x 49"	G		20	.800		297	40.50		337.50	385
0260	37" x 53"	G		18	.889		320	45		365	420
0270	37" x 57"	G		17	.941		340	47.50		387.50	450
0280	37" x 65"	G		16	1		360	50.50		410.50	470
0282	37" x 69"	G		16	1		365	50.50		415.50	475
0286	37" x 77"	G		16	1		380	50.50		430.50	495
0300	Solid vinyl, average quality, double insulated glass, 2'-0" x 3'-0"	G	1 Carp	10	.800		291	40.50		331.50	380
0310	3'-0" x 4'-0"	G		9	.889		214	45		259	305
0330	Premium, double insulated glass, 2'-6" x 3'-0"	G		10	.800		276	40.50		316.50	365
0340	3'-0" x 3'-6"	G		9	.889		310	45		355	410
0350	3'-0" x 4'-0"	G		9	.889		330	45		375	435
0360	3'-0" x 4'-6"	G		9	.889		335	45		380	440
0370	3'-0" x 5'-0"	G		8	1		360	50.50		410.50	470

For customer support on your Green Building Costs with RSMeans data, call 800.448.8182.

08 53 Plastic Windows

08 53 13 – Vinyl Windows

08 53 13.30 Vinyl Double-Hung Windows

		Crew	Daily Output	Labor-Hours	Unit	Material	2018 Bare Costs Labor	Equipment	Total	Total Incl O&P
0380	3'-6" x 6'-0"	G 1 Carp	8	1	Ea.	395	50.50		445.50	510

08 53 13.40 Vinyl Casement Windows

		Crew	Daily Output	Labor-Hours	Unit	Material	Labor	Equipment	Total	Incl O&P
0010	**VINYL CASEMENT WINDOWS**, insulated glass									
0015	Grids, low E, J fin, extension jambs, screens									
0100	One lite, 21" x 41"	G 2 Carp	20	.800	Ea.	315	40.50		355.50	405
0110	21" x 47"	G	20	.800		330	40.50		370.50	425
0120	21" x 53"	G	20	.800		365	40.50		405.50	460
0128	24" x 35"	G	19	.842		297	42.50		339.50	390
0130	24" x 41"	G	19	.842		320	42.50		362.50	415
0140	24" x 47"	G	19	.842		355	42.50		397.50	455
0150	24" x 53"	G	19	.842		380	42.50		422.50	485
0158	28" x 35"	G	19	.842		310	42.50		352.50	405
0160	28" x 41"	G	19	.842		340	42.50		382.50	440
0170	28" x 47"	G	19	.842		375	42.50		417.50	480
0180	28" x 53"	G	19	.842		405	42.50		447.50	510
0184	28" x 59"	G	19	.842		415	42.50		457.50	525
0188	Two lites, 33" x 35"	G	18	.889		495	45		540	615
0190	33" x 41"	G	18	.889		530	45		575	655
0200	33" x 47"	G	18	.889		565	45		610	690
0210	33" x 53"	G	18	.889		580	45		625	710
0212	33" x 59"	G	18	.889		635	45		680	770
0215	33" x 72"	G	18	.889		665	45		710	805
0220	41" x 41"	G	18	.889		550	45		595	675
0230	41" x 47"	G	18	.889		610	45		655	740
0240	41" x 53"	G	17	.941		650	47.50		697.50	790
0242	41" x 59"	G	17	.941		690	47.50		737.50	830
0246	41" x 72"	G	17	.941		720	47.50		767.50	865
0250	47" x 41"	G	17	.941		585	47.50		632.50	715
0260	47" x 47"	G	17	.941		625	47.50		672.50	765
0270	47" x 53"	G	17	.941		665	47.50		712.50	810
0272	47" x 59"	G	17	.941		725	47.50		772.50	870
0280	56" x 41"	G	15	1.067		625	54		679	775
0290	56" x 47"	G	15	1.067		665	54		719	820
0300	56" x 53"	G	15	1.067		725	54		779	880
0302	56" x 59"	G	15	1.067		750	54		804	910
0310	56" x 72"	G	15	1.067		810	54		864	975
0340	Solid vinyl, premium, double insulated glass, 2'-0" x 3'-0" high	G 1 Carp	10	.800		270	40.50		310.50	360
0360	2'-0" x 4'-0" high	G	9	.889		299	45		344	400
0380	2'-0" x 5'-0" high	G	8	1		335	50.50		385.50	445

08 54 Composite Windows

08 54 13 – Fiberglass Windows

08 54 13.10 Fiberglass Single-Hung Windows

		Crew	Daily Output	Labor-Hours	Unit	Material	Labor	Equipment	Total	Incl O&P
0010	**FIBERGLASS SINGLE-HUNG WINDOWS**									
0100	Grids, low E, 18" x 24"	G 2 Carp	18	.889	Ea.	335	45		380	440
0110	18" x 40"	G	17	.941		340	47.50		387.50	450
0130	24" x 40"	G	20	.800		360	40.50		400.50	455
0230	36" x 36"	G	17	.941		370	47.50		417.50	480
0250	36" x 48"	G	20	.800		405	40.50		445.50	505
0260	36" x 60"	G	18	.889		445	45		490	560
0280	36" x 72"	G	16	1		470	50.50		520.50	590

08 54 Composite Windows

08 54 13 – Fiberglass Windows

08 54 13.10 Fiberglass Single-Hung Windows

			Crew	Daily Output	Labor-Hours	Unit	Material	2018 Bare Costs Labor	Equipment	Total	Total Incl O&P
0290	48" x 40"		G 2 Carp	16	1	Ea.	470	50.50		520.50	590

08 62 Unit Skylights

08 62 13 – Domed Unit Skylights

08 62 13.10 Domed Skylights

			Crew	Daily Output	Labor-Hours	Unit	Material	Labor	Equipment	Total	Total Incl O&P
0010	**DOMED SKYLIGHTS**										
0020	Skylight, fixed dome type, 22" x 22"	G	G-3	12	2.667	Ea.	216	133		349	440
0030	22" x 46"	G		10	3.200		269	159		428	540
0040	30" x 30"	G		12	2.667		286	133		419	520
0050	30" x 46"	G		10	3.200		380	159		539	665
0110	Fixed, double glazed, 22" x 27"	G		12	2.667		275	133		408	510
0120	22" x 46"	G		10	3.200		293	159		452	565
0130	44" x 46"	G		10	3.200		430	159		589	720
0210	Operable, double glazed, 22" x 27"	G		12	2.667		405	133		538	650
0220	22" x 46"	G		10	3.200		465	159		624	760
0230	44" x 46"	G		10	3.200		925	159		1,084	1,275

08 62 13.20 Skylights

			Crew	Daily Output	Labor-Hours	Unit	Material	Labor	Equipment	Total	Total Incl O&P
0010	**SKYLIGHTS**, flush or curb mounted										
2120	Ventilating insulated plexiglass dome with										
2130	curb mounting, 36" x 36"	G	G-3	12	2.667	Ea.	480	133		613	735
2150	52" x 52"	G		12	2.667		670	133		803	940
2160	28" x 52"	G		10	3.200		495	159		654	790
2170	36" x 52"	G		10	3.200		545	159		704	840
2180	For electric opening system, add	G					315			315	350
2210	Operating skylight, with thermopane glass, 24" x 48"	G	G-3	10	3.200		595	159		754	900
2220	32" x 48"	G		9	3.556		620	177		797	955
2300	Insulated safety glass with aluminum frame	G		160	.200	S.F.	95	9.95		104.95	120
2310	Non venting insulated plexiglass dome skylight with										
2320	Flush mount 22" x 46"	G	G-3	15.23	2.101	Ea.	335	105		440	525
2330	30" x 30"	G		16	2		310	99.50		409.50	490
2340	46" x 46"	G		13.91	2.301		570	115		685	800
2350	Curb mount 22" x 46"	G		15.23	2.101		365	105		470	560
2360	30" x 30"	G		16	2		405	99.50		504.50	600
2370	46" x 46"	G		13.91	2.301		625	115		740	865
4000	Skylight, solar tube kit, incl. dome, flashing, diffuser, 1 pipe, 10" diam.	G	1 Carp	2	4		300	203		503	640
4010	14" diam.	G		2	4		400	203		603	750
4020	21" diam.	G		2	4		490	203		693	850
4030	Accessories for, 1' long x 9" diam. pipe	G		24	.333		50	16.90		66.90	80.50
4040	2' long x 9" diam. pipe	G		24	.333		43	16.90		59.90	73
4050	4' long x 9" diam. pipe	G		20	.400		75	20.50		95.50	114
4060	1' long x 13" diam. pipe	G		24	.333		70	16.90		86.90	103
4070	2' long x 13" diam. pipe	G		24	.333		55	16.90		71.90	86
4080	4' long x 13" diam. pipe	G		20	.400		102	20.50		122.50	143
4090	6.5" turret ext. for 21" diam. pipe	G		16	.500		110	25.50		135.50	160
4100	12' long x 21" diam. flexible pipe	G		12	.667		90	34		124	151
4110	45 degree elbow, 10"	G		16	.500		155	25.50		180.50	210
4120	14"	G		16	.500		85	25.50		110.50	132
4130	Interior decorative ring, 9"	G		20	.400		45	20.50		65.50	80.50
4140	13"	G		20	.400		60	20.50		80.50	97

08 81 Glass Glazing

08 81 30 – Insulating Glass

08 81 30.10 Reduce Heat Transfer Glass

		Crew	Daily Output	Labor-Hours	Unit	Material	2018 Bare Costs Labor	Equipment	Total	Total Incl O&P
0010	REDUCE HEAT TRANSFER GLASS	R088110-10								
0015	2 lites 1/8" float, 1/2" thk under 15 S.F.									
0020	Clear	G	2 Glaz	95	.168	S.F.	10.35	8.15		18.50	24
0100	Tinted	G		95	.168		14.50	8.15		22.65	28.50
0150	2 lites, 3/8" thick, clear, glass sealed edges	G		76	.211		16.90	10.20		27.10	34
0200	2 lites 3/16" float, for 5/8" thk unit, 15 to 30 S.F., clear	G		90	.178		13.80	8.60		22.40	28
0300	Tinted	G		90	.178		13.85	8.60		22.45	28.50
0400	1" thk, dbl. glazed, 1/4" float, 30 to 70 S.F., clear	G		75	.213		17.35	10.35		27.70	35
0500	Tinted			75	.213		23.50	10.35		33.85	41.50
0600	1" thk, dbl. glazed, 1/4" float, 1/4" wire			75	.213		24.50	10.35		34.85	42.50
0700	1/4" float, 1/4" tempered			75	.213		33.50	10.35		43.85	52
0800	1/4" wire, 1/4" tempered			75	.213		32	10.35		42.35	51
2000	Both lites, light & heat reflective	G		85	.188		31.50	9.15		40.65	49
2500	Heat reflective, film inside, 1" thick unit, clear	G		85	.188		27.50	9.15		36.65	44.50
2600	Tinted	G		85	.188		30	9.15		39.15	47.50
3000	Film on weatherside, clear, 1/2" thick unit	G		95	.168		19.75	8.15		27.90	34
3100	5/8" thick unit	G		90	.178		20.50	8.60		29.10	35.50
3200	1" thick unit	G		85	.188		27.50	9.15		36.65	44
3350	Clear heat reflective film on inside	G	1 Glaz	50	.160		13.35	7.75		21.10	26.50
3360	Heat reflective film on inside, tinted	G		25	.320		14.15	15.50		29.65	39
3370	Heat reflective film on the inside, metalized	G		20	.400		15.35	19.40		34.75	46.50
5000	Spectrally selective film, on ext., blocks solar gain/allows 70% of light	G	2 Glaz	95	.168		15.20	8.15		23.35	29

08 83 Mirrors

08 83 13 – Mirrored Glass Glazing

08 83 13.15 Reflective Glass

		Crew	Daily Output	Labor-Hours	Unit	Material	Labor	Equipment	Total	Total Incl O&P
0010	REFLECTIVE GLASS									
0100	1/4" float with fused metallic oxide fixed	G	2 Glaz	115	.139	S.F.	17.90	6.75		24.65	30
0500	1/4" float glass with reflective applied coating	G	"	115	.139	"	14.50	6.75		21.25	26

08 84 Plastic Glazing

08 84 10 – Plexiglass Glazing

08 84 10.10 Plexiglass Acrylic

		Crew	Daily Output	Labor-Hours	Unit	Material	Labor	Equipment	Total	Total Incl O&P
0010	PLEXIGLASS ACRYLIC, clear, masked,									
0020	1/8" thick, cut sheets		2 Glaz	170	.094	S.F.	11.35	4.56		15.91	19.40
0200	Full sheets			195	.082		5.75	3.98		9.73	12.35
0500	1/4" thick, cut sheets			165	.097		13.35	4.70		18.05	22
0600	Full sheets			185	.086		9.30	4.19		13.49	16.60
0900	3/8" thick, cut sheets			155	.103		21	5		26	30.50
1000	Full sheets			180	.089		16.75	4.31		21.06	25
1300	1/2" thick, cut sheets			135	.119		31.50	5.75		37.25	43
1400	Full sheets			150	.107		18.85	5.15		24	28.50
1700	3/4" thick, cut sheets			115	.139		31	6.75		37.75	44.50
1800	Full sheets			130	.123		18	5.95		23.95	29
2100	1" thick, cut sheets			105	.152		35	7.40		42.40	49.50
2200	Full sheets			125	.128		22	6.20		28.20	33.50
3000	Colored, 1/8" thick, cut sheets			170	.094		20	4.56		24.56	29
3200	Full sheets			195	.082		11.40	3.98		15.38	18.60
3500	1/4" thick, cut sheets			165	.097		22	4.70		26.70	31.50

08 84 Plastic Glazing

08 84 10 – Plexiglass Glazing

08 84 10.10 Plexiglass Acrylic

		Crew	Daily Output	Labor-Hours	Unit	Material	2018 Bare Costs Labor	Equipment	Total	Total Incl O&P
3600	Full sheets	2 Glaz	185	.086	S.F.	14.80	4.19		18.99	22.50
4000	Mirrors, untinted, cut sheets, 1/8" thick		185	.086		13.30	4.19		17.49	21
4200	1/4" thick		180	.089		17.15	4.31		21.46	25.50

08 87 Glazing Surface Films

08 87 13 – Solar Control Films

08 87 13.10 Solar Films On Glass

		Crew	Daily Output	Labor-Hours	Unit	Material	Labor	Equipment	Total	Total Incl O&P
0010	**SOLAR FILMS ON GLASS** (glass not included) R088110-10									
1000	Bronze, 20% VLT	H-2	180	.133	S.F.	1.60	6.10		7.70	11
1020	50% VLT		180	.133		1.80	6.10		7.90	11.25
1050	Neutral, 20% VLT		180	.133		1.80	6.10		7.90	11.25
1100	Silver, 15% VLT		180	.133		1.04	6.10		7.14	10.40
1120	35% VLT		180	.133		3.02	6.10		9.12	12.55
1150	68% VLT		180	.133		.40	6.10		6.50	9.70
3000	One way mirror with night vision 5% in and 15% out VLT		180	.133		3.03	6.10		9.13	12.60

08 87 16 – Glass Safety Films

08 87 16.10 Safety Films On Glass

		Crew	Daily Output	Labor-Hours	Unit	Material	Labor	Equipment	Total	Total Incl O&P
0010	**SAFETY FILMS ON GLASS** (glass not included)									
0015	Safety film helps hold glass together when broken									
0050	Safety film, clear, 2 mil	H-2	180	.133	S.F.	1.21	6.10		7.31	10.60
0100	Safety film, clear, 4 mil		180	.133		1.81	6.10		7.91	11.25
0110	Safety film, tinted, 4 mil		180	.133		3.46	6.10		9.56	13.05
0150	Safety film, black tint, 8 mil		180	.133		2.23	6.10		8.33	11.70

Division Notes

	CREW	DAILY OUTPUT	LABOR-HOURS	UNIT	MAT.	LABOR	EQUIP.	TOTAL	TOTAL INCL O&P

Estimating Tips
General
- Room Finish Schedule: A complete set of plans should contain a room finish schedule. If one is not available, it would be well worth the time and effort to obtain one.

09 20 00 Plaster and Gypsum Board
- Lath is estimated by the square yard plus a 5% allowance for waste. Furring, channels, and accessories are measured by the linear foot. An extra foot should be allowed for each accessory miter or stop.
- Plaster is also estimated by the square yard. Deductions for openings vary by preference, from zero deduction to 50% of all openings over 2 feet in width. The estimator should allow one extra square foot for each linear foot of horizontal interior or exterior angle located below the ceiling level. Also, double the areas of small radius work.
- Drywall accessories, studs, track, and acoustical caulking are all measured by the linear foot. Drywall taping is figured by the square foot. Gypsum wallboard is estimated by the square foot. No material deductions should be made for door or window openings under 32 S.F.

09 60 00 Flooring
- Tile and terrazzo areas are taken off on a square foot basis. Trim and base materials are measured by the linear foot. Accent tiles are listed per each. Two basic methods of installation are used. Mud set is approximately 30% more expensive than thin set. The cost of grout is included with tile unit price lines unless otherwise noted. In terrazzo work, be sure to include the linear footage of embedded decorative strips, grounds, machine rubbing, and power cleanup.
- Wood flooring is available in strip, parquet, or block configuration. The latter two types are set in adhesives with quantities estimated by the square foot. The laying pattern will influence labor costs and material waste. In addition to the material and labor for laying wood floors, the estimator must make allowances for sanding and finishing these areas, unless the flooring is prefinished.
- Sheet flooring is measured by the square yard. Roll widths vary, so consideration should be given to use the most economical width, as waste must be figured into the total quantity. Consider also the installation methods available—direct glue down or stretched. Direct glue-down installation is assumed with sheet carpet unit price lines unless otherwise noted.

09 70 00 Wall Finishes
- Wall coverings are estimated by the square foot. The area to be covered is measured—length by height of the wall above the baseboards—to calculate the square footage of each wall. This figure is divided by the number of square feet in the single roll which is being used. Deduct, in full, the areas of openings such as doors and windows. Where a pattern match is required allow 25%–30% waste.

09 80 00 Acoustic Treatment
- Acoustical systems fall into several categories. The takeoff of these materials should be by the square foot of area with a 5% allowance for waste. Do not forget about scaffolding, if applicable, when estimating these systems.

09 90 00 Painting and Coating
- A major portion of the work in painting involves surface preparation. Be sure to include cleaning, sanding, filling, and masking costs in the estimate.
- Protection of adjacent surfaces is not included in painting costs. When considering the method of paint application, an important factor is the amount of protection and masking required. These must be estimated separately and may be the determining factor in choosing the method of application.

Reference Numbers
Reference numbers are shown at the beginning of some major classifications. These numbers refer to related items in the Reference Section. The reference information may be an estimating procedure, an alternate pricing method, or technical information.

Note: Not all subdivisions listed here necessarily appear. ∎

Did you know?

RSMeans data is available through our online application with 24/7 access:
- Search for unit prices by keyword
- Leverage the most up-to-date data
- Build and export estimates

Try it free for 30 days!
www.rsmeans.com/2018freetrial

No part of this cost data may be reproduced, stored in a retrieval system, or transmitted in any form or by any means without prior written permission of Gordian.

09 05 Common Work Results for Finishes

09 05 05 – Selective Demolition for Finishes

09 05 05.20 Selective Demolition, Flooring

		Crew	Daily Output	Labor-Hours	Unit	Material	2018 Bare Costs Labor	Equipment	Total	Total Incl O&P
0010	**SELECTIVE DEMOLITION, FLOORING** R024119-10									
0200	Brick with mortar	2 Clab	475	.034	S.F.		1.34		1.34	2.04
0400	Carpet, bonded, including surface scraping		2000	.008			.32		.32	.49
0440	Scrim applied		8000	.002			.08		.08	.12
0480	Tackless		9000	.002			.07		.07	.11
0550	Carpet tile, releasable adhesive		5000	.003			.13		.13	.19
0560	Permanent adhesive		1850	.009			.34		.34	.53
0600	Composition, acrylic or epoxy		400	.040			1.59		1.59	2.43
0700	Concrete, scarify skin	A-1A	225	.036			1.86	.95	2.81	3.90
0800	Resilient, sheet goods	2 Clab	1400	.011			.46		.46	.69
0820	For gym floors	"	900	.018			.71		.71	1.08
0850	Vinyl or rubber cove base	1 Clab	1000	.008	L.F.		.32		.32	.49
0860	Vinyl or rubber cove base, molded corner	"	1000	.008	Ea.		.32		.32	.49
0870	For glued and caulked installation, add to labor						50%			
0900	Vinyl composition tile, 12" x 12"	2 Clab	1000	.016	S.F.		.64		.64	.97
2000	Tile, ceramic, thin set		675	.024			.94		.94	1.44
2020	Mud set		625	.026			1.02		1.02	1.55
2200	Marble, slate, thin set		675	.024			.94		.94	1.44
2220	Mud set		625	.026			1.02		1.02	1.55
2600	Terrazzo, thin set		450	.036			1.42		1.42	2.16
2620	Mud set		425	.038			1.50		1.50	2.29
2640	Terrazzo, cast in place		300	.053			2.13		2.13	3.24
2710	With brass dividers	1 Clab	250	.032			1.28		1.28	1.94
3000	Wood, block, on end	1 Carp	400	.020			1.01		1.01	1.54
3200	Parquet		450	.018			.90		.90	1.37
3400	Strip flooring, interior, 2-1/4" x 25/32" thick		325	.025			1.25		1.25	1.90
3500	Exterior, porch flooring, 1" x 4"		220	.036			1.84		1.84	2.81
3800	Subfloor, tongue and groove, 1" x 6"		325	.025			1.25		1.25	1.90
3820	1" x 8"		430	.019			.94		.94	1.44
3840	1" x 10"		520	.015			.78		.78	1.19
4000	Plywood, nailed		600	.013			.68		.68	1.03
4100	Glued and nailed		400	.020			1.01		1.01	1.54
4200	Hardboard, 1/4" thick		760	.011			.53		.53	.81
5000	Slate flooring	1 Clab	280	.029			1.14		1.14	1.73
5010	Granite flooring		340	.024			.94		.94	1.43
5100	Vapor barrier, felt		4300	.002			.07		.07	.11
8000	Remove flooring, bead blast, simple floor plan	A-1A	1000	.008		.05	.42	.21	.68	.94
8100	Complex floor plan		400	.020		.05	1.05	.54	1.64	2.25
8150	Mastic only		1500	.005		.05	.28	.14	.47	.65

09 05 05.30 Selective Demolition, Walls and Partitions

		Crew	Daily Output	Labor-Hours	Unit	Material	2018 Bare Costs Labor	Equipment	Total	Total Incl O&P
0010	**SELECTIVE DEMOLITION, WALLS AND PARTITIONS** R024119-10									
0020	Walls, concrete, reinforced	B-39	120	.400	C.F.		16.85	1.95	18.80	27.50
0025	Plain	"	160	.300			12.65	1.46	14.11	21
0100	Brick, 4" to 12" thick	B-9	220	.182			7.30	1.06	8.36	12.30
0200	Concrete block, 4" thick		1150	.035	S.F.		1.40	.20	1.60	2.35
0203	Remove damaged blocks		769.23	.052			2.09	.30	2.39	3.52
0280	8" thick		1050	.038			1.53	.22	1.75	2.59
0300	Exterior stucco 1" thick over mesh		3200	.013			.50	.07	.57	.85
1000	Gypsum wallboard, nailed or screwed	1 Clab	1000	.008			.32		.32	.49
1010	2 layers		400	.020			.80		.80	1.21
1020	Glued and nailed		900	.009			.35		.35	.54
1500	Fiberboard, nailed		900	.009			.35		.35	.54

09 05 Common Work Results for Finishes

09 05 05 – Selective Demolition for Finishes

09 05 05.30 Selective Demolition, Walls and Partitions

		Crew	Daily Output	Labor-Hours	Unit	Material	2018 Bare Costs Labor	Equipment	Total	Total Incl O&P
1520	Glued and nailed	1 Clab	800	.010	S.F.		.40		.40	.61
1540	Insulation, fiberglass batts or blankets, 15" wide		3200	.003			.10		.10	.15
1550	Rigid insulation, 1" thick		2000	.004			.16		.16	.24
1552	Fiberboard, low density, 1/2" thick		2000	.004			.16		.16	.24
1554	Rigid isocyanurate, foil faced		1500	.005			.21		.21	.32
1556	Blown, to R19		2500	.003			.13		.13	.19
1568	Plenum barrier, sheet lead		300	.027			1.06		1.06	1.62
1600	Glass block		65	.123			4.90		4.90	7.45
2000	Movable walls, metal, 5' high		300	.027			1.06		1.06	1.62
2020	8' high		400	.020			.80		.80	1.21
2200	Metal or wood studs, finish 2 sides, fiberboard	B-1	520	.046			1.87		1.87	2.85
2250	Lath and plaster		260	.092			3.74		3.74	5.70
2300	Gypsum wallboard		520	.046			1.87		1.87	2.85
2350	Plywood		450	.053			2.16		2.16	3.29
2500	Mirror or mirror tile	1 Clab	525	.015			.61		.61	.93
2800	Paneling, 4' x 8' sheets		475	.017			.67		.67	1.02
3000	Plaster, lime and horsehair, on wood lath		400	.020			.80		.80	1.21
3020	On metal lath		335	.024			.95		.95	1.45
3400	Gypsum or perlite, on gypsum lath		410	.020			.78		.78	1.18
3420	On metal lath		300	.027			1.06		1.06	1.62
3450	Plaster, interior gypsum, acoustic, or cement		60	.133	S.Y.		5.30		5.30	8.10
3500	Stucco, on masonry		145	.055			2.20		2.20	3.35
3510	Commercial 3-coat		80	.100			3.99		3.99	6.05
3515	Thin coat		60	.133			5.30		5.30	8.10
3520	Interior stucco		25	.320			12.75		12.75	19.40
3750	Terra cotta block and plaster, to 6" thick	B-1	175	.137	S.F.		5.55		5.55	8.45
3760	Tile, ceramic, on walls, thin set	1 Clab	300	.027			1.06		1.06	1.62
3765	Mud set		250	.032			1.28		1.28	1.94
3800	Toilet partitions, slate or marble		5	1.600	Ea.		64		64	97
3820	Metal or plastic		8	1	"		40		40	60.50
4060	Vapor barrier, polyethylene		7400	.001	S.F.		.04		.04	.07
5000	Wallcovering, vinyl	1 Pape	700	.011			.49		.49	.73
5010	With release agent		1500	.005			.23		.23	.34
5025	Wallpaper, 2 layers or less, by hand		250	.032			1.36		1.36	2.05
5035	3 layers or more		165	.048			2.07		2.07	3.11
6000	Acoustic barrier, panels and matts	1 Clab	4000	.002			.08		.08	.12

09 25 Other Plastering

09 25 23 – Lime Based Plastering

09 25 23.10 Venetian Plaster

		Crew	Daily Output	Labor-Hours	Unit	Material	2018 Bare Costs Labor	Equipment	Total	Total Incl O&P
0010	**VENETIAN PLASTER**									
0100	Walls, 1 coat primer, roller applied	1 Plas	950	.008	S.F.	.17	.39		.56	.78
0200	Plaster, 3 coats, incl. sanding	2 Plas	700	.023		.42	1.06		1.48	2.05
0210	For pigment, light colors add per S.F. plaster					.02			.02	.02
0220	For pigment, dark colors add per S.F. plaster					.04			.04	.04
0300	For sealer/wax coat incl. burnishing, add	1 Plas	300	.027		.38	1.24		1.62	2.27

09 29 Gypsum Board

09 29 10 – Gypsum Board Panels

09 29 10.33 Gypsum Board, Synthetic		Crew	Daily Output	Labor-Hours	Unit	Material	2018 Bare Costs Labor	Equipment	Total	Total Incl O&P
0010	**GYPSUM BOARD, SYNTHETIC** gypsum plasterboard, nailed or screwed									
0100	to studs unless otherwise noted									
0150	3/8" thick, on walls, standard, no finish included	G	2 Carp	2000	.008	S.F.	.36	.41		.77	1.02
0200	On ceilings, standard, no finish included	G		1800	.009		.36	.45		.81	1.09
0250	On beams, columns, or soffits, no finish included	G		675	.024		.36	1.20		1.56	2.23
0300	1/2" thick, on walls, standard, no finish included	G		2000	.008		.34	.41		.75	.99
0350	Taped and finished (level 4 finish)	G		965	.017		.39	.84		1.23	1.71
0390	With compound skim coat (level 5 finish)	G		775	.021		.44	1.05		1.49	2.07
0400	Fire resistant, no finish included	G		2000	.008		.37	.41		.78	1.03
0450	Taped and finished (level 4 finish)	G		965	.017		.42	.84		1.26	1.74
0490	With compound skim coat (level 5 finish)	G		775	.021		.52	1.05		1.57	2.16
0500	Water resistant, no finish included	G		2000	.008		.42	.41		.83	1.08
0550	Taped and finished (level 4 finish)	G		965	.017		.47	.84		1.31	1.79
0590	With compound skim coat (level 5 finish)	G		775	.021		.52	1.05		1.57	2.16
0600	Prefinished, vinyl, clipped to studs	G		900	.018		.51	.90		1.41	1.93
0700	Mold resistant, no finish included	G		2000	.008		.44	.41		.85	1.10
0710	Taped and finished (level 4 finish)	G		965	.017		.49	.84		1.33	1.82
0720	With compound skim coat (level 5 finish)	G		775	.021		.54	1.05		1.59	2.18
1000	On ceilings, standard, no finish included	G		1800	.009		.34	.45		.79	1.06
1050	Taped and finished (level 4 finish)	G		765	.021		.39	1.06		1.45	2.05
1090	With compound skim coat (level 5 finish)	G		610	.026		.44	1.33		1.77	2.51
1100	Fire resistant, no finish included	G		1800	.009		.37	.45		.82	1.10
1150	Taped and finished (level 4 finish)	G		765	.021		.42	1.06		1.48	2.08
1195	With compound skim coat (level 5 finish)	G		610	.026		.47	1.33		1.80	2.55
1200	Water resistant, no finish included	G		1800	.009		.42	.45		.87	1.15
1250	Taped and finished (level 4 finish)	G		765	.021		.47	1.06		1.53	2.13
1290	With compound skim coat (level 5 finish)	G		610	.026		.52	1.33		1.85	2.60
1310	Mold resistant, no finish included	G		1800	.009		.44	.45		.89	1.17
1320	Taped and finished (level 4 finish)	G		765	.021		.49	1.06		1.55	2.16
1330	With compound skim coat (level 5 finish)	G		610	.026		.54	1.33		1.87	2.62
1500	On beams, columns, or soffits, standard, no finish included	G		675	.024		.37	1.20		1.57	2.24
1550	Taped and finished (level 4 finish)	G		475	.034		.39	1.71		2.10	3.03
1590	With compound skim coat (level 5 finish)	G		540	.030		.44	1.50		1.94	2.77
1600	Fire resistant, no finish included	G		675	.024		.37	1.20		1.57	2.24
1650	Taped and finished (level 4 finish)	G		475	.034		.42	1.71		2.13	3.06
1690	With compound skim coat (level 5 finish)	G		540	.030		.47	1.50		1.97	2.81
1700	Water resistant, no finish included	G		675	.024		.42	1.20		1.62	2.29
1750	Taped and finished (level 4 finish)	G		475	.034		.47	1.71		2.18	3.11
1790	With compound skim coat (level 5 finish)	G		540	.030		.52	1.50		2.02	2.86
1800	Mold resistant, no finish included	G		675	.024		.46	1.20		1.66	2.33
1810	Taped and finished (level 4 finish)	G		475	.034		.49	1.71		2.20	3.14
1820	With compound skim coat (level 5 finish)	G		540	.030		.54	1.50		2.04	2.88
2000	5/8" thick, on walls, standard, no finish included	G		2000	.008		.35	.41		.76	1.01
2050	Taped and finished (level 4 finish)	G		965	.017		.40	.84		1.24	1.72
2090	With compound skim coat (level 5 finish)	G		775	.021		.45	1.05		1.50	2.08
2100	Fire resistant, no finish included	G		2000	.008		.36	.41		.77	1.02
2150	Taped and finished (level 4 finish)	G		965	.017		.41	.84		1.25	1.73
2195	With compound skim coat (level 5 finish)	G		775	.021		.46	1.05		1.51	2.09
2200	Water resistant, no finish included	G		2000	.008		.44	.41		.85	1.10
2250	Taped and finished (level 4 finish)	G		965	.017		.49	.84		1.33	1.82
2290	With compound skim coat (level 5 finish)	G		775	.021		.54	1.05		1.59	2.18
2300	Prefinished, vinyl, clipped to studs	G		900	.018		.79	.90		1.69	2.24
2510	Mold resistant, no finish included	G		2000	.008		.49	.41		.90	1.16

09 29 Gypsum Board

09 29 10 – Gypsum Board Panels

09 29 10.33 Gypsum Board, Synthetic

		Crew	Daily Output	Labor-Hours	Unit	Material	2018 Bare Costs Labor	Equipment	Total	Total Incl O&P
2520	Taped and finished (level 4 finish)	G 2 Carp	965	.017	S.F.	.54	.84		1.38	1.87
2530	With compound skim coat (level 5 finish)	G	775	.021		.59	1.05		1.64	2.24
3000	On ceilings, standard, no finish included	G	1800	.009		.35	.45		.80	1.08
3050	Taped and finished (level 4 finish)	G	765	.021		.40	1.06		1.46	2.06
3090	With compound skim coat (level 5 finish)	G	615	.026		.45	1.32		1.77	2.50
3100	Fire resistant, no finish included	G	1800	.009		.36	.45		.81	1.09
3150	Taped and finished (level 4 finish)	G	765	.021		.41	1.06		1.47	2.07
3190	With compound skim coat (level 5 finish)	G	615	.026		.46	1.32		1.78	2.51
3200	Water resistant, no finish included	G	1800	.009		.44	.45		.89	1.17
3250	Taped and finished (level 4 finish)	G	765	.021		.49	1.06		1.55	2.16
3290	With compound skim coat (level 5 finish)	G	615	.026		.54	1.32		1.86	2.60
3300	Mold resistant, no finish included	G	1800	.009		.49	.45		.94	1.23
3310	Taped and finished (level 4 finish)	G	765	.021		.54	1.06		1.60	2.21
3320	With compound skim coat (level 5 finish)	G	615	.026		.59	1.32		1.91	2.66
3500	On beams, columns, or soffits, no finish included	G	675	.024		.40	1.20		1.60	2.27
3550	Taped and finished (level 4 finish)	G	475	.034		.46	1.71		2.17	3.10
3590	With compound skim coat (level 5 finish)	G	380	.042		.52	2.14		2.66	3.82
3600	Fire resistant, no finish included	G	675	.024		.41	1.20		1.61	2.29
3650	Taped and finished (level 4 finish)	G	475	.034		.47	1.71		2.18	3.11
3690	With compound skim coat (level 5 finish)	G	380	.042		.46	2.14		2.60	3.75
3700	Water resistant, no finish included	G	675	.024		.46	1.20		1.66	2.34
3750	Taped and finished (level 4 finish)	G	475	.034		.51	1.71		2.22	3.16
3790	With compound skim coat (level 5 finish)	G	380	.042		.56	2.14		2.70	3.87
3800	Mold resistant, no finish included	G	675	.024		.56	1.20		1.76	2.45
3810	Taped and finished (level 4 finish)	G	475	.034		.62	1.71		2.33	3.28
3820	With compound skim coat (level 5 finish)	G	380	.042		.64	2.14		2.78	3.96
4000	Fireproofing, beams or columns, 2 layers, 1/2" thick, incl. finish	G	330	.048		.79	2.46		3.25	4.61
4010	Mold resistant	G	330	.048		.93	2.46		3.39	4.76
4050	5/8" thick	G	300	.053		.81	2.70		3.51	5
4060	Mold resistant	G	300	.053		1.07	2.70		3.77	5.30
4100	3 layers, 1/2" thick	G	225	.071		1.16	3.61		4.77	6.75
4110	Mold resistant	G	225	.071		1.37	3.61		4.98	7
4150	5/8" thick	G	210	.076		1.22	3.86		5.08	7.25
4160	Mold resistant	G	210	.076		1.61	3.86		5.47	7.65
5050	For 1" thick coreboard on columns	G	480	.033		.77	1.69		2.46	3.42
5100	For foil-backed board, add	G				.18			.18	.20
5200	For work over 8' high, add	G 2 Carp	3060	.005			.27		.27	.40
5270	For textured spray, add	G 2 Lath	1600	.010		.04	.49		.53	.77
5300	For 3 stories and above, add per story	G 2 Carp	6100	.003			.13		.13	.20
5350	For finishing inner corners, add	G	950	.017	L.F.	.10	.85		.95	1.41
5355	For finishing outer corners, add		1250	.013		.23	.65		.88	1.24
5500	For acoustical sealant, add per bead	G 1 Carp	500	.016		.04	.81		.85	1.29
5550	Sealant, 1 quart tube	G			Ea.	7.05			7.05	7.80

167

09 31 Thin-Set Tiling

09 31 13 – Thin-Set Ceramic Tiling

09 31 13.10 Thin-Set Ceramic Tile

			Crew	Daily Output	Labor-Hours	Unit	Material	2018 Bare Costs Labor	Equipment	Total	Total Incl O&P
0010	**THIN-SET CERAMIC TILE**										
9300	Ceramic tiles, recycled glass, standard colors, 2" x 2" thru 6" x 6"	G	D-7	190	.084	S.F.	22	3.54		25.54	30
9310	6" x 6"	G		175	.091		22	3.84		25.84	30
9320	8" x 8"	G		170	.094		23.50	3.96		27.46	32
9330	12" x 12"	G		160	.100		23.50	4.20		27.70	32
9340	Earthtones, 2" x 2" to 4" x 8"	G		190	.084		26	3.54		29.54	34
9350	6" x 6"	G		175	.091		26	3.84		29.84	34
9360	8" x 8"	G		170	.094		27	3.96		30.96	35.50
9370	12" x 12"	G		160	.100		27	4.20		31.20	35.50
9380	Deep colors, 2" x 2" to 4" x 8"	G		190	.084		30.50	3.54		34.04	39.50
9390	6" x 6"	G		175	.091		30.50	3.84		34.34	39.50
9400	8" x 8"	G		170	.094		32	3.96		35.96	41.50
9410	12" x 12"	G		160	.100		32	4.20		36.20	41.50

09 51 Acoustical Ceilings

09 51 23 – Acoustical Tile Ceilings

09 51 23.10 Suspended Acoustic Ceiling Tiles

			Crew	Daily Output	Labor-Hours	Unit	Material	Labor	Equipment	Total	Total Incl O&P
0010	**SUSPENDED ACOUSTIC CEILING TILES**, not including										
0100	suspension system										
5000	Acoustic ceiling tiles, 100% recycled glass, 5/8" thick	G	1 Carp	600	.013	S.F.	5	.68		5.68	6.55
5010	3/4" thick	G		600	.013		7	.68		7.68	8.75
5020	66-78% recycled content, 3/4" thick	G		600	.013		2.08	.68		2.76	3.32
5040	Mylar, 42% recycled content, 3/4" thick	G		600	.013		5	.68		5.68	6.55

09 53 Acoustical Ceiling Suspension Assemblies

09 53 23 – Metal Acoustical Ceiling Suspension Assemblies

09 53 23.30 Ceiling Suspension Systems

			Crew	Daily Output	Labor-Hours	Unit	Material	Labor	Equipment	Total	Total Incl O&P
0010	**CEILING SUSPENSION SYSTEMS** for boards and tile										
0310	25% recycled steel, 2' x 4' grid	G	1 Carp	800	.010	S.F.	.83	.51		1.34	1.68
0320	2' x 2' grid	G		650	.012		1.04	.62		1.66	2.09
0500	Suspension systems, sealed, heavy duty, 2", for clean room, excl. panels			450	.018		16	.90		16.90	18.95
1400	50% recycled aluminum, 15/16" T bar, 2' x 4' grid	G		800	.010		1.81	.51		2.32	2.77
1500	2' x 2' grid	G		650	.012		2.30	.62		2.92	3.48

09 62 Specialty Flooring

09 62 19 – Laminate Flooring

09 62 19.10 Floating Floor

			Crew	Daily Output	Labor-Hours	Unit	Material	Labor	Equipment	Total	Total Incl O&P
0010	**FLOATING FLOOR**										
8300	Floating floor, laminate, wood pattern strip, complete		1 Clab	133	.060	S.F.	4.32	2.40		6.72	8.40
8310	Components, T&G wood composite strips						3.83			3.83	4.22
8320	Film						.17			.17	.18
8330	Foam						.26			.26	.29
8340	Adhesive						.43			.43	.47
8350	Installation kit						.19			.19	.21
8360	Trim, 2" wide x 3' long					L.F.	4.30			4.30	4.73
8370	Reducer moulding					"	5.70			5.70	6.25

09 62 Specialty Flooring

09 62 23 – Bamboo Flooring

09 62 23.10 Flooring, Bamboo

		Crew	Daily Output	Labor-Hours	Unit	Material	2018 Bare Costs Labor	Equipment	Total	Total Incl O&P
0010	**FLOORING, BAMBOO**									
8600	Flooring, wood, bamboo strips, unfinished, 5/8" x 4" x 3' G	1 Carp	255	.031	S.F.	5.70	1.59		7.29	8.65
8610	5/8" x 4" x 4' G		275	.029		5.90	1.47		7.37	8.75
8620	5/8" x 4" x 6' G		295	.027		6.45	1.38		7.83	9.20
8630	Finished, 5/8" x 4" x 3' G		255	.031		6.25	1.59		7.84	9.30
8640	5/8" x 4" x 4' G		275	.029		6.55	1.47		8.02	9.45
8650	5/8" x 4" x 6' G		295	.027		4.99	1.38		6.37	7.60
8660	Stair treads, unfinished, 1-1/16" x 11-1/2" x 4' G		18	.444	Ea.	54.50	22.50		77	94.50
8670	Finished, 1-1/16" x 11-1/2" x 4' G		18	.444		83	22.50		105.50	126
8680	Stair risers, unfinished, 5/8" x 7-1/2" x 4' G		18	.444		20	22.50		42.50	56.50
8690	Finished, 5/8" x 7-1/2" x 4' G		18	.444		38	22.50		60.50	76.50
8700	Stair nosing, unfinished, 6' long G		16	.500		44.50	25.50		70	87.50
8710	Finished, 6' long G		16	.500		42	25.50		67.50	85

09 62 29 – Cork Flooring

09 62 29.10 Cork Tile Flooring

		Crew	Daily Output	Labor-Hours	Unit	Material	Labor	Equipment	Total	Total Incl O&P
0010	**CORK TILE FLOORING**									
2200	Cork tile, standard finish, 1/8" thick G	1 Tilf	315	.025	S.F.	5.25	1.19		6.44	7.50
2250	3/16" thick G		315	.025		5.80	1.19		6.99	8.10
2300	5/16" thick G		315	.025		6.45	1.19		7.64	8.85
2350	1/2" thick G		315	.025		7	1.19		8.19	9.45
2500	Urethane finish, 1/8" thick G		315	.025		5.25	1.19		6.44	7.55
2550	3/16" thick G		315	.025		7.30	1.19		8.49	9.80
2600	5/16" thick G		315	.025		7.25	1.19		8.44	9.70
2650	1/2" thick G		315	.025		7.20	1.19		8.39	9.65

09 63 Masonry Flooring

09 63 13 – Brick Flooring

09 63 13.10 Miscellaneous Brick Flooring

		Crew	Daily Output	Labor-Hours	Unit	Material	Labor	Equipment	Total	Total Incl O&P
0010	**MISCELLANEOUS BRICK FLOORING**									
0020	Acid-proof shales, red, 8" x 3-3/4" x 1-1/4" thick	D-7	.43	37.209	M	715	1,575		2,290	3,100
0050	2-1/4" thick	D-1	.40	40	"	1,050	1,800		2,850	3,900
0150	Clay brick floor, 8" x 3-3/4" x 2-1/4"		95	.168	S.F.	4.13	7.55		11.68	16.10
0200	Acid-proof clay brick, 8" x 3-3/4" x 2-1/4" thick G		.40	40	M	1,000	1,800		2,800	3,850
0250	9" x 4-1/2" x 3" G		95	.168	S.F.	4.41	7.55		11.96	16.40
0260	Cast ceramic, pressed, 4" x 8" x 1/2", unglazed	D-7	100	.160		6.85	6.70		13.55	17.50
0270	Glazed		100	.160		9.15	6.70		15.85	20
0280	Hand molded flooring, 4" x 8" x 3/4", unglazed		95	.168		9.05	7.10		16.15	20.50
0290	Glazed		95	.168		11.40	7.10		18.50	23
0300	8" hexagonal, 3/4" thick, unglazed		85	.188		9.95	7.90		17.85	22.50
0310	Glazed		85	.188		17.95	7.90		25.85	31.50
0400	Heavy duty industrial, cement mortar bed, 2" thick, not incl. brick	D-1	80	.200		1.13	8.95		10.08	14.95
0450	Acid-proof joints, 1/4" wide	"	65	.246		1.58	11.05		12.63	18.65
0500	Pavers, 8" x 4", 1" to 1-1/4" thick, red	D-7	95	.168		3.99	7.10		11.09	14.90
0510	Ironspot	"	95	.168		5.65	7.10		12.75	16.70
0540	1-3/8" to 1-3/4" thick, red	D-1	95	.168		3.85	7.55		11.40	15.80
0560	Ironspot		95	.168		5.60	7.55		13.15	17.70
0580	2-1/4" thick, red		90	.178		3.92	7.95		11.87	16.50
0590	Ironspot		90	.178		6.10	7.95		14.05	18.90
0700	Paver, adobe brick, 6" x 12", 1/2" joint G		42	.381		1.44	17.05		18.49	27.50
0710	Mexican red, 12" x 12" G	1 Tilf	48	.167		1.85	7.80		9.65	13.60

For customer support on your Green Building Costs with RSMeans data, call 800.448.8182.

09 63 Masonry Flooring

09 63 13 – Brick Flooring

09 63 13.10 Miscellaneous Brick Flooring

		Crew	Daily Output	Labor-Hours	Unit	Material	2018 Bare Costs Labor	Equipment	Total	Total Incl O&P
0720	Saltillo, 12" x 12" [G]	1 Tilf	48	.167	S.F.	1.49	7.80		9.29	13.20
0870	For epoxy joints, add	D-1	600	.027		3.05	1.19		4.24	5.20
0880	For Furan underlayment, add	"	600	.027		2.53	1.19		3.72	4.61
0890	For waxed surface, steam cleaned, add	A-1H	1000	.008		.21	.32	.07	.60	.80

09 64 Wood Flooring

09 64 23 – Wood Parquet Flooring

09 64 23.10 Wood Parquet

		Crew	Daily Output	Labor-Hours	Unit	Material	Labor	Equipment	Total	Total Incl O&P
0010	**WOOD PARQUET** flooring									
5200	Parquetry, 5/16" thk, no finish, oak, plain pattern	1 Carp	160	.050	S.F.	5.45	2.54		7.99	9.85
5300	Intricate pattern		100	.080		9.90	4.06		13.96	17.05
5500	Teak, plain pattern		160	.050		6.35	2.54		8.89	10.80
5600	Intricate pattern		100	.080		10.75	4.06		14.81	18.05
5650	13/16" thick, select grade oak, plain pattern		160	.050		11.85	2.54		14.39	16.85
5700	Intricate pattern		100	.080		17.35	4.06		21.41	25.50
5800	Custom parquetry, including finish, plain pattern		100	.080		17.10	4.06		21.16	25
5900	Intricate pattern		50	.160		25	8.10		33.10	40
6700	Parquetry, prefinished white oak, 5/16" thick, plain pattern		160	.050		8	2.54		10.54	12.65
6800	Intricate pattern		100	.080		8.65	4.06		12.71	15.70
7000	Walnut or teak, parquetry, plain pattern		160	.050		8.50	2.54		11.04	13.20
7100	Intricate pattern		100	.080		13.65	4.06		17.71	21
7200	Acrylic wood parquet blocks, 12" x 12" x 5/16",									
7210	Irradiated, set in epoxy	1 Carp	160	.050	S.F.	10.45	2.54		12.99	15.35

09 64 29 – Wood Strip and Plank Flooring

09 64 29.10 Wood

		Crew	Daily Output	Labor-Hours	Unit	Material	Labor	Equipment	Total	Total Incl O&P
0010	**WOOD** R061110-30									
0020	Fir, vertical grain, 1" x 4", not incl. finish, grade B & better	1 Carp	255	.031	S.F.	3.45	1.59		5.04	6.20
0100	Grade C & better		255	.031		3.25	1.59		4.84	6
0300	Flat grain, 1" x 4", not incl. finish, grade B & better		255	.031		3.94	1.59		5.53	6.75
0400	Grade C & better		255	.031		3.79	1.59		5.38	6.60
4000	Maple, strip, 25/32" x 2-1/4", not incl. finish, select		170	.047		4.93	2.39		7.32	9.05
4100	#2 & better		170	.047		4.84	2.39		7.23	8.95
4300	33/32" x 3-1/4", not incl. finish, #1 grade		170	.047		5.65	2.39		8.04	9.85
4400	#2 & better		170	.047		5	2.39		7.39	9.15
4600	Oak, white or red, 25/32" x 2-1/4", not incl. finish									
4700	#1 common	1 Carp	170	.047	S.F.	3.42	2.39		5.81	7.40
4900	Select quartered, 2-1/4" wide		170	.047		4.29	2.39		6.68	8.35
5000	Clear		170	.047		4.23	2.39		6.62	8.30
6100	Prefinished, white oak, prime grade, 2-1/4" wide		170	.047		5.25	2.39		7.64	9.40
6200	3-1/4" wide		185	.043		5.70	2.19		7.89	9.65
6400	Ranch plank		145	.055		7.30	2.80		10.10	12.25
6500	Hardwood blocks, 9" x 9", 25/32" thick		160	.050		7.45	2.54		9.99	12
7300	Walnut, 25/32" thick, 3"-7" wide, random lengths		240	.033		15.85	1.69		17.54	20
7400	Yellow pine, 3/4" x 3-1/8", T&G, C & better, not incl. finish		200	.040		1.67	2.03		3.70	4.93
7500	Refinish wood floor, sand, 2 coats poly, wax, soft wood	1 Clab	400	.020		.21	.80		1.01	1.44
7600	Hardwood		130	.062		.21	2.45		2.66	3.97
7800	Sanding and finishing, 2 coats polyurethane		295	.027		.21	1.08		1.29	1.88
7900	Subfloor and underlayment, see Section 06 16									
8015	Transition molding, 2-1/4" wide, 5" long	1 Carp	19.20	.417	Ea.	18.65	21		39.65	52.50
8920	Laminate flooring, wood pattern	1 Tilf	140	.057	S.F.	3.65	2.68		6.33	8

09 65 Resilient Flooring

09 65 13 – Resilient Base and Accessories

09 65 13.23 Stair Treads

		Crew	Daily Output	Labor-Hours	Unit	Material	2018 Bare Costs Labor	Equipment	Total	Total Incl O&P
0012	**STAIR TREADS**									
3000	Rubber stair treads, black, recycled rubber, sq. nose, 12" D x 36" W	G 1 Tilf	125	.064	L.F.	16.95	3		19.95	23
3010	12" D x 42" W	G	128	.063		17.05	2.93		19.98	23
3020	12" D x 48" W	G	136	.059		17.10	2.76		19.86	23

09 65 16 – Resilient Sheet Flooring

09 65 16.10 Rubber and Vinyl Sheet Flooring

		Crew	Daily Output	Labor-Hours	Unit	Material	Labor	Equipment	Total	Total Incl O&P
0010	**RUBBER AND VINYL SHEET FLOORING**									
5500	Linoleum, sheet goods	G 1 Tilf	360	.022	S.F.	3.59	1.04		4.63	5.50

09 65 19 – Resilient Tile Flooring

09 65 19.33 Rubber Tile Flooring

		Crew	Daily Output	Labor-Hours	Unit	Material	Labor	Equipment	Total	Total Incl O&P
0010	**RUBBER TILE FLOORING**									
6050	Rubber tile, marbleized colors, 12" x 12", 1/8" thick	1 Tilf	400	.020	S.F.	5.80	.94		6.74	7.75
6100	3/16" thick		400	.020		8	.94		8.94	10.20
6300	Special tile, plain colors, 1/8" thick		400	.020		8.15	.94		9.09	10.35
6350	3/16" thick		400	.020		9.75	.94		10.69	12.10
6410	Raised, radial or square, .5 mm black		400	.020		7.75	.94		8.69	9.95
6430	.5 mm colored		400	.020		7.75	.94		8.69	9.95
6450	For golf course, skating rink, etc., 1/4" thick		275	.029		10.45	1.36		11.81	13.45

09 65 66 – Resilient Athletic Flooring

09 65 66.10 Resilient Athletic Flooring

		Crew	Daily Output	Labor-Hours	Unit	Material	Labor	Equipment	Total	Total Incl O&P
0010	**RESILIENT ATHLETIC FLOORING**									
1000	Recycled rubber rolled goods, for weight rooms, 3/8" thk.	1 Tilf	315	.025	S.F.	2.66	1.19		3.85	4.69
1050	Interlocking 2'x2' squares, rubber, 1/4" thk.		310	.026		1.89	1.21		3.10	3.87
1055	5/16" thk.		310	.026		2.29	1.21		3.50	4.31
1060	3/8" thk.		300	.027		2.98	1.25		4.23	5.15
1065	1/2" thk.		310	.026		3.08	1.21		4.29	5.20
2000	Vinyl sheet flooring, 1/4" thk.		315	.025		4.28	1.19		5.47	6.45

09 68 Carpeting

09 68 10 – Carpet Pad

09 68 10.20 Recycled Padding and Carpet Leasing

		Crew	Daily Output	Labor-Hours	Unit	Material	Labor	Equipment	Total	Total Incl O&P
0010	**RECYCLED PADDING AND CARPET LEASING**									
2000	Carpet padding, recycled waste carpet, 5/16" thick	G 1 Tilf	150	.053	S.Y.	1.96	2.50		4.46	5.85
2010	3/8" thick	G	150	.053		2.36	2.50		4.86	6.30
2020	7/16" thick	G	150	.053		2.47	2.50		4.97	6.40
2030	Carpet, commercial, 25% recycled nylon, 26 oz., medium traffic	G	75	.107		14.05	5		19.05	23
2040	32 oz., medium to heavy traffic	G	75	.107		19.60	5		24.60	29
2050	42 oz., heavy traffic	G	70	.114		23	5.35		28.35	33
2300	Carpet leasing, avg 5 year lease, install, maint. & removal, min								20.90	21
2310	Maximum								27	25.50

09 68 16 – Sheet Carpeting

09 68 16.10 Sheet Carpet

		Crew	Daily Output	Labor-Hours	Unit	Material	Labor	Equipment	Total	Total Incl O&P
0010	**SHEET CARPET**									
0100	Natural fiber, sisal, reed, or hemp, 38 oz., medium traffic	G 1 Tilf	75	.107	S.Y.	57	5		62	70
0110	45 oz., medium to heavy traffic	G	75	.107		54.50	5		59.50	67.50
0120	60 oz., heavy traffic	G	70	.114		63.50	5.35		68.85	77.50

09 72 Wall Coverings

09 72 19 – Textile Wall Coverings

09 72 19.10 Textile Wall Covering

		Crew	Daily Output	Labor-Hours	Unit	Material	2018 Bare Costs Labor	Equipment	Total	Total Incl O&P
0010	**TEXTILE WALL COVERING**, including sizing; add 10-30% waste @ takeoff									
0090	Grass cloth, natural fabric [G]	1 Pape	400	.020	S.F.	1.79	.85		2.64	3.25
0100	Grass cloths with lining paper [G]		400	.020		1.38	.85		2.23	2.80
0110	Premium texture/color [G]	↓	350	.023	↓	3.15	.97		4.12	4.94

09 72 23 – Wallpapering

09 72 23.10 Wallpaper

		Crew	Daily Output	Labor-Hours	Unit	Material	Labor	Equipment	Total	Incl O&P
0010	**WALLPAPER** including sizing; add 10-30% waste @ takeoff R097223-10									
5400	Wallpaper, 100% recycled content, textured, paintable, average [G]	1 Pape	540	.015	S.F.	.63	.63		1.26	1.64

09 81 Acoustic Insulation

09 81 13 – Acoustic Board Insulation

09 81 13.10 Acoustic Board Insulation

		Crew	Daily Output	Labor-Hours	Unit	Material	Labor	Equipment	Total	Incl O&P
0010	**ACOUSTIC BOARD INSULATION**									
0020	Cellulose fiber board, 1/2" thk.	1 Carp	800	.010	S.F.	.88	.51		1.39	1.74

09 91 Painting

09 91 03 – Paint Restoration

09 91 03.30 Exterior Surface Preparation

		Crew	Daily Output	Labor-Hours	Unit	Material	Labor	Equipment	Total	Incl O&P
0010	**EXTERIOR SURFACE PREPARATION** R099100-10									
0015	Doors, per side, not incl. frames or trim									
0020	Scrape & sand									
0030	Wood, flush	1 Pord	616	.013	S.F.		.55		.55	.83
0040	Wood, detail		496	.016			.69		.69	1.03
0050	Wood, louvered		280	.029			1.22		1.22	1.83
0060	Wood, overhead	↓	616	.013	↓		.55		.55	.83
0070	Wire brush									
0080	Metal, flush	1 Pord	640	.013	S.F.		.53		.53	.80
0090	Metal, detail		520	.015			.65		.65	.99
0100	Metal, louvered		360	.022			.95		.95	1.42
0110	Metal or fibr., overhead		640	.013			.53		.53	.80
0120	Metal, roll up		560	.014			.61		.61	.92
0130	Metal, bulkhead	↓	640	.013	↓		.53		.53	.80
0140	Power wash, based on 2500 lb. operating pressure									
0150	Metal, flush	A-1H	2240	.004	S.F.		.14	.03	.17	.26
0160	Metal, detail		2120	.004			.15	.04	.19	.27
0170	Metal, louvered		2000	.004			.16	.04	.20	.28
0180	Metal or fibr., overhead		2400	.003			.13	.03	.16	.23
0190	Metal, roll up		2400	.003			.13	.03	.16	.23
0200	Metal, bulkhead	↓	2200	.004	↓		.15	.03	.18	.26
0400	Windows, per side, not incl. trim									
0410	Scrape & sand									
0420	Wood, 1-2 lite	1 Pord	320	.025	S.F.		1.06		1.06	1.60
0430	Wood, 3-6 lite		280	.029			1.22		1.22	1.83
0440	Wood, 7-10 lite		240	.033			1.42		1.42	2.13
0450	Wood, 12 lite		200	.040			1.70		1.70	2.56
0460	Wood, Bay/Bow	↓	320	.025	↓		1.06		1.06	1.60
0470	Wire brush									
0480	Metal, 1-2 lite	1 Pord	480	.017	S.F.		.71		.71	1.07
0490	Metal, 3-6 lite	↓	400	.020	↓		.85		.85	1.28

09 91 Painting

09 91 03 – Paint Restoration

09 91 03.30 Exterior Surface Preparation

		Crew	Daily Output	Labor-Hours	Unit	Material	2018 Bare Costs Labor	Equipment	Total	Total Incl O&P
0500	Metal, Bay/Bow	1 Pord	480	.017	S.F.		.71		.71	1.07
0510	Power wash, based on 2500 lb. operating pressure									
0520	1-2 lite	A-1H	4400	.002	S.F.		.07	.02	.09	.13
0530	3-6 lite		4320	.002			.07	.02	.09	.13
0540	7-10 lite		4240	.002			.08	.02	.10	.13
0550	12 lite		4160	.002			.08	.02	.10	.14
0560	Bay/Bow	↓	4400	.002	↓		.07	.02	.09	.13
0600	Siding, scrape and sand, light=10-30%, med.=30-70%									
0610	Heavy=70-100% of surface to sand									
0650	Texture 1-11, light	1 Pord	480	.017	S.F.		.71		.71	1.07
0660	Med.		440	.018			.77		.77	1.16
0670	Heavy		360	.022			.95		.95	1.42
0680	Wood shingles, shakes, light		440	.018			.77		.77	1.16
0690	Med.		360	.022			.95		.95	1.42
0700	Heavy		280	.029			1.22		1.22	1.83
0710	Clapboard, light		520	.015			.65		.65	.99
0720	Med.		480	.017			.71		.71	1.07
0730	Heavy	↓	400	.020	↓		.85		.85	1.28
0740	Wire brush									
0750	Aluminum, light	1 Pord	600	.013	S.F.		.57		.57	.85
0760	Med.		520	.015			.65		.65	.99
0770	Heavy	↓	440	.018	↓		.77		.77	1.16
0780	Pressure wash, based on 2500 lb. operating pressure									
0790	Stucco	A-1H	3080	.003	S.F.		.10	.02	.12	.19
0800	Aluminum or vinyl		3200	.003			.10	.02	.12	.18
0810	Siding, masonry, brick & block	↓	2400	.003			.13	.03	.16	.23

09 91 03.40 Interior Surface Preparation

		Crew	Daily Output	Labor-Hours	Unit	Material	Labor	Equipment	Total	Total Incl O&P
0010	**INTERIOR SURFACE PREPARATION** R099100-10									
0020	Doors, per side, not incl. frames or trim									
0030	Scrape & sand									
0040	Wood, flush	1 Pord	616	.013	S.F.		.55		.55	.83
0050	Wood, detail		496	.016			.69		.69	1.03
0060	Wood, louvered	↓	280	.029	↓		1.22		1.22	1.83
0070	Wire brush									
0080	Metal, flush	1 Pord	640	.013	S.F.		.53		.53	.80
0090	Metal, detail		520	.015			.65		.65	.99
0100	Metal, louvered	↓	360	.022	↓		.95		.95	1.42
0110	Hand wash									
0120	Wood, flush	1 Pord	2160	.004	S.F.		.16		.16	.24
0130	Wood, detail		2000	.004			.17		.17	.26
0140	Wood, louvered		1360	.006			.25		.25	.38
0150	Metal, flush		2160	.004			.16		.16	.24
0160	Metal, detail		2000	.004			.17		.17	.26
0170	Metal, louvered	↓	1360	.006	↓		.25		.25	.38
0400	Windows, per side, not incl. trim									
0410	Scrape & sand									
0420	Wood, 1-2 lite	1 Pord	360	.022	S.F.		.95		.95	1.42
0430	Wood, 3-6 lite		320	.025			1.06		1.06	1.60
0440	Wood, 7-10 lite		280	.029			1.22		1.22	1.83
0450	Wood, 12 lite		240	.033			1.42		1.42	2.13
0460	Wood, Bay/Bow	↓	360	.022	↓		.95		.95	1.42
0470	Wire brush									

For customer support on your Green Building Costs with RSMeans data, call 800.448.8182.

09 91 Painting

09 91 03 – Paint Restoration

09 91 03.40 Interior Surface Preparation

		Crew	Daily Output	Labor-Hours	Unit	Material	2018 Bare Costs Labor	Equipment	Total	Total Incl O&P
0480	Metal, 1-2 lite	1 Pord	520	.015	S.F.		.65		.65	.99
0490	Metal, 3-6 lite		440	.018			.77		.77	1.16
0500	Metal, Bay/Bow		520	.015			.65		.65	.99
0600	Walls, sanding, light=10-30%, medium=30-70%,									
0610	heavy=70-100% of surface to sand									
0650	Walls, sand									
0660	Gypsum board or plaster, light	1 Pord	3077	.003	S.F.		.11		.11	.17
0670	Gypsum board or plaster, medium		2160	.004			.16		.16	.24
0680	Gypsum board or plaster, heavy		923	.009			.37		.37	.56
0690	Wood, T&G, light		2400	.003			.14		.14	.21
0700	Wood, T&G, medium		1600	.005			.21		.21	.32
0710	Wood, T&G, heavy		800	.010			.43		.43	.64
0715	Ceiling, sand, medium		2160	.004			.16		.16	.24
0720	Walls, wash									
0730	Gypsum board or plaster	1 Pord	3200	.003	S.F.		.11		.11	.16
0735	Gypsum board or plaster, heavy		2500	.003			.14		.14	.21
0740	Wood, T&G		3200	.003			.11		.11	.16
0750	Masonry, brick & block, smooth		2800	.003			.12		.12	.18
0760	Masonry, brick & block, coarse		2000	.004			.17		.17	.26
0770	Ceilings, wash, light		1500	.005			.23		.23	.34
0775	Heavy		1000	.008			.34		.34	.51

09 91 23 – Interior Painting

09 91 23.39 Doors and Windows, Interior Latex, Zero Voc

			Crew	Daily Output	Labor-Hours	Unit	Material	Labor	Equipment	Total	Total Incl O&P
0010	**DOORS & WINDOWS, INTERIOR LATEX, ZERO VOC**										
0100	Doors flush, both sides, incl. frame & trim										
0110	Roll & brush, primer	G	1 Pord	10	.800	Ea.	6.30	34		40.30	58
0120	Finish coat, latex	G		10	.800		6.95	34		40.95	58.50
0130	Primer & 1 coat latex	G		7	1.143		13.25	48.50		61.75	87.50
0140	Primer & 2 coats latex	G		5	1.600		19.80	68		87.80	124
0160	Spray, both sides, primer	G		20	.400		6.65	17		23.65	33
0170	Finish coat, latex	G		20	.400		7.30	17		24.30	33.50
0180	Primer & 1 coat latex	G		11	.727		14.05	31		45.05	62
0190	Primer & 2 coats latex	G		8	1		21	42.50		63.50	87
0200	Doors, French, both sides, 10-15 lite, incl. frame & trim										
0210	Roll & brush, primer	G	1 Pord	6	1.333	Ea.	3.15	56.50		59.65	89
0220	Finish coat, latex	G		6	1.333		3.48	56.50		59.98	89.50
0230	Primer & 1 coat latex	G		3	2.667		6.65	113		119.65	178
0240	Primer & 2 coats latex	G		2	4		9.90	170		179.90	267
0360	Doors, panel, both sides, incl. frame & trim										
0370	Roll & brush, primer	G	1 Pord	6	1.333	Ea.	6.65	56.50		63.15	93
0380	Finish coat, latex	G		6	1.333		6.95	56.50		63.45	93
0390	Primer & 1 coat, latex	G		3	2.667		13.25	113		126.25	186
0400	Primer & 2 coats, latex	G		2.50	3.200		20	136		156	227
0420	Spray, both sides, primer	G		10	.800		6.65	34		40.65	58.50
0430	Finish coat, latex	G		10	.800		7.30	34		41.30	59
0440	Primer & 1 coat, latex	G		5	1.600		14.05	68		82.05	117
0450	Primer & 2 coats, latex	G		4	2		21.50	85		106.50	152
0460	Windows, per interior side, based on 15 S.F.										
0470	1 to 6 lite										
0480	Brushwork, primer	G	1 Pord	13	.615	Ea.	1.24	26		27.24	41
0490	Finish coat, enamel	G		13	.615		1.37	26		27.37	41
0500	Primer & 1 coat enamel	G		8	1		2.62	42.50		45.12	67

09 91 Painting

09 91 23 – Interior Painting

09 91 23.39 Doors and Windows, Interior Latex, Zero Voc

		Crew	Daily Output	Labor-Hours	Unit	Material	2018 Bare Costs Labor	Equipment	Total	Total Incl O&P
0510	Primer & 2 coats enamel	1 Pord [G]	6	1.333	Ea.	3.99	56.50		60.49	90

09 91 23.72 Walls and Ceilings, Interior

		Crew	Daily Output	Labor-Hours	Unit	Material	Labor	Equipment	Total	Total Incl O&P
0010	**WALLS AND CEILINGS, INTERIOR** R099100-10									
0100	Concrete, drywall or plaster, latex, primer or sealer coat R099100-20									
0200	Smooth finish, brushwork	1 Pord	1150	.007	S.F.	.06	.30		.36	.52
0800	Paint 2 coats, smooth finish, brushwork		680	.012		.14	.50		.64	.91
0880	Spray		1625	.005		.13	.21		.34	.47

09 91 23.74 Walls and Ceilings, Interior, Zero VOC Latex

		Crew	Daily Output	Labor-Hours	Unit	Material	Labor	Equipment	Total	Total Incl O&P
0010	**WALLS AND CEILINGS, INTERIOR, ZERO VOC LATEX** R099100-10									
0100	Concrete, dry wall or plaster, latex, primer or sealer coat R099100-20									
0200	Smooth finish, brushwork [G]	1 Pord	1150	.007	S.F.	.08	.30		.38	.54
0240	Roller [G]		1350	.006		.08	.25		.33	.47
0280	Spray [G]		2750	.003		.06	.12		.18	.26
0300	Sand finish, brushwork [G]		975	.008		.08	.35		.43	.62
0340	Roller [G]		1150	.007		.09	.30		.39	.55
0380	Spray [G]		2275	.004		.07	.15		.22	.30
0400	Paint 1 coat, smooth finish, brushwork [G]		1200	.007		.09	.28		.37	.53
0440	Roller [G]		1300	.006		.09	.26		.35	.49
0480	Spray [G]		2275	.004		.08	.15		.23	.32
0500	Sand finish, brushwork [G]		1050	.008		.09	.32		.41	.59
0540	Roller [G]		1600	.005		.09	.21		.30	.42
0580	Spray [G]		2100	.004		.08	.16		.24	.33
0800	Paint 2 coats, smooth finish, brushwork [G]		680	.012		.18	.50		.68	.95
0840	Roller [G]		800	.010		.19	.43		.62	.84
0880	Spray [G]		1625	.005		.16	.21		.37	.50
0900	Sand finish, brushwork [G]		605	.013		.18	.56		.74	1.04
0940	Roller [G]		1020	.008		.19	.33		.52	.70
0980	Spray [G]		1700	.005		.16	.20		.36	.48
1200	Paint 3 coats, smooth finish, brushwork [G]		510	.016		.26	.67		.93	1.29
1240	Roller [G]		650	.012		.28	.52		.80	1.10
1280	Spray [G]		850	.009		.24	.40		.64	.86
1800	For ceiling installations, add [G]						25%			
8200	For work 8'- 15' H, add						10%			
8300	For work over 15' H, add						20%			

Division Notes

	CREW	DAILY OUTPUT	LABOR-HOURS	UNIT	BARE COSTS MAT.	LABOR	EQUIP.	TOTAL	TOTAL INCL O&P

Division 10 Specialties

Estimating Tips
General
- The items in this division are usually priced per square foot or each.
- Many items in Division 10 require some type of support system or special anchors that are not usually furnished with the item. The required anchors must be added to the estimate in the appropriate division.
- Some items in Division 10, such as lockers, may require assembly before installation. Verify the amount of assembly required. Assembly can often exceed installation time.

10 20 00 Interior Specialties
- Support angles and blocking are not included in the installation of toilet compartments, shower/dressing compartments, or cubicles. Appropriate line items from Division 5 or 6 may need to be added to support the installations.
- Toilet partitions are priced by the stall. A stall consists of a side wall, pilaster, and door with hardware. Toilet tissue holders and grab bars are extra.
- The required acoustical rating of a folding partition can have a significant impact on costs. Verify the sound transmission coefficient rating of the panel priced against the specification requirements.
- Grab bar installation does not include supplemental blocking or backing to support the required load. When grab bars are installed at an existing facility, provisions must be made to attach the grab bars to a solid structure.

Reference Numbers
Reference numbers are shown at the beginning of some major classifications. These numbers refer to related items in the Reference Section. The reference information may be an estimating procedure, an alternate pricing method, or technical information.

Note: Not all subdivisions listed here necessarily appear. ■

Did you know?

RSMeans data is available through our online application with 24/7 access:
- Search for unit prices by keyword
- Leverage the most up-to-date data
- Build and export estimates

Try it free for 30 days!
www.rsmeans.com/2018freetrial

No part of this cost data may be reproduced, stored in a retrieval system, or transmitted in any form or by any means without prior written permission of Gordian.

10 21 Compartments and Cubicles

10 21 13 – Toilet Compartments

10 21 13.19 Plastic Toilet Compartments

		Crew	Daily Output	Labor-Hours	Unit	Material	2018 Bare Costs Labor	Equipment	Total	Total Incl O&P
0010	**PLASTIC TOILET COMPARTMENTS**									
3600	Polymer plastic	G 2 Carp	6	2.667	Ea.	860	135		995	1,150
3810	Entrance screen, polymer plastic, flr. mtd., 48"x58"		6	2.667		505	135		640	760
3820	Entrance screen, polymer plastic, flr. to clg pilaster, 48"x58"		6	2.667		600	135		735	865
6110	Urinal screen, polymer plastic, pilaster flush, 18" w		6	2.667		435	135		570	685
7110	Wall hung		6	2.667		745	135		880	1,025
7710	Flange mounted		6	2.667		930	135		1,065	1,225
8500	Urinal screen, recycled plastic, headrail braced, floor mtd	G	10	1.600		179	81		260	320

10 35 Stoves

10 35 13 – Heating Stoves

10 35 13.10 Wood Burning Stoves

		Crew	Daily Output	Labor-Hours	Unit	Material	Labor	Equipment	Total	Total Incl O&P
0010	**WOOD BURNING STOVES**									
2000	Stoves, wood/gas burning, free standing, recycled cast iron, minimum	G 2 Clab	2	8	Ea.	1,100	320		1,420	1,675
2010	Maximum	G "	1	16	"	2,900	640		3,540	4,175

10 51 Lockers

10 51 26 – Plastic Lockers

10 51 26.13 Recycled Plastic Lockers

		Crew	Daily Output	Labor-Hours	Unit	Material	Labor	Equipment	Total	Total Incl O&P
0011	**RECYCLED PLASTIC LOCKERS**, 30% recycled									
0110	Single tier box locker, 12" x 12" x 72"	G 1 Shee	8	1	Ea.	420	60		480	555
0120	12" x 15" x 72"	G	8	1		450	60		510	585
0130	12" x 18" x 72"	G	8	1		425	60		485	560
0410	Double tier, 12" x 12" x 72"	G	21	.381		455	23		478	535
0420	12" x 15" x 72"	G	21	.381		485	23		508	570
0430	12" x 18" x 72"	G	21	.381		450	23		473	530

10 56 Storage Assemblies

10 56 13 – Metal Storage Shelving

10 56 13.10 Shelving, Plastic

		Crew	Daily Output	Labor-Hours	Unit	Material	Labor	Equipment	Total	Total Incl O&P
0012	**SHELVING, PLASTIC**									
6000	Shelving, industrial, recycled plastic, 2 shelf kit, 16" W x 27" H x 8' L	G 1 Clab	350	.023	SF Shlf	10.50	.91		11.41	12.95
6010	1 shelf add-on kit, 16" W x 24" H x 8' L	G	350	.023		14.30	.91		15.21	17.10
6020	Extra shelf, 16" W x 8' L	G	350	.023		14.65	.91		15.56	17.55
6030	2 shelf kit, 24" W x 27" H x 8' L	G	350	.023		8	.91		8.91	10.20
6040	1 shelf add-on kit, 24" W x 24" H x 8' L	G	350	.023		11.05	.91		11.96	13.55
6050	Extra shelf, 24" W x 8' L	G	350	.023		11.30	.91		12.21	13.85
6060	36" W x 27" H x 8' L	G	350	.023		8.50	.91		9.41	10.75
6070	1 shelf add-on kit, 36" W x 24" H x 8' L	G	350	.023		13.15	.91		14.06	15.85
6080	Extra shelf, 36" W x 8' L	G	350	.023		12.75	.91		13.66	15.45
6090	Post for plastic shelving, 2' H	G	32	.250	Ea.	8.85	9.95		18.80	25
6100	3' H	G	32	.250		13.25	9.95		23.20	30
6110	4' H	G	32	.250		16.25	9.95		26.20	33

10 71 Exterior Protection

10 71 13 – Exterior Sun Control Devices

10 71 13.43 Fixed Sun Screens	Crew	Daily Output	Labor-Hours	Unit	Material	2018 Bare Costs Labor	Equipment	Total	Total Incl O&P
0010 **FIXED SUN SCREENS**									
0020　24" projection	E-24	40	.800	L.F.	62.50	43.50	14.75	120.75	155
0030　30" projection		35	.914		71	50	16.90	137.90	177
0040　36" projection		30	1.067		89	58	19.70	166.70	213
0050　42" projection		25	1.280		104	69.50	23.50	197	252
0060　48" projection		20	1.600		119	87	29.50	235.50	305

Division Notes

		CREW	DAILY OUTPUT	LABOR-HOURS	UNIT	BARE COSTS MAT.	LABOR	EQUIP.	TOTAL	TOTAL INCL O&P

Division 11 Equipment

Estimating Tips
General
- The items in this division are usually priced per square foot or each. Many of these items are purchased by the owner for installation by the contractor. Check the specifications for responsibilities and include time for receiving, storage, installation, and mechanical and electrical hookups in the appropriate divisions.
- Many items in Division 11 require some type of support system that is not usually furnished with the item. Examples of these systems include blocking for the attachment of casework and support angles for ceiling-hung projection screens. The required blocking or supports must be added to the estimate in the appropriate division.
- Some items in Division 11 may require assembly or electrical hookups. Verify the amount of assembly required or the need for a hard electrical connection and add the appropriate costs.

Reference Numbers
Reference numbers are shown at the beginning of some major classifications. These numbers refer to related items in the Reference Section. The reference information may be an estimating procedure, an alternate pricing method, or technical information.

Note: Not all subdivisions listed here necessarily appear. ■

Did you know?
RSMeans data is available through our online application with 24/7 access:
- Search for unit prices by keyword
- Leverage the most up-to-date data
- Build and export estimates

Try it free for 30 days!
www.rsmeans.com/2018freetrial

No part of this cost data may be reproduced, stored in a retrieval system, or transmitted in any form or by any means without prior written permission of Gordian.

11 13 Loading Dock Equipment

11 13 13 – Loading Dock Bumpers

11 13 13.10 Dock Bumpers

		Crew	Daily Output	Labor-Hours	Unit	Material	2018 Bare Costs Labor	Equipment	Total	Total Incl O&P
0010	**DOCK BUMPERS** Bolts not included									
1200	Bumpers, recycled rubber blocks 4-1/2" thick, 10" high, 14" long [G]	1 Carp	26	.308	Ea.	52	15.60		67.60	81.50
1210	36" long [G]		17	.471		122	24		146	171
1220	12" high, 36" long [G]		16	.500		149	25.50		174.50	203
1248	Bumpers, vertical rubber blocks 6" thick, 20" high, 24" wide		22	.364		650	18.45		668.45	745
1249	Bumpers, vertical rubber blocks 6" thick, 10" high, 11" wide		22	.364		118	18.45		136.45	157
1250	6" thick, 10" high, 14" long [G]		22	.364		59.50	18.45		77.95	93.50
1260	36" long [G]		13	.615		157	31		188	221
1270	12" high, 36" long [G]		12	.667		176	34		210	246
1290	Welded installation of above bumpers [G]	E-14	8	1		3.90	56.50	12.30	72.70	110
1295	For drilled anchors, add per anchor [G]	1 Carp	36	.222		7	11.25		18.25	25

11 30 Residential Equipment

11 30 13 – Residential Appliances

11 30 13.16 Refrigeration Equipment

		Crew	Daily Output	Labor-Hours	Unit	Material	Labor	Equipment	Total	Total Incl O&P
0010	**REFRIGERATION EQUIPMENT**									
6790	Energy-star qualified, 18 C.F., minimum [G]	2 Carp	4	4	Ea.	535	203		738	900
6795	Maximum [G]		2	8		1,600	405		2,005	2,375
6797	21.7 C.F., minimum [G]		4	4		1,400	203		1,603	1,850
6799	Maximum [G]		4	4		1,875	203		2,078	2,375

11 30 13.17 Kitchen Cleaning Equipment

		Crew	Daily Output	Labor-Hours	Unit	Material	Labor	Equipment	Total	Total Incl O&P
0010	**KITCHEN CLEANING EQUIPMENT**									
2750	Dishwasher, built-in, 2 cycles, minimum	L-1	4	4	Ea.	296	241		537	685
2800	Maximum		2	8		455	480		935	1,225
2950	4 or more cycles, minimum		4	4		400	241		641	800
2960	Average		4	4		535	241		776	945
3000	Maximum		2	8		1,175	480		1,655	2,025
3100	Energy-star qualified, minimum [G]		4	4		380	241		621	780
3110	Maximum [G]		2	8		1,700	480		2,180	2,600

11 30 13.24 Washers

		Crew	Daily Output	Labor-Hours	Unit	Material	Labor	Equipment	Total	Total Incl O&P
0010	**WASHERS**									
6650	Washing machine, automatic, minimum	1 Plum	3	2.667	Ea.	645	166		811	960
6700	Maximum		1	8		1,350	495		1,845	2,225
6750	Energy star qualified, front loading, minimum [G]		3	2.667		700	166		866	1,025
6760	Maximum [G]		1	8		1,800	495		2,295	2,725
6764	Top loading, minimum [G]		3	2.667		640	166		806	955
6766	Maximum [G]		3	2.667		1,000	166		1,166	1,350

11 30 13.25 Dryers

		Crew	Daily Output	Labor-Hours	Unit	Material	Labor	Equipment	Total	Total Incl O&P
0010	**DRYERS**									
6770	Electric, front loading, energy-star qualified, minimum [G]	L-2	3	5.333	Ea.	405	236		641	805
6780	Maximum [G]	"	2	8	"	1,475	355		1,830	2,150

11 41 Foodservice Storage Equipment

11 41 13 – Refrigerated Food Storage Cases

11 41 13.20 Refrigerated Food Storage Equipment

		Crew	Daily Output	Labor-Hours	Unit	Material	2018 Bare Costs Labor	Equipment	Total	Total Incl O&P
0010	**REFRIGERATED FOOD STORAGE EQUIPMENT**									
4300	Freezers, reach-in, 44 C.F.	Q-1	4	4	Ea.	4,725	224		4,949	5,525
4500	68 C.F.	"	3	5.333		5,800	298		6,098	6,825
4600	Freezer, pre-fab, 8' x 8' w/refrigeration	2 Carp	.45	35.556		10,500	1,800		12,300	14,400
4620	8' x 12'		.35	45.714		11,400	2,325		13,725	16,000
4640	8' x 16'		.25	64		13,800	3,250		17,050	20,200
4660	8' x 20'		.17	94.118		19,700	4,775		24,475	29,000
4680	Reach-in, 1 compartment	Q-1	4	4		3,225	224		3,449	3,875
4685	Energy star rated [G]	R-18	7.80	3.333		2,900	170		3,070	3,450
4700	2 compartment	Q-1	3	5.333		4,450	298		4,748	5,325
4705	Energy star rated [G]	R-18	6.20	4.194		3,575	214		3,789	4,275
4710	3 compartment	Q-1	3	5.333		6,150	298		6,448	7,200
4715	Energy star rated [G]	R-18	5.60	4.643		4,925	237		5,162	5,750
8320	Refrigerator, reach-in, 1 compartment		7.80	3.333		2,925	170		3,095	3,450
8325	Energy star rated [G]		7.80	3.333		2,900	170		3,070	3,450
8330	2 compartment		6.20	4.194		4,175	214		4,389	4,925
8335	Energy star rated [G]		6.20	4.194		3,575	214		3,789	4,275
8340	3 compartment		5.60	4.643		5,650	237		5,887	6,550
8345	Energy star rated [G]		5.60	4.643		4,925	237		5,162	5,750

11 44 Food Cooking Equipment

11 44 13 – Commercial Ranges

11 44 13.10 Cooking Equipment

		Crew	Daily Output	Labor-Hours	Unit	Material	Labor	Equipment	Total	Total Incl O&P
0010	**COOKING EQUIPMENT**									
4750	Fryer, with twin baskets, modular model	Q-1	7	2.286	Ea.	1,375	128		1,503	1,725
5000	Floor model, on 6" legs	"	5	3.200		2,575	179		2,754	3,100
5100	Extra single basket, large					50			50	55
5170	Energy star rated, 50 lb. capacity [G]	R-18	4	6.500		4,750	330		5,080	5,725
5175	85 lb. capacity [G]	"	4	6.500		9,900	330		10,230	11,400

11 48 Foodservice Cleaning and Disposal Equipment

11 48 13 – Commercial Dishwashers

11 48 13.10 Dishwashers

		Crew	Daily Output	Labor-Hours	Unit	Material	Labor	Equipment	Total	Total Incl O&P
0010	**DISHWASHERS**									
2700	Dishwasher, commercial, rack type									
2720	10 to 12 racks/hour	Q-1	3.20	5	Ea.	3,400	280		3,680	4,150
2730	Energy star rated, 35 to 40 racks/hour [G]		1.30	12.308		4,250	690		4,940	5,700
2740	50 to 60 racks/hour [G]		1.30	12.308		11,100	690		11,790	13,200

11 68 Play Field Equipment and Structures

11 68 13 – Playground Equipment

11 68 13.10 Free-Standing Playground Equipment		Crew	Daily Output	Labor-Hours	Unit	Material	2018 Bare Costs Labor	Equipment	Total	Total Incl O&P
0010	**FREE-STANDING PLAYGROUND EQUIPMENT** See also individual items									
0200	Bike rack, 10' long, permanent	G	B-1	12	2	Ea.	570	81		651	750

Division 12 Furnishings

Estimating Tips
General
- The items in this division are usually priced per square foot or each. Most of these items are purchased by the owner and installed by the contractor. Do not assume the items in Division 12 will be purchased and installed by the contractor. Check the specifications for responsibilities and include receiving, storage, installation, and mechanical and electrical hookups in the appropriate divisions.
- Some items in this division require some type of support system that is not usually furnished with the item. Examples of these systems include blocking for the attachment of casework and heavy drapery rods. The required blocking must be added to the estimate in the appropriate division.

Reference Numbers
Reference numbers are shown at the beginning of some major classifications. These numbers refer to related items in the Reference Section. The reference information may be an estimating procedure, an alternate pricing method, or technical information.

Note: Not all subdivisions listed here necessarily appear. ■

Did you know?
RSMeans data is available through our online application with 24/7 access:
- Search for unit prices by keyword
- Leverage the most up-to-date data
- Build and export estimates

Try it free for 30 days!
www.rsmeans.com/2018freetrial

No part of this cost data may be reproduced, stored in a retrieval system, or transmitted in any form or by any means without prior written permission of Gordian.

12 24 Window Shades

12 24 13 – Roller Window Shades

12 24 13.10 Shades

		Crew	Daily Output	Labor-Hours	Unit	Material	2018 Bare Costs Labor	Equipment	Total	Total Incl O&P
0010	**SHADES**									
0900	Mylar, single layer, non-heat reflective	1 Carp	685	.012	S.F.	3	.59		3.59	4.20
0910	Mylar, single layer, heat reflective		685	.012		2.54	.59		3.13	3.70
1000	Double layered, heat reflective		685	.012		6.05	.59		6.64	7.55
1100	Triple layered, heat reflective	↓	685	.012	↓	7.60	.59		8.19	9.25
1200	For metal roller instead of wood, add per				Shade	6.35			6.35	6.95
5011	Insulative shades	G	1 Carp	125	.064	S.F.	15.60	3.24		18.84	22
6011	Solar screening, fiberglass	G	"	85	.094	"	7.65	4.77		12.42	15.65
8011	Interior insulative shutter										
8111	Stock unit, 15" x 60"	G	1 Carp	17	.471	Pr.	15.75	24		39.75	54

12 36 Countertops

12 36 23 – Plastic Countertops

12 36 23.20 Countertops

		Crew	Daily Output	Labor-Hours	Unit	Material	Labor	Equipment	Total	Incl O&P
0010	**COUNTERTOPS**									
6000	Countertops, recycled glass, steel/brass chips, w/binder, 1-1/2"T x 25"W	G	1 Carp	40	.200	S.F.	147	10.15		157.15	176
6010	Countertops, recycled waste paper, 1-1/2"T x 25"D	G		40	.200	L.F.	110	10.15		120.15	136
6020	Backsplash for, 1" x 4"	G		60	.133	"	5.90	6.75		12.65	16.80

12 46 Furnishing Accessories

12 46 33 – Waste Receptacles

12 46 33.13 Trash Receptacles

		Crew	Daily Output	Labor-Hours	Unit	Material	Labor	Equipment	Total	Incl O&P
0010	**TRASH RECEPTACLES**									
5550	Plastic recycling barrel, w/lid & wheels, 32 gal.	G	1 Clab	60	.133	Ea.	94	5.30		99.30	111
5560	65 gal.	G		60	.133		605	5.30		610.30	675
5570	95 gal.	G		60	.133		1,125	5.30		1,130.30	1,250

12 48 Rugs and Mats

12 48 13 – Entrance Floor Mats and Frames

12 48 13.13 Entrance Floor Mats

		Crew	Daily Output	Labor-Hours	Unit	Material	Labor	Equipment	Total	Incl O&P
0010	**ENTRANCE FLOOR MATS**									
2000	Recycled rubber tire tile, 12" x 12" x 3/8" thick	G	1 Clab	125	.064	S.F.	9.95	2.55		12.50	14.85
2510	Natural cocoa fiber, 1/2" thick	G		125	.064		7.10	2.55		9.65	11.70
2520	3/4" thick	G		125	.064		6.45	2.55		9	10.95
2530	1" thick	G	↓	125	.064	↓	12.90	2.55		15.45	18.10

12 92 Interior Planters and Artificial Plants

12 92 33 – Interior Planters

12 92 33.10 Planters		Crew	Daily Output	Labor-Hours	Unit	Material	2018 Bare Costs Labor	Equipment	Total	Total Incl O&P
0010	**PLANTERS**									
1000	Fiberglass, hanging, 12" diameter, 7" high				Ea.	112			112	123
1100	15" diameter, 7" high					162			162	178
1200	36" diameter, 8" high					223			223	246
1500	Rectangular, 48" long, 16" high, 15" wide					605			605	665
1550	16" high, 24" wide					660			660	725
1600	24" high, 24" wide					965			965	1,075
1650	60" long, 30" high, 28" wide					1,025			1,025	1,125
1700	72" long, 16" high, 15" wide					860			860	945
1750	21" high, 24" wide					1,050			1,050	1,150
1800	30" high, 24" wide					1,200			1,200	1,325
2000	Round, 12" diameter, 13" high					161			161	177
2050	25" high					212			212	233
2150	14" diameter, 15" high					174			174	191
2200	16" diameter, 16" high					197			197	216
2250	18" diameter, 19" high					237			237	261
2300	23" high					310			310	340
2350	20" diameter, 16" high					217			217	239
2400	18" high					239			239	262
2450	21" high					310			310	340
2500	22" diameter, 10" high					242			242	266
2550	24" diameter, 16" high					288			288	315
2600	19" high					345			345	380
2650	25" high					400			400	435
2700	36" high					620			620	680
2750	48" high					865			865	950
2800	30" diameter, 16" high					340			340	375
2850	18" high					345			345	380
2900	21" high					385			385	425
3000	24" high					395			395	435
3350	27" high					440			440	480
3400	36" diameter, 16" high					415			415	455
3450	18" high					430			430	475
3500	21" high					465			465	510
3550	24" high					495			495	545
3600	27" high					540			540	590
3650	30" high					585			585	640
3700	48" diameter, 16" high					670			670	735
3750	21" high					720			720	795
3800	24" high					810			810	890
3850	27" high					850			850	935
3900	30" high					925			925	1,025
3950	36" high					970			970	1,075
4000	60" diameter, 16" high					985			985	1,075
4100	21" high					1,125			1,125	1,225
4150	27" high					1,250			1,250	1,375
4200	30" high					1,375			1,375	1,525
4250	33" high					1,575			1,575	1,725
4300	36" high					1,925			1,925	2,100
4400	39" high					2,075			2,075	2,275
5000	Square, 10" side, 20" high					199			199	219
5100	14" side, 15" high					214			214	235
5200	18" side, 19" high					241			241	265

For customer support on your Green Building Costs with RSMeans data, call 800.448.8182.

12 92 Interior Planters and Artificial Plants

12 92 33 – Interior Planters

12 92 33.10 Planters		Crew	Daily Output	Labor-Hours	Unit	Material	2018 Bare Costs Labor	Equipment	Total	Total Incl O&P
5300	20" side, 16" high				Ea.	289			289	320
5320	18" high					485			485	535
5340	21" high					390			390	425
5400	24" side, 16" high					295			295	325
5420	21" high					565			565	620
5440	25" high					530			530	580
5460	30" side, 16" high					490			490	540
5480	24" high					725			725	800
5490	27" high					905			905	1,000
6000	Metal bowl, 32" diameter, 8" high, minimum					570			570	630
6050	Maximum					795			795	875
6100	Rectangle, 30" long x 12" wide, 6" high, minimum					445			445	490
6200	Maximum					615			615	675
6300	36" long x 12" wide, 6" high, minimum					875			875	965
6400	Maximum					490			490	535
6500	Square, 15" side, minimum					625			625	690
6600	Maximum					960			960	1,050
6700	20" side, minimum					1,375			1,375	1,525
6800	Maximum					585			585	645
6900	Round, 6" diameter x 6" high, minimum					64			64	70.50
7000	Maximum					76			76	84
7100	8" diameter x 8" high, minimum					85			85	93.50
7200	Maximum					91.50			91.50	101
7300	10" diameter x 11" high, minimum					109			109	120
7400	Maximum					161			161	177
7420	12" diameter x 13" high, minimum					101			101	111
7440	Maximum					204			204	225
7500	14" diameter x 15" high, minimum					136			136	150
7550	Maximum					239			239	263
7580	16" diameter x 17" high, minimum					147			147	162
7600	Maximum					262			262	288
7620	18" diameter x 19" high, minimum					178			178	196
7640	Maximum					320			320	350
7680	22" diameter x 20" high, minimum					225			225	247
7700	Maximum					410			410	450
7750	24" diameter x 21" high, minimum					292			292	320
7800	Maximum					545			545	600
7850	31" diameter x 18" high, minimum					635			635	700
7900	Maximum					1,625			1,625	1,775
7950	38" diameter x 24" high, minimum					1,075			1,075	1,175
8000	Maximum					2,725			2,725	2,975
8050	48" diameter x 24" high, minimum					1,425			1,425	1,550
8150	Maximum					2,800			2,800	3,075
8750	Wood, fiberglass liner, square									
8780	14" square, 15" high, minimum				Ea.	430			430	475
8800	Maximum					530			530	580
8820	24" square, 16" high, minimum					530			530	580
8840	Maximum					700			700	770
8860	36" square, 21" high, minimum					680			680	745
8880	Maximum					1,025			1,025	1,125
9000	Rectangle, 36" long x 12" wide, 10" high, minimum					485			485	535
9050	Maximum					630			630	695
9100	48" long x 12" wide, 10" high, minimum					525			525	575

12 92 Interior Planters and Artificial Plants

12 92 33 – Interior Planters

12 92 33.10 Planters		Crew	Daily Output	Labor-Hours	Unit	Material	2018 Bare Costs Labor	Equipment	Total	Total Incl O&P
9120	Maximum				Ea.	660			660	725
9200	48" long x 12" wide, 24" high, minimum					630			630	695
9300	Maximum					930			930	1,025
9400	Plastic cylinder, molded, 10" diameter, 10" high					47			47	51.50
9500	11" diameter, 11" high					89.50			89.50	98
9600	13" diameter, 12" high					146			146	160
9700	16" diameter, 14" high					169			169	186

12 93 Interior Public Space Furnishings

12 93 13 – Bicycle Racks

12 93 13.10 Bicycle Racks

		Crew	Daily Output	Labor-Hours	Unit	Material	Labor	Equipment	Total	Total Incl O&P
0010	**BICYCLE RACKS**									
0020	Single side, grid, 1-5/8" OD stl. pipe, w/1/2" bars, galv, 5 bike cap	2 Clab	10	1.600	Ea.	315	64		379	440
0025	Powder coat finish		10	1.600		320	64		384	445
0030	Single side, grid, 1-5/8" OD stl. pipe, w/1/2" bars, galv, 9 bike cap		8	2		400	79.50		479.50	560
0035	Powder coat finish		8	2		415	79.50		494.50	575
0040	Single side, grid, 1-5/8" OD stl. pipe, w/1/2" bars, galv, 18 bike cap		4	4		465	159		624	755
0045	Powder coat finish		4	4		525	159		684	820
0050	S curve, 1-7/8" OD stl. pipe, 11 ga., galv, 5 bike cap		10	1.600		157	64		221	270
0055	Powder coat finish		10	1.600		157	64		221	270
0060	S curve, 1-7/8" OD stl. pipe, 11 ga., galv, 7 bike cap		9	1.778		167	71		238	292
0065	Powder coat finish		9	1.778		212	71		283	340
0070	S curve, 1-7/8" OD stl. pipe, 11 ga., galv, 9 bike cap		8	2		320	79.50		399.50	470
0075	Powder coat finish		8	2		310	79.50		389.50	460
0080	S curve, 1-7/8" OD stl. pipe, 11 ga., galv, 11 bike cap		6	2.667		430	106		536	635
0085	Powder coat finish		6	2.667		415	106		521	615

12 93 23 – Trash and Litter Receptacles

12 93 23.10 Trash Receptacles

			Crew	Daily Output	Labor-Hours	Unit	Material	Labor	Equipment	Total	Total Incl O&P
0010	**TRASH RECEPTACLES**										
0500	Recycled plastic, var colors, round, 32 gal., 28" x 38" high	G	2 Clab	5	3.200	Ea.	660	128		788	920
0510	32 gal., 31" x 32" high	G		5	3.200		770	128		898	1,050
9110	Plastic, with dome lid, 32 gal. capacity			35	.457		62.50	18.20		80.70	96.50
9120	Recycled plastic slats, plastic dome lid, 32 gal. capacity			35	.457		297	18.20		315.20	355

Division Notes

	CREW	DAILY OUTPUT	LABOR-HOURS	UNIT	BARE COSTS MAT.	LABOR	EQUIP.	TOTAL	TOTAL INCL O&P

Division 13 Special Construction

Estimating Tips
General
- The items and systems in this division are usually estimated, purchased, supplied, and installed as a unit by one or more subcontractors. The estimator must ensure that all parties are operating from the same set of specifications and assumptions, and that all necessary items are estimated and will be provided. Many times the complex items and systems are covered, but the more common ones, such as excavation or a crane, are overlooked for the very reason that everyone assumes nobody could miss them. The estimator should be the central focus and be able to ensure that all systems are complete.
- Another area where problems can develop in this division is at the interface between systems. The estimator must ensure, for instance, that anchor bolts, nuts, and washers are estimated and included for the air-supported structures and pre-engineered buildings to be bolted to their foundations. Utility supply is a common area where essential items or pieces of equipment can be missed or overlooked, because each subcontractor may feel it is another's responsibility. The estimator should also be aware of certain items which may be supplied as part of a package but installed by others, and ensure that the installing contractor's estimate includes the cost of installation. Conversely, the estimator must also ensure that items are not costed by two different subcontractors, resulting in an inflated overall estimate.

13 30 00 Special Structures
- The foundations and floor slab, as well as rough mechanical and electrical, should be estimated, as this work is required for the assembly and erection of the structure. Generally, as noted in the data set, the pre-engineered building comes as a shell. Pricing is based on the size and structural design parameters stated in the reference section. Additional features, such as windows and doors with their related structural framing, must also be included by the estimator. Here again, the estimator must have a clear understanding of the scope of each portion of the work and all the necessary interfaces.

Reference Numbers
Reference numbers are shown at the beginning of some major classifications. These numbers refer to related items in the Reference Section. The reference information may be an estimating procedure, an alternate pricing method, or technical information.

Note: Not all subdivisions listed here necessarily appear. ■

Did you know?

RSMeans data is available through our online application with 24/7 access:
- Search for unit prices by keyword
- Leverage the most up-to-date data
- Build and export estimates

Try it free for 30 days!
www.rsmeans.com/2018freetrial

13 05 Common Work Results for Special Construction

13 05 05 – Selective Demolition for Special Construction

13 05 05.10 Selective Demolition, Air Supported Structures

		Crew	Daily Output	Labor-Hours	Unit	Material	2018 Bare Costs Labor	Equipment	Total	Total Incl O&P
0010	**SELECTIVE DEMOLITION, AIR SUPPORTED STRUCTURES**									
0050	Round and rectangular R024119-10	B-2	9000	.004	S.F.		.18		.18	.27
0100	Warehouse structures									
0150	Reinforced vinyl, 12 oz., 3,000 S.F.	4 Clab	5000	.006	SF Flr.		.26		.26	.39
0200	12,000 to 24,000 S.F.	8 Clab	20000	.003			.13		.13	.19
0250	Tedlar vinyl fabric, 28 oz. w/liner, to 3,000 S.F.	4 Clab	5000	.006			.26		.26	.39
0300	12,000 to 24,000 S.F.	8 Clab	20000	.003			.13		.13	.19
0350	Greenhouse/shelter, woven polyethylene with liner									
0400	3,000 S.F.	4 Clab	5000	.006	SF Flr.		.26		.26	.39
0450	12,000 to 24,000 S.F.	8 Clab	20000	.003	"		.13		.13	.19

13 05 05.75 Selective Demolition, Storage Tanks

		Crew	Daily Output	Labor-Hours	Unit	Material	Labor	Equipment	Total	Total Incl O&P
0010	**SELECTIVE DEMOLITION, STORAGE TANKS**									
0510	Single wall, 275 gallon R024119-10	Q-1	3	5.333	Ea.		298		298	450
0520	550 thru 2,000 gallon	B-34P	2	12			645	275	920	1,275
0530	5,000 thru 10,000 gallon	B-34Q	2	12			655	530	1,185	1,575
0540	15,000 thru 30,000 gallon	B-34S	2	16			910	1,625	2,535	3,150
0620	500 thru 2,000 gallon	B-34P	2	12			645	275	920	1,275

13 12 Fountains

13 12 13 – Exterior Fountains

13 12 13.10 Outdoor Fountains

		Crew	Daily Output	Labor-Hours	Unit	Material	Labor	Equipment	Total	Total Incl O&P
0010	**OUTDOOR FOUNTAINS**									
0100	Outdoor fountain, 48" high with bowl and figures	2 Clab	2	8	Ea.	570	320		890	1,100
0200	Commercial, concrete or cast stone, 40-60" H, simple		2	8		775	320		1,095	1,350
0220	Average		2	8		1,350	320		1,670	1,950
0240	Ornate		2	8		2,625	320		2,945	3,350
0260	Metal, 72" high		2	8		1,200	320		1,520	1,800
0280	90" high		2	8		1,875	320		2,195	2,550
0300	120" high		2	8		5,000	320		5,320	5,975
0320	Resin or fiberglass, 40-60" H, wall type		2	8		480	320		800	1,025
0340	Waterfall type		2	8		1,000	320		1,320	1,575

13 12 13.54 Garden Ponds

		Crew	Daily Output	Labor-Hours	Unit	Material	Labor	Equipment	Total	Total Incl O&P
0010	**GARDEN PONDS**									
0011	Made from 100% recycled plastic									
4000	185 gal., 18" deep				Ea.	241			241	265
4010	245 gal., 36" deep					375			375	415
4020	Pump kit for					179			179	197

13 12 23 – Interior Fountains

13 12 23.10 Indoor Fountains

		Crew	Daily Output	Labor-Hours	Unit	Material	Labor	Equipment	Total	Total Incl O&P
0010	**INDOOR FOUNTAINS**									
0100	Commercial, floor type, resin or fiberglass, lighted, cascade type	2 Clab	2	8	Ea.	286	320		606	800
0120	Tiered type		2	8		285	320		605	800
0140	Waterfall type		2	8		275	320		595	785

13 31 Fabric Structures

13 31 13 – Air-Supported Fabric Structures

13 31 13.09 Air Supported Tank Covers

		Crew	Daily Output	Labor-Hours	Unit	Material	2018 Bare Costs Labor	Equipment	Total	Total Incl O&P
0010	**AIR SUPPORTED TANK COVERS**, vinyl polyester									
0100	Scrim, double layer, with hardware, blower, standby & controls									
0200	Round, 75' diameter	B-2	4500	.009	S.F.	12.15	.36		12.51	13.95
0300	100' diameter		5000	.008		11.05	.32		11.37	12.70
0400	150' diameter		5000	.008		8.75	.32		9.07	10.15
0500	Rectangular, 20' x 20'		4500	.009		24	.36		24.36	27
0600	30' x 40'		4500	.009		24	.36		24.36	27
0700	50' x 60'		4500	.009		24	.36		24.36	27
0800	For single wall construction, deduct, minimum					.82			.82	.90
0900	Maximum					2.43			2.43	2.67
1000	For maximum resistance to atmosphere or cold, add					1.18			1.18	1.30
1100	For average shipping charges, add				Total	2,025			2,025	2,225

13 31 13.13 Single-Walled Air-Supported Structures

		Crew	Daily Output	Labor-Hours	Unit	Material	Labor	Equipment	Total	Total Incl O&P
0010	**SINGLE-WALLED AIR-SUPPORTED STRUCTURES** R133113-10									
0020	Site preparation, incl. anchor placement and utilities	B-11B	1000	.016	SF Flr.	1.18	.73	.29	2.20	2.71
0050	Warehouse, polyester/vinyl fabric, 28 oz., over 10 yr. life, welded									
0060	Seams, tension cables, primary & auxiliary inflation system,									
0070	airlock, personnel doors and liner									
0100	5,000 S.F.	4 Clab	5000	.006	SF Flr.	27	.26		27.26	30.50
0250	12,000 S.F.	"	6000	.005		19.55	.21		19.76	22
0400	24,000 S.F.	8 Clab	12000	.005		13.75	.21		13.96	15.45
0500	50,000 S.F.	"	12500	.005		12.75	.20		12.95	14.35
0700	12 oz. reinforced vinyl fabric, 5 yr. life, sewn seams,									
0710	accordion door, including liner									
0750	3,000 S.F.	4 Clab	3000	.011	SF Flr.	13.45	.43		13.88	15.45
0800	12,000 S.F.	"	6000	.005		11.45	.21		11.66	12.90
0850	24,000 S.F.	8 Clab	12000	.005		9.70	.21		9.91	11
0950	Deduct for single layer					1.06			1.06	1.17
1000	Add for welded seams					1.53			1.53	1.68
1050	Add for double layer, welded seams included					3.06			3.06	3.37
1250	Tedlar/vinyl fabric, 28 oz., with liner, over 10 yr. life,									
1260	incl. overhead and personnel doors									
1300	3,000 S.F.	4 Clab	3000	.011	SF Flr.	25.50	.43		25.93	28.50
1450	12,000 S.F.	"	6000	.005		17.80	.21		18.01	19.90
1550	24,000 S.F.	8 Clab	12000	.005		13.75	.21		13.96	15.45
1700	Deduct for single layer					2.04			2.04	2.24
2250	Greenhouse/shelter, woven polyethylene with liner, 2 yr. life,									
2260	sewn seams, including doors									
2300	3,000 S.F.	4 Clab	3000	.011	SF Flr.	16.30	.43		16.73	18.60
2350	12,000 S.F.	"	6000	.005		14.30	.21		14.51	16
2450	24,000 S.F.	8 Clab	12000	.005		12.25	.21		12.46	13.75
2550	Deduct for single layer					1			1	1.10
2600	Tennis/gymnasium, polyester/vinyl fabric, 28 oz., over 10 yr. life,									
2610	including thermal liner, heat and lights									
2650	7,200 S.F.	4 Clab	6000	.005	SF Flr.	24.50	.21		24.71	27
2750	13,000 S.F.	"	6500	.005		18.60	.20		18.80	21
2850	Over 24,000 S.F.	8 Clab	12000	.005		17	.21		17.21	19
2860	For low temperature conditions, add					1.17			1.17	1.29
2870	For average shipping charges, add				Total	5,700			5,700	6,275
2900	Thermal liner, translucent reinforced vinyl				SF Flr.	1.17			1.17	1.29
2950	Metalized mylar fabric and mesh, double liner				"	2.42			2.42	2.66
3050	Stadium/convention center, teflon coated fiberglass, heavy weight,									

13 31 Fabric Structures

13 31 13 – Air-Supported Fabric Structures

13 31 13.13 Single-Walled Air-Supported Structures

		Crew	Daily Output	Labor-Hours	Unit	Material	2018 Bare Costs Labor	Equipment	Total	Total Incl O&P
3060	over 20 yr. life, incl. thermal liner and heating system									
3100	Minimum	9 Clab	26000	.003	SF Flr.	59.50	.11		59.61	65
3110	Maximum	"	19000	.004	"	70.50	.15		70.65	77.50
3400	Doors, air lock, 15' long, 10' x 10'	2 Carp	.80	20	Ea.	21,100	1,025		22,125	24,800
3600	15' x 15'	"	.50	32		31,400	1,625		33,025	37,000
3700	For each added 5' length, add					5,600			5,600	6,175
3900	Revolving personnel door, 6' diameter, 6'-6" high	2 Carp	.80	20		15,700	1,025		16,725	18,900

13 33 Geodesic Structures

13 33 13 – Geodesic Domes

13 33 13.35 Geodesic Domes

		Crew	Daily Output	Labor-Hours	Unit	Material	Labor	Equipment	Total	Total Incl O&P
0010	**GEODESIC DOMES** Shell only, interlocking plywood panels R133423-30									
0400	30' diameter	F-5	1.60	20	Ea.	24,400	1,025		25,425	28,400
0500	33' diameter		1.14	28.070		25,800	1,425		27,225	30,500
0600	40' diameter		1	32		29,900	1,650		31,550	35,400
0700	45' diameter	F-3	1.13	35.556		31,400	1,850	440	33,690	37,800
0750	56' diameter		1	40		55,000	2,075	495	57,570	64,000
0800	60' diameter		1	40		62,500	2,075	495	65,070	72,000
0850	67' diameter		.80	50		87,500	2,600	620	90,720	101,000
1100	Aluminum panel, with 6" insulation									
1200	100' diameter				SF Flr.	26			26	29
1300	500' diameter				"	25.50			25.50	28
1600	Aluminum framed, plexiglass closure panels									
1700	40' diameter				SF Flr.	64.50			64.50	71
1800	200' diameter				"	60			60	65.50
2100	Aluminum framed, aluminum closure panels									
2200	40' diameter				SF Flr.	21			21	23.50
2300	100' diameter					20.50			20.50	22.50
2400	200' diameter					20.50			20.50	22.50
2500	For VRP faced bonded fiberglass insulation, add					10				10
2700	Aluminum framed, fiberglass sandwich panel closure									
2800	6' diameter	2 Carp	150	.107	SF Flr.	28.50	5.40		33.90	39.50
2900	28' diameter	"	350	.046	"	25.50	2.32		27.82	32

13 34 Fabricated Engineered Structures

13 34 13 – Glazed Structures

13 34 13.13 Greenhouses

		Crew	Daily Output	Labor-Hours	Unit	Material	Labor	Equipment	Total	Total Incl O&P
0010	**GREENHOUSES**, Shell only, stock units, not incl. 2' stub walls,									
0020	foundation, floors, heat or compartments									
0300	Residential type, free standing, 8'-6" long x 7'-6" wide	2 Carp	59	.271	SF Flr.	24	13.75		37.75	47.50
0400	10'-6" wide		85	.188		44.50	9.55		54.05	63.50
0600	13'-6" wide		108	.148		46	7.50		53.50	62
0700	17'-0" wide		160	.100		46	5.05		51.05	58
0900	Lean-to type, 3'-10" wide		34	.471		44	24		68	84.50
1000	6'-10" wide		58	.276		29	14		43	53.50
1050	8'-0" wide		60	.267		64	13.50		77.50	91
1100	Wall mounted to existing window, 3' x 3'	1 Carp	4	2	Ea.	2,125	101		2,226	2,475
1120	4' x 5'	"	3	2.667	"	2,325	135		2,460	2,750
1200	Deluxe quality, free standing, 7'-6" wide	2 Carp	55	.291	SF Flr.	86	14.75		100.75	117

13 34 Fabricated Engineered Structures

13 34 13 – Glazed Structures

13 34 13.13 Greenhouses

		Crew	Daily Output	Labor-Hours	Unit	Material	2018 Bare Costs Labor	Equipment	Total	Total Incl O&P
1220	10'-6" wide	2 Carp	81	.198	SF Flr.	64.50	10		74.50	86.50
1240	13'-6" wide		104	.154		53.50	7.80		61.30	71
1260	17'-0" wide		150	.107		49	5.40		54.40	62
1400	Lean-to type, 3'-10" wide		31	.516		105	26		131	156
1420	6'-10" wide		55	.291		70.50	14.75		85.25	100
1440	8'-0" wide		97	.165		60	8.35		68.35	79
1500	Commercial, custom, truss frame, incl. equip., plumbing, elec.,									
1550	benches and controls, under 2,000 S.F.				SF Flr.	13.40			13.40	14.75
1700	Over 5,000 S.F.				"	12.35			12.35	13.55
2000	Institutional, custom, rigid frame, including compartments and									
2050	multi-controls, under 500 S.F.				SF Flr.	30			30	33
2150	Over 2,000 S.F.				"	11.20			11.20	12.35
3700	For 1/4" tempered glass, add				SF Surf	1.57			1.57	1.73
3900	Cooling, 1,200 CFM exhaust fan, add				Ea.	330			330	360
4000	7,850 CFM					1,050			1,050	1,150
4200	For heaters, 10 MBH, add					230			230	253
4300	60 MBH, add					800			800	880
4500	For benches, 2' x 8', add					175			175	192
4600	4' x 10', add					213			213	234
4800	For ventilation & humidity control w/4 integrated outlets, add				Total	262			262	288
4900	For environmental controls and automation, 8 outputs, 9 stages, add				"	1,050			1,050	1,150
5100	For humidification equipment, add				Ea.	325			325	360
5200	For vinyl shading, add				S.F.	.42			.42	.46
6000	Geodesic hemisphere, 1/8" plexiglass glazing									
6050	8' diameter	2 Carp	2	8	Ea.	6,450	405		6,855	7,725
6150	24' diameter		.35	45.714		15,000	2,325		17,325	19,900
6250	48' diameter		.20	80		35,000	4,050		39,050	44,600

13 34 63 – Natural Fiber Construction

13 34 63.50 Straw Bale Construction

			Crew	Daily Output	Labor-Hours	Unit	Material	Labor	Equipment	Total	Total Incl O&P
0010	**STRAW BALE CONSTRUCTION**										
2020	Straw bales in walls w/modified post and beam frame	G	2 Carp	320	.050	S.F.	6.35	2.54		8.89	10.80

13 48 Sound, Vibration, and Seismic Control

13 48 13 – Manufactured Sound and Vibration Control Components

13 48 13.50 Audio Masking

		Crew	Daily Output	Labor-Hours	Unit	Material	Labor	Equipment	Total	Total Incl O&P
0010	**AUDIO MASKING**, acoustical enclosure, 4" thick wall and ceiling									
3100	Audio masking system, including speakers, amplification									
3110	and signal generator									
3200	Ceiling mounted, 5,000 S.F.	2 Elec	2400	.007	S.F.	1.21	.39		1.60	1.91
3300	10,000 S.F.		2800	.006		.97	.33		1.30	1.57
3400	Plenum mounted, 5,000 S.F.		3800	.004		1.04	.25		1.29	1.51
3500	10,000 S.F.		4400	.004		.70	.21		.91	1.09

For customer support on your Green Building Costs with RSMeans data, call 800.448.8182.

Division Notes

	CREW	DAILY OUTPUT	LABOR-HOURS	UNIT	BARE COSTS MAT.	LABOR	EQUIP.	TOTAL	TOTAL INCL O&P

Estimating Tips
22 10 00 Plumbing Piping and Pumps
This subdivision is primarily basic pipe and related materials. The pipe may be used by any of the mechanical disciplines, i.e., plumbing, fire protection, heating, and air conditioning.

Note: CPVC plastic piping approved for fire protection is located in 21 11 13.

- The labor adjustment factors listed in Subdivision 22 01 02.20 apply throughout Divisions 21, 22, and 23. CAUTION: the correct percentage may vary for the same items. For example, the percentage add for the basic pipe installation should be based on the maximum height that the installer must install for that particular section. If the pipe is to be located 14' above the floor but it is suspended on threaded rod from beams, the bottom flange of which is 18' high (4' rods), then the height is actually 18' and the add is 20%. The pipe cover, however, does not have to go above the 14', and so the add should be 10%.
- Most pipe is priced first as straight pipe with a joint (coupling, weld, etc.) every 10' and a hanger usually every 10'. There are exceptions with hanger spacing such as for cast iron pipe (5') and plastic pipe (3 per 10'). Following each type of pipe there are several lines listing sizes and the amount to be subtracted to delete couplings and hangers. This is for pipe that is to be buried or supported together on trapeze hangers. The reason that the couplings are deleted is that these runs are usually long, and frequently longer lengths of pipe are used. By deleting the couplings, the estimator is expected to look up and add back the correct reduced number of couplings.
- When preparing an estimate, it may be necessary to approximate the fittings. Fittings usually run between 25% and 50% of the cost of the pipe. The lower percentage is for simpler runs, and the higher number is for complex areas, such as mechanical rooms.
- For historic restoration projects, the systems must be as invisible as possible, and pathways must be sought for pipes, conduit, and ductwork. While installations in accessible spaces (such as basements and attics) are relatively straightforward to estimate, labor costs may be more difficult to determine when delivery systems must be concealed.

22 40 00 Plumbing Fixtures
- Plumbing fixture costs usually require two lines: the fixture itself and its "rough-in, supply, and waste."
- In the Assemblies Section (Plumbing D2010) for the desired fixture, the System Components Group at the center of the page shows the fixture on the first line. The rest of the list (fittings, pipe, tubing, etc.) will total up to what we refer to in the Unit Price section as "Rough-in, supply, waste, and vent." Note that for most fixtures we allow a nominal 5' of tubing to reach from the fixture to a main or riser.
- Remember that gas- and oil-fired units need venting.

Reference Numbers
Reference numbers are shown at the beginning of some major classifications. These numbers refer to related items in the Reference Section. The reference information may be an estimating procedure, an alternate pricing method, or technical information.

Note: Not all subdivisions listed here necessarily appear. ■

Did you know?

RSMeans data is available through our online application with 24/7 access:
- Search for unit prices by keyword
- Leverage the most up-to-date data
- Build and export estimates

Try it free for 30 days!
www.rsmeans.com/2018freetrial

No part of this cost data may be reproduced, stored in a retrieval system, or transmitted in any form or by any means without prior written permission of Gordian.

22 07 Plumbing Insulation

22 07 16 – Plumbing Equipment Insulation

22 07 16.10 Insulation for Plumbing Equipment

		Crew	Daily Output	Labor-Hours	Unit	Material	2018 Bare Costs Labor	Equipment	Total	Total Incl O&P
0010	**INSULATION FOR PLUMBING EQUIPMENT**									
2900	Domestic water heater wrap kit									
2920	1-1/2" with vinyl jacket, 20 to 60 gal.	G	1 Plum	8	1	Ea.	16.50	62		78.50	112
2925	50 to 80 gal.	G	"	8	1	"	27.50	62		89.50	124

22 07 19 – Plumbing Piping Insulation

22 07 19.10 Piping Insulation

		Crew	Daily Output	Labor-Hours	Unit	Material	Labor	Equipment	Total	Total Incl O&P
0010	**PIPING INSULATION**									
0110	Insulation req'd. is based on the surface size/area to be covered									
0230	Insulated protectors (ADA)									
0235	For exposed piping under sinks or lavatories									
0240	Vinyl coated foam, velcro tabs									
0245	P Trap, 1-1/4" or 1-1/2"		1 Plum	32	.250	Ea.	15.90	15.55		31.45	41
0260	Valve and supply cover									
0265	1/2", 3/8", and 7/16" pipe size		1 Plum	32	.250	Ea.	15.60	15.55		31.15	40.50
0280	Tailpiece offset (wheelchair)									
0285	1-1/4" pipe size		1 Plum	32	.250	Ea.	12.90	15.55		28.45	37.50
0600	Pipe covering (price copper tube one size less than IPS)									
1000	Mineral wool									
1010	Preformed, 1200°F, plain									
1014	1" wall									
1016	1/2" iron pipe size	G	Q-14	230	.070	L.F.	1.65	3.53		5.18	7.25
1018	3/4" iron pipe size	G		220	.073		1.72	3.69		5.41	7.60
1022	1" iron pipe size	G		210	.076		1.77	3.86		5.63	7.95
1024	1-1/4" iron pipe size	G		205	.078		1.82	3.96		5.78	8.15
1026	1-1/2" iron pipe size	G		205	.078		1.90	3.96		5.86	8.25
1028	2" iron pipe size	G		200	.080		2.32	4.05		6.37	8.85
1030	2-1/2" iron pipe size	G		190	.084		2.46	4.27		6.73	9.30
1032	3" iron pipe size	G		180	.089		2.55	4.50		7.05	9.80
1034	4" iron pipe size	G		150	.107		3.14	5.40		8.54	11.85
1036	5" iron pipe size	G		140	.114		3.55	5.80		9.35	12.90
1038	6" iron pipe size	G		120	.133		3.79	6.75		10.54	14.65
1040	7" iron pipe size	G		110	.145		4.43	7.35		11.78	16.30
1042	8" iron pipe size	G		100	.160		6.10	8.10		14.20	19.30
1044	9" iron pipe size	G		90	.178		6.65	9		15.65	21.50
1046	10" iron pipe size	G		90	.178		7.50	9		16.50	22.50
1050	1-1/2" wall									
1052	1/2" iron pipe size	G	Q-14	225	.071	L.F.	2.82	3.60		6.42	8.70
1054	3/4" iron pipe size	G		215	.074		2.89	3.77		6.66	9.05
1056	1" iron pipe size			205	.078		2.93	3.96		6.89	9.35
1058	1-1/4" iron pipe size	G		200	.080		2.99	4.05		7.04	9.60
1060	1-1/2" iron pipe size	G		200	.080		3.14	4.05		7.19	9.75
1062	2" iron pipe size	G		190	.084		3.32	4.27		7.59	10.25
1064	2-1/2" iron pipe size	G		180	.089		3.62	4.50		8.12	11
1066	3" iron pipe size	G		165	.097		3.77	4.91		8.68	11.80
1068	4" iron pipe size	G		140	.114		4.53	5.80		10.33	14
1070	5" iron pipe size	G		130	.123		4.84	6.25		11.09	15
1072	6" iron pipe size	G		110	.145		4.99	7.35		12.34	16.95
1074	7" iron pipe size	G		100	.160		5.90	8.10		14	19.10
1076	8" iron pipe size	G		90	.178		6.55	9		15.55	21
1078	9" iron pipe size	G		85	.188		7.55	9.55		17.10	23
1080	10" iron pipe size	G		80	.200		8.30	10.15		18.45	25
1082	12" iron pipe size	G		75	.213		9.45	10.80		20.25	27

22 07 Plumbing Insulation

22 07 19 – Plumbing Piping Insulation

22 07 19.10 Piping Insulation		Crew	Daily Output	Labor-Hours	Unit	Material	2018 Bare Costs Labor	Equipment	Total	Total Incl O&P
1084	14" iron pipe size G	Q-14	70	.229	L.F.	10.80	11.60		22.40	30
1086	16" iron pipe size G		65	.246		12.30	12.45		24.75	33
1088	18" iron pipe size G		60	.267		13.85	13.50		27.35	36.50
1090	20" iron pipe size G		55	.291		15.25	14.75		30	40
1092	22" iron pipe size G		50	.320		17.45	16.20		33.65	44
1094	24" iron pipe size		45	.356		18.65	18		36.65	48.50
1100	2" wall									
1102	1/2" iron pipe size G	Q-14	220	.073	L.F.	3.65	3.69		7.34	9.70
1104	3/4" iron pipe size G		210	.076		3.78	3.86		7.64	10.15
1106	1" iron pipe size G		200	.080		4.01	4.05		8.06	10.70
1108	1-1/4" iron pipe size G		190	.084		4.30	4.27		8.57	11.35
1110	1-1/2" iron pipe size G		190	.084		4.48	4.27		8.75	11.55
1112	2" iron pipe size G		180	.089		4.70	4.50		9.20	12.15
1114	2-1/2" iron pipe size G		170	.094		5.30	4.77		10.07	13.25
1116	3" iron pipe size G		160	.100		5.70	5.05		10.75	14.10
1118	4" iron pipe size G		130	.123		6.60	6.25		12.85	17
1120	5" iron pipe size G		120	.133		7.35	6.75		14.10	18.60
1122	6" iron pipe size G		100	.160		7.65	8.10		15.75	21
1124	8" iron pipe size G		80	.200		9.25	10.15		19.40	26
1126	10" iron pipe size G		70	.229		11.35	11.60		22.95	30.50
1128	12" iron pipe size G		65	.246		12.55	12.45		25	33
1130	14" iron pipe size G		60	.267		14.05	13.50		27.55	36.50
1132	16" iron pipe size G		55	.291		15.90	14.75		30.65	40.50
1134	18" iron pipe size G		50	.320		17.20	16.20		33.40	44
1136	20" iron pipe size G		45	.356		19.80	18		37.80	50
1138	22" iron pipe size G		45	.356		21.50	18		39.50	51.50
1140	24" iron pipe size G		40	.400		22.50	20.50		43	56.50
1150	4" wall									
1152	1-1/4" iron pipe size G	Q-14	170	.094	L.F.	11.65	4.77		16.42	20
1154	1-1/2" iron pipe size G		165	.097		12.10	4.91		17.01	21
1156	2" iron pipe size G		155	.103		12.35	5.25		17.60	21.50
1158	4" iron pipe size G		105	.152		15.60	7.70		23.30	29
1160	6" iron pipe size G		75	.213		18.40	10.80		29.20	37
1162	8" iron pipe size G		60	.267		21	13.50		34.50	44
1164	10" iron pipe size G		50	.320		25	16.20		41.20	52.50
1166	12" iron pipe size G		45	.356		27.50	18		45.50	58.50
1168	14" iron pipe size G		40	.400		29.50	20.50		50	64
1170	16" iron pipe size G		35	.457		33.50	23		56.50	72.50
1172	18" iron pipe size G		32	.500		36	25.50		61.50	79
1174	20" iron pipe size G		30	.533		38.50	27		65.50	84.50
1176	22" iron pipe size G		28	.571		43.50	29		72.50	92.50
1178	24" iron pipe size G		26	.615		46	31		77	99
4280	Cellular glass, closed cell foam, all service jacket, sealant,									
4281	working temp. (-450°F to +900°F), 0 water vapor transmission									
4284	1" wall									
4286	1/2" iron pipe size G	Q-14	120	.133	L.F.	8.50	6.75		15.25	19.85
4300	1-1/2" wall									
4301	1" iron pipe size G	Q-14	105	.152	L.F.	10	7.70		17.70	23
4304	2-1/2" iron pipe size G		90	.178		13.65	9		22.65	29
4306	3" iron pipe size G		85	.188		16.95	9.55		26.50	33.50
4308	4" iron pipe size G		70	.229		20.50	11.60		32.10	40.50
4310	5" iron pipe size G		65	.246		21	12.45		33.45	43
4320	2" wall									

For customer support on your Green Building Costs with RSMeans data, call 800.448.8182.

199

22 07 Plumbing Insulation

22 07 19 – Plumbing Piping Insulation

22 07 19.10 Piping Insulation		Crew	Daily Output	Labor-Hours	Unit	Material	2018 Bare Costs Labor	Equipment	Total	Total Incl O&P
4322	1" iron pipe size	Q-14 G	100	.160	L.F.	13.35	8.10		21.45	27.50
4324	2-1/2" iron pipe size	G	85	.188		20.50	9.55		30.05	37.50
4326	3" iron pipe size	G	80	.200		20.50	10.15		30.65	38.50
4328	4" iron pipe size	G	65	.246		25	12.45		37.45	47
4330	5" iron pipe size	G	60	.267		26	13.50		39.50	49.50
4332	6" iron pipe size	G	50	.320		30	16.20		46.20	58
4336	8" iron pipe size	G	40	.400		35.50	20.50		56	70.50
4338	10" iron pipe size	G	35	.457		43.50	23		66.50	84
4350	2-1/2" wall									
4360	12" iron pipe size	Q-14 G	32	.500	L.F.	62	25.50		87.50	108
4362	14" iron pipe size	" G	28	.571	"	68	29		97	120
4370	3" wall									
4378	6" iron pipe size	Q-14 G	48	.333	L.F.	44	16.90		60.90	74.50
4380	8" iron pipe size	G	38	.421		55.50	21.50		77	94
4382	10" iron pipe size	G	33	.485		57.50	24.50		82	102
4384	16" iron pipe size	G	25	.640		81	32.50		113.50	140
4386	18" iron pipe size	G	22	.727		103	37		140	171
4388	20" iron pipe size	G	20	.800		113	40.50		153.50	187
4400	3-1/2" wall									
4412	12" iron pipe size	Q-14 G	27	.593	L.F.	69	30		99	122
4414	14" iron pipe size	" G	25	.640	"	71	32.50		103.50	129
4430	4" wall									
4446	16" iron pipe size	Q-14 G	22	.727	L.F.	92.50	37		129.50	159
4448	18" iron pipe size	G	20	.800		101	40.50		141.50	174
4450	20" iron pipe size	G	18	.889		114	45		159	195
4480	Fittings, average with fabric and mastic									
4484	1" wall									
4486	1/2" iron pipe size	1 Asbe G	40	.200	Ea.	5.65	11.25		16.90	23.50
4500	1-1/2" wall									
4502	1" iron pipe size	1 Asbe G	38	.211	Ea.	7.50	11.85		19.35	26.50
4504	2-1/2" iron pipe size	G	32	.250		13.60	14.10		27.70	37
4506	3" iron pipe size	G	30	.267		13.60	15		28.60	38.50
4508	4" iron pipe size	G	28	.286		17.15	16.10		33.25	44
4510	5" iron pipe size	G	24	.333		21	18.75		39.75	52
4520	2" wall									
4522	1" iron pipe size	1 Asbe G	36	.222	Ea.	10.90	12.50		23.40	31.50
4524	2-1/2" iron pipe size	G	30	.267		17.15	15		32.15	42.50
4526	3" iron pipe size	G	28	.286		17.15	16.10		33.25	44
4528	4" iron pipe size	G	24	.333		21	18.75		39.75	52
4530	5" iron pipe size	G	22	.364		31	20.50		51.50	66
4532	6" iron pipe size	G	20	.400		44	22.50		66.50	83
4536	8" iron pipe size	G	12	.667		73.50	37.50		111	139
4538	10" iron pipe size	G	8	1		85	56.50		141.50	181
4550	2-1/2" wall									
4560	12" iron pipe size	1 Asbe G	6	1.333	Ea.	156	75		231	289
4562	14" iron pipe size	" G	4	2	"	206	113		319	400
4570	3" wall									
4578	6" iron pipe size	1 Asbe G	16	.500	Ea.	63	28		91	113
4580	8" iron pipe size	G	10	.800		94.50	45		139.50	174
4582	10" iron pipe size	G	6	1.333		128	75		203	257
4900	Calcium silicate, with 8 oz. canvas cover									
5100	1" wall, 1/2" iron pipe size	Q-14 G	170	.094	L.F.	4.02	4.77		8.79	11.80
5130	3/4" iron pipe size	G	170	.094		4.05	4.77		8.82	11.85

22 07 Plumbing Insulation

22 07 19 – Plumbing Piping Insulation

22 07 19.10 Piping Insulation

			Crew	Daily Output	Labor-Hours	Unit	Material	2018 Bare Costs Labor	Equipment	Total	Total Incl O&P
5140	1" iron pipe size	G	Q-14	170	.094	L.F.	3.96	4.77		8.73	11.75
5150	1-1/4" iron pipe size	G		165	.097		4.02	4.91		8.93	12.05
5160	1-1/2" iron pipe size	G		165	.097		4.07	4.91		8.98	12.15
5170	2" iron pipe size	G		160	.100		4.71	5.05		9.76	13.05
5180	2-1/2" iron pipe size	G		160	.100		4.99	5.05		10.04	13.35
5190	3" iron pipe size	G		150	.107		5.40	5.40		10.80	14.35
5200	4" iron pipe size	G		140	.114		6.70	5.80		12.50	16.35
5210	5" iron pipe size	G		135	.119		7.05	6		13.05	17.05
5220	6" iron pipe size	G		130	.123		7.50	6.25		13.75	17.95
5280	1-1/2" wall, 1/2" iron pipe size	G		150	.107		4.36	5.40		9.76	13.20
5310	3/4" iron pipe size	G		150	.107		4.44	5.40		9.84	13.30
5320	1" iron pipe size	G		150	.107		4.83	5.40		10.23	13.70
5330	1-1/4" iron pipe size	G		145	.110		5.20	5.60		10.80	14.40
5340	1-1/2" iron pipe size	G		145	.110		5.55	5.60		11.15	14.85
5350	2" iron pipe size	G		140	.114		6.15	5.80		11.95	15.75
5360	2-1/2" iron pipe size	G		140	.114		6.70	5.80		12.50	16.35
5370	3" iron pipe size	G		135	.119		7.05	6		13.05	17.05
5380	4" iron pipe size	G		125	.128		8.15	6.50		14.65	19
5390	5" iron pipe size	G		120	.133		9.15	6.75		15.90	20.50
5400	6" iron pipe size	G		110	.145		9.50	7.35		16.85	22
5402	8" iron pipe size	G		95	.168		12.40	8.55		20.95	27
5404	10" iron pipe size	G		85	.188		16.25	9.55		25.80	32.50
5406	12" iron pipe size	G		80	.200		19.55	10.15		29.70	37.50
5408	14" iron pipe size	G		75	.213		21.50	10.80		32.30	40.50
5410	16" iron pipe size	G		70	.229		24	11.60		35.60	44.50
5412	18" iron pipe size	G		65	.246		26.50	12.45		38.95	49
5460	2" wall, 1/2" iron pipe size	G		135	.119		6.75	6		12.75	16.70
5490	3/4" iron pipe size	G		135	.119		7.10	6		13.10	17.10
5500	1" iron pipe size	G		135	.119		7.45	6		13.45	17.50
5510	1-1/4" iron pipe size	G		130	.123		8	6.25		14.25	18.50
5520	1-1/2" iron pipe size	G		130	.123		8.35	6.25		14.60	18.85
5530	2" iron pipe size	G		125	.128		8.80	6.50		15.30	19.75
5540	2-1/2" iron pipe size	G		125	.128		10.45	6.50		16.95	21.50
5550	3" iron pipe size	G		120	.133		10.55	6.75		17.30	22
5560	4" iron pipe size	G		115	.139		12.15	7.05		19.20	24.50
5570	5" iron pipe size	G		110	.145		13.85	7.35		21.20	26.50
5580	6" iron pipe size	G		105	.152		15.15	7.70		22.85	28.50
5581	8" iron pipe size	G		95	.168		18.05	8.55		26.60	33
5582	10" iron pipe size	G		85	.188		22.50	9.55		32.05	40
5583	12" iron pipe size	G		80	.200		25	10.15		35.15	43.50
5584	14" iron pipe size	G		75	.213		27.50	10.80		38.30	47.50
5585	16" iron pipe size	G		70	.229		30.50	11.60		42.10	51.50
5586	18" iron pipe size	G		65	.246		33	12.45		45.45	56
5587	3" wall, 1-1/4" iron pipe size	G		100	.160		12.35	8.10		20.45	26
5588	1-1/2" iron pipe size	G		100	.160		12.45	8.10		20.55	26.50
5589	2" iron pipe size	G		95	.168		12.90	8.55		21.45	27.50
5590	2-1/2" iron pipe size	G		95	.168		15	8.55		23.55	30
5591	3" iron pipe size	G		90	.178		15.20	9		24.20	30.50
5592	4" iron pipe size	G		85	.188		19.20	9.55		28.75	36
5593	6" iron pipe size	G		80	.200		23.50	10.15		33.65	42
5594	8" iron pipe size	G		75	.213		28	10.80		38.80	47.50
5595	10" iron pipe size	G		65	.246		33.50	12.45		45.95	56.50
5596	12" iron pipe size	G		60	.267		37	13.50		50.50	62

For customer support on your Green Building Costs with RSMeans data, call 800.448.8182.

22 07 Plumbing Insulation

22 07 19 – Plumbing Piping Insulation

22 07 19.10 Piping Insulation

		Crew	Daily Output	Labor-Hours	Unit	Material	2018 Bare Costs Labor	Equipment	Total	Total Incl O&P
5597	14" iron pipe size	Q-14 G	55	.291	L.F.	41.50	14.75		56.25	68.50
5598	16" iron pipe size	G	50	.320		46	16.20		62.20	75.50
5599	18" iron pipe size	G	45	.356		50.50	18		68.50	83.50
5600	Calcium silicate, no cover									
5720	1" wall, 1/2" iron pipe size	Q-14 G	180	.089	L.F.	3.67	4.50		8.17	11.05
5740	3/4" iron pipe size	G	180	.089		3.67	4.50		8.17	11.05
5750	1" iron pipe size	G	180	.089		3.51	4.50		8.01	10.85
5760	1-1/4" iron pipe size	G	175	.091		3.58	4.63		8.21	11.15
5770	1-1/2" iron pipe size	G	175	.091		3.61	4.63		8.24	11.15
5780	2" iron pipe size	G	170	.094		4.15	4.77		8.92	11.95
5790	2-1/2" iron pipe size	G	170	.094		4.39	4.77		9.16	12.25
5800	3" iron pipe size	G	160	.100		4.72	5.05		9.77	13.05
5810	4" iron pipe size	G	150	.107		5.90	5.40		11.30	14.90
5820	5" iron pipe size	G	145	.110		6.15	5.60		11.75	15.45
5830	6" iron pipe size	G	140	.114		6.45	5.80		12.25	16.10
5900	1-1/2" wall, 1/2" iron pipe size	G	160	.100		3.88	5.05		8.93	12.10
5920	3/4" iron pipe size	G	160	.100		3.94	5.05		8.99	12.20
5930	1" iron pipe size	G	160	.100		4.29	5.05		9.34	12.55
5940	1-1/4" iron pipe size	G	155	.103		4.63	5.25		9.88	13.20
5950	1-1/2" iron pipe size	G	155	.103		4.98	5.25		10.23	13.60
5960	2" iron pipe size	G	150	.107		5.50	5.40		10.90	14.45
5970	2-1/2" iron pipe size	G	150	.107		6	5.40		11.40	15
5980	3" iron pipe size	G	145	.110		6.25	5.60		11.85	15.60
5990	4" iron pipe size	G	135	.119		7.25	6		13.25	17.25
6000	5" iron pipe size	G	130	.123		8.15	6.25		14.40	18.70
6010	6" iron pipe size	G	120	.133		8.35	6.75		15.10	19.65
6020	7" iron pipe size	G	115	.139		9.80	7.05		16.85	21.50
6030	8" iron pipe size	G	105	.152		11.05	7.70		18.75	24
6040	9" iron pipe size	G	100	.160		13.25	8.10		21.35	27
6050	10" iron pipe size	G	95	.168		14.60	8.55		23.15	29.50
6060	12" iron pipe size	G	90	.178		17.35	9		26.35	33
6070	14" iron pipe size	G	85	.188		19.60	9.55		29.15	36.50
6080	16" iron pipe size	G	80	.200		22	10.15		32.15	40
6090	18" iron pipe size	G	75	.213		24.50	10.80		35.30	43.50
6120	2" wall, 1/2" iron pipe size	G	145	.110		6.10	5.60		11.70	15.45
6140	3/4" iron pipe size	G	145	.110		6.45	5.60		12.05	15.80
6150	1" iron pipe size	G	145	.110		6.80	5.60		12.40	16.20
6160	1-1/4" iron pipe size	G	140	.114		7.30	5.80		13.10	17
6170	1-1/2" iron pipe size	G	140	.114		7.60	5.80		13.40	17.35
6180	2" iron pipe size	G	135	.119		8	6		14	18.10
6190	2-1/2" iron pipe size	G	135	.119		9.60	6		15.60	19.85
6200	3" iron pipe size	G	130	.123		9.65	6.25		15.90	20.50
6210	4" iron pipe size	G	125	.128		11.15	6.50		17.65	22.50
6220	5" iron pipe size	G	120	.133		12.70	6.75		19.45	24.50
6230	6" iron pipe size	G	115	.139		13.90	7.05		20.95	26.50
6240	7" iron pipe size	G	110	.145		15.05	7.35		22.40	28
6250	8" iron pipe size	G	105	.152		16.90	7.70		24.60	30.50
6260	9" iron pipe size	G	100	.160		18.75	8.10		26.85	33
6270	10" iron pipe size	G	95	.168		21	8.55		29.55	36.50
6280	12" iron pipe size	G	90	.178		23	9		32	39.50
6290	14" iron pipe size	G	85	.188		25.50	9.55		35.05	43
6300	16" iron pipe size	G	80	.200		28	10.15		38.15	47
6310	18" iron pipe size	G	75	.213		30.50	10.80		41.30	50.50

For customer support on your Green Building Costs with RSMeans data, call 800.448.8182.

22 07 Plumbing Insulation

22 07 19 – Plumbing Piping Insulation

22 07 19.10 Piping Insulation		Crew	Daily Output	Labor-Hours	Unit	Material	2018 Bare Costs Labor	Equipment	Total	Total Incl O&P
6320	20" iron pipe size G	Q-14	65	.246	L.F.	37.50	12.45		49.95	61
6330	22" iron pipe size G		60	.267		41.50	13.50		55	67
6340	24" iron pipe size G		55	.291		42.50	14.75		57.25	70
6360	3" wall, 1/2" iron pipe size G		115	.139		11.10	7.05		18.15	23
6380	3/4" iron pipe size G		115	.139		11.20	7.05		18.25	23.50
6390	1" iron pipe size G		115	.139		11.25	7.05		18.30	23.50
6400	1-1/4" iron pipe size G		110	.145		11.40	7.35		18.75	24
6410	1-1/2" iron pipe size G		110	.145		11.45	7.35		18.80	24
6420	2" iron pipe size G		105	.152		11.85	7.70		19.55	25
6430	2-1/2" iron pipe size G		105	.152		13.95	7.70		21.65	27.50
6440	3" iron pipe size G		100	.160		14.05	8.10		22.15	28
6450	4" iron pipe size G		95	.168		18	8.55		26.55	33
6460	5" iron pipe size G		90	.178		19.50	9		28.50	35.50
6470	6" iron pipe size G		90	.178		22	9		31	38
6480	7" iron pipe size G		85	.188		24.50	9.55		34.05	42
6490	8" iron pipe size G		85	.188		26	9.55		35.55	43.50
6500	9" iron pipe size G		80	.200		29.50	10.15		39.65	48.50
6510	10" iron pipe size G		75	.213		31.50	10.80		42.30	51.50
6520	12" iron pipe size G		70	.229		35	11.60		46.60	56.50
6530	14" iron pipe size G		65	.246		39	12.45		51.45	62.50
6540	16" iron pipe size G		60	.267		43	13.50		56.50	68.50
6550	18" iron pipe size G		55	.291		47.50	14.75		62.25	75
6560	20" iron pipe size G		50	.320		56.50	16.20		72.70	87
6570	22" iron pipe size G		45	.356		61	18		79	95.50
6580	24" iron pipe size G		40	.400		66	20.50		86.50	104
6600	Fiberglass, with all service jacket									
6640	1/2" wall, 1/2" iron pipe size G	Q-14	250	.064	L.F.	.69	3.24		3.93	5.80
6660	3/4" iron pipe size G		240	.067		.79	3.38		4.17	6.10
6670	1" iron pipe size G		230	.070		.82	3.53		4.35	6.35
6680	1-1/4" iron pipe size G		220	.073		.87	3.69		4.56	6.65
6690	1-1/2" iron pipe size G		220	.073		1	3.69		4.69	6.80
6700	2" iron pipe size G		210	.076		1.07	3.86		4.93	7.20
6710	2-1/2" iron pipe size G		200	.080		1.11	4.05		5.16	7.50
6840	1" wall, 1/2" iron pipe size G		240	.067		.85	3.38		4.23	6.20
6860	3/4" iron pipe size G		230	.070		.92	3.53		4.45	6.45
6870	1" iron pipe size G		220	.073		.99	3.69		4.68	6.80
6880	1-1/4" iron pipe size G		210	.076		1.07	3.86		4.93	7.20
6890	1-1/2" iron pipe size G		210	.076		1.15	3.86		5.01	7.25
6900	2" iron pipe size G		200	.080		1.53	4.05		5.58	8
6910	2-1/2" iron pipe size G		190	.084		1.73	4.27		6	8.50
6920	3" iron pipe size G		180	.089		1.86	4.50		6.36	9.05
6930	3-1/2" iron pipe size G		170	.094		2.01	4.77		6.78	9.60
6940	4" iron pipe size G		150	.107		2.48	5.40		7.88	11.15
6950	5" iron pipe size G		140	.114		2.74	5.80		8.54	12
6960	6" iron pipe size G		120	.133		2.95	6.75		9.70	13.75
6970	7" iron pipe size G		110	.145		3.51	7.35		10.86	15.30
6980	8" iron pipe size G		100	.160		4.81	8.10		12.91	17.90
6990	9" iron pipe size G		90	.178		5.05	9		14.05	19.60
7000	10" iron pipe size G		90	.178		5.15	9		14.15	19.70
7010	12" iron pipe size G		80	.200		5.60	10.15		15.75	22
7020	14" iron pipe size G		80	.200		6.75	10.15		16.90	23
7030	16" iron pipe size G		70	.229		8.55	11.60		20.15	27.50
7040	18" iron pipe size G		70	.229		9.50	11.60		21.10	28.50

For customer support on your Green Building Costs with RSMeans data, call 800.448.8182.

22 07 Plumbing Insulation

22 07 19 – Plumbing Piping Insulation

22 07 19.10 Piping Insulation		Crew	Daily Output	Labor-Hours	Unit	Material	2018 Bare Costs Labor	Equipment	Total	Total Incl O&P
7050	20" iron pipe size	G Q-14	60	.267	L.F.	10.60	13.50		24.10	32.50
7060	24" iron pipe size	G	60	.267		12.90	13.50		26.40	35
7080	1-1/2" wall, 1/2" iron pipe size	G	230	.070		1.98	3.53		5.51	7.65
7100	3/4" iron pipe size	G	220	.073		1.98	3.69		5.67	7.90
7110	1" iron pipe size	G	210	.076		2.12	3.86		5.98	8.35
7120	1-1/4" iron pipe size	G	200	.080		2.31	4.05		6.36	8.85
7130	1-1/2" iron pipe size	G	200	.080		2.42	4.05		6.47	8.95
7140	2" iron pipe size	G	190	.084		2.67	4.27		6.94	9.55
7150	2-1/2" iron pipe size	G	180	.089		2.86	4.50		7.36	10.15
7160	3" iron pipe size	G	170	.094		2.99	4.77		7.76	10.70
7170	3-1/2" iron pipe size	G	160	.100		3.28	5.05		8.33	11.45
7180	4" iron pipe size	G	140	.114		3.40	5.80		9.20	12.75
7190	5" iron pipe size	G	130	.123		3.81	6.25		10.06	13.90
7200	6" iron pipe size	G	110	.145		4.03	7.35		11.38	15.90
7210	7" iron pipe size	G	100	.160		4.47	8.10		12.57	17.50
7220	8" iron pipe size	G	90	.178		5.65	9		14.65	20
7230	9" iron pipe size	G	85	.188		5.90	9.55		15.45	21.50
7240	10" iron pipe size	G	80	.200		6.10	10.15		16.25	22.50
7250	12" iron pipe size	G	75	.213		6.90	10.80		17.70	24.50
7260	14" iron pipe size	G	70	.229		8.25	11.60		19.85	27
7270	16" iron pipe size	G	65	.246		10.75	12.45		23.20	31
7280	18" iron pipe size	G	60	.267		12.05	13.50		25.55	34.50
7290	20" iron pipe size	G	55	.291		12.30	14.75		27.05	36.50
7300	24" iron pipe size	G	50	.320		15.05	16.20		31.25	41.50
7320	2" wall, 1/2" iron pipe size	G	220	.073		3.07	3.69		6.76	9.10
7340	3/4" iron pipe size	G	210	.076		3.17	3.86		7.03	9.50
7350	1" iron pipe size	G	200	.080		3.37	4.05		7.42	10
7360	1-1/4" iron pipe size	G	190	.084		3.56	4.27		7.83	10.50
7370	1-1/2" iron pipe size	G	190	.084		3.99	4.27		8.26	11
7380	2" iron pipe size	G	180	.089		3.91	4.50		8.41	11.30
7390	2-1/2" iron pipe size	G	170	.094		4.21	4.77		8.98	12.05
7400	3" iron pipe size	G	160	.100		4.47	5.05		9.52	12.75
7410	3-1/2" iron pipe size	G	150	.107		4.85	5.40		10.25	13.75
7420	4" iron pipe size	G	130	.123		5.60	6.25		11.85	15.85
7430	5" iron pipe size	G	120	.133		5.95	6.75		12.70	17.05
7440	6" iron pipe size	G	100	.160		6.40	8.10		14.50	19.60
7450	7" iron pipe size	G	90	.178		7	9		16	21.50
7460	8" iron pipe size	G	80	.200		7.50	10.15		17.65	24
7470	9" iron pipe size	G	75	.213		8.20	10.80		19	26
7480	10" iron pipe size	G	70	.229		8.95	11.60		20.55	28
7490	12" iron pipe size	G	65	.246		10.05	12.45		22.50	30.50
7500	14" iron pipe size	G	60	.267		12.90	13.50		26.40	35
7510	16" iron pipe size	G	55	.291		14.20	14.75		28.95	38.50
7520	18" iron pipe size	G	50	.320		15.85	16.20		32.05	42.50
7530	20" iron pipe size	G	45	.356		17.95	18		35.95	48
7540	24" iron pipe size	G	40	.400		19.25	20.50		39.75	52.50
7560	2-1/2" wall, 1/2" iron pipe size	G	210	.076		3.63	3.86		7.49	10
7562	3/4" iron pipe size	G	200	.080		3.80	4.05		7.85	10.50
7564	1" iron pipe size	G	190	.084		3.96	4.27		8.23	10.95
7566	1-1/4" iron pipe size	G	185	.086		4.10	4.38		8.48	11.30
7568	1-1/2" iron pipe size	G	180	.089		4.31	4.50		8.81	11.75
7570	2" iron pipe size	G	170	.094		4.53	4.77		9.30	12.40
7572	2-1/2" iron pipe size	G	160	.100		5.20	5.05		10.25	13.60

22 07 Plumbing Insulation

22 07 19 – Plumbing Piping Insulation

22 07 19.10 Piping Insulation

			Crew	Daily Output	Labor-Hours	Unit	Material	2018 Bare Costs Labor	Equipment	Total	Total Incl O&P
7574		3" iron pipe size	G Q-14	150	.107	L.F.	5.50	5.40		10.90	14.45
7576		3-1/2" iron pipe size	G	140	.114		5.95	5.80		11.75	15.55
7578		4" iron pipe size	G	120	.133		6.30	6.75		13.05	17.40
7580		5" iron pipe size	G	110	.145		7.50	7.35		14.85	19.70
7582		6" iron pipe size	G	90	.178		9.05	9		18.05	24
7584		7" iron pipe size	G	80	.200		9.10	10.15		19.25	26
7586		8" iron pipe size	G	70	.229		9.65	11.60		21.25	28.50
7588		9" iron pipe size	G	65	.246		10.55	12.45		23	31
7590		10" iron pipe size	G	60	.267		11.50	13.50		25	33.50
7592		12" iron pipe size	G	55	.291		13.95	14.75		28.70	38.50
7594		14" iron pipe size	G	50	.320		16.30	16.20		32.50	43
7596		16" iron pipe size	G	45	.356		18.70	18		36.70	48.50
7598		18" iron pipe size	G	40	.400		20.50	20.50		41	54
7602		24" iron pipe size	G	30	.533		27	27		54	71.50
7620	3" wall, 1/2" iron pipe size		G	200	.080		4.65	4.05		8.70	11.40
7622		3/4" iron pipe size	G	190	.084		4.92	4.27		9.19	12
7624		1" iron pipe size	G	180	.089		5.20	4.50		9.70	12.75
7626		1-1/4" iron pipe size	G	175	.091		5.30	4.63		9.93	13.05
7628		1-1/2" iron pipe size	G	170	.094		5.55	4.77		10.32	13.50
7630		2" iron pipe size	G	160	.100		6	5.05		11.05	14.45
7632		2-1/2" iron pipe size	G	150	.107		6.25	5.40		11.65	15.30
7634		3" iron pipe size	G	140	.114		6.65	5.80		12.45	16.30
7636		3-1/2" iron pipe size	G	130	.123		7.35	6.25		13.60	17.75
7638		4" iron pipe size	G	110	.145		7.90	7.35		15.25	20
7640		5" iron pipe size	G	100	.160		8.90	8.10		17	22.50
7642		6" iron pipe size	G	80	.200		9.55	10.15		19.70	26.50
7644		7" iron pipe size	G	70	.229		10.90	11.60		22.50	30
7646		8" iron pipe size	G	60	.267		11.90	13.50		25.40	34
7648		9" iron pipe size	G	55	.291		12.80	14.75		27.55	37
7650		10" iron pipe size	G	50	.320		13.75	16.20		29.95	40
7652		12" iron pipe size	G	45	.356		17.10	18		35.10	47
7654		14" iron pipe size	G	40	.400		19.70	20.50		40.20	53
7656		16" iron pipe size	G	35	.457		22.50	23		45.50	60.50
7658		18" iron pipe size	G	32	.500		24	25.50		49.50	66
7660		20" iron pipe size	G	30	.533		26	27		53	70.50
7662		24" iron pipe size	G	28	.571		33	29		62	81.50
7664		26" iron pipe size	G	26	.615		36.50	31		67.50	88.50
7666		30" iron pipe size	G	24	.667		43	34		77	100
7800		For fiberglass with standard canvas jacket, deduct					5%				
7802		For fittings, add 3 L.F. for each fitting									
7804		plus 4 L.F. for each flange of the fitting									
7810		Finishes									
7812		For .016" aluminum jacket, add	G Q-14	200	.080	S.F.	1.01	4.05		5.06	7.40
7813		For .010" stainless steel, add	G "	160	.100	"	3.15	5.05		8.20	11.30
7820	Polyethylene tubing flexible closed cell foam, UV resistant										
7828		Standard temperature (-90°F to +212°F)									
7830		3/8" wall, 1/8" iron pipe size	G 1 Asbe	130	.062	L.F.	.27	3.46		3.73	5.70
7831		1/4" iron pipe size	G	130	.062		.28	3.46		3.74	5.70
7832		3/8" iron pipe size	G	130	.062		.31	3.46		3.77	5.75
7833		1/2" iron pipe size	G	126	.063		.35	3.57		3.92	5.95
7834		3/4" iron pipe size	G	122	.066		.41	3.69		4.10	6.20
7835		1" iron pipe size	G	120	.067		.46	3.75		4.21	6.35
7836		1-1/4" iron pipe size	G	118	.068		.57	3.82		4.39	6.60

For customer support on your Green Building Costs with RSMeans data, call 800.448.8182.

22 07 Plumbing Insulation

22 07 19 – Plumbing Piping Insulation

22 07 19.10 Piping Insulation		Crew	Daily Output	Labor-Hours	Unit	Material	2018 Bare Costs Labor	Equipment	Total	Total Incl O&P
7837	1-1/2" iron pipe size [G]	1 Asbe	118	.068	L.F.	.71	3.82		4.53	6.75
7838	2" iron pipe size [G]		116	.069		.95	3.88		4.83	7.10
7839	2-1/2" iron pipe size [G]		114	.070		1.21	3.95		5.16	7.50
7840	3" iron pipe size [G]		112	.071		1.86	4.02		5.88	8.30
7842	1/2" wall, 1/8" iron pipe size [G]		120	.067		.39	3.75		4.14	6.30
7843	1/4" iron pipe size [G]		120	.067		.42	3.75		4.17	6.30
7844	3/8" iron pipe size [G]		120	.067		.46	3.75		4.21	6.35
7845	1/2" iron pipe size [G]		118	.068		.52	3.82		4.34	6.50
7846	3/4" iron pipe size [G]		116	.069		.59	3.88		4.47	6.70
7847	1" iron pipe size [G]		114	.070		.66	3.95		4.61	6.90
7848	1-1/4" iron pipe size [G]		112	.071		.77	4.02		4.79	7.10
7849	1-1/2" iron pipe size [G]		110	.073		.92	4.09		5.01	7.35
7850	2" iron pipe size [G]		108	.074		1.32	4.17		5.49	7.90
7851	2-1/2" iron pipe size [G]		106	.075		1.63	4.25		5.88	8.40
7852	3" iron pipe size [G]		104	.077		2.25	4.33		6.58	9.20
7853	3-1/2" iron pipe size [G]		102	.078		2.55	4.42		6.97	9.65
7854	4" iron pipe size [G]		100	.080		2.90	4.50		7.40	10.20
7855	3/4" wall, 1/8" iron pipe size [G]		110	.073		.59	4.09		4.68	7
7856	1/4" iron pipe size [G]		110	.073		.63	4.09		4.72	7.05
7857	3/8" iron pipe size [G]		108	.074		.73	4.17		4.90	7.25
7858	1/2" iron pipe size [G]		106	.075		.87	4.25		5.12	7.55
7859	3/4" iron pipe size [G]		104	.077		1.05	4.33		5.38	7.85
7860	1" iron pipe size [G]		102	.078		1.21	4.42		5.63	8.20
7861	1-1/4" iron pipe size [G]		100	.080		1.64	4.50		6.14	8.80
7862	1-1/2" iron pipe size [G]		100	.080		1.86	4.50		6.36	9.05
7863	2" iron pipe size [G]		98	.082		2.36	4.60		6.96	9.75
7864	2-1/2" iron pipe size [G]		96	.083		2.85	4.69		7.54	10.45
7865	3" iron pipe size [G]		94	.085		3.76	4.79		8.55	11.60
7866	3-1/2" iron pipe size [G]		92	.087		4.18	4.90		9.08	12.20
7867	4" iron pipe size [G]		90	.089		4.67	5		9.67	12.90
7868	1" wall, 1/4" iron pipe size [G]		100	.080		1.27	4.50		5.77	8.40
7869	3/8" iron pipe size [G]		98	.082		1.29	4.60		5.89	8.55
7870	1/2" iron pipe size [G]		96	.083		1.61	4.69		6.30	9.05
7871	3/4" iron pipe size [G]		94	.085		1.87	4.79		6.66	9.50
7872	1" iron pipe size [G]		92	.087		2.27	4.90		7.17	10.10
7873	1-1/4" iron pipe size [G]		90	.089		2.59	5		7.59	10.60
7874	1-1/2" iron pipe size [G]		90	.089		2.96	5		7.96	11
7875	2" iron pipe size [G]		88	.091		3.85	5.10		8.95	12.20
7876	2-1/2" iron pipe size [G]		86	.093		5.05	5.25		10.30	13.70
7877	3" iron pipe size [G]		84	.095		5.65	5.35		11	14.50
7878	Contact cement, quart can [G]				Ea.	12.50			12.50	13.75
7879	Rubber tubing, flexible closed cell foam									
7880	3/8" wall, 1/4" iron pipe size [G]	1 Asbe	120	.067	L.F.	.31	3.75		4.06	6.20
7900	3/8" iron pipe size [G]		120	.067		.44	3.75		4.19	6.35
7910	1/2" iron pipe size [G]		115	.070		.47	3.92		4.39	6.60
7920	3/4" iron pipe size [G]		115	.070		.54	3.92		4.46	6.70
7930	1" iron pipe size [G]		110	.073		.57	4.09		4.66	7
7940	1-1/4" iron pipe size [G]		110	.073		.65	4.09		4.74	7.05
7950	1-1/2" iron pipe size [G]		110	.073		.75	4.09		4.84	7.20
8100	1/2" wall, 1/4" iron pipe size [G]		90	.089		.72	5		5.72	8.55
8120	3/8" iron pipe size [G]		90	.089		.77	5		5.77	8.60
8130	1/2" iron pipe size [G]		89	.090		.84	5.05		5.89	8.75
8140	3/4" iron pipe size [G]		89	.090		.95	5.05		6	8.90

206   For customer support on your Green Building Costs with RSMeans data, call 800.448.8182.

22 07 Plumbing Insulation

22 07 19 – Plumbing Piping Insulation

22 07 19.10 Piping Insulation		Crew	Daily Output	Labor-Hours	Unit	Material	2018 Bare Costs Labor	Equipment	Total	Total Incl O&P
8150	1" iron pipe size	G 1 Asbe	88	.091	L.F.	.82	5.10		5.92	8.85
8160	1-1/4" iron pipe size	G	87	.092		1.17	5.20		6.37	9.35
8170	1-1/2" iron pipe size	G	87	.092		1.49	5.20		6.69	9.70
8180	2" iron pipe size	G	86	.093		1.91	5.25		7.16	10.25
8190	2-1/2" iron pipe size	G	86	.093		2.22	5.25		7.47	10.60
8200	3" iron pipe size	G	85	.094		2.37	5.30		7.67	10.85
8210	3-1/2" iron pipe size	G	85	.094		3.31	5.30		8.61	11.90
8220	4" iron pipe size	G	80	.100		3.57	5.65		9.22	12.70
8230	5" iron pipe size	G	80	.100		4.87	5.65		10.52	14.10
8240	6" iron pipe size	G	75	.107		4.87	6		10.87	14.65
8300	3/4" wall, 1/4" iron pipe size	G	90	.089		.89	5		5.89	8.75
8320	3/8" iron pipe size	G	90	.089		1	5		6	8.85
8330	1/2" iron pipe size	G	89	.090		1.09	5.05		6.14	9.05
8340	3/4" iron pipe size	G	89	.090		1.54	5.05		6.59	9.55
8350	1" iron pipe size	G	88	.091		1.77	5.10		6.87	9.90
8360	1-1/4" iron pipe size	G	87	.092		2.39	5.20		7.59	10.70
8370	1-1/2" iron pipe size	G	87	.092		2.62	5.20		7.82	10.95
8380	2" iron pipe size	G	86	.093		3.04	5.25		8.29	11.50
8390	2-1/2" iron pipe size	G	86	.093		4.22	5.25		9.47	12.80
8400	3" iron pipe size	G	85	.094		4.77	5.30		10.07	13.50
8410	3-1/2" iron pipe size	G	85	.094		4.81	5.30		10.11	13.55
8420	4" iron pipe size	G	80	.100		6	5.65		11.65	15.35
8430	5" iron pipe size	G	80	.100		7.15	5.65		12.80	16.60
8440	6" iron pipe size	G	80	.100		8.70	5.65		14.35	18.30
8444	1" wall, 1/2" iron pipe size	G	86	.093		2.32	5.25		7.57	10.70
8445	3/4" iron pipe size	G	84	.095		2.81	5.35		8.16	11.40
8446	1" iron pipe size	G	84	.095		3.39	5.35		8.74	12.05
8447	1-1/4" iron pipe size	G	82	.098		3.75	5.50		9.25	12.70
8448	1-1/2" iron pipe size	G	82	.098		4.88	5.50		10.38	13.90
8449	2" iron pipe size	G	80	.100		6.10	5.65		11.75	15.45
8450	2-1/2" iron pipe size	G	80	.100		7.45	5.65		13.10	16.95
8456	Rubber insulation tape, 1/8" x 2" x 30'	G			Ea.	21			21	23
8460	Polyolefin tubing, flexible closed cell foam, UV stabilized, work									
8462	temp. -165°F to +210°F, 0 water vapor transmission									
8464	3/8" wall, 1/8" iron pipe size	G 1 Asbe	140	.057	L.F.	.48	3.22		3.70	5.50
8466	1/4" iron pipe size	G	140	.057		.50	3.22		3.72	5.55
8468	3/8" iron pipe size	G	140	.057		.55	3.22		3.77	5.60
8470	1/2" iron pipe size	G	136	.059		.62	3.31		3.93	5.85
8472	3/4" iron pipe size	G	132	.061		.62	3.41		4.03	6
8474	1" iron pipe size	G	130	.062		.83	3.46		4.29	6.30
8476	1-1/4" iron pipe size	G	128	.063		1.02	3.52		4.54	6.55
8478	1-1/2" iron pipe size	G	128	.063		1.25	3.52		4.77	6.85
8480	2" iron pipe size	G	126	.063		1.50	3.57		5.07	7.20
8482	2-1/2" iron pipe size	G	123	.065		2.17	3.66		5.83	8.10
8484	3" iron pipe size	G	121	.066		2.42	3.72		6.14	8.45
8486	4" iron pipe size	G	118	.068		4.52	3.82		8.34	10.90
8500	1/2" wall, 1/8" iron pipe size	G	130	.062		.71	3.46		4.17	6.20
8502	1/4" iron pipe size	G	130	.062		.76	3.46		4.22	6.25
8504	3/8" iron pipe size	G	130	.062		.82	3.46		4.28	6.30
8506	1/2" iron pipe size	G	128	.063		.88	3.52		4.40	6.40
8508	3/4" iron pipe size	G	126	.063		1.02	3.57		4.59	6.65
8510	1" iron pipe size	G	123	.065		1.18	3.66		4.84	7
8512	1-1/4" iron pipe size	G	121	.066		1.39	3.72		5.11	7.35

For customer support on your Green Building Costs with RSMeans data, call 800.448.8182.

22 07 Plumbing Insulation

22 07 19 – Plumbing Piping Insulation

22 07 19.10 Piping Insulation

			Crew	Daily Output	Labor-Hours	Unit	Material	2018 Bare Costs Labor	Equipment	Total	Total Incl O&P
8514	1-1/2" iron pipe size	G	1 Asbe	119	.067	L.F.	1.67	3.79		5.46	7.75
8516	2" iron pipe size	G		117	.068		2.11	3.85		5.96	8.30
8518	2-1/2" iron pipe size	G		114	.070		2.85	3.95		6.80	9.30
8520	3" iron pipe size	G		112	.071		3.72	4.02		7.74	10.35
8522	4" iron pipe size	G		110	.073		5.15	4.09		9.24	12
8534	3/4" wall, 1/8" iron pipe size	G		120	.067		1.08	3.75		4.83	7.05
8536	1/4" iron pipe size	G		120	.067		1.14	3.75		4.89	7.10
8538	3/8" iron pipe size	G		117	.068		1.31	3.85		5.16	7.45
8540	1/2" iron pipe size	G		114	.070		1.45	3.95		5.40	7.75
8542	3/4" iron pipe size	G		112	.071		1.57	4.02		5.59	8
8544	1" iron pipe size	G		110	.073		2.20	4.09		6.29	8.75
8546	1-1/4" iron pipe size	G		108	.074		2.86	4.17		7.03	9.60
8548	1-1/2" iron pipe size	G		108	.074		3.44	4.17		7.61	10.25
8550	2" iron pipe size	G		106	.075		4.35	4.25		8.60	11.40
8552	2-1/2" iron pipe size	G		104	.077		5.50	4.33		9.83	12.75
8554	3" iron pipe size	G		102	.078		6.85	4.42		11.27	14.35
8556	4" iron pipe size	G		100	.080		9	4.50		13.50	16.90
8570	1" wall, 1/8" iron pipe size	G		110	.073		1.95	4.09		6.04	8.50
8572	1/4" iron pipe size	G		108	.074		2.06	4.17		6.23	8.70
8574	3/8" iron pipe size	G		106	.075		2.04	4.25		6.29	8.85
8576	1/2" iron pipe size	G		104	.077		2.16	4.33		6.49	9.10
8578	3/4" iron pipe size	G		102	.078		2.83	4.42		7.25	9.95
8580	1" iron pipe size	G		100	.080		3.27	4.50		7.77	10.60
8582	1-1/4" iron pipe size	G		97	.082		3.72	4.64		8.36	11.30
8584	1-1/2" iron pipe size	G		97	.082		4.25	4.64		8.89	11.90
8586	2" iron pipe size	G		95	.084		6	4.74		10.74	13.95
8588	2-1/2" iron pipe size	G		93	.086		7.85	4.84		12.69	16.15
8590	3" iron pipe size	G		91	.088		9.55	4.95		14.50	18.20
8606	Contact adhesive (R-320)	G				Qt.	18.20			18.20	20
8608	Contact adhesive (R-320)	G				Gal.	73			73	80.50
8610	NOTE: Preslit/preglued vs unslit, same price										

22 07 19.30 Piping Insulation Protective Jacketing, PVC

0010	**PIPING INSULATION PROTECTIVE JACKETING, PVC**										
0100	PVC, white, 48" lengths cut from roll goods										
0120	20 mil thick										
0140	Size based on OD of insulation										
0150	1-1/2" ID		Q-14	270	.059	L.F.	.24	3		3.24	4.92
0152	2" ID			260	.062		.32	3.12		3.44	5.20
0154	2-1/2" ID			250	.064		.38	3.24		3.62	5.45
0156	3" ID			240	.067		.46	3.38		3.84	5.75
0158	3-1/2" ID			230	.070		.52	3.53		4.05	6
0160	4" ID			220	.073		.59	3.69		4.28	6.35
0162	4-1/2" ID			210	.076		.66	3.86		4.52	6.75
0164	5" ID			200	.080		.72	4.05		4.77	7.10
0166	5-1/2" ID			190	.084		.79	4.27		5.06	7.45
0168	6" ID			180	.089		.86	4.50		5.36	7.95
0170	6-1/2" ID			175	.091		.93	4.63		5.56	8.20
0172	7" ID			170	.094		.99	4.77		5.76	8.50
0174	7-1/2" ID			164	.098		1.07	4.94		6.01	8.85
0176	8" ID			161	.099		1.13	5.05		6.18	9.05
0178	8-1/2" ID			158	.101		1.20	5.15		6.35	9.25
0180	9" ID			155	.103		1.27	5.25		6.52	9.50

22 07 Plumbing Insulation

22 07 19 – Plumbing Piping Insulation

22 07 19.30 Piping Insulation Protective Jacketing, PVC

		Crew	Daily Output	Labor-Hours	Unit	Material	2018 Bare Costs Labor	Equipment	Total	Total Incl O&P
0182	9-1/2" ID	Q-14	152	.105	L.F.	1.34	5.35		6.69	9.75
0184	10" ID		149	.107		1.40	5.45		6.85	10
0186	10-1/2" ID		146	.110		1.47	5.55		7.02	10.20
0188	11" ID		143	.112		1.54	5.65		7.19	10.50
0190	11-1/2" ID		140	.114		1.61	5.80		7.41	10.75
0192	12" ID		137	.117		1.67	5.90		7.57	11.05
0194	12-1/2" ID		134	.119		1.75	6.05		7.80	11.35
0195	13" ID		132	.121		1.81	6.15		7.96	11.55
0196	13-1/2" ID		132	.121		1.88	6.15		8.03	11.60
0198	14" ID		130	.123		1.95	6.25		8.20	11.85
0200	15" ID		128	.125		2.09	6.35		8.44	12.15
0202	16" ID		126	.127		2.22	6.45		8.67	12.45
0204	17" ID		124	.129		2.36	6.55		8.91	12.75
0206	18" ID		122	.131		2.50	6.65		9.15	13.05
0208	19" ID		120	.133		2.63	6.75		9.38	13.40
0210	20" ID		118	.136		2.77	6.85		9.62	13.70
0212	21" ID		116	.138		2.90	7		9.90	14.05
0214	22" ID		114	.140		3.04	7.10		10.14	14.40
0216	23" ID		112	.143		3.17	7.25		10.42	14.75
0218	24" ID		110	.145		3.31	7.35		10.66	15.10
0220	25" ID		108	.148		3.45	7.50		10.95	15.45
0222	26" ID		106	.151		3.58	7.65		11.23	15.80
0224	27" ID		104	.154		3.72	7.80		11.52	16.20
0226	28" ID		102	.157		3.85	7.95		11.80	16.60
0228	29" ID		100	.160		3.99	8.10		12.09	17
0230	30" ID		98	.163		4.13	8.25		12.38	17.40
0300	For colors, add				Ea.	10%				
1000	30 mil thick									
1010	Size based on OD of insulation									
1020	2" ID	Q-14	260	.062	L.F.	.47	3.12		3.59	5.35
1022	2-1/2" ID		250	.064		.57	3.24		3.81	5.70
1024	3" ID		240	.067		.68	3.38		4.06	6
1026	3-1/2" ID		230	.070		.77	3.53		4.30	6.30
1028	4" ID		220	.073		.87	3.69		4.56	6.65
1030	4-1/2" ID		210	.076		.97	3.86		4.83	7.05
1032	5" ID		200	.080		1.07	4.05		5.12	7.50
1034	5-1/2" ID		190	.084		1.17	4.27		5.44	7.90
1036	6" ID		180	.089		1.27	4.50		5.77	8.40
1038	6-1/2" ID		175	.091		1.37	4.63		6	8.70
1040	7" ID		170	.094		1.47	4.77		6.24	9
1042	7-1/2" ID		164	.098		1.58	4.94		6.52	9.40
1044	8" ID		161	.099		1.68	5.05		6.73	9.65
1046	8-1/2" ID		158	.101		1.78	5.15		6.93	9.90
1048	9" ID		155	.103		1.88	5.25		7.13	10.15
1050	9-1/2" ID		152	.105		1.98	5.35		7.33	10.50
1052	10" ID		149	.107		2.08	5.45		7.53	10.75
1054	10-1/2" ID		146	.110		2.18	5.55		7.73	11
1056	11" ID		143	.112		2.28	5.65		7.93	11.30
1058	11-1/2" ID		140	.114		2.38	5.80		8.18	11.60
1060	12" ID		137	.117		2.48	5.90		8.38	11.95
1062	12-1/2" ID		134	.119		2.59	6.05		8.64	12.25
1063	13" ID		132	.121		2.69	6.15		8.84	12.50
1064	13-1/2" ID		132	.121		2.79	6.15		8.94	12.60

22 07 Plumbing Insulation

22 07 19 – Plumbing Piping Insulation

22 07 19.30 Piping Insulation Protective Jacketing, PVC		Crew	Daily Output	Labor-Hours	Unit	Material	2018 Bare Costs Labor	Equipment	Total	Total Incl O&P
1066	14" ID	Q-14	130	.123	L.F.	2.89	6.25		9.14	12.90
1068	15" ID		128	.125		3.09	6.35		9.44	13.25
1070	16" ID		126	.127		3.29	6.45		9.74	13.60
1072	17" ID		124	.129		3.49	6.55		10.04	14
1074	18" ID		122	.131		3.70	6.65		10.35	14.35
1076	19" ID		120	.133		3.90	6.75		10.65	14.80
1078	20" ID		118	.136		4.10	6.85		10.95	15.15
1080	21" ID		116	.138		4.30	7		11.30	15.60
1082	22" ID		114	.140		4.50	7.10		11.60	16
1084	23" ID		112	.143		4.70	7.25		11.95	16.40
1086	24" ID		110	.145		4.90	7.35		12.25	16.85
1088	25" ID		108	.148		5.10	7.50		12.60	17.25
1090	26" ID		106	.151		5.30	7.65		12.95	17.70
1092	27" ID		104	.154		5.50	7.80		13.30	18.15
1094	28" ID		102	.157		5.70	7.95		13.65	18.65
1096	29" ID		100	.160		5.90	8.10		14	19.10
1098	30" ID	↓	98	.163	↓	6.10	8.25		14.35	19.55
1300	For colors, add				Ea.	10%				
2000	PVC, white, fitting covers									
2020	Fiberglass insulation inserts included with sizes 1-3/4" thru 9-3/4"									
2030	Size is based on OD of insulation									
2040	90° elbow fitting									
2060	1-3/4"	Q-14	135	.119	Ea.	.55	6		6.55	9.90
2062	2"		130	.123		.68	6.25		6.93	10.45
2064	2-1/4"		128	.125		.76	6.35		7.11	10.70
2068	2-1/2"		126	.127		.84	6.45		7.29	10.90
2070	2-3/4"		123	.130		.91	6.60		7.51	11.25
2072	3"		120	.133		.96	6.75		7.71	11.55
2074	3-3/8"		116	.138		1.09	7		8.09	12.05
2076	3-3/4"		113	.142		1.22	7.20		8.42	12.50
2078	4-1/8"		110	.145		1.54	7.35		8.89	13.15
2080	4-3/4"		105	.152		1.86	7.70		9.56	14.05
2082	5-1/4"		100	.160		2.17	8.10		10.27	15
2084	5-3/4"		95	.168		2.86	8.55		11.41	16.40
2086	6-1/4"		90	.178		4.77	9		13.77	19.25
2088	6-3/4"		87	.184		5	9.30		14.30	19.95
2090	7-1/4"		85	.188		6.30	9.55		15.85	21.50
2092	7-3/4"		83	.193		6.60	9.75		16.35	22.50
2094	8-3/4"		80	.200		8.50	10.15		18.65	25
2096	9-3/4"		77	.208		11.35	10.55		21.90	29
2098	10-7/8"		74	.216		12.65	10.95		23.60	31
2100	11-7/8"		71	.225		14.50	11.40		25.90	33.50
2102	12-7/8"		68	.235		18.30	11.90		30.20	38.50
2104	14-1/8"		66	.242		21	12.30		33.30	42
2106	15-1/8"		64	.250		22.50	12.65		35.15	44.50
2108	16-1/8"		63	.254		24.50	12.85		37.35	47
2110	17-1/8"		62	.258		27.50	13.10		40.60	50.50
2112	18-1/8"		61	.262		35	13.30		48.30	59
2114	19-1/8"		60	.267		47.50	13.50		61	73.50
2116	20-1/8"	↓	59	.271	↓	61.50	13.75		75.25	89
2200	45° elbow fitting									
2220	1-3/4" thru 9-3/4" same price as 90° elbow fitting									
2320	10-7/8"	Q-14	74	.216	Ea.	12.65	10.95		23.60	31

22 07 Plumbing Insulation

22 07 19 – Plumbing Piping Insulation

22 07 19.30 Piping Insulation Protective Jacketing, PVC

		Crew	Daily Output	Labor-Hours	Unit	Material	2018 Bare Costs Labor	Equipment	Total	Total Incl O&P
2322	11-7/8"	Q-14	71	.225	Ea.	13.95	11.40		25.35	33
2324	12-7/8"		68	.235		15.55	11.90		27.45	35.50
2326	14-1/8"		66	.242		17.80	12.30		30.10	38.50
2328	15-1/8"		64	.250		19.10	12.65		31.75	40.50
2330	16-1/8"		63	.254		22	12.85		34.85	44
2332	17-1/8"		62	.258		24.50	13.10		37.60	47.50
2334	18-1/8"		61	.262		30	13.30		43.30	53.50
2336	19-1/8"		60	.267		41	13.50		54.50	66
2338	20-1/8"		59	.271		46.50	13.75		60.25	72.50
2400	Tee fitting									
2410	1-3/4"	Q-14	96	.167	Ea.	1.04	8.45		9.49	14.25
2412	2"		94	.170		1.18	8.65		9.83	14.70
2414	2-1/4"		91	.176		1.28	8.90		10.18	15.25
2416	2-1/2"		88	.182		1.40	9.20		10.60	15.85
2418	2-3/4"		85	.188		1.54	9.55		11.09	16.50
2420	3"		82	.195		1.67	9.90		11.57	17.20
2422	3-3/8"		79	.203		1.92	10.25		12.17	18.05
2424	3-3/4"		76	.211		2.18	10.65		12.83	18.95
2426	4-1/8"		73	.219		2.58	11.10		13.68	20
2428	4-3/4"		70	.229		3.21	11.60		14.81	21.50
2430	5-1/4"		67	.239		3.86	12.10		15.96	23
2432	5-3/4"		63	.254		5.15	12.85		18	25.50
2434	6-1/4"		60	.267		6.75	13.50		20.25	28.50
2436	6-3/4"		59	.271		8.35	13.75		22.10	30.50
2438	7-1/4"		57	.281		13.50	14.25		27.75	37
2440	7-3/4"		54	.296		14.80	15		29.80	40
2442	8-3/4"		52	.308		18	15.60		33.60	44
2444	9-3/4"		50	.320		21	16.20		37.20	48.50
2446	10-7/8"		48	.333		21.50	16.90		38.40	49.50
2448	11-7/8"		47	.340		24	17.25		41.25	53
2450	12-7/8"		46	.348		26	17.65		43.65	56.50
2452	14-1/8"		45	.356		28.50	18		46.50	59.50
2454	15-1/8"		44	.364		31	18.45		49.45	62.50
2456	16-1/8"		43	.372		33.50	18.85		52.35	66
2458	17-1/8"		42	.381		35.50	19.30		54.80	69.50
2460	18-1/8"		41	.390		39.50	19.80		59.30	74
2462	19-1/8"		40	.400		43	20.50		63.50	78.50
2464	20-1/8"		39	.410		47.50	21		68.50	84.50
4000	Mechanical grooved fitting cover, including insert									
4020	90° elbow fitting									
4030	3/4" & 1"	Q-14	140	.114	Ea.	4.35	5.80		10.15	13.80
4040	1-1/4" & 1-1/2"		135	.119		5.50	6		11.50	15.35
4042	2"		130	.123		8.70	6.25		14.95	19.25
4044	2-1/2"		125	.128		9.65	6.50		16.15	20.50
4046	3"		120	.133		10.80	6.75		17.55	22.50
4048	3-1/2"		115	.139		12.50	7.05		19.55	24.50
4050	4"		110	.145		13.95	7.35		21.30	27
4052	5"		100	.160		17.35	8.10		25.45	31.50
4054	6"		90	.178		25.50	9		34.50	42
4056	8"		80	.200		28	10.15		38.15	46.50
4058	10"		75	.213		35.50	10.80		46.30	56
4060	12"		68	.235		51.50	11.90		63.40	75
4062	14"		65	.246		51.50	12.45		63.95	76

For customer support on your Green Building Costs with RSMeans data, call 800.448.8182.

22 07 Plumbing Insulation

22 07 19 – Plumbing Piping Insulation

22 07 19.30 Piping Insulation Protective Jacketing, PVC

		Crew	Daily Output	Labor-Hours	Unit	Material	2018 Bare Costs Labor	Equipment	Total	Total Incl O&P
4064	16"	Q-14	63	.254	Ea.	70	12.85		82.85	97
4066	18"		61	.262		96	13.30		109.30	127
4100	45° elbow fitting									
4120	3/4" & 1"	Q-14	140	.114	Ea.	3.87	5.80		9.67	13.25
4130	1-1/4" & 1-1/2"		135	.119		4.93	6		10.93	14.70
4140	2"		130	.123		7.75	6.25		14	18.20
4142	2-1/2"		125	.128		8.60	6.50		15.10	19.50
4144	3"		120	.133		9.65	6.75		16.40	21
4146	3-1/2"		115	.139		10.20	7.05		17.25	22
4148	4"		110	.145		12.40	7.35		19.75	25
4150	5"		100	.160		15.40	8.10		23.50	29.50
4152	6"		90	.178		23	9		32	39
4154	8"		80	.200		25	10.15		35.15	43.50
4156	10"		75	.213		32	10.80		42.80	52
4158	12"		68	.235		45.50	11.90		57.40	69
4160	14"		65	.246		59.50	12.45		71.95	85
4162	16"		63	.254		72	12.85		84.85	99
4164	18"		61	.262		85	13.30		98.30	114
4200	Tee fitting									
4220	3/4" & 1"	Q-14	93	.172	Ea.	5.65	8.70		14.35	19.80
4230	1-1/4" & 1-1/2"		90	.178		7.15	9		16.15	22
4240	2"		87	.184		11.30	9.30		20.60	27
4242	2-1/2"		84	.190		12.55	9.65		22.20	29
4244	3"		80	.200		14.05	10.15		24.20	31
4246	3-1/2"		77	.208		14.90	10.55		25.45	33
4248	4"		73	.219		18.20	11.10		29.30	37.50
4250	5"		67	.239		20	12.10		32.10	41
4252	6"		60	.267		29.50	13.50		43	53.50
4254	8"		54	.296		32	15		47	59
4256	10"		50	.320		46.50	16.20		62.70	76
4258	12"		46	.348		66.50	17.65		84.15	101
4260	14"		43	.372		80.50	18.85		99.35	118
4262	16"		42	.381		96.50	19.30		115.80	136
4264	18"		41	.390		106	19.80		125.80	148

22 07 19.40 Pipe Insulation Protective Jacketing, Aluminum

		Crew	Daily Output	Labor-Hours	Unit	Material	Labor	Equipment	Total	Total Incl O&P
0010	**PIPE INSULATION PROTECTIVE JACKETING, ALUMINUM**									
0100	Metal roll jacketing									
0120	Aluminum with polykraft moisture barrier									
0140	Smooth, based on OD of insulation, .016" thick									
0180	1/2" ID	Q-14	220	.073	L.F.	.27	3.69		3.96	6
0190	3/4" ID		215	.074		.35	3.77		4.12	6.25
0200	1" ID		210	.076		.43	3.86		4.29	6.45
0210	1-1/4" ID		205	.078		.51	3.96		4.47	6.70
0220	1-1/2" ID		202	.079		.59	4.01		4.60	6.90
0230	1-3/4" ID		199	.080		.67	4.07		4.74	7.05
0240	2" ID		195	.082		.75	4.16		4.91	7.30
0250	2-1/4" ID		191	.084		.83	4.25		5.08	7.50
0260	2-1/2" ID		187	.086		.92	4.34		5.26	7.75
0270	2-3/4" ID		184	.087		1	4.41		5.41	7.95
0280	3" ID		180	.089		1.09	4.50		5.59	8.20
0290	3-1/4" ID		176	.091		1.17	4.61		5.78	8.45
0300	3-1/2" ID		172	.093		1.25	4.71		5.96	8.70

22 07 Plumbing Insulation

22 07 19 – Plumbing Piping Insulation

22 07 19.40 Pipe Insulation Protective Jacketing, Aluminum	Crew	Daily Output	Labor-Hours	Unit	Material	2018 Bare Costs Labor	Equipment	Total	Total Incl O&P
0310	3-3/4" ID	Q-14	169	.095	L.F.	1.33	4.80		6.13	8.90
0320	4" ID		165	.097		1.41	4.91		6.32	9.20
0330	4-1/4" ID		161	.099		1.49	5.05		6.54	9.45
0340	4-1/2" ID		157	.102		1.58	5.15		6.73	9.75
0350	4-3/4" ID		154	.104		1.66	5.25		6.91	10
0360	5" ID		150	.107		1.74	5.40		7.14	10.30
0370	5-1/4" ID		146	.110		1.82	5.55		7.37	10.60
0380	5-1/2" ID		143	.112		1.90	5.65		7.55	10.90
0390	5-3/4" ID		139	.115		1.99	5.85		7.84	11.25
0400	6" ID		135	.119		2.07	6		8.07	11.60
0410	6-1/4" ID		133	.120		2.15	6.10		8.25	11.80
0420	6-1/2" ID		131	.122		2.23	6.20		8.43	12.05
0430	7" ID		128	.125		2.38	6.35		8.73	12.45
0440	7-1/4" ID		125	.128		2.46	6.50		8.96	12.75
0450	7-1/2" ID		123	.130		2.54	6.60		9.14	13.05
0460	8" ID		121	.132		2.70	6.70		9.40	13.35
0470	8-1/2" ID		119	.134		2.86	6.80		9.66	13.70
0480	9" ID		116	.138		3.02	7		10.02	14.15
0490	9-1/2" ID		114	.140		3.19	7.10		10.29	14.55
0500	10" ID		112	.143		3.35	7.25		10.60	14.95
0510	10-1/2" ID		110	.145		3.51	7.35		10.86	15.30
0520	11" ID		107	.150		3.67	7.60		11.27	15.80
0530	11-1/2" ID		105	.152		3.84	7.70		11.54	16.20
0540	12" ID		103	.155		4	7.85		11.85	16.60
0550	12-1/2" ID		100	.160		4.16	8.10		12.26	17.20
0560	13" ID		99	.162		4.32	8.20		12.52	17.45
0570	14" ID		98	.163		4.65	8.25		12.90	17.95
0580	15" ID		96	.167		4.97	8.45		13.42	18.55
0590	16" ID		95	.168		5.30	8.55		13.85	19.10
0600	17" ID		93	.172		5.60	8.70		14.30	19.75
0610	18" ID		92	.174		5.85	8.80		14.65	20
0620	19" ID		90	.178		6.25	9		15.25	21
0630	20" ID		89	.180		6.60	9.10		15.70	21.50
0640	21" ID		87	.184		6.90	9.30		16.20	22
0650	22" ID		86	.186		7.25	9.45		16.70	22.50
0660	23" ID		84	.190		7.55	9.65		17.20	23.50
0670	24" ID		83	.193		7.90	9.75		17.65	24
0710	For smooth .020" thick, add					27%	10%			
0720	For smooth .024" thick, add					52%	20%			
0730	For smooth .032" thick, add					104%	33%			
0800	For stucco embossed, add					1%				
0820	For corrugated, add					2.50%				
0900	White aluminum with polysurlyn moisture barrier									
0910	Smooth, % is an add to polykraft lines of same thickness									
0940	For smooth .016" thick, add				L.F.	35%				
0960	For smooth .024" thick, add				"	22%				
1000	Aluminum fitting covers									
1010	Size is based on OD of insulation									
1020	90° LR elbow, 2 piece									
1100	1-1/2"	Q-14	140	.114	Ea.	4.06	5.80		9.86	13.45
1110	1-3/4"		135	.119		4.06	6		10.06	13.75
1120	2"		130	.123		5.10	6.25		11.35	15.30
1130	2-1/4"		128	.125		5.10	6.35		11.45	15.45

22 07 Plumbing Insulation

22 07 19 – Plumbing Piping Insulation

22 07 19.40 Pipe Insulation Protective Jacketing, Aluminum		Crew	Daily Output	Labor-Hours	Unit	Material	2018 Bare Costs Labor	Equipment	Total	Total Incl O&P
1140	2-1/2"	Q-14	126	.127	Ea.	5.10	6.45		11.55	15.60
1150	2-3/4"		123	.130		5.10	6.60		11.70	15.85
1160	3"		120	.133		5.55	6.75		12.30	16.60
1170	3-1/4"		117	.137		5.55	6.95		12.50	16.85
1180	3-1/2"		115	.139		6.55	7.05		13.60	18.15
1190	3-3/4"		113	.142		6.70	7.20		13.90	18.55
1200	4"		110	.145		7.05	7.35		14.40	19.20
1210	4-1/4"		108	.148		7.25	7.50		14.75	19.60
1220	4-1/2"		106	.151		7.25	7.65		14.90	19.80
1230	4-3/4"		104	.154		7.25	7.80		15.05	20
1240	5"		102	.157		8.15	7.95		16.10	21.50
1250	5-1/4"		100	.160		9.40	8.10		17.50	23
1260	5-1/2"		97	.165		11.70	8.35		20.05	26
1270	5-3/4"		95	.168		11.70	8.55		20.25	26
1280	6"		92	.174		10	8.80		18.80	24.50
1290	6-1/4"		90	.178		10	9		19	25
1300	6-1/2"		87	.184		12.05	9.30		21.35	27.50
1310	7"		85	.188		14.60	9.55		24.15	31
1320	7-1/4"		84	.190		14.60	9.65		24.25	31
1330	7-1/2"		83	.193		21.50	9.75		31.25	38.50
1340	8"		82	.195		16	9.90		25.90	33
1350	8-1/2"		80	.200		29.50	10.15		39.65	48.50
1360	9"		78	.205		29.50	10.40		39.90	48.50
1370	9-1/2"		77	.208		22	10.55		32.55	40.50
1380	10"		76	.211		22	10.65		32.65	40.50
1390	10-1/2"		75	.213		22	10.80		32.80	41.50
1400	11"		74	.216		22	10.95		32.95	41.50
1410	11-1/2"		72	.222		25.50	11.25		36.75	45.50
1420	12"		71	.225		25.50	11.40		36.90	45.50
1430	12-1/2"		69	.232		45	11.75		56.75	68
1440	13"		68	.235		45	11.90		56.90	68
1450	14"		66	.242		60.50	12.30		72.80	85.50
1460	15"		64	.250		63	12.65		75.65	89
1470	16"		63	.254		69	12.85		81.85	95.50
2000	45° elbow, 2 piece									
2010	2-1/2"	Q-14	126	.127	Ea.	4.22	6.45		10.67	14.65
2020	2-3/4"		123	.130		4.22	6.60		10.82	14.90
2030	3"		120	.133		4.77	6.75		11.52	15.75
2040	3-1/4"		117	.137		4.77	6.95		11.72	16
2050	3-1/2"		115	.139		5.45	7.05		12.50	16.95
2060	3-3/4"		113	.142		5.45	7.20		12.65	17.15
2070	4"		110	.145		5.55	7.35		12.90	17.55
2080	4-1/4"		108	.148		6.30	7.50		13.80	18.60
2090	4-1/2"		106	.151		6.30	7.65		13.95	18.80
2100	4-3/4"		104	.154		6.30	7.80		14.10	19.05
2110	5"		102	.157		7.40	7.95		15.35	20.50
2120	5-1/4"		100	.160		7.40	8.10		15.50	21
2130	5-1/2"		97	.165		7.75	8.35		16.10	21.50
2140	6"		92	.174		7.75	8.80		16.55	22.50
2150	6-1/2"		87	.184		10.75	9.30		20.05	26.50
2160	7"		85	.188		10.75	9.55		20.30	26.50
2170	7-1/2"		83	.193		10.85	9.75		20.60	27
2180	8"		82	.195		10.85	9.90		20.75	27.50

22 07 Plumbing Insulation

22 07 19 – Plumbing Piping Insulation

22 07 19.40 Pipe Insulation Protective Jacketing, Aluminum

		Crew	Daily Output	Labor-Hours	Unit	Material	2018 Bare Costs Labor	Equipment	Total	Total Incl O&P
2190	8-1/2"	Q-14	80	.200	Ea.	13.45	10.15		23.60	30.50
2200	9"		78	.205		13.45	10.40		23.85	31
2210	9-1/2"		77	.208		18.70	10.55		29.25	37
2220	10"		76	.211		18.70	10.65		29.35	37
2230	10-1/2"		75	.213		17.50	10.80		28.30	36
2240	11"		74	.216		17.50	10.95		28.45	36.50
2250	11-1/2"		72	.222		21	11.25		32.25	40.50
2260	12"		71	.225		21	11.40		32.40	40.50
2270	13"		68	.235		24.50	11.90		36.40	45.50
2280	14"		66	.242		30.50	12.30		42.80	52.50
2290	15"		64	.250		46.50	12.65		59.15	71
2300	16"		63	.254		50.50	12.85		63.35	75.50
2310	17"		62	.258		49.50	13.10		62.60	75
2320	18"		61	.262		56.50	13.30		69.80	82.50
2330	19"		60	.267		69	13.50		82.50	96.50
2340	20"		59	.271		66.50	13.75		80.25	94.50
2350	21"		58	.276		72	14		86	101
3000	Tee, 4 piece									
3010	2-1/2"	Q-14	88	.182	Ea.	29	9.20		38.20	46.50
3020	2-3/4"		86	.186		29	9.45		38.45	46.50
3030	3"		84	.190		32.50	9.65		42.15	51
3040	3-1/4"		82	.195		32.50	9.90		42.40	51.50
3050	3-1/2"		80	.200		34.50	10.15		44.65	53.50
3060	4"		78	.205		34.50	10.40		44.90	54
3070	4-1/4"		76	.211		36.50	10.65		47.15	56.50
3080	4-1/2"		74	.216		36.50	10.95		47.45	57
3090	4-3/4"		72	.222		36.50	11.25		47.75	57.50
3100	5"		70	.229		37.50	11.60		49.10	59.50
3110	5-1/4"		68	.235		37.50	11.90		49.40	60
3120	5-1/2"		66	.242		39.50	12.30		51.80	62.50
3130	6"		64	.250		39.50	12.65		52.15	63
3140	6-1/2"		60	.267		43.50	13.50		57	68.50
3150	7"		58	.276		43.50	14		57.50	69
3160	7-1/2"		56	.286		48	14.50		62.50	75.50
3170	8"		54	.296		48	15		63	76.50
3180	8-1/2"		52	.308		49.50	15.60		65.10	78.50
3190	9"		50	.320		49.50	16.20		65.70	79.50
3200	9-1/2"		49	.327		36.50	16.55		53.05	66
3210	10"		48	.333		36.50	16.90		53.40	66.50
3220	10-1/2"		47	.340		39	17.25		56.25	70
3230	11"		46	.348		39	17.65		56.65	70.50
3240	11-1/2"		45	.356		41	18		59	73.50
3250	12"		44	.364		41	18.45		59.45	74
3260	13"		43	.372		43	18.85		61.85	77
3270	14"		42	.381		45.50	19.30		64.80	80
3280	15"		41	.390		49	19.80		68.80	84.50
3290	16"		40	.400		50.50	20.50		71	87
3300	17"		39	.410		58	21		79	96
3310	18"		38	.421		60	21.50		81.50	99
3320	19"		37	.432		66.50	22		88.50	107
3330	20"		36	.444		68	22.50		90.50	110
3340	22"		35	.457		86.50	23		109.50	131
3350	23"		34	.471		89	24		113	135

For customer support on your Green Building Costs with RSMeans data, call 800.448.8182.

22 07 Plumbing Insulation

22 07 19 – Plumbing Piping Insulation

22 07 19.40 Pipe Insulation Protective Jacketing, Aluminum		Crew	Daily Output	Labor-Hours	Unit	Material	2018 Bare Costs Labor	Equipment	Total	Total Incl O&P
3360	24"	Q-14	31	.516	Ea.	91	26		117	141

22 11 Facility Water Distribution

22 11 19 – Domestic Water Piping Specialties

22 11 19.42 Backflow Preventers

		Crew	Daily Output	Labor-Hours	Unit	Material	Labor	Equipment	Total	Total Incl O&P
0010	**BACKFLOW PREVENTERS**, Includes valves									
0020	and four test cocks, corrosion resistant, automatic operation									
1000	Double check principle									
1010	Threaded, with ball valves									
1020	3/4" pipe size	1 Plum	16	.500	Ea.	231	31		262	300
1030	1" pipe size		14	.571		265	35.50		300.50	345
1040	1-1/2" pipe size		10	.800		565	49.50		614.50	695
1050	2" pipe size		7	1.143		655	71		726	825
1080	Threaded, with gate valves									
1100	3/4" pipe size	1 Plum	16	.500	Ea.	1,025	31		1,056	1,175
1120	1" pipe size		14	.571		1,025	35.50		1,060.50	1,175
1140	1-1/2" pipe size		10	.800		1,175	49.50		1,224.50	1,375
1160	2" pipe size		7	1.143		1,625	71		1,696	1,875
1200	Flanged, valves are gate									
1210	3" pipe size	Q-1	4.50	3.556	Ea.	2,800	199		2,999	3,375
1220	4" pipe size	"	3	5.333		2,900	298		3,198	3,650
1230	6" pipe size	Q-2	3	8		4,300	465		4,765	5,425
1240	8" pipe size		2	12		7,800	695		8,495	9,625
1250	10" pipe size		1	24		11,600	1,400		13,000	14,800
1300	Flanged, valves are OS&Y									
1370	1" pipe size	1 Plum	5	1.600	Ea.	1,125	99.50		1,224.50	1,400
1374	1-1/2" pipe size		5	1.600		1,300	99.50		1,399.50	1,575
1378	2" pipe size		4.80	1.667		1,725	104		1,829	2,050
1380	3" pipe size	Q-1	4.50	3.556		2,625	199		2,824	3,175
1400	4" pipe size	"	3	5.333		3,850	298		4,148	4,700
1420	6" pipe size	Q-2	3	8		6,375	465		6,840	7,700
1430	8" pipe size	"	2	12		13,600	695		14,295	16,000
4000	Reduced pressure principle									
4100	Threaded, bronze, valves are ball									
4120	3/4" pipe size	1 Plum	16	.500	Ea.	455	31		486	545
4140	1" pipe size		14	.571		480	35.50		515.50	585
4150	1-1/4" pipe size		12	.667		895	41.50		936.50	1,050
4160	1-1/2" pipe size		10	.800		985	49.50		1,034.50	1,150
4180	2" pipe size		7	1.143		1,100	71		1,171	1,325
5000	Flanged, bronze, valves are OS&Y									
5060	2-1/2" pipe size	Q-1	5	3.200	Ea.	5,325	179		5,504	6,125
5080	3" pipe size		4.50	3.556		6,050	199		6,249	6,950
5100	4" pipe size		3	5.333		7,550	298		7,848	8,775
5120	6" pipe size	Q-2	3	8		11,000	465		11,465	12,800
5200	Flanged, iron, valves are gate									
5210	2-1/2" pipe size	Q-1	5	3.200	Ea.	2,675	179		2,854	3,200
5220	3" pipe size		4.50	3.556		2,775	199		2,974	3,350
5230	4" pipe size		3	5.333		3,750	298		4,048	4,600
5240	6" pipe size	Q-2	3	8		5,300	465		5,765	6,525
5250	8" pipe size		2	12		9,525	695		10,220	11,600
5260	10" pipe size		1	24		15,300	1,400		16,700	19,000

22 11 Facility Water Distribution

22 11 19 – Domestic Water Piping Specialties

22 11 19.42 Backflow Preventers

		Crew	Daily Output	Labor-Hours	Unit	Material	2018 Bare Costs Labor	Equipment	Total	Total Incl O&P
5600	Flanged, iron, valves are OS&Y									
5660	2-1/2" pipe size	Q-1	5	3.200	Ea.	3,025	179		3,204	3,600
5680	3" pipe size		4.50	3.556		3,175	199		3,374	3,800
5700	4" pipe size		3	5.333		4,000	298		4,298	4,850
5720	6" pipe size	Q-2	3	8		5,800	465		6,265	7,075
5740	8" pipe size		2	12		10,200	695		10,895	12,300
5760	10" pipe size		1	24		19,500	1,400		20,900	23,500

22 12 Facility Potable-Water Storage Tanks

22 12 21 – Facility Underground Potable-Water Storage Tanks

22 12 21.13 Fiberglass, Undrgrnd Pot.-Water Storage Tanks

		Crew	Daily Output	Labor-Hours	Unit	Material	Labor	Equipment	Total	Total Incl O&P
0010	**FIBERGLASS, UNDERGROUND POTABLE-WATER STORAGE TANKS**									
0020	Excludes excavation, backfill, & piping									
0030	Single wall									
2000	600 gallon capacity	B-21B	3.75	10.667	Ea.	3,625	465	132	4,222	4,850
2010	1,000 gallon capacity		3.50	11.429		4,700	495	142	5,337	6,075
2020	2,000 gallon capacity		3.25	12.308		6,825	535	153	7,513	8,475
2030	4,000 gallon capacity		3	13.333		9,450	580	165	10,195	11,500
2040	6,000 gallon capacity		2.65	15.094		10,600	655	187	11,442	12,900
2050	8,000 gallon capacity		2.30	17.391		12,700	755	216	13,671	15,400
2060	10,000 gallon capacity		2	20		14,600	870	248	15,718	17,600
2070	12,000 gallon capacity		1.50	26.667		20,100	1,150	330	21,580	24,200
2080	15,000 gallon capacity		1	40		23,400	1,750	495	25,645	28,900
2090	20,000 gallon capacity		.75	53.333		30,100	2,325	660	33,085	37,400
2100	25,000 gallon capacity		.50	80		44,900	3,475	990	49,365	56,000
2110	30,000 gallon capacity		.35	114		54,500	4,975	1,425	60,900	69,000
2120	40,000 gallon capacity		.30	133		79,000	5,800	1,650	86,450	97,500

22 13 Facility Sanitary Sewerage

22 13 19 – Sanitary Waste Piping Specialties

22 13 19.39 Floor Drain Trap Seal

		Crew	Daily Output	Labor-Hours	Unit	Material	Labor	Equipment	Total	Total Incl O&P
0010	**FLOOR DRAIN TRAP SEAL**									
0100	Inline									
0110	2"	1 Plum	20	.400	Ea.	38	25		63	79.50
0120	3"		16	.500		41	31		72	92
0130	3.5"		14	.571		45	35.50		80.50	103
0140	4"		10	.800		50	49.50		99.50	130

22 13 63 – Facility Gray Water Tanks

22 13 63.10 Graywater Recovery Systems

		Crew	Daily Output	Labor-Hours	Unit	Material	Labor	Equipment	Total	Total Incl O&P
0010	**GRAYWATER RECOVERY SYSTEMS**, for ext. irrigation									
1000	Resi syst, avg home, incl. tank, pump & dist lines, easy access, layout				System				5,000	5,500
1010	Difficult access or complex layout				"				10,000	11,000
2010	Residential system, sink to toilet	Q-1	2	8	Ea.	296	445		741	1,000
2020	Toilet top sink	1 Plum	8	1		159	62		221	269
3010	Prepackaged residential system, 6 people	Q-2	5	4.800		2,000	278		2,278	2,625
3020	9 people		4	6		2,200	350		2,550	2,950
3030	12 people		3.50	6.857		2,350	400		2,750	3,200
3040	for irrigation supply	1 Plum	3	2.667		700	166		866	1,025
4010	Prepackaged commercial system, 1,530 gal.	Q-3	4.25	7.529		30,800	445		31,245	34,600

For customer support on your Green Building Costs with RSMeans data, call 800.448.8182.

22 13 Facility Sanitary Sewerage

22 13 63 – Facility Gray Water Tanks

22 13 63.10 Graywater Recovery Systems

		Crew	Daily Output	Labor-Hours	Unit	Material	2018 Bare Costs Labor	Equipment	Total	Total Incl O&P
4020	3,060 gal.	Q-3	3.50	9.143	Ea.	41,800	540		42,340	46,800
4030	4,590 gal.	"	2.50	12.800		52,000	755		52,755	58,500
5010	Lift station 75 GPM	Q-1	3	5.333		1,450	298		1,748	2,050
5020	100 GPM	"	2.80	5.714		1,700	320		2,020	2,350
6010	System components									
6020	Sand filter	1 Plum	8	1	Ea.	91.50	62		153.50	195
6040	4 in. bull run valve		12	.667		132	41.50		173.50	208
6050	1.5 in. flow splitter		12	.667		15	41.50		56.50	79
6052	2 in. flow splitter		12	.667		15	41.50		56.50	79
6060	Sediment trap filter - 2"		8	1		117	62		179	223
6070	Dye injection unit		4	2		1,300	124		1,424	1,600

22 14 Facility Storm Drainage

22 14 53 – Rainwater Storage Tanks

22 14 53.13 Fiberglass, Rainwater Storage Tank

		Crew	Daily Output	Labor-Hours	Unit	Material	2018 Bare Costs Labor	Equipment	Total	Total Incl O&P
0010	**FIBERGLASS, RAINWATER STORAGE TANK**									
2000	600 gallon	B-21B	3.75	10.667	Ea.	3,625	465	132	4,222	4,850
2010	1,000 gallon		3.50	11.429		4,700	495	142	5,337	6,075
2020	2,000 gallon		3.25	12.308		6,825	535	153	7,513	8,475
2030	4,000 gallon		3	13.333		9,450	580	165	10,195	11,500
2040	6,000 gallon		2.65	15.094		10,600	655	187	11,442	12,900
2050	8,000 gallon		2.30	17.391		12,700	755	216	13,671	15,400
2060	10,000 gallon		2	20		14,600	870	248	15,718	17,600
2070	12,000 gallon		1.50	26.667		20,100	1,150	330	21,580	24,200
2080	15,000 gallon		1	40		23,400	1,750	495	25,645	28,900
2090	20,000 gallon		.75	53.333		30,100	2,325	660	33,085	37,400
2100	25,000 gallon		.50	80		44,900	3,475	990	49,365	56,000
2110	30,000 gallon		.35	114		54,500	4,975	1,425	60,900	69,000
2120	40,000 gallon		.30	133		79,000	5,800	1,650	86,450	97,500

22 14 55 – Rainwater Harvesting Systems

22 14 55.10 Rainwater Systems and Components

		Crew	Daily Output	Labor-Hours	Unit	Material	2018 Bare Costs Labor	Equipment	Total	Total Incl O&P
0010	**RAINWATER SYSTEMS AND COMPONENTS**									
0020	Prepackaged rainwater systems									
2010	Storage, rain barrel 50 gal.	1 Clab	10	.800	Ea.	139	32		171	202
2020	60 gal.		10	.800		123	32		155	184
2025	60 gal. wood		10	.800		375	32		407	465
2030	100 gal.	Q-2	6	4		159	232		391	525
2040	Aboveground storage tank 500 gal.	"	3	8		465	465		930	1,225
2050	1,000 gal.	B-21	6	4.667		660	216	21.50	897.50	1,075
2060	5,000 gal.	"	3.20	8.750		2,200	405	40.50	2,645.50	3,075
2070	Underground storage tank 500 gal.	Q-2	2.67	8.989		660	520		1,180	1,500
2080	1,000 gal.	B-21	5	5.600		1,575	259	26	1,860	2,150
2090	5,000 gal.	"	2.50	11.200		7,000	520	52	7,572	8,550
3010	Aboveground system with 1,200 gal. tank & pump	Q-3	5	6.400		745	380		1,125	1,400
3020	Underground system with 1,200 gal. tank & pump	"	4.25	7.529		1,600	445		2,045	2,425
3100	Rainwater system components									
3110	Leaf diverter	1 Shee	60	.133	Ea.	29	7.95		36.95	44
3120	First flush diverter, 2-3 gal.		30	.267		30	15.95		45.95	57.50
3130	3-6 gal.		30	.267		35	15.95		50.95	63
3140	6-10 gal.		30	.267		66	15.95		81.95	97

22 14 Facility Storm Drainage

22 14 55 – Rainwater Harvesting Systems

22 14 55.10 Rainwater Systems and Components

		Crew	Daily Output	Labor-Hours	Unit	Material	2018 Bare Costs Labor	Equipment	Total	Total Incl O&P
3150	12-36 gal.	1 Shee	20	.400	Ea.	80	24		104	125
3160	Inground first flush diverter	1 Plum	5	1.600		79	99.50		178.50	237
3170	Basket strainers for rain tank	1 Shee	30	.267		45	15.95		60.95	74
3180	12" collection screen	"	16	.500		13.95	30		43.95	61
3190	Filter-inline downspout	1 Clab	10	.800		400	32		432	490
3200	Vortex rainwater filter: 2,200 S.F. in-ground	Q-1	4	4		595	224		819	990
3210	5,500 S.F. in-ground	"	4	4		780	224		1,004	1,200
3220	Floating filter coarse 1.25"	1 Plum	20	.400		180	25		205	236
3230	Coarse 2"		20	.400		300	25		325	370
3240	Fine 1.25"		20	.400		300	25		325	370
3250	Smoothing or calming Inlet		13	.615		296	38.50		334.50	385
3260	HDPE drywell 2' diam. x 2'	1 Clab	6	1.333		94	53		147	184
3270	Rainwater tank level monitor	Q-1	4	4		248	224		472	605
3280	Rainwater digital level indicator	"	4	4		300	224		524	665

22 32 Domestic Water Filtration Equipment

22 32 19 – Domestic-Water Off-Floor Cartridge Filters

22 32 19.10 Water Filters

		Crew	Daily Output	Labor-Hours	Unit	Material	Labor	Equipment	Total	Total Incl O&P
0010	**WATER FILTERS**, Purification and treatment									
1000	Cartridge style, dirt and rust type	1 Plum	12	.667	Ea.	90.50	41.50		132	162
1200	Replacement cartridge		32	.250		18.40	15.55		33.95	44
1600	Taste and odor type		12	.667		123	41.50		164.50	198
1700	Replacement cartridge		32	.250		42.50	15.55		58.05	70
3000	Central unit, dirt/rust/odor/taste/scale		4	2		270	124		394	485
3100	Replacement cartridge, standard		20	.400		79	25		104	125
3600	Replacement cartridge, heavy duty		20	.400		99.50	25		124.50	147
8000	Commercial, fully automatic or push button automatic									
8200	Iron removal, 660 GPH, 1" pipe size	Q-1	1.50	10.667	Ea.	1,625	595		2,220	2,675
8240	1,500 GPH, 1-1/4" pipe size		1	16		2,725	895		3,620	4,350
8280	2,340 GPH, 1-1/2" pipe size		.80	20		3,000	1,125		4,125	4,975
8320	3,420 GPH, 2" pipe size		.60	26.667		5,525	1,500		7,025	8,325
8360	4,620 GPH, 2-1/2" pipe size		.50	32		8,800	1,800		10,600	12,400
8500	Neutralizer for acid water, 780 GPH, 1" pipe size		1.50	10.667		1,575	595		2,170	2,625
8540	1,140 GPH, 1-1/4" pipe size		1	16		1,750	895		2,645	3,275
8580	1,740 GPH, 1-1/2" pipe size		.80	20		2,550	1,125		3,675	4,500
8620	2,520 GPH, 2" pipe size		.60	26.667		3,325	1,500		4,825	5,900
8660	3,480 GPH, 2-1/2" pipe size		.50	32		5,525	1,800		7,325	8,775
8800	Sediment removal, 780 GPH, 1" pipe size		1.50	10.667		1,500	595		2,095	2,550
8840	1,140 GPH, 1-1/4" pipe size		1	16		1,775	895		2,670	3,300
8880	1,740 GPH, 1-1/2" pipe size		.80	20		2,375	1,125		3,500	4,275
8920	2,520 GPH, 2" pipe size		.60	26.667		3,425	1,500		4,925	6,025
8960	3,480 GPH, 2-1/2" pipe size		.50	32		5,375	1,800		7,175	8,625
9200	Taste and odor removal, 660 GPH, 1" pipe size		1.50	10.667		2,075	595		2,670	3,200
9240	1,500 GPH, 1-1/4" pipe size		1	16		3,575	895		4,470	5,300
9280	2,340 GPH, 1-1/2" pipe size		.80	20		4,075	1,125		5,200	6,175
9320	3,420 GPH, 2" pipe size		.60	26.667		6,250	1,500		7,750	9,125
9360	4,620 GPH, 2-1/2" pipe size		.50	32		9,675	1,800		11,475	13,300

22 34 Fuel-Fired Domestic Water Heaters

22 34 13 – Instantaneous, Tankless, Gas Domestic Water Heaters

22 34 13.10 Instantaneous, Tankless, Gas Water Heaters

			Crew	Daily Output	Labor-Hours	Unit	Material	2018 Bare Costs Labor	Equipment	Total	Total Incl O&P
0010	**INSTANTANEOUS, TANKLESS, GAS WATER HEATERS**										
9410	Natural gas/propane, 3.2 GPM	G	1 Plum	2	4	Ea.	500	249		749	925
9420	6.4 GPM	G		1.90	4.211		715	262		977	1,175
9430	8.4 GPM	G		1.80	4.444		855	276		1,131	1,350
9440	9.5 GPM	G	↓	1.60	5	↓	1,000	310		1,310	1,575

22 35 Domestic Water Heat Exchangers

22 35 43 – Domestic Water Heat Reclaimers

22 35 43.10 Drainwater Heat Recovery

			Crew	Daily Output	Labor-Hours	Unit	Material	Labor	Equipment	Total	Total Incl O&P
0010	**DRAINWATER HEAT RECOVERY**										
9005	Drainwater heat recov unit, copp coil type, for 1/2" supply, 3" waste		1 Plum	3	2.667	Ea.	505	166		671	805
9010	For 1/2" supply, 4" waste			3	2.667		560	166		726	865
9020	For 3/4" supply, 3" waste			3	2.667		695	166		861	1,025
9030	For 3/4" supply, 4" waste			3	2.667		730	166		896	1,050
9040	For 1" supply, 4" waste, double manifold		↓	3	2.667	↓	1,375	166		1,541	1,775

22 41 Residential Plumbing Fixtures

22 41 13 – Residential Water Closets, Urinals, and Bidets

22 41 13.13 Water Closets

			Crew	Daily Output	Labor-Hours	Unit	Material	Labor	Equipment	Total	Total Incl O&P
0010	**WATER CLOSETS**										
0032	For automatic flush, see Line 22 42 39.10 0972										
0150	Tank type, vitreous china, incl. seat, supply pipe w/stop, 1.6 gpf or noted										
0999	Floor mounted										
1140	Two piece, close coupled, 1.28 gpf, ADA	G	Q-1	5.30	3.019	Ea.	310	169		479	595
3700	Toilets, composting, material only, non-electric	G				↓	1,825			1,825	2,000
3710	120 VAC electric	G					2,000			2,000	2,200

22 41 23 – Residential Showers

22 41 23.40 Shower System Components

			Crew	Daily Output	Labor-Hours	Unit	Material	Labor	Equipment	Total	Total Incl O&P
0010	**SHOWER SYSTEM COMPONENTS**										
5500	Head, water economizer, 1.6 GPM	G	1 Plum	24	.333	Ea.	49.50	20.50		70	85.50

22 41 39 – Residential Faucets, Supplies and Trim

22 41 39.10 Faucets and Fittings

			Crew	Daily Output	Labor-Hours	Unit	Material	Labor	Equipment	Total	Total Incl O&P
0010	**FAUCETS AND FITTINGS**										
2100	Lavatory faucet, centerset, without drain		1 Plum	10	.800	Ea.	67	49.50		116.50	149
2810	Automatic sensor and operator, with faucet head	G		6.15	1.301		480	81		561	650
7800	Water closet, wax gasket			96	.083		1.73	5.20		6.93	9.70
7830	Replacement diaphragm washer assy for ballcock valve			12	.667		2.89	41.50		44.39	65.50
7850	Dual flush valve		↓	12	.667	↓	127	41.50		168.50	203

22 42 Commercial Plumbing Fixtures

22 42 13 – Commercial Water Closets, Urinals, and Bidets

22 42 13.13 Water Closets

		Crew	Daily Output	Labor-Hours	Unit	Material	2018 Bare Costs Labor	Equipment	Total	Total Incl O&P
0010	**WATER CLOSETS**									
3360	With floor outlet, 1.28 gpf	G Q-1	5.80	2.759	Ea.	550	154		704	835
3362	With floor outlet, 1.28 gpf, ADA	G "	5.80	2.759		575	154		729	860
7000	Toilets, water-saving dams for tank	G 1 Clab	24	.333		4.73	13.30		18.03	25

22 42 13.16 Urinals

		Crew	Daily Output	Labor-Hours	Unit	Material	Labor	Equipment	Total	Total Incl O&P
0010	**URINALS**									
3140	Water saving .5 gpf	G Q-1	3	5.333	Ea.	555	298		853	1,050
8000	Waterless (no flush) urinal									
8010	Wall hung									
8014	Fiberglass reinforced polyester									
8020	Standard unit	G Q-1	21.30	.751	Ea.	385	42		427	485
8030	ADA compliant unit	G "	21.30	.751		400	42		442	505
8070	For solid color, add	G				60			60	66
8080	For 2" brass flange (new const.), add	G Q-1	96	.167		19.20	9.30		28.50	35
8200	Vitreous china									
8220	ADA compliant unit, 14"	G Q-1	21.30	.751	Ea.	198	42		240	282
8250	ADA compliant unit, 15.5"	"	21.30	.751		230	42		272	315
8270	For solid color, add	G				60			60	66
8290	Rough-in, supply, waste & vent	G Q-1	2.92	5.479		635	305		940	1,150
8400	Trap liquid									
8410	1 quart	G			Ea.	17.35			17.35	19.10
8420	1 gallon	G			"	61			61	67

22 42 16 – Commercial Lavatories and Sinks

22 42 16.40 Service Sinks

		Crew	Daily Output	Labor-Hours	Unit	Material	Labor	Equipment	Total	Total Incl O&P
0010	**SERVICE SINKS**									
9400	Kitchen/bath faucet aerator, water saving	G 1 Clab	24	.333	Ea.	9.95	13.30		23.25	31

22 42 39 – Commercial Faucets, Supplies, and Trim

22 42 39.10 Faucets and Fittings

		Crew	Daily Output	Labor-Hours	Unit	Material	Labor	Equipment	Total	Total Incl O&P
0010	**FAUCETS AND FITTINGS**									
0910	Dual flush flushometer	1 Plum	12	.667	Ea.	223	41.50		264.50	310
0912	Flushometer retrofit kit	"	18	.444	"	17.60	27.50		45.10	61
0971	Automatic flush sensor and operator for									
0972	urinals or water closets, standard	G 1 Plum	8	1	Ea.	475	62		537	615
0980	High efficiency water saving									
0984	Water closets, 1.28 gpf	G 1 Plum	8	1	Ea.	415	62		477	555
0988	Urinals, .5 gpf	G "	8	1	"	415	62		477	555
2790	Faucets for lavatories									
2810	Automatic sensor and operator, with faucet head	1 Plum	6.15	1.301	Ea.	480	81		561	650

Division Notes

		CREW	DAILY OUTPUT	LABOR-HOURS	UNIT	BARE COSTS MAT.	LABOR	EQUIP.	TOTAL	TOTAL INCL O&P

Estimating Tips
The labor adjustment factors listed in Subdivision 22 01 02.20 also apply to Division 23.

23 10 00 Facility Fuel Systems
- The prices in this subdivision for above- and below-ground storage tanks do not include foundations or hold-down slabs, unless noted. The estimator should refer to Divisions 3 and 31 for foundation system pricing. In addition to the foundations, required tank accessories, such as tank gauges, leak detection devices, and additional manholes and piping, must be added to the tank prices.

23 50 00 Central Heating Equipment
- When estimating the cost of an HVAC system, check to see who is responsible for providing and installing the temperature control system. It is possible to overlook controls, assuming that they would be included in the electrical estimate.
- When looking up a boiler, be careful on specified capacity. Some manufacturers rate their products on output while others use input.
- Include HVAC insulation for pipe, boiler, and duct (wrap and liner).
- Be careful when looking up mechanical items to get the correct pressure rating and connection type (thread, weld, flange).

23 70 00 Central HVAC Equipment
- Combination heating and cooling units are sized by the air conditioning requirements. (See Reference No. R236000-20 for the preliminary sizing guide.)
- A ton of air conditioning is nominally 400 CFM.
- Rectangular duct is taken off by the linear foot for each size, but its cost is usually estimated by the pound. Remember that SMACNA standards now base duct on internal pressure.
- Prefabricated duct is estimated and purchased like pipe: straight sections and fittings.
- Note that cranes or other lifting equipment are not included on any lines in Division 23. For example, if a crane is required to lift a heavy piece of pipe into place high above a gym floor, or to put a rooftop unit on the roof of a four-story building, etc., it must be added. Due to the potential for extreme variation—from nothing additional required to a major crane or helicopter—we feel that including a nominal amount for "lifting contingency" would be useless and detract from the accuracy of the estimate. When using equipment rental cost data from RSMeans, do not forget to include the cost of the operator(s).

Reference Numbers
Reference numbers are shown at the beginning of some major classifications. These numbers refer to related items in the Reference Section. The reference information may be an estimating procedure, an alternate pricing method, or technical information.

Note: Not all subdivisions listed here necessarily appear. ■

No part of this cost data may be reproduced, stored in a retrieval system, or transmitted in any form or by any means without prior written permission of Gordian.

Note: Trade Service, in part, has been used as a reference source for some of the material prices used in Division 23.

Did you know?
RSMeans data is available through our online application with 24/7 access:
- Search for unit prices by keyword
- Leverage the most up-to-date data
- Build and export estimates

Try it free for 30 days!
www.rsmeans.com/2018freetrial

23 07 HVAC Insulation

23 07 13 – Duct Insulation

23 07 13.10 Duct Thermal Insulation		Crew	Daily Output	Labor-Hours	Unit	Material	2018 Bare Costs Labor	Equipment	Total	Total Incl O&P
0010	**DUCT THERMAL INSULATION**									
0110	Insulation req'd. is based on the surface size/area to be covered									
3000	Ductwork									
3020	Blanket type, fiberglass, flexible									
3030	Fire rated for grease and hazardous exhaust ducts									
3060	1-1/2" thick		Q-14	84	.190	S.F.	4.54	9.65		14.19	20
3090	Fire rated for plenums									
3100	1/2" x 24" x 25'		Q-14	1.94	8.247	Roll	167	420		587	835
3110	1/2" x 24" x 25'			98	.163	S.F.	3.35	8.25		11.60	16.55
3120	1/2" x 48" x 25'			1.04	15.385	Roll	335	780		1,115	1,575
3126	1/2" x 48" x 25'			104	.154	S.F.	3.35	7.80		11.15	15.80
3140	FSK vapor barrier wrap, .75 lb. density									
3160	1" thick	G	Q-14	350	.046	S.F.	.22	2.32		2.54	3.84
3170	1-1/2" thick	G		320	.050		.27	2.53		2.80	4.23
3180	2" thick	G		300	.053		.32	2.70		3.02	4.54
3190	3" thick	G		260	.062		.45	3.12		3.57	5.35
3200	4" thick	G		242	.066		.64	3.35		3.99	5.90
3210	Vinyl jacket, same as FSK									
3280	Unfaced, 1 lb. density									
3310	1" thick	G	Q-14	360	.044	S.F.	.24	2.25		2.49	3.76
3320	1-1/2" thick	G		330	.048		.36	2.46		2.82	4.21
3330	2" thick	G		310	.052		.44	2.62		3.06	4.54
3400	FSK facing, 1 lb. density									
3420	1-1/2" thick	G	Q-14	310	.052	S.F.	.36	2.62		2.98	4.46
3430	2" thick	G	"	300	.053	"	.44	2.70		3.14	4.67
3450	FSK facing, 1.5 lb. density									
3470	1-1/2" thick	G	Q-14	300	.053	S.F.	.45	2.70		3.15	4.69
3480	2" thick	G	"	290	.055		.54	2.80		3.34	4.93
3730	Sheet insulation									
3760	Polyethylene foam, closed cell, UV resistant									
3770	Standard temperature (-90°F to +212°F)									
3771	1/4" thick	G	Q-14	450	.036	S.F.	1.74	1.80		3.54	4.71
3772	3/8" thick	G		440	.036		2.49	1.84		4.33	5.60
3773	1/2" thick	G		420	.038		3.05	1.93		4.98	6.35
3774	3/4" thick	G		400	.040		4.36	2.03		6.39	7.95
3775	1" thick	G		380	.042		5.90	2.13		8.03	9.80
3776	1-1/2" thick	G		360	.044		9.30	2.25		11.55	13.75
3777	2" thick	G		340	.047		12.30	2.39		14.69	17.25
3778	2-1/2" thick	G		320	.050		15.80	2.53		18.33	21.50
3779	Adhesive (see line 7878)									
3780	Foam, rubber									
3782	1" thick	G	1 Stpi	50	.160	S.F.	2.92	10.10		13.02	18.40
3795	Finishes									
3800	Stainless steel woven mesh		Q-14	100	.160	S.F.	.93	8.10		9.03	13.60
3810	For .010" stainless steel, add			160	.100		3.15	5.05		8.20	11.30
3820	18 oz. fiberglass cloth, pasted on			170	.094		.84	4.77		5.61	8.30
3900	8 oz. canvas, pasted on			180	.089		.26	4.50		4.76	7.30
3940	For .016" aluminum jacket, add			200	.080		1.01	4.05		5.06	7.40
7000	Board insulation									
7020	Mineral wool, 1200° F									
7022	6 lb. density, plain									
7024	1" thick	G	Q-14	370	.043	S.F.	.34	2.19		2.53	3.77
7026	1-1/2" thick	G		350	.046		.50	2.32		2.82	4.15

23 07 HVAC Insulation

23 07 13 – Duct Insulation

23 07 13.10 Duct Thermal Insulation

			Crew	Daily Output	Labor-Hours	Unit	Material	2018 Bare Costs Labor	Equipment	Total	Total Incl O&P
7028		2" thick	G	Q-14	330	.048	S.F.	.67	2.46		3.13	4.55
7030		3" thick	G		300	.053		.84	2.70		3.54	5.10
7032		4" thick	G		280	.057		1.34	2.90		4.24	5.95
7038	8 lb. density, plain											
7040		1" thick	G	Q-14	360	.044	S.F.	.41	2.25		2.66	3.95
7042		1-1/2" thick	G		340	.047		.61	2.39		3	4.37
7044		2" thick	G		320	.050		.81	2.53		3.34	4.82
7046		3" thick	G		290	.055		1.22	2.80		4.02	5.70
7048		4" thick	G		270	.059		1.63	3		4.63	6.45
7060	10 lb. density, plain											
7062		1" thick	G	Q-14	350	.046	S.F.	.56	2.32		2.88	4.22
7064		1-1/2" thick	G		330	.048		.84	2.46		3.30	4.73
7066		2" thick	G		310	.052		1.12	2.62		3.74	5.30
7068		3" thick	G		280	.057		1.68	2.90		4.58	6.35
7070		4" thick	G		260	.062		2.23	3.12		5.35	7.30
7878	Contact cement, quart can						Ea.	12.50			12.50	13.75

23 07 16 – HVAC Equipment Insulation

23 07 16.10 HVAC Equipment Thermal Insulation

			Crew	Daily Output	Labor-Hours	Unit	Material	Labor	Equipment	Total	Total Incl O&P
0010	**HVAC EQUIPMENT THERMAL INSULATION**											
0110	Insulation req'd. is based on the surface size/area to be covered											
1000	Boiler, 1-1/2" calcium silicate only	G	Q-14	110	.145	S.F.	3.65	7.35		11	15.45
1020	Plus 2" fiberglass	G	"	80	.200	"	5.15	10.15		15.30	21.50
2000	Breeching, 2" calcium silicate										
2020	Rectangular	G	Q-14	42	.381	S.F.	7.15	19.30		26.45	38
2040	Round	G	"	38.70	.413	"	7.45	21		28.45	40.50
2300	Calcium silicate block, +200°F to +1,200°F										
2310	On irregular surfaces, valves and fittings										
2340	1" thick	G	Q-14	30	.533	S.F.	3.23	27		30.23	45.50
2360	1-1/2" thick	G		25	.640		3.65	32.50		36.15	54.50
2380	2" thick	G		22	.727		3.83	37		40.83	61
2400	3" thick	G		18	.889		5.90	45		50.90	76.50
2410	On plane surfaces										
2420	1" thick	G	Q-14	126	.127	S.F.	3.23	6.45		9.68	13.55
2430	1-1/2" thick	G		120	.133		3.65	6.75		10.40	14.50
2440	2" thick	G		100	.160		3.83	8.10		11.93	16.80
2450	3" thick	G		70	.229		5.90	11.60		17.50	24.50

23 09 Instrumentation and Control for HVAC

23 09 23 – Direct-Digital Control System for HVAC

23 09 23.10 Control Components/DDC Systems

		Crew	Daily Output	Labor-Hours	Unit	Material	Labor	Equipment	Total	Total Incl O&P
0010	**CONTROL COMPONENTS/DDC SYSTEMS** (Sub's quote incl. M & L)									
0100	Analog inputs									
0110	Sensors (avg. 50' run in 1/2" EMT)									
0120	Duct temperature				Ea.				415	415
0130	Space temperature								665	665
0140	Duct humidity, +/- 3%								695	695
0150	Space humidity, +/- 2%								1,075	1,075
0160	Duct static pressure								565	565
0170	CFM/transducer								765	765
0180	KW/transducer								1,350	1,350

For customer support on your Green Building Costs with RSMeans data, call 800.448.8182.

23 09 Instrumentation and Control for HVAC

23 09 23 – Direct-Digital Control System for HVAC

23 09 23.10 Control Components/DDC Systems		Crew	Daily Output	Labor-Hours	Unit	Material	2018 Bare Costs Labor	Equipment	Total	Total Incl O&P
0182	KWH totalization (not incl. elec. meter pulse xmtr.)				Ea.				625	625
0190	Space static pressure								1,075	1,075
1000	Analog outputs (avg. 50' run in 1/2" EMT)									
1010	P/I transducer				Ea.				635	635
1020	Analog output, matl. in MUX								305	305
1030	Pneumatic (not incl. control device)								645	645
1040	Electric (not incl. control device)								380	380
2000	Status (alarms)									
2100	Digital inputs (avg. 50' run in 1/2" EMT)									
2110	Freeze				Ea.				435	435
2120	Fire								395	395
2130	Differential pressure (air)								595	595
2140	Differential pressure (water)								975	975
2150	Current sensor								435	435
2160	Duct high temperature thermostat								570	570
2170	Duct smoke detector								705	705
2200	Digital output (avg. 50' run in 1/2" EMT)									
2210	Start/stop				Ea.				340	340
2220	On/off (maintained contact)				"				585	585
3000	Controller MUX panel, incl. function boards									
3100	48 point				Ea.				5,275	5,275
3110	128 point				"				7,225	7,225
3200	DDC controller (avg. 50' run in conduit)									
3210	Mechanical room									
3214	16 point controller (incl. 120 volt/1 phase power supply)				Ea.				3,275	3,275
3229	32 point controller (incl. 120 volt/1 phase power supply)				"				5,425	5,425
3230	Includes software programming and checkout									
3260	Space									
3266	VAV terminal box (incl. space temp. sensor)				Ea.				840	840
3280	Host computer (avg. 50' run in conduit)									
3281	Package complete with PC, keyboard,									
3282	printer, monitor, basic software				Ea.				3,150	3,150
4000	Front end costs									
4100	Computer (P.C.) with software program				Ea.				6,350	6,350
4200	Color graphics software								3,925	3,925
4300	Color graphics slides								490	490
4350	Additional printer								980	980
4400	Communications trunk cable				L.F.				3.80	3.80
4500	Engineering labor (not incl. dftg.)				Point				94	94
4600	Calibration labor								120	120
4700	Start-up, checkout labor								120	120
4800	Programming labor, as req'd									
5000	Communications bus (data transmission cable)									
5010	#18 twisted shielded pair in 1/2" EMT conduit				C.L.F.				380	380
8000	Applications software									
8050	Basic maintenance manager software (not incl. data base entry)				Ea.				1,950	1,950
8100	Time program				Point				6.85	6.85
8120	Duty cycle								13.65	13.65
8140	Optimum start/stop								41.50	41.50
8160	Demand limiting								20.50	20.50
8180	Enthalpy program								41.50	41.50
8200	Boiler optimization				Ea.				1,225	1,225
8220	Chiller optimization				"				1,625	1,625

23 09 Instrumentation and Control for HVAC

23 09 23 – Direct-Digital Control System for HVAC

23 09 23.10 Control Components/DDC Systems

		Crew	Daily Output	Labor-Hours	Unit	Material	2018 Bare Costs Labor	Equipment	Total	Total Incl O&P
8240	Custom applications									
8260	Cost varies with complexity									

23 09 33 – Electric and Electronic Control System for HVAC

23 09 33.10 Electronic Control Systems

0010	ELECTRONIC CONTROL SYSTEMS	R230500-10								
0020	For electronic costs, add to Section 23 09 43.10				Ea.				15%	15%

23 09 43 – Pneumatic Control System for HVAC

23 09 43.10 Pneumatic Control Systems

0010	PNEUMATIC CONTROL SYSTEMS										
0011	Including a nominal 50' of tubing. Add control panelboard if req'd.										
0100	Heating and ventilating, split system	R230500-10									
0200	Mixed air control, economizer cycle, panel readout, tubing										
0220	Up to 10 tons	G	Q-19	.68	35.294	Ea.	4,450	2,025		6,475	7,925
0240	For 10 to 20 tons	G		.63	37.915		4,750	2,175		6,925	8,450
0260	For over 20 tons	G		.58	41.096		5,125	2,350		7,475	9,175
0270	Enthalpy cycle, up to 10 tons			.50	48.387		4,900	2,775		7,675	9,525
0280	For 10 to 20 tons			.46	52.174		5,275	2,975		8,250	10,300
0290	For over 20 tons			.42	56.604		5,750	3,250		9,000	11,200
0300	Heating coil, hot water, 3 way valve,										
0320	Freezestat, limit control on discharge, readout		Q-5	.69	23.088	Ea.	3,300	1,300		4,600	5,625
0500	Cooling coil, chilled water, room										
0520	Thermostat, 3 way valve		Q-5	2	8	Ea.	1,475	455		1,930	2,300
0600	Cooling tower, fan cycle, damper control,										
0620	Control system including water readout in/out at panel		Q-19	.67	35.821	Ea.	5,850	2,050		7,900	9,525
1000	Unit ventilator, day/night operation,										
1100	freezestat, ASHRAE, cycle 2		Q-19	.91	26.374	Ea.	3,250	1,500		4,750	5,850
2000	Compensated hot water from boiler, valve control,										
2100	readout and reset at panel, up to 60 GPM		Q-19	.55	43.956	Ea.	6,025	2,525		8,550	10,400
2120	For 120 GPM			.51	47.059		6,500	2,700		9,200	11,200
2140	For 240 GPM			.49	49.180		6,750	2,825		9,575	11,700
3000	Boiler room combustion air, damper to 5 S.F., controls			1.37	17.582		2,925	1,000		3,925	4,725
3500	Fan coil, heating and cooling valves, 4 pipe control system			3	8		1,300	460		1,760	2,125
3600	Heat exchanger system controls			.86	27.907		2,850	1,600		4,450	5,525
3900	Multizone control (one per zone), includes thermostat, damper										
3910	motor and reset of discharge temperature		Q-5	.51	31.373	Ea.	2,925	1,775		4,700	5,900
4000	Pneumatic thermostat, including controlling room radiator valve		"	2.43	6.593		880	375		1,255	1,525
4040	Program energy saving optimizer	G	Q-19	1.21	19.786		7,325	1,125		8,450	9,750
4060	Pump control system		"	3	8		1,350	460		1,810	2,175
4080	Reheat coil control system, not incl. coil		Q-5	2.43	6.593		1,150	375		1,525	1,825
4500	Air supply for pneumatic control system										
4600	Tank mounted duplex compressor, starter, alternator,										
4620	piping, dryer, PRV station and filter										
4630	1/2 HP		Q-19	.68	35.139	Ea.	10,800	2,000		12,800	14,900
4640	3/4 HP			.64	37.383		11,400	2,150		13,550	15,800
4650	1 HP			.61	39.539		12,500	2,250		14,750	17,100
4660	1-1/2 HP			.58	41.739		13,300	2,375		15,675	18,200
4680	3 HP			.55	43.956		18,100	2,525		20,625	23,700
4690	5 HP			.42	57.143		31,400	3,275		34,675	39,400
4800	Main air supply, includes 3/8" copper main and labor		Q-5	1.82	8.791	C.L.F.	365	500		865	1,150
4810	If poly tubing used, deduct									30%	30%
7000	Static pressure control for air handling unit, includes pressure										
7010	sensor, receiver controller, readout and damper motors		Q-19	.64	37.383	Ea.	8,600	2,150		10,750	12,700

23 09 Instrumentation and Control for HVAC

23 09 43 – Pneumatic Control System for HVAC

23 09 43.10 Pneumatic Control Systems

		Crew	Daily Output	Labor-Hours	Unit	Material	2018 Bare Costs Labor	Equipment	Total	Total Incl O&P
7020	If return air fan requires control, add				Ea.				70%	70%
8600	VAV boxes, incl. thermostat, damper motor, reheat coil & tubing	Q-5	1.46	10.989		1,350	625		1,975	2,450
8610	If no reheat coil, deduct								204	204

23 09 53 – Pneumatic and Electric Control System for HVAC

23 09 53.10 Control Components

		Crew	Daily Output	Labor-Hours	Unit	Material	Labor	Equipment	Total	Total Incl O&P
0010	**CONTROL COMPONENTS** R230500-10									
0700	Controller, receiver									
0730	Pneumatic, panel mount, single input	1 Plum	8	1	Ea.	475	62		537	615
0740	With conversion mounting bracket		8	1		475	62		537	615
0750	Dual input, with control point adjustment		7	1.143		655	71		726	825
0850	Electric, single snap switch	1 Elec	4	2		490	116		606	710
0860	Dual snap switches	"	3	2.667		655	155		810	950
1000	Enthalpy control, boiler water temperature control									
1010	governed by outdoor temperature, with timer	1 Elec	3	2.667	Ea.	365	155		520	635
2000	Gauges, pressure or vacuum									
2100	2" diameter dial	1 Stpi	32	.250	Ea.	10	15.75		25.75	34.50
2200	2-1/2" diameter dial		32	.250		12.15	15.75		27.90	37
2300	3-1/2" diameter dial		32	.250		18.70	15.75		34.45	44
2400	4-1/2" diameter dial		32	.250		21.50	15.75		37.25	47
2700	Flanged iron case, black ring									
2800	3-1/2" diameter dial	1 Stpi	32	.250	Ea.	102	15.75		117.75	136
2900	4-1/2" diameter dial		32	.250		105	15.75		120.75	140
3000	6" diameter dial		32	.250		168	15.75		183.75	209
3300	For compound pressure-vacuum, add					18%				
3350	Humidistat									
3390	Electric operated	1 Shee	8	1	Ea.	45	60		105	141
3400	Relays									
3430	Pneumatic/electric	1 Plum	16	.500	Ea.	305	31		336	380
3440	Pneumatic proportioning		8	1		237	62		299	355
3450	Pneumatic switching		12	.667		156	41.50		197.50	235
3460	Selector, 3 point		6	1.333		111	83		194	247
3470	Pneumatic time delay		8	1		300	62		362	425
3500	Sensor, air operated									
3520	Humidity	1 Plum	16	.500	Ea.	385	31		416	470
3540	Pressure		16	.500		69	31		100	123
3560	Temperature		12	.667		167	41.50		208.50	247
3600	Electric operated									
3620	Humidity	1 Elec	8	1	Ea.	262	58		320	375
3650	Pressure		8	1		271	58		329	385
3680	Temperature		10	.800		119	46.50		165.50	201
4000	Thermometers									
4100	Dial type, 3-1/2" diameter, vapor type, union connection	1 Stpi	32	.250	Ea.	215	15.75		230.75	261
4120	Liquid type, union connection		32	.250		415	15.75		430.75	480
4500	Stem type, 6-1/2" case, 2" stem, 1/2" NPT		32	.250		57	15.75		72.75	86
4520	4" stem, 1/2" NPT		32	.250		70	15.75		85.75	101
4600	9" case, 3-1/2" stem, 3/4" NPT		28	.286		92	18		110	128
4620	6" stem, 3/4" NPT		28	.286		110	18		128	148
4640	8" stem, 3/4" NPT		28	.286		182	18		200	228
4660	12" stem, 1" NPT		26	.308		147	19.40		166.40	191
5000	Thermostats									
5030	Manual	1 Stpi	8	1	Ea.	43	63		106	142
5040	1 set back, electric, timed [G]		8	1		76.50	63		139.50	180

23 09 Instrumentation and Control for HVAC

23 09 53 – Pneumatic and Electric Control System for HVAC

23 09 53.10	Control Components	Crew	Daily Output	Labor-Hours	Unit	Material	2018 Bare Costs Labor	Equipment	Total	Total Incl O&P
5050	2 set back, electric, timed G	1 Stpi	8	1	Ea.	228	63		291	345
5100	Locking cover	▼	20	.400		24	25		49	64.50
5200	24 hour, automatic, clock G	1 Shee	8	1		235	60		295	350
5220	Electric, low voltage, 2 wire	1 Elec	13	.615		62	36		98	122
5230	3 wire	"	10	.800	▼	54.50	46.50		101	130
5300	Transmitter, pneumatic									
5320	Temperature averaging element	Q-1	8	2	Ea.	132	112		244	315
5350	Pressure differential	1 Plum	7	1.143		1,100	71		1,171	1,325
5370	Humidity, duct		8	1		350	62		412	480
5380	Room		12	.667		355	41.50		396.50	455
5390	Temperature, with averaging element	▼	6	1.333	▼	180	83		263	325
6000	Valves, motorized zone									
6100	Sweat connections, 1/2" C x C	1 Stpi	20	.400	Ea.	156	25		181	210
6110	3/4" C x C		20	.400		151	25		176	204
6120	1" C x C		19	.421		204	26.50		230.50	264
6140	1/2" C x C, with end switch, 2 wire		20	.400		148	25		173	201
6150	3/4" C x C, with end switch, 2 wire		20	.400		130	25		155	181
6160	1" C x C, with end switch, 2 wire	▼	19	.421	▼	190	26.50		216.50	249
7090	Valves, motor controlled, including actuator									
7100	Electric motor actuated									
7200	Brass, two way, screwed									
7210	1/2" pipe size	L-6	36	.333	Ea.	355	20.50		375.50	420
7220	3/4" pipe size		30	.400		600	24.50		624.50	695
7230	1" pipe size		28	.429		715	26		741	825
7240	1-1/2" pipe size		19	.632		820	38.50		858.50	960
7250	2" pipe size	▼	16	.750	▼	1,150	45.50		1,195.50	1,350
7350	Brass, three way, screwed									
7360	1/2" pipe size	L-6	33	.364	Ea.	325	22		347	390
7370	3/4" pipe size		27	.444		355	27		382	430
7380	1" pipe size		25.50	.471		405	28.50		433.50	490
7384	1-1/4" pipe size		21	.571		460	35		495	560
7390	1-1/2" pipe size		17	.706		505	43		548	620
7400	2" pipe size		14	.857		765	52		817	920
7550	Iron body, two way, flanged									
7560	2-1/2" pipe size	L-6	4	3	Ea.	1,150	182		1,332	1,525
7570	3" pipe size		3	4		1,175	243		1,418	1,650
7580	4" pipe size		2	6		2,250	365		2,615	3,000
7850	Iron body, three way, flanged									
7860	2-1/2" pipe size	L-6	3	4	Ea.	1,150	243		1,393	1,650
7870	3" pipe size		2.50	4.800		1,300	292		1,592	1,900
7880	4" pipe size	▼	2	6	▼	1,675	365		2,040	2,400
8000	Pneumatic, air operated									
8050	Brass, two way, screwed									
8060	1/2" pipe size, class 250	1 Plum	24	.333	Ea.	179	20.50		199.50	227
8070	3/4" pipe size, class 250		20	.400		214	25		239	273
8080	1" pipe size, class 250		19	.421		250	26		276	315
8090	1-1/4" pipe size, class 125		15	.533		310	33		343	390
8100	1-1/2" pipe size, class 125		13	.615		395	38.50		433.50	495
8110	2" pipe size, class 125	▼	11	.727	▼	460	45		505	575
8180	Brass, three way, screwed									
8190	1/2" pipe size, class 250	1 Plum	22	.364	Ea.	179	22.50		201.50	230
8200	3/4" pipe size, class 250		18	.444		214	27.50		241.50	277
8210	1" pipe size, class 250	▼	17	.471		250	29.50		279.50	320

23 09 Instrumentation and Control for HVAC

23 09 53 – Pneumatic and Electric Control System for HVAC

23 09 53.10 Control Components

		Crew	Daily Output	Labor-Hours	Unit	Material	2018 Bare Costs Labor	Equipment	Total	Total Incl O&P
8214	1-1/4" pipe size, class 250	1 Plum	14	.571	Ea.	310	35.50		345.50	395
8220	1-1/2" pipe size, class 125		11	.727		395	45		440	505
8230	2" pipe size, class 125		9	.889		460	55		515	590
8450	Iron body, two way, flanged									
8560	Iron body, three way, flanged									
8570	2-1/2" pipe size, class 125	Q-1	4.50	3.556	Ea.	990	199		1,189	1,400
8580	3" pipe size, class 125		4	4		1,225	224		1,449	1,675
8590	4" pipe size, class 125		2.50	6.400		2,300	360		2,660	3,100
8600	6" pipe size, class 125	Q-2	3	8		3,500	465		3,965	4,550

23 21 Hydronic Piping and Pumps

23 21 23 – Hydronic Pumps

23 21 23.13 In-Line Centrifugal Hydronic Pumps

		Crew	Daily Output	Labor-Hours	Unit	Material	Labor	Equipment	Total	Total Incl O&P
0010	**IN-LINE CENTRIFUGAL HYDRONIC PUMPS**									
7010	Domestic hot water recirculating pump	1 Plum	5.33	1.500	Ea.	460	93		553	650

23 21 29 – Automatic Condensate Pump Units

23 21 29.10 Condensate Removal Pump System

			Crew	Daily Output	Labor-Hours	Unit	Material	Labor	Equipment	Total	Total Incl O&P
0010	**CONDENSATE REMOVAL PUMP SYSTEM**										
0020	Pump with 1 gal. ABS tank										
0100	115 V										
0120	1/50 HP, 200 GPH	G	1 Stpi	12	.667	Ea.	187	42		229	269
0140	1/18 HP, 270 GPH	G		10	.800		192	50.50		242.50	287
0160	1/5 HP, 450 GPH	G		8	1		435	63		498	575
0200	230 V										
0240	1/18 HP, 270 GPH		1 Stpi	10	.800	Ea.	206	50.50		256.50	305
0260	1/5 HP, 450 GPH	G	"	8	1	"	490	63		553	635

23 33 Air Duct Accessories

23 33 46 – Flexible Ducts

23 33 46.10 Flexible Air Ducts

			Crew	Daily Output	Labor-Hours	Unit	Material	Labor	Equipment	Total	Total Incl O&P
0010	**FLEXIBLE AIR DUCTS**										
1300	Flexible, coated fiberglass fabric on corr. resist. metal helix										
1400	pressure to 12" (WG) UL-181										
1900	Insulated, 1" thick, PE jacket, 3" diameter	G	Q-9	380	.042	L.F.	2.62	2.27		4.89	6.35
1910	4" diameter	G		340	.047		2.80	2.53		5.33	6.95
1920	5" diameter	G		300	.053		2.93	2.87		5.80	7.60
1940	6" diameter	G		260	.062		3.11	3.31		6.42	8.45
1960	7" diameter	G		220	.073		3.60	3.92		7.52	9.90
1980	8" diameter	G		180	.089		3.80	4.78		8.58	11.50
2000	9" diameter	G		160	.100		4.18	5.40		9.58	12.80
2020	10" diameter	G		140	.114		4.55	6.15		10.70	14.40
2040	12" diameter	G		100	.160		5.25	8.60		13.85	18.95
2060	14" diameter	G		80	.200		6.40	10.75		17.15	23.50
2080	16" diameter	G		60	.267		9	14.35		23.35	32
2100	18" diameter	G		45	.356		10.65	19.15		29.80	40.50
2120	20" diameter	G	Q-10	65	.369		10.65	20.50		31.15	43
2500	Insulated, heavy duty, coated fiberglass fabric										
2520	4" diameter	G	Q-9	340	.047	L.F.	3.78	2.53		6.31	8.05
2540	5" diameter	G		300	.053		4.52	2.87		7.39	9.35

23 33 Air Duct Accessories

23 33 46 – Flexible Ducts

23 33 46.10 Flexible Air Ducts		Crew	Daily Output	Labor-Hours	Unit	Material	2018 Bare Costs Labor	Equipment	Total	Total Incl O&P
2560	6" diameter G	Q-9	260	.062	L.F.	4.52	3.31		7.83	10
2580	7" diameter G		220	.073		5.70	3.92		9.62	12.20
2600	8" diameter G		180	.089		5.70	4.78		10.48	13.55
2620	9" diameter G		160	.100		7.05	5.40		12.45	15.95
2640	10" diameter G		140	.114		7.05	6.15		13.20	17.15
2660	12" diameter G		100	.160		8.30	8.60		16.90	22.50
2680	14" diameter G		80	.200		10	10.75		20.75	27.50
2700	16" diameter G		60	.267		13.20	14.35		27.55	36.50
2720	18" diameter G		45	.356		15.35	19.15		34.50	46
2800	Flexible, aluminum, pressure to 12" (WG) UL-181									
2880	Insulated, 1" thick with 3/4 lb., PE jacket									
2890	3" diameter G	Q-9	380	.042	L.F.	3.17	2.27		5.44	6.95
2891	4" diameter G		340	.047		3.47	2.53		6	7.70
2892	5" diameter G		300	.053		3.96	2.87		6.83	8.75
2893	6" diameter G		260	.062		4.68	3.31		7.99	10.20
2894	7" diameter G		220	.073		5.65	3.92		9.57	12.20
2895	8" diameter G		180	.089		5.80	4.78		10.58	13.65
2896	9" diameter G		160	.100		6.70	5.40		12.10	15.60
2897	10" diameter G		140	.114		7.90	6.15		14.05	18.10
2898	12" diameter G		100	.160		9.25	8.60		17.85	23.50
2899	14" diameter G		80	.200		10.45	10.75		21.20	28
2900	15" diameter G		70	.229		11.75	12.30		24.05	31.50
2901	16" diameter G		60	.267		14.80	14.35		29.15	38.50
2902	18" diameter G		45	.356		17.35	19.15		36.50	48
5000	Flexible, aluminum, acoustical, pressure to 2" (WG), NFPA-90A									
5010	Fiberglass insulation 1-1/2" thick, 1/2 lb. density									
5020	Polyethylene jacket, UL approved									
5026	5" diameter G	Q-9	300	.053	L.F.	4.73	2.87		7.60	9.60
5030	6" diameter G		260	.062		5.60	3.31		8.91	11.20
5034	7" diameter G		220	.073		6.80	3.92		10.72	13.45
5038	8" diameter G		180	.089		6.95	4.78		11.73	14.90
5042	9" diameter G		160	.100		8.05	5.40		13.45	17.05
5046	10" diameter G		140	.114		9.55	6.15		15.70	19.95
5050	12" diameter G		100	.160		11.10	8.60		19.70	25.50
5054	14" diameter G		80	.200		13.30	10.75		24.05	31
5058	16" diameter G		60	.267		17.70	14.35		32.05	41.50
5072	Hospital grade, PE jacket, UL approved									
5076	5" diameter G	Q-9	300	.053	L.F.	5.05	2.87		7.92	9.95
5080	6" diameter G		260	.062		6.05	3.31		9.36	11.70
5084	7" diameter G		220	.073		7.35	3.92		11.27	14.05
5088	8" diameter G		180	.089		7.50	4.78		12.28	15.55
5092	9" diameter G		160	.100		8.60	5.40		14	17.65
5096	10" diameter G		140	.114		10.35	6.15		16.50	21
5100	12" diameter G		100	.160		12	8.60		20.60	26.50
5104	14" diameter G		80	.200		14.30	10.75		25.05	32
5108	16" diameter G		60	.267		19.15	14.35		33.50	43
5140	Flexible, aluminum, silencer, pressure to 12" (WG), NFPA-90A									
5144	Fiberglass insulation 1-1/2" thick, 1/2 lb. density									
5148	Aluminum outer shell, UL approved									
5152	5" diameter G	Q-9	290	.055	L.F.	13.50	2.97		16.47	19.40
5156	6" diameter G		250	.064		13.50	3.45		16.95	20
5160	7" diameter G		210	.076		16.85	4.10		20.95	25
5164	8" diameter G		170	.094		16.85	5.05		21.90	26.50

For customer support on your Green Building Costs with RSMeans data, call 800.448.8182.

231

23 33 Air Duct Accessories

23 33 46 – Flexible Ducts

23 33 46.10 Flexible Air Ducts

		Crew	Daily Output	Labor-Hours	Unit	Material	2018 Bare Costs Labor	Equipment	Total	Total Incl O&P
5168	9" diameter G	Q-9	150	.107	L.F.	20.50	5.75		26.25	31.50
5172	10" diameter G		130	.123		20.50	6.65		27.15	32.50
5176	12" diameter G		90	.178		24	9.55		33.55	41
5180	14" diameter G		70	.229		29.50	12.30		41.80	51.50
5184	16" diameter G		50	.320		38	17.25		55.25	68
5200	Hospital grade, aluminum shell, UL approved									
5204	5" diameter G	Q-9	280	.057	L.F.	14.05	3.08		17.13	20
5208	6" diameter G		240	.067		14.05	3.59		17.64	21
5212	7" diameter G		200	.080		17.50	4.31		21.81	26
5216	8" diameter G		160	.100		17.50	5.40		22.90	27.50
5220	9" diameter G		140	.114		21.50	6.15		27.65	33
5224	10" diameter G		130	.123		21.50	6.65		28.15	33.50
5228	12" diameter G		80	.200		25	10.75		35.75	44
5232	14" diameter G		60	.267		30.50	14.35		44.85	56
5236	16" diameter G		40	.400		39.50	21.50		61	76.50

23 33 53 – Duct Liners

23 33 53.10 Duct Liner Board

		Crew	Daily Output	Labor-Hours	Unit	Material	Labor	Equipment	Total	Total Incl O&P
0010	**DUCT LINER BOARD**									
3340	Board type fiberglass liner, FSK, 1-1/2 lb. density									
3344	1" thick G	Q-14	150	.107	S.F.	.97	5.40		6.37	9.45
3345	1-1/2" thick G		130	.123		1.06	6.25		7.31	10.85
3346	2" thick G		120	.133		1.24	6.75		7.99	11.85
3348	3" thick G		110	.145		1.60	7.35		8.95	13.20
3350	4" thick G		100	.160		1.96	8.10		10.06	14.75
3356	3 lb. density, 1" thick G		150	.107		1.24	5.40		6.64	9.75
3358	1-1/2" thick G		130	.123		1.56	6.25		7.81	11.40
3360	2" thick G		120	.133		1.90	6.75		8.65	12.60
3362	2-1/2" thick G		110	.145		2.23	7.35		9.58	13.90
3364	3" thick G		100	.160		2.57	8.10		10.67	15.45
3366	4" thick G		90	.178		3.22	9		12.22	17.55
3370	6 lb. density, 1" thick G		140	.114		1.75	5.80		7.55	10.95
3374	1-1/2" thick G		120	.133		2.35	6.75		9.10	13.10
3378	2" thick G		100	.160		2.94	8.10		11.04	15.85
3490	Board type, fiberglass liner, 3 lb. density									
3680	No finish									
3700	1" thick G	Q-14	170	.094	S.F.	.69	4.77		5.46	8.15
3710	1-1/2" thick G		140	.114		1.03	5.80		6.83	10.15
3720	2" thick G		130	.123		1.38	6.25		7.63	11.20
3940	Board type, non-fibrous foam									
3950	Temperature, bacteria and fungi resistant									
3960	1" thick G	Q-14	150	.107	S.F.	2.57	5.40		7.97	11.25
3970	1-1/2" thick G		130	.123		4.03	6.25		10.28	14.15
3980	2" thick G		120	.133		4.02	6.75		10.77	14.90

23 34 HVAC Fans

23 34 23 – HVAC Power Ventilators

23 34 23.10 HVAC Power Circulators and Ventilators

			Crew	Daily Output	Labor-Hours	Unit	Material	2018 Bare Costs Labor	Equipment	Total	Total Incl O&P
0010	**HVAC POWER CIRCULATORS AND VENTILATORS**										
3000	Paddle blade air circulator, 3 speed switch										
3020	42", 5,000 CFM high, 3,000 CFM low	G	1 Elec	2.40	3.333	Ea.	123	194		317	425
3040	52", 6,500 CFM high, 4,000 CFM low	G	"	2.20	3.636	"	156	212		368	485
3100	For antique white motor, same cost										
3200	For brass plated motor, same cost										
3300	For light adaptor kit, add	G				Ea.	39.50			39.50	43.50
3310	Industrial grade, reversible, 4 blade										
3312	5,500 CFM		Q-20	5	4	Ea.	159	219		378	505
3314	7,600 CFM			5	4		177	219		396	525
3316	21,015 CFM			4	5		194	274		468	630
4000	High volume, low speed (HVLS), paddle blade air circulator										
4010	Variable speed, reversible, 1 HP motor, motor control panel,										
4020	motor drive cable, control cable with remote, and safety cable.										
4140	8' diameter		Q-5	1.50	10.667	Ea.	4,775	605		5,380	6,150
4150	10' diameter			1.45	11.034		4,800	625		5,425	6,250
4160	12' diameter			1.40	11.429		5,025	650		5,675	6,500
4170	14' diameter			1.35	11.852		5,100	670		5,770	6,625
4180	16' diameter			1.30	12.308		5,150	700		5,850	6,725
4190	18' diameter			1.25	12.800		5,200	725		5,925	6,825
4200	20' diameter			1.20	13.333		5,525	755		6,280	7,250
4210	24' diameter			1	16		5,675	905		6,580	7,600
8150	Attic fan, roof mtd, solar powered w/panel, 800 CFM, w/control	G	1 Carp	2	4		274	203		477	610

23 41 Particulate Air Filtration

23 41 13 – Panel Air Filters

23 41 13.10 Panel Type Air Filters

			Crew	Daily Output	Labor-Hours	Unit	Material	Labor	Equipment	Total	Total Incl O&P
0010	**PANEL TYPE AIR FILTERS**										
2950	Mechanical media filtration units										
3000	High efficiency type, with frame, non-supported	G				MCFM	35			35	38.50
3100	Supported type	G				"	55			55	60.50

23 41 16 – Renewable-Media Air Filters

23 41 16.10 Disposable Media Air Filters

			Crew	Daily Output	Labor-Hours	Unit	Material	Labor	Equipment	Total	Total Incl O&P
0010	**DISPOSABLE MEDIA AIR FILTERS**										
5000	Renewable disposable roll					C.S.F.	5.25			5.25	5.75
5505	Air filter, glass/paper media					Ea.	2.39			2.39	2.63
5610	Filter for 37,570 CFM, 0.15 S.P. drop, w/detergent wash		Q-10	.40	60		1,275	3,350		4,625	6,500
5620	46,650 CFM, 0.15 S.P. drop, w/detergent wash		"	.40	60		1,550	3,350		4,900	6,800
5800	Filter, bag type										
5810	90-95% efficiency										
5820	24" x 12" x 29", 0.75-1.25 MCFM		1 Shee	1.90	4.211	Ea.	60.50	252		312.50	450
5830	24" x 24" x 29", 1.5-2.5 MCFM		"	1.90	4.211	"	107	252		359	500
5850	80-85% efficiency										
5860	24" x 12" x 29", 0.75-1.25 MCFM		1 Shee	1.90	4.211	Ea.	54	252		306	445
5870	24" x 24" x 29", 1.5-2.5 MCFM		"	1.90	4.211	"	99	252		351	495

23 41 Particulate Air Filtration

23 41 19 – Washable Air Filters

23 41 19.10 Permanent Air Filters

		Crew	Daily Output	Labor-Hours	Unit	Material	2018 Bare Costs Labor	Equipment	Total	Total Incl O&P
0010	**PERMANENT AIR FILTERS**									
4500	Permanent washable	G			MCFM	25			25	27.50

23 41 23 – Extended Surface Filters

23 41 23.10 Expanded Surface Filters

		Crew	Daily Output	Labor-Hours	Unit	Material	Labor	Equipment	Total	Total Incl O&P
0010	**EXPANDED SURFACE FILTERS**									
4000	Medium efficiency, extended surface	G			MCFM	6			6	6.60

23 41 33 – High-Efficiency Particulate Filtration

23 41 33.10 HEPA Filters

		Crew	Daily Output	Labor-Hours	Unit	Material	Labor	Equipment	Total	Total Incl O&P
0010	**HEPA FILTERS**									
6000	HEPA filter complete w/particle board,									
6010	kraft paper frame, separator material									
6020	95% DOP efficiency									
6030	12" x 12" x 6", 150 CFM	1 Shee	3.70	2.162	Ea.	44.50	129		173.50	246
6034	24" x 12" x 6", 375 CFM		1.90	4.211		74	252		326	465
6038	24" x 18" x 6", 450 CFM		1.90	4.211		90.50	252		342.50	485
6042	24" x 24" x 6", 700 CFM		1.90	4.211		102	252		354	495
6046	12" x 12" x 12", 250 CFM		3.70	2.162		75	129		204	280
6050	24" x 12" x 12", 500 CFM		1.90	4.211		106	252		358	500
6054	24" x 18" x 12", 875 CFM		1.90	4.211		148	252		400	550
6058	24" x 24" x 12", 1,000 CFM		1.90	4.211		159	252		411	560
6100	99% DOP efficiency									
6110	12" x 12" x 6", 150 CFM	1 Shee	3.70	2.162	Ea.	46.50	129		175.50	248
6114	24" x 12" x 6", 325 CFM		1.90	4.211		77	252		329	470
6118	24" x 18" x 6", 550 CFM		1.90	4.211		94	252		346	490
6122	24" x 24" x 6", 775 CFM		1.90	4.211		106	252		358	500
6124	24" x 48" x 6", 775 CFM		1.30	6.154		203	370		573	785
6126	12" x 12" x 12", 250 CFM		3.60	2.222		78	133		211	289
6130	24" x 12" x 12", 500 CFM		1.90	4.211		110	252		362	505
6134	24" x 18" x 12", 775 CFM		1.90	4.211		154	252		406	555
6138	24" x 24" x 12", 1,100 CFM		1.90	4.211		165	252		417	565
6500	HEPA filter housing, 14 ga. galv. sheet metal									
6510	12" x 12" x 6"	1 Shee	2.50	3.200	Ea.	670	191		861	1,025
6514	24" x 12" x 6"		2	4		745	239		984	1,175
6518	12" x 12" x 12"		2.40	3.333		670	199		869	1,050
6522	14" x 12" x 12"		2.30	3.478		670	208		878	1,050
6526	24" x 18" x 6"		1.90	4.211		950	252		1,202	1,425
6530	24" x 24" x 6"		1.80	4.444		865	266		1,131	1,350
6534	24" x 48" x 6"		1.70	4.706		1,150	281		1,431	1,700
6538	24" x 72" x 6"		1.60	5		1,475	299		1,774	2,075
6542	24" x 18" x 12"		1.80	4.444		950	266		1,216	1,450
6546	24" x 24" x 12"		1.70	4.706		1,075	281		1,356	1,600
6550	24" x 48" x 12"		1.60	5		1,250	299		1,549	1,825
6554	24" x 72" x 12"		1.50	5.333		1,550	320		1,870	2,175
6558	48" x 48" x 6"	Q-9	2.80	5.714		1,700	310		2,010	2,350
6562	48" x 72" x 6"		2.60	6.154		2,050	330		2,380	2,750
6566	48" x 96" x 6"		2.40	6.667		2,600	360		2,960	3,400
6570	48" x 48" x 12"		2.70	5.926		1,700	320		2,020	2,350
6574	48" x 72" x 12"		2.50	6.400		2,050	345		2,395	2,775
6578	48" x 96" x 12"		2.30	6.957		2,600	375		2,975	3,425
6582	114" x 72" x 12"		2	8		3,600	430		4,030	4,600

23 42 Gas-Phase Air Filtration

23 42 13 – Activated-Carbon Air Filtration

23 42 13.10 Charcoal Type Air Filtration

		Crew	Daily Output	Labor-Hours	Unit	Material	2018 Bare Costs Labor	Equipment	Total	Total Incl O&P
0010	**CHARCOAL TYPE AIR FILTRATION**									
0050	Activated charcoal type, full flow				MCFM	650			650	715
0060	Full flow, impregnated media 12" deep					225			225	248
0070	HEPA filter & frame for field erection					450			450	495
0080	HEPA filter-diffuser, ceiling install.				↓	350			350	385

23 43 Electronic Air Cleaners

23 43 13 – Washable Electronic Air Cleaners

23 43 13.10 Electronic Air Cleaners

		Crew	Daily Output	Labor-Hours	Unit	Material	Labor	Equipment	Total	Total Incl O&P
0010	**ELECTRONIC AIR CLEANERS**									
2000	Electronic air cleaner, duct mounted									
2150	1,000 CFM	1 Shee	4	2	Ea.	430	120		550	660
2200	1,200 CFM		3.80	2.105		505	126		631	745
2250	1,400 CFM		3.60	2.222		530	133		663	790
2260	2,000 CFM	↓	3.20	2.500	↓	565	150		715	855

23 52 Heating Boilers

23 52 16 – Condensing Boilers

23 52 16.24 Condensing Boilers

			Crew	Daily Output	Labor-Hours	Unit	Material	Labor	Equipment	Total	Total Incl O&P
0010	**CONDENSING BOILERS**, Cast iron, high efficiency										
0020	Packaged with standard controls, circulator and trim										
0030	Intermittent (spark) pilot, natural or LP gas										
0040	Hot water, DOE MBH output (AFUE %)										
0100	42 MBH (84.0%)	G	Q-5	1.80	8.889	Ea.	1,550	505		2,055	2,450
0120	57 MBH (84.3%)	G		1.60	10		1,675	565		2,240	2,700
0140	85 MBH (84.0%)	G		1.40	11.429		1,875	650		2,525	3,050
0160	112 MBH (83.7%)	G	↓	1.20	13.333		2,125	755		2,880	3,475
0180	140 MBH (83.3%)	G	Q-6	1.60	15		2,350	880		3,230	3,925
0200	167 MBH (83.0%)	G		1.40	17.143		2,650	1,000		3,650	4,425
0220	194 MBH (82.7%)	G	↓	1.20	20		2,925	1,175		4,100	5,000

23 52 19 – Pulse Combustion Boilers

23 52 19.20 Pulse Type Combustion Boilers

			Crew	Daily Output	Labor-Hours	Unit	Material	Labor	Equipment	Total	Total Incl O&P
0010	**PULSE TYPE COMBUSTION BOILERS**, High efficiency										
8000	Pulse combustion, standard controls/trim										
8010	Hot water, DOE MBH output (AFUE %)										
8030	71 MBH (95.2%)		Q-5	1.60	10	Ea.	3,325	565		3,890	4,500
8050	94 MBH (95.3%)	G		1.40	11.429		3,700	650		4,350	5,050
8080	139 MBH (95.6%)	G		1.20	13.333		4,125	755		4,880	5,700
8090	207 MBH (95.4%)			1.16	13.793		4,900	780		5,680	6,575
8120	270 MBH (96.4%)			1.12	14.286		6,500	810		7,310	8,375
8130	365 MBH (91.7%)		↓	1.07	14.953	↓	7,300	850		8,150	9,325

23 52 23 – Cast-Iron Boilers

23 52 23.20 Gas-Fired Boilers

			Crew	Daily Output	Labor-Hours	Unit	Material	Labor	Equipment	Total	Total Incl O&P
0010	**GAS-FIRED BOILERS**, Natural or propane, standard controls, packaged R235000-10										
3023	Install medium efficiency propane boiler, 29.3 kW	G	Q-5	.68	23.704	Ea.	2,450	1,350		3,800	4,725
3025	Install high efficiency gas boiler, 29.3 kW	G		.68	23.704		2,450	1,350		3,800	4,725
3027	Install high efficiency propane boiler, 29.3 kW	G	↓	.68	23.704	↓	2,450	1,350		3,800	4,725

For customer support on your Green Building Costs with RSMeans data, call 800.448.8182.

23 52 Heating Boilers

23 52 88 – Burners

23 52 88.10 Replacement Type Burners

		Crew	Daily Output	Labor-Hours	Unit	Material	2018 Bare Costs Labor	Equipment	Total	Total Incl O&P
0010	**REPLACEMENT TYPE BURNERS**									
0990	Residential, conversion, gas fired, LP or natural									
1000	Gun type, atmospheric input 50 to 225 MBH	Q-1	2.50	6.400	Ea.	1,000	360		1,360	1,650
1020	100 to 400 MBH		2	8		1,675	445		2,120	2,525
1040	300 to 1,000 MBH		1.70	9.412		5,100	525		5,625	6,400
1043	Replace burner G		1.30	12.298		5,100	690		5,790	6,625
2000	Commercial and industrial, gas/oil, input									
2050	400 MBH	Q-1	1.50	10.667	Ea.	4,450	595		5,045	5,800
2090	670 MBH		1.40	11.429		4,450	640		5,090	5,875
2140	1,155 MBH		1.30	12.308		4,950	690		5,640	6,475
2200	1,800 MBH		1.20	13.333		4,975	745		5,720	6,600
2260	3,000 MBH		1.10	14.545		5,050	815		5,865	6,775
2320	4,100 MBH		1	16		6,875	895		7,770	8,900
3000	Flame retention oil fired assembly, input									
3020	.50 to 2.25 GPH	Q-1	2.40	6.667	Ea.	350	375		725	945
3040	2.0 to 5.0 GPH		2	8		340	445		785	1,050
3060	3.0 to 7.0 GPH		1.80	8.889		580	495		1,075	1,375
3080	6.0 to 12.0 GPH		1.60	10		930	560		1,490	1,875
4100	Replace burner fireye G	1 Stpi	26.67	.300		248	18.90		266.90	300
4500	Replace burner blower bearing G		4	2		64	126		190	261
4510	Replace conveyor bearing G		3.60	2.222		72	140		212	290
4520	Replace fan bearings G		3.40	2.353		188	148		336	430
4525	Fan bearing G					188			188	206
4600	Gas safety, shut off valve, 3/4" threaded	1 Stpi	20	.400		186	25		211	243
4610	1" threaded		19	.421		180	26.50		206.50	238
4620	1-1/4" threaded		15	.533		202	33.50		235.50	274
4630	1-1/2" threaded		13	.615		219	39		258	300
4640	2" threaded		11	.727		246	46		292	340
4650	2-1/2" threaded	Q-1	15	1.067		281	59.50		340.50	400
4660	3" threaded		13	1.231		385	69		454	530
4670	4" flanged		3	5.333		2,750	298		3,048	3,475
4680	6" flanged	Q-2	3	8		6,150	465		6,615	7,450
4700	Replace burner ignition transformer G	1 Stpi	16	.500		98.50	31.50		130	156
4705	Burner ignition transformer G					98.50			98.50	108
4710	Replace burner ignition electrode G	1 Stpi	20	.400		14.10	25		39.10	53.50
4715	Burner ignition electrode G					14.10			14.10	15.50
4720	Replace burner oil pump G	1 Stpi	11.43	.700		127	44		171	207
4725	Burner oil pump G					127			127	140
4730	Replace burner nozzle G	1 Stpi	26.66	.300		6.45	18.90		25.35	35.50
4735	Burner nozzle G					6.45			6.45	7.05
4750	Replace burner ignition transformer G	1 Stpi	14	.571		98.50	36		134.50	162
4755	Burner ignition transformer G					98.50			98.50	108
4760	Replace burner ignition electrode G	1 Stpi	20	.400		14.10	25		39.10	53.50
4765	Burner ignition electrode G					14.10			14.10	15.50
4770	Replace burner oil pump G	1 Stpi	10	.800		150	50.50		200.50	241
4775	Burner oil pump G					150			150	165
4780	Replace burner nozzle G	1 Stpi	24	.333		9.10	21		30.10	41.50
4785	Burner nozzle G					9.10			9.10	10
4800	Replace burner ignition transformer G	1 Stpi	12	.667		98.50	42		140.50	172
4805	Burner ignition transformer G					98.50			98.50	108
4810	Replace burner ignition electrode G	1 Stpi	18	.444		14.10	28		42.10	57.50
4815	Burner ignition electrode G					14.10			14.10	15.50

23 52 Heating Boilers

23 52 88 – Burners

23 52 88.10 Replacement Type Burners

		Crew	Daily Output	Labor-Hours	Unit	Material	2018 Bare Costs Labor	Equipment	Total	Total Incl O&P
4820	Replace burner oil pump	G 1 Stpi	8	1	Ea.	127	63		190	235
4825	Burner oil pump	G				127			127	140
4830	Replace burner nozzle	G 1 Stpi	20	.400		9.10	25		34.10	48
4835	Burner nozzle	G				9.10			9.10	10
4850	Replace burner oil pump	G Q-5	6.15	2.602		168	148		316	405
4855	Burner oil pump	G				168			168	185
4860	Replace burner nozzle	G 1 Stpi	14	.571		9.10	36		45.10	64
4865	Burner nozzle	G				9.10			9.10	10
4880	Replace spreader	G 4 Stpi	.25	130		7,575	8,200		15,775	20,600
4885	Pneumatic coal spreader	G				7,575			7,575	8,325
4900	Replace pump seals/bearings	G 1 Stpi	5.33	1.500		31.50	94.50		126	177
4905	Pump seals/bearings	G				31.50			31.50	34.50

23 54 Furnaces

23 54 16 – Fuel-Fired Furnaces

23 54 16.14 Condensing Furnaces

		Crew	Daily Output	Labor-Hours	Unit	Material	Labor	Equipment	Total	Total Incl O&P
0010	**CONDENSING FURNACES**, High efficiency									
0020	Oil fired, packaged, complete									
0030	Upflow									
0040	Output @ 95% A.F.U.E.									
0100	49 MBH @ 1,000 CFM	Q-9	3.70	4.324	Ea.	6,200	233		6,433	7,175
0110	73.5 MBH @ 2,000 CFM		3.60	4.444		6,250	239		6,489	7,250
0120	96 MBH @ 2,000 CFM		3.40	4.706		6,250	253		6,503	7,250
0130	115.6 MBH @ 2,000 CFM		3.40	4.706		6,250	253		6,503	7,250
0140	147 MBH @ 2,000 CFM		3.30	4.848		16,500	261		16,761	18,500
0150	192 MBH @ 4,000 CFM		2.60	6.154		18,000	330		18,330	20,300
0170	231.5 MBH @ 4,000 CFM		2.30	6.957		18,000	375		18,375	20,400
0260	For variable speed motor, add					725			725	800
0270	Note: Also available in horizontal, counterflow and lowboy configurations.									

23 54 16.21 Solid Fuel-Fired Furnaces

		Crew	Daily Output	Labor-Hours	Unit	Material	Labor	Equipment	Total	Total Incl O&P
0010	**SOLID FUEL-FIRED FURNACES**									
6020	Wood fired furnaces									
6030	Includes hot water coil, thermostat, and auto draft control									
6040	24" long firebox	G Q-9	4	4	Ea.	4,375	215		4,590	5,150
6050	30" long firebox	G	3.60	4.444		5,100	239		5,339	6,000
6060	With fireplace glass doors	G	3.20	5		6,450	269		6,719	7,500
6200	Wood/oil fired furnaces, includes two thermostats									
6210	Includes hot water coil and auto draft control									
6240	24" long firebox	G Q-9	3.40	4.706	Ea.	5,375	253		5,628	6,275
6250	30" long firebox	G	3	5.333		5,975	287		6,262	7,025
6260	With fireplace glass doors	G	2.80	5.714		7,325	310		7,635	8,525
6400	Wood/gas fired furnaces, includes two thermostats									
6410	Includes hot water coil and auto draft control									
6440	24" long firebox	G Q-9	2.80	5.714	Ea.	6,000	310		6,310	7,075
6450	30" long firebox	G	2.40	6.667		6,700	360		7,060	7,925
6460	With fireplace glass doors	G	2	8		8,025	430		8,455	9,475
6600	Wood/oil/gas fired furnaces, optional accessories									
6610	Hot air plenum	Q-9	16	1	Ea.	108	54		162	201
6620	Safety heat dump		24	.667		94	36		130	158
6630	Auto air intake		18	.889		148	48		196	236
6640	Cold air return package		14	1.143		159	61.50		220.50	269

For customer support on your Green Building Costs with RSMeans data, call 800.448.8182.

23 54 Furnaces

23 54 16 – Fuel-Fired Furnaces

23 54 16.21 Solid Fuel-Fired Furnaces

		Crew	Daily Output	Labor-Hours	Unit	Material	2018 Bare Costs Labor	Equipment	Total	Total Incl O&P
6650	Wood fork				Ea.	51			51	56
6700	Wood fired outdoor furnace									
6740	24" long firebox [G]	Q-9	3.80	4.211	Ea.	4,000	227		4,227	4,750
6760	Wood fired outdoor furnace, optional accessories									
6770	Chimney section, stainless steel, 6" ID x 3' long [G]	Q-9	36	.444	Ea.	176	24		200	231
6780	Chimney cap, stainless steel [G]	"	40	.400	"	104	21.50		125.50	147
6800	Wood fired hot water furnace									
6820	Includes 200 gal. hot water storage, thermostat, and auto draft control									
6840	30" long firebox [G]	Q-9	2.10	7.619	Ea.	8,350	410		8,760	9,825
6850	Water to air heat exchanger									
6870	Includes mounting kit and blower relay									
6880	140 MBH, 18.75" W x 18.75" L	Q-9	7.50	2.133	Ea.	375	115		490	590
6890	200 MBH, 24" W x 24" L	"	7	2.286	"	535	123		658	775
6900	Water to water heat exchanger									
6940	100 MBH	Q-9	6.50	2.462	Ea.	380	133		513	615
6960	290 MBH	"	6	2.667	"	545	144		689	815
7000	Optional accessories									
7010	Large volume circulation pump (2 included)	Q-9	14	1.143	Ea.	246	61.50		307.50	365
7020	Air bleed fittings (package)		24	.667		51.50	36		87.50	112
7030	Domestic water preheater		6	2.667		222	144		366	465
7040	Smoke pipe kit		4	4		92	215		307	430

23 55 Fuel-Fired Heaters

23 55 23 – Gas-Fired Radiant Heaters

23 55 23.10 Infrared Type Heating Units

		Crew	Daily Output	Labor-Hours	Unit	Material	Labor	Equipment	Total	Total Incl O&P
0010	**INFRARED TYPE HEATING UNITS**									
0020	Gas fired, unvented, electric ignition, 100% shutoff.									
0030	Piping and wiring not included									
0100	Input, 30 MBH	Q-5	6	2.667	Ea.	1,000	151		1,151	1,325
0120	45 MBH		5	3.200		955	181		1,136	1,325
0140	50 MBH		4.50	3.556		955	202		1,157	1,350
0160	60 MBH		4	4		955	227		1,182	1,400
0180	75 MBH		3	5.333		955	300		1,255	1,500
0200	90 MBH		2.50	6.400		955	365		1,320	1,600
0220	105 MBH		2	8		955	455		1,410	1,725
0240	120 MBH		2	8		1,575	455		2,030	2,400
1000	Gas fired, vented, electric ignition, tubular									
1020	Piping and wiring not included, 20' to 80' lengths									
1030	Single stage, input, 60 MBH	Q-6	4.50	5.333	Ea.	1,450	315		1,765	2,075
1040	80 MBH		3.90	6.154		1,450	360		1,810	2,150
1050	100 MBH		3.40	7.059		1,450	415		1,865	2,225
1060	125 MBH		2.90	8.276		1,450	485		1,935	2,325
1070	150 MBH		2.70	8.889		1,450	525		1,975	2,375
1080	170 MBH		2.50	9.600		1,450	565		2,015	2,450
1090	200 MBH		2.20	10.909		1,650	640		2,290	2,800
1100	Note: Final pricing may vary due to									
1110	tube length and configuration package selected									
1130	Two stage, input, 60 MBH high, 45 MBH low	Q-6	4.50	5.333	Ea.	1,775	315		2,090	2,425
1140	80 MBH high, 60 MBH low		3.90	6.154		1,775	360		2,135	2,500
1150	100 MBH high, 65 MBH low		3.40	7.059		1,775	415		2,190	2,575
1160	125 MBH high, 95 MBH low		2.90	8.276		1,775	485		2,260	2,675

23 55 Fuel-Fired Heaters

23 55 23 – Gas-Fired Radiant Heaters

23 55 23.10 Infrared Type Heating Units

		Crew	Daily Output	Labor-Hours	Unit	Material	2018 Bare Costs Labor	Equipment	Total	Total Incl O&P
1170	150 MBH high, 100 MBH low	Q-6	2.70	8.889	Ea.	1,775	525		2,300	2,725
1180	170 MBH high, 125 MBH low		2.50	9.600		2,000	565		2,565	3,050
1190	200 MBH high, 150 MBH low	↓	2.20	10.909	↓	2,000	640		2,640	3,175
1220	Note: Final pricing may vary due to									
1230	tube length and configuration package selected									

23 56 Solar Energy Heating Equipment

23 56 16 – Packaged Solar Heating Equipment

23 56 16.40 Solar Heating Systems

			Crew	Daily Output	Labor-Hours	Unit	Material	Labor	Equipment	Total	Total Incl O&P
0010	**SOLAR HEATING SYSTEMS**	R235616-60									
0020	System/package prices, not including connecting										
0030	pipe, insulation, or special heating/plumbing fixtures										
0500	Hot water, standard package, low temperature										
0540	1 collector, circulator, fittings, 65 gal. tank	G	Q-1	.50	32	Ea.	3,950	1,800		5,750	7,050
0560	2 collectors, circulator, fittings, 100 gal. tank	G	1 Plum	.22	36.364		5,125	2,250		7,375	9,050
0580	2 collectors, circulator, fittings, 120 gal. tank	G	Q-1	.40	40		5,400	2,225		7,625	9,325
0620	3 collectors, circulator, fittings, 120 gal. tank	G	"	.34	47.059	↓	7,375	2,625		10,000	12,100
0700	Medium temperature package										
0720	1 collector, circulator, fittings, 80 gal. tank	G	Q-1	.50	32	Ea.	5,350	1,800		7,150	8,600
0740	2 collectors, circulator, fittings, 120 gal. tank	G		.40	40		6,900	2,225		9,125	11,000
0780	3 collectors, circulator, fittings, 120 gal. tank	G	↓	.30	53.333		7,825	2,975		10,800	13,100
0980	For each additional 120 gal. tank, add	G				↓	1,850			1,850	2,050

23 56 16.50 Packaged Solar Heating Systems

0010	**PACKAGED SOLAR HEATING SYSTEMS**										
9000	Alt energy sources, evac tube solar collector, 20 tube unit, excl. labor	G				System	1,800			1,800	1,975
9010	30 tube unit, excl. labor	G					2,000			2,000	2,200
9020	Simple inst only, incl. collector, piping, pump, wiring & tank							5,000		5,000	5,500
9040	Complex inst only, incl. collector, piping, pump, wiring & tank					↓		7,000		7,000	7,700

23 56 19 – Solar Heating Components

23 56 19.50 Solar Heating Ancillary

0010	**SOLAR HEATING ANCILLARY**										
2300	Circulators, air										
2310	Blowers										
2330	100-300 S.F. system, 1/10 HP	G	Q-9	16	1	Ea.	249	54		303	355
2340	300-500 S.F. system, 1/5 HP	G		15	1.067		330	57.50		387.50	450
2350	Two speed, 100-300 S.F., 1/10 HP	G		14	1.143		144	61.50		205.50	253
2400	Reversible fan, 20" diameter, 2 speed	G		18	.889		114	48		162	199
2550	Booster fan 6" diameter, 120 CFM	G		16	1		37	54		91	123
2570	6" diameter, 225 CFM	G		16	1		45.50	54		99.50	132
2580	8" diameter, 150 CFM	G		16	1		41.50	54		95.50	128
2590	8" diameter, 310 CFM	G		14	1.143		64	61.50		125.50	165
2600	8" diameter, 425 CFM	G		14	1.143		72	61.50		133.50	174
2650	Rheostat	G		32	.500		15.70	27		42.70	58.50
2660	Shutter/damper	G		12	1.333		57	72		129	173
2670	Shutter motor	G	↓	16	1		141	54		195	237
2800	Circulators, liquid, 1/25 HP, 5.3 GPM	G	Q-1	14	1.143		193	64		257	310
2820	1/20 HP, 17 GPM	G		12	1.333		267	74.50		341.50	405
2850	1/20 HP, 17 GPM, stainless steel	G		12	1.333		257	74.50		331.50	395
2870	1/12 HP, 30 GPM	G	↓	10	1.600	↓	350	89.50		439.50	520
3000	Collector panels, air with aluminum absorber plate										

For customer support on your Green Building Costs with RSMeans data, call 800.448.8182.

23 56 Solar Energy Heating Equipment

23 56 19 – Solar Heating Components

23 56 19.50 Solar Heating Ancillary

			Crew	Daily Output	Labor-Hours	Unit	Material	2018 Bare Costs Labor	Equipment	Total	Total Incl O&P
3010	Wall or roof mount										
3040	Flat black, plastic glazing										
3080	4' x 8'	G	Q-9	6	2.667	Ea.	670	144		814	960
3100	4' x 10'	G		5	3.200	"	825	172		997	1,175
3200	Flush roof mount, 10' to 16' x 22" wide	G		96	.167	L.F.	142	8.95		150.95	170
3210	Manifold, by L.F. width of collectors	G		160	.100	"	153	5.40		158.40	176
3300	Collector panels, liquid with copper absorber plate										
3320	Black chrome, tempered glass glazing										
3330	Alum. frame, 4' x 8', 5/32" single glazing	G	Q-1	9.50	1.684	Ea.	1,025	94		1,119	1,275
3360	Solar panel liquid 3'-8" x 6', copper, 5/32" glazing	G		9	1.778		855	99.50		954.50	1,100
3390	Alum. frame, 4' x 10', 5/32" single glazing	G		6	2.667		1,175	149		1,324	1,500
3450	Flat black, alum. frame, 3.5' x 7.5'	G		9	1.778		880	99.50		979.50	1,125
3500	4' x 8'	G		5.50	2.909		1,050	163		1,213	1,400
3520	4' x 10'	G		10	1.600		1,250	89.50		1,339.50	1,500
3540	4' x 12.5'	G		5	3.200		1,275	179		1,454	1,675
3550	Liquid with fin tube absorber plate										
3560	Alum. frame 4' x 8' tempered glass	G	Q-1	10	1.600	Ea.	595	89.50		684.50	790
3580	Liquid with vacuum tubes, 4' x 6'-10"	G		9	1.778		915	99.50		1,014.50	1,150
3600	Liquid, full wetted, plastic, alum. frame, 4' x 10'	G		5	3.200		330	179		509	630
3610	Price per S.F. (collector panels)	G	1 Plum	152	.053	S.F.	31.50	3.27		34.77	40
3650	Collector panel mounting, flat roof or ground rack	G	Q-1	7	2.286	Ea.	248	128		376	465
3670	Roof clamps	G	"	70	.229	Set	2.87	12.80		15.67	22.50
3700	Roof strap, teflon	G	1 Plum	205	.039	L.F.	25	2.43		27.43	31
3900	Differential controller with two sensors										
3930	Thermostat, hard wired	G	1 Plum	8	1	Ea.	103	62		165	207
3950	Line cord and receptacle	G		12	.667		134	41.50		175.50	210
4050	Pool valve system	G		2.50	3.200		163	199		362	480
4070	With 12 VAC actuator	G		2	4		330	249		579	735
4080	Pool pump system, 2" pipe size	G		6	1.333		197	83		280	340
4100	Five station with digital read-out	G		3	2.667		267	166		433	545
4150	Sensors										
4200	Brass plug, 1/2" MPT	G	1 Plum	32	.250	Ea.	16.20	15.55		31.75	41.50
4210	Brass plug, reversed	G		32	.250		27	15.55		42.55	53
4220	Freeze prevention	G		32	.250		23	15.55		38.55	49
4240	Screw attached	G		32	.250		9.90	15.55		25.45	34.50
4250	Brass, immersion	G		32	.250		13.60	15.55		29.15	38.50
4300	Heat exchanger										
4315	includes coil, blower, circulator										
4316	and controller for DHW and space hot air										
4330	Fluid to air coil, up flow, 45 MBH	G	Q-1	4	4	Ea.	320	224		544	690
4380	70 MBH	G		3.50	4.571		360	256		616	785
4400	80 MBH	G		3	5.333		485	298		783	980
4580	Fluid to fluid package includes two circulating pumps										
4590	expansion tank, check valve, relief valve										
4600	controller, high temperature cutoff and sensors	G	Q-1	2.50	6.400	Ea.	810	360		1,170	1,425
4650	Heat transfer fluid										
4700	Propylene glycol, inhibited anti-freeze	G	1 Plum	28	.286	Gal.	23.50	17.75		41.25	52.50
4800	Solar storage tanks, knocked down										
4810	Air, galvanized steel clad, double wall, 4" fiberglass insulation										
5120	45 mil reinforced polypropylene lining,										
5140	4' high, 4' x 4' = 64 C.F./450 gallons	G	Q-9	2	8	Ea.	3,700	430		4,130	4,700
5150	4' x 8' = 128 C.F./900 gallons	G		1.50	10.667		5,525	575		6,100	6,950
5160	4' x 12' = 190 C.F./1,300 gallons	G		1.30	12.308		7,375	665		8,040	9,125

23 56 Solar Energy Heating Equipment

23 56 19 – Solar Heating Components

23 56 19.50 Solar Heating Ancillary

			Crew	Daily Output	Labor-Hours	Unit	Material	2018 Bare Costs Labor	Equipment	Total	Total Incl O&P
5170		8' x 8' = 250 C.F./1,700 gallons	G	Q-9	1	16	Ea.	7,375	860		8,235	9,450
5190		6'-3" high, 7' x 7' = 306 C.F./2,000 gallons	G	Q-10	1.20	20		14,400	1,125		15,525	17,600
5200		7' x 10'-6" = 459 C.F./3,000 gallons	G		.80	30		18,000	1,675		19,675	22,400
5210		7' x 14' = 613 C.F./4,000 gallons	G		.60	40		21,600	2,225		23,825	27,200
5220		10'-6" x 10'-6" = 689 C.F./4,500 gallons	G		.50	48		21,600	2,675		24,275	27,900
5230		10'-6" x 14' = 919 C.F./6,000 gallons	G		.40	60		25,300	3,350		28,650	32,900
5240		14' x 14' = 1,225 C.F./8,000 gallons	G	Q-11	.40	80		28,900	4,550		33,450	38,700
5250		14' x 17'-6" = 1,531 C.F./10,000 gallons	G		.30	107		32,500	6,075		38,575	45,100
5260		17'-6" x 17'-6" = 1,914 C.F./12,500 gallons	G		.25	128		36,100	7,300		43,400	51,000
5270		17'-6" x 21' = 2,297 C.F./15,000 gallons	G		.20	160		39,600	9,100		48,700	57,500
5280		21' x 21' = 2,756 C.F./18,000 gallons	G		.18	178		43,300	10,100		53,400	63,000
5290		30 mil reinforced Hypalon lining, add						.02%				
7000	Solar control valves and vents											
7050		Air purger, 1" pipe size	G	1 Plum	12	.667	Ea.	47.50	41.50		89	115
7070		Air eliminator, automatic 3/4" size	G		32	.250		30	15.55		45.55	56.50
7090		Air vent, automatic, 1/8" fitting	G		32	.250		18.55	15.55		34.10	44
7100		Manual, 1/8" NPT	G		32	.250		2.63	15.55		18.18	26.50
7120		Backflow preventer, 1/2" pipe size	G		16	.500		83	31		114	139
7130		3/4" pipe size	G		16	.500		85	31		116	141
7150		Balancing valve, 3/4" pipe size	G		20	.400		63	25		88	107
7180		Draindown valve, 1/2" copper tube	G		9	.889		215	55		270	320
7200		Flow control valve, 1/2" pipe size	G		22	.364		138	22.50		160.50	186
7220		Expansion tank, up to 5 gal.	G		32	.250		69	15.55		84.55	99.50
7250		Hydronic controller (aquastat)	G		8	1		177	62		239	288
7400		Pressure gauge, 2" dial	G		32	.250		24.50	15.55		40.05	50
7450		Relief valve, temp. and pressure 3/4" pipe size	G		30	.267		24	16.55		40.55	51.50
7500	Solenoid valve, normally closed											
7520		Brass, 3/4" NPT, 24V	G	1 Plum	9	.889	Ea.	136	55		191	233
7530		1" NPT, 24V	G		9	.889		221	55		276	325
7750		Vacuum relief valve, 3/4" pipe size	G		32	.250		30	15.55		45.55	56.50
7800	Thermometers											
7820		Digital temperature monitoring, 4 locations	G	1 Plum	2.50	3.200	Ea.	139	199		338	455
7900		Upright, 1/2" NPT	G		8	1		39.50	62		101.50	137
7970		Remote probe, 2" dial	G		8	1		33.50	62		95.50	131
7990		Stem, 2" dial, 9" stem	G		16	.500		22	31		53	71
8250	Water storage tank with heat exchanger and electric element											
8270		66 gal. with 2" x 2 lb. density insulation	G	1 Plum	1.60	5	Ea.	1,675	310		1,985	2,325
8300		80 gal. with 2" x 2 lb. density insulation	G		1.60	5		1,675	310		1,985	2,325
8320		100 gal. with 2" x 1/2 lb. density insulation	G		1.50	5.333		1,600	330		1,930	2,275
8380		120 gal. with 2" x 2 lb. density insulation	G		1.40	5.714		1,925	355		2,280	2,650
8400		120 gal. with 2" x 2 lb. density insul., 40 S.F. heat coil	G		1.40	5.714		2,425	355		2,780	3,200
8460		Insulated wrap for water heater, 2" x 1/2 lb.	G		32	.250		18.40	15.55		33.95	43.50
8500	Water storage module, plastic											
8600		Tubular, 12" diameter, 4' high	G	1 Carp	48	.167	Ea.	89	8.45		97.45	111
8610		12" diameter, 8' high	G		40	.200		143	10.15		153.15	172
8620		18" diameter, 5' high	G		38	.211		161	10.65		171.65	193
8630		18" diameter, 10' high	G		32	.250		269	12.70		281.70	315
8640		58" diameter, 5' high	G	2 Carp	32	.500		695	25.50		720.50	805
8650		Cap, 12" diameter	G					19.80			19.80	22
8660		18" diameter	G					25			25	27.50

23 72 Air-to-Air Energy Recovery Equipment

23 72 13 – Heat-Wheel Air-to-Air Energy-Recovery Equipment

23 72 13.10 Heat-Wheel Air-to-Air Energy Recovery Equip.

			Crew	Daily Output	Labor-Hours	Unit	Material	2018 Bare Costs Labor	Equipment	Total	Total Incl O&P
0010	**HEAT-WHEEL AIR-TO-AIR ENERGY RECOVERY EQUIPMENT**										
0100	Air to air										
4000	Enthalpy recovery wheel										
4010	1,000 max CFM	G	Q-9	1.20	13.333	Ea.	7,025	720		7,745	8,825
4020	2,000 max CFM	G		1	16		8,225	860		9,085	10,400
4030	4,000 max CFM	G		.80	20		9,525	1,075		10,600	12,200
4040	6,000 max CFM	G		.70	22.857		11,100	1,225		12,325	14,100
4050	8,000 max CFM	G	Q-10	1	24		12,300	1,350		13,650	15,600
4060	10,000 max CFM	G		.90	26.667		14,700	1,500		16,200	18,500
4070	20,000 max CFM	G		.80	30		26,700	1,675		28,375	31,900
4080	25,000 max CFM	G		.70	34.286		32,600	1,925		34,525	38,700
4090	30,000 max CFM	G		.50	48		36,200	2,675		38,875	43,900
4100	40,000 max CFM	G		.45	53.333		49,900	2,975		52,875	59,500
4110	50,000 max CFM	G		.40	60		58,000	3,350		61,350	68,500

23 74 Packaged Outdoor HVAC Equipment

23 74 33 – Dedicated Outdoor-Air Units

23 74 33.10 Rooftop Air Conditioners

			Crew	Daily Output	Labor-Hours	Unit	Material	Labor	Equipment	Total	Total Incl O&P
0010	**ROOFTOP AIR CONDITIONERS**, Standard controls, curb, economizer										
1112	3 ton cooling, 60 MBH heating SEER 14	G	Q-5	.70	22.857	Ea.	3,950	1,300		5,250	6,300
1130	4 ton cooling, 95 MBH heating SEER 14	G		.61	26.403		5,000	1,500		6,500	7,725
1142	5 ton cooling, 112 MBH heating SEER 14	G		.56	28.521		5,200	1,625		6,825	8,150
1146	6 ton cooling, 140 MBH heating SEER 14	G		.52	30.769		6,450	1,750		8,200	9,700
1152	7.5 ton cooling, 170 MBH heating, SEER 14	G		.50	32.258		7,900	1,825		9,725	11,400
1154	8.5 ton cooling, 170 MBH heating SEER 14			.46	34.783		9,975	1,975		11,950	14,000
1162	10 ton cooling, 200 MBH heating SEER 14	G	Q-6	.67	35.982		10,200	2,125		12,325	14,400
1174	12.5 ton cooling, 230 MBH heating, SEER 14	G		.63	37.975		12,700	2,225		14,925	17,300
1182	15 ton cooling, 270 MBH heating SEER 14	G		.57	42.032		13,500	2,475		15,975	18,600
1194	17.5 ton cooling, 330 MBH heating, SEER 14	G		.52	45.889		15,400	2,700		18,100	21,000
1212	20 ton cooling, 360 MBH heating SEER 14	G	Q-7	.67	47.976		25,900	2,875		28,775	32,800
1222	30 ton cooling, 540 MBH heating SEER 14	G		.47	68.376		53,500	4,100		57,600	65,000
1242	40 ton cooling, 675 MBH heating SEER 14	G		.35	91.168		66,000	5,475		71,475	80,500
1262	50 ton cooling, 810 MBH heating SEER 14	G		.28	114		75,000	6,825		81,825	93,000
1272	80 ton cooling, 1,000 MBH heating SEER 14	G		.20	160		116,000	9,600		125,600	142,000
2000	Multizone, electric cool, gas heat, economizer										
2102	15 ton cooling, 360 MBH heating SEER 14	G	Q-7	.61	52.545	Ea.	99,500	3,150		102,650	114,500
2122	20 ton cooling, 360 MBH heating SEER 14	G		.53	60.038		106,000	3,600		109,600	122,000
2142	25 ton cooling, 450 MBH heating SEER 14	G		.45	71.910		128,500	4,325		132,825	148,000
2162	30 ton cooling, 450 MBH heating SEER 14	G		.41	79.012		149,500	4,750		154,250	171,500
2182	35 ton cooling, 540 MBH heating SEER 14	G		.37	85.562		163,500	5,125		168,625	187,500
2202	40 ton cooling, 540 MBH heating SEER 14	G		.28	114		187,000	6,825		193,825	216,000
2222	70 ton cooling, 1,500 MBH heating SEER 14	G		.16	199		251,000	11,900		262,900	294,000
2242	80 ton cooling, 1,500 MBH heating SEER 14	G		.14	229		287,000	13,700		300,700	336,000
2262	90 ton cooling, 1,500 MBH heating SEER 14	G		.13	256		294,500	15,400		309,900	347,000
2282	105 ton cooling, 1,500 MBH heating SEER 14	G		.11	291		327,500	17,400		344,900	386,500

23 76 Evaporative Air-Cooling Equipment

23 76 13 – Direct Evaporative Air Coolers

23 76 13.10 Evaporative Coolers

			Crew	Daily Output	Labor-Hours	Unit	Material	2018 Bare Costs Labor	Equipment	Total	Total Incl O&P
0010	**EVAPORATIVE COOLERS** (Swamp Coolers) ducted, not incl. duct.										
0100	Side discharge style, capacities at 0.25" S.P.										
0120	1,785 CFM, 1/3 HP, 115 V	G	Q-9	5	3.200	Ea.	465	172		637	775
0140	2,740 CFM, 1/3 HP, 115 V	G		4.50	3.556		550	191		741	895
0160	3,235 CFM, 1/2 HP, 115 V	G		4	4		555	215		770	940
0180	3,615 CFM, 1/2 HP, 230 V	G		3.60	4.444		685	239		924	1,125
0200	4,215 CFM, 3/4 HP, 230 V	G		3.20	5		725	269		994	1,200
0220	5,255 CFM, 1 HP, 115/230 V	G		3	5.333		1,275	287		1,562	1,850
0240	6,090 CFM, 1 HP, 230/460 V	G		2.80	5.714		1,925	310		2,235	2,575
0260	8,300 CFM, 1-1/2 HP, 230/460 V	G		2.60	6.154		1,925	330		2,255	2,600
0280	8,360 CFM, 1-1/2 HP, 230/460 V	G		2.20	7.273		1,925	390		2,315	2,700
0300	9,725 CFM, 2 HP, 230/460 V	G		1.80	8.889		2,175	480		2,655	3,125
0320	11,715 CFM, 3 HP, 230/460 V	G		1.40	11.429		2,425	615		3,040	3,625
0340	14,410 CFM, 5 HP, 230/460 V	G		1	16		2,625	860		3,485	4,200
0400	For two-speed motor, add						5%				
0500	For down discharge style, add						10%				

23 81 Decentralized Unitary HVAC Equipment

23 81 29 – Variable Refrigerant Flow HVAC Systems

23 81 29.10 Heat Pump, Gas Driven

		Crew	Daily Output	Labor-Hours	Unit	Material	Labor	Equipment	Total	Total Incl O&P
0010	**HEAT PUMP, GAS DRIVEN**, Variable refrigerant volume (VRV) type									
0020	Not including interconnecting tubing or multi-zone controls									
1000	For indoor fan VRV type AHU see 23 82 19.40									
1010	Multi-zone split									
1020	Outdoor unit									
1100	8 tons cooling, for up to 17 zones	Q-5	1.30	12.308	Ea.	29,100	700		29,800	33,100
1110	Isolation rails		2.60	6.154	Pair	1,025	350		1,375	1,650
1160	15 tons cooling, for up to 33 zones		1	16	Ea.	34,800	905		35,705	39,600
1170	Isolation rails		2.60	6.154	Pair	1,200	350		1,550	1,850
2000	Packaged unit									
2020	Outdoor unit									
2200	11 tons cooling	Q-5	1.30	12.308	Ea.	37,500	700		38,200	42,400
2210	Roof curb adapter	"	2.60	6.154		650	350		1,000	1,250
2220	Thermostat	1 Stpi	1.30	6.154		390	390		780	1,025

23 81 43 – Air-Source Unitary Heat Pumps

23 81 43.10 Air-Source Heat Pumps

		Crew	Daily Output	Labor-Hours	Unit	Material	Labor	Equipment	Total	Total Incl O&P
0010	**AIR-SOURCE HEAT PUMPS**, Not including interconnecting tubing									
1000	Air to air, split system, not including curbs, pads, fan coil and ductwork									
1012	Outside condensing unit only, for fan coil see Section 23 82 19.10									
1015	1.5 ton cooling, 7 MBH heat @ 0°F	Q-5	2.40	6.667	Ea.	1,600	380		1,980	2,350
1020	2 ton cooling, 8.5 MBH heat @ 0°F		2	8		1,650	455		2,105	2,475
1030	2.5 ton cooling, 10 MBH heat @ 0°F		1.60	10		1,800	565		2,365	2,850
1040	3 ton cooling, 13 MBH heat @ 0°F		1.20	13.333		2,100	755		2,855	3,475
1050	3.5 ton cooling, 18 MBH heat @ 0°F		1	16		2,250	905		3,155	3,850
1054	4 ton cooling, 24 MBH heat @ 0°F		.80	20		2,450	1,125		3,575	4,400
1060	5 ton cooling, 27 MBH heat @ 0°F		.50	32		2,675	1,825		4,500	5,650
1080	7.5 ton cooling, 33 MBH heat @ 0°F		.45	35.556		3,875	2,025		5,900	7,275
1100	10 ton cooling, 50 MBH heat @ 0°F	Q-6	.64	37.500		6,275	2,200		8,475	10,300
1120	15 ton cooling, 64 MBH heat @ 0°F		.50	48		8,725	2,825		11,550	13,800
1130	20 ton cooling, 85 MBH heat @ 0°F		.35	68.571		17,900	4,025		21,925	25,800

23 81 Decentralized Unitary HVAC Equipment

23 81 43 – Air-Source Unitary Heat Pumps

23 81 43.10 Air-Source Heat Pumps

		Crew	Daily Output	Labor-Hours	Unit	Material	2018 Bare Costs Labor	Equipment	Total	Total Incl O&P
1140	25 ton cooling, 119 MBH heat @ 0°F	Q-6	.25	96	Ea.	21,100	5,650		26,750	31,700
1500	Single package, not including curbs, pads, or plenums									
1502	0.5 ton cooling, supplementary heat included	Q-5	8	2	Ea.	3,275	113		3,388	3,775
1504	0.75 ton cooling, supplementary heat included		6	2.667		3,450	151		3,601	4,025
1506	1 ton cooling, supplementary heat included		4	4		3,200	227		3,427	3,875
1510	1.5 ton cooling, 5 MBH heat @ 0°F		1.55	10.323		3,225	585		3,810	4,425
1520	2 ton cooling, 6.5 MBH heat @ 0°F		1.50	10.667		3,200	605		3,805	4,425
1540	2.5 ton cooling, 8 MBH heat @ 0°F		1.40	11.429		3,250	650		3,900	4,550
1560	3 ton cooling, 10 MBH heat @ 0°F		1.20	13.333		3,675	755		4,430	5,175
1570	3.5 ton cooling, 11 MBH heat @ 0°F		1	16		4,000	905		4,905	5,775
1580	4 ton cooling, 13 MBH heat @ 0°F		.96	16.667		4,300	945		5,245	6,150
1620	5 ton cooling, 27 MBH heat @ 0°F		.65	24.615		4,925	1,400		6,325	7,500
1640	7.5 ton cooling, 35 MBH heat @ 0°F		.40	40		7,225	2,275		9,500	11,400
1648	10 ton cooling, 45 MBH heat @ 0°F	Q-6	.40	60		10,100	3,525		13,625	16,400
1652	12 ton cooling, 50 MBH heat @ 0°F	"	.36	66.667		10,700	3,925		14,625	17,600
1696	Supplementary electric heat coil incl., unless noted otherwise									
6000	Air to water, single package, excluding storage tank and ductwork									
6010	Includes circulating water pump, air duct connections, digital temperature									
6020	controller with remote tank temp. probe and sensor for storage tank.									
6040	Water heating - air cooling capacity									
6110	35.5 MBH heat water, 2.3 ton cool air	Q-5	1.60	10	Ea.	17,100	565		17,665	19,700
6120	58 MBH heat water, 3.8 ton cool air		1.10	14.545		19,500	825		20,325	22,800
6130	76 MBH heat water, 4.9 ton cool air		.87	18.391		23,300	1,050		24,350	27,200
6140	98 MBH heat water, 6.5 ton cool air		.62	25.806		30,100	1,475		31,575	35,300
6150	113 MBH heat water, 7.4 ton cool air		.59	27.119		33,000	1,550		34,550	38,600
6160	142 MBH heat water, 9.2 ton cool air		.52	30.769		40,000	1,750		41,750	46,600
6170	171 MBH heat water, 11.1 ton cool air		.49	32.653		47,100	1,850		48,950	55,000

23 81 46 – Water-Source Unitary Heat Pumps

23 81 46.10 Water Source Heat Pumps

		Crew	Daily Output	Labor-Hours	Unit	Material	Labor	Equipment	Total	Total Incl O&P
0010	**WATER SOURCE HEAT PUMPS**, Not incl. connecting tubing or water source									
2000	Water source to air, single package									
2100	1 ton cooling, 13 MBH heat @ 75°F	Q-5	2	8	Ea.	1,900	455		2,355	2,750
2120	1.5 ton cooling, 17 MBH heat @ 75°F		1.80	8.889		1,900	505		2,405	2,825
2140	2 ton cooling, 19 MBH heat @ 75°F		1.70	9.412		2,225	535		2,760	3,250
2160	2.5 ton cooling, 25 MBH heat @ 75°F		1.60	10		2,425	565		2,990	3,500
2180	3 ton cooling, 27 MBH heat @ 75°F		1.40	11.429		2,475	650		3,125	3,700
2190	3.5 ton cooling, 29 MBH heat @ 75°F		1.30	12.308		2,700	700		3,400	4,025
2200	4 ton cooling, 31 MBH heat @ 75°F		1.20	13.333		3,000	755		3,755	4,450
2220	5 ton cooling, 29 MBH heat @ 75°F		.90	17.778		3,300	1,000		4,300	5,175
2240	7.5 ton cooling, 35 MBH heat @ 75°F		.60	26.667		6,750	1,500		8,250	9,700
2250	8 ton cooling, 40 MBH heat @ 75°F		.58	27.586		6,900	1,575		8,475	9,925
2260	10 ton cooling, 50 MBH heat @ 75°F		.53	30.189		7,550	1,700		9,250	10,900
2280	15 ton cooling, 64 MBH heat @ 75°F	Q-6	.47	51.064		14,500	3,000		17,500	20,500
2300	20 ton cooling, 100 MBH heat @ 75°F		.41	58.537		15,800	3,450		19,250	22,600
2310	25 ton cooling, 100 MBH heat @ 75°F		.32	75		21,600	4,400		26,000	30,400
2320	30 ton cooling, 128 MBH heat @ 75°F		.24	102		23,700	6,000		29,700	35,100
2340	40 ton cooling, 200 MBH heat @ 75°F		.21	117		33,400	6,875		40,275	47,200
2360	50 ton cooling, 200 MBH heat @ 75°F		.15	160		37,800	9,400		47,200	55,500
3960	For supplementary heat coil, add					10%				
4000	For increase in capacity thru use									
4020	of solar collector, size boiler at 60%									

23 82 Convection Heating and Cooling Units

23 82 19 – Fan Coil Units

23 82 19.10 Fan Coil Air Conditioning

		Crew	Daily Output	Labor-Hours	Unit	Material	Labor	Equipment	Total	Total Incl O&P
0010	**FAN COIL AIR CONDITIONING**									
0100	Chilled water, 1/2 ton cooling	Q-5	8	2	Ea.	555	113		668	780
0120	1 ton cooling		6	2.667		830	151		981	1,150
0180	3 ton cooling		4	4		1,950	227		2,177	2,500
0262	For hot water coil, add					40%	10%			
0320	1 ton cooling	Q-5	6	2.667	Ea.	1,625	151		1,776	2,000
0940	Direct expansion, for use w/air cooled condensing unit, 1-1/2 ton cooling		5	3.200		610	181		791	950
1000	5 ton cooling		3	5.333		1,075	300		1,375	1,625

23 82 19.40 Fan Coil Air Conditioning

			Crew	Daily Output	Labor-Hours	Unit	Material	Labor	Equipment	Total	Total Incl O&P
0010	**FAN COIL AIR CONDITIONING**, Variable refrigerant volume (VRV) type										
0020	Not including interconnecting tubing or multi-zone controls										
0030	For VRV condensing unit see section 23 81 29.10										
0050	Indoor type, ducted										
0100	Vertical concealed										
0130	1 ton cooling	G	Q-5	2.97	5.387	Ea.	2,475	305		2,780	3,175
0140	1.5 ton cooling	G		2.77	5.776		2,525	330		2,855	3,275
0150	2 ton cooling	G		2.70	5.926		2,725	335		3,060	3,500
0160	2.5 ton cooling	G		2.60	6.154		2,875	350		3,225	3,675
0170	3 ton cooling	G		2.50	6.400		2,925	365		3,290	3,750
0180	3.5 ton cooling	G		2.30	6.957		3,075	395		3,470	3,975
0190	4 ton cooling	G		2.19	7.306		3,075	415		3,490	4,025
0200	4.5 ton cooling	G		2.08	7.692		3,400	435		3,835	4,375
0230	Outside air connection possible										
1100	Ceiling concealed										
1130	0.6 ton cooling	G	Q-5	2.60	6.154	Ea.	1,625	350		1,975	2,300
1140	0.75 ton cooling	G		2.60	6.154		1,675	350		2,025	2,375
1150	1 ton cooling	G		2.60	6.154		1,775	350		2,125	2,475
1152	Screening door	G	1 Stpi	5.20	1.538		99	97		196	255
1160	1.5 ton cooling	G	Q-5	2.60	6.154		1,825	350		2,175	2,550
1162	Screening door	G	1 Stpi	5.20	1.538		114	97		211	272
1170	2 ton cooling	G	Q-5	2.60	6.154		2,175	350		2,525	2,900
1172	Screening door	G	1 Stpi	5.20	1.538		99	97		196	255
1180	2.5 ton cooling	G	Q-5	2.60	6.154		2,500	350		2,850	3,275
1182	Screening door	G	1 Stpi	5.20	1.538		172	97		269	335
1190	3 ton cooling	G	Q-5	2.60	6.154		2,650	350		3,000	3,450
1192	Screening door	G	1 Stpi	5.20	1.538		172	97		269	335
1200	4 ton cooling	G	Q-5	2.30	6.957		2,725	395		3,120	3,575
1202	Screening door	G	1 Stpi	5.20	1.538		172	97		269	335
1220	6 ton cooling	G	Q-5	2.08	7.692		4,625	435		5,060	5,725
1230	8 ton cooling	G	"	1.89	8.466		5,200	480		5,680	6,450
1260	Outside air connection possible										
4050	Indoor type, duct-free										
4100	Ceiling mounted cassette										
4130	0.75 ton cooling	G	Q-5	3.46	4.624	Ea.	1,875	262		2,137	2,475
4140	1 ton cooling	G		2.97	5.387		2,000	305		2,305	2,650
4150	1.5 ton cooling	G		2.77	5.776		2,075	330		2,405	2,775
4160	2 ton cooling	G		2.60	6.154		2,200	350		2,550	2,950
4170	2.5 ton cooling	G		2.50	6.400		2,250	365		2,615	3,025
4180	3 ton cooling	G		2.30	6.957		2,425	395		2,820	3,250
4190	4 ton cooling	G		2.08	7.692		2,700	435		3,135	3,625
4198	For ceiling cassette decoration panel, add	G	1 Stpi	5.20	1.538		296	97		393	470
4230	Outside air connection possible										

For customer support on your Green Building Costs with RSMeans data, call 800.448.8182.

23 82 Convection Heating and Cooling Units

23 82 19 – Fan Coil Units

23 82 19.40 Fan Coil Air Conditioning

		Crew	Daily Output	Labor-Hours	Unit	Material	2018 Bare Costs Labor	Equipment	Total	Total Incl O&P
4500	Wall mounted									
4530	0.6 ton cooling G	Q-5	5.20	3.077	Ea.	995	174		1,169	1,375
4540	0.75 ton cooling G		5.20	3.077		1,050	174		1,224	1,425
4550	1 ton cooling G		4.16	3.846		1,200	218		1,418	1,625
4560	1.5 ton cooling G		3.77	4.244		1,300	241		1,541	1,800
4570	2 ton cooling G		3.46	4.624		1,400	262		1,662	1,950
4590	Condensate pump for the above air handlers G	1 Stpi	6.46	1.238		213	78		291	355
4700	Floor standing unit									
4730	1 ton cooling G	Q-5	2.60	6.154	Ea.	1,675	350		2,025	2,375
4740	1.5 ton cooling G		2.60	6.154		1,900	350		2,250	2,625
4750	2 ton cooling G		2.60	6.154		2,050	350		2,400	2,775
4800	Floor standing unit, concealed									
4830	1 ton cooling G	Q-5	2.60	6.154	Ea.	1,600	350		1,950	2,300
4840	1.5 ton cooling G		2.60	6.154		1,825	350		2,175	2,525
4850	2 ton cooling G		2.60	6.154		1,950	350		2,300	2,675
4880	Outside air connection possible									
8000	Accessories									
8100	Branch divergence pipe fitting									
8110	Capacity under 76 MBH	1 Stpi	2.50	3.200	Ea.	151	202		353	470
8120	76 MBH to 112 MBH		2.50	3.200		178	202		380	500
8130	112 MBH to 234 MBH		2.50	3.200		505	202		707	860
8200	Header pipe fitting									
8210	Max 4 branches									
8220	Capacity under 76 MBH	1 Stpi	1.70	4.706	Ea.	221	296		517	690
8260	Max 8 branches									
8270	76 MBH to 112 MBH	1 Stpi	1.70	4.706	Ea.	450	296		746	940
8280	112 MBH to 234 MBH	"	1.30	6.154	"	720	390		1,110	1,375

23 83 Radiant Heating Units

23 83 16 – Radiant-Heating Hydronic Piping

23 83 16.10 Radiant Floor Heating

		Crew	Daily Output	Labor-Hours	Unit	Material	Labor	Equipment	Total	Total Incl O&P
0010	**RADIANT FLOOR HEATING**									
0100	Tubing, PEX (cross-linked polyethylene)									
0110	Oxygen barrier type for systems with ferrous materials									
0120	1/2"	Q-5	800	.020	L.F.	1.05	1.13		2.18	2.87
0130	3/4"		535	.030		1.48	1.70		3.18	4.18
0140	1"		400	.040		2.31	2.27		4.58	5.95
0200	Non barrier type for ferrous free systems									
0210	1/2"	Q-5	800	.020	L.F.	.50	1.13		1.63	2.26
0220	3/4"		535	.030		.92	1.70		2.62	3.56
0230	1"		400	.040		1.58	2.27		3.85	5.15
1000	Manifolds									
1110	Brass									
1120	With supply and return valves, flow meter, thermometer,									
1122	auto air vent and drain/fill valve.									
1130	1", 2 circuit	Q-5	14	1.143	Ea.	298	65		363	430
1140	1", 3 circuit		13.50	1.185		340	67		407	475
1150	1", 4 circuit		13	1.231		370	70		440	510
1154	1", 5 circuit		12.50	1.280		440	72.50		512.50	595
1158	1", 6 circuit		12	1.333		480	75.50		555.50	645
1162	1", 7 circuit		11.50	1.391		525	79		604	700

23 83 Radiant Heating Units

23 83 16 – Radiant-Heating Hydronic Piping

23 83 16.10 Radiant Floor Heating		Crew	Daily Output	Labor-Hours	Unit	Material	2018 Bare Costs Labor	Equipment	Total	Total Incl O&P
1166	1", 8 circuit	Q-5	11	1.455	Ea.	565	82.50		647.50	750
1172	1", 9 circuit		10.50	1.524		625	86.50		711.50	820
1174	1", 10 circuit		10	1.600		670	90.50		760.50	875
1178	1", 11 circuit		9.50	1.684		700	95.50		795.50	915
1182	1", 12 circuit		9	1.778		775	101		876	1,000
1610	Copper manifold header (cut to size)									
1620	1" header, 12 circuit 1/2" sweat outlets	Q-5	3.33	4.805	Ea.	102	272		374	520
1630	1-1/4" header, 12 circuit 1/2" sweat outlets		3.20	5		118	284		402	555
1640	1-1/4" header, 12 circuit 3/4" sweat outlets		3	5.333		128	300		428	595
1650	1-1/2" header, 12 circuit 3/4" sweat outlets		3.10	5.161		153	293		446	610
1660	2" header, 12 circuit 3/4" sweat outlets		2.90	5.517		226	315		541	720
3000	Valves									
3110	Thermostatic zone valve actuator with end switch	Q-5	40	.400	Ea.	44.50	22.50		67	83
3114	Thermostatic zone valve actuator	"	36	.444	"	91	25		116	138
3120	Motorized straight zone valve with operator complete									
3130	3/4"	Q-5	35	.457	Ea.	146	26		172	200
3140	1"		32	.500		158	28.50		186.50	217
3150	1-1/4"		29.60	.541		200	30.50		230.50	266
3500	4 way mixing valve, manual, brass									
3530	1"	Q-5	13.30	1.203	Ea.	203	68		271	325
3540	1-1/4"		11.40	1.404		220	79.50		299.50	360
3550	1-1/2"		11	1.455		281	82.50		363.50	435
3560	2"		10.60	1.509		395	85.50		480.50	565
3800	Mixing valve motor, 4 way for valves, 1" and 1-1/4"		34	.471		405	26.50		431.50	485
3810	Mixing valve motor, 4 way for valves, 1-1/2" and 2"		30	.533		400	30		430	490
5000	Radiant floor heating, zone control panel									
5120	4 zone actuator valve control, expandable	Q-5	20	.800	Ea.	159	45.50		204.50	244
5130	6 zone actuator valve control, expandable		18	.889		253	50.50		303.50	355
6070	Thermal track, straight panel for long continuous runs, 5.333 S.F.		40	.400		31	22.50		53.50	68
6080	Thermal track, utility panel, for direction reverse at run end, 5.333 S.F.		40	.400		31	22.50		53.50	68
6090	Combination panel, for direction reverse plus straight run, 5.333 S.F.		40	.400		31	22.50		53.50	68
7000	PEX tubing fittings									
7100	Compression type									
7116	Coupling									
7120	1/2" x 1/2"	1 Stpi	27	.296	Ea.	6.75	18.65		25.40	35.50
7124	3/4" x 3/4"	"	23	.348	"	13.05	22		35.05	47.50
7130	Adapter									
7132	1/2" x female sweat 1/2"	1 Stpi	27	.296	Ea.	4.37	18.65		23.02	33
7134	1/2" x female sweat 3/4"		26	.308		4.89	19.40		24.29	34.50
7136	5/8" x female sweat 3/4"		24	.333		7	21		28	39
7140	Elbow									
7142	1/2" x female sweat 1/2"	1 Stpi	27	.296	Ea.	6.70	18.65		25.35	35.50
7144	1/2" x female sweat 3/4"		26	.308		7.80	19.40		27.20	37.50
7146	5/8" x female sweat 3/4"		24	.333		8.75	21		29.75	41
7200	Insert type									
7206	PEX x male NPT									
7210	1/2" x 1/2"	1 Stpi	29	.276	Ea.	2.73	17.40		20.13	29
7220	3/4" x 3/4"		27	.296		4.02	18.65		22.67	32.50
7230	1" x 1"		26	.308		6.80	19.40		26.20	36.50
7300	PEX coupling									
7310	1/2" x 1/2"	1 Stpi	30	.267	Ea.	.54	16.80		17.34	26
7320	3/4" x 3/4"		29	.276		.76	17.40		18.16	27
7330	1" x 1"		28	.286		1.35	18		19.35	28.50

For customer support on your Green Building Costs with RSMeans data, call 800.448.8182.

23 83 Radiant Heating Units

23 83 16 – Radiant-Heating Hydronic Piping

23 83 16.10 Radiant Floor Heating

		Crew	Daily Output	Labor-Hours	Unit	Material	2018 Bare Costs Labor	Equipment	Total	Total Incl O&P
7400	PEX stainless crimp ring									
7410	1/2" x 1/2"	1 Stpi	86	.093	Ea.	.46	5.85		6.31	9.35
7420	3/4" x 3/4"		84	.095		.63	6		6.63	9.75
7430	1" x 1"		82	.098		.90	6.15		7.05	10.25

23 83 33 – Electric Radiant Heaters

23 83 33.10 Electric Heating

		Crew	Daily Output	Labor-Hours	Unit	Material	Labor	Equipment	Total	Total Incl O&P
0010	**ELECTRIC HEATING**, not incl. conduit or feed wiring									
3160	Recessed, residential, 750 watt	1 Elec	6	1.333	Ea.	93	77.50		170.50	218
3170	1,000 watt		6	1.333		93	77.50		170.50	218
3180	1,250 watt		5	1.600		100	93		193	249
3190	1,500 watt		4	2		100	116		216	284
5300	Infrared quartz heaters, 120 volts, 1,000 watt		6.70	1.194		335	69.50		404.50	475
5350	1,500 watt		5	1.600		335	93		428	510
5400	240 volts, 1,500 watt		5	1.600		335	93		428	510
5450	2,000 watt		4	2		335	116		451	545
5500	3,000 watt		3	2.667		385	155		540	650
5550	4,000 watt		2.60	3.077		385	179		564	690
5570	Modulating control		.80	10		134	580		714	1,025
9210	1 kW, 3,400 BTU		2.40	3.333		281	194		475	600
9220	3.2 kW, 10,900 BTU		2.40	3.333		292	194		486	610
9230	13.5 kW, 40,956 BTU		2.20	3.636		1,550	212		1,762	2,025
9250	24 kW, 81,912 BTU		2	4		1,600	233		1,833	2,125

23 84 Humidity Control Equipment

23 84 13 – Humidifiers

23 84 13.10 Humidifier Units

			Crew	Daily Output	Labor-Hours	Unit	Material	Labor	Equipment	Total	Total Incl O&P
0010	**HUMIDIFIER UNITS**										
0520	Steam, room or duct, filter, regulators, auto. controls, 220 V										
0540	11 lb./hr.	R236000-30	Q-5	6	2.667	Ea.	2,725	151		2,876	3,225
0560	22 lb./hr.			5	3.200		3,000	181		3,181	3,575
0580	33 lb./hr.			4	4		3,100	227		3,327	3,750
0600	50 lb./hr.			4	4		3,575	227		3,802	4,300
0620	100 lb./hr.			3	5.333		4,525	300		4,825	5,425
0640	150 lb./hr.			2.50	6.400		6,475	365		6,840	7,650
0660	200 lb./hr.			2	8		8,100	455		8,555	9,600
0700	With blower										
0720	11 lb./hr.		Q-5	5.50	2.909	Ea.	4,350	165		4,515	5,025
0740	22 lb./hr.			4.75	3.368		4,550	191		4,741	5,325
0760	33 lb./hr.			3.75	4.267		4,700	242		4,942	5,550
0780	50 lb./hr.			3.50	4.571		5,375	259		5,634	6,325
0800	100 lb./hr.			2.75	5.818		6,000	330		6,330	7,100
0820	150 lb./hr.			2	8		8,750	455		9,205	10,300
0840	200 lb./hr.			1.50	10.667		9,800	605		10,405	11,700
5000	Furnace type, wheel bypass										
5020	10 GPD		1 Stpi	4	2	Ea.	186	126		312	395
5040	14 GPD			3.80	2.105		204	133		337	425
5060	19 GPD			3.60	2.222		330	140		470	570

23 84 Humidity Control Equipment

23 84 16 – Mechanical Dehumidification Units

23 84 16.10 Dehumidifier Units		Crew	Daily Output	Labor-Hours	Unit	Material	2018 Bare Costs Labor	Equipment	Total	Total Incl O&P
0010	**DEHUMIDIFIER UNITS** R236000-30									
6000	Self contained with filters and standard controls									
6040	1.5 lb./hr., 50 CFM	1 Plum	8	1	Ea.	8,175	62		8,237	9,100
6060	3 lb./hr., 150 CFM	Q-1	12	1.333		8,900	74.50		8,974.50	9,875
6065	6 lb./hr., 150 CFM		9	1.778		14,500	99.50		14,599.50	16,100
6070	16 to 20 lb./hr., 600 CFM		5	3.200		27,500	179		27,679	30,600
6080	30 to 40 lb./hr., 1,125 CFM		4	4		42,800	224		43,024	47,400
6090	60 to 75 lb./hr., 2,250 CFM		3	5.333		56,000	298		56,298	62,000
6100	120 to 155 lb./hr., 4,500 CFM		2	8		99,000	445		99,445	109,500
6110	240 to 310 lb./hr., 9,000 CFM		1.50	10.667		142,000	595		142,595	157,000
6120	400 to 515 lb./hr., 15,000 CFM	Q-2	1.60	15		178,500	870		179,370	197,500
6130	530 to 690 lb./hr., 20,000 CFM		1.40	17.143		193,500	995		194,495	214,000
6140	800 to 1030 lb./hr., 30,000 CFM		1.20	20		220,000	1,150		221,150	244,000
6150	1060 to 1375 lb./hr., 40,000 CFM		1	24		306,000	1,400		307,400	339,000

Division Notes

		CREW	DAILY OUTPUT	LABOR-HOURS	UNIT	BARE COSTS MAT.	LABOR	EQUIP.	TOTAL	TOTAL INCL O&P

Estimating Tips
26 05 00 Common Work Results for Electrical
- Conduit should be taken off in three main categories—power distribution, branch power, and branch lighting—so the estimator can concentrate on systems and components, therefore making it easier to ensure all items have been accounted for.
- For cost modifications for elevated conduit installation, add the percentages to labor according to the height of installation and only to the quantities exceeding the different height levels, not to the total conduit quantities. Refer to 26 01 02.20 for labor adjustment factors.
- Remember that aluminum wiring of equal ampacity is larger in diameter than copper and may require larger conduit.
- If more than three wires at a time are being pulled, deduct percentages from the labor hours of that grouping of wires.
- When taking off grounding systems, identify separately the type and size of wire, and list each unique type of ground connection.
- The estimator should take the weights of materials into consideration when completing a takeoff. Topics to consider include: How will the materials be supported? What methods of support are available? How high will the support structure have to reach? Will the final support structure be able to withstand the total burden? Is the support material included or separate from the fixture, equipment, and material specified?
- Do not overlook the costs for equipment used in the installation. If scaffolding or highlifts are available in the field, contractors may use them in lieu of the proposed ladders and rolling staging.

26 20 00 Low-Voltage Electrical Transmission
- Supports and concrete pads may be shown on drawings for the larger equipment, or the support system may be only a piece of plywood for the back of a panelboard. In either case, they must be included in the costs.

26 40 00 Electrical and Cathodic Protection
- When taking off cathodic protection systems, identify the type and size of cable, and list each unique type of anode connection.

26 50 00 Lighting
- Fixtures should be taken off room by room using the fixture schedule, specifications, and the ceiling plan. For large concentrations of lighting fixtures in the same area, deduct the percentages from labor hours.

Reference Numbers
Reference numbers are shown at the beginning of some major classifications. These numbers refer to related items in the Reference Section. The reference information may be an estimating procedure, an alternate pricing method, or technical information.

Note: Not all subdivisions listed here necessarily appear. ■

No part of this cost data may be reproduced, stored in a retrieval system, or transmitted in any form or by any means without prior written permission of Gordian.

Note: Trade Service, in part, has been used as a reference source for some of the material prices used in Division 26.

Did you know?
RSMeans data is available through our online application with 24/7 access:
- Search for unit prices by keyword
- Leverage the most up-to-date data
- Build and export estimates

Try it free for 30 days!
www.rsmeans.com/2018freetrial

26 05 Common Work Results for Electrical

26 05 33 – Raceway and Boxes for Electrical Systems

26 05 33.17 Outlet Boxes, Plastic

		Crew	Daily Output	Labor-Hours	Unit	Material	2018 Bare Costs Labor	Equipment	Total	Total Incl O&P
0010	**OUTLET BOXES, PLASTIC**									
4000	Air/vapor barrier boxes, plastic, for electrical work boxes	G 1 Elec	40	.200	Ea.	4.97	11.65		16.62	23

26 09 Instrumentation and Control for Electrical Systems

26 09 13 – Electrical Power Monitoring

26 09 13.30 Smart Metering

		Crew	Daily Output	Labor-Hours	Unit	Material	Labor	Equipment	Total	Total Incl O&P
0010	**SMART METERING**, In panel									
0100	Single phase, 120/208 volt, 100 amp	G 1 Elec	8.78	.911	Ea.	325	53		378	435
0120	200 amp	G	8.78	.911		335	53		388	450
0200	277 volt, 100 amp	G	8.78	.911		360	53		413	475
0220	200 amp	G	8.78	.911		395	53		448	510
1100	Three phase, 120/208 volt, 100 amp	G	4.69	1.706		675	99.50		774.50	890
1120	200 amp	G	4.69	1.706		800	99.50		899.50	1,025
1130	400 amp	G	4.69	1.706		800	99.50		899.50	1,025
1140	800 amp	G	4.69	1.706		805	99.50		904.50	1,025
1150	1,600 amp	G	4.69	1.706		830	99.50		929.50	1,050
1200	277/480 volt, 100 amp	G	4.69	1.706		870	99.50		969.50	1,100
1220	200 amp	G	4.69	1.706		880	99.50		979.50	1,125
1230	400 amp	G	4.69	1.706		880	99.50		979.50	1,125
1240	800 amp	G	4.69	1.706		850	99.50		949.50	1,075
1250	1,600 amp	G	4.69	1.706		865	99.50		964.50	1,100
2000	Data recorder, 8 meters	G	10.97	.729		1,450	42.50		1,492.50	1,650
2100	16 meters	G	8.53	.938		3,600	54.50		3,654.50	4,025
3000	Software package, per meter, basic	G				254			254	279
3100	Premium	G				665			665	735

26 09 23 – Lighting Control Devices

26 09 23.10 Energy Saving Lighting Devices

		Crew	Daily Output	Labor-Hours	Unit	Material	Labor	Equipment	Total	Total Incl O&P
0010	**ENERGY SAVING LIGHTING DEVICES**									
0100	Occupancy sensors, passive infrared ceiling mounted	G 1 Elec	7	1.143	Ea.	75	66.50		141.50	182
0110	Ultrasonic ceiling mounted	G	7	1.143		85.50	66.50		152	194
0120	Dual technology ceiling mounted	G	6.50	1.231		125	71.50		196.50	244
0150	Automatic wall switches	G	24	.333		75	19.40		94.40	112
0160	Daylighting sensor, manual control, ceiling mounted	G	7	1.143		108	66.50		174.50	218
0170	Remote and dimming control with remote controller	G	6.50	1.231		168	71.50		239.50	292
0200	Passive infrared ceiling mounted		6.50	1.231		33	71.50		104.50	143
0400	Remote power pack	G	10	.800		33	46.50		79.50	106
0450	Photoelectric control, S.P.S.T. 120 V	G	8	1		21	58		79	110
0500	S.P.S.T. 208 V/277 V	G	8	1		27	58		85	117
0550	D.P.S.T. 120 V	G	6	1.333		194	77.50		271.50	330
0600	D.P.S.T. 208 V/277 V	G	6	1.333		204	77.50		281.50	340
0650	S.P.D.T. 208 V/277 V	G	6	1.333		212	77.50		289.50	350
0660	Daylight level sensor, wall mounted, on/off or dimming	G	8	1		197	58		255	305

26 09 26 – Lighting Control Panelboards

26 09 26.10 Lighting Control Relay Panel

		Crew	Daily Output	Labor-Hours	Unit	Material	Labor	Equipment	Total	Total Incl O&P
0010	**LIGHTING CONTROL RELAY PANEL** with timeclock									
0100	4 Relay	G 1 Elec	2.50	3.200	Ea.	1,100	186		1,286	1,500
0110	8 Relay	G	2.30	3.478		1,225	202		1,427	1,650
0120	16 Relay	G	1.80	4.444		1,375	259		1,634	1,900
0130	24 Relay	G	1.50	5.333		1,600	310		1,910	2,225
0140	48 Relay	G	1	8		1,450	465		1,915	2,275

26 09 Instrumentation and Control for Electrical Systems

26 09 26 – Lighting Control Panelboards

26 09 26.10 Lighting Control Relay Panel

		Crew	Daily Output	Labor-Hours	Unit	Material	2018 Bare Costs Labor	Equipment	Total	Total Incl O&P
0200	Room Controller, switching only									
0210	1 Relay	G	1 Elec	3	2.667	Ea.	1,425	155		1,580	1,775
0220	2 Relay	G		3	2.667		1,350	155		1,505	1,700
0230	3 Relay	G		3	2.667		1,450	155		1,605	1,800
0240	Dimming									
0250	1 Relay	G	1 Elec	3	2.667	Ea.	1,275	155		1,430	1,625
0260	2 Relay	G		3	2.667		1,325	155		1,480	1,700
0270	3 Relay	G		3	2.667		1,450	155		1,605	1,800

26 09 36 – Modular Dimming Controls

26 09 36.13 Manual Modular Dimming Controls

		Crew	Daily Output	Labor-Hours	Unit	Material	Labor	Equipment	Total	Total Incl O&P
0010	**MANUAL MODULAR DIMMING CONTROLS**									
2000	Lighting control module	G	1 Elec	2	4	Ea.	315	233		548	695

26 27 Low-Voltage Distribution Equipment

26 27 26 – Wiring Devices

26 27 26.20 Wiring Devices Elements

			Crew	Daily Output	Labor-Hours	Unit	Material	Labor	Equipment	Total	Total Incl O&P
0010	**WIRING DEVICES ELEMENTS**	R262726-90									
1650	Dimmer switch, 120 volt, incandescent, 600 watt, 1 pole	G	1 Elec	16	.500	Ea.	22.50	29		51.50	68.50
1700	600 watt, 3 way	G		12	.667		10.30	39		49.30	69.50
1750	1,000 watt, 1 pole	G		16	.500		40	29		69	88
1800	1,000 watt, 3 way	G		12	.667		73	39		112	139
2000	1,500 watt, 1 pole	G		11	.727		84	42.50		126.50	156
2100	2,000 watt, 1 pole	G		8	1		129	58		187	229
2110	Fluorescent, 600 watt	G		15	.533		109	31		140	167
2120	1,000 watt	G		15	.533		133	31		164	193
2130	1,500 watt	G		10	.800		246	46.50		292.50	340

26 29 Low-Voltage Controllers

26 29 23 – Variable-Frequency Motor Controllers

26 29 23.10 Variable Frequency Drives/Adj. Frequency Drives

		Crew	Daily Output	Labor-Hours	Unit	Material	Labor	Equipment	Total	Total Incl O&P
0010	**VARIABLE FREQUENCY DRIVES/ADJ. FREQUENCY DRIVES**									
0100	Enclosed (NEMA 1), 460 volt, for 3 HP motor size	G	1 Elec	.80	10	Ea.	1,950	580		2,530	3,025
0110	5 HP motor size	G		.80	10		2,225	580		2,805	3,325
0120	7.5 HP motor size	G		.67	11.940		2,700	695		3,395	4,025
0130	10 HP motor size	G		.67	11.940		2,975	695		3,670	4,325
0140	15 HP motor size	G	2 Elec	.89	17.978		3,825	1,050		4,875	5,775
0150	20 HP motor size	G		.89	17.978		4,525	1,050		5,575	6,550
0160	25 HP motor size	G		.67	23.881		5,550	1,400		6,950	8,200
0170	30 HP motor size	G		.67	23.881		6,950	1,400		8,350	9,725
0180	40 HP motor size	G		.67	23.881		8,025	1,400		9,425	10,900
0190	50 HP motor size	G		.53	30.189		10,300	1,750		12,050	13,900
0200	60 HP motor size	G	R-3	.56	35.714		12,400	2,075	231	14,706	17,100
0210	75 HP motor size	G		.56	35.714		14,400	2,075	231	16,706	19,200
0220	100 HP motor size	G		.50	40		18,500	2,325	259	21,084	24,200
0230	125 HP motor size	G		.50	40		20,100	2,325	259	22,684	25,900
0240	150 HP motor size	G		.50	40		24,300	2,325	259	26,884	30,500
0250	200 HP motor size	G		.42	47.619		27,700	2,750	310	30,760	35,000
1100	Custom-engineered, 460 volt, for 3 HP motor size	G	1 Elec	.56	14.286		3,050	830		3,880	4,600
1110	5 HP motor size	G		.56	14.286		3,050	830		3,880	4,600

For customer support on your Green Building Costs with RSMeans data, call 800.448.8182.

26 29 Low-Voltage Controllers

26 29 23 – Variable-Frequency Motor Controllers

26 29 23.10 Variable Frequency Drives/Adj. Frequency Drives		Crew	Daily Output	Labor-Hours	Unit	Material	2018 Bare Costs Labor	Equipment	Total	Total Incl O&P
1120	7.5 HP motor size	G	1 Elec	.47	17.021	Ea.	3,200	990		4,190	4,975
1130	10 HP motor size	G		.47	17.021		3,350	990		4,340	5,150
1140	15 HP motor size	G	2 Elec	.62	25.806		4,175	1,500		5,675	6,850
1150	20 HP motor size	G		.62	25.806		4,700	1,500		6,200	7,425
1160	25 HP motor size	G		.47	34.043		5,500	1,975		7,475	9,000
1170	30 HP motor size	G		.47	34.043		6,875	1,975		8,850	10,500
1180	40 HP motor size	G		.47	34.043		8,125	1,975		10,100	11,900
1190	50 HP motor size	G		.37	43.243		9,325	2,525		11,850	14,100
1200	60 HP motor size	G	R-3	.39	51.282		14,100	2,975	330	17,405	20,300
1210	75 HP motor size	G		.39	51.282		15,000	2,975	330	18,305	21,300
1220	100 HP motor size	G		.35	57.143		16,400	3,325	370	20,095	23,400
1230	125 HP motor size	G		.35	57.143		17,500	3,325	370	21,195	24,700
1240	150 HP motor size	G		.35	57.143		20,100	3,325	370	23,795	27,500
1250	200 HP motor size	G		.29	68.966		26,200	4,000	445	30,645	35,300
2000	For complex & special design systems to meet specific										
2010	requirements, obtain quote from vendor.										

26 31 Photovoltaic Collectors

26 31 13 – Photovoltaics

26 31 13.50 Solar Energy - Photovoltaics

			Crew	Daily Output	Labor-Hours	Unit	Material	Labor	Equipment	Total	Total Incl O&P
0010	**SOLAR ENERGY - PHOTOVOLTAICS**										
0220	Alt. energy source, photovoltaic module, 6 watt, 15 V	G	1 Elec	8	1	Ea.	50	58		108	143
0230	10 watt, 16.3 V	G		8	1		117	58		175	215
0240	20 watt, 14.5 V	G		8	1		180	58		238	285
0250	36 watt, 17 V	G		8	1		170	58		228	275
0260	55 watt, 17 V	G		8	1		238	58		296	350
0270	75 watt, 17 V	G		8	1		395	58		453	520
0280	130 watt, 33 V	G		8	1		620	58		678	765
0290	140 watt, 33 V	G		8	1		475	58		533	610
0300	150 watt, 33 V	G		8	1		400	58		458	520
0310	DC to AC inverter for, 12 V, 2,000 watt	G		4	2		1,725	116		1,841	2,075
0320	12 V, 2,500 watt	G		4	2		1,075	116		1,191	1,375
0330	24 V, 2,500 watt	G		4	2		1,500	116		1,616	1,825
0340	12 V, 3,000 watt	G		3	2.667		1,500	155		1,655	1,875
0350	24 V, 3,000 watt	G		3	2.667		2,375	155		2,530	2,850
0360	24 V, 4,000 watt	G		2	4		3,025	233		3,258	3,675
0370	48 V, 4,000 watt	G		2	4		2,525	233		2,758	3,125
0380	48 V, 5,500 watt	G		2	4		2,975	233		3,208	3,625
0390	PV components, combiner box, 10 lug, NEMA 3R enclosure	G		4	2		270	116		386	470
0400	Fuse, 15 A for combiner box	G		40	.200		21.50	11.65		33.15	41
0410	Battery charger controller w/temperature sensor	G		4	2		495	116		611	715
0420	Digital readout panel, displays hours, volts, amps, etc.	G		4	2		218	116		334	415
0430	Deep cycle solar battery, 6 V, 180 Ah (C/20)	G		8	1		305	58		363	420
0440	Battery interconn, 15" AWG #2/0, sealed w/copper ring lugs	G		16	.500		18.10	29		47.10	63.50
0442	Battery interconn, 24" AWG #2/0, sealed w/copper ring lugs	G		16	.500		23.50	29		52.50	69.50
0444	Battery interconn, 60" AWG #2/0, sealed w/copper ring lugs	G		16	.500		59.50	29		88.50	109
0446	Batt temp computer probe, RJ11 jack, 15' cord	G		16	.500		22	29		51	68
0450	System disconnect, DC 175 amp circuit breaker	G		8	1		226	58		284	335
0460	Conduit box for inverter	G		8	1		62.50	58		120.50	156
0470	Low voltage disconnect	G		8	1		57	58		115	150
0480	Vented battery enclosure, wood	G	1 Carp	2	4		281	203		484	620

26 31 Photovoltaic Collectors

26 31 13 – Photovoltaics

26 31 13.50 Solar Energy - Photovoltaics

		Crew	Daily Output	Labor-Hours	Unit	Material	2018 Bare Costs Labor	Equipment	Total	Total Incl O&P
0490	PV rack system, roof, non-penetrating ballast, 1 panel G	R-1A	30.50	.525	Ea.	965	27.50		992.50	1,100
0500	Penetrating surface mount, on steel framing, 1 panel		5.13	3.122		56	164		220	305
0510	On wood framing, 1 panel		11	1.455		54.50	76		130.50	174
0520	With standoff, 1 panel		11	1.455		64	76		140	185
0530	Ground, ballast, fixed, 3 panel		20.50	.780		1,025	41		1,066	1,175
0540	4 panel		20.50	.780		1,400	41		1,441	1,575
0550	5 panel		20.50	.780		1,850	41		1,891	2,075
0560	6 panel		20.50	.780		2,125	41		2,166	2,375
0570	Adjustable, 3 panel		20.50	.780		1,075	41		1,116	1,250
0580	4 panel		20.50	.780		1,475	41		1,516	1,675
0590	5 panel		20.50	.780		1,975	41		2,016	2,200
0600	6 panel		20.50	.780		2,250	41		2,291	2,525
0610	Passive tracking, 1 panel		20.50	.780		580	41		621	695
0620	2 panel		20.50	.780		1,175	41		1,216	1,350
0630	3 panel		20.50	.780		1,700	41		1,741	1,925
0640	4 panel		20.50	.780		1,850	41		1,891	2,075
0650	6 panel		20.50	.780		2,100	41		2,141	2,375
0660	8 panel		20.50	.780		3,125	41		3,166	3,475
1020	Photovoltaic module, Thin film	1 Elec	8	1		180	58		238	285
1040	Photovoltaic module, Cadium telluride		8	1		238	58		296	350
1060	Photovoltaic module, Polycrystalline		8	1		180	58		238	285
1080	Photovoltaic module, Monocrystalline		8	1		620	58		678	765

26 33 Battery Equipment

26 33 43 – Battery Chargers

26 33 43.55 Electric Vehicle Charging

		Crew	Daily Output	Labor-Hours	Unit	Material	Labor	Equipment	Total	Total Incl O&P
0010	**ELECTRIC VEHICLE CHARGING**									
0020	Level 2, wall mounted									
2200	Heavy duty G	R-1A	15.36	1.042	Ea.	1,575	54.50		1,629.50	1,825
2210	with RFID G		12.29	1.302		3,175	68		3,243	3,600
2300	Free standing, single connector G		10.24	1.563		1,800	82		1,882	2,125
2310	with RFID G		8.78	1.822		3,625	95.50		3,720.50	4,125
2320	Double connector G		7.68	2.083		3,350	109		3,459	3,850
2330	with RFID G		6.83	2.343		6,725	123		6,848	7,575

26 51 Interior Lighting

26 51 13 – Interior Lighting Fixtures, Lamps, and Ballasts

26 51 13.50 Interior Lighting Fixtures

		Crew	Daily Output	Labor-Hours	Unit	Material	Labor	Equipment	Total	Total Incl O&P
0010	**INTERIOR LIGHTING FIXTURES** Including lamps, mounting R265113-40									
0030	hardware and connections									
0100	Fluorescent, C.W. lamps, troffer, recess mounted in grid, RS									
0130	Grid ceiling mount									
0910	Acrylic lens, 1' W x 4' L, two 32 watt T8 G	1 Elec	5.70	1.404	Ea.	61.50	81.50		143	190
0930	2' W x 2' L, two U32 watt T8 G		5.70	1.404		96	81.50		177.50	227
0940	2' W x 4' L, two 32 watt T8 G		5.30	1.509		79	88		167	218
0950	2' W x 4' L, three 32 watt T8 G		5	1.600		70	93		163	216
0960	2' W x 4' L, four 32 watt T8 G		4.70	1.702		74.50	99		173.50	230
2100	Strip fixture									
2130	Surface mounted									

For customer support on your Green Building Costs with RSMeans data, call 800.448.8182.

26 51 Interior Lighting

26 51 13 – Interior Lighting Fixtures, Lamps, and Ballasts

26 51 13.50 Interior Lighting Fixtures		Crew	Daily Output	Labor-Hours	Unit	Material	2018 Bare Costs Labor	Equipment	Total	Total Incl O&P
2310	4' long, two 32 watt T8, RS	G	1 Elec	8	1	Ea.	65.50	58		123.50	159
2580	8' long, one 60 watt T8, SL	G	2 Elec	13.40	1.194		112	69.50		181.50	227
2590	8' long, two 60 watt T8, SL	G	"	12.40	1.290		92.50	75		167.50	214
2704	8' long, 2 lamp & armored cable	G	1 Elec	3.65	2.192		80.50	128		208.50	280
2800	4' long, two 60 watt, HO			6.70	1.194		107	69.50		176.50	222
2810	4' long, two 54 watt, T5HO	G		6.70	1.194		174	69.50		243.50	295
2900	8' long, two 110 watt, HO		2 Elec	10.60	1.509		108	88		196	250
2910	4' long, two 115 watt, VHO		1 Elec	6.50	1.231		142	71.50		213.50	263
2920	8' long, two 215 watt, VHO		2 Elec	10.40	1.538		153	89.50		242.50	305
2930	4' long, one 32 watt T8, staggered cove mtd.	G	1 Elec	8	1		90	58		148	186
2950	High bay pendent mounted, 16" W x 4' L, four 54 watt, T5HO	G	2 Elec	8.90	1.798		244	105		349	425
2952	2' W x 4' L, six 54 watt, T5HO	G		8.50	1.882		310	110		420	505
2954	2' W x 4' L, six 32 watt, T8	G		8.50	1.882		179	110		289	360
3000	Strip, pendent mounted, industrial, white porcelain enamel										
3110	4' long, two 32 watt T8, RS	G	1 Elec	5.70	1.404	Ea.	72	81.50		153.50	201
3200	4' long, two 60 watt, HO		"	5	1.600		83	93		176	231
3290	8' long, two 60 watt T8, SL	G	2 Elec	8.80	1.818		118	106		224	288
3400	8' long, two 110 watt, HO		"	8	2		126	116		242	315
3410	Acrylic finish, 4' long, two 40 watt, RS		1 Elec	5.70	1.404		86.50	81.50		168	217
3420	4' long, two 60 watt, HO			5	1.600		161	93		254	315
3430	4' long, two 115 watt, VHO			4.80	1.667		208	97		305	375
3440	8' long, two 75 watt, SL		2 Elec	8.80	1.818		170	106		276	345
3450	8' long, two 110 watt, HO			8	2		193	116		309	385
3460	8' long, two 215 watt, VHO			7.60	2.105		273	123		396	485
3470	Troffer, air handling, 2' W x 4' L with four 32 watt T8	G	1 Elec	4	2		116	116		232	300
3480	2' W x 2' L with two U32 watt T8	G		5.50	1.455		111	84.50		195.50	250
3490	Air connector insulated, 5" diameter			20	.400		68	23.50		91.50	110
3500	6" diameter			20	.400		69	23.50		92.50	111
3502	Troffer, direct/indirect, 2' W x 4' L with two 32 W T8			5.30	1.509		282	88		370	440
3510	Troffer parabolic lay-in, 1' W x 4' L with one 32 W T8	G		5.70	1.404		117	81.50		198.50	251
3520	1' W x 4' L with two 32 W T8	G		5.30	1.509		140	88		228	285
3525	2' W x 2' L with two U32 W T8	G		5.70	1.404		118	81.50		199.50	252
3530	2' W x 4' L with three 32 W T8	G		5	1.600		131	93		224	283
3531	Intr fxtr, fluor, troffer prismatic lay-in, 2' W x 4'l w/three 32 W T8			5	1.600		152	93		245	305
3535	Downlight, recess mounted	G		8	1		148	58		206	249
3540	Wall wash reflector, recess mounted	G		8	1		105	58		163	203
3550	Direct/indirect, 4' long, stl., pendent mtd.	G		5	1.600		163	93		256	320
3560	4' long, alum., pendent mtd.	G		5	1.600		335	93		428	510
3565	Prefabricated cove, 4' long, stl. continuous row	G		5	1.600		204	93		297	365
3570	4' long, alum. continuous row	G		5	1.600		350	93		443	525
3580	Wet location, recess mounted, 2' W x 4' L with two 32 watt T8	G		5.30	1.509		243	88		331	400
3590	Pendent mounted, 2' W x 4' L with two 32 watt T8	G		5.70	1.404		375	81.50		456.50	535
4220	Metal halide, integral ballast, ceiling, recess mounted										
4230	prismatic glass lens, floating door										
4240	2' W x 2' L, 250 watt		1 Elec	3.20	2.500	Ea.	255	146		401	500
4250	2' W x 2' L, 400 watt		2 Elec	5.80	2.759		365	161		526	645
4260	Surface mounted, 2' W x 2' L, 250 watt		1 Elec	2.70	2.963		345	172		517	640
4270	400 watt		2 Elec	4.80	3.333		405	194		599	740
4280	High bay, aluminum reflector,										
4290	Single unit, 400 watt		2 Elec	4.60	3.478	Ea.	415	202		617	760
4300	Single unit, 1,000 watt			4	4		595	233		828	1,000
4310	Twin unit, 400 watt			3.20	5		825	291		1,116	1,350
4320	Low bay, aluminum reflector, 250W DX lamp		1 Elec	3.20	2.500		365	146		511	620

26 51 Interior Lighting

26 51 13 – Interior Lighting Fixtures, Lamps, and Ballasts

26 51 13.50 Interior Lighting Fixtures		Crew	Daily Output	Labor-Hours	Unit	Material	2018 Bare Costs Labor	Equipment	Total	Total Incl O&P
4330	400 watt lamp	2 Elec	5	3.200	Ea.	530	186		716	860
4340	High pressure sodium integral ballast ceiling, recess mounted									
4350	prismatic glass lens, floating door									
4360	2' W x 2' L, 150 watt lamp	1 Elec	3.20	2.500	Ea.	390	146		536	645
4370	2' W x 2' L, 400 watt lamp	2 Elec	5.80	2.759		465	161		626	750
4380	Surface mounted, 2' W x 2' L, 150 watt lamp	1 Elec	2.70	2.963		475	172		647	780
4390	400 watt lamp	2 Elec	4.80	3.333		530	194		724	875
4400	High bay, aluminum reflector,									
4410	Single unit, 400 watt lamp	2 Elec	4.60	3.478	Ea.	380	202		582	725
4430	Single unit, 1,000 watt lamp	"	4	4		550	233		783	955
4440	Low bay, aluminum reflector, 150 watt lamp	1 Elec	3.20	2.500		330	146		476	580
4445	High bay H.I.D. quartz restrike	"	16	.500		164	29		193	224
4450	Incandescent, high hat can, round alzak reflector, prewired									
4470	100 watt	1 Elec	8	1	Ea.	64.50	58		122.50	158
4480	150 watt		8	1		105	58		163	202
4500	300 watt		6.70	1.194		242	69.50		311.50	370
4520	Round with reflector and baffles, 150 watt		8	1		51.50	58		109.50	144
4540	Round with concentric louver, 150 watt PAR		8	1		79	58		137	174
4600	Square glass lens with metal trim, prewired									
4630	100 watt	1 Elec	6.70	1.194	Ea.	55.50	69.50		125	165
4680	150 watt		6.70	1.194		98	69.50		167.50	212
4700	200 watt		6.70	1.194		98	69.50		167.50	212
4800	300 watt		5.70	1.404		146	81.50		227.50	282
4810	500 watt		5	1.600		286	93		379	455
4900	Ceiling/wall, surface mounted, metal cylinder, 75 watt		10	.800		50.50	46.50		97	126
4920	150 watt		10	.800		81	46.50		127.50	159
4930	300 watt		8	1		168	58		226	272
5000	500 watt		6.70	1.194		365	69.50		434.50	505
5010	Square, 100 watt		8	1		113	58		171	211
5020	150 watt		8	1		124	58		182	223
5030	300 watt		7	1.143		340	66.50		406.50	470
5040	500 watt		6	1.333		345	77.50		422.50	495
5200	Ceiling, surface mounted, opal glass drum									
5300	8", one 60 watt lamp	1 Elec	10	.800	Ea.	65.50	46.50		112	142
5400	10", two 60 watt lamps		8	1		72.50	58		130.50	167
5500	12", four 60 watt lamps		6.70	1.194		103	69.50		172.50	217
5510	Pendent, round, 100 watt		8	1		113	58		171	211
5520	150 watt		8	1		123	58		181	222
5530	300 watt		6.70	1.194		171	69.50		240.50	292
5540	500 watt		5.50	1.455		325	84.50		409.50	480
5550	Square, 100 watt		6.70	1.194		152	69.50		221.50	271
5560	150 watt		6.70	1.194		158	69.50		227.50	278
5570	300 watt		5.70	1.404		231	81.50		312.50	375
5580	500 watt		5	1.600		315	93		408	485
5600	Wall, round, 100 watt		8	1		65.50	58		123.50	159
5620	300 watt		8	1		143	58		201	244
5630	500 watt		6.70	1.194		380	69.50		449.50	520
5640	Square, 100 watt		8	1		104	58		162	201
5650	150 watt		8	1		106	58		164	203
5660	300 watt		7	1.143		166	66.50		232.50	283
5670	500 watt		6	1.333		283	77.50		360.50	425
6010	Vapor tight, incandescent, ceiling mounted, 200 watt		6.20	1.290		78.50	75		153.50	198
6020	Recessed, 200 watt		6.70	1.194		124	69.50		193.50	240

For customer support on your Green Building Costs with RSMeans data, call 800.448.8182.

26 51 Interior Lighting

26 51 13 – Interior Lighting Fixtures, Lamps, and Ballasts

26 51 13.50 Interior Lighting Fixtures

		Crew	Daily Output	Labor-Hours	Unit	Material	2018 Bare Costs Labor	Equipment	Total	Total Incl O&P
6030	Pendent, 200 watt	1 Elec	6.70	1.194	Ea.	78.50	69.50		148	190
6040	Wall, 200 watt		8	1		80	58		138	175
6100	Fluorescent, surface mounted, 2 lamps, 4' L, RS, 40 watt		3.20	2.500		116	146		262	345
6110	Industrial, 2 lamps, 4' L in tandem, 430 MA		2.20	3.636		213	212		425	550
6130	2 lamps, 4' L, 800 MA		1.90	4.211		182	245		427	565
6160	Pendent, indust, 2 lamps, 4' L in tandem, 430 MA		1.90	4.211		248	245		493	640
6170	2 lamps, 4' L, 430 MA		2.30	3.478		166	202		368	490
6180	2 lamps, 4' L, 800 MA		1.70	4.706		209	274		483	640
6850	Vandalproof, surface mounted, fluorescent, two 32 watt T8 G		3.20	2.500		252	146		398	495
6860	Incandescent, one 150 watt		8	1		90	58		148	186
6900	Mirror light, fluorescent, RS, acrylic enclosure, two 40 watt		8	1		116	58		174	215
6910	One 40 watt		8	1		96	58		154	193
6920	One 20 watt		12	.667		82.50	39		121.50	149
7000	Low bay, aluminum reflector, 70 watt, high pressure sodium		4	2		275	116		391	480
7010	250 watt		3.20	2.500		365	146		511	625
7020	400 watt	2 Elec	5	3.200		385	186		571	700
7500	Ballast replacement, by weight of ballast, to 15' high									
7640	Dimmable ballast one-lamp G	1 Elec	8	1	Ea.	108	58		166	206
7650	Dimmable ballast two-lamp G		7.60	1.053		108	61.50		169.50	210
7660	Dimmable ballast three-lamp G		6.90	1.159		130	67.50		197.50	244
7990	Decorator									
8000	Pendent RLM in colors, shallow dome, 12" diam., 100 watt	1 Elec	8	1	Ea.	80.50	58		138.50	176
8010	Regular dome, 12" diam., 100 watt		8	1		83	58		141	179
8020	16" diam., 200 watt		7	1.143		84.50	66.50		151	193
8030	18" diam., 300 watt		6	1.333		93	77.50		170.50	218
8100	Picture framing light		16	.500		96	29		125	150
8150	Miniature low voltage, recessed, pinhole		8	1		129	58		187	229
8160	Star		8	1		134	58		192	234
8170	Adjustable cone		8	1		166	58		224	270
8180	Eyeball		8	1		107	58		165	204
8190	Cone		8	1		130	58		188	230
8200	Coilex baffle		8	1		118	58		176	217
8210	Surface mounted, adjustable cylinder		8	1		125	58		183	224
8250	Chandeliers, incandescent									
8260	24" diam. x 42" high, 6 light candle	1 Elec	6	1.333	Ea.	420	77.50		497.50	580
8270	24" diam. x 42" high, 6 light candle w/glass shade		6	1.333		430	77.50		507.50	590
8280	17" diam. x 12" high, 8 light w/glass panels		8	1		257	58		315	370
8300	27" diam. x 29" high, 10 light bohemian lead crystal		4	2		560	116		676	790
8310	21" diam. x 9" high, 6 light sculptured ice crystal		8	1		400	58		458	525
8500	Accent lights, on floor or edge, 0.5 W low volt incandescent									
8520	incl. transformer & fastenings, based on 100' lengths									
8550	Lights in clear tubing, 12" OC	1 Elec	230	.035	L.F.	8.35	2.02		10.37	12.25
8560	6" OC		160	.050		10.90	2.91		13.81	16.35
8570	4" OC		130	.062		16.70	3.58		20.28	23.50
8580	3" OC		125	.064		18.50	3.72		22.22	26
8590	2" OC		100	.080		27	4.66		31.66	36.50
8600	Carpet, lights both sides 6" OC, in alum. extrusion		270	.030		25.50	1.72		27.22	30.50
8610	In bronze extrusion		270	.030		28.50	1.72		30.22	34
8620	Carpet-bare floor, lights 18" OC, in alum. extrusion		270	.030		20	1.72		21.72	24.50
8630	In bronze extrusion		270	.030		23.50	1.72		25.22	28.50
8640	Carpet edge-wall, lights 6" OC in alum. extrusion		270	.030		25.50	1.72		27.22	30.50
8650	In bronze extrusion		270	.030		28.50	1.72		30.22	34
8660	Bare floor, lights 18" OC, in alum. extrusion		300	.027		20	1.55		21.55	24.50

26 51 Interior Lighting

26 51 13 – Interior Lighting Fixtures, Lamps, and Ballasts

26 51 13.50 Interior Lighting Fixtures

		Crew	Daily Output	Labor-Hours	Unit	Material	2018 Bare Costs Labor	Equipment	Total	Total Incl O&P
8670	In bronze extrusion	1 Elec	300	.027	L.F.	23.50	1.55		25.05	28.50
8680	Bare floor conduit, alum. extrusion		300	.027		6.65	1.55		8.20	9.65
8690	In bronze extrusion		300	.027		13.35	1.55		14.90	16.95
8700	Step edge to 36", lights 6" OC, in alum. extrusion		100	.080	Ea.	67	4.66		71.66	81
8710	In bronze extrusion		100	.080		70	4.66		74.66	84
8720	Step edge to 54", lights 6" OC, in alum. extrusion		100	.080		101	4.66		105.66	118
8730	In bronze extrusion		100	.080		106	4.66		110.66	124
8740	Step edge to 72", lights 6" OC, in alum. extrusion		100	.080		134	4.66		138.66	155
8750	In bronze extrusion		100	.080		146	4.66		150.66	168
8760	Connector, male		32	.250		2.48	14.55		17.03	24.50
8770	Female with pigtail		32	.250		5.20	14.55		19.75	28
8780	Clamps		400	.020		.49	1.16		1.65	2.28
8790	Transformers, 50 watt		8	1		89.50	58		147.50	186
8800	250 watt		4	2		285	116		401	490
8810	1,000 watt		2.70	2.963		325	172		497	620

26 51 13.55 Interior LED Fixtures

			Crew	Daily Output	Labor-Hours	Unit	Material	Labor	Equipment	Total	Total Incl O&P
0010	**INTERIOR LED FIXTURES** Incl. lamps and mounting hardware										
0100	Downlight, recess mounted, 7.5" diameter, 25 watt	G	1 Elec	8	1	Ea.	335	58		393	450
0120	10" diameter, 36 watt	G		8	1		360	58		418	480
0160	cylinder, 10 watts	G		8	1		103	58		161	200
0180	20 watts	G		8	1		129	58		187	229
1000	Troffer, recess mounted, 2' x 4', 3,200 lumens	G		5.30	1.509		138	88		226	282
1010	4,800 lumens	G		5	1.600		179	93		272	335
1020	6,400 lumens	G		4.70	1.702		198	99		297	365
1100	Troffer retrofit lamp, 38 watt	G		21	.381		69.50	22		91.50	110
1110	60 watt	G		20	.400		141	23.50		164.50	191
1120	100 watt	G		18	.444		206	26		232	265
1200	Troffer, volumetric recess mounted, 2' x 2'	G		5.70	1.404		305	81.50		386.50	455
2000	Strip, surface mounted, one light bar 4' long, 3,500 K	G		8.50	.941		260	55		315	370
2010	5,000 K	G		8	1		260	58		318	375
2020	Two light bar 4' long, 5,000 K	G		7	1.143		410	66.50		476.50	550
3000	Linear, suspended mounted, one light bar 4' long, 37 watt	G		6.70	1.194		153	69.50		222.50	272
3010	One light bar 8' long, 74 watt	G	2 Elec	12.20	1.311		283	76.50		359.50	425
3020	Two light bar 4' long, 74 watt	G	1 Elec	5.70	1.404		305	81.50		386.50	455
3030	Two light bar 8' long, 148 watt	G	2 Elec	8.80	1.818		350	106		456	545
4000	High bay, surface mounted, round, 150 watts	G		5.41	2.959		425	172		597	725
4010	2 bars, 164 watts	G		5.41	2.959		385	172		557	680
4020	3 bars, 246 watts	G		5.01	3.197		515	186		701	845
4030	4 bars, 328 watts	G		4.60	3.478		715	202		917	1,100
4040	5 bars, 410 watts	G	3 Elec	4.20	5.716		810	335		1,145	1,400
4050	6 bars, 492 watts	G		3.80	6.324		910	370		1,280	1,550
4060	7 bars, 574 watts	G		3.39	7.075		990	410		1,400	1,725
4070	8 bars, 656 watts	G		2.99	8.029		1,050	465		1,515	1,850
5000	Track, lighthead, 6 watt	G	1 Elec	32	.250		54.50	14.55		69.05	82
5010	9 watt	G	"	32	.250		61.50	14.55		76.05	89.50
6000	Garage, surface mounted, 103 watts	G	2 Elec	6.50	2.462		970	143		1,113	1,300
6100	pendent mounted, 80 watts	G		6.50	2.462		660	143		803	940
6200	95 watts	G		6.50	2.462		780	143		923	1,075
6300	125 watts	G		6.50	2.462		820	143		963	1,125

26 51 Interior Lighting

26 51 13 – Interior Lighting Fixtures, Lamps, and Ballasts

26 51 13.90 Ballast, Replacement HID

		Crew	Daily Output	Labor-Hours	Unit	Material	2018 Bare Costs Labor	Equipment	Total	Total Incl O&P
0010	**BALLAST, REPLACEMENT HID**									
7510	Multi-tap 120/208/240/277 V									
7550	High pressure sodium, 70 watt	1 Elec	10	.800	Ea.	116	46.50		162.50	197
7560	100 watt		9.40	.851		82.50	49.50		132	165
7570	150 watt		9	.889		130	51.50		181.50	221
7580	250 watt		8.50	.941		193	55		248	295
7590	400 watt		7	1.143		171	66.50		237.50	288
7600	1,000 watt		6	1.333		183	77.50		260.50	320
7610	Metal halide, 175 watt		8	1		60.50	58		118.50	154
7620	250 watt		8	1		79	58		137	174
7630	400 watt		7	1.143		98.50	66.50		165	208
7640	1,000 watt		6	1.333		161	77.50		238.50	293
7650	1,500 watt	▼	5	1.600	▼	194	93		287	350

26 52 Safety Lighting

26 52 13 – Emergency and Exit Lighting

26 52 13.10 Emergency Lighting and Battery Units

		Crew	Daily Output	Labor-Hours	Unit	Material	Labor	Equipment	Total	Total Incl O&P
0010	**EMERGENCY LIGHTING AND BATTERY UNITS**									
0300	Emergency light units, battery operated									
0350	Twin sealed beam light, 25 W, 6 V each									
0500	Lead battery operated	1 Elec	4	2	Ea.	144	116		260	330
0700	Nickel cadmium battery operated		4	2		345	116		461	550
0780	Additional remote mount, sealed beam, 25 W 6 V		26.70	.300		29.50	17.45		46.95	58.50
0790	Twin sealed beam light, 25 W 6 V each		26.70	.300		62.50	17.45		79.95	94.50
0900	Self-contained fluorescent lamp pack	▼	10	.800		191	46.50		237.50	280
2030	3 heads, nickel cadmium	R-19	6.67	2.999		875	175		1,050	1,225
2040	Lead acid	"	6.67	2.999		540	175		715	855
3000	Solid state battery charger, 1 ph., w/wall brkt, 208/240/480 V, 6 cell	R-22	3.25	11.471		1,150	610		1,760	2,175
3020	9 cell		3	12.427		1,450	660		2,110	2,600
3040	12 cell		2.75	13.556		1,600	720		2,320	2,825
3060	18 cell	▼	2.50	14.912		1,725	795		2,520	3,100

26 52 13.16 Exit Signs

			Crew	Daily Output	Labor-Hours	Unit	Material	Labor	Equipment	Total	Total Incl O&P
0010	**EXIT SIGNS**										
0080	Exit light ceiling or wall mount, incandescent, single face		1 Elec	8	1	Ea.	70	58		128	164
0084	Exit light w/armored cable			4	2		91	116		207	274
0100	Double face			6.70	1.194		50	69.50		119.50	159
0120	Explosion proof			3.80	2.105		550	123		673	790
0150	Fluorescent, single face			8	1		81	58		139	176
0160	Double face			6.70	1.194		75	69.50		144.50	187
0200	LED standard, single face	G		8	1		47.50	58		105.50	139
0220	Double face	G		6.70	1.194		51	69.50		120.50	160
0230	LED vandal-resistant, single face	G		7.27	1.100		212	64		276	330
0240	LED w/battery unit, single face	G		4.40	1.818		184	106		290	360
0260	Double face	G		4	2		188	116		304	380
0262	LED w/battery unit, vandal-resistant, single face	G		4.40	1.818		245	106		351	430
0290	LED retrofit kits	G	▼	60	.133		50	7.75		57.75	66.50

26 54 Classified Location Lighting

26 54 13 – Incandescent Classified Location Lighting

26 54 13.20 Explosion Proof

		Crew	Daily Output	Labor-Hours	Unit	Material	2018 Bare Costs Labor	Equipment	Total	Total Incl O&P
0010	**EXPLOSION PROOF**, incl. lamps, mounting hardware and connections									
6310	Metal halide with ballast, ceiling, surface mounted, 175 watt	1 Elec	2.90	2.759	Ea.	1,300	161		1,461	1,675
6320	250 watt	"	2.70	2.963		1,575	172		1,747	1,975
6330	400 watt	2 Elec	4.80	3.333		1,675	194		1,869	2,150
6340	Ceiling, pendent mounted, 175 watt	1 Elec	2.60	3.077		1,250	179		1,429	1,650
6350	250 watt	"	2.40	3.333		1,500	194		1,694	1,950
6360	400 watt	2 Elec	4.20	3.810		1,625	222		1,847	2,100
6370	Wall, surface mounted, 175 watt	1 Elec	2.90	2.759		1,400	161		1,561	1,800
6380	250 watt	"	2.70	2.963		1,650	172		1,822	2,075
6390	400 watt	2 Elec	4.80	3.333		1,775	194		1,969	2,250
6400	High pressure sodium, ceiling surface mounted, 70 watt	1 Elec	3	2.667		2,200	155		2,355	2,650
6410	100 watt		3	2.667		2,275	155		2,430	2,725
6420	150 watt		2.70	2.963		2,350	172		2,522	2,825
6430	Pendent mounted, 70 watt		2.70	2.963		2,100	172		2,272	2,550
6440	100 watt		2.70	2.963		2,175	172		2,347	2,650
6450	150 watt		2.40	3.333		1,875	194		2,069	2,350
6460	Wall mounted, 70 watt		3	2.667		2,350	155		2,505	2,800
6470	100 watt		3	2.667		2,425	155		2,580	2,900
6480	150 watt		2.70	2.963		2,500	172		2,672	3,000
6510	Incandescent, ceiling mounted, 200 watt		4	2		1,550	116		1,666	1,875
6520	Pendent mounted, 200 watt		3.50	2.286		1,325	133		1,458	1,650
6530	Wall mounted, 200 watt		4	2		1,525	116		1,641	1,850
6600	Fluorescent, RS, 4' long, ceiling mounted, two 40 watt		2.70	2.963		4,075	172		4,247	4,725
6610	Three 40 watt		2.20	3.636		5,900	212		6,112	6,800
6620	Four 40 watt		1.90	4.211		7,575	245		7,820	8,700
6630	Pendent mounted, two 40 watt		2.30	3.478		4,725	202		4,927	5,500
6640	Three 40 watt		1.90	4.211		6,725	245		6,970	7,775
6650	Four 40 watt		1.70	4.706		8,850	274		9,124	10,200

26 55 Special Purpose Lighting

26 55 33 – Hazard Warning Lighting

26 55 33.10 Warning Beacons

		Crew	Daily Output	Labor-Hours	Unit	Material	Labor	Equipment	Total	Total Incl O&P
0010	**WARNING BEACONS**									
0015	Surface mount with colored or clear lens									
0100	Rotating beacon									
0110	120V, 40 watt halogen	1 Elec	3.50	2.286	Ea.	106	133		239	315
0120	24V, 20 watt halogen	"	3.50	2.286	"	228	133		361	450
0200	Steady beacon									
0210	120V, 40 watt halogen	1 Elec	3.50	2.286	Ea.	108	133		241	320
0220	24V, 20 watt		3.50	2.286		112	133		245	320
0230	12V DC, incandescent		3.50	2.286		103	133		236	315
0300	Flashing beacon									
0310	120V, 40 watt halogen	1 Elec	3.50	2.286	Ea.	106	133		239	315
0320	24V, 20 watt halogen		3.50	2.286		106	133		239	315
0410	12V DC with two 6V lantern batteries		7	1.143		107	66.50		173.50	218

26 56 Exterior Lighting

26 56 13 – Lighting Poles and Standards

26 56 13.10 Lighting Poles		Crew	Daily Output	Labor-Hours	Unit	Material	2018 Bare Costs Labor	Equipment	Total	Total Incl O&P
0010	**LIGHTING POLES**									
2800	Light poles, anchor base									
2820	not including concrete bases									
2840	Aluminum pole, 8' high	1 Elec	4	2	Ea.	785	116		901	1,025
2850	10' high		4	2		825	116		941	1,075
2860	12' high		3.80	2.105		860	123		983	1,125
2870	14' high		3.40	2.353		895	137		1,032	1,200
2880	16' high		3	2.667		980	155		1,135	1,300
3000	20' high	R-3	2.90	6.897		1,050	400	44.50	1,494.50	1,800
3200	30' high		2.60	7.692		1,975	445	50	2,470	2,900
3400	35' high		2.30	8.696		2,150	505	56.50	2,711.50	3,175
3600	40' high		2	10		2,450	580	65	3,095	3,650
3800	Bracket arms, 1 arm	1 Elec	8	1		134	58		192	235
4000	2 arms		8	1		270	58		328	385
4200	3 arms		5.30	1.509		405	88		493	575
4400	4 arms		4.80	1.667		540	97		637	740
4500	Steel pole, galvanized, 8' high		3.80	2.105		680	123		803	930
4510	10' high		3.70	2.162		710	126		836	970
4520	12' high		3.40	2.353		765	137		902	1,050
4530	14' high		3.10	2.581		815	150		965	1,125
4540	16' high		2.90	2.759		865	161		1,026	1,200
4550	18' high		2.70	2.963		910	172		1,082	1,250
4600	20' high	R-3	2.60	7.692		1,050	445	50	1,545	1,900
4800	30' high		2.30	8.696		1,450	505	56.50	2,011.50	2,425
5000	35' high		2.20	9.091		1,600	525	59	2,184	2,600
5200	40' high		1.70	11.765		1,975	680	76	2,731	3,275
5400	Bracket arms, 1 arm	1 Elec	8	1		201	58		259	310
5600	2 arms		8	1		310	58		368	425
5800	3 arms		5.30	1.509		225	88		313	380
6000	4 arms		5.30	1.509		320	88		408	480
6100	Fiberglass pole, 1 or 2 fixtures, 20' high	R-3	4	5		795	290	32.50	1,117.50	1,350
6200	30' high		3.60	5.556		985	320	36	1,341	1,600
6300	35' high		3.20	6.250		1,550	360	40.50	1,950.50	2,300
6400	40' high		2.80	7.143		1,800	415	46.50	2,261.50	2,650
6420	Wood pole, 4-1/2" x 5-1/8", 8' high	1 Elec	6	1.333		375	77.50		452.50	530
6430	10' high		6	1.333		430	77.50		507.50	585
6440	12' high		5.70	1.404		540	81.50		621.50	715
6450	15' high		5	1.600		630	93		723	835
6460	20' high		4	2		765	116		881	1,025
6461	Light poles, anchor base, w/o conc base, pwdr ct stl, 16' H	2 Elec	3.10	5.161		865	300		1,165	1,400
6462	20' high	R-3	2.90	6.897		1,050	400	44.50	1,494.50	1,825
6463	30' high		2.30	8.696		1,450	505	56.50	2,011.50	2,425
6464	35' high		2.40	8.333		1,600	485	54	2,139	2,525
6465	25' high		2.70	7.407		1,050	430	48	1,528	1,875
7300	Transformer bases, not including concrete bases									
7320	Maximum pole size, steel, 40' high	1 Elec	2	4	Ea.	1,600	233		1,833	2,100
7340	Cast aluminum, 30' high		3	2.667		840	155		995	1,150
7350	40' high		2.50	3.200		1,275	186		1,461	1,675

26 56 Exterior Lighting

26 56 19 – LED Exterior Lighting

26 56 19.55 Roadway LED Luminaire

		Crew	Daily Output	Labor-Hours	Unit	Material	2018 Bare Costs Labor	Equipment	Total	Total Incl O&P
0010	**ROADWAY LED LUMINAIRE**									
0100	LED fixture, 72 LEDs, 120 V AC or 12 V DC, equal to 60 watt	G 1 Elec	2.70	2.963	Ea.	585	172		757	905
0110	108 LEDs, 120 V AC or 12 V DC, equal to 90 watt	G	2.70	2.963		690	172		862	1,025
0120	144 LEDs, 120 V AC or 12 V DC, equal to 120 watt	G	2.70	2.963		845	172		1,017	1,200
0130	252 LEDs, 120 V AC or 12 V DC, equal to 210 watt	G 2 Elec	4.40	3.636		1,175	212		1,387	1,625
0140	Replaces high pressure sodium fixture, 75 watt	G 1 Elec	2.70	2.963		395	172		567	695
0150	125 watt	G	2.70	2.963		450	172		622	755
0160	150 watt	G	2.70	2.963		530	172		702	840
0170	175 watt	G	2.70	2.963		780	172		952	1,125
0180	200 watt	G	2.70	2.963		745	172		917	1,075
0190	250 watt	G 2 Elec	4.40	3.636		850	212		1,062	1,250
0200	320 watt	G "	4.40	3.636		930	212		1,142	1,350

26 56 19.60 Parking LED Lighting

		Crew	Daily Output	Labor-Hours	Unit	Material	Labor	Equipment	Total	Total Incl O&P
0010	**PARKING LED LIGHTING**									
0100	Round pole mounting, 88 lamp watts	G 1 Elec	2	4	Ea.	1,150	233		1,383	1,600

26 56 21 – HID Exterior Lighting

26 56 21.20 Roadway Luminaire

		Crew	Daily Output	Labor-Hours	Unit	Material	Labor	Equipment	Total	Total Incl O&P
0010	**ROADWAY LUMINAIRE**									
2650	Roadway area luminaire, low pressure sodium, 135 watt	1 Elec	2	4	Ea.	840	233		1,073	1,275
2700	180 watt	"	2	4		900	233		1,133	1,350
2750	Metal halide, 400 watt	2 Elec	4.40	3.636		650	212		862	1,025
2760	1,000 watt		4	4		730	233		963	1,150
2780	High pressure sodium, 400 watt		4.40	3.636		775	212		987	1,175
2790	1,000 watt		4	4		880	233		1,113	1,325

26 56 23 – Area Lighting

26 56 23.10 Exterior Fixtures

		Crew	Daily Output	Labor-Hours	Unit	Material	Labor	Equipment	Total	Total Incl O&P
0010	**EXTERIOR FIXTURES** With lamps									
0200	Wall mounted, incandescent, 100 watt	1 Elec	8	1	Ea.	40.50	58		98.50	132
0400	Quartz, 500 watt		5.30	1.509		61.50	88		149.50	199
0420	1,500 watt		4.20	1.905		101	111		212	277
1100	Wall pack, low pressure sodium, 35 watt		4	2		191	116		307	385
1150	55 watt		4	2		227	116		343	425
1160	High pressure sodium, 70 watt		4	2		187	116		303	380
1170	150 watt		4	2		205	116		321	400
1175	High pressure sodium, 250 watt		4	2		205	116		321	400
1180	Metal halide, 175 watt		4	2		210	116		326	405
1190	250 watt		4	2		236	116		352	435
1195	400 watt		4	2		415	116		531	630
1250	Induction lamp, 40 watt		4	2		470	116		586	690
1260	80 watt		4	2		560	116		676	790
1278	LED, poly lens, 26 watt		4	2		315	116		431	525
1280	110 watt		4	2		775	116		891	1,025
1500	LED, glass lens, 13 watt		4	2		315	116		431	525

26 56 23.55 Exterior LED Fixtures

		Crew	Daily Output	Labor-Hours	Unit	Material	Labor	Equipment	Total	Total Incl O&P
0010	**EXTERIOR LED FIXTURES**									
0100	Wall mounted, indoor/outdoor, 12 watt	G 1 Elec	10	.800	Ea.	216	46.50		262.50	310
0110	32 watt	G	10	.800		465	46.50		511.50	580
0120	66 watt	G	10	.800		470	46.50		516.50	585
0200	outdoor, 110 watt	G	10	.800		1,200	46.50		1,246.50	1,400
0210	220 watt	G	10	.800		1,750	46.50		1,796.50	2,000

For customer support on your Green Building Costs with RSMeans data, call 800.448.8182.

26 56 Exterior Lighting

26 56 23 – Area Lighting

26 56 23.55 Exterior LED Fixtures

		Crew	Daily Output	Labor-Hours	Unit	Material	2018 Bare Costs Labor	Equipment	Total	Total Incl O&P
0300	modular, type IV, 120 V, 50 lamp watts	1 Elec [G]	9	.889	Ea.	1,150	51.50		1,201.50	1,350
0310	101 lamp watts	[G]	9	.889		1,300	51.50		1,351.50	1,500
0320	126 lamp watts	[G]	9	.889		1,625	51.50		1,676.50	1,850
0330	202 lamp watts	[G]	9	.889		1,850	51.50		1,901.50	2,100
0340	240 V, 50 lamp watts	[G]	8	1		1,200	58		1,258	1,400
0350	101 lamp watts	[G]	8	1		1,350	58		1,408	1,550
0360	126 lamp watts	[G]	8	1		1,450	58		1,508	1,675
0370	202 lamp watts	[G]	8	1		1,900	58		1,958	2,150
0400	wall pack, glass, 13 lamp watts	[G]	4	2		445	116		561	665
0410	poly w/photocell, 26 lamp watts	[G]	4	2		340	116		456	550
0420	50 lamp watts	[G]	4	2		775	116		891	1,025
0430	replacement, 40 watts	[G]	4	2		390	116		506	605
0440	60 watts	[G]	4	2		400	116		516	615

26 56 26 – Landscape Lighting

26 56 26.20 Landscape Fixtures

		Crew	Daily Output	Labor-Hours	Unit	Material	Labor	Equipment	Total	Incl O&P
0010	**LANDSCAPE FIXTURES**									
0012	Incl. conduit, wire, trench									
0960	Landscape lights, solar powered, 6" diam. x 12" H, one piece w/stake [G]	1 Clab	80	.100	Ea.	29	3.99		32.99	38
7380	Landscape recessed uplight, incl. housing, ballast, transformer									
7390	& reflector, not incl. conduit, wire, trench									
7420	Incandescent, 250 watt	1 Elec	5	1.600	Ea.	655	93		748	860
7440	Quartz, 250 watt		5	1.600		620	93		713	820
7460	500 watt		4	2		635	116		751	875

26 56 26.50 Landscape LED Fixtures

		Crew	Daily Output	Labor-Hours	Unit	Material	Labor	Equipment	Total	Incl O&P
0010	**LANDSCAPE LED FIXTURES**									
0100	12 volt alum bullet hooded-BLK	1 Elec	5	1.600	Ea.	96	93		189	245
0200	12 volt alum bullet hooded-BRZ		5	1.600		96	93		189	245
0300	12 volt alum bullet hooded-GRN		5	1.600		96	93		189	245
1000	12 volt alum large bullet hooded-BLK		5	1.600		71	93		164	217
1100	12 volt alum large bullet hooded-BRZ		5	1.600		71	93		164	217
1200	12 volt alum large bullet hooded-GRN		5	1.600		71	93		164	217
2000	12 volt large bullet landscape light fixture		5	1.600		71	93		164	217
2100	12 volt alum light large bullet		5	1.600		71	93		164	217
2200	12 volt alum bullet light		5	1.600		71	93		164	217

26 56 33 – Walkway Lighting

26 56 33.10 Walkway Luminaire

		Crew	Daily Output	Labor-Hours	Unit	Material	Labor	Equipment	Total	Incl O&P
0010	**WALKWAY LUMINAIRE**									
6500	Bollard light, lamp & ballast, 42" high with polycarbonate lens									
6800	Metal halide, 175 watt	1 Elec	3	2.667	Ea.	915	155		1,070	1,225
6900	High pressure sodium, 70 watt		3	2.667		935	155		1,090	1,250
7000	100 watt		3	2.667		935	155		1,090	1,250
7100	150 watt		3	2.667		915	155		1,070	1,225
7200	Incandescent, 150 watt		3	2.667		670	155		825	965
7810	Walkway luminaire, square 16", metal halide 250 watt		2.70	2.963		715	172		887	1,050
7820	High pressure sodium, 70 watt		3	2.667		820	155		975	1,125
7830	100 watt		3	2.667		835	155		990	1,150
7840	150 watt		3	2.667		835	155		990	1,150
7850	200 watt		3	2.667		840	155		995	1,150
7910	Round 19", metal halide, 250 watt		2.70	2.963		1,050	172		1,222	1,400
7920	High pressure sodium, 70 watt		3	2.667		1,150	155		1,305	1,500
7930	100 watt		3	2.667		1,150	155		1,305	1,500

26 56 Exterior Lighting

26 56 33 – Walkway Lighting

26 56 33.10 Walkway Luminaire

		Crew	Daily Output	Labor-Hours	Unit	Material	2018 Bare Costs Labor	Equipment	Total	Total Incl O&P
7940	150 watt	1 Elec	3	2.667	Ea.	1,150	155		1,305	1,500
7950	250 watt		2.70	2.963		1,200	172		1,372	1,575
8000	Sphere 14" opal, incandescent, 200 watt		4	2		330	116		446	540
8020	Sphere 18" opal, incandescent, 300 watt		3.50	2.286		400	133		533	640
8040	Sphere 16" clear, high pressure sodium, 70 watt		3	2.667		695	155		850	995
8050	100 watt		3	2.667		740	155		895	1,050
8100	Cube 16" opal, incandescent, 300 watt		3.50	2.286		440	133		573	685
8120	High pressure sodium, 70 watt		3	2.667		645	155		800	940
8130	100 watt		3	2.667		660	155		815	955
8230	Lantern, high pressure sodium, 70 watt		3	2.667		575	155		730	865
8240	100 watt		3	2.667		620	155		775	910
8250	150 watt		3	2.667		580	155		735	870
8260	250 watt		2.70	2.963		810	172		982	1,150
8270	Incandescent, 300 watt		3.50	2.286		430	133		563	670
8330	Reflector 22" w/globe, high pressure sodium, 70 watt		3	2.667		555	155		710	840
8340	100 watt		3	2.667		560	155		715	845
8350	150 watt		3	2.667		570	155		725	855
8360	250 watt		2.70	2.963		725	172		897	1,050

26 56 33.55 Walkway LED Luminaire

			Crew	Daily Output	Labor-Hours	Unit	Material	Labor	Equipment	Total	Total Incl O&P
0010	**WALKWAY LED LUMINAIRE**										
0100	Pole mounted, 86 watts, 4,350 lumens	G	1 Elec	3	2.667	Ea.	1,325	155		1,480	1,700
0110	4,630 lumens	G		3	2.667		2,250	155		2,405	2,700
0120	80 watts, 4,000 lumens	G		3	2.667		2,025	155		2,180	2,450

26 56 36 – Flood Lighting

26 56 36.20 Floodlights

			Crew	Daily Output	Labor-Hours	Unit	Material	Labor	Equipment	Total	Total Incl O&P
0010	**FLOODLIGHTS** with ballast and lamp,										
1400	Pole mounted, pole not included										
1950	Metal halide, 175 watt		1 Elec	2.70	2.963	Ea.	210	172		382	490
2000	400 watt		2 Elec	4.40	3.636		224	212		436	560
2200	1,000 watt			4	4		790	233		1,023	1,225
2210	1,500 watt			3.70	4.324		420	252		672	835
2250	Low pressure sodium, 55 watt		1 Elec	2.70	2.963		425	172		597	725
2270	90 watt			2	4		575	233		808	985
2290	180 watt			2	4		635	233		868	1,050
2340	High pressure sodium, 70 watt			2.70	2.963		250	172		422	535
2360	100 watt			2.70	2.963		256	172		428	540
2380	150 watt			2.70	2.963		310	172		482	600
2400	400 watt		2 Elec	4.40	3.636		315	212		527	665
2600	1,000 watt		"	4	4		580	233		813	985
9005	Solar powered floodlight, w/motion det, incl. batt pack for cloudy days	G	1 Elec	8	1		60	58		118	153
9020	Replacement battery pack	G	"	8	1		19.90	58		77.90	109

26 56 36.55 LED Floodlights

			Crew	Daily Output	Labor-Hours	Unit	Material	Labor	Equipment	Total	Total Incl O&P
0010	**LED FLOODLIGHTS** with ballast and lamp,										
0020	Pole mounted, pole not included										
0100	11 watt	G	1 Elec	4	2	Ea.	435	116		551	655
0110	46 watt	G		4	2		1,450	116		1,566	1,775
0120	90 watt	G		4	2		2,000	116		2,116	2,375
0130	288 watt	G		4	2		1,800	116		1,916	2,150

26 61 Lighting Systems and Accessories

26 61 23 – Lamps Applications

26 61 23.10 Lamps		Crew	Daily Output	Labor-Hours	Unit	Material	2018 Bare Costs Labor	Equipment	Total	Total Incl O&P
0010	**LAMPS**									
0080	Fluorescent, rapid start, cool white, 2' long, 20 watt	1 Elec	1	8	C	305	465		770	1,025
0120	3' long, 30 watt		.90	8.889		365	515		880	1,175
0125	3' long, 25 watt energy saver R265723-10 G		.90	8.889		1,050	515		1,565	1,950
0155	U-34 watt energy saver G		.80	10		12.05	580		592.05	885
0170	4' long, 34 watt energy saver G		.90	8.889		820	515		1,335	1,675
0176	2' long, T8, 17 watt energy saver G		1	8		335	465		800	1,075
0178	3' long, T8, 25 watt energy saver G		.90	8.889		365	515		880	1,175
0180	4' long, T8, 32 watt energy saver G		.90	8.889		223	515		738	1,025
0200	Slimline, 4' long, 40 watt		.90	8.889		840	515		1,355	1,700
0210	4' long, 30 watt energy saver G		.90	8.889		840	515		1,355	1,700
0300	8' long, 75 watt		.80	10		1,050	580		1,630	2,025
0350	8' long, 60 watt energy saver G		.80	10		410	580		990	1,325
0400	High output, 4' long, 60 watt		.90	8.889		545	515		1,060	1,375
0410	8' long, 95 watt energy saver		.80	10		505	580		1,085	1,425
0500	8' long, 110 watt		.80	10		505	580		1,085	1,425
0512	2' long, T5, 14 watt energy saver G		1	8		159	465		624	870
0514	3' long, T5, 21 watt energy saver G		.90	8.889		180	515		695	975
0516	4' long, T5, 28 watt energy saver G		.90	8.889		180	515		695	975
0517	4' long, T5, 54 watt energy saver G		.90	8.889		555	515		1,070	1,375
0520	Very high output, 4' long, 110 watt		.90	8.889		1,225	515		1,740	2,125
0525	8' long, 195 watt energy saver G		.70	11.429		1,150	665		1,815	2,275
0550	8' long, 215 watt		.70	11.429		1,100	665		1,765	2,200
0554	Full spectrum, 4' long, 60 watt		.90	8.889		665	515		1,180	1,500
0556	6' long, 85 watt		.90	8.889		580	515		1,095	1,400
0558	8' long, 110 watt		.80	10		1,825	580		2,405	2,875
0560	Twin tube compact lamp G		.90	8.889		450	515		965	1,275
0570	Double twin tube compact lamp G		.80	10		985	580		1,565	1,950
0580	Compact fluorescents, 15 watt, replaces standard 25 watt bulb G		.90	8.889		930	515		1,445	1,800
0582	20 watt, replaces standard 75 watt bulb G		.90	8.889		895	515		1,410	1,750
0584	23 watt, replaces standard 90 watt bulb G		.90	8.889		1,050	515		1,565	1,950
0586	26 watt, replaces standard 100 watt bulb G		.90	8.889		2,825	515		3,340	3,875
0600	Mercury vapor, mogul base, deluxe white, 100 watt		.30	26.667		5,325	1,550		6,875	8,175
0650	175 watt		.30	26.667		3,250	1,550		4,800	5,900
0700	250 watt		.30	26.667		5,200	1,550		6,750	8,025
0800	400 watt		.30	26.667		5,200	1,550		6,750	8,050
0900	1,000 watt		.20	40		13,800	2,325		16,125	18,700
1000	Metal halide, mogul base, 175 watt		.30	26.667		1,075	1,550		2,625	3,525
1100	250 watt		.30	26.667		1,725	1,550		3,275	4,225
1200	400 watt		.30	26.667		1,900	1,550		3,450	4,400
1300	1,000 watt		.20	40		3,350	2,325		5,675	7,150
1320	1,000 watt, 125,000 initial lumens		.20	40		11,400	2,325		13,725	16,000
1330	1,500 watt		.20	40		3,700	2,325		6,025	7,550
1350	High pressure sodium, 70 watt		.30	26.667		1,650	1,550		3,200	4,125
1360	100 watt		.30	26.667		1,575	1,550		3,125	4,075
1370	150 watt		.30	26.667		1,675	1,550		3,225	4,175
1380	250 watt		.30	26.667		2,225	1,550		3,775	4,775
1400	400 watt		.30	26.667		1,675	1,550		3,225	4,150
1450	1,000 watt		.20	40		4,450	2,325		6,775	8,350
1500	Low pressure sodium, 35 watt		.30	26.667		16,500	1,550		18,050	20,400
1550	55 watt		.30	26.667		18,800	1,550		20,350	22,900
1600	90 watt		.30	26.667		6,500	1,550		8,050	9,475
1650	135 watt		.20	40		27,300	2,325		29,625	33,500

For customer support on your Green Building Costs with RSMeans data, call 800.448.8182.

26 61 Lighting Systems and Accessories

26 61 23 – Lamps Applications

26 61 23.10 Lamps

		Crew	Daily Output	Labor-Hours	Unit	Material	2018 Bare Costs Labor	Equipment	Total	Total Incl O&P
1700	180 watt	1 Elec	.20	40	C	30,900	2,325		33,225	37,500
1750	Quartz line, clear, 500 watt		1.10	7.273		580	425		1,005	1,275
1760	1,500 watt		.20	40		1,675	2,325		4,000	5,300
1762	Spot, MR 16, 50 watt		1.30	6.154		1,075	360		1,435	1,700
1770	Tungsten halogen, T4, 400 watt		1.10	7.273		3,975	425		4,400	5,000
1775	T3, 1,200 watt		.30	26.667		4,900	1,550		6,450	7,725
1778	PAR 30, 50 watt		1.30	6.154		1,125	360		1,485	1,775
1780	PAR 38, 90 watt		1.30	6.154		9,650	360		10,010	11,100
1800	Incandescent, interior, A21, 100 watt		1.60	5		2,800	291		3,091	3,500
1900	A21, 150 watt		1.60	5		16,600	291		16,891	18,700
2000	A23, 200 watt		1.60	5		335	291		626	805
2200	PS 35, 300 watt		1.60	5		1,000	291		1,291	1,525
2210	PS 35, 500 watt		1.60	5		1,425	291		1,716	1,975
2230	PS 52, 1,000 watt		1.30	6.154		2,550	360		2,910	3,325
2240	PS 52, 1,500 watt		1.30	6.154		6,825	360		7,185	8,050
2300	R30, 75 watt		1.30	6.154		615	360		975	1,225
2400	R40, 100 watt		1.30	6.154		620	360		980	1,225
2500	Exterior, PAR 38, 75 watt		1.30	6.154		1,900	360		2,260	2,600
2600	PAR 38, 150 watt		1.30	6.154		2,200	360		2,560	2,925
2700	PAR 46, 200 watt		1.10	7.273		3,875	425		4,300	4,900
2800	PAR 56, 300 watt		1.10	7.273		2,650	425		3,075	3,550

Division Notes

	CREW	DAILY OUTPUT	LABOR-HOURS	UNIT	BARE COSTS MAT.	LABOR	EQUIP.	TOTAL	TOTAL INCL O&P

Division 28 Electronic Safety & Security

Estimating Tips

- When estimating material costs for electronic safety and security systems, it is always prudent to obtain manufacturers' quotations for equipment prices and special installation requirements that may affect the total cost.

- Fire alarm systems consist of control panels, annunciator panels, batteries with rack, charger, and fire alarm actuating and indicating devices. Some fire alarm systems include speakers, telephone lines, door closer controls, and other components. Be careful not to overlook the costs related to installation for these items. Also be aware of costs for integrated automation instrumentation and terminal devices, control equipment, control wiring, and programming. Insurance underwriters may have specific requirements for the type of materials to be installed or design requirements based on the hazard to be protected. Local jurisdictions may have requirements not covered by code. It is advisable to be aware of any special conditions.

- Security equipment includes items such as CCTV, access control, and other detection and identification systems to perform alert and alarm functions. Be sure to consider the costs related to installation for this security equipment, such as for integrated automation instrumentation and terminal devices, control equipment, control wiring, and programming.

Reference Numbers

Reference numbers are shown at the beginning of some major classifications. These numbers refer to related items in the Reference Section. The reference information may be an estimating procedure, an alternate pricing method, or technical information.

Note: Not all subdivisions listed here necessarily appear. ■

No part of this cost data may be reproduced, stored in a retrieval system, or transmitted in any form or by any means without prior written permission of Gordian.

Note: Trade Service, in part, has been used as a reference source for some of the material prices used in Division 28.

Did you know?

RSMeans data is available through our online application with 24/7 access:

- Search for unit prices by keyword
- Leverage the most up-to-date data
- Build and export estimates

Try it free for 30 days!
www.rsmeans.com/2018freetrial

28 42 Gas Detection and Alarm

28 42 15 – Gas Detection Sensors

28 42 15.50 Tank Leak Detection Systems

		Crew	Daily Output	Labor-Hours	Unit	Material	2018 Bare Costs Labor	Equipment	Total	Total Incl O&P
0010	**TANK LEAK DETECTION SYSTEMS** Liquid and vapor									
0100	For hydrocarbons and hazardous liquids/vapors									
0120	Controller, data acquisition, incl. printer, modem, RS232 port									
0140	24 channel, for use with all probes				Ea.	2,925			2,925	3,200
0160	9 channel, for external monitoring				"	1,175			1,175	1,300
0170	Integrated control panel with monitoring system and printer									
0180	1 to 2 tanks, double wall	2 Elec	4	4	Ea.	2,325	233		2,558	2,900
0181	1 to 8 tanks, single wall		4	4		2,325	233		2,558	2,900
0190	2 to 8 tanks, double wall		2.50	6.400		4,400	370		4,770	5,400
0200	Probes									
0210	Well monitoring									
0220	Liquid phase detection				Ea.	660			660	725
0230	Hydrocarbon vapor, fixed position					630			630	690
0240	Hydrocarbon vapor, float mounted					550			550	605
0250	Both liquid and vapor hydrocarbon					540			540	595
0300	Secondary containment, liquid phase									
0310	Pipe trench/manway sump				Ea.	595			595	655
0320	Double wall pipe and manual sump					500			500	550
0330	Double wall fiberglass annular space					375			375	410
0340	Double wall steel tank annular space					299			299	330
0500	Accessories									
0510	Modem, non-dedicated phone line				Ea.	274			274	300
0600	Monitoring, internal									
0610	Automatic tank gauge, incl. overfill				Ea.	1,225			1,225	1,350
0620	Product line				"	1,275			1,275	1,400
0700	Monitoring, special									
0710	Cathodic protection				Ea.	690			690	760
0720	Annular space chemical monitor				"	940			940	1,025

28 46 Fire Detection and Alarm

28 46 11 – Fire Sensors and Detectors

28 46 11.21 Carbon-Monoxide Detection Sensors

		Crew	Daily Output	Labor-Hours	Unit	Material	Labor	Equipment	Total	Total Incl O&P
0010	**CARBON-MONOXIDE DETECTION SENSORS**									
8400	Smoke and carbon monoxide alarm battery operated photoelectric low profile	1 Elec	24	.333	Ea.	54.50	19.40		73.90	88.50
8410	low profile photoelectric battery powered		24	.333		28.50	19.40		47.90	60.50
8700	Carbon monoxide detector, battery operated, wall mounted		16	.500		52	29		81	101
8710	Hardwired, wall and ceiling mounted		8	1		99.50	58		157.50	196
8720	Duct mounted		8	1		345	58		403	460

28 46 11.27 Other Sensors

		Crew	Daily Output	Labor-Hours	Unit	Material	Labor	Equipment	Total	Total Incl O&P
0010	**OTHER SENSORS**									
8300	Smoke alarm with integrated strobe light 120 V 16DB 60 fpm flash rate	1 Elec	16	.500	Ea.	103	29		132	157
8310	Photoelectric smoke detector with strobe 120 V 90 DB ceiling mount		12	.667		158	39		197	232
8320	120 V, 90 DB wall mount		12	.667		166	39		205	240
8440	Fire alarm beam detector, motorised reflective, infrared optical beam	2 Elec	1.60	10		800	580		1,380	1,750
8450	Fire alarm beam detector, motorised reflective, IR/UV optical beam	"	1.60	10		1,025	580		1,605	2,000

Division 31 Earthwork

Estimating Tips
31 05 00 Common Work Results for Earthwork

- Estimating the actual cost of performing earthwork requires careful consideration of the variables involved. This includes items such as type of soil, whether water will be encountered, dewatering, whether banks need bracing, disposal of excavated earth, and length of haul to fill or spoil sites, etc. If the project has large quantities of cut or fill, consider raising or lowering the site to reduce costs, while paying close attention to the effect on site drainage and utilities.
- If the project has large quantities of fill, creating a borrow pit on the site can significantly lower the costs.
- It is very important to consider what time of year the project is scheduled for completion. Bad weather can create large cost overruns from dewatering, site repair, and lost productivity from cold weather.

Reference Numbers
Reference numbers are shown at the beginning of some major classifications. These numbers refer to related items in the Reference Section. The reference information may be an estimating procedure, an alternate pricing method, or technical information.

Note: Not all subdivisions listed here necessarily appear. ■

Did you know?

RSMeans data is available through our online application with 24/7 access:

- Search for unit prices by keyword
- Leverage the most up-to-date data
- Build and export estimates

Try it free for 30 days!
www.rsmeans.com/2018freetrial

No part of this cost data may be reproduced, stored in a retrieval system, or transmitted in any form or by any means without prior written permission of Gordian.

31 05 Common Work Results for Earthwork

31 05 23 – Cement and Concrete for Earthwork

31 05 23.30 Plant Mixed Bituminous Concrete

		Crew	Daily Output	Labor-Hours	Unit	Material	2018 Bare Costs Labor	Equipment	Total	Total Incl O&P
0010	**PLANT MIXED BITUMINOUS CONCRETE**									
0020	Asphaltic concrete plant mix (145 lb./C.F.)				Ton	65			65	71.50
0040	Asphaltic concrete less than 300 tons add trucking costs									

31 05 23.40 Recycled Plant Mixed Bituminous Concrete

			Crew	Daily Output	Labor-Hours	Unit	Material	Labor	Equipment	Total	Total Incl O&P
0010	**RECYCLED PLANT MIXED BITUMINOUS CONCRETE**										
0200	Reclaimed pavement in stockpile	G				Ton	22			22	24
0400	Recycled pavement, at plant, ratio old:new, 70:30	G					35			35	38.50
0600	Ratio old:new, 30:70	G					52.50			52.50	57.50

31 23 Excavation and Fill

31 23 23 – Fill

31 23 23.16 Fill By Borrow and Utility Bedding

0010	**FILL BY BORROW AND UTILITY BEDDING**										
0600	If material source exceeds 2 miles, add for extra mileage.										

31 25 Erosion and Sedimentation Controls

31 25 14 – Stabilization Measures for Erosion and Sedimentation Control

31 25 14.16 Rolled Erosion Control Mats and Blankets

			Crew	Daily Output	Labor-Hours	Unit	Material	Labor	Equipment	Total	Total Incl O&P
0010	**ROLLED EROSION CONTROL MATS AND BLANKETS**										
0020	Jute mesh, 100 S.Y. per roll, 4' wide, stapled	G	B-80A	2400	.010	S.Y.	.91	.40	.10	1.41	1.72
0060	Polyethylene 3 dimensional geomatrix, 50 mil thick	G	"	700	.034		2.93	1.37	.34	4.64	5.65
0062	120 mil thick	G	"	515	.047		5.70	1.86	.46	8.02	9.65
0068	Slope stakes (placed @ 3' - 5' intervals)	G				Ea.	.13			.13	.14
0070	Paper biodegradable mesh	G	B-1	2500	.010	S.Y.	.18	.39		.57	.79
0080	Paper mulch	G	B-64	20000	.001		.14	.03	.02	.19	.22
0100	Plastic netting, stapled, 2" x 1" mesh, 20 mil	G	B-1	2500	.010		.29	.39		.68	.91
0120	Revegetation mat, webbed	G	2 Clab	1000	.016		2.91	.64		3.55	4.17
0160	Underdrain fabric, 18" x 100' roll	G	"	32	.500	Roll	27.50	19.95		47.45	61
0200	Polypropylene mesh, stapled, 6.5 oz./S.Y.	G	B-1	2500	.010	S.Y.	1.63	.39		2.02	2.38
0300	Tobacco netting, or jute mesh #2, stapled	G	"	2500	.010		.25	.39		.64	.87
0400	Soil sealant, liquid sprayed from truck	G	B-81	5000	.005		.38	.22	.11	.71	.89
1000	Silt fence, install and maintain, remove	G	B-62	1300	.018	L.F.	.46	.81	.13	1.40	1.88
1100	Allow 10% per month for maintenance; 6-month max life										
1130	Cellular confinement, poly, 3-dimen, 8' x 20' panels, 4" deep cell	G	B-6	1600	.015	S.F.	1.33	.66	.20	2.19	2.66
1140	8" deep cells	G	"	1200	.020	"	2.49	.87	.26	3.62	4.36
1200	Place and remove hay bales, staked	G	A-2	3	8	Ton	288	330	63	681	885
1250	Place and remove hay bales, staked (alt. pricing)	G	"	2500	.010	L.F.	4.78	.40	.08	5.26	5.95
1300	Soil cement, 7% Portland cement	G	B-70A	40	1	E.C.Y.	13.20	51	63	127.20	161
1305	For less than 3 to 1 slope, add							15%			
1310	For greater than 3 to 1 slope, add							25%			
1400	Barriers, w/degradable component, 3' H, incl. wd stakes	G	2 Clab	1600	.010	L.F.	.69	.40		1.09	1.37

31 31 Soil Treatment

31 31 16 – Termite Control

31 31 16.13 Chemical Termite Control

		Crew	Daily Output	Labor-Hours	Unit	Material	2018 Bare Costs Labor	Equipment	Total	Total Incl O&P
0010	**CHEMICAL TERMITE CONTROL**									
0030	SS mesh, no chemicals, avg 1,400 S.F. home, min	G 1 Skwk	1000	.008	SF Flr.	.32	.42		.74	.99
0040	Max	G "	500	.016	"	.32	.84		1.16	1.63

31 32 Soil Stabilization

31 32 19 – Geosynthetic Soil Stabilization and Layer Separation

31 32 19.16 Geotextile Soil Stabilization

		Crew	Daily Output	Labor-Hours	Unit	Material	Labor	Equipment	Total	Incl O&P
0010	**GEOTEXTILE SOIL STABILIZATION**									
1500	Geotextile fabric, woven, 200 lb. tensile strength	2 Clab	2500	.006	S.Y.	.94	.26		1.20	1.42
1510	Heavy duty, 600 lb. tensile strength		2400	.007		1.77	.27		2.04	2.35
1550	Non-woven, 120 lb. tensile strength		2500	.006		.84	.26		1.10	1.31

31 62 Driven Piles

31 62 23 – Composite Piles

31 62 23.10 Recycled Plastic and Fiberglass Piles

		Crew	Daily Output	Labor-Hours	Unit	Material	Labor	Equipment	Total	Incl O&P
0010	**RECYCLED PLASTIC AND FIBERGLASS PILES**, 200 PILES									
5000	Marine pilings, recycled plastic w/fiberglass reinf, up to 90' L, 8" diam.	G B-19	500	.128	V.L.F.	31.50	6.70	3.86	42.06	49
5010	10" diam.	G	500	.128		36	6.70	3.86	46.56	54.50
5020	13" diam.	G	400	.160		53	8.40	4.82	66.22	76.50
5030	16" diam.	G	400	.160		76.50	8.40	4.82	89.72	103
5040	20" diam.	G	350	.183		84.50	9.60	5.50	99.60	113
5050	24" diam.	G	350	.183		106	9.60	5.50	121.10	137

31 62 23.12 Marine Recycled Plastic and Fiberglass Piles

		Crew	Daily Output	Labor-Hours	Unit	Material	Labor	Equipment	Total	Incl O&P
0010	**MARINE RECYCLED PLASTIC AND FIBERGLASS PILES**, 200 PILES									
0040	Friction or end bearing, not including									
0050	mobilization or demobilization									
0055	Marine piles include production adjusted									
0060	due to thickness of silt layers									
0090	Shore driven piles with silt layer									
0100	Marine pilings, recycled plastic w/fiberglass, 50' long, 8" diam., 10' silt	G B-19	595	.108	V.L.F.	31.50	5.65	3.24	40.39	47
0110	50' long, 10" diam.	G	595	.108		36	5.65	3.24	44.89	52.50
0120	50' long, 13" diam.	G	476	.134		53	7.05	4.05	64.10	73.50
0130	50' long, 16" diam.	G	476	.134		76.50	7.05	4.05	87.60	100
0140	50' long, 20" diam.	G	417	.153		84.50	8.05	4.62	97.17	110
0150	50' long, 24" diam.	G	417	.153		106	8.05	4.62	118.67	134
0210	55' long, 8" diam.	G	585	.109		31.50	5.75	3.30	40.55	47
0220	55' long, 10" diam.	G	585	.109		36	5.75	3.30	45.05	52.50
0230	55' long, 13" diam.	G	468	.137		53	7.15	4.12	64.27	73.50
0240	55' long, 16" diam.	G	468	.137		76.50	7.15	4.12	87.77	100
0250	55' long, 20" diam.	G	410	.156		84.50	8.20	4.70	97.40	110
0260	55' long, 24" diam.	G	410	.156		106	8.20	4.70	118.90	134
0310	60' long, 8" diam.	G	576	.111		31.50	5.80	3.35	40.65	47
0320	60' long, 10" diam.	G	577	.111		36	5.80	3.34	45.14	52.50
0330	60' long, 13" diam.	G	462	.139		53	7.25	4.17	64.42	74
0340	60' long, 16" diam.	G	462	.139		76.50	7.25	4.17	87.92	100
0350	60' long, 20" diam.	G	404	.158		84.50	8.30	4.77	97.57	111
0360	60' long, 24" diam.	G	404	.158		106	8.30	4.77	119.07	134
0410	65' long, 8" diam.	G	570	.112		31.50	5.90	3.38	40.78	47.50
0420	65' long, 10" diam.	G	570	.112		36	5.90	3.38	45.28	53

For customer support on your Green Building Costs with RSMeans data, call 800.448.8182.

31 62 Driven Piles

31 62 23 – Composite Piles

31 62 23.12 Marine Recycled Plastic and Fiberglass Piles

		Crew	Daily Output	Labor-Hours	Unit	Material	2018 Bare Costs Labor	Equipment	Total	Total Incl O&P
0430	65' long, 13" diam. G	B-19	456	.140	V.L.F.	53	7.35	4.23	64.58	74
0440	65' long, 16" diam. G		456	.140		76.50	7.35	4.23	88.08	101
0450	65' long, 20" diam. G		399	.160		84.50	8.40	4.83	97.73	111
0460	65' long, 24" diam. G		399	.160		106	8.40	4.83	119.23	134
0510	70' long, 8" diam. G		565	.113		31.50	5.95	3.41	40.86	47.50
0520	70' long, 10" diam. G		565	.113		36	5.95	3.41	45.36	53
0530	70' long, 13" diam. G		452	.142		53	7.40	4.27	64.67	74
0540	70' long, 16" diam. G		452	.142		76.50	7.40	4.27	88.17	101
0550	70' long, 20" diam. G		395	.162		84.50	8.50	4.88	97.88	111
0560	70' long, 24" diam. G		399	.160		106	8.40	4.83	119.23	134
0610	75' long, 8" diam. G		560	.114		31.50	6	3.44	40.94	47.50
0620	75' long, 10" diam. G		560	.114		36	6	3.44	45.44	53
0630	75' long, 13" diam. G		448	.143		53	7.50	4.30	64.80	74.50
0640	75' long, 16" diam. G		448	.143		76.50	7.50	4.30	88.30	101
0650	75' long, 20" diam. G		392	.163		84.50	8.55	4.92	97.97	111
0660	75' long, 24" diam. G		392	.163		106	8.55	4.92	119.47	135
0710	80' long, 8" diam. G		556	.115		31.50	6.05	3.47	41.02	47.50
0720	80' long, 10" diam. G		556	.115		36	6.05	3.47	45.52	53
0730	80' long, 13" diam. G		444	.144		53	7.55	4.34	64.89	74.50
0740	80' long, 16" diam. G		444	.144		76.50	7.55	4.34	88.39	101
0750	80' long, 20" diam. G		389	.165		84.50	8.60	4.96	98.06	111
0760	80' long, 24" diam. G		389	.165		106	8.60	4.96	119.56	135
1000	Marine pilings, recycled plastic w/fiberglass, 50' long, 8" diam., 15' silt G		658	.097		31.50	5.10	2.93	39.53	45.50
1010	50' long, 10" diam. G		658	.097		36	5.10	2.93	44.03	51
1020	50' long, 13" diam. G		526	.122		53	6.40	3.67	63.07	72
1030	50' long, 16" diam. G		526	.122		76.50	6.40	3.67	86.57	98.50
1040	50' long, 20" diam. G		461	.139		84.50	7.30	4.18	95.98	108
1050	50' long, 24" diam. G		461	.139		106	7.30	4.18	117.48	132
1210	55' long, 8" diam. G		640	.100		31.50	5.25	3.01	39.76	46
1220	55' long, 10" diam. G		640	.100		36	5.25	3.01	44.26	51.50
1230	55' long, 13" diam. G		512	.125		53	6.55	3.77	63.32	72.50
1240	55' long, 16" diam. G		512	.125		76.50	6.55	3.77	86.82	99
1250	55' long, 20" diam. G		448	.143		84.50	7.50	4.30	96.30	109
1260	55' long, 24" diam. G		448	.143		106	7.50	4.30	117.80	132
1310	60' long, 8" diam. G		625	.102		31.50	5.35	3.09	39.94	46
1320	60' long, 10" diam. G		625	.102		36	5.35	3.09	44.44	51.50
1330	60' long, 13" diam. G		500	.128		53	6.70	3.86	63.56	72.50
1340	60' long, 16" diam. G		500	.128		76.50	6.70	3.86	87.06	99
1350	60' long, 20" diam. G		438	.146		84.50	7.65	4.40	96.55	109
1360	60' long, 24" diam. G		438	.146		106	7.65	4.40	118.05	133
1410	65' long, 8" diam. G		613	.104		31.50	5.45	3.15	40.10	46.50
1420	65' long, 10" diam. G		613	.104		36	5.45	3.15	44.60	52
1430	65' long, 13" diam. G		491	.130		53	6.85	3.93	63.78	73
1440	65' long, 16" diam. G		491	.130		76.50	6.85	3.93	87.28	99.50
1450	65' long, 20" diam. G		429	.149		84.50	7.80	4.49	96.79	110
1460	65' long, 24" diam. G		429	.149		106	7.80	4.49	118.29	133
1510	70' long, 8" diam. G		603	.106		31.50	5.55	3.20	40.25	46.50
1520	70' long, 10" diam. G		603	.106		36	5.55	3.20	44.75	52
1530	70' long, 13" diam. G		483	.133		53	6.95	3.99	63.94	73
1540	70' long, 16" diam. G		483	.133		76.50	6.95	3.99	87.44	99.50
1550	70' long, 20" diam. G		422	.152		84.50	7.95	4.57	97.02	110
1560	70' long, 24" diam. G		422	.152		106	7.95	4.57	118.52	133
1610	75' long, 8" diam. G		595	.108		31.50	5.65	3.24	40.39	47

31 62 Driven Piles

31 62 23 – Composite Piles

31 62 23.12 Marine Recycled Plastic and Fiberglass Piles

		Crew	Daily Output	Labor-Hours	Unit	Material	2018 Bare Costs Labor	Equipment	Total	Total Incl O&P
1620	75' long, 10" diam. G	B-19	595	.108	V.L.F.	36	5.65	3.24	44.89	52.50
1630	75' long, 13" diam. G		476	.134		53	7.05	4.05	64.10	73.50
1640	75' long, 16" diam. G		476	.134		76.50	7.05	4.05	87.60	100
1650	75' long, 20" diam. G		417	.153		84.50	8.05	4.62	97.17	110
1660	75' long, 24" diam. G		417	.153		106	8.05	4.62	118.67	134
1710	80' long, 8" diam. G		588	.109		31.50	5.70	3.28	40.48	47
1720	80' long, 10" diam. G		588	.109		36	5.70	3.28	44.98	52.50
1730	80' long, 13" diam. G		471	.136		53	7.10	4.09	64.19	73.50
1740	80' long, 16" diam. G		471	.136		76.50	7.10	4.09	87.69	100
1750	80' long, 20" diam. G		412	.155		84.50	8.15	4.68	97.33	110
1760	80' long, 24" diam. G		412	.155		106	8.15	4.68	118.83	134
2000	Marine pilings, recycled plastic w/fiberglass, 50' long, 8" diam., 20' silt G		735	.087		31.50	4.56	2.62	38.68	44.50
2010	50' long, 10" diam. G		735	.087		36	4.56	2.62	43.18	50
2020	50' long, 13" diam. G		588	.109		53	5.70	3.28	61.98	70.50
2030	50' long, 16" diam. G		588	.109		76.50	5.70	3.28	85.48	97
2040	50' long, 20" diam. G		515	.124		84.50	6.50	3.74	94.74	107
2050	50' long, 24" diam. G		515	.124		106	6.50	3.74	116.24	130
2210	55' long, 8" diam. G		705	.091		31.50	4.76	2.74	39	45
2220	55' long, 10" diam. G		705	.091		36	4.76	2.74	43.50	50.50
2230	55' long, 13" diam. G		564	.113		53	5.95	3.42	62.37	71
2240	55' long, 16" diam. G		564	.113		76.50	5.95	3.42	85.87	97.50
2250	55' long, 20" diam. G		494	.130		84.50	6.80	3.90	95.20	107
2260	55' long, 24" diam. G		494	.130		106	6.80	3.90	116.70	131
2310	60' long, 8" diam. G		682	.094		31.50	4.92	2.83	39.25	45.50
2320	60' long, 10" diam. G		682	.094		36	4.92	2.83	43.75	51
2330	60' long, 13" diam. G		546	.117		53	6.15	3.53	62.68	71.50
2340	60' long, 16" diam. G		546	.117		76.50	6.15	3.53	86.18	98
2350	60' long, 20" diam. G		477	.134		84.50	7.05	4.04	95.59	108
2360	60' long, 24" diam. G		477	.134		106	7.05	4.04	117.09	131
2410	65' long, 8" diam. G		663	.097		31.50	5.05	2.91	39.46	45.50
2420	65' long, 10" diam. G		663	.097		36	5.05	2.91	43.96	51
2430	65' long, 13" diam. G		531	.121		53	6.30	3.63	62.93	72
2440	65' long, 16" diam. G		531	.121		76.50	6.30	3.63	86.43	98.50
2450	65' long, 20" diam. G		464	.138		84.50	7.25	4.16	95.91	108
2460	65' long, 24" diam. G		464	.138		106	7.25	4.16	117.41	132
2510	70' long, 8" diam. G		648	.099		31.50	5.20	2.98	39.68	46
2520	70' long, 10" diam. G		648	.099		36	5.20	2.98	44.18	51.50
2530	70' long, 13" diam. G		518	.124		53	6.50	3.72	63.22	72
2540	70' long, 16" diam. G		518	.124		76.50	6.50	3.72	86.72	98.50
2550	70' long, 20" diam. G		454	.141		84.50	7.40	4.25	96.15	109
2560	70' long, 24" diam. G		454	.141		106	7.40	4.25	117.65	132
2610	75' long, 8" diam. G		636	.101		31.50	5.25	3.03	39.78	46
2620	75' long, 10" diam. G		636	.101		36	5.25	3.03	44.28	51.50
2630	75' long, 13" diam. G		508	.126		53	6.60	3.80	63.40	72.50
2640	75' long, 16" diam. G		508	.126		76.50	6.60	3.80	86.90	99
2650	75' long, 20" diam. G		445	.144		84.50	7.55	4.33	96.38	109
2660	75' long, 24" diam. G		445	.144		106	7.55	4.33	117.88	132
2710	80' long, 8" diam. G		625	.102		31.50	5.35	3.09	39.94	46
2720	80' long, 10" diam. G		625	.102		36	5.35	3.09	44.44	51.50
2730	80' long, 13" diam. G		500	.128		53	6.70	3.86	63.56	72.50
2740	80' long, 16" diam. G		500	.128		76.50	6.70	3.86	87.06	99
2750	80' long, 20" diam. G		437	.146		84.50	7.70	4.41	96.61	109
2760	80' long, 24" diam. G		437	.146		106	7.70	4.41	118.11	133

For customer support on your Green Building Costs with RSMeans data, call 800.448.8182.

31 62 Driven Piles

31 62 23 – Composite Piles

	31 62 23.12 Marine Recycled Plastic and Fiberglass Piles		Crew	Daily Output	Labor-Hours	Unit	Material	2018 Bare Costs Labor	Equipment	Total	Total Incl O&P
4990	Barge driven piles with silt layer										
5100	Marine pilings, recycled plastic w/fiberglass, 50' long, 8" diam.,10' silt	G	B-19B	476	.134	V.L.F.	31.50	7.05	5.80	44.35	52
5110	50' long, 10" diam.	G		476	.134		36	7.05	5.80	48.85	57.50
5120	50' long, 13" diam.	G		381	.168		53	8.80	7.25	69.05	79.50
5130	50' long, 16" diam.	G		381	.168		76.50	8.80	7.25	92.55	106
5140	50' long, 20" diam.	G		333	.192		84.50	10.05	8.30	102.85	117
5150	50' long, 24" diam.	G		333	.192		106	10.05	8.30	124.35	141
5210	55' long, 8" diam.	G		468	.137		31.50	7.15	5.90	44.55	52
5220	55' long, 10" diam.	G		468	.137		36	7.15	5.90	49.05	57.50
5230	55' long, 13" diam.	G		374	.171		53	8.95	7.40	69.35	80
5240	55' long, 16" diam.	G		374	.171		76.50	8.95	7.40	92.85	107
5250	55' long, 20" diam.	G		328	.195		84.50	10.25	8.45	103.20	118
5260	55' long, 24" diam.	G		328	.195		106	10.25	8.45	124.70	141
5310	60' long, 8" diam.	G		461	.139		31.50	7.30	6	44.80	52.50
5320	60' long, 10" diam.	G		461	.139		36	7.30	6	49.30	58
5330	60' long, 13" diam.	G		369	.173		53	9.10	7.50	69.60	80.50
5340	60' long, 16" diam.	G		369	.173		76.50	9.10	7.50	93.10	107
5350	60' long, 20" diam.	G		323	.198		84.50	10.40	8.55	103.45	118
5360	60' long, 24" diam.	G		323	.198		106	10.40	8.55	124.95	142
5410	65' long, 8" diam.	G		456	.140		31.50	7.35	6.05	44.90	52.50
5420	65' long, 10" diam.	G		456	.140		36	7.35	6.05	49.40	58
5430	65' long, 13" diam.	G		365	.175		53	9.20	7.55	69.75	80.50
5440	65' long, 16" diam.	G		365	.175		76.50	9.20	7.55	93.25	107
5450	65' long, 20" diam.	G		319	.201		84.50	10.50	8.65	103.65	118
5460	65' long, 24" diam.	G		319	.201		106	10.50	8.65	125.15	142
5510	70' long, 8" diam.	G		452	.142		31.50	7.40	6.10	45	53
5520	70' long, 10" diam.	G		452	.142		36	7.40	6.10	49.50	58.50
5530	70' long, 13" diam.	G		361	.177		53	9.30	7.65	69.95	81
5540	70' long, 16" diam.	G		361	.177		76.50	9.30	7.65	93.45	107
5550	70' long, 20" diam.	G		316	.203		84.50	10.60	8.75	103.85	119
5560	70' long, 24" diam.	G		316	.203		106	10.60	8.75	125.35	142
5610	75' long, 8" diam.	G		448	.143		31.50	7.50	6.15	45.15	53
5620	75' long, 10" diam.	G		448	.143		36	7.50	6.15	49.65	58.50
5630	75' long, 13" diam.	G		358	.179		53	9.35	7.70	70.05	81
5640	75' long, 16" diam.	G		358	.179		76.50	9.35	7.70	93.55	108
5650	75' long, 20" diam.	G		313	.204		84.50	10.70	8.85	104.05	119
5660	75' long, 24" diam.	G		313	.204		106	10.70	8.85	125.55	142
5710	80' long, 8" diam.	G		444	.144		31.50	7.55	6.25	45.30	53
5720	80' long, 10" diam.	G		444	.144		36	7.55	6.25	49.80	58.50
5730	80' long, 13" diam.	G		356	.180		53	9.40	7.75	70.15	81
5740	80' long, 16" diam.	G		356	.180		76.50	9.40	7.75	93.65	108
5750	80' long, 20" diam.	G		311	.206		84.50	10.80	8.90	104.20	119
5760	80' long, 24" diam.	G		311	.206		106	10.80	8.90	125.70	143
6100	Marine pilings, recycled plastic w/fiberglass, 50' long, 8" diam.,15' silt	G		526	.122		31.50	6.40	5.25	43.15	50
6110	50' long, 10" diam.	G		526	.122		36	6.40	5.25	47.65	55.50
6120	50' long, 13" diam.	G		421	.152		53	7.95	6.55	67.50	77.50
6130	50' long, 16" diam.	G		421	.152		76.50	7.95	6.55	91	104
6140	50' long, 20" diam.	G		368	.174		84.50	9.10	7.50	101.10	115
6150	50' long, 24" diam.	G		368	.174		106	9.10	7.50	122.60	138
6210	55' long, 8" diam.	G		512	.125		31.50	6.55	5.40	43.45	50.50
6220	55' long, 10" diam.	G		512	.125		36	6.55	5.40	47.95	56
6230	55' long, 13" diam.	G		409	.156		53	8.20	6.75	67.95	78
6240	55' long, 16" diam.	G		409	.156		76.50	8.20	6.75	91.45	105

31 62 Driven Piles

31 62 23 – Composite Piles

31 62 23.12 Marine Recycled Plastic and Fiberglass Piles		Crew	Daily Output	Labor-Hours	Unit	Material	2018 Bare Costs Labor	Equipment	Total	Total Incl O&P
6250	55' long, 20" diam. G	B-19B	358	.179	V.L.F.	84.50	9.35	7.70	101.55	116
6260	55' long, 24" diam. G		358	.179		106	9.35	7.70	123.05	139
6310	60' long, 8" diam. G		500	.128		31.50	6.70	5.55	43.75	51
6320	60' long, 10" diam. G		500	.128		36	6.70	5.55	48.25	56.50
6330	60' long, 13" diam. G		400	.160		53	8.40	6.90	68.30	78.50
6340	60' long, 16" diam. G		400	.160		76.50	8.40	6.90	91.80	105
6350	60' long, 20" diam. G		350	.183		84.50	9.60	7.90	102	116
6360	60' long, 24" diam. G		350	.183		106	9.60	7.90	123.50	140
6410	65' long, 8" diam. G		491	.130		31.50	6.85	5.65	44	51.50
6420	65' long, 10" diam. G		491	.130		36	6.85	5.65	48.50	57
6430	65' long, 13" diam. G		392	.163		53	8.55	7.05	68.60	79
6440	65' long, 16" diam. G		392	.163		76.50	8.55	7.05	92.10	106
6450	65' long, 20" diam. G		343	.187		84.50	9.80	8.05	102.35	117
6460	65' long, 24" diam. G		343	.187		106	9.80	8.05	123.85	140
6510	70' long, 8" diam. G		483	.133		31.50	6.95	5.70	44.15	51.50
6520	70' long, 10" diam. G		483	.133		36	6.95	5.70	48.65	57
6530	70' long, 13" diam. G		386	.166		53	8.70	7.15	68.85	79.50
6540	70' long, 16" diam. G		386	.166		76.50	8.70	7.15	92.35	106
6550	70' long, 20" diam. G		338	.189		84.50	9.90	8.20	102.60	117
6560	70' long, 24" diam. G		338	.189		106	9.90	8.20	124.10	140
6610	75' long, 8" diam. G		476	.134		31.50	7.05	5.80	44.35	52
6620	75' long, 10" diam. G		476	.134		36	7.05	5.80	48.85	57.50
6630	75' long, 13" diam. G		381	.168		53	8.80	7.25	69.05	79.50
6640	75' long, 16" diam. G		381	.168		76.50	8.80	7.25	92.55	106
6650	75' long, 20" diam. G		333	.192		84.50	10.05	8.30	102.85	117
6660	75' long, 24" diam. G		333	.192		106	10.05	8.30	124.35	141
6710	80' long, 8" diam. G		471	.136		31.50	7.10	5.85	44.45	52
6720	80' long, 10" diam. G		471	.136		36	7.10	5.85	48.95	57.50
6730	80' long, 13" diam. G		376	.170		53	8.90	7.35	69.25	80
6740	80' long, 16" diam. G		376	.170		76.50	8.90	7.35	92.75	106
6750	80' long, 20" diam. G		329	.195		84.50	10.20	8.40	103.10	118
6760	80' long, 24" diam. G		329	.195		106	10.20	8.40	124.60	141
7100	Marine pilings, recycled plastic w/fiberglass, 50' long, 8" diam., 20' silt G		588	.109		31.50	5.70	4.70	41.90	48.50
7110	50' long, 10" diam. G		588	.109		36	5.70	4.70	46.40	54
7120	50' long, 13" diam. G		471	.136		53	7.10	5.85	65.95	75.50
7130	50' long, 16" diam. G		471	.136		76.50	7.10	5.85	89.45	102
7140	50' long, 20" diam. G		412	.155		84.50	8.15	6.70	99.35	113
7150	50' long, 24" diam. G		412	.155		106	8.15	6.70	120.85	136
7210	55' long, 8" diam. G		564	.113		31.50	5.95	4.90	42.35	49
7220	55' long, 10" diam. G		564	.113		36	5.95	4.90	46.85	54.50
7230	55' long, 13" diam. G		451	.142		53	7.45	6.15	66.60	76.50
7240	55' long, 16" diam. G		451	.142		76.50	7.45	6.15	90.10	103
7250	55' long, 20" diam. G		395	.162		84.50	8.50	7	100	113
7260	55' long, 24" diam. G		395	.162		106	8.50	7	121.50	137
7310	60' long, 8" diam. G		545	.117		31.50	6.15	5.05	42.70	49.50
7320	60' long, 10" diam. G		545	.117		36	6.15	5.05	47.20	55
7330	60' long, 13" diam. G		436	.147		53	7.70	6.35	67.05	77
7340	60' long, 16" diam. G		436	.147		76.50	7.70	6.35	90.55	103
7350	60' long, 20" diam. G		382	.168		84.50	8.80	7.25	100.55	114
7360	60' long, 24" diam. G		382	.168		106	8.80	7.25	122.05	138
7410	65' long, 8" diam. G		531	.121		31.50	6.30	5.20	43	50
7420	65' long, 10" diam. G		531	.121		36	6.30	5.20	47.50	55.50
7430	65' long, 13" diam. G		424	.151		53	7.90	6.50	67.40	77.50

For customer support on your Green Building Costs with RSMeans data, call 800.448.8182.

31 62 Driven Piles

31 62 23 – Composite Piles

31 62 23.12 Marine Recycled Plastic and Fiberglass Piles

		Crew	Daily Output	Labor-Hours	Unit	Material	2018 Bare Costs Labor	Equipment	Total	Total Incl O&P
7440	65' long, 16" diam. G	B-19B	424	.151	V.L.F.	76.50	7.90	6.50	90.90	104
7450	65' long, 20" diam. G		371	.173		84.50	9.05	7.45	101	115
7460	65' long, 24" diam. G		371	.173		106	9.05	7.45	122.50	138
7510	70' long, 8" diam. G		518	.124		31.50	6.50	5.35	43.35	50.50
7520	70' long, 10" diam. G		518	.124		36	6.50	5.35	47.85	56
7530	70' long, 13" diam. G		415	.154		53	8.10	6.65	67.75	78
7540	70' long, 16" diam. G		415	.154		76.50	8.10	6.65	91.25	104
7550	70' long, 20" diam. G		363	.176		84.50	9.25	7.60	101.35	115
7560	70' long, 24" diam. G		363	.176		106	9.25	7.60	122.85	139
7610	75' long, 8" diam. G		508	.126		31.50	6.60	5.45	43.55	51
7620	75' long, 10" diam. G		508	.126		36	6.60	5.45	48.05	56.50
7630	75' long, 13" diam. G		407	.157		53	8.25	6.80	68.05	78.50
7640	75' long, 16" diam. G		407	.157		76.50	8.25	6.80	91.55	105
7650	75' long, 20" diam. G		356	.180		84.50	9.40	7.75	101.65	116
7660	75' long, 24" diam. G		356	.180		106	9.40	7.75	123.15	139
7710	80' long, 8" diam. G		500	.128		31.50	6.70	5.55	43.75	51
7720	80' long, 10" diam. G		500	.128		36	6.70	5.55	48.25	56.50
7730	80' long, 13" diam. G		400	.160		53	8.40	6.90	68.30	78.50
7740	80' long, 16" diam. G		400	.160		76.50	8.40	6.90	91.80	105
7750	80' long, 20" diam. G		350	.183		84.50	9.60	7.90	102	116
7760	80' long, 24" diam. G		350	.183		106	9.60	7.90	123.50	140

Estimating Tips

32 01 00 Operations and Maintenance of Exterior Improvements

- Recycling of asphalt pavement is becoming very popular and is an alternative to removal and replacement. It can be a good value engineering proposal if removed pavement can be recycled, either at the project site or at another site that is reasonably close to the project site. Sections on repair of flexible and rigid pavement are included.

32 10 00 Bases, Ballasts, and Paving

- When estimating paving, keep in mind the project schedule. Also note that prices for asphalt and concrete are generally higher in the cold seasons. Lines for pavement markings, including tactile warning systems and fence lines, are included.

32 90 00 Planting

- The timing of planting and guarantee specifications often dictate the costs for establishing tree and shrub growth and a stand of grass or ground cover. Establish the work performance schedule to coincide with the local planting season. Maintenance and growth guarantees can add from 20%–100% to the total landscaping cost and can be contractually cumbersome. The cost to replace trees and shrubs can be as high as 5% of the total cost, depending on the planting zone, soil conditions, and time of year.

Reference Numbers

Reference numbers are shown at the beginning of some major classifications. These numbers refer to related items in the Reference Section. The reference information may be an estimating procedure, an alternate pricing method, or technical information.

Note: Not all subdivisions listed here necessarily appear. ∎

Did you know?

RSMeans data is available through our online application with 24/7 access:

- Search for unit prices by keyword
- Leverage the most up-to-date data
- Build and export estimates

Try it free for 30 days!
www.rsmeans.com/2018freetrial

No part of this cost data may be reproduced, stored in a retrieval system, or transmitted in any form or by any means without prior written permission of Gordian.

32 01 Operation and Maintenance of Exterior Improvements

32 01 13 – Flexible Paving Surface Treatment

32 01 13.66 Fog Seal

		Crew	Daily Output	Labor-Hours	Unit	Material	2018 Bare Costs Labor	Equipment	Total	Total Incl O&P
0010	**FOG SEAL**									
0012	Sealcoating, 2 coat coal tar pitch emulsion over 10,000 S.Y.	B-45	5000	.003	S.Y.	.85	.16	.16	1.17	1.36
0030	1,000 to 10,000 S.Y.	"	3000	.005		.85	.27	.27	1.39	1.63
0100	Under 1,000 S.Y.	B-1	1050	.023		.85	.93		1.78	2.35
0160	Small area	"	8500	.003	S.F.	.09	.11		.20	.27

32 01 16 – Flexible Paving Rehabilitation

32 01 16.74 In Place Hot Reused Asphalt Paving

			Crew	Daily Output	Labor-Hours	Unit	Material	Labor	Equipment	Total	Incl O&P
0010	**IN PLACE HOT REUSED ASPHALT PAVING**										
5500	Recycle asphalt pavement at site										
5520	Remove, rejuvenate and spread 4" deep	G	B-72	2500	.026	S.Y.	4.38	1.20	4.40	9.98	11.50
5521	6" deep	G	"	2000	.032	"	6.40	1.51	5.50	13.41	15.40

32 11 Base Courses

32 11 23 – Aggregate Base Courses

32 11 23.23 Base Course Drainage Layers

			Crew	Daily Output	Labor-Hours	Unit	Material	Labor	Equipment	Total	Incl O&P
0010	**BASE COURSE DRAINAGE LAYERS**										
0011	For roadways and large areas										
0025	Red brick dust, from recycled brick, for bases/ballasts, mat only	G				C.Y.	41.50			41.50	45.50
0035	Red brick, 3/8" nuggets, recycled brick, bases/ballast, mat only	G					41.50			41.50	45.50
0045	1-1/4" nuggets, recycled brick, bases/ballasts, mat only	G					73.50			73.50	81
0050	Crushed 3/4" stone base, compacted, 3" deep		B-36C	5200	.008	S.Y.	2.71	.38	.74	3.83	4.38
0080	4" deep			5100	.008		3.61	.39	.76	4.76	5.40
0100	6" deep			5000	.008		5.40	.40	.77	6.57	7.40
0200	9" deep			4600	.009		8.15	.43	.84	9.42	10.50
0300	12" deep			4200	.010		10.85	.47	.92	12.24	13.65
0301	Crushed 1-1/2" stone base, compacted to 4" deep		B-36B	6000	.011		4.52	.51	.75	5.78	6.55
0302	6" deep			5400	.012		6.80	.57	.83	8.20	9.25
0303	8" deep			4500	.014		9.05	.68	1	10.73	12.10
0304	12" deep			3800	.017		13.55	.81	1.19	15.55	17.45
0320	12" deep		B-36C	4200	.010		10.85	.47	.92	12.24	13.65
0350	Bank run gravel, spread and compacted										
0360	4" deep		B-32	7200	.004	S.Y.	2.43	.22	.30	2.95	3.34
0370	6" deep			6000	.005		3.60	.27	.36	4.23	4.75
0390	9" deep			4900	.007		5.40	.33	.44	6.17	6.95
0400	12" deep			4200	.008		7.20	.38	.51	8.09	9.10
1500	Alternate method to figure base course										
1505	Sand, washed & graded, compacted, 6" deep		B-36C	835	.048	E.C.Y.	36	2.39	4.63	43.02	48
1510	Crushed stone, 3/4", compacted, 3" deep		"	435	.092		28	4.58	8.90	41.48	47
1511	6" deep		B-36B	835	.077		28	3.67	5.40	37.07	42
1512	9" deep			1150	.056		28	2.66	3.92	34.58	39
1513	12" deep			1400	.046		28	2.19	3.22	33.41	37.50
1520	Crushed stone, 1-1/2", compacted, 4" deep			665	.096		28	4.60	6.80	39.40	45
1521	6" deep			900	.071		28	3.40	5	36.40	41
1522	8" deep			1000	.064		28	3.06	4.51	35.57	40
1523	12" deep			1265	.051		28	2.42	3.56	33.98	38
1530	Gravel, bank run, compacted, 6" deep		B-36C	835	.048		18.50	2.39	4.63	25.52	29
1531	9" deep			1150	.035		18.50	1.73	3.36	23.59	27
1532	12" deep			1400	.029		18.50	1.42	2.76	22.68	25.50
2010	Crushed stone, 3/4" maximum size, 3" deep		B-36	540	.074	Ton	18.05	3.39	2.85	24.29	28
2011	6" deep			1625	.025		18.05	1.13	.95	20.13	22.50

32 11 Base Courses

32 11 23 – Aggregate Base Courses

32 11 23.23 Base Course Drainage Layers

		Crew	Daily Output	Labor-Hours	Unit	Material	2018 Bare Costs Labor	Equipment	Total	Total Incl O&P
2012	9" deep	B-36	1785	.022	Ton	18.05	1.03	.86	19.94	22.50
2013	12" deep		1950	.021		18.05	.94	.79	19.78	22
2020	Crushed stone, 1-1/2" maximum size, 4" deep		720	.056		18.05	2.55	2.14	22.74	26
2021	6" deep		815	.049		18.05	2.25	1.89	22.19	25.50
2022	8" deep		835	.048		18.05	2.19	1.85	22.09	25
2023	12" deep		975	.041		18.05	1.88	1.58	21.51	24.50
2030	Bank run gravel, 6" deep	B-32A	875	.027		12.45	1.35	1.49	15.29	17.40
2031	9" deep		970	.025		12.45	1.22	1.34	15.01	17
2032	12" deep		1060	.023		12.45	1.11	1.23	14.79	16.75
6000	Stabilization fabric, polypropylene, 6 oz./S.Y.	B-6	10000	.002	S.Y.	.73	.10	.03	.86	.99
6900	For small and irregular areas, add						50%	50%		
7000	Prepare and roll sub-base, small areas to 2,500 S.Y.	B-32A	1500	.016	S.Y.		.79	.87	1.66	2.15
8000	Large areas over 2,500 S.Y.	"	3500	.007			.34	.37	.71	.92
8050	For roadways	B-32	4000	.008			.40	.54	.94	1.20
8200	Capillary water barrier, 4" compacted thickness	B-14	450	.107	C.Y.	190	4.49	.69	195.18	217
8210	6" compacted thickness		500	.096		190	4.04	.63	194.67	216
8220	8" compacted thickness		600	.080		190	3.37	.52	193.89	215

32 11 26 – Asphaltic Base Courses

32 11 26.13 Plant Mix Asphaltic Base Courses

		Crew	Daily Output	Labor-Hours	Unit	Material	Labor	Equipment	Total	Total Incl O&P
0010	**PLANT MIX ASPHALTIC BASE COURSES**									
0011	Roadways and large paved areas									
1600	Macadam base, crushed stone or slag, dry-bound	B-36D	1400	.023	E.C.Y.	47.50	1.16	2.24	50.90	56.50
1610	Water-bound	B-36C	1400	.029	"	47.50	1.42	2.76	51.68	57.50
2000	Alternate method to figure base course									
2005	Bituminous concrete, 4" thick	B-25	1000	.088	Ton	65	3.86	2.69	71.55	80.50
2006	6" thick		1220	.072		65	3.16	2.21	70.37	78.50
2007	8" thick		1320	.067		65	2.92	2.04	69.96	78
2008	10" thick		1400	.063		65	2.75	1.92	69.67	78

32 12 Flexible Paving

32 12 16 – Asphalt Paving

32 12 16.13 Plant-Mix Asphalt Paving

		Crew	Daily Output	Labor-Hours	Unit	Material	Labor	Equipment	Total	Total Incl O&P
0010	**PLANT-MIX ASPHALT PAVING**									
0600	Porous pvmnt, 1" open graded friction course over 3" bitum course	B-25	7725	.011	S.Y.	4.76	.50	.35	5.61	6.40

32 12 16.14 Asphaltic Concrete Paving

		Crew	Daily Output	Labor-Hours	Unit	Material	Labor	Equipment	Total	Total Incl O&P
0011	**ASPHALTIC CONCRETE PAVING**, parking lots & driveways									
0015	No asphalt hauling included									
2000	From 60% recycled content, base course 3" thick [G]	B-25	800	.110	Ton	43	4.82	3.37	51.19	58

32 14 Unit Paving

32 14 13 – Precast Concrete Unit Paving

32 14 13.18 Precast Concrete Plantable Pavers

		Crew	Daily Output	Labor-Hours	Unit	Material	2018 Bare Costs Labor	Equipment	Total	Total Incl O&P
0010	**PRECAST CONCRETE PLANTABLE PAVERS** (50% grass)									
0015	Subgrade preparation and grass planting not included									
0100	Precast concrete plantable pavers with topsoil, 24" x 16"	B-63	800	.050	S.F.	4.38	2.11	.22	6.71	8.25
0200	Less than 600 S.F. or irregular area	"	500	.080	"	4.38	3.37	.35	8.10	10.30
0300	3/4" crushed stone base for plantable pavers, 6" depth	B-62	1000	.024	S.Y.	4.22	1.05	.17	5.44	6.40
0400	8" depth		900	.027		5.60	1.16	.19	6.95	8.20
0500	10" depth		800	.030		7.05	1.31	.22	8.58	10
0600	12" depth		700	.034		8.40	1.50	.25	10.15	11.80
0700	Hydro seeding plantable pavers	B-81A	20	.800	M.S.F.	11.40	33.50	17.95	62.85	83.50
0800	Apply fertilizer and seed to plantable pavers	1 Clab	8	1	"	41.50	40		81.50	106

32 14 16 – Brick Unit Paving

32 14 16.10 Brick Paving

			Crew	Daily Output	Labor-Hours	Unit	Material	Labor	Equipment	Total	Total Incl O&P
0010	**BRICK PAVING**										
1810	Brick paving, reprocessed clay and soil, 4" x 8" x 2-1/4"	G	D-1	110	.145	S.F.	2.52	6.50		9.02	12.75

32 17 Paving Specialties

32 17 13 – Parking Bumpers

32 17 13.16 Plastic Parking Bumpers

			Crew	Daily Output	Labor-Hours	Unit	Material	Labor	Equipment	Total	Total Incl O&P
0010	**PLASTIC PARKING BUMPERS**										
1600	Bollards, recycled plastic, 5" x 5" x 5' L	G	B-6	20	1.200	Ea.	115	52.50	15.60	183.10	223
1610	Wheel stops, recycled plastic, yellow, 4" x 6" x 6' L	G		20	1.200		51	52.50	15.60	119.10	153
1620	Speed bumps, recycled plastic, yellow, 3" H x 10" W x 6' L	G		20	1.200		144	52.50	15.60	212.10	255
1630	3" H x 10" W x 9' L	G		20	1.200		217	52.50	15.60	285.10	335

32 17 13.26 Wood Parking Bumpers

		Crew	Daily Output	Labor-Hours	Unit	Material	Labor	Equipment	Total	Total Incl O&P
0010	**WOOD PARKING BUMPERS**									
0020	Parking barriers, timber w/saddles, treated type									
0100	4" x 4" for cars	B-2	520	.077	L.F.	3.07	3.10		6.17	8.10
0200	6" x 6" for trucks	"	520	.077	"	6.45	3.10		9.55	11.80

32 31 Fences and Gates

32 31 23 – Plastic Fences and Gates

32 31 23.20 Fence, Recycled Plastic

			Crew	Daily Output	Labor-Hours	Unit	Material	Labor	Equipment	Total	Total Incl O&P
0010	**FENCE, RECYCLED PLASTIC**										
9015	Fence rail, made from recycled plastic, various colors, 2 rail	G	B-1	150	.160	L.F.	10.05	6.50		16.55	21
9018	3 rail	G		150	.160		12.80	6.50		19.30	24
9020	4 rail	G		150	.160		15.55	6.50		22.05	27
9030	Fence pole, made from recycled plastic, various colors, 7'	G		96	.250	Ea.	50	10.15		60.15	70.50
9040	Stockade fence, made from recycled plastic, various colors, 4' high	G	B-80C	160	.150	L.F.	33.50	6.20	1.22	40.92	48
9050	6' high	G		160	.150	"	36	6.20	1.22	43.42	50.50
9060	6' pole	G		96	.250	Ea.	38	10.35	2.04	50.39	60
9070	9' pole	G		96	.250	"	43.50	10.35	2.04	55.89	66
9080	Picket fence, made from recycled plastic, various colors, 3' high	G		160	.150	L.F.	22.50	6.20	1.22	29.92	35.50
9090	4' high	G		160	.150	"	33	6.20	1.22	40.42	47
9100	3' high gate	G		8	3	Ea.	22	124	24.50	170.50	240
9110	4' high gate	G		8	3		29	124	24.50	177.50	247
9120	5' high pole	G		96	.250		36	10.35	2.04	48.39	58
9130	6' high pole	G		96	.250		42	10.35	2.04	54.39	64
9140	Pole cap only	G					5.25			5.25	5.80

32 31 Fences and Gates

32 31 23 – Plastic Fences and Gates

32 31 23.20 Fence, Recycled Plastic

		Crew	Daily Output	Labor-Hours	Unit	Material	2018 Bare Costs Labor	Equipment	Total	Total Incl O&P
9150	Keeper pins only	G			Ea.	.41			.41	.45

32 32 Retaining Walls

32 32 29 – Timber Retaining Walls

32 32 29.10 Landscape Timber Retaining Walls

		Crew	Daily Output	Labor-Hours	Unit	Material	Labor	Equipment	Total	Total Incl O&P
0010	**LANDSCAPE TIMBER RETAINING WALLS**									
0100	Treated timbers, 6" x 6"	1 Clab	265	.030	L.F.	2.47	1.20		3.67	4.55
0110	6" x 8"	"	200	.040	"	5.40	1.59		6.99	8.35
0120	Drilling holes in timbers for fastening, 1/2"	1 Carp	450	.018	Inch		.90		.90	1.37
0130	5/8"	"	450	.018	"		.90		.90	1.37
0140	Reinforcing rods for fastening, 1/2"	1 Clab	312	.026	L.F.	.35	1.02		1.37	1.95
0150	5/8"	"	312	.026	"	.55	1.02		1.57	2.16
0160	Reinforcing fabric	2 Clab	2500	.006	S.Y.	2.13	.26		2.39	2.73
0170	Gravel backfill		28	.571	C.Y.	16.80	23		39.80	53
0180	Perforated pipe, 4" diameter with silt sock		1200	.013	L.F.	1	.53		1.53	1.91
0190	Galvanized 60d common nails	1 Clab	625	.013	Ea.	.18	.51		.69	.98
0200	20d common nails	"	3800	.002	"	.04	.08		.12	.17

32 33 Site Furnishings

32 33 33 – Site Manufactured Planters

32 33 33.10 Planters

			Crew	Daily Output	Labor-Hours	Unit	Material	Labor	Equipment	Total	Total Incl O&P
0010	**PLANTERS**										
1710	Tree grates, recycled plastic, 2-piece, black, 4' x 4' square	G	B-6	25	.960	Ea.	261	42	12.50	315.50	365
1720	5' x 5' square	G		25	.960		355	42	12.50	409.50	465
1730	3' round	G		25	.960		243	42	12.50	297.50	345
1740	4' round	G		25	.960		267	42	12.50	321.50	370
1750	5' round	G		25	.960		390	42	12.50	444.50	505

32 33 43 – Site Seating and Tables

32 33 43.13 Site Seating

			Crew	Daily Output	Labor-Hours	Unit	Material	Labor	Equipment	Total	Total Incl O&P
0010	**SITE SEATING**										
1000	Picnic tables, recycled plastic, various colors, 4'	G	2 Clab	5	3.200	Ea.	750	128		878	1,025
1010	6'	G		5	3.200		845	128		973	1,125
1020	8'	G		4	4		1,275	159		1,434	1,650
1030	Classic park bench, recycled plastic, various colors, 4' long	G		5	3.200		620	128		748	875
1040	6' long	G		5	3.200		735	128		863	1,000
1050	8' long	G		4	4		895	159		1,054	1,225
1060	Backless mall bench, recycled plastic, various colors, 4' long	G		5	3.200		254	128		382	475
1070	6' long	G		5	3.200		300	128		428	525
1080	8' long	G		4	4		385	159		544	665

32 84 Planting Irrigation

32 84 13 – Drip Irrigation

32 84 13.10 Subsurface Drip Irrigation

		Crew	Daily Output	Labor-Hours	Unit	Material	2018 Bare Costs Labor	Equipment	Total	Total Incl O&P
0010	**SUBSURFACE DRIP IRRIGATION**									
0011	Looped grid, pressure compensating									
0100	Preinserted PE emitter, line, hand bury, irregular area, small	G	3 Skwk	1200	.020	L.F.	.26	1.05		1.31	1.89
0150	Medium	G		1800	.013		.26	.70		.96	1.36
0200	Large	G		2520	.010		.26	.50		.76	1.05
0250	Rectangular area, small	G		2040	.012		.26	.62		.88	1.23
0300	Medium	G		2640	.009		.26	.48		.74	1.02
0350	Large	G		3600	.007		.26	.35		.61	.82
0400	Install in trench, irregular area, small	G		4050	.006		.26	.31		.57	.77
0450	Medium	G		7488	.003		.26	.17		.43	.55
0500	Large	G		16560	.001		.26	.08		.34	.41
0550	Rectangular area, small	G		8100	.003		.26	.16		.42	.53
0650	Large	G		33264	.001		.26	.04		.30	.35
0700	Trenching and backfill	G	B-53	500	.016			.82	.12	.94	1.38
0750	For vinyl tubing, 1/4", add to above						25%	10%			
0800	Vinyl tubing, 1/4", material only	G					.09			.09	.10
0850	Supply tubing, 1/2", material only, 100' coil	G					.13			.13	.14
0900	500' coil	G					.12			.12	.13
0950	Compression fittings	G	1 Skwk	90	.089	Ea.	1.74	4.65		6.39	9
1000	Barbed fittings, 1/4"	G		360	.022		.12	1.16		1.28	1.91
1100	Flush risers	G		60	.133		3.48	7		10.48	14.55
1150	Flush ends, figure eight	G		180	.044		.53	2.33		2.86	4.14
1300	Auto flush, spring loaded	G		90	.089		2.25	4.65		6.90	9.60
1350	Volumetric	G		90	.089		7.65	4.65		12.30	15.55
1400	Air relief valve, inline with compensation tee, 1/2"	G		45	.178		17.30	9.30		26.60	33.50
1450	1"	G		30	.267		17.30	13.95		31.25	40.50
1500	Round box for flush ends, 6"	G		30	.267		7.90	13.95		21.85	30
1600	Screen filter, 3/4" screen	G		12	.667		10.75	35		45.75	65.50
1650	1" disk	G		8	1		26.50	52.50		79	110
1700	1-1/2" disk	G		4	2		87	105		192	256
1750	2" disk	G		3	2.667		124	140		264	350
1800	Typical installation 18" OC, small, minimum					S.F.				1.53	2.35
1850	Maximum									1.78	2.75
1900	Large, minimum									1.48	2.28
2000	Maximum									1.71	2.64
2100	For non-pressure compensating systems, deduct						10%				10%

32 91 Planting Preparation

32 91 13 – Soil Preparation

32 91 13.16 Mulching

		Crew	Daily Output	Labor-Hours	Unit	Material	Labor	Equipment	Total	Total Incl O&P
0010	**MULCHING**									
0100	Aged barks, 3" deep, hand spread	1 Clab	100	.080	S.Y.	3.80	3.19		6.99	9.05
0150	Skid steer loader	B-63	13.50	2.963	M.S.F.	420	125	12.90	557.90	670
0200	Hay, 1" deep, hand spread	1 Clab	475	.017	S.Y.	.45	.67		1.12	1.52
0250	Power mulcher, small	B-64	180	.089	M.S.F.	50	3.75	1.82	55.57	62.50
0350	Large	B-65	530	.030	"	50	1.27	.86	52.13	58
0370	Fiber mulch recycled newsprint hand spread	1 Clab	500	.016	S.Y.	.23	.64		.87	1.22
0380	Power mulcher small	B-64	200	.080	M.S.F.	25.50	3.37	1.64	30.51	35
0390	Power mulcher large	B-65	600	.027	"	25.50	1.12	.76	27.38	30.50
0400	Humus peat, 1" deep, hand spread	1 Clab	700	.011	S.Y.	2.96	.46		3.42	3.95
0450	Push spreader	"	2500	.003	"	2.96	.13		3.09	3.45

32 91 Planting Preparation

32 91 13 – Soil Preparation

32 91 13.16 Mulching

		Crew	Daily Output	Labor-Hours	Unit	Material	2018 Bare Costs Labor	Equipment	Total	Total Incl O&P
0550	Tractor spreader	B-66	700	.011	M.S.F.	330	.59	.35	330.94	360
0600	Oat straw, 1" deep, hand spread	1 Clab	475	.017	S.Y.	.56	.67		1.23	1.64
0650	Power mulcher, small	B-64	180	.089	M.S.F.	62	3.75	1.82	67.57	76
0700	Large	B-65	530	.030	"	62	1.27	.86	64.13	71.50
0750	Add for asphaltic emulsion	B-45	1770	.009	Gal.	5.80	.45	.45	6.70	7.60
0760	Pine straw, 1" deep, hand spread	1 Clab	1950	.004	S.F.	.11	.16		.27	.37
0800	Peat moss, 1" deep, hand spread		900	.009	S.Y.	4.90	.35		5.25	5.95
0850	Push spreader		2500	.003	"	4.90	.13		5.03	5.60
0950	Tractor spreader	B-66	700	.011	M.S.F.	545	.59	.35	545.94	600
1000	Polyethylene film, 6 mil	2 Clab	2000	.008	S.Y.	.53	.32		.85	1.07
1010	4 mil		2300	.007		.39	.28		.67	.85
1020	1-1/2 mil		2500	.006		.22	.26		.48	.63
1050	Filter fabric weed barrier		2000	.008		.68	.32		1	1.24
1100	Redwood nuggets, 3" deep, hand spread	1 Clab	150	.053		3.12	2.13		5.25	6.65
1150	Skid steer loader	B-63	13.50	2.963	M.S.F.	345	125	12.90	482.90	585
1200	Stone mulch, hand spread, ceramic chips, economy	1 Clab	125	.064	S.Y.	7	2.55		9.55	11.60
1250	Deluxe	"	95	.084	"	10.60	3.36		13.96	16.75
1300	Granite chips	B-1	10	2.400	C.Y.	72.50	97.50		170	228
1400	Marble chips		10	2.400		215	97.50		312.50	385
1600	Pea gravel		28	.857		111	34.50		145.50	175
1700	Quartz		10	2.400		190	97.50		287.50	355
1760	Landscape mulch, 100% recycld tires, var colors, hand spread, 3" deep		10	2.400		283	97.50		380.50	460
1800	Tar paper, 15 lb. felt	1 Clab	800	.010	S.Y.	.48	.40		.88	1.14
1900	Wood chips, 2" deep, hand spread	"	220	.036	"	1.58	1.45		3.03	3.95
1950	Skid steer loader	B-63	20.30	1.970	M.S.F.	176	83	8.55	267.55	330

32 93 Plants

32 93 13 – Ground Covers

32 93 13.20 Ground Cover and Vines

		Crew	Daily Output	Labor-Hours	Unit	Material	Labor	Equipment	Total	Total Incl O&P
0010	**GROUND COVER AND VINES** Planting only, no preparation									
0100	Ajuga, 1 year, bare root	B-1	9	2.667	C	350	108		458	550
0150	Potted, 2 year		6	4	"	800	162		962	1,125
0160	Andora Creeping Juniper, 2 gal. cont		62	.387	Ea.	44.50	15.70		60.20	73
0200	Berberis, potted, 2 year		6	4	C	1,275	162		1,437	1,650
0250	Cotoneaster, 15" to 18", shady areas, B&B		.60	40		3,000	1,625		4,625	5,775
0300	Boston ivy, on bank, 1 year, bare root		6	4		320	162		482	595
0350	Potted, 2 year		6	4		560	162		722	860
0400	English ivy, 1 year, bare root		9	2.667		94.50	108		202.50	269
0450	Potted, 2 year		6	4		340	162		502	620
0460	12" to 15" runners		496	.048	Ea.	31.50	1.96		33.46	38
0500	Halls honeysuckle, 1 year, bare root		5	4.800	C	370	195		565	705
0550	Potted, 2 year		4	6	"	795	243		1,038	1,250
0560	Liriope, Big Blue, 1 gal. cont		94	.255	Ea.	9.90	10.35		20.25	26.50
0600	Memorial rose, 9" to 12", 1 gallon cont		3	8	C	122	325		447	630
0650	Potted, 2 gallon cont		2	12	"	210	485		695	970
0660	Oregon Holly-grape, 2' to 3'		62	.387	Ea.	32	15.70		47.70	59.50
0700	Pachysandra, 1 year, bare root		10	2.400	C	110	97.50		207.50	269
0750	Potted, 2 year		6	4	"	225	162		387	495
0760	Variegated Liriope, 1 gal. cont		94	.255	Ea.	24.50	10.35		34.85	43
0770	Viburnum, Sweet, 24" to 30"		62	.387	"	31.50	15.70		47.20	58.50
0800	Vinca minor, 1 year, bare root		10	2.400	C	178	97.50		275.50	345

For customer support on your Green Building Costs with RSMeans data, call 800.448.8182.

32 93 Plants

32 93 13 – Ground Covers

32 93 13.20 Ground Cover and Vines

		Crew	Daily Output	Labor-Hours	Unit	Material	2018 Bare Costs Labor	Equipment	Total	Total Incl O&P
0850	Potted, 2 year	B-1	6	4	C	227	162		389	495
0900	Woodbine, on bank, 1/2 year, bare root		6	4		217	162		379	485
0950	Potted, 2 year		4	6		565	243		808	995
2000	Alternate method of figuring									
2100	Ajuga, field division, 4,000/M.S.F.	B-1	.23	104	M.S.F.	5,000	4,225		9,225	12,000
2300	Boston ivy, 1 year, 60/M.S.F.		10	2.400		200	97.50		297.50	370
2400	English ivy, 1 year, 500/M.S.F.		1.80	13.333		500	540		1,040	1,375
2500	Halls honeysuckle, 1 year, 333/M.S.F.		1.50	16		500	650		1,150	1,550
2600	Memorial rose, 9" to 12", 1 gal., 333/M.S.F.		.90	26.667		1,000	1,075		2,075	2,750
2700	Pachysandra, 1 year, 4,000/M.S.F.		.25	96		1,600	3,900		5,500	7,675
2800	Vinca minor, rooted cutting, 2,000/M.S.F.		1	24		1,000	970		1,970	2,575
2900	Woodbine, 1 year, 60/M.S.F.		10	2.400		35	97.50		132.50	187

32 93 33 – Shrubs

32 93 33.10 Shrubs and Trees

		Crew	Daily Output	Labor-Hours	Unit	Material	Labor	Equipment	Total	Total Incl O&P
0010	**SHRUBS AND TREES**									
0011	Evergreen, in prepared beds, B&B									
0100	Arborvitae pyramidal, 4'-5'	B-17	30	1.067	Ea.	103	47	21.50	171.50	209
0150	Globe, 12"-15"	B-1	96	.250		26	10.15		36.15	44
0200	Balsam, fraser, 6'-7'	B-17	30	1.067		142	47	21.50	210.50	252
0300	Cedar, blue, 8'-10'		18	1.778		239	78.50	36	353.50	420
0350	Japanese, 4'-5'		55	.582		112	26	11.85	149.85	176
0400	Cypress, hinoki, 15"-18"	B-1	80	.300		79.50	12.15		91.65	106
0500	Hemlock, Canadian, 2-1/2'-3'		36	.667		32.50	27		59.50	76.50
0550	Holly, Savannah, 8'-10' H		9.68	2.479		300	100		400	485
0560	Yaupon, 6'-7'	B-17	10	3.200		176	142	65	383	480
0570	Burford, 3'-4'		37	.865		58	38.50	17.60	114.10	141
0580	Dwarf Burford, 2'-3'		21	1.524		53.50	67.50	31	152	195
0590	Dwarf Chinese, 2'-3'		40	.800		61	35.50	16.25	112.75	138
0600	Juniper, andorra, 18"-24"	B-1	80	.300		50	12.15		62.15	73.50
0620	Wiltoni, 15"-18"	"	80	.300		26.50	12.15		38.65	48
0640	Skyrocket, 4-1/2'-5'	B-17	55	.582		110	26	11.85	147.85	173
0660	Blue pfitzer, 2'-2-1/2'	B-1	44	.545		39.50	22		61.50	77
0670	Repandens holly, 15" to 18" H, in place		37	.649		52.50	26.50		79	98
0675	Pfitzer juniper, 18"-24"		26	.923		34.50	37.50		72	95
0680	Ketleerie, 2-1/2'-3'		50	.480		56	19.45		75.45	91
0700	Pine, black, 2-1/2'-3'		50	.480		62	19.45		81.45	98
0720	Mugo, 18"-24"		60	.400		56	16.20		72.20	86.50
0740	White, 4'-5'	B-17	75	.427		53	18.90	8.70	80.60	96.50
0750	5'-6'	B-1	22	1.091		37.50	44		81.50	109
0760	Jack, 5'-6'	B-17	22	1.455		38	64.50	29.50	132	172
0800	Spruce, blue, 18"-24"	B-1	60	.400		69	16.20		85.20	101
0820	Dwarf alberta, 18"-24"	"	60	.400		59	16.20		75.20	89.50
0840	Norway, 4'-5'	B-17	75	.427		86	18.90	8.70	113.60	133
0900	Yew, denisforma, 12"-15"	B-1	60	.400		36.50	16.20		52.70	65
1000	Capitata, 18"-24"		30	.800		34	32.50		66.50	87
1100	Hicksi, 2'-2-1/2'		30	.800		103	32.50		135.50	164

32 93 33.20 Shrubs

		Crew	Daily Output	Labor-Hours	Unit	Material	Labor	Equipment	Total	Total Incl O&P
0010	**SHRUBS**									
0011	Broadleaf Evergreen, planted in prepared beds									
0100	Andromeda, 15"-18", cont	B-1	96	.250	Ea.	33.50	10.15		43.65	52.50
0150	Aucuba, 3'-4'		32	.750		19.55	30.50		50.05	68
0200	Azalea, 15"-18", cont		96	.250		30.50	10.15		40.65	49.50

32 93 Plants

32 93 33 – Shrubs

32 93 33.20 Shrubs

		Crew	Daily Output	Labor-Hours	Unit	Material	Labor	Equipment	Total	Total Incl O&P
0300	Barberry, 9"-12", cont	B-1	130	.185	Ea.	18.70	7.50		26.20	32
0400	Boxwood, 15"-18", B&B		96	.250		44.50	10.15		54.65	64.50
0450	Cast Iron Plant, 12"-15" H		41.92	.573		15	23		38	52
0470	Cleyera, 3'-4' H, B&B		32.48	.739		30	30		60	78.50
0480	Creeping gardenia, 2 gal. cont		98.48	.244		11	9.85		20.85	27
0500	Euonymus, emerald gaiety, 12"-15", cont		115	.209		24.50	8.45		32.95	40
0520	Glossy Abelia, 2'-3'		33	.727		28.50	29.50		58	76.50
0600	Holly, 15"-18", B&B		96	.250		40	10.15		50.15	59.50
0650	Indian Hawthorn, 18"-24"		29.40	.816		23	33		56	75.50
0700	Leucothoe, 15"-18", cont		96	.250		19.20	10.15		29.35	36.50
0800	Mahonia, 18"-24", cont		80	.300		33.50	12.15		45.65	55
0900	Mount laurel, 18"-24", B&B		80	.300		72.50	12.15		84.65	98.50
1000	Paxistema, 9"-12" H		130	.185		22	7.50		29.50	35.50
1100	Rhododendron, 18"-24", cont		48	.500		38.50	20.50		59	73.50
1200	Rosemary, 1 gal. cont		600	.040		18.55	1.62		20.17	23
1300	Wax Myrtle, 3'-4'		32	.750		66	30.50		96.50	119
2000	Deciduous, planted in prepared beds, amelanchier, 2'-3', B&B		57	.421		123	17.05		140.05	161
2100	Azalea, 15"-18", B&B		96	.250		30.50	10.15		40.65	49
2120	Kurume, 18"-24"		29.80	.805		37	32.50		69.50	90
2200	Barberry, 2'-3', B&B		57	.421		23.50	17.05		40.55	52
2300	Bayberry, 2'-3', B&B		57	.421		30	17.05		47.05	59
2400	Boston ivy, 2 year, cont		600	.040		20.50	1.62		22.12	25
2500	Corylus, 3'-4', B&B	B-17	75	.427		24	18.90	8.70	51.60	64.50
2600	Cotoneaster, 15"-18", B&B	B-1	80	.300		27	12.15		39.15	48.50
2650	Crape Myrtle, 8'-9'	B-17	10.50	3.048		230	135	62	427	525
2700	Deutzia, 12"-15", B&B	B-1	96	.250		12.70	10.15		22.85	29.50
2800	Dogwood, 3'-4', B&B	B-17	40	.800		33	35.50	16.25	84.75	108
2900	Euonymus, alatus compacta, 15"-18", cont	B-1	80	.300		27	12.15		39.15	48
3000	Flowering almond, 2'-3', cont	"	36	.667		22.50	27		49.50	65.50
3100	Flowering currant, 3'-4', cont	B-17	75	.427		27.50	18.90	8.70	55.10	68.50
3200	Forsythia, 2'-3', cont	B-1	60	.400		17.80	16.20		34	44
3300	Hibiscus, 3'-4', B&B	B-17	75	.427		42	18.90	8.70	69.60	84
3400	Honeysuckle, 3'-4', B&B	B-1	60	.400		27.50	16.20		43.70	55
3500	Hydrangea, 2'-3', B&B	"	57	.421		31	17.05		48.05	60
3550	Ligustrum, 2'-3'	B-17	10.50	3.048		29.50	135	62	226.50	305
3600	Lilac, 3'-4', B&B	"	40	.800		27.50	35.50	16.25	79.25	101
3700	Mockorange, 3'-4', B&B	B-1	36	.667		29	27		56	73
3800	Osier willow, 2'-3', B&B		57	.421		35.50	17.05		52.55	65
3850	Pampas Grass, 3'-4'		58	.414		23.50	16.75		40.25	51.50
3900	Privet, bare root, 18"-24"		80	.300		15.15	12.15		27.30	35
4000	Pyracantha, 2'-3', cont		80	.300		41	12.15		53.15	63.50
4100	Quince, 2'-3', B&B		57	.421		29	17.05		46.05	58
4200	Russian olive, 3'-4', B&B	B-17	75	.427		25	18.90	8.70	52.60	65.50
4300	Snowberry, 2'-3', B&B	B-1	57	.421		20	17.05		37.05	48
4400	Spirea, 3'-4', B&B	"	70	.343		20.50	13.90		34.40	43.50
4500	Viburnum, 3'-4', B&B	B-17	40	.800		26	35.50	16.25	77.75	100
4510	12"-15"	"	62	.516		19.60	23	10.50	53.10	67.50
4600	Weigela, 3'-4', B&B	B-1	70	.343		15.35	13.90		29.25	38

32 93 Plants

32 93 43 – Trees

32 93 43.20 Trees

			Crew	Daily Output	Labor-Hours	Unit	Material	2018 Bare Costs Labor	Equipment	Total	Total Incl O&P
0010	**TREES**										
0011	Deciduous, in prep. beds, balled & burlapped (B&B)										
0100	Ash, 2" caliper	G	B-17	8	4	Ea.	200	177	81.50	458.50	580
0200	Beech, 5'-6'	G		50	.640		210	28.50	13	251.50	288
0300	Birch, 6'-8', 3 stems	G		20	1.600		167	71	32.50	270.50	325
0400	Cherry, 6'-8', 1" caliper	G		24	1.333		75	59	27	161	202
0500	Crabapple, 6'-8'	G		20	1.600		139	71	32.50	242.50	296
0600	Dogwood, 4'-5'	G		40	.800		140	35.50	16.25	191.75	225
0610	Kousa, 6'-8'	G		10	3.200		169	142	65	376	470
0700	Eastern redbud, 4'-5'	G		40	.800		148	35.50	16.25	199.75	234
0710	5'-6'	G		9	3.556		169	157	72.50	398.50	505
0800	Elm, 8'-10'	G		20	1.600		325	71	32.50	428.50	505
0810	Camperdown, 12'-15', 3" caliper	G		4	8		390	355	163	908	1,150
0900	Ginkgo, 6'-7'	G		24	1.333		148	59	27	234	283
1000	Hawthorn, 8'-10', 1" caliper	G		20	1.600		161	71	32.50	264.50	320
1100	Honeylocust, 10'-12', 1-1/2" caliper	G		10	3.200		206	142	65	413	510
1200	Laburnum, 6'-8', 1" caliper	G		24	1.333		60	59	27	146	186
1300	Larch, 8'	G		32	1		128	44.50	20.50	193	230
1400	Linden, 8'-10', 1" caliper	G		20	1.600		144	71	32.50	247.50	300
1450	Loquat, 7'-8'	G		10	3.200		53	142	65	260	345
1500	Magnolia, 4'-5'	G		20	1.600		115	71	32.50	218.50	270
1510	10'-12'	G		4	8		250	355	163	768	990
1600	Maple, red, 8'-10', 1-1/2" caliper	G		10	3.200		199	142	65	406	505
1610	16'-18', 4" caliper	G		2.82	11.348		470	500	231	1,201	1,525
1700	Mountain ash, 8'-10', 1" caliper	G		16	2		177	88.50	40.50	306	375
1800	Oak, 2-1/2"-3" caliper	G		6	5.333		320	236	108	664	830
1810	Laurel, 18'-22', 3" caliper	G		2	16		300	710	325	1,335	1,775
1820	18'-22', 5" caliper	G		2	16		420	710	325	1,455	1,900
1830	Live, 15'-20', 4" caliper	G		2	16		810	710	325	1,845	2,325
1840	Willow, 14'-16'	G		3.56	8.989		320	400	183	903	1,150
1900	Pagoda, 6'-8'	G		20	1.600		151	71	32.50	254.50	310
2000	Pear, 6'-8', 1" caliper	G		20	1.600		117	71	32.50	220.50	272
2100	Planetree, 9'-11', 1-1/4" caliper	G		10	3.200		266	142	65	473	580
2200	Plum, 6'-8', 1" caliper	G		20	1.600		79	71	32.50	182.50	230
2300	Poplar, 9'-11', 1-1/4" caliper	G		10	3.200		100	142	65	307	395
2310	14'-16'	G		4	8		192	355	163	710	925
2400	Shadbush, 4'-5'	G		60	.533		65	23.50	10.85	99.35	119
2500	Sumac, 2'-3'	G		75	.427		44.50	18.90	8.70	72.10	87
2600	Tupelo, 5'-6'	G		40	.800		93	35.50	16.25	144.75	173
2700	Tulip, 5'-6'	G		40	.800		46	35.50	16.25	97.75	122
2710	14'-16'	G		6	5.333		242	236	108	586	740
2800	Willow, 6'-8', 1" caliper	G		20	1.600		97	71	32.50	200.50	250
2810	Weeping, 10'-12', 2" caliper	G		6	5.333		160	236	108	504	650

32 94 Planting Accessories

32 94 13 – Landscape Edging

32 94 13.20 Edging

		Crew	Daily Output	Labor-Hours	Unit	Material	2018 Bare Costs Labor	Equipment	Total	Total Incl O&P
0010	**EDGING**									
0780	Landscape timbers, 100% recycled plastic, var colors, 4" x 4" x 8' [G]	2 Carp	250	.064	L.F.	6.50	3.24		9.74	12.10
0790	6" x 6" x 8' [G]	"	250	.064		14.70	3.24		17.94	21
1200	Edging, lawn, made from recycled tires, black, 1" x 6"	B-1	390	.062		1.17	2.49		3.66	5.10

32 94 50 – Tree Guying

32 94 50.10 Tree Guying Systems

		Crew	Daily Output	Labor-Hours	Unit	Material	Labor	Equipment	Total	Total Incl O&P
0010	**TREE GUYING SYSTEMS**									
0015	Tree guying including stakes, guy wire and wrap									
0100	Less than 3" caliper, 2 stakes	2 Clab	35	.457	Ea.	13.10	18.20		31.30	42.50
0200	3" to 4" caliper, 3 stakes	"	21	.762		19.85	30.50		50.35	68.50
0300	6" to 8" caliper, 3 stakes	B-1	8	3		40.50	122		162.50	230
1000	Including arrowhead anchor, cable, turnbuckles and wrap									
1100	Less than 3" caliper, 3" anchors	2 Clab	20	.800	Ea.	21	32		53	72
1200	3" to 6" caliper, 4" anchors		15	1.067		31.50	42.50		74	100
1300	6" caliper, 6" anchors		12	1.333		23.50	53		76.50	107
1400	8" caliper, 8" anchors		9	1.778		116	71		187	236
2000	Tree guard, preformed plastic, 36" high		168	.095		2.77	3.80		6.57	8.85
2010	Snow fence		140	.114		29.50	4.55		34.05	39.50

Division Notes

	CREW	DAILY OUTPUT	LABOR-HOURS	UNIT	BARE COSTS MAT.	LABOR	EQUIP.	TOTAL	TOTAL INCL O&P

Estimating Tips
33 10 00 Water Utilities
33 30 00 Sanitary Sewerage Utilities
33 40 00 Storm Drainage Utilities

- Never assume that the water, sewer, and drainage lines will go in at the early stages of the project. Consider the site access needs before dividing the site in half with open trenches, loose pipe, and machinery obstructions. Always inspect the site to establish that the site drawings are complete. Check off all existing utilities on your drawings as you locate them. Be especially careful with underground utilities because appurtenances are sometimes buried during regrading or repaving operations. If you find any discrepancies, mark up the site plan for further research. Differing site conditions can be very costly if discovered later in the project.
- See also Section 33 01 00 for restoration of pipe where removal/replacement may be undesirable. Use of new types of piping materials can reduce the overall project cost. Owners/design engineers should consider the installing contractor as a valuable source of current information on utility products and local conditions that could lead to significant cost savings.

Reference Numbers
Reference numbers are shown at the beginning of some major classifications. These numbers refer to related items in the Reference Section. The reference information may be an estimating procedure, an alternate pricing method, or technical information.

Note: Not all subdivisions listed here necessarily appear. ■

No part of this cost data may be reproduced, stored in a retrieval system, or transmitted in any form or by any means without prior written permission of Gordian.

Note: Trade Service, in part, has been used as a reference source for some of the material prices used in Division 33.

Did you know?
RSMeans data is available through our online application with 24/7 access:
- Search for unit prices by keyword
- Leverage the most up-to-date data
- Build and export estimates

Try it free for 30 days!
www.rsmeans.com/2018freetrial

33 01 Operation and Maintenance of Utilities

33 01 30 – Operation and Maintenance of Sewer Utilities

33 01 30.11 Television Inspection of Sewers

		Crew	Daily Output	Labor-Hours	Unit	Material	2018 Bare Costs Labor	Equipment	Total	Total Incl O&P
0010	**TELEVISION INSPECTION OF SEWERS**									
0100	Pipe internal cleaning & inspection, cleaning, pressure pipe systems									
0120	Pig method, lengths 1000' to 10,000'									
0140	4" diameter thru 24" diameter, minimum				L.F.				3.60	4.14
0160	Maximum				"				18	21
6000	Sewage/sanitary systems									
6100	Power rodder with header & cutters									
6110	Mobilization charge, minimum				Total				695	800
6120	Mobilization charge, maximum				"				9,125	10,600
6140	Cleaning 4"-12" diameter				L.F.				3.39	3.90
6190	14"-24" diameter								3.98	4.59
6240	30" diameter								5.80	6.65
6250	36" diameter								6.75	7.75
6260	48" diameter								7.70	8.85
6270	60" diameter								8.70	9.95
6280	72" diameter								9.65	11.10
9000	Inspection, television camera with video									
9060	up to 500 linear feet				Total				715	820

33 11 Groundwater Sources

33 11 13 – Potable Water Supply Wells

33 11 13.10 Wells and Accessories

		Crew	Daily Output	Labor-Hours	Unit	Material	Labor	Equipment	Total	Total Incl O&P
0010	**WELLS & ACCESSORIES** R221113-50									
0011	Domestic									
0105	Drill geothermal well 4"-6" diameter, not to exceed 400' depth	B-23	800	.050	L.F.	2.01	3.35		5.36	6.75
0106	4"-6" diameter, medium soil		600	.067		2.68	4.47		7.15	9
0107	4"-6" diameter, dense soil		400	.100		4.03	6.70		10.73	13.55

33 41 Subdrainage

33 41 23 – Drainage Layers

33 41 23.19 Geosynthetic Drainage Layers

		Crew	Daily Output	Labor-Hours	Unit	Material	Labor	Equipment	Total	Total Incl O&P
0010	**GEOSYNTHETIC DRAINAGE LAYERS**									
0100	Fabric, laid in trench, polypropylene, ideal conditions	2 Clab	2400	.007	S.Y.	1.53	.27		1.80	2.08
0110	Adverse conditions	"	1600	.010	"	1.53	.40		1.93	2.29
0150	Plastic filter fabric, in underground drain lines	B-13	22.48	2.491	C.S.F.	6.30	109	26.50	141.80	201
0170	Fabric ply bonded to 3 dimen. nylon mat, 0.4" thick, ideal conditions	2 Clab	2000	.008	S.F.	.26	.32		.58	.77
0180	Adverse conditions		1200	.013	"	.32	.53		.85	1.16
0185	Soil drainage mat on vertical wall, 0.44" thick		265	.060	S.Y.	1.77	2.41		4.18	5.60
0188	0.25" thick		300	.053	"	.84	2.13		2.97	4.17
0190	0.8" thick, ideal conditions		2400	.007	S.F.	.29	.27		.56	.72
0200	Adverse conditions		1600	.010	"	.39	.40		.79	1.04
0300	Drainage material, 3/4" gravel fill in trench	B-6	260	.092	C.Y.	20	4.03	1.20	25.23	29.50
0400	Pea stone	"	260	.092	"	28	4.03	1.20	33.23	38

33 46 Stormwater Management

33 46 11 – Stormwater Ponds

33 46 11.16 Water Retainage Reservoirs

		Crew	Daily Output	Labor-Hours	Unit	Material	2018 Bare Costs Labor	Equipment	Total	Total Incl O&P
0010	**WATER RETAINAGE RESERVOIRS**									
1000	Potable, complete for average size home, minimum				System				18,200	18,200
1010	Maximum								38,100	38,100
1020	Non-potable, complete for average size home, minimum								3,050	3,050
1030	Maximum								8,675	8,675
1040	Irrigation tape, for subsurface/surface, vinyl, flat, material only, 1-1/2"	G			L.F.	.30			.30	.33
1050	2"	G				.45			.45	.50
1060	3"	G				.95			.95	1.05
1070	8 mil	G				.06			.06	.07
1080	10 mil	G				.10			.10	.11
1090	15 mil	G				.12			.12	.13
1100	Couplings for	G	1 Clab	32	.250	Ea.	1.50	9.95		11.45	16.85
1110	Batt oper moisture sensor and control valve for	G	"	8	1	"	75	40		115	143

Division Notes

	CREW	DAILY OUTPUT	LABOR-HOURS	UNIT	BARE COSTS MAT.	LABOR	EQUIP.	TOTAL	TOTAL INCL O&P

Division 46 Water & Wastewater Equipment

Estimating Tips
This division contains information about water and wastewater equipment and systems, which was formerly located in Division 44. The main areas of focus are total wastewater treatment plants and components of wastewater treatment plants. Also included in this section are oil/water separators for wastewater treatment.

Reference Numbers
Reference numbers are shown at the beginning of some major classifications. These numbers refer to related items in the Reference Section. The reference information may be an estimating procedure, an alternate pricing method, or technical information.

Note: Not all subdivisions listed here necessarily appear. ■

Did you know?

RSMeans data is available through our online application with 24/7 access:

- Search for unit prices by keyword
- Leverage the most up-to-date data
- Build and export estimates

Try it free for 30 days!
www.rsmeans.com/2018freetrial

No part of this cost data may be reproduced, stored in a retrieval system, or transmitted in any form or by any means without prior written permission of Gordian.

46 07 Packaged Water and Wastewater Treatment Equipment

46 07 53 – Packaged Wastewater Treatment Equipment

46 07 53.10 Biological Pkg. Wastewater Treatment Plants

		Crew	Daily Output	Labor-Hours	Unit	Material	2018 Bare Costs Labor	Equipment	Total	Total Incl O&P
0010	**BIOLOGICAL PACKAGED WASTEWATER TREATMENT PLANTS**									
0011	Not including fencing or external piping									
0020	Steel packaged, blown air aeration plants									
0100	1,000 GPD				Gal.				55	60.50
0200	5,000 GPD								22	24
0300	15,000 GPD								22	24
0400	30,000 GPD								15.40	16.95
0500	50,000 GPD								11	12.10
0600	100,000 GPD								9.90	10.90
0700	200,000 GPD								8.80	9.70
0800	500,000 GPD				▼				7.70	8.45
1000	Concrete, extended aeration, primary and secondary treatment									
1010	10,000 GPD				Gal.				22	24
1100	30,000 GPD								15.40	16.95
1200	50,000 GPD								11	12.10
1400	100,000 GPD								9.90	10.90
1500	500,000 GPD				▼				7.70	8.45
1700	Municipal wastewater treatment facility									
1720	1.0 MGD				Gal.				11	12.10
1740	1.5 MGD								10.60	11.65
1760	2.0 MGD								10	11
1780	3.0 MGD								7.80	8.60
1800	5.0 MGD				▼				5.80	6.70
2000	Holding tank system, not incl. excavation or backfill									
2010	Recirculating chemical water closet	2 Plum	4	4	Ea.	545	249		794	975
2100	For voltage converter, add	"	16	1		310	62		372	435
2200	For high level alarm, add	1 Plum	7.80	1.026	▼	120	63.50		183.50	228

46 23 Grit Removal And Handling Equipment

46 23 23 – Vortex Grit Removal Equipment

46 23 23.10 Rainwater Filters

		Crew	Daily Output	Labor-Hours	Unit	Material	Labor	Equipment	Total	Total Incl O&P
0010	**RAINWATER FILTERS**									
0100	42 gal./min	B-21	3.50	8	Ea.	39,600	370	37	40,007	44,200
0200	65 gal./min		3.50	8		39,600	370	37	40,007	44,200
0300	208 gal./min	▼	3.50	8	▼	39,700	370	37	40,107	44,300

46 25 Oil and Grease Separation and Removal Equipment

46 25 13 – Coalescing Oil-Water Separators

46 25 13.20 Oil/Water Separators

		Crew	Daily Output	Labor-Hours	Unit	Material	Labor	Equipment	Total	Total Incl O&P
0010	**OIL/WATER SEPARATORS**									
0020	Underground, tank only									
0030	Excludes excavation, backfill, & piping									
0100	200 GPM	B-21	3.50	8	Ea.	39,400	370	37	39,807	43,900
0110	400 GPM		3.25	8.615		76,000	400	40	76,440	84,000
0120	600 GPM		2.75	10.182		82,000	470	47	82,517	91,500
0130	800 GPM		2.50	11.200		95,500	520	52	96,072	106,000
0140	1,000 GPM		2	14		110,000	650	65	110,715	122,000
0150	1,200 GPM		1.50	18.667		119,000	865	86.50	119,951.50	132,500
0160	1,500 GPM	▼	1	28	▼	141,000	1,300	130	142,430	157,000

46 51 Air and Gas Diffusion Equipment

46 51 20 – Air and Gas Handling Equipment

46 51 20.10 Blowers and System Components	Crew	Daily Output	Labor-Hours	Unit	Material	2018 Bare Costs Labor	Equipment	Total	Total Incl O&P
0010 **BLOWERS AND SYSTEM COMPONENTS**									
0020 Rotary lobe blowers									
0030 Medium pressure (7 to 14 PSIG)									
0120 38 CFM, 2.1 BHP	Q-2	2.50	9.600	Ea.	1,300	555		1,855	2,275
0130 125 CFM, 5.5 BHP		2.40	10		1,525	580		2,105	2,550
0140 245 CFM, 10.2 BHP		2	12		1,875	695		2,570	3,125
0150 363 CFM, 14.5 BHP		1.80	13.333		2,725	775		3,500	4,175
0160 622 CFM, 24.5 BHP		1.40	17.143		4,525	995		5,520	6,475
0170 1,125 CFM, 42.8 BHP		1.10	21.818		7,025	1,275		8,300	9,625
0180 1,224 CFM, 47.4 BHP		1	24		9,975	1,400		11,375	13,100
0400 Prepackaged medium pressure (7 to 14 PSIG) blower									
0405 incl. 3 ph. motor, filter, silencer, valves, check valve, press. gage									
0420 38 CFM, 2.1 BHP	Q-2	2.50	9.600	Ea.	3,475	555		4,030	4,675
0430 125 CFM, 5.5 BHP		2.40	10		3,725	580		4,305	4,975
0440 245 CFM, 10.2 BHP		2	12		4,525	695		5,220	6,025
0450 363 CFM, 14.5 BHP		1.80	13.333		6,575	775		7,350	8,400
0460 521 CFM, 20 BHP		1.50	16		6,625	930		7,555	8,700
1010 Filters and silencers									
1100 Silencer with paper filter									
1105 1" connection	1 Plum	14	.571	Ea.	35	35.50		70.50	92
1110 1.5" connection		11	.727		38.50	45		83.50	110
1115 2" connection		9	.889		143	55		198	240
1120 2.5" connection		8	1		143	62		205	251
1125 3" connection	Q-1	8	2		148	112		260	330
1130 4" connection	"	5	3.200		305	179		484	610
1135 5" connection	Q-2	5	4.800		335	278		613	790
1140 6" connection	"	5	4.800		375	278		653	835
1300 Silencer with polyester filter									
1305 1" connection	1 Plum	14	.571	Ea.	39.50	35.50		75	97
1315 2" connection		9	.889		155	55		210	254
1320 2.5" connection		8	1		155	62		217	265
1325 3" connection	Q-1	8	2		160	112		272	345
1330 4" connection	"	5	3.200		310	179		489	610
1335 5" connection	Q-2	5	4.800		300	278		578	750
1340 6" connection	"	5	4.800		345	278		623	800
1500 Chamber silencers									
1505 1" connection	1 Plum	14	.571	Ea.	79	35.50		114.50	141
1510 1.5" connection		11	.727		97.50	45		142.50	175
1515 2" connection		9	.889		121	55		176	216
1520 2.5" connection		8	1		200	62		262	315
1525 3" connection	Q-1	8	2		283	112		395	480
1530 4" connection	"	5	3.200		365	179		544	675
1700 Blower couplings									
1701 Blower flexible coupling									
1710 1.5" connection	Q-1	71	.225	Ea.	30	12.60		42.60	52
1715 2" connection		67	.239		33	13.35		46.35	56.50
1720 2.5" connection		65	.246		38	13.75		51.75	62.50
1725 3" connection		64	.250		51	14		65	77
1730 4" connection		58	.276		61	15.45		76.45	90
1735 5" connection	Q-2	83	.289		66	16.75		82.75	98
1740 6" connection		79	.304		91	17.60		108.60	127
1745 8" connection		69	.348		150	20		170	196

46 51 Air and Gas Diffusion Equipment

46 51 20 – Air and Gas Handling Equipment

46 51 20.20 Aeration System Air Process Piping

		Crew	Daily Output	Labor-Hours	Unit	Material	2018 Bare Costs Labor	2018 Bare Costs Equipment	Total	Total Incl O&P
0010	**AERATION SYSTEM AIR PROCESS PIPING**									
0100	Blower pressure relief valves-adjustable									
0105	1" diameter	1 Plum	14	.571	Ea.	115	35.50		150.50	181
0110	2" diameter		9	.889		125	55		180	221
0115	2.5" diameter	↓	8	1		175	62		237	287
0120	3" diameter	Q-1	8	2		180	112		292	365
0125	4" diameter	"	5	3.200	↓	201	179		380	490
0200	Blower pressure relief valves - weight loaded									
0205	1" diameter	1 Plum	14	.571	Ea.	160	35.50		195.50	230
0210	2" diameter	"	9	.889		190	55		245	292
0220	3" diameter	Q-1	8	2		270	112		382	465
0225	4" diameter	"	5	3.200	↓	290	179		469	590
0300	Pressure relief valves - preset high flow									
0310	2" diameter	1 Plum	9	.889	Ea.	305	55		360	420
0320	3" diameter	Q-1	8	2	"	650	112		762	885
1000	Check valves, wafer style									
1110	2" diameter	1 Plum	9	.889	Ea.	135	55		190	231
1120	3" diameter	Q-1	8	2		167	112		279	350
1125	4" diameter	"	5	3.200		225	179		404	520
1130	5" diameter	Q-2	6	4		310	232		542	690
1135	6" diameter		5	4.800		370	278		648	825
1140	8" diameter	↓	4.50	5.333	↓	515	310		825	1,025
1200	Check valves, flanged steel									
1210	2" diameter	1 Plum	8	1	Ea.	350	62		412	485
1220	3" diameter	Q-1	4.50	3.556		370	199		569	710
1225	4" diameter	"	3	5.333		475	298		773	970
1230	5" diameter	Q-2	3	8		590	465		1,055	1,350
1235	6" diameter		3	8		770	465		1,235	1,550
1240	8" diameter	↓	2.50	9.600	↓	1,200	555		1,755	2,175
2100	Butterfly valves, lever operated - wafer style									
2110	2" diameter	1 Plum	14	.571	Ea.	48.50	35.50		84	107
2120	3" diameter	Q-1	8	2		61	112		173	235
2130	5" diameter	Q-2	6	4		106	232		338	465
2135	6" diameter		5	4.800		124	278		402	555
2140	8" diameter		4.50	5.333		187	310		497	670
2145	10" diameter	↓	4	6	↓	258	350		608	810
2200	Butterfly valves, gear operated - wafer style									
2210	2" diameter	1 Plum	14	.571	Ea.	86.50	35.50		122	149
2220	3" diameter	Q-1	8	2		97	112		209	275
2225	4" diameter	"	5	3.200		117	179		296	400
2230	5" diameter	Q-2	6	4		141	232		373	505
2235	6" diameter		5	4.800		160	278		438	595
2240	8" diameter		4.50	5.333		244	310		554	735
2245	10" diameter		4	6		299	350		649	855
2250	12" diameter	↓	3	8	↓	390	465		855	1,125

46 51 20.30 Aeration System Blower Control Panels

		Crew	Daily Output	Labor-Hours	Unit	Material	Labor	Equipment	Total	Total Incl O&P
0010	**AERATION SYSTEM BLOWER CONTROL PANELS**									
0020	Single phase simplex									
0030	7 to 10 overload amp range	1 Elec	2.70	2.963	Ea.	820	172		992	1,150
0040	9 to 13 overload amp range		2.70	2.963		820	172		992	1,150
0050	12 to 18 overload amp range		2.70	2.963		820	172		992	1,150
0060	16 to 24 overload amp range		2.70	2.963		820	172		992	1,150

46 51 Air and Gas Diffusion Equipment

46 51 20 – Air and Gas Handling Equipment

46 51 20.30 Aeration System Blower Control Panels	Crew	Daily Output	Labor-Hours	Unit	Material	2018 Bare Costs Labor	Equipment	Total	Total Incl O&P
0070 23 to 32 overload amp range	1 Elec	2.70	2.963	Ea.	910	172		1,082	1,250
0080 30 to 40 overload amp range	↓	2.70	2.963	↓	1,050	172		1,222	1,400
0090 Single phase duplex									
0100 7 to 10 overload amp range	1 Elec	2	4	Ea.	1,275	233		1,508	1,750
0110 9 to 13 overload amp range		2	4		1,275	233		1,508	1,750
0120 12 to 18 overload amp range		2	4		1,275	233		1,508	1,750
0130 16 to 24 overload amp range		2	4		1,350	233		1,583	1,825
0140 23 to 32 overload amp range		2	4		1,400	233		1,633	1,900
0150 30 to 40 overload amp range	↓	2	4	↓	1,450	233		1,683	1,950
0160 Three phase simplex									
0170 1.6 to 2.5 overload amp range	1 Elec	2.50	3.200	Ea.	955	186		1,141	1,325
0180 2.5 to 4 overload amp range		2.50	3.200		955	186		1,141	1,325
0190 4 to 6.3 overload amp range		2.50	3.200		955	186		1,141	1,325
0200 6 to 10 overload amp range		2.50	3.200		955	186		1,141	1,325
0210 9 to 14 overload amp range		2.50	3.200		990	186		1,176	1,375
0220 13 to 18 overload amp range		2.50	3.200		990	186		1,176	1,375
0230 17 to 23 overload amp range		2.50	3.200		1,000	186		1,186	1,375
0240 20 to 25 overload amp range		2.50	3.200		1,000	186		1,186	1,375
0250 23 to 32 overload amp range		2.50	3.200		1,125	186		1,311	1,525
0260 37 to 50 overload amp range	↓	2.50	3.200	↓	1,375	186		1,561	1,775
0270 Three phase duplex									
0280 1.6 to 2.5 overload amp range	1 Elec	1.90	4.211	Ea.	1,300	245		1,545	1,800
0290 2.5 to 4 overload amp range		1.90	4.211		1,325	245		1,570	1,825
0300 4 to 6.3 overload amp range		1.90	4.211		1,325	245		1,570	1,825
0310 6 to 10 overload amp range		1.90	4.211		1,325	245		1,570	1,825
0320 9 to 14 overload amp range		1.90	4.211		1,375	245		1,620	1,875
0330 13 to 18 overload amp range		1.90	4.211		1,425	245		1,670	1,950
0340 17 to 23 overload amp range		1.90	4.211		1,450	245		1,695	1,975
0350 20 to 25 overload amp range		1.90	4.211		1,450	245		1,695	1,975
0360 23 to 32 overload amp range		1.90	4.211		1,650	245		1,895	2,200
0370 37 to 50 overload amp range	↓	1.90	4.211	↓	2,150	245		2,395	2,750

46 51 36 – Ceramic Disc Fine Bubble Diffusers

46 51 36.10 Ceramic Disc Air Diffuser Systems

0010	**CERAMIC DISC AIR DIFFUSER SYSTEMS**									
0020	Price for air diffuser pipe system by cell size excluding concrete work									
0030	Price for air diffuser pipe system by cell size excluding air supply									
0040	Depth of 12' is the waste depth, not the cell dimensions									
0100	Ceramic disc air diffuser system, cell size 20' x 20' x 12'	2 Plum	.38	42.667	Ea.	10,300	2,650		12,950	15,300
0120	20' x 30' x 12'		.26	61.326		15,200	3,800		19,000	22,500
0140	20' x 40' x 12'		.20	80		20,100	4,975		25,075	29,600
0160	20' x 50' x 12'		.16	98.644		25,000	6,125		31,125	36,700
0180	20' x 60' x 12'		.14	117		29,900	7,300		37,200	43,900
0200	20' x 70' x 12'		.12	136		34,900	8,450		43,350	51,000
0220	20' x 80' x 12'		.10	155		39,800	9,625		49,425	58,500
0240	20' x 90' x 12'		.09	173		44,700	10,800		55,500	65,500
0260	20' x 100' x 12'		.08	192		49,600	11,900		61,500	72,500
0280	20' x 120' x 12'		.07	229		59,500	14,200		73,700	87,000
0300	20' x 140' x 12'		.06	267		69,500	16,600		86,100	101,000
0320	20' x 160' x 12'		.05	304		79,000	18,900		97,900	115,500
0340	20' x 180' x 12'		.05	341		89,000	21,200		110,200	130,000
0360	20' x 200' x 12'		.04	378		99,000	23,500		122,500	144,000
0380	20' x 250' x 12'	↓	.03	472	↓	123,500	29,300		152,800	179,500

46 51 Air and Gas Diffusion Equipment

46 51 36 – Ceramic Disc Fine Bubble Diffusers

46 51 36.10 Ceramic Disc Air Diffuser Systems		Crew	Daily Output	Labor-Hours	Unit	Material	2018 Bare Costs Labor	Equipment	Total	Total Incl O&P
0400	20' x 300' x 12'	2 Plum	.03	565	Ea.	148,000	35,100		183,100	216,000
0420	20' x 350' x 12'		.02	658		172,500	40,900		213,400	251,500
0440	20' x 400' x 12'		.02	751		197,000	46,700		243,700	287,500
0460	20' x 450' x 12'		.02	847		222,000	52,500		274,500	323,000
0480	20' x 500' x 12'		.02	941		246,500	58,500		305,000	359,000

46 53 Biological Treatment Systems

46 53 17 – Activated Sludge Treatment

46 53 17.10 Activated Sludge Treatment Cells

		Crew	Daily Output	Labor-Hours	Unit	Material	Labor	Equipment	Total	Incl O&P
0010	**ACTIVATED SLUDGE TREATMENT CELLS**									
0015	Price for cell construction excluding aerator piping & drain									
0020	Cell construction by dimensions									
0100	Treatment cell, end or single, 20' x 20' x 14' high (2' freeboard)	C-14D	.46	434	Ea.	19,700	21,800	1,975	43,475	57,000
0120	20' x 30' x 14' high		.35	568		25,600	28,500	2,575	56,675	74,500
0140	20' x 40' x 14' high		.29	702		31,500	35,200	3,175	69,875	91,500
0160	20' x 50' x 14' high		.24	835		37,400	42,000	3,800	83,200	109,500
0180	20' x 60' x 14' high		.21	969		43,300	48,700	4,400	96,400	126,500
0200	20' x 70' x 14' high		.18	1103		49,200	55,500	5,000	109,700	144,000
0220	20' x 80' x 14' high		.16	1237		55,000	62,000	5,625	122,625	161,000
0240	20' x 90' x 14' high		.15	1371		61,000	69,000	6,225	136,225	178,500
0260	20' x 100' x 14' high		.13	1504		67,000	75,500	6,825	149,325	196,000
0280	20' x 120' x 14' high		.11	1771		78,500	89,000	8,050	175,550	231,000
0300	20' x 140' x 14' high		.10	2039		90,500	102,500	9,250	202,250	265,000
0320	20' x 160' x 14' high		.09	2307		102,000	116,000	10,500	228,500	300,000
0340	20' x 180' x 14' high		.08	2574		114,000	129,500	11,700	255,200	335,000
0360	20' x 200' x 14' high		.07	2841		126,000	142,500	12,900	281,400	369,500
0380	20' x 250' x 14' high		.06	3509		155,500	176,000	15,900	347,400	456,500
0400	20' x 300' x 14' high		.05	4175		185,000	209,500	19,000	413,500	543,500
0420	20' x 350' x 14' high		.04	4843		214,500	243,000	22,000	479,500	629,500
0440	20' x 400' x 14' high		.04	5510		244,000	276,500	25,000	545,500	716,500
0460	20' x 450' x 14' high		.03	6192		273,500	311,000	28,100	612,600	804,500
0480	20' x 500' x 14' high		.03	6849		303,000	344,000	31,100	678,100	890,000
0500	Treatment cell, end or single, 20' x 20' x 12' high (2' freeboard)		.48	414		18,600	20,800	1,875	41,275	54,500
0520	20' x 30' x 12' high		.37	543		24,300	27,300	2,475	54,075	71,000
0540	20' x 40' x 12' high		.30	672		29,900	33,700	3,050	66,650	88,000
0560	20' x 50' x 12' high		.25	800		35,500	40,200	3,625	79,325	104,000
0580	20' x 60' x 12' high		.22	929		41,200	46,700	4,225	92,125	121,000
0600	20' x 70' x 12' high		.19	1058		46,800	53,000	4,800	104,600	138,000
0620	20' x 80' x 12' high		.17	1186		52,500	59,500	5,375	117,375	154,000
0640	20' x 90' x 12' high		.15	1315		58,000	66,000	5,975	129,975	171,000
0660	20' x 100' x 12' high		.14	1444		63,500	72,500	6,550	142,550	187,500
0680	20' x 120' x 12' high		.12	1701		75,000	85,500	7,725	168,225	221,000
0700	20' x 140' x 12' high		.10	1959		86,000	98,500	8,900	193,400	254,500
0720	20' x 160' x 12' high		.09	2215		97,500	111,000	10,100	218,600	287,000
0740	20' x 180' x 12' high		.08	2472		109,000	124,000	11,200	244,200	321,000
0760	20' x 200' x 12' high		.07	2732		120,000	137,000	12,400	269,400	354,000
0780	20' x 250' x 12' high		.06	3373		148,000	169,500	15,300	332,800	437,500
0800	20' x 300' x 12' high		.05	4016		176,500	201,500	18,200	396,200	521,000
0820	20' x 350' x 12' high		.04	4662		204,500	234,000	21,200	459,700	604,500
0840	20' x 400' x 12' high		.04	5305		232,500	266,500	24,100	523,100	688,000
0860	20' x 450' x 12' high		.03	5952		261,000	299,000	27,000	587,000	771,000

46 53 Biological Treatment Systems

46 53 17 – Activated Sludge Treatment

46 53 17.10 Activated Sludge Treatment Cells

		Crew	Daily Output	Labor-Hours	Unit	Material	2018 Bare Costs Labor	Equipment	Total	Total Incl O&P
0880	20' x 500' x 12' high	C-14D	.03	6601	Ea.	289,000	331,500	30,000	650,500	855,000
1100	Treatment cell, connecting, 20' x 20' x 14' high (2' freeboard)		.57	351		15,700	17,600	1,600	34,900	45,900
1120	20' x 30' x 14' high		.45	443		19,700	22,200	2,000	43,900	57,500
1140	20' x 40' x 14' high		.37	535		23,600	26,900	2,425	52,925	69,500
1160	20' x 50' x 14' high		.32	627		27,600	31,500	2,850	61,950	81,500
1180	20' x 60' x 14' high		.28	719		31,400	36,100	3,275	70,775	93,000
1200	20' x 70' x 14' high		.25	811		35,400	40,700	3,675	79,775	105,000
1220	20' x 80' x 14' high		.22	903		39,300	45,300	4,100	88,700	116,500
1240	20' x 90' x 14' high		.20	995		43,200	49,900	4,525	97,625	128,500
1260	20' x 100' x 14' high		.18	1086		47,100	54,500	4,925	106,525	140,500
1280	20' x 120' x 14' high		.16	1271		55,000	64,000	5,775	124,775	164,000
1300	20' x 140' x 14' high		.14	1455		63,000	73,000	6,600	142,600	187,500
1320	20' x 160' x 14' high		.12	1638		70,500	82,500	7,425	160,425	211,000
1340	20' x 180' x 14' high		.11	1823		78,500	91,500	8,275	178,275	235,000
1360	20' x 200' x 14' high		.10	2006		86,500	100,500	9,100	196,100	258,000
1380	20' x 250' x 14' high		.08	2466		106,000	124,000	11,200	241,200	317,500
1400	20' x 300' x 14' high		.07	2924		125,500	147,000	13,300	285,800	376,000
1420	20' x 350' x 14' high		.06	3384		145,500	170,000	15,400	330,900	435,500
1440	20' x 400' x 14' high		.05	3846		165,000	193,000	17,500	375,500	494,500
1460	20' x 450' x 14' high		.05	4301		184,500	216,000	19,500	420,000	553,000
1480	20' x 500' x 14' high		.04	4762		204,000	239,000	21,600	464,600	612,500
1500	Treatment cell, connecting, 20' x 20' x 12' high (2' freeboard)		.60	336		14,900	16,900	1,525	33,325	43,800
1520	20' x 30' x 12' high		.47	425		18,700	21,400	1,925	42,025	55,000
1540	20' x 40' x 12' high		.39	515		22,500	25,900	2,325	50,725	66,500
1560	20' x 50' x 12' high		.33	604		26,300	30,300	2,750	59,350	78,000
1580	20' x 60' x 12' high		.29	694		30,100	34,800	3,150	68,050	89,500
1600	20' x 70' x 12' high		.26	783		33,900	39,300	3,550	76,750	101,000
1620	20' x 80' x 12' high		.23	873		37,700	43,800	3,950	85,450	112,500
1640	20' x 90' x 12' high		.21	962		41,500	48,300	4,375	94,175	124,000
1660	20' x 100' x 12' high		.19	1052		45,300	53,000	4,775	103,075	135,500
1680	20' x 120' x 12' high		.16	1230		53,000	62,000	5,575	120,575	158,000
1700	20' x 140' x 12' high		.14	1409		60,500	71,000	6,400	137,900	181,000
1720	20' x 160' x 12' high		.13	1589		68,000	80,000	7,200	155,200	204,500
1740	20' x 180' x 12' high		.11	1767		75,500	88,500	8,025	172,025	227,000
1760	20' x 200' x 12' high		.10	1946		83,000	97,500	8,825	189,325	249,500
1780	20' x 250' x 12' high		.08	2392		102,000	120,000	10,900	232,900	307,500
1800	20' x 300' x 12' high		.07	2841		121,000	142,500	12,900	276,400	364,500
1820	20' x 350' x 12' high		.06	3289		140,000	165,000	14,900	319,900	422,000
1840	20' x 400' x 12' high		.05	3738		159,000	187,500	17,000	363,500	479,000
1860	20' x 450' x 12' high		.05	4184		178,000	210,000	19,000	407,000	536,500
1880	20' x 500' x 12' high		.04	5571		197,000	280,000	25,300	502,300	670,500
1996	Price for aerator curb per cell excluding aerator piping & drain									
2000	Treatment cell, 20' x 20' aerator curb	F-7	1.88	17.067	Ea.	650	775		1,425	1,900
2010	20' x 30'		1.25	25.600		975	1,150		2,125	2,850
2020	20' x 40'		.94	34.133		1,300	1,550		2,850	3,775
2030	20' x 50'		.75	42.667		1,625	1,925		3,550	4,725
2040	20' x 60'		.63	51.200		1,950	2,325		4,275	5,675
2050	20' x 70'		.54	59.735		2,275	2,700		4,975	6,625
2060	20' x 80'		.47	68.259		2,600	3,100		5,700	7,550
2070	20' x 90'		.42	76.794		2,925	3,475		6,400	8,525
2080	20' x 100'		.38	85.333		3,250	3,875		7,125	9,450
2090	20' x 120'		.31	102		3,900	4,625		8,525	11,400
2100	20' x 140'		.27	119		4,550	5,400		9,950	13,200

46 53 Biological Treatment Systems

46 53 17 – Activated Sludge Treatment

46 53 17.10 Activated Sludge Treatment Cells		Crew	Daily Output	Labor-Hours	Unit	Material	2018 Bare Costs Labor	Equipment	Total	Total Incl O&P
2110	20' x 160'	F-7	.23	137	Ea.	5,200	6,175		11,375	15,200
2120	20' x 180'		.21	154		5,850	6,950		12,800	17,000
2130	20' x 200'		.19	171		6,500	7,725		14,225	19,000
2160	20' x 250'		.15	213		8,125	9,650		17,775	23,600
2190	20' x 300'		.13	256		9,750	11,600		21,350	28,400
2220	20' x 350'		.11	299		11,400	13,500		24,900	33,100
2250	20' x 400'		.09	341		13,000	15,400		28,400	37,800
2280	20' x 450'		.08	384		14,600	17,400		32,000	42,600
2310	20' x 500'	↓	.08	427	↓	16,200	19,300		35,500	47,300

Division 48 — Electrical Power Generation

Estimating Tips

- When estimating costs for the installation of electrical power generation equipment, factors to review include access to the job site, access and setting up at the installation site, required connections, uncrating pads, anchors, leveling, final assembly of the components, and temporary protection from physical damage, such as environmental exposure.

- Be aware of the costs of equipment supports, concrete pads, and vibration isolators. Cross-reference them against other trades' specifications. Also, review site and structural drawings for items that must be included in the estimates.

- It is important to include items that are not documented in the plans and specifications but must be priced. These items include, but are not limited to, testing, dust protection, roof penetration, core drilling concrete floors and walls, patching, cleanup, and final adjustments. Add a contingency or allowance for utility company fees for power hookups, if needed.

- The project size and scope of electrical power generation equipment will have a significant impact on cost. The intent of RSMeans cost data is to provide a benchmark cost so that owners, engineers, and electrical contractors will have a comfortable number with which to start a project. Additionally, there are many websites available to use for research and to obtain a vendor's quote to finalize costs.

Reference Numbers

Reference numbers are shown at the beginning of some major classifications. These numbers refer to related items in the Reference Section. The reference information may be an estimating procedure, an alternate pricing method, or technical information.

Note: Not all subdivisions listed here necessarily appear. ■

No part of this cost data may be reproduced, stored in a retrieval system, or transmitted in any form or by any means without prior written permission of Gordian.

Note: Trade Service, in part, has been used as a reference source for some of the material prices used in Division 48.

Did you know?

RSMeans data is available through our online application with 24/7 access:

- Search for unit prices by keyword
- Leverage the most up-to-date data
- Build and export estimates

Try it free for 30 days!
www.rsmeans.com/2018freetrial

48 15 Wind Energy Electrical Power Generation Equipment

48 15 13 – Wind Turbines

48 15 13.50 Wind Turbines and Components

		Crew	Daily Output	Labor-Hours	Unit	Material	2018 Bare Costs Labor	Equipment	Total	Total Incl O&P
0010	**WIND TURBINES & COMPONENTS**									
0500	Complete system, grid connected									
1000	20 kW, 31' diam., incl. labor & material	G			System				49,900	49,900
1010	Enhanced	G							92,000	92,000
1500	10 kW, 23' diam., incl. labor & material	G							74,000	74,000
2000	2.4 kW, 12' diam., incl. labor & material	G							18,000	18,000
2900	Component system									
3200	1,000 W, 9' diam.	G	1 Elec	2.05	3.902	Ea.	1,500	227		1,727	2,000
3400	Mounting hardware									
3500	30' guyed tower kit	G	2 Clab	5.12	3.125	Ea.	395	125		520	620
3505	3' galvanized helical earth screw	G	1 Clab	8	1		48	40		88	113
3510	Attic mount kit	G	1 Rofc	2.56	3.125		202	137		339	455
3520	Roof mount kit	G	1 Clab	3.41	2.346		292	93.50		385.50	460
8900	Equipment									
9100	DC to AC inverter for, 48 V, 4,000 W	G	1 Elec	2	4	Ea.	2,275	233		2,508	2,850

48 18 Fuel Cell Electrical Power Generation Equipment

48 18 13 – Electrical Power Generation Fuel Cells

48 18 13.10 Fuel Cells

		Crew	Daily Output	Labor-Hours	Unit	Material	Labor	Equipment	Total	Total Incl O&P
0010	**FUEL CELLS**									
2001	Complete system, natural gas, installed, 200 kW	G			System				1,150,000	1,150,000
2002	400 kW	G							2,168,000	2,168,000
2003	600 kW	G							3,060,000	3,060,000
2004	800 kW	G							4,000,000	4,000,000
2005	1,000 kW	G							5,005,000	5,005,000
2010	Comm type, for battery charging, uses hydrogen, 100 W, 12 V	G			Ea.	2,350			2,350	2,575
2020	500 W, 12 V	G				4,575			4,575	5,025
2030	1,000 W, 48 V	G				7,250			7,250	7,975
2040	Small, for demonstration or battery charging units, 12 V	G				159			159	175
2050	Spare anode set for unit	G				39			39	43
2060	3 W, uses hydrogen gas	G				299			299	330
2070	6 W, uses hydrogen gas	G				520			520	570
2080	10 W, uses hydrogen gas	G				1,325			1,325	1,450

Assemblies Section

Table of Contents

Table No.	Page
B3010 000	
B3010 Roof Coverings	
B3010 125 Green Roof	312
B3020 Roof Openings	
B3020 110 Skylights	314
D2020 000	
D2020 Domestic Water Distribution	
D2020 265 Solar, Closed Loop, Add-On Hot Water Systems	317
D2020 270 Solar, Drainback, Hot Water Systems	319
D2020 275 Solar, Draindown, Hot Water Systems	321
D2020 295 Solar, Closed Loop, Hot Water Systems	323
D3010 Energy Supply	
D3010 660 Solar Swimming Pool Heater Systems	325
D3010 682 Solar Direct Gain Glazing, Door Panels	326
D3010 684 Solar Direct Gain Glazing-Window Panels	327
D3010 686 Passive Solar Indirect Gain Wall	328

Table No.	Page
D3010 688 Passive Solar Indirect Gain Panel	329
D3010 690 Passive Solar Sunspace	330
D3030 Cooling Generating Systems	
D3030 214 Heating/Cooling System	331
D3050 Terminal & Package Units	
D3050 152 Rooftop Single Zone Unit Systems SEER 14	332
D3050 157 Rooftop Multizone Unit Systems SEER 14	334
D3050 248 Geothermal Heat Pump System	337
D5020 Lighting and Branch Wiring	
D5020 218 Fluorescent Fixture, High Bay, 8'-10' (by Wattage)	339
D5020 290 Daylight Dimming System	340
D5020 295 Lighting On/Off Control System	341
D5090 Other Electrical Systems	
D5090 420 Photovoltaic Power System, Stand Alone	343
D5090 430 Photovoltaic Power System, Grid Connected	344
D5090 480 Energy Monitoring Systems	345

RSMeans data: Assemblies—How They Work

Assemblies estimating provides a fast and reasonably accurate way to develop construction costs. An assembly is the grouping of individual work items—with appropriate quantities—to provide a cost for a major construction component in a convenient unit of measure.

An assemblies estimate is often used during early stages of design development to compare the cost impact of various design alternatives on total building cost.

Assemblies estimates are also used as an efficient tool to verify construction estimates.

Assemblies estimates do not require a completed design or detailed drawings. Instead, they are based on the general size of the structure and other known parameters of the project. The degree of accuracy of an assemblies estimate is generally within +/- 15%.

Most assemblies consist of three major elements: a graphic, the system components, and the cost data itself. The **Graphic** is a visual representation showing the typical appearance of the assembly

① Unique 12-character Identifier

Our assemblies are identified by a **unique 12-character identifier**. The assemblies are numbered using UNIFORMAT II, ASTM Standard E1557. The first 5 characters represent this system to Level 3. The last 7 characters represent further breakdown in order to arrange items in understandable groups of similar tasks. Line numbers are consistent across all of our publications, so a line number in any assemblies data set will always refer to the same item.

② Narrative Descriptions

Our assemblies descriptions appear in two formats: narrative and table. **Narrative descriptions** are shown in a hierarchical structure to make them readable. In order to read a complete description, read up through the indents to the top of the section. Include everything that is above and to the left that is not contradicted by information below.

B30 Roofing
B3010 Roof Coverings

Green Roof

System Components ①

	QUANTITY	UNIT	MAT.	INST.	TOTAL
SYSTEM B3010 125 1400					
GREEN ROOF, 4 INCH SOIL DEPTH WITH SEDUM PLANTS					
Mobilization/Demob crane driver	2.000	Ea.		.09	.09
Green roof edging treated lumber 4" x 4", no hoisting included	280.000	L.F.	.09	.22	.31
Hoist and spread soil mixture 4" depth up to 5 stories tall roof	1.000	S.F.	.25	1.20	1.45
Planting sedum, light soil, potted, 2-1/4" diameter, 2 per S.F.	1.000	S.F.	6.70	1.16	7.86
Hoist plants & edging to roof	1.000	Day		1.21	1.21
TOTAL			7.04	3.88	10.92

B3010 125	Green Roof	MAT.	INST.	TOTAL
1200	Green roof with wood edging, soil, sedum plants, up to five stories height			
1400	Green roof, 4 inch soil depth with treated wood edging and sedum plants	7.05	3.88	10.93
1500	6 inch soil depth	7.25	4.48	11.73
1600	② 8 inch soil depth	7.50	5.10	12.60
1700	10 inch soil depth	7.65	5.75	13.40
1800	12 inch soil depth	7.75	6.35	14.10
2000	Green roof, 4 inch soil depth with redwood edging and sedum plants	7.45	3.88	11.33
2100	6 inch soil depth	8.05	4.48	12.53
2200	8 inch soil depth	9.05	5.10	14.15
2300	10 inch soil depth	9.25	5.75	15

For supplemental customizable square foot estimating forms, visit: **www.RSMeans.com/2018books**

in question. It is frequently accompanied by additional explanatory technical information describing the class of items. The **System Components** is a listing of the individual tasks that make up the assembly, including the quantity and unit of measure for each item, along with the cost of material and installation. The **Assemblies Data** below lists prices for other similar systems with dimensional and/or size variations.

All of our assemblies costs represent the cost for the installing contractor. An allowance for profit has been added to all material, labor, and equipment rental costs. A markup for labor burdens, including workers' compensation, fixed overhead, and business overhead, is included with installation costs.

The information in RSMeans cost data represents a "national average" cost. This data should be modified to the project location using the **City Cost Indexes** or **Location Factors** tables found in the Reference Section.

B30 Roofing
B3010 Roof Coverings

Green Roof

System Components	QUANTITY	UNIT	COST PER S.F. MAT.	INST.	TOTAL
SYSTEM B3010 125 1400					
GREEN ROOF, 4 INCH SOIL DEPTH WITH SEDUM PLANTS					
Mobilization/Demob crane driver	2.000	Ea.		.09	.09
Green roof edging treated lumber 4" x 4", no hoisting included	280.000	L.F.	.09	.22	.31
Hoist and spread soil mixture 4" depth up to 5 stories tall roof	1.000	S.F.	.25	1.20	1.45
Planting sedum, light soil, potted, 2-1/4" diameter, 2 per S.F.	1.000	S.F.	6.70	1.16	7.86
Hoist plants & edging to roof	1.000	Day		1.21	1.21
TOTAL			7.04	3.88	10.92

B3010 125	Green Roof	COST PER S.F. MAT.	INST.	TOTAL
1200	Green roof with wood edging, soil, sedum plants, up to five stories height			
1400	Green roof, 4 inch soil depth with treated wood edging and sedum plants	7.05	3.88	10.93
1500	6 inch soil depth	7.25	4.48	11.73
1600	8 inch soil depth	7.50	5.10	12.60
1700	10 inch soil depth	7.65	5.75	13.40
1800	12 inch soil depth	7.75	6.35	14.10
2000	Green roof, 4 inch soil depth with redwood edging and sedum plants	7.45	3.88	11.33
2100	6 inch soil depth	8.05	4.48	12.53
2200	8 inch soil depth	9.05	5.10	14.15
2300	10 inch soil depth	9.25	5.75	15

Unit of Measure
All RSMeans data: Assemblies include a typical **Unit of Measure** used for estimating that item. For instance, for continuous footings or foundation walls the unit is linear feet (L.F.). For spread footings the unit is each (Ea.). The estimator needs to take special care that the unit in the data matches the unit in the takeoff. Abbreviations and unit conversions can be found in the Reference Section.

System Components
System components are listed separately to detail what is included in the development of the total system price.

References
Information is available in the Reference Section to assist the estimator with estimating procedures, alternate pricing methods, and additional technical information.

RSMeans data: Assemblies—How They Work (Continued)

Sample Estimate

This sample demonstrates the elements of an estimate, including a tally of the RSMeans data lines. Published assemblies costs include all markups for labor burden and profit for the installing contractor. This estimate adds a summary of the markups applied by a general contractor on the installing contractor's work. These figures represent the total cost to the owner. The location factor with RSMeans data is applied at the bottom of the estimate to adjust the cost of the work to a specific location.

Project Name:	Interior Fit-out, ABC Office			
Location:	Anywhere, USA		Date: 1/1/2018	STD
Assembly Number	**Description**	**Qty.**	**Unit**	**Subtotal**
C1010 124 1200	Wood partition, 2 x 4 @ 16" OC w/5/8" FR gypsum board	560.000	S.F.	$2,856.00
C1020 114 1800	Metal door & frame, flush hollow core, 3'-0" x 7'-0"	2.000	Ea.	$2,510.00
C3010 230 0080	Painting, brushwork, primer & 2 coats	1,120.000	S.F.	$1,422.40
C3020 410 0140	Carpet, tufted, nylon, roll goods, 12' wide, 26 oz	240.000	S.F.	$842.40
C3030 210 6000	Acoustic ceilings, 24" x 48" tile, tee grid suspension	200.000	S.F.	$1,260.00
D5020 125 0560	Receptacles incl plate, box, conduit, wire, 20 A duplex	8.000	Ea.	$2,320.00
D5020 125 0720	Light switch incl plate, box, conduit, wire, 20 A single pole	2.000	Ea.	$566.00
D5020 210 0560	Fluorescent fixtures, recess mounted, 20 per 1000 SF	200.000	S.F.	$2,226.00
	Assembly Subtotal			**$14,002.80**
	Sales Tax @ ❷	5 %		$ 350.07
	General Requirements @ ❸	7 %		$ 980.20
	Subtotal A			**$15,333.07**
	GC Overhead @ ❹	5 %		$ 766.65
	Subtotal B			**$16,099.72**
	GC Profit @ ❺	5 %		$ 804.99
	Subtotal C			**$16,904.71**
	Adjusted by Location Factor ❻	115.2		$ 19,474.22
	Architects Fee @ ❼	8 %		$ 1,557.94
	Contingency @ ❽	15 %		$ 2,921.13
	Project Total Cost			**$ 23,953.29**

This estimate is based on an interactive spreadsheet. You are free to download it and adjust it to your methodology. A copy of this spreadsheet is available at **www.RSMeans.com/2018books**.

① Work Performed
The body of the estimate shows the RSMeans data selected, including line numbers, a brief description of each item, its takeoff quantity and unit, and the total installed cost, including the installing contractor's overhead and profit.

② Sales Tax
If the work is subject to state or local sales taxes, the amount must be added to the estimate. In a conceptual estimate it can be assumed that one half of the total represents material costs. Therefore, apply the sales tax rate to 50% of the assembly subtotal.

③ General Requirements
This item covers project-wide needs provided by the general contractor. These items vary by project but may include temporary facilities and utilities, security, testing, project cleanup, etc. In assemblies estimates a percentage is used—typically between 5% and 15% of project cost.

④ General Contractor Overhead
This entry represents the general contractor's markup on all work to cover project administration costs.

⑤ General Contractor Profit
This entry represents the GC's profit on all work performed. The value included here can vary widely by project and is influenced by the GC's perception of the project's financial risk and market conditions.

⑥ Location Factor
RSMeans published data are based on national average costs. If necessary, adjust the total cost of the project using a location factor from the "Location Factor" table or the "City Cost Indexes" table found in the Reference Section. Use location factors if the work is general, covering the work of multiple trades. If the work is by a single trade (e.g., masonry) use the more specific data found in the City Cost Indexes.

To adjust costs by location factors, multiply the base cost by the factor and divide by 100.

⑦ Architect's Fee
If appropriate, add the design cost to the project estimate. These fees vary based on project complexity and size. Typical design and engineering fees can be found in the Reference Section.

⑧ Contingency
A factor for contingency may be added to any estimate to represent the cost of unknowns that may occur between the time that the estimate is performed and the time the project is constructed. The amount of the allowance will depend on the stage of design at which the estimate is done, and the contractor's assessment of the risk involved.

B Shell

Did you know?

RSMeans data is available through our online application with 24/7 access:
- Search for unit prices by keyword
- Leverage the most up-to-date data
- Build and export estimates

Try it free for 30 days!
www.rsmeans.com/2018freetrial

No part of this cost data may be reproduced, stored in a retrieval system, or transmitted in any form or by any means without prior written permission of Gordian.

B30 Roofing

B3010 Roof Coverings

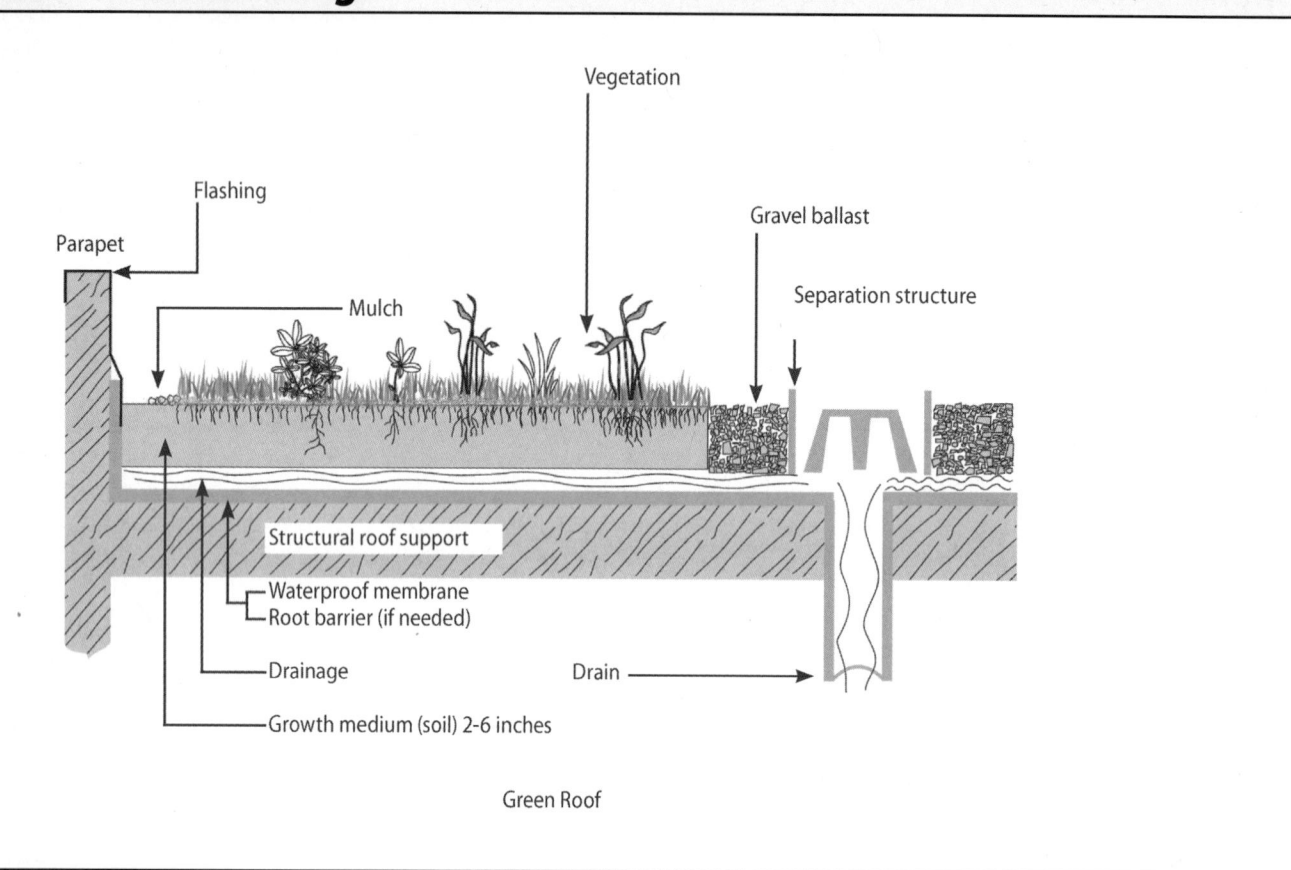

Green Roof

System Components	QUANTITY	UNIT	COST PER S.F. MAT.	COST PER S.F. INST.	COST PER S.F. TOTAL
SYSTEM B3010 125 1400					
GREEN ROOF, 4 INCH SOIL DEPTH WITH SEDUM PLANTS					
Mobilization/Demob crane driver	2.000	Ea.		.09	.09
Green roof edging treated lumber 4" x 4", no hoisting included	280.000	L.F.	.09	.22	.31
Hoist and spread soil mixture 4" depth up to 5 stories tall roof	1.000	S.F.	.25	1.20	1.45
Planting sedum, light soil, potted, 2-1/4" diameter, 2 per S.F.	1.000	S.F.	6.70	1.16	7.86
Hoist plants & edging to roof	1.000	Day		1.21	1.21
TOTAL			7.04	3.88	10.92

B3010 125	Green Roof	COST PER S.F. MAT.	COST PER S.F. INST.	COST PER S.F. TOTAL
1200	Green roof with wood edging, soil, sedum plants, up to five stories height			
1400	Green roof, 4 inch soil depth with treated wood edging and sedum plants	7.05	3.88	10.93
1500	6 inch soil depth	7.25	4.48	11.73
1600	8 inch soil depth	7.50	5.10	12.60
1700	10 inch soil depth	7.65	5.75	13.40
1800	12 inch soil depth	7.75	6.35	14.10
2000	Green roof, 4 inch soil depth with redwood edging and sedum plants	7.45	3.88	11.33
2100	6 inch soil depth	8.05	4.48	12.53
2200	8 inch soil depth	9.05	5.10	14.15
2300	10 inch soil depth	9.25	5.75	15
2400	12 inch soil depth	9.40	6.35	15.75
3000	Green roof, 4 inch soil depth with treated wood edging and sedum mats	8.40	3.21	11.61
3100	6 inch soil depth	8.60	3.81	12.41
3200	8 inch soil depth	8.85	4.44	13.29
3300	10 inch soil depth	9	5.10	14.10
3400	12 inch soil depth	9.10	5.70	14.80

B30 Roofing

B3010 Roof Coverings

B3010 125	Green Roof	MAT.	INST.	TOTAL
4000	Green roof, 4 inch soil depth with redwood edging and sedum mats	8.80	3.21	12.01
4100	6 inch soil depth	9.40	3.81	13.21
4200	8 inch soil depth	10.40	4.44	14.84
4300	10 inch soil depth	10.60	5.10	15.70
4400	12 inch soil depth	10.75	5.70	16.45
5000	Green roof with treated wood enclosure & sedum mat system (no soil)	11.30	2.01	13.31
5100	Green roof with redwood enclosure & sedum mat system (no soil)	11.70	2.01	13.71
6000	Green roof with wood edging, soil, sedum plants, six to ten stories			
6100	Green roof, 4 inch soil depth with treated wood edging and sedum plants	7.05	4.54	11.59
6110	6 inch soil depth	7.25	5.25	12.50
6120	8 inch soil depth	7.50	6	13.50
6130	10 inch soil depth	7.65	6.80	14.45
6140	12 inch soil depth	7.75	7.50	15.25
6200	Green roof, 4 inch soil depth with redwood edging and sedum plants	7.45	4.54	11.99
6210	6 inch soil depth	8.05	5.25	13.30
6220	8 inch soil depth	8.90	5.30	14.20
6230	10 inch soil depth	9.25	6.80	16.05
6240	12 inch soil depth	9.40	7.50	16.90
6300	Green roof, 4 inch soil depth with treated wood edging and sedum mats	8.40	3.87	12.27
6310	6 inch soil depth	8.60	4.59	13.19
6320	8 inch soil depth	8.85	5.35	14.20
6330	10 inch soil depth	9	6.10	15.10
6340	12 inch soil depth	9.10	6.80	15.90
6400	Green roof, 4 inch soil depth with redwood edging and sedum mats	8.80	3.87	12.67
6410	6 inch soil depth	9.40	4.59	13.99
6420	8 inch soil depth	10.40	5.35	15.75
6430	10 inch soil depth	10.60	6.10	16.70
6440	12 inch soil depth	10.75	6.80	17.55
6500	Green roof with treated wood enclosure & sedum mat system (no soil)	11.30	2.43	13.73
6600	Green roof with redwood enclosure & sedum mat system (no soil)	11.70	2.43	14.13

COST PER S.F.

B30 Roofing

B3020 Roof Openings

Roof Hatch 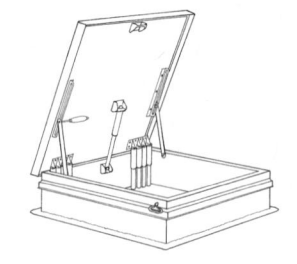   Smoke Hatch 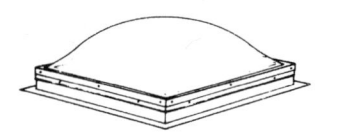   Skylight

B3020 110	Skylights	COST PER S.F.		
		MAT.	INST.	TOTAL
5100	Skylights, plastic domes, insul curbs, nom. size to 10 S.F., single glaze	33	15.20	48.20
5200	Double glazing	38	18.70	56.70
5300	10 S.F. to 20 S.F., single glazing	35	6.15	41.15
5400	Double glazing	32.50	7.70	40.20
5500	20 S.F. to 30 S.F., single glazing	26	5.25	31.25
5600	Double glazing	30	6.15	36.15
5700	30 S.F. to 65 S.F., single glazing	25	3.99	28.99
5800	Double glazing	31	5.25	36.25
6000	Sandwich panels fiberglass, 1-9/16" thick, 2 S.F. to 10 S.F.	20.50	12.15	32.65
6100	10 S.F. to 18 S.F.	18.45	9.15	27.60
6200	2-3/4" thick, 25 S.F. to 40 S.F.	29.50	8.25	37.75
6300	40 S.F. to 70 S.F.	24	7.35	31.35

D Services

Did you know?

RSMeans data is available through our online application with 24/7 access:
- Search for unit prices by keyword
- Leverage the most up-to-date data
- Build and export estimates

Try it free for 30 days!
www.rsmeans.com/2018freetrial

No part of this cost data may be reproduced, stored in a retrieval system, or transmitted in any form or by any means without prior written permission of Gordian.

D20 Plumbing

D2020 Domestic Water Distribution

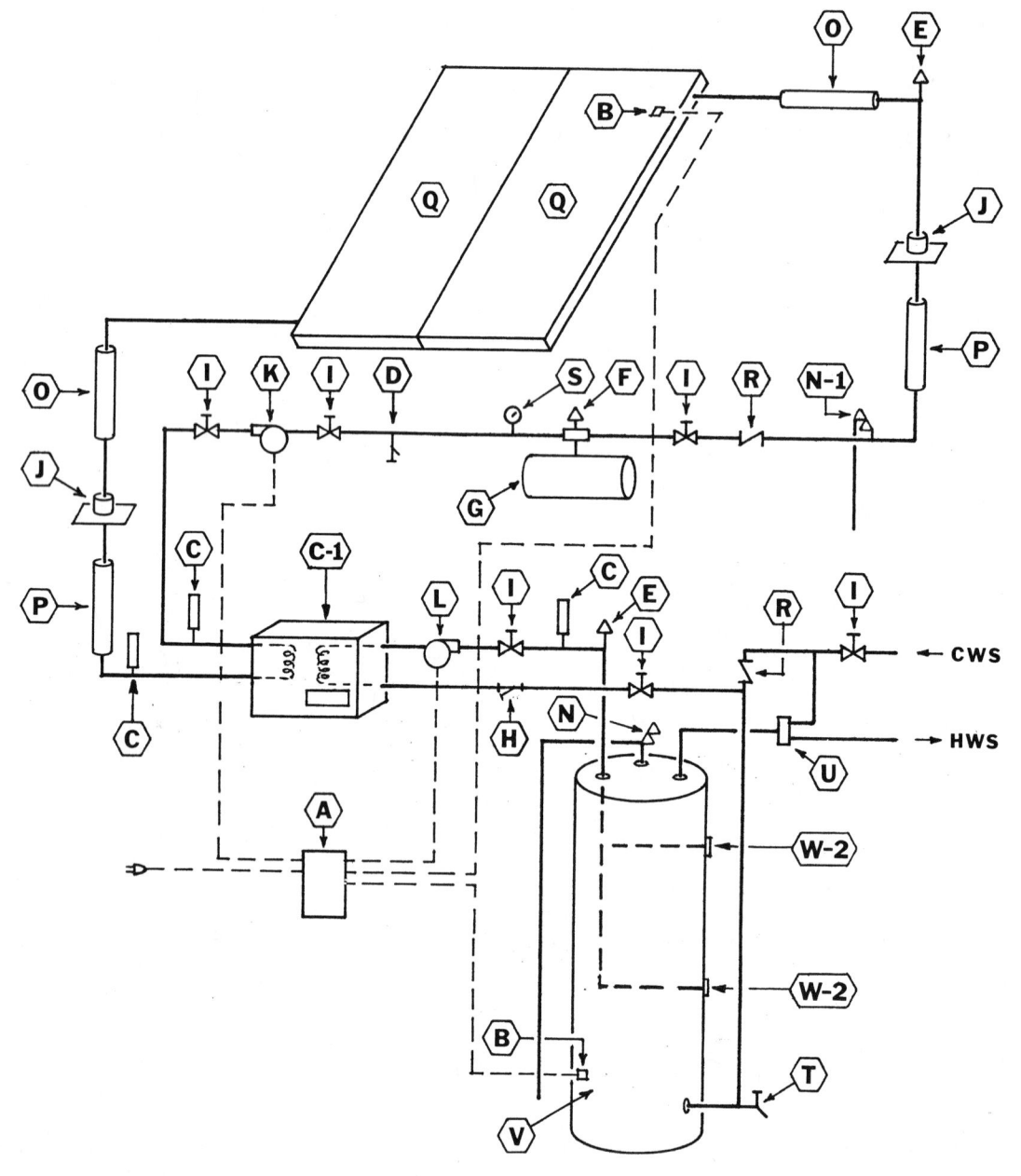

In this closed-loop indirect collection system, fluid with a low freezing temperature, such as propylene glycol, transports heat from the collectors to water storage. The transfer fluid is contained in a closed-loop consisting of collectors, supply and return piping, and a remote heat exchanger. The heat exchanger transfers heat energy from the fluid in the collector loop to potable water circulated in a storage loop. A typical two-or-three panel system contains 5 to 6 gallons of heat transfer fluid.

When the collectors become approximately 20°F warmer than the storage temperature, a controller activates the circulator on the collector and storage loops. The circulators will move the fluid and potable water through the heat exchanger until heat collection no longer occurs. At that point, the system shuts down. Since the heat transfer medium is a fluid with a very low freezing temperature, there is no need for it to be drained from the system between periods of collection.

316

For customer support on your Green Building Costs with RSMeans data, call 800.448.8182.

D20 Plumbing

D2020 Domestic Water Distribution

System Components		QUANTITY	UNIT	COST EACH MAT.	COST EACH INST.	TOTAL
	SYSTEM D2020 265 2760					
	SOLAR, CLOSED LOOP, ADD-ON HOT WATER SYS., EXTERNAL HEAT EXCHANGER					
	3/4" TUBING, TWO 3'X7' BLACK CHROME COLLECTORS					
A,B,G,L,K,M	Heat exchanger fluid-fluid pkg incl 2 circulators, expansion tank, Check valve, relief valve, controller, hi temp cutoff, & 2 sensors	1.000	Ea.	895	540	1,435
C	Thermometer, 2" dial	3.000	Ea.	72	141	213
D, T	Fill & drain valve, brass, 3/4" connection	1.000	Ea.	11.60	31	42.60
E	Air vent, manual, 1/8" fitting	2.000	Ea.	5.78	47	52.78
F	Air purger	1.000	Ea.	52	62.50	114.50
H	Strainer, Y type, bronze body, 3/4" IPS	1.000	Ea.	49.50	40	89.50
I	Valve, gate, bronze, NRS, soldered 3/4" diam	6.000	Ea.	420	225	645
J	Neoprene vent flashing	2.000	Ea.	21	75	96
N-1, N	Relief valve temp & press, 150 psi 210°F self-closing 3/4" IPS	1.000	Ea.	26.50	25	51.50
O	Pipe covering, urethane, ultraviolet cover, 1" wall 3/4" diam	20.000	L.F.	62.20	137	199.20
P	Pipe covering, fiberglass, all service jacket, 1" wall, 3/4" diam	50.000	L.F.	50.50	272.50	323
Q	Collector panel solar energy blk chrome on copper, 1/8" temp glass 3'x7'	2.000	Ea.	2,250	284	2,534
	Roof clamps for solar energy collector panels	2.000	Set	6.32	38.50	44.82
R	Valve, swing check, bronze, regrinding disc, 3/4" diam	2.000	Ea.	190	75	265
S	Pressure gauge, 60 psi, 2" dial	1.000	Ea.	26.50	23.50	50
U	Valve, water tempering, bronze, sweat connections, 3/4" diam	1.000	Ea.	153	37.50	190.50
W-2, V	Tank water storage w/heating element, drain, relief valve, existing	1.000	Ea.			
	Copper tubing type L, solder joint, hanger 10' OC 3/4" diam	20.000	L.F.	98.80	197	295.80
	Copper tubing, type M, solder joint, hanger 10' OC 3/4" diam	70.000	L.F.	402.50	672	1,074.50
	Sensor wire, #22-2 conductor multistranded	.500	C.L.F.	5.73	34.75	40.48
	Solar energy heat transfer fluid, propylene glycol anti-freeze	6.000	Gal.	156	159	315
	Wrought copper fittings & solder, 3/4" diam	76.000	Ea.	210.52	3,002	3,212.52
	TOTAL			**5,165.45**	**6,119.25**	**11,284.70**

D2020 265	Solar, Closed Loop, Add-On Hot Water Systems		MAT.	INST.	TOTAL
2550	Solar, closed loop, add-on hot water system, external heat exchanger				
2700	3/4" tubing, 3 ea. 3'x7' black chrome collectors		6,300	6,275	12,575
2720	3 ea. 3'x7' flat black absorber plate collectors	R235616-60	5,825	6,300	12,125
2740	2 ea. 4'x9' flat black w/plastic glazing collectors		5,225	6,325	11,550
2760	2 ea. 3'x7' black chrome collectors		5,175	6,125	11,300
2780	1" tubing, 4 ea 2'x9' plastic absorber & glazing collectors		6,350	7,125	13,475
2800	4 ea. 3'x7' black chrome absorber collectors		8,225	7,150	15,375
2820	4 ea. 3'x7' flat black absorber collectors		7,600	7,175	14,775

For customer support on your Green Building Costs with RSMeans data, call 800.448.8182.

D20 Plumbing

D2020 Domestic Water Distribution

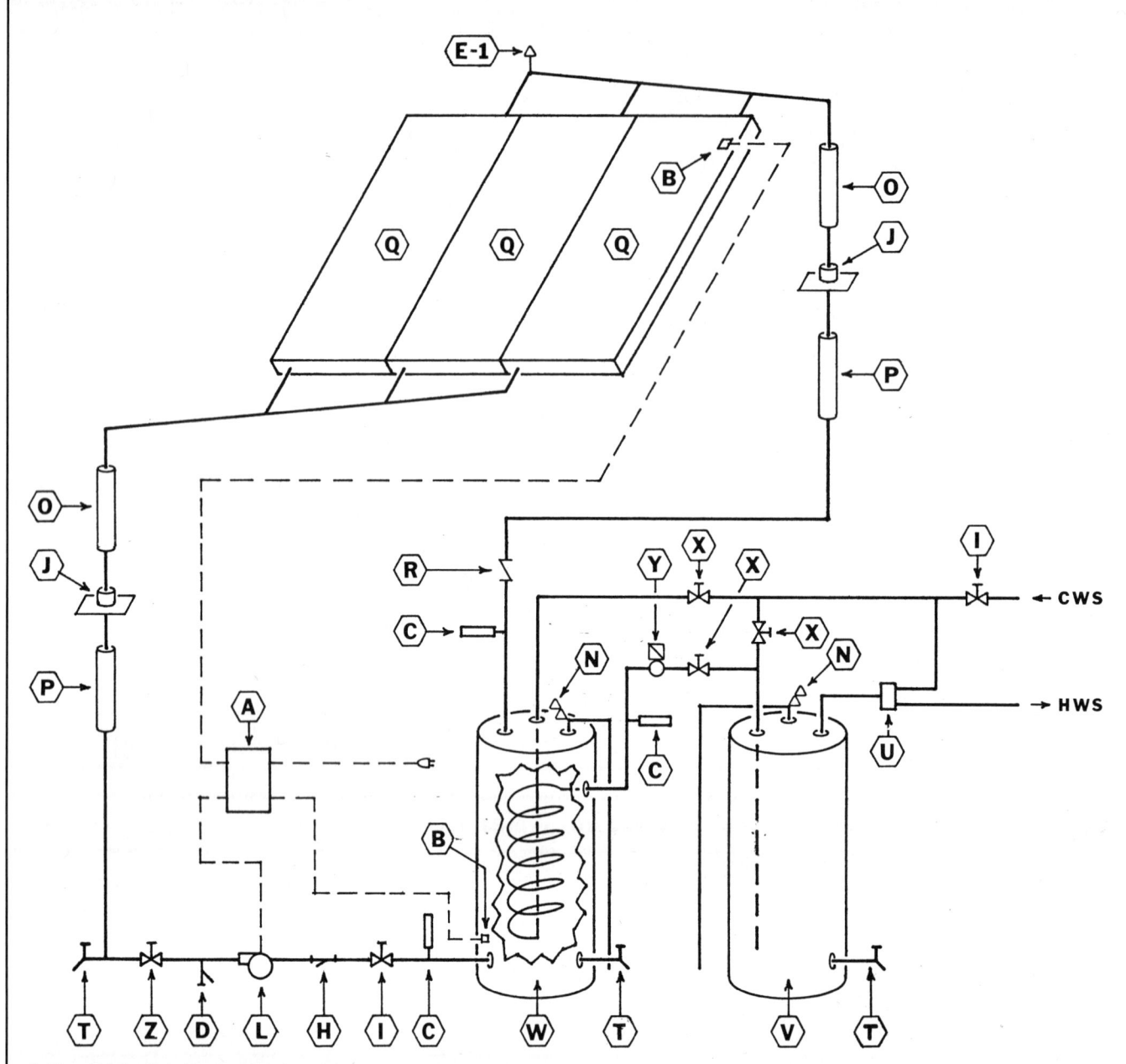

In the drainback indirect-collection system, the heat transfer fluid is distilled water contained in a loop consisting of collectors, supply and return piping, and an unpressurized holding tank. A large heat exchanger containing incoming potable water is immersed in the holding tank. When a controller activates solar collection, the distilled water is pumped through the collectors and heated and pumped back down to the holding tank. When the temperature differential between the water in the collectors and water in storage is such that collection no longer occurs, the pump turns off and gravity causes the distilled water in the collector loop to drain back to the holding tank. All the loop piping is pitched so that the water can drain out of the collectors and piping and not freeze there. As hot water is needed in the home, incoming water first flows through the holding tank with the immersed heat exchanger and is warmed and then flows through a conventional heater for any supplemental heating that is necessary.

D20 Plumbing

D2020 Domestic Water Distribution

System Components	QUANTITY	UNIT	COST EACH MAT.	COST EACH INST.	COST EACH TOTAL
SYSTEM D2020 270 2760					
SOLAR, DRAINBACK, ADD ON, HOT WATER, IMMERSED HEAT EXCHANGER					
3/4" TUBING, THREE EA 3'X7' BLACK CHROME COLLECTOR					
A, B Differential controller 2 sensors, thermostat, solar energy system	1.000	Ea.	147	62.50	209.50
C Thermometer 2" dial	3.000	Ea.	72	141	213
D, T Fill & drain valve, brass, 3/4" connection	1.000	Ea.	11.60	31	42.60
E-1 Automatic air vent 1/8" fitting	1.000	Ea.	20.50	23.50	44
H Strainer, Y type, bronze body, 3/4" IPS	1.000	Ea.	49.50	40	89.50
I Valve, gate, bronze, NRS, soldered 3/4" diam	2.000	Ea.	140	75	215
J Neoprene vent flashing	2.000	Ea.	21	75	96
L Circulator, solar heated liquid, 1/20 HP	1.000	Ea.	293	112	405
N Relief valve temp. & press. 150 psi 210°F self-closing 3/4" IPS	1.000	Ea.	26.50	25	51.50
O Pipe covering, urethane, ultraviolet cover, 1" wall, 3/4" diam	20.000	L.F.	62.20	137	199.20
P Pipe covering, fiberglass, all service jacket, 1" wall, 3/4" diam	50.000	L.F.	50.50	272.50	323
Q Collector panel solar energy blk chrome on copper, 1/8" temp glas 3'x7'	3.000	Ea.	3,375	426	3,801
Roof clamps for solar energy collector panels	3.000	Set	9.48	57.75	67.23
R Valve, swing check, bronze, regrinding disc, 3/4" diam	1.000	Ea.	95	37.50	132.50
U Valve, water tempering, bronze sweat connections, 3/4" diam	1.000	Ea.	153	37.50	190.50
V Tank, water storage w/heating element, drain, relief valve, existing	1.000	Ea.			
W Tank, water storage immersed heat exchr elec 2"x1/2# insul 120 gal	1.000	Ea.	2,125	535	2,660
X Valve, globe, bronze, rising stem, 3/4" diam, soldered	3.000	Ea.	450	112.50	562.50
Y Flow control valve	1.000	Ea.	152	34	186
Z Valve, ball, bronze, solder 3/4" diam, solar loop flow control	1.000	Ea.	26.50	37.50	64
Copper tubing, type L, solder joint, hanger 10' OC 3/4" diam	20.000	L.F.	98.80	197	295.80
Copper tubing, type M, solder joint, hanger 10' OC 3/4" diam	70.000	L.F.	402.50	672	1,074.50
Sensor wire, #22-2 conductor, multistranded	.500	C.L.F.	5.73	34.75	40.48
Wrought copper fittings & solder, 3/4" diam	76.000	Ea.	210.52	3,002	3,212.52
TOTAL			7,997.33	6,178	14,175.33

D2020 270	Solar, Drainback, Hot Water Systems		MAT.	INST.	TOTAL
2550	Solar, drainback, hot water, immersed heat exchanger				
2560	3/8" tubing, 3 ea. 4' x 4'-4" vacuum tube collectors		7,075	5,550	12,625
2760	3/4" tubing, 3 ea 3'x7' black chrome collectors, 120 gal tank	R235616-60	8,000	6,175	14,175
2780	3 ea. 3'x7' flat black absorber collectors, 120 gal tank		7,525	6,200	13,725
2800	2 ea. 4'x9' flat blk w/plastic glazing collectors 120 gal tank		6,925	6,225	13,150
2840	1" tubing, 4 ea. 2'x9' plastic absorber & glazing collectors, 120 gal tank		8,175	7,025	15,200
2860	4 ea. 3'x7' black chrome absorber collectors, 120 gal tank		10,100	7,050	17,150
2880	4 ea. 3'x7' flat black absorber collectors, 120 gal tank		9,425	7,075	16,500

D20 Plumbing

D2020 Domestic Water Distribution

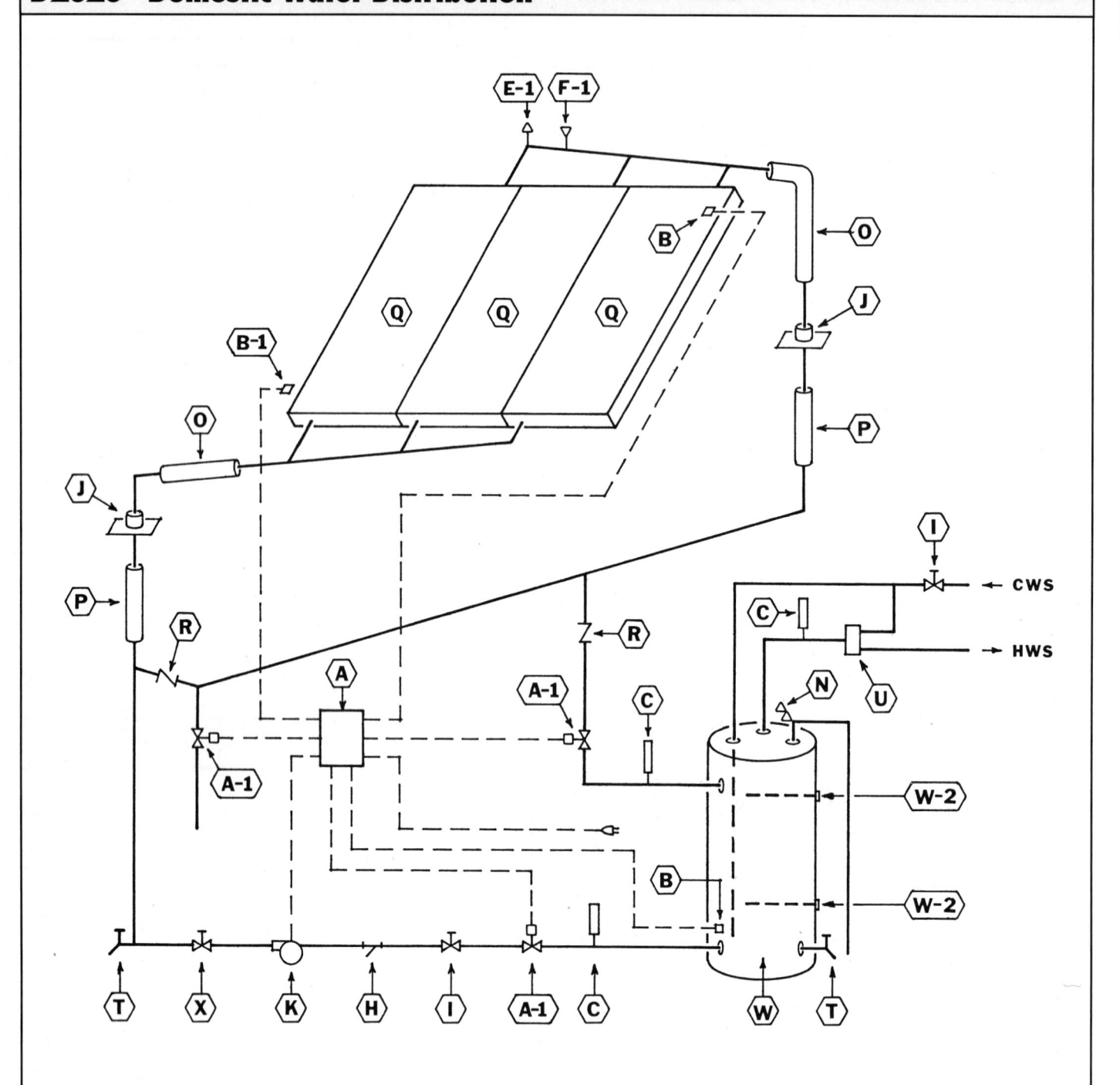

In the draindown direct-collection system, incoming domestic water is heated in the collectors. When the controller activates solar collection, domestic water is first heated as it flows through the collectors and is then pumped to storage. When conditions are no longer suitable for heat collection, the pump shuts off and the water in the loop drains down and out of the system by means of solenoid valves and properly pitched piping.

D20 Plumbing

D2020 Domestic Water Distribution

System Components	QUANTITY	UNIT	MAT.	INST.	TOTAL
SYSTEM D2020 275 2760					
SOLAR, DRAINDOWN, HOT WATER, DIRECT COLLECTION					
3/4" TUBING, THREE 3'X7' BLACK CHROME COLLECTORS					
A, B Differential controller, 2 sensors, thermostat, solar energy system	1.000	Ea.	147	62.50	209.50
A-1 Solenoid valve, solar heating loop, brass, 3/4" diam, 24 volts	3.000	Ea.	450	249	699
B-1 Solar energy sensor, freeze prevention	1.000	Ea.	25.50	23.50	49
C Thermometer, 2" dial	3.000	Ea.	72	141	213
E-1 Vacuum relief valve, 3/4" diam	1.000	Ea.	33	23.50	56.50
F-1 Air vent, automatic, 1/8" fitting	1.000	Ea.	20.50	23.50	44
H Strainer, Y type, bronze body, 3/4" IPS	1.000	Ea.	49.50	40	89.50
I Valve, gate, bronze, NRS, soldered, 3/4" diam	2.000	Ea.	140	75	215
J Vent flashing neoprene	2.000	Ea.	21	75	96
K Circulator, solar heated liquid, 1/25 HP	1.000	Ea.	212	96.50	308.50
N Relief valve temp & press 150 psi 210°F self-closing 3/4" IPS	1.000	Ea.	26.50	25	51.50
O Pipe covering, urethane, ultraviolet cover, 1" wall, 3/4" diam	20.000	L.F.	62.20	137	199.20
P Pipe covering, fiberglass, all service jacket, 1" wall, 3/4" diam	50.000	L.F.	50.50	272.50	323
Roof clamps for solar energy collector panels	3.000	Set	9.48	57.75	67.23
Q Collector panel solar energy blk chrome on copper, 1/8" temp glass 3'x7'	3.000	Ea.	3,375	426	3,801
R Valve, swing check, bronze, regrinding disc, 3/4" diam, soldered	2.000	Ea.	190	75	265
T Drain valve, brass, 3/4" connection	2.000	Ea.	23.20	62	85.20
U Valve, water tempering, bronze, sweat connections, 3/4" diam	1.000	Ea.	153	37.50	190.50
W-2, W Tank, water storage elec elem 2"x1/2# insul 120 gal	1.000	Ea.	2,125	535	2,660
X Valve, globe, bronze, rising stem, 3/4" diam, soldered	1.000	Ea.	150	37.50	187.50
Copper tubing, type L, solder joints, hangers 10' OC 3/4" diam	20.000	L.F.	98.80	197	295.80
Copper tubing, type M, solder joints, hangers 10' OC 3/4" diam	70.000	L.F.	402.50	672	1,074.50
Sensor wire, #22-2 conductor, multistranded	.500	C.L.F.	5.73	34.75	40.48
Wrought copper fittings & solder, 3/4" diam	76.000	Ea.	210.52	3,002	3,212.52
TOTAL			8,052.93	6,380.50	14,433.43

D2020 275	Solar, Draindown, Hot Water Systems		MAT.	INST.	TOTAL
2550	Solar, draindown, hot water				
2580	1/2" tubing, 4 ea. 4' x 4'-4" vacuum tube collectors, 80 gal tank		7,975	6,250	14,225
2760	3/4" tubing, 3 ea. 3'x7' black chrome collectors, 120 gal tank	R235616 -60	8,050	6,375	14,425
2780	3 ea. 3'x7' flat collectors, 120 gal tank		7,575	6,400	13,975
2800	2 ea. 4'x9' flat black & plastic glazing collectors, 120 gal tank		6,975	6,425	13,400
2840	1" tubing, 4 ea. 2'x9' plastic absorber & glazing collectors, 120 gal tank		11,900	8,475	20,375
2860	4 ea. 3'x7' black chrome absorber collectors, 120 gal tank		11,400	8,025	19,425
2880	4 ea. 3'x7' flat black absorber collectors, 120 gal tank		9,650	7,275	16,925

For customer support on your Green Building Costs with RSMeans data, call 800.448.8182.

D20 Plumbing

D2020 Domestic Water Distribution

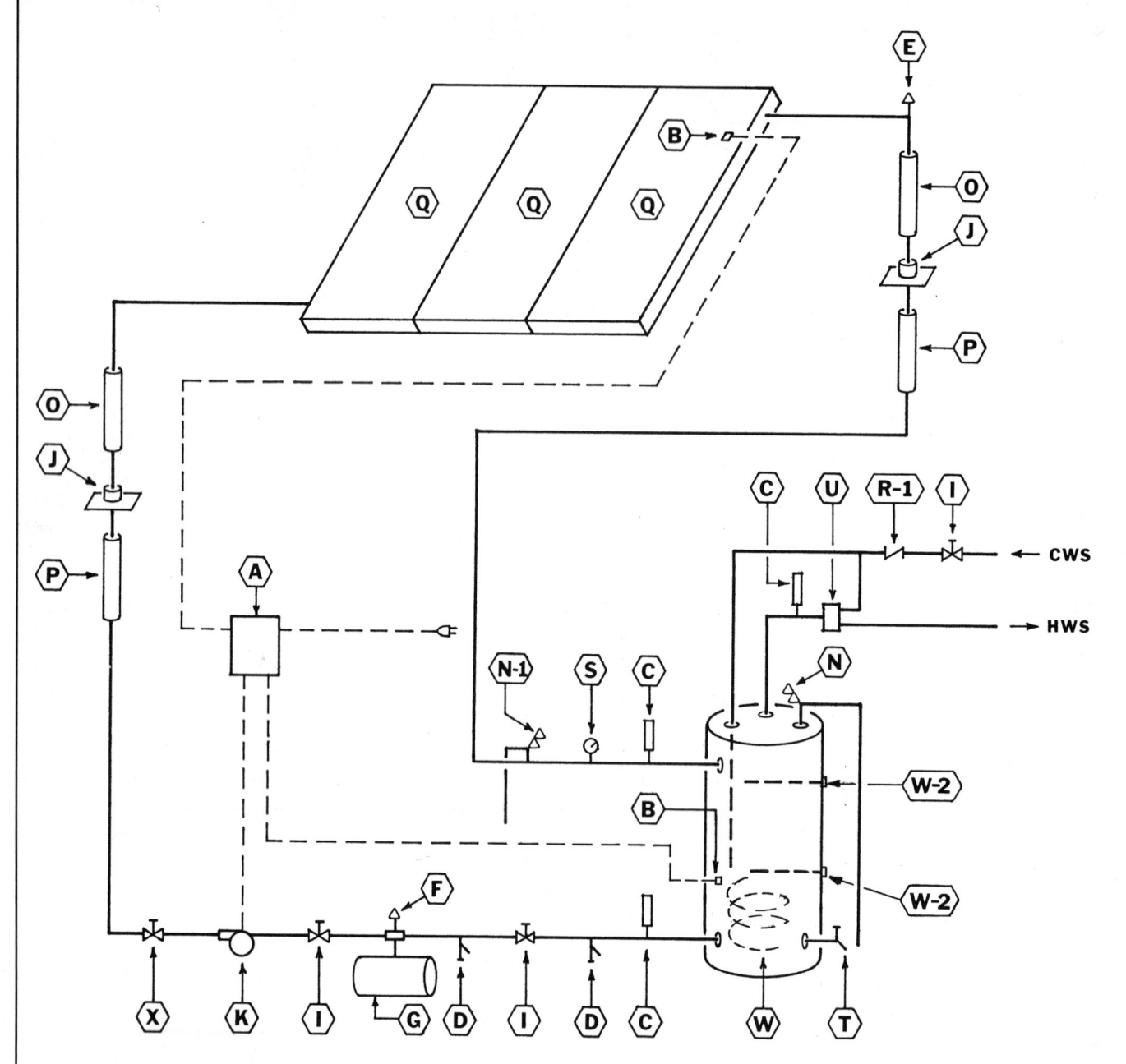

In this closed-loop indirect collection system, fluid with a low freezing temperature, such as propylene glycol, transports heat from the collectors to water storage. The transfer fluid is contained in a closed-loop consisting of collectors, supply and return piping, and a heat exchanger immersed in the storage tank. A typical two-or-three panel system contains 5 to 6 gallons of heat transfer fluid.

When the collectors become approximately 20°F warmer than the storage temperature, a controller activates the circulator. The circulator moves the fluid continuously through the collectors until the temperature difference between the collectors and storage is such that heat collection no longer occurs; at that point, the circulator shuts off. Since the heat transfer fluid has a very low freezing temperature, there is no need for it to be drained from the collectors between periods of collection.

322

For customer support on your Green Building Costs with RSMeans data, call 800.448.8182.

D20 Plumbing

D2020 Domestic Water Distribution

System Components		QUANTITY	UNIT	COST EACH MAT.	COST EACH INST.	TOTAL
	SYSTEM D2020 295 2760					
	SOLAR, CLOSED LOOP, HOT WATER SYSTEM, IMMERSED HEAT EXCHANGER					
	3/4" TUBING, THREE 3' X 7' BLACK CHROME COLLECTORS					
A, B	Differential controller, 2 sensors, thermostat, solar energy system	1.000	Ea.	147	62.50	209.50
C	Thermometer 2" dial	3.000	Ea.	72	141	213
D, T	Fill & drain valves, brass, 3/4" connection	3.000	Ea.	34.80	93	127.80
E	Air vent, manual, 1/8" fitting	1.000	Ea.	2.89	23.50	26.39
F	Air purger	1.000	Ea.	52	62.50	114.50
G	Expansion tank	1.000	Ea.	76	23.50	99.50
I	Valve, gate, bronze, NRS, soldered 3/4" diam	3.000	Ea.	210	112.50	322.50
J	Neoprene vent flashing	2.000	Ea.	21	75	96
K	Circulator, solar heated liquid, 1/25 HP	1.000	Ea.	212	96.50	308.50
N-1, N	Relief valve, temp & press 150 psi 210°F self-closing 3/4" IPS	2.000	Ea.	53	50	103
O	Pipe covering, urethane ultraviolet cover, 1" wall, 3/4" diam	20.000	L.F.	62.20	137	199.20
P	Pipe covering, fiberglass, all service jacket, 1" wall, 3/4" diam	50.000	L.F.	50.50	272.50	323
	Roof clamps for solar energy collector panel	3.000	Set	9.48	57.75	67.23
Q	Collector panel solar blk chrome on copper, 1/8" temp glass, 3'x7'	3.000	Ea.	3,375	426	3,801
R-1	Valve, swing check, bronze, regrinding disc, 3/4" diam, soldered	1.000	Ea.	95	37.50	132.50
S	Pressure gauge, 60 psi, 2-1/2" dial	1.000	Ea.	26.50	23.50	50
U	Valve, water tempering, bronze, sweat connections, 3/4" diam	1.000	Ea.	153	37.50	190.50
W-2, W	Tank, water storage immersed heat exchr elec elem 2"x2# insul 120 Gal	1.000	Ea.	2,125	535	2,660
X	Valve, globe, bronze, rising stem, 3/4" diam, soldered	1.000	Ea.	150	37.50	187.50
	Copper tubing type L, solder joint, hanger 10' OC 3/4" diam	20.000	L.F.	98.80	197	295.80
	Copper tubing, type M, solder joint, hanger 10' OC 3/4" diam	70.000	L.F.	402.50	672	1,074.50
	Sensor wire, #22-2 conductor multistranded	.500	C.L.F.	5.73	34.75	40.48
	Solar energy heat transfer fluid, propylene glycol, anti-freeze	6.000	Gal.	156	159	315
	Wrought copper fittings & solder, 3/4" diam	76.000	Ea.	210.52	3,002	3,212.52
	TOTAL			7,800.92	6,369	14,169.92

D2020 295	Solar, Closed Loop, Hot Water Systems		MAT.	INST.	TOTAL
2550	Solar, closed loop, hot water system, immersed heat exchanger				
2560	3/8" tubing, 3 ea. 4' x 4'-4" vacuum tube collectors, 80 gal. tank		6,975	5,775	12,750
2580	1/2" tubing, 4 ea. 4' x 4'-4" vacuum tube collectors, 80 gal. tank	R235616 -60	7,750	6,225	13,975
2600	120 gal. tank		8,025	6,300	14,325
2640	2 ea. 3'x7' black chrome collectors, 80 gal. tank		6,075	5,950	12,025
2660	120 gal. tank		6,275	5,950	12,225
2760	3/4" tubing, 3 ea. 3'x7' black chrome collectors, 120 gal. tank		7,800	6,375	14,175
2840	1" tubing, 4 ea. 2'x9' plastic absorber & glazing collectors 120 gal. tank		7,775	7,175	14,950
2860	4 ea. 3'x7' black chrome collectors, 120 gal. tank		9,650	7,200	16,850

D30 HVAC

D3010 Energy Supply

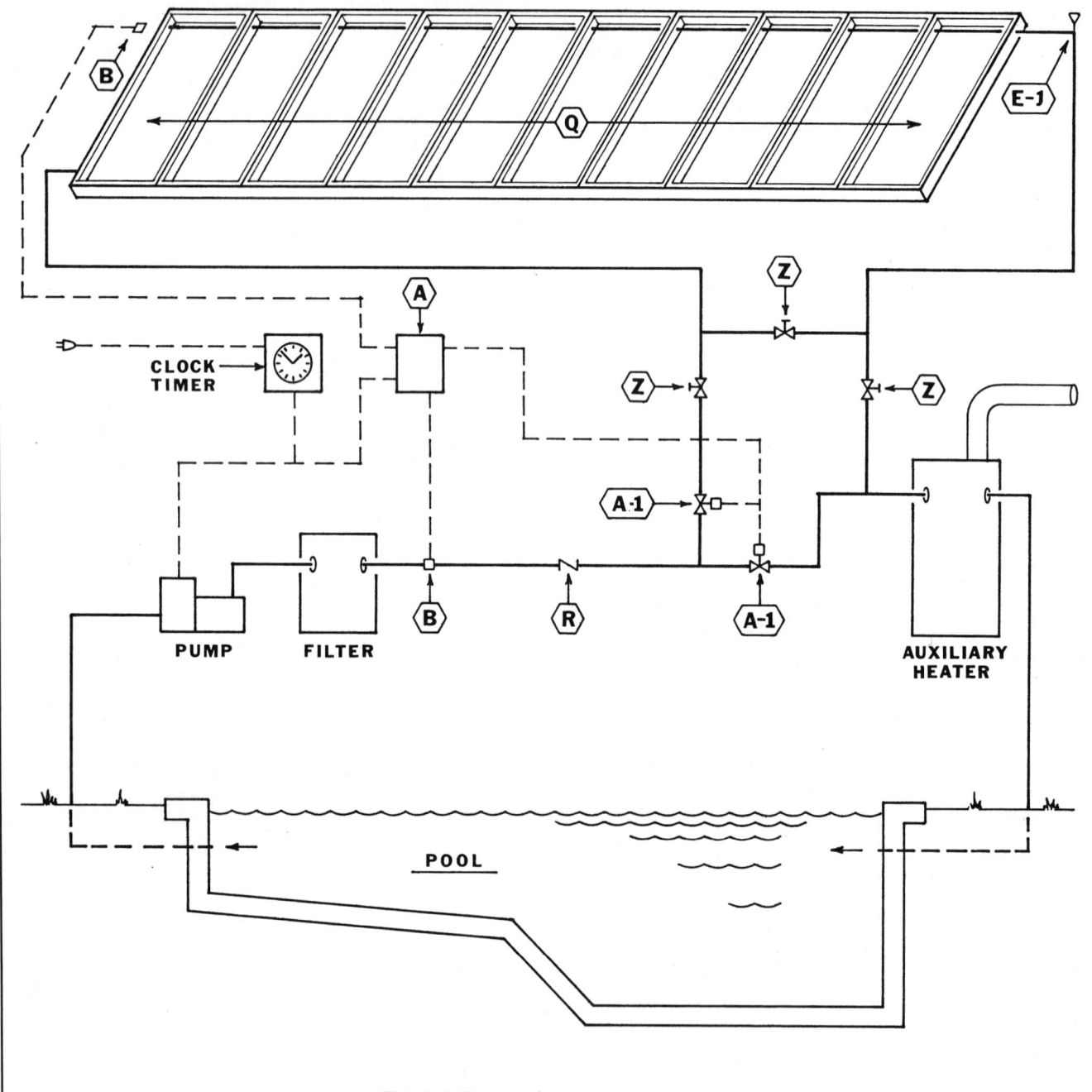

This draindown pool system uses a differential thermostat similar to those used in solar domestic hot water and space heating applications. To heat the pool, the pool water passes through the conventional pump-filter loop and then flows through the collectors. When collection is not possible, or when the pool temperature is reached, all water drains from the solar loop back to the pool through the existing piping. The modes are controlled by solenoid valves or other automatic valves in conjunction with a vacuum breaker relief valve, which facilitates draindown.

D30 HVAC

D3010 Energy Supply

System Components	QUANTITY	UNIT	COST EACH MAT.	COST EACH INST.	TOTAL
SYSTEM D3010 660 2640					
SOLAR SWIMMING POOL HEATER, ROOF MOUNTED COLLECTORS					
TEN 4' X 10' FULLY WETTED UNGLAZED PLASTIC ABSORBERS					
A Differential thermostat/controller, 110V, adj pool pump system	1.000	Ea.	360	375	735
A-1 Solenoid valve, PVC, normally 1 open 1 closed (included)	2.000	Ea.			
B Sensor, thermistor type (included)	2.000	Ea.			
E-1 Valve, vacuum relief	1.000	Ea.	33	23.50	56.50
Q Collector panel, solar energy, plastic, liquid full wetted, 4' x 10'	10.000	Ea.	3,600	2,700	6,300
R Valve, ball check, PVC, socket, 1-1/2" diam	1.000	Ea.	113	37.50	150.50
Z Valve, ball, PVC, socket, 1-1/2" diam	3.000	Ea.	265.50	112.50	378
Pipe, PVC, sch 40, 1-1/2" diam	80.000	L.F.	844	1,680	2,524
Pipe fittings, PVC sch 40, socket joint, 1-1/2" diam	10.000	Ea.	21.30	375	396.30
Sensor wire, #22-2 conductor, multistranded	.500	C.L.F.	5.73	34.75	40.48
Roof clamps for solar energy collector panels	10.000	Set	31.60	192.50	224.10
Roof strap, teflon for solar energy collector panels	26.000	L.F.	715	94.90	809.90
TOTAL			5,989.13	5,625.65	11,614.78

D3010 660	Solar Swimming Pool Heater Systems		MAT.	INST.	TOTAL
2530	Solar swimming pool heater systems, roof mounted collectors				
2540	10 ea. 3'x7' black chrome absorber, 1/8" temp. glass		13,600	4,350	17,950
2560	10 ea. 4'x8' black chrome absorber, 3/16" temp. glass	R235616 -60	15,100	5,175	20,275
2580	10 ea. 3'8"x6' flat black absorber, 3/16" temp. glass		12,000	4,425	16,425
2600	10 ea. 4'x9' flat black absorber, plastic glazing		13,900	5,375	19,275
2620	10 ea. 2'x9' rubber absorber, plastic glazing		15,500	5,825	21,325
2640	10 ea. 4'x10' fully wetted unglazed plastic absorber		6,000	5,625	11,625
2660	Ground mounted collectors				
2680	10 ea. 3'x7' black chrome absorber, 1/8" temp. glass		13,600	4,850	18,450
2700	10 ea. 4'x8' black chrome absorber, 3/16" temp. glass		15,100	5,675	20,775
2720	10 ea. 3'8"x6' flat blk absorber, 3/16" temp. glass		12,000	4,925	16,925
2740	10 ea. 4'x9' flat blk absorber, plastic glazing		13,900	5,875	19,775
2760	10 ea. 2'x9' rubber absorber, plastic glazing		15,500	6,125	21,625
2780	10 ea. 4'x10' fully wetted unglazed plastic absorber		5,975	6,125	12,100

D30 HVAC

D3010 Energy Supply

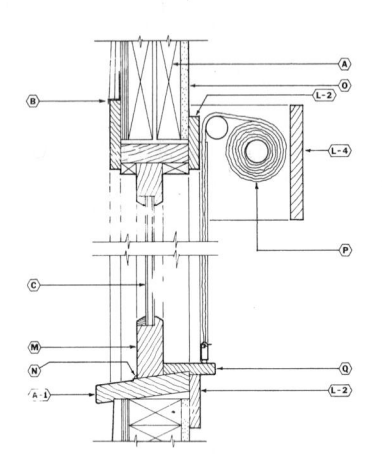

Solar Direct Gain Glazing — Door Panels: In a Direct Gain System the collection, absorption, and storage of solar energy occur directly within the building's living space. In this system, a section of the building's south wall is removed and replaced with glazing. The glazing in the System Component example consists of three standard insulating glass door panels preassembled in wood frames. A direct gain system also includes a thermal storage mass and night insulation.

During the heating season, solar radiation enters the living space directly through the glazing and is converted to heat, which either warms the air or is stored in the mass. The storage mass is typically masonry or water. Masonry often serves as a basic structural component of the building (e.g., a wall or floor). In this system the cost of adding mass to the building is not included. To reduce heat loss through the south facing glass, thereby increasing overall thermal performance, night insulation is included in this system.

System Components		QUANTITY	UNIT	COST EACH MAT.	COST EACH INST.	TOTAL
SYSTEM D3010 682 2600						
SOLAR PASSIVE HEATING, DIRECT GAIN, 3'X6'8" DOUBLE GLAZED DOOR PANEL						
3 PANELS WIDE						
A	Framing headers over openings, fir 2" x 12"	.025	M.B.F.	29.55	53.25	82.80
A-1	Treated wood sleeper, 1" x 2"	.002	M.B.F.	3.95	6.35	10.30
B	Aluminum flashing, mill finish, .013 thick	5.000	S.F.	7.28	32.64	39.92
	Studs, 8' high wall, 2" x 4"	.020	M.B.F.	13.80	27	40.80
L-2	Interior casing, stock pine, 11/16" x 2-1/2"	25.000	L.F.	39	61.75	100.75
L-4	Valance 1" x 8"	12.000	L.F.	17.52	37.08	54.60
M	Vinyl clad sliding door, insulated glass, 6' wide	1.000	Ea.	2,368	396.80	2,764.80
N	Caulking/sealants, silicone rubber, cartridges	.250	Gal.	14.38		14.38
O	Drywall, gypsum plasterboard, nailed to studs, 5/8" standard	39.000	S.F.	15.21	24.18	39.39
O	For taping and finishing, add	39.000	S.F.	1.95	24.18	26.13
P	Mylar shade, dbl. layer heat reflective	49.640	S.F.	330.11	44.68	374.79
Q	Stool cap, pine, 11/16" x 3-1/2"	12.000	L.F.	28.68	37.08	65.76
	Paint wood trim	40.000	S.F.	6	25.60	31.60
	Demolition, framing	84.000	S.F.		20.58	20.58
	Demolition, shingles	84.000	S.F.		116.76	116.76
	Demolition, drywall	84.000	S.F.		41.16	41.16
	TOTAL			2,875.43	949.09	3,824.52

D3010 682	Solar Direct Gain Glazing, Door Panels	COST EACH MAT.	COST EACH INST.	TOTAL
2550	Solar passive heating, direct gain, 3'x6'8", double glazed door			
2560	One panel wide	1,450	515	1,965
2580	Two panels wide	2,200	740	2,940
2600	Three panels wide	2,875	950	3,825

D30 HVAC

D3010 Energy Supply

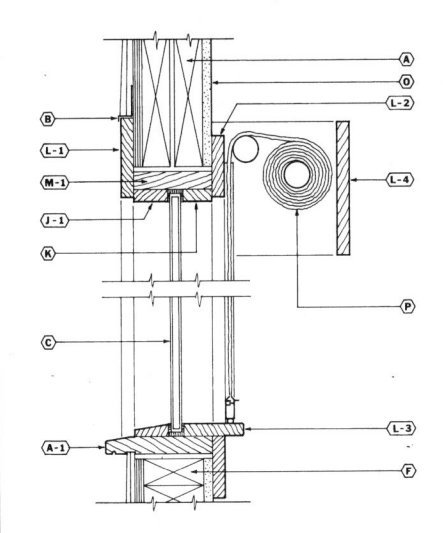

Solar Direct Gain Glazing — Window Units: In a Direct Gain System, collection, absorption, and storage of solar energy occur directly within the building's living space. In this system, a section of the building's south wall is removed and replaced with glazing. The glazing consists of standard insulating replacement glass units in wood site-built frames. A direct gain system also includes a thermal storage mass and night insulation.

During the heating season, solar radiation enters the living space directly through the glazing and is converted to heat, which either warms the air or is stored in the mass. The thermal storage mass is typically masonry or water. Masonry often serves as a basic structural component of the building (e.g., a wall or floor). In this system the cost of adding mass to the building is not included. To reduce heat loss through the south facing glass, thereby increasing overall thermal performance, night insulation is included in this system.

	System Components	QUANTITY	UNIT	MAT.	INST.	TOTAL
	SYSTEM D3010 684 2600 **SOLAR PASSIVE HEATING, DIRECT GAIN, 2'-6"X5' DBL. GLAZED WINDOW PANEL** **3 PANELS WIDE**					
A	Framing headers over openings, fir 2" x 8"	.022	M.B.F.	16.17	60.50	76.67
A-1	Wood exterior sill, oak, no horns, 8/4 x 8" deep	8.000	L.F.	62.80	98.80	161.60
B	Aluminum flashing, mill finish, .013 thick	4.160	S.F.	3.79	16.97	20.76
C	Glazing, insul glass 2 lite 3/16" float 5/8" thick unit, 15-30 S.F.	38.000	S.F.	575.70	495.90	1,071.60
F	2"x4" sill blocking	.013	M.B.F.	8.97	47.13	56.10
	Mullion	.027	M.B.F.	18.63	36.45	55.08
J-1	Exterior window stop 1" x 2"	45.000	L.F.	13.95	84.15	98.10
	Exterior sill stock water repellent 1" x 3"	8.000	L.F.	19.12	24.72	43.84
K	Interior window stop 1" x 3"	45.000	L.F.	65.25	115.65	180.90
L-1	Exterior trim and molding, corner board, pine, D & better, 1" x 6"	28.000	L.F.	28.08	74.16	102.24
L-2	Interior casing, 1" x 4"	28.000	L.F.	55.16	78.68	133.84
L-3	Apron	8.000	L.F.	17.04	22.48	39.52
L-4	Valance 1" x 8"	10.000	L.F.	14.60	30.90	45.50
M-1	Window frame	52.000	L.F.	280.80	133.64	414.44
O	Drywall, gypsum plasterboard, nailed/screw to studs, 5/8" standard	39.000	S.F.	15.21	24.18	39.39
O	For taping and finishing, add	39.000	S.F.	1.95	24.18	26.13
	Demolition, wall framing	60.000	S.F.		16.66	16.66
	Demolition, shingles	60.000	S.F.		83.40	83.40
P	Mylar triple layer heat reflective shade (see desc. sheet)	37.500	S.F.	313.13	33.75	346.88
	Demolition, drywall	60.000	S.F.		29.40	29.40
	Paint interior & exterior trim	200.000	L.F.	30	128	158
	TOTAL			1,540.35	1,659.70	3,200.05

D3010 684	Solar Direct Gain Glazing-Window Panels	MAT.	INST.	TOTAL
2550	Solar passive heating, direct gain, 2'-6"x5', double glazed window			
2560	One panel wide	555	605	1,160
2580	Two panels wide	1,125	1,625	2,750
2600	Three panels wide	1,550	1,650	3,200

D30 HVAC

D3010 Energy Supply

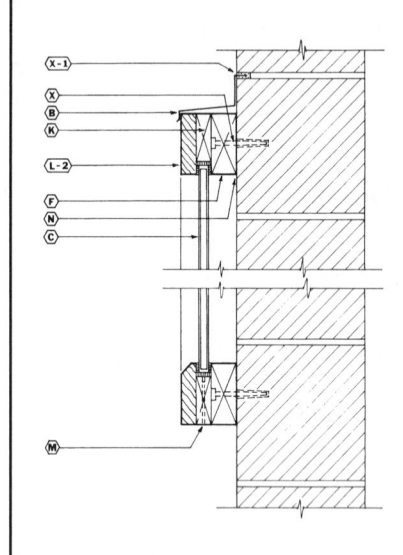

Solar Indirect Gain — Thermal Wall: The thermal storage wall is an Indirect Gain System because collection, absorption, and storage of solar energy occur outside the living space. This system consists of an unvented existing masonry wall located between south facing glazing and the space to be heated. The outside surface of the masonry wall is painted black to enable it to absorb maximum thermal energy. Standard double glazed units in wooden site-built frames are added to the south side of the building.

Thermal energy conducts through the masonry wall and radiates into the living space. A masonry thermal storage wall can also contain vents that allow warm air to flow into the living space through convection.

Indirect gain solar systems can be retrofitted to masonry walls constructed from a wide variety of building materials, including concrete, concrete block (solid and filled), brick, stone and adobe.

System Components	QUANTITY	UNIT	MAT.	INST.	TOTAL
SYSTEM D3010 686 2600					
SOLAR PASSIVE HEATING, INDIRECT GAIN, THERMAL STORAGE WALL					
3' X 6'-8" DOUBLE GLAZED PANEL, THREE PANELS WIDE					
B Aluminum flashing, mill finish, .013 thick	5.500	S.F.	5.01	22.44	27.45
C Glazing, insul glass 2 lite 3/16" float 5/8" thick unit, 15-30 S.F.	54.000	S.F.	818.10	704.70	1,522.80
F Framing 2" x 4" lumber	.030	M.B.F.	20.70	74.25	94.95
K Molding, miscellaneous, 1" x 3"	44.000	L.F.	63.80	113.08	176.88
L-2 Wood batten, 1" x 4", custom pine or cedar	44.000	L.F.	39.60	135.96	175.56
M Drill holes, 4 per panel 1/2" diameter	30.000	Inch		41.10	41.10
N Caulking/sealants, silicone rubber, cartridges	.250	Gal.	14.38		14.38
X Lag screws 3/8" x 3" long	20.000	Ea.	6.20	82.40	88.60
X-1 Reglet	8.000	L.F.	.40	36.08	36.48
Trim, primer & 1 coat	44.000	L.F.	10.12	35.64	45.76
Layout and drill holes for lag screws	20.000	Ea.	1.20	196	197.20
Expansion shields for lag screws	20.000	Ea.	9	77.20	86.20
TOTAL			988.51	1,518.85	2,507.36

D3010 686	Passive Solar Indirect Gain Wall	MAT.	INST.	TOTAL
2550	Solar passive heating, indirect gain			
2560	3'x6'8", double glazed thermal storage wall, one panel wide	355	580	935
2580	Two panels wide	670	1,025	1,695
2600	Three panels wide	990	1,525	2,515

D30 HVAC

D3010 Energy Supply

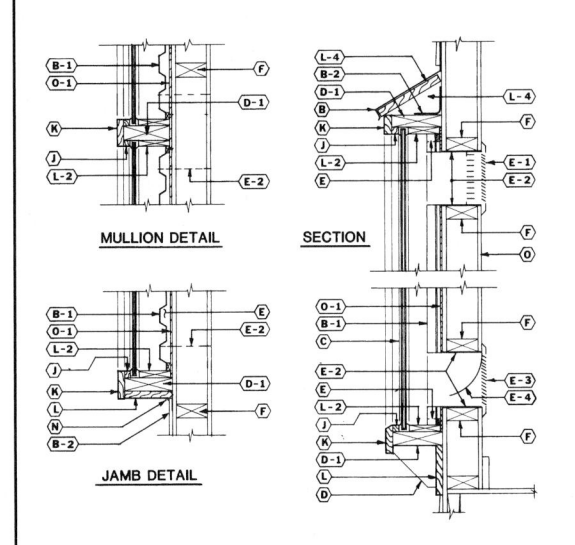

Solar Indirect Gain — Thermosyphon Panel: The Thermosyphon Air Panel (TAP) System is an indirect gain system used primarily for daytime heating because it does not include thermal mass. This site-built TAP System makes use of double glazing and a ribbed aluminum absorber plate. The panel is framed in wood and attached to the south side of a building. Solar radiation passes through the glass and is absorbed by the absorber plate. As the absorber plate heats, the air between it and the glass also heats. Vents cut through the building's south wall and the absorber plate near the top and bottom of the TAP allow hot air to circulate into the building by means of natural convection.

	System Components	QUANTITY	UNIT	MAT.	INST.	TOTAL
	SYSTEM D3010 688 2600					
	SOLAR PASSIVE HEATING, INDIRECT GAIN, THERMOSYPHON PANEL					
	3'X6'8" DOUBLE GLAZED PANEL, THREE PANELS WIDE					
B	Aluminum flashing and sleeves, mill finish, .013 thick	8.000	S.F.	20.93	93.84	114.77
B-1	Aluminum ribbed, 4" pitch, on steel frame .032" mill finish	45.000	S.F.	129.60	141.30	270.90
B-2	Angle brackets	9.000	Ea.	7.47	31.77	39.24
C	Glazing, insul glass 2 lite 3/16" float 5/8" thick unit, 15-30 S.F.	45.000	S.F.	681.75	587.25	1,269
D	Support brackets, fir 2"x6"	.003	M.B.F.	2.07	10.88	12.95
D-1	Framing fir 2" x 6"	.040	M.B.F.	32.40	124	156.40
E	Corrugated end closure	15.000	L.F.	15.75	45.60	61.35
E-1	Register, multilouvre operable 6" x 30"	3.000	Ea.	93	121.50	214.50
E-3	Grille 6" x 30"	3.000	Ea.	76.50	94.50	171
E-4	Waterproofed kraft with sisal or fiberglass fibers	.038	C.S.F.	.87	.63	1.50
F	House wall blocking 2" x 4"	.012	M.B.F.	27.60	60	87.60
J	Absorber supports & glass stop	54.000	L.F.	25.92	123.66	149.58
K	Exterior & bottom trim & interior glazing stop	40.000	L.F.	56.40	232.18	288.58
L	Exterior trim and molding, cornice board, pine, #2, 1" x 6"	24.000	L.F.	21.60	59.28	80.88
L-2	Trim cap	8.000	L.F.	11.68	24.72	36.40
N	Caulking/sealants, silicone rubber, cartridges	.250	Gal.	14.38		14.38
O	Drywall, nailed & taped, 5/8" thick	60.000	S.F.	23.40	37.20	60.60
O	For taping and finishing, add	60.000	S.F.	3	37.20	40.20
O-1	Insulation foil faced exterior wall	45.000	S.F.	21.60	20.70	42.30
	Demolition, framing	60.000	S.F.		20.58	20.58
	Demolition, drywall	60.000	S.F.		29.40	29.40
	Paint absorber plate black	45.000	S.F.	6.30	57.60	63.90
	Finish paint	125.000	S.F.	18.75	80	98.75
	Paint walls & ceiling with roller, primer & 1 coat	60.000	S.F.	8.40	31.80	40.20
	TOTAL			**1,299.37**	**2,065.59**	**3,364.96**

D3010 688	Passive Solar Indirect Gain Panel	MAT.	INST.	TOTAL
2550	Solar passive heating, indirect gain			
2560	3'x6'8", double glazed thermosyphon panel, one panel wide	445	730	1,175
2580	Two panels wide	870	1,400	2,270
2600	Three panels wide	1,300	2,075	3,375

D30 HVAC

D3010 Energy Supply

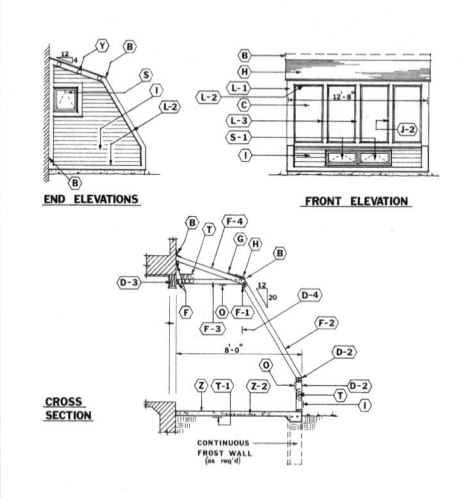

Solar Attached Sunspace: The attached sunspace, a room adjacent to the south side of a building, is designed solely for heat collection. During the heating season, solar radiation enters the sunspace through south facing glass. Radiation is absorbed by elements in the space and converted to heat. This sunspace is thermally isolated from the building. A set of sliding glass doors connecting the sunspace to the building space is closed to prevent night heat losses from the living space. This attached sunspace uses standard size, double glazed units and has a concrete slab floor. Since the required depth of footings (if required) is dependent on local frost conditions, costs of footings at depths of 2′, 3′ and 4′ are provided with the base cost of system as shown.

	System Components	QUANTITY	UNIT	MAT.	INST.	TOTAL
	SYSTEM D3010 690 2560					
	SOLAR PASSIVE HEATING, DIRECT GAIN, ATTACHED SUNSPACE					
	WOOD FRAMED, SLAB ON GRADE					
B	Aluminum, flashing, mill finish	21.000	S.F.	19.11	85.68	104.79
C	Glazing, double, tempered glass	72.000	S.F.	1,090.80	939.60	2,030.40
D-2-4	Knee & end wall framing	.188	M.B.F.	133.48	230.30	363.78
F	Ledgers, headers and rafters	.028	M.B.F.	124.89	271.50	396.39
	Building paper, asphalt felt sheathing paper 15 lb	240.000	S.F.	14.16	40.08	54.24
G	Sheathing plywood on roof CDX 1/2"	240.000	S.F.	163.20	211.20	374.40
H	Asphalt shingles inorganic class A 210-235 lb/sq	1.000	Sq.	82.50	108	190.50
I	Wood siding, match existing	164.000	S.F.	797.04	342.76	1,139.80
	Window stop, interior or external	96.000	L.F.	59.52	359.04	418.56
L-1	Exterior trim and molding, fascia, pine, D & better, 1" x 6"	44.000	L.F.	51.48	108.68	160.16
L-2, L-3	Exterior trim 1" x 4"	206.000	L.F.	185.40	636.54	821.94
O	Drywall, taping & finishing joints	200.000	S.F.	10	124	134
O	Drywall, 1/2" on walls, standard, no finish	200.000	S.F.	74	124	198
S, S-1	Windows, wood, awning type, double glazed, with screens	4.000	Ea.	2,440	308	2,748
T	Insulation batts, fiberglass, faced	210.000	S.F.	142.80	96.60	239.40
T-1	Polyethylene vapor barrier, standard, 4 mil	2.500	C.S.F.	5.68	33.40	39.08
Y	Button vents	6.000	Ea.	19.38	61.80	81.18
Z	Slab on grade, not including finish, 4" thick	1.234	C.Y.	197.44	133.84	331.28
	Floor finishing, steel trowel	100.000	S.F.		97	97
Z-2	Mesh, welded wire 6 x 6, #10/10	1.000	C.S.F.	16.60	38	54.60
	Paint interior, exterior and trim	330.000	S.F.	49.50	280.50	330
	TOTAL			5,676.98	4,630.52	10,307.50

D3010 690	Passive Solar Sunspace	MAT.	INST.	TOTAL
2550	Solar passive heating, direct gain, attached sunspace, 100 S.F.			
2560	Wood framed, slab on grade	5,675	4,625	10,300
2580	2′ deep frost wall	6,125	5,675	11,800
2600	3′ deep frost wall	6,275	6,100	12,375
2620	4′ deep frost wall	6,450	6,500	12,950

D30 HVAC

D3030 Cooling Generating Systems

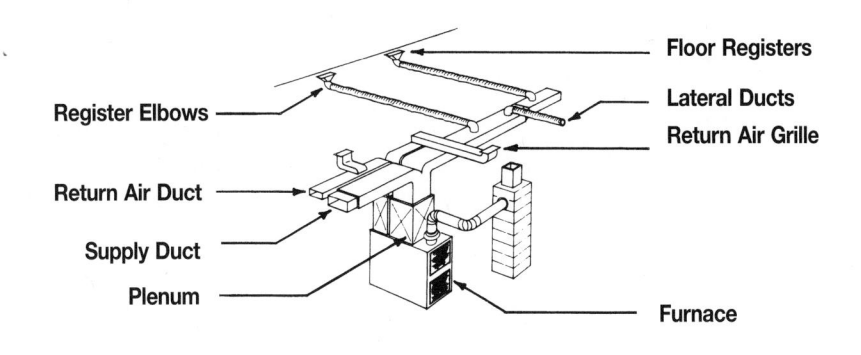

System Components	QUANTITY	UNIT	COST EACH MAT.	COST EACH INST.	COST EACH TOTAL
SYSTEM D3030 214 1200 HEATING/COOLING, GAS FIRED FORCED AIR, ONE ZONE, 1200 S.F. BLDG, SEER 14					
Thermostat manual	1.000	Ea.	47	95	142
Intermittent pilot	1.000	Ea.	273		273
Furnace, 3 Ton cooling, 115 MBH	1.000	Ea.	2,625	440	3,065
Cooling tubing 25 feet	1.000	Ea.	320		320
Ductwork	158.000	Lb.	99.54	1,374.60	1,474.14
Ductwork connection	12.000	Ea.	195	528	723
Supply ductwork	176.000	SF Surf	174.24	1,029.60	1,203.84
Supply grill	2.000	Ea.	62	66	128
Duct insulation	1.000	L.F.	492.48	727.20	1,219.68
Return register	1.000	Ea.	167.40	276	443.40
TOTAL			4,455.66	4,536.40	8,992.06

D3030 214	Heating/Cooling System	COST EACH MAT.	COST EACH INST.	COST EACH TOTAL
1200	Heating/Cooling system, gas fired, 3 ton, SEER 14, 1200 S.F. Bldg	4,450	4,525	8,975
1300	5 ton, 2000 S.F. Bldg	5,400	7,200	12,600
1400	Heating/Cooling system, heat pump 3 ton, SEER 14, 1200 S.F. Bldg	5,575	5,800	11,375
1500	5 ton, SEER 14, 2000 S.F. Bldg	7,375	6,750	14,125

For customer support on your Green Building Costs with RSMeans data, call 800.448.8182.

D30 HVAC

D3050 Terminal & Package Units

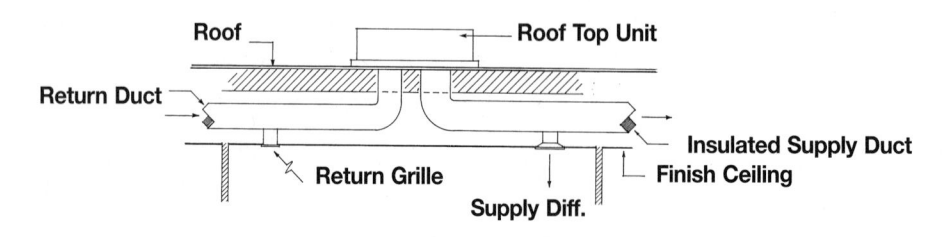

System Description: Rooftop single zone units are electric cooling and gas heat. Duct systems are low velocity, galvanized steel supply and return. Price variations between sizes are due to several factors. Jumps in the cost of the rooftop unit occur when the manufacturer shifts from the largest capacity unit on a small frame to the smallest capacity on the next larger frame, or changes from one compressor to two. As the unit capacity increases for larger areas the duct distribution grows in proportion. For most applications there is a tradeoff point where it is less expensive and more efficient to utilize smaller units with short simple distribution systems. Larger units also require larger initial supply and return ducts which can create a space problem. Supplemental heat may be desired in colder locations. The table below is based on one unit supplying the area listed. The 10,000 S.F. unit for bars and taverns is not listed because a nominal 110 ton unit would be required and this is above the normal single zone rooftop capacity.

System Components	QUANTITY	UNIT	MAT.	INST.	TOTAL
SYSTEM D3050 152 1280					
ROOFTOP, SINGLE ZONE, AIR CONDITIONER SEER 14					
APARTMENT CORRIDORS, 500 S.F., .92 TON					
Roof top AC, curb, econ, sgl zone, elec cool, gas ht, 3 ton, 60 MBH, SEER14	1.000	Ea.	2,001	897	2,898
Ductwork package for rooftop single zone units	1.000	System	205.16	1,265	1,470.16
TOTAL			2,206.16	2,162	4,368.16
COST PER S.F.			4.41	4.32	8.73

D3050 152	Rooftop Single Zone Unit Systems SEER 14	MAT.	INST.	TOTAL
1260	Rooftop, single zone, air conditioner SEER 14			
1280	Apartment corridors, 500 S.F., .92 ton SEER 14	4.40	4.30	8.70
1320	1,000 S.F., 1.83 ton	4.39	4.30	8.69
1360	1500 S.F., 2.75 ton	2.92	3.55	6.47
1400	3,000 S.F., 5.50 ton	2.51	3.41	5.92
1440	5,000 S.F., 9.17 ton	2.46	3.10	5.56
1480	10,000 S.F., 18.33 ton	3.02	2.92	5.94
1560	Banks or libraries, 500 S.F., 2.08 ton SEER 14	10	9.80	19.80
1600	1,000 S.F., 4.17 ton	6.65	8.05	14.70
1640	1,500 S.F., 6.25 ton	5.70	7.75	13.45
1680	3,000 S.F., 12.50 ton	5.60	7.05	12.65
1720	5,000 S.F., 20.80 ton	6.85	6.60	13.45
1760	10,000 S.F., 41.67 ton	8.50	6.60	15.10
1840	Bars and taverns, 500 S.F. 5.54 ton SEER 14	13.95	13	26.95
1880	1,000 S.F., 11.08 ton	13.65	11.15	24.80
1920	1,500 S.F., 16.62 ton	12.25	10.35	22.60
1960	3,000 S.F., 33.25 ton	23	9.90	32.90
2000	5,000 S.F., 55.42 ton	19.50	9.90	29.40
2080	Bowling alleys, 500 S.F., 2.83 ton SEER 14	9	10.95	19.95
2120	1,000 S.F., 5.67 ton	7.75	10.55	18.30
2160	1,500 S.F., 8.50 ton	7.60	9.60	17.20
2200	3,000 S.F., 17.00 ton	6.90	9.20	16.10
2240	5,000 S.F., 28.33 ton	12.40	8.95	21.35
2280	10,000 S.F., 56.67 ton	10.60	8.95	19.55
2360	Department stores, 500 S.F., 1.46 ton SEER 14	7	6.85	13.85
2400	1,000 S.F., 2.92 ton	4.64	5.65	10.29

D30 HVAC

D3050 Terminal & Package Units

D3050 152 Rooftop Single Zone Unit Systems SEER 14

		COST PER S.F.		
		MAT.	INST.	TOTAL
2440	1,500 S.F., 4.37 ton	3.99	5.40	9.39
2480	3,000 S.F., 8.75 ton	3.92	4.94	8.86
2520	5,000 S.F., 14.58 ton	3.55	4.73	8.28
2560	10,000 S.F., 29.17 ton	6.40	4.61	11.01
2640	Drug stores, 500 S.F., 3.33 ton SEER 14	10.60	12.90	23.50
2680	1,000 S.F., 6.67 ton	9.10	12.40	21.50
2720	1,500 S.F., 10.00 ton	8.95	11.30	20.25
2760	3,000 S.F., 20.00 ton	11	10.60	21.60
2800	5,000 S.F., 33.33 ton	14.60	10.55	25.15
2840	10,000 S.F., 66.67 ton	12.50	10.55	23.05
2920	Factories, 500 S.F., 1.67 ton SEER 14	7.95	7.85	15.80
2960	1,000 S.F., 3.33 ton	5.30	6.45	11.75
3000	1,500 S.F., 5.00 ton	4.56	6.20	10.76
3040	3,000 S.F., 10.00 ton	4.47	5.65	10.12
3080	5,000 S.F., 16.67 ton	4.05	5.40	9.45
3120	10,000 S.F., 33.33 ton	7.30	5.25	12.55
3200	Food supermarkets, 500 S.F., 1.42 ton SEER 14	6.80	6.65	13.45
3240	1,000 S.F., 2.83 ton	4.46	5.45	9.91
3280	1,500 S.F., 4.25 ton	3.87	5.25	9.12
3320	3,000 S.F., 8.50 ton	3.80	4.80	8.60
3360	5,000 S.F., 14.17 ton	3.44	4.60	8.04
3400	10,000 S.F., 28.33 ton	6.20	4.48	10.68
3480	Medical centers, 500 S.F., 1.17 ton SEER 14	5.60	5.50	11.10
3520	1,000 S.F., 2.33 ton	5.60	5.45	11.05
3560	1,500 S.F., 3.50 ton	3.71	4.52	8.23
3600	3,000 S.F., 7.00 ton	3.19	4.34	7.53
3640	5,000 S.F., 11.67 ton	3.13	3.95	7.08
3680	10,000 S.F., 23.33 ton	3.85	3.71	7.56
3760	Offices, 500 S.F., 1.58 ton SEER 14	7.60	7.45	15.05
3800	1,000 S.F., 3.17 ton	5.05	6.15	11.20
3840	1,500 S.F., 4.75 ton	4.34	5.90	10.24
3880	3,000 S.F., 9.50 ton	4.26	5.35	9.61
3920	5,000 S.F., 15.83 ton	3.86	5.15	9.01
3960	10,000 S.F., 31.67 ton	6.95	5	11.95
4000	Restaurants, 500 S.F., 2.50 ton SEER 14	12	11.75	23.75
4040	1,000 S.F., 5.00 ton	6.85	9.30	16.15
4080	1,500 S.F., 7.50 ton	6.70	8.45	15.15
4120	3,000 S.F., 15.00 ton	6.10	8.10	14.20
4160	5,000 S.F., 25.00 ton	8.25	7.95	16.20
4200	10,000 S.F., 50.00 ton	9.35	7.90	17.25
4240	Schools and colleges, 500 S.F., 1.92 ton SEER 14	9.20	9	18.20
4280	1,000 S.F., 3.83 ton	6.10	7.45	13.55
4320	1,500 S.F., 5.75 ton	5.25	7.15	12.40
4360	3,000 S.F., 11.50 ton	5.15	6.50	11.65
4400	5,000 S.F., 19.17 ton	6.30	6.10	12.40
4440	10,000 S.F., 38.33 ton	7.80	6.05	13.85

D30 HVAC

D3050 Terminal & Package Units

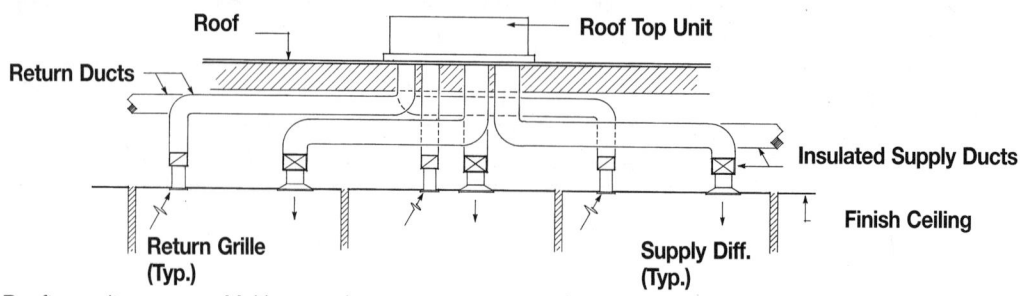

System Description: Rooftop units are multizone with up to 12 zones, and include electric cooling, gas heat, thermostats, filters, supply and return fans complete. Duct systems are low velocity, galvanized steel supply and return with insulated supplies.

Multizone units cost more per ton of cooling than single zone. However, they offer flexibility where load conditions are varied due to heat generating areas or exposure to radiational heating. For example, perimeter offices on the "sunny side" may require cooling at the same time "shady side" or central offices may require heating. It is possible to accomplish similar results using duct heaters in branches of the single zone unit. However, heater location could be a problem and total system operating energy efficiency could be lower.

System Components	QUANTITY	UNIT	MAT.	INST.	TOTAL
SYSTEM D3050 157 1280					
ROOFTOP, MULTIZONE, AIR CONDITIONER SEER 14					
APARTMENT CORRIDORS, 3,000 S.F., 5.50 TON					
Rooftop multizone unit, standard controls, curb	1.000	Ea.	48,180	2,090	50,270
Ductwork package for rooftop multizone units	1.000	System	1,732.50	14,437.50	16,170
TOTAL			49,912.50	16,527.50	66,440
COST PER S.F.			16.64	5.51	22.15

Note A: Small single zone unit recommended.
Note B: A combination of multizone units recommended.

D3050 157	Rooftop Multizone Unit Systems SEER 14	MAT.	INST.	TOTAL
1240	Rooftop, multizone, air conditioner SEER 14			
1260	Apartment corridors, 1,500 S.F., 2.75 ton. See Note A. SEER 14			
1280	3,000 S.F., 5.50 ton	16.63	5.50	22.13
1320	10,000 S.F., 18.30 ton	11.25	5.30	16.55
1360	15,000 S.F., 27.50 ton	11.35	5.30	16.65
1400	20,000 S.F., 36.70 ton	11.60	5.30	16.90
1440	25,000 S.F., 45.80 ton	10.75	5.30	16.05
1520	Banks or libraries, 1,500 S.F., 6.25 ton, SEER 14	38	12.50	50.50
1560	3,000 S.F., 12.50 ton	31.50	12.25	43.75
1600	10,000 S.F., 41.67 ton	24.50	12.10	36.60
1640	15,000 S.F., 62.50 ton	17.75	12	29.75
1680	20,000 S.F., 83.33 ton	17.75	12	29.75
1720	25,000 S.F., 104.00 ton	15.55	11.95	27.50
1800	Bars and taverns, 1,500 S.F., 16.62 ton, SEER 14	82.50	18.05	100.55
1840	3,000 S.F., 33.24 ton	68	17.40	85.40
1880	10,000 S.F., 110.83 ton	39.50	17.30	56.80
1920	15,000 S.F., 165 ton, See Note B.			
1960	20,000 S.F., 220 ton, See Note B.			
2000	25,000 S.F., 275 ton, See Note B.			
2080	Bowling alleys, 1,500 S.F., 8.50 ton, SEER 14	51.50	17.05	68.55
2120	3,000 S.F., 17.00 ton	43	16.65	59.65
2160	10,000 S.F., 56.70 ton	33.50	16.45	49.95
2200	15,000 S.F., 85.00 ton	24	16.35	40.35
2240	20,000 S.F., 113.00 ton	21	16.25	37.25
2280	25,000 S.F., 140.00 ton see Note B.			
2360	Department stores, 1,500 S.F., 4.37 ton, See Note A. SEER 14			

D30 HVAC

D3050 Terminal & Package Units

D3050 157	Rooftop Multizone Unit Systems SEER 14	MAT.	INST.	TOTAL
2400	3,000 S.F., 8.75 ton	26.50	8.75	35.25
2440	10,000 S.F., 29.17 ton	18.40	8.40	26.80
2480	15,000 S.F., 43.75 ton	17.10	8.45	25.55
2520	20,000 S.F., 58.33 ton	12.40	8.40	20.80
2560	25,000 S.F., 72.92 ton	12.40	8.40	20.80
2640	Drug stores, 1,500 S.F., 10.00 ton SEER 14	60.50	20	80.50
2680	3,000 S.F., 20.00 ton	41	19.30	60.30
2720	10,000 S.F., 66.66 ton	28.50	19.20	47.70
2760	15,000 S.F., 100.00 ton	25	19.15	44.15
2800	20,000 S.F., 135 ton, See Note B.			
2840	25,000 S.F., 165 ton, See Note B.			
2920	Factories, 1,500 S.F., 5 ton, See Note A SEER 14			
2960	3,000 S.F., 10.00 ton	30.50	10	40.50
3000	10,000 S.F., 33.33 ton	21	9.60	30.60
3040	15,000 S.F., 50.00 ton	19.55	9.70	29.25
3080	20,000 S.F., 66.66 ton	14.20	9.60	23.80
3120	25,000 S.F., 83.33 ton	14.20	9.60	23.80
3200	Food supermarkets, 1,500 S.F., 4.25 ton, See Note A. SEER 14			
3240	3,000 S.F., 8.50 ton	25.50	8.50	34
3280	10,000 S.F., 28.33 ton	17.55	8.15	25.70
3320	15,000 S.F., 42.50 ton	16.65	8.25	24.90
3360	20,000 S.F., 56.67 ton	12.05	8.15	20.20
3400	25,000 S.F., 70.83 ton	12.05	8.15	20.20
3480	Medical centers, 1,500 S.F., 3.5 ton, See Note A. SEER 14			
3520	3,000 S.F., 7.00 ton	21	7	28
3560	10,000 S.F., 23.33 ton	13.95	6.75	20.70
3600	15,000 S.F., 35.00 ton	14.75	6.75	21.50
3640	20,000 S.F., 46.66 ton	13.70	6.75	20.45
3680	25,000 S.F., 58.33 ton	9.95	6.70	16.65
3760	Offices, 1,500 S.F., 4.75 ton, See Note A. SEER 14			
3800	3,000 S.F., 9.50 ton	28.50	9.50	38
3840	10,000 S.F., 31.66 ton	20	9.15	29.15
3880	15,000 S.F., 47.50 ton	18.60	9.20	27.80
3920	20,000 S.F., 63.33 ton	13.50	9.10	22.60
3960	25,000 S.F., 79.16 ton	13.50	9.10	22.60
4000	Restaurants, 1,500 S.F., 7.50 ton	45.50	15.05	60.55
4040	3,000 S.F., 15.00 ton	38	14.70	52.70
4080	10,000 S.F., 50.00 ton	29.50	14.50	44
4120	15,000 S.F., 75.00 ton	21.50	14.40	35.90
4160	20,000 S.F., 100.00 ton	18.70	14.40	33.10
4200	25,000 S.F., 125 ton, See Note B..			
4240	Schools and colleges, 1,500 S.F., 5.75 ton	35	11.50	46.50
4280	3,000 S.F., 11.50 ton	29	11.25	40.25
4320	10,000 S.F., 38.33 ton	22.50	11.15	33.65
4360	15,000 S.F., 57.50 ton	16.30	11.05	27.35
4400	20,000 S.F., 76.66 ton	16.30	11.05	27.35
4440	25,000 S.F., 95.83 ton	15	11.05	26.05
4450				

D30 HVAC

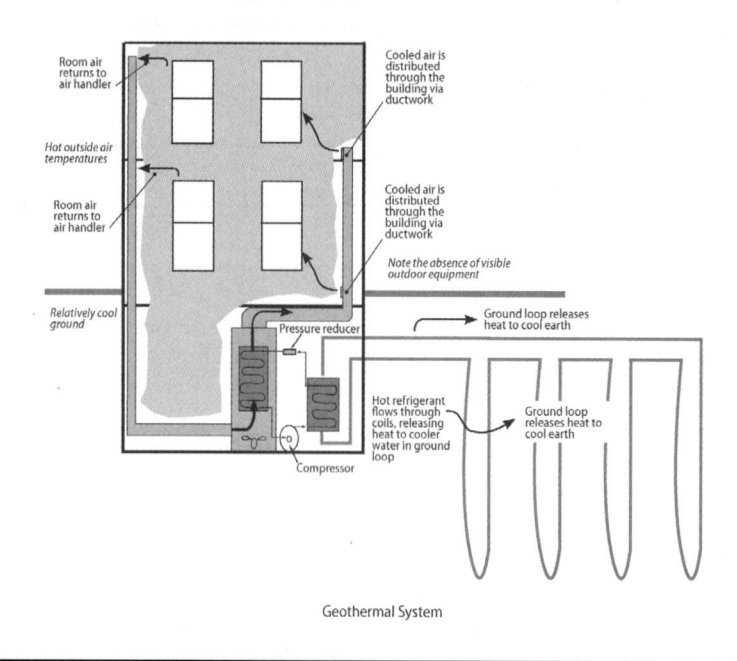

D3050 Terminal & Package Units

Geothermal System

System Components	QUANTITY	UNIT	COST EACH MAT.	COST EACH INST.	COST EACH TOTAL
SYSTEM D3050 248 1000					
GEOTHERMAL HEAT PUMP SYSTEM 50 TON, VERTICAL LOOP, 200 LF PER TON					
Mobilization excavator	2.000	Ea.		1,636	1,636
Mobilization support crew and equipment	2.000	Ea.		589	589
Mobilization drill rig	2.000	Ea.		338	338
Drill wells 6" diameter	100.000	C.L.F.		67,600	67,600
Pipe loops 1 1/2" diameter	200.000	C.L.F.	19,400	41,800	61,200
Pipe headers 2" diameter	1600.000	L.F.	3,216	4,128	7,344
U-fittings for pipe loops	50.000	Ea.	287.50	922.50	1,210
Header tee fittings	100.000	Ea.	1,165	3,150	4,315
Header elbow fittings	10.000	Ea.	77	196	273
Excavate trench for pipe header	475.000	B.C.Y.		3,690.75	3,690.75
Backfill trench for pipe header	655.000	L.C.Y.		1,984.65	1,984.65
Compact trench for pipe header	475.000	E.C.Y.		1,235	1,235
Circulation pump 5 HP	1.000	Ea.	12,100	900	13,000
Pump control system	1.000	Ea.	1,300	1,125	2,425
Pump gauges	2.000	Ea.	41	47	88
Pump gauge fittings	2.000	Ea.	109	47	156
Pipe insulation for pump connection	12.000	L.F.	39.48	88.80	128.28
Pipe for pump connection	12.000	L.F.	224.40	396.12	620.52
Pipe fittings for pump connection	1.000	Ea.	32	202.30	234.30
Install thermostat wells	2.000	Ea.	16.40	122.66	139.06
Install gauge wells	2.000	Ea.	16.40	128.92	145.32
Thermometers, stem type, 9" case, 8" stem, 3/4" NPT	8.000	Ea.	308	809.20	1,117.20
Gauges, pressure or vacuum, 3-1/2" diameter dial	1.000	Ea.	750	299	1,049
Pipe strainer for pump	1.000	Ea.	196	305	501
Shut valve for pump	1.000	Ea.	690	325	1,015
Expansion joints for pump	2.000	Ea.	660	240	900
Heat pump 50 tons	1.000	Ea.	41,500	14,200	55,700
TOTAL			82,128.18	146,505.90	228,634.08

For customer support on your Green Building Costs with RSMeans data, call 800.448.8182.

D30 HVAC

D3050 Terminal & Package Units

D3050 248	Geothermal Heat Pump System	COST EACH		
		MAT.	INST.	TOTAL
0990	Geothermal heat pump system, vertical loops 200' depth, 200 LF/4 gpm per ton			
1000	50 tons, vertical loops 200' depth, soft soil	82,000	146,500	228,500
1050	50 tons common soil	82,000	169,000	251,000
1075	50 tons dense soil	82,000	214,500	296,500
1100	40 tons, vertical loops 200' depth, soft soil	73,000	119,000	192,000
1150	40 tons common soil	77,000	163,500	240,500
1175	40 tons dense soil	73,000	173,500	246,500
1200	30 tons, vertical loops 200' depth, soft soil	55,000	93,500	148,500
1250	30 tons, common soil	55,000	107,000	162,000
1275	30 tons, dense soil	55,000	134,500	189,500
1300	25 tons, vertical loops 200' depth, soft soil	50,500	79,500	130,000
1350	25 tons, common soil	50,500	90,500	141,000
1375	25 tons, dense soil	50,500	113,500	164,000
1390	Geothermal heat pump system, vertical loops 250' depth, 250 LF/4 gpm per ton			
1400	50 tons, vertical loops 250' depth, soft soil	87,000	174,000	261,000
1450	50 tons common soil	87,000	202,000	289,000
1475	50 tons dense soil	87,000	259,000	346,000
1500	40 tons, vertical loops 250' depth, soft soil	77,000	141,000	218,000
1550	40 tons common soil	77,000	163,500	240,500
1575	40 tons dense soil	77,000	208,500	285,500
1600	30 tons, vertical loops 250' depth, soft soil	58,000	109,500	167,500
1650	30 tons, common soil	58,000	127,000	185,000
1675	30 tons, dense soil	58,000	161,000	219,000
1700	25 tons, vertical loops 250' depth, soft soil	53,000	93,000	146,000
1750	25 tons, common soil	53,000	107,000	160,000
1775	25 tons, dense soil	53,000	135,000	188,000
1998	Geothermal heat pump system, vertical loops 200' depth, 200 LF/4 gpm per ton			
1999	Includes pumping of wells and adding 1:1 cement grout mix with 5% waste factor			
2000	50 tons, vertical loops 200' depth, soft soil	112,500	170,000	282,500
2050	50 tons common soil	112,500	192,000	304,500
2075	50 tons dense soil	112,500	237,500	350,000
2100	40 tons, vertical loops 200' depth, soft soil	97,500	137,500	235,000
2150	40 tons common soil	101,500	182,000	283,500
2175	40 tons dense soil	97,500	192,000	289,500
2200	30 tons, vertical loops 200' depth, soft soil	73,500	107,000	180,500
2250	30 tons, common soil	73,500	121,000	194,500
2275	30 tons, dense soil	73,500	148,000	221,500
2300	25 tons, vertical loops 200' depth, soft soil	66,000	90,500	156,500
2350	25 tons, common soil	66,000	102,000	168,000
2375	25 tons, dense soil	66,000	125,000	191,000
2390	Geothermal heat pump system, vertical loops 250' depth, 250 LF/4 gpm per ton			
2391	Includes pumping of wells and adding 1:1 cement grout mix with 5% waste factor			
2400	50 tons, vertical loops 250' depth, soft soil	125,000	203,000	328,000
2450	50 tons common soil	125,000	231,000	356,000
2475	50 tons dense soil	125,000	287,500	412,500
2500	40 tons, vertical loops 250' depth, soft soil	107,500	164,000	271,500
2550	40 tons common soil	107,500	186,500	294,000
2575	40 tons dense soil	107,500	232,000	339,500
2600	30 tons, vertical loops 250' depth, soft soil	81,000	127,000	208,000
2650	30 tons, common soil	81,000	144,000	225,000
2675	30 tons, dense soil	81,000	178,000	259,000
2700	25 tons, vertical loops 250' depth, soft soil	72,000	107,000	179,000
2750	25 tons, common soil	72,000	121,500	193,500
2775	25 tons, dense soil	72,000	150,000	222,000
2998	Geothermal heat pump system, vertical loops 200' depth, 200 LF/4 gpm per ton			
2999	Includes pumping of wells and adding bentonite mix with 5% waste factor			
3000	50 tons, vertical loops 200' depth, soft soil	101,500	170,000	271,500
3050	50 tons common soil	101,500	192,000	293,500

D30 HVAC

D3050 Terminal & Package Units

D3050 248	Geothermal Heat Pump System	MAT.	INST.	TOTAL
3075	50 tons dense soil	101,500	237,500	339,000
3100	40 tons, vertical loops 200' depth, soft soil	88,500	137,500	226,000
3150	40 tons common soil	92,000	182,000	274,000
3175	40 tons dense soil	88,500	192,000	280,500
3200	30 tons, vertical loops 200' depth, soft soil	66,500	107,000	173,500
3250	30 tons, common soil	66,500	121,000	187,500
3275	30 tons, dense soil	66,500	148,000	214,500
3300	25 tons, vertical loops 200' depth, soft soil	60,000	90,500	150,500
3350	25 tons, common soil	60,000	102,000	162,000
3375	25 tons, dense soil	60,000	125,000	185,000
3390	Geothermal heat pump system, vertical loops 250' depth, 250 LF/4 gpm per ton			
3391	Includes pumping of wells and adding bentonite mix with 5% waste factor			
3400	50 tons, vertical loops 250' depth, soft soil	111,000	203,000	314,000
3450	50 tons common soil	111,000	231,000	342,000
3475	50 tons dense soil	111,000	287,500	398,500
3500	40 tons, vertical loops 250' depth, soft soil	96,000	164,000	260,000
3550	40 tons common soil	96,000	186,500	282,500
3575	40 tons dense soil	96,000	232,000	328,000
3600	30 tons, vertical loops 250' depth, soft soil	72,500	127,000	199,500
3650	30 tons, common soil	72,500	144,000	216,500
3675	30 tons, dense soil	72,500	178,000	250,500
3700	25 tons, vertical loops 250' depth, soft soil	65,000	107,000	172,000
3750	25 tons, common soil	65,000	121,500	186,500
3775	25 tons, dense soil	65,000	150,000	215,000

For customer support on your Green Building Costs with RSMeans data, call 800.448.8182.

D50 Electrical

D5020 Lighting and Branch Wiring

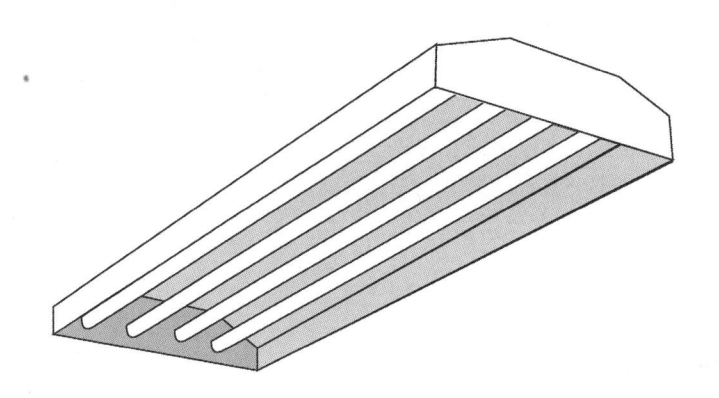

High Bay Fluorescent Fixtures
Four T5 HO/54 watt lamps

System Components	QUANTITY	UNIT	COST PER S.F. MAT.	COST PER S.F. INST.	COST PER S.F. TOTAL
SYSTEM D5020 218 0200					
FLUORESCENT HIGH BAY FIXTURE, 4 LAMP, 8'-10' ABOVE WORK PLANE					
0.5 WATT/S.F., 29 FC, 2 FIXTURES/1000 S.F.					
Steel intermediate conduit, (IMC) 1/2" diam	.100	L.F.	.19	.70	.89
Wire, 600V, type THWN-THHN, copper, solid, #10	.002	C.L.F.	.03	.14	.17
Steel outlet box 4" concrete	.002	Ea.	.02	.07	.09
Steel outlet box plate with stud, 4" concrete	.002	Ea.	.02	.02	.04
Flourescent, hi bay, 4 lamp, T-5 fixture	.002	Ea.	.54	.31	.85
TOTAL			.80	1.24	2.04

D5020 218	Fluorescent Fixture, High Bay, 8'-10' (by Wattage)	MAT.	INST.	TOTAL
0190	Fluorescent high bay-4 lamp fixture, 8'-10' above work plane			
0200	.5 watt/SF, 29 FC, 2 fixtures per 1000 S.F.	.80	1.24	2.04
0400	1 watt/SF, 59 FC, 4 fixtures per 1000 S.F.	1.55	2.36	3.91
0600	1.5 watt/SF, 103 FC, 7 fixtures per 1000 S.F.	2.61	3.70	6.31
0800	2 watt/SF, 133 FC, 9 fixtures per 1000 S.F.	3.39	4.88	8.27
1000	2.5 watt/SF, 162 FC, 11 fixtures per 1000 S.F.	4.17	6.05	10.22

For customer support on your Green Building Costs with RSMeans data, call 800.448.8182.

D50 Electrical

D5020 Lighting and Branch Wiring

Daylight Dimming System

System Components	QUANTITY	UNIT	COST PER S.F. MAT.	COST PER S.F. INST.	COST PER S.F. TOTAL
SYSTEM D5020 290 0800					
DAYLIGHT DIMMING CONTROL SYSTEM					
5 FIXTURES PER 1000 S.F.					
Tray cable, type TC, copper #16-4 conductor	.300	C.L.F.	.01	.03	.04
Wire, 600 volt, type THWN-THHN, copper, solid, #12	.320	C.L.F.		.02	.02
Conduit (EMT), to 10' H, incl 2 termn, 2 elb&11 bm clp per 100', 3/4"	10.000	L.F.	.01	.05	.06
Cabinet, hinged, steel, NEMA 1, 12"W x 12"H x 4"D	.200	Ea.	.01	.02	.03
Lighting control module	.200	Ea.	.07	.07	.14
Dimmable ballast three-lamp	5.000	Ea.	.72	.51	1.23
Daylight level sensor, wall mounted, on/off or dimming	.200	Ea.	.04	.02	.06
Automatic wall switches	.200	Ea.	.02	.01	.03
Remote power pack	.100	Ea.		.01	.01
TOTAL			.88	.74	1.62

D5020 290	Daylight Dimming System	MAT.	INST.	TOTAL
0500	Daylight Dimming System (no fixtures or fixture power)			
0800	5 fixtures per 1000 S.F.	.88	.74	1.62
1000	10 fixtures per 1000 S.F.	1.75	1.38	3.13
2000	12 fixtures per 1000 S.F.	2.11	1.65	3.76
3000	15 fixtures per 1000 S.F.	2.62	2.05	4.67
4000	20 fixtures per 1000 S.F.	3.49	2.69	6.18
5000	25 fixtures per 1000 S.F.	4.36	3.36	7.72
6000	50 fixtures per 1000 S.F.	8.70	6.65	15.35

D50 Electrical

D5020 Lighting and Branch Wiring

Lighting AC Control System

System Components	QUANTITY	UNIT	COST PER S.F. MAT.	COST PER S.F. INST.	COST PER S.F. TOTAL
SYSTEM D5020 295 0800					
LIGHTING ON/OFF CONTROL SYSTEM					
5 FIXTURES PER 1000 S.F.					
Tray cable, type TC, copper #16-4 conductor	.600	C.L.F.	.03	.06	.09
Wire, 600 volt, type THWN-THHN, copper, solid, #12	.320	C.L.F.		.02	.02
Conduit (EMT), to 10' H, incl 2 termn,2 elb&11 bm clp per 100', 3/4"	10.000	L.F.	.01	.05	.06
Cabinet, hinged, steel, NEMA 1, 12"W x 12"H x 4"D	.400	Ea.	.01	.05	.06
Relays, 120 V or 277 V standard	.800	Ea.	.04	.05	.09
24 hour dial with reserve power	.400	Ea.	.25	.08	.33
Lighting control module	.200	Ea.	.07	.07	.14
Occupancy sensors, passive infrared ceiling mounted	.400	Ea.	.03	.04	.07
Automatic wall switches	.400	Ea.	.03	.01	.04
Remote power pack	.200	Ea.	.01	.01	.02
TOTAL			.48	.44	.92

D5020 295	Lighting On/Off Control System	MAT.	INST.	TOTAL
0500	Includes occupancy and time switching (no fixtures or fixture power)			
0800	5 fixtures per 1000 SF	.48	.44	.92
1000	10 fixtures per 1000 S.F.	.55	.51	1.06
2000	12 fixtures per 1000 S.F.	.67	.60	1.27
3000	15 fixtures per 1000 S.F.	.81	.73	1.54
4000	20 fixtures per 1000 S.F.	1.10	.92	2.02
5000	25 fixtures per 1000 S.F.	1.35	1.15	2.50
6000	50 fixtures per 1000 S.F.	2.71	2.24	4.95

D50 Electrical

D5090 Other Electrical Systems

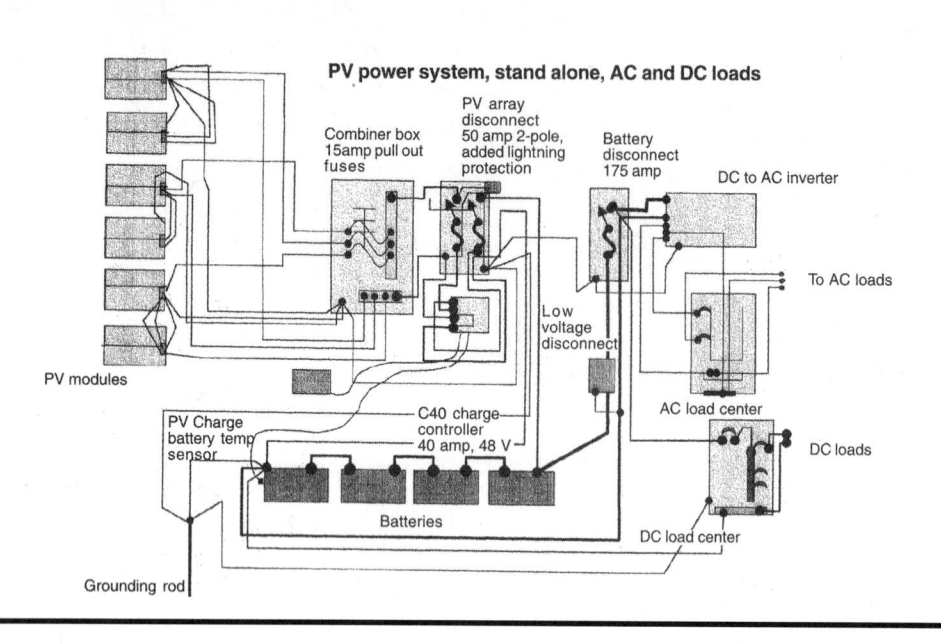

PV power system, stand alone, AC and DC loads

System Components	QUANTITY	UNIT	MAT.	INST.	TOTAL
SYSTEM D5090 420 0100					
PHOTOVOLTAIC POWER SYSTEM, STAND ALONE					
Alternative energy sources, photovoltaic module, 75 watt, 17 V	12.000	Ea.	5,220	1,044	6,264
PV rack system, roof, penetrating surface mount, on wood framing, 1 panel	12.000	Ea.	720	1,368	2,088
DC to AC inverter for, 24 V, 2,500 watt	1.000	Ea.	1,650	174	1,824
PV components, combiner box, 10 lug, NEMA 3R enclosure	1.000	Ea.	297	174	471
Alternative energy sources, PV components, fuse, 15 A for combiner box	10.000	Ea.	235	174	409
Battery charger controller w/temperature sensor	1.000	Ea.	540	174	714
Digital readout panel, displays hours, volts, amps, etc.	1.000	Ea.	240	174	414
Deep cycle solar battery, 6 V, 180 Ah (C/20)	4.000	Ea.	1,340	348	1,688
Battery interconnection, 15" AWG #2/0, sealed w/copper ring lugs	3.000	Ea.	59.70	130.50	190.20
Battery interconn, 24" AWG #2/0, sealed w/copper ring lugs	2.000	Ea.	52	87	139
Battery interconn, 60" AWG #2/0, sealed w/copper ring lugs	2.000	Ea.	130	87	217
Batt temp computer probe, RJ11 jack, 15' cord	1.000	Ea.	24.50	43.50	68
System disconnect, DC 175 amp circuit breaker	1.000	Ea.	248	87	335
Conduit box for inverter	1.000	Ea.	69	87	156
Low voltage disconnect	1.000	Ea.	63	87	150
Vented battery enclosure, wood	1.000	Ea.	310	310	620
Grounding, rod, copper clad, 8' long, 5/8" diameter	1.000	Ea.	23.50	127	150.50
Grounding, clamp, bronze, 5/8" dia	1.000	Ea.	5.30	22	27.30
Bare copper wire, stranded, #8	1.000	C.L.F.	47.50	63.50	111
Wire, 600 volt, type THW, copper, stranded, #12	3.600	C.L.F.	52.20	228.60	280.80
Wire, 600 volt, type THW, copper, stranded, #10	1.050	C.L.F.	24.15	72.98	97.13
Cond to 10' H,incl 2 termn,2 elb&11 bm CLP per 100',galv stl,1/2" dia	120.000	L.F.	304.80	930	1,234.80
Conduit,to 10' H,incl 2 termn,2 elb&11 bm clp per 100',(EMT), 1" dia	30.000	L.F.	60.90	181.50	242.40
Lightning surge suppressor	1.000	Ea.	84	22	106
General duty 240 volt, 2 pole, nonfusible, NEMA 3R, 60 amp	1.000	Ea.	137	305	442
Load centers, 3 wire, 120/240V, 100 amp main lugs, indoor, 8 circuits	2.000	Ea.	188	990	1,178
Circuit breaker, Plug-in, 120/240 volt, to 60 amp, 1 pole	5.000	Ea.	33.75	290	323.75
Fuses, dual element, time delay, 250 volt, 50 amp	2.000	Ea.	25.10	27.80	52.90
TOTAL			12,184.40	7,809.38	19,993.78

D50 Electrical

D5090 Other Electrical Systems

D5090 420	Photovoltaic Power System, Stand Alone	MAT.	INST.	TOTAL
0050	24 V capacity, 900 W (~102 SF)			
0100	Roof mounted, on wood framing	12,200	7,800	20,000
0150	with standoff	12,300	7,800	20,100
0200	Ground placement, ballast, fixed	17,100	8,325	25,425
0250	Adjustable	17,400	8,325	25,725
0300	Top of pole, passive tracking	17,100	8,325	25,425
0350	1.8 kW (~204 SF)			
0400	Roof mounted, on wood framing	19,700	12,400	32,100
0450	with standoff	20,000	12,400	32,400
0500	Ground placement, ballast, fixed	28,600	11,700	40,300
0550	Adjustable	29,200	11,700	40,900
0600	Top of pole, passive tracking	29,600	11,700	41,300
0650	3.2 kW (~408 SF)			
0700	Roof mounted, on wood framing	35,800	21,300	57,100
0750	with standoff	36,300	21,300	57,600
0800	Ground placement, ballast, fixed	52,500	18,200	70,700
0850	Adjustable	54,000	18,200	72,200
0900	Top of pole, passive tracking	54,500	18,000	72,500

COST EACH

For customer support on your Green Building Costs with RSMeans data, call 800.448.8182.

D50 Electrical

D5090 Other Electrical Systems

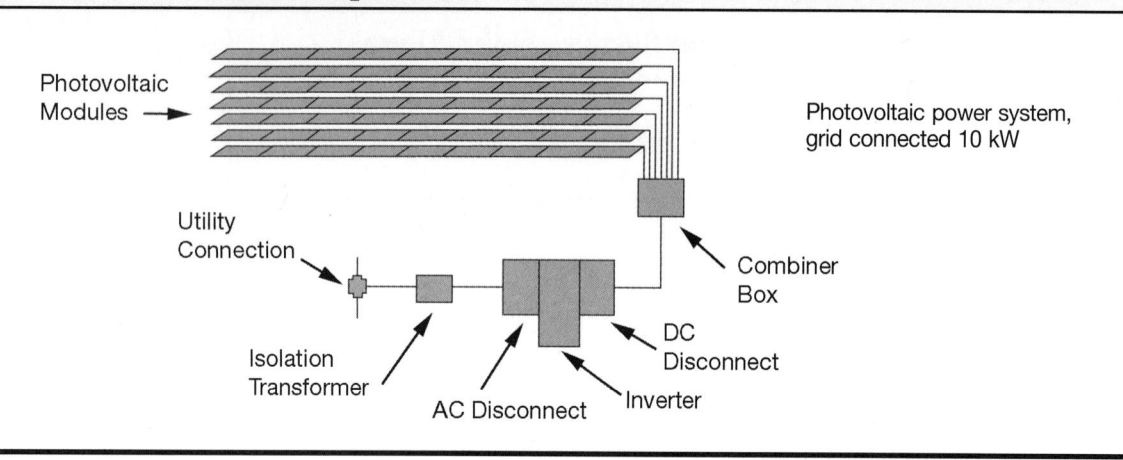

Photovoltaic power system, grid connected 10 kW

System Components	QUANTITY	UNIT	MAT.	INST.	TOTAL
SYSTEM D5090 430 0100					
PHOTOVOLTAIC POWER SYSTEM, GRID CONNECTED 10 kW					
Photovoltaic module, 150 watt, 33 V	60.000	Ea.	26,100	5,220	31,320
PV rack system, roof, non-penetrating ballast, 1 panel	60.000	Ea.	63,000	2,460	65,460
DC to AC inverter for, 24 V, 4,000 watt	3.000	Ea.	9,975	1,050	11,025
Combiner box 10 lug, NEMA 3R	1.000	Ea.	297	174	471
15 amp fuses	10.000	Ea.	235	174	409
Safety switch, 60 amp	1.000	Ea.	281	315	596
Safety switch, 100 amp	1.000	Ea.	480	385	865
Utility connection, 3 pole breaker	1.000	Ea.	253	112	365
Fuse, 60 A	3.000	Ea.	38.40	41.70	80.10
Fuse, 100 A	3.000	Ea.	93	52.20	145.20
10 kVA isolation tranformer	1.000	Ea.	1,950	870	2,820
EMT Conduit w/fittings & support	1.000	L.F.	365.40	1,089	1,454.40
RGS Conduit w/fittings & support	267.000	L.F.	1,989.15	2,856.90	4,846.05
Enclosure 24" x 24" x 10", NEMA 4	1.000	Ea.	5,400	1,400	6,800
Wire, 600 volt, type THWN-THHN, copper, stranded, #6	8.000	C.L.F.	424	856	1,280
Wire, 600 volt, copper type XLPE-USE(RHW), stranded, #12	18.000	C.L.F.	360	1,143	1,503
Grounding, bare copper wire stranded, 4/0	2.000	C.L.F.	970	488	1,458
Grounding, exothermic weld, 4/0 wire to building steel	4.000	Ea.	42.20	398	440.20
Grounding, brazed connections, #6 wire	2.000	Ea.	35.60	116	151.60
Insulated ground wire, copper, #6	.400	C.L.F.	21.20	42.80	64
TOTAL			112,309.95	19,243.60	131,553.55

D5090 430	Photovoltaic Power System, Grid Connected	MAT.	INST.	TOTAL
0050	10 kW			
0100	Roof mounted, non-penetrating ballast	112,500	19,200	131,700
0200	Penetrating surface mount, on steel framing	53,000	31,400	84,400
0300	on wood framing	53,000	23,600	76,600
0400	with standoff	53,500	23,700	77,200
0500	Ground placement, ballast, fixed	73,500	19,100	92,600
0600	adjustable	75,000	19,100	94,100
0700	Top of pole, passive tracking	75,000	19,500	94,500
1050	20 kW			
1100	Roof mounted, non-penetrating ballast	217,000	32,200	249,200
1200	Penetrating surface mount, on steel framing	98,500	56,500	155,000
1300	on wood framing	98,500	41,000	139,500
1400	with standoff	99,500	41,000	140,500
1500	Ground placement, ballast, fixed	139,000	31,000	170,000
1600	adjustable	142,000	31,000	173,000
1700	Top of pole, passive tracking	142,000	31,900	173,900

D50 Electrical

D5090 Other Electrical Systems

System Components	QUANTITY	UNIT	COST EACH MAT.	COST EACH INST.	COST EACH TOTAL
SYSTEM D5090 480 1100					
ELECTRICAL, SINGLE PHASE, 1 METER					
#18 twisted shielded pair in 1/2" EMT conduit	.050	C.L.F.	7.85	11.60	19.45
Wire, 600 volt, type THW, copper, solid, #12	.150	C.L.F.	1.59	9.53	11.12
Conduit (EMT), to 10' H, incl 2 termn,2 elb&11 bm clp per 100', 3/4"	5.000	L.F.	6.20	26.75	32.95
Outlet boxes, pressed steel, handy box	1.000	Ea.	2.19	26	28.19
Outlet boxes, pressed steel, handy box, covers, device	1.000	Ea.	1.10	10.90	12
Wiring devices, receptacle, duplex, 120 volt, ground, 20 amp	1.000	Ea.	10	26	36
Single phase, 277 volt, 200 amp	1.000	Ea.	430	79.50	509.50
Data recorder, 8 meters	1.000	Ea.	1,575	63.50	1,638.50
Software package, per meter, premium	1.000	Ea.	735		735
TOTAL			2,768.93	253.78	3,022.71

D5090 480	Energy Monitoring Systems	MAT.	INST.	TOTAL
1000	Electrical			
1100	Single phase, 1 meter	2,775	254	3,029
1110	4 meters	6,925	1,925	8,850
1120	8 meters	13,900	3,950	17,850
1200	Three phase, 1 meter	3,250	320	3,570
1210	5 meters	10,800	3,000	13,800
1220	10 meters	22,200	6,150	28,350
1230	25 meters	52,500	12,200	64,700
2000	Mechanical			
2100	BTU, 1 meter	3,550	925	4,475
2110	w/1 duct sensor	3,750	1,150	4,900
2120	& 1 space sensor	4,250	1,300	5,550
2130	& 5 space sensors	6,275	1,925	8,200
2140	& 10 space sensors	11,200	2,700	13,900
2200	BTU, 3 meters	7,525	2,650	10,175
2210	w/3 duct sensors	8,125	3,300	11,425
2220	& 3 space sensors	9,625	3,775	13,400
2230	& 15 space sensors	15,700	5,625	21,325
2240	& 30 space sensors	25,600	7,975	33,575
9000	Front end display	525	136	661
9100	Computer workstation	1,225	1,800	3,025

Green Commercial/Industrial/Institutional Section

Table of Contents

Table No.	Page
Green Models	
Building Types	
G.050 Bank	356
G.120 College, Classroom, 2-3 Story	358
G.130 College, Dorm., 2-3 Story	360
G.140 College, Dorm., 4-8 Story	362
G.150 College, Laboratory	364
G.220 Fire Station, 1 Story	366
G.230 Fire Station, 2 Story	368
G.250 Funeral Home	370
G.390 Library	372
G.400 Medical Office, 1 Story	374
G.410 Medical Office, 2 Story	376
G.420 Motel, 1 Story	378
G.430 Motel, 2-3 Story	380
G.455 Office, 1 Story	382
G.460 Office, 2-4 Story	384
G.470 Office, 5-10 Story	386
G.480 Office, 11-20 Story	388
G.490 Police Station	390
G.530 Restaurant	392
G.560 School, Elementary	394
G.570 School, High, 2-3 Story	396
G.580 School, Jr. High, 2-3 Story	398
G.590 School, Vocational	400
G.640 Supermarket	402
G.690 Warehouse	404

Introduction to the Commercial/Industrial/Institutional Section

General
The Commercial/Industrial/Institutional section contains base building costs per square foot of floor area for 77 model buildings. Each model has a table of square foot costs for combinations of exterior wall and framing systems. This table is supplemented by a list of common additives and their unit costs. In printed versions, a breakdown of all component costs used to develop the base cost for the model is included. In electronic products, the cost breakdown is available as a printable report. Modifications to the standard models can be performed manually in printed products and automatically using the "swapper" feature in electronic products.

This data may be used directly to estimate the construction cost of most types of buildings when only the floor area, exterior wall construction, and framing systems are known. To adjust the base cost for components that are different than the model, use the tables from the Assemblies Section.

Building Identification & Model Selection
The building models in this section represent structures by use. Occupancy, however, does not necessarily identify the building, i.e., a restaurant could be a converted warehouse. In all instances, the building should be described and identified by its own physical characteristics. The model selection should also be guided by comparing specifications with the model. In the case of converted use, data from one model may be used to supplement data from another.

Green Models
Consistent with expanding green trends in the design and construction industry, 25 green building models are currently included. Although similar to our standard models in building type and structural system, the new green models align with Energy Star requirements and address many of the items necessary to obtain LEED certification. Although our models do not include site-specific information, our design assumption is that they are located in climate zone 5. DOE's eQuest software was used to perform an energy analysis of the model buildings. By reducing energy use, we were able to reduce the size of the service entrances, switchgear, power feeds, and generators. Each of the following building systems was researched and analyzed: building envelope, HVAC, plumbing fixtures, lighting, and electrical service. These systems were targeted because of their impact on energy usage and green building.

Wall and roof insulation was increased to reduce heat loss and a recycled vapor barrier was added to the foundation. White roofs were specified for models with flat roofs. Interior finishes include materials with recycled content and low VOC paint. Stainless steel toilet partitions were selected because the recycled material is easy to maintain. Plumbing fixtures were selected to conserve water. Water closets are low-flow and equipped with auto-sensor valves. Waterless urinals are specified throughout. Faucets use auto-sensor flush valves and are powered by a hydroelectric power unit inside the faucet. Energy-efficient, low-flow water coolers were specified to reduce energy consumption and water usage throughout each building model.

Lighting efficiency was achieved by specifying LED fixtures in place of standard fluorescents. Daylight on/off lighting control systems were incorporated into the models. These controls are equipped with sensors that automatically turn off the lights when sufficient daylight is available. Energy monitoring systems were also included in all green models.

Adjustments
The base cost tables represent the base cost per square foot of floor area for buildings without a basement and without unusual special features. Basement costs and other common additives are available. Cost adjustments can also be made to the model by using the tables from the Assemblies Section.

Dimensions
All base cost tables are developed so that measurements can be readily made during the inspection process. Areas are calculated from exterior dimensions and story heights are measured from the top surface of one floor to the top surface of the floor above. Roof areas are measured by horizontal area covered and costs related to inclines are converted with appropriate factors. The precision of measurement is a matter of the user's choice and discretion. For ease in calculation, consideration should be given to measuring in tenths of a foot, i.e., 9 ft. 6 in. = 9.5 ft., 9 ft. 4 in. = 9.3 ft.

Floor Area
The term "Floor Area" as used in this section includes the sum of floor plate at grade level and above. This dimension is measured from the outside face of the foundation wall. Basement costs are calculated separately. The user must exercise his/her own judgment, where the lowest level floor is slightly below grade, whether to consider it at grade level or make the basement adjustment.

How to Use the Commercial/Industrial/Institutional Section

The following is a detailed explanation of a sample entry in the Commercial/Industrial/Institutional Square Foot Cost Section. Each bold number below corresponds to the described item on the following page with the appropriate component or cost of the sample entry following in parentheses.

Prices listed are costs that include overhead and profit of the installing contractor and additional markups for General Conditions and Architects' Fees.

COMMERCIAL/INDUSTRIAL/INSTITUTIONAL | **G.460** ❶ | **G Office, 2-4 Story** ❷

Costs per square foot of floor area

Exterior Wall ❸	S.F. Area	5000	8000	12000	16000	20000	35000	50000	65000	80000
	L.F. Perimeter	220	260	310	330	360 ❹	440	550	600	675
Face Brick and Concrete Block	Wood Joists	279.60	243.65	223.05	208.35	200.70	185.35	180.65	175.90	173.70
	Steel Joists	291.30	255.35	234.75	220.05	212.40 ❺	197.05	192.30	187.60	185.40
Curtain Wall	Rigid Steel	323.95	280.95	256.30	238.40	229.10	210.45	204.85	199.00	196.35
	Reinforced Concrete	326.65	283.65	259.00	241.10	231.80	213.15	207.50	201.75	199.05
Wood Clapboard	Wood Frame	236.55	209.60	194.25	183.65	178.05	166.95	163.45	160.15	158.60
Brick Veneer	Wood Frame	246.75	217.15	200.20	188.40	182.20	169.85	166.00	162.30	160.55
Perimeter Adj., Add or Deduct ❻	Per 100 L.F.	47.20	29.45	19.65	14.75	11.75 ❼	6.75	4.70	3.60	2.95
Story Hgt. Adj., Add or Deduct	Per 1 Ft.	7.75	5.70	4.50	3.55	3.10	2.20	1.90	1.65	1.50

❽ **For Basement**, add $42.72 per square foot of basement area

The above costs were calculated using the basic specifications shown on the facing page. These costs should be adjusted where necessary for design alternatives and owner's requirements.

Common additives ❾

Description	Unit	$ Cost
Closed Circuit Surveillance, one station, camera and monitor	Ea.	1475
For additional camera stations, add	Ea.	665
Directory Boards, plastic, glass covered, 30" x 20"	Ea.	640
36" x 48"	Ea.	1625
Aluminum, 36" x 24"	Ea.	790
48" x 32"	Ea.	1025
Electronic, wall mounted	S.F.	4625
Escalators, 10' rise, 32" wide, glass balustrade	Ea.	153,500
48" wide, glass balustrade	Ea.	161,000
Pedestal access flr sys w/PLAM cover, comp rm,		
Less than 6000 SF	S.F.	22
Greater than 6000 SF	S.F.	21.50
Office, greater than 6000 S.F.	S.F.	17.95
Uninterruptible power supply, 15 kVA/12.75 kW	kW	1.28

Description	Unit	$ Cost
Commissioning Fees, sustainable commercial construction	S.F.	0.24 - 3.04
Energy Modelling Fees, commercial buildings to 10,000 SF	Ea.	11,000
Greater than 10,000 SF add	S.F.	0.04
Green Bldg Cert Fees for comm construction project reg	Project	900
Photovoltaic Pwr Sys, grid connected, 20 kW (~2400 SF), roof	Ea.	249,200
Green Roofs, 6" soil depth, w/treated wd edging & sedum mats	S.F.	12.41
10" Soil depth, with treated wood edging & sedum mats	S.F.	14.10
Greywater Recovery Systems, prepackaged comm, 3060 gal.	Ea.	45,900
4590 gal.	Ea.	57,625
Rainwater Harvest Sys, prepckged comm, 10,000 gal, sys contrller	Ea.	37,550
20,000 gal. w/system controller	Ea.	61,000
30,000 gal. w/system controller	Ea.	97,350
Solar Domestic HW, closed loop, add-on sys, ext heat exchanger	Ea.	11,300
Drainback, hot water system, 120 gal tank	Ea.	14,175
Draindown, hot water system, 120 gal tank	Ea.	14,425

① Model Number (G.460)
"G" distinguishes this section of the data and stands for green and is followed by the sequential building type number.

② Type of Building (G Office, 2-4 Story)
There are 25 different types of commercial/industrial/institutional buildings highlighted in this section.

③ Exterior Wall Construction and Building Framing Options (Face Brick with Concrete Block Back-up and Open Web Steel Bar Joists)
Three or more commonly used exterior walls and, in most cases, two typical building framing systems are presented for each type of building. The model selected should be based on the actual characteristics of the building being estimated.

④ Total Square Foot of Floor Area and Perimeter Used to Compute Base Costs (20,000 Square Feet and 360 Linear Feet)
Square foot of floor area is the total gross area of all floors at grade and above and does not include a basement. The perimeter in linear feet used for the base cost is generally for a rectangular, economical building shape.

⑤ Cost per Square Foot of Floor Area ($212.40)
The highlighted cost is for a building of the selected exterior wall and framing system and floor area. Costs for buildings with floor areas other than those calculated may be interpolated between the costs shown.

⑥ Building Perimeter and Story Height Adjustments
Square foot costs for a building with a perimeter or floor-to-floor story height significantly different from the model used to calculate the base cost may be adjusted (add or deduct) to reflect the actual building geometry.

⑦ Cost per Square Foot of Floor Area for the Perimeter and/or Height Adjustment ($11.75 for Perimeter Difference and $3.10 for Story Height Difference)
Add (or deduct) $11.75 to the base square foot cost for each 100 feet of perimeter difference between the model and the actual building. Add (or deduct) $3.10 to the base square foot cost for each 1 foot of story height difference between the model and the actual building.

⑧ Optional Cost per Square Foot of Basement Floor Area ($42.72)
The cost of an unfinished basement for the building being estimated is $41.45 times the gross area of the basement.

⑨ Common Additives
Common components and/or systems used in this type of building are listed. These costs should be added to the total building cost. Additional selections may be found in the Assemblies Section.

How to Use the Commercial/Industrial/Institutional Section (Cont.)

The following is a detailed explanation of the specification and costs for a model building in the Commercial/Industrial/Institutional Square Foot Cost Section. Each bold number below corresponds to the described item on the following page with the appropriate component of the sample entry following in parentheses.

Prices listed in the specification are costs that include overhead and profit of the installing contractor but not the general contractor's markup or Architects' Fees.

Model costs calculated for a 3 story building ❶ with 12' story height and 20,000 square feet of floor area

❷ G Office, 2-4 Story

				Unit	Unit Cost	Cost Per S.F.	% Of Sub-Total
A.	**SUBSTRUCTURE**						
1010	Standard Foundations	Poured concrete; strip and spread footings		S.F. Ground	8.31	2.77	
1020	Special Foundations	N/A		—	—	—	
1030	Slab on Grade	4" reinforced concrete with recycled vapor barrier and granular base		S.F. Slab	5.84	1.95	4.4%
2010	Basement Excavation	Site preparation for slab and trench for foundation wall and footing		S.F. Ground	.33	.11	
2020	Basement Walls	4' foundation wall		L.F. Wall	186	2.08	
B.	**SHELL**						
	B10 Superstructure						
1010	Floor Construction	Open web steel joists, slab form, concrete, columns		S.F. Floor	20.63	13.75	10.3%
1020	Roof Construction	Metal deck, open web steel joists, columns		S.F. Roof	7.92	2.64	
	B20 Exterior Enclosure						
2010	Exterior Walls	Face brick with concrete block backup	80% of wall	S.F. Wall	41.20	21.36	
2020	Exterior Windows	Aluminum outward projecting	20% of wall	Each	755	4.25	17.0%
2030	Exterior Doors	Aluminum and glass, hollow metal		Each	4565	1.38	
	B30 Roofing						
3010	Roof Coverings	Single-ply, TPO membrane, 60 mils, heat welded seams w/R-20 insul.		S.F. Roof	8.88	2.96	1.9%
3020	Roof Openings	N/A		—	—	—	
C.	**INTERIORS** ❸						
1010	Partitions	Gypsum board on metal studs ❹	❺ 20 SF Flr/LF Part.	S.F. Partition	11.43	4.57	
1020	Interior Doors	Single leaf hollow metal, low VOC paint	❻ 200 S.F. Floor/Door	Each ❼	1222	6.11 ❽	
1030	Fittings	Toilet partitions		S.F. Floor	1.87	1.87	
2010	Stair Construction	Concrete filled metal pan		Flight	15,800	5.53	20.2% ❾
3010	Wall Finishes	60% vinyl wall covering, 40% paint, low VOC		S.F. Surface	1.65	1.32	
3020	Floor Finishes	60% carpet tile, 30% vinyl composition tile, recycled content, 10% ceramic tile		S.F. Floor	5.08	5.08	
3030	Ceiling Finishes	Mineral fiber tile on concealed zee bars		S.F. Ceiling	7.60	7.60	
D.	**SERVICES**						
	D10 Conveying						
1010	Elevators & Lifts	Two hydraulic passenger elevators		Each	125,900	12.59	7.9%
1020	Escalators & Moving Walks	N/A		—	—	—	
	D20 Plumbing						
2010	Plumbing Fixtures	Toilet, low flow, auto sensor, & service fixt., supply & drain.	1 Fixt./1320 SF Flr.	Each	5900	4.47	
2020	Domestic Water Distribution	Gas fired, tankless water heater		S.F. Floor	.22	.22	3.5%
2040	Rain Water Drainage	Roof drains		S.F. Roof	2.82	.94	
	D30 HVAC						
3010	Energy Supply	N/A		—	—	—	
3020	Heat Generating Systems	Included in D3050		—	—	—	
3040	Distribution Systems	Enthalpy heat recovery packages		Each	18,475	2.77	12.2 %
3050	Terminal & Package Units	Multizone rooftop air conditioner. SEER 14		S.F. Floor	16.65	16.65	
3090	Other HVAC Sys. & Equipment	N/A		—	—	—	
	D40 Fire Protection						
4010	Sprinklers	Wet pipe sprinkler system		S.F. Floor	4.02	4.02	3.2%
4020	Standpipes	Standpipes and hose systems		S.F. Floor	1.07	1.07	
	D50 Electrical						
5010	Electrical Service/Distribution	1000 ampere service, panel board and feeders		S.F. Floor	2.86	2.86	
5020	Lighting & Branch Wiring	LED fixtures, daylt. dim., ltg. on/off, recept., switches, and A.C. power		S.F. Floor	16.63	16.63	19.1%
5030	Communications & Security	Addressable alarm systems, internet and phone wiring, & emergency ltg.		S.F. Floor	9.57	9.57	
5090	Other Electrical Systems	Emergency generator, 7.5 kW, UPS, energy monitoring systems		S.F. Floor	1.33	1.33	
E.	**EQUIPMENT & FURNISHINGS**						
1010	Commercial Equipment	N/A		—	—	—	
1020	Institutional Equipment	N/A		—	—	—	0.2 %
1090	Other Equipment	Waste handling recycling tilt truck		S.F. Floor	.31	.31	
2020	Moveable Furnishings	No smoking signage		S.F. Floor	.02	.02	
F.	**SPECIAL CONSTRUCTION**						
1020	Integrated Construction	N/A		—	—	—	0.0%
1040	Special Facilities	N/A		—	—	—	
G.	**BUILDING SITEWORK**	N/A					

❿ **Sub-Total**		158.78	100%
CONTRACTOR FEES (General Requirements: 10%, Overhead: 5%, Profit: 10%) ⓫	25%	39.73	
ARCHITECT FEES	7%	13.89	
⓬ **Total Building Cost**		**212.40**	

352

1 Building Description (Model costs are calculated for a 3-story building building with a 12' story height and 20,000 square feet of floor area)
The model highlighted is described in terms of building type, number of stories, typical story height, and square footage.

2 Type of Building
(G Office, 2-4 Story)

3 Division C Interiors
(C1020 Interior Doors)
System costs are presented in divisions according to the 7-element UNIFORMAT II classifications. Each of the component systems is listed.

4 Specification Highlights
(Single leaf hollow metal, low VOC paint)
All systems in each subdivision are described with the material and proportions used.

5 Quantity Criteria (200 S.F. Floor/Door)
The criteria used in determining quantities for the calculations are shown.

6 Unit (Each)
The unit of measure shown in this column is the unit of measure of the particular system shown that corresponds to the unit cost.

7 Unit Cost ($1222)
The cost per unit of measure of each system subdivision.

8 Cost per Square Foot ($6.11)
The cost per square foot for each system is the unit cost of the system times the total number of units, divided by the total square feet of building area.

9 % of Sub-Total (20.2%)
The percent of sub-total is the total cost per square foot of all systems in the division divided by the sub-total cost per square foot of the building.

10 Sub-Total ($158.78)
The sub-total is the total of all the system costs per square foot.

11 Project Fees
(Contractor Fees) (25%);
(Architects' Fee) (7%)
Contractor fees to cover the general requirements, overhead, and profit of the General Contractor are added as a percentage of the sub-total. An Architect's Fee, also as a percentage of the sub-total, is also added. These values vary with the building type.

12 Total Building Cost ($212.40)
The total building cost per square foot of building area is the sum of the square foot costs of all the systems, the General Contractor's general requirements, overhead and profit, and the Architect's fee. The total building cost is the amount that appears shaded in the Cost per Square Foot of Floor Area table shown previously.

Example

Example 1

This example illustrates the use of the base cost tables. The base cost is adjusted for different exterior wall systems, different story height and a partial basement.

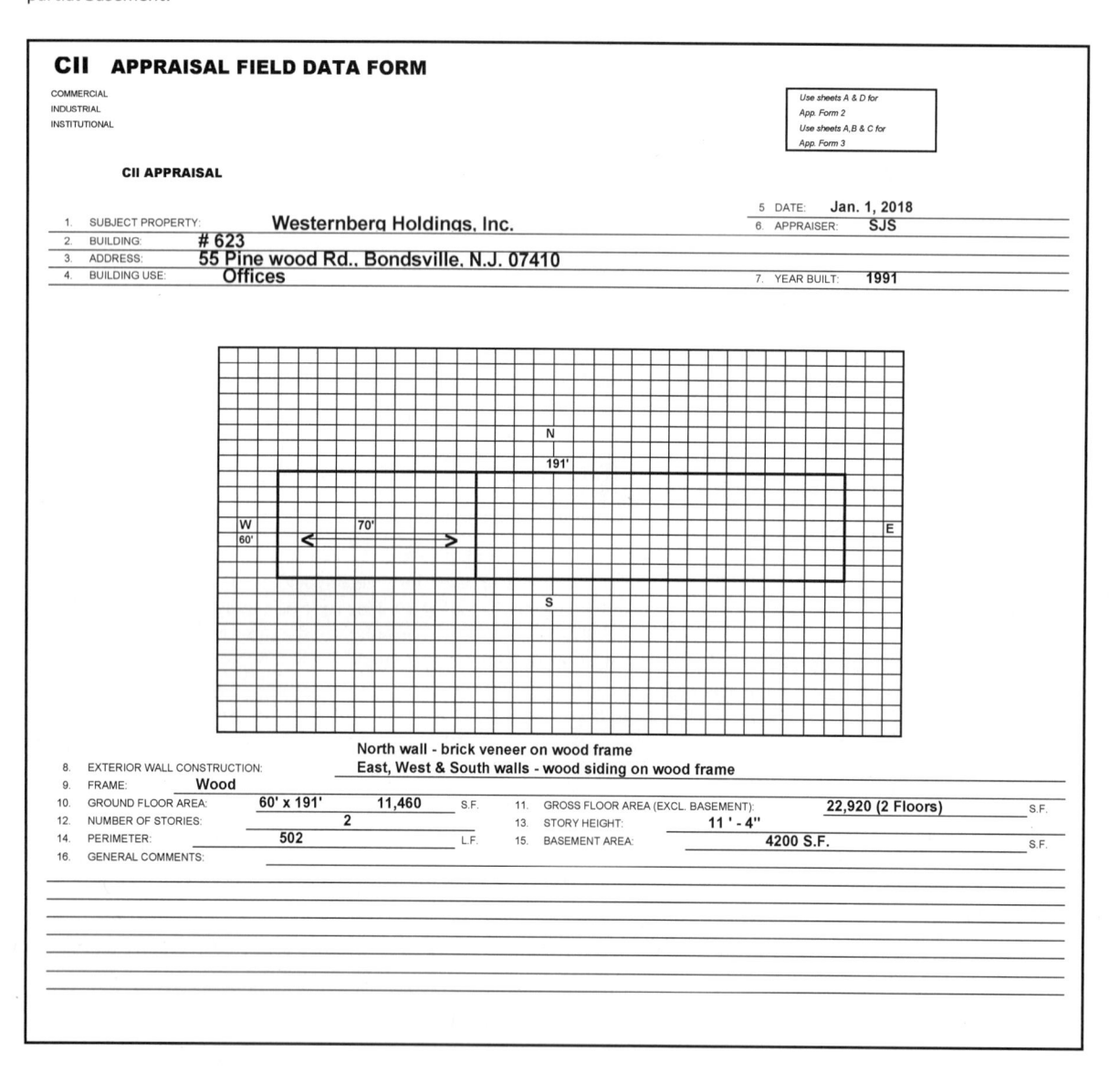

CII APPRAISAL FIELD DATA FORM

COMMERCIAL
INDUSTRIAL
INSTITUTIONAL

Use sheets A & D for App. Form 2
Use sheets A, B & C for App. Form 3

CII APPRAISAL

1. SUBJECT PROPERTY: Westernberg Holdings, Inc.
2. BUILDING: # 623
3. ADDRESS: 55 Pine wood Rd., Bondsville, N.J. 07410
4. BUILDING USE: Offices
5. DATE: Jan. 1, 2018
6. APPRAISER: SJS
7. YEAR BUILT: 1991

Diagram:
- N: 191'
- W: 60', 70'
- E
- S

8. EXTERIOR WALL CONSTRUCTION: North wall - brick veneer on wood frame; East, West & South walls - wood siding on wood frame
9. FRAME: Wood
10. GROUND FLOOR AREA: 60' x 191'   11,460 S.F.
11. GROSS FLOOR AREA (EXCL. BASEMENT): 22,920 (2 Floors) S.F.
12. NUMBER OF STORIES: 2
13. STORY HEIGHT: 11' - 4"
14. PERIMETER: 502 L.F.
15. BASEMENT AREA: 4200 S.F.
16. GENERAL COMMENTS:

354

Example 1 (continued)

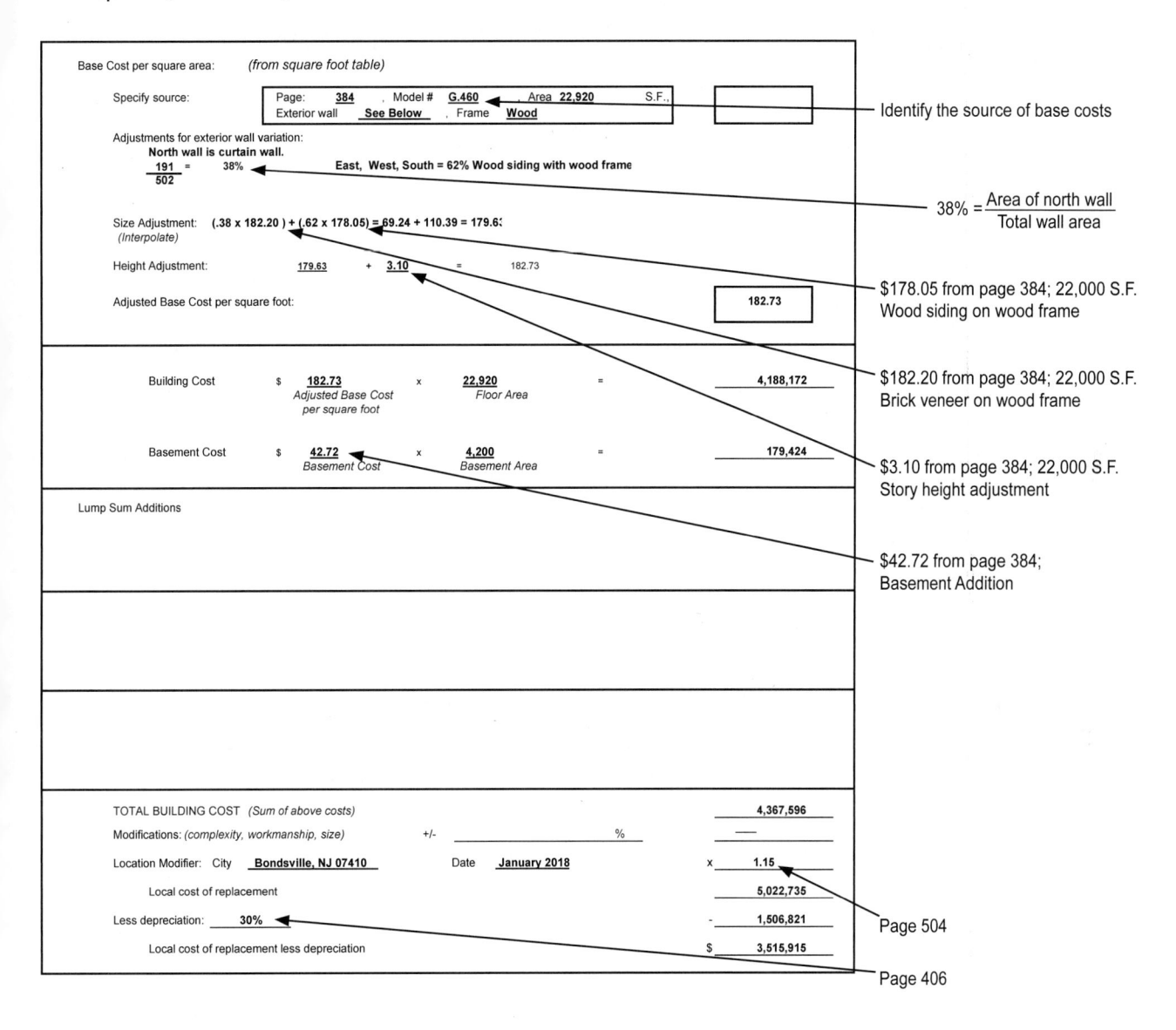

Base Cost per square area: *(from square foot table)*

Specify source: Page: **384**, Model # **G.460**, Area **22,920** S.F., Exterior wall **See Below**, Frame **Wood** ← Identify the source of base costs

Adjustments for exterior wall variation:
North wall is curtain wall.
$\frac{191}{502}$ = 38%   East, West, South = 62% Wood siding with wood frame

$38\% = \frac{\text{Area of north wall}}{\text{Total wall area}}$

Size Adjustment: (.38 x 182.20) + (.62 x 178.05) = 69.24 + 110.39 = 179.6(3)
(Interpolate)

Height Adjustment: 179.63 + **3.10** = 182.73

Adjusted Base Cost per square foot: 182.73

$178.05 from page 384; 22,000 S.F. Wood siding on wood frame

$182.20 from page 384; 22,000 S.F. Brick veneer on wood frame

Building Cost	$ **182.73** Adjusted Base Cost per square foot	x	**22,920** Floor Area	=	4,188,172
Basement Cost	$ **42.72** Basement Cost	x	**4,200** Basement Area	=	179,424

$3.10 from page 384; 22,000 S.F. Story height adjustment

$42.72 from page 384; Basement Addition

Lump Sum Additions

TOTAL BUILDING COST *(Sum of above costs)*   4,367,596

Modifications: *(complexity, workmanship, size)* +/- _____ %   _____

Location Modifier: City **Bondsville, NJ 07410**   Date **January 2018**   x **1.15** ← Page 504

Local cost of replacement   5,022,735

Less depreciation: **30%** ←   - 1,506,821

Local cost of replacement less depreciation $ 3,515,915 ← Page 406

COMMERCIAL/INDUSTRIAL/INSTITUTIONAL

G.050 G Bank

Costs per square foot of floor area

Exterior Wall	S.F. Area	2000	2700	3400	4100	4800	5500	6200	6900	7600
	L.F. Perimeter	180	208	236	256	280	303	317	337	357
Face Brick and Concrete Block	Rigid Steel	307.90	287.65	275.80	265.65	259.55	254.65	249.20	245.90	243.20
	Reinforced Concrete	325.55	305.30	293.50	**283.35**	277.20	272.30	266.85	263.55	260.85
Precast Concrete	Rigid Steel	301.40	279.65	266.90	255.90	249.35	244.00	238.10	234.55	231.60
	Reinforced Concrete	336.25	314.45	301.75	290.75	284.15	278.85	272.95	269.35	266.45
Limestone and Concrete Block	Rigid Steel	334.35	310.45	296.50	284.45	277.20	271.40	264.85	260.95	257.70
	Reinforced Concrete	350.50	326.60	312.65	300.60	293.35	287.55	281.00	277.05	273.85
Perimeter Adj., Add or Deduct	Per 100 L.F.	58.70	43.45	34.50	28.65	24.40	21.30	18.90	17.00	15.40
Story Hgt. Adj., Add or Deduct	Per 1 Ft.	5.65	4.80	4.35	3.90	3.65	3.40	3.20	3.05	2.90

For Basement, add $39.57 per square foot of basement area

The above costs were calculated using the basic specifications shown on the facing page. These costs should be adjusted where necessary for design alternatives and owner's requirements.

Common additives

Description	Unit	$ Cost
Bulletproof Teller Window, 44" x 60"	Ea.	5850
60" x 48"	Ea.	7700
Closed Circuit Surveillance, one station, camera & monitor	Ea.	1475
For additional camera stations, add	Ea.	665
Counters, complete, dr & frame, 3' x 6'-8", bullet resist stl with vision panel	Ea.	7375 - 9525
Drive-up Window, drawer & micr., not incl. glass	Ea.	9525 - 13,300
Night Depository	Ea.	10,000 - 15,200
Package Receiver, painted	Ea.	1975
Stainless steel	Ea.	3050
Partitions, bullet resistant to 8' high	L.F.	345 - 545
Pneumatic Tube Systems, 2 station	Ea.	34,200
With TV viewer	Ea.	62,500
Service Windows, pass thru, steel, 24" x 36"	Ea.	4100
48" x 48"	Ea.	4175
Twenty-four Hour Teller, automatic deposit cash & memo	Ea.	54,500
Vault Front, door & frame, 2 hour test, 32" door	Opng.	9800
4 hour test, 40" door	Opng.	13,800
Time lock, two movement, add	Ea.	2400

Description	Unit	$ Cost
Commissioning Fees, sustainable commercial construction	S.F.	0.24 - 3.04
Energy Modelling Fees, banks to 10,000 SF	Ea.	11,000
Green Bldg Cert Fees for comm construction project reg	Project	900
Photovoltaic Pwr Sys, grid connected, 20 kW (~2400 SF), roof	Ea.	249,200
Green Roofs, 6" soil depth, w/treated wd edging & sedum mats	S.F.	12.41
10" Soil depth, with treated wood edging & sedum mats	S.F.	14.10
Greywater Recovery Systems, prepackaged comm, 1530 gal	Ea.	33,855
Rainwater Harvest Sys, prepckged comm, 10,000 gal, sys contrller	Ea.	37,550
20,000 gal. w/system controller	Ea.	61,000
30,000 gal. w/system controller	Ea.	97,350
Solar Domestic HW, closed loop, add-on sys, ext heat exchanger	Ea.	11,300
Draindown, hot water system, 120 gal tank	Ea.	14,425

Important: See the Reference Section for Location Factors.

Model costs calculated for a 1 story building with 14' story height and 4,100 square feet of floor area

G Bank

			Unit	Unit Cost	Cost Per S.F.	% Of Sub-Total
A. SUBSTRUCTURE						
1010	Standard Foundations	Poured concrete; strip and spread footings	S.F. Ground	4.62	4.62	
1020	Special Foundations	N/A	—	—	—	
1030	Slab on Grade	4" reinforced concrete with recycled vapor barrier and granular base	S.F. Slab	5.84	5.84	8.9%
2010	Basement Excavation	Site preparation for slab and trench for foundation wall and footing	S.F. Ground	.33	.33	
2020	Basement Walls	4' Foundation wall	L.F. Wall	98	7.34	
B. SHELL						
B10 Superstructure						
1010	Floor Construction	Cast-in-place columns	L.F. Column	6.39	6.39	11.6%
1020	Roof Construction	Cast-in-place concrete flat plate	S.F. Roof	17.25	17.25	
B20 Exterior Enclosure						
2010	Exterior Walls	Face brick with concrete block backup 80% of wall	S.F. Wall	41.20	28.81	
2020	Exterior Windows	Horizontal aluminum sliding 20% of wall	Each	589	6.86	18.6%
2030	Exterior Doors	Double aluminum and glass and hollow metal, low VOC paint	Each	4560	2.22	
B30 Roofing						
3010	Roof Coverings	Single-ply TPO membrane, 60 mils, heat welded seams w/4" thk. R20 insul.	S.F. Roof	8.77	8.77	4.3%
3020	Roof Openings	N/A	—	—	—	
C. INTERIORS						
1010	Partitions	Gypsum board on metal studs w/sound attenuation 20 SF of Flr./LF Part.	S.F. Partition	13.32	6.66	
1020	Interior Doors	Single leaf hollow metal, low VOC paint 200 S.F. Floor/Door	Each	1222	6.11	
1030	Fittings	N/A	—	—	—	
2010	Stair Construction	N/A	—	—	—	13.7%
3010	Wall Finishes	50% vinyl wall covering, 50% paint, low VOC	S.F. Surface	1.57	1.57	
3020	Floor Finishes	50% carpet tile, 40% vinyl composition tile, recycled, 10% quarry tile	S.F. Floor	6.10	6.10	
3030	Ceiling Finishes	Mineral fiber tile on concealed zee bars	S.F. Ceiling	7.60	7.60	
D. SERVICES						
D10 Conveying						
1010	Elevators & Lifts	N/A	—	—	—	0.0 %
1020	Escalators & Moving Walks	N/A	—	—	—	
D20 Plumbing						
2010	Plumbing Fixtures	Toilet low flow, auto sensor and service fixt., supply and drainage 1 Fixt./580 SF Flr.	Each	6247	10.77	
2020	Domestic Water Distribution	Tankless, on demand water heaters, natural gas/propane	S.F. Floor	1.06	1.06	6.6%
2040	Rain Water Drainage	Roof drains	S.F. Roof	1.67	1.67	
D30 HVAC						
3010	Energy Supply	N/A	—	—	—	
3020	Heat Generating Systems	Included in D3050	—	—	—	
3040	Distribution Systems	Enthalpy heat recovery packages	Each	15,550	3.79	6.1 %
3050	Terminal & Package Units	Single zone rooftop air conditioner	S.F. Floor	8.67	8.67	
3090	Other HVAC Sys. & Equipment	N/A	—	—	—	
D40 Fire Protection						
4010	Sprinklers	Wet pipe sprinkler system	S.F. Floor	5.13	5.13	4.1%
4020	Standpipes	Standpipe	S.F. Floor	3.25	3.25	
D50 Electrical						
5010	Electrical Service/Distribution	200 ampere service, panel board and feeders	S.F. Floor	1.51	1.51	
5020	Lighting & Branch Wiring	LED fixtures, daylt. dimming & ltg. on/off control, receptacles, switches, A.C.	S.F. Floor	11.50	11.50	13.8%
5030	Communications & Security	Alarm systems, internet/phone wiring, and security television	S.F. Floor	11.15	11.15	
5090	Other Electrical Systems	Emergency generator, 15 kW, UPS, energy monitoring systems	S.F. Floor	4	4	
E. EQUIPMENT & FURNISHINGS						
1010	Commercial Equipment	Automatic teller, drive up window, night depository	S.F. Floor	8.37	8.37	
1020	Institutional Equipment	Closed circuit TV monitoring system	S.F. Floor	2.95	2.95	6.3%
1090	Other Equipment	Waste handling recycling tilt truck	S.F. Floor	1.52	1.52	
2020	Moveable Furnishings	No smoking signage	S.F. Floor	.04	.04	
F. SPECIAL CONSTRUCTION						
1020	Integrated Construction	N/A	—	—	—	6.1 %
1040	Special Facilities	Security vault door	S.F. Floor	12.36	12.36	
G. BUILDING SITEWORK	N/A					

		Sub-Total	204.21	**100%**
CONTRACTOR FEES (General Requirements: 10%, Overhead: 5%, Profit: 10%)		25%	51.06
ARCHITECT FEES		11%	28.08
	Total Building Cost		**283.35**

For customer support on your Green Building Costs with RSMeans data, call 800.448.8182.

COMMERCIAL/INDUSTRIAL/INSTITUTIONAL

G.120   G College, Classroom, 2-3 Story

Costs per square foot of floor area

Exterior Wall	S.F. Area	15000	20000	28000	38000	50000	65000	85000	100000	150000
	L.F. Perimeter	350	400	480	550	630	660	750	825	1035
Face Brick and Concrete Block	Rigid Steel	266.10	253.35	242.45	233.35	227.05	219.80	215.50	213.70	209.35
	Bearing Walls	257.95	244.95	233.85	224.50	218.10	210.65	206.30	204.35	199.95
Decorative Concrete Block	Rigid Steel	256.75	245.35	235.60	227.55	221.95	215.70	211.95	210.35	206.60
	Bearing Walls	246.75	235.15	225.15	216.90	211.25	204.80	200.95	199.30	195.40
Stucco and Concrete Block	Rigid Steel	269.80	256.50	245.15	235.60	229.00	221.40	216.90	215.00	210.45
	Bearing Walls	261.65	248.10	236.55	226.80	220.10	212.25	207.65	205.70	201.05
Perimeter Adj., Add or Deduct	Per 100 L.F.	16.35	12.30	8.80	6.45	4.90	3.80	2.95	2.40	1.70
Story Hgt. Adj., Add or Deduct	Per 1 Ft.	3.00	2.55	2.25	1.85	1.60	1.30	1.15	1.00	0.90

For Basement, add $42.46 per square foot of basement area

The above costs were calculated using the basic specifications shown on the facing page. These costs should be adjusted where necessary for design alternatives and owner's requirements.

Common additives

Description	Unit	$ Cost
Clock System, 20 room	Ea.	20,200
50 room	Ea.	48,200
Elevators, hydraulic passenger, 2 stops, 2000# capacity	Ea.	74,100
3500# capacity	Ea.	81,600
Additional stop, add	Ea.	8375
Seating, auditorium chair, all veneer	Ea.	355
Veneer back, padded seat	Ea.	380
Upholstered, spring seat	Ea.	335
Classroom, movable chair & desk	Set	81 - 171
Lecture hall, pedestal type	Ea.	350 - 650
Sound System, amplifier, 250 watts	Ea.	2025
Speaker, ceiling or wall	Ea.	240
Trumpet	Ea.	460
TV Antenna, Master system, 30 outlet	Outlet	335
100 outlet	Outlet	370

Description	Unit	$ Cost
Commissioning Fees, sustainable institutional construction	S.F.	0.58 - 2.47
Energy Modelling Fees, academic buildings to 10,000 SF	Ea.	9000
Greater than 10,000 SF add	S.F.	0.20
Green Bldg Cert Fees for school construction project reg	Project	900
Photovoltaic Pwr Sys, grid connected, 20 kW (~2400 SF), roof	Ea.	249,200
Green Roofs, 6" soil depth, w/treated wd edging & sedum mats	S.F.	12.41
10" Soil depth, with treated wood edging & sedum mats	S.F.	14.10
Greywater Recovery Systems, prepackaged comm, 3060 gal.	Ea.	45,900
4590 gal.	Ea.	57,625
Rainwater Harvest Sys, prepckged comm, 10,000 gal, sys contrller	Ea.	37,550
20,000 gal. w/system controller	Ea.	61,000
30,000 gal. w/system controller	Ea.	97,350
Solar Domestic HW, closed loop, add-on sys, ext heat exchanger	Ea.	11,300
Drainback, hot water system, 120 gal tank	Ea.	14,175
Draindown, hot water system, 120 gal tank	Ea.	14,425

Important: See the Reference Section for Location Factors.

G College, Classroom, 2-3 Story

Model costs calculated for a 2 story building with 12' story height and 50,000 square feet of floor area

				Unit	Unit Cost	Cost Per S.F.	% Of Sub-Total
A.	**SUBSTRUCTURE**						
1010	Standard Foundations	Poured concrete; strip and spread footings		S.F. Ground	1.38	.69	
1020	Special Foundations	N/A		—	—	—	3.6%
1030	Slab on Grade	4" reinforced concrete with vapor barrier and granular base		S.F. Slab	5.84	2.93	
2010	Basement Excavation	Site preparation for slab and trench for foundation wall and footing		S.F. Ground	.31	.16	
2020	Basement Walls	4' Foundation wall		L.F. Wall	186	1.91	
B.	**SHELL**						
	B10 Superstructure						
1010	Floor Construction	Open web steel joists, slab form, concrete		S.F. Floor	18.66	9.33	9.3%
1020	Roof Construction	Metal deck on open web steel joists, columns		S.F. Roof	10.84	5.42	
	B20 Exterior Enclosure						
2010	Exterior Walls	Decorative concrete block	65% of wall	S.F. Wall	21.83	4.29	
2020	Exterior Windows	Window wall	35% of wall	Each	58	5.77	6.9%
2030	Exterior Doors	Double glass and aluminum with transom		Each	7200	.87	
	B30 Roofing						
3010	Roof Coverings	Built-up tar and gravel with flashing; perlite/EPS composite insulation		S.F. Roof	7.06	3.53	2.2%
3020	Roof Openings	N/A		—	—	—	
C.	**INTERIORS**						
1010	Partitions	Concrete block	20 SF Flr.LF Part.	S.F. Partition	24.16	12.08	
1020	Interior Doors	Single leaf hollow metal	200 S.F. Floor/Door	Each	1222	6.11	
1030	Fittings	Chalkboards, counters, cabinets		S.F. Floor	6.31	6.31	
2010	Stair Construction	Concrete filled metal pan		Flight	18,900	3.78	28.4%
3010	Wall Finishes	95% paint, 5% ceramic tile		S.F. Surface	4.53	4.53	
3020	Floor Finishes	70% vinyl composition tile, 25% carpet, 5% ceramic tile		S.F. Floor	4.42	4.42	
3030	Ceiling Finishes	Mineral fiber tile on concealed zee bars		S.F. Ceiling	7.60	7.60	
D.	**SERVICES**						
	D10 Conveying						
1010	Elevators & Lifts	Two hydraulic passenger elevators		Each	91,250	3.65	2.3%
1020	Escalators & Moving Walks	N/A		—	—	—	
	D20 Plumbing						
2010	Plumbing Fixtures	Toilet, low flow, auto sensor & service fixt., supply & drain.	1 Fixt./455 SF Flr.	Each	8959	19.69	
2020	Domestic Water Distribution	Oil fired hot water heater		S.F. Floor	.84	.84	13.5%
2040	Rain Water Drainage	Roof drains		S.F. Roof	1.66	.83	
	D30 HVAC						
3010	Energy Supply	N/A		—	—	—	
3020	Heat Generating Systems	Included in D3050		—	—	—	
3040	Distribution Systems	Enthalpy heat recovery packages		Each	38,725	2.33	14.3%
3050	Terminal & Package Units	Multizone unit, gas heating, electric cooling, SEER 14		S.F. Floor	20.20	20.20	
3090	Other HVAC Sys. & Equipment	N/A		—	—	—	
	D40 Fire Protection						
4010	Sprinklers	Sprinklers, light hazard		S.F. Floor	3.30	3.30	2.3%
4020	Standpipes	Standpipe, dry, Class III		S.F. Floor	.39	.39	
	D50 Electrical						
5010	Electrical Service/Distribution	2000 ampere service, panel board and feeders		S.F. Floor	3.02	3.02	
5020	Lighting & Branch Wiring	LED fixtures, receptacles, switches, A.C. & misc. power		S.F. Floor	14.62	14.62	17.0%
5030	Communications & Security	Addressable alarm sys., internet wiring, comm. sys. & emerg. ltg.		S.F. Floor	7.43	7.43	
5090	Other Electrical Systems	Emergency generator, 100 kW		S.F. Floor	1.77	1.77	
E.	**EQUIPMENT & FURNISHINGS**						
1010	Commercial Equipment	N/A		—	—	—	
1020	Institutional Equipment	N/A		—	—	—	0.1%
1090	Other Equipment	Waste handling recycling tilt truck		S.F. Floor	.13	.13	
2020	Moveable Furnishings	No smoking signage		S.F. Floor			
F.	**SPECIAL CONSTRUCTION**						
1020	Integrated Construction	N/A		—	—	—	0.0%
1040	Special Facilities	N/A		—	—	—	
G.	**BUILDING SITEWORK**	N/A					

	Sub-Total	157.93	100%
CONTRACTOR FEES (General Requirements: 10%, Overhead: 5%, Profit: 10%)	25%	39.50	
ARCHITECT FEES	7%	13.82	
	Total Building Cost	**211.25**	

For customer support on your Green Building Costs with RSMeans data, call 800.448.8182.

COMMERCIAL/INDUSTRIAL/INSTITUTIONAL

G.130 — G College, Dormitory, 2-3 Story

Costs per square foot of floor area

Exterior Wall	S.F. Area	10000	15000	25000	40000	55000	70000	80000	90000	100000
	L.F. Perimeter	260	320	400	476	575	628	684	721	772
Face Brick and Concrete Block	Reinforced Concrete	270.95	255.50	239.45	227.95	223.70	219.75	218.45	217.05	216.20
	Rigid Steel	283.10	267.65	251.65	240.15	235.85	231.90	230.65	229.20	228.35
Decorative Concrete Block	Reinforced Concrete	251.55	239.60	227.55	219.10	215.85	213.05	212.10	211.10	210.45
	Rigid Steel	263.70	251.75	239.70	231.25	228.00	225.25	224.30	223.25	222.60
Precast Concrete	Reinforced Concrete	290.25	271.35	251.35	236.80	231.40	226.40	224.85	223.00	221.90
	Rigid Steel	302.45	283.50	263.50	249.00	243.60	238.60	237.05	235.15	234.10
Perimeter Adj., Add or Deduct	Per 100 L.F.	22.85	15.25	9.15	5.75	4.10	3.25	2.95	2.55	2.30
Story Hgt. Adj., Add or Deduct	Per 1 Ft.	4.40	3.65	2.75	2.05	1.75	1.50	1.50	1.35	1.30

For Basement, add $41.33 per square foot of basement area

The above costs were calculated using the basic specifications shown on the facing page. These costs should be adjusted where necessary for design alternatives and owner's requirements.

Common additives

Description	Unit	$ Cost
Closed Circuit Surveillance, one station, camera & monitor	Ea.	1475
For additional camera stations, add	Ea.	665
Elevators, hydraulic passenger, 2 stops, 3500# capacity	Ea.	81,600
Additional stop, add	Ea.	8375
Furniture	Student	2800 - 5350
Intercom System, 25 station capacity		
Master station	Ea.	3225
Intercom outlets	Ea.	212
Kitchen Equipment		
Broiler	Ea.	4425
Coffee urn, twin 6 gallon	Ea.	2900
Cooler, 6 ft. long	Ea.	3750
Dishwasher, 10-12 racks per hr.	Ea.	4150
Food warmer	Ea.	790
Freezer, 44 C.F., reach-in	Ea.	5525
Ice cube maker, 50 lb. per day	Ea.	2100
Range with 1 oven	Ea.	3575
Laundry Equipment, dryer, 30 lb. capacity	Ea.	4100
Washer, commercial	Ea.	1700
TV Antenna, Master system, 30 outlet	Outlet	335
100 outlet	Outlet	370

Description	Unit	$ Cost
Commissioning Fees, sustainable institutional construction	S.F.	0.58 - 2.47
Energy Modelling Fees, academic buildings to 10,000 SF	Ea.	9000
Greater than 10,000 SF add	S.F.	0.20
Green Bldg Cert Fees for school construction project reg	Project	900
Photovoltaic Pwr Sys, grid connected, 20 kW (~2400 SF), roof	Ea.	249,200
Green Roofs, 6" soil depth, w/treated wd edging & sedum mats	S.F.	12.41
10" Soil depth, with treated wood edging & sedum mats	S.F.	14.10
Greywater Recovery Systems, prepackaged comm, 3060 gal.	Ea.	45,900
4590 gal.	Ea.	57,625
Rainwater Harvest Sys, prepckged comm, 30,000 gal, sys contrller	Ea.	97,350
Solar Domestic HW, closed loop, add-on sys, ext heat exchanger	Ea.	11,300
Drainback, hot water system, 120 gal tank	Ea.	14,175
Draindown, hot water system, 120 gal tank	Ea.	14,425

Important: See the Reference Section for Location Factors.

Model costs calculated for a 3 story building with 12' story height and 25,000 square feet of floor area

G College, Dormitory, 2-3 Story

				Unit	Unit Cost	Cost Per S.F.	% Of Sub-Total
A.	**SUBSTRUCTURE**						
1010	Standard Foundations	Poured concrete; strip and spread footings		S.F. Ground	6.81	2.27	
1020	Special Foundations	N/A		—	—	—	
1030	Slab on Grade	4" reinforced concrete with recycled vapor barrier and granular base		S.F. Slab	5.84	1.95	3.3%
2010	Basement Excavation	Site preparation for slab and trench for foundation wall and footing		S.F. Ground	.18	.06	
2020	Basement Walls	4' Foundation wall		L.F. Wall	98	1.57	
B.	**SHELL**						
	B10 Superstructure						
1010	Floor Construction	Concrete flat plate		S.F. Floor	27.21	18.14	12.9%
1020	Roof Construction	Concrete flat plate		S.F. Roof	14.88	4.96	
	B20 Exterior Enclosure						
2010	Exterior Walls	Face brick with concrete block backup	80% of wall	S.F. Wall	41.19	18.98	
2020	Exterior Windows	Aluminum horizontal sliding	20% of wall	Each	755	3.78	13.8%
2030	Exterior Doors	Double glass & aluminum doors		Each	7800	1.88	
	B30 Roofing						
3010	Roof Coverings	Single-ply TPO membrane, heat welded w/R-20 insul.		S.F. Roof	8.10	2.70	1.5%
3020	Roof Openings	N/A		—	—	—	
C.	**INTERIORS**						
1010	Partitions	Gypsum board on metal studs, CMU w/foamed-in insul.	9 SF Flr./LF Part.	S.F. Partition	8.20	9.11	
1020	Interior Doors	Single leaf wood, low VOC paint	90 S.F. Floor/Door	Each	720	8	
1030	Fittings	Closet shelving, mirrors, bathroom accessories		S.F. Floor	1.78	1.78	
2010	Stair Construction	Cast in place concrete		Flight	5850	3.05	18.6%
3010	Wall Finishes	95% paint, low VOC paint, 5% ceramic tile		S.F. Surface	2.20	4.89	
3020	Floor Finishes	80% carpet tile, 10% vinyl comp. tile, recycled content, 10% ceramic tile		S.F. Floor	5.23	5.23	
3030	Ceiling Finishes	90% paint, low VOC, 10% suspended fiberglass board		S.F. Ceiling	1.31	1.32	
D.	**SERVICES**						
	D10 Conveying						
1010	Elevators & Lifts	One hydraulic passenger elevator		Each	124,000	4.96	2.8%
1020	Escalators & Moving Walks	N/A		—	—	—	
	D20 Plumbing						
2010	Plumbing Fixtures	Toilet, low flow, auto sensor, & service fixt., supply & drain.	1 Fixt./455 SF Flr.	Each	12,221	26.86	
2020	Domestic Water Distribution	Electric, point-of-use water heater		S.F. Floor	1.31	1.31	16.1%
2040	Rain Water Drainage	Roof drains		S.F. Roof	1.89	.63	
	D30 HVAC						
3010	Energy Supply	N/A		—	—	—	
3020	Heat Generating Systems	Included in D3050		—	—	—	
3040	Distribution Systems	Enthalpy heat recovery packages		Each	31,850	1.27	8.1%
3050	Terminal & Package Units	Rooftop multizone unit system, SEER 14		S.F. Floor	13.31	13.31	
3090	Other HVAC Sys. & Equipment	N/A		—	—	—	
	D40 Fire Protection						
4010	Sprinklers	Wet pipe sprinkler system		S.F. Floor	3.12	3.12	2.3%
4020	Standpipes	Standpipe, dry, Class III		S.F. Floor	1	1	
	D50 Electrical						
5010	Electrical Service/Distribution	800 ampere service, panel board and feeders		S.F. Floor	1.58	1.58	
5020	Lighting & Branch Wiring	LED fixtures, daylt. dim., ltg. on/off, recept., switches, and A.C. power		S.F. Floor	19.83	19.83	18.3%
5030	Communications & Security	Alarm sys., internet & phone wiring, comm. sys. and emergency ltg.		S.F. Floor	10.28	10.28	
5090	Other Electrical Systems	Emergency generator, 7.5 kW, energy monitoring systems		S.F. Floor	1.11	1.11	
E.	**EQUIPMENT & FURNISHINGS**						
1010	Commercial Equipment	N/A		—	—	—	
1020	Institutional Equipment	N/A		—	—	—	2.3%
1090	Other Equipment	Waste handling recycling tilt truck		S.F. Floor	.25	.25	
2020	Moveable Furnishings	Dormitory furniture, no smoking signage		S.F. Floor	3.86	3.86	
F.	**SPECIAL CONSTRUCTION**						
1020	Integrated Construction	N/A		—	—	—	0.0%
1040	Special Facilities	N/A		—	—	—	
G.	**BUILDING SITEWORK**	N/A					

	Sub-Total	179.04	100%
CONTRACTOR FEES (General Requirements: 10%, Overhead: 5%, Profit: 10%)	25%	44.74	
ARCHITECT FEES	7%	15.67	
	Total Building Cost	**239.45**	

For customer support on your Green Building Costs with RSMeans data, call 800.448.8182.

COMMERCIAL/INDUSTRIAL/INSTITUTIONAL

G.140 G College, Dormitory, 4-8 Story

Costs per square foot of floor area

Exterior Wall	S.F. Area	20000	35000	45000	65000	85000	110000	135000	160000	200000
	L.F. Perimeter	260	340	400	440	500	540	560	590	640
Face Brick and Concrete Block	Reinforced Concrete	269.60	250.20	245.05	234.10	229.35	224.40	220.65	218.35	215.90
	Rigid Steel	282.85	263.50	258.35	247.35	242.60	237.70	233.90	231.60	229.15
Decorative Concrete Block	Reinforced Concrete	252.05	237.05	233.05	224.90	221.40	217.80	215.05	213.35	211.60
	Rigid Steel	265.30	250.35	246.30	238.20	234.65	231.05	228.30	226.60	224.85
Precast Concrete	Reinforced Concrete	274.95	254.15	248.65	236.85	231.75	226.45	222.30	219.85	217.25
	Rigid Steel	288.20	267.45	261.90	250.10	245.00	239.70	235.55	233.10	230.50
Perimeter Adj., Add or Deduct	Per 100 L.F.	22.25	12.75	9.90	6.85	5.20	4.10	3.30	2.80	2.25
Story Hgt. Adj., Add or Deduct	Per 1 Ft.	4.45	3.30	3.05	2.35	2.00	1.70	1.45	1.30	1.10

For Basement, add $41.33 per square foot of basement area

The above costs were calculated using the basic specifications shown on the facing page. These costs should be adjusted where necessary for design alternatives and owner's requirements.

Common additives

Description	Unit	$ Cost
Closed Circuit Surveillance, one station, camera & monitor	Ea.	1475
For additional camera stations, add	Ea.	665
Elevators, electric passenger, 5 stops, 3500# capacity	Ea.	193,000
Additional stop, add	Ea.	10,900
Furniture	Student	2800 - 5350
Intercom System, 25 station capacity		
Master station	Ea.	3225
Intercom outlets	Ea.	212
Kitchen Equipment		
Broiler	Ea.	4425
Coffee urn, twin, 6 gallon	Ea.	2900
Cooler, 6 ft. long	Ea.	3750
Dishwasher, 10-12 racks per hr.	Ea.	4150
Food warmer	Ea.	790
Freezer, 44 C.F., reach-in	Ea.	5525
Ice cube maker, 50 lb. per day	Ea.	2100
Range with 1 oven	Ea.	3575
Laundry Equipment, dryer, 30 lb. capacity	Ea.	4100
Washer, commercial	Ea.	1700
TV Antenna, Master system, 30 outlet	Outlet	335
100 outlet	Outlet	370

Description	Unit	$ Cost
Commissioning Fees, sustainable institutional construction	S.F.	0.58 - 2.47
Energy Modelling Fees, academic buildings to 10,000 SF	Ea.	9000
Greater than 10,000 SF add	S.F.	0.20
Green Bldg Cert Fees for school construction project reg	Project	900
Photovoltaic Pwr Sys, grid connected, 20 kW (~2400 SF), roof	Ea.	249,200
Green Roofs, 6" soil depth, w/treated wd edging & sedum mats	S.F.	12.41
10" Soil depth, with treated wood edging & sedum mats	S.F.	14.10
Greywater Recovery Systems, prepackaged comm, 3060 gal.	Ea.	45,900
4590 gal.	Ea.	57,625
Rainwater Harvest Sys, prepckged comm, 30,000 gal, sys contrller	Ea.	97,350
Solar Domestic HW, closed loop, add-on sys, ext heat exchanger	Ea.	11,300
Drainback, hot water system, 120 gal tank	Ea.	14,175
Draindown, hot water system, 120 gal tank	Ea.	14,425

Important: See the Reference Section for Location Factors.

Model costs calculated for a 6 story building with 12' story height and 85,000 square feet of floor area

G College, Dormitory, 4-8 Story

				Unit	Unit Cost	Cost Per S.F.	% Of Sub-Total
A.	**SUBSTRUCTURE**						
1010	Standard Foundations	Poured concrete; strip and spread footings		S.F. Ground	10.14	1.69	
1020	Special Foundations	N/A		—	—	—	2.0%
1030	Slab on Grade	4" reinforced concrete with recycled vapor barrier and granular base		S.F. Slab	5.84	.98	
2010	Basement Excavation	Site preparation for slab and trench for foundation wall and footing		S.F. Ground	.31	.05	
2020	Basement Walls	4' foundation wall		L.F. Wall	186	.81	
B.	**SHELL**						
	B10 Superstructure						
1010	Floor Construction	Concrete slab with metal deck and beams		S.F. Floor	30.46	25.38	16.6%
1020	Roof Construction	Concrete slab with metal deck and beams		S.F. Roof	22.86	3.81	
	B20 Exterior Enclosure						
2010	Exterior Walls	Decorative concrete block	80% of wall	S.F. Wall	23.67	8.02	
2020	Exterior Windows	Aluminum horizontal sliding	20% of wall	Each	529	2.99	6.5%
2030	Exterior Doors	Double glass & aluminum doors		Each	4663	.44	
	B30 Roofing						
3010	Roof Coverings	Single-ply TPO membrane, 60 mils, heat welded seams w/R-20 insul.		S.F. Roof	7.56	1.26	0.7%
3020	Roof Openings	N/A		—	—	—	
C.	**INTERIORS**						
1010	Partitions	Concrete block w/foamed-in insulation	9 SF Floor/LF Part.	S.F. Partition	13.20	14.67	
1020	Interior Doors	Single leaf wood, low VOC paint	90 S.F. Floor/Door	Each	725	8.06	
1030	Fittings	Closet shelving, mirrors, bathroom accessories		S.F. Floor	1.46	1.46	
2010	Stair Construction	Concrete filled metal pan		Flight	18,900	4	23.5%
3010	Wall Finishes	95% paint, low VOC, 5% ceramic tile		S.F. Surface	2.95	6.55	
3020	Floor Finishes	80% carpet tile, 10% vinyl comp. tile, recycled, 10% ceramic tile		S.F. Floor	5.23	5.23	
3030	Ceiling Finishes	Mineral fiber tile on concealed zee bars, paint		S.F. Ceiling	1.31	1.32	
D.	**SERVICES**						
	D10 Conveying						
1010	Elevators & Lifts	Four geared passenger elevators		Each	267,113	12.57	7.2%
1020	Escalators & Moving Walks	N/A		—	—	—	
	D20 Plumbing						
2010	Plumbing Fixtures	Toilet, low flow, auto sensor, & service fixt., supply & drain.	1 Fixt./390 SF Flr.	Each	10,417	26.71	
2020	Domestic Water Distribution	Electric water heater, point-of-use, energy saver		S.F. Floor	.74	.74	15.9%
2040	Rain Water Drainage	Roof drains		S.F. Roof	2.28	.38	
	D30 HVAC						
3010	Energy Supply	N/A		—	—	—	
3020	Heat Generating Systems	N/A		—	—	—	
3040	Distribution Systems	Enthalpy heat recovery packages		Each	31,850	.37	7.8%
3050	Terminal & Package Units	Multizone rooftop air conditioner, SEER 14		S.F. Floor	13.31	13.31	
3090	Other HVAC Sys. & Equipment	N/A					
	D40 Fire Protection						
4010	Sprinklers	Sprinklers, light hazard		S.F. Floor	3.06	3.06	2.1%
4020	Standpipes	Standpipe, dry, Class III		S.F. Floor	.71	.71	
	D50 Electrical						
5010	Electrical Service/Distribution	1200 ampere service, panel board and feeders		S.F. Floor	.83	.83	
5020	Lighting & Branch Wiring	LED fixtures, daylt. dim., ltg. on/off, recept. switches, and A.C. power		S.F. Floor	18.50	18.50	15.8%
5030	Communications & Security	Alarm systems, internet & phone wiring, comm. systems and emerg. ltg.		S.F. Floor	7.44	7.44	
5090	Other Electrical Systems	Emergency generator, 30 kW, energy monitoring systems		S.F. Floor	.88	.88	
E.	**EQUIPMENT & FURNISHINGS**						
1010	Commercial Equipment	N/A		—	—	—	
1020	Institutional Equipment	N/A		—	—	—	1.8%
1090	Other Equipment	Waste handling recycling tilt truck		S.F. Floor	.08	.08	
2020	Moveable Furnishings	Built-in dormitory furnishings, no smoking signage		S.F. Floor	3.14	3.14	
F.	**SPECIAL CONSTRUCTION**						
1020	Integrated Construction	N/A		—	—	—	0.0%
1040	Special Facilities	N/A		—	—	—	
G.	**BUILDING SITEWORK**	N/A					

		Sub-Total	175.44	100%
CONTRACTOR FEES (General Requirements: 10%, Overhead: 5%, Profit: 10%)		25%	43.86	
ARCHITECT FEES		7%	15.35	
	Total Building Cost		**234.65**	

For customer support on your Green Building Costs with RSMeans data, call 800.448.8182.

COMMERCIAL/INDUSTRIAL/INSTITUTIONAL

G.150 G College, Laboratory

Costs per square foot of floor area

Exterior Wall	S.F. Area	12000	20000	28000	37000	45000	57000	68000	80000	92000
	L.F. Perimeter	470	600	698	793	900	1000	1075	1180	1275
Face Brick and Concrete Block	Rigid Steel	353.50	297.50	271.55	255.20	246.95	237.20	230.85	226.50	223.05
	Bearing Walls	348.20	292.25	266.25	249.90	241.65	231.90	225.55	221.25	217.75
Decorative Concrete Block	Rigid Steel	344.95	290.95	266.15	250.50	242.60	233.35	227.40	223.25	220.00
	Bearing Walls	339.95	285.95	261.10	245.50	237.60	228.35	222.40	218.25	215.00
Stucco and Concrete Block	Rigid Steel	357.20	300.35	273.95	257.20	248.80	238.90	232.40	227.90	224.35
	Bearing Walls	352.15	295.30	268.85	252.15	243.80	233.85	227.30	222.85	219.35
Perimeter Adj., Add or Deduct	Per 100 L.F.	13.40	8.00	5.75	4.35	3.55	2.85	2.40	2.00	1.70
Story Hgt. Adj., Add or Deduct	Per 1 Ft.	2.60	1.95	1.65	1.35	1.30	1.20	1.05	1.00	0.90

For Basement, add $26.69 per square foot of basement area

The above costs were calculated using the basic specifications shown on the facing page. These costs should be adjusted where necessary for design alternatives and owner's requirements.

Common additives

Description	Unit	$ Cost
Cabinets, Base, door units, metal	L.F.	350
Drawer units	L.F.	690
Tall storage cabinets, open	L.F.	640
With doors	L.F.	1025
Wall, metal 12-1/2" deep, open	L.F.	294
With doors	L.F.	520
Countertops, not incl. base cabinets, acid proof	S.F.	67 - 70
Stainless steel	S.F.	196
Fume Hood, Not incl. ductwork	L.F.	845 - 2000
Ductwork	Hood	6450 - 10,200
Glassware Washer, Distilled water rinse	Ea.	8150 - 17,500
Seating, auditorium chair, veneer back, padded seat	Ea.	380
Upholstered, spring seat	Ea.	335
Classroom, movable chair & desk	Set	81 - 171
Lecture hall, pedestal type	Ea.	350 - 650
Safety Equipment, Eye wash, hand held	Ea.	455
Deluge shower	Ea.	900
Tables, acid resist. top, drawers	L.F.	229
Titration Unit, Four 2000 ml reservoirs	Ea.	6650

Description	Unit	$ Cost
Commissioning Fees, sustainable institutional construction	S.F.	0.58 - 2.47
Energy Modelling Fees, academic buildings to 10,000 SF	Ea.	9000
Greater than 10,000 SF add	S.F.	0.20
Green Bldg Cert Fees for school construction project reg	Project	900
Photovoltaic Pwr Sys, grid connected, 20 kW (~2400 SF), roof	Ea.	249,200
Green Roofs, 6" soil depth, w/treated wd edging & sedum mats	S.F.	12.41
10" Soil depth, with treated wood edging & sedum mats	S.F.	14.10
Greywater Recovery Systems, prepackaged comm, 3060 gal.	Ea.	45,900
4590 gal.	Ea.	57,625
Rainwater Harvest Sys, prepckged comm, 30,000 gal, sys contrller	Ea.	97,350
Solar Domestic HW, closed loop, add-on sys, ext heat exchanger	Ea.	11,300
Drainback, hot water system, 120 gal tank	Ea.	14,175
Draindown, hot water system, 120 gal tank	Ea.	14,425

Important: See the Reference Section for Location Factors.

Model costs calculated for a 1 story building with 12' story height and 45,000 square feet of floor area

G College, Laboratory

				Unit	Unit Cost	Cost Per S.F.	% Of Sub-Total
A.	**SUBSTRUCTURE**						
1010	Standard Foundations	Poured concrete; strip and spread footings		S.F. Ground	3.41	3.41	
1020	Special Foundations	N/A		—	—	—	9.7%
1030	Slab on Grade	4" reinforced concrete with recycled vapor barrier and granular base		S.F. Slab	5.84	5.84	
2010	Basement Excavation	Site preparation for slab and trench for foundation wall and footing		S.F. Ground	.18	.18	
2020	Basement Walls	4' foundation wall		L.F. Wall	186	7.64	
B.	**SHELL**						
	B10 Superstructure						
1010	Floor Construction	Metal deck on open web steel joists	(5680 S.F.)	S.F. Floor	2.42	2.42	4.6%
1020	Roof Construction	Metal deck on open web steel joists		S.F. Roof	5.59	5.59	
	B20 Exterior Enclosure						
2010	Exterior Walls	Face brick with concrete block backup	75% of wall	S.F. Wall	41.22	7.42	
2020	Exterior Windows	Window wall	25% of wall	Each	58	3.27	7.6%
2030	Exterior Doors	Glass and metal doors and entrances with transom		Each	6168	2.74	
	B30 Roofing						
3010	Roof Coverings	Single-ply TPO membrane, 60 mils, heat welded w/R-20 insul.		S.F. Roof	6.80	6.80	4.1%
3020	Roof Openings	Skylight		S.F. Roof	.43	.43	
C.	**INTERIORS**						
1010	Partitions	Concrete block, foamed-in insulation	10 SF Flr./LF Part.	S.F. Partition	15.15	15.15	
1020	Interior Doors	Single leaf-kalamein fire doors, low VOC paint	820 S.F. Floor/Door	Each	1452	1.77	
1030	Fittings	Lockers		S.F. Floor	.05	.05	
2010	Stair Construction	N/A		—	—	—	21.0%
3010	Wall Finishes	60% paint, low VOC, 40% epoxy coating		S.F. Surface	2.92	5.83	
3020	Floor Finishes	60% epoxy, 20% carpet, 20% vinyl composition tile, recycled content		S.F. Floor	6.57	6.57	
3030	Ceiling Finishes	Mineral fiber tile on concealed zee runners		S.F. Ceiling	7.60	7.60	
D.	**SERVICES**						
	D10 Conveying						
1010	Elevators & Lifts	N/A		—	—	—	0.0 %
1020	Escalators & Moving Walks	N/A		—	—	—	
	D20 Plumbing						
2010	Plumbing Fixtures	Toilet, low flow, auto sensor & service fixt., supply & drain.	1 Fixt./260 SF Flr.	Each	8445	32.48	
2020	Domestic Water Distribution	Electric, point-of-use water heater		S.F. Floor	1.67	1.67	19.9%
2040	Rain Water Drainage	Roof drains		S.F. Roof	.90	.90	
	D30 HVAC						
3010	Energy Supply	N/A		—	—	—	
3020	Heat Generating Systems	Included in D3050					
3040	Distribution Systems	Enthalpy heat recovery packages		Each	38,725	.87	12.0 %
3050	Terminal & Package Units	Multizone rooftop air conditioner, SEER 14		S.F. Floor	20.20	20.20	
3090	Other HVAC Sys. & Equipment	N/A		—	—	—	
	D40 Fire Protection						
4010	Sprinklers	Sprinklers, light hazard		S.F. Floor	2.93	2.93	1.9%
4020	Standpipes	Standpipe, wet, Class III		S.F. Floor	.35	.35	
	D50 Electrical						
5010	Electrical Service/Distribution	1000 ampere service, panel board and feeders		S.F. Floor	1.38	1.38	
5020	Lighting & Branch Wiring	LED fixtures, daylt. dim., ltg. on/off, recept., switches, & A.C. power		S.F. Floor	26.37	26.37	18.2%
5030	Communications & Security	Addressable alarm systems, internet wiring, & emergency lighting		S.F. Floor	3.39	3.39	
5090	Other Electrical Systems	Emergency generator, 11.5 kW, UPS, and energy monitoring systems		S.F. Floor	.79	.79	
E.	**EQUIPMENT & FURNISHINGS**						
1010	Commercial Equipment	N/A		—	—	—	
1020	Institutional Equipment	Cabinets, fume hoods, lockers, glassware washer		S.F. Floor	1.54	1.54	1.0%
1090	Other Equipment	Waste handling recycling tilt truck		S.F. Floor	.14	.14	
2020	Moveable Furnishings	No smoking signage		S.F. Floor	.02	.02	
F.	**SPECIAL CONSTRUCTION**						
1020	Integrated Construction	N/A		—	—	—	0.0 %
1040	Special Facilities	N/A		—	—	—	
G.	**BUILDING SITEWORK**	N/A					

	Sub-Total	175.74	100%
CONTRACTOR FEES (General Requirements: 10%, Overhead: 5%, Profit: 10%)	25%	43.94	
ARCHITECT FEES	10%	21.97	
	Total Building Cost	**241.65**	

For customer support on your Green Building Costs with RSMeans data, call 800.448.8182.

COMMERCIAL/INDUSTRIAL/INSTITUTIONAL

G.220 G Fire Station, 1 Story

Costs per square foot of floor area

Exterior Wall	S.F. Area	4000	4500	5000	5500	6000	6500	7000	7500	8000
	L.F. Perimeter	260	280	300	310	320	336	353	370	386
Face Brick and Concrete Block	Steel Joists	232.05	227.55	224.00	219.15	215.15	212.75	210.85	209.15	207.50
	Bearing Walls	224.35	219.80	216.30	211.45	207.45	205.05	203.15	201.45	199.80
Decorative Concrete Block	Steel Joists	214.25	210.45	207.55	203.70	200.55	198.60	197.00	195.60	194.30
	Bearing Walls	208.15	204.35	201.45	197.60	194.40	192.50	190.90	189.50	188.20
Limestone and Concrete Block	Steel Joists	248.45	243.25	239.20	233.35	228.60	225.85	223.55	221.60	219.70
	Bearing Walls	242.35	237.15	233.10	227.25	222.50	219.70	217.45	215.50	213.60
Perimeter Adj., Add or Deduct	Per 100 L.F.	25.35	22.60	20.35	18.45	16.95	15.60	14.50	13.50	12.75
Story Hgt. Adj., Add or Deduct	Per 1 Ft.	3.40	3.20	3.10	2.90	2.75	2.70	2.60	2.55	2.55

For Basement, add $45.29 per square foot of basement area

The above costs were calculated using the basic specifications shown on the facing page. These costs should be adjusted where necessary for design alternatives and owner's requirements.

Common additives

Description	Unit	$ Cost
Appliances, cooking range, 30" free standing		
1 oven	Ea.	610 - 2775
2 oven	Ea.	1200 - 3725
Microwave oven	Ea.	281 - 855
Compactor, residential, 4-1 compaction	Ea.	885 - 1475
Dishwasher, built-in, 2 cycles	Ea.	685 - 1225
4 cycles	Ea.	800 - 2025
Garbage disposer, sink type	Ea.	260 - 370
Hood for range, 2 speed, vented, 30" wide	Ea.	370 - 1450
Refrigerator, no frost 10-12 C.F.	Ea.	580 - 750
14-16 C.F.	Ea.	720 - 1025
18-20 C.F.	Ea.	895 - 2075
Lockers, Steel, single tier, 60" or 72"	Opng.	232 - 395
Locker bench, lam. maple top only	L.F.	36.50
Pedestals, steel pipe	Ea.	79
Sound System, amplifier, 250 watts	Ea.	2025
Speaker, ceiling or wall	Ea.	240
Trumpet	Ea.	460

Description	Unit	$ Cost
Commissioning Fees, sustainable commercial construction	S.F.	0.24 - 3.04
Energy Modelling Fees, Fire Stations to 10,000 SF	Ea.	11,000
Green Bldg Cert Fees for comm construction project reg	Project	900
Photovoltaic Pwr Sys, grid connected, 20 kW (~2400 SF), roof	Ea.	249,200
Green Roofs, 6" soil depth, w/treated wd edging & sedum mats	S.F.	12.41
10" Soil depth, with treated wood edging & sedum mats	S.F.	14.10
Greywater Recovery Systems, prepackaged comm, 3060 gal.	Ea.	45,900
4590 gal.	Ea.	57,625
Rainwater Harvest Sys, prepckged comm, 10,000 gal, sys contrller	Ea.	37,550
20,000 gal. w/system controller	Ea.	61,000
30,000 gal. w/system controller	Ea.	97,350
Solar Domestic HW, closed loop, add-on sys, ext heat exchanger	Ea.	11,300
Drainback, hot water system, 120 gal tank	Ea.	14,175

Important: See the Reference Section for Location Factors.

Model costs calculated for a 1 story building with 14' story height and 6,000 square feet of floor area

G Fire Station, 1 Story

				Unit	Unit Cost	Cost Per S.F.	% Of Sub-Total
A.	**SUBSTRUCTURE**						
1010	Standard Foundations	Poured concrete; strip and spread footings		S.F. Ground	3.63	3.63	
1020	Special Foundations	N/A		—	—	—	
1030	Slab on Grade	6" reinforced concrete with recycled vapor barrier and granular base		S.F. Slab	7.51	7.51	10.6%
2010	Basement Excavation	Site preparation for slab and trench for foundation wall and footing		S.F. Ground	.57	.57	
2020	Basement Walls	4' foundation wall		L.F. Wall	98	5.22	
B.	**SHELL**						
	B10 Superstructure						
1010	Floor Construction	N/A		—	—	—	6.8 %
1020	Roof Construction	Metal deck, open web steel joists, beams on columns		S.F. Roof	10.90	10.90	
	B20 Exterior Enclosure						
2010	Exterior Walls	Face brick with concrete block backup	75% of wall	S.F. Wall	41.20	23.07	
2020	Exterior Windows	Aluminum insulated glass	10% of wall	Each	873	2.04	19.3%
2030	Exterior Doors	Single aluminum and glass, overhead, hollow metal, low VOC paint	15% of wall	S.F. Door	3678	5.58	
	B30 Roofing						
3010	Roof Coverings	Single-ply TPO membrane, 60 mil, with flashing, R-20 insulation and roof edges		S.F. Roof	8.34	8.34	5.4%
3020	Roof Openings	Skylights, roof hatches		S.F. Roof	.19	.19	
C.	**INTERIORS**						
1010	Partitions	Concrete block w/foamed-in insulation	17 S.F. Floor/LF Part.	S.F. Partition	12.04	7.08	
1020	Interior Doors	Single leaf hollow metal, low VOC paint	500 S.F. Floor/Door	Each	1222	2.44	
1030	Fittings	Toilet partitions		S.F. Floor	.52	.52	
2010	Stair Construction	N/A		—	—	—	12.4%
3010	Wall Finishes	Paint, low VOC		S.F. Surface	2.55	3	
3020	Floor Finishes	50% vinyl tile with recycled content, 50% paint, low VOC		S.F. Floor	2.99	2.99	
3030	Ceiling Finishes	Mineral board acoustic ceiling tiles, concealed grid, suspended	50% of area	S.F. Ceiling	3.80	3.81	
D.	**SERVICES**						
	D10 Conveying						
1010	Elevators & Lifts	N/A		—	—	—	0.0 %
1020	Escalators & Moving Walks	N/A		—	—	—	
	D20 Plumbing						
2010	Plumbing Fixtures	Kitchen, toilet, low flow, auto sensor & service fixt., supply & drain.	1 Fixt./375 SF Flr.	Each	4586	12.23	
2020	Domestic Water Distribution	Water heater, tankless, on-demand, natural gas/propane		S.F. Floor	2.23	2.23	10.2%
2040	Rain Water Drainage	Roof drains		S.F. Roof	1.75	1.75	
	D30 HVAC						
3010	Energy Supply	N/A		—	—	—	
3020	Heat Generating Systems	Included in D3050		—	—	—	
3040	Distribution Systems	Enthalpy heat recovery packages		Each	15,550	2.59	15.9 %
3050	Terminal & Package Units	Multizone rooftop air conditioner, SEER 14		S.F. Floor	22.78	22.78	
3090	Other HVAC Sys. & Equipment	N/A		—	—	—	
	D40 Fire Protection						
4010	Sprinklers	Wet pipe sprinkler system		S.F. Floor	5.13	5.13	4.2%
4020	Standpipes	Standpipe, wet, Class III		S.F. Floor	1.59	1.59	
	D50 Electrical						
5010	Electrical Service/Distribution	200 ampere service, panel board and feeders		S.F. Floor	1.41	1.41	
5020	Lighting & Branch Wiring	LED fixt., daylt. dimming & ltg. on/off control, receptacles, switches, A.C. & misc. pwr.		S.F. Floor	15.38	15.38	14.5%
5030	Communications & Security	Addressable alarm systems		S.F. Floor	2.03	2.03	
5090	Other Electrical Systems	Energy monitoring systems		S.F. Floor	4.28	4.28	
E.	**EQUIPMENT & FURNISHINGS**						
1010	Commercial Equipment	N/A		—	—	—	
1020	Institutional Equipment	N/A		—	—	—	0.7%
1090	Other Equipment	Waste handling recycling tilt truck		S.F. Floor	1.04	1.04	
2020	Moveable Furnishings	No smoking signage		S.F. Floor	.04	.04	
F.	**SPECIAL CONSTRUCTION**						
1020	Integrated Construction	N/A		—	—	—	0.0 %
1040	Special Facilities	N/A		—	—	—	
G.	**BUILDING SITEWORK**	N/A					

	Sub-Total	159.37	100%
CONTRACTOR FEES (General Requirements: 10%, Overhead: 5%, Profit: 10%)	25%	39.84	
ARCHITECT FEES	8%	15.94	
Total Building Cost		**215.15**	

For customer support on your Green Building Costs with RSMeans data, call 800.448.8182.

COMMERCIAL/INDUSTRIAL/INSTITUTIONAL

G.230 G Fire Station, 2 Story

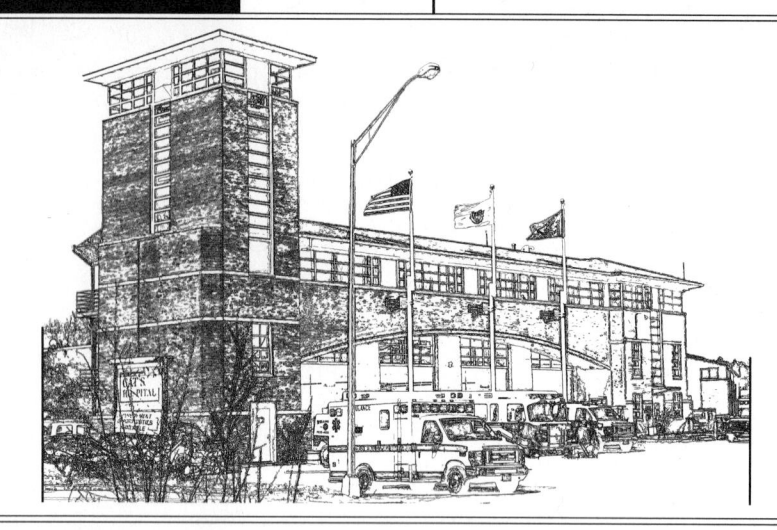

Costs per square foot of floor area

Exterior Wall	S.F. Area	6000	7000	8000	9000	10000	11000	12000	13000	14000
	L.F. Perimeter	220	240	260	280	286	303	320	336	353
Face Brick and Concrete Block	Steel Joists	240.10	233.15	227.85	223.80	218.10	215.15	212.75	210.65	208.85
	Precast Concrete	253.60	246.65	241.45	237.40	231.75	228.85	226.45	224.35	222.65
Decorative Concrete Block	Steel Joists	214.55	208.65	204.20	200.80	196.20	193.75	191.70	190.00	188.45
	Precast Concrete	236.95	231.10	226.70	223.30	218.85	216.35	214.35	212.65	211.15
Limestone and Concrete Block	Steel Joists	258.60	250.45	244.25	239.55	232.50	229.10	226.20	223.70	221.60
	Precast Concrete	272.10	263.95	257.85	253.10	246.20	242.80	239.90	237.40	235.30
Perimeter Adj., Add or Deduct	Per 100 L.F.	29.40	25.20	22.05	19.65	17.70	16.10	14.70	13.50	12.60
Story Hgt. Adj., Add or Deduct	Per 1 Ft.	3.85	3.65	3.45	3.30	3.05	2.90	2.80	2.65	2.70

For Basement, add $44.01 per square foot of basement area

The above costs were calculated using the basic specifications shown on the facing page. These costs should be adjusted where necessary for design alternatives and owner's requirements.

Common additives

Description	Unit	$ Cost
Appliances		
Cooking range, 30" free standing		
1 oven	Ea.	610 - 2775
2 oven	Ea.	1200 - 3725
Microwave oven	Ea.	281 - 855
Compactor, residential, 4-1 compaction	Ea.	885 - 1475
Dishwasher, built-in, 2 cycles	Ea.	685 - 1225
4 cycles	Ea.	800 - 2025
Garbage diposer, sink type	Ea.	260 - 370
Hood for range, 2 speed, vented, 30" wide	Ea.	370 - 1450
Refrigerator, no frost 10-12 C.F.	Ea.	580 - 750
14-16 C.F.	Ea.	720 - 1025
18-20 C.F.	Ea.	895 - 2075
Elevators, hydraulic passenger, 2 stops, 2500# capacity	Ea.	76,600
3500# capacity	Ea.	81,600
Lockers, Steel, single tier, 60" or 72"	Opng.	232 - 395
Locker bench, lam. maple top only	L.F.	36.50
Pedestals, steel pipe	Ea.	79
Sound System, amplifier, 250 watts	Ea.	2025
Speaker, ceiling or wall	Ea.	240
Trumpet	Ea.	460

Description	Unit	$ Cost
Commissioning Fees, sustainable commercial construction	S.F.	0.24 - 3.04
Energy Modelling Fees, Fire Stations to 10,000 SF	Ea.	11,000
Greater than 10,000 SF add	S.F.	0.04
Green Bldg Cert Fees for comm construction project reg	Project	900
Photovoltaic Pwr Sys, grid connected, 20 kW (~2400 SF), roof	Ea.	249,200
Green Roofs, 6" soil depth, w/treated wd edging & sedum mats	S.F.	12.41
10" Soil depth, with treated wood edging & sedum mats	S.F.	14.10
Greywater Recovery Systems, prepackaged comm, 3060 gal.	Ea.	45,900
4590 gal.	Ea.	57,625
Rainwater Harvest Sys, prepckged comm, 10,000 gal, sys contrller	Ea.	37,550
20,000 gal. w/system controller	Ea.	61,000
30,000 gal. w/system controller	Ea.	97,350
Solar Domestic HW, closed loop, add-on sys, ext heat exchanger	Ea.	11,300
Drainback, hot water system, 120 gal tank	Ea.	14,175

Important: See the Reference Section for Location Factors.

Model costs calculated for a 2 story building with 14' story height and 10,000 square feet of floor area

G Fire Station, 2 Story

					Unit	Unit Cost	Cost Per S.F.	% Of Sub-Total
A.	**SUBSTRUCTURE**							
1010	Standard Foundations	Poured concrete; strip and spread footings			S.F. Ground	3.40	1.70	
1020	Special Foundations	N/A			—	—	—	6.1%
1030	Slab on Grade	6" reinforced concrete with recycled vapor barrier and granular base			S.F. Slab	7.51	3.76	
2010	Basement Excavation	Site preparation for slab and trench for foundation wall and footing			S.F. Ground	.57	.29	
2020	Basement Walls	4' foundation wall with insulation			L.F. Wall	108	3.07	
B.	**SHELL**							
	B10 Superstructure							
1010	Floor Construction	Open web steel joists, slab form, concrete			S.F. Floor	15.96	7.98	7.4%
1020	Roof Construction	Metal deck on open web steel joists			S.F. Roof	5.60	2.80	
	B20 Exterior Enclosure							
2010	Exterior Walls	Decorative concrete block, insul.	75% of wall		S.F. Wall	25.21	15.14	
2020	Exterior Windows	Aluminum insulated glass	10% of wall		Each	755	2.63	15.3%
2030	Exterior Doors	Single aluminum and glass, steel overhead, hollow metal, low VOC paint	15% of wall		S.F. Door	2815	4.47	
	B30 Roofing							
3010	Roof Coverings	Single-ply TPO, 60 mils, heat welded seams w/R-20 insul.			S.F. Roof	8.52	4.26	2.9%
3020	Roof Openings	N/A			—	—	—	
C.	**INTERIORS**							
1010	Partitions	Concrete block, foamed-in insul.	10 SF Floor/LF Part.		S.F. Partition	12.04	7.08	
1020	Interior Doors	Single leaf hollow metal, low VOC paint	500 S.F. Floor/Door		Each	1452	2.90	
1030	Fittings	Toilet partitions			S.F. Floor	.47	.47	
2010	Stair Construction	Concrete filled metal pan			Flight	22,075	4.42	17.8%
3010	Wall Finishes	Paint, low VOC			S.F. Surface	4.10	4.82	
3020	Floor Finishes	50% vinyl tile, (recycled content) 50% paint (low VOC)			S.F. Floor	2.99	2.99	
3030	Ceiling Finishes	Fiberglass board on exposed grid, suspended	50% of area		S.F. Ceiling	3.15	3.16	
D.	**SERVICES**							
	D10 Conveying							
1010	Elevators & Lifts	One hydraulic passenger elevator			Each	91,200	9.12	6.3%
1020	Escalators & Moving Walks	N/A			—	—	—	
	D20 Plumbing							
2010	Plumbing Fixtures	Kitchen, toilet low flow, auto sensor & service fixt., supply & drain.	1 Fixt./400 SF Flr.		Each	4528	11.32	
2020	Domestic Water Distribution	Gas fired tankless water heater			S.F. Floor	.88	.88	9.1%
2040	Rain Water Drainage	Roof drains			S.F. Roof	2.18	1.09	
	D30 HVAC							
3010	Energy Supply	N/A			—	—	—	
3020	Heat Generating Systems	Included in D3050						
3040	Distribution Systems	Enthalpy heat recovery packages			Each	15,550	1.56	16.7%
3050	Terminal & Package Units	Multizone rooftop air conditioner, SEER 14			S.F. Floor	22.78	22.78	
3090	Other HVAC Sys. & Equipment	N/A						
	D40 Fire Protection							
4010	Sprinklers	Wet pipe sprinkler system			S.F. Floor	4.08	4.08	3.9%
4020	Standpipes	Standpipe, wet, Class III			S.F. Floor	1.64	1.64	
	D50 Electrical							
5010	Electrical Service/Distribution	400 ampere service, panel board and feeders			S.F. Floor	1.14	1.14	
5020	Lighting & Branch Wiring	LED fixt., daylt. dimming & ltg. on/off control., receptacles, switches, A.C. and misc. pwr.			S.F. Floor	15.61	15.61	14.1%
5030	Communications & Security	Addressable alarm systems and emergency lighting			S.F. Floor	1.58	1.58	
5090	Other Electrical Systems	Emergency generator, 15 kW, and energy monitoring systems			S.F. Floor	2.21	2.21	
E.	**EQUIPMENT & FURNISHINGS**							
1010	Commercial Equipment	N/A			—	—	—	
1020	Institutional Equipment	N/A			—	—	—	0.3%
1090	Other Equipment	Waste handling recycling tilt truck			S.F. Floor	.37	.37	
2020	Moveable Furnishings	No smoking signage			S.F. Floor	.02	.02	
F.	**SPECIAL CONSTRUCTION**							
1020	Integrated Construction	N/A			—	—	—	0.0%
1040	Special Facilities	N/A			—	—	—	
G.	**BUILDING SITEWORK**	N/A						

Sub-Total	145.34	**100%**
CONTRACTOR FEES (General Requirements: 10%, Overhead: 5%, Profit: 10%)	25%	36.33
ARCHITECT FEES	8%	14.53
Total Building Cost		**196.20**

For customer support on your Green Building Costs with RSMeans data, call 800.448.8182.

COMMERCIAL/INDUSTRIAL/INSTITUTIONAL

G.250 G Funeral Home

Costs per square foot of floor area

Exterior Wall	S.F. Area	4000	6000	8000	10000	12000	14000	16000	18000	20000
	L.F. Perimeter	260	320	384	424	460	484	510	540	576
Wood Board and Batten	Wood Frame	175.80	163.50	157.70	152.70	149.20	146.20	143.90	142.45	141.30
Brick Veneer	Wood Frame	186.05	172.20	165.65	159.90	155.85	152.35	149.70	147.95	146.70
Aluminum Clapboard	Wood Frame	170.70	159.60	154.30	149.90	146.80	144.15	142.15	140.85	139.90
Face Brick and Concrete Block	Wood Truss	201.15	185.25	177.80	171.05	166.30	162.10	159.05	157.00	155.50
Limestone and Concrete Block	Wood Truss	221.00	201.55	192.45	184.00	178.05	172.65	168.75	166.10	164.25
Stucco and Concrete Block	Wood Truss	209.25	191.65	183.35	175.80	170.50	165.70	162.20	159.90	158.25
Perimeter Adj., Add or Deduct	Per 100 L.F.	15.30	10.20	7.65	6.15	5.10	4.40	3.90	3.35	3.05
Story Hgt. Adj., Add or Deduct	Per 1 Ft.	2.00	1.65	1.45	1.30	1.20	1.05	1.00	0.90	0.90

For Basement, add $37.31 per square foot of basement area

The above costs were calculated using the basic specifications shown on the facing page. These costs should be adjusted where necessary for design alternatives and owner's requirements.

Common additives

Description	Unit	$ Cost
Autopsy Table, standard	Ea.	11,600
Deluxe	Ea.	19,400
Directory Boards, plastic, glass covered, 30" x 20"	Ea.	640
36" x 48"	Ea.	1625
Aluminum, 24" x 18"	Ea.	630
36" x 24"	Ea.	790
48" x 32"	Ea.	1025
Mortuary Refrigerator, end operated		
Two capacity	Ea.	9800
Six capacity	Ea.	18,400
Planters, precast concrete, 48" diam., 24" high	Ea.	790
7" diam., 36" high	Ea.	1850
Fiberglass, 36" diam., 24" high	Ea.	825
60" diam., 24" high	Ea.	1350

Description	Unit	$ Cost
Commissioning Fees, sustainable commercial construction	S.F.	0.24 - 3.04
Energy Modelling Fees, commercial buildings to 10,000 SF	Ea.	11,000
Greater than 10,000 SF add	S.F.	0.04
Green Bldg Cert Fees for comm construction project reg	Project	900
Photovoltaic Pwr Sys, grid connected, 20 kW (~2400 SF), roof	Ea.	249,200
Green Roofs, 6" soil depth, w/treated wd edging & sedum mats	S.F.	12.41
10" Soil depth, with treated wood edging & sedum mats	S.F.	14.10
Greywater Recovery Systems, prepackaged comm, 3060 gal.	Ea.	45,900
4590 gal.	Ea.	57,625
Rainwater Harvest Sys, prepckged comm, 10,000 gal, sys contrller	Ea.	37,550
20,000 gal. w/system controller	Ea.	61,000
30,000 gal. w/system controller	Ea.	97,350
Solar Domestic HW, closed loop, add-on sys, ext heat exchanger	Ea.	11,300
Drainback, hot water system, 120 gal tank	Ea.	14,175
Draindown, hot water system, 120 gal tank	Ea.	14,425

Important: See the Reference Section for Location Factors.

Model costs calculated for a 1 story building with 12' story height and 10,000 square feet of floor area

G Funeral Home

			Unit	Unit Cost	Cost Per S.F.	% Of Sub-Total

A. SUBSTRUCTURE

1010	Standard Foundations	Poured concrete; strip and spread footings	S.F. Ground	1.98	1.98	
1020	Special Foundations	N/A	—	—	—	
1030	Slab on Grade	4" reinforced concrete with recycled plastic vapor barrier and granular base	S.F. Slab	5.84	5.84	10.9%
2010	Basement Excavation	Site preparation for slab and trench for foundation wall and footing	S.F. Ground	.33	.33	
2020	Basement Walls	4' foundation wall	L.F. Wall	88	4.10	

B. SHELL

B10 Superstructure

1010	Floor Construction	N/A	—	—	—	3.5%
1020	Roof Construction	Plywood on wood truss	S.F. Roof	3.91	3.91	

B20 Exterior Enclosure

2010	Exterior Walls	1" x 4" vertical T & G redwood siding on 2x6 wood studs with insul. 90% of wall	S.F. Wall	17.71	8.11	
2020	Exterior Windows	Double hung wood 10% of wall	Each	533	2.26	11.1%
2030	Exterior Doors	Wood swinging double doors, single leaf hollow metal, low VOC paint	Each	3360	2.02	

B30 Roofing

3010	Roof Coverings	Single ply membrane, TPO, 45 mil, fully adhered; polyisocyanurate sheets	S.F. Roof	6.27	6.27	5.6%
3020	Roof Openings	N/A	—	—	—	

C. INTERIORS

1010	Partitions	Gypsum board on wood studs with sound deadening board 15 SF Flr./LF Part.	S.F. Partition	10.58	5.64	
1020	Interior Doors	Single leaf wood, low VOC paint 150 S.F. Floor/Door	Each	725	4.83	
1030	Fittings	N/A	—	—	—	
2010	Stair Construction	N/A	—	—	—	25.0%
3010	Wall Finishes	50% wallpaper, 25% wood paneling, 25% paint (low VOC)	S.F. Surface	3.46	3.69	
3020	Floor Finishes	70% carpet tile, 30% ceramic tile	S.F. Floor	7.61	7.61	
3030	Ceiling Finishes	Fiberglass board on exposed grid, suspended	S.F. Ceiling	6.30	6.30	

D. SERVICES

D10 Conveying

1010	Elevators & Lifts	N/A	—	—	—	0.0%
1020	Escalators & Moving Walks	N/A	—	—	—	

D20 Plumbing

2010	Plumbing Fixtures	Toilets, low flow, auto sensor, urinals & service fixt., supply & drain. 1 Fixt./770 SF Flr.	Each	3573	4.64	
2020	Domestic Water Distribution	Electric water heater, point-of-use	S.F. Floor	.49	.49	5.5%
2040	Rain Water Drainage	Roof drain	S.F. Roof	1.08	1.08	

D30 HVAC

3010	Energy Supply	N/A	—	—	—	
3020	Heat Generating Systems	Included in D3050	—	—	—	
3040	Distribution Systems	Enthalpy heat recovery packages	Each	38,725	3.87	19.5%
3050	Terminal & Package Units	Multizone rooftop air conditioner, SEER 14	S.F. Floor	18.02	18.02	
3090	Other HVAC Sys. & Equipment	N/A	—	—	—	

D40 Fire Protection

4010	Sprinklers	Wet pipe sprinkler system	S.F. Floor	3.79	3.79	4.2%
4020	Standpipes	Standpipe, wet, Class III	S.F. Floor	.95	.95	

D50 Electrical

5010	Electrical Service/Distribution	400 ampere service, panel board and feeders	S.F. Floor	1.60	1.60	
5020	Lighting & Branch Wiring	LED light fixtures, daylt. dimming control & ltg. on/off sys., recept., switches, & A.C. power	S.F. Floor	10.53	10.53	14.0%
5030	Communications & Security	Addressable alarm systems	S.F. Floor	1.58	1.58	
5090	Other Electrical Systems	Emergency generator, 15 kW and energy monitoring systems	S.F. Floor	1.96	1.96	

E. EQUIPMENT & FURNISHINGS

1010	Commercial Equipment	N/A	—	—	—	
1020	Institutional Equipment	N/A	—	—	—	0.6%
1090	Other Equipment	Waste handling recycling tilt truck	S.F. Floor	.63	.63	
2020	Moveable Furnishings	No smoking signage	S.F. Floor	.04	.04	

F. SPECIAL CONSTRUCTION

1020	Integrated Construction	N/A	—	—	—	0.0%
1040	Special Facilities	N/A	—	—	—	

G. BUILDING SITEWORK   N/A

	Sub-Total	112.07	100%
CONTRACTOR FEES (General Requirements: 10%, Overhead: 5%, Profit: 10%)	25%	28.02	
ARCHITECT FEES	9%	12.61	
	Total Building Cost	**152.70**	

For customer support on your Green Building Costs with RSMeans data, call 800.448.8182.

COMMERCIAL/INDUSTRIAL/INSTITUTIONAL G.390 G Library

Costs per square foot of floor area

Exterior Wall	S.F. Area	7000	10000	13000	16000	19000	22000	25000	28000	31000
	L.F. Perimeter	240	300	336	386	411	435	472	510	524
Face Brick and Concrete Block	Reinforced Concrete	225.00	213.65	203.95	199.55	193.95	189.85	187.75	186.10	183.30
	Rigid Steel	221.95	210.55	200.85	196.45	190.85	186.75	184.65	183.00	180.20
Limestone and Concrete Block	Reinforced Concrete	251.60	236.10	222.95	217.00	209.45	203.80	200.95	198.75	194.95
	Rigid Steel	246.15	231.70	219.05	213.45	206.10	200.70	198.00	195.85	192.15
Precast Concrete	Reinforced Concrete	252.70	237.10	223.80	217.80	210.10	204.50	201.60	199.30	195.50
	Rigid Steel	249.60	234.00	220.65	214.70	207.00	201.40	198.50	196.20	192.40
Perimeter Adj., Add or Deduct	Per 100 L.F.	27.80	19.45	14.95	12.15	10.30	8.85	7.80	6.90	6.25
Story Hgt. Adj., Add or Deduct	Per 1 Ft.	4.20	3.65	3.15	3.00	2.70	2.45	2.30	2.25	2.10

For Basement, add $55.65 per square foot of basement area

The above costs were calculated using the basic specifications shown on the facing page. These costs should be adjusted where necessary for design alternatives and owner's requirements.

Common additives

Description	Unit	$ Cost
Carrels Hardwood	Ea.	740 - 1925
Closed Circuit Surveillance, one station, camera and monitor	Ea.	1475
For additional camera stations, add	Ea.	665
Elevators, hydraulic passenger, 2 stops, 1500# capacity	Ea.	73,100
2500# capacity	Ea.	76,600
3500# capacity	Ea.	81,600
Library Furnishings, bookshelf, 90" high, 10" shelf double face	L.F.	260
Single face	L.F.	181
Charging desk, built-in with counter		
Plastic laminated top	L.F.	600
Reading table, laminated		
Top 60" x 36"	Ea.	505

Description	Unit	$ Cost
Commissioning Fees, sustainable institutional construction	S.F.	0.58 - 2.47
Energy Modelling Fees, commercial buildings to 10,000 SF	Ea.	11,000
Greater than 10,000 SF add	S.F.	0.04
Green Bldg Cert Fees for comm construction project reg	Project	900
Photovoltaic Pwr Sys, grid connected, 20 kW (~2400 SF), roof	Ea.	249,200
Green Roofs, 6" soil depth, w/treated wd edging & sedum mats	S.F.	12.41
10" Soil depth, with treated wood edging & sedum mats	S.F.	14.10
Greywater Recovery Systems, prepackaged comm, 3060 gal.	Ea.	45,900
4590 gal.	Ea.	57,625
Rainwater Harvest Sys, prepckged comm, 10,000 gal, sys contrller	Ea.	37,550
20,000 gal. w/system controller	Ea.	61,000
30,000 gal. w/system controller	Ea.	97,350
Solar Domestic HW, closed loop, add-on sys, ext heat exchanger	Ea.	11,300
Drainback, hot water system, 120 gal tank	Ea.	14,175
Draindown, hot water system, 120 gal tank	Ea.	14,425

Important: See the Reference Section for Location Factors.

G Library

Model costs calculated for a 2 story building with 14' story height and 22,000 square feet of floor area

				Unit	Unit Cost	Cost Per S.F.	% Of Sub-Total
A.	**SUBSTRUCTURE**						
1010	Standard Foundations	Poured concrete; strip and spread footings		S.F. Ground	4.24	2.12	
1020	Special Foundations	N/A		—	—	—	
1030	Slab on Grade	4" reinforced concrete with recycled vapor barrier and granular base		S.F. Slab	5.84	2.93	5.1%
2010	Basement Excavation	Site preparation for slab and trench for foundation wall and footing		S.F. Ground	.33	.17	
2020	Basement Walls	4' foundation wall		L.F. Wall	98	1.94	
B.	**SHELL**						
	B10 Superstructure						
1010	Floor Construction	Concrete waffle slab		S.F. Floor	30.96	15.48	19.1%
1020	Roof Construction	Concrete waffle slab		S.F. Roof	22.80	11.40	
	B20 Exterior Enclosure						
2010	Exterior Walls	Face brick with concrete block backup	90% of wall	S.F. Wall	38.73	19.30	
2020	Exterior Windows	Window wall	10% of wall	Each	58	3.19	16.5%
2030	Exterior Doors	Double aluminum and glass, single leaf hollow metal, low VOC paint		Each	7200	.66	
	B30 Roofing						
3010	Roof Coverings	Single-ply TPO membrane, 60 mil, heat welded w/R-20 insulation		S.F. Roof	7.50	3.75	2.7%
3020	Roof Openings	Roof hatches		S.F. Roof	.10	.05	
C.	**INTERIORS**						
1010	Partitions	Gypsum board on metal studs w/sound attenuation insul.	30 SF Flr./LF Part.	S.F. Partition	14.70	5.88	
1020	Interior Doors	Single leaf wood, low VOC paint	300 S.F. Floor/Door	Each	725	2.42	
1030	Fittings	N/A		—	—	—	
2010	Stair Construction	Concrete filled metal pan		Flight	10,475	.96	16.4%
3010	Wall Finishes	Paint, low VOC		S.F. Surface	2.10	1.68	
3020	Floor Finishes	50% carpet tile, 50% vinyl composition tile, recycled content		S.F. Floor	4.54	4.54	
3030	Ceiling Finishes	Mineral fiber on concealed zee bars		S.F. Ceiling	7.60	7.60	
D.	**SERVICES**						
	D10 Conveying						
1010	Elevators & Lifts	One hydraulic passenger elevator		Each	94,820	4.31	3.1%
1020	Escalators & Moving Walks	N/A		—	—	—	
	D20 Plumbing						
2010	Plumbing Fixtures	Toilet, low flow, auto sensor & service fixt., supply & drain.	1 Fixt./1835 SF.Flr.	Each	8680	4.73	
2020	Domestic Water Distribution	Tankless, on demand water heater, gas/propane		S.F. Floor	.60	.60	4.4%
2040	Rain Water Drainage	Roof drains		S.F. Roof	1.62	.81	
	D30 HVAC						
3010	Energy Supply	N/A		—	—	—	
3020	Heat Generating Systems	Included in D3050		—	—	—	
3040	Distribution Systems	Enthalpy heat recovery packages		Each	38,725	1.76	16.0%
3050	Terminal & Package Units	Multizone rooftop air conditioner, SEER 14		S.F. Floor	20.80	20.80	
3090	Other HVAC Sys. & Equipment	N/A		—	—	—	
	D40 Fire Protection						
4010	Sprinklers	Wet pipe sprinkler system		S.F. Floor	3.30	3.30	3.1%
4020	Standpipes	Standpipe		S.F. Floor	1.09	1.09	
	D50 Electrical						
5010	Electrical Service/Distribution	400 ampere service, panel board and feeders		S.F. Floor	.55	.55	
5020	Lighting & Branch Wiring	LED fixtures, daylt. dim., ltg. on/off, recept., switches, and A.C. power		S.F. Floor	14.95	14.95	13.4%
5030	Communications & Security	Addressable alarm systems, internet wiring, and emergency lighting		S.F. Floor	2.15	2.15	
5090	Other Electrical Systems	Emergency generator, 7.5 kW, UPS, energy monitoring systems		S.F. Floor	1.23	1.23	
E.	**EQUIPMENT & FURNISHINGS**						
1010	Commercial Equipment	N/A		—	—	—	
1020	Institutional Equipment	N/A		—	—	—	0.2%
1090	Other Equipment	Waste handling recycling tilt truck		S.F. Floor	.28	.28	
2020	Moveable Furnishings	No smoking signage		S.F. Floor			
F.	**SPECIAL CONSTRUCTION**						
1020	Integrated Construction	N/A		—	—	—	0.0%
1040	Special Facilities	N/A		—	—	—	
G.	**BUILDING SITEWORK**	N/A					

	Sub-Total	140.63	100%
CONTRACTOR FEES (General Requirements: 10%, Overhead: 5%, Profit: 10%)	25%	35.16	
ARCHITECT FEES	8%	14.06	
Total Building Cost		**189.85**	

For customer support on your Green Building Costs with RSMeans data, call 800.448.8182.

COMMERCIAL/INDUSTRIAL/INSTITUTIONAL

G.400 G Medical Office, 1 Story

Costs per square foot of floor area

Exterior Wall	S.F. Area	4000	5500	7000	8500	10000	11500	13000	14500	16000
	L.F. Perimeter	280	320	380	440	453	503	510	522	560
Face Brick and Concrete Block	Steel Joists	269.60	257.80	253.45	250.55	244.75	243.05	239.15	236.30	235.25
	Wood Truss	266.60	254.80	250.45	247.55	241.75	240.10	236.15	233.30	232.25
Stucco and Concrete Block	Steel Joists	274.10	261.15	256.45	253.35	246.95	245.05	240.70	237.55	236.40
	Wood Truss	273.30	260.40	255.60	252.55	246.05	244.30	239.90	236.75	235.60
Brick Veneer	Wood Truss	257.45	247.05	243.10	240.50	235.50	233.95	230.50	228.05	227.10
Wood Clapboard	Wood Frame	247.75	239.15	235.80	233.65	229.60	228.35	225.60	223.60	222.80
Perimeter Adj., Add or Deduct	Per 100 L.F.	19.95	14.55	11.40	9.40	8.05	7.00	6.10	5.50	5.00
Story Hgt. Adj., Add or Deduct	Per 1 Ft.	4.00	3.40	3.10	3.00	2.65	2.55	2.25	2.10	2.05

For Basement, add $36.22 per square foot of basement area

The above costs were calculated using the basic specifications shown on the facing page. These costs should be adjusted where necessary for design alternatives and owner's requirements.

Common additives

Description	Unit	$ Cost
Cabinets, hospital, base, laminated plastic	L.F.	530
Counter top, laminated plastic	L.F.	87.50
Nurses station, door type, laminated plastic	L.F.	595
Wall cabinets, laminated plastic	L.F.	390
Directory Boards, plastic, glass covered, 30" x 20"	Ea.	640
36" x 48"	Ea.	1625
Aluminum, 36" x 24"	Ea.	790
48" x 32"	Ea.	1025
Heat Therapy Unit, humidified, 26" x 78" x 28"	Ea.	3675
Tables, examining, vinyl top, with base cabinets	Ea.	1575 - 6525
Utensil Washer, Sanitizer	Ea.	10,300
X-Ray, Mobile	Ea.	20,800 - 105,000

Description	Unit	$ Cost
Commissioning Fees, sustainable commercial construction	S.F.	0.24 - 3.04
Energy Modelling Fees, commercial buildings to 10,000 SF	Ea.	11,000
Greater than 10,000 SF add	S.F.	0.04
Green Bldg Cert Fees for comm construction project reg	Project	900
Photovoltaic Pwr Sys, grid connected, 20 kW (~2400 SF), roof	Ea.	249,200
Green Roofs, 6" soil depth, w/treated wd edging & sedum mats	S.F.	12.41
10" Soil depth, with treated wood edging & sedum mats	S.F.	14.10
Greywater Recovery Systems, prepackaged comm, 3060 gal.	Ea.	45,900
4590 gal.	Ea.	57,625
Rainwater Harvest Sys, prepckged comm, 10,000 gal, sys contrller	Ea.	37,550
20,000 gal. w/system controller	Ea.	61,000
30,000 gal. w/system controller	Ea.	97,350
Solar Domestic HW, closed loop, add-on sys, ext heat exchanger	Ea.	11,300
Drainback, hot water system, 120 gal tank	Ea.	14,175
Draindown, hot water system, 120 gal tank	Ea.	14,425

Important: See the Reference Section for Location Factors.

Model costs calculated for a 1 story building with 10' story height and 7,000 square feet of floor area

G Medical Office, 1 Story

				Unit	Unit Cost	Cost Per S.F.	% Of Sub-Total
A.	**SUBSTRUCTURE**						
1010	Standard Foundations	Poured concrete; strip and spread footings		S.F. Ground	2.31	2.31	
1020	Special Foundations	N/A		—	—	—	
1030	Slab on Grade	4" reinforced concrete with recycled vapor barrier and granular base		S.F. Slab	5.84	5.84	7.5%
2010	Basement Excavation	Site preparation for slab and trench for foundation wall and footing		S.F. Ground	.33	.33	
2020	Basement Walls	4' foundation wall		L.F. Wall	98	5.32	
B.	**SHELL**						
	B10 Superstructure						
1010	Floor Construction	N/A		—	—	—	4.2%
1020	Roof Construction	Plywood on wood trusses		S.F. Roof	7.76	7.76	
	B20 Exterior Enclosure						
2010	Exterior Walls	Face brick with concrete block backup	70% of wall	S.F. Wall	42.95	16.32	
2020	Exterior Windows	Wood double hung	30% of wall	Each	665	6.37	14.6%
2030	Exterior Doors	Aluminum and glass doors and entrance with transoms		Each	2385	4.08	
	B30 Roofing						
3010	Roof Coverings	Asphalt shingles with flashing (Pitched); rigid fiber glass insulation, gutters		S.F. Roof	3.33	3.33	1.8%
3020	Roof Openings	N/A		—	—	—	
C.	**INTERIORS**						
1010	Partitions	Gypsum bd. & sound deadening bd. on wood studs w/insul.	6 SF Flr./LF Part.	S.F. Partition	10.29	13.72	
1020	Interior Doors	Single leaf wood, low VOC paint	60 S.F. Floor/Door	Each	725	12.08	
1030	Fittings	N/A		—	—	—	
2010	Stair Construction	N/A		—	—	—	22.2%
3010	Wall Finishes	50% paint, low VOC, 50% vinyl wall covering		S.F. Surface	1.48	3.94	
3020	Floor Finishes	50% carpet tile, 50% vinyl composition tile, recycled content		S.F. Floor	4.21	4.21	
3030	Ceiling Finishes	Mineral fiber tile on concealed zee bars		S.F. Ceiling	6.86	6.86	
D.	**SERVICES**						
	D10 Conveying						
1010	Elevators & Lifts	N/A		—	—	—	0.0%
1020	Escalators & Moving Walks	N/A		—	—	—	
	D20 Plumbing						
2010	Plumbing Fixtures	Toilet, low flow, auto sensor, exam room & service fixt., supply & drain.	1 Fixt./195 SF Flr.	Each	5117	26.24	
2020	Domestic Water Distribution	Gas fired tankless water heater		S.F. Floor	3.02	3.02	16.7%
2040	Rain Water Drainage	Roof drains		S.F. Roof	1.37	1.37	
	D30 HVAC						
3010	Energy Supply	N/A		—	—	—	
3020	Heat Generating Systems	Included in D3050		—	—	—	
3040	Distribution Systems	Enthalpy heat recovery packages		Each	14,075	2.01	8.9%
3050	Terminal & Package Units	Multizone rooftop air conditioner, SEER 14		S.F. Floor	14.43	14.43	
3090	Other HVAC Sys. & Equipment	N/A		—	—	—	
	D40 Fire Protection						
4010	Sprinklers	Wet pipe sprinkler system		S.F. Floor	5.13	5.13	3.5%
4020	Standpipes	Standpipe		S.F. Floor	1.36	1.36	
	D50 Electrical						
5010	Electrical Service/Distribution	200 ampere service, panel board and feeders		S.F. Floor	1.33	1.33	
5020	Lighting & Branch Wiring	LED fixtures, daylt. dim., ltg. on/off, recept., switches, and A.C. power		S.F. Floor	13.46	13.46	14.3%
5030	Communications & Security	Alarm systems, internet & phone wiring, intercom system, & emerg. ltg.		S.F. Floor	8.24	8.24	
5090	Other Electrical Systems	Emergency generator, 7.5 kW, and energy monitoring systems		S.F. Floor	3.17	3.17	
E.	**EQUIPMENT & FURNISHINGS**						
1010	Commercial Equipment	N/A		—	—	—	
1020	Institutional Equipment	Exam room casework and countertops		S.F. Floor	10.58	10.58	6.3%
1090	Other Equipment	Waste handling recycling tilt truck		S.F. Floor	.89	.89	
2020	Moveable Furnishings	No smoking signage		S.F. Floor	.11	.11	
F.	**SPECIAL CONSTRUCTION**						
1020	Integrated Construction	N/A		—	—	—	0.0%
1040	Special Facilities	N/A		—	—	—	
G.	**BUILDING SITEWORK**	N/A					

		Sub-Total	183.81	**100%**
CONTRACTOR FEES (General Requirements: 10%, Overhead: 5%, Profit: 10%)		25%	45.96
ARCHITECT FEES		9%	20.68
	Total Building Cost		**250.45**

For customer support on your Green Building Costs with RSMeans data, call 800.448.8182.

COMMERCIAL/INDUSTRIAL/INSTITUTIONAL

G.410 | G Medical Office, 2 Story

Costs per square foot of floor area

Exterior Wall	S.F. Area	4000	5500	7000	8500	10000	11500	13000	14500	16000
	L.F. Perimeter	180	210	240	270	286	311	336	361	386
Face Brick and Concrete Block	Steel Joists	302.35	289.95	282.85	278.25	273.00	270.25	268.15	266.45	265.10
	Wood Joists	301.15	288.75	281.70	277.05	271.80	269.05	266.95	265.25	263.90
Stucco and Concrete Block	Steel Joists	284.80	275.05	269.50	265.85	261.85	259.65	258.05	256.70	255.70
	Wood Joists	283.65	273.85	268.30	264.65	260.70	258.55	256.85	255.55	254.50
Brick Veneer	Wood Frame	288.90	278.30	272.25	268.35	264.00	261.70	259.90	258.45	257.30
Wood Clapboard	Wood Frame	283.75	273.90	268.35	264.75	260.75	258.60	256.90	255.55	254.55
Perimeter Adj., Add or Deduct	Per 100 L.F.	35.95	26.05	20.50	16.85	14.35	12.45	11.00	9.85	8.95
Story Hgt. Adj., Add or Deduct	Per 1 Ft.	5.30	4.45	4.00	3.70	3.35	3.20	3.00	2.90	2.85

For Basement, add $40.19 per square foot of basement area

The above costs were calculated using the basic specifications shown on the facing page. These costs should be adjusted where necessary for design alternatives and owner's requirements.

Common additives

Description	Unit	$ Cost
Cabinets, hospital, base, laminated plastic	L.F.	530
Counter top, laminated plastic	L.F.	87.50
Nurses station, door type, laminated plastic	L.F.	595
Wall cabinets, laminated plastic	L.F.	390
Elevators, hydraulic passenger, 2 stops, 2500# capacity	Ea.	76,600
3500# capacity	Ea.	81,600
Directory Boards, plastic, glass covered, 30" x 20"	Ea.	640
36" x 48"	Ea.	1625
Aluminum, 36" x 24"	Ea.	790
48" x 32"	Ea.	1025
Heat Therapy Unit, humidified, 26" x 78" x 28"	Ea.	3675
Tables, examining, vinyl top, with base cabinets	Ea.	1575 - 6525
Utensil Washer, Sanitizer	Ea.	10,300
X-Ray, Mobile	Ea.	20,800 - 105,000

Description	Unit	$ Cost
Commissioning Fees, sustainable commercial construction	S.F.	0.24 - 3.04
Energy Modelling Fees, commercial buildings to 10,000 SF	Ea.	11,000
Greater than 10,000 SF add	S.F.	0.04
Green Bldg Cert Fees for comm construction project reg	Project	900
Photovoltaic Pwr Sys, grid connected, 20 kW (~2400 SF), roof	Ea.	249,200
Green Roofs, 6" soil depth, w/treated wd edging & sedum mats	S.F.	12.41
10" Soil depth, with treated wood edging & sedum mats	S.F.	14.10
Greywater Recovery Systems, prepackaged comm, 3060 gal.	Ea.	45,900
4590 gal.	Ea.	57,625
Rainwater Harvest Sys, prepckged comm, 10,000 gal, sys contrller	Ea.	37,550
20,000 gal. w/system controller	Ea.	61,000
30,000 gal. w/system controller	Ea.	97,350
Solar Domestic HW, closed loop, add-on sys, ext heat exchanger	Ea.	11,300
Drainback, hot water system, 120 gal tank	Ea.	14,175
Draindown, hot water system, 120 gal tank	Ea.	14,425

Important: See the Reference Section for Location Factors.

G Medical Office, 2 Story

Model costs calculated for a 2 story building with 10' story height and 7,000 square feet of floor area

				Unit	Unit Cost	Cost Per S.F.	% Of Sub-Total
A.	**SUBSTRUCTURE**						
1010	Standard Foundations	Poured concrete; strip and spread footings		S.F. Ground	3.72	1.86	
1020	Special Foundations	N/A		—	—	—	
1030	Slab on Grade	4" reinforced concrete with vapor barrier and granular base		S.F. Slab	5.84	2.93	4.3%
2010	Basement Excavation	Site preparation for slab and trench for foundation wall and footing		S.F. Ground	.57	.29	
2020	Basement Walls	4' foundation wall		L.F. Wall	98	3.36	
B.	**SHELL**						
	B10 Superstructure						
1010	Floor Construction	Open web steel joists, slab form, concrete, columns		S.F. Floor	14.62	7.31	5.4%
1020	Roof Construction	Metal deck, open web steel joists, beams, columns		S.F. Roof	6.64	3.32	
	B20 Exterior Enclosure						
2010	Exterior Walls	Stucco on concrete block		S.F. Wall	20.75	9.96	
2020	Exterior Windows	Outward projecting metal	30% of wall	Each	529	7.25	9.7%
2030	Exterior Doors	Aluminum and glass doors with transoms		Each	7200	2.05	
	B30 Roofing						
3010	Roof Coverings	Built-up tar and gravel with flashing; perlite/EPS composite insulation		S.F. Roof	8.68	4.34	2.3%
3020	Roof Openings	Roof hatches		S.F. Roof	.32	.16	
C.	**INTERIORS**						
1010	Partitions	Gypsum bd. & acous. insul. on metal studs	6 SF Floor/LF Part.	S.F. Partition	8.44	11.25	
1020	Interior Doors	Single leaf wood	60 S.F. Floor/Door	Each	725	12.08	
1030	Fittings	N/A		—	—	—	
2010	Stair Construction	Concrete filled metal pan		Flight	15,800	4.52	21.7%
3010	Wall Finishes	45% paint, 50% vinyl wall coating, 5% ceramic tile		S.F. Surface	1.48	3.94	
3020	Floor Finishes	50% carpet, 50% vinyl composition tile		S.F. Floor	4.21	4.21	
3030	Ceiling Finishes	Mineral fiber tile on concealed zee bars		S.F. Ceiling	6.86	6.86	
D.	**SERVICES**						
	D10 Conveying						
1010	Elevators & Lifts	One hydraulic hospital elevator		Each	116,690	16.67	8.4%
1020	Escalators & Moving Walks	N/A		—	—	—	
	D20 Plumbing						
2010	Plumbing Fixtures	Toilet, exam room & service fixt., supply & drain.	1 Fixt./160 SF Flr.	Each	4752	29.70	
2020	Domestic Water Distribution	Gas fired water heater		S.F. Floor	3.02	3.02	17.3%
2040	Rain Water Drainage	Roof drains		S.F. Roof	2.96	1.48	
	D30 HVAC						
3010	Energy Supply	N/A		—	—	—	
3020	Heat Generating Systems	Included in D3050		—	—	—	
3040	Distribution Systems	Enthalpy heat recovery packages		Each	14,075	2.01	8.3%
3050	Terminal & Package Units	Multizone rooftop air conditioner, SEER 14		S.F. Floor	14.43	14.43	
3090	Other HVAC Sys. & Equipment	N/A		—	—	—	
	D40 Fire Protection						
4010	Sprinklers	Wet pipe sprinkler system		S.F. Floor	4.08	4.08	3.1%
4020	Standpipes	Standpipe		S.F. Floor	2.06	2.06	
	D50 Electrical						
5010	Electrical Service/Distribution	400 ampere service, panel board and feeders		S.F. Floor	1.65	1.65	
5020	Lighting & Branch Wiring	LED fixtures, receptacles, switches, A.C. and misc. power		S.F. Floor	14.36	14.36	13.9%
5030	Communications & Security	Alarm system, internet & phone wiring, intercom system, & emergency ltg.		S.F. Floor	8.24	8.24	
5090	Other Electrical Systems	Emergency generator, 7.5 kW		S.F. Floor	3.26	3.26	
E.	**EQUIPMENT & FURNISHINGS**						
1010	Commercial Equipment	N/A		—	—	—	
1020	Institutional Equipment	Exam room casework and contertops		S.F. Floor	10.58	10.58	5.6%
1090	Other Equipment	Waste handling recycling tilt truck		S.F. Floor	.52	.52	
2020	Moveable Furnishings	No smoking signage		S.F. Floor	.02	.02	
F.	**SPECIAL CONSTRUCTION**						
1020	Integrated Construction	N/A		—	—	—	0.0%
1040	Special Facilities	N/A		—	—	—	
G.	**BUILDING SITEWORK**	N/A					

	Sub-Total	197.77	100%
CONTRACTOR FEES (General Requirements: 10%, Overhead: 5%, Profit: 10%)	25%	49.48	
ARCHITECT FEES	9%	22.25	
Total Building Cost		**269.50**	

For customer support on your Green Building Costs with RSMeans data, call 800.448.8182.

COMMERCIAL/INDUSTRIAL/INSTITUTIONAL — G.420 G Motel, 1 Story

Costs per square foot of floor area

Exterior Wall	S.F. Area	2000	3000	4000	6000	8000	10000	12000	14000	16000
	L.F. Perimeter	240	260	280	380	480	560	580	660	740
Brick Veneer	Wood Frame	239.70	210.75	196.25	188.50	184.60	181.00	175.10	173.95	172.90
Aluminum Clapboard	Wood Frame	221.15	197.40	185.45	178.70	175.35	172.35	167.70	166.60	165.80
Wood Clapboard	Wood Frame	220.80	197.15	185.25	178.50	175.20	172.20	167.50	166.45	165.60
Wood Shingles	Wood Frame	224.65	199.90	187.50	180.60	177.10	173.95	169.10	168.05	167.10
Precast Concrete	Wood Truss	224.65	199.85	187.45	180.55	177.10	173.95	169.05	168.00	167.10
Face Brick and Concrete Block	Wood Truss	256.25	222.70	205.95	197.25	192.90	188.75	181.80	180.40	179.30
Perimeter Adj., Add or Deduct	Per 100 L.F.	33.55	22.40	16.75	11.20	8.40	6.70	5.65	4.80	4.20
Story Hgt. Adj., Add or Deduct	Per 1 Ft.	5.30	3.80	3.10	2.80	2.70	2.40	2.20	2.00	2.05

For Basement, add $ 27.67 per square foot of basement area

The above costs were calculated using the basic specifications shown on the facing page. These costs should be adjusted where necessary for design alternatives and owner's requirements.

Common additives

Description	Unit	$ Cost
Closed Circuit Surveillance, one station, camera & monitor	Ea.	1475
For additional camera stations, add	Ea.	665
Laundry Equipment, dryer, gas, 30 lb. capacity	Ea.	4100
Washer, commercial	Ea.	1700
Sauna, prefabricated, complete, 6' x 9'	Ea.	10,000
8' x 8'	Ea.	10,600
Swimming Pools, Complete, gunite	S.F.	106 - 132
TV Antenna, Master system, 12 outlet	Outlet	242
30 outlet	Outlet	335
100 outlet	Outlet	370

Description	Unit	$ Cost
Commissioning Fees, sustainable commercial construction	S.F.	0.24 - 3.04
Energy Modelling Fees, commercial buildings to 10,000 SF	Ea.	11,000
Greater than 10,000 SF add	S.F.	0.04
Green Bldg Cert Fees for comm construction project reg	Project	900
Photovoltaic Pwr Sys, grid connected, 20 kW (~2400 SF), roof	Ea.	249,200
Green Roofs, 6" soil depth, w/treated wd edging & sedum mats	S.F.	12.41
10" Soil depth, with treated wood edging & sedum mats	S.F.	14.10
Greywater Recovery Systems, prepackaged comm, 3060 gal.	Ea.	45,900
4590 gal.	Ea.	57,625
Rainwater Harvest Sys, prepckged comm, 10,000 gal, sys contrller	Ea.	37,550
20,000 gal. w/system controller	Ea.	61,000
30,000 gal. w/system controller	Ea.	97,350
Solar Domestic HW, closed loop, add-on sys, ext heat exchanger	Ea.	11,300
Drainback, hot water system, 120 gal tank	Ea.	14,175
Draindown, hot water system, 120 gal tank	Ea.	14,425

Important: See the Reference Section for Location Factors.

Model costs calculated for a 1 story building with 9' story height and 8,000 square feet of floor area

G Motel, 1 Story

			Unit	Unit Cost	Cost Per S.F.	% Of Sub-Total
A.	**SUBSTRUCTURE**					
1010	Standard Foundations	Poured concrete; strip and spread footings	S.F. Ground	3.50	3.50	
1020	Special Foundations	N/A	—	—	—	
1030	Slab on Grade	4" reinforced concrete with recycled vapor barrier and granular base	S.F. Slab	5.84	5.84	12.8%
2010	Basement Excavation	Site preparation for slab and trench for foundation wall and footing	S.F. Ground	.33	.33	
2020	Basement Walls	4' foundation wall	L.F. Wall	98	8.06	
B.	**SHELL**					
	B10 Superstructure					
1010	Floor Construction	N/A	—	—	—	5.6 %
1020	Roof Construction	Plywood on wood trusses	S.F. Roof	7.76	7.76	
	B20 Exterior Enclosure					
2010	Exterior Walls	Face brick on wood studs with sheathing, insulation and paper 80% of wall	S.F. Wall	26.85	11.60	
2020	Exterior Windows	Wood double hung 20% of wall	Each	533	4.11	16.1%
2030	Exterior Doors	Wood solid core	Each	2385	6.56	
	B30 Roofing					
3010	Roof Coverings	Asphalt strip shingles, 210-235 lbs/Sq., R-10 insul. & weather barrier-recycled	S.F. Roof	8.65	8.65	6.3%
3020	Roof Openings	N/A	—	—	—	
C.	**INTERIORS**					
1010	Partitions	Gypsum bd. and sound deadening bd. on wood studs 9 SF Flr./LF Part.	S.F. Partition	11.04	9.81	
1020	Interior Doors	Single leaf hollow core wood, low VOC paint 300 S.F. Floor/Door	Each	645	2.15	
1030	Fittings	N/A	—	—	—	
2010	Stair Construction	N/A	—	—	—	18.6%
3010	Wall Finishes	90% paint, low VOC, 10% ceramic tile	S.F. Surface	1.76	3.12	
3020	Floor Finishes	85% carpet tile, 15% ceramic tile	S.F. Floor	5.65	5.65	
3030	Ceiling Finishes	Painted gypsum board on furring, low VOC paint	S.F. Ceiling	4.94	4.94	
D.	**SERVICES**					
	D10 Conveying					
1010	Elevators & Lifts	N/A	—	—	—	0.0 %
1020	Escalators & Moving Walks	N/A	—	—	—	
	D20 Plumbing					
2010	Plumbing Fixtures	Toilet, low flow, auto sensor, & service fixt., supply & drainage 1 Fixt./90 SF Flr.	Each	2276	25.29	
2020	Domestic Water Distribution	Gas fired tankless water heater	S.F. Floor	.43	.43	20.1%
2040	Rain Water Drainage	Roof Drains	S.F. Roof	2.05	2.05	
	D30 HVAC					
3010	Energy Supply	N/A	—	—	—	
3020	Heat Generating Systems	Included in D3050	—	—	—	
3030	Cooling Generating Systems	N/A	—	—	—	2.2 %
3050	Terminal & Package Units	Through the wall electric heating and cooling units	S.F. Floor	3.08	3.08	
3090	Other HVAC Sys. & Equipment	N/A	—	—	—	
	D40 Fire Protection					
4010	Sprinklers	Wet pipe sprinkler system	S.F. Floor	5.13	5.13	4.6%
4020	Standpipes	Standpipe, wet, Class III	S.F. Floor	1.19	1.19	
	D50 Electrical					
5010	Electrical Service/Distribution	200 ampere service, panel board and feeders	S.F. Floor	1.31	1.31	
5020	Lighting & Branch Wiring	LED fixt., daylit. dim., ltg. on/off control, recept., switches and misc. pwr.	S.F. Floor	10.56	10.56	12.2%
5030	Communications & Security	Addressable alarm systems	S.F. Floor	2.80	2.80	
5090	Other Electrical Systems	Emergency generator, 7.5 kW, and energy monitoring systems	S.F. Floor	2.14	2.14	
E.	**EQUIPMENT & FURNISHINGS**					
1010	Commercial Equipment	Laundry equipment	S.F. Floor	1.02	1.02	
1020	Institutional Equipment	N/A	—	—	—	1.4%
1090	Other Equipment	Waste handling recycling tilt truck	S.F. Floor	.78	.78	
2020	Moveable Furnishings	No smoking signage	S.F. Floor	.18	.18	
F.	**SPECIAL CONSTRUCTION**					
1020	Integrated Construction	N/A	—	—	—	0.0 %
1040	Special Facilities	N/A	—	—	—	
G.	**BUILDING SITEWORK**	N/A				

		Sub-Total		138.04	**100%**
	CONTRACTOR FEES (General Requirements:10%, Overhead: 5%, Profit:10%)		25%	34.48	
	ARCHITECT FEES		7%	12.08	
		Total Building Cost		**184.60**	

COMMERCIAL/INDUSTRIAL/INSTITUTIONAL G.430 G Motel, 2-3 Story

Costs per square foot of floor area

Exterior Wall	S.F. Area	25000	37000	49000	61000	73000	81000	88000	96000	104000
	L.F. Perimeter	433	593	606	720	835	911	978	1054	1074
Decorative Concrete Block	Wood Joists	197.45	192.85	185.95	184.35	183.20	182.65	182.25	181.80	180.65
	Precast Concrete	213.45	208.80	202.00	200.30	199.20	198.65	198.20	197.85	196.65
Stucco and Concrete Block	Wood Joists	198.20	193.45	186.30	184.60	183.40	182.85	182.40	182.00	180.80
	Precast Concrete	215.10	210.35	203.20	201.50	200.35	199.75	199.30	198.90	197.65
Wood Clapboard	Wood Frame	193.70	189.30	183.10	181.60	180.50	179.95	179.50	179.15	178.10
Brick Veneer	Wood Frame	198.25	193.50	186.35	184.65	183.50	182.90	182.50	182.10	180.85
Perimeter Adj., Add or Deduct	Per 100 L.F.	5.95	3.90	3.05	2.35	2.00	1.80	1.65	1.55	1.45
Story Hgt. Adj., Add or Deduct	Per 1 Ft.	2.05	1.90	1.50	1.40	1.40	1.35	1.30	1.35	1.25

For Basement, add $36.28 per square foot of basement area

The above costs were calculated using the basic specifications shown on the facing page. These costs should be adjusted where necessary for design alternatives and owner's requirements.

Common additives

Description	Unit	$ Cost
Closed Circuit Surveillance, one station, camera & monitor	Ea.	1475
For additional camera station, add	Ea.	665
Elevators, hydraulic passenger, 2 stops, 2500# capacity	Ea.	76,600
3500# capacity	Ea.	81,600
Additional stop, add	Ea.	8375
Laundry Equipment, dryer, gas, 30 lb. capacity	Ea.	4100
Washer, commercial	Ea.	1700
Sauna, prefabricated, complete, 6' x 9'	Ea.	10,000
8' x 8'	Ea.	10,600
Swimming Pools, Complete, gunite	S.F.	106 - 132
TV Antenna, Master system, 12 outlet	Outlet	242
30 outlet	Outlet	335
100 outlet	Outlet	370

Description	Unit	$ Cost
Commissioning Fees, sustainable commercial construction	S.F.	0.24 - 3.04
Energy Modelling Fees, commercial buildings to 10,000 SF	Ea.	11,000
Greater than 10,000 SF add	S.F.	0.04
Green Bldg Cert Fees for comm construction project reg	Project	900
Photovoltaic Pwr Sys, grid connected, 20 kW (~2400 SF), roof	Ea.	249,200
Green Roofs, 6" soil depth, w/treated wd edging & sedum mats	S.F.	12.41
10" Soil depth, with treated wood edging & sedum mats	S.F.	14.10
Greywater Recovery Systems, prepackaged comm, 3060 gal.	Ea.	45,900
4590 gal.	Ea.	57,625
Rainwater Harvest Sys, prepckged comm, 10,000 gal, sys contrller	Ea.	37,550
20,000 gal. w/system controller	Ea.	61,000
30,000 gal. w/system controller	Ea.	97,350
Solar Domestic HW, closed loop, add-on sys, ext heat exchanger	Ea.	11,300
Drainback, hot water system, 120 gal tank	Ea.	14,175
Draindown, hot water system, 120 gal tank	Ea.	14,425

Model costs calculated for a 3 story building with 9' story height and 49,000 square feet of floor area

G Motel, 2-3 Story

			Unit	Unit Cost	Cost Per S.F.	% Of Sub-Total
A. SUBSTRUCTURE						
1010	Standard Foundations	Poured concrete; strip and spread footings	S.F. Ground	1.62	.54	
1020	Special Foundations	N/A	—	—	—	
1030	Slab on Grade	4" reinforced concrete with recycled vapor barrier and granular base	S.F. Slab	5.84	1.95	3.3%
2010	Basement Excavation	Site preparation for slab and trench for foundation wall and footing	S.F. Ground	.18	.06	
2020	Basement Walls	4' foundation wall	L.F. Wall	98	2.43	
B. SHELL						
	B10 Superstructure					
1010	Floor Construction	Precast concrete plank	S.F. Floor	13.65	9.10	8.8%
1020	Roof Construction	Precast concrete plank	S.F. Roof	12.87	4.29	
	B20 Exterior Enclosure					
2010	Exterior Walls	Decorative concrete block 85% of wall	S.F. Wall	23.64	6.71	
2020	Exterior Windows	Aluminum sliding 15% of wall	Each	589	1.97	11.9%
2030	Exterior Doors	Aluminum and glass doors and entrance with transom	Each	2872	9.50	
	B30 Roofing					
3010	Roof Coverings	Single-ply TPO membrane, 60 mils w/R-20 insul.	S.F. Roof	7.86	2.62	1.8%
3020	Roof Openings	Roof hatches	S.F. Roof	.15	.05	
C. INTERIORS						
1010	Partitions	Concrete block w/foamed-in insul. 7 SF Flr./LF Part.	S.F. Partition	24.16	27.61	
1020	Interior Doors	Wood hollow core, low VOC paint 70 S.F. Floor/Door	Each	645	9.21	
1030	Fittings	N/A	—	—	—	
2010	Stair Construction	Concrete filled metal pan	Flight	15,800	3.87	36.1%
3010	Wall Finishes	90% paint, low VOC, 10% ceramic tile	S.F. Surface	1.76	4.02	
3020	Floor Finishes	85% carpet tile, 5% vinyl composition tile, recycled content, 10% ceramic tile	S.F. Floor	5.65	5.65	
3030	Ceiling Finishes	Textured finish	S.F. Ceiling	4.66	4.66	
D. SERVICES						
	D10 Conveying					
1010	Elevators & Lifts	Two hydraulic passenger elevators	Each	117,845	4.81	3.2%
1020	Escalators & Moving Walks	N/A	—	—	—	
	D20 Plumbing					
2010	Plumbing Fixtures	Toilet, low flow, auto sensor & service fixtures, supply & drain. 1 Fixt./180 SF Flr.	Each	5443	30.24	
2020	Domestic Water Distribution	Gas fired, tankless water heater	S.F. Floor	.32	.32	20.5%
2040	Rain Water Drainage	Roof drains	S.F. Roof	1.86	.62	
	D30 HVAC					
3010	Energy Supply	N/A	—	—	—	
3020	Heat Generating Systems	Included in D3050	—	—	—	
3030	Cooling Generating Systems	N/A	—	—	—	1.8%
3050	Terminal & Package Units	Through the wall electric heating and cooling units	S.F. Floor	2.79	2.79	
3090	Other HVAC Sys. & Equipment	N/A	—	—	—	
	D40 Fire Protection					
4010	Sprinklers	Sprinklers, wet, light hazard	S.F. Floor	3.12	3.12	2.2%
4020	Standpipes	Standpipe, wet, Class III	S.F. Floor	.29	.29	
	D50 Electrical					
5010	Electrical Service/Distribution	800 ampere service, panel board and feeders	S.F. Floor	1.23	1.23	
5020	Lighting & Branch Wiring	LED fixtures, daylt. dim., ltg. on/off, recept., switches and misc. power	S.F. Floor	11.35	11.35	10.2%
5030	Communications & Security	Addressable alarm systems and emergency lighting	S.F. Floor	1.93	1.93	
5090	Other Electrical Systems	Emergency generator, 7.5 kW, energy monitoring systems	S.F. Floor	1.07	1.07	
E. EQUIPMENT & FURNISHINGS						
1010	Commercial Equipment	Commercial laundry equipment	S.F. Floor	.34	.34	
1020	Institutional Equipment	N/A	—	—	—	0.3%
1090	Other Equipment	Waste handling recycling tilt truck	S.F. Floor	.07	.07	
2020	Moveable Furnishings	No smoking signage	S.F. Floor	.02	.02	
F. SPECIAL CONSTRUCTION						
1020	Integrated Construction	N/A	—	—	—	0.0%
1040	Special Facilities	N/A	—	—	—	
G. BUILDING SITEWORK	N/A					

		Sub-Total	152.44	**100%**
CONTRACTOR FEES (General Requirements: 10%, Overhead: 5%, Profit: 10%)		25%	38.13
ARCHITECT FEES		6%	11.43
	Total Building Cost		**202**

For customer support on your Green Building Costs with RSMeans data, call 800.448.8182.

COMMERCIAL/INDUSTRIAL/INSTITUTIONAL

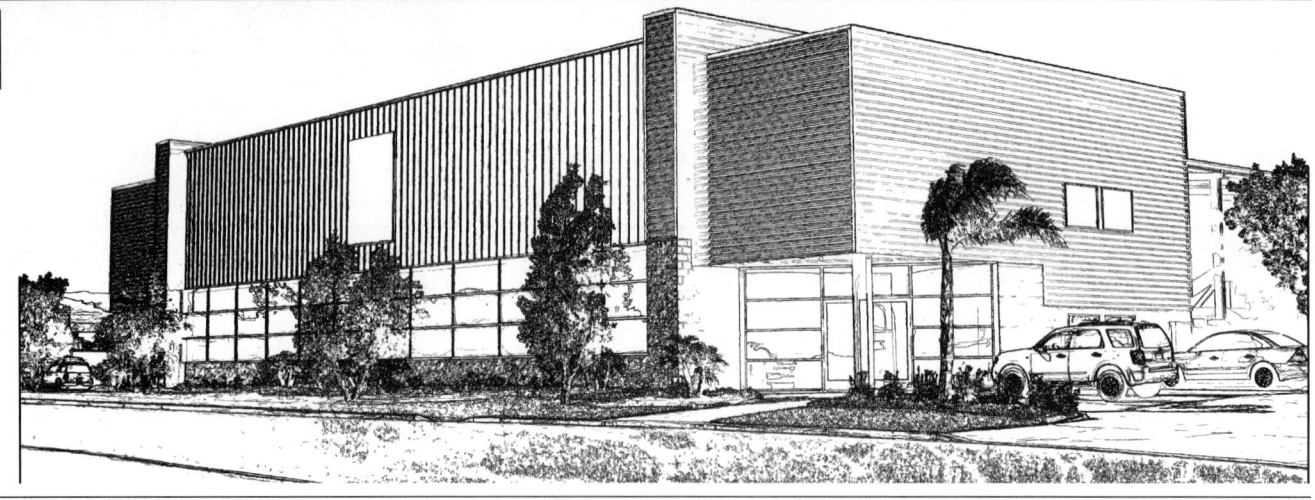

G.455 G Office, 1 Story

Costs per square foot of floor area

Exterior Wall	S.F. Area	2000	3000	5000	7000	9000	12000	15000	20000	25000
	L.F. Perimeter	220	260	320	360	420	480	520	640	700
Wood Clapboard	Wood Truss	236.75	213.95	193.30	182.55	178.00	172.40	168.25	165.75	162.75
Brick Veneer	Wood Truss	243.70	219.30	197.05	185.45	180.60	174.50	170.00	167.30	164.05
Face Brick and Concrete Block	Wood Truss	262.00	233.85	208.00	194.35	188.75	181.60	176.25	173.10	169.15
	Steel Roof Deck	279.05	249.25	221.80	207.35	201.40	193.75	188.10	184.75	180.60
E.I.F.S. and Metal Studs	Steel Roof Deck	255.55	231.70	210.10	198.90	194.15	188.25	183.95	181.30	178.20
Tilt-up Concrete Panels	Steel Roof Deck	262.45	237.45	214.65	202.85	197.80	191.60	187.05	184.25	180.95
Perimeter Adj., Add or Deduct	Per 100 L.F.	31.85	21.30	12.70	9.10	7.10	5.30	4.35	3.20	2.55
Story Hgt. Adj., Add or Deduct	Per 1 Ft.	4.00	3.20	2.35	1.85	1.70	1.45	1.35	1.20	1.05

For Basement, add $38.18 per square foot of basement area

The above costs were calculated using the basic specifications shown on the facing page. These costs should be adjusted where necessary for design alternatives and owner's requirements.

Common additives

Description	Unit	$ Cost
Closed Circuit Surveillance, one station, camera & monitor	Ea.	1475
For additional camera stations, add	Ea.	665
Directory boards, plastic, glass covered, 30" x 20"	Ea.	640
36" x 48"	Ea.	1625
Aluminum, 36" x 24"	Ea.	790
48" x 32"	Ea.	1025
Electronic, wall mounted	S.F.	4625
Pedestal access flr sys w/PLAM cover, comp rm,		
Less than 6000 SF	S.F.	22
Greater than 6000 SF	S.F.	21.50
Office, greater than 6000 S.F.	S.F.	17.95
Uninterruptible power supply, 15 kVA/12.75 kW	kW	1.28

Description	Unit	$ Cost
Commissioning Fees, sustainable commercial construction	S.F.	0.24 - 3.04
Energy Modelling Fees, commercial buildings to 10,000 SF	Ea.	11,000
Greater than 10,000 SF add	S.F.	0.04
Green Bldg Cert Fees for comm construction project reg	Project	900
Photovoltaic Pwr Sys, grid connected, 20 kW (~2400 SF), roof	Ea.	249,200
Green Roofs, 6" soil depth, w/treated wd edging & sedum mats	S.F.	12.41
10" Soil depth, with treated wood edging & sedum mats	S.F.	14.10
Greywater Recovery Systems, prepackaged comm, 3060 gal.	Ea.	45,900
4590 gal.	Ea.	57,625
Rainwater Harvest Sys, prepckged comm, 10,000 gal, sys contrller	Ea.	37,550
20,000 gal. w/system controller	Ea.	61,000
30,000 gal. w/system controller	Ea.	97,350
Solar Domestic HW, closed loop, add-on sys, ext heat exchanger	Ea.	11,300
Drainback, hot water system, 120 gal tank	Ea.	14,175
Draindown, hot water system, 120 gal tank	Ea.	14,425

Model costs calculated for a 1 story building with 12' story height and 7,000 square feet of floor area							**G Office, 1 Story**	
					Unit	Unit Cost	Cost Per S.F.	% Of Sub-Total

A. SUBSTRUCTURE

1010	Standard Foundations	Poured concrete; strip and spread footings	S.F. Ground	3.04	3.04	
1020	Special Foundations	N/A	—	—	—	
1030	Slab on Grade	4" reinforced concrete with recycled vapor barrier and granular base	S.F. Slab	5.84	5.84	9.8%
2010	Basement Excavation	Site preparation for slab and trench for foundation wall and footing	S.F. Ground	.33	.33	
2020	Basement Walls	4' foundation wall	L.F. Wall	186	5.29	

B. SHELL

B10 Superstructure

1010	Floor Construction	N/A	—	—	—	7.4%
1020	Roof Construction	Steel joists, girders & deck on columns	S.F. Roof	10.96	10.96	

B20 Exterior Enclosure

2010	Exterior Walls	E.I.F.S. on metal studs		S.F. Wall	18.70	9.23	
2020	Exterior Windows	Aluminum outward projecting	20% of wall	Each	755	4.05	11.6%
2030	Exterior Doors	Aluminum and glass, hollow metal		Each	4565	3.91	

B30 Roofing

3010	Roof Coverings	Single-ply TPO membrane, 45 mils, heat welded seams w/R-20 insul.	S.F. Roof	13	13	8.9%
3020	Roof Openings	Roof hatch	S.F. Roof	.21	.21	

C. INTERIORS

1010	Partitions	Gyp. bd. on mtl. studs w/sound attenuation	20 SF Flr/LF Part.	S.F. Partition	11.08	5.54	
1020	Interior Doors	Single leaf hollow metal, low VOC paint	200 S.F. Floor/Door	Each	1222	6.11	
1030	Fittings	Toilet partitions		S.F. Floor	.89	.89	
2010	Stair Construction	N/A		—	—	—	18.1%
3010	Wall Finishes	60% vinyl wall covering, 40% paint, low VOC		S.F. Surface	1.66	1.66	
3020	Floor Finishes	60% carpet tile, 30% vinyl composition tile, recycled content, 10% ceramic tile		S.F. Floor	5.08	5.08	
3030	Ceiling Finishes	Mineral fiber tile on concealed zee bars		S.F. Ceiling	7.60	7.60	

D. SERVICES

D10 Conveying

1010	Elevators & Lifts	N/A	—	—	—	0.0%
1020	Escalators & Moving Walks	N/A	—	—	—	

D20 Plumbing

2010	Plumbing Fixtures	Toilet, low flow, auto sensor, & service fixt., supply & drain.	1 Fixt./1320 SF Flr.	Each	10,019	7.59	
2020	Domestic Water Distribution	Tankless, on-demand water heater, gas/propane		S.F. Floor	.96	.96	6.4%
2040	Rain Water Drainage	Roof drains		S.F. Roof	.90	.90	

D30 HVAC

3010	Energy Supply	N/A	—	—	—	
3020	Heat Generating Systems	Included in D3050	—	—	—	
3040	Distribution Systems	Enthalpy heat recovery packages	Each	10,375	1.48	14.9%
3050	Terminal & Package Units	Multizone rooftop air conditioner, SEER 14	S.F. Floor	20.70	20.70	
3090	Other HVAC Sys. & Equipment	N/A	—	—	—	

D40 Fire Protection

4010	Sprinklers	Sprinkler system, light hazard	S.F. Floor	3.79	3.79	3.6%
4020	Standpipes	Standpipes and hose systems	S.F. Floor	1.63	1.63	

D50 Electrical

5010	Electrical Service/Distribution	400 ampere service, panel board and feeders	S.F. Floor	2.06	2.06	
5020	Lighting & Branch Wiring	LED fixtures, daylt. dim., ltg. on/off, recept., switches, and A.C. power	S.F. Floor	15.96	15.96	18.8%
5030	Communications & Security	Addressable alarm systems, internet and phone wiring, and emergency lighting	S.F. Floor	7.49	7.49	
5090	Other Electrical Systems	Emergency generator, 7.5 kW, energy monitoring systems	S.F. Floor	2.45	2.45	

E. EQUIPMENT & FURNISHINGS

1010	Commercial Equipment	N/A	—	—	—	
1020	Institutional Equipment	N/A	—	—	—	0.6%
1090	Other Equipment	Waste handling recycling tilt truck	S.F. Floor	.89	.89	
2020	Moveable Furnishings	No smoking signage	S.F. Floor	.06	.06	

F. SPECIAL CONSTRUCTION

1020	Integrated Construction	N/A	—	—	—	0.0%
1040	Special Facilities	N/A	—	—	—	

G. BUILDING SITEWORK   N/A

Sub-Total	148.70	100%
CONTRACTOR FEES (General Requirements: 10%, Overhead: 5%, Profit: 10%)	25%	37.19
ARCHITECT FEES	7%	13.01
Total Building Cost		**198.90**

For customer support on your Green Building Costs with RSMeans data, call 800.448.8182.

COMMERCIAL/INDUSTRIAL/INSTITUTIONAL

G.460 G Office, 2-4 Story

Costs per square foot of floor area

Exterior Wall	S.F. Area	5000	8000	12000	16000	20000	35000	50000	65000	80000
	L.F. Perimeter	220	260	310	330	360	440	550	600	675
Face Brick and Concrete Block	Wood Joists	279.60	243.65	223.05	208.35	200.70	185.35	180.65	175.90	173.70
	Steel Joists	291.30	255.35	234.75	220.05	212.40	197.05	192.30	187.60	185.40
Curtain Wall	Rigid Steel	323.95	280.95	256.30	238.40	229.10	210.45	204.85	199.00	196.35
	Reinforced Concrete	326.65	283.65	259.00	241.10	231.80	213.15	207.50	201.75	199.05
Wood Clapboard	Wood Frame	236.55	209.60	194.25	183.65	178.05	166.95	163.45	160.15	158.60
Brick Veneer	Wood Frame	246.75	217.15	200.20	188.40	182.20	169.85	166.00	162.30	160.55
Perimeter Adj., Add or Deduct	Per 100 L.F.	47.20	29.45	19.65	14.75	11.75	6.75	4.70	3.60	2.95
Story Hgt. Adj., Add or Deduct	Per 1 Ft.	7.75	5.70	4.50	3.55	3.10	2.20	1.90	1.65	1.50

For Basement, add $42.72 per square foot of basement area

The above costs were calculated using the basic specifications shown on the facing page. These costs should be adjusted where necessary for design alternatives and owner's requirements.

Common additives

Description	Unit	$ Cost
Closed Circuit Surveillance, one station, camera and monitor	Ea.	1475
For additional camera stations, add	Ea.	665
Directory Boards, plastic, glass covered, 30" x 20"	Ea.	640
36" x 48"	Ea.	1625
Aluminum, 36" x 24"	Ea.	790
48" x 32"	Ea.	1025
Electronic, wall mounted	S.F.	4625
Escalators, 10' rise, 32" wide, glass balustrade	Ea.	153,500
48" wide, glass balustrade	Ea.	161,000
Pedestal access flr sys w/PLAM cover, comp rm,		
Less than 6000 SF	S.F.	22
Greater than 6000 SF	S.F.	21.50
Office, greater than 6000 S.F.	S.F.	17.95
Uninterruptible power supply, 15 kVA/12.75 kW	kW	1.28

Description	Unit	$ Cost
Commissioning Fees, sustainable commercial construction	S.F.	0.24 - 3.04
Energy Modelling Fees, commercial buildings to 10,000 SF	Ea.	11,000
Greater than 10,000 SF add	S.F.	0.04
Green Bldg Cert Fees for comm construction project reg	Project	900
Photovoltaic Pwr Sys, grid connected, 20 kW (~2400 SF), roof	Ea.	249,200
Green Roofs, 6" soil depth, w/treated wd edging & sedum mats	S.F.	12.41
10" Soil depth, with treated wood edging & sedum mats	S.F.	14.10
Greywater Recovery Systems, prepackaged comm, 3060 gal.	Ea.	45,900
4590 gal.	Ea.	57,625
Rainwater Harvest Sys, prepckged comm, 10,000 gal, sys contrller	Ea.	37,550
20,000 gal. w/system controller	Ea.	61,000
30,000 gal. w/system controller	Ea.	97,350
Solar Domestic HW, closed loop, add-on sys, ext heat exchanger	Ea.	11,300
Drainback, hot water system, 120 gal tank	Ea.	14,175
Draindown, hot water system, 120 gal tank	Ea.	14,425

Important: See the Reference Section for Location Factors.

Model costs calculated for a 3 story building with 12' story height and 20,000 square feet of floor area

G Office, 2-4 Story

			Unit	Unit Cost	Cost Per S.F.	% Of Sub-Total
A. SUBSTRUCTURE						
1010	Standard Foundations	Poured concrete; strip and spread footings	S.F. Ground	8.31	2.77	
1020	Special Foundations	N/A	—	—	—	
1030	Slab on Grade	4" reinforced concrete with recycled vapor barrier and granular base	S.F. Slab	5.84	1.95	4.4%
2010	Basement Excavation	Site preparation for slab and trench for foundation wall and footing	S.F. Ground	.33	.11	
2020	Basement Walls	4' foundation wall	L.F. Wall	186	2.08	
B. SHELL						
B10 Superstructure						
1010	Floor Construction	Open web steel joists, slab form, concrete, columns	S.F. Floor	20.63	13.75	10.3%
1020	Roof Construction	Metal deck, open web steel joists, columns	S.F. Roof	7.92	2.64	
B20 Exterior Enclosure						
2010	Exterior Walls	Face brick with concrete block backup — 80% of wall	S.F. Wall	41.20	21.36	
2020	Exterior Windows	Aluminum outward projecting — 20% of wall	Each	755	4.25	17.0%
2030	Exterior Doors	Aluminum and glass, hollow metal	Each	4565	1.38	
B30 Roofing						
3010	Roof Coverings	Single-ply, TPO membrane, 60 mils, heat welded seams w/R-20 insul.	S.F. Roof	8.88	2.96	1.9%
3020	Roof Openings	N/A	—	—	—	
C. INTERIORS						
1010	Partitions	Gypsum board on metal studs — 20 SF Flr/LF Part.	S.F. Partition	11.43	4.57	
1020	Interior Doors	Single leaf hollow metal, low VOC paint — 200 S.F. Floor/Door	Each	1222	6.11	
1030	Fittings	Toilet partitions	S.F. Floor	1.87	1.87	
2010	Stair Construction	Concrete filled metal pan	Flight	15,800	5.53	20.2%
3010	Wall Finishes	60% vinyl wall covering, 40% paint, low VOC	S.F. Surface	1.65	1.32	
3020	Floor Finishes	60% carpet tile, 30% vinyl composition tile, recycled content, 10% ceramic tile	S.F. Floor	5.08	5.08	
3030	Ceiling Finishes	Mineral fiber tile on concealed zee bars	S.F. Ceiling	7.60	7.60	
D. SERVICES						
D10 Conveying						
1010	Elevators & Lifts	Two hydraulic passenger elevators	Each	125,900	12.59	7.9%
1020	Escalators & Moving Walks	N/A	—	—	—	
D20 Plumbing						
2010	Plumbing Fixtures	Toilet, low flow, auto sensor, & service fixt., supply & drain. — 1 Fixt./1320 SF Flr.	Each	5900	4.47	
2020	Domestic Water Distribution	Gas fired, tankless water heater	S.F. Floor	.22	.22	3.5%
2040	Rain Water Drainage	Roof drains	S.F. Roof	2.82	.94	
D30 HVAC						
3010	Energy Supply	N/A	—	—	—	
3020	Heat Generating Systems	Included in D3050	—	—	—	
3040	Distribution Systems	Enthalpy heat recovery packages	Each	18,475	2.77	12.2%
3050	Terminal & Package Units	Multizone rooftop air conditioner. SEER 14	S.F. Floor	16.65	16.65	
3090	Other HVAC Sys. & Equipment	N/A	—	—	—	
D40 Fire Protection						
4010	Sprinklers	Wet pipe sprinkler system	S.F. Floor	4.02	4.02	3.2%
4020	Standpipes	Standpipes and hose systems	S.F. Floor	1.07	1.07	
D50 Electrical						
5010	Electrical Service/Distribution	1000 ampere service, panel board and feeders	S.F. Floor	2.86	2.86	
5020	Lighting & Branch Wiring	LED fixtures, daylt. dim., ltg. on/off, recept., switches, and A.C. power	S.F. Floor	16.63	16.63	19.1%
5030	Communications & Security	Addressable alarm systems, internet and phone wiring, & emergency ltg.	S.F. Floor	9.57	9.57	
5090	Other Electrical Systems	Emergency generator, 7.5 kW, UPS, energy monitoring systems	S.F. Floor	1.33	1.33	
E. EQUIPMENT & FURNISHINGS						
1010	Commercial Equipment	N/A	—	—	—	
1020	Institutional Equipment	N/A	—	—	—	0.2%
1090	Other Equipment	Waste handling recycling tilt truck	S.F. Floor	.31	.31	
2020	Moveable Furnishings	No smoking signage	S.F. Floor	.02	.02	
F. SPECIAL CONSTRUCTION						
1020	Integrated Construction	N/A	—	—	—	0.0%
1040	Special Facilities	N/A	—	—	—	
G. BUILDING SITEWORK	N/A					

Sub-Total	158.78	100%
CONTRACTOR FEES (General Requirements: 10%, Overhead: 5%, Profit: 10%)	25%	39.73
ARCHITECT FEES	7%	13.89
Total Building Cost	**212.40**	

COMMERCIAL/INDUSTRIAL/INSTITUTIONAL — G.470 — G Office, 5-10 Story

Costs per square foot of floor area

Exterior Wall	S.F. Area	20000	40000	60000	80000	100000	150000	200000	250000	300000
	L.F. Perimeter	260	360	400	420	460	520	650	720	800
Precast Concrete	Rigid Steel	269.15	230.10	209.00	196.40	190.45	180.40	178.20	174.90	172.95
	Reinforced Concrete	268.35	229.35	208.15	195.60	189.65	179.55	177.40	174.05	172.10
Face Brick and Concrete Block	Rigid Steel	241.50	210.95	194.80	185.25	180.65	173.00	171.25	168.75	167.25
	Reinforced Concrete	240.75	210.15	194.00	184.40	179.85	172.15	170.45	167.95	166.45
Limestone and Concrete Block	Rigid Steel	271.00	231.35	209.90	197.15	191.15	180.85	178.60	175.30	173.30
	Reinforced Concrete	270.20	230.60	209.15	196.30	190.30	180.05	177.85	174.50	172.50
Perimeter Adj., Add or Deduct	Per 100 L.F.	40.75	20.40	13.55	10.20	8.10	5.40	4.05	3.25	2.70
Story Hgt. Adj., Add or Deduct	Per 1 Ft.	8.50	5.90	4.35	3.45	3.00	2.25	2.10	1.85	1.75

For Basement, add $46.07 per square foot of basement area

The above costs were calculated using the basic specifications shown on the facing page. These costs should be adjusted where necessary for design alternatives and owner's requirements.

Common additives

Description	Unit	$ Cost
Closed Circuit Surveillance, one station, camera and monitor	Ea.	1475
For additional camera stations, add	Ea.	665
Directory Boards, plastic, glass covered, 30" x 20"	Ea.	640
36" x 48"	Ea.	1625
Aluminum, 36" x 24"	Ea.	790
48" x 32"	Ea.	1025
Electronic, wall mounted	S.F.	4625
Escalators, 10' rise, 32" wide, glass balustrade	Ea.	153,500
48" wide, glass balustrade	Ea.	161,000
Pedestal access flr sys w/PLAM cover, comp rm,		
Less than 6000 SF	S.F.	22
Greater than 6000 SF	S.F.	21.50
Office, greater than 6000 S.F.	S.F.	17.95
Uninterruptible power supply, 15 kVA/12.75 kW	kW	1.28

Description	Unit	$ Cost
Commissioning Fees, sustainable commercial construction	S.F.	0.24 - 3.04
Energy Modelling Fees, commercial buildings to 10,000 SF	Ea.	11,000
Greater than 10,000 SF add	S.F.	0.04
Green Bldg Cert Fees for comm construction project reg	Project	900
Photovoltaic Pwr Sys, grid connected, 20 kW (~2400 SF), roof	Ea.	249,200
Green Roofs, 6" soil depth, w/treated wd edging & sedum mats	S.F.	12.41
10" Soil depth, with treated wood edging & sedum mats	S.F.	14.10
Greywater Recovery Systems, prepackaged comm, 3060 gal.	Ea.	45,900
4590 gal.	Ea.	57,625
Rainwater Harvest Sys, prepckged comm, 10,000 gal, sys contrller	Ea.	37,550
20,000 gal. w/system controller	Ea.	61,000
30,000 gal. w/system controller	Ea.	97,350
Solar Domestic HW, closed loop, add-on sys, ext heat exchanger	Ea.	11,300
Drainback, hot water system, 120 gal tank	Ea.	14,175
Draindown, hot water system, 120 gal tank	Ea.	14,425

Important: See the Reference Section for Location Factors.

Model costs calculated for a 8 story building with 12' story height and 80,000 square feet of floor area

G Office, 5-10 Story

				Unit	Unit Cost	Cost Per S.F.	% Of Sub-Total
A.	**SUBSTRUCTURE**						
1010	Standard Foundations	Poured concrete; strip and spread footings		S.F. Ground	13.36	1.67	
1020	Special Foundations	N/A		—	—	—	
1030	Slab on Grade	4" reinforced concrete with recycled vapor barrier and granular base		S.F. Slab	5.84	.73	2.1%
2010	Basement Excavation	Site preparation for slab and trench for foundation wall and footing		S.F. Ground	.33	.04	
2020	Basement Walls	4' foundation wall		L.F. Wall	98	.66	
B.	**SHELL**						
	B10 Superstructure						
1010	Floor Construction	Concrete slab with metal deck and beams		S.F. Floor	25.26	22.10	15.6%
1020	Roof Construction	Metal deck, open web steel joists, interior columns		S.F. Roof	7.60	.95	
	B20 Exterior Enclosure						
2010	Exterior Walls	Precast concrete panels	80% of wall	S.F. Wall	62	25.04	
2020	Exterior Windows	Vertical pivoted steel	20% of wall	Each	589	3.96	19.8%
2030	Exterior Doors	Double aluminum and glass doors and entrance with transoms		Each	5428	.34	
	B30 Roofing						
3010	Roof Coverings	Single-ply TPO membrane, 60 mils, welded seams w/R-20 insul.		S.F. Roof	7.36	.92	0.6%
3020	Roof Openings	N/A		—	—	—	
C.	**INTERIORS**						
1010	Partitions	Gypsum board on metal studs w/sound attenuation	30 SF Flr./LF Part.	S.F. Partition	12.27	4.09	
1020	Interior Doors	Single leaf hollow metal, low VOC paint	400 S.F. Floor/Door	Each	1222	3.06	
1030	Fittings	Toilet Partitions		S.F. Floor	1.25	1.25	
2010	Stair Construction	Concrete filled metal pan		Flight	15,800	3.36	17.2%
3010	Wall Finishes	60% vinyl wall covering, 40% paint, low VOC paint		S.F. Surface	1.67	1.11	
3020	Floor Finishes	60% carpet tile, 30% vinyl composition tile, recycled content, 10% ceramic tile		S.F. Floor	5.08	5.08	
3030	Ceiling Finishes	Mineral fiber tile on concealed zee bars		S.F. Ceiling	7.60	7.60	
D.	**SERVICES**						
	D10 Conveying						
1010	Elevators & Lifts	Four geared passenger elevators		Each	324,600	16.23	10.9%
1020	Escalators & Moving Walks	N/A		—	—	—	
	D20 Plumbing						
2010	Plumbing Fixtures	Toilet, low flow, auto sensor, & service fixt., supply & drain.	1 Fixt./1370 SF Flr.	Each	4302	3.14	
2020	Domestic Water Distribution	Gas fired tankless water heater		S.F. Floor	.42	.42	2.7%
2040	Rain Water Drainage	Roof drains		S.F. Roof	3.36	.42	
	D30 HVAC						
3010	Energy Supply	N/A		—	—	—	
3020	Heat Generating Systems	Included in D3050		—	—	—	
3040	Distribution Systems	Enthalpy heat recovery packages		Each	38,725	1.94	12.5%
3050	Terminal & Package Units	Multizone rooftop air conditioner, SEER 14		S.F. Floor	16.65	16.65	
3090	Other HVAC Sys. & Equipment	N/A		—	—	—	
	D40 Fire Protection						
4010	Sprinklers	Wet pipe sprinkler system		S.F. Floor	3.06	3.06	2.9%
4020	Standpipes	Standpipes and hose systems		S.F. Floor	1.17	1.17	
	D50 Electrical						
5010	Electrical Service/Distribution	1600 ampere service, panel board and feeders		S.F. Floor	1.10	1.10	
5020	Lighting & Branch Wiring	LED fixtures, daylt. dim., ltg. on/off, recept., switches, and A.C. power		S.F. Floor	15.39	15.39	15.6%
5030	Communications & Security	Addressable alarm systems, internet and phone wiring, emergency lighting		S.F. Floor	5.51	5.51	
5090	Other Electrical Systems	Emergency generator, 100 kW, UPS, energy monitoring systems		S.F. Floor	1.19	1.19	
E.	**EQUIPMENT & FURNISHINGS**						
1010	Commercial Equipment	N/A		—	—	—	
1020	Institutional Equipment	N/A		—	—	—	0.0%
1090	Other Equipment	Waste handling recycling tilt truck		S.F. Floor	.04	.04	
2020	Moveable Furnishings	No smoking signage		S.F. Floor			
F.	**SPECIAL CONSTRUCTION**						
1020	Integrated Construction	N/A		—	—	—	0.0%
1040	Special Facilities	N/A		—	—	—	
G.	**BUILDING SITEWORK**	N/A					

	Sub-Total	148.22	100%
CONTRACTOR FEES (General Requirements: 10%, Overhead: 5%, Profit: 10%)	25%	37.06	
ARCHITECT FEES	6%	11.12	
	Total Building Cost	**196.40**	

For customer support on your Green Building Costs with RSMeans data, call 800.448.8182.

COMMERCIAL/INDUSTRIAL/INSTITUTIONAL

G.480 G Office, 11-20 Story

Costs per square foot of floor area

Exterior Wall	S.F. Area	120000	145000	170000	200000	230000	260000	400000	600000	800000
	L.F. Perimeter	420	450	470	490	510	530	650	800	900
Curtain Wall	Rigid Steel	224.35	215.00	207.40	200.40	195.20	191.20	181.75	175.20	170.75
	Reinforced Concrete	215.00	205.90	198.40	191.50	186.40	182.50	173.20	166.85	162.45
Face Brick and Concrete Block	Rigid Steel	196.95	190.75	185.80	181.25	177.90	175.25	169.00	164.80	162.00
	Reinforced Concrete	187.60	181.60	176.80	172.35	169.10	166.55	160.50	156.40	153.70
Precast Concrete	Rigid Steel	207.10	199.75	193.80	188.30	184.25	181.15	173.75	168.65	165.25
	Reinforced Concrete	197.75	190.60	184.80	179.50	175.50	172.50	165.20	160.30	156.95
Perimeter Adj., Add or Deduct	Per 100 L.F.	15.40	12.80	10.95	9.20	8.05	7.15	4.60	3.15	2.40
Story Hgt. Adj., Add or Deduct	Per 1 Ft.	6.20	5.55	4.95	4.35	3.95	3.65	2.90	2.40	2.05

For Basement, add $46.07 per square foot of basement area

The above costs were calculated using the basic specifications shown on the facing page. These costs should be adjusted where necessary for design alternatives and owner's requirements.

Common additives

Description	Unit	$ Cost
Closed Circuit Surveillance, one station, camera and monitor	Ea.	1475
For additional camera stations, add	Ea.	665
Directory Boards, plastic, glass covered, 30" x 20"	Ea.	640
36" x 48"	Ea.	1625
Aluminum, 36" x 24"	Ea.	790
48" x 32"	Ea.	1025
Electronic, wall mounted	S.F.	4625
Escalators, 10' rise, 32" wide, glass balustrade	Ea.	153,500
48" wide, glass balustrade	Ea.	161,000
Pedestal access flr sys w/PLAM cover, comp rm,		
Less than 6000 SF	S.F.	22
Greater than 6000 SF	S.F.	21.50
Office, greater than 6000 S.F.	S.F.	17.95
Uninterruptible power supply, 15 kVA/12.75 kW	kW	1.28

Description	Unit	$ Cost
Commissioning Fees, sustainable commercial construction	S.F.	0.24 - 3.04
Energy Modelling Fees, commercial buildings to 10,000 SF	Ea.	11,000
Greater than 10,000 SF add	S.F.	0.04
Green Bldg Cert Fees for comm construction project reg	Project	900
Photovoltaic Pwr Sys, grid connected, 20 kW (~2400 SF), roof	Ea.	249,200
Green Roofs, 6" soil depth, w/treated wd edging & sedum mats	S.F.	12.41
10" Soil depth, with treated wood edging & sedum mats	S.F.	14.10
Greywater Recovery Systems, prepackaged comm, 3060 gal.	Ea.	45,900
4590 gal.	Ea.	57,625
Rainwater Harvest Sys, prepckged comm, 10,000 gal, sys contrller	Ea.	37,550
20,000 gal. w/system controller	Ea.	61,000
30,000 gal. w/system controller	Ea.	97,350
Solar Domestic HW, closed loop, add-on sys, ext heat exchanger	Ea.	11,300
Drainback, hot water system, 120 gal tank	Ea.	14,175
Draindown, hot water system, 120 gal tank	Ea.	14,425

Important: See the Reference Section for Location Factors.

Model costs calculated for a 16 story building with 10' story height and 260,000 square feet of floor area

G Office, 11-20 Story

	Unit	Unit Cost	Cost Per S.F.	% Of Sub-Total

A. SUBSTRUCTURE

1010	Standard Foundations	CIP concrete pile caps	S.F. Ground	11.20	.70	
1020	Special Foundations	Steel H-piles, concrete grade beams	S.F. Ground	65	4.06	
1030	Slab on Grade	4" reinforced concrete with recycled vapor barrier and granular base	S.F. Slab	5.84	.36	3.9%
2010	Basement Excavation	Site preparation for slab, piles and grade beams	S.F. Ground	.33	.02	
2020	Basement Walls	4' foundation wall	L.F. Wall	98	.48	

B. SHELL

B10 Superstructure

1010	Floor Construction	Concrete slab, metal deck, beams	S.F. Floor	29.69	27.83	19.7%
1020	Roof Construction	Metal deck, open web steel joists, beams, columns	S.F. Roof	9.12	.57	

B20 Exterior Enclosure

2010	Exterior Walls	N/A		—	—	—
2020	Exterior Windows	Double glazed heat absorbing, tinted plate glass wall panels 100% of wall	Each	86	26.17	18.7 %
2030	Exterior Doors	Double aluminum & glass doors	Each	8111	.88	

B30 Roofing

3010	Roof Coverings	Single ply membrane, fully adhered; perlite/EPS R-20 insulation	S.F. Roof	8	.50	0.3%
3020	Roof Openings	N/A	—	—	—	

C. INTERIORS

1010	Partitions	Gypsum board on metal studs, sound attenuation 30 SF Flr./LF Part.	S.F. Partition	13.88	3.70	
1020	Interior Doors	Single leaf hollow metal, low VOC paint 400 S.F. Floor/Door	Each	1222	3.06	
1030	Fittings	Toilet partitions	S.F. Floor	.72	.72	
2010	Stair Construction	Concrete filled metal pan	Flight	18,900	2.54	16.6%
3010	Wall Finishes	60% vinyl wall covering, 40% paint, low VOC	S.F. Surface	1.65	.88	
3020	Floor Finishes	60% carpet tile, 30% vinyl composition tile, recycled content, 10% ceramic tile	S.F. Floor	5.48	5.48	
3030	Ceiling Finishes	Mineral fiber tile on concealed zee bars	S.F. Ceiling	7.60	7.60	

D. SERVICES

D10 Conveying

1010	Elevators & Lifts	Four geared passenger elevators	Each	505,050	7.77	5.4%
1020	Escalators & Moving Walks	N/A	—	—	—	

D20 Plumbing

2010	Plumbing Fixtures	Toilet, low flow, auto sensor, & service fixt., supply & drain. 1 Fixt./1345 SF Flr.	Each	7021	5.22	
2020	Domestic Water Distribution	Gas fired, tankless water heater	S.F. Floor	.19	.19	3.9%
2040	Rain Water Drainage	Roof drains	S.F. Roof	4.32	.27	

D30 HVAC

3010	Energy Supply	N/A	—	—	—	
3020	Heat Generating Systems	N/A	—	—	—	
3040	Distribution Systems	Enthalpy heat recovery packages	Each	38,725	1.63	12.7 %
3050	Terminal & Package Units	Multizone rooftop air conditioner	S.F. Floor	16.65	16.65	
3090	Other HVAC Sys. & Equipment	N/A	—	—	—	

D40 Fire Protection

4010	Sprinklers	Sprinkler system, light hazard	S.F. Floor	2.95	2.95	2.5%
4020	Standpipes	Standpipes and hose systems	S.F. Floor	.60	.60	

D50 Electrical

5010	Electrical Service/Distribution	2400 ampere service, panel board and feeders	S.F. Floor	.69	.69	
5020	Lighting & Branch Wiring	LED fixtures, daylt. dim., ltg. on/off, recept., switches, and A.C. power	S.F. Floor	16.27	16.27	16.3%
5030	Communications & Security	Addressable alarm systems, internet & phone wiring, emergency ltg.	S.F. Floor	5.85	5.85	
5090	Other Electrical Systems	Emergency generator, 200 kW, UPS, energy monitoring systems	S.F. Floor	.65	.65	

E. EQUIPMENT & FURNISHINGS

1010	Commercial Equipment	N/A	—	—	—	
1020	Institutional Equipment	N/A	—	—	—	0.0%
1090	Other Equipment	Waste handling recycling tilt truck	S.F. Floor	.01	.01	
2020	Moveable Furnishings	No smoking signage	S.F. Floor			

F. SPECIAL CONSTRUCTION

1020	Integrated Construction	N/A	—	—	—	0.0 %
1040	Special Facilities	N/A	—	—	—	

G. BUILDING SITEWORK   N/A

Sub-Total	144.30	100%
CONTRACTOR FEES (General Requirements: 10%, Overhead: 5%, Profit: 10%)	25%	36.08
ARCHITECT FEES	6%	10.82
Total Building Cost		**191.20**

For customer support on your Green Building Costs with RSMeans data, call 800.448.8182.

COMMERCIAL/INDUSTRIAL/INSTITUTIONAL

G.490 G Police Station

Costs per square foot of floor area

Exterior Wall	S.F. Area	7000	9000	11000	13000	15000	17000	19000	21000	23000
	L.F. Perimeter	240	280	303	325	354	372	397	422	447
Limestone and Concrete Block	Bearing Walls	280.65	264.85	251.35	241.80	235.85	229.85	225.95	222.75	220.20
	Reinforced Concrete	303.75	288.00	274.45	264.90	259.00	253.00	249.05	245.90	243.30
Face Brick and Concrete Block	Bearing Walls	260.60	246.75	235.30	227.20	222.10	217.10	213.75	211.05	208.85
	Reinforced Concrete	283.75	269.80	258.40	250.30	245.20	240.25	236.90	234.15	232.00
Decorative Concrete Block	Bearing Walls	246.25	233.65	223.75	216.75	212.25	207.95	205.00	202.65	200.75
	Reinforced Concrete	269.40	256.80	246.85	239.85	235.30	231.05	228.15	225.80	223.85
Perimeter Adj., Add or Deduct	Per 100 L.F.	31.90	24.90	20.35	17.20	14.95	13.15	11.75	10.70	9.70
Story Hgt. Adj., Add or Deduct	Per 1 Ft.	5.45	5.00	4.40	4.05	3.80	3.50	3.35	3.25	3.05

For Basement, add $36.22 per square foot of basement area

The above costs were calculated using the basic specifications shown on the facing page. These costs should be adjusted where necessary for design alternatives and owner's requirements.

Common additives

Description	Unit	$ Cost
Cells Prefabricated, 5'-6" x 7'-8", 7'-8' high	Ea.	12,700
Elevators, hydraulic passenger, 2 stops, 2500# capacity	Ea.	76,600
3500# capacity	Ea.	81,600
Lockers, Steel, Single tier, 60" to 72"	Opng.	232 - 395
Locker bench, lam. maple top only	L.F.	36.50
Pedestals, steel pipe	Ea.	79
Safe, Office type, 1 hr rating, 60"x36"x18", double door	Ea.	10,200
Shooting Range, incl. bullet traps, Target provisions & controls, excl. struct shell	Ea.	57,500
Sound System, amplifier, 250 watts	Ea.	2025
Speaker, ceiling or wall	Ea.	240
Trumpet	Ea.	460

Description	Unit	$ Cost
Commissioning Fees, sustainable commercial construction	S.F.	0.24 - 3.04
Energy Modelling Fees, commercial buildings to 10,000 SF	Ea.	11,000
Greater than 10,000 SF add	S.F.	0.04
Green Bldg Cert Fees for comm construction project reg	Project	900
Photovoltaic Pwr Sys, grid connected, 20 kW (~2400 SF), roof	Ea.	249,200
Green Roofs, 6" soil depth, w/treated wd edging & sedum mats	S.F.	12.41
10" Soil depth, with treated wood edging & sedum mats	S.F.	14.10
Greywater Recovery Systems, prepackaged comm, 3060 gal.	Ea.	45,900
4590 gal.	Ea.	57,625
Rainwater Harvest Sys, prepckged comm, 10,000 gal, sys contrller	Ea.	37,550
20,000 gal. w/system controller	Ea.	61,000
30,000 gal. w/system controller	Ea.	97,350
Solar Domestic HW, closed loop, add-on sys, ext heat exchanger	Ea.	11,300
Drainback, hot water system, 120 gal tank	Ea.	14,175
Draindown, hot water system, 120 gal tank	Ea.	14,425

Important: See the Reference Section for Location Factors.

G Police Station

Model costs calculated for a 2 story building with 12' story height and 11,000 square feet of floor area

				Unit	Unit Cost	Cost Per S.F.	% Of Sub-Total
A.	**SUBSTRUCTURE**						
1010	Standard Foundations	Poured concrete; strip and spread footings		S.F. Ground	3.12	1.56	
1020	Special Foundations	N/A		—	—	—	
1030	Slab on Grade	4" reinforced concrete with recycled vapor barrier and granular base		S.F. Slab	5.84	2.93	4.5%
2010	Basement Excavation	Site preparation for slab and trench for foundation wall and footing		S.F. Ground	.33	.17	
2020	Basement Walls	4' foundation wall		L.F. Wall	98	3.59	
B.	**SHELL**						
	B10 Superstructure						
1010	Floor Construction	Open web steel joists, slab form, concrete		S.F. Floor	13.46	6.73	5.1%
1020	Roof Construction	Metal deck on open web steel joists		S.F. Roof	5.40	2.70	
	B20 Exterior Enclosure						
2010	Exterior Walls	Limestone with concrete block backup	80% of wall	S.F. Wall	63	33.58	
2020	Exterior Windows	Metal horizontal sliding	20% of wall	Each	529	4.66	22.1%
2030	Exterior Doors	Hollow metal		Each	3506	2.55	
	B30 Roofing						
3010	Roof Coverings	Single-ply TPO membrane, 60 mils, heat welded w/R-20 insul.		S.F. Roof	8.44	4.22	2.3%
3020	Roof Openings	N/A		—	—	—	
C.	**INTERIORS**						
1010	Partitions	Concrete block w/foamed-in insul.	20 SF Flr./LF Part.	S.F. Partition	12.06	6.03	
1020	Interior Doors	Single leaf kalamein fire door, low VOC paint	200 S.F. Floor/Door	Each	1222	6.11	
1030	Fittings	Toilet partitions		S.F. Floor	.98	.98	
2010	Stair Construction	Concrete filled metal pan		Flight	18,900	3.43	17.4%
3010	Wall Finishes	90% paint, low VOC, 10% ceramic tile		S.F. Surface	2.97	2.97	
3020	Floor Finishes	70% vinyl composition tile, recycled content, 20% carpet tile, 10% ceramic tile		S.F. Floor	4.94	4.94	
3030	Ceiling Finishes	Mineral fiber tile on concealed zee bars		S.F. Ceiling	7.60	7.60	
D.	**SERVICES**						
	D10 Conveying						
1010	Elevators & Lifts	One hydraulic passenger elevator		Each	91,190	8.29	4.5%
1020	Escalators & Moving Walks	N/A		—	—	—	
	D20 Plumbing						
2010	Plumbing Fixtures	Toilet, low flow, auto sensor, & service fixt., supply & drainage	1 Fixt./580 SF Flr.	Each	5823	10.04	
2020	Domestic Water Distribution	Electric water heater, point-of-use, energy saver		S.F. Floor	1.28	1.28	7.1%
2040	Rain Water Drainage	Roof drains		S.F. Roof	3.44	1.72	
	D30 HVAC						
3010	Energy Supply	N/A		—	—	—	
3020	Heat Generating Systems	N/A		—	—	—	
3040	Distribution Systems	Enthalpy heat recovery packages		Each	15,550	1.42	12.0%
3050	Terminal & Package Units	Multizone rooftop air conditioner, SEER 14		S.F. Floor	20.70	20.70	
3090	Other HVAC Sys. & Equipment	N/A		—	—	—	
	D40 Fire Protection						
4010	Sprinklers	Wet pipe sprinkler system		S.F. Floor	4.08	4.08	2.8%
4020	Standpipes	Standpipe		S.F. Floor	1.15	1.15	
	D50 Electrical						
5010	Electrical Service/Distribution	400 ampere service, panel board and feeders		S.F. Floor	1.03	1.03	
5020	Lighting & Branch Wiring	LED fixtures, daylt. dim., ltg. on/off cntrl., recept., switches, & A.C. pwr.		S.F. Floor	13.60	13.60	12.9%
5030	Communications & Security	Addressable alarm systems, internet wiring, intercom & emergency ltg.		S.F. Floor	7.52	7.52	
5090	Other Electrical Systems	Emergency generator, 15 kW, energy monitoring systems		S.F. Floor	1.71	1.71	
E.	**EQUIPMENT & FURNISHINGS**						
1020	Institutional Equipment	Lockers, detention rooms, cells, gasoline dispensers		S.F. Floor	13.65	13.65	
1030	Vehicular Equipment	Gasoline dispenser system		S.F. Floor	2.54	2.54	9.1%
1090	Other Equipment	Waste handling recycling tilt truck		S.F. Floor	.57	.57	
2020	Moveable Furnishings	No smoking signage		S.F. Floor	.04	.04	
F.	**SPECIAL CONSTRUCTION**						
1020	Integrated Construction	N/A		—	—	—	0.0%
1040	Special Facilities	N/A		—	—	—	
G.	**BUILDING SITEWORK**	N/A					

		Sub-Total	184.47	**100%**
CONTRACTOR FEES (General Requirements: 10%, Overhead: 5%, Profit: 10%)		25%	46.13
ARCHITECT FEES		9%	20.75
	Total Building Cost		**251.35**

For customer support on your Green Building Costs with RSMeans data, call 800.448.8182.

COMMERCIAL/INDUSTRIAL/INSTITUTIONAL G.530 G Restaurant

Costs per square foot of floor area

Exterior Wall	S.F. Area	2000	2800	3500	4200	5000	5800	6500	7200	8000
	L.F. Perimeter	180	212	240	268	300	314	336	344	368
Wood Clapboard	Wood Frame	284.55	269.70	262.25	257.30	253.40	248.40	246.15	242.95	241.20
Brick Veneer	Wood Frame	297.75	280.75	272.30	266.60	262.15	256.30	253.65	249.95	247.95
Face Brick and Concrete Block	Wood Joists	312.25	293.00	283.35	276.90	271.85	265.00	262.00	257.65	255.35
	Steel Joists	305.40	286.10	276.50	270.05	264.95	258.15	255.15	250.75	248.45
Stucco and Concrete Block	Wood Joists	300.40	283.50	275.00	269.35	264.95	259.05	256.40	252.70	250.70
	Steel Joists	290.70	273.80	265.30	259.65	255.20	249.35	246.75	242.95	241.00
Perimeter Adj., Add or Deduct	Per 100 L.F.	33.40	23.85	19.15	15.95	13.35	11.50	10.25	9.25	8.40
Story Hgt. Adj., Add or Deduct	Per 1 Ft.	3.45	2.85	2.65	2.45	2.30	2.10	1.95	1.80	1.85

For Basement, add $41.33 per square foot of basement area

The above costs were calculated using the basic specifications shown on the facing page. These costs should be adjusted where necessary for design alternatives and owner's requirements.

Common additives

Description	Unit	$ Cost
Bar, Front Bar	L.F.	450
Back bar	L.F.	360
Booth, Upholstered, custom straight	L.F.	258 - 475
"L" or "U" shaped	L.F.	267 - 450
Fireplace, brick, excl. chimney or foundation, 30"x29" opening	Ea.	3400
Chimney, standard brick, single flue, 16" x 20"	V.L.F.	113
2 Flue, 20" x 24"	V.L.F.	165
Kitchen Equipment		
Broiler	Ea.	4425
Coffee urn, twin 6 gallon	Ea.	2900
Cooler, 6 ft. long	Ea.	3750
Dishwasher, 10-12 racks per hr.	Ea.	4150
Food warmer, counter, 1.2 KW	Ea.	790
Freezer, 44 C.F., reach-in	Ea.	5525
Ice cube maker, 50 lb. per day	Ea.	2100
Range with 1 oven	Ea.	3575
Refrigerators, prefabricated, walk-in, 7'-6" high, 6' x 6'	S.F.	145
10' x 10'	S.F.	114
12' x 14'	S.F.	99.50
12' x 20'	S.F.	137

Description	Unit	$ Cost
Commissioning Fees, sustainable commercial construction	S.F.	0.24 - 3.04
Energy Modelling Fees, commercial buildings to 10,000 SF	Ea.	11,000
Greater than 10,000 SF add	S.F.	0.04
Green Bldg Cert Fees for comm construction project reg	Project	900
Photovoltaic Pwr Sys, grid connected, 20 kW (~2400 SF), roof	Ea.	249,200
Green Roofs, 6" soil depth, w/treated wd edging & sedum mats	S.F.	12.41
10" Soil depth, with treated wood edging & sedum mats	S.F.	14.10
Greywater Recovery Systems, prepackaged comm, 3060 gal.	Ea.	45,900
4590 gal.	Ea.	57,625
Rainwater Harvest Sys, prepckged comm, 10,000 gal, sys contrller	Ea.	37,550
20,000 gal. w/system controller	Ea.	61,000
30,000 gal. w/system controller	Ea.	97,350
Solar Domestic HW, closed loop, add-on sys, ext heat exchanger	Ea.	11,300
Drainback, hot water system, 120 gal tank	Ea.	14,175
Draindown, hot water system, 120 gal tank	Ea.	14,425

G Restaurant

Model costs calculated for a 1 story building with 12' story height and 5,000 square feet of floor area

				Unit	Unit Cost	Cost Per S.F.	% Of Sub-Total
A. SUBSTRUCTURE							
1010	Standard Foundations	Poured concrete; strip and spread footings		S.F. Ground	2.87	2.87	
1020	Special Foundations	N/A		—	—	—	
1030	Slab on Grade	4" reinforced concrete with recycled vapor barrier and granular base		S.F. Slab	5.84	5.84	8.0%
2010	Basement Excavation	Site preparation for slab and trench for foundation wall and footing		S.F. Ground	.57	.57	
2020	Basement Walls	4' foundation wall		L.F. Wall	98	5.88	
B. SHELL							
B10 Superstructure							
1010	Floor Construction	Wood columns		S.F. Floor	.93	.93	5.1%
1020	Roof Construction	Plywood on wood truss (pitched)		S.F. Roof	8.68	8.68	
B20 Exterior Enclosure							
2010	Exterior Walls	Cedar siding on wood studs with insulation	70% of wall	S.F. Wall	17	8.57	
2020	Exterior Windows	Storefront windows	30% of wall	Each	54	11.06	14.0%
2030	Exterior Doors	Aluminum and glass doors and entrance with transom		Each	6939	6.95	
B30 Roofing							
3010	Roof Coverings	Cedar shingles with flashing (pitched); rigid fiberglass insulation		S.F. Roof	7.59	7.59	4.1%
3020	Roof Openings	Skylights		S.F. Roof	.10	.10	
C. INTERIORS							
1010	Partitions	Gypsum board on wood studs	25 SF Floor/LF Part.	S.F. Partition	13.15	5.26	
1020	Interior Doors	Hollow core wood, low VOC paint	250 S.F. Floor/Door	Each	645	2.58	
1030	Fittings	Toilet partitions		S.F. Floor	1.25	1.25	
2010	Stair Construction	N/A		—	—	—	15.1%
3010	Wall Finishes	75% paint, low VOC, 25% ceramic tile		S.F. Surface	2.81	2.25	
3020	Floor Finishes	65% carpet, 35% quarry tile		S.F. Floor	9.64	9.64	
3030	Ceiling Finishes	Mineral fiber tile on concealed zee bars		S.F. Ceiling	7.60	7.60	
D. SERVICES							
D10 Conveying							
1010	Elevators & Lifts	N/A		—	—	—	0.0%
1020	Escalators & Moving Walks	N/A		—	—	—	
D20 Plumbing							
2010	Plumbing Fixtures	Kitchen, toilet, low flow, auto sensor, & service fixt., supply & drain.	1 Fixt./335 SF Flr.	Each	3969	11.18	
2020	Domestic Water Distribution	Tankless, on-demand water heater gas/propane		S.F. Floor	2.81	2.81	8.6%
2040	Rain Water Drainage	Roof drains		S.F. Roof	2.34	2.34	
D30 HVAC							
3010	Energy Supply	N/A		—	—	—	
3020	Heat Generating Systems	Included in D3050		—	—	—	
3040	Distribution Systems	Enthalpy heat recovery packages and kitchen exhaust/make-up air system		Each	46,050	9.21	26.2%
3050	Terminal & Package Units	Multizone rooftop air conditioner, SEER 14		S.F. Floor	40.50	40.50	
3090	Other HVAC Sys. & Equipment	N/A		—	—	—	
D40 Fire Protection							
4010	Sprinklers	Sprinklers, light hazard and ordinary hazard kitchen		S.F. Floor	9.18	9.18	6.1%
4020	Standpipes	Standpipe		S.F. Floor	2.29	2.29	
D50 Electrical							
5010	Electrical Service/Distribution	400 ampere service, panel board and feeders		S.F. Floor	2.37	2.37	
5020	Lighting & Branch Wiring	LED fixtures, daylt. dim., ltg. on/off, receptacles, switches, and A.C. power		S.F. Floor	13.48	13.48	12.2%
5030	Communications & Security	Addressable alarm systems and emergency lighting		S.F. Floor	3.70	3.70	
5090	Other Electrical Systems	Emergency generator, 15 kW and energy monitoring systems		S.F. Floor	3.48	3.48	
E. EQUIPMENT & FURNISHINGS							
1010	Commercial Equipment	N/A		—	—	—	
1020	Institutional Equipment	N/A		—	—	—	0.7%
1090	Other Equipment	Waste handling recycling tilt truck		S.F. Floor	1.24	1.24	
2020	Moveable Furnishings	No smoking signage		S.F. Floor	.06	.06	
F. SPECIAL CONSTRUCTION							
1020	Integrated Construction	N/A		—	—	—	0.0%
1040	Special Facilities	N/A		—	—	—	
G. BUILDING SITEWORK	N/A						

Sub-Total	189.46	100%
CONTRACTOR FEES (General Requirements: 10%, Overhead: 5%, Profit: 10%)	25%	47.36
ARCHITECT FEES	7%	16.58
Total Building Cost	**253.40**	

COMMERCIAL/INDUSTRIAL/INSTITUTIONAL

G.560 G School, Elementary

Costs per square foot of floor area

Exterior Wall	S.F. Area	25000	30000	35000	40000	45000	50000	55000	60000	65000
	L.F. Perimeter	900	1050	1200	1350	1510	1650	1800	1970	2100
Face Brick and Concrete Block	Rigid Steel	208.80	206.50	204.85	203.55	202.90	201.85	201.15	201.10	200.25
	Bearing Walls	200.65	198.50	197.10	196.00	195.45	194.45	193.90	193.85	193.05
Stucco and Concrete Block	Rigid Steel	201.50	199.40	197.80	196.70	196.05	195.10	194.50	194.40	193.65
	Bearing Walls	194.85	192.75	191.20	190.05	189.45	188.50	187.85	187.75	187.00
Decorative Concrete Block	Rigid Steel	200.75	198.60	197.10	196.00	195.35	194.40	193.85	193.70	192.95
	Bearing Walls	194.10	191.95	190.50	189.35	188.70	187.75	187.20	187.05	186.35
Perimeter Adj., Add or Deduct	Per 100 L.F.	5.30	4.40	3.75	3.30	2.95	2.60	2.45	2.20	2.00
Story Hgt. Adj., Add or Deduct	Per 1 Ft.	2.05	1.95	1.85	1.85	1.85	1.80	1.85	1.75	1.75

For Basement, add $30.61 per square foot of basement area

The above costs were calculated using the basic specifications shown on the facing page. These costs should be adjusted where necessary for design alternatives and owner's requirements.

Common additives

Description	Unit	$ Cost
Bleachers, Telescoping, manual, 16-20 tier	Seat	340 - 405
21-30 tier	Seat	340 - 460
For power operation, add	Seat	63 - 101
Carrels Hardwood	Ea.	740 - 1925
Clock System, 20 room	Ea.	20,200
50 room	Ea.	48,200
Kitchen Equipment		
Broiler	Ea.	4425
Cooler, 6 ft. long, reach-in	Ea.	3750
Dishwasher, 10-12 racks per hr.	Ea.	4150
Food warmer, counter, 1.2 KW	Ea.	790
Freezer, 44 C.F., reach-in	Ea.	5525
Ice cube maker, 50 lb. per day	Ea.	2100
Range with 1 oven	Ea.	3575
Lockers, Steel, single tier, 60" to 72"	Opng.	232 - 395
2 tier, 60" to 72" total	Opng.	139 - 172
Locker bench, lam. maple top only	L.F.	36.50
Pedestals, steel pipe	Ea.	79
Seating, auditorium chair, veneer back, padded seat	Ea.	380
Classroom, movable chair & desk	Set	81 - 171
Lecture hall, pedestal type	Ea.	350 - 650

Description	Unit	$ Cost
Sound System, amplifier, 250 watts	Ea.	2025
Speaker, ceiling or wall	Ea.	240
Commissioning Fees, sustainable institutional construction	S.F.	0.58 - 2.47
Energy Modelling Fees, academic buildings to 10,000 SF	Ea.	9000
Greater than 10,000 SF add	S.F.	0.20
Green Bldg Cert Fees for school construction project reg	Project	900
Photovoltaic Pwr Sys, grid connected, 20 kW (~2400 SF), roof	Ea.	249,200
Green Roofs, 6" soil depth; w/treated wd edging & sedum mats	S.F.	12.41
10" Soil depth, with treated wood edging & sedum mats	S.F.	14.10
Greywater Recovery Systems, prepackaged comm, 3060 gal.	Ea.	45,900
4590 gal.	Ea.	57,625
Rainwater Harvest Sys, prepckged comm, 10,000 gal, sys contrller	Ea.	37,550
20,000 gal. w/system controller	Ea.	61,000
30,000 gal. w/system controller	Ea.	97,350
Solar Domestic HW, closed loop, add-on sys, ext heat exchanger	Ea.	11,300
Drainback, hot water system, 120 gal tank	Ea.	14,175
Draindown, hot water system, 120 gal tank	Ea.	14,425

Important: See the Reference Section for Location Factors.

Model costs calculated for a 1 story building with 15' story height and 45,000 square feet of floor area

G School, Elementary

				Unit	Unit Cost	Cost Per S.F.	% Of Sub-Total
A.	**SUBSTRUCTURE**						
1010	Standard Foundations	Poured concrete; strip and spread footings		S.F. Ground	5.43	5.43	
1020	Special Foundations	N/A		—	—	—	
1030	Slab on Grade	4" reinforced concrete with recycled vapor barrier and granular base		S.F. Slab	5.84	5.84	11.7%
2010	Basement Excavation	Site preparation for slab and trench for foundation wall and footing		S.F. Ground	.18	.18	
2020	Basement Walls	4' foundation wall		L.F. Wall	98	5.60	
B.	**SHELL**						
	B10 Superstructure						
1010	Floor Construction	N/A		—	—	—	3.4 %
1020	Roof Construction	Metal deck on open web steel joists		S.F. Roof	4.92	4.92	
	B20 Exterior Enclosure						
2010	Exterior Walls	Face brick with concrete block backup	70% of wall	S.F. Wall	41.21	14.52	
2020	Exterior Windows	Steel outward projecting	25% of wall	Each	755	4.96	13.9%
2030	Exterior Doors	Metal and glass	5% of wall	Each	4985	.89	
	B30 Roofing						
3010	Roof Coverings	Single-ply TPO membrane, 60 mils, w/flashing; polyiso. insulation		S.F. Roof	10.08	10.08	6.9%
3020	Roof Openings	N/A		—	—	—	
C.	**INTERIORS**						
1010	Partitions	Concrete block w/foamed-in insul.	20 SF Flr./LF Part.	S.F. Partition	12.56	6.28	
1020	Interior Doors	Single leaf kalamein fire doors, low VOC paint	700 S.F. Floor/Door	Each	1222	1.75	
1030	Fittings	Toilet partitions		S.F. Floor	2.04	2.04	
2010	Stair Construction	N/A		—	—	—	20.1%
3010	Wall Finishes	75% paint, low VOC, 15% glazed coating, 10% ceramic tile		S.F. Surface	5.17	5.17	
3020	Floor Finishes	65% vinyl composition tile, recycled content, 25% carpet tile, 10% terrazzo		S.F. Floor	6.60	6.60	
3030	Ceiling Finishes	Mineral fiber tile on concealed zee bars		S.F. Ceiling	7.60	7.60	
D.	**SERVICES**						
	D10 Conveying						
1010	Elevators & Lifts	N/A		—	—	—	0.0 %
1020	Escalators & Moving Walks	N/A		—	—	—	
	D20 Plumbing						
2010	Plumbing Fixtures	Kitchen, toilet, low flow, auto sensor, & service fixt., supply & drain.	1 Fixt./625 SF Flr.	Each	9994	15.99	
2020	Domestic Water Distribution	Gas fired, tankless water heater		S.F. Floor	.17	.17	12.2%
2040	Rain Water Drainage	Roof drains		S.F. Roof	1.72	1.72	
	D30 HVAC						
3010	Energy Supply	N/A		—	—	—	
3020	Heat Generating Systems	N/A		—	—	—	
3040	Distribution Systems	Enthalpy heat recovery packages		Each	31,850	.71	14.3 %
3050	Terminal & Package Units	Multizone rooftop air conditioner		S.F. Floor	20.20	20.20	
3090	Other HVAC Sys. & Equipment	N/A		—	—	—	
	D40 Fire Protection						
4010	Sprinklers	Sprinklers, light hazard		S.F. Floor	2.93	2.93	2.3%
4020	Standpipes	Standpipe		S.F. Floor	.46	.46	
	D50 Electrical						
5010	Electrical Service/Distribution	800 ampere service, panel board and feeders		S.F. Floor	.86	.86	
5020	Lighting & Branch Wiring	LED fixtures, daylt. dim., ltg. on/off, recept., switches, and A.C. power		S.F. Floor	14.51	14.51	14.9%
5030	Communications & Security	Addressable alarm systems, internet wiring, comm. systems & emerg. ltg.		S.F. Floor	5.34	5.34	
5090	Other Electrical Systems	Emergency generator, 15 kW, energy monitoring systems		S.F. Floor	1.06	1.06	
E.	**EQUIPMENT & FURNISHINGS**						
1010	Commercial Equipment	N/A		—	—	—	
1020	Institutional Equipment	Chalkboards		S.F. Floor	.22	.22	0.2 %
1090	Other Equipment	Waste handling recycling tilt truck		S.F. Floor	.08	.08	
2020	Moveable Furnishings	No smoking signage		S.F. Floor	.02	.02	
F.	**SPECIAL CONSTRUCTION**						
1020	Integrated Construction	N/A		—	—	—	0.0 %
1040	Special Facilities	N/A		—	—	—	
G.	**BUILDING SITEWORK**	N/A					

		Sub-Total	146.13	**100%**
CONTRACTOR FEES (General Requirements: 10%, Overhead: 5%, Profit: 10%)		25%	36.53
ARCHITECT FEES		7%	12.79
	Total Building Cost		**195.45**

For customer support on your Green Building Costs with RSMeans data, call 800.448.8182.

COMMERCIAL/INDUSTRIAL/INSTITUTIONAL G.570 G School, High, 2-3 Story

Costs per square foot of floor area

Exterior Wall	S.F. Area	50000	70000	90000	110000	130000	150000	170000	190000	210000
	L.F. Perimeter	850	1140	1420	1700	1980	2280	2560	2840	3120
Face Brick and Concrete Block	Rigid Steel	195.45	192.45	190.45	189.25	188.30	188.05	187.45	187.05	186.75
	Reinforced Concrete	199.35	196.30	194.35	193.10	192.20	191.95	191.35	190.95	190.65
Decorative Concrete Block	Rigid Steel	187.30	184.60	182.85	181.80	181.00	180.70	180.20	179.85	179.60
	Reinforced Concrete	191.20	188.45	186.70	185.65	184.80	184.60	184.10	183.75	183.45
Limestone and Concrete Block	Rigid Steel	206.85	203.35	201.00	199.60	198.50	198.25	197.60	197.10	196.70
	Reinforced Concrete	215.15	211.60	209.30	207.85	206.80	206.50	205.90	205.35	205.00
Perimeter Adj., Add or Deduct	Per 100 L.F.	4.85	3.40	2.70	2.15	1.85	1.55	1.45	1.35	1.10
Story Hgt. Adj., Add or Deduct	Per 1 Ft.	2.45	2.30	2.20	2.20	2.20	2.15	2.20	2.15	2.15

For Basement, add $39.99 per square foot of basement area

The above costs were calculated using the basic specifications shown on the facing page. These costs should be adjusted where necessary for design alternatives and owner's requirements.

Common additives

Description	Unit	$ Cost
Bleachers, Telescoping, manual, 16-20 tier	Seat	340 - 405
21-30 tier	Seat	340 - 460
For power operation, add	Seat	63 - 101
Carrels Hardwood	Ea.	740 - 1925
Clock System, 20 room	Ea.	20,200
50 room	Ea.	48,200
Elevators, hydraulic passenger, 2 stops, 2500# capacity	Ea.	76,600
3500# capacity	Ea.	81,600
Kitchen Equipment		
Broiler	Ea.	4425
Cooler, 6 ft. long, reach-in	Ea.	3750
Dishwasher, 10-12 racks per hr.	Ea.	4150
Food warmer, counter, 1.2 KW	Ea.	790
Freezer, 44 C.F., reach-in	Ea.	5525
Lockers, Steel, single tier, 60" or 72"	Opng.	232 - 395
2 tier, 60" or 72" total	Opng.	139 - 172
Locker bench, lam. maple top only	L.F.	36.50
Pedestals, steel pipe	Ea.	79
Seat, auditorium chair, veneer back, padded seat	Ea.	380
Classroom, movable chair & desk	Set	81 - 171
Lecture hall, pedestal type	Ea.	350 - 650

Description	Unit	$ Cost
Sound System, amplifier, 250 watts	Ea.	2025
Speaker, ceiling or wall	Ea.	240
Commissioning Fees, sustainable institutional construction	S.F.	0.58 - 2.47
Energy Modelling Fees, academic buildings to 10,000 SF	Ea.	9000
Greater than 10,000 SF add	S.F.	0.20
Green Bldg Cert Fees for school construction project reg	Project	900
Photovoltaic Pwr Sys, grid connected, 20 kW (~2400 SF), roof	Ea.	249,200
Green Roofs, 6" soil depth, w/treated wd edging & sedum mats	S.F.	12.41
10" Soil depth, with treated wood edging & sedum mats	S.F.	14.10
Greywater Recovery Systems, prepackaged comm, 3060 gal.	Ea.	45,900
4590 gal.	Ea.	57,625
Rainwater Harvest Sys, prepckged comm, 10,000 gal, sys contrller	Ea.	37,550
20,000 gal. w/system controller	Ea.	61,000
30,000 gal. w/system controller	Ea.	97,350
Solar Domestic HW, closed loop, add-on sys, ext heat exchanger	Ea.	11,300
Drainback, hot water system, 120 gal tank	Ea.	14,175
Draindown, hot water system, 120 gal tank	Ea.	14,425

G School, High, 2-3 Story

Model costs calculated for a 2 story building with 15' story height and 130,000 square feet of floor area

				Unit	Unit Cost	Cost Per S.F.	% Of Sub-Total
A.	**SUBSTRUCTURE**						
1010	Standard Foundations	Poured concrete; strip and spread footings		S.F. Ground	2.94	1.47	
1020	Special Foundations	N/A		—	—	—	
1030	Slab on Grade	4" reinforced concrete with recycled vapor barrier and granular base		S.F. Slab	5.84	2.93	4.2%
2010	Basement Excavation	Site preparation for slab and trench for foundation wall and footing		S.F. Ground	.18	.09	
2020	Basement Walls	4' foundation wall		L.F. Wall	98	1.49	
B.	**SHELL**						
	B10 Superstructure						
1010	Floor Construction	Concrete slab without drop panel, concrete columns		S.F. Floor	23.92	11.96	14.1%
1020	Roof Construction	Concrete slab without drop panel		S.F. Roof	16.62	8.31	
	B20 Exterior Enclosure						
2010	Exterior Walls	Face brick with concrete block backup	75% of wall	S.F. Wall	41.20	14.12	
2020	Exterior Windows	Window wall	25% of wall	Each	77	8.73	16.4%
2030	Exterior Doors	Metal and glass		Each	3156	.71	
	B30 Roofing						
3010	Roof Coverings	Single-ply TPO membrane and standing seam metal; polyiso. insulation		S.F. Roof	13.82	6.91	4.9%
3020	Roof Openings	Roof hatches		S.F. Roof	.14	.07	
C.	**INTERIORS**						
1010	Partitions	Concrete block w/foamed-in insul.	25 SF Flr./LF Part.	S.F. Partition	15.85	7.61	
1020	Interior Doors	Single leaf kalamein fire doors, low VOC paint	700 S.F. Floor/Door	Each	1222	1.75	
1030	Fittings	Toilet partitions, chalkboards		S.F. Floor	1.60	1.60	
2010	Stair Construction	Concrete filled metal pan		Flight	15,800	.73	20.4%
3010	Wall Finishes	75% paint, low VOC. 15% glazed coating, 10% ceramic tile		S.F. Surface	3.66	3.51	
3020	Floor Finishes	70% vinyl comp. tile, recycled content, 20% carpet tile, 10% terrazzo		S.F. Floor	6.57	6.57	
3030	Ceiling Finishes	Mineral fiber tile on concealed zee bars		S.F. Ceiling	7.60	7.60	
D.	**SERVICES**						
	D10 Conveying						
1010	Elevators & Lifts	One hydraulic passenger elevator		Each	91,000	.70	0.5%
1020	Escalators & Moving Walks	N/A		—	—	—	
	D20 Plumbing						
2010	Plumbing Fixtures	Kitchen, toilet, low flow, auto sensor & service fixt., supply & drain.	1 Fixt./860 SF Flr.	Each	5315	6.18	
2020	Domestic Water Distribution	Gas fired, tankless water heater		S.F. Floor	.32	.32	5.2%
2040	Rain Water Drainage	Roof drains		S.F. Roof	2	1	
	D30 HVAC						
3010	Energy Supply	N/A		—	—	—	
3020	Heat Generating Systems	N/A		—	—	—	
3040	Distribution Systems	Enthalpy heat recovery packages		Each	31,850	.74	14.6%
3050	Terminal & Package Units	Multizone rooftop air conditioner, SEER 14		S.F. Floor	20.20	20.20	
3090	Other HVAC Sys. & Equipment	N/A		—	—	—	
	D40 Fire Protection						
4010	Sprinklers	Sprinklers, light hazard		S.F. Floor	2.57	2.57	2.1%
4020	Standpipes	Standpipe, wet, Class III		S.F. Floor	.39	.39	
	D50 Electrical						
5010	Electrical Service/Distribution	2000 ampere service, panel board and feeders		S.F. Floor	.86	.86	
5020	Lighting & Branch Wiring	LED fixtures, daylt. dim., ltg. on/off, recept., switches, and A.C. power		S.F. Floor	15.42	15.42	15.3%
5030	Communications & Security	Addressable alarm systems, internet wiring, comm. systems and emerg. ltg.		S.F. Floor	4.83	4.83	
5090	Other Electrical Systems	Emergency generator, 250 kW, and energy monitoring systems		S.F. Floor	.85	.85	
E.	**EQUIPMENT & FURNISHINGS**						
1010	Commercial Equipment	N/A		—	—	—	
1020	Institutional Equipment	Laboratory casework and counters		S.F. Floor	2.25	2.25	2.4%
1090	Other Equipment	Waste handlg. recyc. tilt truck, built-in athletic equip., bleachers & backstp.		S.F. Floor	1.15	1.15	
2020	Moveable Furnishings	No smoking signage		S.F. Floor	.02	.02	
F.	**SPECIAL CONSTRUCTION**						
1020	Integrated Construction	N/A		—	—	—	0.0%
1040	Special Facilities	N/A		—	—	—	
G.	**BUILDING SITEWORK**	N/A					

	Sub-Total	143.69	100%
CONTRACTOR FEES (General Requirements: 10%, Overhead: 5%, Profit: 10%)	25%	35.94	
ARCHITECT FEES	7%	12.57	
	Total Building Cost	**192.20**	

COMMERCIAL/INDUSTRIAL/INSTITUTIONAL

G.580 G School, Jr High, 2-3 Story

Costs per square foot of floor area

Exterior Wall	S.F. Area	50000	65000	80000	95000	110000	125000	140000	155000	170000
	L.F. Perimeter	850	1060	1280	1490	1700	1920	2140	2340	2560
Face Brick and Concrete Block	Rigid Steel	202.75	200.20	198.90	197.70	197.00	196.50	196.15	195.55	195.35
	Bearing Walls	194.90	192.30	191.00	189.85	189.10	188.65	188.25	187.70	187.50
Stone and Concrete Block	Rigid Steel	208.85	206.05	204.65	203.35	202.55	202.00	201.60	200.95	200.75
	Bearing Walls	201.00	198.20	196.75	195.50	194.65	194.15	193.75	193.10	192.90
Decorative Concrete Block	Rigid Steel	194.55	192.35	191.20	190.20	189.55	189.10	188.80	188.30	188.10
	Bearing Walls	187.00	184.80	183.60	182.55	181.95	181.55	181.15	180.65	180.50
Perimeter Adj., Add or Deduct	Per 100 L.F.	4.45	3.45	2.80	2.40	2.05	1.75	1.60	1.45	1.35
Story Hgt. Adj., Add or Deduct	Per 1 Ft.	2.25	2.20	2.10	2.05	2.05	2.05	1.95	2.05	2.05

For Basement, add $41.63 per square foot of basement area

The above costs were calculated using the basic specifications shown on the facing page. These costs should be adjusted where necessary for design alternatives and owner's requirements.

Common additives

Description	Unit	$ Cost
Bleachers, Telescoping, manual, 16-20 tier	Seat	340 - 405
21-30 tier	Seat	340 - 460
For power operation, add	Seat	63 - 101
Carrels Hardwood	Ea.	740 - 1925
Clock System, 20 room	Ea.	20,200
50 room	Ea.	48,200
Elevators, hydraulic passenger, 2 stops, 2500# capacity	Ea.	76,600
3500# capacity	Ea.	81,600
Kitchen Equipment		
Broiler	Ea.	4425
Cooler, 6 ft. long, reach-in	Ea.	3750
Dishwasher, 10-12 racks per hr.	Ea.	4150
Food warmer, counter, 1.2 KW	Ea.	790
Freezer, 44 C.F., reach-in	Ea.	5525
Lockers, Steel, single tier, 60" to 72"	Opng.	232 - 395
2 tier, 60" to 72" total	Opng.	139 - 172
Locker bench, lam. maple top only	L.F.	36.50
Pedestals, steel pipe	Ea.	79

Description	Unit	$ Cost
Seating, auditorium chair, veneer back, padded seat	Ea.	380
Upholstered, spring seat	Ea.	335
Classroom, movable chair & desk	Set	81 - 171
Lecture hall, pedestal type	Ea.	350 - 650
Sound System, amplifier, 250 watts	Ea.	2025
Speaker, ceiling or wall	Ea.	240
Commissioning Fees, sustainable institutional construction	S.F.	0.58 - 2.47
Energy Modelling Fees, academic buildings to 10,000 SF	Ea.	9000
Greater than 10,000 SF add	S.F.	0.20
Green Bldg Cert Fees for school construction project reg	Project	900
Photovoltaic Pwr Sys, grid connected, 20 kW (~2400 SF), roof	Ea.	249,200
Green Roofs, 6" soil depth, w/treated wd edging & sedum mats	S.F.	12.41
10" Soil depth, with treated wood edging & sedum mats	S.F.	14.10
Greywater Recovery Systems, prepackaged comm, 3060 gal.	Ea.	45,900
4590 gal.	Ea.	57,625
Rainwater Harvest Sys, prepckged comm, 10,000 gal, sys contrller	Ea.	37,550
20,000 gal. w/system controller	Ea.	61,000
30,000 gal. w/system controller	Ea.	97,350
Solar Domestic HW, closed loop, add-on sys, ext heat exchanger	Ea.	11,300
Drainback, hot water system, 120 gal tank	Ea.	14,175
Draindown, hot water system, 120 gal tank	Ea.	14,425

Model costs calculated for a 2 story building with 15' story height and 110,000 square feet of floor area

G School, Jr High, 2-3 Story

				Unit	Unit Cost	Cost Per S.F.	% Of Sub-Total
A.	**SUBSTRUCTURE**						
1010	Standard Foundations	Poured concrete; strip and spread footings		S.F. Ground	2.72	1.36	
1020	Special Foundations	N/A		—	—	—	
1030	Slab on Grade	4" reinforced concrete with recycled vapor barrier and granular base		S.F. Slab	5.84	2.93	4.0%
2010	Basement Excavation	Site preparation for slab and trench for foundation wall and footing		S.F. Ground	.18	.09	
2020	Basement Walls	4' foundation wall		L.F. Wall	98	1.52	
B.	**SHELL**						
	B10 Superstructure						
1010	Floor Construction	Open web steel joists, slab form, concrete, columns		S.F. Floor	30.22	15.11	14.5%
1020	Roof Construction	Metal deck, open web steel joists, columns		S.F. Roof	12.58	6.29	
	B20 Exterior Enclosure						
2010	Exterior Walls	Face brick with concrete block backup	75% of wall	S.F. Wall	41.21	14.33	
2020	Exterior Windows	Window wall	25% of wall	Each	65	7.21	15.2%
2030	Exterior Doors	Double aluminum & glass		Each	3355	.89	
	B30 Roofing						
3010	Roof Coverings	Single-ply TPO membrane & standing seam metal; polyiso. insulation		S.F. Roof	14	7	4.8%
3020	Roof Openings	Roof hatches		S.F. Roof	.06	.03	
C.	**INTERIORS**						
1010	Partitions	Concrete block w/foamed-in insul.	20 SF Flr./LF Part.	S.F. Partition	13.22	7.93	
1020	Interior Doors	Single leaf kalamein fire doors, low VOC paint	750 S.F. Floor/Door	Each	1222	1.63	
1030	Fittings	Toilet partitions, chalkboards		S.F. Floor	1.75	1.75	
2010	Stair Construction	Concrete filled metal pan		Flight	15,800	.86	23.0%
3010	Wall Finishes	50% paint, low VOC, 40% glazed coatings, 10% ceramic tile		S.F. Surface	4.04	4.85	
3020	Floor Finishes	50% vinyl comp. tile, recycled content, 30% carpet tile, 20% terrrazzo		S.F. Floor	9.24	9.24	
3030	Ceiling Finishes	Mineral fiberboard on concealed zee bars		S.F. Ceiling	7.60	7.60	
D.	**SERVICES**						
	D10 Conveying						
1010	Elevators & Lifts	One hydraulic passenger elevator		Each	91,300	.83	0.6%
1020	Escalators & Moving Walks	N/A		—	—	—	
	D20 Plumbing						
2010	Plumbing Fixtures	Kitchen, toilet, low flow, auto sensor, & service fixt., supply & drain.	1 Fixt./1170 SF Flr.	Each	7675	6.56	
2020	Domestic Water Distribution	Gas fired, tankless water heater		S.F. Floor	.38	.38	5.4%
2040	Rain Water Drainage	Roof drains		S.F. Roof	2.02	1.01	
	D30 HVAC						
3010	Energy Supply	N/A		—	—	—	
3020	Heat Generating Systems	Included in D3050		—	—	—	
3040	Distribution Systems	Enthalpy heat recovery packages		Each	38,725	.70	14.2%
3050	Terminal & Package Units	Multizone rooftop air conditioner, SEER 14		S.F. Floor	20.20	20.20	
3090	Other HVAC Sys. & Equipment	N/A		—	—	—	
	D40 Fire Protection						
4010	Sprinklers	Sprinklers, light hazard	10% of area	S.F. Floor	2.57	2.57	2.1%
4020	Standpipes	Standpipe, wet, Class III		S.F. Floor	.45	.45	
	D50 Electrical						
5010	Electrical Service/Distribution	1600 ampere service, panel board and feeders		S.F. Floor	.75	.75	
5020	Lighting & Branch Wiring	LED fixtures, daylt. dim., ltg. on/off, recept., switches, and A.C. power		S.F. Floor	13.28	13.28	13.5%
5030	Communications & Security	Addressable alarm systems, internet wiring, comm. systems and emerg. ltg.		S.F. Floor	5.11	5.11	
5090	Other Electrical Systems	Emergency generator, 100 kW, and energy monitoring systems		S.F. Floor	.80	.80	
E.	**EQUIPMENT & FURNISHINGS**						
1010	Commercial Equipment	N/A		—	—	—	
1020	Institutional Equipment	Laboratory casework and counters		S.F. Floor	2.65	2.65	2.7%
1090	Other Equipment	Waste handlg. recyc. tilt truck, built-in athletic equip., bleachers & backstps.		S.F. Floor	1.35	1.35	
2020	Moveable Furnishings	No smoking signage		S.F. Floor	.02	.02	
F.	**SPECIAL CONSTRUCTION**						
1020	Integrated Construction	N/A		—	—	—	0.0%
1040	Special Facilities	N/A		—	—	—	
G.	**BUILDING SITEWORK**	N/A					

	Sub-Total	147.28	100%
CONTRACTOR FEES (General Requirements: 10%, Overhead: 5%, Profit: 10%)	25%	36.83	
ARCHITECT FEES	7%	12.89	
Total Building Cost		**197**	

For customer support on your Green Building Costs with RSMeans data, call 800.448.8182.

COMMERCIAL/INDUSTRIAL/INSTITUTIONAL — G.590 G School, Vocational

Costs per square foot of floor area

Exterior Wall	S.F. Area	20000	30000	40000	50000	60000	70000	80000	90000	100000
	L.F. Perimeter	440	590	740	900	1050	1200	1360	1510	1660
Face Brick and Concrete Block	Rigid Steel	206.90	199.40	195.70	193.85	192.30	191.15	190.60	189.85	189.35
	Bearing Walls	200.55	193.10	189.35	187.55	186.00	184.85	184.35	183.60	183.05
Decorative Concrete Block	Rigid Steel	191.40	185.55	182.60	181.20	179.95	179.10	178.65	178.10	177.65
	Bearing Walls	184.40	178.55	175.60	174.20	172.95	172.10	171.60	171.10	170.65
Metal Panel and Metal Studs	Rigid Steel	181.85	177.00	174.65	173.40	172.40	171.65	171.30	170.85	170.50
Metal Sandwich Panel	Rigid Steel	209.00	201.30	197.45	195.60	193.95	192.80	192.25	191.50	191.00
Perimeter Adj., Add or Deduct	Per 100 L.F.	11.45	7.60	5.60	4.50	3.80	3.25	2.85	2.55	2.30
Story Hgt. Adj., Add or Deduct	Per 1 Ft.	2.80	2.50	2.35	2.25	2.20	2.15	2.15	2.20	2.10

For Basement, add $40.40 per square foot of basement area

The above costs were calculated using the basic specifications shown on the facing page. These costs should be adjusted where necessary for design alternatives and owner's requirements.

Common additives

Description	Unit	$ Cost
Carrels Hardwood	Ea.	740 - 1925
Clock System, 20 room	Ea.	20,200
50 room	Ea.	48,200
Directory Boards, plastic, glass covered, 36" x 48"	Ea.	1625
Aluminum, 36" x 24"	Ea.	790
48" x 60"	Ea.	2200
Elevators, hydraulic passenger, 2 stops, 2500# capacity	Ea.	76,600
3500# capacity	Ea.	81,600
Seating, auditorium chair, veneer back, padded seat	Ea.	380
Classroom, movable chair & desk	Set	81 - 171
Lecture hall, pedestal type	Ea.	350 - 650
Shops & Workroom, benches, metal	Ea.	740
Parts bins 6'-3" high, 3' wide, 12" deep, 72 bins	Ea.	710
Shelving, metal 1' x 3'	S.F.	13
Wide span 6' wide x 24" deep	S.F.	9.80

Description	Unit	$ Cost
Sound System, amplifier, 250 watts	Ea.	2025
Speaker, ceiling or wall	Ea.	240
Commissioning Fees, sustainable institutional construction	S.F.	0.58 - 2.47
Energy Modelling Fees, academic buildings to 10,000 SF	Ea.	9000
Greater than 10,000 SF add	S.F.	0.20
Green Bldg Cert Fees for school construction project reg	Project	900
Photovoltaic Pwr Sys, grid connected, 20 kW (~2400 SF), roof	Ea.	249,200
Green Roofs, 6" soil depth, w/treated wd edging & sedum mats	S.F.	12.41
10" Soil depth, with treated wood edging & sedum mats	S.F.	14.10
Greywater Recovery Systems, prepackaged comm, 3060 gal.	Ea.	45,900
4590 gal.	Ea.	57,625
Rainwater Harvest Sys, prepckged comm, 10,000 gal, sys contrller	Ea.	37,550
20,000 gal. w/system controller	Ea.	61,000
30,000 gal. w/system controller	Ea.	97,350
Solar Domestic HW, closed loop, add-on sys, ext heat exchanger	Ea.	11,300
Drainback, hot water system, 120 gal tank	Ea.	14,175
Draindown, hot water system, 120 gal tank	Ea.	14,425

G School, Vocational

Model costs calculated for a 2 story building with 16' story height and 40,000 square feet of floor area

				Unit	Unit Cost	Cost Per S.F.	% Of Sub-Total
A.	**SUBSTRUCTURE**						
1010	Standard Foundations	Poured concrete; strip and spread footings		S.F. Ground	3.04	1.52	
1020	Special Foundations	N/A		—	—	—	
1030	Slab on Grade	5" reinforced concrete with recycled vapor barrier and granular base		S.F. Slab	13.99	7	7.4%
2010	Basement Excavation	Site preparation for slab and trench for foundation wall and footing		S.F. Ground	.18	.09	
2020	Basement Walls	4' foundation wall		L.F. Wall	98	1.82	
B.	**SHELL**						
	B10 Superstructure						
1010	Floor Construction	Open web steel joists, slab form, concrete, beams, columns		S.F. Floor	20.10	10.05	9.6%
1020	Roof Construction	Metal deck, open web steel joists, beams, columns		S.F. Roof	7.08	3.54	
	B20 Exterior Enclosure						
2010	Exterior Walls	Face brick with concrete block backup	85% of wall	S.F. Wall	41.20	20.73	
2020	Exterior Windows	Tubular aluminum framing with insulated glass	15% of wall	Each	65	5.53	19.1%
2030	Exterior Doors	Metal and glass doors, low VOC paint		Each	3682	.74	
	B30 Roofing						
3010	Roof Coverings	Single-ply TPO membrane, 60 mils, heat welded seams w/polyiso. insul.		S.F. Roof	9.16	4.58	3.4%
3020	Roof Openings	Roof hatches		S.F. Roof	.40	.20	
C.	**INTERIORS**						
1010	Partitions	Concrete block w/foamed-in insul.	20 SF Flr./LF Part.	S.F. Partition	12.03	7.22	
1020	Interior Doors	Single leaf kalamein fire doors, low VOC paint	600 S.F. Floor/Door	Each	1222	2.03	
1030	Fittings	Toilet partitions, chalkboards		S.F. Floor	1.70	1.70	
2010	Stair Construction	Concrete filled metal pan		Flight	15,800	1.58	20.9%
3010	Wall Finishes	50% paint, low VOC, 40% glazed coating, 10% ceramic tile		S.F. Surface	4.90	5.88	
3020	Floor Finishes	70% vinyl comp. tile, recycled content, 20% carpet tile, 10% terrazzo		S.F. Floor	6.57	6.57	
3030	Ceiling Finishes	Mineral fiber tile on concealed zee bars	60% of area	S.F. Ceiling	4.56	4.56	
D.	**SERVICES**						
	D10 Conveying						
1010	Elevators & Lifts	One hydraulic passenger elevator		Each	91,200	2.28	1.6%
1020	Escalators & Moving Walks	N/A		—	—	—	
	D20 Plumbing						
2010	Plumbing Fixtures	Toilet, low flow, auto sensor, & service fixt., supply & drain.	1 Fixt./700 SF.Flr.	Each	3626	5.18	
2020	Domestic Water Distribution	Gas fired, tankless water heater		S.F. Floor	.33	.33	4.8%
2040	Rain Water Drainage	Roof drains		S.F. Roof	2.62	1.31	
	D30 HVAC						
3010	Energy Supply	N/A		—	—	—	
3020	Heat Generating Systems	N/A		—	—	—	
3040	Distribution Systems	Enthalpy heat recovery packages		Each	31,850	.79	14.8%
3050	Terminal & Package Units	Multizone rooftop air conditioner, SEER 14		S.F. Floor	20.20	20.20	
3090	Other HVAC Sys. & Equipment	N/A		—	—	—	
	D40 Fire Protection						
4010	Sprinklers	Sprinklers, light hazard		S.F. Floor	3.30	3.30	3.1%
4020	Standpipes	Standpipe, wet, Class III		S.F. Floor	1.05	1.05	
	D50 Electrical						
5010	Electrical Service/Distribution	800 ampere service, panel board and feeders		S.F. Floor	.96	.96	
5020	Lighting & Branch Wiring	LED fixtures, daylt. dim.; ltg. on/off, recept., switches, and A.C. power		S.F. Floor	14.24	14.24	15.1%
5030	Communications & Security	Addressable alarm systems, internet wiring, comm. systems & emerg. ltg.		S.F. Floor	5	5	
5090	Other Electrical Systems	Emergency generator, 11.5 kW, and energy monitoring systems		S.F. Floor	1.23	1.23	
E.	**EQUIPMENT & FURNISHINGS**						
1010	Commercial Equipment	N/A		—	—	—	
1020	Institutional Equipment	Stainless steel countertops		S.F. Floor	.20	.20	0.3%
1090	Other Equipment	Waste handling recycling tilt truck		S.F. Floor	.15	.15	
2020	Moveable Furnishings	No smoking signage		S.F. Floor	.02	.02	
F.	**SPECIAL CONSTRUCTION**						
1020	Integrated Construction	N/A		—	—	—	0.0%
1040	Special Facilities	N/A		—	—	—	
G.	**BUILDING SITEWORK**	N/A					

	Sub-Total	141.58	100%
CONTRACTOR FEES (General Requirements: 10%, Overhead: 5%, Profit: 10%)	25%	35.38	
ARCHITECT FEES	7%	12.39	
Total Building Cost		**189.35**	

COMMERCIAL/INDUSTRIAL/INSTITUTIONAL

G.640 G Supermarket

Costs per square foot of floor area

Exterior Wall	S.F. Area	12000	16000	20000	26000	32000	38000	44000	52000	60000
	L.F. Perimeter	450	510	570	650	716	780	840	920	1020
Face Brick and Concrete Block	Rigid Steel	190.30	178.80	171.85	164.85	159.90	156.40	153.80	151.20	149.75
	Bearing Walls	184.45	172.95	166.00	159.00	154.05	150.50	147.95	145.35	143.90
Stucco and Concrete Block	Rigid Steel	179.15	169.35	163.40	157.45	153.25	150.30	148.15	145.95	144.75
	Bearing Walls	176.60	166.75	160.80	154.90	150.70	147.70	145.55	143.40	142.10
Precast Concrete	Rigid Steel	202.75	189.35	181.30	173.20	167.30	163.20	160.15	157.10	155.40
Metal Sandwich Panel	Rigid Steel	188.75	177.50	170.65	163.85	158.95	155.55	153.05	150.50	149.05
Perimeter Adj., Add or Deduct	Per 100 L.F.	11.65	8.60	6.95	5.40	4.30	3.70	3.15	2.70	2.35
Story Hgt. Adj., Add or Deduct	Per 1 Ft.	2.45	2.00	1.80	1.65	1.40	1.30	1.25	1.15	1.10

For Basement, add $30.66 per square foot of basement area

The above costs were calculated using the basic specifications shown on the facing page. These costs should be adjusted where necessary for design alternatives and owner's requirements.

Common additives

Description	Unit	$ Cost
Check Out Counter, single belt	Ea.	3850
Scanner, registers, guns & memory 10 lanes	Ea.	186,000
Power take away	Ea.	6475
Refrigerators, prefabricated, walk-in, 7'-6" High, 10' x 10'	S.F.	114
12' x 14'	S.F.	99.50
12' x 20'	S.F.	137
Refrigerated Food Cases, dairy, multi deck, 12' long	Ea.	12,300
Delicatessen case, multi deck, 18 S.F. shelf display	Ea.	9200
Freezer, glass door upright, 78 C.F.	Ea.	10,600
Frozen food, chest type, 12' long	Ea.	9025
Glass door reach in, 5 door	Ea.	11,300
Island case 12' long, multi deck	Ea.	10,300
Meat case, 12' long, multi deck	Ea.	11,300
Produce, 12' long multi deck	Ea.	9575
Safe, Office type, 1 hr rating, 60"x36"x18", double door	Ea.	10,200

Description	Unit	$ Cost
Sound System, amplifier, 250 watts	Ea.	2025
Speaker, ceiling or wall	Ea.	240
Commissioning Fees, sustainable commercial construction	S.F.	0.24 - 3.04
Energy Modelling Fees, commercial buildings to 10,000 SF	Ea.	11,000
Greater than 10,000 SF add	S.F.	0.04
Green Bldg Cert Fees for comm construction project reg	Project	900
Photovoltaic Pwr Sys, grid connected, 20 kW (~2400 SF), roof	Ea.	249,200
Green Roofs, 6" soil depth, w/treated wd edging & sedum mats	S.F.	12.41
10" Soil depth, with treated wood edging & sedum mats	S.F.	14.10
Greywater Recovery Systems, prepackaged comm, 3060 gal.	Ea.	45,900
4590 gal.	Ea.	57,625
Rainwater Harvest Sys, prepckged comm, 10,000 gal, sys contrller	Ea.	37,550
20,000 gal. w/system controller	Ea.	61,000
30,000 gal. w/system controller	Ea.	97,350
Solar Domestic HW, closed loop, add-on sys, ext heat exchanger	Ea.	11,300
Drainback, hot water system, 120 gal tank	Ea.	14,175
Draindown, hot water system, 120 gal tank	Ea.	14,425

Important: See the Reference Section for Location Factors.

G Supermarket

Model costs calculated for a 1 story building with 18' story height and 44,000 square feet of floor area

				Unit	Unit Cost	Cost Per S.F.	% Of Sub-Total
A. SUBSTRUCTURE							
1010	Standard Foundations	Poured concrete; strip and spread footings		S.F. Ground	1.25	1.25	
1020	Special Foundations	N/A		—	—	—	
1030	Slab on Grade	4" reinforced concrete with recycled vapor barrier and granular base		S.F. Slab	5.84	5.84	8.3%
2010	Basement Excavation	Site preparation for slab and trench for foundation wall and footing		S.F. Ground	.18	.18	
2020	Basement Walls	4' foundation wall		L.F. Wall	98	1.87	
B. SHELL							
B10 Superstructure							
1010	Floor Construction	N/A		—	—	—	7.9%
1020	Roof Construction	Metal deck, open web steel joists, beams, interior columns		S.F. Roof	8.70	8.70	
B20 Exterior Enclosure							
2010	Exterior Walls	Face brick with concrete block backup	85% of wall	S.F. Wall	41.22	12.04	
2020	Exterior Windows	Storefront windows	15% of wall	Each	65	3.36	15.3%
2030	Exterior Doors	Sliding entrance doors with electrical operator, hollow metal		Each	5986	1.49	
B30 Roofing							
3010	Roof Coverings	Single-ply TPO membrane, 60 mils, heat welded seams w/R-20 insul.		S.F. Roof	6.67	6.67	6.2%
3020	Roof Openings	Roof hatches		S.F. Roof	.16	.16	
C. INTERIORS							
1010	Partitions	50% CMU w/foamed-in insul., 50% gyp. bd. on mtl. studs	50 SF Flr./LF Part.	S.F. Partition	10.04	2.41	
1020	Interior Doors	Single leaf hollow metal, low VOC paint	2000 S.F. Floor/Door	Each	1222	.61	
1030	Fittings	N/A		—	—	—	
2010	Stair Construction	N/A		—	—	—	15.6%
3010	Wall Finishes	Paint, low VOC		S.F. Surface	5.79	2.78	
3020	Floor Finishes	Vinyl composition tile, recycled content		S.F. Floor	3.84	3.84	
3030	Ceiling Finishes	Mineral fiber tile on concealed zee bars		S.F. Ceiling	7.60	7.60	
D. SERVICES							
D10 Conveying							
1010	Elevators & Lifts	N/A		—	—	—	0.0%
1020	Escalators & Moving Walks	N/A		—	—	—	
D20 Plumbing							
2010	Plumbing Fixtures	Toilet, low flow, auto sensor, & service fixt., supply & drain.	1 Fixt./1820 SF Flr.	Each	2639	1.45	
2020	Domestic Water Distribution	Point of use water heater, electric, energy saver		S.F. Floor	.22	.22	2.6%
2040	Rain Water Drainage	Roof drains		S.F. Roof	1.23	1.23	
D30 HVAC							
3010	Energy Supply	N/A		—	—	—	
3020	Heat Generating Systems	Included in D3050		—	—	—	
3040	Distribution Systems	Enthalpy heat recovery packages		Each	31,850	.79	4.7%
3050	Terminal & Package Units	Single zone rooftop air conditioner		S.F. Floor	4.39	4.39	
3090	Other HVAC Sys. & Equipment	N/A		—	—	—	
D40 Fire Protection							
4010	Sprinklers	Sprinklers, light hazard		S.F. Floor	3.79	3.79	4.0%
4020	Standpipes	Standpipe		S.F. Floor	.60	.60	
D50 Electrical							
5010	Electrical Service/Distribution	1600 ampere service, panel board and feeders		S.F. Floor	1.89	1.89	
5020	Lighting & Branch Wiring	LED fixtures, daylt. dim., ltg. on/off, receptacles, switches, and A.C.power		S.F. Floor	32.43	32.43	35.4%
5030	Communications & Security	Addressable alarm systems, partial internet wiring and emergency lighting		S.F. Floor	3.80	3.80	
5090	Other Electrical Systems	Emergency generator, 15 kW and energy monitoring systems		S.F. Floor	1.06	1.06	
E. EQUIPMENT & FURNISHINGS							
1010	Commercial Equipment	N/A		—	—	—	
1020	Institutional Equipment	N/A		—	—	—	0.1%
1090	Other Equipment	Waste handling recycling tilt truck		S.F. Floor	.14	.14	
2020	Moveable Furnishings	No smoking signage		S.F. Floor	.02	.02	
F. SPECIAL CONSTRUCTION							
1020	Integrated Construction	N/A		—	—	—	0.0%
1040	Special Facilities	N/A		—	—	—	
G. BUILDING SITEWORK	N/A						

Sub-Total	110.61	100%
CONTRACTOR FEES (General Requirements: 10%, Overhead: 5%, Profit: 10%)	25%	27.66
ARCHITECT FEES	7%	9.68
Total Building Cost		**147.95**

For customer support on your Green Building Costs with RSMeans data, call 800.448.8182.

COMMERCIAL/INDUSTRIAL/INSTITUTIONAL | G.690 | G Warehouse

Costs per square foot of floor area

Exterior Wall	S.F. Area	10000	15000	20000	25000	30000	35000	40000	50000	60000
	L.F. Perimeter	410	500	600	640	700	766	833	966	1000
Tilt-up Concrete Panels	Rigid Steel	161.50	150.35	145.15	139.80	136.85	134.95	133.50	131.50	128.55
Face Brick and Concrete Block	Bearing Walls	186.00	169.40	161.90	153.45	148.90	145.95	143.75	140.65	135.85
Concrete Block	Rigid Steel	161.50	150.15	145.00	139.55	136.55	134.60	133.15	131.10	128.15
	Bearing Walls	157.20	145.90	140.70	135.30	132.30	130.35	128.90	126.85	123.90
Metal Panel	Rigid Steel	162.35	150.90	145.60	140.10	137.05	135.10	133.60	131.55	128.50
Metal Sandwich Panel	Rigid Steel	169.30	156.50	150.75	144.45	141.00	138.80	137.10	134.80	131.30
Perimeter Adj., Add or Deduct	Per 100 L.F.	9.60	6.35	4.80	3.85	3.20	2.75	2.45	1.85	1.55
Story Hgt. Adj., Add or Deduct	Per 1 Ft.	1.15	0.90	0.85	0.70	0.60	0.55	0.55	0.50	0.40

For Basement, add $33.96 per square foot of basement area

The above costs were calculated using the basic specifications shown on the facing page. These costs should be adjusted where necessary for design alternatives and owner's requirements.

Common additives

Description	Unit	$ Cost
Dock Leveler, 10 ton cap., 6' x 8'	Ea.	6250
7' x 8'	Ea.	8625
Fence, Chain link, 6' high, 9 ga. wire	L.F.	29
6 ga. wire	L.F.	34.50
Gate	Ea.	400
Paving, Bituminous, wearing course plus base course	S.Y.	7.40
Sidewalks, Concrete 4" thick	S.F.	4.99
Sound System, amplifier, 250 watts	Ea.	2025
Speaker, ceiling or wall	Ea.	240
Yard Lighting, 20' aluminum pole, 400W, HP sodium fixture	Ea.	3600

Description	Unit	$ Cost
Commissioning Fees, sustainable industrial construction	S.F.	0.20 - 1.06
Energy Modelling Fees, commercial buildings to 10,000 SF	Ea.	11,000
Greater than 10,000 SF add	S.F.	0.04
Green Bldg Cert Fees for comm construction project reg	Project	900
Photovoltaic Pwr Sys, grid connected, 20 kW (~2400 SF), roof	Ea.	249,200
Green Roofs, 6" soil depth, w/treated wd edging & sedum mats	S.F.	12.41
10" Soil depth, with treated wood edging & sedum mats	S.F.	14.10
Greywater Recovery Systems, prepackaged comm, 3060 gal.	Ea.	45,900
4590 gal.	Ea.	57,625
Rainwater Harvest Sys, prepckged comm, 10,000 gal, sys contrller	Ea.	37,550
20,000 gal. w/system controller	Ea.	61,000
30,000 gal. w/system controller	Ea.	97,350
Solar Domestic HW, closed loop, add-on sys, ext heat exchanger	Ea.	11,300
Drainback, hot water system, 120 gal tank	Ea.	14,175
Draindown, hot water system, 120 gal tank	Ea.	14,425

Important: See the Reference Section for Location Factors.

G Warehouse

Model costs calculated for a 1 story building with 24' story height and 30,000 square feet of floor area

				Unit	Unit Cost	Cost Per S.F.	% Of Sub-Total
A.	**SUBSTRUCTURE**						
1010	Standard Foundations	Poured concrete; strip and spread footings		S.F. Ground	1.57	1.57	
1020	Special Foundations	N/A		—	—	—	18.9%
1030	Slab on Grade	5" reinforced concrete with recycled vapor barrier and granular base		S.F. Slab	13.99	13.99	
2010	Basement Excavation	Site preparation for slab and trench for foundation wall and footing		S.F. Ground	.18	.18	
2020	Basement Walls	4' foundation wall		L.F. Wall	98	2.98	
B.	**SHELL**						
	B10 Superstructure						
1010	Floor Construction	Mezzanine: open web steel joists, slab form, concrete beams, columns	10% of area	S.F. Floor	2.33	2.33	10.4%
1020	Roof Construction	Metal deck, open web steel joists, beams, columns		S.F. Roof	7.92	7.92	
	B20 Exterior Enclosure						
2010	Exterior Walls	Concrete block	95% of wall	S.F. Wall	18.59	9.89	
2020	Exterior Windows	N/A		—	—	—	11.4%
2030	Exterior Doors	Steel overhead, hollow metal	5% of wall	Each	3857	1.42	
	B30 Roofing						
3010	Roof Coverings	Single-ply TPO membrane, 60 mils, heat welded w/R-20 insul.		S.F. Roof	6.84	6.84	7.3%
3020	Roof Openings	Roof hatches and skylight		S.F. Roof	.42	.42	
C.	**INTERIORS**						
1010	Partitions	Concrete block w/foamed-in insul. (office and washrooms)	100 SF Flr./LF Part.	S.F. Partition	12.13	.97	
1020	Interior Doors	Single leaf hollow metal, low VOC paint	5000 S.F. Floor/Door	Each	1222	.25	
1030	Fittings	N/A		—	—	—	
2010	Stair Construction	Steel gate with rails		Flight	13,950	.93	7.4%
3010	Wall Finishes	Paint, low VOC		S.F. Surface	15.06	2.41	
3020	Floor Finishes	90% hardener, 10% vinyl composition tile, recycled content		S.F. Floor	1.97	1.97	
3030	Ceiling Finishes	Suspended mineral tile on zee channels in office area	10% of area	S.F. Ceiling	.76	.77	
D.	**SERVICES**						
	D10 Conveying						
1010	Elevators & Lifts	N/A		—	—	—	0.0 %
1020	Escalators & Moving Walks	N/A		—	—	—	
	D20 Plumbing						
2010	Plumbing Fixtures	Toilet, low flow, auto sensor & service fixt., supply & drainage	1 Fixt./2500 SF Flr.	Each	4625	1.85	
2020	Domestic Water Distribution	Tankless, on-demand water heater, gas/propane		S.F. Floor	.45	.45	3.8%
2040	Rain Water Drainage	Roof drains		S.F. Roof	1.46	1.46	
	D30 HVAC						
3010	Energy Supply	N/A		—	—	—	
3020	Heat Generating Systems	Ventilation with heat		Each	151,400	5.45	
3030	Cooling Generating Systems	N/A		—	—	—	6.3 %
3050	Terminal & Package Units	Single zone rooftop air conditioner, SEER 14		S.F. Floor	.75	.75	
3090	Other HVAC Sys. & Equipment	N/A		—	—	—	
	D40 Fire Protection						
4010	Sprinklers	Sprinklers, ordinary hazard		S.F. Floor	4.36	4.36	5.0%
4020	Standpipes	Standpipe		S.F. Floor	.54	.54	
	D50 Electrical						
5010	Electrical Service/Distribution	200 ampere service, panel board and feeders		S.F. Floor	.30	.30	
5020	Lighting & Branch Wiring	LED fixtures, daylt. dim., ltg. on/off, receptacles, switches, and A.C. power		S.F. Floor	17.18	17.18	21.8%
5030	Communications & Security	Addressable alarm systems		S.F. Floor	2.83	2.83	
5090	Other Electrical Systems	Energy monitoring systems		S.F. Floor	1.24	1.24	
E.	**EQUIPMENT & FURNISHINGS**						
1010	Commercial Equipment	N/A		—	—	—	
1030	Vehicular Equipment	Dock boards, dock levelers		S.F. Floor	1.87	1.87	2.1 %
1090	Other Equipment	Waste handling recycling tilt truck		S.F. Floor	.21	.21	
2020	Moveable Furnishings	No smoking signage		S.F. Floor	.02	.02	
F.	**SPECIAL CONSTRUCTION**						
1020	Integrated Construction	Shipping & receiving air curtain		S.F. Floor	5.56	5.56	5.6%
1040	Special Facilities	N/A		—	—	—	
G.	**BUILDING SITEWORK**	N/A					

	Sub-Total	98.91	100%
CONTRACTOR FEES (General Requirements: 10%, Overhead: 5%, Profit: 10%)	25%	24.74	
ARCHITECT FEES	7%	8.65	
Total Building Cost		**132.30**	

COMMERCIAL/INDUSTRIAL/INSTITUTIONAL
Adjustments: Depreciation

Deterioration occurs within the structure itself and is determined by the observation of both materials and equipment.

Curable deterioration can be remedied either by maintenance, repair or replacement, within prudent economic limits.

Incurable deterioration that has progressed to the point of actually affecting the structural integrity of the structure, making repair or replacement not economically feasible.

Actual Versus Observed Age

The observed age of a structure refers to the age that the structure appears to be. Periodic maintenance, remodeling, and renovation all tend to reduce the amount of deterioration that has taken place, thereby decreasing the observed age. Actual age, on the other hand, relates solely to the year that the structure was built.

The Depreciation Table shown here relates to the observed age.

Obsolescence arises from conditions either occurring within the structure (functional) or caused by factors outside the limits of the structure (economic).

Functional obsolescence is any inadequacy caused by outmoded design, dated construction materials, or oversized or undersized areas, all of which cause excessive operation costs.

Incurable is so costly as not to economically justify the capital expenditure required to correct the deficiency.

Economic obsolescence is caused by factors outside the limits of the structure. The prime causes of economic obsolescence are:

- zoning and environmental laws
- government legislation
- negative neighborhood influences
- business climate
- proximity to transportation facilities

Depreciation Table
Commercial/Industrial/Institutional

Observed Age (Years)	Frame	Masonry On Wood	Masonry On Masonry Or Steel
1	1%	0%	0%
2	2	1	0
3	3	2	1
4	4	3	2
5	6	5	3
10	20	15	8
15	25	20	15
20	30	25	20
25	35	30	25
30	40	35	30
35	45	40	35
40	50	45	40
45	55	50	45
50	60	55	50
55	65	60	55
60	70	65	60

Reference Section

All the reference information is in one section, making it easy to find what you need to know ... and easy to use the data set on a daily basis. This section is visually identified by a vertical black bar on the page edges.

In this Reference Section, we've included Equipment Rental Costs, a listing of rental and operating costs; Crew Listings, a full listing of all crews and equipment, and their costs; Historical Cost Indexes for cost comparisons over time; City Cost Indexes and Location Factors for adjusting costs to the region you are in; Reference Tables, where you will find explanations, estimating information and procedures, or technical data; Change Orders, information on pricing changes to contract documents; and an explanation of all the Abbreviations in the data set.

Table of Contents

Construction Equipment Rental Costs	409
Crew Listings	421
Historical Cost Indexes	458
City Cost Indexes	459
Location Factors	502
Reference Tables	508
R01 General Requirements	508
R02 Existing Conditions	515
R03 Concrete	517
R04 Masonry	531
R05 Metals	532
R06 Wood, Plastics & Composites	538
R07 Thermal & Moisture Protection	538
R08 Openings	539
R09 Finishes	540
R13 Special Construction	541

Reference Tables (cont.)

R22 Plumbing	542
R23 Heating, Ventilating & Air Conditioning	542
R26 Electrical	546
Change Orders	548
Project Costs	551
Abbreviations	556

Equipment Rental Costs

Estimating Tips
- This section contains the average costs to rent and operate hundreds of pieces of construction equipment. This is useful information when estimating the time and material requirements of any particular operation in order to establish a unit or total cost. Bare equipment costs shown on a unit cost line include not only rental, but also operating costs for equipment under normal use.

Rental Costs
- Equipment rental rates are obtained from the following industry sources throughout North America: contractors, suppliers, dealers, manufacturers, and distributors.
- Rental rates vary throughout the country, with larger cities generally having lower rates. Lease plans for new equipment are available for periods in excess of six months, with a percentage of payments applying toward purchase.
- Monthly rental rates vary from 2% to 5% of the purchase price of the equipment depending on the anticipated life of the equipment and its wearing parts.
- Weekly rental rates are about 1/3 of the monthly rates, and daily rental rates are about 1/3 of the weekly rate.
- Rental rates can also be treated as reimbursement costs for contractor-owned equipment. Owned equipment costs include depreciation, loan payments, interest, taxes, insurance, storage, and major repairs.

Operating Costs
- The operating costs include parts and labor for routine servicing, such as the repair and replacement of pumps, filters, and worn lines. Normal operating expendables, such as fuel, lubricants, tires, and electricity (where applicable), are also included.
- Extraordinary operating expendables with highly variable wear patterns, such as diamond bits and blades, are excluded. These costs can be found as material costs in the Unit Price section.
- The hourly operating costs listed do not include the operator's wages.

Equipment Cost/Day
- Any power equipment required by a crew is shown in the Crew Listings with a daily cost.
- This daily cost of equipment needed by a crew includes both the rental cost and the operating cost and is based on dividing the weekly rental rate by 5 (number of working days in the week), and then adding the hourly operating cost times 8 (the number of hours in a day). This "Equipment Cost/Day" is shown in the far right column of the Equipment Rental section.
- If equipment is needed for only one or two days, it is best to develop your own cost by including components for daily rent and hourly operating costs. This is important when the listed Crew for a task does not contain the equipment needed, such as a crane for lifting mechanical heating/cooling equipment up onto a roof.
- If the quantity of work is less than the crew's Daily Output shown for a Unit Price line item that includes a bare unit equipment cost, the recommendation is to estimate one day's rental cost and operating cost for equipment shown in the Crew Listing for that line item.

Mobilization, Demobilization Costs
- The cost to move construction equipment from an equipment yard or rental company to the job site and back again is not included in equipment rental costs listed in the Reference Section, nor in the bare equipment cost of any unit price line item, nor in any equipment costs shown in the Crew Listings.
- Mobilization (to the site) and demobilization (from the site) costs can be found in the Unit Price section.
- If a piece of equipment is already at the job site, it is not appropriate to utilize mobilization, demobilization costs again in an estimate. ■

Did you know?
RSMeans data is available through our online application with 24/7 access:
- Search for unit prices by keyword
- Leverage the most up-to-date data
- Build and export estimates

Try it free for 30 days!
www.rsmeans.com/2018freetrial

No part of this cost data may be reproduced, stored in a retrieval system, or transmitted in any form or by any means without prior written permission of Gordian.

01 54 | Construction Aids

01 54 33 | Equipment Rental

		UNIT	HOURLY OPER. COST	RENT PER DAY	RENT PER WEEK	RENT PER MONTH	EQUIPMENT COST/DAY
10 0010	**CONCRETE EQUIPMENT RENTAL** without operators R015433-10						
0200	Bucket, concrete lightweight, 1/2 C.Y.	Ea.	.85	24.50	73	219	21.40
0300	1 C.Y.		.95	28.50	85	255	24.60
0400	1-1/2 C.Y.		1.20	38.50	115	345	32.60
0500	2 C.Y.		1.30	46.50	140	420	38.40
0580	8 C.Y.		6.35	263	790	2,375	208.80
0600	Cart, concrete, self-propelled, operator walking, 10 C.F.		2.85	58.50	175	525	57.80
0700	Operator riding, 18 C.F.		4.80	98.50	295	885	97.40
0800	Conveyer for concrete, portable, gas, 16" wide, 26' long		10.60	130	390	1,175	162.80
0900	46' long		11.00	155	465	1,400	181
1000	56' long		11.15	163	490	1,475	187.20
1100	Core drill, electric, 2-1/2 H.P., 1" to 8" bit diameter		1.56	58.50	175	525	47.50
1150	11 H.P., 8" to 18" cores		5.40	115	345	1,025	112.20
1200	Finisher, concrete floor, gas, riding trowel, 96" wide		9.65	148	445	1,325	166.20
1300	Gas, walk-behind, 3 blade, 36" trowel		2.15	23	69	207	31
1400	4 blade, 48" trowel		3.05	28	84	252	41.20
1500	Float, hand-operated (Bull float), 48" wide		.08	13.65	41	123	8.85
1570	Curb builder, 14 H.P., gas, single screw		13.90	275	825	2,475	276.20
1590	Double screw		14.80	330	995	2,975	317.40
1600	Floor grinder, concrete and terrazzo, electric, 22" path		2.95	183	550	1,650	133.60
1700	Edger, concrete, electric, 7" path		1.12	56.50	170	510	42.95
1750	Vacuum pick-up system for floor grinders, wet/dry		1.62	90	270	810	66.95
1800	Mixer, powered, mortar and concrete, gas, 6 C.F., 18 H.P.		7.40	123	370	1,100	133.20
1900	10 C.F., 25 H.P.		9.00	148	445	1,325	161
2000	16 C.F.		9.35	172	515	1,550	177.80
2100	Concrete, stationary, tilt drum, 2 C.Y.		7.40	242	725	2,175	204.20
2120	Pump, concrete, truck mounted, 4" line, 80' boom		29.20	1,075	3,240	9,725	881.60
2140	5" line, 110' boom		36.60	1,375	4,115	12,300	1,116
2160	Mud jack, 50 C.F. per hr.		6.45	128	385	1,150	128.60
2180	225 C.F. per hr.		8.80	147	440	1,325	158.40
2190	Shotcrete pump rig, 12 C.Y./hr.		13.95	225	675	2,025	246.60
2200	35 C.Y./hr.		15.65	242	725	2,175	270.20
2600	Saw, concrete, manual, gas, 18 H.P.		5.40	46.50	140	420	71.20
2650	Self-propelled, gas, 30 H.P.		7.55	70	210	630	102.40
2675	V-groove crack chaser, manual, gas, 6 H.P.		1.80	18.35	55	165	25.40
2700	Vibrators, concrete, electric, 60 cycle, 2 H.P.		.47	9	27	81	9.15
2800	3 H.P.		.60	11.65	35	105	11.80
2900	Gas engine, 5 H.P.		1.50	16.35	49	147	21.80
3000	8 H.P.		2.00	16	48	144	25.60
3050	Vibrating screed, gas engine, 8 H.P.		2.82	88	264	790	75.35
3120	Concrete transit mixer, 6 x 4, 250 H.P., 8 C.Y., rear discharge		48.75	600	1,805	5,425	751
3200	Front discharge		56.60	735	2,205	6,625	893.80
3300	6 x 6, 285 H.P., 12 C.Y., rear discharge		55.65	700	2,095	6,275	864.20
3400	Front discharge		57.95	735	2,210	6,625	905.60
20 0010	**EARTHWORK EQUIPMENT RENTAL** without operators R015433-10						
0040	Aggregate spreader, push type, 8' to 12' wide	Ea.	2.60	26.50	80	240	36.80
0045	Tailgate type, 8' wide		2.55	33.50	100	300	40.40
0055	Earth auger, truck mounted, for fence & sign posts, utility poles		12.60	455	1,365	4,100	373.80
0060	For borings and monitoring wells		42.60	695	2,090	6,275	758.80
0070	Portable, trailer mounted		2.30	33	99	297	38.20
0075	Truck mounted, for caissons, water wells		85.75	2,925	8,790	26,400	2,444
0080	Horizontal boring machine, 12" to 36" diameter, 45 H.P.		22.70	197	590	1,775	299.60
0090	12" to 48" diameter, 65 H.P.		30.60	340	1,020	3,050	448.80
0095	Auger, for fence posts, gas engine, hand held		.45	6.35	19	57	7.40
0100	Excavator, diesel hydraulic, crawler mounted, 1/2 C.Y. cap.		21.30	440	1,325	3,975	435.40
0120	5/8 C.Y. capacity		28.60	580	1,740	5,225	576.80
0140	3/4 C.Y. capacity		31.95	690	2,070	6,200	669.60
0150	1 C.Y. capacity		39.90	705	2,115	6,350	742.20

01 54 | Construction Aids

01 54 33 | Equipment Rental

		UNIT	HOURLY OPER. COST	RENT PER DAY	RENT PER WEEK	RENT PER MONTH	EQUIPMENT COST/DAY
0200	1-1/2 C.Y. capacity	Ea.	47.45	855	2,570	7,700	893.60
0300	2 C.Y. capacity		54.15	1,025	3,095	9,275	1,052
0320	2-1/2 C.Y. capacity		78.90	1,300	3,900	11,700	1,411
0325	3-1/2 C.Y. capacity		113.65	2,150	6,430	19,300	2,195
0330	4-1/2 C.Y. capacity		143.70	2,650	7,925	23,800	2,735
0335	6 C.Y. capacity		181.40	3,400	10,180	30,500	3,487
0340	7 C.Y. capacity		175.20	3,125	9,365	28,100	3,275
0342	Excavator attachments, bucket thumbs		3.35	252	755	2,275	177.80
0345	Grapples		3.05	220	660	1,975	156.40
0346	Hydraulic hammer for boom mounting, 4000 ft lb.		13.20	365	1,095	3,275	324.60
0347	5000 ft lb.		15.50	450	1,350	4,050	394
0348	8000 ft lb.		22.85	655	1,970	5,900	576.80
0349	12,000 ft lb.		24.90	785	2,350	7,050	669.20
0350	Gradall type, truck mounted, 3 ton @ 15' radius, 5/8 C.Y.		44.95	850	2,550	7,650	869.60
0370	1 C.Y. capacity		60.20	1,275	3,805	11,400	1,243
0400	Backhoe-loader, 40 to 45 H.P., 5/8 C.Y. capacity		12.25	248	745	2,225	247
0450	45 H.P. to 60 H.P., 3/4 C.Y. capacity		17.80	283	850	2,550	312.40
0460	80 H.P., 1-1/4 C.Y. capacity		19.50	380	1,145	3,425	385
0470	112 H.P., 1-1/2 C.Y. capacity		31.90	605	1,820	5,450	619.20
0482	Backhoe-loader attachment, compactor, 20,000 lb.		6.25	148	445	1,325	139
0485	Hydraulic hammer, 750 ft lb.		3.55	102	305	915	89.40
0486	Hydraulic hammer, 1200 ft lb.		6.55	208	625	1,875	177.40
0500	Brush chipper, gas engine, 6" cutter head, 35 H.P.		9.15	110	330	990	139.20
0550	Diesel engine, 12" cutter head, 130 H.P.		24.00	335	1,005	3,025	393
0600	15" cutter head, 165 H.P.		26.05	400	1,200	3,600	448.40
0750	Bucket, clamshell, general purpose, 3/8 C.Y.		1.40	40	120	360	35.20
0800	1/2 C.Y.		1.50	48.50	145	435	41
0850	3/4 C.Y.		1.65	56.50	170	510	47.20
0900	1 C.Y.		1.70	61.50	185	555	50.60
0950	1-1/2 C.Y.		2.75	85	255	765	73
1000	2 C.Y.		2.90	93.50	280	840	79.20
1010	Bucket, dragline, medium duty, 1/2 C.Y.		.80	24.50	73	219	21
1020	3/4 C.Y.		.80	25.50	77	231	21.80
1030	1 C.Y.		.85	27	81	243	23
1040	1-1/2 C.Y.		1.30	41.50	125	375	35.40
1050	2 C.Y.		1.35	45	135	405	37.80
1070	3 C.Y.		2.10	65	195	585	55.80
1200	Compactor, manually guided 2-drum vibratory smooth roller, 7.5 H.P.		7.20	203	610	1,825	179.60
1250	Rammer/tamper, gas, 8"		2.25	46.50	140	420	46
1260	15"		2.50	53.50	160	480	52
1300	Vibratory plate, gas, 18" plate, 3000 lb. blow		2.15	24.50	73	219	31.80
1350	21" plate, 5000 lb. blow		2.60	33	99	297	40.60
1370	Curb builder/extruder, 14 H.P., gas, single screw		13.90	275	825	2,475	276.20
1390	Double screw		14.80	330	995	2,975	317.40
1500	Disc harrow attachment, for tractor		.47	78.50	235	705	50.75
1810	Feller buncher, shearing & accumulating trees, 100 H.P.		40.55	810	2,430	7,300	810.40
1860	Grader, self-propelled, 25,000 lb.		32.75	745	2,235	6,700	709
1910	30,000 lb.		32.35	640	1,925	5,775	643.80
1920	40,000 lb.		54.75	1,250	3,765	11,300	1,191
1930	55,000 lb.		67.80	1,650	4,975	14,900	1,537
1950	Hammer, pavement breaker, self-propelled, diesel, 1000 to 1250 lb.		28.40	460	1,380	4,150	503.20
2000	1300 to 1500 lb.		42.60	920	2,760	8,275	892.80
2050	Pile driving hammer, steam or air, 4150 ft lb. @ 225 bpm		11.80	565	1,695	5,075	433.40
2100	8750 ft lb. @ 145 bpm		14.30	805	2,410	7,225	596.40
2150	15,000 ft lb. @ 60 bpm		14.65	845	2,530	7,600	623.20
2200	24,450 ft lb. @ 111 bpm		15.65	935	2,800	8,400	685.20
2250	Leads, 60' high for pile driving hammers up to 20,000 ft lb.		3.60	84.50	253	760	79.40
2300	90' high for hammers over 20,000 ft lb.		5.35	148	444	1,325	131.60

For customer support on your Green Building Costs with RSMeans data, call 800.448.8182.

01 54 | Construction Aids

01 54 33 | Equipment Rental

		Description	UNIT	HOURLY OPER. COST	RENT PER DAY	RENT PER WEEK	RENT PER MONTH	EQUIPMENT COST/DAY
20	2350	Diesel type hammer, 22,400 ft lb.	Ea.	18.25	470	1,405	4,225	427
	2400	41,300 ft lb.		26.50	600	1,800	5,400	572
	2450	141,000 ft lb.		41.80	945	2,840	8,525	902.40
	2500	Vib. elec. hammer/extractor, 200 kW diesel generator, 34 H.P.		40.35	695	2,080	6,250	738.80
	2550	80 H.P.		70.10	1,000	3,000	9,000	1,161
	2600	150 H.P.		129.40	1,925	5,780	17,300	2,191
	2800	Log chipper, up to 22" diameter, 600 H.P.		46.10	660	1,980	5,950	764.80
	2850	Logger, for skidding & stacking logs, 150 H.P.		44.05	830	2,485	7,450	849.40
	2860	Mulcher, diesel powered, trailer mounted		17.10	220	660	1,975	268.80
	2900	Rake, spring tooth, with tractor		14.54	360	1,075	3,225	331.30
	3000	Roller, vibratory, tandem, smooth drum, 20 H.P.		7.65	150	450	1,350	151.20
	3050	35 H.P.		10.05	252	755	2,275	231.40
	3100	Towed type vibratory compactor, smooth drum, 50 H.P.		25.25	370	1,105	3,325	423
	3150	Sheepsfoot, 50 H.P.		25.35	370	1,115	3,350	425.80
	3170	Landfill compactor, 220 H.P.		71.35	1,575	4,710	14,100	1,513
	3200	Pneumatic tire roller, 80 H.P.		12.90	390	1,175	3,525	338.20
	3250	120 H.P.		19.45	645	1,930	5,800	541.60
	3300	Sheepsfoot vibratory roller, 240 H.P.		62.05	1,375	4,100	12,300	1,316
	3320	340 H.P.		83.10	2,025	6,075	18,200	1,880
	3350	Smooth drum vibratory roller, 75 H.P.		23.30	650	1,950	5,850	576.40
	3400	125 H.P.		27.60	730	2,195	6,575	659.80
	3410	Rotary mower, brush, 60", with tractor		19.00	340	1,025	3,075	357
	3420	Rototiller, walk-behind, gas, 5 H.P.		2.21	76.50	229	685	63.50
	3422	8 H.P.		2.80	87	261	785	74.60
	3440	Scrapers, towed type, 7 C.Y. capacity		6.30	122	365	1,100	123.40
	3450	10 C.Y. capacity		7.10	165	495	1,475	155.80
	3500	15 C.Y. capacity		7.60	192	575	1,725	175.80
	3525	Self-propelled, single engine, 14 C.Y. capacity		131.25	2,400	7,200	21,600	2,490
	3550	Dual engine, 21 C.Y. capacity		137.25	2,275	6,850	20,600	2,468
	3600	31 C.Y. capacity		184.55	3,500	10,500	31,500	3,576
	3640	44 C.Y. capacity		225.40	4,425	13,270	39,800	4,457
	3650	Elevating type, single engine, 11 C.Y. capacity		61.05	1,100	3,335	10,000	1,155
	3700	22 C.Y. capacity		114.65	2,275	6,835	20,500	2,284
	3710	Screening plant, 110 H.P. w/5' x 10' screen		20.55	385	1,160	3,475	396.40
	3720	5' x 16' screen		25.96	495	1,480	4,450	503.70
	3850	Shovel, crawler-mounted, front-loading, 7 C.Y. capacity		204.00	3,750	11,240	33,700	3,880
	3855	12 C.Y. capacity		332.00	5,200	15,567	46,700	5,769
	3860	Shovel/backhoe bucket, 1/2 C.Y.		2.70	71.50	215	645	64.60
	3870	3/4 C.Y.		2.75	78.50	235	705	69
	3880	1 C.Y.		2.85	88.50	265	795	75.80
	3890	1-1/2 C.Y.		3.00	102	305	915	85
	3910	3 C.Y.		3.35	137	410	1,225	108.80
	3950	Stump chipper, 18" deep, 30 H.P.		6.93	214	643	1,925	184.05
	4110	Dozer, crawler, torque converter, diesel 80 H.P.		25.05	440	1,320	3,950	464.40
	4150	105 H.P.		34.25	555	1,670	5,000	608
	4200	140 H.P.		42.20	845	2,540	7,625	845.60
	4260	200 H.P.		61.65	1,300	3,900	11,700	1,273
	4310	300 H.P.		82.45	1,950	5,845	17,500	1,829
	4360	410 H.P.		109.35	2,350	7,080	21,200	2,291
	4370	500 H.P.		137.25	2,875	8,600	25,800	2,818
	4380	700 H.P.		229.75	5,275	15,805	47,400	4,999
	4400	Loader, crawler, torque conv., diesel 1-1/2 C.Y., 80 H.P.		29.60	570	1,715	5,150	579.80
	4450	1-1/2 to 1-3/4 C.Y., 95 H.P.		30.55	670	2,005	6,025	645.40
	4510	1-3/4 to 2-1/4 C.Y., 130 H.P.		47.50	1,000	2,995	8,975	979
	4530	2-1/2 to 3-1/4 C.Y., 190 H.P.		57.55	1,250	3,720	11,200	1,204
	4560	3-1/2 to 5 C.Y., 275 H.P.		71.55	1,475	4,435	13,300	1,459
	4610	Front end loader, 4WD, articulated frame, diesel, 1 to 1-1/4 C.Y., 70 H.P.		16.10	270	810	2,425	290.80
	4620	1-1/2 to 1-3/4 C.Y., 95 H.P.		19.35	315	940	2,825	342.80

01 54 | Construction Aids

01 54 33 | Equipment Rental

			UNIT	HOURLY OPER. COST	RENT PER DAY	RENT PER WEEK	RENT PER MONTH	EQUIPMENT COST/DAY	
20	4650	1-3/4 to 2 C.Y., 130 H.P.	Ea.	20.50	380	1,140	3,425	392	20
	4710	2-1/2 to 3-1/2 C.Y., 145 H.P.		29.15	485	1,450	4,350	523.20	
	4730	3 to 4-1/2 C.Y., 185 H.P.		32.20	530	1,585	4,750	574.60	
	4760	5-1/4 to 5-3/4 C.Y., 270 H.P.		53.15	930	2,785	8,350	982.20	
	4810	7 to 9 C.Y., 475 H.P.		90.60	1,750	5,275	15,800	1,780	
	4870	9 to 11 C.Y., 620 H.P.		131.70	2,625	7,880	23,600	2,630	
	4880	Skid-steer loader, wheeled, 10 C.F., 30 H.P. gas		9.50	163	490	1,475	174	
	4890	1 C.Y., 78 H.P., diesel		18.35	365	1,090	3,275	364.80	
	4892	Skid-steer attachment, auger		.82	136	408	1,225	88.15	
	4893	Backhoe		.74	123	369	1,100	79.70	
	4894	Broom		.71	118	355	1,075	76.70	
	4895	Forks		.16	27	81	243	17.50	
	4896	Grapple		.69	115	346	1,050	74.70	
	4897	Concrete hammer		1.05	175	526	1,575	113.60	
	4898	Tree spade		.60	100	300	900	64.80	
	4899	Trencher		.69	115	344	1,025	74.30	
	4900	Trencher, chain, boom type, gas, operator walking, 12 H.P.		4.10	48.50	145	435	61.80	
	4910	Operator riding, 40 H.P.		16.30	345	1,030	3,100	336.40	
	5000	Wheel type, diesel, 4' deep, 12" wide		69.35	900	2,700	8,100	1,095	
	5100	6' deep, 20" wide		87.50	2,100	6,285	18,900	1,957	
	5150	Chain type, diesel, 5' deep, 8" wide		16.30	345	1,030	3,100	336.40	
	5200	Diesel, 8' deep, 16" wide		95.25	2,150	6,430	19,300	2,048	
	5202	Rock trencher, wheel type, 6" wide x 18" deep		43.65	925	2,775	8,325	904.20	
	5206	Chain type, 18" wide x 7' deep		106.10	3,050	9,160	27,500	2,681	
	5210	Tree spade, self-propelled		14.24	390	1,167	3,500	347.30	
	5250	Truck, dump, 2-axle, 12 ton, 8 C.Y. payload, 220 H.P.		23.95	245	735	2,200	338.60	
	5300	Three axle dump, 16 ton, 12 C.Y. payload, 400 H.P.		41.60	350	1,050	3,150	542.80	
	5310	Four axle dump, 25 ton, 18 C.Y. payload, 450 H.P.		50.00	510	1,530	4,600	706	
	5350	Dump trailer only, rear dump, 16-1/2 C.Y.		5.75	145	435	1,300	133	
	5400	20 C.Y.		6.20	163	490	1,475	147.60	
	5450	Flatbed, single axle, 1-1/2 ton rating		18.30	70	210	630	188.40	
	5500	3 ton rating		22.25	100	300	900	238	
	5550	Off highway rear dump, 25 ton capacity		61.80	1,425	4,245	12,700	1,343	
	5600	35 ton capacity		66.10	1,525	4,595	13,800	1,448	
	5610	50 ton capacity		81.20	1,675	5,060	15,200	1,662	
	5620	65 ton capacity		84.95	1,950	5,820	17,500	1,844	
	5630	100 ton capacity		119.60	2,850	8,560	25,700	2,669	
	6000	Vibratory plow, 25 H.P., walking		6.80	61.50	185	555	91.40	
40	0010	**GENERAL EQUIPMENT RENTAL** without operators	R015433-10						40
	0020	Aerial lift, scissor type, to 20' high, 1200 lb. capacity, electric	Ea.	3.40	51.50	155	465	58.20	
	0030	To 30' high, 1200 lb. capacity		3.85	68.50	205	615	71.80	
	0040	Over 30' high, 1500 lb. capacity		5.15	122	365	1,100	114.20	
	0070	Articulating boom, to 45' high, 500 lb. capacity, diesel	R015433-15	9.70	273	820	2,450	241.60	
	0075	To 60' high, 500 lb. capacity		13.70	470	1,410	4,225	391.60	
	0080	To 80' high, 500 lb. capacity		16.10	560	1,685	5,050	465.80	
	0085	To 125' high, 500 lb. capacity		18.40	780	2,335	7,000	614.20	
	0100	Telescoping boom to 40' high, 500 lb. capacity, diesel		11.60	315	950	2,850	282.80	
	0105	To 45' high, 500 lb. capacity		12.40	320	958	2,875	290.80	
	0110	To 60' high, 500 lb. capacity		16.20	540	1,625	4,875	454.60	
	0115	To 80' high, 500 lb. capacity		21.70	625	1,875	5,625	548.60	
	0120	To 100' high, 500 lb. capacity		28.80	805	2,420	7,250	714.40	
	0125	To 120' high, 500 lb. capacity		29.25	845	2,530	7,600	740	
	0195	Air compressor, portable, 6.5 CFM, electric		.91	13	39	117	15.10	
	0196	Gasoline		.66	19.65	59	177	17.10	
	0200	Towed type, gas engine, 60 CFM		9.30	51.50	155	465	105.40	
	0300	160 CFM		10.65	53.50	160	480	117.20	
	0400	Diesel engine, rotary screw, 250 CFM		12.05	118	355	1,075	167.40	
	0500	365 CFM		15.80	142	425	1,275	211.40	

For customer support on your Green Building Costs with RSMeans data, call 800.448.8182

01 54 | Construction Aids

01 54 33 | Equipment Rental

		UNIT	HOURLY OPER. COST	RENT PER DAY	RENT PER WEEK	RENT PER MONTH	EQUIPMENT COST/DAY
0550	450 CFM	Ea.	19.70	177	530	1,600	263.60
0600	600 CFM		33.90	243	730	2,200	417.20
0700	750 CFM		34.10	252	755	2,275	423.80
0930	Air tools, breaker, pavement, 60 lb.		.55	10.35	31	93	10.60
0940	80 lb.		.55	10.65	32	96	10.80
0950	Drills, hand (jackhammer), 65 lb.		.65	17.65	53	159	15.80
0960	Track or wagon, swing boom, 4" drifter		54.80	925	2,775	8,325	993.40
0970	5" drifter		63.45	1,100	3,325	9,975	1,173
0975	Track mounted quarry drill, 6" diameter drill		104.15	1,650	4,945	14,800	1,822
0980	Dust control per drill		1.04	24.50	74	222	23.10
0990	Hammer, chipping, 12 lb.		.60	27	81	243	21
1000	Hose, air with couplings, 50' long, 3/4" diameter		.07	11.35	34	102	7.35
1100	1" diameter		.08	13	39	117	8.45
1200	1-1/2" diameter		.21	35	105	315	22.70
1300	2" diameter		.24	40	120	360	25.90
1400	2-1/2" diameter		.35	58.50	175	525	37.80
1410	3" diameter		.40	66.50	200	600	43.20
1450	Drill, steel, 7/8" x 2'		.08	13.65	41	123	8.85
1460	7/8" x 6'		.11	17.65	53	159	11.50
1520	Moil points		.03	4.67	14	42	3.05
1525	Pneumatic nailer w/accessories		.48	32	96	288	23.05
1530	Sheeting driver for 60 lb. breaker		.04	7.35	22	66	4.70
1540	For 90 lb. breaker		.15	9.65	29	87	7
1550	Spade, 25 lb.		.50	7.35	22	66	8.40
1560	Tamper, single, 35 lb.		.59	39.50	118	355	28.30
1570	Triple, 140 lb.		.89	59	177	530	42.50
1580	Wrenches, impact, air powered, up to 3/4" bolt		.45	13	39	117	11.40
1590	Up to 1-1/4" bolt		.55	23.50	71	213	18.60
1600	Barricades, barrels, reflectorized, 1 to 99 barrels		.03	5.35	16	48	3.45
1610	100 to 200 barrels		.02	4.13	12.40	37	2.65
1620	Barrels with flashers, 1 to 99 barrels		.04	6	18	54	3.90
1630	100 to 200 barrels		.03	4.80	14.40	43	3.10
1640	Barrels with steady burn type C lights		.05	8	24	72	5.20
1650	Illuminated board, trailer mounted, with generator		3.30	133	400	1,200	106.40
1670	Portable barricade, stock, with flashers, 1 to 6 units		.04	6	18	54	3.90
1680	25 to 50 units		.03	5.60	16.80	50.50	3.60
1685	Butt fusion machine, wheeled, 1.5 H.P. electric, 2" - 8" diameter pipe		2.63	167	500	1,500	121.05
1690	Tracked, 20 H.P. diesel, 4" - 12" diameter pipe		11.21	560	1,680	5,050	425.70
1695	83 H.P. diesel, 8" - 24" diameter pipe		49.46	2,525	7,560	22,700	1,908
1700	Carts, brick, gas engine, 1000 lb. capacity		2.95	61.50	185	555	60.60
1800	1500 lb., 7-1/2' lift		3.00	65	195	585	63
1822	Dehumidifier, medium, 6 lb./hr., 150 CFM		1.16	72.50	218	655	52.90
1824	Large, 18 lb./hr., 600 CFM		2.20	138	413	1,250	100.20
1830	Distributor, asphalt, trailer mounted, 2000 gal., 38 H.P. diesel		10.75	350	1,050	3,150	296
1840	3000 gal., 38 H.P. diesel		12.35	380	1,140	3,425	326.80
1850	Drill, rotary hammer, electric		1.12	27	81	243	25.15
1860	Carbide bit, 1-1/2" diameter, add to electric rotary hammer		.03	5	15	45	3.25
1865	Rotary, crawler, 250 H.P.		136.15	2,225	6,690	20,100	2,427
1870	Emulsion sprayer, 65 gal., 5 H.P. gas engine		2.77	103	309	925	83.95
1880	200 gal., 5 H.P. engine		7.30	172	515	1,550	161.40
1900	Floor auto-scrubbing machine, walk-behind, 28" path		5.41	350	1,055	3,175	254.30
1930	Floodlight, mercury vapor, or quartz, on tripod, 1000 watt		.46	22	66	198	16.90
1940	2000 watt		.63	27.50	82	246	21.45
1950	Floodlights, trailer mounted with generator, 1 - 300 watt light		3.60	76.50	230	690	74.80
1960	2 - 1000 watt lights		4.50	102	305	915	97
2000	4 - 300 watt lights		4.25	96.50	290	870	92
2005	Foam spray rig, incl. box trailer, compressor, generator, proportioner		23.78	515	1,545	4,625	499.25
2015	Forklift, pneumatic tire, rough terr, straight mast, 5000 lb, 12' lift, gas		19.00	212	635	1,900	279

For customer support on your Green Building Costs with RSMeans data, call 800.448.8182.

01 54 | Construction Aids

01 54 33 | Equipment Rental

			UNIT	HOURLY OPER. COST	RENT PER DAY	RENT PER WEEK	RENT PER MONTH	EQUIPMENT COST/DAY
40	2025	8000 lb., 12' lift	Ea.	22.75	283	850	2,550	352
	2030	5000 lb., 12' lift, diesel		15.70	237	710	2,125	267.60
	2035	8000 lb., 12' lift, diesel		16.75	268	805	2,425	295
	2045	All terrain, telescoping boom, diesel, 5000 lb., 10' reach, 19' lift		17.25	325	980	2,950	334
	2055	6600 lb., 29' reach, 42' lift		21.10	380	1,140	3,425	396.80
	2065	10,000 lb., 31' reach, 45' lift		23.65	490	1,475	4,425	484.20
	2070	Cushion tire, smooth floor, gas, 5000 lb. capacity		8.25	76.50	230	690	112
	2075	8000 lb. capacity		11.40	95	285	855	148.20
	2085	Diesel, 5000 lb. capacity		7.75	83.50	250	750	112
	2090	12,000 lb. capacity		12.05	130	390	1,175	174.40
	2095	20,000 lb. capacity		17.00	165	495	1,475	235
	2100	Generator, electric, gas engine, 1.5 kW to 3 kW		2.70	11.35	34	102	28.40
	2200	5 kW		3.35	14.35	43	129	35.40
	2300	10 kW		6.25	35	105	315	71
	2400	25 kW		7.60	86.50	260	780	112.80
	2500	Diesel engine, 20 kW		9.20	76.50	230	690	119.60
	2600	50 kW		15.85	100	300	900	186.80
	2700	100 kW		28.20	137	410	1,225	307.60
	2800	250 kW		56.05	260	780	2,350	604.40
	2850	Hammer, hydraulic, for mounting on boom, to 500 ft lb.		2.85	86.50	260	780	74.80
	2860	1000 ft lb.		4.70	133	400	1,200	117.60
	2900	Heaters, space, oil or electric, 50 MBH		1.47	8	24	72	16.55
	3000	100 MBH		2.73	11.35	34	102	28.65
	3100	300 MBH		7.84	40	120	360	86.70
	3150	500 MBH		12.75	45	135	405	129
	3200	Hose, water, suction with coupling, 20' long, 2" diameter		.02	3	9	27	1.95
	3210	3" diameter		.03	4.33	13	39	2.85
	3220	4" diameter		.03	5	15	45	3.25
	3230	6" diameter		.11	17.65	53	159	11.50
	3240	8" diameter		.28	46.50	140	420	30.25
	3250	Discharge hose with coupling, 50' long, 2" diameter		.01	1.33	4	12	.90
	3260	3" diameter		.01	2.33	7	21	1.50
	3270	4" diameter		.02	3.67	11	33	2.35
	3280	6" diameter		.06	9.35	28	84	6.10
	3290	8" diameter		.24	40	120	360	25.90
	3295	Insulation blower		.83	6	18	54	10.25
	3300	Ladders, extension type, 16' to 36' long		.18	30	90	270	19.45
	3400	40' to 60' long		.67	112	335	1,000	72.35
	3405	Lance for cutting concrete		2.23	58.50	176	530	53.05
	3407	Lawn mower, rotary, 22", 5 H.P.		1.15	25	75	225	24.20
	3408	48" self-propelled		2.86	90	270	810	76.90
	3410	Level, electronic, automatic, with tripod and leveling rod		1.05	70	210	630	50.40
	3430	Laser type, for pipe and sewer line and grade		2.13	142	425	1,275	102.05
	3440	Rotating beam for interior control		.90	60	180	540	43.20
	3460	Builder's optical transit, with tripod and rod		.10	16.35	49	147	10.60
	3500	Light towers, towable, with diesel generator, 2000 watt		4.25	96.50	290	870	92
	3600	4000 watt		4.50	102	305	915	97
	3700	Mixer, powered, plaster and mortar, 6 C.F., 7 H.P.		2.05	20.50	62	186	28.80
	3800	10 C.F., 9 H.P.		2.20	33.50	100	300	37.60
	3850	Nailer, pneumatic		.48	32	96	288	23.05
	3900	Paint sprayers complete, 8 CFM		.94	62.50	188	565	45.10
	4000	17 CFM		1.69	112	337	1,000	80.90
	4020	Pavers, bituminous, rubber tires, 8' wide, 50 H.P., diesel		31.55	550	1,645	4,925	581.40
	4030	10' wide, 150 H.P.		96.50	1,875	5,655	17,000	1,903
	4050	Crawler, 8' wide, 100 H.P., diesel		87.60	2,025	6,105	18,300	1,922
	4060	10' wide, 150 H.P.		104.50	2,350	7,015	21,000	2,239
	4070	Concrete paver, 12' to 24' wide, 250 H.P.		87.45	1,625	4,875	14,600	1,675
	4080	Placer-spreader-trimmer, 24' wide, 300 H.P.		117.20	2,375	7,115	21,300	2,361

For customer support on your Green Building Costs with RSMeans data, call 800.448.8182.

01 54 | Construction Aids

01 54 33 | Equipment Rental

		UNIT	HOURLY OPER. COST	RENT PER DAY	RENT PER WEEK	RENT PER MONTH	EQUIPMENT COST/DAY
4100	Pump, centrifugal gas pump, 1-1/2" diameter, 65 GPM	Ea.	3.90	53.50	160	480	63.20
4200	2" diameter, 130 GPM		5.00	63.50	190	570	78
4300	3" diameter, 250 GPM		5.15	63.50	190	570	79.20
4400	6" diameter, 1500 GPM		22.30	197	590	1,775	296.40
4500	Submersible electric pump, 1-1/4" diameter, 55 GPM		.41	17.65	53	159	13.90
4600	1-1/2" diameter, 83 GPM		.45	20.50	61	183	15.80
4700	2" diameter, 120 GPM		1.65	25.50	76	228	28.40
4800	3" diameter, 300 GPM		2.94	45	135	405	50.50
4900	4" diameter, 560 GPM		14.70	167	500	1,500	217.60
5000	6" diameter, 1590 GPM		21.94	218	655	1,975	306.50
5100	Diaphragm pump, gas, single, 1-1/2" diameter		1.12	54.50	164	490	41.75
5200	2" diameter		4.00	68.50	205	615	73
5300	3" diameter		4.05	68.50	205	615	73.40
5400	Double, 4" diameter		5.85	113	340	1,025	114.80
5450	Pressure washer 5 GPM, 3000 psi		3.95	53.50	160	480	63.60
5460	7 GPM, 3000 psi		4.90	63.50	190	570	77.20
5500	Trash pump, self-priming, gas, 2" diameter		3.80	23.50	70	210	44.40
5600	Diesel, 4" diameter		6.95	95	285	855	112.60
5650	Diesel, 6" diameter		16.90	167	500	1,500	235.20
5655	Grout pump		19.50	275	825	2,475	321
5700	Salamanders, L.P. gas fired, 100,000 BTU		2.93	14	42	126	31.85
5705	50,000 BTU		1.67	11.35	34	102	20.15
5720	Sandblaster, portable, open top, 3 C.F. capacity		.60	27	81	243	21
5730	6 C.F. capacity		1.00	40	120	360	32
5740	Accessories for above		.14	22.50	68	204	14.70
5750	Sander, floor		.77	17.65	53	159	16.75
5760	Edger		.52	15	45	135	13.15
5800	Saw, chain, gas engine, 18" long		1.80	22.50	67	201	27.80
5900	Hydraulic powered, 36" long		.80	66.50	200	600	46.40
5950	60" long		.80	68.50	205	615	47.40
6000	Masonry, table mounted, 14" diameter, 5 H.P.		1.32	56.50	170	510	44.55
6050	Portable cut-off, 8 H.P.		1.85	33.50	100	300	34.80
6100	Circular, hand held, electric, 7-1/4" diameter		.23	5	15	45	4.85
6200	12" diameter		.23	8	24	72	6.65
6250	Wall saw, w/hydraulic power, 10 H.P.		3.30	33.50	100	300	46.40
6275	Shot blaster, walk-behind, 20" wide		4.85	293	880	2,650	214.80
6280	Sidewalk broom, walk-behind		2.39	85	255	765	70.10
6300	Steam cleaner, 100 gallons per hour		3.35	80	240	720	74.80
6310	200 gallons per hour		4.40	96.50	290	870	93.20
6340	Tar kettle/pot, 400 gallons		15.15	76.50	230	690	167.20
6350	Torch, cutting, acetylene-oxygen, 150' hose, excludes gases		.45	15	45	135	12.60
6360	Hourly operating cost includes tips and gas		21.00				168
6410	Toilet, portable chemical		.13	22	66	198	14.25
6420	Recycle flush type		.16	27	81	243	17.50
6430	Toilet, fresh water flush, garden hose,		.19	32.50	97	291	20.90
6440	Hoisted, non-flush, for high rise		.16	26.50	79	237	17.10
6465	Tractor, farm with attachment		17.80	340	1,025	3,075	347.40
6480	Trailers, platform, flush deck, 2 axle, 3 ton capacity		1.60	21	63	189	25.40
6500	25 ton capacity		6.25	138	415	1,250	133
6600	40 ton capacity		8.00	193	580	1,750	180
6700	3 axle, 50 ton capacity		8.65	215	645	1,925	198.20
6800	75 ton capacity		10.90	285	855	2,575	258.20
6810	Trailer mounted cable reel for high voltage line work		5.79	276	827	2,475	211.70
6820	Trailer mounted cable tensioning rig		11.48	545	1,640	4,925	419.85
6830	Cable pulling rig		72.98	3,075	9,210	27,600	2,426
6850	Portable cable/wire puller, 8000 lb. max pulling capacity		3.72	167	502	1,500	130.15
6900	Water tank trailer, engine driven discharge, 5000 gallons		7.20	150	450	1,350	147.60
6925	10,000 gallons		9.70	207	620	1,850	201.60

01 54 | Construction Aids

01 54 33 | Equipment Rental

		Description	UNIT	HOURLY OPER. COST	RENT PER DAY	RENT PER WEEK	RENT PER MONTH	EQUIPMENT COST/DAY	
40	6950	Water truck, off highway, 6000 gallons	Ea.	70.16	805	2,420	7,250	1,045	40
	7010	Tram car for high voltage line work, powered, 2 conductor		6.85	150	449	1,350	144.60	
	7020	Transit (builder's level) with tripod		.10	16.35	49	147	10.60	
	7030	Trench box, 3000 lb., 6' x 8'		.56	93.50	280	840	60.50	
	7040	7200 lb., 6' x 20'		.75	125	375	1,125	81	
	7050	8000 lb., 8' x 16'		1.08	180	540	1,625	116.65	
	7060	9500 lb., 8' x 20'		1.21	201	603	1,800	130.30	
	7065	11,000 lb., 8' x 24'		1.27	211	633	1,900	136.75	
	7070	12,000 lb., 10' x 20'		1.50	251	752	2,250	162.40	
	7100	Truck, pickup, 3/4 ton, 2 wheel drive		9.90	60	180	540	115.20	
	7200	4 wheel drive		10.20	75	225	675	126.60	
	7250	Crew carrier, 9 passenger		14.00	90	270	810	166	
	7290	Flat bed truck, 20,000 lb. GVW		14.90	130	390	1,175	197.20	
	7300	Tractor, 4 x 2, 220 H.P.		21.00	203	610	1,825	290	
	7410	330 H.P.		30.80	280	840	2,525	414.40	
	7500	6 x 4, 380 H.P.		35.15	325	975	2,925	476.20	
	7600	450 H.P.		43.30	395	1,185	3,550	583.40	
	7610	Tractor, with A frame, boom and winch, 225 H.P.		24.10	282	845	2,525	361.80	
	7620	Vacuum truck, hazardous material, 2500 gallons		12.85	305	910	2,725	284.80	
	7625	5000 gallons		13.11	425	1,270	3,800	358.90	
	7650	Vacuum, HEPA, 16 gallon, wet/dry		.90	18	54	162	18	
	7655	55 gallon, wet/dry		.81	27	81	243	22.70	
	7660	Water tank, portable		.74	123	370	1,100	79.90	
	7690	Sewer/catch basin vacuum, 14 C.Y., 1500 gallons		17.59	635	1,910	5,725	522.70	
	7700	Welder, electric, 200 amp		3.99	16.35	49	147	41.70	
	7800	300 amp		5.90	20	60	180	59.20	
	7900	Gas engine, 200 amp		9.10	24.50	74	222	87.60	
	8000	300 amp		10.35	26	78	234	98.40	
	8100	Wheelbarrow, any size		.06	10.65	32	96	6.90	
	8200	Wrecking ball, 4000 lb.		2.45	71.50	215	645	62.60	
50	0010	**HIGHWAY EQUIPMENT RENTAL** without operators	R015433 -10						50
	0050	Asphalt batch plant, portable drum mixer, 100 ton/hr.	Ea.	85.49	1,500	4,505	13,500	1,585	
	0060	200 ton/hr.		97.81	1,600	4,800	14,400	1,742	
	0070	300 ton/hr.		116.21	1,875	5,625	16,900	2,055	
	0100	Backhoe attachment, long stick, up to 185 H.P., 10.5' long		.37	24.50	73	219	17.55	
	0140	Up to 250 H.P., 12' long		.41	27	81	243	19.50	
	0180	Over 250 H.P., 15' long		.56	37	111	335	26.70	
	0200	Special dipper arm, up to 100 H.P., 32' long		1.14	75.50	227	680	54.50	
	0240	Over 100 H.P., 33' long		1.42	94.50	284	850	68.15	
	0280	Catch basin/sewer cleaning truck, 3 ton, 9 C.Y., 1000 gal.		35.10	405	1,210	3,625	522.80	
	0300	Concrete batch plant, portable, electric, 200 C.Y./hr.		24.34	545	1,630	4,900	520.70	
	0520	Grader/dozer attachment, ripper/scarifier, rear mounted, up to 135 H.P.		3.15	61.50	185	555	62.20	
	0540	Up to 180 H.P.		4.10	91.50	275	825	87.80	
	0580	Up to 250 H.P.		5.70	145	435	1,300	132.60	
	0700	Pvmt. removal bucket, for hyd. excavator, up to 90 H.P.		2.10	56.50	170	510	50.80	
	0740	Up to 200 H.P.		2.25	71.50	215	645	61	
	0780	Over 200 H.P.		2.45	88.50	265	795	72.60	
	0900	Aggregate spreader, self-propelled, 187 H.P.		50.00	730	2,185	6,550	837	
	1000	Chemical spreader, 3 C.Y.		3.15	45	135	405	52.20	
	1900	Hammermill, traveling, 250 H.P.		68.23	2,200	6,620	19,900	1,870	
	2000	Horizontal borer, 3" diameter, 13 H.P. gas driven		5.50	56.50	170	510	78	
	2150	Horizontal directional drill, 20,000 lb. thrust, 78 H.P. diesel		27.50	680	2,045	6,125	629	
	2160	30,000 lb. thrust, 115 H.P.		33.65	1,050	3,135	9,400	896.20	
	2170	50,000 lb. thrust, 170 H.P.		48.35	1,325	4,005	12,000	1,188	
	2190	Mud trailer for HDD, 1500 gallons, 175 H.P., gas		24.10	158	475	1,425	287.80	
	2200	Hydromulcher, diesel, 3000 gallon, for truck mounting		16.35	253	760	2,275	282.80	
	2300	Gas, 600 gallon		7.40	103	310	930	121.20	
	2400	Joint & crack cleaner, walk behind, 25 H.P.		3.10	51.50	155	465	55.80	

For customer support on your Green Building Costs with RSMeans data, call 800.448.8182.

417

01 54 | Construction Aids

01 54 33 | Equipment Rental

		UNIT	HOURLY OPER. COST	RENT PER DAY	RENT PER WEEK	RENT PER MONTH	EQUIPMENT COST/DAY	
50 2500	Filler, trailer mounted, 400 gallons, 20 H.P.	Ea.	8.40	218	655	1,975	198.20	50
3000	Paint striper, self-propelled, 40 gallon, 22 H.P.		6.75	162	485	1,450	151	
3100	120 gallon, 120 H.P.		18.90	405	1,220	3,650	395.20	
3200	Post drivers, 6" I-Beam frame, for truck mounting		12.45	390	1,175	3,525	334.60	
3400	Road sweeper, self-propelled, 8' wide, 90 H.P.		35.95	670	2,005	6,025	688.60	
3450	Road sweeper, vacuum assisted, 4 C.Y., 220 gallons		56.05	655	1,960	5,875	840.40	
4000	Road mixer, self-propelled, 130 H.P.		45.95	800	2,405	7,225	848.60	
4100	310 H.P.		75.55	2,150	6,425	19,300	1,889	
4220	Cold mix paver, incl. pug mill and bitumen tank, 165 H.P.		94.60	2,300	6,915	20,700	2,140	
4240	Pavement brush, towed		3.40	96.50	290	870	85.20	
4250	Paver, asphalt, wheel or crawler, 130 H.P., diesel		94.25	2,275	6,845	20,500	2,123	
4300	Paver, road widener, gas, 1' to 6', 67 H.P.		46.65	940	2,825	8,475	938.20	
4400	Diesel, 2' to 14', 88 H.P.		56.75	1,125	3,355	10,100	1,125	
4600	Slipform pavers, curb and gutter, 2 track, 75 H.P.		56.30	1,200	3,615	10,800	1,173	
4700	4 track, 165 H.P.		36.95	825	2,470	7,400	789.60	
4800	Median barrier, 215 H.P.		57.45	1,275	3,805	11,400	1,221	
4901	Trailer, low bed, 75 ton capacity		11.05	268	805	2,425	249.40	
5000	Road planer, walk behind, 10" cutting width, 10 H.P.		2.50	33.50	100	300	40	
5100	Self-propelled, 12" cutting width, 64 H.P.		8.00	115	345	1,025	133	
5120	Traffic line remover, metal ball blaster, truck mounted, 115 H.P.		46.70	800	2,395	7,175	852.60	
5140	Grinder, truck mounted, 115 H.P.		51.05	850	2,555	7,675	919.40	
5160	Walk-behind, 11 H.P.		3.55	55	165	495	61.40	
5200	Pavement profiler, 4' to 6' wide, 450 H.P.		218.90	3,450	10,350	31,100	3,821	
5300	8' to 10' wide, 750 H.P.		336.50	4,550	13,635	40,900	5,419	
5400	Roadway plate, steel, 1" x 8' x 20'		.09	14.35	43	129	9.30	
5600	Stabilizer, self-propelled, 150 H.P.		41.50	680	2,045	6,125	741	
5700	310 H.P.		77.65	1,825	5,485	16,500	1,718	
5800	Striper, truck mounted, 120 gallon paint, 460 H.P.		48.50	505	1,510	4,525	690	
5900	Thermal paint heating kettle, 115 gallons		7.73	26.50	80	240	77.85	
6000	Tar kettle, 330 gallon, trailer mounted		11.65	60	180	540	129.20	
7000	Tunnel locomotive, diesel, 8 to 12 ton		29.90	600	1,800	5,400	599.20	
7005	Electric, 10 ton		28.40	685	2,060	6,175	639.20	
7010	Muck cars, 1/2 C.Y. capacity		2.25	26	78	234	33.60	
7020	1 C.Y. capacity		2.45	33.50	100	300	39.60	
7030	2 C.Y. capacity		2.60	38.50	115	345	43.80	
7040	Side dump, 2 C.Y. capacity		2.80	46.50	140	420	50.40	
7050	3 C.Y. capacity		3.80	51.50	155	465	61.40	
7060	5 C.Y. capacity		5.50	66.50	200	600	84	
7100	Ventilating blower for tunnel, 7-1/2 H.P.		2.16	51.50	155	465	48.30	
7110	10 H.P.		2.39	53.50	160	480	51.10	
7120	20 H.P.		3.56	69.50	208	625	70.10	
7140	40 H.P.		6.02	80	240	720	96.15	
7160	60 H.P.		8.75	98.50	295	885	129	
7175	75 H.P.		10.31	153	460	1,375	174.50	
7180	200 H.P.		20.73	305	920	2,750	349.85	
7800	Windrow loader, elevating		54.10	1,350	4,045	12,100	1,242	
60 0010	**LIFTING AND HOISTING EQUIPMENT RENTAL** without operators	R015433-10						60
0150	Crane, flatbed mounted, 3 ton capacity	Ea.	14.10	205	615	1,850	235.80	
0200	Crane, climbing, 106' jib, 6000 lb. capacity, 410 fpm	R312316-45	41.13	1,750	5,260	15,800	1,381	
0300	101' jib, 10,250 lb. capacity, 270 fpm		48.18	2,225	6,670	20,000	1,719	
0500	Tower, static, 130' high, 106' jib, 6200 lb. capacity at 400 fpm		45.23	2,025	6,080	18,200	1,578	
0520	Mini crawler spider crane, up to 24" wide, 1990 lb. lifting capacity		12.54	755	2,265	6,800	553.30	
0525	Up to 30" wide, 6450 lb. lifting capacity		14.57	840	2,520	7,550	620.55	
0530	Up to 52" wide, 6680 lb. lifting capacity		23.17	1,325	3,960	11,900	977.35	
0535	Up to 55" wide, 8920 lb. lifting capacity		25.87	1,500	4,500	13,500	1,107	
0540	Up to 66" wide, 13,350 lb. lifting capacity		35.03	2,050	6,120	18,400	1,504	
0600	Crawler mounted, lattice boom, 1/2 C.Y., 15 tons at 12' radius		37.10	885	2,660	7,975	828.80	
0700	3/4 C.Y., 20 tons at 12' radius		49.46	1,100	3,320	9,950	1,060	

01 54 | Construction Aids

01 54 33 | Equipment Rental

		UNIT	HOURLY OPER. COST	RENT PER DAY	RENT PER WEEK	RENT PER MONTH	EQUIPMENT COST/DAY
0800	1 C.Y., 25 tons at 12' radius	Ea.	65.95	1,375	4,100	12,300	1,348
0900	1-1/2 C.Y., 40 tons at 12' radius		66.45	1,400	4,190	12,600	1,370
1000	2 C.Y., 50 tons at 12' radius		88.90	2,050	6,145	18,400	1,940
1100	3 C.Y., 75 tons at 12' radius		76.00	1,825	5,500	16,500	1,708
1200	100 ton capacity, 60' boom		86.05	1,975	5,920	17,800	1,872
1300	165 ton capacity, 60' boom		105.00	2,325	6,970	20,900	2,234
1400	200 ton capacity, 70' boom		140.85	3,125	9,385	28,200	3,004
1500	350 ton capacity, 80' boom		182.50	4,125	12,375	37,100	3,935
1600	Truck mounted, lattice boom, 6 x 4, 20 tons at 10' radius		37.84	1,300	3,900	11,700	1,083
1700	25 tons at 10' radius		40.92	1,425	4,240	12,700	1,175
1800	8 x 4, 30 tons at 10' radius		44.29	1,500	4,520	13,600	1,258
1900	40 tons at 12' radius		47.09	1,575	4,720	14,200	1,321
2000	60 tons at 15' radius		52.56	1,675	5,000	15,000	1,420
2050	82 tons at 15' radius		58.46	1,775	5,340	16,000	1,536
2100	90 tons at 15' radius		65.33	1,950	5,820	17,500	1,687
2200	115 tons at 15' radius		73.60	2,175	6,500	19,500	1,889
2300	150 tons at 18' radius		80.95	2,275	6,845	20,500	2,017
2350	165 tons at 18' radius		85.95	2,425	7,260	21,800	2,140
2400	Truck mounted, hydraulic, 12 ton capacity		31.00	415	1,240	3,725	496
2500	25 ton capacity		37.45	485	1,455	4,375	590.60
2550	33 ton capacity		50.70	890	2,675	8,025	940.60
2560	40 ton capacity		51.00	905	2,710	8,125	950
2600	55 ton capacity		56.60	900	2,705	8,125	993.80
2700	80 ton capacity		77.85	1,500	4,475	13,400	1,518
2720	100 ton capacity		76.80	1,525	4,595	13,800	1,533
2740	120 ton capacity		101.90	1,825	5,460	16,400	1,907
2760	150 ton capacity		107.85	1,975	5,960	17,900	2,055
2800	Self-propelled, 4 x 4, with telescoping boom, 5 ton		15.00	232	695	2,075	259
2900	12-1/2 ton capacity		20.45	335	1,000	3,000	363.60
3000	15 ton capacity		33.95	520	1,560	4,675	583.60
3050	20 ton capacity		25.40	615	1,840	5,525	571.20
3100	25 ton capacity		37.30	615	1,850	5,550	668.40
3150	40 ton capacity		44.10	635	1,910	5,725	734.80
3200	Derricks, guy, 20 ton capacity, 60' boom, 75' mast		23.07	430	1,288	3,875	442.15
3300	100' boom, 115' mast		36.55	735	2,210	6,625	734.40
3400	Stiffleg, 20 ton capacity, 70' boom, 37' mast		25.74	555	1,670	5,000	539.90
3500	100' boom, 47' mast		39.84	895	2,680	8,050	854.70
3550	Helicopter, small, lift to 1250 lb. maximum, w/pilot		97.10	3,475	10,400	31,200	2,857
3600	Hoists, chain type, overhead, manual, 3/4 ton		.15	.33	1	3	1.40
3900	10 ton		.80	6	18	54	10
4000	Hoist and tower, 5000 lb. cap., portable electric, 40' high		5.19	247	742	2,225	189.90
4100	For each added 10' section, add		.12	19.35	58	174	12.55
4200	Hoist and single tubular tower, 5000 lb. electric, 100' high		7.03	345	1,036	3,100	263.45
4300	For each added 6'-6" section, add		.20	33.50	101	305	21.80
4400	Hoist and double tubular tower, 5000 lb., 100' high		7.56	380	1,141	3,425	288.70
4500	For each added 6'-6" section, add		.22	37	111	335	23.95
4550	Hoist and tower, mast type, 6000 lb., 100' high		8.14	395	1,183	3,550	301.70
4570	For each added 10' section, add		.14	22.50	68	204	14.70
4600	Hoist and tower, personnel, electric, 2000 lb., 100' @ 125 fpm		17.23	1,050	3,150	9,450	767.85
4700	3000 lb., 100' @ 200 fpm		19.70	1,200	3,570	10,700	871.60
4800	3000 lb., 150' @ 300 fpm		21.85	1,325	4,000	12,000	974.80
4900	4000 lb., 100' @ 300 fpm		22.62	1,350	4,080	12,200	996.95
5000	6000 lb., 100' @ 275 fpm		24.32	1,425	4,270	12,800	1,049
5100	For added heights up to 500', add	L.F.	.01	1.67	5	15	1.10
5200	Jacks, hydraulic, 20 ton	Ea.	.05	2	6	18	1.60
5500	100 ton		.40	12	36	108	10.40
6100	Jacks, hydraulic, climbing w/50' jackrods, control console, 30 ton cap.		2.13	142	426	1,275	102.25
6150	For each added 10' jackrod section, add		.05	3.33	10	30	2.40

For customer support on your Green Building Costs with RSMeans data, call 800.448.8182.

01 54 | Construction Aids

01 54 33 | Equipment Rental

		Unit	Hourly Oper. Cost	Rent Per Day	Rent Per Week	Rent Per Month	Equipment Cost/Day
6300	50 ton capacity	Ea.	3.43	228	685	2,050	164.45
6350	For each added 10' jackrod section, add		.06	4	12	36	2.90
6500	125 ton capacity		8.95	595	1,790	5,375	429.60
6550	For each added 10' jackrod section, add		.61	40.50	121	365	29.10
6600	Cable jack, 10 ton capacity with 200' cable		1.79	119	357	1,075	85.70
6650	For each added 50' of cable, add		.22	14.35	43	129	10.35
0010	**WELLPOINT EQUIPMENT RENTAL** without operators	R015433-10					
0020	Based on 2 months rental						
0100	Combination jetting & wellpoint pump, 60 H.P. diesel	Ea.	15.83	350	1,057	3,175	338.05
0200	High pressure gas jet pump, 200 H.P., 300 psi	"	34.42	300	903	2,700	455.95
0300	Discharge pipe, 8" diameter	L.F.	.01	.57	1.71	5.15	.40
0350	12" diameter		.01	.84	2.53	7.60	.60
0400	Header pipe, flows up to 150 GPM, 4" diameter		.01	.52	1.56	4.68	.40
0500	400 GPM, 6" diameter		.01	.61	1.83	5.50	.45
0600	800 GPM, 8" diameter		.01	.84	2.53	7.60	.60
0700	1500 GPM, 10" diameter		.01	.89	2.66	8	.60
0800	2500 GPM, 12" diameter		.03	1.68	5.03	15.10	1.25
0900	4500 GPM, 16" diameter		.03	2.15	6.44	19.30	1.55
0950	For quick coupling aluminum and plastic pipe, add		.03	2.22	6.67	20	1.55
1100	Wellpoint, 25' long, with fittings & riser pipe, 1-1/2" or 2" diameter	Ea.	.07	4.44	13.31	40	3.20
1200	Wellpoint pump, diesel powered, 4" suction, 20 H.P.		7.07	203	609	1,825	178.35
1300	6" suction, 30 H.P.		9.51	252	756	2,275	227.30
1400	8" suction, 40 H.P.		12.87	345	1,036	3,100	310.15
1500	10" suction, 75 H.P.		19.01	405	1,211	3,625	394.30
1600	12" suction, 100 H.P.		27.56	645	1,930	5,800	606.50
1700	12" suction, 175 H.P.		39.50	710	2,130	6,400	742
0010	**MARINE EQUIPMENT RENTAL** without operators	R015433-10					
0200	Barge, 400 ton, 30' wide x 90' long	Ea.	18.05	1,150	3,455	10,400	835.40
0240	800 ton, 45' wide x 90' long		21.95	1,425	4,240	12,700	1,024
2000	Tugboat, diesel, 100 H.P.		28.80	228	685	2,050	367.40
2040	250 H.P.		54.40	410	1,225	3,675	680.20
2080	380 H.P.		122.45	1,225	3,685	11,100	1,717
3000	Small work boat, gas, 16-foot, 50 H.P.		12.50	63.50	190	570	138
4000	Large, diesel, 48-foot, 200 H.P.		74.90	1,300	3,930	11,800	1,385

Crews - Standard

Crew No.	Bare Costs Hr.	Bare Costs Daily	Incl. Subs O&P Hr.	Incl. Subs O&P Daily	Cost Per Labor-Hour Bare Costs	Cost Per Labor-Hour Incl. O&P
Crew A-1						
1 Building Laborer	$39.85	$318.80	$60.70	$485.60	$39.85	$60.70
1 Concrete Saw, Gas Manual		71.20		78.32	8.90	9.79
8 L.H., Daily Totals		$390.00		$563.92	$48.75	$70.49
Crew A-1A						
1 Skilled Worker	$52.35	$418.80	$80.15	$641.20	$52.35	$80.15
1 Shot Blaster, 20"		214.80		236.28	26.85	29.54
8 L.H., Daily Totals		$633.60		$877.48	$79.20	$109.69
Crew A-1B						
1 Building Laborer	$39.85	$318.80	$60.70	$485.60	$39.85	$60.70
1 Concrete Saw		102.40		112.64	12.80	14.08
8 L.H., Daily Totals		$421.20		$598.24	$52.65	$74.78
Crew A-1C						
1 Building Laborer	$39.85	$318.80	$60.70	$485.60	$39.85	$60.70
1 Chain Saw, Gas, 18"		27.80		30.58	3.48	3.82
8 L.H., Daily Totals		$346.60		$516.18	$43.33	$64.52
Crew A-1D						
1 Building Laborer	$39.85	$318.80	$60.70	$485.60	$39.85	$60.70
1 Vibrating Plate, Gas, 18"		31.80		34.98	3.98	4.37
8 L.H., Daily Totals		$350.60		$520.58	$43.83	$65.07
Crew A-1E						
1 Building Laborer	$39.85	$318.80	$60.70	$485.60	$39.85	$60.70
1 Vibrating Plate, Gas, 21"		40.60		44.66	5.08	5.58
8 L.H., Daily Totals		$359.40		$530.26	$44.92	$66.28
Crew A-1F						
1 Building Laborer	$39.85	$318.80	$60.70	$485.60	$39.85	$60.70
1 Rammer/Tamper, Gas, 8"		46.00		50.60	5.75	6.33
8 L.H., Daily Totals		$364.80		$536.20	$45.60	$67.03
Crew A-1G						
1 Building Laborer	$39.85	$318.80	$60.70	$485.60	$39.85	$60.70
1 Rammer/Tamper, Gas, 15"		52.00		57.20	6.50	7.15
8 L.H., Daily Totals		$370.80		$542.80	$46.35	$67.85
Crew A-1H						
1 Building Laborer	$39.85	$318.80	$60.70	$485.60	$39.85	$60.70
1 Exterior Steam Cleaner		74.80		82.28	9.35	10.29
8 L.H., Daily Totals		$393.60		$567.88	$49.20	$70.98
Crew A-1J						
1 Building Laborer	$39.85	$318.80	$60.70	$485.60	$39.85	$60.70
1 Cultivator, Walk-Behind, 5 H.P.		63.50		69.85	7.94	8.73
8 L.H., Daily Totals		$382.30		$555.45	$47.79	$69.43
Crew A-1K						
1 Building Laborer	$39.85	$318.80	$60.70	$485.60	$39.85	$60.70
1 Cultivator, Walk-Behind, 8 H.P.		74.60		82.06	9.32	10.26
8 L.H., Daily Totals		$393.40		$567.66	$49.17	$70.96
Crew A-1M						
1 Building Laborer	$39.85	$318.80	$60.70	$485.60	$39.85	$60.70
1 Snow Blower, Walk-Behind		70.10		77.11	8.76	9.64
8 L.H., Daily Totals		$388.90		$562.71	$48.61	$70.34

Crew No.	Bare Costs Hr.	Bare Costs Daily	Incl. Subs O&P Hr.	Incl. Subs O&P Daily	Cost Per Labor-Hour Bare Costs	Cost Per Labor-Hour Incl. O&P
Crew A-2						
2 Laborers	$39.85	$637.60	$60.70	$971.20	$41.40	$62.80
1 Truck Driver (light)	44.50	356.00	67.00	536.00		
1 Flatbed Truck, Gas, 1.5 Ton		188.40		207.24	7.85	8.63
24 L.H., Daily Totals		$1182.00		$1714.44	$49.25	$71.44
Crew A-2A						
2 Laborers	$39.85	$637.60	$60.70	$971.20	$41.40	$62.80
1 Truck Driver (light)	44.50	356.00	67.00	536.00		
1 Flatbed Truck, Gas, 1.5 Ton		188.40		207.24		
1 Concrete Saw		102.40		112.64	12.12	13.33
24 L.H., Daily Totals		$1284.40		$1827.08	$53.52	$76.13
Crew A-2B						
1 Truck Driver (light)	$44.50	$356.00	$67.00	$536.00	$44.50	$67.00
1 Flatbed Truck, Gas, 1.5 Ton		188.40		207.24	23.55	25.91
8 L.H., Daily Totals		$544.40		$743.24	$68.05	$92.91
Crew A-3A						
1 Equip. Oper. (light)	$51.30	$410.40	$77.35	$618.80	$51.30	$77.35
1 Pickup Truck, 4x4, 3/4 Ton		126.60		139.26	15.82	17.41
8 L.H., Daily Totals		$537.00		$758.06	$67.13	$94.76
Crew A-3B						
1 Equip. Oper. (medium)	$53.75	$430.00	$81.05	$648.40	$49.88	$75.17
1 Truck Driver (heavy)	46.00	368.00	69.30	554.40		
1 Dump Truck, 12 C.Y., 400 H.P.		542.80		597.08		
1 F.E. Loader, W.M., 2.5 C.Y.		523.20		575.52	66.63	73.29
16 L.H., Daily Totals		$1864.00		$2375.40	$116.50	$148.46
Crew A-3C						
1 Equip. Oper. (light)	$51.30	$410.40	$77.35	$618.80	$51.30	$77.35
1 Loader, Skid Steer, 78 H.P.		364.80		401.28	45.60	50.16
8 L.H., Daily Totals		$775.20		$1020.08	$96.90	$127.51
Crew A-3D						
1 Truck Driver (light)	$44.50	$356.00	$67.00	$536.00	$44.50	$67.00
1 Pickup Truck, 4x4, 3/4 Ton		126.60		139.26		
1 Flatbed Trailer, 25 Ton		133.00		146.30	32.45	35.70
8 L.H., Daily Totals		$615.60		$821.56	$76.95	$102.69
Crew A-3E						
1 Equip. Oper. (crane)	$56.10	$448.80	$84.60	$676.80	$51.05	$76.95
1 Truck Driver (heavy)	46.00	368.00	69.30	554.40		
1 Pickup Truck, 4x4, 3/4 Ton		126.60		139.26	7.91	8.70
16 L.H., Daily Totals		$943.40		$1370.46	$58.96	$85.65
Crew A-3F						
1 Equip. Oper. (crane)	$56.10	$448.80	$84.60	$676.80	$51.05	$76.95
1 Truck Driver (heavy)	46.00	368.00	69.30	554.40		
1 Pickup Truck, 4x4, 3/4 Ton		126.60		139.26		
1 Truck Tractor, 6x4, 380 H.P.		476.20		523.82		
1 Lowbed Trailer, 75 Ton		249.40		274.34	53.26	58.59
16 L.H., Daily Totals		$1669.00		$2168.62	$104.31	$135.54

Crews - Standard

Crew No.	Bare Costs Hr.	Bare Costs Daily	Incl. Subs O&P Hr.	Incl. Subs O&P Daily	Cost Per Labor-Hour Bare Costs	Cost Per Labor-Hour Incl. O&P
Crew A-3G						
1 Equip. Oper. (crane)	$56.10	$448.80	$84.60	$676.80	$51.05	$76.95
1 Truck Driver (heavy)	46.00	368.00	69.30	554.40		
1 Pickup Truck, 4x4, 3/4 Ton		126.60		139.26		
1 Truck Tractor, 6x4, 450 H.P.		583.40		641.74		
1 Lowbed Trailer, 75 Ton		249.40		274.34	59.96	65.96
16 L.H., Daily Totals		$1776.20		$2286.54	$111.01	$142.91
Crew A-3H						
1 Equip. Oper. (crane)	$56.10	$448.80	$84.60	$676.80	$56.10	$84.60
1 Hyd. Crane, 12 Ton (Daily)		628.60		691.46	78.58	86.43
8 L.H., Daily Totals		$1077.40		$1368.26	$134.68	$171.03
Crew A-3I						
1 Equip. Oper. (crane)	$56.10	$448.80	$84.60	$676.80	$56.10	$84.60
1 Hyd. Crane, 25 Ton (Daily)		759.40		835.34	94.92	104.42
8 L.H., Daily Totals		$1208.20		$1512.14	$151.03	$189.02
Crew A-3J						
1 Equip. Oper. (crane)	$56.10	$448.80	$84.60	$676.80	$56.10	$84.60
1 Hyd. Crane, 40 Ton (Daily)		1313.00		1444.30	164.13	180.54
8 L.H., Daily Totals		$1761.80		$2121.10	$220.22	$265.14
Crew A-3K						
1 Equip. Oper. (crane)	$56.10	$448.80	$84.60	$676.80	$52.35	$78.95
1 Equip. Oper. (oiler)	48.60	388.80	73.30	586.40		
1 Hyd. Crane, 55 Ton (Daily)		1353.00		1488.30		
1 P/U Truck, 3/4 Ton (Daily)		139.20		153.12	93.26	102.59
16 L.H., Daily Totals		$2329.80		$2904.62	$145.61	$181.54
Crew A-3L						
1 Equip. Oper. (crane)	$56.10	$448.80	$84.60	$676.80	$52.35	$78.95
1 Equip. Oper. (oiler)	48.60	388.80	73.30	586.40		
1 Hyd. Crane, 80 Ton (Daily)		2113.00		2324.30		
1 P/U Truck, 3/4 Ton (Daily)		139.20		153.12	140.76	154.84
16 L.H., Daily Totals		$3089.80		$3740.62	$193.11	$233.79
Crew A-3M						
1 Equip. Oper. (crane)	$56.10	$448.80	$84.60	$676.80	$52.35	$78.95
1 Equip. Oper. (oiler)	48.60	388.80	73.30	586.40		
1 Hyd. Crane, 100 Ton (Daily)		2144.00		2358.40		
1 P/U Truck, 3/4 Ton (Daily)		139.20		153.12	142.70	156.97
16 L.H., Daily Totals		$3120.80		$3774.72	$195.05	$235.92
Crew A-3N						
1 Equip. Oper. (crane)	$56.10	$448.80	$84.60	$676.80	$56.10	$84.60
1 Tower Crane (monthly)		1180.00		1298.00	147.50	162.25
8 L.H., Daily Totals		$1628.80		$1974.80	$203.60	$246.85
Crew A-3P						
1 Equip. Oper. (light)	$51.30	$410.40	$77.35	$618.80	$51.30	$77.35
1 A.T. Forklift, 31' reach, 45' lift		484.20		532.62	60.52	66.58
8 L.H., Daily Totals		$894.60		$1151.42	$111.83	$143.93
Crew A-3Q						
1 Equip. Oper. (light)	$51.30	$410.40	$77.35	$618.80	$51.30	$77.35
1 Pickup Truck, 4x4, 3/4 Ton		126.60		139.26		
1 Flatbed Trailer, 3 Ton		25.40		27.94	19.00	20.90
8 L.H., Daily Totals		$562.40		$786.00	$70.30	$98.25

Crew No.	Bare Costs Hr.	Bare Costs Daily	Incl. Subs O&P Hr.	Incl. Subs O&P Daily	Cost Per Labor-Hour Bare Costs	Cost Per Labor-Hour Incl. O&P
Crew A-3R						
1 Equip. Oper. (light)	$51.30	$410.40	$77.35	$618.80	$51.30	$77.35
1 Forklift, Smooth Floor, 8,000 Lb.		148.20		163.02	18.52	20.38
8 L.H., Daily Totals		$558.60		$781.82	$69.83	$97.73
Crew A-4						
2 Carpenters	$50.70	$811.20	$77.20	$1235.20	$47.98	$72.82
1 Painter, Ordinary	42.55	340.40	64.05	512.40		
24 L.H., Daily Totals		$1151.60		$1747.60	$47.98	$72.82
Crew A-5						
2 Laborers	$39.85	$637.60	$60.70	$971.20	$40.37	$61.40
.25 Truck Driver (light)	44.50	89.00	67.00	134.00		
.25 Flatbed Truck, Gas, 1.5 Ton		47.10		51.81	2.62	2.88
18 L.H., Daily Totals		$773.70		$1157.01	$42.98	$64.28
Crew A-6						
1 Instrument Man	$52.35	$418.80	$80.15	$641.20	$50.42	$76.80
1 Rodman/Chainman	48.50	388.00	73.45	587.60		
1 Level, Electronic		50.40		55.44	3.15	3.46
16 L.H., Daily Totals		$857.20		$1284.24	$53.58	$80.27
Crew A-7						
1 Chief of Party	$63.65	$509.20	$96.45	$771.60	$54.83	$83.35
1 Instrument Man	52.35	418.80	80.15	641.20		
1 Rodman/Chainman	48.50	388.00	73.45	587.60		
1 Level, Electronic		50.40		55.44	2.10	2.31
24 L.H., Daily Totals		$1366.40		$2055.84	$56.93	$85.66
Crew A-8						
1 Chief of Party	$63.65	$509.20	$96.45	$771.60	$53.25	$80.88
1 Instrument Man	52.35	418.80	80.15	641.20		
2 Rodmen/Chainmen	48.50	776.00	73.45	1175.20		
1 Level, Electronic		50.40		55.44	1.58	1.73
32 L.H., Daily Totals		$1754.40		$2643.44	$54.83	$82.61
Crew A-9						
1 Asbestos Foreman	$56.80	$454.40	$88.15	$705.20	$56.36	$87.49
7 Asbestos Workers	56.30	3152.80	87.40	4894.40		
64 L.H., Daily Totals		$3607.20		$5599.60	$56.36	$87.49
Crew A-10A						
1 Asbestos Foreman	$56.80	$454.40	$88.15	$705.20	$56.47	$87.65
2 Asbestos Workers	56.30	900.80	87.40	1398.40		
24 L.H., Daily Totals		$1355.20		$2103.60	$56.47	$87.65
Crew A-10B						
1 Asbestos Foreman	$56.80	$454.40	$88.15	$705.20	$56.42	$87.59
3 Asbestos Workers	56.30	1351.20	87.40	2097.60		
32 L.H., Daily Totals		$1805.60		$2802.80	$56.42	$87.59
Crew A-10C						
3 Asbestos Workers	$56.30	$1351.20	$87.40	$2097.60	$56.30	$87.40
1 Flatbed Truck, Gas, 1.5 Ton		188.40		207.24	7.85	8.63
24 L.H., Daily Totals		$1539.60		$2304.84	$64.15	$96.03

Crews - Standard

Crew No.		Bare Costs		Incl. Subs O&P		Cost Per Labor-Hour	
Crew A-10D	Hr.	Daily	Hr.	Daily	Bare Costs	Incl. O&P
2 Asbestos Workers	$56.30	$900.80	$87.40	$1398.40	$54.33	$83.17
1 Equip. Oper. (crane)	56.10	448.80	84.60	676.80		
1 Equip. Oper. (oiler)	48.60	388.80	73.30	586.40		
1 Hydraulic Crane, 33 Ton		940.60		1034.66	29.39	32.33
32 L.H., Daily Totals		$2679.00		$3696.26	$83.72	$115.51
Crew A-11	Hr.	Daily	Hr.	Daily	Bare Costs	Incl. O&P
1 Asbestos Foreman	$56.80	$454.40	$88.15	$705.20	$56.36	$87.49
7 Asbestos Workers	56.30	3152.80	87.40	4894.40		
2 Chip. Hammers, 12 Lb., Elec.		42.00		46.20	.66	.72
64 L.H., Daily Totals		$3649.20		$5645.80	$57.02	$88.22
Crew A-12	Hr.	Daily	Hr.	Daily	Bare Costs	Incl. O&P
1 Asbestos Foreman	$56.80	$454.40	$88.15	$705.20	$56.36	$87.49
7 Asbestos Workers	56.30	3152.80	87.40	4894.40		
1 Trk-Mtd Vac, 14 CY, 1500 Gal.		522.70		574.97		
1 Flatbed Truck, 20,000 GVW		197.20		216.92	11.25	12.37
64 L.H., Daily Totals		$4327.10		$6391.49	$67.61	$99.87
Crew A-13	Hr.	Daily	Hr.	Daily	Bare Costs	Incl. O&P
1 Equip. Oper. (light)	$51.30	$410.40	$77.35	$618.80	$51.30	$77.35
1 Trk-Mtd Vac, 14 CY, 1500 Gal.		522.70		574.97		
1 Flatbed Truck, 20,000 GVW		197.20		216.92	89.99	98.99
8 L.H., Daily Totals		$1130.30		$1410.69	$141.29	$176.34
Crew B-1	Hr.	Daily	Hr.	Daily	Bare Costs	Incl. O&P
1 Labor Foreman (outside)	$41.85	$334.80	$63.75	$510.00	$40.52	$61.72
2 Laborers	39.85	637.60	60.70	971.20		
24 L.H., Daily Totals		$972.40		$1481.20	$40.52	$61.72
Crew B-1A	Hr.	Daily	Hr.	Daily	Bare Costs	Incl. O&P
1 Labor Foreman (outside)	$41.85	$334.80	$63.75	$510.00	$40.52	$61.72
2 Laborers	39.85	637.60	60.70	971.20		
2 Cutting Torches		25.20		27.72		
2 Sets of Gases		336.00		369.60	15.05	16.56
24 L.H., Daily Totals		$1333.60		$1878.52	$55.57	$78.27
Crew B-1B	Hr.	Daily	Hr.	Daily	Bare Costs	Incl. O&P
1 Labor Foreman (outside)	$41.85	$334.80	$63.75	$510.00	$44.41	$67.44
2 Laborers	39.85	637.60	60.70	971.20		
1 Equip. Oper. (crane)	56.10	448.80	84.60	676.80		
2 Cutting Torches		25.20		27.72		
2 Sets of Gases		336.00		369.60		
1 Hyd. Crane, 12 Ton		496.00		545.60	26.79	29.47
32 L.H., Daily Totals		$2278.40		$3100.92	$71.20	$96.90
Crew B-1C	Hr.	Daily	Hr.	Daily	Bare Costs	Incl. O&P
1 Labor Foreman (outside)	$41.85	$334.80	$63.75	$510.00	$40.52	$61.72
2 Laborers	39.85	637.60	60.70	971.20		
1 Telescoping Boom Lift, to 60'		454.60		500.06	18.94	20.84
24 L.H., Daily Totals		$1427.00		$1981.26	$59.46	$82.55
Crew B-1D	Hr.	Daily	Hr.	Daily	Bare Costs	Incl. O&P
2 Laborers	$39.85	$637.60	$60.70	$971.20	$39.85	$60.70
1 Small Work Boat, Gas, 50 H.P.		138.00		151.80		
1 Pressure Washer, 7 GPM		77.20		84.92	13.45	14.80
16 L.H., Daily Totals		$852.80		$1207.92	$53.30	$75.50

Crew No.		Bare Costs		Incl. Subs O&P		Cost Per Labor-Hour	
Crew B-1E	Hr.	Daily	Hr.	Daily	Bare Costs	Incl. O&P
1 Labor Foreman (outside)	$41.85	$334.80	$63.75	$510.00	$40.35	$61.46
3 Laborers	39.85	956.40	60.70	1456.80		
1 Work Boat, Diesel, 200 H.P.		1385.00		1523.50		
2 Pressure Washers, 7 GPM		154.40		169.84	48.11	52.92
32 L.H., Daily Totals		$2830.60		$3660.14	$88.46	$114.38
Crew B-1F	Hr.	Daily	Hr.	Daily	Bare Costs	Incl. O&P
2 Skilled Workers	$52.35	$837.60	$80.15	$1282.40	$48.18	$73.67
1 Laborer	39.85	318.80	60.70	485.60		
1 Small Work Boat, Gas, 50 H.P.		138.00		151.80		
1 Pressure Washer, 7 GPM		77.20		84.92	8.97	9.86
24 L.H., Daily Totals		$1371.60		$2004.72	$57.15	$83.53
Crew B-1G	Hr.	Daily	Hr.	Daily	Bare Costs	Incl. O&P
2 Laborers	$39.85	$637.60	$60.70	$971.20	$39.85	$60.70
1 Small Work Boat, Gas, 50 H.P.		138.00		151.80	8.63	9.49
16 L.H., Daily Totals		$775.60		$1123.00	$48.48	$70.19
Crew B-1H	Hr.	Daily	Hr.	Daily	Bare Costs	Incl. O&P
2 Skilled Workers	$52.35	$837.60	$80.15	$1282.40	$48.18	$73.67
1 Laborer	39.85	318.80	60.70	485.60		
1 Small Work Boat, Gas, 50 H.P.		138.00		151.80	5.75	6.33
24 L.H., Daily Totals		$1294.40		$1919.80	$53.93	$79.99
Crew B-1J	Hr.	Daily	Hr.	Daily	Bare Costs	Incl. O&P
1 Labor Foreman (inside)	$40.35	$322.80	$61.45	$491.60	$40.10	$61.08
1 Laborer	39.85	318.80	60.70	485.60		
16 L.H., Daily Totals		$641.60		$977.20	$40.10	$61.08
Crew B-1K	Hr.	Daily	Hr.	Daily	Bare Costs	Incl. O&P
1 Carpenter Foreman (inside)	$51.20	$409.60	$78.00	$624.00	$50.95	$77.60
1 Carpenter	50.70	405.60	77.20	617.60		
16 L.H., Daily Totals		$815.20		$1241.60	$50.95	$77.60
Crew B-2	Hr.	Daily	Hr.	Daily	Bare Costs	Incl. O&P
1 Labor Foreman (outside)	$41.85	$334.80	$63.75	$510.00	$40.25	$61.31
4 Laborers	39.85	1275.20	60.70	1942.40		
40 L.H., Daily Totals		$1610.00		$2452.40	$40.25	$61.31
Crew B-2A	Hr.	Daily	Hr.	Daily	Bare Costs	Incl. O&P
1 Labor Foreman (outside)	$41.85	$334.80	$63.75	$510.00	$40.52	$61.72
2 Laborers	39.85	637.60	60.70	971.20		
1 Telescoping Boom Lift, to 60'		454.60		500.06	18.94	20.84
24 L.H., Daily Totals		$1427.00		$1981.26	$59.46	$82.55
Crew B-3	Hr.	Daily	Hr.	Daily	Bare Costs	Incl. O&P
1 Labor Foreman (outside)	$41.85	$334.80	$63.75	$510.00	$44.55	$67.47
2 Laborers	39.85	637.60	60.70	971.20		
1 Equip. Oper. (medium)	53.75	430.00	81.05	648.40		
2 Truck Drivers (heavy)	46.00	736.00	69.30	1108.80		
1 Crawler Loader, 3 C.Y.		1204.00		1324.40		
2 Dump Trucks, 12 C.Y., 400 H.P.		1085.60		1194.16	47.70	52.47
48 L.H., Daily Totals		$4428.00		$5756.96	$92.25	$119.94
Crew B-3A	Hr.	Daily	Hr.	Daily	Bare Costs	Incl. O&P
4 Laborers	$39.85	$1275.20	$60.70	$1942.40	$42.63	$64.77
1 Equip. Oper. (medium)	53.75	430.00	81.05	648.40		
1 Hyd. Excavator, 1.5 C.Y.		893.60		982.96	22.34	24.57
40 L.H., Daily Totals		$2598.80		$3573.76	$64.97	$89.34

Crews - Standard

Crew No.		Bare Costs		Incl. Subs O&P		Cost Per Labor-Hour	
Crew B-3B	**Hr.**	**Daily**	**Hr.**	**Daily**	**Bare Costs**	**Incl. O&P**	
2 Laborers	$39.85	$637.60	$60.70	$971.20	$44.86	$67.94	
1 Equip. Oper. (medium)	53.75	430.00	81.05	648.40			
1 Truck Driver (heavy)	46.00	368.00	69.30	554.40			
1 Backhoe Loader, 80 H.P.		385.00		423.50			
1 Dump Truck, 12 C.Y., 400 H.P.		542.80		597.08	28.99	31.89	
32 L.H., Daily Totals		$2363.40		$3194.58	$73.86	$99.83	

Crew B-3C	**Hr.**	**Daily**	**Hr.**	**Daily**	**Bare Costs**	**Incl. O&P**
3 Laborers	$39.85	$956.40	$60.70	$1456.80	$43.33	$65.79
1 Equip. Oper. (medium)	53.75	430.00	81.05	648.40		
1 Crawler Loader, 4 C.Y.		1459.00		1604.90	45.59	50.15
32 L.H., Daily Totals		$2845.40		$3710.10	$88.92	$115.94

Crew B-4	**Hr.**	**Daily**	**Hr.**	**Daily**	**Bare Costs**	**Incl. O&P**
1 Labor Foreman (outside)	$41.85	$334.80	$63.75	$510.00	$41.21	$62.64
4 Laborers	39.85	1275.20	60.70	1942.40		
1 Truck Driver (heavy)	46.00	368.00	69.30	554.40		
1 Truck Tractor, 220 H.P.		290.00		319.00		
1 Flatbed Trailer, 40 Ton		180.00		198.00	9.79	10.77
48 L.H., Daily Totals		$2448.00		$3523.80	$51.00	$73.41

Crew B-5	**Hr.**	**Daily**	**Hr.**	**Daily**	**Bare Costs**	**Incl. O&P**
1 Labor Foreman (outside)	$41.85	$334.80	$63.75	$510.00	$44.11	$66.95
4 Laborers	39.85	1275.20	60.70	1942.40		
2 Equip. Oper. (medium)	53.75	860.00	81.05	1296.80		
1 Air Compressor, 250 cfm		167.40		184.14		
2 Breakers, Pavement, 60 lb.		21.20		23.32		
2 -50' Air Hoses, 1.5"		45.40		49.94		
1 Crawler Loader, 3 C.Y.		1204.00		1324.40	25.68	28.25
56 L.H., Daily Totals		$3908.00		$5331.00	$69.79	$95.20

Crew B-5A	**Hr.**	**Daily**	**Hr.**	**Daily**	**Bare Costs**	**Incl. O&P**
1 Labor Foreman (outside)	$41.85	$334.80	$63.75	$510.00	$44.31	$67.17
6 Laborers	39.85	1912.80	60.70	2913.60		
2 Equip. Oper. (medium)	53.75	860.00	81.05	1296.80		
1 Equip. Oper. (light)	51.30	410.40	77.35	618.80		
2 Truck Drivers (heavy)	46.00	736.00	69.30	1108.80		
1 Air Compressor, 365 cfm		211.40		232.54		
2 Breakers, Pavement, 60 lb.		21.20		23.32		
8 -50' Air Hoses, 1"		67.60		74.36		
2 Dump Trucks, 8 C.Y., 220 H.P.		677.20		744.92	10.18	11.20
96 L.H., Daily Totals		$5231.40		$7523.14	$54.49	$78.37

Crew B-5B	**Hr.**	**Daily**	**Hr.**	**Daily**	**Bare Costs**	**Incl. O&P**
1 Powderman	$52.35	$418.80	$80.15	$641.20	$49.64	$75.03
2 Equip. Oper. (medium)	53.75	860.00	81.05	1296.80		
3 Truck Drivers (heavy)	46.00	1104.00	69.30	1663.20		
1 F.E. Loader, W.M., 2.5 C.Y.		523.20		575.52		
3 Dump Trucks, 12 C.Y., 400 H.P.		1628.40		1791.24		
1 Air Compressor, 365 cfm		211.40		232.54	49.23	54.15
48 L.H., Daily Totals		$4745.80		$6200.50	$98.87	$129.18

Crew B-5C	**Hr.**	**Daily**	**Hr.**	**Daily**	**Bare Costs**	**Incl. O&P**
3 Laborers	$39.85	$956.40	$60.70	$1456.80	$46.25	$69.96
1 Equip. Oper. (medium)	53.75	430.00	81.05	648.40		
2 Truck Drivers (heavy)	46.00	736.00	69.30	1108.80		
1 Equip. Oper. (crane)	56.10	448.80	84.60	676.80		
1 Equip. Oper. (oiler)	48.60	388.80	73.30	586.40		
2 Dump Trucks, 12 C.Y., 400 H.P.		1085.60		1194.16		
1 Crawler Loader, 4 C.Y.		1459.00		1604.90		
1 S.P. Crane, 4x4, 25 Ton		668.40		735.24	50.20	55.22
64 L.H., Daily Totals		$6173.00		$8011.50	$96.45	$125.18

Crew B-5D	**Hr.**	**Daily**	**Hr.**	**Daily**	**Bare Costs**	**Incl. O&P**
1 Labor Foreman (outside)	$41.85	$334.80	$63.75	$510.00	$44.34	$67.24
4 Laborers	39.85	1275.20	60.70	1942.40		
2 Equip. Oper. (medium)	53.75	860.00	81.05	1296.80		
1 Truck Driver (heavy)	46.00	368.00	69.30	554.40		
1 Air Compressor, 250 cfm		167.40		184.14		
2 Breakers, Pavement, 60 lb.		21.20		23.32		
2 -50' Air Hoses, 1.5"		45.40		49.94		
1 Crawler Loader, 3 C.Y.		1204.00		1324.40		
1 Dump Truck, 12 C.Y., 400 H.P.		542.80		597.08	30.95	34.05
64 L.H., Daily Totals		$4818.80		$6482.48	$75.29	$101.29

Crew B-6	**Hr.**	**Daily**	**Hr.**	**Daily**	**Bare Costs**	**Incl. O&P**
2 Laborers	$39.85	$637.60	$60.70	$971.20	$43.67	$66.25
1 Equip. Oper. (light)	51.30	410.40	77.35	618.80		
1 Backhoe Loader, 48 H.P.		312.40		343.64	13.02	14.32
24 L.H., Daily Totals		$1360.40		$1933.64	$56.68	$80.57

Crew B-6A	**Hr.**	**Daily**	**Hr.**	**Daily**	**Bare Costs**	**Incl. O&P**
.5 Labor Foreman (outside)	$41.85	$167.40	$63.75	$255.00	$45.81	$69.45
1 Laborer	39.85	318.80	60.70	485.60		
1 Equip. Oper. (medium)	53.75	430.00	81.05	648.40		
1 Vacuum Truck, 5000 Gal.		358.90		394.79	17.95	19.74
20 L.H., Daily Totals		$1275.10		$1783.79	$63.76	$89.19

Crew B-6B	**Hr.**	**Daily**	**Hr.**	**Daily**	**Bare Costs**	**Incl. O&P**
2 Labor Foremen (outside)	$41.85	$669.60	$63.75	$1020.00	$40.52	$61.72
4 Laborers	39.85	1275.20	60.70	1942.40		
1 S.P. Crane, 4x4, 5 Ton		259.00		284.90		
1 Flatbed Truck, Gas, 1.5 Ton		188.40		207.24		
1 Butt Fusion Mach., 4"-12" diam.		425.70		468.27	18.19	20.01
48 L.H., Daily Totals		$2817.90		$3922.81	$58.71	$81.73

Crew B-6C	**Hr.**	**Daily**	**Hr.**	**Daily**	**Bare Costs**	**Incl. O&P**
2 Labor Foremen (outside)	$41.85	$669.60	$63.75	$1020.00	$40.52	$61.72
4 Laborers	39.85	1275.20	60.70	1942.40		
1 S.P. Crane, 4x4, 12 Ton		363.60		399.96		
1 Flatbed Truck, Gas, 3 Ton		238.00		261.80		
1 Butt Fusion Mach., 8"-24" diam.		1908.00		2098.80	52.28	57.51
48 L.H., Daily Totals		$4454.40		$5722.96	$92.80	$119.23

Crew B-7	**Hr.**	**Daily**	**Hr.**	**Daily**	**Bare Costs**	**Incl. O&P**
1 Labor Foreman (outside)	$41.85	$334.80	$63.75	$510.00	$42.50	$64.60
4 Laborers	39.85	1275.20	60.70	1942.40		
1 Equip. Oper. (medium)	53.75	430.00	81.05	648.40		
1 Brush Chipper, 12", 130 H.P.		393.00		432.30		
1 Crawler Loader, 3 C.Y.		1204.00		1324.40		
2 Chain Saws, Gas, 36" Long		92.80		102.08	35.20	38.72
48 L.H., Daily Totals		$3729.80		$4959.58	$77.70	$103.32

Crews - Standard

Crew No.	Bare Costs Hr.	Bare Costs Daily	Incl. Subs O&P Hr.	Incl. Subs O&P Daily	Cost Per Labor-Hour Bare Costs	Cost Per Labor-Hour Incl. O&P
Crew B-7A						
2 Laborers	$39.85	$637.60	$60.70	$971.20	$43.67	$66.25
1 Equip. Oper. (light)	51.30	410.40	77.35	618.80		
1 Rake w/Tractor		331.30		364.43		
2 Chain Saws, Gas, 18"		55.60		61.16	16.12	17.73
24 L.H., Daily Totals		$1434.90		$2015.59	$59.79	$83.98
Crew B-7B	Hr.	Daily	Hr.	Daily	Bare Costs	Incl. O&P
1 Labor Foreman (outside)	$41.85	$334.80	$63.75	$510.00	$43.00	$65.27
4 Laborers	39.85	1275.20	60.70	1942.40		
1 Equip. Oper. (medium)	53.75	430.00	81.05	648.40		
1 Truck Driver (heavy)	46.00	368.00	69.30	554.40		
1 Brush Chipper, 12", 130 H.P.		393.00		432.30		
1 Crawler Loader, 3 C.Y.		1204.00		1324.40		
2 Chain Saws, Gas, 36" Long		92.80		102.08		
1 Dump Truck, 8 C.Y., 220 H.P.		338.60		372.46	36.22	39.84
56 L.H., Daily Totals		$4436.40		$5886.44	$79.22	$105.11
Crew B-7C	Hr.	Daily	Hr.	Daily	Bare Costs	Incl. O&P
1 Labor Foreman (outside)	$41.85	$334.80	$63.75	$510.00	$43.00	$65.27
4 Laborers	39.85	1275.20	60.70	1942.40		
1 Equip. Oper. (medium)	53.75	430.00	81.05	648.40		
1 Truck Driver (heavy)	46.00	368.00	69.30	554.40		
1 Brush Chipper, 12", 130 H.P.		393.00		432.30		
1 Crawler Loader, 3 C.Y.		1204.00		1324.40		
2 Chain Saws, Gas, 36" Long		92.80		102.08		
1 Dump Truck, 12 C.Y., 400 H.P.		542.80		597.08	39.87	43.85
56 L.H., Daily Totals		$4640.60		$6111.06	$82.87	$109.13
Crew B-8	Hr.	Daily	Hr.	Daily	Bare Costs	Incl. O&P
1 Labor Foreman (outside)	$41.85	$334.80	$63.75	$510.00	$46.21	$69.89
2 Laborers	39.85	637.60	60.70	971.20		
2 Equip. Oper. (medium)	53.75	860.00	81.05	1296.80		
1 Equip. Oper. (oiler)	48.60	388.80	73.30	586.40		
2 Truck Drivers (heavy)	46.00	736.00	69.30	1108.80		
1 Hyd. Crane, 25 Ton		590.60		649.66		
1 Crawler Loader, 3 C.Y.		1204.00		1324.40		
2 Dump Trucks, 12 C.Y., 400 H.P.		1085.60		1194.16	45.00	49.50
64 L.H., Daily Totals		$5837.40		$7641.42	$91.21	$119.40
Crew B-9	Hr.	Daily	Hr.	Daily	Bare Costs	Incl. O&P
1 Labor Foreman (outside)	$41.85	$334.80	$63.75	$510.00	$40.25	$61.31
4 Laborers	39.85	1275.20	60.70	1942.40		
1 Air Compressor, 250 cfm		167.40		184.14		
2 Breakers, Pavement, 60 lb.		21.20		23.32		
2 -50' Air Hoses, 1.5"		45.40		49.94	5.85	6.43
40 L.H., Daily Totals		$1844.00		$2709.80	$46.10	$67.75
Crew B-9A	Hr.	Daily	Hr.	Daily	Bare Costs	Incl. O&P
2 Laborers	$39.85	$637.60	$60.70	$971.20	$41.90	$63.57
1 Truck Driver (heavy)	46.00	368.00	69.30	554.40		
1 Water Tank Trailer, 5000 Gal.		147.60		162.36		
1 Truck Tractor, 220 H.P.		290.00		319.00		
2 -50' Discharge Hoses, 3"		3.00		3.30	18.36	20.19
24 L.H., Daily Totals		$1446.20		$2010.26	$60.26	$83.76

Crew No.	Bare Costs Hr.	Bare Costs Daily	Incl. Subs O&P Hr.	Incl. Subs O&P Daily	Cost Per Labor-Hour Bare Costs	Cost Per Labor-Hour Incl. O&P
Crew B-9B						
2 Laborers	$39.85	$637.60	$60.70	$971.20	$41.90	$63.57
1 Truck Driver (heavy)	46.00	368.00	69.30	554.40		
2 -50' Discharge Hoses, 3"		3.00		3.30		
1 Water Tank Trailer, 5000 Gal.		147.60		162.36		
1 Truck Tractor, 220 H.P.		290.00		319.00		
1 Pressure Washer		63.60		69.96	21.01	23.11
24 L.H., Daily Totals		$1509.80		$2080.22	$62.91	$86.68
Crew B-9D	Hr.	Daily	Hr.	Daily	Bare Costs	Incl. O&P
1 Labor Foreman (outside)	$41.85	$334.80	$63.75	$510.00	$40.25	$61.31
4 Common Laborers	39.85	1275.20	60.70	1942.40		
1 Air Compressor, 250 cfm		167.40		184.14		
2 -50' Air Hoses, 1.5"		45.40		49.94		
2 Air Powered Tampers		56.60		62.26	6.74	7.41
40 L.H., Daily Totals		$1879.40		$2748.74	$46.98	$68.72
Crew B-10	Hr.	Daily	Hr.	Daily	Bare Costs	Incl. O&P
1 Equip. Oper. (medium)	$53.75	$430.00	$81.05	$648.40	$49.12	$74.27
.5 Laborer	39.85	159.40	60.70	242.80		
12 L.H., Daily Totals		$589.40		$891.20	$49.12	$74.27
Crew B-10A	Hr.	Daily	Hr.	Daily	Bare Costs	Incl. O&P
1 Equip. Oper. (medium)	$53.75	$430.00	$81.05	$648.40	$49.12	$74.27
.5 Laborer	39.85	159.40	60.70	242.80		
1 Roller, 2-Drum, W.B., 7.5 H.P.		179.60		197.56	14.97	16.46
12 L.H., Daily Totals		$769.00		$1088.76	$64.08	$90.73
Crew B-10B	Hr.	Daily	Hr.	Daily	Bare Costs	Incl. O&P
1 Equip. Oper. (medium)	$53.75	$430.00	$81.05	$648.40	$49.12	$74.27
.5 Laborer	39.85	159.40	60.70	242.80		
1 Dozer, 200 H.P.		1273.00		1400.30	106.08	116.69
12 L.H., Daily Totals		$1862.40		$2291.50	$155.20	$190.96
Crew B-10C	Hr.	Daily	Hr.	Daily	Bare Costs	Incl. O&P
1 Equip. Oper. (medium)	$53.75	$430.00	$81.05	$648.40	$49.12	$74.27
.5 Laborer	39.85	159.40	60.70	242.80		
1 Dozer, 200 H.P.		1273.00		1400.30		
1 Vibratory Roller, Towed, 23 Ton		423.00		465.30	141.33	155.47
12 L.H., Daily Totals		$2285.40		$2756.80	$190.45	$229.73
Crew B-10D	Hr.	Daily	Hr.	Daily	Bare Costs	Incl. O&P
1 Equip. Oper. (medium)	$53.75	$430.00	$81.05	$648.40	$49.12	$74.27
.5 Laborer	39.85	159.40	60.70	242.80		
1 Dozer, 200 H.P.		1273.00		1400.30		
1 Sheepsft. Roller, Towed		425.80		468.38	141.57	155.72
12 L.H., Daily Totals		$2288.20		$2759.88	$190.68	$229.99
Crew B-10E	Hr.	Daily	Hr.	Daily	Bare Costs	Incl. O&P
1 Equip. Oper. (medium)	$53.75	$430.00	$81.05	$648.40	$49.12	$74.27
.5 Laborer	39.85	159.40	60.70	242.80		
1 Tandem Roller, 5 Ton		151.20		166.32	12.60	13.86
12 L.H., Daily Totals		$740.60		$1057.52	$61.72	$88.13
Crew B-10F	Hr.	Daily	Hr.	Daily	Bare Costs	Incl. O&P
1 Equip. Oper. (medium)	$53.75	$430.00	$81.05	$648.40	$49.12	$74.27
.5 Laborer	39.85	159.40	60.70	242.80		
1 Tandem Roller, 10 Ton		231.40		254.54	19.28	21.21
12 L.H., Daily Totals		$820.80		$1145.74	$68.40	$95.48

Crews - Standard

Crew No.	Bare Costs		Incl. Subs O&P		Cost Per Labor-Hour	
Crew B-10G	Hr.	Daily	Hr.	Daily	Bare Costs	Incl. O&P
1 Equip. Oper. (medium)	$53.75	$430.00	$81.05	$648.40	$49.12	$74.27
.5 Laborer	39.85	159.40	60.70	242.80		
1 Sheepsfoot Roller, 240 H.P.		1316.00		1447.60	109.67	120.63
12 L.H., Daily Totals		$1905.40		$2338.80	$158.78	$194.90
Crew B-10H	Hr.	Daily	Hr.	Daily	Bare Costs	Incl. O&P
1 Equip. Oper. (medium)	$53.75	$430.00	$81.05	$648.40	$49.12	$74.27
.5 Laborer	39.85	159.40	60.70	242.80		
1 Diaphragm Water Pump, 2"		73.00		80.30		
1 -20' Suction Hose, 2"		1.95		2.15		
2 -50' Discharge Hoses, 2"		1.80		1.98	6.40	7.04
12 L.H., Daily Totals		$666.15		$975.63	$55.51	$81.30
Crew B-10I	Hr.	Daily	Hr.	Daily	Bare Costs	Incl. O&P
1 Equip. Oper. (medium)	$53.75	$430.00	$81.05	$648.40	$49.12	$74.27
.5 Laborer	39.85	159.40	60.70	242.80		
1 Diaphragm Water Pump, 4"		114.80		126.28		
1 -20' Suction Hose, 4"		3.25		3.58		
2 -50' Discharge Hoses, 4"		4.70		5.17	10.23	11.25
12 L.H., Daily Totals		$712.15		$1026.22	$59.35	$85.52
Crew B-10J	Hr.	Daily	Hr.	Daily	Bare Costs	Incl. O&P
1 Equip. Oper. (medium)	$53.75	$430.00	$81.05	$648.40	$49.12	$74.27
.5 Laborer	39.85	159.40	60.70	242.80		
1 Centrifugal Water Pump, 3"		79.20		87.12		
1 -20' Suction Hose, 3"		2.85		3.13		
2 -50' Discharge Hoses, 3"		3.00		3.30	7.09	7.80
12 L.H., Daily Totals		$674.45		$984.76	$56.20	$82.06
Crew B-10K	Hr.	Daily	Hr.	Daily	Bare Costs	Incl. O&P
1 Equip. Oper. (medium)	$53.75	$430.00	$81.05	$648.40	$49.12	$74.27
.5 Laborer	39.85	159.40	60.70	242.80		
1 Centr. Water Pump, 6"		296.40		326.04		
1 -20' Suction Hose, 6"		11.50		12.65		
2 -50' Discharge Hoses, 6"		12.20		13.42	26.68	29.34
12 L.H., Daily Totals		$909.50		$1243.31	$75.79	$103.61
Crew B-10L	Hr.	Daily	Hr.	Daily	Bare Costs	Incl. O&P
1 Equip. Oper. (medium)	$53.75	$430.00	$81.05	$648.40	$49.12	$74.27
.5 Laborer	39.85	159.40	60.70	242.80		
1 Dozer, 80 H.P.		464.40		510.84	38.70	42.57
12 L.H., Daily Totals		$1053.80		$1402.04	$87.82	$116.84
Crew B-10M	Hr.	Daily	Hr.	Daily	Bare Costs	Incl. O&P
1 Equip. Oper. (medium)	$53.75	$430.00	$81.05	$648.40	$49.12	$74.27
.5 Laborer	39.85	159.40	60.70	242.80		
1 Dozer, 300 H.P.		1829.00		2011.90	152.42	167.66
12 L.H., Daily Totals		$2418.40		$2903.10	$201.53	$241.93
Crew B-10N	Hr.	Daily	Hr.	Daily	Bare Costs	Incl. O&P
1 Equip. Oper. (medium)	$53.75	$430.00	$81.05	$648.40	$49.12	$74.27
.5 Laborer	39.85	159.40	60.70	242.80		
1 F.E. Loader, T.M., 1.5 C.Y.		579.80		637.78	48.32	53.15
12 L.H., Daily Totals		$1169.20		$1528.98	$97.43	$127.42
Crew B-10O	Hr.	Daily	Hr.	Daily	Bare Costs	Incl. O&P
1 Equip. Oper. (medium)	$53.75	$430.00	$81.05	$648.40	$49.12	$74.27
.5 Laborer	39.85	159.40	60.70	242.80		
1 F.E. Loader, T.M., 2.25 C.Y.		979.00		1076.90	81.58	89.74
12 L.H., Daily Totals		$1568.40		$1968.10	$130.70	$164.01

Crew No.	Bare Costs		Incl. Subs O&P		Cost Per Labor-Hour	
Crew B-10P	Hr.	Daily	Hr.	Daily	Bare Costs	Incl. O&P
1 Equip. Oper. (medium)	$53.75	$430.00	$81.05	$648.40	$49.12	$74.27
.5 Laborer	39.85	159.40	60.70	242.80		
1 Crawler Loader, 3 C.Y.		1204.00		1324.40	100.33	110.37
12 L.H., Daily Totals		$1793.40		$2215.60	$149.45	$184.63
Crew B-10Q	Hr.	Daily	Hr.	Daily	Bare Costs	Incl. O&P
1 Equip. Oper. (medium)	$53.75	$430.00	$81.05	$648.40	$49.12	$74.27
.5 Laborer	39.85	159.40	60.70	242.80		
1 Crawler Loader, 4 C.Y.		1459.00		1604.90	121.58	133.74
12 L.H., Daily Totals		$2048.40		$2496.10	$170.70	$208.01
Crew B-10R	Hr.	Daily	Hr.	Daily	Bare Costs	Incl. O&P
1 Equip. Oper. (medium)	$53.75	$430.00	$81.05	$648.40	$49.12	$74.27
.5 Laborer	39.85	159.40	60.70	242.80		
1 F.E. Loader, W.M., 1 C.Y.		290.80		319.88	24.23	26.66
12 L.H., Daily Totals		$880.20		$1211.08	$73.35	$100.92
Crew B-10S	Hr.	Daily	Hr.	Daily	Bare Costs	Incl. O&P
1 Equip. Oper. (medium)	$53.75	$430.00	$81.05	$648.40	$49.12	$74.27
.5 Laborer	39.85	159.40	60.70	242.80		
1 F.E. Loader, W.M., 1.5 C.Y.		342.80		377.08	28.57	31.42
12 L.H., Daily Totals		$932.20		$1268.28	$77.68	$105.69
Crew B-10T	Hr.	Daily	Hr.	Daily	Bare Costs	Incl. O&P
1 Equip. Oper. (medium)	$53.75	$430.00	$81.05	$648.40	$49.12	$74.27
.5 Laborer	39.85	159.40	60.70	242.80		
1 F.E. Loader, W.M., 2.5 C.Y.		523.20		575.52	43.60	47.96
12 L.H., Daily Totals		$1112.60		$1466.72	$92.72	$122.23
Crew B-10U	Hr.	Daily	Hr.	Daily	Bare Costs	Incl. O&P
1 Equip. Oper. (medium)	$53.75	$430.00	$81.05	$648.40	$49.12	$74.27
.5 Laborer	39.85	159.40	60.70	242.80		
1 F.E. Loader, W.M., 5.5 C.Y.		982.20		1080.42	81.85	90.03
12 L.H., Daily Totals		$1571.60		$1971.62	$130.97	$164.30
Crew B-10V	Hr.	Daily	Hr.	Daily	Bare Costs	Incl. O&P
1 Equip. Oper. (medium)	$53.75	$430.00	$81.05	$648.40	$49.12	$74.27
.5 Laborer	39.85	159.40	60.70	242.80		
1 Dozer, 700 H.P.		4999.00		5498.90	416.58	458.24
12 L.H., Daily Totals		$5588.40		$6390.10	$465.70	$532.51
Crew B-10W	Hr.	Daily	Hr.	Daily	Bare Costs	Incl. O&P
1 Equip. Oper. (medium)	$53.75	$430.00	$81.05	$648.40	$49.12	$74.27
.5 Laborer	39.85	159.40	60.70	242.80		
1 Dozer, 105 H.P.		608.00		668.80	50.67	55.73
12 L.H., Daily Totals		$1197.40		$1560.00	$99.78	$130.00
Crew B-10X	Hr.	Daily	Hr.	Daily	Bare Costs	Incl. O&P
1 Equip. Oper. (medium)	$53.75	$430.00	$81.05	$648.40	$49.12	$74.27
.5 Laborer	39.85	159.40	60.70	242.80		
1 Dozer, 410 H.P.		2291.00		2520.10	190.92	210.01
12 L.H., Daily Totals		$2880.40		$3411.30	$240.03	$284.27
Crew B-10Y	Hr.	Daily	Hr.	Daily	Bare Costs	Incl. O&P
1 Equip. Oper. (medium)	$53.75	$430.00	$81.05	$648.40	$49.12	$74.27
.5 Laborer	39.85	159.40	60.70	242.80		
1 Vibr. Roller, Towed, 12 Ton		576.40		634.04	48.03	52.84
12 L.H., Daily Totals		$1165.80		$1525.24	$97.15	$127.10

Crews - Standard

Crew No.		Bare Costs		Incl. Subs O&P		Cost Per Labor-Hour	
Crew B-11A	Hr.	Daily	Hr.	Daily	Bare Costs	Incl. O&P
1 Equipment Oper. (med.)	$53.75	$430.00	$81.05	$648.40	$46.80	$70.88
1 Laborer	39.85	318.80	60.70	485.60		
1 Dozer, 200 H.P.		1273.00		1400.30	79.56	87.52
16 L.H., Daily Totals		$2021.80		$2534.30	$126.36	$158.39
Crew B-11B	Hr.	Daily	Hr.	Daily	Bare Costs	Incl. O&P
1 Equipment Oper. (light)	$51.30	$410.40	$77.35	$618.80	$45.58	$69.03
1 Laborer	39.85	318.80	60.70	485.60		
1 Air Powered Tamper		28.30		31.13		
1 Air Compressor, 365 cfm		211.40		232.54		
2 -50' Air Hoses, 1.5"		45.40		49.94	17.82	19.60
16 L.H., Daily Totals		$1014.30		$1418.01	$63.39	$88.63
Crew B-11C	Hr.	Daily	Hr.	Daily	Bare Costs	Incl. O&P
1 Equipment Oper. (med.)	$53.75	$430.00	$81.05	$648.40	$46.80	$70.88
1 Laborer	39.85	318.80	60.70	485.60		
1 Backhoe Loader, 48 H.P.		312.40		343.64	19.52	21.48
16 L.H., Daily Totals		$1061.20		$1477.64	$66.33	$92.35
Crew B-11J	Hr.	Daily	Hr.	Daily	Bare Costs	Incl. O&P
1 Equipment Oper. (med.)	$53.75	$430.00	$81.05	$648.40	$46.80	$70.88
1 Laborer	39.85	318.80	60.70	485.60		
1 Grader, 30,000 Lbs.		643.80		708.18		
1 Ripper, Beam & 1 Shank		87.80		96.58	45.73	50.30
16 L.H., Daily Totals		$1480.40		$1938.76	$92.53	$121.17
Crew B-11K	Hr.	Daily	Hr.	Daily	Bare Costs	Incl. O&P
1 Equipment Oper. (med.)	$53.75	$430.00	$81.05	$648.40	$46.80	$70.88
1 Laborer	39.85	318.80	60.70	485.60		
1 Trencher, Chain Type, 8' D		2048.00		2252.80	128.00	140.80
16 L.H., Daily Totals		$2796.80		$3386.80	$174.80	$211.68
Crew B-11L	Hr.	Daily	Hr.	Daily	Bare Costs	Incl. O&P
1 Equipment Oper. (med.)	$53.75	$430.00	$81.05	$648.40	$46.80	$70.88
1 Laborer	39.85	318.80	60.70	485.60		
1 Grader, 30,000 Lbs.		643.80		708.18	40.24	44.26
16 L.H., Daily Totals		$1392.60		$1842.18	$87.04	$115.14
Crew B-11M	Hr.	Daily	Hr.	Daily	Bare Costs	Incl. O&P
1 Equipment Oper. (med.)	$53.75	$430.00	$81.05	$648.40	$46.80	$70.88
1 Laborer	39.85	318.80	60.70	485.60		
1 Backhoe Loader, 80 H.P.		385.00		423.50	24.06	26.47
16 L.H., Daily Totals		$1133.80		$1557.50	$70.86	$97.34
Crew B-11N	Hr.	Daily	Hr.	Daily	Bare Costs	Incl. O&P
1 Labor Foreman (outside)	$41.85	$334.80	$63.75	$510.00	$47.26	$71.29
2 Equipment Operators (med.)	53.75	860.00	81.05	1296.80		
6 Truck Drivers (heavy)	46.00	2208.00	69.30	3326.40		
1 F.E. Loader, W.M., 5.5 C.Y.		982.20		1080.42		
1 Dozer, 410 H.P.		2291.00		2520.10		
6 Dump Trucks, Off Hwy., 50 Ton		9972.00		10969.20	183.96	202.36
72 L.H., Daily Totals		$16648.00		$19702.92	$231.22	$273.65
Crew B-11Q	Hr.	Daily	Hr.	Daily	Bare Costs	Incl. O&P
1 Equipment Operator (med.)	$53.75	$430.00	$81.05	$648.40	$49.12	$74.27
.5 Laborer	39.85	159.40	60.70	242.80		
1 Dozer, 140 H.P.		845.60		930.16	70.47	77.51
12 L.H., Daily Totals		$1435.00		$1821.36	$119.58	$151.78

Crew No.		Bare Costs		Incl. Subs O&P		Cost Per Labor-Hour	
Crew B-11R	Hr.	Daily	Hr.	Daily	Bare Costs	Incl. O&P
1 Equipment Operator (med.)	$53.75	$430.00	$81.05	$648.40	$49.12	$74.27
.5 Laborer	39.85	159.40	60.70	242.80		
1 Dozer, 200 H.P.		1273.00		1400.30	106.08	116.69
12 L.H., Daily Totals		$1862.40		$2291.50	$155.20	$190.96
Crew B-11S	Hr.	Daily	Hr.	Daily	Bare Costs	Incl. O&P
1 Equipment Operator (med.)	$53.75	$430.00	$81.05	$648.40	$49.12	$74.27
.5 Laborer	39.85	159.40	60.70	242.80		
1 Dozer, 300 H.P.		1829.00		2011.90		
1 Ripper, Beam & 1 Shank		87.80		96.58	159.73	175.71
12 L.H., Daily Totals		$2506.20		$2999.68	$208.85	$249.97
Crew B-11T	Hr.	Daily	Hr.	Daily	Bare Costs	Incl. O&P
1 Equipment Operator (med.)	$53.75	$430.00	$81.05	$648.40	$49.12	$74.27
.5 Laborer	39.85	159.40	60.70	242.80		
1 Dozer, 410 H.P.		2291.00		2520.10		
1 Ripper, Beam & 2 Shanks		132.60		145.86	201.97	222.16
12 L.H., Daily Totals		$3013.00		$3557.16	$251.08	$296.43
Crew B-11U	Hr.	Daily	Hr.	Daily	Bare Costs	Incl. O&P
1 Equipment Operator (med.)	$53.75	$430.00	$81.05	$648.40	$49.12	$74.27
.5 Laborer	39.85	159.40	60.70	242.80		
1 Dozer, 520 H.P.		2818.00		3099.80	234.83	258.32
12 L.H., Daily Totals		$3407.40		$3991.00	$283.95	$332.58
Crew B-11V	Hr.	Daily	Hr.	Daily	Bare Costs	Incl. O&P
3 Laborers	$39.85	$956.40	$60.70	$1456.80	$39.85	$60.70
1 Roller, 2-Drum, W.B., 7.5 H.P.		179.60		197.56	7.48	8.23
24 L.H., Daily Totals		$1136.00		$1654.36	$47.33	$68.93
Crew B-11W	Hr.	Daily	Hr.	Daily	Bare Costs	Incl. O&P
1 Equipment Operator (med.)	$53.75	$430.00	$81.05	$648.40	$46.13	$69.56
1 Common Laborer	39.85	318.80	60.70	485.60		
10 Truck Drivers (heavy)	46.00	3680.00	69.30	5544.00		
1 Dozer, 200 H.P.		1273.00		1400.30		
1 Vibratory Roller, Towed, 23 Ton		423.00		465.30		
10 Dump Trucks, 8 C.Y., 220 H.P.		3386.00		3724.60	52.94	58.23
96 L.H., Daily Totals		$9510.80		$12268.20	$99.07	$127.79
Crew B-11Y	Hr.	Daily	Hr.	Daily	Bare Costs	Incl. O&P
1 Labor Foreman (outside)	$41.85	$334.80	$63.75	$510.00	$44.71	$67.82
5 Common Laborers	39.85	1594.00	60.70	2428.00		
3 Equipment Operators (med.)	53.75	1290.00	81.05	1945.20		
1 Dozer, 80 H.P.		464.40		510.84		
2 Rollers, 2-Drums, W.B., 7.5 H.P.		359.20		395.12		
4 Vibrating Plates, Gas, 21"		162.40		178.64	13.69	15.06
72 L.H., Daily Totals		$4204.80		$5967.80	$58.40	$82.89
Crew B-12A	Hr.	Daily	Hr.	Daily	Bare Costs	Incl. O&P
1 Equip. Oper. (crane)	$56.10	$448.80	$84.60	$676.80	$47.98	$72.65
1 Laborer	39.85	318.80	60.70	485.60		
1 Hyd. Excavator, 1 C.Y.		742.20		816.42	46.39	51.03
16 L.H., Daily Totals		$1509.80		$1978.82	$94.36	$123.68
Crew B-12B	Hr.	Daily	Hr.	Daily	Bare Costs	Incl. O&P
1 Equip. Oper. (crane)	$56.10	$448.80	$84.60	$676.80	$47.98	$72.65
1 Laborer	39.85	318.80	60.70	485.60		
1 Hyd. Excavator, 1.5 C.Y.		893.60		982.96	55.85	61.44
16 L.H., Daily Totals		$1661.20		$2145.36	$103.83	$134.09

Crews - Standard

Crew No.	Bare Costs Hr.	Bare Costs Daily	Incl. Subs O&P Hr.	Incl. Subs O&P Daily	Cost Per Labor-Hour Bare Costs	Cost Per Labor-Hour Incl. O&P
Crew B-12C					Bare Costs	Incl. O&P
1 Equip. Oper. (crane)	$56.10	$448.80	$84.60	$676.80	$47.98	$72.65
1 Laborer	39.85	318.80	60.70	485.60		
1 Hyd. Excavator, 2 C.Y.		1052.00		1157.20	65.75	72.33
16 L.H., Daily Totals		$1819.60		$2319.60	$113.72	$144.97
Crew B-12D					Bare Costs	Incl. O&P
1 Equip. Oper. (crane)	$56.10	$448.80	$84.60	$676.80	$47.98	$72.65
1 Laborer	39.85	318.80	60.70	485.60		
1 Hyd. Excavator, 3.5 C.Y.		2195.00		2414.50	137.19	150.91
16 L.H., Daily Totals		$2962.60		$3576.90	$185.16	$223.56
Crew B-12E					Bare Costs	Incl. O&P
1 Equip. Oper. (crane)	$56.10	$448.80	$84.60	$676.80	$47.98	$72.65
1 Laborer	39.85	318.80	60.70	485.60		
1 Hyd. Excavator, .5 C.Y.		435.40		478.94	27.21	29.93
16 L.H., Daily Totals		$1203.00		$1641.34	$75.19	$102.58
Crew B-12F					Bare Costs	Incl. O&P
1 Equip. Oper. (crane)	$56.10	$448.80	$84.60	$676.80	$47.98	$72.65
1 Laborer	39.85	318.80	60.70	485.60		
1 Hyd. Excavator, .75 C.Y.		669.60		736.56	41.85	46.03
16 L.H., Daily Totals		$1437.20		$1898.96	$89.83	$118.69
Crew B-12G					Bare Costs	Incl. O&P
1 Equip. Oper. (crane)	$56.10	$448.80	$84.60	$676.80	$47.98	$72.65
1 Laborer	39.85	318.80	60.70	485.60		
1 Crawler Crane, 15 Ton		828.80		911.68		
1 Clamshell Bucket, .5 C.Y.		41.00		45.10	54.36	59.80
16 L.H., Daily Totals		$1637.40		$2119.18	$102.34	$132.45
Crew B-12H					Bare Costs	Incl. O&P
1 Equip. Oper. (crane)	$56.10	$448.80	$84.60	$676.80	$47.98	$72.65
1 Laborer	39.85	318.80	60.70	485.60		
1 Crawler Crane, 25 Ton		1348.00		1482.80		
1 Clamshell Bucket, 1 C.Y.		50.60		55.66	87.41	96.15
16 L.H., Daily Totals		$2166.20		$2700.86	$135.39	$168.80
Crew B-12I					Bare Costs	Incl. O&P
1 Equip. Oper. (crane)	$56.10	$448.80	$84.60	$676.80	$47.98	$72.65
1 Laborer	39.85	318.80	60.70	485.60		
1 Crawler Crane, 20 Ton		1060.00		1166.00		
1 Dragline Bucket, .75 C.Y.		21.80		23.98	67.61	74.37
16 L.H., Daily Totals		$1849.40		$2352.38	$115.59	$147.02
Crew B-12J					Bare Costs	Incl. O&P
1 Equip. Oper. (crane)	$56.10	$448.80	$84.60	$676.80	$47.98	$72.65
1 Laborer	39.85	318.80	60.70	485.60		
1 Gradall, 5/8 C.Y.		869.60		956.56	54.35	59.78
16 L.H., Daily Totals		$1637.20		$2118.96	$102.33	$132.44
Crew B-12K					Bare Costs	Incl. O&P
1 Equip. Oper. (crane)	$56.10	$448.80	$84.60	$676.80	$47.98	$72.65
1 Laborer	39.85	318.80	60.70	485.60		
1 Gradall, 3 Ton, 1 C.Y.		1243.00		1367.30	77.69	85.46
16 L.H., Daily Totals		$2010.60		$2529.70	$125.66	$158.11

Crew No.	Bare Costs Hr.	Bare Costs Daily	Incl. Subs O&P Hr.	Incl. Subs O&P Daily	Cost Per Labor-Hour Bare Costs	Cost Per Labor-Hour Incl. O&P
Crew B-12L					Bare Costs	Incl. O&P
1 Equip. Oper. (crane)	$56.10	$448.80	$84.60	$676.80	$47.98	$72.65
1 Laborer	39.85	318.80	60.70	485.60		
1 Crawler Crane, 15 Ton		828.80		911.68		
1 F.E. Attachment, .5 C.Y.		64.60		71.06	55.84	61.42
16 L.H., Daily Totals		$1661.00		$2145.14	$103.81	$134.07
Crew B-12M					Bare Costs	Incl. O&P
1 Equip. Oper. (crane)	$56.10	$448.80	$84.60	$676.80	$47.98	$72.65
1 Laborer	39.85	318.80	60.70	485.60		
1 Crawler Crane, 20 Ton		1060.00		1166.00		
1 F.E. Attachment, .75 C.Y.		69.00		75.90	70.56	77.62
16 L.H., Daily Totals		$1896.60		$2404.30	$118.54	$150.27
Crew B-12N					Bare Costs	Incl. O&P
1 Equip. Oper. (crane)	$56.10	$448.80	$84.60	$676.80	$47.98	$72.65
1 Laborer	39.85	318.80	60.70	485.60		
1 Crawler Crane, 25 Ton		1348.00		1482.80		
1 F.E. Attachment, 1 C.Y.		75.80		83.38	88.99	97.89
16 L.H., Daily Totals		$2191.40		$2728.58	$136.96	$170.54
Crew B-12O					Bare Costs	Incl. O&P
1 Equip. Oper. (crane)	$56.10	$448.80	$84.60	$676.80	$47.98	$72.65
1 Laborer	39.85	318.80	60.70	485.60		
1 Crawler Crane, 40 Ton		1370.00		1507.00		
1 F.E. Attachment, 1.5 C.Y.		85.00		93.50	90.94	100.03
16 L.H., Daily Totals		$2222.60		$2762.90	$138.91	$172.68
Crew B-12P					Bare Costs	Incl. O&P
1 Equip. Oper. (crane)	$56.10	$448.80	$84.60	$676.80	$47.98	$72.65
1 Laborer	39.85	318.80	60.70	485.60		
1 Crawler Crane, 40 Ton		1370.00		1507.00		
1 Dragline Bucket, 1.5 C.Y.		35.40		38.94	87.84	96.62
16 L.H., Daily Totals		$2173.00		$2708.34	$135.81	$169.27
Crew B-12Q					Bare Costs	Incl. O&P
1 Equip. Oper. (crane)	$56.10	$448.80	$84.60	$676.80	$47.98	$72.65
1 Laborer	39.85	318.80	60.70	485.60		
1 Hyd. Excavator, 5/8 C.Y.		576.80		634.48	36.05	39.66
16 L.H., Daily Totals		$1344.40		$1796.88	$84.03	$112.31
Crew B-12S					Bare Costs	Incl. O&P
1 Equip. Oper. (crane)	$56.10	$448.80	$84.60	$676.80	$47.98	$72.65
1 Laborer	39.85	318.80	60.70	485.60		
1 Hyd. Excavator, 2.5 C.Y.		1411.00		1552.10	88.19	97.01
16 L.H., Daily Totals		$2178.60		$2714.50	$136.16	$169.66
Crew B-12T					Bare Costs	Incl. O&P
1 Equip. Oper. (crane)	$56.10	$448.80	$84.60	$676.80	$47.98	$72.65
1 Laborer	39.85	318.80	60.70	485.60		
1 Crawler Crane, 75 Ton		1708.00		1878.80		
1 F.E. Attachment, 3 C.Y.		108.80		119.68	113.55	124.91
16 L.H., Daily Totals		$2584.40		$3160.88	$161.53	$197.56
Crew B-12V					Bare Costs	Incl. O&P
1 Equip. Oper. (crane)	$56.10	$448.80	$84.60	$676.80	$47.98	$72.65
1 Laborer	39.85	318.80	60.70	485.60		
1 Crawler Crane, 75 Ton		1708.00		1878.80		
1 Dragline Bucket, 3 C.Y.		55.80		61.38	110.24	121.26
16 L.H., Daily Totals		$2531.40		$3102.58	$158.21	$193.91

Crews - Standard

Crew No.		Bare Costs		Incl. Subs O&P		Cost Per Labor-Hour	
Crew B-12Y	**Hr.**	**Daily**	**Hr.**	**Daily**	**Bare Costs**	**Incl. O&P**	
1 Equip. Oper. (crane)	$56.10	$448.80	$84.60	$676.80	$45.27	$68.67	
2 Laborers	39.85	637.60	60.70	971.20			
1 Hyd. Excavator, 3.5 C.Y.		2195.00		2414.50	91.46	100.60	
24 L.H., Daily Totals		$3281.40		$4062.50	$136.72	$169.27	
Crew B-12Z	**Hr.**	**Daily**	**Hr.**	**Daily**	**Bare Costs**	**Incl. O&P**	
1 Equip. Oper. (crane)	$56.10	$448.80	$84.60	$676.80	$45.27	$68.67	
2 Laborers	39.85	637.60	60.70	971.20			
1 Hyd. Excavator, 2.5 C.Y.		1411.00		1552.10	58.79	64.67	
24 L.H., Daily Totals		$2497.40		$3200.10	$104.06	$133.34	
Crew B-13	**Hr.**	**Daily**	**Hr.**	**Daily**	**Bare Costs**	**Incl. O&P**	
1 Labor Foreman (outside)	$41.85	$334.80	$63.75	$510.00	$43.71	$66.35	
4 Laborers	39.85	1275.20	60.70	1942.40			
1 Equip. Oper. (crane)	56.10	448.80	84.60	676.80			
1 Equip. Oper. (oiler)	48.60	388.80	73.30	586.40			
1 Hyd. Crane, 25 Ton		590.60		649.66	10.55	11.60	
56 L.H., Daily Totals		$3038.20		$4365.26	$54.25	$77.95	
Crew B-13A	**Hr.**	**Daily**	**Hr.**	**Daily**	**Bare Costs**	**Incl. O&P**	
1 Labor Foreman (outside)	$41.85	$334.80	$63.75	$510.00	$45.86	$69.41	
2 Laborers	39.85	637.60	60.70	971.20			
2 Equipment Operators (med.)	53.75	860.00	81.05	1296.80			
2 Truck Drivers (heavy)	46.00	736.00	69.30	1108.80			
1 Crawler Crane, 75 Ton		1708.00		1878.80			
1 Crawler Loader, 4 C.Y.		1459.00		1604.90			
2 Dump Trucks, 8 C.Y., 220 H.P.		677.20		744.92	68.65	75.51	
56 L.H., Daily Totals		$6412.60		$8115.42	$114.51	$144.92	
Crew B-13B	**Hr.**	**Daily**	**Hr.**	**Daily**	**Bare Costs**	**Incl. O&P**	
1 Labor Foreman (outside)	$41.85	$334.80	$63.75	$510.00	$43.71	$66.35	
4 Laborers	39.85	1275.20	60.70	1942.40			
1 Equip. Oper. (crane)	56.10	448.80	84.60	676.80			
1 Equip. Oper. (oiler)	48.60	388.80	73.30	586.40			
1 Hyd. Crane, 55 Ton		993.80		1093.18	17.75	19.52	
56 L.H., Daily Totals		$3441.40		$4808.78	$61.45	$85.87	
Crew B-13C	**Hr.**	**Daily**	**Hr.**	**Daily**	**Bare Costs**	**Incl. O&P**	
1 Labor Foreman (outside)	$41.85	$334.80	$63.75	$510.00	$43.71	$66.35	
4 Laborers	39.85	1275.20	60.70	1942.40			
1 Equip. Oper. (crane)	56.10	448.80	84.60	676.80			
1 Equip. Oper. (oiler)	48.60	388.80	73.30	586.40			
1 Crawler Crane, 100 Ton		1872.00		2059.20	33.43	36.77	
56 L.H., Daily Totals		$4319.60		$5774.80	$77.14	$103.12	
Crew B-13D	**Hr.**	**Daily**	**Hr.**	**Daily**	**Bare Costs**	**Incl. O&P**	
1 Laborer	$39.85	$318.80	$60.70	$485.60	$47.98	$72.65	
1 Equip. Oper. (crane)	56.10	448.80	84.60	676.80			
1 Hyd. Excavator, 1 C.Y.		742.20		816.42			
1 Trench Box		81.00		89.10	51.45	56.59	
16 L.H., Daily Totals		$1590.80		$2067.92	$99.42	$129.25	
Crew B-13E	**Hr.**	**Daily**	**Hr.**	**Daily**	**Bare Costs**	**Incl. O&P**	
1 Laborer	$39.85	$318.80	$60.70	$485.60	$47.98	$72.65	
1 Equip. Oper. (crane)	56.10	448.80	84.60	676.80			
1 Hyd. Excavator, 1.5 C.Y.		893.60		982.96			
1 Trench Box		81.00		89.10	60.91	67.00	
16 L.H., Daily Totals		$1742.20		$2234.46	$108.89	$139.65	

Crew No.		Bare Costs		Incl. Subs O&P		Cost Per Labor-Hour	
Crew B-13F	**Hr.**	**Daily**	**Hr.**	**Daily**	**Bare Costs**	**Incl. O&P**	
1 Laborer	$39.85	$318.80	$60.70	$485.60	$47.98	$72.65	
1 Equip. Oper. (crane)	56.10	448.80	84.60	676.80			
1 Hyd. Excavator, 3.5 C.Y.		2195.00		2414.50			
1 Trench Box		81.00		89.10	142.25	156.47	
16 L.H., Daily Totals		$3043.60		$3666.00	$190.22	$229.13	
Crew B-13G	**Hr.**	**Daily**	**Hr.**	**Daily**	**Bare Costs**	**Incl. O&P**	
1 Laborer	$39.85	$318.80	$60.70	$485.60	$47.98	$72.65	
1 Equip. Oper. (crane)	56.10	448.80	84.60	676.80			
1 Hyd. Excavator, .75 C.Y.		669.60		736.56			
1 Trench Box		81.00		89.10	46.91	51.60	
16 L.H., Daily Totals		$1518.20		$1988.06	$94.89	$124.25	
Crew B-13H	**Hr.**	**Daily**	**Hr.**	**Daily**	**Bare Costs**	**Incl. O&P**	
1 Laborer	$39.85	$318.80	$60.70	$485.60	$47.98	$72.65	
1 Equip. Oper. (crane)	56.10	448.80	84.60	676.80			
1 Gradall, 5/8 C.Y.		869.60		956.56			
1 Trench Box		81.00		89.10	59.41	65.35	
16 L.H., Daily Totals		$1718.20		$2208.06	$107.39	$138.00	
Crew B-13I	**Hr.**	**Daily**	**Hr.**	**Daily**	**Bare Costs**	**Incl. O&P**	
1 Laborer	$39.85	$318.80	$60.70	$485.60	$47.98	$72.65	
1 Equip. Oper. (crane)	56.10	448.80	84.60	676.80			
1 Gradall, 3 Ton, 1 C.Y.		1243.00		1367.30			
1 Trench Box		81.00		89.10	82.75	91.03	
16 L.H., Daily Totals		$2091.60		$2618.80	$130.72	$163.68	
Crew B-13J	**Hr.**	**Daily**	**Hr.**	**Daily**	**Bare Costs**	**Incl. O&P**	
1 Laborer	$39.85	$318.80	$60.70	$485.60	$47.98	$72.65	
1 Equip. Oper. (crane)	56.10	448.80	84.60	676.80			
1 Hyd. Excavator, 2.5 C.Y.		1411.00		1552.10			
1 Trench Box		81.00		89.10	93.25	102.58	
16 L.H., Daily Totals		$2259.60		$2803.60	$141.22	$175.22	
Crew B-13K	**Hr.**	**Daily**	**Hr.**	**Daily**	**Bare Costs**	**Incl. O&P**	
2 Equip. Opers. (crane)	$56.10	$897.60	$84.60	$1353.60	$56.10	$84.60	
1 Hyd. Excavator, .75 C.Y.		669.60		736.56			
1 Hyd. Hammer, 4000 ft-lb		324.60		357.06			
1 Hyd. Excavator, .75 C.Y.		669.60		736.56	103.99	114.39	
16 L.H., Daily Totals		$2561.40		$3183.78	$160.09	$198.99	
Crew B-13L	**Hr.**	**Daily**	**Hr.**	**Daily**	**Bare Costs**	**Incl. O&P**	
2 Equip. Opers. (crane)	$56.10	$897.60	$84.60	$1353.60	$56.10	$84.60	
1 Hyd. Excavator, 1.5 C.Y.		893.60		982.96			
1 Hyd. Hammer, 5000 ft-lb		394.00		433.40			
1 Hyd. Excavator, .75 C.Y.		669.60		736.56	122.33	134.56	
16 L.H., Daily Totals		$2854.80		$3506.52	$178.43	$219.16	
Crew B-13M	**Hr.**	**Daily**	**Hr.**	**Daily**	**Bare Costs**	**Incl. O&P**	
2 Equip. Opers. (crane)	$56.10	$897.60	$84.60	$1353.60	$56.10	$84.60	
1 Hyd. Excavator, 2.5 C.Y.		1411.00		1552.10			
1 Hyd. Hammer, 8000 ft-lb		576.80		634.48			
1 Hyd. Excavator, 1.5 C.Y.		893.60		982.96	180.09	198.10	
16 L.H., Daily Totals		$3779.00		$4523.14	$236.19	$282.70	

Crews - Standard

Crew No.		Bare Costs		Incl. Subs O&P		Cost Per Labor-Hour	
Crew B-13N	Hr.	Daily	Hr.	Daily	Bare Costs	Incl. O&P
2 Equip. Opers. (crane)	$56.10	$897.60	$84.60	$1353.60	$56.10	$84.60
1 Hyd. Excavator, 3.5 C.Y.		2195.00		2414.50		
1 Hyd. Hammer, 12,000 ft-lb		669.20		736.12		
1 Hyd. Excavator, 1.5 C.Y.		893.60		982.96	234.86	258.35
16 L.H., Daily Totals		$4655.40		$5487.18	$290.96	$342.95
Crew B-14	Hr.	Daily	Hr.	Daily	Bare Costs	Incl. O&P
1 Labor Foreman (outside)	$41.85	$334.80	$63.75	$510.00	$42.09	$63.98
4 Laborers	39.85	1275.20	60.70	1942.40		
1 Equip. Oper. (light)	51.30	410.40	77.35	618.80		
1 Backhoe Loader, 48 H.P.		312.40		343.64	6.51	7.16
48 L.H., Daily Totals		$2332.80		$3414.84	$48.60	$71.14
Crew B-14A	Hr.	Daily	Hr.	Daily	Bare Costs	Incl. O&P
1 Equip. Oper. (crane)	$56.10	$448.80	$84.60	$676.80	$50.68	$76.63
.5 Laborer	39.85	159.40	60.70	242.80		
1 Hyd. Excavator, 4.5 C.Y.		2735.00		3008.50	227.92	250.71
12 L.H., Daily Totals		$3343.20		$3928.10	$278.60	$327.34
Crew B-14B	Hr.	Daily	Hr.	Daily	Bare Costs	Incl. O&P
1 Equip. Oper. (crane)	$56.10	$448.80	$84.60	$676.80	$50.68	$76.63
.5 Laborer	39.85	159.40	60.70	242.80		
1 Hyd. Excavator, 6 C.Y.		3487.00		3835.70	290.58	319.64
12 L.H., Daily Totals		$4095.20		$4755.30	$341.27	$396.27
Crew B-14C	Hr.	Daily	Hr.	Daily	Bare Costs	Incl. O&P
1 Equip. Oper. (crane)	$56.10	$448.80	$84.60	$676.80	$50.68	$76.63
.5 Laborer	39.85	159.40	60.70	242.80		
1 Hyd. Excavator, 7 C.Y.		3275.00		3602.50	272.92	300.21
12 L.H., Daily Totals		$3883.20		$4522.10	$323.60	$376.84
Crew B-14F	Hr.	Daily	Hr.	Daily	Bare Costs	Incl. O&P
1 Equip. Oper. (crane)	$56.10	$448.80	$84.60	$676.80	$50.68	$76.63
.5 Laborer	39.85	159.40	60.70	242.80		
1 Hyd. Shovel, 7 C.Y.		3880.00		4268.00	323.33	355.67
12 L.H., Daily Totals		$4488.20		$5187.60	$374.02	$432.30
Crew B-14G	Hr.	Daily	Hr.	Daily	Bare Costs	Incl. O&P
1 Equip. Oper. (crane)	$56.10	$448.80	$84.60	$676.80	$50.68	$76.63
.5 Laborer	39.85	159.40	60.70	242.80		
1 Hyd. Shovel, 12 C.Y.		5769.00		6345.90	480.75	528.83
12 L.H., Daily Totals		$6377.20		$7265.50	$531.43	$605.46
Crew B-14J	Hr.	Daily	Hr.	Daily	Bare Costs	Incl. O&P
1 Equip. Oper. (medium)	$53.75	$430.00	$81.05	$648.40	$49.12	$74.27
.5 Laborer	39.85	159.40	60.70	242.80		
1 F.E. Loader, 8 C.Y.		1780.00		1958.00	148.33	163.17
12 L.H., Daily Totals		$2369.40		$2849.20	$197.45	$237.43
Crew B-14K	Hr.	Daily	Hr.	Daily	Bare Costs	Incl. O&P
1 Equip. Oper. (medium)	$53.75	$430.00	$81.05	$648.40	$49.12	$74.27
.5 Laborer	39.85	159.40	60.70	242.80		
1 F.E. Loader, 10 C.Y.		2630.00		2893.00	219.17	241.08
12 L.H., Daily Totals		$3219.40		$3784.20	$268.28	$315.35

Crew No.		Bare Costs		Incl. Subs O&P		Cost Per Labor-Hour	
Crew B-15	Hr.	Daily	Hr.	Daily	Bare Costs	Incl. O&P
1 Equipment Oper. (med.)	$53.75	$430.00	$81.05	$648.40	$47.34	$71.43
.5 Laborer	39.85	159.40	60.70	242.80		
2 Truck Drivers (heavy)	46.00	736.00	69.30	1108.80		
2 Dump Trucks, 12 C.Y., 400 H.P.		1085.60		1194.16		
1 Dozer, 200 H.P.		1273.00		1400.30	84.24	92.66
28 L.H., Daily Totals		$3684.00		$4594.46	$131.57	$164.09
Crew B-16	Hr.	Daily	Hr.	Daily	Bare Costs	Incl. O&P
1 Labor Foreman (outside)	$41.85	$334.80	$63.75	$510.00	$41.89	$63.61
2 Laborers	39.85	637.60	60.70	971.20		
1 Truck Driver (heavy)	46.00	368.00	69.30	554.40		
1 Dump Truck, 12 C.Y., 400 H.P.		542.80		597.08	16.96	18.66
32 L.H., Daily Totals		$1883.20		$2632.68	$58.85	$82.27
Crew B-17	Hr.	Daily	Hr.	Daily	Bare Costs	Incl. O&P
2 Laborers	$39.85	$637.60	$60.70	$971.20	$44.25	$67.01
1 Equip. Oper. (light)	51.30	410.40	77.35	618.80		
1 Truck Driver (heavy)	46.00	368.00	69.30	554.40		
1 Backhoe Loader, 48 H.P.		312.40		343.64		
1 Dump Truck, 8 C.Y., 220 H.P.		338.60		372.46	20.34	22.38
32 L.H., Daily Totals		$2067.00		$2860.50	$64.59	$89.39
Crew B-17A	Hr.	Daily	Hr.	Daily	Bare Costs	Incl. O&P
2 Labor Foremen (outside)	$41.85	$669.60	$63.75	$1020.00	$42.95	$65.50
6 Laborers	39.85	1912.80	60.70	2913.60		
1 Skilled Worker Foreman (out)	54.35	434.80	83.20	665.60		
1 Skilled Worker	52.35	418.80	80.15	641.20		
80 L.H., Daily Totals		$3436.00		$5240.40	$42.95	$65.50
Crew B-17B	Hr.	Daily	Hr.	Daily	Bare Costs	Incl. O&P
2 Laborers	$39.85	$637.60	$60.70	$971.20	$44.25	$67.01
1 Equip. Oper. (light)	51.30	410.40	77.35	618.80		
1 Truck Driver (heavy)	46.00	368.00	69.30	554.40		
1 Backhoe Loader, 48 H.P.		312.40		343.64		
1 Dump Truck, 12 C.Y., 400 H.P.		542.80		597.08	26.73	29.40
32 L.H., Daily Totals		$2271.20		$3085.12	$70.97	$96.41
Crew B-18	Hr.	Daily	Hr.	Daily	Bare Costs	Incl. O&P
1 Labor Foreman (outside)	$41.85	$334.80	$63.75	$510.00	$40.52	$61.72
2 Laborers	39.85	637.60	60.70	971.20		
1 Vibrating Plate, Gas, 21"		40.60		44.66	1.69	1.86
24 L.H., Daily Totals		$1013.00		$1525.86	$42.21	$63.58
Crew B-19	Hr.	Daily	Hr.	Daily	Bare Costs	Incl. O&P
1 Pile Driver Foreman (outside)	$53.30	$426.40	$84.05	$672.40	$52.41	$81.27
4 Pile Drivers	51.30	1641.60	80.90	2588.80		
2 Equip. Oper. (crane)	56.10	897.60	84.60	1353.60		
1 Equip. Oper. (oiler)	48.60	388.80	73.30	586.40		
1 Crawler Crane, 40 Ton		1370.00		1507.00		
1 Lead, 90' High		131.60		144.76		
1 Hammer, Diesel, 22k ft-lb		427.00		469.70	30.13	33.15
64 L.H., Daily Totals		$5283.00		$7322.66	$82.55	$114.42

Crews - Standard

Crew No.	Bare Costs Hr.	Bare Costs Daily	Incl. Subs O&P Hr.	Incl. Subs O&P Daily	Cost Per Labor-Hour Bare Costs	Cost Per Labor-Hour Incl. O&P
Crew B-19A						
1 Pile Driver Foreman (outside)	$53.30	$426.40	$84.05	$672.40	$52.41	$81.27
4 Pile Drivers	51.30	1641.60	80.90	2588.80		
2 Equip. Oper. (crane)	56.10	897.60	84.60	1353.60		
1 Equip. Oper. (oiler)	48.60	388.80	73.30	586.40		
1 Crawler Crane, 75 Ton		1708.00		1878.80		
1 Lead, 90' High		131.60		144.76		
1 Hammer, Diesel, 41k ft-lb		572.00		629.20	37.68	41.45
64 L.H., Daily Totals		$5766.00		$7853.96	$90.09	$122.72
Crew B-19B						
1 Pile Driver Foreman (outside)	$53.30	$426.40	$84.05	$672.40	$52.41	$81.27
4 Pile Drivers	51.30	1641.60	80.90	2588.80		
2 Equip. Oper. (crane)	56.10	897.60	84.60	1353.60		
1 Equip. Oper. (oiler)	48.60	388.80	73.30	586.40		
1 Crawler Crane, 40 Ton		1370.00		1507.00		
1 Lead, 90' High		131.60		144.76		
1 Hammer, Diesel, 22k ft-lb		427.00		469.70		
1 Barge, 400 Ton		835.40		918.94	43.19	47.51
64 L.H., Daily Totals		$6118.40		$8241.60	$95.60	$128.78
Crew B-19C						
1 Pile Driver Foreman (outside)	$53.30	$426.40	$84.05	$672.40	$52.41	$81.27
4 Pile Drivers	51.30	1641.60	80.90	2588.80		
2 Equip. Oper. (crane)	56.10	897.60	84.60	1353.60		
1 Equip. Oper. (oiler)	48.60	388.80	73.30	586.40		
1 Crawler Crane, 75 Ton		1708.00		1878.80		
1 Lead, 90' High		131.60		144.76		
1 Hammer, Diesel, 41k ft-lb		572.00		629.20		
1 Barge, 400 Ton		835.40		918.94	50.73	55.81
64 L.H., Daily Totals		$6601.40		$8772.90	$103.15	$137.08
Crew B-20						
1 Labor Foreman (outside)	$41.85	$334.80	$63.75	$510.00	$44.68	$68.20
1 Skilled Worker	52.35	418.80	80.15	641.20		
1 Laborer	39.85	318.80	60.70	485.60		
24 L.H., Daily Totals		$1072.40		$1636.80	$44.68	$68.20
Crew B-20A						
1 Labor Foreman (outside)	$41.85	$334.80	$63.75	$510.00	$48.39	$73.22
1 Laborer	39.85	318.80	60.70	485.60		
1 Plumber	62.15	497.20	93.60	748.80		
1 Plumber Apprentice	49.70	397.60	74.85	598.80		
32 L.H., Daily Totals		$1548.40		$2343.20	$48.39	$73.22
Crew B-21						
1 Labor Foreman (outside)	$41.85	$334.80	$63.75	$510.00	$46.31	$70.54
1 Skilled Worker	52.35	418.80	80.15	641.20		
1 Laborer	39.85	318.80	60.70	485.60		
.5 Equip. Oper. (crane)	56.10	224.40	84.60	338.40		
.5 S.P. Crane, 4x4, 5 Ton		129.50		142.45	4.63	5.09
28 L.H., Daily Totals		$1426.30		$2117.65	$50.94	$75.63
Crew B-21A						
1 Labor Foreman (outside)	$41.85	$334.80	$63.75	$510.00	$49.93	$75.50
1 Laborer	39.85	318.80	60.70	485.60		
1 Plumber	62.15	497.20	93.60	748.80		
1 Plumber Apprentice	49.70	397.60	74.85	598.80		
1 Equip. Oper. (crane)	56.10	448.80	84.60	676.80		
1 S.P. Crane, 4x4, 12 Ton		363.60		399.96	9.09	10.00
40 L.H., Daily Totals		$2360.80		$3419.96	$59.02	$85.50

Crew No.	Bare Costs Hr.	Bare Costs Daily	Incl. Subs O&P Hr.	Incl. Subs O&P Daily	Cost Per Labor-Hour Bare Costs	Cost Per Labor-Hour Incl. O&P
Crew B-21B						
1 Labor Foreman (outside)	$41.85	$334.80	$63.75	$510.00	$43.50	$66.09
3 Laborers	39.85	956.40	60.70	1456.80		
1 Equip. Oper. (crane)	56.10	448.80	84.60	676.80		
1 Hyd. Crane, 12 Ton		496.00		545.60	12.40	13.64
40 L.H., Daily Totals		$2236.00		$3189.20	$55.90	$79.73
Crew B-21C						
1 Labor Foreman (outside)	$41.85	$334.80	$63.75	$510.00	$43.71	$66.35
4 Laborers	39.85	1275.20	60.70	1942.40		
1 Equip. Oper. (crane)	56.10	448.80	84.60	676.80		
1 Equip. Oper. (oiler)	48.60	388.80	73.30	586.40		
2 Cutting Torches		25.20		27.72		
2 Sets of Gases		336.00		369.60		
1 Lattice Boom Crane, 90 Ton		1687.00		1855.70	36.58	40.23
56 L.H., Daily Totals		$4495.80		$5968.62	$80.28	$106.58
Crew B-22						
1 Labor Foreman (outside)	$41.85	$334.80	$63.75	$510.00	$46.97	$71.48
1 Skilled Worker	52.35	418.80	80.15	641.20		
1 Laborer	39.85	318.80	60.70	485.60		
.75 Equip. Oper. (crane)	56.10	336.60	84.60	507.60		
.75 S.P. Crane, 4x4, 5 Ton		194.25		213.68	6.47	7.12
30 L.H., Daily Totals		$1603.25		$2358.07	$53.44	$78.60
Crew B-22A						
1 Labor Foreman (outside)	$41.85	$334.80	$63.75	$510.00	$46.00	$69.98
1 Skilled Worker	52.35	418.80	80.15	641.20		
2 Laborers	39.85	637.60	60.70	971.20		
1 Equipment Operator, Crane	56.10	448.80	84.60	676.80		
1 S.P. Crane, 4x4, 5 Ton		259.00		284.90		
1 Butt Fusion Mach., 4"-12" diam.		425.70		468.27	17.12	18.83
40 L.H., Daily Totals		$2524.70		$3552.37	$63.12	$88.81
Crew B-22B						
1 Labor Foreman (outside)	$41.85	$334.80	$63.75	$510.00	$46.00	$69.98
1 Skilled Worker	52.35	418.80	80.15	641.20		
2 Laborers	39.85	637.60	60.70	971.20		
1 Equip. Oper. (crane)	56.10	448.80	84.60	676.80		
1 S.P. Crane, 4x4, 5 Ton		259.00		284.90		
1 Butt Fusion Mach., 8"-24" diam.		1908.00		2098.80	54.17	59.59
40 L.H., Daily Totals		$4007.00		$5182.90	$100.18	$129.57
Crew B-22C						
1 Skilled Worker	$52.35	$418.80	$80.15	$641.20	$46.10	$70.42
1 Laborer	39.85	318.80	60.70	485.60		
1 Butt Fusion Mach., 2"-8" diam.		121.05		133.16	7.57	8.32
16 L.H., Daily Totals		$858.65		$1259.95	$53.67	$78.75
Crew B-23						
1 Labor Foreman (outside)	$41.85	$334.80	$63.75	$510.00	$40.25	$61.31
4 Laborers	39.85	1275.20	60.70	1942.40		
1 Drill Rig, Truck-Mounted		2444.00		2688.40		
1 Flatbed Truck, Gas, 3 Ton		238.00		261.80	67.05	73.75
40 L.H., Daily Totals		$4292.00		$5402.60	$107.30	$135.07

Crews - Standard

Crew No.	Bare Costs Hr.	Bare Costs Daily	Incl. Subs O&P Hr.	Incl. Subs O&P Daily	Cost Per Labor-Hour Bare Costs	Cost Per Labor-Hour Incl. O&P
Crew B-23A						
1 Labor Foreman (outside)	$41.85	$334.80	$63.75	$510.00	$45.15	$68.50
1 Laborer	39.85	318.80	60.70	485.60		
1 Equip. Oper. (medium)	53.75	430.00	81.05	648.40		
1 Drill Rig, Truck-Mounted		2444.00		2688.40		
1 Pickup Truck, 3/4 Ton		115.20		126.72	106.63	117.30
24 L.H., Daily Totals		$3642.80		$4459.12	$151.78	$185.80
Crew B-23B						
1 Labor Foreman (outside)	$41.85	$334.80	$63.75	$510.00	$45.15	$68.50
1 Laborer	39.85	318.80	60.70	485.60		
1 Equip. Oper. (medium)	53.75	430.00	81.05	648.40		
1 Drill Rig, Truck-Mounted		2444.00		2688.40		
1 Pickup Truck, 3/4 Ton		115.20		126.72		
1 Centr. Water Pump, 6"		296.40		326.04	118.98	130.88
24 L.H., Daily Totals		$3939.20		$4785.16	$164.13	$199.38
Crew B-24						
1 Cement Finisher	$47.55	$380.40	$70.45	$563.60	$46.03	$69.45
1 Laborer	39.85	318.80	60.70	485.60		
1 Carpenter	50.70	405.60	77.20	617.60		
24 L.H., Daily Totals		$1104.80		$1666.80	$46.03	$69.45
Crew B-25						
1 Labor Foreman (outside)	$41.85	$334.80	$63.75	$510.00	$43.82	$66.53
7 Laborers	39.85	2231.60	60.70	3399.20		
3 Equip. Oper. (medium)	53.75	1290.00	81.05	1945.20		
1 Asphalt Paver, 130 H.P.		2123.00		2335.30		
1 Tandem Roller, 10 Ton		231.40		254.54		
1 Roller, Pneum. Whl., 12 Ton		338.20		372.02	30.60	33.66
88 L.H., Daily Totals		$6549.00		$8816.26	$74.42	$100.18
Crew B-25B						
1 Labor Foreman (outside)	$41.85	$334.80	$63.75	$510.00	$44.65	$67.74
7 Laborers	39.85	2231.60	60.70	3399.20		
4 Equip. Oper. (medium)	53.75	1720.00	81.05	2593.60		
1 Asphalt Paver, 130 H.P.		2123.00		2335.30		
2 Tandem Rollers, 10 Ton		462.80		509.08		
1 Roller, Pneum. Whl., 12 Ton		338.20		372.02	30.46	33.50
96 L.H., Daily Totals		$7210.40		$9719.20	$75.11	$101.24
Crew B-25C						
1 Labor Foreman (outside)	$41.85	$334.80	$63.75	$510.00	$44.82	$67.99
3 Laborers	39.85	956.40	60.70	1456.80		
2 Equip. Oper. (medium)	53.75	860.00	81.05	1296.80		
1 Asphalt Paver, 130 H.P.		2123.00		2335.30		
1 Tandem Roller, 10 Ton		231.40		254.54	49.05	53.95
48 L.H., Daily Totals		$4505.60		$5853.44	$93.87	$121.95
Crew B-25D						
1 Labor Foreman (outside)	$41.85	$334.80	$63.75	$510.00	$45.02	$68.28
3 Laborers	39.85	956.40	60.70	1456.80		
2.125 Equip. Oper. (medium)	53.75	913.75	81.05	1377.85		
.125 Truck Driver (heavy)	46.00	46.00	69.30	69.30		
.125 Truck Tractor, 6x4, 380 H.P.		59.52		65.48		
.125 Dist. Tanker, 3000 Gallon		40.85		44.94		
1 Asphalt Paver, 130 H.P.		2123.00		2335.30		
1 Tandem Roller, 10 Ton		231.40		254.54	49.10	54.01
50 L.H., Daily Totals		$4705.73		$6114.20	$94.11	$122.28
Crew B-25E						
1 Labor Foreman (outside)	$41.85	$334.80	$63.75	$510.00	$45.21	$68.54
3 Laborers	39.85	956.40	60.70	1456.80		
2.250 Equip. Oper. (medium)	53.75	967.50	81.05	1458.90		
.25 Truck Driver (heavy)	46.00	92.00	69.30	138.60		
.25 Truck Tractor, 6x4, 380 H.P.		119.05		130.96		
.25 Dist. Tanker, 3000 Gallon		81.70		89.87		
1 Asphalt Paver, 130 H.P.		2123.00		2335.30		
1 Tandem Roller, 10 Ton		231.40		254.54	49.14	54.05
52 L.H., Daily Totals		$4905.85		$6374.97	$94.34	$122.60
Crew B-26						
1 Labor Foreman (outside)	$41.85	$334.80	$63.75	$510.00	$44.60	$67.63
6 Laborers	39.85	1912.80	60.70	2913.60		
2 Equip. Oper. (medium)	53.75	860.00	81.05	1296.80		
1 Rodman (reinf.)	54.65	437.20	83.45	667.60		
1 Cement Finisher	47.55	380.40	70.45	563.60		
1 Grader, 30,000 Lbs.		643.80		708.18		
1 Paving Mach. & Equip.		2361.00		2597.10	34.15	37.56
88 L.H., Daily Totals		$6930.00		$9256.88	$78.75	$105.19
Crew B-26A						
1 Labor Foreman (outside)	$41.85	$334.80	$63.75	$510.00	$44.60	$67.63
6 Laborers	39.85	1912.80	60.70	2913.60		
2 Equip. Oper. (medium)	53.75	860.00	81.05	1296.80		
1 Rodman (reinf.)	54.65	437.20	83.45	667.60		
1 Cement Finisher	47.55	380.40	70.45	563.60		
1 Grader, 30,000 Lbs.		643.80		708.18		
1 Paving Mach. & Equip.		2361.00		2597.10		
1 Concrete Saw		102.40		112.64	35.31	38.84
88 L.H., Daily Totals		$7032.40		$9369.52	$79.91	$106.47
Crew B-26B						
1 Labor Foreman (outside)	$41.85	$334.80	$63.75	$510.00	$45.37	$68.75
6 Laborers	39.85	1912.80	60.70	2913.60		
3 Equip. Oper. (medium)	53.75	1290.00	81.05	1945.20		
1 Rodman (reinf.)	54.65	437.20	83.45	667.60		
1 Cement Finisher	47.55	380.40	70.45	563.60		
1 Grader, 30,000 Lbs.		643.80		708.18		
1 Paving Mach. & Equip.		2361.00		2597.10		
1 Concrete Pump, 110' Boom		1116.00		1227.60	42.92	47.22
96 L.H., Daily Totals		$8476.00		$11132.88	$88.29	$115.97
Crew B-26C						
1 Labor Foreman (outside)	$41.85	$334.80	$63.75	$510.00	$43.69	$66.29
6 Laborers	39.85	1912.80	60.70	2913.60		
1 Equip. Oper. (medium)	53.75	430.00	81.05	648.40		
1 Rodman (reinf.)	54.65	437.20	83.45	667.60		
1 Cement Finisher	47.55	380.40	70.45	563.60		
1 Paving Mach. & Equip.		2361.00		2597.10		
1 Concrete Saw		102.40		112.64	30.79	33.87
80 L.H., Daily Totals		$5958.60		$8012.94	$74.48	$100.16
Crew B-27						
1 Labor Foreman (outside)	$41.85	$334.80	$63.75	$510.00	$40.35	$61.46
3 Laborers	39.85	956.40	60.70	1456.80		
1 Berm Machine		317.40		349.14	9.92	10.91
32 L.H., Daily Totals		$1608.60		$2315.94	$50.27	$72.37

Crews - Standard

Crew No.		Bare Costs	Incl. Subs O&P		Cost Per Labor-Hour	
Crew B-28	Hr.	Daily	Hr.	Daily	Bare Costs	Incl. O&P
2 Carpenters	$50.70	$811.20	$77.20	$1235.20	$47.08	$71.70
1 Laborer	39.85	318.80	60.70	485.60		
24 L.H., Daily Totals		$1130.00		$1720.80	$47.08	$71.70
Crew B-29	Hr.	Daily	Hr.	Daily	Bare Costs	Incl. O&P
1 Labor Foreman (outside)	$41.85	$334.80	$63.75	$510.00	$43.71	$66.35
4 Laborers	39.85	1275.20	60.70	1942.40		
1 Equip. Oper. (crane)	56.10	448.80	84.60	676.80		
1 Equip. Oper. (oiler)	48.60	388.80	73.30	586.40		
1 Gradall, 5/8 C.Y.		869.60		956.56	15.53	17.08
56 L.H., Daily Totals		$3317.20		$4672.16	$59.24	$83.43
Crew B-30	Hr.	Daily	Hr.	Daily	Bare Costs	Incl. O&P
1 Equip. Oper. (medium)	$53.75	$430.00	$81.05	$648.40	$48.58	$73.22
2 Truck Drivers (heavy)	46.00	736.00	69.30	1108.80		
1 Hyd. Excavator, 1.5 C.Y.		893.60		982.96		
2 Dump Trucks, 12 C.Y., 400 H.P.		1085.60		1194.16	82.47	90.71
24 L.H., Daily Totals		$3145.20		$3934.32	$131.05	$163.93
Crew B-31	Hr.	Daily	Hr.	Daily	Bare Costs	Incl. O&P
1 Labor Foreman (outside)	$41.85	$334.80	$63.75	$510.00	$42.42	$64.61
3 Laborers	39.85	956.40	60.70	1456.80		
1 Carpenter	50.70	405.60	77.20	617.60		
1 Air Compressor, 250 cfm		167.40		184.14		
1 Sheeting Driver		7.00		7.70		
2 -50' Air Hoses, 1.5"		45.40		49.94	5.50	6.04
40 L.H., Daily Totals		$1916.60		$2826.18	$47.91	$70.65
Crew B-32	Hr.	Daily	Hr.	Daily	Bare Costs	Incl. O&P
1 Laborer	$39.85	$318.80	$60.70	$485.60	$50.27	$75.96
3 Equip. Oper. (medium)	53.75	1290.00	81.05	1945.20		
1 Grader, 30,000 Lbs.		643.80		708.18		
1 Tandem Roller, 10 Ton		231.40		254.54		
1 Dozer, 200 H.P.		1273.00		1400.30	67.13	73.84
32 L.H., Daily Totals		$3757.00		$4793.82	$117.41	$149.81
Crew B-32A	Hr.	Daily	Hr.	Daily	Bare Costs	Incl. O&P
1 Laborer	$39.85	$318.80	$60.70	$485.60	$49.12	$74.27
2 Equip. Oper. (medium)	53.75	860.00	81.05	1296.80		
1 Grader, 30,000 Lbs.		643.80		708.18		
1 Roller, Vibratory, 25 Ton		659.80		725.78	54.32	59.75
24 L.H., Daily Totals		$2482.40		$3216.36	$103.43	$134.01
Crew B-32B	Hr.	Daily	Hr.	Daily	Bare Costs	Incl. O&P
1 Laborer	$39.85	$318.80	$60.70	$485.60	$49.12	$74.27
2 Equip. Oper. (medium)	53.75	860.00	81.05	1296.80		
1 Dozer, 200 H.P.		1273.00		1400.30		
1 Roller, Vibratory, 25 Ton		659.80		725.78	80.53	88.59
24 L.H., Daily Totals		$3111.60		$3908.48	$129.65	$162.85
Crew B-32C	Hr.	Daily	Hr.	Daily	Bare Costs	Incl. O&P
1 Labor Foreman (outside)	$41.85	$334.80	$63.75	$510.00	$47.13	$71.38
2 Laborers	39.85	637.60	60.70	971.20		
3 Equip. Oper. (medium)	53.75	1290.00	81.05	1945.20		
1 Grader, 30,000 Lbs.		643.80		708.18		
1 Tandem Roller, 10 Ton		231.40		254.54		
1 Dozer, 200 H.P.		1273.00		1400.30	44.75	49.23
48 L.H., Daily Totals		$4410.60		$5789.42	$91.89	$120.61

Crew No.		Bare Costs	Incl. Subs O&P		Cost Per Labor-Hour	
Crew B-33A	Hr.	Daily	Hr.	Daily	Bare Costs	Incl. O&P
1 Equip. Oper. (medium)	$53.75	$430.00	$81.05	$648.40	$49.78	$75.24
.5 Laborer	39.85	159.40	60.70	242.80		
.25 Equip. Oper. (medium)	53.75	107.50	81.05	162.10		
1 Scraper, Towed, 7 C.Y.		123.40		135.74		
1.25 Dozers, 300 H.P.		2286.25		2514.88	172.12	189.33
14 L.H., Daily Totals		$3106.55		$3703.92	$221.90	$264.57
Crew B-33B	Hr.	Daily	Hr.	Daily	Bare Costs	Incl. O&P
1 Equip. Oper. (medium)	$53.75	$430.00	$81.05	$648.40	$49.78	$75.24
.5 Laborer	39.85	159.40	60.70	242.80		
.25 Equip. Oper. (medium)	53.75	107.50	81.05	162.10		
1 Scraper, Towed, 10 C.Y.		155.80		171.38		
1.25 Dozers, 300 H.P.		2286.25		2514.88	174.43	191.88
14 L.H., Daily Totals		$3138.95		$3739.55	$224.21	$267.11
Crew B-33C	Hr.	Daily	Hr.	Daily	Bare Costs	Incl. O&P
1 Equip. Oper. (medium)	$53.75	$430.00	$81.05	$648.40	$49.78	$75.24
.5 Laborer	39.85	159.40	60.70	242.80		
.25 Equip. Oper. (medium)	53.75	107.50	81.05	162.10		
1 Scraper, Towed, 15 C.Y.		175.80		193.38		
1.25 Dozers, 300 H.P.		2286.25		2514.88	175.86	193.45
14 L.H., Daily Totals		$3158.95		$3761.55	$225.64	$268.68
Crew B-33D	Hr.	Daily	Hr.	Daily	Bare Costs	Incl. O&P
1 Equip. Oper. (medium)	$53.75	$430.00	$81.05	$648.40	$49.78	$75.24
.5 Laborer	39.85	159.40	60.70	242.80		
.25 Equip. Oper. (medium)	53.75	107.50	81.05	162.10		
1 S.P. Scraper, 14 C.Y.		2490.00		2739.00		
.25 Dozer, 300 H.P.		457.25		502.98	210.52	231.57
14 L.H., Daily Totals		$3644.15		$4295.27	$260.30	$306.81
Crew B-33E	Hr.	Daily	Hr.	Daily	Bare Costs	Incl. O&P
1 Equip. Oper. (medium)	$53.75	$430.00	$81.05	$648.40	$49.78	$75.24
.5 Laborer	39.85	159.40	60.70	242.80		
.25 Equip. Oper. (medium)	53.75	107.50	81.05	162.10		
1 S.P. Scraper, 21 C.Y.		2468.00		2714.80		
.25 Dozer, 300 H.P.		457.25		502.98	208.95	229.84
14 L.H., Daily Totals		$3622.15		$4271.07	$258.73	$305.08
Crew B-33F	Hr.	Daily	Hr.	Daily	Bare Costs	Incl. O&P
1 Equip. Oper. (medium)	$53.75	$430.00	$81.05	$648.40	$49.78	$75.24
.5 Laborer	39.85	159.40	60.70	242.80		
.25 Equip. Oper. (medium)	53.75	107.50	81.05	162.10		
1 Elev. Scraper, 11 C.Y.		1155.00		1270.50		
.25 Dozer, 300 H.P.		457.25		502.98	115.16	126.68
14 L.H., Daily Totals		$2309.15		$2826.78	$164.94	$201.91
Crew B-33G	Hr.	Daily	Hr.	Daily	Bare Costs	Incl. O&P
1 Equip. Oper. (medium)	$53.75	$430.00	$81.05	$648.40	$49.78	$75.24
.5 Laborer	39.85	159.40	60.70	242.80		
.25 Equip. Oper. (medium)	53.75	107.50	81.05	162.10		
1 Elev. Scraper, 22 C.Y.		2284.00		2512.40		
.25 Dozer, 300 H.P.		457.25		502.98	195.80	215.38
14 L.H., Daily Totals		$3438.15		$4068.68	$245.58	$290.62

For customer support on your Green Building Costs with RSMeans data, call 800.448.8182.

Crews - Standard

Crew No.	Bare Costs Hr.	Bare Costs Daily	Incl. Subs O&P Hr.	Incl. Subs O&P Daily	Cost Per Labor-Hour Bare Costs	Cost Per Labor-Hour Incl. O&P
Crew B-33H						
.5 Laborer	$39.85	$159.40	$60.70	$242.80	$49.78	$75.24
1 Equipment Operator (med.)	53.75	430.00	81.05	648.40		
.25 Equipment Operator (med.)	53.75	107.50	81.05	162.10		
1 S.P. Scraper, 44 C.Y.		4457.00		4902.70		
.25 Dozer, 410 H.P.		572.75		630.02	359.27	395.19
14 L.H., Daily Totals		$5726.65		$6586.02	$409.05	$470.43
Crew B-33J						
1 Equipment Operator (med.)	$53.75	$430.00	$81.05	$648.40	$53.75	$81.05
1 S.P. Scraper, 14 C.Y.		2490.00		2739.00	311.25	342.38
8 L.H., Daily Totals		$2920.00		$3387.40	$365.00	$423.43
Crew B-33K						
1 Equipment Operator (med.)	$53.75	$430.00	$81.05	$648.40	$49.78	$75.24
.25 Equipment Operator (med.)	53.75	107.50	81.05	162.10		
.5 Laborer	39.85	159.40	60.70	242.80		
1 S.P. Scraper, 31 C.Y.		3576.00		3933.60		
.25 Dozer, 410 H.P.		572.75		630.02	296.34	325.97
14 L.H., Daily Totals		$4845.65		$5616.93	$346.12	$401.21
Crew B-34A						
1 Truck Driver (heavy)	$46.00	$368.00	$69.30	$554.40	$46.00	$69.30
1 Dump Truck, 8 C.Y., 220 H.P.		338.60		372.46	42.33	46.56
8 L.H., Daily Totals		$706.60		$926.86	$88.33	$115.86
Crew B-34B						
1 Truck Driver (heavy)	$46.00	$368.00	$69.30	$554.40	$46.00	$69.30
1 Dump Truck, 12 C.Y., 400 H.P.		542.80		597.08	67.85	74.64
8 L.H., Daily Totals		$910.80		$1151.48	$113.85	$143.94
Crew B-34C						
1 Truck Driver (heavy)	$46.00	$368.00	$69.30	$554.40	$46.00	$69.30
1 Truck Tractor, 6x4, 380 H.P.		476.20		523.82		
1 Dump Trailer, 16.5 C.Y.		133.00		146.30	76.15	83.77
8 L.H., Daily Totals		$977.20		$1224.52	$122.15	$153.07
Crew B-34D						
1 Truck Driver (heavy)	$46.00	$368.00	$69.30	$554.40	$46.00	$69.30
1 Truck Tractor, 6x4, 380 H.P.		476.20		523.82		
1 Dump Trailer, 20 C.Y.		147.60		162.36	77.97	85.77
8 L.H., Daily Totals		$991.80		$1240.58	$123.97	$155.07
Crew B-34E						
1 Truck Driver (heavy)	$46.00	$368.00	$69.30	$554.40	$46.00	$69.30
1 Dump Truck, Off Hwy., 25 Ton		1343.00		1477.30	167.88	184.66
8 L.H., Daily Totals		$1711.00		$2031.70	$213.88	$253.96
Crew B-34F						
1 Truck Driver (heavy)	$46.00	$368.00	$69.30	$554.40	$46.00	$69.30
1 Dump Truck, Off Hwy., 35 Ton		1448.00		1592.80	181.00	199.10
8 L.H., Daily Totals		$1816.00		$2147.20	$227.00	$268.40
Crew B-34G						
1 Truck Driver (heavy)	$46.00	$368.00	$69.30	$554.40	$46.00	$69.30
1 Dump Truck, Off Hwy., 50 Ton		1662.00		1828.20	207.75	228.53
8 L.H., Daily Totals		$2030.00		$2382.60	$253.75	$297.82

Crew No.	Bare Costs Hr.	Bare Costs Daily	Incl. Subs O&P Hr.	Incl. Subs O&P Daily	Cost Per Labor-Hour Bare Costs	Cost Per Labor-Hour Incl. O&P
Crew B-34H						
1 Truck Driver (heavy)	$46.00	$368.00	$69.30	$554.40	$46.00	$69.30
1 Dump Truck, Off Hwy., 65 Ton		1844.00		2028.40	230.50	253.55
8 L.H., Daily Totals		$2212.00		$2582.80	$276.50	$322.85
Crew B-34I						
1 Truck Driver (heavy)	$46.00	$368.00	$69.30	$554.40	$46.00	$69.30
1 Dump Truck, 18 C.Y., 450 H.P.		706.00		776.60	88.25	97.08
8 L.H., Daily Totals		$1074.00		$1331.00	$134.25	$166.38
Crew B-34J						
1 Truck Driver (heavy)	$46.00	$368.00	$69.30	$554.40	$46.00	$69.30
1 Dump Truck, Off Hwy., 100 Ton		2669.00		2935.90	333.63	366.99
8 L.H., Daily Totals		$3037.00		$3490.30	$379.63	$436.29
Crew B-34K						
1 Truck Driver (heavy)	$46.00	$368.00	$69.30	$554.40	$46.00	$69.30
1 Truck Tractor, 6x4, 450 H.P.		583.40		641.74		
1 Lowbed Trailer, 75 Ton		249.40		274.34	104.10	114.51
8 L.H., Daily Totals		$1200.80		$1470.48	$150.10	$183.81
Crew B-34L						
1 Equip. Oper. (light)	$51.30	$410.40	$77.35	$618.80	$51.30	$77.35
1 Flatbed Truck, Gas, 1.5 Ton		188.40		207.24	23.55	25.91
8 L.H., Daily Totals		$598.80		$826.04	$74.85	$103.26
Crew B-34M						
1 Equip. Oper. (light)	$51.30	$410.40	$77.35	$618.80	$51.30	$77.35
1 Flatbed Truck, Gas, 3 Ton		238.00		261.80	29.75	32.73
8 L.H., Daily Totals		$648.40		$880.60	$81.05	$110.08
Crew B-34N						
1 Truck Driver (heavy)	$46.00	$368.00	$69.30	$554.40	$49.88	$75.17
1 Equip. Oper. (medium)	53.75	430.00	81.05	648.40		
1 Truck Tractor, 6x4, 380 H.P.		476.20		523.82		
1 Flatbed Trailer, 40 Ton		180.00		198.00	41.01	45.11
16 L.H., Daily Totals		$1454.20		$1924.62	$90.89	$120.29
Crew B-34P						
1 Pipe Fitter	$63.00	$504.00	$94.90	$759.20	$53.75	$80.98
1 Truck Driver (light)	44.50	356.00	67.00	536.00		
1 Equip. Oper. (medium)	53.75	430.00	81.05	648.40		
1 Flatbed Truck, Gas, 3 Ton		238.00		261.80		
1 Backhoe Loader, 48 H.P.		312.40		343.64	22.93	25.23
24 L.H., Daily Totals		$1840.40		$2549.04	$76.68	$106.21
Crew B-34Q						
1 Pipe Fitter	$63.00	$504.00	$94.90	$759.20	$54.53	$82.17
1 Truck Driver (light)	44.50	356.00	67.00	536.00		
1 Equip. Oper. (crane)	56.10	448.80	84.60	676.80		
1 Flatbed Trailer, 25 Ton		133.00		146.30		
1 Dump Truck, 8 C.Y., 220 H.P.		338.60		372.46		
1 Hyd. Crane, 25 Ton		590.60		649.66	44.26	48.68
24 L.H., Daily Totals		$2371.00		$3140.42	$98.79	$130.85

Crews - Standard

Crew No.	Bare Costs Hr.	Bare Costs Daily	Incl. Subs O&P Hr.	Incl. Subs O&P Daily	Cost Per Labor-Hour Bare Costs	Cost Per Labor-Hour Incl. O&P
Crew B-34R						
1 Pipe Fitter	$63.00	$504.00	$94.90	$759.20	$54.53	$82.17
1 Truck Driver (light)	44.50	356.00	67.00	536.00		
1 Equip. Oper. (crane)	56.10	448.80	84.60	676.80		
1 Flatbed Trailer, 25 Ton		133.00		146.30		
1 Dump Truck, 8 C.Y., 220 H.P.		338.60		372.46		
1 Hyd. Crane, 25 Ton		590.60		649.66		
1 Hyd. Excavator, 1 C.Y.		742.20		816.42	75.18	82.70
24 L.H., Daily Totals		$3113.20		$3956.84	$129.72	$164.87
Crew B-34S	Hr.	Daily	Hr.	Daily	Bare Costs	Incl. O&P
2 Pipe Fitters	$63.00	$1008.00	$94.90	$1518.40	$57.02	$85.92
1 Truck Driver (heavy)	46.00	368.00	69.30	554.40		
1 Equip. Oper. (crane)	56.10	448.80	84.60	676.80		
1 Flatbed Trailer, 40 Ton		180.00		198.00		
1 Truck Tractor, 6x4, 380 H.P.		476.20		523.82		
1 Hyd. Crane, 80 Ton		1518.00		1669.80		
1 Hyd. Excavator, 2 C.Y.		1052.00		1157.20	100.82	110.90
32 L.H., Daily Totals		$5051.00		$6298.42	$157.84	$196.83
Crew B-34T	Hr.	Daily	Hr.	Daily	Bare Costs	Incl. O&P
2 Pipe Fitters	$63.00	$1008.00	$94.90	$1518.40	$57.02	$85.92
1 Truck Driver (heavy)	46.00	368.00	69.30	554.40		
1 Equip. Oper. (crane)	56.10	448.80	84.60	676.80		
1 Flatbed Trailer, 40 Ton		180.00		198.00		
1 Truck Tractor, 6x4, 380 H.P.		476.20		523.82		
1 Hyd. Crane, 80 Ton		1518.00		1669.80	67.94	74.74
32 L.H., Daily Totals		$3999.00		$5141.22	$124.97	$160.66
Crew B-34U	Hr.	Daily	Hr.	Daily	Bare Costs	Incl. O&P
1 Truck Driver (heavy)	$46.00	$368.00	$69.30	$554.40	$48.65	$73.33
1 Equip. Oper. (light)	51.30	410.40	77.35	618.80		
1 Truck Tractor, 220 H.P.		290.00		319.00		
1 Flatbed Trailer, 25 Ton		133.00		146.30	26.44	29.08
16 L.H., Daily Totals		$1201.40		$1638.50	$75.09	$102.41
Crew B-34V	Hr.	Daily	Hr.	Daily	Bare Costs	Incl. O&P
1 Truck Driver (heavy)	$46.00	$368.00	$69.30	$554.40	$51.13	$77.08
1 Equip. Oper. (crane)	56.10	448.80	84.60	676.80		
1 Equip. Oper. (light)	51.30	410.40	77.35	618.80		
1 Truck Tractor, 6x4, 450 H.P.		583.40		641.74		
1 Equipment Trailer, 50 Ton		198.20		218.02		
1 Pickup Truck, 4x4, 3/4 Ton		126.60		139.26	37.84	41.63
24 L.H., Daily Totals		$2135.40		$2849.02	$88.97	$118.71
Crew B-34W	Hr.	Daily	Hr.	Daily	Bare Costs	Incl. O&P
5 Truck Drivers (heavy)	$46.00	$1840.00	$69.30	$2772.00	$48.71	$73.48
2 Equip. Opers. (crane)	56.10	897.60	84.60	1353.60		
1 Equip. Oper. (mechanic)	56.30	450.40	84.90	679.20		
1 Laborer	39.85	318.80	60.70	485.60		
4 Truck Tractors, 6x4, 380 H.P.		1904.80		2095.28		
2 Equipment Trailers, 50 Ton		396.40		436.04		
2 Flatbed Trailers, 40 Ton		360.00		396.00		
1 Pickup Truck, 4x4, 3/4 Ton		126.60		139.26		
1 S.P. Crane, 4x4, 20 Ton		571.20		628.32	46.65	51.32
72 L.H., Daily Totals		$6865.80		$8985.30	$95.36	$124.80

Crew No.	Bare Costs Hr.	Bare Costs Daily	Incl. Subs O&P Hr.	Incl. Subs O&P Daily	Cost Per Labor-Hour Bare Costs	Cost Per Labor-Hour Incl. O&P
Crew B-35						
1 Labor Foreman (outside)	$41.85	$334.80	$63.75	$510.00	$50.15	$76.02
1 Skilled Worker	52.35	418.80	80.15	641.20		
1 Welder (plumber)	62.15	497.20	93.60	748.80		
1 Laborer	39.85	318.80	60.70	485.60		
1 Equip. Oper. (crane)	56.10	448.80	84.60	676.80		
1 Equip. Oper. (oiler)	48.60	388.80	73.30	586.40		
1 Welder, Electric, 300 amp		59.20		65.12		
1 Hyd. Excavator, .75 C.Y.		669.60		736.56	15.18	16.70
48 L.H., Daily Totals		$3136.00		$4450.48	$65.33	$92.72
Crew B-35A	Hr.	Daily	Hr.	Daily	Bare Costs	Incl. O&P
1 Labor Foreman (outside)	$41.85	$334.80	$63.75	$510.00	$48.68	$73.83
2 Laborers	39.85	637.60	60.70	971.20		
1 Skilled Worker	52.35	418.80	80.15	641.20		
1 Welder (plumber)	62.15	497.20	93.60	748.80		
1 Equip. Oper. (crane)	56.10	448.80	84.60	676.80		
1 Equip. Oper. (oiler)	48.60	388.80	73.30	586.40		
1 Welder, Gas Engine, 300 amp		98.40		108.24		
1 Crawler Crane, 75 Ton		1708.00		1878.80	32.26	35.48
56 L.H., Daily Totals		$4532.40		$6121.44	$80.94	$109.31
Crew B-36	Hr.	Daily	Hr.	Daily	Bare Costs	Incl. O&P
1 Labor Foreman (outside)	$41.85	$334.80	$63.75	$510.00	$45.81	$69.45
2 Laborers	39.85	637.60	60.70	971.20		
2 Equip. Oper. (medium)	53.75	860.00	81.05	1296.80		
1 Dozer, 200 H.P.		1273.00		1400.30		
1 Aggregate Spreader		36.80		40.48		
1 Tandem Roller, 10 Ton		231.40		254.54	38.53	42.38
40 L.H., Daily Totals		$3373.60		$4473.32	$84.34	$111.83
Crew B-36A	Hr.	Daily	Hr.	Daily	Bare Costs	Incl. O&P
1 Labor Foreman (outside)	$41.85	$334.80	$63.75	$510.00	$48.08	$72.76
2 Laborers	39.85	637.60	60.70	971.20		
4 Equip. Oper. (medium)	53.75	1720.00	81.05	2593.60		
1 Dozer, 200 H.P.		1273.00		1400.30		
1 Aggregate Spreader		36.80		40.48		
1 Tandem Roller, 10 Ton		231.40		254.54		
1 Roller, Pneum. Whl., 12 Ton		338.20		372.02	33.56	36.92
56 L.H., Daily Totals		$4571.80		$6142.14	$81.64	$109.68
Crew B-36B	Hr.	Daily	Hr.	Daily	Bare Costs	Incl. O&P
1 Labor Foreman (outside)	$41.85	$334.80	$63.75	$510.00	$47.82	$72.33
2 Laborers	39.85	637.60	60.70	971.20		
4 Equip. Oper. (medium)	53.75	1720.00	81.05	2593.60		
1 Truck Driver (heavy)	46.00	368.00	69.30	554.40		
1 Grader, 30,000 Lbs.		643.80		708.18		
1 F.E. Loader, Crl, 1.5 C.Y.		645.40		709.94		
1 Dozer, 300 H.P.		1829.00		2011.90		
1 Roller, Vibratory, 25 Ton		659.80		725.78		
1 Truck Tractor, 6x4, 450 H.P.		583.40		641.74		
1 Water Tank Trailer, 5000 Gal.		147.60		162.36	70.45	77.50
64 L.H., Daily Totals		$7569.40		$9589.10	$118.27	$149.83

435

Crews - Standard

Crew No.		Bare Costs		Incl. Subs O&P		Cost Per Labor-Hour	
Crew B-36C	Hr.	Daily	Hr.	Daily	Bare Costs	Incl. O&P
1 Labor Foreman (outside)	$41.85	$334.80	$63.75	$510.00	$49.82	$75.24
3 Equip. Oper. (medium)	53.75	1290.00	81.05	1945.20		
1 Truck Driver (heavy)	46.00	368.00	69.30	554.40		
1 Grader, 30,000 Lbs.		643.80		708.18		
1 Dozer, 300 H.P.		1829.00		2011.90		
1 Roller, Vibratory, 25 Ton		659.80		725.78		
1 Truck Tractor, 6x4, 450 H.P.		583.40		641.74		
1 Water Tank Trailer, 5000 Gal.		147.60		162.36	96.59	106.25
40 L.H., Daily Totals		$5856.40		$7259.56	$146.41	$181.49
Crew B-36D	Hr.	Daily	Hr.	Daily	Bare Costs	Incl. O&P
1 Labor Foreman (outside)	$41.85	$334.80	$63.75	$510.00	$50.77	$76.72
3 Equip. Oper. (medium)	53.75	1290.00	81.05	1945.20		
1 Grader, 30,000 Lbs.		643.80		708.18		
1 Dozer, 300 H.P.		1829.00		2011.90		
1 Roller, Vibratory, 25 Ton		659.80		725.78	97.89	107.68
32 L.H., Daily Totals		$4757.40		$5901.06	$148.67	$184.41
Crew B-37	Hr.	Daily	Hr.	Daily	Bare Costs	Incl. O&P
1 Labor Foreman (outside)	$41.85	$334.80	$63.75	$510.00	$42.09	$63.98
4 Laborers	39.85	1275.20	60.70	1942.40		
1 Equip. Oper. (light)	51.30	410.40	77.35	618.80		
1 Tandem Roller, 5 Ton		151.20		166.32	3.15	3.46
48 L.H., Daily Totals		$2171.60		$3237.52	$45.24	$67.45
Crew B-37A	Hr.	Daily	Hr.	Daily	Bare Costs	Incl. O&P
2 Laborers	$39.85	$637.60	$60.70	$971.20	$41.40	$62.80
1 Truck Driver (light)	44.50	356.00	67.00	536.00		
1 Flatbed Truck, Gas, 1.5 Ton		188.40		207.24		
1 Tar Kettle, T.M.		129.20		142.12	13.23	14.56
24 L.H., Daily Totals		$1311.20		$1856.56	$54.63	$77.36
Crew B-37B	Hr.	Daily	Hr.	Daily	Bare Costs	Incl. O&P
3 Laborers	$39.85	$956.40	$60.70	$1456.80	$41.01	$62.27
1 Truck Driver (light)	44.50	356.00	67.00	536.00		
1 Flatbed Truck, Gas, 1.5 Ton		188.40		207.24		
1 Tar Kettle, T.M.		129.20		142.12	9.93	10.92
32 L.H., Daily Totals		$1630.00		$2342.16	$50.94	$73.19
Crew B-37C	Hr.	Daily	Hr.	Daily	Bare Costs	Incl. O&P
2 Laborers	$39.85	$637.60	$60.70	$971.20	$42.17	$63.85
2 Truck Drivers (light)	44.50	712.00	67.00	1072.00		
2 Flatbed Trucks, Gas, 1.5 Ton		376.80		414.48		
1 Tar Kettle, T.M.		129.20		142.12	15.81	17.39
32 L.H., Daily Totals		$1855.60		$2599.80	$57.99	$81.24
Crew B-37D	Hr.	Daily	Hr.	Daily	Bare Costs	Incl. O&P
1 Laborer	$39.85	$318.80	$60.70	$485.60	$42.17	$63.85
1 Truck Driver (light)	44.50	356.00	67.00	536.00		
1 Pickup Truck, 3/4 Ton		115.20		126.72	7.20	7.92
16 L.H., Daily Totals		$790.00		$1148.32	$49.38	$71.77

Crew No.		Bare Costs		Incl. Subs O&P		Cost Per Labor-Hour	
Crew B-37E	Hr.	Daily	Hr.	Daily	Bare Costs	Incl. O&P
3 Laborers	$39.85	$956.40	$60.70	$1456.80	$44.80	$67.79
1 Equip. Oper. (light)	51.30	410.40	77.35	618.80		
1 Equip. Oper. (medium)	53.75	430.00	81.05	648.40		
2 Truck Drivers (light)	44.50	712.00	67.00	1072.00		
4 Barrels w/Flasher		15.60		17.16		
1 Concrete Saw		102.40		112.64		
1 Rotary Hammer Drill		25.15		27.66		
1 Hammer Drill Bit		3.25		3.58		
1 Loader, Skid Steer, 30 H.P.		174.00		191.40		
1 Conc. Hammer Attach.		113.60		124.96		
1 Vibrating Plate, Gas, 18"		31.80		34.98		
2 Flatbed Trucks, Gas, 1.5 Ton		376.80		414.48	15.05	16.55
56 L.H., Daily Totals		$3351.40		$4722.86	$59.85	$84.34
Crew B-37F	Hr.	Daily	Hr.	Daily	Bare Costs	Incl. O&P
3 Laborers	$39.85	$956.40	$60.70	$1456.80	$41.01	$62.27
1 Truck Driver (light)	44.50	356.00	67.00	536.00		
4 Barrels w/Flasher		15.60		17.16		
1 Concrete Mixer, 10 C.F.		161.00		177.10		
1 Air Compressor, 60 cfm		105.40		115.94		
1 -50' Air Hose, 3/4"		7.35		8.09		
1 Spade (Chipper)		8.40		9.24		
1 Flatbed Truck, Gas, 1.5 Ton		188.40		207.24	15.19	16.71
32 L.H., Daily Totals		$1798.55		$2527.57	$56.20	$78.99
Crew B-37G	Hr.	Daily	Hr.	Daily	Bare Costs	Incl. O&P
1 Labor Foreman (outside)	$41.85	$334.80	$63.75	$510.00	$42.09	$63.98
4 Laborers	39.85	1275.20	60.70	1942.40		
1 Equip. Oper. (light)	51.30	410.40	77.35	618.80		
1 Berm Machine		317.40		349.14		
1 Tandem Roller, 5 Ton		151.20		166.32	9.76	10.74
48 L.H., Daily Totals		$2489.00		$3586.66	$51.85	$74.72
Crew B-37H	Hr.	Daily	Hr.	Daily	Bare Costs	Incl. O&P
1 Labor Foreman (outside)	$41.85	$334.80	$63.75	$510.00	$42.09	$63.98
4 Laborers	39.85	1275.20	60.70	1942.40		
1 Equip. Oper. (light)	51.30	410.40	77.35	618.80		
1 Tandem Roller, 5 Ton		151.20		166.32		
1 Flatbed Truck, Gas, 1.5 Ton		188.40		207.24		
1 Tar Kettle, T.M.		129.20		142.12	9.77	10.74
48 L.H., Daily Totals		$2489.20		$3586.88	$51.86	$74.73
Crew B-37I	Hr.	Daily	Hr.	Daily	Bare Costs	Incl. O&P
3 Laborers	$39.85	$956.40	$60.70	$1456.80	$44.80	$67.79
1 Equip. Oper. (light)	51.30	410.40	77.35	618.80		
1 Equip. Oper. (medium)	53.75	430.00	81.05	648.40		
2 Truck Drivers (light)	44.50	712.00	67.00	1072.00		
4 Barrels w/Flasher		15.60		17.16		
1 Concrete Saw		102.40		112.64		
1 Rotary Hammer Drill		25.15		27.66		
1 Hammer Drill Bit		3.25		3.58		
1 Air Compressor, 60 cfm		105.40		115.94		
1 -50' Air Hose, 3/4"		7.35		8.09		
1 Spade (Chipper)		8.40		9.24		
1 Loader, Skid Steer, 30 H.P.		174.00		191.40		
1 Conc. Hammer Attach.		113.60		124.96		
1 Concrete Mixer, 10 C.F.		161.00		177.10		
1 Vibrating Plate, Gas, 18"		31.80		34.98		
2 Flatbed Trucks, Gas, 1.5 Ton		376.80		414.48	20.08	22.09
56 L.H., Daily Totals		$3633.55		$5033.23	$64.88	$89.88

Crews - Standard

Crew No.		Bare Costs		Incl. Subs O&P		Cost Per Labor-Hour	
Crew B-37J	Hr.	Daily	Hr.	Daily	Bare Costs	Incl. O&P
1 Labor Foreman (outside)	$41.85	$334.80	$63.75	$510.00	$42.09	$63.98
4 Laborers	39.85	1275.20	60.70	1942.40		
1 Equip. Oper. (light)	51.30	410.40	77.35	618.80		
1 Air Compressor, 60 cfm		105.40		115.94		
1 -50' Air Hose, 3/4"		7.35		8.09		
2 Concrete Mixers, 10 C.F.		322.00		354.20		
2 Flatbed Trucks, Gas, 1.5 Ton		376.80		414.48		
1 Shot Blaster, 20"		214.80		236.28	21.38	23.52
48 L.H., Daily Totals		$3046.75		$4200.19	$63.47	$87.50
Crew B-37K	Hr.	Daily	Hr.	Daily	Bare Costs	Incl. O&P
1 Labor Foreman (outside)	$41.85	$334.80	$63.75	$510.00	$42.09	$63.98
4 Laborers	39.85	1275.20	60.70	1942.40		
1 Equip. Oper. (light)	51.30	410.40	77.35	618.80		
1 Air Compressor, 60 cfm		105.40		115.94		
1 -50' Air Hose, 3/4"		7.35		8.09		
2 Flatbed Trucks, Gas, 1.5 Ton		376.80		414.48		
1 Shot Blaster, 20"		214.80		236.28	14.67	16.14
48 L.H., Daily Totals		$2724.75		$3845.99	$56.77	$80.12
Crew B-38	Hr.	Daily	Hr.	Daily	Bare Costs	Incl. O&P
1 Labor Foreman (outside)	$41.85	$334.80	$63.75	$510.00	$45.32	$68.71
2 Laborers	39.85	637.60	60.70	971.20		
1 Equip. Oper. (light)	51.30	410.40	77.35	618.80		
1 Equip. Oper. (medium)	53.75	430.00	81.05	648.40		
1 Backhoe Loader, 48 H.P.		312.40		343.64		
1 Hyd. Hammer (1200 lb.)		177.40		195.14		
1 F.E. Loader, W.M., 4 C.Y.		574.60		632.06		
1 Pvmt. Rem. Bucket		61.00		67.10	28.14	30.95
40 L.H., Daily Totals		$2938.20		$3986.34	$73.45	$99.66
Crew B-39	Hr.	Daily	Hr.	Daily	Bare Costs	Incl. O&P
1 Labor Foreman (outside)	$41.85	$334.80	$63.75	$510.00	$42.09	$63.98
4 Laborers	39.85	1275.20	60.70	1942.40		
1 Equip. Oper. (light)	51.30	410.40	77.35	618.80		
1 Air Compressor, 250 cfm		167.40		184.14		
2 Breakers, Pavement, 60 lb.		21.20		23.32		
2 -50' Air Hoses, 1.5"		45.40		49.94	4.88	5.36
48 L.H., Daily Totals		$2254.40		$3328.60	$46.97	$69.35
Crew B-40	Hr.	Daily	Hr.	Daily	Bare Costs	Incl. O&P
1 Pile Driver Foreman (outside)	$53.30	$426.40	$84.05	$672.40	$52.41	$81.27
4 Pile Drivers	51.30	1641.60	80.90	2588.80		
2 Equip. Oper. (crane)	56.10	897.60	84.60	1353.60		
1 Equip. Oper. (oiler)	48.60	388.80	73.30	586.40		
1 Crawler Crane, 40 Ton		1370.00		1507.00		
1 Vibratory Hammer & Gen.		2191.00		2410.10	55.64	61.20
64 L.H., Daily Totals		$6915.40		$9118.30	$108.05	$142.47
Crew B-40B	Hr.	Daily	Hr.	Daily	Bare Costs	Incl. O&P
1 Labor Foreman (outside)	$41.85	$334.80	$63.75	$510.00	$44.35	$67.29
3 Laborers	39.85	956.40	60.70	1456.80		
1 Equip. Oper. (crane)	56.10	448.80	84.60	676.80		
1 Equip. Oper. (oiler)	48.60	388.80	73.30	586.40		
1 Lattice Boom Crane, 40 Ton		1321.00		1453.10	27.52	30.27
48 L.H., Daily Totals		$3449.80		$4683.10	$71.87	$97.56

Crew No.		Bare Costs		Incl. Subs O&P		Cost Per Labor-Hour	
Crew B-41	Hr.	Daily	Hr.	Daily	Bare Costs	Incl. O&P
1 Labor Foreman (outside)	$41.85	$334.80	$63.75	$510.00	$41.35	$62.91
4 Laborers	39.85	1275.20	60.70	1942.40		
.25 Equip. Oper. (crane)	56.10	112.20	84.60	169.20		
.25 Equip. Oper. (oiler)	48.60	97.20	73.30	146.60		
.25 Crawler Crane, 40 Ton		342.50		376.75	7.78	8.56
44 L.H., Daily Totals		$2161.90		$3144.95	$49.13	$71.48
Crew B-42	Hr.	Daily	Hr.	Daily	Bare Costs	Incl. O&P
1 Labor Foreman (outside)	$41.85	$334.80	$63.75	$510.00	$45.08	$69.22
4 Laborers	39.85	1275.20	60.70	1942.40		
1 Equip. Oper. (crane)	56.10	448.80	84.60	676.80		
1 Equip. Oper. (oiler)	48.60	388.80	73.30	586.40		
1 Welder	54.65	437.20	89.35	714.80		
1 Hyd. Crane, 25 Ton		590.60		649.66		
1 Welder, Gas Engine, 300 amp		98.40		108.24		
1 Horz. Boring Csg. Mch.		448.80		493.68	17.78	19.56
64 L.H., Daily Totals		$4022.60		$5681.98	$62.85	$88.78
Crew B-43	Hr.	Daily	Hr.	Daily	Bare Costs	Incl. O&P
1 Labor Foreman (outside)	$41.85	$334.80	$63.75	$510.00	$44.35	$67.29
3 Laborers	39.85	956.40	60.70	1456.80		
1 Equip. Oper. (crane)	56.10	448.80	84.60	676.80		
1 Equip. Oper. (oiler)	48.60	388.80	73.30	586.40		
1 Drill Rig, Truck-Mounted		2444.00		2688.40	50.92	56.01
48 L.H., Daily Totals		$4572.80		$5918.40	$95.27	$123.30
Crew B-44	Hr.	Daily	Hr.	Daily	Bare Costs	Incl. O&P
1 Pile Driver Foreman (outside)	$53.30	$426.40	$84.05	$672.40	$51.32	$79.69
4 Pile Drivers	51.30	1641.60	80.90	2588.80		
2 Equip. Oper. (crane)	56.10	897.60	84.60	1353.60		
1 Laborer	39.85	318.80	60.70	485.60		
1 Crawler Crane, 40 Ton		1370.00		1507.00		
1 Lead, 60' High		79.40		87.34		
1 Hammer, Diesel, 15K ft.-lbs.		623.20		685.52	32.38	35.62
64 L.H., Daily Totals		$5357.00		$7380.26	$83.70	$115.32
Crew B-45	Hr.	Daily	Hr.	Daily	Bare Costs	Incl. O&P
1 Equip. Oper. (medium)	$53.75	$430.00	$81.05	$648.40	$49.88	$75.17
1 Truck Driver (heavy)	46.00	368.00	69.30	554.40		
1 Dist. Tanker, 3000 Gallon		326.80		359.48		
1 Truck Tractor, 6x4, 380 H.P.		476.20		523.82	50.19	55.21
16 L.H., Daily Totals		$1601.00		$2086.10	$100.06	$130.38
Crew B-46	Hr.	Daily	Hr.	Daily	Bare Costs	Incl. O&P
1 Pile Driver Foreman (outside)	$53.30	$426.40	$84.05	$672.40	$45.91	$71.33
2 Pile Drivers	51.30	820.80	80.90	1294.40		
3 Laborers	39.85	956.40	60.70	1456.80		
1 Chain Saw, Gas, 36" Long		46.40		51.04	.97	1.06
48 L.H., Daily Totals		$2250.00		$3474.64	$46.88	$72.39
Crew B-47	Hr.	Daily	Hr.	Daily	Bare Costs	Incl. O&P
1 Blast Foreman (outside)	$41.85	$334.80	$63.75	$510.00	$44.33	$67.27
1 Driller	39.85	318.80	60.70	485.60		
1 Equip. Oper. (light)	51.30	410.40	77.35	618.80		
1 Air Track Drill, 4"		993.40		1092.74		
1 Air Compressor, 600 cfm		417.20		458.92		
2 -50' Air Hoses, 3"		86.40		95.04	62.38	68.61
24 L.H., Daily Totals		$2561.00		$3261.10	$106.71	$135.88

Crews - Standard

Crew No.	Bare Costs Hr.	Daily	Incl. Subs O&P Hr.	Daily	Cost Per Labor-Hour Bare Costs	Incl. O&P
Crew B-47A	Hr.	Daily	Hr.	Daily	Bare Costs	Incl. O&P
1 Drilling Foreman (outside)	$41.85	$334.80	$63.75	$510.00	$48.85	$73.88
1 Equip. Oper. (heavy)	56.10	448.80	84.60	676.80		
1 Equip. Oper. (oiler)	48.60	388.80	73.30	586.40		
1 Air Track Drill, 5"		1173.00		1290.30	48.88	53.76
24 L.H., Daily Totals		$2345.40		$3063.50	$97.72	$127.65
Crew B-47C	Hr.	Daily	Hr.	Daily	Bare Costs	Incl. O&P
1 Laborer	$39.85	$318.80	$60.70	$485.60	$45.58	$69.03
1 Equip. Oper. (light)	51.30	410.40	77.35	618.80		
1 Air Compressor, 750 cfm		423.80		466.18		
2 -50' Air Hoses, 3"		86.40		95.04		
1 Air Track Drill, 4"		993.40		1092.74	93.97	103.37
16 L.H., Daily Totals		$2232.80		$2758.36	$139.55	$172.40
Crew B-47E	Hr.	Daily	Hr.	Daily	Bare Costs	Incl. O&P
1 Labor Foreman (outside)	$41.85	$334.80	$63.75	$510.00	$40.35	$61.46
3 Laborers	39.85	956.40	60.70	1456.80		
1 Flatbed Truck, Gas, 3 Ton		238.00		261.80	7.44	8.18
32 L.H., Daily Totals		$1529.20		$2228.60	$47.79	$69.64
Crew B-47G	Hr.	Daily	Hr.	Daily	Bare Costs	Incl. O&P
1 Labor Foreman (outside)	$41.85	$334.80	$63.75	$510.00	$43.21	$65.63
2 Laborers	39.85	637.60	60.70	971.20		
1 Equip. Oper. (light)	51.30	410.40	77.35	618.80		
1 Air Track Drill, 4"		993.40		1092.74		
1 Air Compressor, 600 cfm		417.20		458.92		
2 -50' Air Hoses, 3"		86.40		95.04		
1 Gunite Pump Rig		321.00		353.10	56.81	62.49
32 L.H., Daily Totals		$3200.80		$4099.80	$100.03	$128.12
Crew B-47H	Hr.	Daily	Hr.	Daily	Bare Costs	Incl. O&P
1 Skilled Worker Foreman (out)	$54.35	$434.80	$83.20	$665.60	$52.85	$80.91
3 Skilled Workers	52.35	1256.40	80.15	1923.60		
1 Flatbed Truck, Gas, 3 Ton		238.00		261.80	7.44	8.18
32 L.H., Daily Totals		$1929.20		$2851.00	$60.29	$89.09
Crew B-48	Hr.	Daily	Hr.	Daily	Bare Costs	Incl. O&P
1 Labor Foreman (outside)	$41.85	$334.80	$63.75	$510.00	$45.34	$68.73
3 Laborers	39.85	956.40	60.70	1456.80		
1 Equip. Oper. (crane)	56.10	448.80	84.60	676.80		
1 Equip. Oper. (oiler)	48.60	388.80	73.30	586.40		
1 Equip. Oper. (light)	51.30	410.40	77.35	618.80		
1 Centr. Water Pump, 6"		296.40		326.04		
1 -20' Suction Hose, 6"		11.50		12.65		
1 -50' Discharge Hose, 6"		6.10		6.71		
1 Drill Rig, Truck-Mounted		2444.00		2688.40	49.25	54.17
56 L.H., Daily Totals		$5297.20		$6882.60	$94.59	$122.90
Crew B-49	Hr.	Daily	Hr.	Daily	Bare Costs	Incl. O&P
1 Labor Foreman (outside)	$41.85	$334.80	$63.75	$510.00	$47.70	$72.80
3 Laborers	39.85	956.40	60.70	1456.80		
2 Equip. Oper. (crane)	56.10	897.60	84.60	1353.60		
2 Equip. Oper. (oilers)	48.60	777.60	73.30	1172.80		
1 Equip. Oper. (light)	51.30	410.40	77.35	618.80		
2 Pile Drivers	51.30	820.80	80.90	1294.40		
1 Hyd. Crane, 25 Ton		590.60		649.66		
1 Centr. Water Pump, 6"		296.40		326.04		
1 -20' Suction Hose, 6"		11.50		12.65		
1 -50' Discharge Hose, 6"		6.10		6.71		
1 Drill Rig, Truck-Mounted		2444.00		2688.40	38.05	41.86
88 L.H., Daily Totals		$7546.20		$10089.86	$85.75	$114.66

Crew No.	Bare Costs Hr.	Daily	Incl. Subs O&P Hr.	Daily	Cost Per Labor-Hour Bare Costs	Incl. O&P
Crew B-50	Hr.	Daily	Hr.	Daily	Bare Costs	Incl. O&P
2 Pile Driver Foremen (outside)	$53.30	$852.80	$84.05	$1344.80	$49.63	$77.01
6 Pile Drivers	51.30	2462.40	80.90	3883.20		
2 Equip. Oper. (crane)	56.10	897.60	84.60	1353.60		
1 Equip. Oper. (oiler)	48.60	388.80	73.30	586.40		
3 Laborers	39.85	956.40	60.70	1456.80		
1 Crawler Crane, 40 Ton		1370.00		1507.00		
1 Lead, 60' High		79.40		87.34		
1 Hammer, Diesel, 15K ft.-lbs.		623.20		685.52		
1 Air Compressor, 600 cfm		417.20		458.92		
2 -50' Air Hoses, 3"		86.40		95.04		
1 Chain Saw, Gas, 36" Long		46.40		51.04	23.42	25.76
112 L.H., Daily Totals		$8180.60		$11509.66	$73.04	$102.76
Crew B-51	Hr.	Daily	Hr.	Daily	Bare Costs	Incl. O&P
1 Labor Foreman (outside)	$41.85	$334.80	$63.75	$510.00	$40.96	$62.26
4 Laborers	39.85	1275.20	60.70	1942.40		
1 Truck Driver (light)	44.50	356.00	67.00	536.00		
1 Flatbed Truck, Gas, 1.5 Ton		188.40		207.24	3.92	4.32
48 L.H., Daily Totals		$2154.40		$3195.64	$44.88	$66.58
Crew B-52	Hr.	Daily	Hr.	Daily	Bare Costs	Incl. O&P
1 Carpenter Foreman (outside)	$52.70	$421.60	$80.25	$642.00	$46.39	$70.32
1 Carpenter	50.70	405.60	77.20	617.60		
3 Laborers	39.85	956.40	60.70	1456.80		
1 Cement Finisher	47.55	380.40	70.45	563.60		
.5 Rodman (reinf.)	54.65	218.60	83.45	333.80		
.5 Equip. Oper. (medium)	53.75	215.00	81.05	324.20		
.5 Crawler Loader, 3 C.Y.		602.00		662.20	10.75	11.82
56 L.H., Daily Totals		$3199.60		$4600.20	$57.14	$82.15
Crew B-53	Hr.	Daily	Hr.	Daily	Bare Costs	Incl. O&P
1 Equip. Oper. (light)	$51.30	$410.40	$77.35	$618.80	$51.30	$77.35
1 Trencher, Chain, 12 H.P.		61.80		67.98	7.72	8.50
8 L.H., Daily Totals		$472.20		$686.78	$59.02	$85.85
Crew B-54	Hr.	Daily	Hr.	Daily	Bare Costs	Incl. O&P
1 Equip. Oper. (light)	$51.30	$410.40	$77.35	$618.80	$51.30	$77.35
1 Trencher, Chain, 40 H.P.		336.40		370.04	42.05	46.26
8 L.H., Daily Totals		$746.80		$988.84	$93.35	$123.61
Crew B-54A	Hr.	Daily	Hr.	Daily	Bare Costs	Incl. O&P
.17 Labor Foreman (outside)	$41.85	$56.92	$63.75	$86.70	$52.02	$78.54
1 Equipment Operator (med.)	53.75	430.00	81.05	648.40		
1 Wheel Trencher, 67 H.P.		1095.00		1204.50	116.99	128.69
9.36 L.H., Daily Totals		$1581.92		$1939.60	$169.01	$207.22
Crew B-54B	Hr.	Daily	Hr.	Daily	Bare Costs	Incl. O&P
.25 Labor Foreman (outside)	$41.85	$83.70	$63.75	$127.50	$51.37	$77.59
1 Equipment Operator (med.)	53.75	430.00	81.05	648.40		
1 Wheel Trencher, 150 H.P.		1957.00		2152.70	195.70	215.27
10 L.H., Daily Totals		$2470.70		$2928.60	$247.07	$292.86
Crew B-54C	Hr.	Daily	Hr.	Daily	Bare Costs	Incl. O&P
1 Laborer	$39.85	$318.80	$60.70	$485.60	$46.80	$70.88
1 Equipment Operator (med.)	53.75	430.00	81.05	648.40		
1 Wheel Trencher, 67 H.P.		1095.00		1204.50	68.44	75.28
16 L.H., Daily Totals		$1843.80		$2338.50	$115.24	$146.16

Crews - Standard

Crew No.		Bare Costs		Incl. Subs O&P		Cost Per Labor-Hour	
Crew B-54D	Hr.	Daily	Hr.	Daily	Bare Costs	Incl. O&P
1 Laborer	$39.85	$318.80	$60.70	$485.60	$46.80	$70.88
1 Equipment Operator (med.)	53.75	430.00	81.05	648.40		
1 Rock Trencher, 6" Width		904.20		994.62	56.51	62.16
16 L.H., Daily Totals		$1653.00		$2128.62	$103.31	$133.04
Crew B-54E	Hr.	Daily	Hr.	Daily	Bare Costs	Incl. O&P
1 Laborer	$39.85	$318.80	$60.70	$485.60	$46.80	$70.88
1 Equipment Operator (med.)	53.75	430.00	81.05	648.40		
1 Rock Trencher, 18" Width		2681.00		2949.10	167.56	184.32
16 L.H., Daily Totals		$3429.80		$4083.10	$214.36	$255.19
Crew B-55	Hr.	Daily	Hr.	Daily	Bare Costs	Incl. O&P
2 Laborers	$39.85	$637.60	$60.70	$971.20	$41.40	$62.80
1 Truck Driver (light)	44.50	356.00	67.00	536.00		
1 Truck-Mounted Earth Auger		758.80		834.68		
1 Flatbed Truck, Gas, 3 Ton		238.00		261.80	41.53	45.69
24 L.H., Daily Totals		$1990.40		$2603.68	$82.93	$108.49
Crew B-56	Hr.	Daily	Hr.	Daily	Bare Costs	Incl. O&P
1 Laborer	$39.85	$318.80	$60.70	$485.60	$45.58	$69.03
1 Equip. Oper. (light)	51.30	410.40	77.35	618.80		
1 Air Track Drill, 4"		993.40		1092.74		
1 Air Compressor, 600 cfm		417.20		458.92		
1 -50' Air Hose, 3"		43.20		47.52	90.86	99.95
16 L.H., Daily Totals		$2183.00		$2703.58	$136.44	$168.97
Crew B-57	Hr.	Daily	Hr.	Daily	Bare Costs	Incl. O&P
1 Labor Foreman (outside)	$41.85	$334.80	$63.75	$510.00	$46.26	$70.07
2 Laborers	39.85	637.60	60.70	971.20		
1 Equip. Oper. (crane)	56.10	448.80	84.60	676.80		
1 Equip. Oper. (light)	51.30	410.40	77.35	618.80		
1 Equip. Oper. (oiler)	48.60	388.80	73.30	586.40		
1 Crawler Crane, 25 Ton		1348.00		1482.80		
1 Clamshell Bucket, 1 C.Y.		50.60		55.66		
1 Centr. Water Pump, 6"		296.40		326.04		
1 -20' Suction Hose, 6"		11.50		12.65		
20 -50' Discharge Hoses, 6"		122.00		134.20	38.09	41.90
48 L.H., Daily Totals		$4048.90		$5374.55	$84.35	$111.97
Crew B-58	Hr.	Daily	Hr.	Daily	Bare Costs	Incl. O&P
2 Laborers	$39.85	$637.60	$60.70	$971.20	$43.67	$66.25
1 Equip. Oper. (light)	51.30	410.40	77.35	618.80		
1 Backhoe Loader, 48 H.P.		312.40		343.64		
1 Small Helicopter, w/ Pilot		2857.00		3142.70	132.06	145.26
24 L.H., Daily Totals		$4217.40		$5076.34	$175.72	$211.51
Crew B-59	Hr.	Daily	Hr.	Daily	Bare Costs	Incl. O&P
1 Truck Driver (heavy)	$46.00	$368.00	$69.30	$554.40	$46.00	$69.30
1 Truck Tractor, 220 H.P.		290.00		319.00		
1 Water Tank Trailer, 5000 Gal.		147.60		162.36	54.70	60.17
8 L.H., Daily Totals		$805.60		$1035.76	$100.70	$129.47
Crew B-59A	Hr.	Daily	Hr.	Daily	Bare Costs	Incl. O&P
2 Laborers	$39.85	$637.60	$60.70	$971.20	$41.90	$63.57
1 Truck Driver (heavy)	46.00	368.00	69.30	554.40		
1 Water Tank Trailer, 5000 Gal.		147.60		162.36		
1 Truck Tractor, 220 H.P.		290.00		319.00	18.23	20.06
24 L.H., Daily Totals		$1443.20		$2006.96	$60.13	$83.62

Crew No.		Bare Costs		Incl. Subs O&P		Cost Per Labor-Hour	
Crew B-60	Hr.	Daily	Hr.	Daily	Bare Costs	Incl. O&P
1 Labor Foreman (outside)	$41.85	$334.80	$63.75	$510.00	$46.98	$71.11
2 Laborers	39.85	637.60	60.70	971.20		
1 Equip. Oper. (crane)	56.10	448.80	84.60	676.80		
2 Equip. Oper. (light)	51.30	820.80	77.35	1237.60		
1 Equip. Oper. (oiler)	48.60	388.80	73.30	586.40		
1 Crawler Crane, 40 Ton		1370.00		1507.00		
1 Lead, 60' High		79.40		87.34		
1 Hammer, Diesel, 15K ft.-lbs.		623.20		685.52		
1 Backhoe Loader, 48 H.P.		312.40		343.64	42.59	46.85
56 L.H., Daily Totals		$5015.80		$6605.50	$89.57	$117.96
Crew B-61	Hr.	Daily	Hr.	Daily	Bare Costs	Incl. O&P
1 Labor Foreman (outside)	$41.85	$334.80	$63.75	$510.00	$42.54	$64.64
3 Laborers	39.85	956.40	60.70	1456.80		
1 Equip. Oper. (light)	51.30	410.40	77.35	618.80		
1 Cement Mixer, 2 C.Y.		204.20		224.62		
1 Air Compressor, 160 cfm		117.20		128.92	8.04	8.84
40 L.H., Daily Totals		$2023.00		$2939.14	$50.58	$73.48
Crew B-62	Hr.	Daily	Hr.	Daily	Bare Costs	Incl. O&P
2 Laborers	$39.85	$637.60	$60.70	$971.20	$43.67	$66.25
1 Equip. Oper. (light)	51.30	410.40	77.35	618.80		
1 Loader, Skid Steer, 30 H.P.		174.00		191.40	7.25	7.97
24 L.H., Daily Totals		$1222.00		$1781.40	$50.92	$74.22
Crew B-62A	Hr.	Daily	Hr.	Daily	Bare Costs	Incl. O&P
2 Laborers	$39.85	$637.60	$60.70	$971.20	$43.67	$66.25
1 Equip. Oper. (light)	51.30	410.40	77.35	618.80		
1 Loader, Skid Steer, 30 H.P.		174.00		191.40		
1 Trencher Attachment		74.30		81.73	10.35	11.38
24 L.H., Daily Totals		$1296.30		$1863.13	$54.01	$77.63
Crew B-63	Hr.	Daily	Hr.	Daily	Bare Costs	Incl. O&P
4 Laborers	$39.85	$1275.20	$60.70	$1942.40	$42.14	$64.03
1 Equip. Oper. (light)	51.30	410.40	77.35	618.80		
1 Loader, Skid Steer, 30 H.P.		174.00		191.40	4.35	4.79
40 L.H., Daily Totals		$1859.60		$2752.60	$46.49	$68.81
Crew B-63B	Hr.	Daily	Hr.	Daily	Bare Costs	Incl. O&P
1 Labor Foreman (inside)	$40.35	$322.80	$61.45	$491.60	$42.84	$65.05
2 Laborers	39.85	637.60	60.70	971.20		
1 Equip. Oper. (light)	51.30	410.40	77.35	618.80		
1 Loader, Skid Steer, 78 H.P.		364.80		401.28	11.40	12.54
32 L.H., Daily Totals		$1735.60		$2482.88	$54.24	$77.59
Crew B-64	Hr.	Daily	Hr.	Daily	Bare Costs	Incl. O&P
1 Laborer	$39.85	$318.80	$60.70	$485.60	$42.17	$63.85
1 Truck Driver (light)	44.50	356.00	67.00	536.00		
1 Power Mulcher (small)		139.20		153.12		
1 Flatbed Truck, Gas, 1.5 Ton		188.40		207.24	20.48	22.52
16 L.H., Daily Totals		$1002.40		$1381.96	$62.65	$86.37
Crew B-65	Hr.	Daily	Hr.	Daily	Bare Costs	Incl. O&P
1 Laborer	$39.85	$318.80	$60.70	$485.60	$42.17	$63.85
1 Truck Driver (light)	44.50	356.00	67.00	536.00		
1 Power Mulcher (Large)		268.80		295.68		
1 Flatbed Truck, Gas, 1.5 Ton		188.40		207.24	28.57	31.43
16 L.H., Daily Totals		$1132.00		$1524.52	$70.75	$95.28

Crews - Standard

Crew No.	Bare Costs Hr.	Bare Costs Daily	Incl. Subs O&P Hr.	Incl. Subs O&P Daily	Cost Per Labor-Hour Bare Costs	Cost Per Labor-Hour Incl. O&P
Crew B-66					Bare Costs	Incl. O&P
1 Equip. Oper. (light)	$51.30	$410.40	$77.35	$618.80	$51.30	$77.35
1 Loader-Backhoe, 40 H.P.		247.00		271.70	30.88	33.96
8 L.H., Daily Totals		$657.40		$890.50	$82.17	$111.31
Crew B-67	Hr.	Daily	Hr.	Daily	Bare Costs	Incl. O&P
1 Millwright	$52.75	$422.00	$76.95	$615.60	$52.02	$77.15
1 Equip. Oper. (light)	51.30	410.40	77.35	618.80		
1 R.T. Forklift, 5,000 Lb., diesel		267.60		294.36	16.73	18.40
16 L.H., Daily Totals		$1100.00		$1528.76	$68.75	$95.55
Crew B-67B	Hr.	Daily	Hr.	Daily	Bare Costs	Incl. O&P
1 Millwright Foreman (inside)	$53.25	$426.00	$77.70	$621.60	$53.00	$77.33
1 Millwright	52.75	422.00	76.95	615.60		
16 L.H., Daily Totals		$848.00		$1237.20	$53.00	$77.33
Crew B-68	Hr.	Daily	Hr.	Daily	Bare Costs	Incl. O&P
2 Millwrights	$52.75	$844.00	$76.95	$1231.20	$52.27	$77.08
1 Equip. Oper. (light)	51.30	410.40	77.35	618.80		
1 R.T. Forklift, 5,000 Lb., diesel		267.60		294.36	11.15	12.27
24 L.H., Daily Totals		$1522.00		$2144.36	$63.42	$89.35
Crew B-68A	Hr.	Daily	Hr.	Daily	Bare Costs	Incl. O&P
1 Millwright Foreman (inside)	$53.25	$426.00	$77.70	$621.60	$52.92	$77.20
2 Millwrights	52.75	844.00	76.95	1231.20		
1 Forklift, Smooth Floor, 8,000 Lb.		148.20		163.02	6.17	6.79
24 L.H., Daily Totals		$1418.20		$2015.82	$59.09	$83.99
Crew B-68B	Hr.	Daily	Hr.	Daily	Bare Costs	Incl. O&P
1 Millwright Foreman (inside)	$53.25	$426.00	$77.70	$621.60	$57.06	$84.69
2 Millwrights	52.75	844.00	76.95	1231.20		
2 Electricians	58.20	931.20	87.00	1392.00		
2 Plumbers	62.15	994.40	93.60	1497.60		
1 R.T. Forklift, 5,000 Lb., gas		279.00		306.90	4.98	5.48
56 L.H., Daily Totals		$3474.60		$5049.30	$62.05	$90.17
Crew B-68C	Hr.	Daily	Hr.	Daily	Bare Costs	Incl. O&P
1 Millwright Foreman (inside)	$53.25	$426.00	$77.70	$621.60	$56.59	$83.81
1 Millwright	52.75	422.00	76.95	615.60		
1 Electrician	58.20	465.60	87.00	696.00		
1 Plumber	62.15	497.20	93.60	748.80		
1 R.T. Forklift, 5,000 Lb., gas		279.00		306.90	8.72	9.59
32 L.H., Daily Totals		$2089.80		$2988.90	$65.31	$93.40
Crew B-68D	Hr.	Daily	Hr.	Daily	Bare Costs	Incl. O&P
1 Labor Foreman (inside)	$40.35	$322.80	$61.45	$491.60	$43.83	$66.50
1 Laborer	39.85	318.80	60.70	485.60		
1 Equip. Oper. (light)	51.30	410.40	77.35	618.80		
1 R.T. Forklift, 5,000 Lb., gas		279.00		306.90	11.63	12.79
24 L.H., Daily Totals		$1331.00		$1902.90	$55.46	$79.29
Crew B-68E	Hr.	Daily	Hr.	Daily	Bare Costs	Incl. O&P
1 Struc. Steel Foreman (inside)	$55.15	$441.20	$90.15	$721.20	$54.75	$89.51
3 Struc. Steel Workers	54.65	1311.60	89.35	2144.40		
1 Welder	54.65	437.20	89.35	714.80		
1 Forklift, Smooth Floor, 8,000 Lb.		148.20		163.02	3.71	4.08
40 L.H., Daily Totals		$2338.20		$3743.42	$58.45	$93.59

Crew No.	Bare Costs Hr.	Bare Costs Daily	Incl. Subs O&P Hr.	Incl. Subs O&P Daily	Cost Per Labor-Hour Bare Costs	Cost Per Labor-Hour Incl. O&P
Crew B-68F	Hr.	Daily	Hr.	Daily	Bare Costs	Incl. O&P
1 Skilled Worker Foreman (out)	$54.35	$434.80	$83.20	$665.60	$53.02	$81.17
2 Skilled Workers	52.35	837.60	80.15	1282.40		
1 R.T. Forklift, 5,000 Lb., gas		279.00		306.90	11.63	12.79
24 L.H., Daily Totals		$1551.40		$2254.90	$64.64	$93.95
Crew B-68G	Hr.	Daily	Hr.	Daily	Bare Costs	Incl. O&P
2 Structural Steel Workers	$54.65	$874.40	$89.35	$1429.60	$54.65	$89.35
1 R.T. Forklift, 5,000 Lb., gas		279.00		306.90	17.44	19.18
16 L.H., Daily Totals		$1153.40		$1736.50	$72.09	$108.53
Crew B-69	Hr.	Daily	Hr.	Daily	Bare Costs	Incl. O&P
1 Labor Foreman (outside)	$41.85	$334.80	$63.75	$510.00	$44.35	$67.29
3 Laborers	39.85	956.40	60.70	1456.80		
1 Equip. Oper. (crane)	56.10	448.80	84.60	676.80		
1 Equip. Oper. (oiler)	48.60	388.80	73.30	586.40		
1 Hyd. Crane, 80 Ton		1518.00		1669.80	31.63	34.79
48 L.H., Daily Totals		$3646.80		$4899.80	$75.97	$102.08
Crew B-69A	Hr.	Daily	Hr.	Daily	Bare Costs	Incl. O&P
1 Labor Foreman (outside)	$41.85	$334.80	$63.75	$510.00	$43.78	$66.22
3 Laborers	39.85	956.40	60.70	1456.80		
1 Equip. Oper. (medium)	53.75	430.00	81.05	648.40		
1 Concrete Finisher	47.55	380.40	70.45	563.60		
1 Curb/Gutter Paver, 2-Track		1173.00		1290.30	24.44	26.88
48 L.H., Daily Totals		$3274.60		$4469.10	$68.22	$93.11
Crew B-69B	Hr.	Daily	Hr.	Daily	Bare Costs	Incl. O&P
1 Labor Foreman (outside)	$41.85	$334.80	$63.75	$510.00	$43.78	$66.22
3 Laborers	39.85	956.40	60.70	1456.80		
1 Equip. Oper. (medium)	53.75	430.00	81.05	648.40		
1 Cement Finisher	47.55	380.40	70.45	563.60		
1 Curb/Gutter Paver, 4-Track		789.60		868.56	16.45	18.09
48 L.H., Daily Totals		$2891.20		$4047.36	$60.23	$84.32
Crew B-70	Hr.	Daily	Hr.	Daily	Bare Costs	Incl. O&P
1 Labor Foreman (outside)	$41.85	$334.80	$63.75	$510.00	$46.09	$69.86
3 Laborers	39.85	956.40	60.70	1456.80		
3 Equip. Oper. (medium)	53.75	1290.00	81.05	1945.20		
1 Grader, 30,000 Lbs.		643.80		708.18		
1 Ripper, Beam & 1 Shank		87.80		96.58		
1 Road Sweeper, S.P., 8' wide		688.60		757.46		
1 F.E. Loader, W.M., 1.5 C.Y.		342.80		377.08	31.48	34.63
56 L.H., Daily Totals		$4344.20		$5851.30	$77.58	$104.49
Crew B-70A	Hr.	Daily	Hr.	Daily	Bare Costs	Incl. O&P
1 Laborer	$39.85	$318.80	$60.70	$485.60	$50.97	$76.98
4 Equip. Oper. (medium)	53.75	1720.00	81.05	2593.60		
1 Grader, 40,000 Lbs.		1191.00		1310.10		
1 F.E. Loader, W.M., 2.5 C.Y.		523.20		575.52		
1 Dozer, 80 H.P.		464.40		510.84		
1 Roller, Pneum. Whl., 12 Ton		338.20		372.02	62.92	69.21
40 L.H., Daily Totals		$4555.60		$5847.68	$113.89	$146.19
Crew B-71	Hr.	Daily	Hr.	Daily	Bare Costs	Incl. O&P
1 Labor Foreman (outside)	$41.85	$334.80	$63.75	$510.00	$46.09	$69.86
3 Laborers	39.85	956.40	60.70	1456.80		
3 Equip. Oper. (medium)	53.75	1290.00	81.05	1945.20		
1 Pvmt. Profiler, 750 H.P.		5419.00		5960.90		
1 Road Sweeper, S.P., 8' wide		688.60		757.46		
1 F.E. Loader, W.M., 1.5 C.Y.		342.80		377.08	115.19	126.70
56 L.H., Daily Totals		$9031.60		$11007.44	$161.28	$196.56

For customer support on your Green Building Costs with RSMeans data, call 800.448.8182.

Crews - Standard

Crew No.	Bare Costs Hr.	Daily	Incl. Subs O&P Hr.	Daily	Cost Per Labor-Hour Bare Costs	Incl. O&P
Crew B-72						
1 Labor Foreman (outside)	$41.85	$334.80	$63.75	$510.00	$47.05	$71.26
3 Laborers	39.85	956.40	60.70	1456.80		
4 Equip. Oper. (medium)	53.75	1720.00	81.05	2593.60		
1 Pvmt. Profiler, 750 H.P.		5419.00		5960.90		
1 Hammermill, 250 H.P.		1870.00		2057.00		
1 Windrow Loader		1242.00		1366.20		
1 Mix Paver, 165 H.P.		2140.00		2354.00		
1 Roller, Pneum. Whl., 12 Ton		338.20		372.02	172.02	189.22
64 L.H., Daily Totals		$14020.40		$16670.52	$219.07	$260.48
Crew B-73						
1 Labor Foreman (outside)	$41.85	$334.80	$63.75	$510.00	$48.79	$73.80
2 Laborers	39.85	637.60	60.70	971.20		
5 Equip. Oper. (medium)	53.75	2150.00	81.05	3242.00		
1 Road Mixer, 310 H.P.		1889.00		2077.90		
1 Tandem Roller, 10 Ton		231.40		254.54		
1 Hammermill, 250 H.P.		1870.00		2057.00		
1 Grader, 30,000 Lbs.		643.80		708.18		
.5 F.E. Loader, W.M., 1.5 C.Y.		171.40		188.54		
.5 Truck Tractor, 220 H.P.		145.00		159.50		
.5 Water Tank Trailer, 5000 Gal.		73.80		81.18	78.51	86.36
64 L.H., Daily Totals		$8146.80		$10250.04	$127.29	$160.16
Crew B-74						
1 Labor Foreman (outside)	$41.85	$334.80	$63.75	$510.00	$48.59	$73.41
1 Laborer	39.85	318.80	60.70	485.60		
4 Equip. Oper. (medium)	53.75	1720.00	81.05	2593.60		
2 Truck Drivers (heavy)	46.00	736.00	69.30	1108.80		
1 Grader, 30,000 Lbs.		643.80		708.18		
1 Ripper, Beam & 1 Shank		87.80		96.58		
2 Stabilizers, 310 H.P.		3436.00		3779.60		
1 Flatbed Truck, Gas, 3 Ton		238.00		261.80		
1 Chem. Spreader, Towed		52.20		57.42		
1 Roller, Vibratory, 25 Ton		659.80		725.78		
1 Water Tank Trailer, 5000 Gal.		147.60		162.36		
1 Truck Tractor, 220 H.P.		290.00		319.00	86.80	95.48
64 L.H., Daily Totals		$8664.80		$10808.72	$135.39	$168.89
Crew B-75						
1 Labor Foreman (outside)	$41.85	$334.80	$63.75	$510.00	$48.96	$73.99
1 Laborer	39.85	318.80	60.70	485.60		
4 Equip. Oper. (medium)	53.75	1720.00	81.05	2593.60		
1 Truck Driver (heavy)	46.00	368.00	69.30	554.40		
1 Grader, 30,000 Lbs.		643.80		708.18		
1 Ripper, Beam & 1 Shank		87.80		96.58		
2 Stabilizers, 310 H.P.		3436.00		3779.60		
1 Dist. Tanker, 3000 Gallon		326.80		359.48		
1 Truck Tractor, 6x4, 380 H.P.		476.20		523.82		
1 Roller, Vibratory, 25 Ton		659.80		725.78	100.54	110.60
56 L.H., Daily Totals		$8372.00		$10337.04	$149.50	$184.59

Crew No.	Bare Costs Hr.	Daily	Incl. Subs O&P Hr.	Daily	Cost Per Labor-Hour Bare Costs	Incl. O&P
Crew B-76						
1 Dock Builder Foreman (outside)	$53.30	$426.40	$84.05	$672.40	$52.29	$81.23
5 Dock Builders	51.30	2052.00	80.90	3236.00		
2 Equip. Oper. (crane)	56.10	897.60	84.60	1353.60		
1 Equip. Oper. (oiler)	48.60	388.80	73.30	586.40		
1 Crawler Crane, 50 Ton		1940.00		2134.00		
1 Barge, 400 Ton		835.40		918.94		
1 Hammer, Diesel, 15K ft.-lbs.		623.20		685.52		
1 Lead, 60' High		79.40		87.34		
1 Air Compressor, 600 cfm		417.20		458.92		
2 -50' Air Hoses, 3"		86.40		95.04	55.30	60.83
72 L.H., Daily Totals		$7746.40		$10228.16	$107.59	$142.06
Crew B-76A						
1 Labor Foreman (outside)	$41.85	$334.80	$63.75	$510.00	$43.23	$65.64
5 Laborers	39.85	1594.00	60.70	2428.00		
1 Equip. Oper. (crane)	56.10	448.80	84.60	676.80		
1 Equip. Oper. (oiler)	48.60	388.80	73.30	586.40		
1 Crawler Crane, 50 Ton		1940.00		2134.00		
1 Barge, 400 Ton		835.40		918.94	43.37	47.70
64 L.H., Daily Totals		$5541.80		$7254.14	$86.59	$113.35
Crew B-77						
1 Labor Foreman (outside)	$41.85	$334.80	$63.75	$510.00	$41.18	$62.57
3 Laborers	39.85	956.40	60.70	1456.80		
1 Truck Driver (light)	44.50	356.00	67.00	536.00		
1 Crack Cleaner, 25 H.P.		55.80		61.38		
1 Crack Filler, Trailer Mtd.		198.20		218.02		
1 Flatbed Truck, Gas, 3 Ton		238.00		261.80	12.30	13.53
40 L.H., Daily Totals		$2139.20		$3044.00	$53.48	$76.10
Crew B-78						
1 Labor Foreman (outside)	$41.85	$334.80	$63.75	$510.00	$40.96	$62.26
4 Laborers	39.85	1275.20	60.70	1942.40		
1 Truck Driver (light)	44.50	356.00	67.00	536.00		
1 Paint Striper, S.P., 40 Gallon		151.00		166.10		
1 Flatbed Truck, Gas, 3 Ton		238.00		261.80		
1 Pickup Truck, 3/4 Ton		115.20		126.72	10.50	11.55
48 L.H., Daily Totals		$2470.20		$3543.02	$51.46	$73.81
Crew B-78A						
1 Equip. Oper. (light)	$51.30	$410.40	$77.35	$618.80	$51.30	$77.35
1 Line Rem. (Metal Balls) 115 H.P.		852.60		937.86	106.58	117.23
8 L.H., Daily Totals		$1263.00		$1556.66	$157.88	$194.58
Crew B-78B						
2 Laborers	$39.85	$637.60	$60.70	$971.20	$41.12	$62.55
.25 Equip. Oper. (light)	51.30	102.60	77.35	154.70		
1 Pickup Truck, 3/4 Ton		115.20		126.72		
1 Line Rem.,11 H.P.,Walk Behind		61.40		67.54		
.25 Road Sweeper, S.P., 8' wide		172.15		189.37	19.38	21.31
18 L.H., Daily Totals		$1088.95		$1509.53	$60.50	$83.86
Crew B-78C						
1 Labor Foreman (outside)	$41.85	$334.80	$63.75	$510.00	$40.96	$62.26
4 Laborers	39.85	1275.20	60.70	1942.40		
1 Truck Driver (light)	44.50	356.00	67.00	536.00		
1 Paint Striper, T.M., 120 Gal.		690.00		759.00		
1 Flatbed Truck, Gas, 3 Ton		238.00		261.80		
1 Pickup Truck, 3/4 Ton		115.20		126.72	21.73	23.91
48 L.H., Daily Totals		$3009.20		$4135.92	$62.69	$86.17

Crews - Standard

Crew No.	Bare Costs		Incl. Subs O&P		Cost Per Labor-Hour	
Crew B-78D	Hr.	Daily	Hr.	Daily	Bare Costs	Incl. O&P
2 Labor Foremen (outside)	$41.85	$669.60	$63.75	$1020.00	$40.72	$61.94
7 Laborers	39.85	2231.60	60.70	3399.20		
1 Truck Driver (light)	44.50	356.00	67.00	536.00		
1 Paint Striper, T.M., 120 Gal.		690.00		759.00		
1 Flatbed Truck, Gas, 3 Ton		238.00		261.80		
3 Pickup Trucks, 3/4 Ton		345.60		380.16		
1 Air Compressor, 60 cfm		105.40		115.94		
1 -50' Air Hose, 3/4"		7.35		8.09		
1 Breaker, Pavement, 60 lb.		10.60		11.66	17.46	19.21
80 L.H., Daily Totals		$4654.15		$6491.85	$58.18	$81.15

Crew B-78E	Hr.	Daily	Hr.	Daily	Bare Costs	Incl. O&P
2 Labor Foremen (outside)	$41.85	$669.60	$63.75	$1020.00	$40.57	$61.73
9 Laborers	39.85	2869.20	60.70	4370.40		
1 Truck Driver (light)	44.50	356.00	67.00	536.00		
1 Paint Striper, T.M., 120 Gal.		690.00		759.00		
1 Flatbed Truck, Gas, 3 Ton		238.00		261.80		
4 Pickup Trucks, 3/4 Ton		460.80		506.88		
2 Air Compressors, 60 cfm		210.80		231.88		
2 -50' Air Hoses, 3/4"		14.70		16.17		
2 Breakers, Pavement, 60 lb.		21.20		23.32	17.04	18.74
96 L.H., Daily Totals		$5530.30		$7725.45	$57.61	$80.47

Crew B-78F	Hr.	Daily	Hr.	Daily	Bare Costs	Incl. O&P
2 Labor Foremen (outside)	$41.85	$669.60	$63.75	$1020.00	$40.47	$61.59
11 Laborers	39.85	3506.80	60.70	5341.60		
1 Truck Driver (light)	44.50	356.00	67.00	536.00		
1 Paint Striper, T.M., 120 Gal.		690.00		759.00		
1 Flatbed Truck, Gas, 3 Ton		238.00		261.80		
7 Pickup Trucks, 3/4 Ton		806.40		887.04		
3 Air Compressors, 60 cfm		316.20		347.82		
3 -50' Air Hoses, 3/4"		22.05		24.25		
3 Breakers, Pavement, 60 lb.		31.80		34.98	18.79	20.67
112 L.H., Daily Totals		$6636.85		$9212.50	$59.26	$82.25

Crew B-79	Hr.	Daily	Hr.	Daily	Bare Costs	Incl. O&P
1 Labor Foreman (outside)	$41.85	$334.80	$63.75	$510.00	$41.18	$62.57
3 Laborers	39.85	956.40	60.70	1456.80		
1 Truck Driver (light)	44.50	356.00	67.00	536.00		
1 Paint Striper, T.M., 120 Gal.		690.00		759.00		
1 Heating Kettle, 115 Gallon		77.85		85.64		
1 Flatbed Truck, Gas, 3 Ton		238.00		261.80		
2 Pickup Trucks, 3/4 Ton		230.40		253.44	30.91	34.00
40 L.H., Daily Totals		$2883.45		$3862.68	$72.09	$96.57

Crew B-79A	Hr.	Daily	Hr.	Daily	Bare Costs	Incl. O&P
1.5 Equip. Oper. (light)	$51.30	$615.60	$77.35	$928.20	$51.30	$77.35
.5 Line Remov. (Grinder) 115 H.P.		459.70		505.67		
1 Line Rem. (Metal Balls) 115 H.P.		852.60		937.86	109.36	120.29
12 L.H., Daily Totals		$1927.90		$2371.73	$160.66	$197.64

Crew B-79B	Hr.	Daily	Hr.	Daily	Bare Costs	Incl. O&P
1 Laborer	$39.85	$318.80	$60.70	$485.60	$39.85	$60.70
1 Set of Gases		168.00		184.80	21.00	23.10
8 L.H., Daily Totals		$486.80		$670.40	$60.85	$83.80

Crew No.	Bare Costs		Incl. Subs O&P		Cost Per Labor-Hour	
Crew B-79C	Hr.	Daily	Hr.	Daily	Bare Costs	Incl. O&P
1 Labor Foreman (outside)	$41.85	$334.80	$63.75	$510.00	$40.80	$62.04
5 Laborers	39.85	1594.00	60.70	2428.00		
1 Truck Driver (light)	44.50	356.00	67.00	536.00		
1 Paint Striper, T.M., 120 Gal.		690.00		759.00		
1 Heating Kettle, 115 Gallon		77.85		85.64		
1 Flatbed Truck, Gas, 3 Ton		238.00		261.80		
3 Pickup Trucks, 3/4 Ton		345.60		380.16		
1 Air Compressor, 60 cfm		105.40		115.94		
1 -50' Air Hose, 3/4"		7.35		8.09		
1 Breaker, Pavement, 60 lb.		10.60		11.66	26.34	28.97
56 L.H., Daily Totals		$3759.60		$5096.28	$67.14	$91.00

Crew B-79D	Hr.	Daily	Hr.	Daily	Bare Costs	Incl. O&P
2 Labor Foremen (outside)	$41.85	$669.60	$63.75	$1020.00	$40.93	$62.25
5 Laborers	39.85	1594.00	60.70	2428.00		
1 Truck Driver (light)	44.50	356.00	67.00	536.00		
1 Paint Striper, T.M., 120 Gal.		690.00		759.00		
1 Heating Kettle, 115 Gallon		77.85		85.64		
1 Flatbed Truck, Gas, 3 Ton		238.00		261.80		
4 Pickup Trucks, 3/4 Ton		460.80		506.88		
1 Air Compressor, 60 cfm		105.40		115.94		
1 -50' Air Hose, 3/4"		7.35		8.09		
1 Breaker, Pavement, 60 lb.		10.60		11.66	24.84	27.33
64 L.H., Daily Totals		$4209.60		$5733.00	$65.78	$89.58

Crew B-79E	Hr.	Daily	Hr.	Daily	Bare Costs	Incl. O&P
2 Labor Foremen (outside)	$41.85	$669.60	$63.75	$1020.00	$40.72	$61.94
7 Laborers	39.85	2231.60	60.70	3399.20		
1 Truck Driver (light)	44.50	356.00	67.00	536.00		
1 Paint Striper, T.M., 120 Gal.		690.00		759.00		
1 Heating Kettle, 115 Gallon		77.85		85.64		
1 Flatbed Truck, Gas, 3 Ton		238.00		261.80		
5 Pickup Trucks, 3/4 Ton		576.00		633.60		
2 Air Compressors, 60 cfm		210.80		231.88		
2 -50' Air Hoses, 3/4"		14.70		16.17		
2 Breakers, Pavement, 60 lb.		21.20		23.32	22.86	25.14
80 L.H., Daily Totals		$5085.75		$6966.60	$63.57	$87.08

Crew B-80	Hr.	Daily	Hr.	Daily	Bare Costs	Incl. O&P
1 Labor Foreman (outside)	$41.85	$334.80	$63.75	$510.00	$44.38	$67.20
1 Laborer	39.85	318.80	60.70	485.60		
1 Truck Driver (light)	44.50	356.00	67.00	536.00		
1 Equip. Oper. (light)	51.30	410.40	77.35	618.80		
1 Flatbed Truck, Gas, 3 Ton		238.00		261.80		
1 Earth Auger, Truck-Mtd.		373.80		411.18	19.12	21.03
32 L.H., Daily Totals		$2031.80		$2823.38	$63.49	$88.23

Crew B-80A	Hr.	Daily	Hr.	Daily	Bare Costs	Incl. O&P
3 Laborers	$39.85	$956.40	$60.70	$1456.80	$39.85	$60.70
1 Flatbed Truck, Gas, 3 Ton		238.00		261.80	9.92	10.91
24 L.H., Daily Totals		$1194.40		$1718.60	$49.77	$71.61

Crew B-80B	Hr.	Daily	Hr.	Daily	Bare Costs	Incl. O&P
3 Laborers	$39.85	$956.40	$60.70	$1456.80	$42.71	$64.86
1 Equip. Oper. (light)	51.30	410.40	77.35	618.80		
1 Crane, Flatbed Mounted, 3 Ton		235.80		259.38	7.37	8.11
32 L.H., Daily Totals		$1602.60		$2334.98	$50.08	$72.97

Crews - Standard

Crew No.	Bare Costs		Incl. Subs O&P		Cost Per Labor-Hour	
Crew B-80C	Hr.	Daily	Hr.	Daily	Bare Costs	Incl. O&P
2 Laborers	$39.85	$637.60	$60.70	$971.20	$41.40	$62.80
1 Truck Driver (light)	44.50	356.00	67.00	536.00		
1 Flatbed Truck, Gas, 1.5 Ton		188.40		207.24		
1 Manual Fence Post Auger, Gas		7.40		8.14	8.16	8.97
24 L.H., Daily Totals		$1189.40		$1722.58	$49.56	$71.77
Crew B-81	Hr.	Daily	Hr.	Daily	Bare Costs	Incl. O&P
1 Laborer	$39.85	$318.80	$60.70	$485.60	$46.53	$70.35
1 Equip. Oper. (medium)	53.75	430.00	81.05	648.40		
1 Truck Driver (heavy)	46.00	368.00	69.30	554.40		
1 Hydromulcher, T.M., 3000 Gal.		282.80		311.08		
1 Truck Tractor, 220 H.P.		290.00		319.00	23.87	26.25
24 L.H., Daily Totals		$1689.60		$2318.48	$70.40	$96.60
Crew B-81A	Hr.	Daily	Hr.	Daily	Bare Costs	Incl. O&P
1 Laborer	$39.85	$318.80	$60.70	$485.60	$42.17	$63.85
1 Truck Driver (light)	44.50	356.00	67.00	536.00		
1 Hydromulcher, T.M., 600 Gal.		121.20		133.32		
1 Flatbed Truck, Gas, 3 Ton		238.00		261.80	22.45	24.70
16 L.H., Daily Totals		$1034.00		$1416.72	$64.63	$88.55
Crew B-82	Hr.	Daily	Hr.	Daily	Bare Costs	Incl. O&P
1 Laborer	$39.85	$318.80	$60.70	$485.60	$45.58	$69.03
1 Equip. Oper. (light)	51.30	410.40	77.35	618.80		
1 Horiz. Borer, 6 H.P.		78.00		85.80	4.88	5.36
16 L.H., Daily Totals		$807.20		$1190.20	$50.45	$74.39
Crew B-82A	Hr.	Daily	Hr.	Daily	Bare Costs	Incl. O&P
2 Laborers	$39.85	$637.60	$60.70	$971.20	$45.58	$69.03
2 Equip. Opers. (light)	51.30	820.80	77.35	1237.60		
2 Dump Trucks, 8 C.Y., 220 H.P.		677.20		744.92		
1 Flatbed Trailer, 25 Ton		133.00		146.30		
1 Horiz. Dir. Drill, 20k lb. Thrust		629.00		691.90		
1 Mud Trailer for HDD, 1500 Gal.		287.80		316.58		
1 Pickup Truck, 4x4, 3/4 Ton		126.60		139.26		
1 Flatbed Trailer, 3 Ton		25.40		27.94		
1 Loader, Skid Steer, 78 H.P.		364.80		401.28	70.12	77.13
32 L.H., Daily Totals		$3702.20		$4676.98	$115.69	$146.16
Crew B-82B	Hr.	Daily	Hr.	Daily	Bare Costs	Incl. O&P
2 Laborers	$39.85	$637.60	$60.70	$971.20	$45.58	$69.03
2 Equip. Opers. (light)	51.30	820.80	77.35	1237.60		
2 Dump Trucks, 8 C.Y., 220 H.P.		677.20		744.92		
1 Flatbed Trailer, 25 Ton		133.00		146.30		
1 Horiz. Dir. Drill, 30k lb. Thrust		896.20		985.82		
1 Mud Trailer for HDD, 1500 Gal.		287.80		316.58		
1 Pickup Truck, 4x4, 3/4 Ton		126.60		139.26		
1 Flatbed Trailer, 3 Ton		25.40		27.94		
1 Loader, Skid Steer, 78 H.P.		364.80		401.28	78.47	86.32
32 L.H., Daily Totals		$3969.40		$4970.90	$124.04	$155.34

Crew No.	Bare Costs		Incl. Subs O&P		Cost Per Labor-Hour	
Crew B-82C	Hr.	Daily	Hr.	Daily	Bare Costs	Incl. O&P
2 Laborers	$39.85	$637.60	$60.70	$971.20	$45.58	$69.03
2 Equip. Opers. (light)	51.30	820.80	77.35	1237.60		
2 Dump Trucks, 8 C.Y., 220 H.P.		677.20		744.92		
1 Flatbed Trailer, 25 Ton		133.00		146.30		
1 Horiz. Dir. Drill, 50k lb. Thrust		1188.00		1306.80		
1 Mud Trailer for HDD, 1500 Gal.		287.80		316.58		
1 Pickup Truck, 4x4, 3/4 Ton		126.60		139.26		
1 Flatbed Trailer, 3 Ton		25.40		27.94		
1 Loader, Skid Steer, 78 H.P.		364.80		401.28	87.59	96.35
32 L.H., Daily Totals		$4261.20		$5291.88	$133.16	$165.37
Crew B-82D	Hr.	Daily	Hr.	Daily	Bare Costs	Incl. O&P
1 Equip. Oper. (light)	$51.30	$410.40	$77.35	$618.80	$51.30	$77.35
1 Mud Trailer for HDD, 1500 Gal.		287.80		316.58	35.98	39.57
8 L.H., Daily Totals		$698.20		$935.38	$87.28	$116.92
Crew B-83	Hr.	Daily	Hr.	Daily	Bare Costs	Incl. O&P
1 Tugboat Captain	$53.75	$430.00	$81.05	$648.40	$46.80	$70.88
1 Tugboat Hand	39.85	318.80	60.70	485.60		
1 Tugboat, 250 H.P.		680.20		748.22	42.51	46.76
16 L.H., Daily Totals		$1429.00		$1882.22	$89.31	$117.64
Crew B-84	Hr.	Daily	Hr.	Daily	Bare Costs	Incl. O&P
1 Equip. Oper. (medium)	$53.75	$430.00	$81.05	$648.40	$53.75	$81.05
1 Rotary Mower/Tractor		357.00		392.70	44.63	49.09
8 L.H., Daily Totals		$787.00		$1041.10	$98.38	$130.14
Crew B-85	Hr.	Daily	Hr.	Daily	Bare Costs	Incl. O&P
3 Laborers	$39.85	$956.40	$60.70	$1456.80	$43.86	$66.49
1 Equip. Oper. (medium)	53.75	430.00	81.05	648.40		
1 Truck Driver (heavy)	46.00	368.00	69.30	554.40		
1 Telescoping Boom Lift, to 80'		548.60		603.46		
1 Brush Chipper, 12", 130 H.P.		393.00		432.30		
1 Pruning Saw, Rotary		6.65		7.32	23.71	26.08
40 L.H., Daily Totals		$2702.65		$3702.68	$67.57	$92.57
Crew B-86	Hr.	Daily	Hr.	Daily	Bare Costs	Incl. O&P
1 Equip. Oper. (medium)	$53.75	$430.00	$81.05	$648.40	$53.75	$81.05
1 Stump Chipper, S.P.		184.05		202.46	23.01	25.31
8 L.H., Daily Totals		$614.05		$850.86	$76.76	$106.36
Crew B-86A	Hr.	Daily	Hr.	Daily	Bare Costs	Incl. O&P
1 Equip. Oper. (medium)	$53.75	$430.00	$81.05	$648.40	$53.75	$81.05
1 Grader, 30,000 Lbs.		643.80		708.18	80.47	88.52
8 L.H., Daily Totals		$1073.80		$1356.58	$134.22	$169.57
Crew B-86B	Hr.	Daily	Hr.	Daily	Bare Costs	Incl. O&P
1 Equip. Oper. (medium)	$53.75	$430.00	$81.05	$648.40	$53.75	$81.05
1 Dozer, 200 H.P.		1273.00		1400.30	159.13	175.04
8 L.H., Daily Totals		$1703.00		$2048.70	$212.88	$256.09
Crew B-87	Hr.	Daily	Hr.	Daily	Bare Costs	Incl. O&P
1 Laborer	$39.85	$318.80	$60.70	$485.60	$50.97	$76.98
4 Equip. Oper. (medium)	53.75	1720.00	81.05	2593.60		
2 Feller Bunchers, 100 H.P.		1620.80		1782.88		
1 Log Chipper, 22" Tree		764.80		841.28		
1 Dozer, 105 H.P.		608.00		668.80		
1 Chain Saw, Gas, 36" Long		46.40		51.04	76.00	83.60
40 L.H., Daily Totals		$5078.80		$6423.20	$126.97	$160.58

Crews - Standard

Crew No.	Bare Costs Hr.	Daily	Incl. Subs O&P Hr.	Daily	Cost Per Labor-Hour Bare Costs	Incl. O&P
Crew B-88						
1 Laborer	$39.85	$318.80	$60.70	$485.60	$51.76	$78.14
6 Equip. Oper. (medium)	53.75	2580.00	81.05	3890.40		
2 Feller Bunchers, 100 H.P.		1620.80		1782.88		
1 Log Chipper, 22" Tree		764.80		841.28		
2 Log Skidders, 50 H.P.		1698.80		1868.68		
1 Dozer, 105 H.P.		608.00		668.80		
1 Chain Saw, Gas, 36" Long		46.40		51.04	84.62	93.08
56 L.H., Daily Totals		$7637.60		$9588.68	$136.39	$171.23
Crew B-89						
1 Equip. Oper. (light)	$51.30	$410.40	$77.35	$618.80	$47.90	$72.17
1 Truck Driver (light)	44.50	356.00	67.00	536.00		
1 Flatbed Truck, Gas, 3 Ton		238.00		261.80		
1 Concrete Saw		102.40		112.64		
1 Water Tank, 65 Gal.		79.90		87.89	26.27	28.90
16 L.H., Daily Totals		$1186.70		$1617.13	$74.17	$101.07
Crew B-89A						
1 Skilled Worker	$52.35	$418.80	$80.15	$641.20	$46.10	$70.42
1 Laborer	39.85	318.80	60.70	485.60		
1 Core Drill (Large)		112.20		123.42	7.01	7.71
16 L.H., Daily Totals		$849.80		$1250.22	$53.11	$78.14
Crew B-89B						
1 Equip. Oper. (light)	$51.30	$410.40	$77.35	$618.80	$47.90	$72.17
1 Truck Driver (light)	44.50	356.00	67.00	536.00		
1 Wall Saw, Hydraulic, 10 H.P.		46.40		51.04		
1 Generator, Diesel, 100 kW		307.60		338.36		
1 Water Tank, 65 Gal.		79.90		87.89		
1 Flatbed Truck, Gas, 3 Ton		238.00		261.80	41.99	46.19
16 L.H., Daily Totals		$1438.30		$1893.89	$89.89	$118.37
Crew B-90						
1 Labor Foreman (outside)	$41.85	$334.80	$63.75	$510.00	$44.50	$67.39
3 Laborers	39.85	956.40	60.70	1456.80		
2 Equip. Oper. (light)	51.30	820.80	77.35	1237.60		
2 Truck Drivers (heavy)	46.00	736.00	69.30	1108.80		
1 Road Mixer, 310 H.P.		1889.00		2077.90		
1 Dist. Truck, 2000 Gal.		296.00		325.60	34.14	37.55
64 L.H., Daily Totals		$5033.00		$6716.70	$78.64	$104.95
Crew B-90A						
1 Labor Foreman (outside)	$41.85	$334.80	$63.75	$510.00	$48.08	$72.76
2 Laborers	39.85	637.60	60.70	971.20		
4 Equip. Oper. (medium)	53.75	1720.00	81.05	2593.60		
2 Graders, 30,000 Lbs.		1287.60		1416.36		
1 Tandem Roller, 10 Ton		231.40		254.54		
1 Roller, Pneum. Whl., 12 Ton		338.20		372.02	33.16	36.48
56 L.H., Daily Totals		$4549.60		$6117.72	$81.24	$109.25
Crew B-90B						
1 Labor Foreman (outside)	$41.85	$334.80	$63.75	$510.00	$47.13	$71.38
2 Laborers	39.85	637.60	60.70	971.20		
3 Equip. Oper. (medium)	53.75	1290.00	81.05	1945.20		
1 Roller, Pneum. Whl., 12 Ton		338.20		372.02		
1 Road Mixer, 310 H.P.		1889.00		2077.90	46.40	51.04
48 L.H., Daily Totals		$4489.60		$5876.32	$93.53	$122.42

Crew No.	Bare Costs Hr.	Daily	Incl. Subs O&P Hr.	Daily	Cost Per Labor-Hour Bare Costs	Incl. O&P
Crew B-90C						
1 Labor Foreman (outside)	$41.85	$334.80	$63.75	$510.00	$45.50	$68.87
4 Laborers	39.85	1275.20	60.70	1942.40		
3 Equip. Oper. (medium)	53.75	1290.00	81.05	1945.20		
3 Truck Drivers (heavy)	46.00	1104.00	69.30	1663.20		
3 Road Mixers, 310 H.P.		5667.00		6233.70	64.40	70.84
88 L.H., Daily Totals		$9671.00		$12294.50	$109.90	$139.71
Crew B-90D						
1 Labor Foreman (outside)	$41.85	$334.80	$63.75	$510.00	$44.63	$67.62
6 Laborers	39.85	1912.80	60.70	2913.60		
3 Equip. Oper. (medium)	53.75	1290.00	81.05	1945.20		
3 Truck Drivers (heavy)	46.00	1104.00	69.30	1663.20		
3 Road Mixers, 310 H.P.		5667.00		6233.70	54.49	59.94
104 L.H., Daily Totals		$10308.60		$13265.70	$99.12	$127.55
Crew B-90E						
1 Labor Foreman (outside)	$41.85	$334.80	$63.75	$510.00	$45.39	$68.78
4 Laborers	39.85	1275.20	60.70	1942.40		
3 Equip. Oper. (medium)	53.75	1290.00	81.05	1945.20		
1 Truck Driver (heavy)	46.00	368.00	69.30	554.40		
1 Road Mixer, 310 H.P.		1889.00		2077.90	26.24	28.86
72 L.H., Daily Totals		$5157.00		$7029.90	$71.63	$97.64
Crew B-91						
1 Labor Foreman (outside)	$41.85	$334.80	$63.75	$510.00	$47.82	$72.33
2 Laborers	39.85	637.60	60.70	971.20		
4 Equip. Oper. (medium)	53.75	1720.00	81.05	2593.60		
1 Truck Driver (heavy)	46.00	368.00	69.30	554.40		
1 Dist. Tanker, 3000 Gallon		326.80		359.48		
1 Truck Tractor, 6x4, 380 H.P.		476.20		523.82		
1 Aggreg. Spreader, S.P.		837.00		920.70		
1 Roller, Pneum. Whl., 12 Ton		338.20		372.02		
1 Tandem Roller, 10 Ton		231.40		254.54	34.52	37.98
64 L.H., Daily Totals		$5270.00		$7059.76	$82.34	$110.31
Crew B-91B						
1 Laborer	$39.85	$318.80	$60.70	$485.60	$46.80	$70.88
1 Equipment Oper. (med.)	53.75	430.00	81.05	648.40		
1 Road Sweeper, Vac. Assist.		840.40		924.44	52.52	57.78
16 L.H., Daily Totals		$1589.20		$2058.44	$99.33	$128.65
Crew B-91C						
1 Laborer	$39.85	$318.80	$60.70	$485.60	$42.17	$63.85
1 Truck Driver (light)	44.50	356.00	67.00	536.00		
1 Catch Basin Cleaning Truck		522.80		575.08	32.67	35.94
16 L.H., Daily Totals		$1197.60		$1596.68	$74.85	$99.79
Crew B-91D						
1 Labor Foreman (outside)	$41.85	$334.80	$63.75	$510.00	$46.30	$70.08
5 Laborers	39.85	1594.00	60.70	2428.00		
5 Equip. Oper. (medium)	53.75	2150.00	81.05	3242.00		
2 Truck Drivers (heavy)	46.00	736.00	69.30	1108.80		
1 Aggreg. Spreader, S.P.		837.00		920.70		
2 Truck Tractors, 6x4, 380 H.P.		952.40		1047.64		
2 Dist. Tankers, 3000 Gallon		653.60		718.96		
2 Pavement Brushes, Towed		170.40		187.44		
2 Rollers Pneum. Whl., 12 Ton		676.40		744.04	31.63	34.80
104 L.H., Daily Totals		$8104.60		$10907.58	$77.93	$104.88

Crews - Standard

Crew No.		Bare Costs		Incl. Subs O&P		Cost Per Labor-Hour	
Crew B-92	Hr.	Daily	Hr.	Daily	Bare Costs	Incl. O&P
1 Labor Foreman (outside)	$41.85	$334.80	$63.75	$510.00	$40.35	$61.46
3 Laborers	39.85	956.40	60.70	1456.80		
1 Crack Cleaner, 25 H.P.		55.80		61.38		
1 Air Compressor, 60 cfm		105.40		115.94		
1 Tar Kettle, T.M.		129.20		142.12		
1 Flatbed Truck, Gas, 3 Ton		238.00		261.80	16.51	18.16
32 L.H., Daily Totals		$1819.60		$2548.04	$56.86	$79.63
Crew B-93	Hr.	Daily	Hr.	Daily	Bare Costs	Incl. O&P
1 Equip. Oper. (medium)	$53.75	$430.00	$81.05	$648.40	$53.75	$81.05
1 Feller Buncher, 100 H.P.		810.40		891.44	101.30	111.43
8 L.H., Daily Totals		$1240.40		$1539.84	$155.05	$192.48
Crew B-94A	Hr.	Daily	Hr.	Daily	Bare Costs	Incl. O&P
1 Laborer	$39.85	$318.80	$60.70	$485.60	$39.85	$60.70
1 Diaphragm Water Pump, 2"		73.00		80.30		
1 -20' Suction Hose, 2"		1.95		2.15		
2 -50' Discharge Hoses, 2"		1.80		1.98	9.59	10.55
8 L.H., Daily Totals		$395.55		$570.02	$49.44	$71.25
Crew B-94B	Hr.	Daily	Hr.	Daily	Bare Costs	Incl. O&P
1 Laborer	$39.85	$318.80	$60.70	$485.60	$39.85	$60.70
1 Diaphragm Water Pump, 4"		114.80		126.28		
1 -20' Suction Hose, 4"		3.25		3.58		
2 -50' Discharge Hoses, 4"		4.70		5.17	15.34	16.88
8 L.H., Daily Totals		$441.55		$620.63	$55.19	$77.58
Crew B-94C	Hr.	Daily	Hr.	Daily	Bare Costs	Incl. O&P
1 Laborer	$39.85	$318.80	$60.70	$485.60	$39.85	$60.70
1 Centrifugal Water Pump, 3"		79.20		87.12		
1 -20' Suction Hose, 3"		2.85		3.13		
2 -50' Discharge Hoses, 3"		3.00		3.30	10.63	11.69
8 L.H., Daily Totals		$403.85		$579.15	$50.48	$72.39
Crew B-94D	Hr.	Daily	Hr.	Daily	Bare Costs	Incl. O&P
1 Laborer	$39.85	$318.80	$60.70	$485.60	$39.85	$60.70
1 Centr. Water Pump, 6"		296.40		326.04		
1 -20' Suction Hose, 6"		11.50		12.65		
2 -50' Discharge Hoses, 6"		12.20		13.42	40.01	44.01
8 L.H., Daily Totals		$638.90		$837.71	$79.86	$104.71
Crew C-1	Hr.	Daily	Hr.	Daily	Bare Costs	Incl. O&P
3 Carpenters	$50.70	$1216.80	$77.20	$1852.80	$47.99	$73.08
1 Laborer	39.85	318.80	60.70	485.60		
32 L.H., Daily Totals		$1535.60		$2338.40	$47.99	$73.08
Crew C-2	Hr.	Daily	Hr.	Daily	Bare Costs	Incl. O&P
1 Carpenter Foreman (outside)	$52.70	$421.60	$80.25	$642.00	$49.23	$74.96
4 Carpenters	50.70	1622.40	77.20	2470.40		
1 Laborer	39.85	318.80	60.70	485.60		
48 L.H., Daily Totals		$2362.80		$3598.00	$49.23	$74.96
Crew C-2A	Hr.	Daily	Hr.	Daily	Bare Costs	Incl. O&P
1 Carpenter Foreman (outside)	$52.70	$421.60	$80.25	$642.00	$48.70	$73.83
3 Carpenters	50.70	1216.80	77.20	1852.80		
1 Cement Finisher	47.55	380.40	70.45	563.60		
1 Laborer	39.85	318.80	60.70	485.60		
48 L.H., Daily Totals		$2337.60		$3544.00	$48.70	$73.83

Crew No.		Bare Costs		Incl. Subs O&P		Cost Per Labor-Hour	
Crew C-3	Hr.	Daily	Hr.	Daily	Bare Costs	Incl. O&P
1 Rodman Foreman (outside)	$56.65	$453.20	$86.50	$692.00	$50.78	$77.38
4 Rodmen (reinf.)	54.65	1748.80	83.45	2670.40		
1 Equip. Oper. (light)	51.30	410.40	77.35	618.80		
2 Laborers	39.85	637.60	60.70	971.20		
3 Stressing Equipment		31.20		34.32		
.5 Grouting Equipment		79.20		87.12	1.73	1.90
64 L.H., Daily Totals		$3360.40		$5073.84	$52.51	$79.28
Crew C-4	Hr.	Daily	Hr.	Daily	Bare Costs	Incl. O&P
1 Rodman Foreman (outside)	$56.65	$453.20	$86.50	$692.00	$55.15	$84.21
3 Rodmen (reinf.)	54.65	1311.60	83.45	2002.80		
3 Stressing Equipment		31.20		34.32	.97	1.07
32 L.H., Daily Totals		$1796.00		$2729.12	$56.13	$85.28
Crew C-4A	Hr.	Daily	Hr.	Daily	Bare Costs	Incl. O&P
2 Rodmen (reinf.)	$54.65	$874.40	$83.45	$1335.20	$54.65	$83.45
4 Stressing Equipment		41.60		45.76	2.60	2.86
16 L.H., Daily Totals		$916.00		$1380.96	$57.25	$86.31
Crew C-5	Hr.	Daily	Hr.	Daily	Bare Costs	Incl. O&P
1 Rodman Foreman (outside)	$56.65	$453.20	$86.50	$692.00	$54.28	$82.60
4 Rodmen (reinf.)	54.65	1748.80	83.45	2670.40		
1 Equip. Oper. (crane)	56.10	448.80	84.60	676.80		
1 Equip. Oper. (oiler)	48.60	388.80	73.30	586.40		
1 Hyd. Crane, 25 Ton		590.60		649.66	10.55	11.60
56 L.H., Daily Totals		$3630.20		$5275.26	$64.83	$94.20
Crew C-6	Hr.	Daily	Hr.	Daily	Bare Costs	Incl. O&P
1 Labor Foreman (outside)	$41.85	$334.80	$63.75	$510.00	$41.47	$62.83
4 Laborers	39.85	1275.20	60.70	1942.40		
1 Cement Finisher	47.55	380.40	70.45	563.60		
2 Gas Engine Vibrators		51.20		56.32	1.07	1.17
48 L.H., Daily Totals		$2041.60		$3072.32	$42.53	$64.01
Crew C-7	Hr.	Daily	Hr.	Daily	Bare Costs	Incl. O&P
1 Labor Foreman (outside)	$41.85	$334.80	$63.75	$510.00	$43.44	$65.78
5 Laborers	39.85	1594.00	60.70	2428.00		
1 Cement Finisher	47.55	380.40	70.45	563.60		
1 Equip. Oper. (medium)	53.75	430.00	81.05	648.40		
1 Equip. Oper. (oiler)	48.60	388.80	73.30	586.40		
2 Gas Engine Vibrators		51.20		56.32		
1 Concrete Bucket, 1 C.Y.		24.60		27.06		
1 Hyd. Crane, 55 Ton		993.80		1093.18	14.86	16.34
72 L.H., Daily Totals		$4197.60		$5912.96	$58.30	$82.12
Crew C-7A	Hr.	Daily	Hr.	Daily	Bare Costs	Incl. O&P
1 Labor Foreman (outside)	$41.85	$334.80	$63.75	$510.00	$41.64	$63.23
5 Laborers	39.85	1594.00	60.70	2428.00		
2 Truck Drivers (heavy)	46.00	736.00	69.30	1108.80		
2 Conc. Transit Mixers		1811.20		1992.32	28.30	31.13
64 L.H., Daily Totals		$4476.00		$6039.12	$69.94	$94.36
Crew C-7B	Hr.	Daily	Hr.	Daily	Bare Costs	Incl. O&P
1 Labor Foreman (outside)	$41.85	$334.80	$63.75	$510.00	$43.23	$65.64
5 Laborers	39.85	1594.00	60.70	2428.00		
1 Equipment Operator, Crane	56.10	448.80	84.60	676.80		
1 Equipment Oiler	48.60	388.80	73.30	586.40		
1 Conc. Bucket, 2 C.Y.		38.40		42.24		
1 Lattice Boom Crane, 165 Ton		2140.00		2354.00	34.04	37.44
64 L.H., Daily Totals		$4944.80		$6597.44	$77.26	$103.09

Crews - Standard

Crew No.	Bare Costs Hr.	Bare Costs Daily	Incl. Subs O&P Hr.	Incl. Subs O&P Daily	Cost Per Labor-Hour Bare Costs	Cost Per Labor-Hour Incl. O&P
Crew C-7C					Bare Costs	Incl. O&P
1 Labor Foreman (outside)	$41.85	$334.80	$63.75	$510.00	$43.58	$66.17
5 Laborers	39.85	1594.00	60.70	2428.00		
2 Equipment Operators (med.)	53.75	860.00	81.05	1296.80		
2 F.E. Loaders, W.M., 4 C.Y.		1149.20		1264.12	17.96	19.75
64 L.H., Daily Totals		$3938.00		$5498.92	$61.53	$85.92
Crew C-7D	Hr.	Daily	Hr.	Daily	Bare Costs	Incl. O&P
1 Labor Foreman (outside)	$41.85	$334.80	$63.75	$510.00	$42.12	$64.04
5 Laborers	39.85	1594.00	60.70	2428.00		
1 Equip. Oper. (medium)	53.75	430.00	81.05	648.40		
1 Concrete Conveyer		187.20		205.92	3.34	3.68
56 L.H., Daily Totals		$2546.00		$3792.32	$45.46	$67.72
Crew C-8	Hr.	Daily	Hr.	Daily	Bare Costs	Incl. O&P
1 Labor Foreman (outside)	$41.85	$334.80	$63.75	$510.00	$44.32	$66.83
3 Laborers	39.85	956.40	60.70	1456.80		
2 Cement Finishers	47.55	760.80	70.45	1127.20		
1 Equip. Oper. (medium)	53.75	430.00	81.05	648.40		
1 Concrete Pump (Small)		881.60		969.76	15.74	17.32
56 L.H., Daily Totals		$3363.60		$4712.16	$60.06	$84.15
Crew C-8A	Hr.	Daily	Hr.	Daily	Bare Costs	Incl. O&P
1 Labor Foreman (outside)	$41.85	$334.80	$63.75	$510.00	$42.75	$64.46
3 Laborers	39.85	956.40	60.70	1456.80		
2 Cement Finishers	47.55	760.80	70.45	1127.20		
48 L.H., Daily Totals		$2052.00		$3094.00	$42.75	$64.46
Crew C-8B	Hr.	Daily	Hr.	Daily	Bare Costs	Incl. O&P
1 Labor Foreman (outside)	$41.85	$334.80	$63.75	$510.00	$43.03	$65.38
3 Laborers	39.85	956.40	60.70	1456.80		
1 Equip. Oper. (medium)	53.75	430.00	81.05	648.40		
1 Vibrating Power Screed		75.35		82.89		
1 Roller, Vibratory, 25 Ton		659.80		725.78		
1 Dozer, 200 H.P.		1273.00		1400.30	50.20	55.22
40 L.H., Daily Totals		$3729.35		$4824.17	$93.23	$120.60
Crew C-8C	Hr.	Daily	Hr.	Daily	Bare Costs	Incl. O&P
1 Labor Foreman (outside)	$41.85	$334.80	$63.75	$510.00	$43.78	$66.22
3 Laborers	39.85	956.40	60.70	1456.80		
1 Cement Finisher	47.55	380.40	70.45	563.60		
1 Equip. Oper. (medium)	53.75	430.00	81.05	648.40		
1 Shotcrete Rig, 12 C.Y./hr		246.60		271.26		
1 Air Compressor, 160 cfm		117.20		128.92		
4 -50' Air Hoses, 1"		33.80		37.18		
4 -50' Air Hoses, 2"		103.60		113.96	10.44	11.49
48 L.H., Daily Totals		$2602.80		$3730.12	$54.23	$77.71
Crew C-8D	Hr.	Daily	Hr.	Daily	Bare Costs	Incl. O&P
1 Labor Foreman (outside)	$41.85	$334.80	$63.75	$510.00	$45.14	$68.06
1 Laborer	39.85	318.80	60.70	485.60		
1 Cement Finisher	47.55	380.40	70.45	563.60		
1 Equipment Oper. (light)	51.30	410.40	77.35	618.80		
1 Air Compressor, 250 cfm		167.40		184.14		
2 -50' Air Hoses, 1"		16.90		18.59	5.76	6.34
32 L.H., Daily Totals		$1628.70		$2380.73	$50.90	$74.40

Crew No.	Bare Costs Hr.	Bare Costs Daily	Incl. Subs O&P Hr.	Incl. Subs O&P Daily	Cost Per Labor-Hour Bare Costs	Cost Per Labor-Hour Incl. O&P
Crew C-8E	Hr.	Daily	Hr.	Daily	Bare Costs	Incl. O&P
1 Labor Foreman (outside)	$41.85	$334.80	$63.75	$510.00	$43.38	$65.61
3 Laborers	39.85	956.40	60.70	1456.80		
1 Cement Finisher	47.55	380.40	70.45	563.60		
1 Equipment Oper. (light)	51.30	410.40	77.35	618.80		
1 Shotcrete Rig, 35 C.Y./hr		270.20		297.22		
1 Air Compressor, 250 cfm		167.40		184.14		
4 -50' Air Hoses, 1"		33.80		37.18		
4 -50' Air Hoses, 2"		103.60		113.96	11.98	13.18
48 L.H., Daily Totals		$2657.00		$3781.70	$55.35	$78.79
Crew C-10	Hr.	Daily	Hr.	Daily	Bare Costs	Incl. O&P
1 Laborer	$39.85	$318.80	$60.70	$485.60	$44.98	$67.20
2 Cement Finishers	47.55	760.80	70.45	1127.20		
24 L.H., Daily Totals		$1079.60		$1612.80	$44.98	$67.20
Crew C-10B	Hr.	Daily	Hr.	Daily	Bare Costs	Incl. O&P
3 Laborers	$39.85	$956.40	$60.70	$1456.80	$42.93	$64.60
2 Cement Finishers	47.55	760.80	70.45	1127.20		
1 Concrete Mixer, 10 C.F.		161.00		177.10		
2 Trowels, 48" Walk-Behind		82.40		90.64	6.09	6.69
40 L.H., Daily Totals		$1960.60		$2851.74	$49.02	$71.29
Crew C-10C	Hr.	Daily	Hr.	Daily	Bare Costs	Incl. O&P
1 Laborer	$39.85	$318.80	$60.70	$485.60	$44.98	$67.20
2 Cement Finishers	47.55	760.80	70.45	1127.20		
1 Trowel, 48" Walk-Behind		41.20		45.32	1.72	1.89
24 L.H., Daily Totals		$1120.80		$1658.12	$46.70	$69.09
Crew C-10D	Hr.	Daily	Hr.	Daily	Bare Costs	Incl. O&P
1 Laborer	$39.85	$318.80	$60.70	$485.60	$44.98	$67.20
2 Cement Finishers	47.55	760.80	70.45	1127.20		
1 Vibrating Power Screed		75.35		82.89		
1 Trowel, 48" Walk-Behind		41.20		45.32	4.86	5.34
24 L.H., Daily Totals		$1196.15		$1741.01	$49.84	$72.54
Crew C-10E	Hr.	Daily	Hr.	Daily	Bare Costs	Incl. O&P
1 Laborer	$39.85	$318.80	$60.70	$485.60	$44.98	$67.20
2 Cement Finishers	47.55	760.80	70.45	1127.20		
1 Vibrating Power Screed		75.35		82.89		
1 Cement Trowel, 96" Ride-On		166.20		182.82	10.06	11.07
24 L.H., Daily Totals		$1321.15		$1878.51	$55.05	$78.27
Crew C-10F	Hr.	Daily	Hr.	Daily	Bare Costs	Incl. O&P
1 Laborer	$39.85	$318.80	$60.70	$485.60	$44.98	$67.20
2 Cement Finishers	47.55	760.80	70.45	1127.20		
1 Telescoping Boom Lift, to 60'		454.60		500.06	18.94	20.84
24 L.H., Daily Totals		$1534.20		$2112.86	$63.92	$88.04
Crew C-11	Hr.	Daily	Hr.	Daily	Bare Costs	Incl. O&P
1 Struc. Steel Foreman (outside)	$56.65	$453.20	$92.60	$740.80	$54.36	$87.40
6 Struc. Steel Workers	54.65	2623.20	89.35	4288.80		
1 Equip. Oper. (crane)	56.10	448.80	84.60	676.80		
1 Equip. Oper. (oiler)	48.60	388.80	73.30	586.40		
1 Lattice Boom Crane, 150 Ton		2017.00		2218.70	28.01	30.82
72 L.H., Daily Totals		$5931.00		$8511.50	$82.38	$118.22

Crews - Standard

Crew No.	Bare Costs Hr.	Daily	Incl. Subs O&P Hr.	Daily	Cost Per Labor-Hour Bare Costs	Incl. O&P
Crew C-12	Hr.	Daily	Hr.	Daily	Bare Costs	Incl. O&P
1 Carpenter Foreman (outside)	$52.70	$421.60	$80.25	$642.00	$50.13	$76.19
3 Carpenters	50.70	1216.80	77.20	1852.80		
1 Laborer	39.85	318.80	60.70	485.60		
1 Equip. Oper. (crane)	56.10	448.80	84.60	676.80		
1 Hyd. Crane, 12 Ton		496.00		545.60	10.33	11.37
48 L.H., Daily Totals		$2902.00		$4202.80	$60.46	$87.56
Crew C-13	Hr.	Daily	Hr.	Daily	Bare Costs	Incl. O&P
1 Struc. Steel Worker	$54.65	$437.20	$89.35	$714.80	$53.33	$85.30
1 Welder	54.65	437.20	89.35	714.80		
1 Carpenter	50.70	405.60	77.20	617.60		
1 Welder, Gas Engine, 300 amp		98.40		108.24	4.10	4.51
24 L.H., Daily Totals		$1378.40		$2155.44	$57.43	$89.81
Crew C-14	Hr.	Daily	Hr.	Daily	Bare Costs	Incl. O&P
1 Carpenter Foreman (outside)	$52.70	$421.60	$80.25	$642.00	$49.11	$74.54
5 Carpenters	50.70	2028.00	77.20	3088.00		
4 Laborers	39.85	1275.20	60.70	1942.40		
4 Rodmen (reinf.)	54.65	1748.80	83.45	2670.40		
2 Cement Finishers	47.55	760.80	70.45	1127.20		
1 Equip. Oper. (crane)	56.10	448.80	84.60	676.80		
1 Equip. Oper. (oiler)	48.60	388.80	73.30	586.40		
1 Hyd. Crane, 80 Ton		1518.00		1669.80	10.54	11.60
144 L.H., Daily Totals		$8590.00		$12403.00	$59.65	$86.13
Crew C-14A	Hr.	Daily	Hr.	Daily	Bare Costs	Incl. O&P
1 Carpenter Foreman (outside)	$52.70	$421.60	$80.25	$642.00	$50.54	$76.89
16 Carpenters	50.70	6489.60	77.20	9881.60		
4 Rodmen (reinf.)	54.65	1748.80	83.45	2670.40		
2 Laborers	39.85	637.60	60.70	971.20		
1 Cement Finisher	47.55	380.40	70.45	563.60		
1 Equip. Oper. (medium)	53.75	430.00	81.05	648.40		
1 Gas Engine Vibrator		25.60		28.16		
1 Concrete Pump (Small)		881.60		969.76	4.54	4.99
200 L.H., Daily Totals		$11015.20		$16375.12	$55.08	$81.88
Crew C-14B	Hr.	Daily	Hr.	Daily	Bare Costs	Incl. O&P
1 Carpenter Foreman (outside)	$52.70	$421.60	$80.25	$642.00	$50.42	$76.64
16 Carpenters	50.70	6489.60	77.20	9881.60		
4 Rodmen (reinf.)	54.65	1748.80	83.45	2670.40		
2 Laborers	39.85	637.60	60.70	971.20		
2 Cement Finishers	47.55	760.80	70.45	1127.20		
1 Equip. Oper. (medium)	53.75	430.00	81.05	648.40		
1 Gas Engine Vibrator		25.60		28.16		
1 Concrete Pump (Small)		881.60		969.76	4.36	4.80
208 L.H., Daily Totals		$11395.60		$16938.72	$54.79	$81.44
Crew C-14C	Hr.	Daily	Hr.	Daily	Bare Costs	Incl. O&P
1 Carpenter Foreman (outside)	$52.70	$421.60	$80.25	$642.00	$48.08	$73.11
6 Carpenters	50.70	2433.60	77.20	3705.60		
2 Rodmen (reinf.)	54.65	874.40	83.45	1335.20		
4 Laborers	39.85	1275.20	60.70	1942.40		
1 Cement Finisher	47.55	380.40	70.45	563.60		
1 Gas Engine Vibrator		25.60		28.16	.23	.25
112 L.H., Daily Totals		$5410.80		$8216.96	$48.31	$73.37

Crew No.	Bare Costs Hr.	Daily	Incl. Subs O&P Hr.	Daily	Cost Per Labor-Hour Bare Costs	Incl. O&P
Crew C-14D	Hr.	Daily	Hr.	Daily	Bare Costs	Incl. O&P
1 Carpenter Foreman (outside)	$52.70	$421.60	$80.25	$642.00	$50.22	$76.39
18 Carpenters	50.70	7300.80	77.20	11116.80		
2 Rodmen (reinf.)	54.65	874.40	83.45	1335.20		
2 Laborers	39.85	637.60	60.70	971.20		
1 Cement Finisher	47.55	380.40	70.45	563.60		
1 Equip. Oper. (medium)	53.75	430.00	81.05	648.40		
1 Gas Engine Vibrator		25.60		28.16		
1 Concrete Pump (Small)		881.60		969.76	4.54	4.99
200 L.H., Daily Totals		$10952.00		$16275.12	$54.76	$81.38
Crew C-14E	Hr.	Daily	Hr.	Daily	Bare Costs	Incl. O&P
1 Carpenter Foreman (outside)	$52.70	$421.60	$80.25	$642.00	$49.07	$74.64
2 Carpenters	50.70	811.20	77.20	1235.20		
4 Rodmen (reinf.)	54.65	1748.80	83.45	2670.40		
3 Laborers	39.85	956.40	60.70	1456.80		
1 Cement Finisher	47.55	380.40	70.45	563.60		
1 Gas Engine Vibrator		25.60		28.16	.29	.32
88 L.H., Daily Totals		$4344.00		$6596.16	$49.36	$74.96
Crew C-14F	Hr.	Daily	Hr.	Daily	Bare Costs	Incl. O&P
1 Labor Foreman (outside)	$41.85	$334.80	$63.75	$510.00	$45.21	$67.54
2 Laborers	39.85	637.60	60.70	971.20		
6 Cement Finishers	47.55	2282.40	70.45	3381.60		
1 Gas Engine Vibrator		25.60		28.16	.36	.39
72 L.H., Daily Totals		$3280.40		$4890.96	$45.56	$67.93
Crew C-14G	Hr.	Daily	Hr.	Daily	Bare Costs	Incl. O&P
1 Labor Foreman (outside)	$41.85	$334.80	$63.75	$510.00	$44.54	$66.71
2 Laborers	39.85	637.60	60.70	971.20		
4 Cement Finishers	47.55	1521.60	70.45	2254.40		
1 Gas Engine Vibrator		25.60		28.16	.46	.50
56 L.H., Daily Totals		$2519.60		$3763.76	$44.99	$67.21
Crew C-14H	Hr.	Daily	Hr.	Daily	Bare Costs	Incl. O&P
1 Carpenter Foreman (outside)	$52.70	$421.60	$80.25	$642.00	$49.36	$74.88
2 Carpenters	50.70	811.20	77.20	1235.20		
1 Rodman (reinf.)	54.65	437.20	83.45	667.60		
1 Laborer	39.85	318.80	60.70	485.60		
1 Cement Finisher	47.55	380.40	70.45	563.60		
1 Gas Engine Vibrator		25.60		28.16	.53	.59
48 L.H., Daily Totals		$2394.80		$3622.16	$49.89	$75.46
Crew C-14L	Hr.	Daily	Hr.	Daily	Bare Costs	Incl. O&P
1 Carpenter Foreman (outside)	$52.70	$421.60	$80.25	$642.00	$46.99	$71.39
6 Carpenters	50.70	2433.60	77.20	3705.60		
4 Laborers	39.85	1275.20	60.70	1942.40		
1 Cement Finisher	47.55	380.40	70.45	563.60		
1 Gas Engine Vibrator		25.60		28.16	.27	.29
96 L.H., Daily Totals		$4536.40		$6881.76	$47.25	$71.69
Crew C-14M	Hr.	Daily	Hr.	Daily	Bare Costs	Incl. O&P
1 Carpenter Foreman (outside)	$52.70	$421.60	$80.25	$642.00	$48.72	$73.88
2 Carpenters	50.70	811.20	77.20	1235.20		
1 Rodman (reinf.)	54.65	437.20	83.45	667.60		
2 Laborers	39.85	637.60	60.70	971.20		
1 Cement Finisher	47.55	380.40	70.45	563.60		
1 Equip. Oper. (medium)	53.75	430.00	81.05	648.40		
1 Gas Engine Vibrator		25.60		28.16		
1 Concrete Pump (Small)		881.60		969.76	14.18	15.59
64 L.H., Daily Totals		$4025.20		$5725.92	$62.89	$89.47

For customer support on your Green Building Costs with RSMeans data, call 800.448.8182.

Crews - Standard

Crew C-15	Hr.	Daily	Hr.	Daily	Bare Costs	Incl. O&P
1 Carpenter Foreman (outside)	$52.70	$421.60	$80.25	$642.00	$47.04	$71.23
2 Carpenters	50.70	811.20	77.20	1235.20		
3 Laborers	39.85	956.40	60.70	1456.80		
2 Cement Finishers	47.55	760.80	70.45	1127.20		
1 Rodman (reinf.)	54.65	437.20	83.45	667.60		
72 L.H., Daily Totals		$3387.20		$5128.80	$47.04	$71.23

Crew C-16	Hr.	Daily	Hr.	Daily	Bare Costs	Incl. O&P
1 Labor Foreman (outside)	$41.85	$334.80	$63.75	$510.00	$44.32	$66.83
3 Laborers	39.85	956.40	60.70	1456.80		
2 Cement Finishers	47.55	760.80	70.45	1127.20		
1 Equip. Oper. (medium)	53.75	430.00	81.05	648.40		
1 Gunite Pump Rig		321.00		353.10		
2 -50' Air Hoses, 3/4"		14.70		16.17		
2 -50' Air Hoses, 2"		51.80		56.98	6.92	7.61
56 L.H., Daily Totals		$2869.50		$4168.65	$51.24	$74.44

Crew C-16A	Hr.	Daily	Hr.	Daily	Bare Costs	Incl. O&P
1 Laborer	$39.85	$318.80	$60.70	$485.60	$47.17	$70.66
2 Cement Finishers	47.55	760.80	70.45	1127.20		
1 Equip. Oper. (medium)	53.75	430.00	81.05	648.40		
1 Gunite Pump Rig		321.00		353.10		
2 -50' Air Hoses, 3/4"		14.70		16.17		
2 -50' Air Hoses, 2"		51.80		56.98		
1 Telescoping Boom Lift, to 60'		454.60		500.06	26.32	28.95
32 L.H., Daily Totals		$2351.70		$3187.51	$73.49	$99.61

Crew C-17	Hr.	Daily	Hr.	Daily	Bare Costs	Incl. O&P
2 Skilled Worker Foremen (out)	$54.35	$869.60	$83.20	$1331.20	$52.75	$80.76
8 Skilled Workers	52.35	3350.40	80.15	5129.60		
80 L.H., Daily Totals		$4220.00		$6460.80	$52.75	$80.76

Crew C-17A	Hr.	Daily	Hr.	Daily	Bare Costs	Incl. O&P
2 Skilled Worker Foremen (out)	$54.35	$869.60	$83.20	$1331.20	$52.79	$80.81
8 Skilled Workers	52.35	3350.40	80.15	5129.60		
.125 Equip. Oper. (crane)	56.10	56.10	84.60	84.60		
.125 Hyd. Crane, 80 Ton		189.75		208.72	2.34	2.58
81 L.H., Daily Totals		$4465.85		$6754.13	$55.13	$83.38

Crew C-17B	Hr.	Daily	Hr.	Daily	Bare Costs	Incl. O&P
2 Skilled Worker Foremen (out)	$54.35	$869.60	$83.20	$1331.20	$52.83	$80.85
8 Skilled Workers	52.35	3350.40	80.15	5129.60		
.25 Equip. Oper. (crane)	56.10	112.20	84.60	169.20		
.25 Hyd. Crane, 80 Ton		379.50		417.45		
.25 Trowel, 48" Walk-Behind		10.30		11.33	4.75	5.23
82 L.H., Daily Totals		$4722.00		$7058.78	$57.59	$86.08

Crew C-17C	Hr.	Daily	Hr.	Daily	Bare Costs	Incl. O&P
2 Skilled Worker Foremen (out)	$54.35	$869.60	$83.20	$1331.20	$52.87	$80.90
8 Skilled Workers	52.35	3350.40	80.15	5129.60		
.375 Equip. Oper. (crane)	56.10	168.30	84.60	253.80		
.375 Hyd. Crane, 80 Ton		569.25		626.17	6.86	7.54
83 L.H., Daily Totals		$4957.55		$7340.77	$59.73	$88.44

Crew C-17D	Hr.	Daily	Hr.	Daily	Bare Costs	Incl. O&P
2 Skilled Worker Foremen (out)	$54.35	$869.60	$83.20	$1331.20	$52.91	$80.94
8 Skilled Workers	52.35	3350.40	80.15	5129.60		
.5 Equip. Oper. (crane)	56.10	224.40	84.60	338.40		
.5 Hyd. Crane, 80 Ton		759.00		834.90	9.04	9.94
84 L.H., Daily Totals		$5203.40		$7634.10	$61.95	$90.88

Crew C-17E	Hr.	Daily	Hr.	Daily	Bare Costs	Incl. O&P
2 Skilled Worker Foremen (out)	$54.35	$869.60	$83.20	$1331.20	$52.75	$80.76
8 Skilled Workers	52.35	3350.40	80.15	5129.60		
1 Hyd. Jack with Rods		102.25		112.47	1.28	1.41
80 L.H., Daily Totals		$4322.25		$6573.27	$54.03	$82.17

Crew C-18	Hr.	Daily	Hr.	Daily	Bare Costs	Incl. O&P
.125 Labor Foreman (outside)	$41.85	$41.85	$63.75	$63.75	$40.07	$61.04
1 Laborer	39.85	318.80	60.70	485.60		
1 Concrete Cart, 10 C.F.		57.80		63.58	6.42	7.06
9 L.H., Daily Totals		$418.45		$612.93	$46.49	$68.10

Crew C-19	Hr.	Daily	Hr.	Daily	Bare Costs	Incl. O&P
.125 Labor Foreman (outside)	$41.85	$41.85	$63.75	$63.75	$40.07	$61.04
1 Laborer	39.85	318.80	60.70	485.60		
1 Concrete Cart, 18 C.F.		97.40		107.14	10.82	11.90
9 L.H., Daily Totals		$458.05		$656.49	$50.89	$72.94

Crew C-20	Hr.	Daily	Hr.	Daily	Bare Costs	Incl. O&P
1 Labor Foreman (outside)	$41.85	$334.80	$63.75	$510.00	$42.80	$64.84
5 Laborers	39.85	1594.00	60.70	2428.00		
1 Cement Finisher	47.55	380.40	70.45	563.60		
1 Equip. Oper. (medium)	53.75	430.00	81.05	648.40		
2 Gas Engine Vibrators		51.20		56.32		
1 Concrete Pump (Small)		881.60		969.76	14.57	16.03
64 L.H., Daily Totals		$3672.00		$5176.08	$57.38	$80.88

Crew C-21	Hr.	Daily	Hr.	Daily	Bare Costs	Incl. O&P
1 Labor Foreman (outside)	$41.85	$334.80	$63.75	$510.00	$42.80	$64.84
5 Laborers	39.85	1594.00	60.70	2428.00		
1 Cement Finisher	47.55	380.40	70.45	563.60		
1 Equip. Oper. (medium)	53.75	430.00	81.05	648.40		
2 Gas Engine Vibrators		51.20		56.32		
1 Concrete Conveyer		187.20		205.92	3.73	4.10
64 L.H., Daily Totals		$2977.60		$4412.24	$46.52	$68.94

Crew C-22	Hr.	Daily	Hr.	Daily	Bare Costs	Incl. O&P
1 Rodman Foreman (outside)	$56.65	$453.20	$86.50	$692.00	$54.92	$83.82
4 Rodmen (reinf.)	54.65	1748.80	83.45	2670.40		
.125 Equip. Oper. (crane)	56.10	56.10	84.60	84.60		
.125 Equip. Oper. (oiler)	48.60	48.60	73.30	73.30		
.125 Hyd. Crane, 25 Ton		73.83		81.21	1.76	1.93
42 L.H., Daily Totals		$2380.53		$3601.51	$56.68	$85.75

Crew C-23	Hr.	Daily	Hr.	Daily	Bare Costs	Incl. O&P
2 Skilled Worker Foremen (out)	$54.35	$869.60	$83.20	$1331.20	$52.75	$80.52
6 Skilled Workers	52.35	2512.80	80.15	3847.20		
1 Equip. Oper. (crane)	56.10	448.80	84.60	676.80		
1 Equip. Oper. (oiler)	48.60	388.80	73.30	586.40		
1 Lattice Boom Crane, 90 Ton		1687.00		1855.70	21.09	23.20
80 L.H., Daily Totals		$5907.00		$8297.30	$73.84	$103.72

Crew C-23A	Hr.	Daily	Hr.	Daily	Bare Costs	Incl. O&P
1 Labor Foreman (outside)	$41.85	$334.80	$63.75	$510.00	$45.25	$68.61
2 Laborers	39.85	637.60	60.70	971.20		
1 Equip. Oper. (crane)	56.10	448.80	84.60	676.80		
1 Equip. Oper. (oiler)	48.60	388.80	73.30	586.40		
1 Crawler Crane, 100 Ton		1872.00		2059.20		
3 Conc. Buckets, 8 C.Y.		626.40		689.04	62.46	68.71
40 L.H., Daily Totals		$4308.40		$5492.64	$107.71	$137.32

Crews - Standard

Crew No.	Bare Costs		Incl. Subs O&P		Cost Per Labor-Hour	
Crew C-24	**Hr.**	**Daily**	**Hr.**	**Daily**	**Bare Costs**	**Incl. O&P**
2 Skilled Worker Foremen (out)	$54.35	$869.60	$83.20	$1331.20	$52.75	$80.52
6 Skilled Workers	52.35	2512.80	80.15	3847.20		
1 Equip. Oper. (crane)	56.10	448.80	84.60	676.80		
1 Equip. Oper. (oiler)	48.60	388.80	73.30	586.40		
1 Lattice Boom Crane, 150 Ton		2017.00		2218.70	25.21	27.73
80 L.H., Daily Totals		$6237.00		$8660.30	$77.96	$108.25
Crew C-25	**Hr.**	**Daily**	**Hr.**	**Daily**	**Bare Costs**	**Incl. O&P**
2 Rodmen (reinf.)	$54.65	$874.40	$83.45	$1335.20	$43.75	$69.38
2 Rodmen Helpers	32.85	525.60	55.30	884.80		
32 L.H., Daily Totals		$1400.00		$2220.00	$43.75	$69.38
Crew C-27	**Hr.**	**Daily**	**Hr.**	**Daily**	**Bare Costs**	**Incl. O&P**
2 Cement Finishers	$47.55	$760.80	$70.45	$1127.20	$47.55	$70.45
1 Concrete Saw		102.40		112.64	6.40	7.04
16 L.H., Daily Totals		$863.20		$1239.84	$53.95	$77.49
Crew C-28	**Hr.**	**Daily**	**Hr.**	**Daily**	**Bare Costs**	**Incl. O&P**
1 Cement Finisher	$47.55	$380.40	$70.45	$563.60	$47.55	$70.45
1 Portable Air Compressor, Gas		17.10		18.81	2.14	2.35
8 L.H., Daily Totals		$397.50		$582.41	$49.69	$72.80
Crew C-29	**Hr.**	**Daily**	**Hr.**	**Daily**	**Bare Costs**	**Incl. O&P**
1 Laborer	$39.85	$318.80	$60.70	$485.60	$39.85	$60.70
1 Pressure Washer		63.60		69.96	7.95	8.74
8 L.H., Daily Totals		$382.40		$555.56	$47.80	$69.44
Crew C-30	**Hr.**	**Daily**	**Hr.**	**Daily**	**Bare Costs**	**Incl. O&P**
1 Laborer	$39.85	$318.80	$60.70	$485.60	$39.85	$60.70
1 Concrete Mixer, 10 C.F.		161.00		177.10	20.13	22.14
8 L.H., Daily Totals		$479.80		$662.70	$59.98	$82.84
Crew C-31	**Hr.**	**Daily**	**Hr.**	**Daily**	**Bare Costs**	**Incl. O&P**
1 Cement Finisher	$47.55	$380.40	$70.45	$563.60	$47.55	$70.45
1 Grout Pump		321.00		353.10	40.13	44.14
8 L.H., Daily Totals		$701.40		$916.70	$87.67	$114.59
Crew C-32	**Hr.**	**Daily**	**Hr.**	**Daily**	**Bare Costs**	**Incl. O&P**
1 Cement Finisher	$47.55	$380.40	$70.45	$563.60	$43.70	$65.58
1 Laborer	39.85	318.80	60.70	485.60		
1 Crack Chaser Saw, Gas, 6 H.P.		25.40		27.94		
1 Vacuum Pick-Up System		66.95		73.64	5.77	6.35
16 L.H., Daily Totals		$791.55		$1150.79	$49.47	$71.92
Crew D-1	**Hr.**	**Daily**	**Hr.**	**Daily**	**Bare Costs**	**Incl. O&P**
1 Bricklayer	$50.30	$402.40	$77.00	$616.00	$44.80	$68.58
1 Bricklayer Helper	39.30	314.40	60.15	481.20		
16 L.H., Daily Totals		$716.80		$1097.20	$44.80	$68.58
Crew D-2	**Hr.**	**Daily**	**Hr.**	**Daily**	**Bare Costs**	**Incl. O&P**
3 Bricklayers	$50.30	$1207.20	$77.00	$1848.00	$46.34	$70.89
2 Bricklayer Helpers	39.30	628.80	60.15	962.40		
.5 Carpenter	50.70	202.80	77.20	308.80		
44 L.H., Daily Totals		$2038.80		$3119.20	$46.34	$70.89

Crew No.	Bare Costs		Incl. Subs O&P		Cost Per Labor-Hour	
Crew D-3	**Hr.**	**Daily**	**Hr.**	**Daily**	**Bare Costs**	**Incl. O&P**
3 Bricklayers	$50.30	$1207.20	$77.00	$1848.00	$46.13	$70.59
2 Bricklayer Helpers	39.30	628.80	60.15	962.40		
.25 Carpenter	50.70	101.40	77.20	154.40		
42 L.H., Daily Totals		$1937.40		$2964.80	$46.13	$70.59
Crew D-4	**Hr.**	**Daily**	**Hr.**	**Daily**	**Bare Costs**	**Incl. O&P**
1 Bricklayer	$50.30	$402.40	$77.00	$616.00	$45.05	$68.66
2 Bricklayer Helpers	39.30	628.80	60.15	962.40		
1 Equip. Oper. (light)	51.30	410.40	77.35	618.80		
1 Grout Pump, 50 C.F./hr.		128.60		141.46	4.02	4.42
32 L.H., Daily Totals		$1570.20		$2338.66	$49.07	$73.08
Crew D-5	**Hr.**	**Daily**	**Hr.**	**Daily**	**Bare Costs**	**Incl. O&P**
1 Bricklayer	50.30	402.40	77.00	616.00	50.30	77.00
8 L.H., Daily Totals		$402.40		$616.00	$50.30	$77.00
Crew D-6	**Hr.**	**Daily**	**Hr.**	**Daily**	**Bare Costs**	**Incl. O&P**
3 Bricklayers	$50.30	$1207.20	$77.00	$1848.00	$45.04	$68.92
3 Bricklayer Helpers	39.30	943.20	60.15	1443.60		
.25 Carpenter	50.70	101.40	77.20	154.40		
50 L.H., Daily Totals		$2251.80		$3446.00	$45.04	$68.92
Crew D-7	**Hr.**	**Daily**	**Hr.**	**Daily**	**Bare Costs**	**Incl. O&P**
1 Tile Layer	$46.85	$374.80	$69.35	$554.80	$42.02	$62.20
1 Tile Layer Helper	37.20	297.60	55.05	440.40		
16 L.H., Daily Totals		$672.40		$995.20	$42.02	$62.20
Crew D-8	**Hr.**	**Daily**	**Hr.**	**Daily**	**Bare Costs**	**Incl. O&P**
3 Bricklayers	$50.30	$1207.20	$77.00	$1848.00	$45.90	$70.26
2 Bricklayer Helpers	39.30	628.80	60.15	962.40		
40 L.H., Daily Totals		$1836.00		$2810.40	$45.90	$70.26
Crew D-9	**Hr.**	**Daily**	**Hr.**	**Daily**	**Bare Costs**	**Incl. O&P**
3 Bricklayers	$50.30	$1207.20	$77.00	$1848.00	$44.80	$68.58
3 Bricklayer Helpers	39.30	943.20	60.15	1443.60		
48 L.H., Daily Totals		$2150.40		$3291.60	$44.80	$68.58
Crew D-10	**Hr.**	**Daily**	**Hr.**	**Daily**	**Bare Costs**	**Incl. O&P**
1 Bricklayer Foreman (outside)	$52.30	$418.40	$80.05	$640.40	$49.50	$75.45
1 Bricklayer	50.30	402.40	77.00	616.00		
1 Bricklayer Helper	39.30	314.40	60.15	481.20		
1 Equip. Oper. (crane)	56.10	448.80	84.60	676.80		
1 S.P. Crane, 4x4, 12 Ton		363.60		399.96	11.36	12.50
32 L.H., Daily Totals		$1947.60		$2814.36	$60.86	$87.95
Crew D-11	**Hr.**	**Daily**	**Hr.**	**Daily**	**Bare Costs**	**Incl. O&P**
1 Bricklayer Foreman (outside)	$52.30	$418.40	$80.05	$640.40	$47.30	$72.40
1 Bricklayer	50.30	402.40	77.00	616.00		
1 Bricklayer Helper	39.30	314.40	60.15	481.20		
24 L.H., Daily Totals		$1135.20		$1737.60	$47.30	$72.40
Crew D-12	**Hr.**	**Daily**	**Hr.**	**Daily**	**Bare Costs**	**Incl. O&P**
1 Bricklayer Foreman (outside)	$52.30	$418.40	$80.05	$640.40	$45.30	$69.34
1 Bricklayer	50.30	402.40	77.00	616.00		
2 Bricklayer Helpers	39.30	628.80	60.15	962.40		
32 L.H., Daily Totals		$1449.60		$2218.80	$45.30	$69.34

Crews - Standard

Crew No.		Bare Costs	Incl. Subs O&P		Cost Per Labor-Hour	
Crew D-13	Hr.	Daily	Hr.	Daily	Bare Costs	Incl. O&P
1 Bricklayer Foreman (outside)	$52.30	$418.40	$80.05	$640.40	$48.00	$73.19
1 Bricklayer	50.30	402.40	77.00	616.00		
2 Bricklayer Helpers	39.30	628.80	60.15	962.40		
1 Carpenter	50.70	405.60	77.20	617.60		
1 Equip. Oper. (crane)	56.10	448.80	84.60	676.80		
1 S.P. Crane, 4x4, 12 Ton		363.60		399.96	7.58	8.33
48 L.H., Daily Totals		$2667.60		$3913.16	$55.58	$81.52
Crew D-14	Hr.	Daily	Hr.	Daily	Bare Costs	Incl. O&P
3 Bricklayers	$50.30	$1207.20	$77.00	$1848.00	$47.55	$72.79
1 Bricklayer Helper	39.30	314.40	60.15	481.20		
32 L.H., Daily Totals		$1521.60		$2329.20	$47.55	$72.79
Crew E-1	Hr.	Daily	Hr.	Daily	Bare Costs	Incl. O&P
1 Welder Foreman (outside)	$56.65	$453.20	$92.60	$740.80	$54.20	$86.43
1 Welder	54.65	437.20	89.35	714.80		
1 Equip. Oper. (light)	51.30	410.40	77.35	618.80		
1 Welder, Gas Engine, 300 amp		98.40		108.24	4.10	4.51
24 L.H., Daily Totals		$1399.20		$2182.64	$58.30	$90.94
Crew E-2	Hr.	Daily	Hr.	Daily	Bare Costs	Incl. O&P
1 Struc. Steel Foreman (outside)	$56.65	$453.20	$92.60	$740.80	$54.28	$86.84
4 Struc. Steel Workers	54.65	1748.80	89.35	2859.20		
1 Equip. Oper. (crane)	56.10	448.80	84.60	676.80		
1 Equip. Oper. (oiler)	48.60	388.80	73.30	586.40		
1 Lattice Boom Crane, 90 Ton		1687.00		1855.70	30.13	33.14
56 L.H., Daily Totals		$4726.60		$6718.90	$84.40	$119.98
Crew E-3	Hr.	Daily	Hr.	Daily	Bare Costs	Incl. O&P
1 Struc. Steel Foreman (outside)	$56.65	$453.20	$92.60	$740.80	$55.32	$90.43
1 Struc. Steel Worker	54.65	437.20	89.35	714.80		
1 Welder	54.65	437.20	89.35	714.80		
1 Welder, Gas Engine, 300 amp		98.40		108.24	4.10	4.51
24 L.H., Daily Totals		$1426.00		$2278.64	$59.42	$94.94
Crew E-3A	Hr.	Daily	Hr.	Daily	Bare Costs	Incl. O&P
1 Struc. Steel Foreman (outside)	$56.65	$453.20	$92.60	$740.80	$55.32	$90.43
1 Struc. Steel Worker	54.65	437.20	89.35	714.80		
1 Welder	54.65	437.20	89.35	714.80		
1 Welder, Gas Engine, 300 amp		98.40		108.24		
1 Telescoping Boom Lift, to 40'		282.80		311.08	15.88	17.47
24 L.H., Daily Totals		$1708.80		$2589.72	$71.20	$107.91
Crew E-4	Hr.	Daily	Hr.	Daily	Bare Costs	Incl. O&P
1 Struc. Steel Foreman (outside)	$56.65	$453.20	$92.60	$740.80	$55.15	$90.16
3 Struc. Steel Workers	54.65	1311.60	89.35	2144.40		
1 Welder, Gas Engine, 300 amp		98.40		108.24	3.08	3.38
32 L.H., Daily Totals		$1863.20		$2993.44	$58.23	$93.55
Crew E-5	Hr.	Daily	Hr.	Daily	Bare Costs	Incl. O&P
2 Struc. Steel Foremen (outside)	$56.65	$906.40	$92.60	$1481.60	$54.59	$87.92
5 Struc. Steel Workers	54.65	2186.00	89.35	3574.00		
1 Equip. Oper. (crane)	56.10	448.80	84.60	676.80		
1 Welder	54.65	437.20	89.35	714.80		
1 Equip. Oper. (oiler)	48.60	388.80	73.30	586.40		
1 Lattice Boom Crane, 90 Ton		1687.00		1855.70		
1 Welder, Gas Engine, 300 amp		98.40		108.24	22.32	24.55
80 L.H., Daily Totals		$6152.60		$8997.54	$76.91	$112.47

Crew No.		Bare Costs	Incl. Subs O&P		Cost Per Labor-Hour	
Crew E-6	Hr.	Daily	Hr.	Daily	Bare Costs	Incl. O&P
3 Struc. Steel Foremen (outside)	$56.65	$1359.60	$92.60	$2222.40	$54.53	$87.91
9 Struc. Steel Workers	54.65	3934.80	89.35	6433.20		
1 Equip. Oper. (crane)	56.10	448.80	84.60	676.80		
1 Welder	54.65	437.20	89.35	714.80		
1 Equip. Oper. (oiler)	48.60	388.80	73.30	586.40		
1 Equip. Oper. (light)	51.30	410.40	77.35	618.80		
1 Lattice Boom Crane, 90 Ton		1687.00		1855.70		
1 Welder, Gas Engine, 300 amp		98.40		108.24		
1 Air Compressor, 160 cfm		117.20		128.92		
2 Impact Wrenches		37.20		40.92	15.15	16.67
128 L.H., Daily Totals		$8919.40		$13386.18	$69.68	$104.58
Crew E-7	Hr.	Daily	Hr.	Daily	Bare Costs	Incl. O&P
1 Struc. Steel Foreman (outside)	$56.65	$453.20	$92.60	$740.80	$54.59	$87.92
4 Struc. Steel Workers	54.65	1748.80	89.35	2859.20		
1 Equip. Oper. (crane)	56.10	448.80	84.60	676.80		
1 Equip. Oper. (oiler)	48.60	388.80	73.30	586.40		
1 Welder Foreman (outside)	56.65	453.20	92.60	740.80		
2 Welders	54.65	874.40	89.35	1429.60		
1 Lattice Boom Crane, 90 Ton		1687.00		1855.70		
2 Welders, Gas Engine, 300 amp		196.80		216.48	23.55	25.90
80 L.H., Daily Totals		$6251.00		$9105.78	$78.14	$113.82
Crew E-8	Hr.	Daily	Hr.	Daily	Bare Costs	Incl. O&P
1 Struc. Steel Foreman (outside)	$56.65	$453.20	$92.60	$740.80	$54.35	$87.33
4 Struc. Steel Workers	54.65	1748.80	89.35	2859.20		
1 Welder Foreman (outside)	56.65	453.20	92.60	740.80		
4 Welders	54.65	1748.80	89.35	2859.20		
1 Equip. Oper. (crane)	56.10	448.80	84.60	676.80		
1 Equip. Oper. (oiler)	48.60	388.80	73.30	586.40		
1 Equip. Oper. (light)	51.30	410.40	77.35	618.80		
1 Lattice Boom Crane, 90 Ton		1687.00		1855.70		
4 Welders, Gas Engine, 300 amp		393.60		432.96	20.01	22.01
104 L.H., Daily Totals		$7732.60		$11370.66	$74.35	$109.33
Crew E-9	Hr.	Daily	Hr.	Daily	Bare Costs	Incl. O&P
2 Struc. Steel Foremen (outside)	$56.65	$906.40	$92.60	$1481.60	$54.53	$87.91
5 Struc. Steel Workers	54.65	2186.00	89.35	3574.00		
1 Welder Foreman (outside)	56.65	453.20	92.60	740.80		
5 Welders	54.65	2186.00	89.35	3574.00		
1 Equip. Oper. (crane)	56.10	448.80	84.60	676.80		
1 Equip. Oper. (oiler)	48.60	388.80	73.30	586.40		
1 Equip. Oper. (light)	51.30	410.40	77.35	618.80		
1 Lattice Boom Crane, 90 Ton		1687.00		1855.70		
5 Welders, Gas Engine, 300 amp		492.00		541.20	17.02	18.73
128 L.H., Daily Totals		$9158.60		$13649.30	$71.55	$106.64
Crew E-10	Hr.	Daily	Hr.	Daily	Bare Costs	Incl. O&P
1 Welder Foreman (outside)	$56.65	$453.20	$92.60	$740.80	$55.65	$90.97
1 Welder	54.65	437.20	89.35	714.80		
1 Welder, Gas Engine, 300 amp		98.40		108.24		
1 Flatbed Truck, Gas, 3 Ton		238.00		261.80	21.02	23.13
16 L.H., Daily Totals		$1226.80		$1825.64	$76.67	$114.10
Crew E-11	Hr.	Daily	Hr.	Daily	Bare Costs	Incl. O&P
2 Painters, Struc. Steel	$43.50	$696.00	$72.45	$1159.20	$44.54	$70.74
1 Building Laborer	39.85	318.80	60.70	485.60		
1 Equip. Oper. (light)	51.30	410.40	77.35	618.80		
1 Air Compressor, 250 cfm		167.40		184.14		
1 Sandblaster, Portable, 3 C.F.		21.00		23.10		
1 Set Sand Blasting Accessories		14.70		16.17	6.35	6.98
32 L.H., Daily Totals		$1628.30		$2487.01	$50.88	$77.72

For customer support on your Green Building Costs with RSMeans data, call 800.448.8182

Crews - Standard

Crew No.	Bare Costs Hr.	Bare Costs Daily	Incl. Subs O&P Hr.	Incl. Subs O&P Daily	Cost Per Labor-Hour Bare Costs	Cost Per Labor-Hour Incl. O&P
Crew E-11A						
2 Painters, Struc. Steel	$43.50	$696.00	$72.45	$1159.20	$44.54	$70.74
1 Building Laborer	39.85	318.80	60.70	485.60		
1 Equip. Oper. (light)	51.30	410.40	77.35	618.80		
1 Air Compressor, 250 cfm		167.40		184.14		
1 Sandblaster, Portable, 3 C.F.		21.00		23.10		
1 Set Sand Blasting Accessories		14.70		16.17		
1 Telescoping Boom Lift, to 60'		454.60		500.06	20.55	22.61
32 L.H., Daily Totals		$2082.90		$2987.07	$65.09	$93.35
Crew E-11B						
2 Painters, Struc. Steel	$43.50	$696.00	$72.45	$1159.20	$42.28	$68.53
1 Building Laborer	39.85	318.80	60.70	485.60		
2 Paint Sprayer, 8 C.F.M.		90.20		99.22		
1 Telescoping Boom Lift, to 60'		454.60		500.06	22.70	24.97
24 L.H., Daily Totals		$1559.60		$2244.08	$64.98	$93.50
Crew E-12						
1 Welder Foreman (outside)	$56.65	$453.20	$92.60	$740.80	$53.98	$84.97
1 Equip. Oper. (light)	51.30	410.40	77.35	618.80		
1 Welder, Gas Engine, 300 amp		98.40		108.24	6.15	6.76
16 L.H., Daily Totals		$962.00		$1467.84	$60.13	$91.74
Crew E-13						
1 Welder Foreman (outside)	$56.65	$453.20	$92.60	$740.80	$54.87	$87.52
.5 Equip. Oper. (light)	51.30	205.20	77.35	309.40		
1 Welder, Gas Engine, 300 amp		98.40		108.24	8.20	9.02
12 L.H., Daily Totals		$756.80		$1158.44	$63.07	$96.54
Crew E-14						
1 Welder Foreman (outside)	$56.65	$453.20	$92.60	$740.80	$56.65	$92.60
1 Welder, Gas Engine, 300 amp		98.40		108.24	12.30	13.53
8 L.H., Daily Totals		$551.60		$849.04	$68.95	$106.13
Crew E-16						
1 Welder Foreman (outside)	$56.65	$453.20	$92.60	$740.80	$55.65	$90.97
1 Welder	54.65	437.20	89.35	714.80		
1 Welder, Gas Engine, 300 amp		98.40		108.24	6.15	6.76
16 L.H., Daily Totals		$988.80		$1563.84	$61.80	$97.74
Crew E-17						
1 Struc. Steel Foreman (outside)	$56.65	$453.20	$92.60	$740.80	$55.65	$90.97
1 Structural Steel Worker	54.65	437.20	89.35	714.80		
16 L.H., Daily Totals		$890.40		$1455.60	$55.65	$90.97
Crew E-18						
1 Struc. Steel Foreman (outside)	$56.65	$453.20	$92.60	$740.80	$54.87	$88.34
3 Structural Steel Workers	54.65	1311.60	89.35	2144.40		
1 Equipment Operator (med.)	53.75	430.00	81.05	648.40		
1 Lattice Boom Crane, 20 Ton		1083.00		1191.30	27.07	29.78
40 L.H., Daily Totals		$3277.80		$4724.90	$81.94	$118.12
Crew E-19						
1 Struc. Steel Foreman (outside)	$56.65	$453.20	$92.60	$740.80	$54.20	$86.43
1 Structural Steel Worker	54.65	437.20	89.35	714.80		
1 Equip. Oper. (light)	51.30	410.40	77.35	618.80		
1 Lattice Boom Crane, 20 Ton		1083.00		1191.30	45.13	49.64
24 L.H., Daily Totals		$2383.80		$3265.70	$99.33	$136.07

Crew No.	Bare Costs Hr.	Bare Costs Daily	Incl. Subs O&P Hr.	Incl. Subs O&P Daily	Cost Per Labor-Hour Bare Costs	Cost Per Labor-Hour Incl. O&P
Crew E-20						
1 Struc. Steel Foreman (outside)	$56.65	$453.20	$92.60	$740.80	$54.33	$87.16
5 Structural Steel Workers	54.65	2186.00	89.35	3574.00		
1 Equip. Oper. (crane)	56.10	448.80	84.60	676.80		
1 Equip. Oper. (oiler)	48.60	388.80	73.30	586.40		
1 Lattice Boom Crane, 40 Ton		1321.00		1453.10	20.64	22.70
64 L.H., Daily Totals		$4797.80		$7031.10	$74.97	$109.86
Crew E-22						
1 Skilled Worker Foreman (out)	$54.35	$434.80	$83.20	$665.60	$53.02	$81.17
2 Skilled Workers	52.35	837.60	80.15	1282.40		
24 L.H., Daily Totals		$1272.40		$1948.00	$53.02	$81.17
Crew E-24						
3 Structural Steel Workers	$54.65	$1311.60	$89.35	$2144.40	$54.42	$87.28
1 Equipment Operator (med.)	53.75	430.00	81.05	648.40		
1 Hyd. Crane, 25 Ton		590.60		649.66	18.46	20.30
32 L.H., Daily Totals		$2332.20		$3442.46	$72.88	$107.58
Crew E-25						
1 Welder Foreman (outside)	$56.65	$453.20	$92.60	$740.80	$56.65	$92.60
1 Cutting Torch		12.60		13.86	1.58	1.73
8 L.H., Daily Totals		$465.80		$754.66	$58.23	$94.33
Crew E-26						
1 Struc. Steel Foreman (outside)	$56.65	$453.20	$92.60	$740.80	$56.01	$90.41
1 Struc. Steel Worker	54.65	437.20	89.35	714.80		
1 Welder	54.65	437.20	89.35	714.80		
.25 Electrician	58.20	116.40	87.00	174.00		
.25 Plumber	62.15	124.30	93.60	187.20		
1 Welder, Gas Engine, 300 amp		98.40		108.24	3.51	3.87
28 L.H., Daily Totals		$1666.70		$2639.84	$59.52	$94.28
Crew E-27						
1 Struc. Steel Foreman (outside)	$56.65	$453.20	$92.60	$740.80	$54.33	$87.16
5 Struc. Steel Workers	54.65	2186.00	89.35	3574.00		
1 Equip. Oper. (crane)	56.10	448.80	84.60	676.80		
1 Equip. Oper. (oiler)	48.60	388.80	73.30	586.40		
1 Hyd. Crane, 12 Ton		496.00		545.60		
1 Hyd. Crane, 80 Ton		1518.00		1669.80	31.47	34.62
64 L.H., Daily Totals		$5490.80		$7793.40	$85.79	$121.77
Crew F-3						
4 Carpenters	$50.70	$1622.40	$77.20	$2470.40	$51.78	$78.68
1 Equip. Oper. (crane)	56.10	448.80	84.60	676.80		
1 Hyd. Crane, 12 Ton		496.00		545.60	12.40	13.64
40 L.H., Daily Totals		$2567.20		$3692.80	$64.18	$92.32
Crew F-4						
4 Carpenters	$50.70	$1622.40	$77.20	$2470.40	$51.25	$77.78
1 Equip. Oper. (crane)	56.10	448.80	84.60	676.80		
1 Equip. Oper. (oiler)	48.60	388.80	73.30	586.40		
1 Hyd. Crane, 55 Ton		993.80		1093.18	20.70	22.77
48 L.H., Daily Totals		$3453.80		$4826.78	$71.95	$100.56
Crew F-5						
1 Carpenter Foreman (outside)	$52.70	$421.60	$80.25	$642.00	$51.20	$77.96
3 Carpenters	50.70	1216.80	77.20	1852.80		
32 L.H., Daily Totals		$1638.40		$2494.80	$51.20	$77.96

Crews - Standard

Crew No.		Bare Costs		Incl. Subs O&P		Cost Per Labor-Hour	
Crew F-6	**Hr.**	**Daily**	**Hr.**	**Daily**	**Bare Costs**	**Incl. O&P**	
2 Carpenters	$50.70	$811.20	$77.20	$1235.20	$47.44	$72.08	
2 Building Laborers	39.85	637.60	60.70	971.20			
1 Equip. Oper. (crane)	56.10	448.80	84.60	676.80			
1 Hyd. Crane, 12 Ton		496.00		545.60	12.40	13.64	
40 L.H., Daily Totals		$2393.60		$3428.80	$59.84	$85.72	
Crew F-7	**Hr.**	**Daily**	**Hr.**	**Daily**	**Bare Costs**	**Incl. O&P**	
2 Carpenters	$50.70	$811.20	$77.20	$1235.20	$45.27	$68.95	
2 Building Laborers	39.85	637.60	60.70	971.20			
32 L.H., Daily Totals		$1448.80		$2206.40	$45.27	$68.95	
Crew G-1	**Hr.**	**Daily**	**Hr.**	**Daily**	**Bare Costs**	**Incl. O&P**	
1 Roofer Foreman (outside)	$45.95	$367.60	$77.35	$618.80	$41.06	$69.11	
4 Roofers Composition	43.95	1406.40	73.95	2366.40			
2 Roofer Helpers	32.85	525.60	55.30	884.80			
1 Application Equipment		181.00		199.10			
1 Tar Kettle/Pot		167.20		183.92			
1 Crew Truck		166.00		182.60	9.18	10.10	
56 L.H., Daily Totals		$2813.80		$4435.62	$50.25	$79.21	
Crew G-2	**Hr.**	**Daily**	**Hr.**	**Daily**	**Bare Costs**	**Incl. O&P**	
1 Plasterer	$46.45	$371.60	$69.70	$557.60	$42.02	$63.35	
1 Plasterer Helper	39.75	318.00	59.65	477.20			
1 Building Laborer	39.85	318.80	60.70	485.60			
1 Grout Pump, 50 C.F./hr.		128.60		141.46	5.36	5.89	
24 L.H., Daily Totals		$1137.00		$1661.86	$47.38	$69.24	
Crew G-2A	**Hr.**	**Daily**	**Hr.**	**Daily**	**Bare Costs**	**Incl. O&P**	
1 Roofer Composition	$43.95	$351.60	$73.95	$591.60	$38.88	$63.32	
1 Roofer Helper	32.85	262.80	55.30	442.40			
1 Building Laborer	39.85	318.80	60.70	485.60			
1 Foam Spray Rig, Trailer-Mtd.		499.25		549.17			
1 Pickup Truck, 3/4 Ton		115.20		126.72	25.60	28.16	
24 L.H., Daily Totals		$1547.65		$2195.49	$64.49	$91.48	
Crew G-3	**Hr.**	**Daily**	**Hr.**	**Daily**	**Bare Costs**	**Incl. O&P**	
2 Sheet Metal Workers	$59.80	$956.80	$91.25	$1460.00	$49.83	$75.97	
2 Building Laborers	39.85	637.60	60.70	971.20			
32 L.H., Daily Totals		$1594.40		$2431.20	$49.83	$75.97	
Crew G-4	**Hr.**	**Daily**	**Hr.**	**Daily**	**Bare Costs**	**Incl. O&P**	
1 Labor Foreman (outside)	$41.85	$334.80	$63.75	$510.00	$40.52	$61.72	
2 Building Laborers	39.85	637.60	60.70	971.20			
1 Flatbed Truck, Gas, 1.5 Ton		188.40		207.24			
1 Air Compressor, 160 cfm		117.20		128.92	12.73	14.01	
24 L.H., Daily Totals		$1278.00		$1817.36	$53.25	$75.72	
Crew G-5	**Hr.**	**Daily**	**Hr.**	**Daily**	**Bare Costs**	**Incl. O&P**	
1 Roofer Foreman (outside)	$45.95	$367.60	$77.35	$618.80	$39.91	$67.17	
2 Roofers Composition	43.95	703.20	73.95	1183.20			
2 Roofer Helpers	32.85	525.60	55.30	884.80			
1 Application Equipment		181.00		199.10	4.53	4.98	
40 L.H., Daily Totals		$1777.40		$2885.90	$44.44	$72.15	
Crew G-6A	**Hr.**	**Daily**	**Hr.**	**Daily**	**Bare Costs**	**Incl. O&P**	
2 Roofers Composition	$43.95	$703.20	$73.95	$1183.20	$43.95	$73.95	
1 Small Compressor, Electric		15.10		16.61			
2 Pneumatic Nailers		46.10		50.71	3.83	4.21	
16 L.H., Daily Totals		$764.40		$1250.52	$47.77	$78.16	

Crew No.		Bare Costs		Incl. Subs O&P		Cost Per Labor-Hour	
Crew G-7	**Hr.**	**Daily**	**Hr.**	**Daily**	**Bare Costs**	**Incl. O&P**	
1 Carpenter	$50.70	$405.60	$77.20	$617.60	$50.70	$77.20	
1 Small Compressor, Electric		15.10		16.61			
1 Pneumatic Nailer		23.05		25.36	4.77	5.25	
8 L.H., Daily Totals		$443.75		$659.57	$55.47	$82.45	
Crew H-1	**Hr.**	**Daily**	**Hr.**	**Daily**	**Bare Costs**	**Incl. O&P**	
2 Glaziers	$48.50	$776.00	$73.45	$1175.20	$51.58	$81.40	
2 Struc. Steel Workers	54.65	874.40	89.35	1429.60			
32 L.H., Daily Totals		$1650.40		$2604.80	$51.58	$81.40	
Crew H-2	**Hr.**	**Daily**	**Hr.**	**Daily**	**Bare Costs**	**Incl. O&P**	
2 Glaziers	$48.50	$776.00	$73.45	$1175.20	$45.62	$69.20	
1 Building Laborer	39.85	318.80	60.70	485.60			
24 L.H., Daily Totals		$1094.80		$1660.80	$45.62	$69.20	
Crew H-3	**Hr.**	**Daily**	**Hr.**	**Daily**	**Bare Costs**	**Incl. O&P**	
1 Glazier	$48.50	$388.00	$73.45	$587.60	$43.15	$65.90	
1 Helper	37.80	302.40	58.35	466.80			
16 L.H., Daily Totals		$690.40		$1054.40	$43.15	$65.90	
Crew H-4	**Hr.**	**Daily**	**Hr.**	**Daily**	**Bare Costs**	**Incl. O&P**	
1 Carpenter	$50.70	$405.60	$77.20	$617.60	$47.04	$71.62	
1 Carpenter Helper	37.80	302.40	58.35	466.80			
.5 Electrician	58.20	232.80	87.00	348.00			
20 L.H., Daily Totals		$940.80		$1432.40	$47.04	$71.62	
Crew J-1	**Hr.**	**Daily**	**Hr.**	**Daily**	**Bare Costs**	**Incl. O&P**	
3 Plasterers	$46.45	$1114.80	$69.70	$1672.80	$43.77	$65.68	
2 Plasterer Helpers	39.75	636.00	59.65	954.40			
1 Mixing Machine, 6 C.F.		133.20		146.52	3.33	3.66	
40 L.H., Daily Totals		$1884.00		$2773.72	$47.10	$69.34	
Crew J-2	**Hr.**	**Daily**	**Hr.**	**Daily**	**Bare Costs**	**Incl. O&P**	
3 Plasterers	$46.45	$1114.80	$69.70	$1672.80	$44.67	$66.84	
2 Plasterer Helpers	39.75	636.00	59.65	954.40			
1 Lather	49.15	393.20	72.65	581.20			
1 Mixing Machine, 6 C.F.		133.20		146.52	2.77	3.05	
48 L.H., Daily Totals		$2277.20		$3354.92	$47.44	$69.89	
Crew J-3	**Hr.**	**Daily**	**Hr.**	**Daily**	**Bare Costs**	**Incl. O&P**	
1 Terrazzo Worker	$47.00	$376.00	$69.55	$556.40	$43.05	$63.70	
1 Terrazzo Helper	39.10	312.80	57.85	462.80			
1 Floor Grinder, 22" Path		133.60		146.96			
1 Terrazzo Mixer		177.80		195.58	19.46	21.41	
16 L.H., Daily Totals		$1000.20		$1361.74	$62.51	$85.11	
Crew J-4	**Hr.**	**Daily**	**Hr.**	**Daily**	**Bare Costs**	**Incl. O&P**	
2 Cement Finishers	$47.55	$760.80	$70.45	$1127.20	$44.98	$67.20	
1 Laborer	39.85	318.80	60.70	485.60			
1 Floor Grinder, 22" Path		133.60		146.96			
1 Floor Edger, 7" Path		42.95		47.24			
1 Vacuum Pick-Up System		66.95		73.64	10.15	11.16	
24 L.H., Daily Totals		$1323.10		$1880.65	$55.13	$78.36	

Crews - Standard

Crew No.		Bare Costs		Incl. Subs O&P		Cost Per Labor-Hour	
Crew J-4A	Hr.	Daily	Hr.	Daily	Bare Costs	Incl. O&P
2 Cement Finishers	$47.55	$760.80	$70.45	$1127.20	$43.70	$65.58
2 Laborers	39.85	637.60	60.70	971.20		
1 Floor Grinder, 22" Path		133.60		146.96		
1 Floor Edger, 7" Path		42.95		47.24		
1 Vacuum Pick-Up System		66.95		73.64		
1 Floor Auto Scrubber		254.30		279.73	15.56	17.11
32 L.H., Daily Totals		$1896.20		$2645.98	$59.26	$82.69
Crew J-4B	Hr.	Daily	Hr.	Daily	Bare Costs	Incl. O&P
1 Laborer	$39.85	$318.80	$60.70	$485.60	$39.85	$60.70
1 Floor Auto Scrubber		254.30		279.73	31.79	34.97
8 L.H., Daily Totals		$573.10		$765.33	$71.64	$95.67
Crew J-6	Hr.	Daily	Hr.	Daily	Bare Costs	Incl. O&P
2 Painters	$42.55	$680.80	$64.05	$1024.80	$44.06	$66.54
1 Building Laborer	39.85	318.80	60.70	485.60		
1 Equip. Oper. (light)	51.30	410.40	77.35	618.80		
1 Air Compressor, 250 cfm		167.40		184.14		
1 Sandblaster, Portable, 3 C.F.		21.00		23.10		
1 Set Sand Blasting Accessories		14.70		16.17	6.35	6.98
32 L.H., Daily Totals		$1613.10		$2352.61	$50.41	$73.52
Crew J-7	Hr.	Daily	Hr.	Daily	Bare Costs	Incl. O&P
2 Painters	$42.55	$680.80	$64.05	$1024.80	$42.55	$64.05
1 Floor Belt Sander		16.75		18.43		
1 Floor Sanding Edger		13.15		14.47	1.87	2.06
16 L.H., Daily Totals		$710.70		$1057.69	$44.42	$66.11
Crew K-1	Hr.	Daily	Hr.	Daily	Bare Costs	Incl. O&P
1 Carpenter	$50.70	$405.60	$77.20	$617.60	$47.60	$72.10
1 Truck Driver (light)	44.50	356.00	67.00	536.00		
1 Flatbed Truck, Gas, 3 Ton		238.00		261.80	14.88	16.36
16 L.H., Daily Totals		$999.60		$1415.40	$62.48	$88.46
Crew K-2	Hr.	Daily	Hr.	Daily	Bare Costs	Incl. O&P
1 Struc. Steel Foreman (outside)	$56.65	$453.20	$92.60	$740.80	$51.93	$82.98
1 Struc. Steel Worker	54.65	437.20	89.35	714.80		
1 Truck Driver (light)	44.50	356.00	67.00	536.00		
1 Flatbed Truck, Gas, 3 Ton		238.00		261.80	9.92	10.91
24 L.H., Daily Totals		$1484.40		$2253.40	$61.85	$93.89
Crew L-1	Hr.	Daily	Hr.	Daily	Bare Costs	Incl. O&P
1 Electrician	$58.20	$465.60	$87.00	$696.00	$60.17	$90.30
1 Plumber	62.15	497.20	93.60	748.80		
16 L.H., Daily Totals		$962.80		$1444.80	$60.17	$90.30
Crew L-2	Hr.	Daily	Hr.	Daily	Bare Costs	Incl. O&P
1 Carpenter	$50.70	$405.60	$77.20	$617.60	$44.25	$67.78
1 Carpenter Helper	37.80	302.40	58.35	466.80		
16 L.H., Daily Totals		$708.00		$1084.40	$44.25	$67.78
Crew L-3	Hr.	Daily	Hr.	Daily	Bare Costs	Incl. O&P
1 Carpenter	$50.70	$405.60	$77.20	$617.60	$54.85	$83.16
.5 Electrician	58.20	232.80	87.00	348.00		
.5 Sheet Metal Worker	59.80	239.20	91.25	365.00		
16 L.H., Daily Totals		$877.60		$1330.60	$54.85	$83.16

Crew No.		Bare Costs		Incl. Subs O&P		Cost Per Labor-Hour	
Crew L-3A	Hr.	Daily	Hr.	Daily	Bare Costs	Incl. O&P
1 Carpenter Foreman (outside)	$52.70	$421.60	$80.25	$642.00	$55.07	$83.92
.5 Sheet Metal Worker	59.80	239.20	91.25	365.00		
12 L.H., Daily Totals		$660.80		$1007.00	$55.07	$83.92
Crew L-4	Hr.	Daily	Hr.	Daily	Bare Costs	Incl. O&P
2 Skilled Workers	$52.35	$837.60	$80.15	$1282.40	$47.50	$72.88
1 Helper	37.80	302.40	58.35	466.80		
24 L.H., Daily Totals		$1140.00		$1749.20	$47.50	$72.88
Crew L-5	Hr.	Daily	Hr.	Daily	Bare Costs	Incl. O&P
1 Struc. Steel Foreman (outside)	$56.65	$453.20	$92.60	$740.80	$55.14	$89.14
5 Struc. Steel Workers	54.65	2186.00	89.35	3574.00		
1 Equip. Oper. (crane)	56.10	448.80	84.60	676.80		
1 Hyd. Crane, 25 Ton		590.60		649.66	10.55	11.60
56 L.H., Daily Totals		$3678.60		$5641.26	$65.69	$100.74
Crew L-5A	Hr.	Daily	Hr.	Daily	Bare Costs	Incl. O&P
1 Struc. Steel Foreman (outside)	$56.65	$453.20	$92.60	$740.80	$55.51	$88.97
2 Structural Steel Workers	54.65	874.40	89.35	1429.60		
1 Equip. Oper. (crane)	56.10	448.80	84.60	676.80		
1 S.P. Crane, 4x4, 25 Ton		668.40		735.24	20.89	22.98
32 L.H., Daily Totals		$2444.80		$3582.44	$76.40	$111.95
Crew L-5B	Hr.	Daily	Hr.	Daily	Bare Costs	Incl. O&P
1 Struc. Steel Foreman (outside)	$56.65	$453.20	$92.60	$740.80	$57.01	$88.11
2 Structural Steel Workers	54.65	874.40	89.35	1429.60		
2 Electricians	58.20	931.20	87.00	1392.00		
2 Steamfitters/Pipefitters	63.00	1008.00	94.90	1518.40		
1 Equip. Oper. (crane)	56.10	448.80	84.60	676.80		
1 Equip. Oper. (oiler)	48.60	388.80	73.30	586.40		
1 Hyd. Crane, 80 Ton		1518.00		1669.80	21.08	23.19
72 L.H., Daily Totals		$5622.40		$8013.80	$78.09	$111.30
Crew L-6	Hr.	Daily	Hr.	Daily	Bare Costs	Incl. O&P
1 Plumber	$62.15	$497.20	$93.60	$748.80	$60.83	$91.40
.5 Electrician	58.20	232.80	87.00	348.00		
12 L.H., Daily Totals		$730.00		$1096.80	$60.83	$91.40
Crew L-7	Hr.	Daily	Hr.	Daily	Bare Costs	Incl. O&P
2 Carpenters	$50.70	$811.20	$77.20	$1235.20	$48.67	$73.89
1 Building Laborer	39.85	318.80	60.70	485.60		
.5 Electrician	58.20	232.80	87.00	348.00		
28 L.H., Daily Totals		$1362.80		$2068.80	$48.67	$73.89
Crew L-8	Hr.	Daily	Hr.	Daily	Bare Costs	Incl. O&P
2 Carpenters	$50.70	$811.20	$77.20	$1235.20	$52.99	$80.48
.5 Plumber	62.15	248.60	93.60	374.40		
20 L.H., Daily Totals		$1059.80		$1609.60	$52.99	$80.48
Crew L-9	Hr.	Daily	Hr.	Daily	Bare Costs	Incl. O&P
1 Labor Foreman (inside)	$40.35	$322.80	$61.45	$491.60	$45.29	$70.16
2 Building Laborers	39.85	637.60	60.70	971.20		
1 Struc. Steel Worker	54.65	437.20	89.35	714.80		
.5 Electrician	58.20	232.80	87.00	348.00		
36 L.H., Daily Totals		$1630.40		$2525.60	$45.29	$70.16

Crews - Standard

Crew No.	Bare Costs Hr.	Bare Costs Daily	Incl. Subs O&P Hr.	Incl. Subs O&P Daily	Cost Per Labor-Hour Bare Costs	Cost Per Labor-Hour Incl. O&P
Crew L-10					Bare Costs	Incl. O&P
1 Struc. Steel Foreman (outside)	$56.65	$453.20	$92.60	$740.80	$55.80	$88.85
1 Structural Steel Worker	54.65	437.20	89.35	714.80		
1 Equip. Oper. (crane)	56.10	448.80	84.60	676.80		
1 Hyd. Crane, 12 Ton		496.00		545.60	20.67	22.73
24 L.H., Daily Totals		$1835.20		$2678.00	$76.47	$111.58
Crew L-11	Hr.	Daily	Hr.	Daily	Bare Costs	Incl. O&P
2 Wreckers	$39.85	$637.60	$62.70	$1003.20	$46.77	$71.84
1 Equip. Oper. (crane)	56.10	448.80	84.60	676.80		
1 Equip. Oper. (light)	51.30	410.40	77.35	618.80		
1 Hyd. Excavator, 2.5 C.Y.		1411.00		1552.10		
1 Loader, Skid Steer, 78 H.P.		364.80		401.28	55.49	61.04
32 L.H., Daily Totals		$3272.60		$4252.18	$102.27	$132.88
Crew M-1	Hr.	Daily	Hr.	Daily	Bare Costs	Incl. O&P
3 Elevator Constructors	$82.20	$1972.80	$122.50	$2940.00	$78.09	$116.36
1 Elevator Apprentice	65.75	526.00	97.95	783.60		
5 Hand Tools		50.00		55.00	1.56	1.72
32 L.H., Daily Totals		$2548.80		$3778.60	$79.65	$118.08
Crew M-3	Hr.	Daily	Hr.	Daily	Bare Costs	Incl. O&P
1 Electrician Foreman (outside)	$60.20	$481.60	$90.00	$720.00	$61.51	$92.10
1 Common Laborer	39.85	318.80	60.70	485.60		
.25 Equipment Operator (med.)	53.75	107.50	81.05	162.10		
1 Elevator Constructor	82.20	657.60	122.50	980.00		
1 Elevator Apprentice	65.75	526.00	97.95	783.60		
.25 S.P. Crane, 4x4, 20 Ton		142.80		157.08	4.20	4.62
34 L.H., Daily Totals		$2234.30		$3288.38	$65.71	$96.72
Crew M-4	Hr.	Daily	Hr.	Daily	Bare Costs	Incl. O&P
1 Electrician Foreman (outside)	$60.20	$481.60	$90.00	$720.00	$60.93	$91.25
1 Common Laborer	39.85	318.80	60.70	485.60		
.25 Equipment Operator, Crane	56.10	112.20	84.60	169.20		
.25 Equip. Oper. (oiler)	48.60	97.20	73.30	146.60		
1 Elevator Constructor	82.20	657.60	122.50	980.00		
1 Elevator Apprentice	65.75	526.00	97.95	783.60		
.25 S.P. Crane, 4x4, 40 Ton		183.70		202.07	5.10	5.61
36 L.H., Daily Totals		$2377.10		$3487.07	$66.03	$96.86
Crew Q-1	Hr.	Daily	Hr.	Daily	Bare Costs	Incl. O&P
1 Plumber	$62.15	$497.20	$93.60	$748.80	$55.92	$84.22
1 Plumber Apprentice	49.70	397.60	74.85	598.80		
16 L.H., Daily Totals		$894.80		$1347.60	$55.92	$84.22
Crew Q-1A	Hr.	Daily	Hr.	Daily	Bare Costs	Incl. O&P
.25 Plumber Foreman (outside)	$64.15	$128.30	$96.60	$193.20	$62.55	$94.20
1 Plumber	62.15	497.20	93.60	748.80		
10 L.H., Daily Totals		$625.50		$942.00	$62.55	$94.20
Crew Q-1C	Hr.	Daily	Hr.	Daily	Bare Costs	Incl. O&P
1 Plumber	$62.15	$497.20	$93.60	$748.80	$55.20	$83.17
1 Plumber Apprentice	49.70	397.60	74.85	598.80		
1 Equip. Oper. (medium)	53.75	430.00	81.05	648.40		
1 Trencher, Chain Type, 8' D		2048.00		2252.80	85.33	93.87
24 L.H., Daily Totals		$3372.80		$4248.80	$140.53	$177.03
Crew Q-2	Hr.	Daily	Hr.	Daily	Bare Costs	Incl. O&P
2 Plumbers	$62.15	$994.40	$93.60	$1497.60	$58.00	$87.35
1 Plumber Apprentice	49.70	397.60	74.85	598.80		
24 L.H., Daily Totals		$1392.00		$2096.40	$58.00	$87.35
Crew Q-3	Hr.	Daily	Hr.	Daily	Bare Costs	Incl. O&P
1 Plumber Foreman (inside)	$62.65	$501.20	$94.35	$754.80	$59.16	$89.10
2 Plumbers	62.15	994.40	93.60	1497.60		
1 Plumber Apprentice	49.70	397.60	74.85	598.80		
32 L.H., Daily Totals		$1893.20		$2851.20	$59.16	$89.10
Crew Q-4	Hr.	Daily	Hr.	Daily	Bare Costs	Incl. O&P
1 Plumber Foreman (inside)	$62.65	$501.20	$94.35	$754.80	$59.16	$89.10
1 Plumber	62.15	497.20	93.60	748.80		
1 Welder (plumber)	62.15	497.20	93.60	748.80		
1 Plumber Apprentice	49.70	397.60	74.85	598.80		
1 Welder, Electric, 300 amp		59.20		65.12	1.85	2.04
32 L.H., Daily Totals		$1952.40		$2916.32	$61.01	$91.14
Crew Q-5	Hr.	Daily	Hr.	Daily	Bare Costs	Incl. O&P
1 Steamfitter	$63.00	$504.00	$94.90	$759.20	$56.70	$85.40
1 Steamfitter Apprentice	50.40	403.20	75.90	607.20		
16 L.H., Daily Totals		$907.20		$1366.40	$56.70	$85.40
Crew Q-6	Hr.	Daily	Hr.	Daily	Bare Costs	Incl. O&P
2 Steamfitters	$63.00	$1008.00	$94.90	$1518.40	$58.80	$88.57
1 Steamfitter Apprentice	50.40	403.20	75.90	607.20		
24 L.H., Daily Totals		$1411.20		$2125.60	$58.80	$88.57
Crew Q-7	Hr.	Daily	Hr.	Daily	Bare Costs	Incl. O&P
1 Steamfitter Foreman (inside)	$63.50	$508.00	$95.65	$765.20	$59.98	$90.34
2 Steamfitters	63.00	1008.00	94.90	1518.40		
1 Steamfitter Apprentice	50.40	403.20	75.90	607.20		
32 L.H., Daily Totals		$1919.20		$2890.80	$59.98	$90.34
Crew Q-8	Hr.	Daily	Hr.	Daily	Bare Costs	Incl. O&P
1 Steamfitter Foreman (inside)	$63.50	$508.00	$95.65	$765.20	$59.98	$90.34
1 Steamfitter	63.00	504.00	94.90	759.20		
1 Welder (steamfitter)	63.00	504.00	94.90	759.20		
1 Steamfitter Apprentice	50.40	403.20	75.90	607.20		
1 Welder, Electric, 300 amp		59.20		65.12	1.85	2.04
32 L.H., Daily Totals		$1978.40		$2955.92	$61.83	$92.37
Crew Q-9	Hr.	Daily	Hr.	Daily	Bare Costs	Incl. O&P
1 Sheet Metal Worker	$59.80	$478.40	$91.25	$730.00	$53.83	$82.13
1 Sheet Metal Apprentice	47.85	382.80	73.00	584.00		
16 L.H., Daily Totals		$861.20		$1314.00	$53.83	$82.13
Crew Q-10	Hr.	Daily	Hr.	Daily	Bare Costs	Incl. O&P
2 Sheet Metal Workers	$59.80	$956.80	$91.25	$1460.00	$55.82	$85.17
1 Sheet Metal Apprentice	47.85	382.80	73.00	584.00		
24 L.H., Daily Totals		$1339.60		$2044.00	$55.82	$85.17
Crew Q-11	Hr.	Daily	Hr.	Daily	Bare Costs	Incl. O&P
1 Sheet Metal Foreman (inside)	$60.30	$482.40	$92.00	$736.00	$56.94	$86.88
2 Sheet Metal Workers	59.80	956.80	91.25	1460.00		
1 Sheet Metal Apprentice	47.85	382.80	73.00	584.00		
32 L.H., Daily Totals		$1822.00		$2780.00	$56.94	$86.88
Crew Q-12	Hr.	Daily	Hr.	Daily	Bare Costs	Incl. O&P
1 Sprinkler Installer	$59.90	$479.20	$90.45	$723.60	$53.90	$81.40
1 Sprinkler Apprentice	47.90	383.20	72.35	578.80		
16 L.H., Daily Totals		$862.40		$1302.40	$53.90	$81.40

Crews - Standard

Crew No.	Bare Costs Hr.	Bare Costs Daily	Incl. Subs O&P Hr.	Incl. Subs O&P Daily	Cost Per Labor-Hour Bare Costs	Cost Per Labor-Hour Incl. O&P
Crew Q-13	Hr.	Daily	Hr.	Daily	Bare Costs	Incl. O&P
1 Sprinkler Foreman (inside)	$60.40	$483.20	$91.20	$729.60	$57.02	$86.11
2 Sprinkler Installers	59.90	958.40	90.45	1447.20		
1 Sprinkler Apprentice	47.90	383.20	72.35	578.80		
32 L.H., Daily Totals		$1824.80		$2755.60	$57.02	$86.11
Crew Q-14	Hr.	Daily	Hr.	Daily	Bare Costs	Incl. O&P
1 Asbestos Worker	$56.30	$450.40	$87.40	$699.20	$50.67	$78.65
1 Asbestos Apprentice	45.05	360.40	69.90	559.20		
16 L.H., Daily Totals		$810.80		$1258.40	$50.67	$78.65
Crew Q-15	Hr.	Daily	Hr.	Daily	Bare Costs	Incl. O&P
1 Plumber	$62.15	$497.20	$93.60	$748.80	$55.92	$84.22
1 Plumber Apprentice	49.70	397.60	74.85	598.80		
1 Welder, Electric, 300 amp		59.20		65.12	3.70	4.07
16 L.H., Daily Totals		$954.00		$1412.72	$59.63	$88.30
Crew Q-16	Hr.	Daily	Hr.	Daily	Bare Costs	Incl. O&P
2 Plumbers	$62.15	$994.40	$93.60	$1497.60	$58.00	$87.35
1 Plumber Apprentice	49.70	397.60	74.85	598.80		
1 Welder, Electric, 300 amp		59.20		65.12	2.47	2.71
24 L.H., Daily Totals		$1451.20		$2161.52	$60.47	$90.06
Crew Q-17	Hr.	Daily	Hr.	Daily	Bare Costs	Incl. O&P
1 Steamfitter	$63.00	$504.00	$94.90	$759.20	$56.70	$85.40
1 Steamfitter Apprentice	50.40	403.20	75.90	607.20		
1 Welder, Electric, 300 amp		59.20		65.12	3.70	4.07
16 L.H., Daily Totals		$966.40		$1431.52	$60.40	$89.47
Crew Q-17A	Hr.	Daily	Hr.	Daily	Bare Costs	Incl. O&P
1 Steamfitter	$63.00	$504.00	$94.90	$759.20	$56.50	$85.13
1 Steamfitter Apprentice	50.40	403.20	75.90	607.20		
1 Equip. Oper. (crane)	56.10	448.80	84.60	676.80		
1 Hyd. Crane, 12 Ton		496.00		545.60		
1 Welder, Electric, 300 amp		59.20		65.12	23.13	25.45
24 L.H., Daily Totals		$1911.20		$2653.92	$79.63	$110.58
Crew Q-18	Hr.	Daily	Hr.	Daily	Bare Costs	Incl. O&P
2 Steamfitters	$63.00	$1008.00	$94.90	$1518.40	$58.80	$88.57
1 Steamfitter Apprentice	50.40	403.20	75.90	607.20		
1 Welder, Electric, 300 amp		59.20		65.12	2.47	2.71
24 L.H., Daily Totals		$1470.40		$2190.72	$61.27	$91.28
Crew Q-19	Hr.	Daily	Hr.	Daily	Bare Costs	Incl. O&P
1 Steamfitter	$63.00	$504.00	$94.90	$759.20	$57.20	$85.93
1 Steamfitter Apprentice	50.40	403.20	75.90	607.20		
1 Electrician	58.20	465.60	87.00	696.00		
24 L.H., Daily Totals		$1372.80		$2062.40	$57.20	$85.93
Crew Q-20	Hr.	Daily	Hr.	Daily	Bare Costs	Incl. O&P
1 Sheet Metal Worker	$59.80	$478.40	$91.25	$730.00	$54.70	$83.10
1 Sheet Metal Apprentice	47.85	382.80	73.00	584.00		
.5 Electrician	58.20	232.80	87.00	348.00		
20 L.H., Daily Totals		$1094.00		$1662.00	$54.70	$83.10
Crew Q-21	Hr.	Daily	Hr.	Daily	Bare Costs	Incl. O&P
2 Steamfitters	$63.00	$1008.00	$94.90	$1518.40	$58.65	$88.17
1 Steamfitter Apprentice	50.40	403.20	75.90	607.20		
1 Electrician	58.20	465.60	87.00	696.00		
32 L.H., Daily Totals		$1876.80		$2821.60	$58.65	$88.17

Crew No.	Bare Costs Hr.	Bare Costs Daily	Incl. Subs O&P Hr.	Incl. Subs O&P Daily	Cost Per Labor-Hour Bare Costs	Cost Per Labor-Hour Incl. O&P
Crew Q-22	Hr.	Daily	Hr.	Daily	Bare Costs	Incl. O&P
1 Plumber	$62.15	$497.20	$93.60	$748.80	$55.92	$84.22
1 Plumber Apprentice	49.70	397.60	74.85	598.80		
1 Hyd. Crane, 12 Ton		496.00		545.60	31.00	34.10
16 L.H., Daily Totals		$1390.80		$1893.20	$86.92	$118.33
Crew Q-22A	Hr.	Daily	Hr.	Daily	Bare Costs	Incl. O&P
1 Plumber	$62.15	$497.20	$93.60	$748.80	$51.95	$78.44
1 Plumber Apprentice	49.70	397.60	74.85	598.80		
1 Laborer	39.85	318.80	60.70	485.60		
1 Equip. Oper. (crane)	56.10	448.80	84.60	676.80		
1 Hyd. Crane, 12 Ton		496.00		545.60	15.50	17.05
32 L.H., Daily Totals		$2158.40		$3055.60	$67.45	$95.49
Crew Q-23	Hr.	Daily	Hr.	Daily	Bare Costs	Incl. O&P
1 Plumber Foreman (outside)	$64.15	$513.20	$96.60	$772.80	$60.02	$90.42
1 Plumber	62.15	497.20	93.60	748.80		
1 Equip. Oper. (medium)	53.75	430.00	81.05	648.40		
1 Lattice Boom Crane, 20 Ton		1083.00		1191.30	45.13	49.64
24 L.H., Daily Totals		$2523.40		$3361.30	$105.14	$140.05
Crew R-1	Hr.	Daily	Hr.	Daily	Bare Costs	Incl. O&P
1 Electrician Foreman	$58.70	$469.60	$87.75	$702.00	$54.40	$81.33
3 Electricians	58.20	1396.80	87.00	2088.00		
2 Electrician Apprentices	46.55	744.80	69.60	1113.60		
48 L.H., Daily Totals		$2611.20		$3903.60	$54.40	$81.33
Crew R-1A	Hr.	Daily	Hr.	Daily	Bare Costs	Incl. O&P
1 Electrician	$58.20	$465.60	$87.00	$696.00	$52.38	$78.30
1 Electrician Apprentice	46.55	372.40	69.60	556.80		
16 L.H., Daily Totals		$838.00		$1252.80	$52.38	$78.30
Crew R-1B	Hr.	Daily	Hr.	Daily	Bare Costs	Incl. O&P
1 Electrician	$58.20	$465.60	$87.00	$696.00	$50.43	$75.45
2 Electrician Apprentices	46.55	744.80	69.60	1113.60		
24 L.H., Daily Totals		$1210.40		$1809.60	$50.43	$75.45
Crew R-1C	Hr.	Daily	Hr.	Daily	Bare Costs	Incl. O&P
2 Electricians	$58.20	$931.20	$87.00	$1392.00	$52.38	$78.30
2 Electrician Apprentices	46.55	744.80	69.60	1113.60		
1 Portable Cable Puller, 8000 lb.		130.15		143.16	4.07	4.47
32 L.H., Daily Totals		$1806.15		$2648.76	$56.44	$82.77
Crew R-2	Hr.	Daily	Hr.	Daily	Bare Costs	Incl. O&P
1 Electrician Foreman	$58.70	$469.60	$87.75	$702.00	$54.64	$81.79
3 Electricians	58.20	1396.80	87.00	2088.00		
2 Electrician Apprentices	46.55	744.80	69.60	1113.60		
1 Equip. Oper. (crane)	56.10	448.80	84.60	676.80		
1 S.P. Crane, 4x4, 5 Ton		259.00		284.90	4.63	5.09
56 L.H., Daily Totals		$3319.00		$4865.30	$59.27	$86.88
Crew R-3	Hr.	Daily	Hr.	Daily	Bare Costs	Incl. O&P
1 Electrician Foreman	$58.70	$469.60	$87.75	$702.00	$57.98	$86.82
1 Electrician	58.20	465.60	87.00	696.00		
.5 Equip. Oper. (crane)	56.10	224.40	84.60	338.40		
.5 S.P. Crane, 4x4, 5 Ton		129.50		142.45	6.47	7.12
20 L.H., Daily Totals		$1289.10		$1878.85	$64.45	$93.94

Crews - Standard

Crew No.		Bare Costs		Incl. Subs O&P		Cost Per Labor-Hour	
Crew R-4	Hr.	Daily	Hr.	Daily	Bare Costs	Incl. O&P
1 Struc. Steel Foreman (outside)	$56.65	$453.20	$92.60	$740.80	$55.76	$89.53
3 Struc. Steel Workers	54.65	1311.60	89.35	2144.40		
1 Electrician	58.20	465.60	87.00	696.00		
1 Welder, Gas Engine, 300 amp		98.40		108.24	2.46	2.71
40 L.H., Daily Totals		$2328.80		$3689.44	$58.22	$92.24
Crew R-5	Hr.	Daily	Hr.	Daily	Bare Costs	Incl. O&P
1 Electrician Foreman	$58.70	$469.60	$87.75	$702.00	$50.83	$76.65
4 Electrician Linemen	58.20	1862.40	87.00	2784.00		
2 Electrician Operators	58.20	931.20	87.00	1392.00		
4 Electrician Groundmen	37.80	1209.60	58.35	1867.20		
1 Crew Truck		166.00		182.60		
1 Flatbed Truck, 20,000 GVW		197.20		216.92		
1 Pickup Truck, 3/4 Ton		115.20		126.72		
.2 Hyd. Crane, 55 Ton		198.76		218.64		
.2 Hyd. Crane, 12 Ton		99.20		109.12		
.2 Earth Auger, Truck-Mtd.		74.76		82.24		
1 Tractor w/Winch		361.80		397.98	13.78	15.16
88 L.H., Daily Totals		$5685.72		$8079.41	$64.61	$91.81
Crew R-6	Hr.	Daily	Hr.	Daily	Bare Costs	Incl. O&P
1 Electrician Foreman	$58.70	$469.60	$87.75	$702.00	$50.83	$76.65
4 Electrician Linemen	58.20	1862.40	87.00	2784.00		
2 Electrician Operators	58.20	931.20	87.00	1392.00		
4 Electrician Groundmen	37.80	1209.60	58.35	1867.20		
1 Crew Truck		166.00		182.60		
1 Flatbed Truck, 20,000 GVW		197.20		216.92		
1 Pickup Truck, 3/4 Ton		115.20		126.72		
.2 Hyd. Crane, 55 Ton		198.76		218.64		
.2 Hyd. Crane, 12 Ton		99.20		109.12		
.2 Earth Auger, Truck-Mtd.		74.76		82.24		
1 Tractor w/Winch		361.80		397.98		
3 Cable Trailers		635.10		698.61		
.5 Tensioning Rig		209.93		230.92		
.5 Cable Pulling Rig		1213.00		1334.30	37.17	40.89
88 L.H., Daily Totals		$7743.74		$10343.24	$88.00	$117.54
Crew R-7	Hr.	Daily	Hr.	Daily	Bare Costs	Incl. O&P
1 Electrician Foreman	$58.70	$469.60	$87.75	$702.00	$41.28	$63.25
5 Electrician Groundmen	37.80	1512.00	58.35	2334.00		
1 Crew Truck		166.00		182.60	3.46	3.80
48 L.H., Daily Totals		$2147.60		$3218.60	$44.74	$67.05
Crew R-8	Hr.	Daily	Hr.	Daily	Bare Costs	Incl. O&P
1 Electrician Foreman	$58.70	$469.60	$87.75	$702.00	$51.48	$77.58
3 Electrician Linemen	58.20	1396.80	87.00	2088.00		
2 Electrician Groundmen	37.80	604.80	58.35	933.60		
1 Pickup Truck, 3/4 Ton		115.20		126.72		
1 Crew Truck		166.00		182.60	5.86	6.44
48 L.H., Daily Totals		$2752.40		$4032.92	$57.34	$84.02
Crew R-9	Hr.	Daily	Hr.	Daily	Bare Costs	Incl. O&P
1 Electrician Foreman	$58.70	$469.60	$87.75	$702.00	$48.06	$72.77
1 Electrician Lineman	58.20	465.60	87.00	696.00		
2 Electrician Operators	58.20	931.20	87.00	1392.00		
4 Electrician Groundmen	37.80	1209.60	58.35	1867.20		
1 Pickup Truck, 3/4 Ton		115.20		126.72		
1 Crew Truck		166.00		182.60	4.39	4.83
64 L.H., Daily Totals		$3357.20		$4966.52	$52.46	$77.60

Crew No.		Bare Costs		Incl. Subs O&P		Cost Per Labor-Hour	
Crew R-10	Hr.	Daily	Hr.	Daily	Bare Costs	Incl. O&P
1 Electrician Foreman	$58.70	$469.60	$87.75	$702.00	$54.88	$82.35
4 Electrician Linemen	58.20	1862.40	87.00	2784.00		
1 Electrician Groundman	37.80	302.40	58.35	466.80		
1 Crew Truck		166.00		182.60		
3 Tram Cars		433.80		477.18	12.50	13.75
48 L.H., Daily Totals		$3234.20		$4612.58	$67.38	$96.10
Crew R-11	Hr.	Daily	Hr.	Daily	Bare Costs	Incl. O&P
1 Electrician Foreman	$58.70	$469.60	$87.75	$702.00	$55.35	$83.01
4 Electricians	58.20	1862.40	87.00	2784.00		
1 Equip. Oper. (crane)	56.10	448.80	84.60	676.80		
1 Common Laborer	39.85	318.80	60.70	485.60		
1 Crew Truck		166.00		182.60		
1 Hyd. Crane, 12 Ton		496.00		545.60	11.82	13.00
56 L.H., Daily Totals		$3761.60		$5376.60	$67.17	$96.01
Crew R-12	Hr.	Daily	Hr.	Daily	Bare Costs	Incl. O&P
1 Carpenter Foreman (inside)	$51.20	$409.60	$78.00	$624.00	$47.44	$72.73
4 Carpenters	50.70	1622.40	77.20	2470.40		
4 Common Laborers	39.85	1275.20	60.70	1942.40		
1 Equip. Oper. (medium)	53.75	430.00	81.05	648.40		
1 Steel Worker	54.65	437.20	89.35	714.80		
1 Dozer, 200 H.P.		1273.00		1400.30		
1 Pickup Truck, 3/4 Ton		115.20		126.72	15.78	17.35
88 L.H., Daily Totals		$5562.60		$7927.02	$63.21	$90.08
Crew R-13	Hr.	Daily	Hr.	Daily	Bare Costs	Incl. O&P
1 Electrician Foreman	$58.70	$469.60	$87.75	$702.00	$56.37	$84.42
3 Electricians	58.20	1396.80	87.00	2088.00		
.25 Equip. Oper. (crane)	56.10	112.20	84.60	169.20		
1 Equipment Oiler	48.60	388.80	73.30	586.40		
.25 Hydraulic Crane, 33 Ton		235.15		258.67	5.60	6.16
42 L.H., Daily Totals		$2602.55		$3804.26	$61.97	$90.58
Crew R-15	Hr.	Daily	Hr.	Daily	Bare Costs	Incl. O&P
1 Electrician Foreman	$58.70	$469.60	$87.75	$702.00	$57.13	$85.52
4 Electricians	58.20	1862.40	87.00	2784.00		
1 Equipment Oper. (light)	51.30	410.40	77.35	618.80		
1 Telescoping Boom Lift, to 40'		282.80		311.08	5.89	6.48
48 L.H., Daily Totals		$3025.20		$4415.88	$63.02	$92.00
Crew R-15A	Hr.	Daily	Hr.	Daily	Bare Costs	Incl. O&P
1 Electrician Foreman	$58.70	$469.60	$87.75	$702.00	$51.02	$76.75
2 Electricians	58.20	931.20	87.00	1392.00		
2 Common Laborers	39.85	637.60	60.70	971.20		
1 Equip. Oper. (light)	51.30	410.40	77.35	618.80		
1 Telescoping Boom Lift, to 40'		282.80		311.08	5.89	6.48
48 L.H., Daily Totals		$2731.60		$3995.08	$56.91	$83.23
Crew R-18	Hr.	Daily	Hr.	Daily	Bare Costs	Incl. O&P
.25 Electrician Foreman	$58.70	$117.40	$87.75	$175.50	$51.07	$76.35
1 Electrician	58.20	465.60	87.00	696.00		
2 Electrician Apprentices	46.55	744.80	69.60	1113.60		
26 L.H., Daily Totals		$1327.80		$1985.10	$51.07	$76.35
Crew R-19	Hr.	Daily	Hr.	Daily	Bare Costs	Incl. O&P
.5 Electrician Foreman	$58.70	$234.80	$87.75	$351.00	$58.30	$87.15
2 Electricians	58.20	931.20	87.00	1392.00		
20 L.H., Daily Totals		$1166.00		$1743.00	$58.30	$87.15

Crews - Standard

Crew No.	Bare Costs		Incl. Subs O & P		Cost Per Labor-Hour	

Crew R-21	Hr.	Daily	Hr.	Daily	Bare Costs	Incl. O&P
1 Electrician Foreman	$58.70	$469.60	$87.75	$702.00	$58.21	$87.04
3 Electricians	58.20	1396.80	87.00	2088.00		
.1 Equip. Oper. (medium)	53.75	43.00	81.05	64.84		
.1 S.P. Crane, 4x4, 25 Ton		66.84		73.52	2.04	2.24
32.8 L.H., Daily Totals		$1976.24		$2928.36	$60.25	$89.28

Crew R-22	Hr.	Daily	Hr.	Daily	Bare Costs	Incl. O&P
.66 Electrician Foreman	$58.70	$309.94	$87.75	$463.32	$53.27	$79.64
2 Electricians	58.20	931.20	87.00	1392.00		
2 Electrician Apprentices	46.55	744.80	69.60	1113.60		
37.28 L.H., Daily Totals		$1985.94		$2968.92	$53.27	$79.64

Crew R-30	Hr.	Daily	Hr.	Daily	Bare Costs	Incl. O&P
.25 Electrician Foreman (outside)	$60.20	$120.40	$90.00	$180.00	$47.06	$71.05
1 Electrician	58.20	465.60	87.00	696.00		
2 Laborers (Semi-Skilled)	39.85	637.60	60.70	971.20		
26 L.H., Daily Totals		$1223.60		$1847.20	$47.06	$71.05

Crew R-31	Hr.	Daily	Hr.	Daily	Bare Costs	Incl. O&P
1 Electrician	$58.20	$465.60	$87.00	$696.00	$58.20	$87.00
1 Core Drill, Electric, 2.5 H.P.		47.50		52.25	5.94	6.53
8 L.H., Daily Totals		$513.10		$748.25	$64.14	$93.53

Crew W-41E	Hr.	Daily	Hr.	Daily	Bare Costs	Incl. O&P
.5 Plumber Foreman (outside)	$64.15	$256.60	$96.60	$386.40	$53.63	$81.04
1 Plumber	62.15	497.20	93.60	748.80		
1 Laborer	39.85	318.80	60.70	485.60		
20 L.H., Daily Totals		$1072.60		$1620.80	$53.63	$81.04

Historical Cost Indexes

The table below lists both the RSMeans® historical cost index based on Jan. 1, 1993 = 100 as well as the computed value of an index based on Jan. 1, 2018 costs. Since the Jan. 1, 2018 figure is estimated, space is left to write in the actual index figures as they become available through the quarterly *RSMeans Construction Cost Indexes*.

To compute the actual index based on Jan. 1, 2018 = 100, divide the historical cost index for a particular year by the actual Jan. 1, 2018 construction cost index. Space has been left to advance the index figures as the year progresses.

Year	Historical Cost Index Jan. 1, 1993 = 100 Est.	Actual	Current Index Based on Jan. 1, 2018 = 100 Est.	Actual	Year	Historical Cost Index Jan. 1, 1993 = 100 Actual	Current Index Based on Jan. 1, 2018 = 100 Est.	Actual	Year	Historical Cost Index Jan. 1, 1993 = 100 Actual	Current Index Based on Jan. 1, 2018 = 100 Est.	Actual
Oct 2018*					July 2003	132.0	61.2		July 1985	82.6	38.3	
July 2018*					2002	128.7	59.6		1984	82.0	38.0	
April 2018*					2001	125.1	58.0		1983	80.2	37.1	
Jan 2018*	215.8		100.0	100.0	2000	120.9	56.0		1982	76.1	35.3	
July 2017		213.6	99.0		1999	117.6	54.5		1981	70.0	32.4	
2016		207.3	96.1		1998	115.1	53.3		1980	62.9	29.1	
2015		206.2	95.6		1997	112.8	52.3		1979	57.8	26.8	
2014		204.9	94.9		1996	110.2	51.1		1978	53.5	24.8	
2013		201.2	93.2		1995	107.6	49.9		1977	49.5	22.9	
2012		194.6	90.2		1994	104.4	48.4		1976	46.9	21.7	
2011		191.2	88.6		1993	101.7	47.1		1975	44.8	20.8	
2010		183.5	85.0		1992	99.4	46.1		1974	41.4	19.2	
2009		180.1	83.5		1991	96.8	44.9		1973	37.7	17.5	
2008		180.4	83.6		1990	94.3	43.7		1972	34.8	16.1	
2007		169.4	78.5		1989	92.1	42.7		1971	32.1	14.9	
2006		162.0	75.1		1988	89.9	41.6		1970	28.7	13.3	
2005		151.6	70.3		1987	87.7	40.6		1969	26.9	12.5	
2004		143.7	66.6		1986	84.2	39.0		1968	24.9	11.5	

Adjustments to Costs

The "Historical Cost Index" can be used to convert national average building costs at a particular time to the approximate building costs for some other time.

Example:

Estimate and compare construction costs for different years in the same city.
To estimate the national average construction cost of a building in 1970, knowing that it cost $900,000 in 2018:

INDEX in 1970 = 28.7
INDEX in 2018 = 215.8

Note: The city cost indexes for Canada can be used to convert U.S. national averages to local costs in Canadian dollars.

Time Adjustment Using the Historical Cost Indexes:

$$\frac{\text{Index for Year A}}{\text{Index for Year B}} \times \text{Cost in Year B} = \text{Cost in Year A}$$

$$\frac{\text{INDEX 1970}}{\text{INDEX 2018}} \times \text{Cost 2018} = \text{Cost 1970}$$

$$\frac{28.7}{215.8} \times \$900,000 = .133 \times \$900,000 = \$119,694$$

The construction cost of the building in 1970 was $119,694.

Example:

To estimate and compare the cost of a building in Toronto, ON in 2018 with the known cost of $600,000 (US$) in New York, NY in 2018:

INDEX Toronto = 110.8
INDEX New York = 134.6

$$\frac{\text{INDEX Toronto}}{\text{INDEX New York}} \times \text{Cost New York} = \text{Cost Toronto}$$

$$\frac{110.8}{134.6} \times \$600,000 = .823 \times \$600,000 = \$493,908$$

The construction cost of the building in Toronto is $493,908 (CN$).

*Historical Cost Index updates and other resources are provided on the following website:
http://info.thegordiangroup.com/RSMeans.html

City Cost Indexes

How to Use the City Cost Indexes

What you should know before you begin

RSMeans City Cost Indexes (CCI) are an extremely useful tool for when you want to compare costs from city to city and region to region.

This publication contains average construction cost indexes for 731 U.S. and Canadian cities covering over 930 three-digit zip code locations, as listed directly under each city.

Keep in mind that a City Cost Index number is a percentage ratio of a specific city's cost to the national average cost of the same item at a stated time period.

In other words, these index figures represent relative construction factors (or, if you prefer, multipliers) for material and installation costs, as well as the weighted average for Total In Place costs for each CSI MasterFormat division. Installation costs include both labor and equipment rental costs. When estimating equipment rental rates only for a specific location, use 01 54 33 EQUIPMENT RENTAL COSTS in the Reference Section.

The 30 City Average Index is the average of 30 major U.S. cities and serves as a national average.

Index figures for both material and installation are based on the 30 major city average of 100 and represent the cost relationship as of July 1, 2017. The index for each division is computed from representative material and labor quantities for that division. The weighted average for each city is a weighted total of the components listed above it. It does not include relative productivity between trades or cities.

As changes occur in local material prices, labor rates, and equipment rental rates (including fuel costs), the impact of these changes should be accurately measured by the change in the City Cost Index for each particular city (as compared to the 30 city average).

Therefore, if you know (or have estimated) building costs in one city today, you can easily convert those costs to expected building costs in another city.

In addition, by using the Historical Cost Index, you can easily convert national average building costs at a particular time to the approximate building costs for some other time. The City Cost Indexes can then be applied to calculate the costs for a particular city.

Quick calculations

Location Adjustment Using the City Cost Indexes:

$$\frac{\text{Index for City A}}{\text{Index for City B}} \times \text{Cost in City B} = \text{Cost in City A}$$

Time Adjustment for the National Average Using the Historical Cost Index:

$$\frac{\text{Index for Year A}}{\text{Index for Year B}} \times \text{Cost in Year B} = \text{Cost in Year A}$$

Adjustment from the National Average:

$$\frac{\text{Index for City A}}{100} \times \text{National Average Cost} = \text{Cost in City A}$$

Since each of the other RSMeans data sets contains many different items, any *one* item multiplied by the particular city index may give incorrect results. However, the larger the number of items compiled, the closer the results should be to actual costs for that particular city.

The City Cost Indexes for Canadian cities are calculated using Canadian material and equipment prices and labor rates in Canadian dollars. Therefore, indexes for Canadian cities can be used to convert U.S. national average prices to local costs in Canadian dollars.

How to use this section

1. Compare costs from city to city.

In using the RSMeans Indexes, remember that an index number is not a fixed number but a ratio: It's a percentage ratio of a building component's cost at any stated time to the national average cost of that same component at the same time period. Put in the form of an equation:

$$\frac{\text{Specific City Cost}}{\text{National Average Cost}} \times 100 = \text{City Index Number}$$

Therefore, when making cost comparisons between cities, do not subtract one city's index number from the index number of another city and read the result as a percentage difference. Instead, divide one city's index number by that of the other city. The resulting number may then be used as a multiplier to calculate cost differences from city to city.

The formula used to find cost differences between cities for the purpose of comparison is as follows:

$$\frac{\text{City A Index}}{\text{City B Index}} \times \text{City B Cost (Known)} = \text{City A Cost (Unknown)}$$

In addition, you can use RSMeans CCI to calculate and compare costs division by division between cities using the same basic formula. (Just be sure that you're comparing similar divisions.)

2. Compare a specific city's construction costs with the national average.

When you're studying construction location feasibility, it's advisable to compare a prospective project's cost index with an index of the national average cost.

For example, divide the weighted average index of construction costs of a specific city by that of the 30 City Average, which = 100.

$$\frac{\text{City Index}}{100} = \% \text{ of National Average}$$

As a result, you get a ratio that indicates the relative cost of construction in that city in comparison with the national average.

3. Convert U.S. national average to actual costs in Canadian City.

$$\frac{\text{Index for Canadian City}}{100} \times \text{National Average Cost} = \text{Cost in Canadian City in \$ CAN}$$

4. Adjust construction cost data based on a national average.
When you use a source of construction cost data which is based on a national average (such as RSMeans cost data), it is necessary to adjust those costs to a specific location.

$$\frac{\text{City Index}}{100} \times \text{Cost Based on National Average Costs} = \text{City Cost (Unknown)}$$

5. When applying the City Cost Indexes to demolition projects, use the appropriate division installation index. For example, for removal of existing doors and windows, use the Division 8 (Openings) index.

What you might like to know about how we developed the Indexes

The information presented in the CCI is organized according to the Construction Specifications Institute (CSI) MasterFormat 2014 classification system.

To create a reliable index, RSMeans researched the building type most often constructed in the United States and Canada. Because it was concluded that no one type of building completely represented the building construction industry, nine different types of buildings were combined to create a composite model.

The exact material, labor, and equipment quantities are based on detailed analyses of these nine building types, and then each quantity is weighted in proportion to expected usage. These various material items, labor hours, and equipment rental rates are thus combined to form a composite building representing as closely as possible the actual usage of materials, labor, and equipment in the North American building construction industry.

The following structures were chosen to make up that composite model:

1. Factory, 1 story
2. Office, 2–4 stories
3. Store, Retail
4. Town Hall, 2–3 stories
5. High School, 2–3 stories
6. Hospital, 4–8 stories
7. Garage, Parking
8. Apartment, 1–3 stories
9. Hotel/Motel, 2–3 stories

For the purposes of ensuring the timeliness of the data, the components of the index for the composite model have been streamlined. They currently consist of:

- specific quantities of 66 commonly used construction materials;
- specific labor-hours for 21 building construction trades; and
- specific days of equipment rental for 6 types of construction equipment (normally used to install the 66 material items by the 21 trades.) Fuel costs and routine maintenance costs are included in the equipment cost.

Material and equipment price quotations are gathered quarterly from cities in the United States and Canada. These prices and the latest negotiated labor wage rates for 21 different building trades are used to compile the quarterly update of the City Cost Index.

The 30 major U.S. cities used to calculate the national average are:

Atlanta, GA
Baltimore, MD
Boston, MA
Buffalo, NY
Chicago, IL
Cincinnati, OH
Cleveland, OH
Columbus, OH
Dallas, TX
Denver, CO
Detroit, MI
Houston, TX
Indianapolis, IN
Kansas City, MO
Los Angeles, CA
Memphis, TN
Milwaukee, WI
Minneapolis, MN
Nashville, TN
New Orleans, LA
New York, NY
Philadelphia, PA
Phoenix, AZ
Pittsburgh, PA
St. Louis, MO
San Antonio, TX
San Diego, CA
San Francisco, CA
Seattle, WA
Washington, DC

What the CCI does not indicate

The weighted average for each city is a total of the divisional components weighted to reflect typical usage. It does not include the productivity variations between trades or cities.

In addition, the CCI does not take into consideration factors such as the following:

- managerial efficiency
- competitive conditions
- automation
- restrictive union practices
- unique local requirements
- regional variations due to specific building codes

City Cost Indexes

DIVISION		UNITED STATES 30 CITY AVERAGE			ALABAMA ANNISTON 362			ALABAMA BIRMINGHAM 350 - 352			ALABAMA BUTLER 369			ALABAMA DECATUR 356			ALABAMA DOTHAN 363		
		MAT.	INST.	TOTAL	MAT.	INST.	TOTAL	MAT.	INST.	TOTAL	MAT.	INST.	TOTAL	MAT.	INST.	TOTAL	MAT.	INST.	TOTAL
015433	CONTRACTOR EQUIPMENT		100.0	100.0		104.4	104.4		104.5	104.5		101.9	101.9		104.4	104.4		101.9	101.9
0241, 31 - 34	SITE & INFRASTRUCTURE, DEMOLITION	100.0	100.0	100.0	86.8	92.4	90.7	93.0	92.8	92.8	99.8	87.9	91.5	86.4	91.9	90.3	97.5	88.2	91.0
0310	Concrete Forming & Accessories	100.0	100.0	100.0	88.7	66.5	69.6	92.5	67.5	70.9	85.3	67.1	69.6	95.0	62.6	67.1	93.9	68.2	71.7
0320	Concrete Reinforcing	100.0	100.0	100.0	87.2	72.0	79.5	95.5	71.9	83.6	92.3	72.2	82.2	89.4	68.9	79.1	92.3	71.6	81.9
0330	Cast-in-Place Concrete	100.0	100.0	100.0	91.6	67.5	82.5	102.4	68.4	89.5	89.3	67.9	81.2	100.5	67.4	87.9	89.3	67.6	81.1
03	CONCRETE	100.0	100.0	100.0	92.3	69.6	81.9	92.6	70.3	82.4	93.2	70.0	82.6	92.4	67.2	80.9	92.5	70.3	82.3
04	MASONRY	100.0	100.0	100.0	92.9	70.6	79.1	90.4	68.0	76.5	97.6	70.6	80.9	88.3	70.1	77.0	99.0	60.0	74.8
05	METALS	100.0	100.0	100.0	92.1	95.2	93.1	92.2	95.4	93.2	91.1	96.3	92.7	94.2	94.2	94.2	91.2	95.7	92.6
06	WOOD, PLASTICS & COMPOSITES	100.0	100.0	100.0	88.9	67.1	76.8	92.2	67.1	78.2	83.7	67.1	74.5	102.1	61.5	79.5	95.3	68.6	80.5
07	THERMAL & MOISTURE PROTECTION	100.0	100.0	100.0	95.4	65.2	82.6	98.3	67.3	85.2	95.4	67.8	83.8	97.3	67.0	84.5	95.4	64.9	82.5
08	OPENINGS	100.0	100.0	100.0	95.8	68.8	89.6	101.0	68.8	93.6	95.8	68.8	89.6	107.7	64.8	97.9	95.8	69.6	89.8
0920	Plaster & Gypsum Board	100.0	100.0	100.0	88.0	66.7	73.7	87.9	66.7	73.7	85.0	66.7	72.7	93.9	60.9	71.8	95.2	68.3	77.1
0950, 0980	Ceilings & Acoustic Treatment	100.0	100.0	100.0	77.6	66.7	70.2	82.6	66.7	71.9	77.6	66.7	70.2	82.9	60.9	68.1	77.6	68.3	71.3
0960	Flooring	100.0	100.0	100.0	80.5	82.5	81.0	92.3	75.9	87.8	84.9	82.5	84.2	87.0	82.5	85.7	90.0	84.1	88.3
0970, 0990	Wall Finishes & Painting/Coating	100.0	100.0	100.0	86.2	60.0	70.9	87.8	60.0	71.6	86.2	48.9	64.5	83.5	62.6	71.3	86.2	80.5	82.9
09	FINISHES	100.0	100.0	100.0	79.2	69.2	73.7	87.3	68.2	76.9	81.9	68.0	74.4	83.4	66.0	74.0	84.6	72.5	78.1
COVERS	DIVS. 10 - 14, 25, 28, 41, 43, 44, 46	100.0	100.0	100.0	100.0	71.6	93.7	100.0	84.9	96.6	100.0	78.5	95.2	100.0	70.8	93.5	100.0	73.0	94.0
21, 22, 23	FIRE SUPPRESSION, PLUMBING & HVAC	100.0	100.0	100.0	100.9	51.3	79.7	100.0	63.1	84.2	98.2	66.9	84.8	100.0	65.9	85.5	98.2	65.3	84.1
26, 27, 3370	ELECTRICAL, COMMUNICATIONS & UTIL.	100.0	100.0	100.0	96.4	60.2	77.6	98.1	61.5	79.1	98.5	67.4	82.3	93.9	66.0	79.4	97.2	76.1	86.3
MF2016	WEIGHTED AVERAGE	100.0	100.0	100.0	94.5	68.5	83.1	95.9	71.4	85.2	94.8	72.8	85.2	96.0	71.3	85.2	94.9	72.9	85.3

DIVISION		ALABAMA EVERGREEN 364			ALABAMA GADSDEN 359			ALABAMA HUNTSVILLE 357 - 358			ALABAMA JASPER 355			ALABAMA MOBILE 365 - 366			ALABAMA MONTGOMERY 360 - 361		
		MAT.	INST.	TOTAL	MAT.	INST.	TOTAL	MAT.	INST.	TOTAL	MAT.	INST.	TOTAL	MAT.	INST.	TOTAL	MAT.	INST.	TOTAL
015433	CONTRACTOR EQUIPMENT		101.9	101.9		104.4	104.4		104.4	104.4		104.4	104.4		101.9	101.9		101.9	101.9
0241, 31 - 34	SITE & INFRASTRUCTURE, DEMOLITION	100.2	87.9	91.6	91.9	92.4	92.3	86.1	92.3	90.4	91.8	92.5	92.3	92.9	89.0	90.1	91.3	88.2	89.1
0310	Concrete Forming & Accessories	82.1	68.0	69.9	87.2	66.9	69.7	95.0	64.3	68.5	92.3	67.2	70.7	93.0	68.0	71.4	94.6	67.0	70.8
0320	Concrete Reinforcing	92.3	72.2	82.2	95.0	71.9	83.3	89.4	71.1	80.2	89.4	72.1	80.7	89.8	71.6	80.6	97.6	71.5	84.5
0330	Cast-in-Place Concrete	89.3	67.6	81.1	100.6	67.5	88.0	97.9	66.6	86.0	111.5	68.3	95.1	93.7	67.6	83.7	90.6	67.7	81.9
03	CONCRETE	93.5	70.3	82.9	96.8	69.7	84.4	91.2	68.1	80.6	100.5	70.2	86.6	89.1	70.2	80.5	87.4	69.8	79.4
04	MASONRY	97.6	70.1	80.6	86.8	66.4	74.2	89.6	65.0	74.4	84.5	71.7	76.6	95.8	60.0	73.6	93.1	60.5	72.9
05	METALS	91.2	96.2	92.7	92.2	95.5	93.2	94.2	94.9	94.4	92.1	95.5	93.2	93.1	95.5	93.8	92.2	95.0	93.1
06	WOOD, PLASTICS & COMPOSITES	80.3	68.6	73.8	92.9	67.1	78.5	102.1	64.3	81.1	99.2	67.1	81.4	93.9	68.6	79.9	92.3	67.1	78.3
07	THERMAL & MOISTURE PROTECTION	95.4	67.8	83.7	97.5	66.6	84.4	97.2	65.7	83.9	97.5	63.7	83.2	95.0	64.9	82.3	93.6	65.0	81.5
08	OPENINGS	95.8	69.6	89.8	104.2	68.8	96.0	107.4	67.0	98.2	104.1	68.8	96.0	98.7	69.6	92.0	97.5	68.8	90.9
0920	Plaster & Gypsum Board	84.4	68.3	73.6	86.7	66.7	73.3	93.9	63.8	73.7	90.7	66.7	74.6	92.1	68.3	76.1	88.8	66.7	74.0
0950, 0980	Ceilings & Acoustic Treatment	77.6	68.3	71.3	80.3	66.7	71.1	84.8	63.8	70.7	80.3	66.7	71.1	82.9	68.3	73.0	84.2	66.7	72.4
0960	Flooring	82.9	82.5	82.8	83.3	77.5	81.7	87.0	77.5	84.3	85.3	82.5	84.5	89.5	65.1	82.8	87.8	65.1	81.5
0970, 0990	Wall Finishes & Painting/Coating	86.2	48.9	64.4	83.5	60.0	69.8	83.5	62.7	71.4	83.5	60.0	69.8	89.4	48.9	65.8	86.5	60.0	71.1
09	FINISHES	81.3	68.8	74.5	81.3	68.1	74.1	83.8	66.4	74.3	82.3	69.5	75.3	84.7	65.2	74.1	85.7	65.7	74.8
COVERS	DIVS. 10 - 14, 25, 28, 41, 43, 44, 46	100.0	71.4	93.6	100.0	84.4	96.5	100.0	83.7	96.4	100.0	72.8	93.9	100.0	85.4	96.8	100.0	84.6	96.6
21, 22, 23	FIRE SUPPRESSION, PLUMBING & HVAC	98.2	66.7	84.7	102.1	62.9	85.3	100.0	62.2	83.8	102.1	63.0	85.4	99.8	66.7	85.6	99.9	65.5	85.2
26, 27, 3370	ELECTRICAL, COMMUNICATIONS & UTIL.	95.8	67.4	81.0	93.8	61.5	77.0	94.8	66.0	79.8	93.6	60.2	76.2	99.1	58.0	77.7	99.6	76.1	87.4
MF2016	WEIGHTED AVERAGE	94.5	72.6	84.9	96.1	71.0	85.1	96.0	70.7	84.9	96.5	71.2	85.5	95.4	70.2	84.4	94.8	72.3	85.0

DIVISION		ALABAMA PHENIX CITY 368			ALABAMA SELMA 367			ALABAMA TUSCALOOSA 354			ALASKA ANCHORAGE 995 - 996			ALASKA FAIRBANKS 997			ALASKA JUNEAU 998		
		MAT.	INST.	TOTAL	MAT.	INST.	TOTAL	MAT.	INST.	TOTAL	MAT.	INST.	TOTAL	MAT.	INST.	TOTAL	MAT.	INST.	TOTAL
015433	CONTRACTOR EQUIPMENT		101.9	101.9		101.9	101.9		104.4	104.4		115.3	115.3		115.3	115.3		115.3	115.3
0241, 31 - 34	SITE & INFRASTRUCTURE, DEMOLITION	103.9	88.2	92.9	97.4	88.2	90.9	86.6	92.5	90.7	127.0	130.4	129.4	126.5	130.4	129.2	147.3	130.4	135.5
0310	Concrete Forming & Accessories	88.7	67.2	70.1	86.4	67.1	69.8	94.9	67.2	71.0	125.4	119.5	120.3	130.1	118.0	119.7	131.0	119.5	121.1
0320	Concrete Reinforcing	92.3	65.9	78.9	92.3	72.1	82.1	89.4	71.9	80.6	158.3	118.8	138.4	152.5	118.8	135.5	137.9	118.8	128.3
0330	Cast-in-Place Concrete	89.3	67.8	81.2	89.3	67.8	81.1	102.0	67.8	89.0	108.1	119.1	112.3	117.0	119.4	117.9	127.8	119.1	124.5
03	CONCRETE	96.2	68.9	83.7	92.0	70.0	81.9	93.1	69.9	82.5	117.6	118.4	118.0	110.2	117.9	113.7	123.5	118.4	121.2
04	MASONRY	97.6	70.6	80.8	100.4	70.6	82.1	88.5	66.8	75.1	175.5	121.0	141.7	185.3	121.0	145.4	165.8	121.0	138.0
05	METALS	91.1	93.6	91.9	91.1	95.8	92.6	93.5	95.6	94.1	120.0	104.9	115.4	121.2	105.0	116.2	117.0	104.9	113.3
06	WOOD, PLASTICS & COMPOSITES	88.6	67.0	76.6	85.7	67.1	75.4	102.1	67.1	82.6	117.8	117.9	117.9	129.1	115.8	121.7	124.7	117.9	120.9
07	THERMAL & MOISTURE PROTECTION	95.8	67.8	84.0	95.3	67.8	83.7	97.3	66.8	84.4	169.2	117.9	147.5	180.8	116.9	153.8	183.4	117.9	155.7
08	OPENINGS	95.8	67.1	89.2	95.8	68.8	89.6	107.4	68.8	98.6	128.9	117.3	126.3	134.8	116.4	130.6	129.7	117.3	126.8
0920	Plaster & Gypsum Board	89.3	66.6	74.1	87.3	66.7	73.5	93.9	66.7	75.6	143.2	118.3	126.5	166.9	116.1	132.8	147.9	118.3	128.0
0950, 0980	Ceilings & Acoustic Treatment	77.6	66.6	70.2	77.6	66.7	70.2	84.8	66.7	72.6	131.3	118.3	122.5	130.9	116.1	120.9	143.6	118.3	126.5
0960	Flooring	86.8	82.5	85.6	85.4	82.5	84.6	87.0	77.5	84.3	119.0	125.1	120.7	117.5	125.1	119.6	125.7	125.1	125.5
0970, 0990	Wall Finishes & Painting/Coating	86.2	80.5	82.9	86.2	60.0	70.9	83.5	60.0	69.8	103.4	115.3	110.3	106.4	119.9	114.3	108.9	115.3	112.6
09	FINISHES	83.5	71.4	76.9	82.1	69.2	75.1	83.8	68.2	75.3	125.6	120.4	122.8	126.1	119.7	122.6	128.4	120.4	124.1
COVERS	DIVS. 10 - 14, 25, 28, 41, 43, 44, 46	100.0	84.6	96.6	100.0	72.1	93.8	100.0	84.6	96.6	100.0	111.1	102.5	100.0	110.9	102.4	100.0	111.1	102.5
21, 22, 23	FIRE SUPPRESSION, PLUMBING & HVAC	98.2	65.4	84.2	98.2	65.5	84.2	100.0	68.3	86.5	100.8	106.4	103.2	100.6	110.1	104.7	100.6	106.4	103.1
26, 27, 3370	ELECTRICAL, COMMUNICATIONS & UTIL.	97.9	67.7	82.2	97.0	76.1	86.1	94.3	61.5	77.3	114.4	111.5	112.9	118.2	111.5	114.7	103.1	111.5	107.5
MF2016	WEIGHTED AVERAGE	95.4	72.7	85.4	94.6	73.6	85.4	96.0	72.3	85.6	118.9	114.8	117.1	120.1	115.3	118.0	118.8	114.8	117.0

461

City Cost Indexes

DIVISION		ALASKA KETCHIKAN 999			ARIZONA CHAMBERS 865			ARIZONA FLAGSTAFF 860			ARIZONA GLOBE 855			ARIZONA KINGMAN 864			ARIZONA MESA/TEMPE 852		
		MAT.	INST.	TOTAL	MAT.	INST.	TOTAL	MAT.	INST.	TOTAL	MAT.	INST.	TOTAL	MAT.	INST.	TOTAL	MAT.	INST.	TOTAL
015433	CONTRACTOR EQUIPMENT		115.3	115.3		90.7	90.7		90.7	90.7		92.0	92.0		90.7	90.7		92.0	92.0
0241, 31 - 34	SITE & INFRASTRUCTURE, DEMOLITION	183.9	130.4	146.4	72.9	94.9	88.3	92.6	94.9	94.2	105.2	95.9	98.7	72.9	94.8	88.3	94.5	95.9	95.5
0310	Concrete Forming & Accessories	121.3	119.5	119.7	97.2	68.7	72.6	102.4	68.7	73.3	93.4	68.7	72.1	95.5	68.6	72.3	96.5	68.8	72.6
0320	Concrete Reinforcing	113.8	118.8	116.3	100.0	81.8	90.9	99.8	81.8	90.8	110.6	81.9	96.1	100.2	81.8	90.9	111.3	81.9	96.5
0330	Cast-in-Place Concrete	236.9	119.1	192.1	89.7	68.4	81.6	89.8	68.4	81.6	82.7	68.1	77.2	89.4	68.4	81.4	83.4	68.1	77.6
03	CONCRETE	187.2	118.4	155.7	92.0	70.8	82.3	111.6	70.8	93.0	103.7	70.8	88.6	91.7	70.8	82.1	94.6	70.8	83.8
04	MASONRY	192.8	121.0	148.2	95.7	59.3	73.1	95.8	58.7	72.8	103.6	59.2	76.0	95.7	59.3	73.1	103.7	59.2	76.1
05	METALS	121.3	104.9	116.3	101.6	73.5	92.9	102.1	73.5	93.3	98.7	74.4	91.3	102.2	73.4	93.4	99.0	74.5	91.5
06	WOOD, PLASTICS & COMPOSITES	119.9	117.8	118.8	100.1	70.5	83.6	105.8	70.5	86.2	97.0	70.7	82.4	95.3	70.5	81.5	100.3	70.7	83.8
07	THERMAL & MOISTURE PROTECTION	185.6	117.9	157.0	93.6	70.1	83.6	95.4	69.8	84.6	99.9	68.8	86.7	93.5	69.9	83.5	99.7	68.5	86.5
08	OPENINGS	130.4	117.3	127.4	105.9	68.4	97.3	106.0	73.0	98.4	96.4	68.8	90.1	106.1	70.8	98.0	96.5	70.9	90.6
0920	Plaster & Gypsum Board	155.6	118.3	130.6	88.6	69.9	76.0	91.8	69.9	77.1	89.0	69.9	76.2	81.2	69.9	73.6	91.3	69.9	76.9
0950, 0980	Ceilings & Acoustic Treatment	124.2	118.3	120.2	105.7	69.9	81.6	106.6	69.9	81.9	95.0	69.9	78.1	106.6	69.9	81.9	95.0	69.9	78.1
0960	Flooring	117.5	125.1	119.6	91.1	60.1	82.5	93.5	60.1	84.3	102.7	60.1	90.9	89.8	60.1	81.6	104.6	60.1	92.3
0970, 0990	Wall Finishes & Painting/Coating	106.4	115.3	111.6	88.8	64.0	74.3	88.8	64.0	74.3	94.1	64.0	76.5	88.8	64.0	74.3	94.1	64.0	76.5
09	FINISHES	127.1	120.4	123.5	90.7	66.4	77.5	93.9	66.4	78.9	97.7	66.6	80.8	89.5	66.4	76.9	97.5	66.6	80.7
COVERS	DIVS. 10 - 14, 25, 28, 41, 43, 44, 46	100.0	111.1	102.5	100.0	84.1	96.5	100.0	84.0	96.4	100.0	84.4	96.5	100.0	84.0	96.4	100.0	84.4	96.5
21, 22, 23	FIRE SUPPRESSION, PLUMBING & HVAC	98.7	106.4	102.0	99.8	77.2	89.1	102.0	78.2	90.8	97.0	77.3	88.6	98.0	78.0	89.4	100.1	77.4	90.4
26, 27, 3370	ELECTRICAL, COMMUNICATIONS & UTIL.	118.2	111.5	114.7	103.2	86.2	94.4	102.2	63.1	81.9	99.0	66.4	82.0	103.2	66.4	84.0	95.9	66.4	80.5
MF2016	WEIGHTED AVERAGE	130.8	114.8	123.8	97.9	75.0	87.9	101.7	72.1	88.8	99.9	72.4	87.4	97.9	72.5	86.8	98.2	72.5	87.0

DIVISION		ARIZONA PHOENIX 850, 853			ARIZONA PRESCOTT 863			ARIZONA SHOW LOW 859			ARIZONA TUCSON 856 - 857			ARKANSAS BATESVILLE 725			ARKANSAS CAMDEN 717		
		MAT.	INST.	TOTAL	MAT.	INST.	TOTAL	MAT.	INST.	TOTAL	MAT.	INST.	TOTAL	MAT.	INST.	TOTAL	MAT.	INST.	TOTAL
015433	CONTRACTOR EQUIPMENT		93.0	93.0		90.7	90.7		92.0	92.0		92.0	92.0		92.2	92.2		92.2	92.2
0241, 31 - 34	SITE & INFRASTRUCTURE, DEMOLITION	95.1	94.5	94.7	79.8	94.8	90.3	107.5	95.9	99.4	90.1	95.9	94.2	73.6	90.1	85.2	82.5	90.1	87.8
0310	Concrete Forming & Accessories	101.4	72.9	76.9	98.7	68.7	72.8	100.5	68.8	73.1	96.9	68.8	72.7	83.8	57.4	61.1	81.0	57.4	60.7
0320	Concrete Reinforcing	109.2	79.3	94.2	99.8	81.8	90.8	111.3	81.9	96.5	92.4	81.8	87.1	90.9	65.5	78.1	94.9	65.2	79.9
0330	Cast-in-Place Concrete	83.0	70.7	78.3	89.7	68.4	81.6	82.8	68.1	77.2	85.9	68.1	79.1	68.9	75.8	71.5	80.4	75.8	78.7
03	CONCRETE	97.2	73.3	86.2	97.4	70.8	85.2	106.1	70.8	89.9	93.2	70.8	83.0	73.3	66.1	70.0	79.5	66.0	73.4
04	MASONRY	96.1	62.9	75.5	95.8	59.3	73.1	103.6	59.2	76.1	90.2	58.5	70.6	92.6	43.2	62.0	109.8	37.7	65.1
05	METALS	100.5	75.7	92.9	102.1	73.4	93.3	98.5	74.4	91.1	99.8	74.5	92.0	99.1	73.7	91.3	100.9	73.3	92.4
06	WOOD, PLASTICS & COMPOSITES	103.4	74.2	87.1	101.4	70.7	84.3	104.6	70.7	85.7	100.6	70.7	83.9	93.1	58.5	73.7	93.0	58.5	73.6
07	THERMAL & MOISTURE PROTECTION	100.9	70.4	88.0	94.1	70.2	84.0	100.1	68.6	86.8	100.8	68.3	87.1	103.1	59.0	84.4	96.4	57.5	79.9
08	OPENINGS	97.7	74.4	92.4	106.0	68.8	97.5	95.7	70.9	90.0	92.9	73.1	88.4	99.7	54.2	89.2	102.6	56.1	91.9
0920	Plaster & Gypsum Board	99.2	73.3	81.8	88.7	70.1	76.2	93.3	69.9	77.6	96.2	69.9	78.5	82.0	57.5	65.5	85.1	57.5	66.5
0950, 0980	Ceilings & Acoustic Treatment	105.6	73.3	83.8	104.9	70.1	81.4	95.0	69.9	78.1	95.8	69.9	78.4	86.7	57.5	67.0	82.1	57.5	65.5
0960	Flooring	106.7	60.1	93.8	92.0	60.1	83.2	106.6	60.1	93.7	95.7	60.1	85.8	84.5	54.2	76.1	92.0	36.3	76.6
0970, 0990	Wall Finishes & Painting/Coating	98.9	66.2	79.8	88.8	64.0	74.3	94.1	64.0	76.5	94.8	64.0	76.8	90.5	36.0	58.7	93.1	50.5	68.3
09	FINISHES	102.2	69.8	84.6	91.4	66.5	77.9	99.7	66.6	81.7	95.5	66.6	79.8	78.4	53.9	65.1	80.9	52.3	65.3
COVERS	DIVS. 10 - 14, 25, 28, 41, 43, 44, 46	100.0	86.5	97.0	100.0	84.1	96.5	100.0	84.4	96.5	100.0	84.4	96.5	100.0	67.2	92.7	100.0	67.2	92.7
21, 22, 23	FIRE SUPPRESSION, PLUMBING & HVAC	99.9	80.2	91.5	100.2	77.2	90.4	97.0	77.3	88.6	100.0	77.5	90.4	97.1	53.2	78.3	97.0	57.9	80.3
26, 27, 3370	ELECTRICAL, COMMUNICATIONS & UTIL.	101.4	63.1	81.5	101.9	66.4	83.4	96.2	66.6	80.7	98.1	61.0	78.8	95.5	62.6	78.4	94.4	59.0	76.0
MF2016	WEIGHTED AVERAGE	99.5	74.1	88.4	99.3	72.2	87.5	99.4	72.5	87.6	97.1	71.8	86.0	92.6	60.8	78.7	95.0	60.5	79.9

DIVISION		ARKANSAS FAYETTEVILLE 727			ARKANSAS FORT SMITH 729			ARKANSAS HARRISON 726			ARKANSAS HOT SPRINGS 719			ARKANSAS JONESBORO 724			ARKANSAS LITTLE ROCK 720 - 722		
		MAT.	INST.	TOTAL	MAT.	INST.	TOTAL	MAT.	INST.	TOTAL	MAT.	INST.	TOTAL	MAT.	INST.	TOTAL	MAT.	INST.	TOTAL
015433	CONTRACTOR EQUIPMENT		92.2	92.2		92.2	92.2		92.2	92.2		92.2	92.2		116.6	116.6		92.2	92.2
0241, 31 - 34	SITE & INFRASTRUCTURE, DEMOLITION	73.0	90.1	85.0	78.1	90.1	86.5	78.5	90.1	86.6	85.8	90.1	88.8	97.6	108.2	105.0	86.4	90.3	89.1
0310	Concrete Forming & Accessories	79.4	57.6	60.6	97.9	57.9	63.5	88.1	57.3	61.5	78.6	57.6	60.5	87.2	57.6	61.7	92.2	59.5	64.0
0320	Concrete Reinforcing	91.0	62.8	76.7	92.1	65.2	78.6	90.6	65.2	78.0	93.1	65.5	79.2	87.8	65.7	76.6	97.4	68.4	82.7
0330	Cast-in-Place Concrete	68.9	75.9	71.6	78.8	76.1	77.7	76.4	75.8	76.2	82.3	75.9	79.9	75.1	77.2	75.9	76.3	76.2	76.3
03	CONCRETE	73.0	65.7	69.7	80.1	66.3	73.8	79.7	66.0	73.4	82.8	66.2	75.2	77.3	67.7	72.9	81.0	67.6	74.9
04	MASONRY	84.0	42.7	58.4	90.9	63.4	73.8	93.0	44.3	62.8	82.3	42.9	57.9	85.2	40.8	57.7	86.7	67.2	74.6
05	METALS	99.1	72.9	91.0	101.4	75.2	93.3	100.2	73.6	92.1	100.9	73.8	92.6	95.6	89.1	93.6	101.6	76.8	94.0
06	WOOD, PLASTICS & COMPOSITES	89.7	58.2	72.2	109.4	58.2	80.9	98.9	58.2	76.3	90.4	58.2	72.5	97.3	58.6	75.7	93.9	59.7	74.9
07	THERMAL & MOISTURE PROTECTION	103.9	58.9	84.8	104.2	64.7	87.5	103.4	59.3	84.7	96.7	58.9	80.7	108.7	58.3	87.4	98.2	65.9	84.5
08	OPENINGS	99.7	56.1	89.7	101.7	56.6	91.4	100.5	53.1	89.6	102.6	56.0	91.9	105.4	57.2	94.3	95.9	58.2	87.2
0920	Plaster & Gypsum Board	81.4	57.5	65.3	88.3	57.5	67.6	87.3	57.5	67.3	83.8	57.5	66.1	96.1	57.5	70.1	95.4	59.0	71.0
0950, 0980	Ceilings & Acoustic Treatment	86.7	57.5	67.0	88.4	57.5	67.5	88.4	57.5	67.5	82.1	57.5	65.5	90.7	57.5	68.3	90.5	59.0	69.3
0960	Flooring	81.7	53.1	73.8	91.0	75.0	86.6	86.7	54.2	77.7	90.9	53.1	80.4	61.2	48.0	57.5	90.9	83.9	88.9
0970, 0990	Wall Finishes & Painting/Coating	90.5	48.2	65.8	90.5	50.8	67.3	90.5	31.1	55.9	93.1	50.5	68.3	80.1	44.1	59.1	88.5	50.5	66.5
09	FINISHES	77.5	54.9	65.2	81.8	60.1	70.0	80.5	53.3	65.7	80.7	55.3	66.9	76.2	53.7	64.0	87.8	62.8	74.2
COVERS	DIVS. 10 - 14, 25, 28, 41, 43, 44, 46	100.0	67.2	92.7	100.0	79.3	95.4	100.0	68.3	92.9	100.0	67.2	92.7	100.0	66.3	92.5	100.0	79.5	95.4
21, 22, 23	FIRE SUPPRESSION, PLUMBING & HVAC	97.2	62.3	82.3	100.3	49.2	78.4	97.1	49.4	76.7	97.0	53.2	78.4	100.6	53.2	80.4	99.9	53.6	80.1
26, 27, 3370	ELECTRICAL, COMMUNICATIONS & UTIL.	90.0	54.7	71.6	93.0	59.0	75.4	94.2	54.7	73.6	96.3	68.8	82.0	98.8	62.9	80.1	99.7	68.8	83.7
MF2016	WEIGHTED AVERAGE	91.5	61.8	78.5	95.0	63.1	81.0	93.9	58.9	78.6	94.3	62.0	80.1	94.5	63.7	81.0	95.3	66.6	82.7

City Cost Indexes

		ARKANSAS													CALIFORNIA					
	DIVISION	PINE BLUFF 716			RUSSELLVILLE 728			TEXARKANA 718			WEST MEMPHIS 723			ALHAMBRA 917 - 918			ANAHEIM 928		
		MAT.	INST.	TOTAL	MAT.	INST.	TOTAL	MAT.	INST.	TOTAL	MAT.	INST.	TOTAL	MAT.	INST.	TOTAL	MAT.	INST.	TOTAL
015433	CONTRACTOR EQUIPMENT		92.2	92.2		92.2	92.2		93.5	93.5		116.6	116.6		95.8	95.8		101.0	101.0
0241, 31 - 34	SITE & INFRASTRUCTURE, DEMOLITION	87.8	90.2	89.4	74.9	90.1	85.5	98.9	92.3	94.3	104.6	108.5	107.3	101.0	109.1	106.7	102.0	109.9	107.5
0310	Concrete Forming & Accessories	78.4	58.2	61.0	84.4	57.3	61.0	84.1	57.5	61.1	92.6	57.9	62.7	116.4	134.6	132.1	104.9	138.5	133.9
0320	Concrete Reinforcing	94.8	68.1	81.3	91.5	65.4	78.4	94.4	65.5	79.8	87.8	63.9	75.7	104.8	128.4	116.7	104.8	128.1	116.6
0330	Cast-in-Place Concrete	82.3	76.2	80.0	72.2	75.8	73.6	89.7	75.9	84.5	78.7	77.3	78.2	82.8	129.0	100.4	87.9	132.7	104.9
03	CONCRETE	83.5	67.0	75.9	76.1	65.9	71.5	81.9	66.1	74.7	83.8	67.5	76.4	94.6	130.3	110.9	95.6	133.4	112.9
04	MASONRY	116.6	63.4	83.6	90.2	41.8	60.2	96.5	42.2	62.8	73.9	40.6	53.3	112.0	141.0	130.0	78.0	136.0	114.0
05	METALS	101.7	76.4	93.9	99.1	73.4	91.2	93.8	73.6	87.6	94.6	88.7	92.8	86.5	109.6	93.6	104.9	111.5	106.9
06	WOOD, PLASTICS & COMPOSITES	89.9	58.2	72.3	94.4	58.2	74.2	97.4	58.2	75.6	102.9	58.6	78.2	99.6	130.3	116.7	99.7	135.3	119.5
07	THERMAL & MOISTURE PROTECTION	96.7	64.6	83.1	104.1	58.6	84.8	97.4	58.7	81.0	109.2	58.2	87.6	98.9	130.1	112.1	106.2	134.4	118.1
08	OPENINGS	103.8	57.4	93.2	99.7	55.3	89.5	108.9	55.3	96.6	102.8	56.0	92.1	91.2	131.2	100.4	107.1	134.0	113.3
0920	Plaster & Gypsum Board	83.5	57.5	66.0	82.0	57.5	65.5	86.5	57.5	67.0	98.4	57.5	70.9	96.2	131.4	119.9	105.7	136.3	126.2
0950, 0980	Ceilings & Acoustic Treatment	82.1	57.5	65.5	86.7	57.5	67.0	85.5	57.5	66.6	88.8	57.5	67.7	110.3	131.4	124.5	111.1	136.3	128.1
0960	Flooring	90.6	75.0	86.3	84.1	54.2	75.8	92.8	45.8	79.8	63.4	48.0	59.2	102.9	116.0	106.5	97.4	118.6	103.3
0970, 0990	Wall Finishes & Painting/Coating	93.1	50.8	68.4	90.5	33.2	57.1	93.1	41.7	63.1	80.1	50.5	62.9	108.0	120.9	115.5	89.3	118.5	106.4
09	FINISHES	80.6	60.1	69.5	78.5	53.6	65.0	82.9	53.1	66.7	77.5	54.6	65.1	102.3	129.3	117.0	97.4	132.8	116.7
COVERS	DIVS. 10 - 14, 25, 28, 41, 43, 44, 46	100.0	79.3	95.4	100.0	67.2	92.7	100.0	67.2	92.7	100.0	68.1	92.9	100.0	119.7	104.4	100.0	120.9	104.6
21, 22, 23	FIRE SUPPRESSION, PLUMBING & HVAC	100.2	53.5	80.2	97.2	52.9	78.2	100.0	56.7	81.6	97.5	65.4	83.8	96.9	125.5	109.1	100.0	133.2	114.2
26, 27, 3370	ELECTRICAL, COMMUNICATIONS & UTIL.	94.6	64.4	78.9	93.0	54.7	73.1	96.2	56.4	75.5	100.3	64.6	81.7	117.8	126.8	122.5	91.1	108.6	100.2
MF2016	WEIGHTED AVERAGE	96.9	65.0	82.9	92.7	59.4	78.1	95.7	60.7	80.3	94.2	66.6	82.1	98.0	125.9	110.2	99.1	125.9	110.8

		CALIFORNIA																		
	DIVISION	BAKERSFIELD 932 - 933			BERKELEY 947			EUREKA 955			FRESNO 936 - 938			INGLEWOOD 903 - 905			LONG BEACH 906 - 908		
		MAT.	INST.	TOTAL	MAT.	INST.	TOTAL	MAT.	INST.	TOTAL	MAT.	INST.	TOTAL	MAT.	INST.	TOTAL	MAT.	INST.	TOTAL
015433	CONTRACTOR EQUIPMENT		98.9	98.9		102.7	102.7		98.7	98.7		98.9	98.9		97.8	97.8		97.8	97.8
0241, 31 - 34	SITE & INFRASTRUCTURE, DEMOLITION	99.6	107.6	105.2	107.4	109.4	108.8	113.2	106.2	108.3	104.1	107.0	106.1	91.7	105.8	101.6	99.1	105.9	103.8
0310	Concrete Forming & Accessories	104.7	134.4	130.3	115.2	165.0	158.2	113.6	150.3	145.2	102.1	149.9	143.3	108.3	134.9	131.2	103.3	135.0	130.6
0320	Concrete Reinforcing	90.0	128.0	109.2	90.6	130.1	110.5	102.9	129.5	116.3	75.5	129.1	102.5	94.7	128.4	111.7	93.9	128.4	111.3
0330	Cast-in-Place Concrete	89.3	131.6	105.4	117.4	133.0	123.3	95.4	129.0	108.2	96.9	128.8	109.0	80.8	131.6	100.1	92.0	131.7	107.1
03	CONCRETE	88.1	131.1	107.8	102.9	145.7	122.5	105.9	137.6	120.4	92.1	137.3	112.8	88.9	131.4	108.3	98.3	131.5	113.4
04	MASONRY	92.0	135.4	118.9	118.6	155.8	141.7	103.0	150.3	132.4	96.7	145.1	126.7	74.2	141.1	115.7	83.2	141.1	119.1
05	METALS	102.6	110.5	105.1	106.6	114.8	109.1	104.7	112.3	107.2	103.0	111.9	105.8	96.3	111.4	100.9	96.2	111.5	100.9
06	WOOD, PLASTICS & COMPOSITES	96.1	130.7	115.4	110.2	170.1	143.5	113.7	153.2	135.7	103.1	153.2	130.9	100.0	130.7	117.1	94.2	130.7	114.5
07	THERMAL & MOISTURE PROTECTION	102.6	124.5	111.9	102.7	153.7	124.3	110.0	145.8	125.1	94.0	133.0	110.5	103.4	130.2	114.7	103.7	131.8	115.6
08	OPENINGS	95.1	130.0	103.1	96.2	158.5	110.5	106.3	140.2	114.1	96.7	142.4	107.2	91.0	131.4	100.3	91.0	131.4	100.3
0920	Plaster & Gypsum Board	95.3	131.4	119.5	107.3	171.5	150.4	110.7	154.5	140.1	92.8	154.5	134.2	103.7	131.4	122.3	100.1	131.4	121.1
0950, 0980	Ceilings & Acoustic Treatment	97.9	131.4	120.5	100.5	171.5	148.4	114.5	154.5	141.5	95.3	154.5	135.2	109.2	131.4	124.2	109.2	131.4	124.2
0960	Flooring	100.9	116.0	105.1	116.9	136.3	122.3	101.2	130.6	109.4	103.5	114.8	106.6	109.0	116.0	110.9	105.7	116.0	108.7
0970, 0990	Wall Finishes & Painting/Coating	91.8	108.5	101.5	108.5	165.7	141.9	90.7	127.2	112.0	103.6	120.9	113.7	107.3	120.9	115.3	107.3	120.9	115.3
09	FINISHES	94.9	128.3	113.1	106.8	161.6	136.6	102.3	146.0	126.0	94.3	142.7	120.6	106.1	129.5	118.8	105.1	129.5	118.4
COVERS	DIVS. 10 - 14, 25, 28, 41, 43, 44, 46	100.0	112.1	102.7	100.0	131.3	107.0	100.0	128.1	106.2	100.0	128.0	106.2	100.0	120.6	104.6	100.0	120.6	104.6
21, 22, 23	FIRE SUPPRESSION, PLUMBING & HVAC	100.0	123.0	109.9	97.1	161.4	124.6	96.9	122.9	108.0	100.2	128.4	112.3	96.6	122.9	107.8	96.6	125.6	109.0
26, 27, 3370	ELECTRICAL, COMMUNICATIONS & UTIL.	106.3	105.1	105.6	102.5	159.0	131.9	97.6	120.7	109.6	96.5	108.5	102.7	100.5	126.8	114.2	100.2	126.8	114.1
MF2016	WEIGHTED AVERAGE	98.3	121.3	108.3	102.5	148.9	122.8	102.4	130.0	114.4	98.2	128.2	111.3	95.5	125.5	108.6	97.1	126.1	109.8

		CALIFORNIA																		
	DIVISION	LOS ANGELES 900 - 902			MARYSVILLE 959			MODESTO 953			MOJAVE 935			OAKLAND 946			OXNARD 930		
		MAT.	INST.	TOTAL	MAT.	INST.	TOTAL	MAT.	INST.	TOTAL	MAT.	INST.	TOTAL	MAT.	INST.	TOTAL	MAT.	INST.	TOTAL
015433	CONTRACTOR EQUIPMENT		103.6	103.6		98.7	98.7		98.7	98.7		98.9	98.9		102.7	102.7		97.8	97.8
0241, 31 - 34	SITE & INFRASTRUCTURE, DEMOLITION	97.7	111.1	107.1	109.7	106.3	107.3	104.3	106.5	105.8	97.3	107.6	104.5	112.3	109.4	110.3	104.3	105.7	105.3
0310	Concrete Forming & Accessories	106.3	138.9	134.4	103.8	150.0	143.7	100.3	149.9	143.1	113.8	134.3	131.5	104.4	165.0	156.7	105.3	138.6	134.0
0320	Concrete Reinforcing	95.4	128.6	112.1	102.9	128.9	116.0	106.6	128.8	117.8	90.4	128.0	109.4	92.7	130.1	111.6	88.8	128.1	108.6
0330	Cast-in-Place Concrete	83.4	132.6	102.1	106.6	128.9	115.1	95.5	128.8	108.1	83.8	131.6	102.0	111.3	133.0	119.6	97.6	132.0	110.7
03	CONCRETE	95.8	133.7	113.1	106.7	137.4	120.7	97.9	137.3	115.9	84.1	131.1	105.6	102.9	145.7	122.5	92.2	133.2	110.9
04	MASONRY	89.0	142.4	122.1	104.0	140.0	126.5	101.3	140.4	125.5	94.8	135.4	120.0	126.1	155.8	144.5	97.8	134.6	120.6
05	METALS	102.8	113.6	106.2	104.2	112.1	106.6	101.0	111.9	104.3	100.6	110.4	103.6	101.9	114.8	105.9	98.3	111.2	102.3
06	WOOD, PLASTICS & COMPOSITES	103.9	135.7	121.6	101.2	153.2	130.1	96.9	153.2	128.2	102.2	130.7	118.1	98.8	170.1	138.5	97.4	135.4	118.5
07	THERMAL & MOISTURE PROTECTION	99.5	134.1	114.1	109.4	135.1	120.3	108.9	132.4	118.9	99.9	122.2	109.3	101.4	153.7	123.6	103.2	132.5	115.6
08	OPENINGS	100.8	134.9	108.6	105.5	143.1	114.1	104.2	143.6	113.3	91.4	130.0	100.3	96.2	158.5	110.6	94.1	134.0	103.3
0920	Plaster & Gypsum Board	99.3	136.3	124.1	103.3	154.5	137.7	105.7	154.5	138.5	102.6	131.4	121.9	101.9	171.5	148.7	96.6	136.3	123.2
0950, 0980	Ceilings & Acoustic Treatment	116.2	136.3	129.7	113.6	154.5	141.2	111.1	154.5	140.4	96.7	131.4	120.1	103.3	171.5	149.3	99.2	136.3	124.2
0960	Flooring	106.9	118.6	110.1	96.9	121.2	103.6	97.3	121.0	103.9	104.5	116.0	107.7	109.7	136.3	117.1	96.7	118.6	102.7
0970, 0990	Wall Finishes & Painting/Coating	103.9	120.9	113.8	90.7	134.7	116.4	90.7	131.9	114.7	88.6	107.0	99.3	108.5	165.7	141.9	88.6	115.4	104.2
09	FINISHES	107.1	133.1	121.3	99.3	145.2	124.3	98.8	144.9	123.9	94.6	128.0	112.8	104.8	161.6	135.7	92.1	132.5	114.1
COVERS	DIVS. 10 - 14, 25, 28, 41, 43, 44, 46	100.0	118.7	104.2	100.0	128.1	106.2	100.0	128.0	106.2	100.0	112.1	102.7	100.0	131.3	107.0	100.0	121.1	104.7
21, 22, 23	FIRE SUPPRESSION, PLUMBING & HVAC	100.0	130.1	112.9	96.9	125.4	109.1	100.0	124.1	110.3	96.9	122.4	107.8	100.0	161.4	126.4	100.0	133.2	114.2
26, 27, 3370	ELECTRICAL, COMMUNICATIONS & UTIL.	98.9	130.6	115.4	94.5	118.3	106.9	96.8	107.3	102.3	95.0	107.9	101.7	101.7	159.0	131.5	100.4	117.2	109.1
MF2016	WEIGHTED AVERAGE	99.9	129.3	112.8	101.6	128.8	113.5	100.4	126.9	112.0	95.2	121.4	106.7	102.5	148.9	122.8	97.6	126.5	110.2

463

City Cost Indexes

CALIFORNIA

DIVISION		PALM SPRINGS 922			PALO ALTO 943			PASADENA 910 - 912			REDDING 960			RICHMOND 948			RIVERSIDE 925		
		MAT.	INST.	TOTAL	MAT.	INST.	TOTAL	MAT.	INST.	TOTAL	MAT.	INST.	TOTAL	MAT.	INST.	TOTAL	MAT.	INST.	TOTAL
015433	CONTRACTOR EQUIPMENT		99.8	99.8		102.7	102.7		95.8	95.8		98.7	98.7		102.7	102.7		99.8	99.8
0241, 31 - 34	SITE & INFRASTRUCTURE, DEMOLITION	93.4	107.9	103.5	103.7	109.4	107.7	97.7	109.1	105.7	133.9	106.3	114.5	111.6	109.4	110.1	100.5	107.9	105.7
0310	Concrete Forming & Accessories	101.7	134.9	130.3	102.6	164.7	156.1	105.4	134.5	130.5	104.3	149.7	143.5	117.8	164.6	158.2	105.4	138.5	133.9
0320	Concrete Reinforcing	108.3	128.2	118.3	90.6	129.6	110.3	105.8	128.4	117.2	127.7	128.9	128.3	90.6	129.6	110.3	105.2	128.1	116.7
0330	Cast-in-Place Concrete	83.8	132.6	102.4	99.3	132.9	112.1	78.6	128.9	97.7	115.6	128.9	120.6	114.2	132.8	121.3	91.2	132.7	106.9
03	CONCRETE	90.1	131.7	109.1	92.6	145.5	116.8	90.4	130.2	108.6	117.1	137.2	126.3	104.8	145.4	123.4	96.0	133.4	113.1
04	MASONRY	76.0	138.5	114.8	100.7	148.3	130.2	97.5	141.0	124.5	132.5	140.4	137.4	118.4	148.3	136.9	77.0	135.7	113.4
05	METALS	105.5	111.5	107.3	99.4	114.0	103.9	86.6	109.5	93.6	106.4	112.1	108.2	99.5	113.8	103.9	104.9	111.5	106.9
06	WOOD, PLASTICS & COMPOSITES	94.7	130.6	114.7	96.4	169.9	137.3	86.5	130.3	110.9	111.3	152.7	134.3	113.4	170.1	145.0	99.7	135.3	119.5
07	THERMAL & MOISTURE PROTECTION	105.5	133.6	117.4	100.6	152.2	122.4	98.5	130.1	111.9	130.6	135.1	132.5	101.3	149.3	121.6	106.4	133.4	117.8
08	OPENINGS	102.8	131.4	109.3	96.2	157.4	110.3	91.2	131.2	100.4	119.0	142.9	124.5	96.2	157.5	110.3	105.7	134.0	112.2
0920	Plaster & Gypsum Board	100.9	131.4	121.4	100.3	171.3	148.0	90.3	131.4	117.9	104.9	154.1	137.9	108.5	171.5	150.8	104.9	136.3	126.0
0950, 0980	Ceilings & Acoustic Treatment	107.7	131.4	123.7	101.4	171.3	148.5	110.3	131.4	124.5	141.6	154.1	150.0	101.4	171.5	148.7	116.3	136.3	129.7
0960	Flooring	99.4	122.3	105.7	108.2	136.3	116.0	96.4	116.0	101.8	91.7	124.9	100.9	119.5	136.3	124.2	101.0	118.6	105.9
0970, 0990	Wall Finishes & Painting/Coating	87.8	118.5	105.7	108.5	165.7	141.9	108.0	120.9	115.5	100.4	134.7	120.4	108.5	165.7	141.9	87.8	118.5	105.7
09	FINISHES	96.0	130.3	114.7	103.2	161.4	134.9	99.3	129.3	115.6	104.6	145.6	126.9	108.3	161.6	137.3	99.1	132.8	117.4
COVERS	DIVS. 10 - 14, 25, 28, 41, 43, 44, 46	100.0	120.4	104.5	100.0	131.3	107.0	100.0	119.7	104.4	100.0	128.0	106.2	100.0	131.2	106.9	100.0	120.9	104.6
21, 22, 23	FIRE SUPPRESSION, PLUMBING & HVAC	96.9	125.3	109.1	97.1	155.6	122.1	96.9	122.8	108.0	100.5	125.4	111.1	97.1	154.1	121.5	100.0	133.2	114.2
26, 27, 3370	ELECTRICAL, COMMUNICATIONS & UTIL.	94.1	110.8	102.8	101.6	169.0	136.6	114.7	126.8	121.0	99.0	118.3	109.1	102.2	136.0	119.8	90.9	108.0	99.8
MF2016	WEIGHTED AVERAGE	97.2	123.9	108.9	98.5	148.0	120.2	96.0	125.3	108.8	109.1	128.8	117.7	101.7	143.0	119.8	99.0	125.6	110.7

CALIFORNIA

DIVISION		SACRAMENTO 942, 956 - 958			SALINAS 939			SAN BERNARDINO 923 - 924			SAN DIEGO 919 - 921			SAN FRANCISCO 940 - 941			SAN JOSE 951		
		MAT.	INST.	TOTAL	MAT.	INST.	TOTAL	MAT.	INST.	TOTAL	MAT.	INST.	TOTAL	MAT.	INST.	TOTAL	MAT.	INST.	TOTAL
015433	CONTRACTOR EQUIPMENT		101.4	101.4		98.9	98.9		99.8	99.8		100.8	100.8		109.7	109.7		100.5	100.5
0241, 31 - 34	SITE & INFRASTRUCTURE, DEMOLITION	93.6	115.5	108.9	118.0	107.1	110.4	79.5	107.9	99.4	106.2	106.5	106.4	113.9	113.0	113.3	135.4	101.4	111.6
0310	Concrete Forming & Accessories	102.5	152.8	145.9	108.4	153.1	147.0	109.2	138.5	134.4	105.3	126.0	123.1	108.4	165.5	157.9	106.2	164.9	156.8
0320	Concrete Reinforcing	86.2	129.3	107.9	89.2	129.4	109.5	105.2	128.3	116.8	102.4	128.3	115.4	105.6	130.3	118.1	94.2	129.7	112.1
0330	Cast-in-Place Concrete	94.2	129.9	107.7	96.4	129.3	108.9	63.0	132.6	89.5	90.0	119.2	101.1	124.3	133.3	127.7	110.9	132.2	119.0
03	CONCRETE	93.9	138.7	114.4	101.1	139.0	118.4	71.0	133.4	99.5	100.6	123.2	110.9	114.2	146.7	129.1	103.9	145.7	123.0
04	MASONRY	101.6	146.1	129.2	94.9	146.5	126.9	83.3	138.5	117.5	89.8	132.5	116.3	135.9	156.5	148.7	131.2	149.8	142.7
05	METALS	97.6	108.5	101.0	103.2	113.2	106.3	104.9	111.6	107.0	102.8	113.0	106.0	107.4	122.2	112.0	99.3	119.1	105.4
06	WOOD, PLASTICS & COMPOSITES	92.2	156.5	128.0	101.8	156.3	132.1	103.2	135.3	121.1	97.9	122.6	111.6	101.1	170.1	139.5	109.7	169.9	143.2
07	THERMAL & MOISTURE PROTECTION	110.6	139.1	122.7	100.5	143.3	118.6	104.5	135.1	117.5	103.6	118.2	109.8	106.5	156.0	127.4	105.4	151.6	125.0
08	OPENINGS	109.6	145.4	117.8	95.3	150.9	108.1	102.8	134.6	110.1	100.1	125.8	106.0	102.2	158.5	115.2	95.7	158.4	110.1
0920	Plaster & Gypsum Board	97.6	157.7	137.9	97.6	157.7	138.0	106.3	136.3	126.4	96.2	123.0	114.2	99.9	171.5	148.0	101.8	171.5	148.6
0950, 0980	Ceilings & Acoustic Treatment	101.4	157.7	139.3	96.7	157.7	137.8	111.1	136.3	128.1	120.8	123.0	122.3	110.6	171.5	151.7	111.2	171.5	151.9
0960	Flooring	108.4	125.7	113.2	98.7	137.9	109.6	102.9	118.6	107.3	106.2	118.6	109.6	110.2	137.9	117.9	90.7	136.3	103.4
0970, 0990	Wall Finishes & Painting/Coating	105.2	134.7	122.4	89.4	165.7	133.9	87.8	120.9	107.1	105.6	120.9	114.5	106.4	175.4	146.7	91.0	165.7	134.6
09	FINISHES	102.1	148.0	127.1	94.0	153.3	126.3	97.4	132.9	116.7	107.0	123.7	116.1	106.4	162.9	137.2	97.8	161.4	132.4
COVERS	DIVS. 10 - 14, 25, 28, 41, 43, 44, 46	100.0	128.9	106.4	100.0	128.4	106.3	100.0	118.5	104.0	100.0	114.5	103.2	100.0	131.4	107.0	100.0	130.8	106.8
21, 22, 23	FIRE SUPPRESSION, PLUMBING & HVAC	100.1	128.1	112.5	96.9	134.5	113.0	96.9	129.9	111.1	99.9	126.5	111.3	100.0	189.7	138.4	100.0	166.0	128.3
26, 27, 3370	ELECTRICAL, COMMUNICATIONS & UTIL.	97.4	122.0	110.2	96.0	128.7	113.0	94.1	111.6	103.2	101.3	103.1	102.2	101.8	174.7	139.7	99.7	170.0	136.3
MF2016	WEIGHTED AVERAGE	100.0	131.6	113.8	98.8	134.8	114.6	94.8	125.7	108.4	101.0	119.5	109.1	106.3	158.5	129.1	102.4	150.4	123.4

CALIFORNIA

DIVISION		SAN LUIS OBISPO 934			SAN MATEO 944			SAN RAFAEL 949			SANTA ANA 926 - 927			SANTA BARBARA 931			SANTA CRUZ 950		
		MAT.	INST.	TOTAL	MAT.	INST.	TOTAL	MAT.	INST.	TOTAL	MAT.	INST.	TOTAL	MAT.	INST.	TOTAL	MAT.	INST.	TOTAL
015433	CONTRACTOR EQUIPMENT		98.9	98.9		102.7	102.7		101.8	101.8		99.8	99.8		98.9	98.9		100.5	100.5
0241, 31 - 34	SITE & INFRASTRUCTURE, DEMOLITION	110.0	107.7	108.4	109.5	109.4	109.4	106.3	115.2	112.5	91.8	107.9	103.1	104.3	107.7	106.7	135.0	101.3	111.4
0310	Concrete Forming & Accessories	115.5	136.8	133.9	108.4	164.9	157.1	112.9	164.9	157.7	109.4	134.7	131.2	106.1	138.6	134.1	106.2	153.5	147.0
0320	Concrete Reinforcing	90.4	128.1	109.4	90.6	129.8	110.4	91.4	129.9	110.8	108.9	128.1	118.6	88.8	128.1	108.6	116.2	129.4	122.9
0330	Cast-in-Place Concrete	103.6	131.8	114.3	110.6	132.9	119.1	128.6	132.0	129.9	80.5	132.5	100.2	97.2	131.9	110.4	110.2	131.1	118.1
03	CONCRETE	99.5	132.3	114.5	101.6	145.6	121.7	122.8	145.1	133.0	87.7	131.6	107.8	92.0	133.1	110.8	106.4	140.1	121.8
04	MASONRY	96.5	135.6	120.7	118.1	151.3	138.8	96.9	152.5	131.4	73.1	138.8	113.8	95.1	135.6	120.2	134.9	146.7	142.2
05	METALS	101.3	110.0	104.3	99.3	114.3	103.9	100.6	110.8	103.7	105.0	111.4	106.9	98.9	111.2	102.7	106.5	117.8	110.0
06	WOOD, PLASTICS & COMPOSITES	104.3	133.2	120.4	103.6	170.1	140.6	99.4	169.9	138.6	105.1	130.6	119.3	97.4	135.4	118.5	109.7	156.4	135.7
07	THERMAL & MOISTURE PROTECTION	100.7	131.7	113.8	101.0	152.4	122.7	105.3	151.9	125.0	105.8	133.7	117.6	100.1	132.6	113.9	105.0	145.8	122.2
08	OPENINGS	93.4	131.4	102.1	96.2	157.5	110.3	107.1	158.0	118.7	102.1	131.4	108.8	95.1	134.4	104.1	97.0	150.9	109.3
0920	Plaster & Gypsum Board	103.5	134.0	124.0	105.2	171.5	149.7	106.9	171.5	150.2	108.0	131.4	123.7	96.6	136.3	123.2	110.4	157.7	142.1
0950, 0980	Ceilings & Acoustic Treatment	96.7	134.0	121.9	101.4	171.5	148.7	108.2	171.5	150.9	111.1	131.4	124.8	99.2	136.3	124.2	111.9	157.7	142.8
0960	Flooring	105.4	116.0	108.4	112.3	136.3	118.9	124.7	130.6	126.3	103.5	116.0	107.0	97.8	118.6	103.6	94.7	137.9	106.7
0970, 0990	Wall Finishes & Painting/Coating	88.6	110.9	101.6	108.5	165.7	141.9	104.6	164.8	139.7	87.8	118.5	105.7	88.6	115.4	104.2	91.2	165.7	134.7
09	FINISHES	96.0	129.9	114.4	105.5	161.6	136.0	108.9	160.3	136.9	98.9	129.2	115.4	92.6	132.3	114.2	100.4	153.4	129.2
COVERS	DIVS. 10 - 14, 25, 28, 41, 43, 44, 46	100.0	127.6	106.2	100.0	131.3	107.0	100.0	130.6	106.8	100.0	120.4	104.5	100.0	118.3	104.1	100.0	128.7	106.4
21, 22, 23	FIRE SUPPRESSION, PLUMBING & HVAC	96.9	127.2	109.9	100.0	157.3	122.9	97.1	185.0	134.7	96.9	122.0	107.6	100.0	133.2	114.2	100.0	134.9	115.0
26, 27, 3370	ELECTRICAL, COMMUNICATIONS & UTIL.	95.0	112.5	104.1	101.6	161.1	132.6	98.8	123.8	111.8	94.1	110.0	102.4	93.9	124.4	104.8	98.9	128.7	114.4
MF2016	WEIGHTED AVERAGE	98.1	124.4	109.6	100.8	147.7	121.3	103.8	148.4	123.3	96.8	122.9	108.3	96.9	126.3	109.8	104.3	135.1	117.8

464

City Cost Indexes

		CALIFORNIA																	COLORADO		
	DIVISION	SANTA ROSA			STOCKTON			SUSANVILLE			VALLEJO			VAN NUYS			ALAMOSA		
		954			952			961			945			913 - 916			811		
		MAT.	INST.	TOTAL	MAT.	INST.	TOTAL	MAT.	INST.	TOTAL	MAT.	INST.	TOTAL	MAT.	INST.	TOTAL	MAT.	INST.	TOTAL
015433	CONTRACTOR EQUIPMENT		99.3	99.3		98.7	98.7		98.7	98.7		101.8	101.8		95.8	95.8		92.8	92.8
0241, 31 - 34	SITE & INFRASTRUCTURE, DEMOLITION	106.1	106.5	106.4	104.0	106.5	105.8	142.3	106.2	117.0	94.8	115.3	109.1	116.1	109.1	111.2	143.5	88.4	104.9
0310	Concrete Forming & Accessories	102.6	164.2	155.7	104.2	152.2	145.6	105.4	141.9	136.9	103.6	163.8	155.5	112.1	134.5	131.4	102.5	63.8	69.1
0320	Concrete Reinforcing	103.8	130.0	117.0	106.6	128.8	117.8	127.7	128.8	128.3	92.5	129.8	111.3	105.8	128.4	117.2	107.9	67.8	87.7
0330	Cast-in-Place Concrete	104.7	130.5	114.5	93.0	128.8	106.6	105.1	128.8	114.1	102.5	131.1	113.4	82.9	128.9	100.4	100.0	73.6	89.9
03	CONCRETE	106.6	144.6	124.0	96.9	138.3	115.9	119.5	133.7	126.0	98.7	144.2	119.5	104.7	130.2	116.4	110.6	68.6	91.4
04	MASONRY	101.8	153.3	133.7	101.2	140.4	125.5	131.1	140.4	136.8	73.7	151.4	121.9	112.0	141.0	130.0	130.4	60.9	87.3
05	METALS	105.3	115.2	108.3	101.2	111.9	104.5	105.2	111.9	107.3	100.5	110.1	103.5	85.7	109.5	93.0	103.7	78.2	95.9
06	WOOD, PLASTICS & COMPOSITES	96.1	169.6	137.0	102.3	156.3	132.3	113.0	142.3	129.3	89.3	169.9	134.1	94.6	130.3	114.5	97.8	64.1	79.0
07	THERMAL & MOISTURE PROTECTION	106.3	152.0	125.6	109.4	134.0	119.8	132.3	131.9	132.1	103.3	151.8	123.8	99.7	130.1	112.6	104.3	69.0	89.4
08	OPENINGS	103.7	158.3	116.3	104.2	143.2	113.2	119.9	137.1	123.9	108.9	156.3	119.8	91.0	131.2	100.3	96.4	67.0	89.6
0920	Plaster & Gypsum Board	102.7	171.5	148.9	105.7	157.7	140.6	105.7	143.4	131.0	101.6	171.5	148.5	94.3	131.4	119.2	78.0	63.0	67.9
0950, 0980	Ceilings & Acoustic Treatment	111.1	171.5	151.8	119.7	157.7	145.3	134.1	143.4	140.3	110.1	171.5	151.5	107.7	131.4	123.7	102.3	63.0	75.8
0960	Flooring	99.9	128.7	107.9	97.3	121.0	103.9	92.1	124.9	101.2	118.0	136.3	123.1	99.8	116.0	104.3	109.3	73.0	99.2
0970, 0990	Wall Finishes & Painting/Coating	87.8	155.6	127.4	90.7	128.3	112.6	100.4	134.7	120.4	105.6	164.8	140.1	108.0	120.9	115.5	103.1	61.9	79.1
09	FINISHES	98.0	158.5	130.9	100.5	146.3	125.4	104.4	139.5	123.5	105.4	161.0	135.6	101.7	129.2	116.7	99.6	64.8	80.7
COVERS	DIVS. 10 - 14, 25, 28, 41, 43, 44, 46	100.0	129.7	106.6	100.0	128.4	106.3	100.0	126.9	106.0	100.0	130.2	106.7	100.0	119.7	104.4	100.0	84.4	96.5
21, 22, 23	FIRE SUPPRESSION, PLUMBING & HVAC	96.9	182.2	133.4	100.0	124.1	110.3	97.4	125.4	109.4	100.2	143.2	118.5	96.9	122.8	108.0	96.9	65.5	83.5
26, 27, 3370	ELECTRICAL, COMMUNICATIONS & UTIL.	94.4	124.4	110.0	96.8	110.8	104.1	99.4	118.3	109.2	95.0	126.8	111.5	114.7	126.8	121.0	97.7	65.1	80.8
MF2016	WEIGHTED AVERAGE	101.1	147.3	121.3	100.5	127.7	112.4	108.8	127.0	116.8	99.5	139.6	117.0	99.1	125.3	110.6	103.3	69.0	88.3

		COLORADO																	
	DIVISION	BOULDER			COLORADO SPRINGS			DENVER			DURANGO			FORT COLLINS			FORT MORGAN		
		803			808 - 809			800 - 802			813			805			807		
		MAT.	INST.	TOTAL	MAT.	INST.	TOTAL	MAT.	INST.	TOTAL	MAT.	INST.	TOTAL	MAT.	INST.	TOTAL	MAT.	INST.	TOTAL
015433	CONTRACTOR EQUIPMENT		94.7	94.7		92.6	92.6		99.1	99.1		92.8	92.8		94.7	94.7		94.7	94.7
0241, 31 - 34	SITE & INFRASTRUCTURE, DEMOLITION	97.3	95.7	96.2	99.1	90.7	93.2	104.2	102.4	102.9	136.6	88.4	102.8	109.6	95.6	99.8	99.5	95.4	96.6
0310	Concrete Forming & Accessories	103.0	74.9	78.8	93.8	60.3	64.9	102.0	63.8	69.1	108.6	63.6	69.8	100.6	69.9	74.1	103.5	53.3	60.2
0320	Concrete Reinforcing	97.7	67.9	82.7	96.9	67.9	82.3	96.9	68.0	82.3	107.9	67.8	87.7	97.8	67.9	82.7	97.9	67.9	82.8
0330	Cast-in-Place Concrete	106.0	74.2	93.9	108.9	73.3	95.4	113.6	72.7	98.0	115.0	73.5	99.2	119.7	72.8	101.9	104.0	72.7	92.1
03	CONCRETE	103.2	73.8	89.7	106.8	66.9	88.6	109.4	68.3	90.6	112.8	68.4	92.5	114.2	71.0	94.5	101.6	63.5	84.2
04	MASONRY	97.3	64.7	77.1	98.9	62.7	76.4	100.1	65.1	78.4	117.1	60.9	82.2	115.2	62.2	82.3	112.5	62.2	81.3
05	METALS	98.1	77.1	91.7	101.3	77.4	93.9	103.8	78.4	96.0	103.7	78.0	95.8	99.4	77.1	92.5	97.8	76.9	91.4
06	WOOD, PLASTICS & COMPOSITES	105.7	77.7	90.1	96.1	59.1	75.5	103.0	63.6	81.1	106.7	64.1	83.0	103.3	72.2	86.0	105.7	49.9	74.6
07	THERMAL & MOISTURE PROTECTION	98.9	73.5	88.1	99.6	70.7	87.4	97.4	71.6	86.5	104.3	69.0	89.4	99.2	71.8	87.6	98.8	69.3	86.3
08	OPENINGS	98.3	74.5	92.8	102.6	64.2	93.8	105.3	66.7	96.4	103.4	67.0	95.0	98.2	71.5	92.1	98.2	59.1	89.2
0920	Plaster & Gypsum Board	116.2	77.5	90.2	100.0	58.2	71.9	111.9	63.0	79.1	90.8	63.0	72.2	110.6	71.8	84.6	116.2	48.9	71.0
0950, 0980	Ceilings & Acoustic Treatment	90.2	77.5	81.6	97.9	58.2	71.1	102.5	63.0	75.9	102.3	63.0	75.8	90.2	71.8	77.8	90.2	48.9	62.4
0960	Flooring	111.8	73.0	101.0	102.8	73.0	94.5	109.0	73.0	99.0	114.7	73.0	103.1	107.7	73.0	98.1	112.3	73.0	101.4
0970, 0990	Wall Finishes & Painting/Coating	101.5	61.9	78.4	101.2	61.9	78.3	108.2	61.9	81.2	103.1	61.9	79.1	101.5	61.9	78.4	101.5	61.9	78.4
09	FINISHES	102.8	73.4	86.8	99.4	61.8	79.0	104.8	64.6	82.9	102.1	64.8	81.8	101.4	69.5	84.0	102.9	56.3	77.6
COVERS	DIVS. 10 - 14, 25, 28, 41, 43, 44, 46	100.0	85.8	96.8	100.0	83.2	96.3	100.0	83.5	96.3	100.0	84.4	96.5	100.0	84.4	96.5	100.0	81.9	96.0
21, 22, 23	FIRE SUPPRESSION, PLUMBING & HVAC	96.9	73.3	86.8	100.1	80.6	91.8	99.9	75.5	89.5	96.9	57.3	80.0	100.0	72.0	88.0	96.9	74.8	87.4
26, 27, 3370	ELECTRICAL, COMMUNICATIONS & UTIL.	95.2	79.5	87.1	98.2	75.8	86.5	99.8	79.6	89.3	97.2	53.1	74.3	95.2	79.5	87.1	95.5	79.4	87.2
MF2016	WEIGHTED AVERAGE	98.8	75.9	88.8	101.0	73.2	88.8	102.8	74.6	90.5	103.7	65.5	87.0	102.1	74.3	89.9	99.4	71.2	87.0

		COLORADO																	
	DIVISION	GLENWOOD SPRINGS			GOLDEN			GRAND JUNCTION			GREELEY			MONTROSE			PUEBLO		
		816			804			815			806			814			810		
		MAT.	INST.	TOTAL	MAT.	INST.	TOTAL	MAT.	INST.	TOTAL	MAT.	INST.	TOTAL	MAT.	INST.	TOTAL	MAT.	INST.	TOTAL
015433	CONTRACTOR EQUIPMENT		96.0	96.0		94.7	94.7		96.0	96.0		94.7	94.7		94.4	94.4		92.8	92.8
0241, 31 - 34	SITE & INFRASTRUCTURE, DEMOLITION	153.2	96.4	113.4	110.6	95.7	100.2	135.9	96.6	108.4	95.9	95.6	95.7	146.3	92.4	108.5	127.3	88.4	100.0
0310	Concrete Forming & Accessories	99.5	53.2	59.6	96.1	59.6	64.6	107.5	74.3	78.9	98.5	73.9	77.3	99.0	53.3	59.8	104.7	60.3	66.4
0320	Concrete Reinforcing	106.7	67.8	87.1	97.9	67.9	82.8	107.0	67.9	87.3	97.7	67.9	82.7	106.5	67.8	87.0	103.1	67.9	85.3
0330	Cast-in-Place Concrete	99.9	72.4	89.5	104.1	74.1	92.7	110.7	73.9	96.7	100.0	72.8	89.7	100.0	73.0	89.7	99.2	73.6	89.5
03	CONCRETE	115.7	63.4	91.8	112.7	66.8	91.7	109.3	73.5	92.9	98.3	72.8	86.6	106.8	63.7	87.1	99.5	67.0	84.7
04	MASONRY	101.7	62.1	77.2	115.6	64.7	84.0	137.4	65.4	92.7	109.0	62.2	80.0	110.2	60.9	79.6	97.9	62.0	75.7
05	METALS	103.4	77.7	95.5	98.0	77.0	91.6	105.1	78.1	96.8	99.3	77.1	92.5	102.5	78.0	95.0	106.8	78.3	98.0
06	WOOD, PLASTICS & COMPOSITES	93.1	50.0	69.2	98.3	57.1	75.4	104.4	71.0	89.2	100.6	77.6	87.8	94.4	50.2	69.8	100.3	59.4	77.5
07	THERMAL & MOISTURE PROTECTION	104.2	67.9	88.8	99.9	71.2	87.8	103.3	72.2	90.1	98.5	72.4	87.4	104.4	67.5	88.8	102.8	69.1	88.5
08	OPENINGS	102.4	59.2	92.5	98.2	63.1	90.2	103.1	74.1	96.5	98.2	74.5	92.8	103.5	59.3	93.4	98.2	64.4	90.5
0920	Plaster & Gypsum Board	120.4	48.9	72.4	108.3	56.4	73.4	132.9	76.7	95.1	109.0	77.4	87.8	77.3	48.9	58.2	82.0	58.2	66.0
0950, 0980	Ceilings & Acoustic Treatment	101.5	48.9	66.0	90.2	56.4	67.4	101.5	76.7	84.7	90.2	77.4	81.6	102.3	48.9	66.3	110.0	58.2	75.1
0960	Flooring	108.4	73.0	98.6	105.2	73.0	96.3	114.0	73.0	102.6	106.5	73.0	97.2	112.0	73.0	101.1	110.6	73.0	100.1
0970, 0990	Wall Finishes & Painting/Coating	103.1	61.9	79.1	101.5	61.9	78.4	103.1	61.9	79.1	101.5	61.9	78.4	103.1	61.9	79.1	103.1	61.9	79.1
09	FINISHES	105.3	56.5	78.8	101.0	61.2	79.4	106.9	73.0	88.5	100.0	72.7	85.2	100.3	56.6	76.5	100.2	62.0	79.4
COVERS	DIVS. 10 - 14, 25, 28, 41, 43, 44, 46	100.0	82.2	96.0	100.0	83.5	96.3	100.0	86.0	96.9	100.0	85.0	96.7	100.0	82.5	96.1	100.0	83.9	96.4
21, 22, 23	FIRE SUPPRESSION, PLUMBING & HVAC	96.9	66.6	83.9	96.9	73.3	86.8	99.9	76.4	89.9	100.0	72.0	88.0	96.9	77.1	88.4	99.9	66.6	85.7
26, 27, 3370	ELECTRICAL, COMMUNICATIONS & UTIL.	94.7	53.1	73.1	95.5	79.5	87.2	96.9	53.1	74.1	95.2	79.5	87.1	96.9	53.1	74.1	97.7	66.2	81.3
MF2016	WEIGHTED AVERAGE	103.5	65.9	87.0	101.0	72.6	88.6	105.5	73.0	91.3	99.3	75.1	88.7	102.4	67.8	87.3	101.3	68.8	87.1

For customer support on your Green Building Costs with RSMeans data, call 800.448.8182.

465

City Cost Indexes

DIVISION		COLORADO SALIDA 812			CONNECTICUT															
					BRIDGEPORT 066			BRISTOL 060			HARTFORD 061			MERIDEN 064			NEW BRITAIN 060		
		MAT.	INST.	TOTAL	MAT.	INST.	TOTAL	MAT.	INST.	TOTAL	MAT.	INST.	TOTAL	MAT.	INST.	TOTAL	MAT.	INST.	TOTAL
015433	CONTRACTOR EQUIPMENT		94.4	94.4		98.8	98.8		98.8	98.8		98.8	98.8		99.3	99.3		98.8	98.8
0241, 31 - 34	SITE & INFRASTRUCTURE, DEMOLITION	136.3	92.4	105.5	105.9	103.2	104.0	105.0	103.2	103.7	100.3	103.2	102.3	102.9	103.9	103.6	105.2	103.2	103.8
0310	Concrete Forming & Accessories	107.4	53.3	60.8	102.2	118.7	116.5	102.2	118.6	116.3	102.1	118.6	116.3	101.9	118.5	116.3	102.6	118.6	116.4
0320	Concrete Reinforcing	106.2	67.8	86.8	117.4	142.1	129.8	117.4	142.1	129.8	112.6	142.1	127.5	117.4	142.1	129.8	117.4	142.1	129.8
0330	Cast-in-Place Concrete	114.5	72.9	98.7	98.7	129.3	110.3	92.5	129.2	106.4	96.9	129.2	109.2	89.0	129.2	104.3	94.0	129.2	107.4
03	CONCRETE	107.8	63.6	87.6	96.2	125.6	109.7	93.3	125.5	108.0	93.5	125.6	108.2	91.6	125.5	107.1	94.0	125.5	108.4
04	MASONRY	138.9	60.9	90.5	113.9	130.1	124.0	105.1	130.1	120.6	104.4	130.1	120.3	104.8	130.1	120.5	107.5	130.1	121.5
05	METALS	102.2	77.8	94.7	96.2	116.4	102.4	96.2	116.2	102.4	101.2	116.3	105.8	93.6	116.2	100.6	92.7	116.3	100.0
06	WOOD, PLASTICS & COMPOSITES	101.3	50.2	72.9	110.3	116.7	113.9	110.3	116.7	113.9	96.7	116.7	107.8	110.3	116.7	113.9	110.3	116.7	113.9
07	THERMAL & MOISTURE PROTECTION	103.2	67.5	88.1	100.1	124.8	110.6	100.3	121.4	109.3	105.4	121.4	112.1	100.3	121.3	109.2	100.3	121.6	109.3
08	OPENINGS	96.5	59.3	87.9	95.5	122.4	101.7	95.5	122.4	101.7	94.0	122.4	100.5	97.8	122.4	103.4	95.5	122.4	101.7
0920	Plaster & Gypsum Board	77.6	48.9	58.3	115.6	116.8	116.4	115.6	116.8	116.4	103.9	116.8	112.5	116.8	116.8	116.8	115.6	116.8	116.4
0950, 0980	Ceilings & Acoustic Treatment	102.3	48.9	66.3	95.3	116.8	109.8	95.3	116.8	109.8	93.2	116.8	109.1	98.5	116.8	110.8	95.3	116.8	109.8
0960	Flooring	117.6	73.0	105.2	87.3	131.6	99.6	87.3	124.4	97.6	90.2	131.6	101.7	87.3	124.4	97.6	87.3	124.4	97.6
0970, 0990	Wall Finishes & Painting/Coating	103.1	61.9	79.1	92.3	128.8	113.6	92.3	128.8	113.6	94.4	128.8	114.5	92.3	128.8	113.6	92.3	128.8	113.6
09	FINISHES	101.0	56.6	76.8	91.4	121.4	107.7	91.4	120.2	107.0	93.6	121.4	108.7	92.2	120.2	107.4	91.4	120.2	107.0
COVERS	DIVS. 10 - 14, 25, 28, 41, 43, 44, 46	100.0	82.6	96.1	100.0	113.2	102.9	100.0	113.2	102.9	100.0	113.2	102.9	100.0	113.2	102.9	100.0	113.2	102.9
21, 22, 23	FIRE SUPPRESSION, PLUMBING & HVAC	96.9	62.9	82.3	100.1	118.8	108.1	100.1	118.7	108.1	100.0	118.8	108.0	97.0	118.7	106.3	100.1	118.7	108.1
26, 27, 3370	ELECTRICAL, COMMUNICATIONS & UTIL.	97.1	60.8	78.2	99.0	108.3	103.8	99.0	106.3	102.8	98.5	110.5	104.8	98.9	105.7	102.5	99.0	106.3	102.8
MF2016	WEIGHTED AVERAGE	103.0	65.8	86.7	98.5	118.4	107.2	97.7	117.9	106.5	98.4	118.6	107.3	96.6	117.8	105.9	97.4	117.9	106.3

DIVISION		CONNECTICUT																	
		NEW HAVEN 065			NEW LONDON 063			NORWALK 068			STAMFORD 069			WATERBURY 067			WILLIMANTIC 062		
		MAT.	INST.	TOTAL	MAT.	INST.	TOTAL	MAT.	INST.	TOTAL	MAT.	INST.	TOTAL	MAT.	INST.	TOTAL	MAT.	INST.	TOTAL
015433	CONTRACTOR EQUIPMENT		99.3	99.3		99.3	99.3		98.8	98.8		98.8	98.8		98.8	98.8		98.8	98.8
0241, 31 - 34	SITE & INFRASTRUCTURE, DEMOLITION	105.1	103.7	104.1	97.4	103.7	101.8	105.6	103.1	103.9	106.3	103.2	104.1	105.7	103.2	103.9	105.6	102.9	103.7
0310	Concrete Forming & Accessories	101.9	118.6	116.3	101.9	118.6	116.3	102.2	118.7	116.4	102.2	119.1	116.7	102.2	118.6	116.4	102.2	118.5	116.2
0320	Concrete Reinforcing	117.4	142.1	129.8	92.0	142.1	117.3	117.4	142.1	129.8	117.4	142.2	129.9	117.4	142.1	129.8	117.4	142.1	129.8
0330	Cast-in-Place Concrete	95.6	129.2	108.4	81.5	129.2	99.6	97.1	129.3	109.3	98.7	129.4	110.4	98.7	129.2	110.3	92.2	129.2	106.2
03	CONCRETE	106.6	125.5	115.3	82.3	125.5	102.1	95.4	125.6	109.2	96.2	125.8	109.8	96.2	125.6	109.6	93.1	125.5	107.9
04	MASONRY	105.4	130.1	120.7	103.7	130.1	120.1	104.8	130.1	120.5	105.6	130.1	120.8	105.6	130.1	120.8	105.0	130.1	120.6
05	METALS	92.9	116.3	100.1	92.7	116.3	99.9	96.2	116.4	102.4	96.2	116.8	102.5	96.2	116.3	102.4	96.0	116.2	102.2
06	WOOD, PLASTICS & COMPOSITES	110.3	116.7	113.9	110.3	116.7	113.9	110.3	116.7	113.9	110.3	116.7	113.9	110.3	116.7	113.9	110.3	116.7	113.9
07	THERMAL & MOISTURE PROTECTION	100.4	121.7	109.4	100.2	121.4	109.1	100.3	124.8	110.7	100.3	124.8	110.7	100.3	121.8	109.4	100.5	121.0	109.2
08	OPENINGS	95.5	122.4	101.7	97.9	122.4	103.5	95.5	122.4	101.7	95.5	122.4	101.7	95.5	122.4	101.7	97.9	122.4	103.5
0920	Plaster & Gypsum Board	115.6	116.8	116.4	115.6	116.8	116.4	115.6	116.8	116.4	115.6	116.8	116.4	115.6	116.8	116.4	115.6	116.8	116.4
0950, 0980	Ceilings & Acoustic Treatment	95.3	116.8	109.8	93.4	116.8	109.2	95.3	116.8	109.8	95.3	116.8	109.8	95.3	116.8	109.8	93.4	116.8	109.2
0960	Flooring	87.3	131.6	99.6	87.3	131.6	99.6	87.3	124.4	97.6	87.3	131.6	99.6	87.3	129.1	98.9	87.3	128.0	98.6
0970, 0990	Wall Finishes & Painting/Coating	92.3	128.8	113.6	92.3	128.8	113.6	92.3	128.8	113.6	92.3	128.8	113.6	92.3	128.8	113.6	92.3	128.8	113.6
09	FINISHES	91.4	121.4	107.7	90.6	121.4	107.3	91.4	120.2	107.1	91.5	121.4	107.7	91.3	121.0	107.4	91.1	120.8	107.3
COVERS	DIVS. 10 - 14, 25, 28, 41, 43, 44, 46	100.0	113.2	102.9	100.0	113.2	102.9	100.0	113.2	102.9	100.0	113.4	103.0	100.0	113.2	102.9	100.0	113.2	102.9
21, 22, 23	FIRE SUPPRESSION, PLUMBING & HVAC	100.1	118.8	108.1	97.0	118.7	106.3	100.1	118.8	108.1	100.1	118.8	108.1	100.1	118.8	108.1	100.1	118.6	108.0
26, 27, 3370	ELECTRICAL, COMMUNICATIONS & UTIL.	98.9	112.0	105.7	96.0	109.6	103.1	99.0	110.7	105.1	99.0	158.5	130.0	98.5	111.4	105.2	99.0	110.5	105.0
MF2016	WEIGHTED AVERAGE	98.9	118.9	107.6	94.7	118.5	105.1	98.0	118.6	107.0	98.1	125.5	110.1	98.1	118.7	107.1	97.9	118.5	106.9

DIVISION		D.C. WASHINGTON 200 - 205			DELAWARE								FLORIDA					
					DOVER 199			NEWARK 197			WILMINGTON 198			DAYTONA BEACH 321			FORT LAUDERDALE 333		
		MAT.	INST.	TOTAL	MAT.	INST.	TOTAL	MAT.	INST.	TOTAL	MAT.	INST.	TOTAL	MAT.	INST.	TOTAL	MAT.	INST.	TOTAL
015433	CONTRACTOR EQUIPMENT		106.4	106.4		122.9	122.9		122.9	122.9		123.1	123.1		101.9	101.9		94.8	94.8
0241, 31 - 34	SITE & INFRASTRUCTURE, DEMOLITION	104.0	96.5	98.7	104.1	114.8	111.6	103.8	114.8	111.5	105.0	115.2	112.1	102.4	88.7	92.8	94.2	76.1	81.5
0310	Concrete Forming & Accessories	99.2	72.3	76.0	95.9	102.3	101.4	98.3	102.3	101.8	96.7	102.3	101.5	97.3	63.6	68.3	95.8	56.5	61.9
0320	Concrete Reinforcing	100.6	87.1	93.8	105.3	114.3	109.9	100.8	114.3	107.6	105.3	114.3	109.9	92.6	65.9	79.2	92.3	57.5	74.7
0330	Cast-in-Place Concrete	109.9	81.0	98.9	101.0	107.7	103.5	88.3	107.7	95.7	98.2	107.7	101.8	88.8	65.8	80.0	88.6	62.7	78.7
03	CONCRETE	107.2	79.0	94.3	96.2	107.4	101.3	91.2	107.4	98.6	95.0	107.4	100.7	86.4	66.5	77.3	87.4	60.7	75.2
04	MASONRY	101.8	82.1	89.6	101.0	100.5	100.7	103.1	100.5	101.5	101.3	100.5	100.8	89.7	59.6	71.0	94.7	63.5	75.4
05	METALS	101.9	96.6	100.3	102.0	124.3	108.9	103.5	124.3	109.9	102.0	124.3	108.9	96.0	90.9	94.5	94.8	87.8	92.7
06	WOOD, PLASTICS & COMPOSITES	99.7	70.2	83.3	91.3	100.3	96.3	96.8	100.3	98.8	87.3	100.3	94.5	100.5	62.9	79.6	90.3	56.4	71.4
07	THERMAL & MOISTURE PROTECTION	99.8	85.6	93.8	100.7	113.2	106.0	105.0	113.2	108.5	100.1	113.2	105.6	97.2	65.8	83.9	98.4	62.2	83.1
08	OPENINGS	99.8	74.6	94.0	90.6	110.5	95.2	91.5	110.5	95.9	88.7	110.5	93.7	95.3	62.0	87.7	96.2	56.3	87.0
0920	Plaster & Gypsum Board	106.2	69.3	81.6	101.9	100.3	100.8	98.9	100.3	99.8	101.3	100.3	100.6	88.7	62.4	71.0	97.7	55.7	69.5
0950, 0980	Ceilings & Acoustic Treatment	99.2	69.3	79.0	94.2	100.3	98.3	96.1	100.3	98.9	91.6	100.3	97.5	83.2	62.4	69.2	87.2	55.7	65.9
0960	Flooring	97.4	79.0	92.3	87.5	111.5	94.1	86.5	111.5	93.4	88.0	111.5	94.5	96.8	58.0	86.0	94.1	78.5	89.8
0970, 0990	Wall Finishes & Painting/Coating	103.1	74.9	86.7	88.0	110.6	101.2	86.7	110.6	100.6	83.9	110.6	99.5	94.7	62.4	75.8	87.8	63.1	73.3
09	FINISHES	96.3	72.8	83.5	92.2	104.0	98.6	88.9	104.0	97.1	91.7	104.0	98.4	88.2	61.9	73.9	88.7	60.9	73.6
COVERS	DIVS. 10 - 14, 25, 28, 41, 43, 44, 46	100.0	95.9	99.1	100.0	106.2	101.4	100.0	106.2	101.4	100.0	106.2	101.4	100.0	82.6	96.1	100.0	81.6	95.9
21, 22, 23	FIRE SUPPRESSION, PLUMBING & HVAC	100.0	89.9	95.7	100.0	122.0	109.4	100.2	122.0	109.5	100.0	122.0	109.4	99.9	76.4	89.8	99.9	58.9	82.4
26, 27, 3370	ELECTRICAL, COMMUNICATIONS & UTIL.	100.6	102.8	101.7	97.3	112.7	105.3	98.9	112.7	106.1	97.3	112.7	105.3	92.7	62.2	76.8	94.6	69.4	81.4
MF2016	WEIGHTED AVERAGE	101.1	87.6	95.2	98.0	112.4	104.3	97.9	112.4	104.3	97.6	112.5	104.1	94.9	71.0	84.4	95.1	66.0	82.4

City Cost Indexes

		FLORIDA																	
DIVISION		FORT MYERS			GAINESVILLE			JACKSONVILLE			LAKELAND			MELBOURNE			MIAMI		
		339, 341			326, 344			320, 322			338			329			330 - 332, 340		
		MAT.	INST.	TOTAL	MAT.	INST.	TOTAL	MAT.	INST.	TOTAL	MAT.	INST.	TOTAL	MAT.	INST.	TOTAL	MAT.	INST.	TOTAL
015433	CONTRACTOR EQUIPMENT		101.9	101.9		101.9	101.9		101.9	101.9		101.9	101.9		101.9	101.9		94.8	94.8
0241, 31 - 34	SITE & INFRASTRUCTURE, DEMOLITION	105.9	88.2	93.5	110.0	88.5	95.0	102.4	88.5	92.7	107.8	88.7	94.4	109.1	88.9	94.9	95.5	76.1	81.9
0310	Concrete Forming & Accessories	91.7	56.5	61.3	92.5	56.6	61.5	97.1	56.6	62.1	88.0	62.5	66.0	93.7	63.6	67.9	100.0	56.2	62.3
0320	Concrete Reinforcing	93.3	56.0	74.5	98.2	58.4	78.1	92.6	58.2	75.3	95.6	76.5	86.0	93.6	65.9	79.7	99.1	56.9	77.8
0330	Cast-in-Place Concrete	92.4	62.6	81.1	101.9	64.0	87.5	89.6	63.9	79.9	94.5	65.3	83.4	107.0	65.9	91.4	85.6	62.5	76.8
03	CONCRETE	88.0	60.4	75.4	97.0	61.4	80.7	86.8	61.3	75.2	89.6	67.6	79.6	97.5	66.6	83.4	85.8	60.5	74.2
04	MASONRY	88.4	63.5	73.0	103.0	56.6	74.2	89.4	54.1	67.6	104.5	58.8	76.2	87.5	59.6	70.2	95.0	54.4	69.8
05	METALS	96.8	87.2	93.8	94.9	87.9	92.8	94.6	87.7	92.5	96.7	94.3	95.9	104.1	91.0	100.1	95.2	86.8	92.6
06	WOOD, PLASTICS & COMPOSITES	87.2	56.4	70.0	94.4	55.5	72.8	100.5	55.5	75.5	82.4	62.1	71.1	96.1	62.9	77.6	96.2	56.4	74.0
07	THERMAL & MOISTURE PROTECTION	98.2	62.5	83.1	97.6	60.9	82.1	97.5	60.2	81.7	98.1	62.6	83.0	97.7	64.6	83.7	98.2	59.7	81.9
08	OPENINGS	97.4	56.0	87.9	94.9	56.2	86.0	95.3	56.2	86.3	97.3	64.0	89.7	94.5	64.6	87.6	98.8	56.3	89.0
0920	Plaster & Gypsum Board	93.8	55.7	68.2	85.5	54.8	64.9	88.7	54.8	65.9	90.5	61.6	71.1	85.5	62.4	70.0	87.7	55.7	66.2
0950, 0980	Ceilings & Acoustic Treatment	82.7	55.7	64.5	77.6	54.8	62.2	83.2	54.8	64.0	82.7	61.6	68.5	82.3	62.4	68.9	86.8	55.7	65.8
0960	Flooring	91.1	76.7	87.1	94.2	58.0	84.2	96.8	58.0	86.0	88.9	58.0	80.3	94.4	58.0	84.3	93.0	58.0	83.3
0970, 0990	Wall Finishes & Painting/Coating	91.7	63.0	75.0	94.7	62.4	75.8	94.7	63.0	76.2	91.7	63.0	75.0	94.7	83.5	88.2	85.8	63.1	72.5
09	FINISHES	88.4	60.5	73.2	86.6	56.7	70.4	88.2	56.8	71.1	87.4	61.2	73.2	87.4	64.2	74.8	87.5	56.7	70.7
COVERS	DIVS. 10 - 14, 25, 28, 41, 43, 44, 46	100.0	78.4	95.2	100.0	80.8	95.7	100.0	79.0	95.3	100.0	80.5	95.7	100.0	82.6	96.1	100.0	81.6	95.9
21, 22, 23	FIRE SUPPRESSION, PLUMBING & HVAC	98.2	57.0	80.6	98.7	61.9	82.9	99.9	61.9	83.6	98.2	59.5	81.7	99.9	76.4	89.8	99.9	57.3	81.7
26, 27, 3370	ELECTRICAL, COMMUNICATIONS & UTIL.	96.4	62.9	79.0	92.9	59.0	75.3	92.4	64.1	77.7	94.8	63.4	78.5	93.7	61.0	76.7	98.2	73.3	85.2
MF2016	WEIGHTED AVERAGE	95.4	65.4	82.3	96.4	65.0	82.7	94.7	65.3	81.8	96.2	67.8	83.7	97.6	71.2	86.0	95.6	64.6	82.0

		FLORIDA																	
DIVISION		ORLANDO			PANAMA CITY			PENSACOLA			SARASOTA			ST. PETERSBURG			TALLAHASSEE		
		327 - 328, 347			324			325			342			337			323		
		MAT.	INST.	TOTAL	MAT.	INST.	TOTAL	MAT.	INST.	TOTAL	MAT.	INST.	TOTAL	MAT.	INST.	TOTAL	MAT.	INST.	TOTAL
015433	CONTRACTOR EQUIPMENT		101.9	101.9		101.9	101.9		101.9	101.9		101.9	101.9		101.9	101.9		101.9	101.9
0241, 31 - 34	SITE & INFRASTRUCTURE, DEMOLITION	99.7	88.7	92.0	113.1	88.0	95.5	113.8	88.5	96.0	113.3	88.7	96.1	109.4	88.3	94.6	101.7	88.5	92.5
0310	Concrete Forming & Accessories	100.1	63.3	68.4	96.4	61.4	66.2	94.5	64.7	68.8	95.4	62.5	67.0	95.2	60.3	65.2	97.1	56.6	62.2
0320	Concrete Reinforcing	96.2	65.9	80.9	96.7	69.1	82.8	99.2	68.6	83.7	93.3	76.5	84.8	95.6	76.5	86.0	99.8	58.4	78.9
0330	Cast-in-Place Concrete	105.9	65.7	90.7	94.2	59.9	81.2	116.4	65.1	96.9	103.2	65.3	88.8	95.5	62.1	82.8	91.4	64.0	81.0
03	CONCRETE	94.1	66.3	81.4	95.1	64.0	80.9	104.9	67.2	87.7	95.2	67.6	82.6	91.1	65.5	79.4	88.3	61.4	76.0
04	MASONRY	95.3	59.6	73.2	94.1	58.6	72.1	114.3	58.7	79.8	92.0	58.8	71.4	144.1	53.2	87.7	91.7	56.6	69.9
05	METALS	95.2	90.6	93.8	95.8	92.1	94.6	96.8	91.4	95.1	98.7	94.3	97.4	97.6	93.2	96.3	92.3	87.9	91.0
06	WOOD, PLASTICS & COMPOSITES	89.8	62.9	74.9	99.3	65.4	80.4	97.3	65.4	79.5	98.1	62.1	78.1	91.7	62.1	75.2	96.0	55.5	73.5
07	THERMAL & MOISTURE PROTECTION	100.0	65.8	85.5	97.8	59.9	81.8	97.7	63.0	83.0	98.2	62.6	83.1	98.3	60.0	82.1	96.9	60.8	81.7
08	OPENINGS	98.1	62.0	89.8	93.3	64.0	86.6	93.3	64.0	86.6	99.5	64.0	91.3	96.1	63.6	88.6	100.1	56.2	90.0
0920	Plaster & Gypsum Board	94.7	62.4	73.0	87.8	64.9	72.4	95.5	64.9	75.0	94.7	61.6	72.5	96.1	61.6	72.9	93.3	54.8	67.4
0950, 0980	Ceilings & Acoustic Treatment	89.4	62.4	71.2	82.3	64.9	70.6	82.3	64.9	70.6	87.1	61.6	69.9	84.6	61.6	69.1	87.9	54.8	65.6
0960	Flooring	91.3	58.0	82.1	96.3	76.7	90.9	92.2	58.0	82.7	101.4	58.0	89.4	93.0	58.0	83.3	92.9	58.0	83.2
0970, 0990	Wall Finishes & Painting/Coating	93.4	63.0	75.7	94.7	60.6	74.8	94.7	62.4	75.8	96.3	63.0	76.9	91.7	63.6	75.3	91.9	63.0	75.1
09	FINISHES	90.4	61.9	74.9	88.8	64.3	75.5	88.4	63.1	74.6	94.3	61.2	76.3	89.9	59.9	73.6	89.8	56.8	71.8
COVERS	DIVS. 10 - 14, 25, 28, 41, 43, 44, 46	100.0	82.6	96.1	100.0	78.0	95.1	100.0	81.1	95.8	100.0	80.5	95.7	100.0	78.6	95.2	100.0	78.6	95.2
21, 22, 23	FIRE SUPPRESSION, PLUMBING & HVAC	100.0	57.8	81.9	99.9	51.9	79.4	99.9	63.0	84.1	99.9	59.5	82.6	99.9	56.6	81.4	99.9	67.8	86.2
26, 27, 3370	ELECTRICAL, COMMUNICATIONS & UTIL.	96.6	62.7	78.9	91.6	59.0	74.6	94.8	53.5	73.3	95.7	63.9	79.2	94.8	64.0	78.8	96.7	59.0	77.1
MF2016	WEIGHTED AVERAGE	96.8	67.0	83.8	96.2	65.1	82.5	98.8	67.1	84.9	98.1	67.9	84.9	99.0	65.9	84.5	95.6	66.2	82.7

		FLORIDA						GEORGIA											
DIVISION		TAMPA			WEST PALM BEACH			ALBANY			ATHENS			ATLANTA			AUGUSTA		
		335 - 336, 346			334, 349			317, 398			306			300 - 303, 399			308 - 309		
		MAT.	INST.	TOTAL	MAT.	INST.	TOTAL	MAT.	INST.	TOTAL	MAT.	INST.	TOTAL	MAT.	INST.	TOTAL	MAT.	INST.	TOTAL
015433	CONTRACTOR EQUIPMENT		101.9	101.9		94.8	94.8		95.7	95.7		94.5	94.5		96.4	96.4		94.5	94.5
0241, 31 - 34	SITE & INFRASTRUCTURE, DEMOLITION	109.9	88.7	95.1	91.1	76.1	80.6	104.3	79.0	86.6	102.6	95.1	97.3	99.4	95.3	96.5	95.6	95.4	95.5
0310	Concrete Forming & Accessories	98.3	62.4	67.4	99.4	56.3	62.2	94.0	68.9	72.4	91.4	45.1	51.5	96.0	71.7	75.1	92.5	72.9	75.6
0320	Concrete Reinforcing	92.3	76.5	84.3	94.9	56.9	75.7	88.1	71.9	79.9	102.0	65.6	83.6	101.2	72.0	86.5	102.4	68.1	85.1
0330	Cast-in-Place Concrete	93.4	65.3	82.7	84.2	62.5	76.0	88.3	69.0	81.0	109.3	69.9	94.3	112.7	71.4	97.0	103.3	70.2	90.7
03	CONCRETE	89.8	67.6	79.7	84.4	60.5	73.5	86.4	71.2	79.5	104.9	58.6	83.7	107.1	72.4	91.2	97.3	71.8	85.6
04	MASONRY	95.7	58.8	72.8	94.3	54.4	69.5	92.2	69.2	77.9	78.5	79.4	79.1	91.9	69.4	77.9	92.2	69.3	78.0
05	METALS	96.7	94.3	96.0	93.9	86.8	91.7	97.8	98.0	97.9	93.1	80.0	89.1	93.9	85.1	91.2	92.8	81.3	89.3
06	WOOD, PLASTICS & COMPOSITES	95.7	62.1	77.0	95.3	56.4	73.6	85.9	69.6	76.8	97.0	37.4	63.9	99.2	73.1	84.7	98.5	75.3	85.6
07	THERMAL & MOISTURE PROTECTION	98.6	62.6	83.3	98.1	61.3	82.5	97.3	68.9	85.3	97.9	70.2	86.2	99.4	72.4	88.0	97.7	71.7	86.7
08	OPENINGS	97.4	64.0	89.7	95.7	56.3	86.7	87.7	71.6	84.0	93.1	52.0	83.6	97.6	73.5	92.1	93.1	73.8	88.7
0920	Plaster & Gypsum Board	98.4	61.6	73.7	102.1	55.7	70.9	103.6	69.3	80.5	93.6	36.1	55.0	96.0	72.5	80.2	94.9	75.0	81.6
0950, 0980	Ceilings & Acoustic Treatment	87.2	61.6	69.9	82.7	55.7	64.5	83.8	69.3	74.0	98.8	36.1	56.6	91.6	72.5	78.7	99.8	75.0	83.1
0960	Flooring	94.1	58.0	84.1	95.9	58.0	85.4	96.9	67.4	88.7	95.8	86.6	93.3	98.8	67.4	90.1	96.0	67.4	88.1
0970, 0990	Wall Finishes & Painting/Coating	91.7	63.0	75.0	87.8	62.4	72.9	89.1	95.9	93.1	97.5	95.9	96.6	101.3	95.9	98.2	97.5	80.4	87.5
09	FINISHES	91.1	61.2	74.9	88.7	56.7	71.3	92.2	71.1	80.7	96.2	56.0	74.4	96.3	73.2	83.7	96.0	72.8	83.4
COVERS	DIVS. 10 - 14, 25, 28, 41, 43, 44, 46	100.0	80.5	95.7	100.0	81.6	95.9	100.0	84.9	96.6	100.0	81.2	95.8	100.0	86.0	96.9	100.0	85.3	96.7
21, 22, 23	FIRE SUPPRESSION, PLUMBING & HVAC	99.9	59.5	82.6	98.2	56.8	80.5	99.9	71.1	87.6	97.0	68.5	84.8	100.0	70.1	87.2	100.1	69.2	86.9
26, 27, 3370	ELECTRICAL, COMMUNICATIONS & UTIL.	94.5	62.2	77.7	95.6	69.4	81.9	95.0	63.6	78.7	99.1	67.5	82.7	98.5	71.4	84.4	99.7	70.5	84.5
MF2016	WEIGHTED AVERAGE	96.6	67.0	83.9	94.2	64.0	81.0	95.0	73.4	85.5	96.6	69.1	84.5	98.7	75.0	88.3	96.6	74.2	86.9

City Cost Indexes

DIVISION		COLUMBUS 318-319 MAT.	INST.	TOTAL	DALTON 307 MAT.	INST.	TOTAL	GAINESVILLE 305 MAT.	INST.	TOTAL	MACON 310-312 MAT.	INST.	TOTAL	SAVANNAH 313-314 MAT.	INST.	TOTAL	STATESBORO 304 MAT.	INST.	TOTAL
							GEORGIA												
015433	CONTRACTOR EQUIPMENT		95.7	95.7		110.4	110.4		94.5	94.5		105.7	105.7		96.6	96.6		97.6	97.6
0241, 31 - 34	SITE & INFRASTRUCTURE, DEMOLITION	104.2	79.1	86.6	102.0	100.6	101.0	102.5	95.0	97.2	106.0	94.5	97.9	104.0	80.6	87.6	103.2	81.3	87.8
0310	Concrete Forming & Accessories	93.9	69.0	72.4	84.4	66.7	69.1	94.9	42.5	49.7	93.6	69.1	72.5	96.1	71.8	75.2	79.2	53.1	56.7
0320	Concrete Reinforcing	87.9	71.9	79.9	101.4	62.7	81.9	101.8	65.5	83.4	89.1	72.0	80.4	94.7	68.2	81.3	101.0	36.7	68.5
0330	Cast-in-Place Concrete	88.0	69.1	80.8	106.2	68.5	91.9	114.9	69.7	97.7	86.8	70.4	80.6	91.7	68.9	83.1	109.1	68.6	93.7
03	CONCRETE	86.2	71.3	79.4	104.1	68.5	87.8	106.7	57.3	84.1	85.8	71.8	79.4	87.7	71.9	80.4	104.5	57.8	83.2
04	MASONRY	92.2	69.2	77.9	79.6	78.7	79.1	87.0	79.4	82.3	104.5	69.3	82.7	87.2	69.2	76.0	81.6	79.4	80.2
05	METALS	97.4	98.3	97.7	94.1	94.7	94.3	92.4	79.4	88.4	93.1	98.4	94.7	94.2	96.4	94.9	97.6	84.9	93.7
06	WOOD, PLASTICS & COMPOSITES	85.9	69.6	76.8	79.7	68.3	73.3	100.8	34.7	64.0	92.6	69.6	79.8	90.3	73.6	81.0	73.6	49.3	60.1
07	THERMAL & MOISTURE PROTECTION	97.2	70.5	85.9	100.0	72.4	88.3	97.9	69.9	86.0	95.7	72.7	85.9	95.3	70.1	84.6	98.6	69.5	86.3
08	OPENINGS	87.7	71.6	84.0	94.1	68.3	88.2	93.1	50.5	83.3	87.5	71.6	83.8	94.4	72.9	89.4	95.0	50.5	84.8
0920	Plaster & Gypsum Board	103.6	69.3	80.5	82.4	67.8	72.6	95.9	33.3	53.9	109.5	69.3	82.5	98.9	73.4	81.8	82.3	48.4	59.6
0950, 0980	Ceilings & Acoustic Treatment	83.8	69.3	74.0	113.1	67.8	82.6	98.8	33.3	54.7	79.0	69.3	72.4	90.3	73.4	78.9	109.4	48.4	68.3
0960	Flooring	96.9	67.4	88.7	96.6	86.6	93.8	97.4	86.6	94.4	76.4	67.4	73.9	92.5	67.4	85.6	113.6	86.6	106.1
0970, 0990	Wall Finishes & Painting/Coating	89.1	95.9	93.1	87.6	73.2	79.2	97.5	95.9	96.6	91.1	95.9	93.9	88.3	87.9	88.1	95.3	73.2	82.4
09	FINISHES	92.1	71.1	80.7	105.3	71.6	87.0	96.9	54.4	73.8	81.9	71.1	76.0	92.1	72.6	81.5	108.8	60.6	82.6
COVERS	DIVS. 10 - 14, 25, 28, 41, 43, 44, 46	100.0	85.0	96.7	100.0	28.8	84.2	100.0	36.8	85.9	100.0	85.0	96.7	100.0	85.0	96.7	100.0	42.9	87.3
21, 22, 23	FIRE SUPPRESSION, PLUMBING & HVAC	100.0	67.4	86.1	97.1	63.2	82.6	97.0	68.3	84.7	100.0	70.5	87.4	100.1	68.3	86.5	97.6	69.1	85.4
26, 27, 3370	ELECTRICAL, COMMUNICATIONS & UTIL.	95.2	71.5	82.9	107.6	65.7	85.8	99.1	71.4	84.7	93.9	66.2	79.5	98.7	72.4	85.0	99.3	55.7	76.6
MF2016	WEIGHTED AVERAGE	94.9	73.8	85.7	98.3	72.2	86.9	97.2	67.6	84.2	93.8	75.1	85.6	95.4	74.4	86.2	98.7	66.3	84.5

DIVISION		VALDOSTA 316 MAT.	INST.	TOTAL	WAYCROSS 315 MAT.	INST.	TOTAL	HILO 967 MAT.	INST.	TOTAL	HONOLULU 968 MAT.	INST.	TOTAL	STATES & POSS., GUAM 969 MAT.	INST.	TOTAL	BOISE 836-837 MAT.	INST.	TOTAL
		GEORGIA						HAWAII									IDAHO		
015433	CONTRACTOR EQUIPMENT		95.7	95.7		95.7	95.7		99.3	99.3		99.3	99.3		165.6	165.6		97.4	97.4
0241, 31 - 34	SITE & INFRASTRUCTURE, DEMOLITION	113.8	79.0	89.4	110.6	80.3	89.4	156.3	106.9	121.7	164.8	106.9	124.2	201.3	102.9	132.3	88.9	96.8	94.5
0310	Concrete Forming & Accessories	84.4	42.8	48.5	86.4	65.9	68.7	107.6	122.5	120.4	118.4	122.5	121.9	110.0	53.9	61.7	98.7	81.3	83.7
0320	Concrete Reinforcing	90.0	61.4	75.5	90.0	61.6	75.7	133.0	113.9	123.4	154.7	113.9	134.1	243.0	28.2	134.7	101.6	77.6	89.5
0330	Cast-in-Place Concrete	86.5	68.9	79.8	97.7	68.7	86.7	194.4	122.0	166.9	156.3	122.0	143.3	168.5	100.5	142.7	90.5	84.8	88.3
03	CONCRETE	91.1	57.5	75.7	94.1	67.7	82.0	151.7	119.9	137.1	142.6	119.8	132.2	153.7	66.6	113.9	96.1	82.0	89.7
04	MASONRY	97.6	79.4	86.3	98.5	79.4	86.7	153.6	121.4	133.6	140.0	121.4	128.5	217.5	36.2	105.2	125.6	89.0	102.9
05	METALS	97.0	94.1	96.1	96.0	89.7	94.1	112.9	102.3	109.6	125.9	102.3	118.7	145.3	77.1	124.4	108.1	82.1	100.1
06	WOOD, PLASTICS & COMPOSITES	74.1	34.5	52.0	75.7	66.4	70.5	114.9	122.4	119.1	129.4	122.4	125.5	126.7	56.3	87.5	92.4	79.9	85.5
07	THERMAL & MOISTURE PROTECTION	97.5	68.6	85.3	97.2	71.1	86.2	130.8	119.0	125.8	148.7	119.0	136.1	153.9	60.9	114.5	94.3	86.3	90.9
08	OPENINGS	84.3	49.2	76.2	84.6	64.2	79.9	117.0	118.9	117.5	131.8	118.9	128.6	121.6	45.9	104.3	97.1	74.3	91.9
0920	Plaster & Gypsum Board	95.7	33.2	53.7	95.7	66.0	75.8	108.1	122.9	118.0	151.3	122.9	132.2	216.4	44.6	101.0	92.4	79.4	83.7
0950, 0980	Ceilings & Acoustic Treatment	81.3	33.2	48.8	79.4	66.0	70.3	131.5	122.9	125.7	140.9	122.9	128.8	246.8	44.6	110.5	102.4	79.4	86.9
0960	Flooring	90.9	88.2	90.2	92.0	86.6	90.5	107.3	136.7	115.5	125.7	136.7	128.8	126.6	41.8	103.1	93.8	81.4	90.4
0970, 0990	Wall Finishes & Painting/Coating	89.1	95.9	93.1	89.1	73.2	79.8	95.6	137.2	119.9	103.4	137.2	123.1	100.4	33.0	61.1	93.6	41.3	63.1
09	FINISHES	89.8	54.6	70.6	89.3	70.6	79.2	108.7	127.1	118.7	124.8	127.1	126.1	178.9	50.4	109.0	92.7	77.2	84.3
COVERS	DIVS. 10 - 14, 25, 28, 41, 43, 44, 46	100.0	80.6	95.7	100.0	50.7	89.0	100.0	112.7	102.7	100.0	112.7	102.7	100.0	68.5	93.0	100.0	90.4	97.9
21, 22, 23	FIRE SUPPRESSION, PLUMBING & HVAC	100.0	70.6	87.4	98.1	65.4	84.1	100.5	109.4	104.3	100.5	109.4	104.3	103.5	34.9	74.2	100.1	74.9	89.3
26, 27, 3370	ELECTRICAL, COMMUNICATIONS & UTIL.	93.5	54.6	73.2	97.3	55.7	75.6	105.3	121.7	113.9	106.9	121.7	114.6	151.8	37.9	92.6	97.9	67.8	82.2
MF2016	WEIGHTED AVERAGE	95.1	67.3	82.9	95.3	69.5	84.0	116.9	116.0	116.5	121.1	116.0	118.9	139.1	53.4	101.6	100.5	79.8	91.4

DIVISION		COEUR D'ALENE 838 MAT.	INST.	TOTAL	IDAHO FALLS 834 MAT.	INST.	TOTAL	LEWISTON 835 MAT.	INST.	TOTAL	POCATELLO 832 MAT.	INST.	TOTAL	TWIN FALLS 833 MAT.	INST.	TOTAL	BLOOMINGTON 617 MAT.	INST.	TOTAL
		IDAHO															ILLINOIS		
015433	CONTRACTOR EQUIPMENT		92.2	92.2		97.4	97.4		92.2	92.2		97.4	97.4		97.4	97.4		105.2	105.2
0241, 31 - 34	SITE & INFRASTRUCTURE, DEMOLITION	87.9	90.9	90.0	86.5	96.8	93.7	94.7	91.8	92.7	89.9	96.8	94.7	97.0	96.6	96.7	95.7	100.5	99.1
0310	Concrete Forming & Accessories	108.9	79.6	83.6	92.8	80.1	81.8	113.9	81.6	86.0	98.8	80.9	83.4	100.0	79.9	82.7	83.4	119.9	114.9
0320	Concrete Reinforcing	110.0	99.2	104.6	103.8	77.7	90.6	110.0	99.3	104.6	102.1	77.7	89.7	104.1	77.7	90.7	96.1	105.6	100.9
0330	Cast-in-Place Concrete	97.8	82.6	92.0	86.2	83.2	85.0	101.7	86.0	95.7	93.0	84.7	89.9	95.5	83.1	90.8	97.7	117.5	105.2
03	CONCRETE	102.6	84.2	94.2	88.3	80.9	84.9	106.0	86.2	97.0	95.3	81.8	89.1	102.9	80.8	92.8	93.2	117.2	104.2
04	MASONRY	127.3	85.4	101.3	120.4	86.3	99.4	127.7	87.7	102.9	123.1	89.0	102.0	125.9	86.4	101.4	115.2	122.8	119.9
05	METALS	101.6	99.5	100.9	116.4	81.9	105.8	101.0	89.8	97.6	116.5	81.8	105.8	116.5	81.7	105.8	99.9	125.4	107.7
06	WOOD, PLASTICS & COMPOSITES	97.5	78.4	86.8	86.7	79.9	82.9	102.5	79.4	89.8	92.4	79.9	85.5	93.5	79.9	85.9	86.7	118.5	104.4
07	THERMAL & MOISTURE PROTECTION	147.3	83.8	120.4	93.5	76.4	86.3	147.6	85.5	121.4	94.0	77.2	86.9	94.9	83.3	90.0	96.9	115.8	104.9
08	OPENINGS	114.3	76.9	105.7	100.1	74.3	94.1	108.0	80.9	101.8	97.8	69.2	91.2	100.9	64.9	92.6	94.5	124.8	101.5
0920	Plaster & Gypsum Board	166.3	77.9	107.0	77.5	79.4	78.8	168.0	79.0	108.2	79.4	79.4	79.4	81.0	79.4	79.9	92.8	119.1	110.4
0950, 0980	Ceilings & Acoustic Treatment	136.6	77.9	97.1	103.2	79.4	87.1	136.6	79.0	97.8	110.0	79.4	89.4	105.7	79.4	88.0	89.2	119.1	109.3
0960	Flooring	132.6	81.4	118.4	93.4	81.4	90.1	136.1	81.4	120.9	97.1	81.4	92.7	98.3	81.4	93.7	84.6	126.3	96.2
0970, 0990	Wall Finishes & Painting/Coating	112.8	75.9	91.3	93.6	41.3	63.1	112.8	75.9	91.3	93.6	41.3	63.0	93.6	41.3	63.1	85.6	140.9	117.8
09	FINISHES	155.8	79.2	114.1	90.3	76.5	82.8	157.2	80.4	115.4	93.4	77.2	84.6	93.9	76.5	84.5	86.9	123.7	106.9
COVERS	DIVS. 10 - 14, 25, 28, 41, 43, 44, 46	100.0	95.0	98.9	100.0	89.5	97.7	100.0	95.9	99.1	100.0	90.4	97.9	100.0	89.5	97.7	100.0	107.6	101.7
21, 22, 23	FIRE SUPPRESSION, PLUMBING & HVAC	99.6	83.2	92.6	100.9	72.3	88.7	100.9	88.1	95.4	99.9	74.8	89.2	99.9	70.1	87.2	96.9	107.5	101.4
26, 27, 3370	ELECTRICAL, COMMUNICATIONS & UTIL.	90.2	86.1	88.1	89.9	68.2	78.6	88.4	82.6	85.4	95.4	69.7	82.0	91.3	68.2	79.3	95.6	95.4	95.5
MF2016	WEIGHTED AVERAGE	108.1	84.7	97.8	100.0	78.5	90.6	108.2	86.3	98.6	101.5	79.5	91.9	102.8	77.8	91.8	96.8	113.0	103.9

City Cost Indexes

ILLINOIS

DIVISION		CARBONDALE 629 MAT.	INST.	TOTAL	CENTRALIA 628 MAT.	INST.	TOTAL	CHAMPAIGN 618 - 619 MAT.	INST.	TOTAL	CHICAGO 606 - 608 MAT.	INST.	TOTAL	DECATUR 625 MAT.	INST.	TOTAL	EAST ST. LOUIS 620 - 622 MAT.	INST.	TOTAL
015433	CONTRACTOR EQUIPMENT		114.0	114.0		114.0	114.0		106.1	106.1		100.2	100.2		106.1	106.1		114.0	114.0
0241, 31 - 34	SITE & INFRASTRUCTURE, DEMOLITION	100.6	101.6	101.3	100.9	102.3	101.9	104.7	101.6	102.5	101.9	104.4	103.6	97.6	101.8	100.5	102.9	102.4	102.5
0310	Concrete Forming & Accessories	90.5	106.1	104.0	92.1	110.8	108.3	89.6	117.8	113.9	99.8	160.4	152.0	92.6	118.2	114.7	88.0	111.9	108.6
0320	Concrete Reinforcing	98.3	102.6	100.5	98.3	102.8	100.6	96.1	100.9	98.6	104.7	150.8	128.0	96.3	101.2	98.8	98.2	103.1	100.7
0330	Cast-in-Place Concrete	90.8	103.6	95.7	91.3	117.2	101.1	113.3	112.9	113.2	123.6	153.6	135.0	99.2	116.5	105.8	92.8	118.0	102.4
03	CONCRETE	83.1	106.3	93.7	83.5	113.2	97.1	105.5	113.8	109.3	109.9	155.7	130.8	93.5	115.2	103.4	84.6	114.0	98.0
04	MASONRY	78.1	109.9	97.8	78.1	112.4	99.4	139.8	121.5	128.5	102.6	164.9	141.2	73.8	122.8	104.2	78.3	117.2	102.4
05	METALS	97.8	130.5	107.9	97.9	132.9	108.6	99.9	121.7	106.6	97.9	146.9	113.0	101.6	121.2	107.6	99.0	133.3	109.5
06	WOOD, PLASTICS & COMPOSITES	90.9	102.7	97.5	93.3	108.3	101.6	93.2	117.1	106.5	104.2	160.0	135.3	91.2	117.1	105.6	88.4	108.9	99.8
07	THERMAL & MOISTURE PROTECTION	93.9	101.4	97.1	93.9	108.0	99.9	97.7	114.6	104.9	96.7	150.2	119.3	99.6	113.2	105.4	94.0	107.6	99.7
08	OPENINGS	89.4	115.7	95.4	89.4	118.8	96.1	95.1	119.4	100.7	109.1	170.3	117.6	100.5	119.5	104.9	89.4	119.1	96.2
0920	Plaster & Gypsum Board	97.3	102.9	101.1	98.3	108.6	105.2	94.7	117.6	110.1	103.3	161.7	142.5	99.7	117.6	111.7	96.3	109.2	105.0
0950, 0980	Ceilings & Acoustic Treatment	87.5	102.9	97.9	87.5	108.6	101.7	89.2	117.6	108.3	102.2	161.7	142.3	93.4	117.6	109.7	87.5	109.2	102.1
0960	Flooring	107.2	116.4	109.8	108.0	112.1	109.2	87.8	117.3	96.0	94.4	163.4	113.5	96.1	117.8	102.2	106.2	112.1	107.9
0970, 0990	Wall Finishes & Painting/Coating	94.5	104.8	100.5	94.5	115.2	106.6	85.6	117.6	104.2	101.4	162.5	137.0	86.5	111.6	101.1	94.5	115.2	106.6
09	FINISHES	91.6	106.6	99.7	92.0	111.1	102.4	88.8	118.3	104.9	99.3	162.1	133.4	91.4	118.1	105.9	91.2	112.4	102.7
COVERS	DIVS. 10 - 14, 25, 28, 41, 43, 44, 46	100.0	103.4	100.8	100.0	104.2	100.9	100.0	106.6	101.5	100.0	127.1	106.0	100.0	107.1	101.6	100.0	104.6	101.0
21, 22, 23	FIRE SUPPRESSION, PLUMBING & HVAC	96.9	105.8	100.7	96.9	94.1	95.7	96.9	105.1	100.4	100.0	138.4	116.4	100.1	98.2	99.3	100.0	97.7	99.0
26, 27, 3370	ELECTRICAL, COMMUNICATIONS & UTIL.	94.9	107.4	101.4	96.2	107.4	102.0	98.7	95.4	97.0	96.4	135.5	116.7	98.6	92.6	95.5	95.8	100.5	98.2
MF2016	WEIGHTED AVERAGE	93.2	108.8	100.0	93.4	108.8	100.1	100.3	110.6	104.8	100.0	145.8	120.5	97.3	109.0	102.4	94.4	109.4	100.9

ILLINOIS

DIVISION		EFFINGHAM 624 MAT.	INST.	TOTAL	GALESBURG 614 MAT.	INST.	TOTAL	JOLIET 604 MAT.	INST.	TOTAL	KANKAKEE 609 MAT.	INST.	TOTAL	LA SALLE 613 MAT.	INST.	TOTAL	NORTH SUBURBAN 600 - 603 MAT.	INST.	TOTAL
015433	CONTRACTOR EQUIPMENT		106.1	106.1		105.2	105.2		96.6	96.6		96.6	96.6		105.2	105.2		96.6	96.6
0241, 31 - 34	SITE & INFRASTRUCTURE, DEMOLITION	101.3	100.6	100.8	98.1	100.1	99.5	97.6	102.8	101.3	91.6	102.0	98.9	97.5	101.1	100.0	96.9	102.6	100.9
0310	Concrete Forming & Accessories	97.1	116.3	113.7	89.5	118.9	114.9	99.1	158.3	150.1	92.7	141.6	134.9	103.1	122.5	119.8	98.4	153.7	146.1
0320	Concrete Reinforcing	99.5	92.1	95.8	95.6	102.9	99.2	104.7	141.0	123.0	105.6	134.9	120.4	95.8	133.8	115.0	104.7	146.1	125.6
0330	Cast-in-Place Concrete	98.8	111.0	103.4	100.6	106.8	103.0	112.4	152.0	127.4	104.8	139.2	117.8	100.5	126.1	110.3	112.5	150.1	126.7
03	CONCRETE	94.3	110.8	101.8	96.0	112.6	103.6	102.8	152.2	125.4	96.7	139.1	116.1	96.8	126.5	110.4	102.8	150.4	124.6
04	MASONRY	82.0	115.2	102.6	115.4	120.6	118.6	101.8	163.4	140.0	98.1	147.8	128.9	115.4	145.7	134.2	98.6	159.1	136.2
05	METALS	98.7	114.1	103.4	99.9	122.9	107.0	95.9	138.4	108.9	95.9	133.9	107.5	100.0	143.1	113.2	97.0	140.1	110.2
06	WOOD, PLASTICS & COMPOSITES	93.5	117.1	106.6	93.0	118.6	107.3	102.9	157.3	133.2	96.1	139.8	120.4	107.7	119.5	114.3	101.3	152.6	129.8
07	THERMAL & MOISTURE PROTECTION	99.1	110.2	103.8	97.1	110.0	102.6	101.1	149.2	121.5	100.2	138.3	116.3	97.3	124.0	108.6	101.4	144.3	119.6
08	OPENINGS	95.3	116.0	100.0	94.5	117.3	99.7	99.5	165.7	114.7	92.7	153.2	106.6	94.5	133.5	103.5	99.6	163.8	114.3
0920	Plaster & Gypsum Board	99.6	117.6	111.7	94.7	119.3	111.2	96.1	159.0	138.3	94.1	141.0	125.6	101.7	120.1	114.1	99.1	154.1	136.0
0950, 0980	Ceilings & Acoustic Treatment	87.5	117.6	107.8	89.2	119.3	109.4	101.8	159.0	140.3	101.8	141.0	128.2	89.2	120.1	110.1	101.8	154.1	137.1
0960	Flooring	97.2	110.9	101.0	87.6	126.3	98.3	92.4	158.3	110.7	89.3	159.3	108.7	94.2	125.7	102.9	92.9	158.3	111.0
0970, 0990	Wall Finishes & Painting/Coating	86.5	109.3	99.8	85.6	99.9	93.9	93.5	170.4	138.4	93.5	140.9	121.2	85.6	139.1	116.8	95.5	159.5	132.9
09	FINISHES	90.6	115.7	104.3	88.2	119.2	105.1	94.7	160.6	130.6	93.2	145.2	121.4	91.1	123.5	108.7	95.4	156.0	128.3
COVERS	DIVS. 10 - 14, 25, 28, 41, 43, 44, 46	100.0	78.1	95.1	100.0	102.4	100.5	100.0	126.9	106.0	100.0	116.9	103.8	100.0	103.1	100.7	100.0	120.6	104.6
21, 22, 23	FIRE SUPPRESSION, PLUMBING & HVAC	97.0	104.2	100.1	96.9	105.2	100.5	100.0	135.4	115.2	96.9	129.7	111.0	96.9	123.8	108.4	99.9	133.2	114.2
26, 27, 3370	ELECTRICAL, COMMUNICATIONS & UTIL.	96.5	107.3	102.2	96.5	86.4	91.2	95.6	127.2	112.0	91.0	126.4	109.5	93.7	126.5	110.8	95.5	132.0	114.5
MF2016	WEIGHTED AVERAGE	95.8	108.7	101.5	97.4	108.9	102.5	98.8	142.0	117.7	95.6	133.5	112.2	97.6	126.5	110.3	98.9	140.6	117.1

ILLINOIS

DIVISION		PEORIA 615 - 616 MAT.	INST.	TOTAL	QUINCY 623 MAT.	INST.	TOTAL	ROCK ISLAND 612 MAT.	INST.	TOTAL	ROCKFORD 610 - 611 MAT.	INST.	TOTAL	SOUTH SUBURBAN 605 MAT.	INST.	TOTAL	SPRINGFIELD 626 - 627 MAT.	INST.	TOTAL
015433	CONTRACTOR EQUIPMENT		105.2	105.2		106.1	106.1		105.2	105.2		105.2	105.2		96.6	96.6		106.1	106.1
0241, 31 - 34	SITE & INFRASTRUCTURE, DEMOLITION	98.4	100.6	99.9	100.2	101.1	100.8	96.2	99.6	98.6	97.9	102.0	100.8	96.9	102.3	100.7	101.2	101.6	101.5
0310	Concrete Forming & Accessories	92.3	120.3	116.4	95.0	114.5	111.8	91.0	102.7	101.1	96.5	132.2	127.3	98.4	153.7	146.1	93.3	117.8	114.4
0320	Concrete Reinforcing	93.2	103.0	98.1	99.1	84.5	91.7	95.6	96.2	95.9	88.2	128.6	108.6	104.7	146.1	125.6	99.6	101.2	100.4
0330	Cast-in-Place Concrete	97.6	120.0	106.1	99.0	101.6	100.0	98.4	102.1	99.8	99.9	131.2	111.8	112.5	150.1	126.7	94.1	110.7	100.4
03	CONCRETE	93.3	117.8	104.5	93.9	105.5	99.2	94.0	102.5	97.8	94.0	131.7	111.2	102.8	150.4	124.6	91.7	113.1	101.4
04	MASONRY	114.5	123.6	120.2	105.4	111.0	108.9	115.2	101.9	106.9	89.1	139.1	120.1	98.6	159.1	136.2	84.6	121.6	107.5
05	METALS	102.6	124.2	109.3	98.7	112.4	102.9	99.9	118.7	105.7	102.6	140.4	114.2	97.0	140.1	110.2	99.1	121.3	105.9
06	WOOD, PLASTICS & COMPOSITES	100.5	118.6	110.6	91.1	117.1	105.5	94.6	102.2	98.8	100.5	129.6	116.7	101.3	152.6	129.8	92.2	117.1	106.1
07	THERMAL & MOISTURE PROTECTION	97.8	116.6	105.8	99.1	105.4	101.8	97.1	100.7	98.6	100.2	132.0	113.7	101.4	144.3	119.6	101.6	114.6	107.1
08	OPENINGS	100.6	124.1	106.0	96.0	113.6	100.0	94.5	106.7	97.3	100.6	140.6	109.7	99.6	163.8	114.3	98.8	118.8	103.4
0920	Plaster & Gypsum Board	98.5	119.3	112.4	98.3	117.6	111.3	94.7	102.4	99.9	98.5	130.5	120.0	99.1	154.1	136.0	100.8	117.6	112.1
0950, 0980	Ceilings & Acoustic Treatment	94.3	119.3	111.1	87.5	117.6	107.8	89.2	102.4	98.1	94.3	130.5	118.7	101.8	154.1	137.1	94.7	117.6	110.2
0960	Flooring	91.1	126.3	100.9	96.1	114.1	101.1	88.7	98.2	91.4	91.1	125.7	100.7	92.9	158.3	111.0	99.3	117.8	104.4
0970, 0990	Wall Finishes & Painting/Coating	85.6	140.9	117.8	86.5	115.2	103.2	85.6	99.9	93.9	85.6	149.2	122.7	95.5	159.5	132.9	84.7	115.2	102.5
09	FINISHES	90.8	123.9	108.8	90.1	115.7	104.0	88.4	101.4	95.5	90.8	132.6	113.6	95.4	156.0	128.3	96.9	118.1	108.4
COVERS	DIVS. 10 - 14, 25, 28, 41, 43, 44, 46	100.0	107.8	101.7	100.0	79.3	95.4	100.0	100.7	100.1	100.0	116.0	103.6	100.0	120.6	104.6	100.0	106.6	101.5
21, 22, 23	FIRE SUPPRESSION, PLUMBING & HVAC	100.0	102.7	101.1	97.0	101.5	98.9	96.9	100.1	98.3	100.1	118.6	108.0	99.9	133.2	114.2	100.0	103.0	101.3
26, 27, 3370	ELECTRICAL, COMMUNICATIONS & UTIL.	97.5	96.6	97.0	94.1	86.8	90.3	89.0	93.8	91.5	97.7	132.6	115.9	95.5	132.0	114.5	101.1	86.8	93.7
MF2016	WEIGHTED AVERAGE	99.3	112.2	104.9	96.7	103.9	99.8	96.4	101.9	98.8	98.2	128.3	111.4	98.9	140.6	117.1	97.8	108.8	102.6

City Cost Indexes

INDIANA

DIVISION		ANDERSON 460 MAT.	INST.	TOTAL	BLOOMINGTON 474 MAT.	INST.	TOTAL	COLUMBUS 472 MAT.	INST.	TOTAL	EVANSVILLE 476 - 477 MAT.	INST.	TOTAL	FORT WAYNE 467 - 468 MAT.	INST.	TOTAL	GARY 463 - 464 MAT.	INST.	TOTAL
015433	CONTRACTOR EQUIPMENT		96.7	96.7		83.4	83.4		83.4	83.4		113.9	113.9		96.7	96.7		96.7	96.7
0241, 31 - 34	SITE & INFRASTRUCTURE, DEMOLITION	97.9	93.4	94.7	87.8	92.1	90.8	84.4	91.9	89.7	93.4	121.8	113.3	98.9	93.2	94.9	98.5	97.1	97.5
0310	Concrete Forming & Accessories	94.6	81.2	83.0	99.0	81.6	84.0	93.2	79.1	81.0	92.6	82.3	83.7	92.7	74.8	77.3	94.7	114.8	112.1
0320	Concrete Reinforcing	90.1	85.7	87.8	87.1	85.3	86.2	87.5	85.4	86.4	95.4	78.6	86.9	90.1	77.1	83.5	90.1	113.1	101.7
0330	Cast-in-Place Concrete	100.6	78.7	92.3	99.1	77.8	91.0	98.7	75.7	89.9	94.7	87.6	92.0	106.9	75.0	94.8	105.1	116.3	109.4
03	CONCRETE	89.8	81.6	86.0	97.8	80.5	89.9	97.1	78.6	88.6	97.9	83.6	91.4	92.6	76.0	85.0	91.9	114.7	102.3
04	MASONRY	88.8	77.2	81.6	91.1	73.5	80.2	91.0	74.6	80.8	86.5	80.6	82.8	91.8	74.5	81.0	90.2	111.7	103.5
05	METALS	96.3	89.9	94.3	98.2	74.8	91.0	98.2	74.2	90.9	91.5	83.2	88.9	96.3	86.6	93.3	96.3	106.3	99.4
06	WOOD, PLASTICS & COMPOSITES	96.5	81.3	88.0	111.0	82.0	94.9	106.1	78.8	90.9	91.8	81.4	86.0	96.3	74.4	84.1	93.8	113.1	104.5
07	THERMAL & MOISTURE PROTECTION	110.1	77.9	96.5	96.6	78.8	89.1	96.0	78.5	88.6	100.9	84.8	94.1	109.8	74.0	94.7	108.5	108.2	108.4
08	OPENINGS	93.5	79.7	90.3	100.3	80.1	95.6	96.4	78.3	92.3	94.2	78.3	90.5	93.5	72.0	88.5	93.5	116.6	98.8
0920	Plaster & Gypsum Board	105.8	81.1	89.2	99.0	82.3	87.8	96.4	78.9	84.7	94.8	80.5	85.2	105.1	74.0	84.2	98.9	113.7	108.8
0950, 0980	Ceilings & Acoustic Treatment	89.7	81.1	83.9	79.8	82.3	81.5	79.8	78.9	79.2	83.6	80.5	81.5	89.7	74.0	79.1	89.7	113.7	105.9
0960	Flooring	94.0	79.3	89.9	98.5	83.7	94.4	93.3	83.7	90.6	93.0	75.5	88.1	94.0	73.2	88.2	94.0	116.8	100.3
0970, 0990	Wall Finishes & Painting/Coating	93.1	68.8	78.9	86.0	79.8	82.4	86.0	79.8	82.4	91.1	88.2	89.4	93.1	73.4	81.6	93.1	123.7	110.9
09	FINISHES	91.2	79.7	85.0	90.6	81.9	85.9	88.6	80.0	83.9	89.2	81.5	85.0	91.0	74.4	82.0	90.2	116.2	104.3
COVERS	DIVS. 10 - 14, 25, 28, 41, 43, 44, 46	100.0	91.0	98.0	100.0	87.5	97.2	100.0	87.2	97.1	100.0	95.1	98.9	100.0	90.5	97.9	100.0	107.2	101.6
21, 22, 23	FIRE SUPPRESSION, PLUMBING & HVAC	100.0	80.2	91.5	99.7	79.3	91.0	96.6	80.1	89.6	100.0	79.3	91.2	100.0	73.3	88.6	100.0	107.1	103.0
26, 27, 3370	ELECTRICAL, COMMUNICATIONS & UTIL.	87.9	87.8	87.9	99.9	88.1	93.8	99.2	87.7	93.2	96.0	86.0	90.8	88.6	76.5	82.3	99.4	114.1	107.0
MF2016	WEIGHTED AVERAGE	95.1	83.3	89.9	97.9	81.3	90.6	96.3	80.8	89.5	95.5	85.5	91.1	95.7	77.7	87.8	96.5	110.4	102.6

INDIANA

DIVISION		INDIANAPOLIS 461 - 462 MAT.	INST.	TOTAL	KOKOMO 469 MAT.	INST.	TOTAL	LAFAYETTE 479 MAT.	INST.	TOTAL	LAWRENCEBURG 470 MAT.	INST.	TOTAL	MUNCIE 473 MAT.	INST.	TOTAL	NEW ALBANY 471 MAT.	INST.	TOTAL
015433	CONTRACTOR EQUIPMENT		84.3	84.3		96.7	96.7		83.4	83.4		103.6	103.6		95.3	95.3		93.1	93.1
0241, 31 - 34	SITE & INFRASTRUCTURE, DEMOLITION	99.0	90.4	93.0	94.3	93.3	93.6	85.3	92.1	90.0	83.1	107.7	100.3	87.7	92.6	91.1	80.1	94.4	90.1
0310	Concrete Forming & Accessories	99.3	84.6	86.6	97.7	75.7	80.2	90.9	82.5	83.6	89.8	78.1	79.7	90.7	80.6	82.0	88.3	78.8	80.1
0320	Concrete Reinforcing	91.1	85.7	88.4	81.4	85.5	83.5	87.1	85.6	86.3	86.4	77.5	81.9	96.4	85.6	90.9	87.7	81.4	84.5
0330	Cast-in-Place Concrete	98.8	86.0	93.9	99.6	82.5	93.1	99.2	81.7	92.6	92.8	75.0	86.0	104.2	77.8	94.2	95.8	74.7	87.8
03	CONCRETE	95.7	84.7	90.7	86.9	81.2	84.3	97.3	82.3	90.4	90.5	77.5	84.6	96.2	81.1	89.3	95.8	78.1	87.7
04	MASONRY	90.5	79.2	83.5	88.5	75.2	80.3	96.5	77.1	84.5	75.7	73.3	74.2	92.9	77.3	83.2	82.3	69.5	74.4
05	METALS	97.1	75.3	90.4	92.7	89.6	91.8	96.6	75.1	90.0	93.3	85.3	90.8	100.0	89.9	96.9	95.2	81.8	91.1
06	WOOD, PLASTICS & COMPOSITES	98.8	85.1	91.2	99.5	76.2	86.5	103.3	83.0	92.0	90.1	77.9	83.3	105.1	80.8	91.6	92.0	80.1	85.4
07	THERMAL & MOISTURE PROTECTION	101.3	81.2	92.8	109.0	77.7	95.8	95.9	81.0	89.6	101.7	77.7	91.5	99.1	79.3	90.7	88.0	72.9	81.6
08	OPENINGS	99.7	81.8	95.6	89.0	76.9	86.2	94.9	80.6	91.6	96.1	74.7	91.2	93.7	79.4	90.4	93.7	78.8	90.3
0920	Plaster & Gypsum Board	94.7	85.0	88.2	110.4	75.8	87.2	94.0	83.3	86.8	73.6	77.9	76.5	94.8	81.1	85.6	92.5	80.0	84.1
0950, 0980	Ceilings & Acoustic Treatment	90.9	86.0	87.6	89.7	75.8	80.4	76.4	83.3	81.0	87.0	77.9	80.9	79.8	81.1	80.7	83.6	80.0	81.2
0960	Flooring	96.2	83.7	92.7	98.2	87.4	95.2	92.2	83.7	89.8	68.4	83.7	72.6	92.3	79.3	88.7	90.4	57.1	81.2
0970, 0990	Wall Finishes & Painting/Coating	98.6	79.8	87.6	93.1	71.0	80.2	86.0	85.1	85.4	86.8	74.5	79.6	86.0	68.8	76.0	91.1	68.2	77.8
09	FINISHES	94.6	84.1	88.9	93.0	78.4	85.0	87.3	83.1	85.0	79.2	79.0	79.1	87.8	79.1	83.1	88.3	73.7	80.4
COVERS	DIVS. 10 - 14, 25, 28, 41, 43, 44, 46	100.0	91.9	98.2	100.0	87.8	97.3	100.0	90.2	97.8	100.0	85.7	96.8	100.0	89.9	97.8	100.0	85.2	96.7
21, 22, 23	FIRE SUPPRESSION, PLUMBING & HVAC	99.9	80.8	91.7	96.9	80.2	89.8	96.6	79.4	89.3	97.6	75.9	88.3	99.7	80.1	91.3	96.9	77.0	88.4
26, 27, 3370	ELECTRICAL, COMMUNICATIONS & UTIL.	102.2	87.8	94.7	92.2	81.5	86.7	98.6	83.0	90.5	93.9	73.7	83.4	91.8	78.2	84.7	94.5	77.1	85.5
MF2016	WEIGHTED AVERAGE	98.3	83.2	91.7	93.5	81.7	88.3	96.0	81.6	89.7	92.8	79.6	87.0	96.3	81.7	89.9	94.0	78.0	87.0

INDIANA / IOWA

DIVISION		SOUTH BEND 465 - 466 MAT.	INST.	TOTAL	TERRE HAUTE 478 MAT.	INST.	TOTAL	WASHINGTON 475 MAT.	INST.	TOTAL	BURLINGTON 526 MAT.	INST.	TOTAL	CARROLL 514 MAT.	INST.	TOTAL	CEDAR RAPIDS 522 - 524 MAT.	INST.	TOTAL
015433	CONTRACTOR EQUIPMENT		108.4	108.4		113.9	113.9		113.9	113.9		101.5	101.5		101.5	101.5		98.2	98.2
0241, 31 - 34	SITE & INFRASTRUCTURE, DEMOLITION	97.4	93.9	94.9	95.2	122.2	114.1	95.0	122.4	114.2	99.5	96.6	97.5	88.3	97.4	94.7	100.7	96.1	97.5
0310	Concrete Forming & Accessories	94.5	79.6	81.6	93.4	80.8	82.6	94.3	82.5	84.1	93.0	82.5	83.9	81.3	80.6	80.7	98.7	87.9	89.4
0320	Concrete Reinforcing	89.4	86.2	87.8	95.4	85.7	90.5	88.2	85.1	86.7	91.7	86.1	88.9	92.4	82.9	87.6	92.4	82.7	87.5
0330	Cast-in-Place Concrete	99.1	81.5	92.4	91.7	82.4	88.2	99.8	87.8	95.3	107.6	57.4	88.5	107.6	58.9	89.1	107.9	85.3	99.3
03	CONCRETE	88.3	83.0	85.9	100.8	82.4	92.4	106.6	84.9	96.7	94.6	75.2	85.7	93.5	74.3	84.7	94.7	86.7	91.0
04	MASONRY	93.4	77.2	83.4	94.2	76.4	83.2	86.7	80.3	82.8	100.4	75.0	84.6	102.1	74.2	84.8	106.2	83.4	92.0
05	METALS	96.3	105.9	99.2	92.2	86.7	90.5	86.7	86.1	86.5	90.2	95.0	91.7	90.2	94.0	91.4	92.7	95.0	93.4
06	WOOD, PLASTICS & COMPOSITES	94.3	78.6	85.6	93.8	80.4	86.3	94.2	81.3	87.0	89.0	81.4	84.8	76.4	84.4	80.9	95.3	87.6	91.1
07	THERMAL & MOISTURE PROTECTION	101.2	82.0	93.1	101.0	83.0	93.4	100.9	84.5	93.9	104.2	78.5	93.3	104.5	73.4	91.4	105.2	83.5	96.0
08	OPENINGS	95.2	78.5	91.4	94.7	79.2	91.1	91.5	80.1	88.9	93.5	84.9	91.5	97.9	82.6	94.4	98.4	85.4	95.4
0920	Plaster & Gypsum Board	95.1	78.3	83.9	94.8	79.4	84.5	95.1	80.4	85.2	109.4	81.0	90.3	104.8	84.1	90.9	113.9	87.7	96.3
0950, 0980	Ceilings & Acoustic Treatment	91.6	78.3	82.7	83.6	79.4	80.8	79.4	80.4	80.1	98.0	81.0	86.5	98.0	84.1	88.7	100.6	87.7	91.9
0960	Flooring	91.6	91.1	91.5	93.0	80.0	89.4	93.9	81.1	90.3	94.1	73.0	88.3	88.2	84.1	87.1	107.9	89.1	102.7
0970, 0990	Wall Finishes & Painting/Coating	86.9	86.3	86.5	91.1	83.4	86.6	91.1	88.2	89.4	94.8	89.1	91.5	94.8	76.1	83.9	96.4	74.0	83.3
09	FINISHES	91.1	82.2	86.2	89.2	80.8	84.6	88.9	82.6	85.5	94.1	81.6	87.3	90.2	81.6	85.5	99.4	86.8	92.6
COVERS	DIVS. 10 - 14, 25, 28, 41, 43, 44, 46	100.0	92.1	98.2	100.0	92.4	98.3	100.0	95.1	98.9	100.0	91.7	98.1	100.0	64.9	92.2	100.0	93.7	98.6
21, 22, 23	FIRE SUPPRESSION, PLUMBING & HVAC	99.9	78.1	90.6	100.0	79.7	91.3	96.9	80.9	90.0	97.1	82.6	90.9	97.1	73.8	87.2	100.2	84.5	93.5
26, 27, 3370	ELECTRICAL, COMMUNICATIONS & UTIL.	100.1	88.6	94.1	94.3	88.1	91.1	94.8	86.0	90.2	100.8	76.3	88.0	101.4	81.2	90.9	100.2	79.6	88.6
MF2016	WEIGHTED AVERAGE	96.3	85.0	91.4	96.3	85.4	91.5	94.8	86.5	91.1	96.0	82.3	90.0	95.8	79.9	88.8	98.2	86.5	93.1

City Cost Indexes

IOWA

DIVISION		COUNCIL BLUFFS 515			CRESTON 508			DAVENPORT 527 - 528			DECORAH 521			DES MOINES 500 - 503, 509			DUBUQUE 520		
		MAT.	INST.	TOTAL	MAT.	INST.	TOTAL	MAT.	INST.	TOTAL	MAT.	INST.	TOTAL	MAT.	INST.	TOTAL	MAT.	INST.	TOTAL
015433	CONTRACTOR EQUIPMENT		97.5	97.5		101.5	101.5		101.5	101.5		101.5	101.5		103.4	103.4		97.0	97.0
0241, 31 - 34	SITE & INFRASTRUCTURE, DEMOLITION	103.5	92.5	95.8	98.0	98.3	98.2	99.8	99.6	99.7	98.1	96.3	96.8	104.4	101.2	102.2	98.5	93.2	94.8
0310	Concrete Forming & Accessories	80.8	76.2	76.8	78.5	83.7	83.0	98.2	100.5	100.2	90.7	74.7	76.9	96.4	86.0	87.4	82.0	85.4	85.0
0320	Concrete Reinforcing	94.3	80.0	87.1	91.5	82.4	86.9	92.4	108.9	100.7	91.7	71.0	81.3	96.0	83.4	89.6	91.1	82.5	86.8
0330	Cast-in-Place Concrete	112.1	81.9	100.7	108.8	63.4	91.6	103.9	100.3	102.5	104.7	79.7	95.2	92.6	93.3	92.9	105.6	87.2	98.6
03	CONCRETE	96.9	79.8	89.1	93.9	77.2	86.3	92.7	102.2	97.1	92.6	76.7	85.3	87.5	89.0	88.2	91.6	86.2	89.2
04	MASONRY	107.2	77.5	88.8	101.9	72.4	83.6	102.8	96.1	98.7	122.3	69.7	89.7	89.0	86.0	87.1	107.1	71.8	85.2
05	METALS	97.7	93.1	96.3	94.5	93.5	94.2	92.7	106.3	96.9	90.3	88.6	89.8	100.5	100.7	100.6	91.2	94.0	92.1
06	WOOD, PLASTICS & COMPOSITES	75.3	75.6	75.5	72.1	84.4	78.9	95.3	99.9	97.9	86.1	74.3	79.5	91.4	84.4	87.5	76.9	86.2	82.0
07	THERMAL & MOISTURE PROTECTION	104.6	76.9	92.9	107.5	80.1	95.9	104.6	95.7	100.9	104.4	72.7	91.0	99.1	86.7	93.9	104.9	80.7	94.6
08	OPENINGS	97.4	78.7	93.1	105.0	84.4	100.3	98.4	100.5	98.9	96.5	77.4	92.1	96.9	87.5	94.7	97.5	86.6	95.0
0920	Plaster & Gypsum Board	104.8	75.3	85.0	102.5	84.1	90.2	113.9	100.0	104.6	108.1	73.7	85.0	94.5	84.1	87.5	104.8	86.2	92.3
0950, 0980	Ceilings & Acoustic Treatment	98.0	75.3	82.7	89.8	84.1	86.0	100.6	100.0	100.2	98.0	73.7	81.6	91.5	84.1	86.5	98.0	86.2	90.0
0960	Flooring	86.8	89.1	87.4	78.6	73.0	77.1	96.6	94.5	96.0	93.5	73.0	87.8	87.5	94.1	89.3	98.8	73.0	91.7
0970, 0990	Wall Finishes & Painting/Coating	90.9	74.0	81.0	84.3	77.7	80.4	94.8	94.6	94.7	94.8	85.0	89.1	85.8	85.0	85.3	95.6	82.0	87.7
09	FINISHES	90.8	78.2	84.0	83.4	81.5	82.4	95.9	98.8	97.5	93.7	75.6	83.9	89.5	87.0	88.1	94.7	82.9	88.3
COVERS	DIVS. 10 - 14, 25, 28, 41, 43, 44, 46	100.0	90.6	97.9	100.0	67.5	92.8	100.0	97.4	99.4	100.0	81.1	95.8	100.0	93.6	98.6	100.0	92.5	98.3
21, 22, 23	FIRE SUPPRESSION, PLUMBING & HVAC	100.2	74.8	89.3	96.9	81.7	90.4	100.2	97.8	99.2	97.1	73.1	86.9	99.9	83.9	93.0	100.2	78.7	91.0
26, 27, 3370	ELECTRICAL, COMMUNICATIONS & UTIL.	103.6	82.8	92.8	93.3	81.2	87.0	96.6	92.5	94.4	98.4	49.9	73.2	104.3	83.8	93.6	102.2	77.1	89.1
MF2016	WEIGHTED AVERAGE	99.0	81.1	91.2	96.2	82.1	90.0	97.3	98.6	97.9	96.8	74.0	86.8	97.2	88.6	93.5	97.3	82.8	91.0

IOWA

DIVISION		FORT DODGE 505			MASON CITY 504			OTTUMWA 525			SHENANDOAH 516			SIBLEY 512			SIOUX CITY 510 - 511		
		MAT.	INST.	TOTAL	MAT.	INST.	TOTAL	MAT.	INST.	TOTAL	MAT.	INST.	TOTAL	MAT.	INST.	TOTAL	MAT.	INST.	TOTAL
015433	CONTRACTOR EQUIPMENT		101.5	101.5		101.5	101.5		97.0	97.0		97.5	97.5		101.5	101.5		101.5	101.5
0241, 31 - 34	SITE & INFRASTRUCTURE, DEMOLITION	107.1	95.1	98.7	107.1	96.2	99.5	99.0	90.9	93.3	102.1	92.9	95.7	109.7	96.3	100.3	111.4	97.5	101.6
0310	Concrete Forming & Accessories	79.1	75.2	75.8	83.1	74.6	75.7	88.7	74.9	76.8	82.3	57.9	61.3	82.7	38.9	44.9	98.7	75.7	78.9
0320	Concrete Reinforcing	91.5	69.0	80.2	91.4	82.4	86.9	91.7	86.1	88.9	94.3	69.4	81.7	94.3	68.9	81.5	92.4	79.6	85.9
0330	Cast-in-Place Concrete	102.2	43.5	79.9	102.2	74.7	91.7	108.3	66.7	92.5	108.5	79.3	97.4	106.3	58.0	87.9	106.9	73.3	94.2
03	CONCRETE	89.5	64.2	77.9	89.8	77.0	83.9	94.2	75.0	85.4	94.4	68.8	82.7	93.4	52.7	74.8	94.0	76.5	86.0
04	MASONRY	100.8	51.7	70.3	114.2	68.4	85.8	103.6	55.1	73.5	106.8	73.2	86.0	126.0	52.0	80.1	94.0	69.6	81.1
05	METALS	94.6	87.6	92.4	94.6	93.4	94.2	90.2	94.8	91.6	96.7	88.1	94.1	90.4	87.1	89.4	92.7	92.5	92.6
06	WOOD, PLASTICS & COMPOSITES	72.5	84.4	79.1	76.3	74.3	75.2	83.5	81.2	82.2	76.9	52.8	63.5	77.6	35.7	54.3	95.3	75.7	84.4
07	THERMAL & MOISTURE PROTECTION	106.8	67.0	90.0	106.3	73.3	92.3	105.0	69.5	90.0	103.8	67.4	88.4	104.1	54.6	83.2	104.6	73.0	91.3
08	OPENINGS	99.0	70.3	92.4	91.4	80.5	88.9	97.9	81.7	94.2	89.1	59.0	82.2	94.6	43.3	82.8	98.4	77.1	93.5
0920	Plaster & Gypsum Board	102.5	84.1	90.2	102.5	73.7	83.2	105.7	81.0	89.1	104.8	51.9	69.2	104.8	34.1	57.3	113.9	75.2	87.9
0950, 0980	Ceilings & Acoustic Treatment	89.8	84.1	86.0	89.8	73.7	79.0	98.0	81.0	86.5	98.0	51.9	66.9	98.0	34.1	54.9	100.6	75.2	83.5
0960	Flooring	79.8	73.0	77.9	81.7	73.0	79.3	102.0	73.0	93.9	87.5	78.1	84.9	89.1	73.0	84.7	96.6	75.7	90.8
0970, 0990	Wall Finishes & Painting/Coating	84.3	85.0	84.7	84.3	85.0	84.7	95.6	85.0	89.4	90.9	63.7	75.0	94.8	59.8	74.4	94.8	69.5	80.0
09	FINISHES	85.3	77.1	80.8	85.9	75.3	80.2	95.9	76.0	85.1	90.7	60.9	74.6	93.4	45.6	67.4	97.4	74.9	85.2
COVERS	DIVS. 10 - 14, 25, 28, 41, 43, 44, 46	100.0	84.1	96.5	100.0	88.5	97.4	100.0	84.5	96.5	100.0	61.7	91.5	100.0	75.9	94.6	100.0	90.6	97.9
21, 22, 23	FIRE SUPPRESSION, PLUMBING & HVAC	96.9	70.6	85.7	96.9	79.5	89.5	97.1	72.7	86.7	97.1	87.1	92.8	97.1	66.3	84.0	100.2	79.5	91.4
26, 27, 3370	ELECTRICAL, COMMUNICATIONS & UTIL.	99.3	73.2	85.7	98.4	49.9	73.2	100.6	74.9	87.2	98.4	79.8	88.7	98.4	49.9	73.2	98.4	72.6	85.0
MF2016	WEIGHTED AVERAGE	95.9	73.0	85.9	95.8	76.0	87.1	96.7	76.2	87.7	96.4	76.5	87.7	97.1	61.0	81.3	97.9	79.2	89.7

IOWA / KANSAS

DIVISION		SPENCER 513			WATERLOO 506 - 507			BELLEVILLE 669			COLBY 677			DODGE CITY 678			EMPORIA 668		
		MAT.	INST.	TOTAL	MAT.	INST.	TOTAL	MAT.	INST.	TOTAL	MAT.	INST.	TOTAL	MAT.	INST.	TOTAL	MAT.	INST.	TOTAL
015433	CONTRACTOR EQUIPMENT		101.5	101.5		101.5	101.5		107.1	107.1		107.1	107.1		107.1	107.1		105.2	105.2
0241, 31 - 34	SITE & INFRASTRUCTURE, DEMOLITION	109.8	95.0	99.5	112.5	97.4	101.9	110.7	97.2	101.3	109.2	97.9	101.3	111.7	96.8	101.3	102.5	94.7	97.0
0310	Concrete Forming & Accessories	88.7	38.7	45.6	94.3	71.6	74.7	93.9	56.2	61.4	99.6	63.6	68.6	92.9	63.3	67.3	85.1	68.2	70.5
0320	Concrete Reinforcing	94.3	68.9	81.5	92.1	82.9	87.5	96.8	63.4	80.0	104.6	63.5	83.9	102.0	63.3	82.5	95.5	63.9	79.6
0330	Cast-in-Place Concrete	106.3	68.7	92.0	109.4	83.4	99.5	120.9	87.7	108.3	115.6	91.6	106.5	117.7	91.3	107.6	116.9	91.7	107.3
03	CONCRETE	93.8	56.3	76.7	95.3	78.7	87.7	111.5	70.0	92.5	108.9	74.7	93.3	110.3	74.4	93.9	104.1	76.9	91.6
04	MASONRY	126.0	52.0	80.1	101.5	77.7	86.7	92.0	55.2	69.2	102.2	61.5	77.0	112.5	59.9	79.9	97.9	68.9	79.9
05	METALS	90.4	87.0	89.3	97.0	94.7	96.3	98.7	86.4	95.0	99.1	87.3	95.5	100.6	86.0	96.1	98.5	87.9	95.2
06	WOOD, PLASTICS & COMPOSITES	83.4	35.7	56.9	89.3	67.4	77.1	98.2	53.6	73.4	107.0	60.1	80.9	99.0	60.1	77.4	89.6	65.9	76.4
07	THERMAL & MOISTURE PROTECTION	105.1	55.2	84.0	106.5	79.9	95.3	93.7	63.5	80.9	95.4	66.9	83.3	95.3	66.1	83.0	91.8	78.4	86.1
08	OPENINGS	105.9	43.3	91.5	91.7	76.7	88.3	98.2	55.9	88.5	103.4	63.3	94.2	103.4	59.5	93.3	96.1	65.2	89.0
0920	Plaster & Gypsum Board	105.7	34.1	57.6	111.0	66.7	81.2	95.4	52.4	66.5	100.6	59.1	72.7	95.0	59.1	70.9	92.7	65.1	74.2
0950, 0980	Ceilings & Acoustic Treatment	98.0	34.1	54.9	92.4	66.7	75.0	84.0	52.4	62.7	81.5	59.1	66.4	81.5	59.1	66.4	84.0	65.1	71.3
0960	Flooring	91.9	73.0	86.7	86.7	83.4	85.8	88.5	70.8	83.6	87.4	70.8	82.8	83.6	70.8	80.1	83.8	70.8	80.2
0970, 0990	Wall Finishes & Painting/Coating	94.8	59.8	74.4	84.3	85.0	84.7	84.5	57.6	68.8	91.7	57.6	71.8	91.7	57.6	71.8	84.5	57.6	68.8
09	FINISHES	94.3	44.4	67.2	89.4	74.3	81.2	86.6	57.8	71.0	86.3	63.3	73.8	84.5	63.3	72.9	83.8	66.7	74.5
COVERS	DIVS. 10 - 14, 25, 28, 41, 43, 44, 46	100.0	74.6	94.4	100.0	91.0	98.0	100.0	85.3	96.7	100.0	88.2	97.4	100.0	88.2	97.4	100.0	88.8	97.5
21, 22, 23	FIRE SUPPRESSION, PLUMBING & HVAC	97.1	70.7	85.9	100.0	83.1	92.8	96.9	71.7	86.1	96.9	72.5	86.5	100.0	72.5	88.2	96.9	75.9	87.9
26, 27, 3370	ELECTRICAL, COMMUNICATIONS & UTIL.	100.1	49.9	74.0	95.1	65.0	79.5	102.2	66.2	83.5	99.6	71.7	85.1	96.8	71.7	83.7	99.5	70.0	84.2
MF2016	WEIGHTED AVERAGE	98.7	62.1	82.7	97.2	80.2	89.7	99.1	69.9	86.3	99.8	73.5	88.3	100.9	72.9	88.7	97.4	75.8	87.9

471

City Cost Indexes

		KANSAS																	
DIVISION		FORT SCOTT 667			HAYS 676			HUTCHINSON 675			INDEPENDENCE 673			KANSAS CITY 660 - 662			LIBERAL 679		
		MAT.	INST.	TOTAL	MAT.	INST.	TOTAL	MAT.	INST.	TOTAL	MAT.	INST.	TOTAL	MAT.	INST.	TOTAL	MAT.	INST.	TOTAL
---	---	---	---	---	---	---	---	---	---	---	---	---	---	---	---	---	---	---	---
015433	CONTRACTOR EQUIPMENT		106.1	106.1		107.1	107.1		107.1	107.1		107.1	107.1		103.6	103.6		107.1	107.1
0241, 31 - 34	SITE & INFRASTRUCTURE, DEMOLITION	99.3	94.7	96.1	114.1	97.4	102.4	93.1	97.9	96.5	112.8	97.9	102.4	93.3	94.9	94.4	113.8	97.5	102.4
0310	Concrete Forming & Accessories	101.8	83.7	86.2	97.1	61.1	66.1	87.6	58.6	62.6	108.3	70.4	75.6	98.5	98.7	98.7	93.4	60.7	65.2
0320	Concrete Reinforcing	94.9	101.7	98.3	102.0	63.4	82.5	102.0	63.3	82.5	101.4	64.9	83.0	92.0	104.4	98.3	103.5	63.3	83.2
0330	Cast-in-Place Concrete	108.4	86.8	100.2	91.2	88.0	90.0	84.5	91.3	87.1	118.2	91.5	108.0	92.8	99.9	95.5	91.2	87.6	89.8
03	CONCRETE	99.3	88.6	94.4	100.4	72.3	87.6	83.7	72.3	78.5	111.4	77.9	96.1	91.4	100.6	95.6	102.3	71.9	88.4
04	MASONRY	99.3	55.9	72.4	111.6	55.3	76.6	102.1	59.9	75.9	99.3	64.6	77.8	99.8	98.2	98.8	110.3	53.6	75.1
05	METALS	98.4	100.3	99.0	98.7	87.0	95.1	98.5	86.0	94.7	98.4	86.5	94.8	106.0	106.3	106.1	99.0	85.8	94.9
06	WOOD, PLASTICS & COMPOSITES	108.2	90.6	98.4	103.6	60.1	79.5	94.1	53.8	71.7	117.3	69.0	90.4	104.1	98.6	101.0	99.6	60.1	77.6
07	THERMAL & MOISTURE PROTECTION	92.8	75.2	85.4	95.7	64.2	82.4	94.2	65.4	82.0	95.4	77.8	88.0	92.5	100.6	95.9	95.9	63.2	82.0
08	OPENINGS	96.1	87.5	94.1	103.3	59.5	93.3	103.3	56.0	92.4	101.1	64.0	92.6	97.4	98.0	97.6	103.4	59.5	93.3
0920	Plaster & Gypsum Board	97.7	90.4	92.8	97.9	59.1	71.8	94.0	52.6	66.2	107.5	68.2	81.1	91.4	98.6	96.2	95.6	59.1	71.1
0950, 0980	Ceilings & Acoustic Treatment	84.0	90.4	88.3	81.5	59.1	66.4	81.5	52.6	62.0	81.5	68.2	72.6	84.0	98.6	93.9	81.5	59.1	66.4
0960	Flooring	97.9	70.7	90.3	86.2	70.8	81.9	80.8	70.8	78.0	91.6	70.7	85.8	78.8	99.7	84.6	83.9	69.7	79.9
0970, 0990	Wall Finishes & Painting/Coating	86.1	81.0	83.1	91.7	57.6	71.8	91.7	57.6	71.8	91.7	57.6	71.8	91.5	102.4	97.8	91.7	57.6	71.8
09	FINISHES	89.0	82.2	85.3	86.0	61.7	72.8	82.0	59.6	69.8	88.6	69.1	78.0	84.1	99.3	92.4	85.3	61.4	72.3
COVERS	DIVS. 10 - 14, 25, 28, 41, 43, 44, 46	100.0	88.5	97.5	100.0	86.1	96.9	100.0	87.5	97.2	100.0	89.2	97.6	100.0	95.9	99.1	100.0	86.1	96.9
21, 22, 23	FIRE SUPPRESSION, PLUMBING & HVAC	96.9	69.0	85.0	96.9	69.3	85.1	96.9	70.4	85.6	96.9	72.9	86.6	99.9	98.8	99.4	96.9	67.9	84.5
26, 27, 3370	ELECTRICAL, COMMUNICATIONS & UTIL.	98.8	71.7	84.7	98.6	71.7	84.6	94.1	64.4	78.6	96.1	72.3	83.7	104.4	98.4	101.3	96.8	71.7	83.7
MF2016	WEIGHTED AVERAGE	97.3	79.1	89.3	99.1	73.1	86.9	95.0	70.5	84.3	99.6	75.6	89.1	98.4	99.0	98.8	99.0	70.6	86.6

		KANSAS						KENTUCKY											
DIVISION		SALINA 674			TOPEKA 664 - 666			WICHITA 670 - 672			ASHLAND 411 - 412			BOWLING GREEN 421 - 422			CAMPTON 413 - 414		
		MAT.	INST.	TOTAL	MAT.	INST.	TOTAL	MAT.	INST.	TOTAL	MAT.	INST.	TOTAL	MAT.	INST.	TOTAL	MAT.	INST.	TOTAL
---	---	---	---	---	---	---	---	---	---	---	---	---	---	---	---	---	---	---	---
015433	CONTRACTOR EQUIPMENT		107.1	107.1		105.2	105.2		107.1	107.1		100.3	100.3		93.1	93.1		99.5	99.5
0241, 31 - 34	SITE & INFRASTRUCTURE, DEMOLITION	102.0	97.4	98.8	96.9	94.5	95.2	98.0	98.6	98.4	115.9	82.6	92.6	80.2	94.2	90.0	89.3	95.5	93.6
0310	Concrete Forming & Accessories	89.4	56.3	60.9	97.2	69.0	72.8	95.7	56.1	61.6	85.8	95.9	94.5	84.7	79.2	79.9	87.7	83.2	83.8
0320	Concrete Reinforcing	101.4	63.4	82.2	91.6	90.6	91.1	99.5	101.3	100.4	89.2	94.7	92.0	86.5	79.1	82.8	87.3	95.2	91.3
0330	Cast-in-Place Concrete	102.1	88.0	96.8	97.5	89.9	94.6	95.5	76.3	88.2	87.2	97.1	91.0	86.5	72.5	81.2	96.5	70.6	86.7
03	CONCRETE	97.4	70.2	85.0	93.2	82.1	87.7	93.2	72.5	83.7	91.7	97.2	94.2	90.1	77.2	84.2	93.7	81.2	88.0
04	MASONRY	127.8	55.3	82.8	93.5	67.0	77.1	99.3	51.5	69.7	93.3	94.3	93.9	95.4	69.8	79.5	92.1	57.1	70.4
05	METALS	100.5	87.0	96.3	102.6	97.7	101.1	102.6	99.3	101.6	94.3	109.5	99.0	95.9	84.4	92.4	95.2	90.8	93.8
06	WOOD, PLASTICS & COMPOSITES	95.6	53.6	72.2	101.0	68.1	82.7	104.0	53.8	76.1	74.4	95.5	86.2	86.9	79.8	83.0	85.5	90.6	88.3
07	THERMAL & MOISTURE PROTECTION	94.8	63.5	81.6	96.5	77.7	88.6	94.1	60.6	79.9	92.0	91.7	91.9	88.0	79.2	84.2	101.0	70.9	88.3
08	OPENINGS	103.3	55.9	92.4	103.3	74.0	96.6	105.7	64.7	96.2	93.0	94.4	93.3	93.7	81.2	90.8	95.0	88.7	93.6
0920	Plaster & Gypsum Board	94.0	52.4	66.1	100.8	67.3	78.3	93.7	52.6	66.1	61.6	95.6	84.4	88.2	79.7	82.5	88.2	89.9	89.4
0950, 0980	Ceilings & Acoustic Treatment	81.5	52.4	61.9	88.7	67.3	74.3	85.3	52.6	63.3	78.9	95.6	90.2	83.6	79.7	81.0	83.6	89.9	87.9
0960	Flooring	82.2	70.8	79.0	89.6	70.8	84.4	92.6	70.8	86.6	73.6	85.9	77.0	88.3	64.4	81.7	90.4	65.7	83.5
0970, 0990	Wall Finishes & Painting/Coating	91.7	57.6	71.8	88.8	70.8	78.3	97.5	57.6	71.9	93.2	91.7	92.3	91.1	89.2	90.0	91.1	56.3	70.8
09	FINISHES	83.2	57.8	69.4	92.1	68.5	79.3	90.3	57.5	72.4	76.5	93.9	85.9	87.0	77.3	81.7	87.8	78.1	82.5
COVERS	DIVS. 10 - 14, 25, 28, 41, 43, 44, 46	100.0	86.1	96.9	100.0	83.3	96.3	100.0	85.4	96.8	100.0	91.7	98.1	100.0	87.4	97.2	100.0	49.5	88.8
21, 22, 23	FIRE SUPPRESSION, PLUMBING & HVAC	100.0	70.3	87.3	100.0	76.0	89.8	99.8	69.8	87.0	96.7	87.6	92.8	100.0	80.2	91.5	96.9	76.8	88.3
26, 27, 3370	ELECTRICAL, COMMUNICATIONS & UTIL.	96.5	74.1	84.8	103.2	73.7	87.8	100.2	74.1	86.6	92.3	93.2	92.8	94.8	78.9	86.5	92.4	93.1	92.8
MF2016	WEIGHTED AVERAGE	99.6	70.8	87.0	99.1	78.1	89.9	99.2	72.1	87.3	93.5	93.4	93.5	94.6	79.9	88.2	94.7	80.2	88.3

		KENTUCKY																	
DIVISION		CORBIN 407 - 409			COVINGTON 410			ELIZABETHTOWN 427			FRANKFORT 406			HAZARD 417 - 418			HENDERSON 424		
		MAT.	INST.	TOTAL	MAT.	INST.	TOTAL	MAT.	INST.	TOTAL	MAT.	INST.	TOTAL	MAT.	INST.	TOTAL	MAT.	INST.	TOTAL
---	---	---	---	---	---	---	---	---	---	---	---	---	---	---	---	---	---	---	---
015433	CONTRACTOR EQUIPMENT		99.5	99.5		103.6	103.6		93.1	93.1		99.5	99.5		99.5	99.5		113.9	113.9
0241, 31 - 34	SITE & INFRASTRUCTURE, DEMOLITION	95.1	96.0	95.7	84.6	107.6	100.7	74.6	93.9	88.1	93.0	96.4	95.4	87.0	96.6	93.7	83.1	121.3	109.9
0310	Concrete Forming & Accessories	83.2	74.4	75.6	83.3	73.1	74.5	79.6	75.4	75.9	94.0	76.0	78.4	84.3	83.8	83.9	90.7	80.5	81.9
0320	Concrete Reinforcing	90.9	62.1	76.4	86.0	81.1	83.5	86.9	82.7	84.8	95.8	80.5	88.1	87.7	62.3	74.9	86.6	77.8	82.2
0330	Cast-in-Place Concrete	91.8	75.2	85.5	92.3	76.3	86.2	78.2	69.9	75.0	90.9	77.4	85.8	92.8	72.9	85.2	76.5	88.8	81.2
03	CONCRETE	87.1	73.1	80.7	92.1	76.5	84.9	82.3	75.2	79.1	89.3	77.7	84.0	90.6	76.6	84.2	87.3	83.2	85.4
04	MASONRY	90.0	62.6	73.0	106.9	75.1	87.1	79.2	64.4	70.0	85.5	73.3	77.9	90.8	59.2	71.2	99.0	82.1	88.5
05	METALS	93.9	78.4	89.1	93.2	89.9	92.2	95.1	85.1	92.0	96.6	86.2	93.4	95.2	78.8	90.2	86.4	84.6	85.9
06	WOOD, PLASTICS & COMPOSITES	72.1	75.0	73.7	83.7	70.2	76.1	82.4	77.5	79.7	89.6	75.0	81.5	82.7	90.6	87.1	89.5	79.4	83.9
07	THERMAL & MOISTURE PROTECTION	105.1	72.2	91.2	101.9	75.1	90.5	87.4	71.1	80.5	102.6	75.7	91.2	100.9	72.7	89.0	100.2	80.7	91.9
08	OPENINGS	89.4	62.5	83.2	97.0	74.1	91.7	93.7	75.6	89.6	95.3	77.2	91.2	95.4	80.7	92.0	91.9	79.8	89.1
0920	Plaster & Gypsum Board	93.1	73.9	80.2	70.8	70.0	70.2	87.5	77.3	80.6	92.5	73.9	80.0	87.5	89.9	89.1	91.5	78.4	82.7
0950, 0980	Ceilings & Acoustic Treatment	80.1	73.9	75.9	86.2	70.0	75.2	83.6	77.3	79.4	88.7	73.9	78.7	83.6	89.9	87.9	79.4	78.4	78.7
0960	Flooring	85.0	65.7	79.6	65.9	85.9	71.4	85.5	78.0	83.5	90.5	65.7	83.6	88.5	65.7	82.2	92.0	80.4	88.8
0970, 0990	Wall Finishes & Painting/Coating	90.9	64.8	75.7	86.8	74.4	79.5	91.1	70.1	78.9	93.2	71.2	80.4	91.1	56.3	70.8	91.1	90.7	90.9
09	FINISHES	83.2	71.9	77.0	78.1	75.0	76.4	85.7	75.0	79.9	89.9	73.6	81.0	87.0	78.6	82.4	87.1	81.8	84.2
COVERS	DIVS. 10 - 14, 25, 28, 41, 43, 44, 46	100.0	90.7	97.9	100.0	89.3	97.6	100.0	72.8	94.0	100.0	59.0	90.9	100.0	50.2	88.9	100.0	58.0	90.6
21, 22, 23	FIRE SUPPRESSION, PLUMBING & HVAC	97.0	76.4	88.2	97.7	79.0	89.7	97.0	77.1	88.5	100.0	80.2	91.5	96.9	77.6	88.7	97.0	79.0	89.3
26, 27, 3370	ELECTRICAL, COMMUNICATIONS & UTIL.	92.6	93.1	92.9	95.8	76.5	85.8	92.2	78.9	85.3	101.1	75.5	87.8	92.4	93.1	92.8	94.3	75.8	84.7
MF2016	WEIGHTED AVERAGE	92.7	77.7	86.2	94.7	80.5	88.5	91.5	77.2	85.3	96.0	78.5	88.3	94.1	78.7	87.4	92.4	83.0	88.3

City Cost Indexes

KENTUCKY

DIVISION		LEXINGTON 403-405 MAT.	INST.	TOTAL	LOUISVILLE 400-402 MAT.	INST.	TOTAL	OWENSBORO 423 MAT.	INST.	TOTAL	PADUCAH 420 MAT.	INST.	TOTAL	PIKEVILLE 415-416 MAT.	INST.	TOTAL	SOMERSET 425-426 MAT.	INST.	TOTAL
015433	CONTRACTOR EQUIPMENT		99.5	99.5		93.1	93.1		113.9	113.9		113.9	113.9		100.3	100.3		99.5	99.5
0241, 31-34	SITE & INFRASTRUCTURE, DEMOLITION	97.2	97.8	97.6	91.6	94.2	93.4	93.3	122.0	113.4	85.9	121.2	110.6	127.4	81.8	95.5	79.6	96.0	91.1
0310	Concrete Forming & Accessories	94.2	76.7	79.1	94.7	78.4	80.7	89.2	80.5	81.7	87.2	82.3	82.9	94.5	78.1	80.3	85.3	74.8	76.3
0320	Concrete Reinforcing	99.8	83.0	91.3	95.8	82.9	89.3	86.6	79.8	83.1	87.1	81.0	84.0	89.7	94.5	92.1	86.9	62.3	74.5
0330	Cast-in-Place Concrete	93.9	80.8	88.9	90.9	71.7	83.6	89.2	88.3	88.9	81.5	84.5	82.6	95.9	92.3	94.5	76.5	92.1	82.4
03	CONCRETE	89.9	79.6	85.2	89.3	77.3	83.8	99.1	83.4	91.9	91.7	83.1	87.8	105.0	87.4	97.0	77.5	79.1	78.2
04	MASONRY	88.2	73.3	79.0	86.5	69.4	75.9	91.3	82.0	85.5	94.1	78.8	84.6	90.8	86.8	88.3	85.7	65.4	73.1
05	METALS	96.4	86.9	93.5	97.5	85.5	93.8	87.9	86.5	87.5	84.9	86.7	85.4	94.2	108.0	98.5	95.1	79.0	90.2
06	WOOD, PLASTICS & COMPOSITES	86.0	75.0	79.8	89.7	79.8	84.2	87.5	79.4	83.0	85.3	82.2	83.6	83.3	77.0	79.8	83.2	75.0	78.6
07	THERMAL & MOISTURE PROTECTION	105.3	76.5	93.1	102.4	74.2	90.5	100.9	80.1	92.1	100.3	84.7	93.7	92.8	82.6	88.5	100.2	73.2	88.8
08	OPENINGS	89.6	77.1	86.8	85.9	76.9	83.9	91.9	80.2	89.2	91.2	82.6	89.2	93.6	76.6	89.7	94.4	69.3	88.7
0920	Plaster & Gypsum Board	102.4	73.9	83.3	92.8	79.7	84.0	90.2	78.4	82.3	89.2	81.3	83.9	64.5	76.6	72.6	87.5	73.9	78.4
0950, 0980	Ceilings & Acoustic Treatment	83.5	73.9	77.0	88.7	79.7	82.6	79.4	78.4	78.7	79.4	81.3	80.7	78.9	76.6	77.3	83.6	73.9	77.1
0960	Flooring	89.9	65.7	83.2	89.8	64.4	82.7	91.3	64.4	83.9	90.3	80.4	87.5	77.9	65.7	74.5	88.9	65.7	82.4
0970, 0990	Wall Finishes & Painting/Coating	90.9	80.9	85.0	92.5	70.1	79.5	91.1	90.7	90.9	91.1	76.5	82.6	93.2	69.9	79.6	91.1	70.1	78.9
09	FINISHES	86.7	74.6	80.1	89.6	74.9	81.6	87.3	78.2	82.3	86.5	81.3	83.7	79.0	74.6	76.6	86.4	72.5	78.8
COVERS	DIVS. 10-14, 25, 28, 41, 43, 44, 46	100.0	91.8	98.2	100.0	89.3	97.6	100.0	96.9	99.3	100.0	88.1	97.3	100.0	48.3	88.5	100.0	90.7	97.9
21, 22, 23	FIRE SUPPRESSION, PLUMBING & HVAC	100.1	79.0	91.1	100.0	78.7	90.9	100.0	80.3	91.6	97.0	79.9	89.7	96.7	82.8	90.8	97.0	75.9	88.0
26, 27, 3370	ELECTRICAL, COMMUNICATIONS & UTIL.	95.2	78.9	86.7	101.1	78.9	89.5	94.3	75.8	84.7	96.5	78.1	87.0	95.1	66.7	80.3	92.8	93.1	93.0
MF2016	WEIGHTED AVERAGE	94.8	80.3	88.5	95.1	79.1	88.1	94.7	84.3	90.2	92.6	84.5	89.1	95.9	81.4	89.6	91.9	79.2	86.4

LOUISIANA

DIVISION		ALEXANDRIA 713-714 MAT.	INST.	TOTAL	BATON ROUGE 707-708 MAT.	INST.	TOTAL	HAMMOND 704 MAT.	INST.	TOTAL	LAFAYETTE 705 MAT.	INST.	TOTAL	LAKE CHARLES 706 MAT.	INST.	TOTAL	MONROE 712 MAT.	INST.	TOTAL
015433	CONTRACTOR EQUIPMENT		93.5	93.5		91.4	91.4		91.9	91.9		91.9	91.9		91.4	91.4		93.5	93.5
0241, 31-34	SITE & INFRASTRUCTURE, DEMOLITION	105.3	92.4	96.3	102.3	91.1	94.5	98.9	90.4	93.0	99.9	92.7	94.9	100.7	91.8	94.5	105.3	92.3	96.2
0310	Concrete Forming & Accessories	80.2	62.9	65.3	95.5	74.7	77.5	77.9	57.3	60.1	95.0	70.9	74.2	95.8	71.0	74.4	79.8	62.2	64.7
0320	Concrete Reinforcing	96.3	65.1	80.5	91.7	55.6	73.5	93.0	53.7	73.2	94.3	54.0	74.0	94.3	54.3	74.1	95.1	65.0	80.0
0330	Cast-in-Place Concrete	93.8	68.2	84.0	93.5	77.2	87.3	90.1	65.7	80.8	89.7	69.5	82.0	94.4	69.5	84.9	93.8	67.4	83.7
03	CONCRETE	87.1	65.8	77.3	88.8	72.5	81.4	86.9	60.4	74.8	87.8	67.9	78.7	90.1	68.0	80.0	86.9	65.2	77.0
04	MASONRY	114.2	62.9	82.4	87.1	64.9	73.4	91.7	54.7	68.8	91.7	65.3	75.4	91.1	69.7	77.8	108.7	61.6	79.5
05	METALS	92.5	75.1	87.2	96.6	70.4	88.5	87.6	69.1	81.9	86.9	69.8	81.7	86.9	70.2	81.8	92.5	75.0	87.1
06	WOOD, PLASTICS & COMPOSITES	92.9	61.6	75.5	102.1	76.5	87.9	85.6	56.8	69.6	105.4	71.3	86.4	103.6	71.3	85.6	92.3	61.6	75.2
07	THERMAL & MOISTURE PROTECTION	97.9	67.4	85.0	95.3	69.9	84.5	97.1	63.7	83.0	97.6	69.5	85.7	97.3	70.5	86.0	97.9	66.6	84.6
08	OPENINGS	110.5	63.8	99.8	99.7	70.4	93.0	95.5	57.0	86.6	99.1	64.9	91.3	99.1	64.9	91.3	110.5	62.2	99.4
0920	Plaster & Gypsum Board	84.0	60.9	68.5	99.3	76.3	83.9	101.2	56.0	70.9	109.0	70.9	83.4	109.0	70.9	83.4	83.7	60.9	68.4
0950, 0980	Ceilings & Acoustic Treatment	83.0	60.9	68.1	94.8	76.3	82.3	101.6	56.0	70.9	99.9	70.9	80.3	100.9	70.9	80.7	83.0	60.9	68.1
0960	Flooring	90.9	64.9	83.7	86.9	60.4	79.6	88.1	58.4	79.8	96.8	64.3	87.8	96.8	67.4	88.6	90.5	58.2	81.5
0970, 0990	Wall Finishes & Painting/Coating	93.1	62.5	75.2	89.4	62.5	73.7	94.9	62.5	76.0	94.9	62.5	76.0	94.9	62.5	76.0	93.1	62.5	75.2
09	FINISHES	82.0	62.8	71.6	89.7	71.2	79.6	91.4	57.6	73.0	94.8	69.0	80.8	95.0	69.7	81.2	81.8	61.1	70.6
COVERS	DIVS. 10-14, 25, 28, 41, 43, 44, 46	100.0	80.6	95.7	100.0	87.2	97.2	100.0	80.4	95.6	100.0	86.8	97.1	100.0	86.9	97.1	100.0	80.1	95.6
21, 22, 23	FIRE SUPPRESSION, PLUMBING & HVAC	100.2	65.4	85.3	100.0	66.4	85.6	97.1	63.0	82.5	100.2	66.6	85.8	100.0	66.6	85.8	100.2	64.6	85.0
26, 27, 3370	ELECTRICAL, COMMUNICATIONS & UTIL.	93.2	64.9	78.5	97.9	59.8	78.1	93.7	70.5	81.7	94.8	67.4	80.5	94.4	69.6	81.5	94.8	60.5	77.0
MF2016	WEIGHTED AVERAGE	96.9	68.2	84.3	96.3	70.1	84.8	93.2	65.1	80.9	94.9	70.1	84.0	95.1	70.9	84.5	96.7	66.9	83.7

LOUISIANA / MAINE

DIVISION		NEW ORLEANS 700-701 MAT.	INST.	TOTAL	SHREVEPORT 710-711 MAT.	INST.	TOTAL	THIBODAUX 703 MAT.	INST.	TOTAL	AUGUSTA 043 MAT.	INST.	TOTAL	BANGOR 044 MAT.	INST.	TOTAL	BATH 045 MAT.	INST.	TOTAL
015433	CONTRACTOR EQUIPMENT		87.5	87.5		93.5	93.5		91.9	91.9		98.8	98.8		98.8	98.8		98.8	98.8
0241, 31-34	SITE & INFRASTRUCTURE, DEMOLITION	99.9	93.5	95.4	107.6	92.3	96.9	101.2	92.4	95.1	90.4	99.3	96.6	93.6	100.7	98.6	91.6	99.3	97.0
0310	Concrete Forming & Accessories	97.3	69.3	73.1	94.8	62.9	67.2	89.4	67.2	70.3	101.1	77.7	80.9	93.8	79.5	81.5	89.7	77.9	79.5
0320	Concrete Reinforcing	96.2	55.0	75.4	96.3	53.8	74.9	93.0	67.5	80.1	102.3	79.0	90.5	92.1	80.8	86.4	91.1	80.2	85.6
0330	Cast-in-Place Concrete	91.1	69.3	82.8	96.7	67.5	85.6	96.8	67.4	85.6	86.7	112.4	96.5	70.0	113.9	86.7	70.0	112.5	86.1
03	CONCRETE	93.1	66.7	81.0	90.5	63.6	78.2	91.7	67.6	80.7	88.1	90.5	89.2	81.7	92.1	86.5	81.7	90.8	85.9
04	MASONRY	96.9	60.6	74.4	98.1	58.9	73.8	114.7	53.9	77.0	102.7	66.6	80.5	118.3	95.5	104.1	125.5	86.9	101.5
05	METALS	96.8	62.7	86.3	96.6	70.8	88.7	87.6	68.9	81.9	101.1	89.5	97.6	91.0	92.7	91.5	89.4	91.2	89.9
06	WOOD, PLASTICS & COMPOSITES	103.7	71.4	85.7	99.1	62.4	78.6	92.8	68.7	79.4	98.6	76.5	86.3	97.9	76.5	86.0	92.5	76.5	83.6
07	THERMAL & MOISTURE PROTECTION	97.9	68.4	85.4	95.6	66.0	83.1	97.0	65.1	83.5	100.6	70.1	90.9	102.8	84.7	95.1	102.8	76.3	93.5
08	OPENINGS	103.1	65.3	94.5	105.4	59.0	94.8	100.0	59.4	90.7	100.6	80.3	96.0	98.0	80.3	94.0	98.0	80.3	93.9
0920	Plaster & Gypsum Board	98.6	70.9	80.0	93.5	61.7	72.2	102.5	68.2	79.5	108.2	75.4	86.2	112.7	75.4	87.7	108.5	75.4	86.3
0950, 0980	Ceilings & Acoustic Treatment	105.8	70.9	82.3	89.7	61.7	70.8	101.6	68.2	79.1	104.0	75.4	84.7	86.6	75.4	79.1	85.6	75.4	78.8
0960	Flooring	103.8	60.4	91.8	94.9	58.2	84.7	94.1	40.3	79.2	88.5	48.4	77.4	85.0	104.4	90.4	83.3	48.4	73.6
0970, 0990	Wall Finishes & Painting/Coating	99.0	62.5	77.7	85.6	62.5	72.1	96.1	62.5	76.5	90.5	93.0	91.9	90.7	93.0	92.0	90.7	93.0	92.0
09	FINISHES	101.3	67.1	82.7	88.7	61.7	74.0	93.7	61.6	76.3	93.1	72.7	82.0	87.4	84.8	86.0	86.1	72.7	78.8
COVERS	DIVS. 10-14, 25, 28, 41, 43, 44, 46	100.0	85.6	96.8	100.0	85.7	96.8	100.0	85.2	96.7	100.0	100.9	100.2	100.0	104.0	100.9	100.0	100.9	100.2
21, 22, 23	FIRE SUPPRESSION, PLUMBING & HVAC	100.1	64.0	84.7	99.9	64.8	84.9	97.1	64.5	83.2	100.0	71.9	88.0	100.2	73.0	88.5	97.1	72.0	86.3
26, 27, 3370	ELECTRICAL, COMMUNICATIONS & UTIL.	98.4	70.5	83.9	100.2	64.5	81.6	92.5	70.5	81.1	101.5	77.6	89.1	99.7	73.2	86.0	97.8	77.6	87.3
MF2016	WEIGHTED AVERAGE	98.7	68.4	85.5	97.9	66.7	84.2	95.6	67.4	83.3	98.4	79.8	90.3	95.8	85.0	91.1	94.8	82.2	89.3

473

City Cost Indexes

DIVISION		MAINE																
		HOULTON 047			KITTERY 039			LEWISTON 042			MACHIAS 046			PORTLAND 040 - 041			ROCKLAND 048		
		MAT.	INST.	TOTAL	MAT.	INST.	TOTAL	MAT.	INST.	TOTAL	MAT.	INST.	TOTAL	MAT.	INST.	TOTAL	MAT.	INST.	TOTAL
015433	CONTRACTOR EQUIPMENT		98.8	98.8		98.8	98.8		98.8	98.8		98.8	98.8		98.8	98.8		98.8	98.8
0241, 31 - 34	SITE & INFRASTRUCTURE, DEMOLITION	93.4	99.3	97.5	82.9	99.3	94.4	91.3	100.7	97.9	92.8	99.3	97.3	91.2	100.7	97.8	89.3	99.3	96.3
0310	Concrete Forming & Accessories	97.6	77.7	80.4	87.8	78.2	79.6	99.4	79.6	82.3	94.7	77.7	80.0	101.1	79.6	82.5	95.7	77.7	80.2
0320	Concrete Reinforcing	92.1	78.7	85.3	85.3	80.3	82.8	113.1	80.8	96.8	92.1	78.7	85.3	102.3	80.8	91.4	92.1	78.7	85.3
0330	Cast-in-Place Concrete	70.0	112.4	86.1	73.3	112.6	88.2	71.4	113.9	87.6	70.0	112.4	86.1	86.7	113.9	97.0	71.5	112.4	87.0
03	CONCRETE	82.6	90.4	86.2	78.8	91.0	84.4	82.1	92.1	86.7	82.1	90.4	85.9	87.4	92.1	89.6	79.8	90.4	84.7
04	MASONRY	100.2	62.4	76.8	115.6	86.9	97.8	100.8	95.5	97.5	100.2	62.4	76.8	106.1	95.5	99.5	93.7	62.4	74.3
05	METALS	89.6	89.1	89.5	85.8	91.5	87.6	94.3	92.7	93.8	89.6	89.1	89.5	101.2	92.7	98.6	89.5	89.1	89.4
06	WOOD, PLASTICS & COMPOSITES	101.8	76.5	87.7	95.8	76.5	85.0	103.6	76.5	88.5	98.8	76.5	86.4	97.3	76.5	85.7	99.6	76.5	86.7
07	THERMAL & MOISTURE PROTECTION	102.9	69.9	89.0	102.4	75.4	91.0	102.6	84.7	95.0	102.8	69.1	88.6	106.5	84.7	97.2	102.5	69.1	88.4
08	OPENINGS	98.1	80.3	94.0	97.4	80.4	93.5	101.3	80.3	96.5	98.1	80.3	94.0	99.9	80.3	95.4	98.0	80.3	94.0
0920	Plaster & Gypsum Board	115.0	75.4	88.4	104.8	75.4	85.1	118.0	75.4	89.4	113.4	75.4	87.9	108.6	75.4	86.3	113.4	75.4	87.9
0950, 0980	Ceilings & Acoustic Treatment	85.6	75.4	78.8	99.5	75.4	83.3	95.1	75.4	81.8	85.6	75.4	78.8	102.2	75.4	84.1	85.6	75.4	78.8
0960	Flooring	86.2	45.2	74.9	85.4	50.4	75.7	87.8	104.4	92.4	85.4	45.2	74.2	89.2	104.4	93.4	85.4	45.2	74.5
0970, 0990	Wall Finishes & Painting/Coating	90.7	93.0	92.0	84.8	106.8	97.6	90.7	93.0	92.0	90.7	93.0	92.0	93.2	93.0	93.1	90.7	93.0	92.0
09	FINISHES	88.0	72.1	79.3	87.8	74.5	80.6	90.3	84.8	87.3	87.4	72.1	79.1	93.7	84.8	88.8	87.2	72.1	79.0
COVERS	DIVS. 10 - 14, 25, 28, 41, 43, 44, 46	100.0	100.9	100.2	100.0	100.9	100.2	100.0	104.1	100.9	100.0	100.9	100.2	100.0	104.1	100.9	100.0	100.9	100.2
21, 22, 23	FIRE SUPPRESSION, PLUMBING & HVAC	97.1	71.9	86.3	97.0	82.6	90.9	100.2	73.0	88.5	97.1	71.9	86.3	100.0	73.0	88.5	97.1	71.9	86.3
26, 27, 3370	ELECTRICAL, COMMUNICATIONS & UTIL.	101.7	77.6	89.2	96.0	77.6	86.4	101.7	77.6	89.2	101.7	77.6	89.2	103.8	77.6	90.2	101.6	77.6	89.1
MF2016	WEIGHTED AVERAGE	94.4	79.2	87.8	93.0	84.9	89.5	96.3	85.6	91.6	94.2	79.2	87.7	98.7	85.6	93.0	93.5	79.2	87.2

DIVISION		MAINE			MARYLAND													
		WATERVILLE 049			ANNAPOLIS 214			BALTIMORE 210 - 212			COLLEGE PARK 207 - 208			CUMBERLAND 215			EASTON 216		
		MAT.	INST.	TOTAL	MAT.	INST.	TOTAL	MAT.	INST.	TOTAL	MAT.	INST.	TOTAL	MAT.	INST.	TOTAL	MAT.	INST.	TOTAL
015433	CONTRACTOR EQUIPMENT		98.8	98.8		105.7	105.7		105.6	105.6		111.0	111.0		105.7	105.7		105.7	105.7
0241, 31 - 34	SITE & INFRASTRUCTURE, DEMOLITION	93.3	99.3	97.5	105.3	94.1	97.5	102.5	98.2	99.4	101.3	98.6	99.4	95.9	95.3	95.5	103.1	92.4	95.6
0310	Concrete Forming & Accessories	89.2	77.7	79.3	97.4	75.7	78.7	98.8	78.3	81.2	85.6	73.8	75.4	90.9	85.8	86.5	89.1	74.1	76.2
0320	Concrete Reinforcing	92.1	79.0	85.5	104.8	90.0	97.3	100.6	90.1	95.3	100.6	89.1	94.8	91.6	85.8	88.7	90.9	87.7	89.3
0330	Cast-in-Place Concrete	70.0	112.4	86.1	110.5	74.5	96.8	109.9	76.3	97.1	116.0	78.2	101.7	94.8	87.3	91.9	105.3	68.1	91.1
03	CONCRETE	83.1	90.5	86.5	98.2	79.3	89.5	107.2	80.7	95.1	106.9	79.7	94.4	89.6	87.6	88.7	97.6	75.8	87.6
04	MASONRY	110.8	66.9	83.6	99.5	70.6	81.6	101.8	70.6	82.5	115.6	76.5	91.4	101.0	87.9	92.9	115.2	61.1	81.6
05	METALS	89.6	89.5	89.6	102.1	105.0	103.0	101.7	99.9	101.1	88.5	107.3	94.3	98.1	105.0	100.2	98.4	101.0	99.2
06	WOOD, PLASTICS & COMPOSITES	92.0	76.5	83.4	94.2	77.4	84.8	101.2	80.7	89.8	83.4	71.7	76.9	90.2	84.9	87.2	88.3	80.9	84.1
07	THERMAL & MOISTURE PROTECTION	102.9	70.1	89.0	103.1	79.8	93.2	101.1	80.8	92.5	100.6	82.9	93.1	99.9	85.6	93.8	100.1	75.8	89.8
08	OPENINGS	98.1	80.3	94.0	97.3	83.0	94.0	99.8	84.8	96.4	95.2	79.6	91.6	100.1	87.8	97.3	98.3	84.3	95.1
0920	Plaster & Gypsum Board	108.5	75.4	86.3	100.1	77.0	84.6	104.3	80.1	88.1	98.7	71.0	80.1	105.7	84.7	91.6	105.7	80.6	88.9
0950, 0980	Ceilings & Acoustic Treatment	85.6	75.4	78.8	91.7	77.0	81.8	100.0	80.1	86.6	101.6	71.0	81.0	103.0	84.7	90.7	103.0	80.6	87.9
0960	Flooring	83.0	48.4	73.4	86.2	80.0	84.5	99.3	80.0	93.9	89.3	80.0	86.7	87.9	96.3	90.2	87.0	80.0	85.1
0970, 0990	Wall Finishes & Painting/Coating	90.7	93.0	92.0	87.3	76.5	81.0	102.9	76.5	87.5	104.1	74.3	86.7	97.3	88.5	92.2	97.3	74.3	83.9
09	FINISHES	86.2	72.7	78.8	86.1	76.2	80.7	99.8	78.2	88.1	92.8	74.1	82.6	94.1	88.0	90.8	94.3	75.7	84.2
COVERS	DIVS. 10 - 14, 25, 28, 41, 43, 44, 46	100.0	100.7	100.2	100.0	87.9	97.3	100.0	89.1	97.6	100.0	84.0	96.4	100.0	92.5	98.3	100.0	70.9	93.5
21, 22, 23	FIRE SUPPRESSION, PLUMBING & HVAC	97.1	71.9	86.3	100.1	82.1	92.4	100.1	82.2	92.4	97.0	86.1	92.3	96.8	74.9	87.5	96.8	75.8	87.8
26, 27, 3370	ELECTRICAL, COMMUNICATIONS & UTIL.	101.7	77.6	89.1	100.1	90.9	95.3	100.7	90.9	95.6	100.2	98.6	99.4	98.1	80.6	89.0	97.6	64.1	80.2
MF2016	WEIGHTED AVERAGE	94.7	79.8	88.2	98.9	84.2	92.4	101.4	84.7	94.1	97.9	86.8	93.0	96.9	86.3	92.3	98.6	76.6	88.9

DIVISION		MARYLAND														MASSACHUSETTS		
		ELKTON 219			HAGERSTOWN 217			SALISBURY 218			SILVER SPRING 209			WALDORF 206			BOSTON 020 - 022, 024		
		MAT.	INST.	TOTAL	MAT.	INST.	TOTAL	MAT.	INST.	TOTAL	MAT.	INST.	TOTAL	MAT.	INST.	TOTAL	MAT.	INST.	TOTAL
015433	CONTRACTOR EQUIPMENT		105.7	105.7		105.7	105.7		105.7	105.7		102.4	102.4		102.4	102.4		103.0	103.0
0241, 31 - 34	SITE & INFRASTRUCTURE, DEMOLITION	89.8	93.9	92.6	94.0	95.2	94.8	103.1	92.4	95.6	89.7	90.0	89.9	96.1	90.1	91.9	95.5	102.1	100.1
0310	Concrete Forming & Accessories	94.8	90.7	91.3	90.0	82.5	83.5	102.8	52.6	59.5	94.1	73.1	75.9	101.3	70.5	74.8	101.6	139.1	133.8
0320	Concrete Reinforcing	90.9	113.2	102.2	91.6	85.8	88.7	90.9	67.3	79.0	99.4	89.0	94.1	100.0	89.0	94.4	101.1	147.6	124.6
0330	Cast-in-Place Concrete	85.3	74.0	81.0	90.3	87.3	89.2	105.3	66.1	90.4	118.8	78.6	103.5	133.1	78.6	112.4	96.0	139.2	112.4
03	CONCRETE	82.3	89.9	85.8	86.0	86.0	86.0	98.4	61.8	81.7	104.8	79.3	93.1	115.7	78.1	98.5	100.9	139.9	118.7
04	MASONRY	99.6	69.9	81.2	106.6	87.9	95.0	114.9	57.5	79.3	115.1	76.9	91.4	98.5	76.9	85.1	112.0	148.2	134.5
05	METALS	98.4	113.6	103.1	98.3	104.9	100.3	98.4	93.0	96.8	92.9	103.1	96.1	92.9	103.1	96.1	101.1	133.3	111.0
06	WOOD, PLASTICS & COMPOSITES	95.3	98.1	96.9	89.5	80.5	84.4	105.3	53.8	76.6	89.9	70.9	79.3	96.8	67.5	80.5	101.9	139.5	122.8
07	THERMAL & MOISTURE PROTECTION	99.6	81.6	92.0	100.3	86.7	94.5	100.3	71.1	87.9	104.3	88.0	97.4	104.8	87.6	97.5	106.0	137.6	119.3
08	OPENINGS	98.3	100.6	98.9	98.3	82.5	94.7	98.6	63.7	90.6	87.4	79.1	85.5	88.1	77.3	85.6	98.7	145.2	109.3
0920	Plaster & Gypsum Board	109.3	98.4	102.0	105.7	80.1	88.5	116.2	52.8	73.6	104.3	71.0	81.9	107.3	67.5	80.6	108.8	140.4	130.0
0950, 0980	Ceilings & Acoustic Treatment	103.0	98.4	99.9	103.9	80.1	87.9	103.0	52.8	69.2	110.1	71.0	83.7	110.1	67.5	81.4	109.4	140.4	130.3
0960	Flooring	89.5	80.0	86.9	87.5	96.3	89.9	93.4	80.0	89.7	95.4	80.0	91.2	99.2	80.0	93.8	95.3	163.7	114.3
0970, 0990	Wall Finishes & Painting/Coating	97.3	74.3	83.9	97.3	74.3	83.9	97.3	74.3	83.9	111.7	74.3	89.9	111.7	74.3	89.9	97.1	158.1	132.7
09	FINISHES	94.7	88.1	91.1	94.0	83.8	88.5	97.7	58.8	76.5	93.8	73.6	82.8	95.6	71.6	82.5	102.7	146.3	126.4
COVERS	DIVS. 10 - 14, 25, 28, 41, 43, 44, 46	100.0	58.1	90.7	100.0	92.0	98.2	100.0	79.7	95.5	100.0	84.4	96.5	100.0	84.0	96.4	100.0	116.7	103.7
21, 22, 23	FIRE SUPPRESSION, PLUMBING & HVAC	96.8	80.5	89.8	99.9	86.5	94.2	96.8	73.7	86.9	97.0	85.9	92.3	97.0	85.8	92.2	100.1	126.1	111.2
26, 27, 3370	ELECTRICAL, COMMUNICATIONS & UTIL.	99.3	89.1	94.0	97.9	80.6	88.9	96.4	63.5	79.3	97.5	98.6	98.1	95.1	98.6	96.9	101.4	129.8	116.2
MF2016	WEIGHTED AVERAGE	95.8	87.4	92.1	97.2	87.7	93.0	99.0	69.8	86.2	97.2	85.8	92.2	97.9	85.2	92.3	101.2	133.1	115.2

474

City Cost Indexes

		MASSACHUSETTS																
		BROCKTON			BUZZARDS BAY			FALL RIVER			FITCHBURG			FRAMINGHAM			GREENFIELD		
	DIVISION	023			025			027			014			017			013		
		MAT.	INST.	TOTAL	MAT.	INST.	TOTAL	MAT.	INST.	TOTAL	MAT.	INST.	TOTAL	MAT.	INST.	TOTAL	MAT.	INST.	TOTAL
015433	CONTRACTOR EQUIPMENT		101.4	101.4		101.4	101.4		102.3	102.3		98.8	98.8		100.7	100.7		98.8	98.8
0241, 31 - 34	SITE & INFRASTRUCTURE, DEMOLITION	94.0	103.8	100.9	84.2	103.8	97.9	93.0	103.9	100.6	85.3	103.7	98.2	82.0	103.8	97.1	88.9	102.5	98.4
0310	Concrete Forming & Accessories	98.6	125.5	121.8	96.3	124.9	120.9	98.6	125.1	121.4	92.9	125.1	120.7	100.3	125.5	122.0	91.3	109.4	106.9
0320	Concrete Reinforcing	102.0	147.3	124.9	81.8	124.4	103.3	102.0	124.5	113.4	84.6	147.0	116.1	84.6	147.1	116.1	88.3	120.1	104.3
0330	Cast-in-Place Concrete	89.4	138.6	108.1	74.3	138.4	98.6	86.5	138.9	106.4	78.7	138.5	101.4	78.7	138.7	101.5	80.9	122.3	96.6
03	CONCRETE	92.2	133.3	111.0	78.1	129.0	101.4	90.8	129.2	108.4	76.7	132.9	102.3	79.2	133.3	103.9	80.0	115.4	96.2
04	MASONRY	103.0	144.1	128.5	96.0	142.3	124.7	103.7	142.3	127.6	102.0	140.7	126.0	108.7	140.8	128.6	106.9	122.8	116.8
05	METALS	97.0	128.7	106.8	91.9	118.8	100.1	97.0	119.2	103.8	94.0	125.0	103.5	94.1	128.3	104.6	96.5	111.5	101.1
06	WOOD, PLASTICS & COMPOSITES	101.4	122.2	113.0	98.3	122.2	111.6	101.4	122.4	113.1	99.7	122.2	112.2	105.9	122.0	114.8	97.8	107.1	103.0
07	THERMAL & MOISTURE PROTECTION	100.1	132.9	114.0	99.0	129.5	111.9	100.0	127.8	111.8	100.8	126.7	111.7	100.9	131.5	113.8	100.8	110.2	104.8
08	OPENINGS	98.8	133.2	106.7	94.6	122.4	101.0	98.8	122.4	104.2	100.1	133.2	107.7	90.9	133.1	100.6	100.5	113.1	103.4
0920	Plaster & Gypsum Board	92.1	122.4	112.5	87.9	122.4	111.1	92.1	122.4	112.5	108.3	122.4	117.8	111.1	122.4	118.6	109.3	106.9	107.7
0950, 0980	Ceilings & Acoustic Treatment	108.7	122.4	117.9	93.3	122.4	112.9	108.7	122.4	117.9	93.1	122.4	112.9	93.1	122.4	112.9	101.6	106.9	105.2
0960	Flooring	90.8	163.7	111.0	88.7	163.7	109.5	89.9	163.7	110.4	86.6	163.7	108.0	88.3	163.7	109.2	85.8	140.4	101.0
0970, 0990	Wall Finishes & Painting/Coating	90.5	137.4	117.9	90.5	137.4	117.9	90.5	137.4	117.9	87.8	137.4	116.7	88.7	137.4	117.1	87.8	114.3	103.3
09	FINISHES	92.8	133.9	115.2	88.0	133.9	112.9	92.6	134.1	115.1	87.5	133.9	112.7	88.2	133.7	113.0	89.4	115.7	103.7
COVERS	DIVS. 10 - 14, 25, 28, 41, 43, 44, 46	100.0	115.1	103.4	100.0	115.1	103.4	100.0	115.7	103.5	100.0	109.7	102.2	100.0	114.7	103.3	100.0	105.3	101.2
21, 22, 23	FIRE SUPPRESSION, PLUMBING & HVAC	100.3	109.7	104.3	97.2	109.2	102.3	100.3	109.3	104.1	97.4	110.4	102.9	97.4	123.4	108.5	97.4	102.4	99.5
26, 27, 3370	ELECTRICAL, COMMUNICATIONS & UTIL.	100.1	103.2	101.7	97.5	103.2	100.4	100.0	103.2	101.6	101.4	102.5	101.9	98.1	129.3	114.3	101.4	98.2	99.7
MF2016	WEIGHTED AVERAGE	97.9	121.8	108.4	92.8	119.5	104.5	97.7	119.6	107.3	94.4	120.8	105.9	93.7	127.9	108.7	95.7	109.0	101.5

		MASSACHUSETTS																
		HYANNIS			LAWRENCE			LOWELL			NEW BEDFORD			PITTSFIELD			SPRINGFIELD		
	DIVISION	026			019			018			027			012			010 - 011		
		MAT.	INST.	TOTAL	MAT.	INST.	TOTAL	MAT.	INST.	TOTAL	MAT.	INST.	TOTAL	MAT.	INST.	TOTAL	MAT.	INST.	TOTAL
015433	CONTRACTOR EQUIPMENT		101.4	101.4		101.4	101.4		98.8	98.8		102.3	102.3		98.8	98.8		98.8	98.8
0241, 31 - 34	SITE & INFRASTRUCTURE, DEMOLITION	90.3	103.8	99.8	94.1	103.8	100.9	93.0	103.8	100.5	91.4	103.9	100.2	94.0	102.2	99.7	93.5	102.5	99.8
0310	Concrete Forming & Accessories	90.9	124.9	120.2	101.5	125.8	122.4	98.0	125.7	121.9	98.6	125.2	121.5	98.0	107.8	106.4	98.2	109.4	107.9
0320	Concrete Reinforcing	81.8	124.4	103.3	104.7	139.0	122.0	105.6	138.7	122.3	102.0	124.5	113.4	87.7	120.8	104.4	105.6	120.1	112.9
0330	Cast-in-Place Concrete	81.6	138.4	103.2	91.0	138.8	109.2	82.8	138.7	104.0	76.2	138.9	100.0	90.3	119.5	101.4	86.1	122.3	99.9
03	CONCRETE	84.0	129.0	104.6	92.4	132.0	110.5	84.7	131.7	106.2	86.0	129.3	105.8	86.0	113.8	98.7	86.3	115.4	99.6
04	MASONRY	102.0	142.3	127.0	114.6	144.9	133.4	100.9	140.7	125.6	101.9	142.3	126.9	101.5	113.8	109.2	101.2	122.8	114.6
05	METALS	93.4	118.8	101.2	96.9	125.7	105.7	96.9	122.2	104.6	97.0	119.3	103.9	96.7	111.5	101.2	99.5	111.5	103.2
06	WOOD, PLASTICS & COMPOSITES	92.1	122.2	108.8	106.1	122.2	115.0	105.6	122.2	114.8	101.4	122.4	113.1	105.6	107.5	106.7	105.6	107.1	106.4
07	THERMAL & MOISTURE PROTECTION	99.5	129.5	112.2	101.5	133.1	114.8	101.2	131.9	114.2	99.9	127.8	111.7	101.3	106.9	103.7	101.2	110.2	105.0
08	OPENINGS	95.2	122.4	101.4	94.8	130.9	103.1	101.6	130.9	108.3	98.8	127.1	105.3	101.6	113.6	104.3	101.6	113.1	104.2
0920	Plaster & Gypsum Board	83.7	122.4	109.7	113.6	122.4	119.5	113.6	122.4	119.5	92.1	122.4	112.5	113.6	107.3	109.4	113.6	106.9	109.1
0950, 0980	Ceilings & Acoustic Treatment	101.9	122.4	115.7	103.5	122.4	116.3	103.5	122.4	116.3	108.7	122.4	117.9	103.5	107.3	106.1	103.5	106.9	105.8
0960	Flooring	86.0	163.7	107.6	88.8	163.7	109.6	88.8	163.7	109.6	89.9	163.7	110.4	89.2	132.9	101.4	88.2	140.4	102.7
0970, 0990	Wall Finishes & Painting/Coating	90.5	137.4	117.9	87.9	137.4	116.8	87.8	137.4	116.7	90.5	137.4	117.9	87.8	114.3	103.3	89.0	114.3	103.7
09	FINISHES	88.6	133.9	113.2	91.4	133.9	114.5	91.4	133.9	114.5	92.4	134.1	115.1	91.5	113.3	103.3	91.3	115.7	104.6
COVERS	DIVS. 10 - 14, 25, 28, 41, 43, 44, 46	100.0	115.1	103.4	100.0	115.2	103.4	100.0	115.2	103.4	100.0	115.7	103.5	100.0	103.7	100.8	100.0	105.3	101.2
21, 22, 23	FIRE SUPPRESSION, PLUMBING & HVAC	100.3	109.2	104.1	100.1	125.9	111.1	100.1	125.8	111.1	100.3	109.3	104.1	100.1	98.1	99.2	100.1	102.4	101.1
26, 27, 3370	ELECTRICAL, COMMUNICATIONS & UTIL.	97.9	103.2	100.6	100.5	129.9	115.7	100.9	126.0	114.0	100.9	103.2	102.1	100.9	98.2	99.5	101.0	98.2	99.5
MF2016	WEIGHTED AVERAGE	95.1	119.5	105.8	98.0	128.5	111.4	97.1	127.1	110.3	97.0	119.8	107.0	97.3	106.5	101.3	97.8	109.0	102.7

		MASSACHUSETTS			MICHIGAN													
		WORCESTER			ANN ARBOR			BATTLE CREEK			BAY CITY			DEARBORN			DETROIT		
	DIVISION	015 - 016			481			490			487			481			482		
		MAT.	INST.	TOTAL	MAT.	INST.	TOTAL	MAT.	INST.	TOTAL	MAT.	INST.	TOTAL	MAT.	INST.	TOTAL	MAT.	INST.	TOTAL
015433	CONTRACTOR EQUIPMENT		98.8	98.8		112.1	112.1		98.9	98.9		112.1	112.1		112.1	112.1		96.3	96.3
0241, 31 - 34	SITE & INFRASTRUCTURE, DEMOLITION	93.4	103.7	100.6	82.2	96.7	92.3	92.1	85.8	87.7	73.6	96.3	89.5	81.9	96.6	92.3	97.3	100.7	99.7
0310	Concrete Forming & Accessories	98.6	125.1	121.5	96.4	106.3	105.0	95.2	80.9	82.9	96.5	82.6	84.5	96.3	107.0	105.5	99.3	107.0	105.9
0320	Concrete Reinforcing	105.6	147.0	126.5	98.4	104.5	101.5	88.6	80.9	84.7	98.4	103.7	101.1	98.4	104.6	101.5	99.3	106.5	102.9
0330	Cast-in-Place Concrete	85.6	138.5	105.7	88.4	101.5	93.3	85.3	95.8	89.3	84.6	87.7	85.7	86.4	102.3	92.5	103.2	101.9	102.8
03	CONCRETE	86.1	132.9	107.5	89.2	105.2	96.5	84.8	85.8	85.3	87.4	89.6	88.4	88.3	105.8	96.3	101.3	104.5	102.8
04	MASONRY	100.7	140.7	125.5	97.8	100.5	99.5	97.3	81.7	87.7	97.4	81.0	87.2	97.7	102.4	100.6	96.1	102.5	100.0
05	METALS	99.5	125.0	107.3	97.2	117.5	103.4	99.2	84.1	94.6	97.8	115.4	103.2	97.2	117.7	103.5	98.5	96.3	97.8
06	WOOD, PLASTICS & COMPOSITES	106.0	122.2	115.0	90.9	107.9	100.4	89.2	79.2	83.6	90.9	82.1	86.0	90.9	107.9	100.4	95.7	107.8	102.4
07	THERMAL & MOISTURE PROTECTION	101.2	126.7	112.0	106.1	102.7	104.6	97.5	81.9	90.9	103.3	84.5	95.4	104.3	106.2	105.1	103.5	106.7	104.9
08	OPENINGS	101.6	133.2	108.8	96.6	103.3	98.1	91.7	77.3	88.4	96.6	85.1	93.9	96.6	102.7	98.0	98.3	103.7	99.5
0920	Plaster & Gypsum Board	113.6	122.4	119.5	105.4	107.8	107.0	98.0	75.2	82.7	105.4	81.3	89.2	105.4	107.8	107.0	100.6	107.8	105.4
0950, 0980	Ceilings & Acoustic Treatment	103.5	122.4	116.3	88.9	107.8	101.6	82.4	75.2	77.5	89.8	81.3	84.0	88.9	107.8	101.6	96.9	107.8	104.3
0960	Flooring	88.8	163.7	109.6	90.1	113.4	96.6	88.3	74.5	84.4	90.1	81.3	87.7	89.6	107.4	94.6	97.6	107.4	100.3
0970, 0990	Wall Finishes & Painting/Coating	87.8	137.4	116.7	82.0	99.9	92.4	86.7	79.7	82.6	82.0	82.7	82.4	82.0	98.1	91.4	92.3	99.8	96.7
09	FINISHES	91.4	133.9	114.5	90.3	107.3	99.5	85.7	79.0	82.0	90.1	81.7	85.5	90.2	106.5	99.0	97.4	106.6	102.4
COVERS	DIVS. 10 - 14, 25, 28, 41, 43, 44, 46	100.0	109.7	102.2	100.0	97.1	99.4	100.0	97.6	99.5	100.0	91.2	98.0	100.0	97.6	99.5	100.0	102.2	100.5
21, 22, 23	FIRE SUPPRESSION, PLUMBING & HVAC	100.1	110.4	104.5	100.2	95.2	98.0	100.2	86.0	94.1	100.2	81.9	92.4	100.2	104.2	101.9	100.2	101.8	100.9
26, 27, 3370	ELECTRICAL, COMMUNICATIONS & UTIL.	101.0	102.5	101.7	96.3	100.9	98.7	93.5	82.1	87.6	95.5	87.1	91.1	96.3	101.9	99.0	99.0	101.4	100.3
MF2016	WEIGHTED AVERAGE	97.7	120.8	107.8	96.2	102.4	98.9	94.8	83.7	89.9	95.7	88.3	92.5	96.1	104.7	99.8	99.2	103.0	100.9

475

City Cost Indexes

DIVISION		MICHIGAN																	
		FLINT			GAYLORD			GRAND RAPIDS			IRON MOUNTAIN			JACKSON			KALAMAZOO		
		484 - 485			497			493, 495			498 - 499			492			491		
		MAT.	INST.	TOTAL	MAT.	INST.	TOTAL	MAT.	INST.	TOTAL	MAT.	INST.	TOTAL	MAT.	INST.	TOTAL	MAT.	INST.	TOTAL
015433	CONTRACTOR EQUIPMENT		112.1	112.1		106.8	106.8		98.9	98.9		93.6	93.6		106.8	106.8		98.9	98.9
0241, 31 - 34	SITE & INFRASTRUCTURE, DEMOLITION	71.5	96.2	88.8	86.6	82.6	83.8	91.0	85.7	87.3	95.1	91.6	92.7	109.1	85.1	92.3	92.4	85.8	87.7
0310	Concrete Forming & Accessories	99.2	85.8	87.6	93.9	73.2	76.0	93.8	79.4	81.4	85.7	79.8	80.6	90.5	84.1	85.0	95.2	80.8	82.8
0320	Concrete Reinforcing	98.4	104.1	101.3	82.6	89.0	85.8	93.0	80.7	86.8	82.5	85.7	84.1	80.2	104.0	92.2	88.6	78.7	83.6
0330	Cast-in-Place Concrete	89.0	90.2	89.4	85.1	82.2	84.0	89.5	94.0	91.2	100.7	70.8	89.3	84.9	92.1	87.6	87.0	95.8	90.3
03	CONCRETE	89.7	91.9	90.7	81.7	81.0	81.4	88.6	84.5	86.7	90.1	78.4	84.8	77.0	91.6	83.7	87.9	85.4	86.7
04	MASONRY	97.9	89.6	92.7	108.0	75.7	88.0	90.2	77.2	82.2	93.2	80.8	85.5	87.5	87.5	87.5	95.8	81.7	87.1
05	METALS	97.2	116.1	103.0	100.6	113.0	104.4	96.3	83.6	92.4	100.0	91.8	97.5	100.8	114.1	104.9	99.2	83.2	94.3
06	WOOD, PLASTICS & COMPOSITES	94.3	84.5	88.9	82.6	71.9	76.6	93.2	77.6	84.5	78.2	79.8	79.1	81.4	82.1	81.8	89.2	79.2	83.6
07	THERMAL & MOISTURE PROTECTION	103.7	88.7	97.3	96.2	70.8	85.4	98.8	74.1	88.3	100.0	76.4	90.0	95.4	89.0	92.7	97.5	81.9	90.9
08	OPENINGS	96.6	86.3	94.2	92.1	80.0	89.3	101.3	77.0	95.8	99.0	71.4	92.7	91.2	88.5	90.6	91.7	77.2	88.4
0920	Plaster & Gypsum Board	107.4	83.8	91.5	97.8	70.1	79.2	101.4	73.6	82.7	52.7	79.8	70.9	96.2	80.6	85.7	98.0	75.2	82.7
0950, 0980	Ceilings & Acoustic Treatment	88.9	83.8	85.4	81.5	70.1	73.8	95.1	73.6	80.6	80.5	79.8	80.0	81.5	80.6	80.9	82.4	75.2	77.5
0960	Flooring	90.1	90.9	90.3	81.8	90.5	84.2	90.3	80.5	87.6	100.0	92.4	97.9	80.5	83.1	81.2	88.3	74.5	84.4
0970, 0990	Wall Finishes & Painting/Coating	82.0	81.9	81.9	83.1	80.9	81.9	87.9	80.4	83.5	100.4	67.9	81.5	83.1	98.1	91.9	86.7	79.7	82.6
09	FINISHES	89.8	85.7	87.5	85.2	76.5	80.5	91.3	79.1	84.7	85.6	80.9	83.1	86.1	84.6	85.3	85.7	79.0	82.0
COVERS	DIVS. 10 - 14, 25, 28, 41, 43, 44, 46	100.0	92.5	98.3	100.0	80.5	95.7	100.0	97.3	99.4	100.0	89.0	97.6	100.0	93.7	98.6	100.0	97.6	99.5
21, 22, 23	FIRE SUPPRESSION, PLUMBING & HVAC	100.2	86.8	94.5	97.3	75.3	87.9	100.0	82.9	92.7	97.2	82.1	90.7	97.3	86.9	92.8	100.2	81.5	92.2
26, 27, 3370	ELECTRICAL, COMMUNICATIONS & UTIL.	96.3	94.1	95.2	91.7	75.9	83.5	98.5	87.6	92.8	97.4	81.3	89.0	95.2	99.8	97.6	93.4	78.3	85.5
MF2016	WEIGHTED AVERAGE	95.9	92.3	94.4	94.1	80.7	88.2	96.4	82.9	90.5	96.0	82.4	90.0	93.4	91.8	92.7	95.1	82.1	89.4

DIVISION		MICHIGAN															MINNESOTA		
		LANSING			MUSKEGON			ROYAL OAK			SAGINAW			TRAVERSE CITY			BEMIDJI		
		488 - 489			494			480, 483			486			496			566		
		MAT.	INST.	TOTAL	MAT.	INST.	TOTAL	MAT.	INST.	TOTAL	MAT.	INST.	TOTAL	MAT.	INST.	TOTAL	MAT.	INST.	TOTAL
015433	CONTRACTOR EQUIPMENT		112.1	112.1		98.9	98.9		91.7	91.7		112.1	112.1		93.6	93.6		100.3	100.3
0241, 31 - 34	SITE & INFRASTRUCTURE, DEMOLITION	94.1	96.5	95.8	90.1	85.7	87.0	86.1	95.8	92.9	74.6	96.2	89.8	80.8	91.1	88.0	96.1	99.6	98.6
0310	Concrete Forming & Accessories	93.3	78.4	80.5	95.5	79.2	81.5	91.7	106.6	104.6	96.4	83.4	85.2	85.7	72.9	74.7	85.0	85.2	85.1
0320	Concrete Reinforcing	101.2	103.8	102.5	89.2	80.6	84.9	89.2	90.0	89.6	98.4	103.6	101.1	83.7	77.9	80.8	94.4	98.7	96.6
0330	Cast-in-Place Concrete	99.3	89.0	95.4	85.0	93.9	88.4	77.3	102.0	86.7	87.3	87.6	87.4	78.5	78.5	78.5	102.1	107.1	104.0
03	CONCRETE	92.1	88.2	90.3	83.2	84.3	83.7	76.7	101.5	88.0	88.7	89.9	89.3	73.9	76.6	75.1	89.9	96.4	92.9
04	MASONRY	96.9	88.1	91.5	94.4	77.2	83.8	91.5	100.8	97.3	99.3	81.0	87.9	91.4	76.9	82.4	100.1	100.9	100.6
05	METALS	96.3	115.5	102.2	96.9	83.4	92.8	100.4	91.8	97.8	97.2	115.3	102.8	99.9	88.6	96.4	93.5	116.4	100.6
06	WOOD, PLASTICS & COMPOSITES	89.9	74.6	81.4	86.0	77.6	81.3	86.7	107.9	98.5	87.3	83.5	85.2	78.2	72.6	75.1	66.8	80.7	74.5
07	THERMAL & MOISTURE PROTECTION	101.7	86.1	95.1	96.4	74.4	87.1	101.9	102.6	102.2	104.6	84.8	96.2	99.0	68.4	86.0	106.1	91.9	100.1
08	OPENINGS	100.4	80.6	95.9	91.0	77.6	87.9	96.4	103.2	98.0	94.6	85.9	92.6	99.0	66.1	91.5	98.8	101.8	99.5
0920	Plaster & Gypsum Board	99.3	73.6	82.0	77.1	73.6	74.7	103.1	107.8	106.2	105.4	82.6	90.1	52.7	72.5	66.0	108.9	80.5	89.9
0950, 0980	Ceilings & Acoustic Treatment	88.7	73.6	78.5	83.2	73.6	76.7	88.1	107.8	101.4	88.9	82.6	84.7	80.5	72.5	75.1	125.3	80.5	95.1
0960	Flooring	91.9	83.1	89.5	87.0	76.4	84.1	87.2	107.4	92.8	90.1	81.3	87.7	100.0	90.5	97.4	90.6	90.4	90.6
0970, 0990	Wall Finishes & Painting/Coating	89.6	80.4	84.2	84.9	79.1	81.5	83.6	98.1	92.0	82.0	82.7	82.4	100.4	41.2	65.9	90.9	108.5	101.1
09	FINISHES	89.4	78.3	83.4	82.0	77.5	79.6	89.2	106.2	98.4	90.0	82.5	85.9	84.6	72.7	78.1	97.8	88.1	92.5
COVERS	DIVS. 10 - 14, 25, 28, 41, 43, 44, 46	100.0	91.7	98.2	100.0	97.3	99.4	100.0	102.4	100.5	100.0	91.4	98.1	100.0	87.2	97.2	100.0	95.3	99.0
21, 22, 23	FIRE SUPPRESSION, PLUMBING & HVAC	100.0	87.1	94.5	99.9	82.9	92.7	97.3	99.9	98.4	100.2	81.4	92.2	97.2	79.0	89.4	97.3	82.8	91.1
26, 27, 3370	ELECTRICAL, COMMUNICATIONS & UTIL.	97.9	92.5	95.1	93.8	77.0	85.1	98.3	101.4	99.9	94.7	89.2	91.8	93.2	75.9	84.2	104.4	104.2	104.3
MF2016	WEIGHTED AVERAGE	97.0	90.1	94.0	93.6	81.2	88.2	94.3	100.5	97.0	95.6	88.7	92.6	92.9	78.4	86.6	97.0	96.0	96.6

DIVISION		MINNESOTA																	
		BRAINERD			DETROIT LAKES			DULUTH			MANKATO			MINNEAPOLIS			ROCHESTER		
		564			565			556 - 558			560			553 - 555			559		
		MAT.	INST.	TOTAL	MAT.	INST.	TOTAL	MAT.	INST.	TOTAL	MAT.	INST.	TOTAL	MAT.	INST.	TOTAL	MAT.	INST.	TOTAL
015433	CONTRACTOR EQUIPMENT		103.0	103.0		100.3	100.3		103.4	103.4		103.0	103.0		107.9	107.9		103.4	103.4
0241, 31 - 34	SITE & INFRASTRUCTURE, DEMOLITION	98.6	104.6	102.8	94.3	99.8	98.2	99.8	102.9	102.0	95.2	104.3	101.6	97.9	108.3	105.2	98.8	102.6	101.4
0310	Concrete Forming & Accessories	85.9	85.7	85.7	82.1	84.9	84.5	99.5	96.7	97.1	93.6	95.3	95.1	98.1	114.7	112.4	98.1	98.9	98.8
0320	Concrete Reinforcing	93.2	98.6	95.9	94.4	98.5	96.5	95.2	99.0	97.2	93.0	106.0	99.6	94.9	106.5	100.8	92.9	106.2	99.6
0330	Cast-in-Place Concrete	111.0	111.6	111.2	99.2	110.0	103.3	102.2	101.6	102.0	102.3	99.2	101.1	101.5	115.9	106.9	99.7	99.9	99.8
03	CONCRETE	93.8	98.2	95.8	87.6	97.3	92.0	95.1	99.9	97.3	89.4	99.6	94.1	98.0	114.3	105.5	91.5	101.6	96.2
04	MASONRY	125.1	106.4	113.5	124.5	103.7	111.6	99.2	110.1	106.0	112.9	104.3	107.6	105.4	118.5	113.5	98.8	107.8	104.4
05	METALS	94.7	116.0	101.2	93.5	115.7	100.3	101.2	118.8	106.6	94.5	119.7	102.2	101.2	124.0	108.2	100.9	122.0	107.4
06	WOOD, PLASTICS & COMPOSITES	83.6	77.8	80.4	64.1	78.0	71.8	93.1	93.6	93.3	92.5	93.3	93.0	95.7	112.1	104.8	95.7	97.4	96.6
07	THERMAL & MOISTURE PROTECTION	104.4	101.8	103.3	105.9	100.6	103.7	105.1	104.0	104.6	104.8	92.8	99.7	103.4	116.7	109.0	110.0	93.5	103.0
08	OPENINGS	85.8	100.2	89.1	98.8	100.3	99.1	105.8	106.0	105.8	90.3	112.2	95.3	101.3	122.6	106.2	100.7	113.5	103.6
0920	Plaster & Gypsum Board	94.8	77.8	83.3	107.9	77.8	87.7	92.7	93.9	93.5	99.4	93.7	95.6	100.8	112.7	108.8	103.6	97.8	99.7
0950, 0980	Ceilings & Acoustic Treatment	57.8	77.8	71.3	125.3	77.8	93.3	94.3	93.9	94.0	57.8	93.7	82.0	99.6	112.7	108.4	96.3	97.8	97.3
0960	Flooring	89.5	90.4	89.7	89.4	90.4	89.7	92.7	122.4	100.9	91.4	86.5	90.0	100.8	116.9	105.3	93.6	86.5	91.6
0970, 0990	Wall Finishes & Painting/Coating	85.3	108.5	98.8	90.9	87.2	88.7	85.5	109.2	99.3	96.2	102.6	100.0	100.9	129.5	117.6	85.7	102.6	95.6
09	FINISHES	81.8	88.0	85.2	97.1	85.5	90.8	90.5	102.2	96.8	83.6	94.7	89.6	99.8	116.7	109.0	91.4	97.5	94.7
COVERS	DIVS. 10 - 14, 25, 28, 41, 43, 44, 46	100.0	96.9	99.3	100.0	96.7	99.3	100.0	97.9	99.5	100.0	97.1	99.4	100.0	105.6	101.2	100.0	98.1	99.6
21, 22, 23	FIRE SUPPRESSION, PLUMBING & HVAC	96.5	86.3	92.1	97.3	85.3	92.2	100.0	96.3	98.4	96.5	86.4	92.2	99.9	108.4	103.6	100.0	93.9	97.4
26, 27, 3370	ELECTRICAL, COMMUNICATIONS & UTIL.	102.1	99.5	100.8	104.2	70.3	86.6	103.1	99.5	101.2	108.5	92.0	99.9	101.2	104.4	102.9	101.6	92.0	96.6
MF2016	WEIGHTED AVERAGE	95.9	97.5	96.6	97.8	92.0	95.3	99.8	102.7	101.1	96.0	98.0	96.9	100.4	113.0	105.9	98.8	100.9	99.7

City Cost Indexes

		MINNESOTA																	MISSISSIPPI		
	DIVISION	SAINT PAUL			ST. CLOUD			THIEF RIVER FALLS			WILLMAR			WINDOM			BILOXI		
		550 - 551			563			567			562			561			395		
		MAT.	INST.	TOTAL	MAT.	INST.	TOTAL	MAT.	INST.	TOTAL	MAT.	INST.	TOTAL	MAT.	INST.	TOTAL	MAT.	INST.	TOTAL
015433	CONTRACTOR EQUIPMENT		103.4	103.4		103.0	103.0		100.3	100.3		103.0	103.0		103.0	103.0		102.5	102.5
0241, 31 - 34	SITE & INFRASTRUCTURE, DEMOLITION	96.0	103.6	101.3	93.7	105.6	102.1	95.1	99.4	98.1	93.2	104.6	101.2	87.0	103.9	98.8	102.9	89.7	93.6
0310	Concrete Forming & Accessories	97.1	114.4	112.0	83.3	113.7	109.5	85.6	84.2	84.4	83.1	89.8	88.9	87.3	85.8	86.0	93.4	66.9	70.5
0320	Concrete Reinforcing	95.5	106.5	101.1	93.2	105.8	99.6	94.8	98.4	96.6	92.8	105.6	99.3	92.8	105.0	99.0	83.1	50.1	66.4
0330	Cast-in-Place Concrete	101.2	114.4	106.2	98.0	114.1	104.1	101.2	83.5	94.5	99.5	82.2	92.9	86.1	87.3	86.5	114.5	67.1	96.5
03	CONCRETE	94.6	113.7	103.3	85.5	113.1	98.1	88.7	87.8	88.3	85.5	91.2	88.1	76.7	91.1	83.3	98.1	65.7	83.3
04	MASONRY	97.7	118.6	110.7	109.0	108.7	108.8	100.1	98.4	99.0	113.0	102.9	106.7	124.2	85.2	100.0	97.5	61.5	75.2
05	METALS	101.2	123.5	108.1	95.3	120.3	103.0	93.7	114.9	100.2	94.4	119.2	102.1	94.4	117.9	101.6	89.4	84.8	88.0
06	WOOD, PLASTICS & COMPOSITES	97.1	111.8	105.3	81.2	111.8	98.2	67.7	80.7	75.0	80.9	83.7	82.5	84.9	83.7	84.2	102.6	67.6	83.1
07	THERMAL & MOISTURE PROTECTION	106.0	116.3	110.4	104.5	106.0	105.1	106.9	87.4	98.6	104.3	97.9	101.6	104.3	83.6	95.5	94.8	63.9	81.7
08	OPENINGS	100.3	121.5	105.2	90.7	121.5	97.8	98.8	101.8	99.5	87.8	106.0	91.9	91.3	106.0	94.7	100.8	57.8	90.9
0920	Plaster & Gypsum Board	102.0	112.7	109.1	94.8	112.7	106.8	108.6	80.5	89.7	94.8	83.8	87.4	94.8	83.8	87.4	97.0	67.2	77.0
0950, 0980	Ceilings & Acoustic Treatment	95.8	112.7	107.2	57.8	112.7	94.8	125.3	80.5	95.1	57.8	83.8	75.4	57.8	83.8	75.4	90.2	67.2	74.7
0960	Flooring	87.7	116.9	95.8	86.3	90.4	87.4	90.3	90.4	90.3	87.6	90.4	88.4	90.2	90.4	90.2	88.6	57.5	80.0
0970, 0990	Wall Finishes & Painting/Coating	88.1	123.2	108.6	96.2	123.2	112.0	90.9	87.2	88.7	90.9	87.2	88.7	90.9	102.6	97.7	81.9	49.0	62.7
09	FINISHES	91.5	115.8	104.7	81.2	111.2	97.5	97.6	85.7	91.1	81.2	89.1	85.5	81.5	88.4	85.2	85.7	63.6	73.7
COVERS	DIVS. 10 - 14, 25, 28, 41, 43, 44, 46	100.0	102.8	100.6	100.0	102.6	100.6	100.0	95.2	98.9	100.0	97.5	99.4	100.0	94.3	98.7	100.0	72.7	93.9
21, 22, 23	FIRE SUPPRESSION, PLUMBING & HVAC	99.9	111.3	104.8	99.6	108.2	103.2	97.3	82.4	91.0	96.5	101.9	98.8	96.5	82.3	90.4	99.9	57.6	81.8
26, 27, 3370	ELECTRICAL, COMMUNICATIONS & UTIL.	101.6	113.2	107.6	102.1	113.2	107.9	101.6	70.2	85.3	102.1	79.7	90.5	108.5	92.0	99.9	100.0	56.7	77.5
MF2016	WEIGHTED AVERAGE	98.9	114.1	105.6	95.2	111.3	102.3	96.6	89.2	93.4	94.3	97.4	95.6	94.6	92.3	93.6	96.7	65.5	83.1

		MISSISSIPPI																	
	DIVISION	CLARKSDALE			COLUMBUS			GREENVILLE			GREENWOOD			JACKSON			LAUREL		
		386			397			387			389			390 - 392			394		
		MAT.	INST.	TOTAL	MAT.	INST.	TOTAL	MAT.	INST.	TOTAL	MAT.	INST.	TOTAL	MAT.	INST.	TOTAL	MAT.	INST.	TOTAL
015433	CONTRACTOR EQUIPMENT		102.5	102.5		102.5	102.5		102.5	102.5		102.5	102.5		102.5	102.5		102.5	102.5
0241, 31 - 34	SITE & INFRASTRUCTURE, DEMOLITION	97.3	88.3	91.0	101.7	89.2	92.9	102.8	89.5	93.5	100.1	88.1	91.7	98.0	89.5	92.1	106.6	88.4	93.9
0310	Concrete Forming & Accessories	84.9	45.7	51.1	82.3	47.6	52.4	81.7	64.5	66.9	94.0	45.5	52.2	90.7	65.5	69.1	82.4	61.8	64.6
0320	Concrete Reinforcing	100.7	64.8	82.6	89.0	35.9	62.2	101.2	51.5	76.1	100.7	44.0	72.1	92.2	51.1	71.5	89.6	32.9	61.0
0330	Cast-in-Place Concrete	102.2	50.8	82.7	116.8	56.1	93.7	105.3	57.2	87.0	109.9	50.4	87.3	99.8	65.7	86.8	114.2	52.1	90.6
03	CONCRETE	93.7	52.9	75.1	99.5	50.8	77.2	99.1	61.5	81.9	99.9	49.1	76.7	92.4	64.8	79.8	102.0	55.2	80.6
04	MASONRY	92.5	41.0	60.6	124.2	47.2	76.4	138.0	69.1	95.3	93.2	40.9	60.8	103.3	59.2	75.9	120.1	43.8	72.8
05	METALS	89.3	87.2	88.6	86.5	79.3	84.3	90.4	85.7	88.9	89.3	77.4	85.7	95.7	85.2	92.5	86.6	76.0	83.3
06	WOOD, PLASTICS & COMPOSITES	85.2	46.4	63.6	88.6	47.3	65.6	82.0	65.8	73.0	97.6	46.4	69.1	97.2	67.0	80.4	89.7	67.6	77.4
07	THERMAL & MOISTURE PROTECTION	95.8	49.5	76.2	94.8	54.5	77.7	96.3	63.8	82.5	96.2	51.8	77.4	93.1	62.4	80.1	94.9	55.5	78.2
08	OPENINGS	96.7	49.8	85.9	100.4	43.3	87.3	96.4	57.1	87.4	96.7	43.6	84.5	101.2	57.8	91.3	97.3	54.4	87.4
0920	Plaster & Gypsum Board	87.5	45.5	59.3	88.0	46.4	60.0	87.2	65.3	72.5	98.1	45.5	62.7	85.8	66.6	72.9	88.0	67.2	74.0
0950, 0980	Ceilings & Acoustic Treatment	84.7	45.5	58.2	84.9	46.4	58.9	88.5	65.3	72.9	84.7	45.5	58.2	90.8	66.6	74.5	84.9	67.2	72.9
0960	Flooring	95.7	47.6	82.3	82.9	53.4	74.7	94.0	47.6	81.1	101.4	47.6	86.5	85.9	57.5	78.1	81.6	47.6	72.1
0970, 0990	Wall Finishes & Painting/Coating	92.1	49.0	67.0	81.9	49.0	62.7	92.1	49.0	67.0	92.1	49.0	67.0	82.6	49.0	63.0	81.9	49.0	62.7
09	FINISHES	88.7	46.0	65.5	81.8	48.4	63.6	89.4	60.0	73.4	92.2	46.0	67.1	85.7	62.7	73.2	81.9	59.2	69.5
COVERS	DIVS. 10 - 14, 25, 28, 41, 43, 44, 46	100.0	49.8	88.8	100.0	50.8	89.1	100.0	71.8	93.7	100.0	49.8	88.8	100.0	71.9	93.7	100.0	35.4	85.6
21, 22, 23	FIRE SUPPRESSION, PLUMBING & HVAC	98.6	53.3	79.2	98.2	54.9	79.7	100.0	58.9	82.4	98.6	53.5	79.3	99.9	58.9	82.4	98.2	43.4	74.8
26, 27, 3370	ELECTRICAL, COMMUNICATIONS & UTIL.	95.6	43.9	68.7	97.5	46.6	71.0	95.6	56.7	75.4	95.6	41.2	67.3	101.5	56.7	78.2	99.0	56.7	77.0
MF2016	WEIGHTED AVERAGE	94.7	55.2	77.4	96.6	55.8	78.7	98.3	65.6	83.9	96.0	53.2	77.3	97.3	65.3	83.3	96.7	56.3	79.0

		MISSISSIPPI						MISSOURI											
	DIVISION	MCCOMB			MERIDIAN			TUPELO			BOWLING GREEN			CAPE GIRARDEAU			CHILLICOTHE		
		396			393			388			633			637			646		
		MAT.	INST.	TOTAL	MAT.	INST.	TOTAL	MAT.	INST.	TOTAL	MAT.	INST.	TOTAL	MAT.	INST.	TOTAL	MAT.	INST.	TOTAL
015433	CONTRACTOR EQUIPMENT		102.5	102.5		102.5	102.5		102.5	102.5		110.5	110.5		110.5	110.5		104.8	104.8
0241, 31 - 34	SITE & INFRASTRUCTURE, DEMOLITION	94.8	88.2	90.2	98.8	89.7	92.4	94.8	88.2	90.2	89.1	94.9	93.1	90.7	94.8	93.6	105.8	92.9	96.8
0310	Concrete Forming & Accessories	82.3	47.0	51.9	79.6	65.3	67.3	82.2	47.4	52.2	93.6	91.5	91.8	86.4	78.3	79.4	82.9	96.1	94.2
0320	Concrete Reinforcing	90.1	34.5	62.1	89.0	51.1	69.9	98.5	44.1	71.0	106.8	96.7	101.7	108.1	78.4	93.1	98.0	101.3	99.7
0330	Cast-in-Place Concrete	101.3	50.3	81.9	108.4	66.7	92.6	102.2	71.0	90.3	91.4	98.5	94.1	90.4	88.1	89.6	94.8	89.0	92.6
03	CONCRETE	89.0	48.1	70.3	93.5	65.0	80.5	93.2	57.0	76.7	92.8	96.4	94.5	92.0	83.7	88.2	98.6	95.3	97.1
04	MASONRY	125.4	40.4	72.7	97.1	60.8	74.6	126.7	43.6	75.2	113.0	93.7	101.0	109.9	79.8	91.2	103.0	92.1	96.3
05	METALS	86.7	75.3	83.2	87.6	85.2	86.8	89.2	77.6	85.7	97.5	119.0	104.1	98.6	110.2	102.2	92.4	110.9	98.1
06	WOOD, PLASTICS & COMPOSITES	88.6	48.9	66.6	86.1	65.8	74.8	82.5	47.3	62.9	99.6	91.5	95.1	92.6	75.3	83.0	93.0	97.5	95.5
07	THERMAL & MOISTURE PROTECTION	94.3	51.9	76.3	94.5	63.0	81.1	95.8	53.1	77.7	100.1	99.3	99.8	99.6	85.4	93.6	92.5	94.5	93.3
08	OPENINGS	100.4	43.3	87.3	100.1	57.1	90.2	96.6	47.0	85.3	102.9	98.4	101.9	102.9	74.4	96.4	92.1	97.6	93.3
0920	Plaster & Gypsum Board	88.0	48.0	61.2	88.0	65.3	72.8	87.2	46.4	59.8	103.9	91.6	95.6	103.2	75.0	84.3	100.6	97.3	98.4
0950, 0980	Ceilings & Acoustic Treatment	84.9	48.0	60.1	86.8	65.3	72.3	84.7	46.4	58.8	91.4	91.6	91.5	91.4	75.0	80.3	91.1	97.3	95.3
0960	Flooring	82.9	47.6	73.1	81.5	57.5	74.9	94.2	47.6	81.3	95.6	98.5	96.4	92.2	87.2	90.8	94.7	104.7	97.5
0970, 0990	Wall Finishes & Painting/Coating	81.9	49.0	62.7	81.9	49.0	62.7	92.1	47.3	66.0	96.0	105.8	101.8	96.0	70.1	80.9	95.5	94.2	94.8
09	FINISHES	81.2	47.4	62.8	81.4	62.4	71.1	88.2	47.0	65.8	97.7	94.0	95.7	96.5	77.7	86.3	97.8	97.8	97.8
COVERS	DIVS. 10 - 14, 25, 28, 41, 43, 44, 46	100.0	52.8	89.5	100.0	72.3	93.8	100.0	50.8	89.1	100.0	82.7	96.2	100.0	92.8	98.4	100.0	83.4	96.3
21, 22, 23	FIRE SUPPRESSION, PLUMBING & HVAC	98.2	52.8	78.8	99.9	59.8	82.7	98.7	54.5	79.8	96.9	79.9	89.6	99.9	99.4	99.7	97.0	100.9	98.7
26, 27, 3370	ELECTRICAL, COMMUNICATIONS & UTIL.	96.1	46.8	70.5	99.0	58.7	78.1	95.3	46.7	70.0	101.8	79.6	90.3	101.7	101.0	101.3	95.9	86.5	86.5
MF2016	WEIGHTED AVERAGE	95.0	53.7	76.9	95.1	65.9	82.3	96.2	55.9	78.6	98.7	95.0	97.1	99.1	91.5	95.8	96.5	95.1	95.9

City Cost Indexes

DIVISION		COLUMBIA 652 MAT.	INST.	TOTAL	FLAT RIVER 636 MAT.	INST.	TOTAL	HANNIBAL 634 MAT.	INST.	TOTAL	HARRISONVILLE 647 MAT.	INST.	TOTAL	JEFFERSON CITY 650 - 651 MAT.	INST.	TOTAL	JOPLIN 648 MAT.	INST.	TOTAL
015433	CONTRACTOR EQUIPMENT		114.0	114.0		110.5	110.5		110.5	110.5		104.8	104.8		114.0	114.0		108.3	108.3
0241, 31 - 34	SITE & INFRASTRUCTURE, DEMOLITION	95.1	99.0	97.8	91.8	94.7	93.9	87.0	94.9	92.5	97.1	94.2	95.1	94.7	99.0	97.7	106.3	97.8	100.4
0310	Concrete Forming & Accessories	83.2	81.6	81.8	99.9	86.0	87.9	91.9	83.2	84.4	80.4	102.0	99.0	94.4	81.6	83.3	93.4	74.5	77.1
0320	Concrete Reinforcing	87.7	96.2	92.0	108.1	103.5	105.8	106.2	96.7	101.4	97.6	106.8	102.3	94.7	96.2	95.5	101.2	86.9	94.0
0330	Cast-in-Place Concrete	83.5	86.5	84.6	94.4	94.3	94.3	86.5	98.4	91.0	97.1	103.1	99.4	88.4	86.5	87.7	102.7	78.1	93.3
03	CONCRETE	80.7	87.8	83.9	95.7	93.7	94.8	89.2	92.7	90.8	94.6	103.9	98.9	87.4	87.8	87.6	97.4	79.2	89.1
04	MASONRY	144.4	87.5	109.1	110.2	78.5	90.5	104.7	93.7	97.9	97.4	102.3	100.4	102.0	87.5	93.0	96.3	81.3	87.0
05	METALS	102.6	118.1	107.4	97.4	120.9	104.6	97.5	118.6	104.0	92.9	114.6	99.5	102.2	118.1	107.1	95.6	101.0	97.2
06	WOOD, PLASTICS & COMPOSITES	85.6	79.1	82.0	107.7	85.2	95.2	97.9	80.8	88.4	89.9	101.6	96.4	97.8	79.1	87.4	103.5	73.0	86.5
07	THERMAL & MOISTURE PROTECTION	93.6	87.7	91.1	100.3	93.1	97.3	100.0	96.2	98.4	91.7	104.2	97.0	100.8	87.7	95.2	91.6	83.1	88.0
08	OPENINGS	99.6	84.1	96.0	102.9	97.0	101.6	102.9	85.0	98.8	92.1	104.5	95.0	97.6	84.1	94.5	93.2	78.0	89.7
0920	Plaster & Gypsum Board	93.1	78.6	83.3	109.8	85.1	93.2	103.6	80.6	88.1	96.2	101.5	99.8	96.8	78.6	84.6	107.0	72.1	83.6
0950, 0980	Ceilings & Acoustic Treatment	93.0	78.6	83.3	91.4	85.1	87.2	91.4	80.6	84.1	91.1	101.5	98.1	92.5	78.6	83.1	91.9	72.1	78.6
0960	Flooring	88.5	75.5	84.9	98.9	87.2	95.6	94.9	100.4	96.5	90.3	106.5	94.8	93.9	75.5	88.8	119.6	75.5	107.4
0970, 0990	Wall Finishes & Painting/Coating	92.4	81.7	86.2	96.0	75.0	83.8	96.0	98.4	97.4	99.8	107.6	104.3	86.0	81.7	83.5	95.1	79.3	85.9
09	FINISHES	85.9	79.9	82.7	99.7	83.9	91.1	97.3	86.7	91.6	95.5	103.4	99.8	91.2	79.9	85.1	104.7	75.4	88.8
COVERS	DIVS. 10 - 14, 25, 28, 41, 43, 44, 46	100.0	96.6	99.3	100.0	93.5	98.5	100.0	81.6	95.9	100.0	85.8	96.8	100.0	96.6	99.3	100.0	82.2	96.0
21, 22, 23	FIRE SUPPRESSION, PLUMBING & HVAC	99.9	99.9	99.9	96.9	99.0	97.8	96.9	99.9	98.2	96.9	102.7	99.4	99.9	100.0	100.0	100.1	71.8	88.0
26, 27, 3370	ELECTRICAL, COMMUNICATIONS & UTIL.	95.4	83.8	89.4	106.3	101.0	103.6	100.5	79.6	89.6	102.1	101.5	101.8	100.6	83.8	91.8	93.9	69.7	81.3
MF2016	WEIGHTED AVERAGE	98.1	92.5	95.7	99.6	95.7	97.9	97.6	93.6	95.9	95.9	102.8	98.9	97.8	92.5	95.5	97.8	79.6	89.8

DIVISION		KANSAS CITY 640 - 641 MAT.	INST.	TOTAL	KIRKSVILLE 635 MAT.	INST.	TOTAL	POPLAR BLUFF 639 MAT.	INST.	TOTAL	ROLLA 654 - 655 MAT.	INST.	TOTAL	SEDALIA 653 MAT.	INST.	TOTAL	SIKESTON 638 MAT.	INST.	TOTAL
015433	CONTRACTOR EQUIPMENT		105.7	105.7		100.2	100.2		102.6	102.6		114.0	114.0		103.6	103.6		102.6	102.6
0241, 31 - 34	SITE & INFRASTRUCTURE, DEMOLITION	98.5	98.4	98.4	90.9	89.6	90.0	78.0	93.5	88.8	94.0	99.4	97.8	93.7	94.1	94.0	81.4	94.1	90.3
0310	Concrete Forming & Accessories	93.3	102.0	100.8	84.6	80.8	81.3	84.8	79.9	80.6	90.2	96.5	95.7	88.0	80.7	81.7	85.9	76.7	78.0
0320	Concrete Reinforcing	96.1	96.9	96.5	107.0	85.9	96.3	110.2	78.3	94.1	88.1	96.4	92.3	86.9	106.2	96.6	109.5	78.3	93.8
0330	Cast-in-Place Concrete	100.6	104.0	101.9	94.3	86.4	91.3	72.6	86.4	77.8	85.4	98.0	90.2	89.2	85.3	87.7	77.5	86.5	80.9
03	CONCRETE	97.4	102.4	99.7	107.7	84.9	97.3	82.9	83.1	83.0	82.3	98.5	89.7	96.0	88.0	92.3	86.6	81.7	84.4
04	MASONRY	103.4	102.3	102.7	116.8	87.6	98.7	108.2	76.1	88.3	117.4	88.2	99.3	123.8	84.1	99.2	107.9	76.1	88.2
05	METALS	102.6	109.1	104.6	97.2	102.8	98.9	97.8	99.5	98.3	102.1	118.7	107.2	100.9	111.9	104.3	98.2	99.7	98.7
06	WOOD, PLASTICS & COMPOSITES	98.5	101.5	100.2	85.3	78.8	81.7	84.4	79.9	81.9	92.9	98.1	95.8	86.0	79.1	82.1	85.9	75.4	80.1
07	THERMAL & MOISTURE PROTECTION	91.8	104.7	97.3	106.8	89.2	99.3	104.9	83.4	95.8	93.8	95.8	94.7	99.7	90.6	95.9	105.1	84.5	96.4
08	OPENINGS	100.1	101.9	100.5	108.2	82.2	102.2	109.3	76.9	101.9	99.6	94.6	98.4	104.5	88.7	100.9	109.3	74.4	101.3
0920	Plaster & Gypsum Board	102.5	101.5	101.8	98.9	78.6	85.3	99.3	79.7	86.1	95.1	98.2	97.2	88.8	78.6	81.9	100.9	75.0	83.5
0950, 0980	Ceilings & Acoustic Treatment	95.1	101.5	99.4	89.7	78.6	82.2	91.4	79.7	83.5	93.0	98.2	96.5	93.0	78.6	83.3	91.4	75.0	80.3
0960	Flooring	96.5	106.5	99.3	74.1	75.5	74.5	87.2	87.2	87.2	92.1	75.5	87.5	71.8	75.5	72.8	87.7	87.2	87.6
0970, 0990	Wall Finishes & Painting/Coating	98.4	107.6	103.7	92.0	81.9	86.1	91.2	70.1	78.9	92.4	94.3	93.5	92.4	81.9	86.3	91.2	70.1	78.9
09	FINISHES	99.1	103.4	101.4	96.4	79.8	87.4	96.2	79.6	87.2	87.4	92.7	90.3	84.7	79.1	81.7	96.8	77.3	86.2
COVERS	DIVS. 10 - 14, 25, 28, 41, 43, 44, 46	100.0	100.3	100.1	100.0	81.4	95.9	100.0	91.9	98.2	100.0	100.3	100.1	100.0	91.4	98.1	100.0	91.6	98.1
21, 22, 23	FIRE SUPPRESSION, PLUMBING & HVAC	99.9	102.6	101.1	96.9	99.3	97.9	96.9	96.8	96.8	96.9	100.4	98.4	96.8	97.4	97.0	96.9	96.8	96.9
26, 27, 3370	ELECTRICAL, COMMUNICATIONS & UTIL.	103.8	101.5	102.6	100.7	77.9	88.8	100.0	100.9	100.5	94.0	83.8	88.7	95.0	101.5	98.4	100.0	100.9	100.5
MF2016	WEIGHTED AVERAGE	100.3	102.7	101.4	101.1	88.5	95.6	97.5	89.7	94.1	96.2	96.9	96.5	98.6	93.2	96.2	98.0	89.1	94.1

DIVISION		MISSOURI SPRINGFIELD 656 - 658 MAT.	INST.	TOTAL	ST. JOSEPH 644 - 645 MAT.	INST.	TOTAL	ST. LOUIS 630 - 631 MAT.	INST.	TOTAL	MONTANA BILLINGS 590 - 591 MAT.	INST.	TOTAL	BUTTE 597 MAT.	INST.	TOTAL	GREAT FALLS 594 MAT.	INST.	TOTAL
015433	CONTRACTOR EQUIPMENT		106.1	106.1		104.8	104.8		111.1	111.1		100.6	100.6		100.3	100.3		100.3	100.3
0241, 31 - 34	SITE & INFRASTRUCTURE, DEMOLITION	96.4	96.6	96.5	100.8	92.0	94.6	96.0	99.4	98.4	90.7	100.6	95.6	95.9	96.4	96.3	99.5	97.4	98.0
0310	Concrete Forming & Accessories	96.1	76.6	79.3	92.2	90.2	90.5	97.1	104.1	103.2	94.7	67.7	71.4	82.8	67.5	69.6	94.6	66.9	70.7
0320	Concrete Reinforcing	84.6	95.8	90.2	94.9	106.4	100.7	98.8	104.9	101.9	95.4	80.9	88.1	103.5	80.8	92.1	95.4	80.8	88.1
0330	Cast-in-Place Concrete	90.7	77.5	85.7	95.4	100.1	97.1	102.1	102.8	102.3	108.9	71.3	94.7	119.9	71.1	101.4	126.7	71.2	105.6
03	CONCRETE	92.2	81.5	87.3	93.6	97.4	95.4	98.6	105.0	101.5	92.4	72.2	83.1	95.9	72.0	85.0	100.6	71.8	87.4
04	MASONRY	94.1	81.7	86.4	99.3	91.8	94.7	94.1	111.1	104.7	127.7	75.4	95.3	123.6	75.4	93.7	127.9	75.4	95.3
05	METALS	107.5	104.0	106.4	98.9	113.4	103.3	103.4	121.5	109.0	105.2	88.1	99.9	99.4	87.9	95.9	102.7	88.0	98.2
06	WOOD, PLASTICS & COMPOSITES	93.4	75.3	83.4	103.5	89.1	95.5	99.9	102.6	101.4	86.5	64.5	74.3	74.6	64.5	69.0	87.6	63.6	74.3
07	THERMAL & MOISTURE PROTECTION	97.9	78.4	89.6	92.1	91.6	91.9	97.9	107.1	101.8	107.6	71.1	92.2	107.4	71.0	92.0	108.0	70.6	92.2
08	OPENINGS	107.0	86.8	102.4	97.3	97.6	97.4	101.5	107.4	102.8	96.8	66.4	89.8	95.1	66.4	88.5	98.0	65.9	90.6
0920	Plaster & Gypsum Board	96.1	74.7	81.7	108.8	88.6	95.3	108.2	103.0	104.7	113.2	63.9	80.1	112.3	63.9	79.8	121.9	62.9	82.3
0950, 0980	Ceilings & Acoustic Treatment	93.0	74.7	80.7	99.6	88.6	92.2	93.1	103.0	99.8	91.9	63.9	73.0	97.8	63.9	74.9	99.5	62.9	74.9
0960	Flooring	91.1	75.5	86.8	99.9	104.7	101.2	98.0	100.4	98.7	93.7	79.7	89.8	91.1	79.7	87.9	97.9	79.7	92.9
0970, 0990	Wall Finishes & Painting/Coating	86.9	103.9	96.8	95.5	107.6	102.5	97.0	108.5	103.7	95.2	70.8	81.0	94.1	70.8	80.5	94.1	70.8	80.5
09	FINISHES	89.6	79.6	84.1	101.5	94.5	97.7	100.1	103.7	102.1	91.6	69.6	79.7	91.6	69.6	79.7	95.6	69.1	81.2
COVERS	DIVS. 10 - 14, 25, 28, 41, 43, 44, 46	100.0	94.0	98.7	100.0	97.4	99.4	100.0	102.2	100.5	100.0	92.2	98.3	100.0	92.2	98.3	100.0	92.1	98.2
21, 22, 23	FIRE SUPPRESSION, PLUMBING & HVAC	100.0	72.3	88.1	100.1	89.0	95.4	99.9	105.2	102.2	100.1	74.4	89.1	100.2	70.8	87.6	100.2	70.8	87.6
26, 27, 3370	ELECTRICAL, COMMUNICATIONS & UTIL.	99.1	71.7	84.8	102.1	77.9	89.5	104.3	101.0	102.6	98.6	72.0	84.7	105.4	72.0	87.6	98.0	71.2	84.1
MF2016	WEIGHTED AVERAGE	99.6	81.7	91.7	98.9	92.8	96.2	100.5	106.0	103.0	100.0	76.4	89.6	99.8	75.3	89.1	101.3	75.3	89.9

City Cost Indexes

MONTANA

DIVISION		HAVRE 595 MAT.	INST.	TOTAL	HELENA 596 MAT.	INST.	TOTAL	KALISPELL 599 MAT.	INST.	TOTAL	MILES CITY 593 MAT.	INST.	TOTAL	MISSOULA 598 MAT.	INST.	TOTAL	WOLF POINT 592 MAT.	INST.	TOTAL
015433	CONTRACTOR EQUIPMENT		100.3	100.3		100.3	100.3		100.3	100.3		100.3	100.3		100.3	100.3		100.3	100.3
0241, 31 - 34	SITE & INFRASTRUCTURE, DEMOLITION	102.8	96.5	98.4	90.0	96.4	94.5	86.6	96.3	93.4	92.5	96.4	95.2	79.6	96.2	91.2	108.8	96.5	100.2
0310	Concrete Forming & Accessories	76.4	67.4	68.6	97.5	67.4	71.6	85.7	67.5	70.0	93.2	67.5	71.0	85.7	67.4	69.9	86.4	66.8	69.5
0320	Concrete Reinforcing	104.3	80.8	92.5	110.2	79.6	94.8	106.2	85.6	95.8	104.0	80.8	92.3	105.2	85.6	95.3	105.4	80.1	92.7
0330	Cast-in-Place Concrete	129.1	71.1	107.1	93.7	71.1	85.1	104.1	71.1	91.6	114.0	71.1	97.7	88.4	71.1	81.8	127.7	71.1	106.2
03	CONCRETE	103.3	72.0	89.0	89.2	71.8	81.2	86.4	72.9	80.2	93.0	72.0	83.4	76.0	72.8	74.5	106.4	71.6	90.5
04	MASONRY	124.6	75.4	94.1	115.4	75.4	90.6	122.6	75.8	93.6	129.9	75.4	96.1	149.3	75.8	103.7	131.0	75.4	96.5
05	METALS	95.7	87.8	93.3	101.4	87.5	97.1	95.5	89.6	93.7	94.8	87.9	92.7	96.1	89.4	94.0	94.9	87.6	92.7
06	WOOD, PLASTICS & COMPOSITES	67.1	64.5	65.7	90.0	64.5	75.8	77.5	64.5	70.3	85.0	64.5	73.6	77.5	64.5	70.3	77.3	63.6	69.7
07	THERMAL & MOISTURE PROTECTION	107.8	66.2	90.2	102.4	71.0	89.1	107.0	73.2	92.7	107.3	66.3	90.0	106.6	70.6	91.3	108.3	66.2	90.5
08	OPENINGS	95.6	66.4	88.9	99.5	66.2	91.9	95.6	67.5	89.1	95.1	66.4	88.5	95.1	67.5	88.8	95.1	65.8	88.4
0920	Plaster & Gypsum Board	108.0	63.9	78.4	106.4	63.9	77.8	112.3	63.9	79.8	121.1	63.9	82.7	112.3	63.9	79.8	115.9	62.9	80.3
0950, 0980	Ceilings & Acoustic Treatment	97.8	63.9	74.9	96.8	63.9	74.6	97.8	63.9	74.9	96.1	63.9	74.4	97.8	63.9	74.9	96.1	62.9	73.7
0960	Flooring	88.6	79.7	86.1	98.9	79.7	93.6	92.8	79.7	89.2	97.7	79.7	92.8	92.8	79.7	89.2	94.3	79.7	90.2
0970, 0990	Wall Finishes & Painting/Coating	94.1	70.8	80.5	94.4	70.8	80.6	94.1	70.8	80.5	94.1	70.8	80.5	94.1	56.0	71.9	94.1	70.8	80.5
09	FINISHES	90.9	69.6	79.3	97.2	69.6	82.2	91.6	69.6	79.7	94.4	69.6	80.9	91.1	68.1	78.6	93.8	69.1	80.4
COVERS	DIVS. 10 - 14, 25, 28, 41, 43, 44, 46	100.0	92.2	98.3	100.0	92.2	98.3	100.0	92.2	98.3	100.0	92.2	98.3	100.0	92.2	98.3	100.0	92.1	98.2
21, 22, 23	FIRE SUPPRESSION, PLUMBING & HVAC	97.1	70.8	85.8	100.2	70.8	87.6	97.1	68.8	85.0	97.1	74.4	87.4	100.2	68.8	86.8	97.1	74.4	87.4
26, 27, 3370	ELECTRICAL, COMMUNICATIONS & UTIL.	98.0	71.2	84.1	104.6	71.2	87.2	102.2	68.7	84.8	98.0	76.6	86.8	103.2	67.7	84.8	98.0	76.6	86.8
MF2016	WEIGHTED AVERAGE	98.9	75.2	88.5	99.6	75.3	88.9	96.8	75.0	87.2	97.8	76.7	88.6	97.4	74.5	87.4	99.9	76.5	89.7

NEBRASKA

DIVISION		ALLIANCE 693 MAT.	INST.	TOTAL	COLUMBUS 686 MAT.	INST.	TOTAL	GRAND ISLAND 688 MAT.	INST.	TOTAL	HASTINGS 689 MAT.	INST.	TOTAL	LINCOLN 683 - 685 MAT.	INST.	TOTAL	McCOOK 690 MAT.	INST.	TOTAL
015433	CONTRACTOR EQUIPMENT		98.2	98.2		105.2	105.2		105.2	105.2		105.2	105.2		105.2	105.2		105.2	105.2
0241, 31 - 34	SITE & INFRASTRUCTURE, DEMOLITION	99.4	101.2	100.6	100.8	95.2	96.9	105.6	95.2	98.3	104.4	95.2	97.9	91.1	95.2	94.0	102.7	95.2	97.4
0310	Concrete Forming & Accessories	86.3	55.8	60.0	95.2	74.8	77.6	94.8	71.2	74.4	98.0	74.3	77.6	93.7	76.4	78.8	91.6	55.9	60.9
0320	Concrete Reinforcing	111.2	88.0	99.5	97.2	86.9	92.0	96.6	76.3	86.4	96.6	73.4	84.9	95.9	76.5	86.2	103.4	69.7	86.4
0330	Cast-in-Place Concrete	107.8	77.3	96.2	110.5	80.9	99.2	117.0	80.3	103.0	117.0	62.2	96.2	91.8	80.4	87.5	116.6	58.6	94.6
03	CONCRETE	115.6	69.7	94.6	100.3	80.2	91.1	105.0	76.5	92.0	105.2	71.2	89.7	88.5	78.9	84.1	105.1	61.0	85.0
04	MASONRY	110.3	75.1	88.5	116.5	78.6	93.0	109.1	75.1	88.0	118.6	75.1	91.6	96.9	78.6	85.6	105.5	75.1	86.6
05	METALS	104.0	84.1	97.9	98.3	98.4	98.3	100.1	94.2	98.3	101.1	92.8	98.5	101.2	94.5	99.8	98.5	90.8	96.2
06	WOOD, PLASTICS & COMPOSITES	86.6	50.1	66.3	99.2	74.1	85.2	98.5	69.4	82.3	102.0	74.1	86.5	98.3	76.3	86.1	95.2	50.1	70.1
07	THERMAL & MOISTURE PROTECTION	102.5	65.9	87.0	101.7	80.5	92.7	101.8	79.1	92.2	101.9	78.7	92.1	98.2	80.9	90.9	97.5	76.1	88.4
08	OPENINGS	94.1	59.7	86.2	93.8	74.2	89.3	93.8	69.7	88.3	93.8	70.9	88.6	101.3	70.3	94.1	94.6	55.1	85.5
0920	Plaster & Gypsum Board	82.7	48.9	60.0	94.6	73.5	80.4	93.9	68.7	77.0	95.6	73.5	80.7	102.7	75.8	84.6	94.7	48.9	63.9
0950, 0980	Ceilings & Acoustic Treatment	93.2	48.9	63.3	85.9	73.5	77.5	85.9	68.7	74.3	85.9	73.5	77.5	95.1	75.8	82.1	89.2	48.9	62.0
0960	Flooring	89.7	83.4	88.0	82.4	89.7	84.5	82.2	83.4	82.5	83.5	83.4	83.5	93.7	89.7	92.6	88.5	83.4	87.1
0970, 0990	Wall Finishes & Painting/Coating	150.3	52.9	93.5	73.3	61.6	66.5	73.3	65.3	68.7	73.3	61.6	66.5	91.4	81.3	85.5	85.6	46.1	62.6
09	FINISHES	91.4	59.5	74.1	83.6	76.0	79.4	83.7	72.3	77.5	84.3	74.7	79.1	94.0	79.4	86.2	89.1	58.8	72.6
COVERS	DIVS. 10 - 14, 25, 28, 41, 43, 44, 46	100.0	60.9	91.3	100.0	84.1	96.5	100.0	89.0	97.5	100.0	84.1	96.5	100.0	89.7	97.7	100.0	60.3	91.2
21, 22, 23	FIRE SUPPRESSION, PLUMBING & HVAC	97.1	73.4	86.9	97.0	76.3	88.2	100.1	80.6	91.8	97.0	76.0	88.0	100.0	80.6	91.7	96.9	76.1	88.0
26, 27, 3370	ELECTRICAL, COMMUNICATIONS & UTIL.	93.5	65.6	79.0	93.7	80.2	86.7	92.4	65.7	78.5	91.8	81.4	86.4	101.4	65.7	82.8	95.5	65.6	80.0
MF2016	WEIGHTED AVERAGE	100.4	71.9	87.9	97.3	81.4	90.3	98.5	78.4	89.7	98.5	79.0	89.9	98.3	80.2	90.4	98.0	71.5	86.4

NEBRASKA / NEVADA

DIVISION		NORFOLK 687 MAT.	INST.	TOTAL	NORTH PLATTE 691 MAT.	INST.	TOTAL	OMAHA 680 - 681 MAT.	INST.	TOTAL	VALENTINE 692 MAT.	INST.	TOTAL	CARSON CITY 897 MAT.	INST.	TOTAL	ELKO 898 MAT.	INST.	TOTAL
015433	CONTRACTOR EQUIPMENT		94.4	94.4		105.2	105.2		94.4	94.4		97.9	97.9		97.4	97.4		97.4	97.4
0241, 31 - 34	SITE & INFRASTRUCTURE, DEMOLITION	83.6	94.3	91.1	103.9	95.2	97.8	90.9	94.3	93.3	87.3	100.3	96.4	89.2	97.8	95.2	110.2	96.1	88.8
0310	Concrete Forming & Accessories	81.9	75.5	76.4	94.1	70.3	73.6	93.3	76.1	78.5	82.7	55.3	59.1	105.0	79.3	83.2	110.2	77.4	82.0
0320	Concrete Reinforcing	97.3	64.6	80.8	102.8	73.3	87.9	95.9	76.5	86.1	103.4	64.2	83.6	99.0	113.3	106.2	106.2	91.7	98.9
0330	Cast-in-Place Concrete	111.1	61.5	92.2	116.6	63.3	96.3	92.1	78.2	86.8	102.8	56.3	85.1	102.5	82.7	94.9	99.2	74.1	89.7
03	CONCRETE	98.9	69.3	85.4	105.2	69.7	89.0	88.6	77.4	83.5	102.5	58.3	82.3	96.7	86.7	92.1	94.4	79.0	87.4
04	MASONRY	123.3	78.6	95.5	93.8	75.1	82.1	97.9	78.6	85.9	105.4	75.0	86.6	115.7	72.4	88.8	122.3	67.3	88.2
05	METALS	101.9	79.4	95.0	97.7	92.2	96.0	102.1	84.3	96.7	110.3	78.2	100.4	105.7	94.4	102.2	109.1	86.6	102.2
06	WOOD, PLASTICS & COMPOSITES	82.5	75.8	78.8	97.1	69.4	81.7	94.5	75.8	84.1	81.0	49.7	63.6	92.3	77.8	84.2	101.7	77.8	88.4
07	THERMAL & MOISTURE PROTECTION	101.6	79.2	92.1	97.4	78.2	89.3	98.1	80.3	90.6	98.3	57.0	80.4	105.7	80.4	95.0	102.3	71.8	89.4
08	OPENINGS	95.4	69.7	89.5	93.9	68.4	88.0	99.3	76.4	94.0	96.3	55.2	86.9	98.7	80.0	94.4	101.5	75.3	95.5
0920	Plaster & Gypsum Board	94.7	75.8	82.0	94.7	68.7	77.2	101.0	75.8	84.0	96.1	48.9	64.4	99.3	77.3	84.5	101.3	77.3	85.2
0950, 0980	Ceilings & Acoustic Treatment	99.8	75.8	83.6	89.2	68.7	75.4	97.2	75.8	82.8	105.6	48.9	67.4	101.4	77.3	85.1	100.1	77.3	84.7
0960	Flooring	102.0	89.7	98.6	89.6	83.4	87.9	94.3	89.7	93.0	114.6	83.4	105.9	96.0	71.0	89.0	101.0	71.0	92.6
0970, 0990	Wall Finishes & Painting/Coating	127.6	61.6	89.1	85.6	61.6	71.6	101.4	75.4	86.2	150.8	63.8	100.0	93.9	80.4	86.0	93.4	80.4	85.8
09	FINISHES	99.9	76.9	87.4	89.4	71.9	79.9	96.1	78.4	86.5	109.6	60.4	82.8	96.1	77.5	86.0	92.8	76.5	84.0
COVERS	DIVS. 10 - 14, 25, 28, 41, 43, 44, 46	100.0	86.1	96.9	100.0	62.4	91.6	100.0	88.7	97.5	100.0	58.3	90.7	100.0	95.2	98.9	100.0	90.5	97.9
21, 22, 23	FIRE SUPPRESSION, PLUMBING & HVAC	96.7	76.7	88.1	100.0	75.6	89.6	100.0	76.9	90.1	96.5	76.2	87.8	100.1	80.1	91.6	98.6	77.7	89.7
26, 27, 3370	ELECTRICAL, COMMUNICATIONS & UTIL.	92.7	83.9	88.1	93.8	65.6	79.2	102.7	83.9	92.9	91.2	66.1	78.2	103.2	93.2	98.0	100.4	93.2	96.7
MF2016	WEIGHTED AVERAGE	98.8	78.6	90.0	97.8	75.2	87.9	98.4	80.8	90.7	100.5	70.5	87.4	101.0	84.9	93.9	100.6	81.2	92.1

479

City Cost Indexes

DIVISION		NEVADA									NEW HAMPSHIRE								
		ELY - 893			LAS VEGAS - 889-891			RENO - 894-895			CHARLESTON - 036			CLAREMONT - 037			CONCORD - 032-033		
		MAT.	INST.	TOTAL	MAT.	INST.	TOTAL	MAT.	INST.	TOTAL	MAT.	INST.	TOTAL	MAT.	INST.	TOTAL	MAT.	INST.	TOTAL
015433	CONTRACTOR EQUIPMENT		97.4	97.4		97.4	97.4		97.4	97.4		98.8	98.8		98.8	98.8		98.8	98.8
0241, 31 - 34	SITE & INFRASTRUCTURE, DEMOLITION	77.9	96.6	91.7	81.2	100.1	94.4	77.6	97.8	91.8	84.9	99.8	95.3	78.8	99.8	93.5	90.2	101.2	97.9
0310	Concrete Forming & Accessories	103.4	99.8	100.3	104.3	108.8	108.1	99.7	79.8	82.5	85.5	78.7	79.6	91.2	78.7	80.4	95.9	93.5	93.9
0320	Concrete Reinforcing	105.0	91.9	98.4	96.5	120.6	108.7	99.2	119.4	109.4	85.3	83.3	84.3	85.3	83.3	84.3	99.6	83.7	91.6
0330	Cast-in-Place Concrete	106.5	100.1	104.1	103.1	106.7	104.5	112.7	82.7	101.3	87.7	104.5	94.1	80.6	104.5	89.7	103.4	115.5	108.0
03	CONCRETE	102.6	98.3	100.6	97.9	109.5	103.2	102.5	87.8	95.8	87.3	88.7	88.0	80.2	88.7	84.1	94.6	99.3	96.7
04	MASONRY	127.9	78.1	97.0	114.8	99.2	105.1	121.5	72.4	91.0	95.6	77.4	84.3	95.9	77.4	84.4	104.0	100.1	101.6
05	METALS	109.1	89.7	103.1	117.6	101.6	112.7	110.8	96.4	106.4	93.0	89.3	91.9	93.0	89.3	91.9	99.6	90.6	96.9
06	WOOD, PLASTICS & COMPOSITES	92.6	101.0	97.3	90.7	106.9	99.7	87.0	77.8	81.9	94.2	83.2	88.1	100.0	83.2	90.7	94.9	92.7	93.7
07	THERMAL & MOISTURE PROTECTION	102.9	95.8	99.9	115.7	100.3	109.2	102.4	80.4	93.1	101.9	97.6	100.1	101.7	97.6	100.0	106.1	108.3	107.0
08	OPENINGS	101.4	88.2	98.4	100.4	111.9	103.0	99.2	81.4	95.1	97.3	82.9	94.0	98.4	82.9	94.8	95.7	88.1	94.0
0920	Plaster & Gypsum Board	96.7	101.1	99.7	91.9	107.2	102.1	87.0	77.3	80.5	104.8	82.4	89.7	106.1	82.4	90.2	107.3	92.1	97.1
0950, 0980	Ceilings & Acoustic Treatment	100.1	101.1	100.8	107.8	107.2	107.4	105.2	77.3	86.4	99.5	82.4	87.9	99.5	82.4	87.9	98.6	92.1	94.2
0960	Flooring	98.4	71.0	90.8	90.1	102.2	93.5	95.0	71.0	88.4	83.9	106.7	90.2	86.4	106.7	92.0	92.5	106.7	96.4
0970, 0990	Wall Finishes & Painting/Coating	93.4	117.1	107.2	95.9	114.9	107.0	93.4	80.4	85.8	84.8	94.1	90.2	84.8	94.1	90.2	88.8	94.1	91.9
09	FINISHES	92.0	96.9	94.7	90.5	108.3	100.1	90.5	77.5	83.4	86.6	85.4	85.9	87.1	85.4	86.2	90.6	95.7	93.3
COVERS	DIVS. 10 - 14, 25, 28, 41, 43, 44, 46	100.0	72.7	93.9	100.0	103.9	100.9	100.0	95.2	98.9	100.0	85.5	96.8	100.0	85.5	96.8	100.0	104.8	101.1
21, 22, 23	FIRE SUPPRESSION, PLUMBING & HVAC	98.6	99.5	99.0	100.3	100.7	100.5	100.2	80.1	91.6	97.0	60.1	81.2	97.0	60.1	81.2	100.0	85.2	93.7
26, 27, 3370	ELECTRICAL, COMMUNICATIONS & UTIL.	100.7	98.2	99.4	104.9	113.8	109.5	101.1	93.2	97.0	97.2	49.1	72.2	97.2	49.1	72.2	98.0	79.5	88.4
MF2016	WEIGHTED AVERAGE	101.9	94.1	98.5	103.1	105.2	104.0	101.8	85.3	94.6	94.3	76.3	86.4	93.5	76.3	86.0	97.9	92.4	95.5

DIVISION		NEW HAMPSHIRE															NEW JERSEY		
		KEENE - 034			LITTLETON - 035			MANCHESTER - 031			NASHUA - 030			PORTSMOUTH - 038			ATLANTIC CITY - 082, 084		
		MAT.	INST.	TOTAL	MAT.	INST.	TOTAL	MAT.	INST.	TOTAL	MAT.	INST.	TOTAL	MAT.	INST.	TOTAL	MAT.	INST.	TOTAL
015433	CONTRACTOR EQUIPMENT		98.8	98.8		98.8	98.8		98.8	98.8		98.8	98.8		98.8	98.8		96.3	96.3
0241, 31 - 34	SITE & INFRASTRUCTURE, DEMOLITION	91.9	100.1	97.6	79.0	100.1	93.7	92.1	101.2	98.5	93.4	101.0	98.7	86.9	101.6	97.2	89.7	104.6	100.2
0310	Concrete Forming & Accessories	89.8	80.3	81.6	102.0	80.3	83.3	95.9	93.7	94.0	97.8	93.6	94.2	86.9	93.5	92.6	110.1	143.9	139.3
0320	Concrete Reinforcing	85.3	83.4	84.3	86.0	83.4	84.7	99.6	83.7	91.6	106.5	83.7	95.0	85.3	83.7	84.5	75.8	142.1	109.2
0330	Cast-in-Place Concrete	88.1	106.5	95.1	79.0	106.6	89.5	103.4	115.6	108.0	83.4	115.4	95.5	79.1	116.0	93.1	77.9	142.7	102.5
03	CONCRETE	87.0	90.2	88.4	79.7	90.2	84.5	94.5	99.4	96.8	87.0	99.3	92.6	79.8	99.5	88.8	82.1	141.5	109.2
04	MASONRY	98.4	80.7	87.4	108.5	80.7	91.2	100.7	100.1	100.4	100.7	100.0	100.3	96.0	100.3	98.7	111.3	140.6	129.5
05	METALS	93.7	89.7	92.5	93.8	89.7	92.5	101.2	90.8	98.0	99.3	90.3	96.6	95.3	91.5	94.2	96.5	115.7	102.4
06	WOOD, PLASTICS & COMPOSITES	98.4	83.2	89.9	109.2	83.2	94.7	95.0	92.7	93.7	107.6	92.7	99.3	95.4	92.7	93.9	118.0	144.6	132.8
07	THERMAL & MOISTURE PROTECTION	102.4	99.1	101.0	101.8	99.1	100.7	106.3	108.3	107.2	102.8	108.3	105.1	102.4	108.3	104.9	101.0	137.4	116.4
08	OPENINGS	96.0	86.5	93.8	99.3	82.9	95.5	96.7	91.8	95.5	100.6	91.1	98.4	100.9	81.2	96.4	96.8	140.3	106.8
0920	Plaster & Gypsum Board	105.1	82.4	89.8	118.9	82.4	94.4	107.3	92.1	97.1	114.5	92.1	99.5	104.8	92.1	96.3	116.0	145.4	135.7
0950, 0980	Ceilings & Acoustic Treatment	99.5	82.4	87.9	99.5	82.4	87.9	99.6	92.1	94.5	111.5	92.1	98.4	100.4	92.1	94.8	91.4	145.4	127.8
0960	Flooring	86.0	106.7	91.8	96.7	105.6	99.2	89.8	106.7	94.5	89.7	106.7	94.4	84.1	106.7	90.4	92.5	168.1	113.4
0970, 0990	Wall Finishes & Painting/Coating	84.8	108.1	98.4	84.8	94.1	90.2	90.8	108.1	100.9	84.8	106.9	97.7	84.8	106.9	97.7	83.0	145.9	119.6
09	FINISHES	88.4	87.8	88.0	91.9	86.0	88.7	91.9	97.2	94.8	93.1	97.1	95.3	87.4	97.1	92.7	89.7	149.9	122.4
COVERS	DIVS. 10 - 14, 25, 28, 41, 43, 44, 46	100.0	93.2	98.5	100.0	98.5	99.7	100.0	104.8	101.1	100.0	104.8	101.1	100.0	104.8	101.1	100.0	119.2	104.3
21, 22, 23	FIRE SUPPRESSION, PLUMBING & HVAC	97.0	63.3	82.6	97.0	69.8	85.4	100.1	85.2	93.7	100.1	85.2	93.7	100.1	85.2	93.7	99.8	131.7	113.4
26, 27, 3370	ELECTRICAL, COMMUNICATIONS & UTIL.	97.2	58.6	77.2	98.2	51.9	74.1	98.1	79.5	88.4	99.4	79.4	89.0	97.7	79.5	88.2	93.2	144.6	119.9
MF2016	WEIGHTED AVERAGE	94.8	79.6	88.1	94.9	79.8	88.3	98.3	92.7	95.9	97.7	92.6	95.5	95.1	92.4	93.9	95.7	134.7	112.8

DIVISION		NEW JERSEY																	
		CAMDEN - 081			DOVER - 078			ELIZABETH - 072			HACKENSACK - 076			JERSEY CITY - 073			LONG BRANCH - 077		
		MAT.	INST.	TOTAL	MAT.	INST.	TOTAL	MAT.	INST.	TOTAL	MAT.	INST.	TOTAL	MAT.	INST.	TOTAL	MAT.	INST.	TOTAL
015433	CONTRACTOR EQUIPMENT		96.3	96.3		98.8	98.8		98.8	98.8		98.8	98.8		96.3	96.3		95.9	95.9
0241, 31 - 34	SITE & INFRASTRUCTURE, DEMOLITION	90.9	104.6	100.5	96.5	106.3	103.4	100.3	106.3	104.5	97.5	106.3	103.6	88.7	106.2	100.9	92.5	105.9	101.9
0310	Concrete Forming & Accessories	101.3	143.8	137.9	99.4	146.5	140.0	111.6	146.5	141.7	99.4	146.4	139.9	103.7	146.4	140.6	104.2	145.6	139.9
0320	Concrete Reinforcing	99.5	132.6	116.2	78.1	150.5	114.6	78.1	150.5	114.6	78.1	150.5	114.6	101.3	150.5	126.1	78.1	150.5	114.6
0330	Cast-in-Place Concrete	75.6	140.8	100.3	85.2	136.1	104.5	73.2	136.1	97.1	83.2	136.1	103.3	66.4	136.1	92.9	73.8	140.8	99.3
03	CONCRETE	82.6	139.1	108.4	84.2	142.1	110.7	80.8	142.1	108.8	82.7	142.1	109.9	76.6	141.9	107.5	82.3	143.1	110.1
04	MASONRY	101.4	140.6	125.7	93.5	143.0	124.2	111.1	143.0	130.9	97.6	143.0	125.8	89.3	143.0	122.6	103.2	141.1	126.7
05	METALS	102.3	112.3	105.3	94.3	123.7	103.4	95.9	123.7	104.4	94.4	123.7	103.4	100.2	120.6	106.4	94.4	120.4	102.4
06	WOOD, PLASTICS & COMPOSITES	106.7	144.6	127.8	102.4	146.2	126.7	117.3	146.2	133.3	102.4	146.2	126.7	103.2	146.2	127.1	104.2	146.1	127.5
07	THERMAL & MOISTURE PROTECTION	100.8	138.4	116.8	108.7	136.4	120.4	108.9	136.4	120.5	108.4	135.6	119.9	108.1	136.4	120.1	108.3	135.2	119.7
08	OPENINGS	99.1	138.1	108.0	104.2	144.2	113.4	102.6	144.2	112.1	102.0	144.2	111.7	100.7	144.2	110.7	96.6	144.2	107.6
0920	Plaster & Gypsum Board	111.5	145.4	134.3	107.2	147.0	133.9	114.4	147.0	136.3	107.2	147.0	133.9	110.2	147.0	134.9	109.1	147.0	134.6
0950, 0980	Ceilings & Acoustic Treatment	101.4	145.4	130.9	87.8	147.0	127.7	89.7	147.0	128.3	87.8	147.0	127.7	97.3	147.0	130.8	87.8	147.0	127.7
0960	Flooring	88.6	168.1	110.6	81.8	191.9	112.4	86.9	191.9	116.0	81.8	191.9	112.4	82.9	191.9	113.1	83.1	187.0	111.9
0970, 0990	Wall Finishes & Painting/Coating	83.0	145.9	119.6	84.0	145.9	120.1	84.0	145.9	120.1	84.0	145.9	120.1	84.1	145.9	120.1	84.1	145.9	120.1
09	FINISHES	89.7	149.9	122.4	85.4	155.4	123.5	88.8	155.4	125.0	85.3	155.4	123.4	87.8	155.4	124.6	86.3	154.2	123.2
COVERS	DIVS. 10 - 14, 25, 28, 41, 43, 44, 46	100.0	119.2	104.3	100.0	131.8	107.1	100.0	131.8	107.1	100.0	131.8	107.1	100.0	131.8	107.1	100.0	119.4	104.3
21, 22, 23	FIRE SUPPRESSION, PLUMBING & HVAC	100.0	131.6	113.5	99.9	137.5	116.0	100.1	137.5	116.1	99.9	137.5	116.0	100.1	137.5	116.0	99.9	136.5	115.6
26, 27, 3370	ELECTRICAL, COMMUNICATIONS & UTIL.	97.7	139.5	119.4	94.8	142.9	119.8	95.4	142.9	120.1	94.8	140.9	118.8	99.5	140.9	121.0	94.4	137.2	116.7
MF2016	WEIGHTED AVERAGE	97.0	133.3	112.9	95.7	138.2	114.3	96.8	138.2	114.9	95.5	137.9	114.0	95.9	137.6	114.1	95.0	136.2	113.1

City Cost Indexes

		NEW JERSEY																	
		NEW BRUNSWICK			NEWARK			PATERSON			POINT PLEASANT			SUMMIT			TRENTON		
	DIVISION	088 - 089			070 - 071			074 - 075			087			079			085 - 086		
		MAT.	INST.	TOTAL	MAT.	INST.	TOTAL	MAT.	INST.	TOTAL	MAT.	INST.	TOTAL	MAT.	INST.	TOTAL	MAT.	INST.	TOTAL
---	---	---	---	---	---	---	---	---	---	---	---	---	---	---	---	---	---	---	---
015433	CONTRACTOR EQUIPMENT		95.9	95.9		98.8	98.8		98.8	98.8		95.9	95.9		98.8	98.8		95.9	95.9
0241, 31 - 34	SITE & INFRASTRUCTURE, DEMOLITION	102.2	106.0	104.9	100.9	106.3	104.7	99.4	106.3	104.2	103.7	105.9	105.3	98.1	106.3	103.9	89.0	105.9	100.9
0310	Concrete Forming & Accessories	104.3	146.4	140.6	104.4	146.5	140.7	101.4	146.4	140.2	98.8	145.5	139.1	102.2	146.5	140.4	100.5	145.3	139.1
0320	Concrete Reinforcing	76.7	150.5	113.9	99.7	150.5	125.3	101.3	150.5	126.1	76.7	150.5	113.9	78.1	150.5	114.6	100.7	119.9	110.4
0330	Cast-in-Place Concrete	96.3	141.9	113.6	93.9	136.1	109.9	84.7	136.1	104.2	96.3	142.9	114.0	70.7	136.1	95.6	94.8	140.6	112.2
03	CONCRETE	97.5	143.8	118.7	91.6	142.1	114.7	87.1	142.1	112.2	97.2	143.8	118.5	78.2	142.1	107.4	91.9	137.6	112.8
04	MASONRY	109.7	143.0	130.4	96.6	143.0	125.4	94.0	143.0	124.4	98.0	141.1	124.7	96.6	143.0	125.4	101.9	141.1	126.2
05	METALS	96.6	120.5	103.9	102.0	123.7	108.7	95.5	123.7	104.2	96.6	120.3	103.9	94.3	123.7	103.4	102.0	109.1	104.2
06	WOOD, PLASTICS & COMPOSITES	111.5	146.1	130.8	100.0	146.2	125.7	105.0	146.2	127.9	104.1	146.1	127.5	106.1	146.2	128.4	93.5	146.1	122.8
07	THERMAL & MOISTURE PROTECTION	101.3	134.8	115.5	109.8	136.4	121.1	108.7	135.6	120.1	101.3	137.6	116.7	109.1	136.4	120.6	101.7	138.6	117.3
08	OPENINGS	92.0	144.2	104.0	100.6	144.2	110.6	107.3	144.2	115.8	93.8	144.2	105.3	108.3	144.2	116.5	98.5	136.7	107.3
0920	Plaster & Gypsum Board	113.3	147.0	136.0	102.5	147.0	132.4	110.2	147.0	134.9	108.4	147.0	134.3	109.1	147.0	134.6	103.4	147.0	132.7
0950, 0980	Ceilings & Acoustic Treatment	91.4	147.0	128.9	98.8	147.0	131.3	97.3	147.0	130.8	91.4	147.0	128.9	87.8	147.0	127.7	97.9	147.0	131.0
0960	Flooring	90.0	191.9	118.3	87.4	191.9	116.3	82.9	191.9	113.1	87.5	168.1	109.8	83.1	191.9	113.3	91.9	187.0	118.2
0970, 0990	Wall Finishes & Painting/Coating	83.0	145.9	119.6	85.4	145.9	120.6	84.0	145.9	120.1	83.0	145.9	119.6	84.0	145.9	120.1	86.6	145.9	121.2
09	FINISHES	89.6	155.3	125.4	90.7	155.4	125.9	88.0	155.4	124.6	88.2	150.9	122.3	86.4	155.4	123.9	92.4	154.2	126.0
COVERS	DIVS. 10 - 14, 25, 28, 41, 43, 44, 46	100.0	131.7	107.0	100.0	131.8	107.1	100.0	131.8	107.1	100.0	116.4	103.7	100.0	131.8	107.1	100.0	119.4	104.3
21, 22, 23	FIRE SUPPRESSION, PLUMBING & HVAC	99.8	137.5	115.9	100.0	137.5	116.1	100.1	137.5	116.1	99.8	136.5	115.5	99.9	137.5	116.0	100.2	136.2	115.6
26, 27, 3370	ELECTRICAL, COMMUNICATIONS & UTIL.	93.9	141.2	118.5	103.1	140.9	122.8	99.5	142.9	122.1	93.2	137.2	116.1	95.4	142.9	120.1	101.2	135.9	119.2
MF2016	WEIGHTED AVERAGE	97.4	137.8	115.1	99.1	137.9	116.1	97.4	138.2	115.3	96.8	135.8	113.9	95.8	138.2	114.3	98.5	133.9	114.0

		NEW JERSEY			NEW MEXICO														
		VINELAND			ALBUQUERQUE			CARRIZOZO			CLOVIS			FARMINGTON			GALLUP		
	DIVISION	080, 083			870 - 872			883			881			874			873		
		MAT.	INST.	TOTAL	MAT.	INST.	TOTAL	MAT.	INST.	TOTAL	MAT.	INST.	TOTAL	MAT.	INST.	TOTAL	MAT.	INST.	TOTAL
---	---	---	---	---	---	---	---	---	---	---	---	---	---	---	---	---	---	---	---
015433	CONTRACTOR EQUIPMENT		96.3	96.3		111.0	111.0		111.0	111.0		111.0	111.0		111.0	111.0		111.0	111.0
0241, 31 - 34	SITE & INFRASTRUCTURE, DEMOLITION	93.9	104.7	101.4	92.3	102.4	99.4	112.0	102.4	105.3	98.8	102.4	101.3	98.8	102.4	101.3	108.5	102.4	104.2
0310	Concrete Forming & Accessories	96.0	144.0	137.4	99.0	64.1	68.9	97.1	64.1	68.6	97.1	64.0	68.5	99.1	64.1	68.9	99.1	64.1	68.9
0320	Concrete Reinforcing	75.8	135.4	105.9	97.0	71.0	83.9	109.7	71.0	90.2	110.9	71.0	90.8	106.1	71.0	88.4	101.5	71.0	86.1
0330	Cast-in-Place Concrete	84.0	140.9	105.6	93.6	70.1	84.7	94.7	70.1	85.3	94.6	70.0	85.3	94.5	70.1	85.2	88.9	70.1	81.8
03	CONCRETE	86.3	139.8	110.8	93.3	68.8	82.1	114.3	68.8	93.5	102.6	68.7	87.1	96.7	68.8	83.9	102.9	68.8	87.3
04	MASONRY	98.6	141.1	125.0	107.3	60.0	78.0	106.9	60.0	77.8	106.9	60.0	77.8	116.9	60.0	81.6	101.6	60.0	75.8
05	METALS	96.5	113.9	101.8	109.2	91.0	103.6	105.2	91.0	100.8	104.8	90.8	100.5	106.8	91.0	101.9	105.9	91.0	101.3
06	WOOD, PLASTICS & COMPOSITES	101.0	144.6	125.2	94.7	64.6	77.9	92.4	64.6	77.0	92.4	64.6	77.0	94.8	64.6	78.0	94.8	64.6	78.0
07	THERMAL & MOISTURE PROTECTION	100.8	137.6	116.4	96.9	70.8	85.8	99.5	70.8	87.3	98.2	70.8	86.6	97.1	70.8	86.0	98.2	70.8	86.6
08	OPENINGS	93.3	139.1	103.8	98.5	65.8	91.0	96.6	65.8	89.5	96.7	65.8	89.7	100.8	65.8	92.8	100.8	65.8	92.8
0920	Plaster & Gypsum Board	106.8	145.4	132.7	100.6	63.4	75.6	77.6	63.4	68.1	77.6	63.4	68.1	92.7	63.4	73.0	92.7	63.4	73.0
0950, 0980	Ceilings & Acoustic Treatment	91.4	145.4	127.8	99.3	63.4	75.1	102.3	63.4	76.1	102.3	63.4	76.1	97.1	63.4	74.4	97.1	63.4	74.4
0960	Flooring	86.6	168.1	109.2	87.7	69.5	82.7	98.5	69.5	90.4	98.5	69.5	90.4	89.3	69.5	83.8	89.3	69.5	83.8
0970, 0990	Wall Finishes & Painting/Coating	83.0	145.9	119.6	95.3	52.8	70.5	93.6	52.8	69.8	93.6	52.8	69.8	89.9	52.8	68.3	89.9	52.8	68.3
09	FINISHES	87.0	150.0	121.3	89.4	63.6	75.4	93.9	63.6	77.4	92.6	63.6	76.8	88.3	63.6	74.9	89.6	63.6	75.4
COVERS	DIVS. 10 - 14, 25, 28, 41, 43, 44, 46	100.0	119.4	104.3	100.0	84.0	96.5	100.0	84.0	96.5	100.0	84.0	96.5	100.0	84.0	96.5	100.0	84.0	96.5
21, 22, 23	FIRE SUPPRESSION, PLUMBING & HVAC	99.8	131.9	113.5	100.2	69.2	86.9	98.1	69.2	85.7	98.1	68.8	85.6	100.0	69.2	86.8	98.1	69.2	85.7
26, 27, 3370	ELECTRICAL, COMMUNICATIONS & UTIL.	93.2	144.6	119.9	88.1	88.5	88.3	91.7	88.5	90.0	89.4	88.5	88.9	86.2	88.5	87.4	85.6	88.5	87.1
MF2016	WEIGHTED AVERAGE	95.0	134.4	112.2	98.5	75.1	88.3	101.1	75.1	89.7	98.9	75.0	88.4	99.1	75.1	88.6	98.9	75.1	88.5

		NEW MEXICO																	
		LAS CRUCES			LAS VEGAS			ROSWELL			SANTA FE			SOCORRO			TRUTH/CONSEQUENCES		
	DIVISION	880			877			882			875			878			879		
		MAT.	INST.	TOTAL	MAT.	INST.	TOTAL	MAT.	INST.	TOTAL	MAT.	INST.	TOTAL	MAT.	INST.	TOTAL	MAT.	INST.	TOTAL
---	---	---	---	---	---	---	---	---	---	---	---	---	---	---	---	---	---	---	---
015433	CONTRACTOR EQUIPMENT		85.7	85.7		111.0	111.0		111.0	111.0		111.0	111.0		111.0	111.0		85.7	85.7
0241, 31 - 34	SITE & INFRASTRUCTURE, DEMOLITION	99.0	80.8	86.3	97.9	102.4	101.1	101.0	102.4	102.0	102.2	102.4	102.3	94.4	102.4	100.0	114.9	80.9	91.0
0310	Concrete Forming & Accessories	93.8	63.0	67.2	99.1	64.1	68.9	97.1	64.1	68.6	97.8	64.1	68.7	99.1	64.1	68.9	96.8	63.0	67.6
0320	Concrete Reinforcing	106.4	70.9	88.5	103.3	71.0	87.0	110.9	71.0	90.8	96.5	71.0	83.7	105.3	71.0	88.0	98.4	70.9	84.5
0330	Cast-in-Place Concrete	89.4	62.6	79.2	91.9	70.1	83.6	94.6	70.1	85.3	97.5	70.1	87.1	90.0	70.1	82.5	98.6	62.6	85.0
03	CONCRETE	81.3	65.3	74.0	94.3	68.8	82.6	103.4	68.8	87.6	93.5	68.8	82.2	93.1	68.8	82.0	87.1	65.3	77.1
04	MASONRY	102.2	59.6	75.8	101.9	60.0	75.9	118.3	60.0	82.1	94.9	60.0	73.2	101.8	60.0	75.9	99.0	59.6	74.6
05	METALS	103.6	83.0	97.2	105.6	91.0	101.1	106.1	91.0	101.4	102.7	91.0	99.1	105.9	91.0	101.3	105.5	83.0	98.6
06	WOOD, PLASTICS & COMPOSITES	81.4	63.5	71.4	94.8	64.6	78.0	92.4	64.6	77.0	93.9	64.6	77.6	94.8	64.6	78.0	85.9	63.5	73.5
07	THERMAL & MOISTURE PROTECTION	85.7	65.9	77.3	96.7	70.8	85.7	98.4	70.8	86.7	99.2	70.8	87.2	96.6	70.8	85.7	85.6	65.9	77.2
08	OPENINGS	92.3	65.2	86.1	97.3	65.8	90.1	96.6	65.8	89.5	100.0	65.8	92.2	97.1	65.8	89.9	90.7	65.2	84.9
0920	Plaster & Gypsum Board	75.9	63.4	67.5	92.7	63.4	73.0	77.6	63.4	68.1	107.8	63.4	78.0	92.7	63.4	73.0	94.1	63.4	73.5
0950, 0980	Ceilings & Acoustic Treatment	88.0	63.4	71.4	97.1	63.4	74.4	102.3	63.4	76.1	97.7	63.4	74.6	97.1	63.4	74.4	85.9	63.4	70.7
0960	Flooring	129.6	69.5	112.9	89.3	69.5	83.8	98.5	69.5	90.4	97.0	69.5	89.4	89.3	69.5	83.8	118.0	69.5	104.5
0970, 0990	Wall Finishes & Painting/Coating	82.8	52.8	65.3	89.9	52.8	68.3	93.6	52.8	69.8	95.9	52.8	70.8	89.9	52.8	68.3	82.3	52.8	65.1
09	FINISHES	102.6	62.7	80.9	88.2	63.6	74.8	92.7	63.6	76.9	96.6	63.6	78.6	88.1	63.6	74.8	100.0	62.8	79.8
COVERS	DIVS. 10 - 14, 25, 28, 41, 43, 44, 46	100.0	81.5	95.9	100.0	84.0	96.5	100.0	84.0	96.5	100.0	84.0	96.5	100.0	84.0	96.5	100.0	81.5	95.9
21, 22, 23	FIRE SUPPRESSION, PLUMBING & HVAC	100.4	68.9	86.9	98.1	69.2	85.7	99.9	69.2	86.8	100.1	69.2	86.9	98.1	69.2	85.7	98.1	68.9	85.6
26, 27, 3370	ELECTRICAL, COMMUNICATIONS & UTIL.	91.4	88.5	89.9	87.7	88.5	88.1	90.8	88.5	89.6	99.8	88.5	93.9	86.0	88.5	87.3	89.6	88.5	89.0
MF2016	WEIGHTED AVERAGE	96.4	71.7	85.6	97.2	75.1	87.5	100.3	75.1	89.3	99.1	75.1	88.6	96.8	75.1	87.3	96.6	71.8	85.7

City Cost Indexes

		NEW MEXICO			NEW YORK													
	DIVISION	TUCUMCARI			ALBANY			BINGHAMTON			BRONX			BROOKLYN			BUFFALO		
		884			120 - 122			137 - 139			104			112			140 - 142		
		MAT.	INST.	TOTAL	MAT.	INST.	TOTAL	MAT.	INST.	TOTAL	MAT.	INST.	TOTAL	MAT.	INST.	TOTAL	MAT.	INST.	TOTAL
015433	CONTRACTOR EQUIPMENT		111.0	111.0		115.8	115.8		121.0	121.0		106.9	106.9		112.3	112.3		98.9	98.9
0241, 31 - 34	SITE & INFRASTRUCTURE, DEMOLITION	98.4	102.4	101.2	83.9	104.7	98.5	96.2	93.2	94.1	92.6	113.7	107.4	120.9	125.5	124.1	99.6	101.6	101.0
0310	Concrete Forming & Accessories	97.1	64.0	68.5	99.3	105.9	105.0	100.6	90.7	92.0	99.1	193.1	180.2	106.7	182.5	172.1	102.3	120.3	117.8
0320	Concrete Reinforcing	108.7	71.0	89.7	103.7	119.5	111.7	100.4	104.2	102.3	96.4	172.4	134.8	101.8	222.6	162.8	108.6	115.3	111.9
0330	Cast-in-Place Concrete	94.6	70.0	85.3	79.7	116.1	93.5	105.1	107.6	106.1	86.4	173.4	119.5	107.2	171.7	131.7	108.3	125.3	114.8
03	CONCRETE	101.9	68.7	86.7	84.1	112.9	97.3	93.4	101.3	97.0	89.4	181.7	131.6	104.6	184.0	140.9	105.1	120.6	112.2
04	MASONRY	118.3	60.0	82.1	90.5	116.0	106.3	106.8	104.1	105.1	90.1	182.8	147.6	117.2	182.8	157.9	113.5	123.6	119.7
05	METALS	104.8	90.8	100.5	101.2	128.8	109.7	94.2	134.4	106.6	90.8	170.3	115.2	102.1	167.5	122.2	99.4	108.2	102.1
06	WOOD, PLASTICS & COMPOSITES	92.4	64.6	77.0	94.4	102.3	98.8	105.6	86.6	95.0	98.0	197.8	153.6	107.2	183.4	149.6	100.9	119.7	111.4
07	THERMAL & MOISTURE PROTECTION	98.2	70.8	86.6	106.6	110.3	108.2	107.1	95.0	102.0	104.4	168.9	131.7	107.3	166.6	132.4	104.8	113.3	108.4
08	OPENINGS	96.5	65.8	89.5	95.4	104.5	97.5	91.9	92.8	92.1	92.8	200.7	117.6	89.4	190.6	112.7	99.8	114.0	103.1
0920	Plaster & Gypsum Board	77.6	63.4	68.1	102.5	102.3	102.3	107.2	85.9	92.9	96.7	200.3	166.3	103.4	185.8	158.7	105.4	120.1	115.3
0950, 0980	Ceilings & Acoustic Treatment	102.3	63.4	76.1	99.6	102.3	101.4	94.1	85.9	88.6	85.2	200.3	162.8	89.9	185.8	154.5	97.3	120.1	112.7
0960	Flooring	98.5	69.5	90.4	90.6	111.1	96.3	99.4	99.2	99.4	92.6	189.9	119.6	106.3	189.9	129.5	95.2	118.5	101.7
0970, 0990	Wall Finishes & Painting/Coating	93.6	52.8	69.8	93.8	102.3	98.8	87.4	99.6	94.5	103.8	159.9	136.5	114.2	159.9	140.8	97.8	115.8	108.3
09	FINISHES	92.5	63.6	76.8	90.3	105.9	98.8	91.4	92.2	91.8	92.6	190.5	145.8	104.3	181.9	146.5	100.1	120.1	111.0
COVERS	DIVS. 10 - 14, 25, 28, 41, 43, 44, 46	100.0	84.0	96.5	100.0	102.0	100.4	100.0	98.8	99.7	100.0	137.9	108.4	100.0	135.5	107.9	100.0	108.1	101.8
21, 22, 23	FIRE SUPPRESSION, PLUMBING & HVAC	98.1	68.8	85.6	100.2	109.0	103.9	100.6	99.6	100.2	100.2	170.4	130.2	99.7	170.2	129.9	100.0	103.4	101.5
26, 27, 3370	ELECTRICAL, COMMUNICATIONS & UTIL.	91.7	88.5	90.0	95.5	110.9	103.5	99.4	100.8	100.1	94.2	181.5	139.6	99.1	181.5	141.9	98.9	106.0	102.6
MF2016	WEIGHTED AVERAGE	99.5	75.0	88.8	95.8	111.2	102.5	97.2	101.7	99.2	94.7	173.4	129.2	101.6	172.5	132.7	101.2	111.6	105.8

		NEW YORK																	
	DIVISION	ELMIRA			FAR ROCKAWAY			FLUSHING			GLENS FALLS			HICKSVILLE			JAMAICA		
		148 - 149			116			113			128			115, 117, 118			114		
		MAT.	INST.	TOTAL	MAT.	INST.	TOTAL	MAT.	INST.	TOTAL	MAT.	INST.	TOTAL	MAT.	INST.	TOTAL	MAT.	INST.	TOTAL
015433	CONTRACTOR EQUIPMENT		123.0	123.0		112.3	112.3		112.3	112.3		115.8	115.8		112.3	112.3		112.3	112.3
0241, 31 - 34	SITE & INFRASTRUCTURE, DEMOLITION	102.2	92.8	95.6	124.2	125.5	125.1	124.2	125.5	125.1	74.3	104.2	95.3	113.8	124.6	121.3	118.4	125.5	123.4
0310	Concrete Forming & Accessories	83.5	96.0	94.3	93.1	193.0	179.2	97.0	193.0	179.8	84.8	96.3	94.8	89.6	162.1	152.1	97.0	193.0	179.8
0320	Concrete Reinforcing	108.1	108.3	108.2	101.8	222.7	162.8	103.5	222.7	163.6	99.3	111.3	105.4	101.8	222.5	162.7	101.8	222.7	162.8
0330	Cast-in-Place Concrete	98.3	106.7	101.5	115.9	171.8	137.1	115.9	171.8	137.1	77.0	110.7	89.8	98.5	168.2	125.0	107.2	171.8	131.7
03	CONCRETE	89.5	104.3	96.2	110.7	188.8	146.4	111.2	188.8	146.7	78.3	105.3	90.6	96.6	173.4	131.7	104.0	188.8	142.8
04	MASONRY	105.1	105.1	105.1	122.0	182.8	159.7	115.9	182.8	157.4	96.6	108.1	103.7	111.7	178.0	152.8	119.9	182.8	158.9
05	METALS	95.2	137.2	108.1	102.1	167.5	122.2	102.1	167.5	122.2	94.6	125.1	104.0	103.6	164.4	122.3	102.1	167.5	122.2
06	WOOD, PLASTICS & COMPOSITES	84.7	94.3	90.0	91.1	197.5	150.3	95.6	197.5	152.3	87.2	92.9	90.4	87.8	159.5	127.7	95.6	197.5	152.3
07	THERMAL & MOISTURE PROTECTION	103.2	95.6	100.0	107.2	168.2	133.0	107.2	168.2	133.0	99.7	105.3	102.1	106.9	161.4	130.0	107.0	168.2	132.9
08	OPENINGS	98.3	97.3	98.0	88.1	198.4	113.5	88.1	198.4	113.5	90.4	98.6	92.3	88.5	177.4	108.9	88.1	198.4	113.5
0920	Plaster & Gypsum Board	101.8	94.1	96.6	92.5	200.3	164.9	94.8	200.3	165.6	95.0	92.6	93.4	92.1	161.2	138.5	94.8	200.3	165.6
0950, 0980	Ceilings & Acoustic Treatment	98.5	94.1	95.5	79.7	200.3	161.0	79.7	200.3	161.0	85.6	92.6	90.3	78.7	161.2	134.4	79.7	200.3	161.0
0960	Flooring	86.5	102.4	90.9	101.1	189.9	125.7	102.6	189.9	126.9	82.3	111.1	90.3	100.0	176.4	121.2	102.6	189.9	126.9
0970, 0990	Wall Finishes & Painting/Coating	94.8	91.5	92.9	114.2	159.9	140.8	114.2	159.9	140.8	89.8	97.3	94.2	114.2	159.9	140.8	114.2	159.9	140.8
09	FINISHES	92.0	96.5	94.5	99.6	190.2	148.8	100.4	190.2	149.3	82.4	98.2	91.0	98.2	164.1	134.1	100.0	190.2	149.1
COVERS	DIVS. 10 - 14, 25, 28, 41, 43, 44, 46	100.0	97.9	99.5	100.0	137.1	108.3	100.0	137.1	108.3	100.0	98.1	99.6	100.0	124.9	105.5	100.0	137.1	108.3
21, 22, 23	FIRE SUPPRESSION, PLUMBING & HVAC	97.1	96.5	96.9	96.6	170.2	128.1	96.6	170.2	128.1	97.1	104.4	100.3	99.7	159.5	125.3	96.6	170.2	128.1
26, 27, 3370	ELECTRICAL, COMMUNICATIONS & UTIL.	97.7	103.8	100.9	105.9	181.5	145.2	105.9	181.5	145.2	90.7	110.9	101.2	98.6	142.4	121.4	97.6	181.5	141.2
MF2016	WEIGHTED AVERAGE	96.5	103.0	99.3	102.0	174.8	133.9	101.9	174.8	133.8	91.4	106.4	98.0	99.6	158.6	125.6	100.2	174.8	132.9

		NEW YORK																	
	DIVISION	JAMESTOWN			KINGSTON			LONG ISLAND CITY			MONTICELLO			MOUNT VERNON			NEW ROCHELLE		
		147			124			111			127			105			108		
		MAT.	INST.	TOTAL	MAT.	INST.	TOTAL	MAT.	INST.	TOTAL	MAT.	INST.	TOTAL	MAT.	INST.	TOTAL	MAT.	INST.	TOTAL
015433	CONTRACTOR EQUIPMENT		91.9	91.9		112.3	112.3		112.3	112.3		112.3	112.3		106.9	106.9		106.9	106.9
0241, 31 - 34	SITE & INFRASTRUCTURE, DEMOLITION	103.7	93.5	96.6	145.6	120.7	128.1	122.0	125.5	124.5	140.6	121.2	127.0	97.5	109.9	106.2	97.3	109.9	106.1
0310	Concrete Forming & Accessories	83.6	89.1	88.3	86.2	128.1	122.4	101.3	193.0	180.4	93.3	128.1	123.3	89.4	140.1	133.1	104.5	140.1	135.2
0320	Concrete Reinforcing	108.3	114.5	111.4	99.8	156.7	128.5	101.8	222.7	162.8	99.0	156.7	128.1	95.2	170.9	133.4	95.3	170.9	133.4
0330	Cast-in-Place Concrete	102.0	85.3	95.7	103.9	145.2	119.6	110.6	171.8	133.8	97.3	145.2	115.5	96.5	150.7	117.0	96.5	150.7	117.1
03	CONCRETE	92.4	92.3	92.4	98.3	138.6	116.7	107.0	188.8	144.4	93.6	138.6	114.2	98.7	149.4	121.9	98.1	149.4	121.5
04	MASONRY	114.6	101.4	106.4	111.3	150.7	135.7	114.0	182.8	156.7	104.2	150.7	133.0	95.9	154.7	132.4	95.9	154.7	132.4
05	METALS	92.7	102.6	95.7	102.8	134.2	112.5	102.1	167.5	122.2	102.9	134.2	112.5	90.6	162.5	112.7	90.8	162.4	112.8
06	WOOD, PLASTICS & COMPOSITES	83.3	86.1	84.8	88.4	122.0	107.1	101.4	197.5	154.9	95.2	122.0	110.1	88.6	134.9	114.3	105.4	134.9	121.8
07	THERMAL & MOISTURE PROTECTION	102.7	94.0	99.0	123.4	143.5	131.9	107.2	168.2	133.0	123.1	143.5	131.7	105.4	146.6	122.8	105.4	146.6	122.9
08	OPENINGS	98.1	94.8	97.3	92.6	140.8	103.7	88.1	198.4	113.4	88.3	140.8	100.3	92.8	165.9	109.6	92.9	165.9	109.6
0920	Plaster & Gypsum Board	88.9	85.6	86.7	97.2	122.8	114.4	99.4	200.3	167.2	97.9	122.8	114.6	91.7	135.6	121.2	104.9	135.6	125.5
0950, 0980	Ceilings & Acoustic Treatment	95.1	85.6	88.7	76.3	122.8	107.6	79.7	200.3	161.0	76.3	122.8	107.6	83.5	135.6	118.6	83.5	135.6	118.6
0960	Flooring	89.0	102.4	92.7	98.7	162.9	116.5	104.3	189.9	128.0	101.1	162.9	118.2	84.6	173.4	109.3	92.0	173.4	114.6
0970, 0990	Wall Finishes & Painting/Coating	96.4	95.1	95.6	118.7	129.0	124.7	114.2	159.9	140.8	118.7	129.0	124.7	102.2	159.9	135.9	102.2	159.9	135.9
09	FINISHES	90.6	91.4	91.0	96.0	134.0	116.7	101.3	190.2	149.7	96.4	134.0	116.9	89.6	147.5	121.1	93.5	147.5	122.8
COVERS	DIVS. 10 - 14, 25, 28, 41, 43, 44, 46	100.0	96.6	99.3	100.0	115.9	103.5	100.0	137.1	108.3	100.0	115.9	103.5	100.0	119.9	104.4	100.0	116.8	103.7
21, 22, 23	FIRE SUPPRESSION, PLUMBING & HVAC	97.0	89.0	93.6	97.1	125.7	109.3	99.7	170.2	129.9	97.1	121.8	107.6	97.2	140.6	115.8	97.2	140.6	115.8
26, 27, 3370	ELECTRICAL, COMMUNICATIONS & UTIL.	96.7	93.8	95.2	92.0	121.0	107.1	98.1	181.5	141.4	92.0	121.0	107.1	92.4	149.6	122.2	92.4	149.6	122.2
MF2016	WEIGHTED AVERAGE	96.6	93.9	95.4	100.0	131.6	113.8	101.2	174.8	133.5	98.5	130.8	112.7	95.1	145.6	117.2	95.5	145.5	117.4

City Cost Indexes

		NEW YORK																		
	DIVISION	NEW YORK			NIAGARA FALLS			PLATTSBURGH			POUGHKEEPSIE			QUEENS			RIVERHEAD		
		100 - 102			143			129			125 - 126			110			119		
		MAT.	INST.	TOTAL	MAT.	INST.	TOTAL	MAT.	INST.	TOTAL	MAT.	INST.	TOTAL	MAT.	INST.	TOTAL	MAT.	INST.	TOTAL
015433	CONTRACTOR EQUIPMENT		104.9	104.9		91.9	91.9		96.6	96.6		112.3	112.3		112.3	112.3		112.3	112.3
0241, 31 - 34	SITE & INFRASTRUCTURE, DEMOLITION	101.4	111.7	108.6	106.0	95.0	98.3	113.2	101.7	105.2	141.7	121.1	127.3	117.1	125.5	123.0	115.0	124.7	121.8
0310	Concrete Forming & Accessories	108.5	196.3	184.2	83.5	118.6	113.8	90.5	95.8	95.1	86.2	175.7	163.3	89.9	193.0	178.8	94.2	162.2	152.8
0320	Concrete Reinforcing	102.0	236.2	169.7	106.8	115.6	111.2	103.8	115.6	109.8	99.8	156.8	128.5	103.5	222.7	163.6	103.7	222.5	163.6
0330	Cast-in-Place Concrete	99.9	181.8	131.0	105.5	130.7	115.1	94.2	106.0	98.7	100.7	142.7	116.6	101.8	171.8	128.4	100.1	168.6	126.1
03	CONCRETE	103.3	195.8	145.6	94.6	121.5	106.9	90.9	102.5	96.2	95.8	159.3	124.8	99.8	188.8	140.5	97.2	173.6	132.1
04	MASONRY	103.5	189.8	157.0	121.8	130.5	127.2	90.9	101.5	97.5	103.8	145.5	129.7	108.1	182.5	154.4	117.5	178.4	155.3
05	METALS	102.0	169.5	122.8	95.3	104.3	98.0	98.8	101.6	99.7	102.9	135.3	112.9	102.1	167.5	122.2	104.1	164.5	122.7
06	WOOD, PLASTICS & COMPOSITES	102.4	197.9	155.5	83.2	113.4	100.0	93.6	92.4	93.0	88.4	188.0	143.9	87.9	197.5	148.9	92.7	159.5	129.9
07	THERMAL & MOISTURE PROTECTION	107.4	173.4	135.3	102.8	115.4	108.1	117.8	102.0	111.1	123.4	148.4	133.9	106.8	168.2	132.8	107.8	161.6	130.6
08	OPENINGS	95.8	201.1	119.9	98.1	110.0	100.9	98.1	99.5	98.5	92.7	177.3	112.1	88.1	198.4	113.4	88.5	177.4	108.9
0920	Plaster & Gypsum Board	102.2	200.3	168.1	88.9	113.7	105.6	114.8	91.7	99.3	97.2	190.6	159.9	92.1	200.3	164.8	93.3	161.2	138.9
0950, 0980	Ceilings & Acoustic Treatment	100.5	200.3	167.8	95.1	113.7	107.7	104.7	91.7	95.9	76.3	190.6	153.3	79.7	200.3	161.0	79.6	161.2	134.6
0960	Flooring	93.9	189.9	120.5	89.0	118.5	97.2	104.6	111.1	106.4	98.7	167.7	117.8	100.0	189.9	125.0	101.1	176.4	122.0
0970, 0990	Wall Finishes & Painting/Coating	100.5	164.8	138.0	96.4	116.5	108.1	114.4	99.5	105.7	118.7	129.0	124.7	114.2	159.9	140.8	114.2	159.9	140.8
09	FINISHES	97.5	192.8	149.3	90.7	118.6	105.9	94.7	98.2	96.6	95.8	172.5	137.5	98.6	190.2	148.4	98.8	163.9	134.2
COVERS	DIVS. 10 - 14, 25, 28, 41, 43, 44, 46	100.0	143.3	109.6	100.0	107.0	101.6	100.0	96.6	99.2	100.0	121.4	104.8	100.0	137.1	108.3	100.0	125.0	105.6
21, 22, 23	FIRE SUPPRESSION, PLUMBING & HVAC	100.1	174.1	131.8	97.0	107.7	101.6	97.1	104.5	100.3	97.1	125.3	109.1	99.7	170.2	129.9	99.9	159.6	125.5
26, 27, 3370	ELECTRICAL, COMMUNICATIONS & UTIL.	100.9	188.1	146.3	95.4	104.4	100.1	88.5	96.9	93.0	92.0	128.0	110.8	98.6	181.5	141.7	100.1	142.4	122.1
MF2016	WEIGHTED AVERAGE	100.6	178.2	134.6	97.6	111.9	103.9	96.6	100.9	98.5	99.2	142.4	118.1	99.6	174.8	132.6	100.4	159.0	126.1

		NEW YORK																		
	DIVISION	ROCHESTER			SCHENECTADY			STATEN ISLAND			SUFFERN			SYRACUSE			UTICA		
		144 - 146			123			103			109			130 - 132			133 - 135		
		MAT.	INST.	TOTAL	MAT.	INST.	TOTAL	MAT.	INST.	TOTAL	MAT.	INST.	TOTAL	MAT.	INST.	TOTAL	MAT.	INST.	TOTAL
015433	CONTRACTOR EQUIPMENT		119.8	119.8		115.8	115.8		106.9	106.9		106.9	106.9		115.8	115.8		115.8	115.8
0241, 31 - 34	SITE & INFRASTRUCTURE, DEMOLITION	94.1	108.8	104.4	84.6	104.7	98.7	101.5	113.7	110.1	94.5	109.2	104.8	94.8	103.5	100.9	73.2	103.1	94.1
0310	Concrete Forming & Accessories	99.8	101.5	101.3	101.1	105.9	105.3	88.9	182.9	169.9	97.8	147.6	140.7	99.7	93.4	94.2	100.8	90.5	91.9
0320	Concrete Reinforcing	110.7	108.4	109.5	98.3	119.5	109.0	96.4	222.7	160.1	95.3	156.9	126.4	101.4	104.2	102.8	101.4	103.5	102.5
0330	Cast-in-Place Concrete	97.7	107.7	101.5	92.9	116.1	101.7	96.5	173.5	125.8	93.6	146.5	113.7	97.6	107.7	101.4	89.3	106.3	95.8
03	CONCRETE	94.3	106.1	99.7	91.2	112.9	101.2	100.5	184.9	139.1	95.3	147.9	119.3	96.0	101.6	98.6	94.0	99.7	96.6
04	MASONRY	99.6	107.8	104.7	93.3	116.0	107.4	102.0	182.8	152.1	95.4	148.3	128.2	99.3	105.3	103.0	90.4	103.7	98.6
05	METALS	101.4	123.2	108.1	98.7	128.8	108.0	88.9	170.5	113.9	88.9	135.0	103.1	97.7	120.4	104.7	95.8	120.0	103.2
06	WOOD, PLASTICS & COMPOSITES	98.0	100.0	99.1	105.3	102.3	103.6	87.1	183.7	140.9	97.8	149.4	126.5	101.9	90.1	95.4	101.9	86.7	93.4
07	THERMAL & MOISTURE PROTECTION	102.5	103.6	102.9	101.2	110.3	105.1	104.8	167.3	131.3	105.3	145.0	122.1	101.7	98.8	100.5	90.1	98.7	93.7
08	OPENINGS	102.3	101.6	102.1	96.1	104.5	98.0	92.8	192.9	115.8	92.9	155.9	107.3	94.2	92.8	93.9	96.9	90.8	95.5
0920	Plaster & Gypsum Board	105.9	100.1	102.0	104.3	102.3	103.0	91.8	185.8	154.9	96.0	150.5	132.6	98.5	89.8	92.7	98.5	86.2	90.3
0950, 0980	Ceilings & Acoustic Treatment	97.0	100.1	99.1	92.4	102.3	99.1	85.2	185.8	153.0	83.5	150.5	128.7	94.1	89.8	91.2	94.1	86.2	88.8
0960	Flooring	90.1	111.0	95.9	89.5	111.1	95.5	88.1	189.9	116.3	88.1	181.4	114.0	88.9	97.6	91.3	86.9	97.7	89.9
0970, 0990	Wall Finishes & Painting/Coating	94.7	102.9	99.5	89.8	102.3	97.1	103.8	159.9	136.5	102.2	132.7	120.0	91.2	103.2	98.2	84.8	103.2	95.5
09	FINISHES	95.2	103.5	99.7	87.8	105.9	97.6	91.3	182.1	140.7	90.9	153.2	124.8	90.5	94.5	92.7	88.9	92.3	90.7
COVERS	DIVS. 10 - 14, 25, 28, 41, 43, 44, 46	100.0	102.0	100.5	100.0	102.0	100.4	100.0	136.3	108.1	100.0	119.5	104.3	100.0	99.0	99.8	100.0	93.5	98.6
21, 22, 23	FIRE SUPPRESSION, PLUMBING & HVAC	100.1	91.8	96.5	100.2	109.0	104.0	100.2	170.4	130.2	97.2	128.8	110.7	100.2	96.7	98.7	100.2	96.4	98.6
26, 27, 3370	ELECTRICAL, COMMUNICATIONS & UTIL.	102.7	94.9	98.6	94.7	110.9	103.1	94.2	181.5	139.6	99.0	121.0	110.5	99.4	106.7	103.2	97.5	106.7	102.3
MF2016	WEIGHTED AVERAGE	99.5	102.7	100.9	96.1	111.2	102.7	96.4	172.2	129.6	95.1	136.0	113.0	97.6	102.0	99.5	95.7	100.8	97.9

		NEW YORK									NORTH CAROLINA								
	DIVISION	WATERTOWN			WHITE PLAINS			YONKERS			ASHEVILLE			CHARLOTTE			DURHAM		
		136			106			107			287 - 288			281 - 282			277		
		MAT.	INST.	TOTAL	MAT.	INST.	TOTAL	MAT.	INST.	TOTAL	MAT.	INST.	TOTAL	MAT.	INST.	TOTAL	MAT.	INST.	TOTAL
015433	CONTRACTOR EQUIPMENT		115.8	115.8		106.9	106.9		106.9	106.9		101.9	101.9		101.9	101.9		107.3	107.3
0241, 31 - 34	SITE & INFRASTRUCTURE, DEMOLITION	80.9	103.6	96.8	92.4	109.9	104.7	99.2	110.0	106.7	97.4	81.6	86.3	99.1	81.8	87.0	101.5	90.7	93.9
0310	Concrete Forming & Accessories	85.8	97.5	95.9	102.8	140.1	135.0	103.0	151.3	144.7	91.1	63.4	67.2	96.1	62.9	67.5	95.2	63.4	67.7
0320	Concrete Reinforcing	102.1	104.2	103.2	95.3	170.9	133.4	99.1	171.0	135.4	94.9	68.0	81.3	99.2	67.0	82.9	98.2	67.0	82.5
0330	Cast-in-Place Concrete	104.0	110.2	106.3	85.7	150.7	110.4	95.9	150.9	116.8	109.3	71.3	94.9	111.5	70.6	95.9	98.2	71.3	88.0
03	CONCRETE	106.4	104.4	105.5	89.1	149.4	116.7	98.1	154.6	124.0	99.5	68.0	85.4	99.2	68.0	84.9	94.2	68.4	82.4
04	MASONRY	91.6	109.3	102.6	94.8	154.7	131.9	98.6	154.7	133.4	90.1	63.7	73.7	93.9	62.3	74.3	86.6	63.7	72.4
05	METALS	95.8	120.4	103.4	90.5	162.5	112.6	98.6	163.0	118.4	97.8	91.7	95.9	98.6	91.4	96.4	113.7	91.3	106.8
06	WOOD, PLASTICS & COMPOSITES	84.4	94.2	89.9	103.1	134.9	120.8	103.0	149.4	128.8	90.7	61.8	74.7	91.2	61.8	74.8	94.9	61.8	76.5
07	THERMAL & MOISTURE PROTECTION	90.4	102.0	95.3	105.1	146.6	122.7	105.4	149.5	124.1	101.0	65.3	85.9	95.4	64.6	82.4	107.4	65.3	89.6
08	OPENINGS	96.9	97.3	97.0	92.9	165.9	109.6	96.5	173.7	114.2	93.7	62.9	86.6	98.6	62.7	90.3	100.8	62.7	92.1
0920	Plaster & Gypsum Board	89.7	94.0	92.6	98.9	135.6	123.6	102.3	150.5	134.7	106.6	60.6	75.7	101.6	60.6	74.1	98.7	60.6	73.1
0950, 0980	Ceilings & Acoustic Treatment	94.1	94.0	94.0	83.5	135.6	118.6	99.7	150.5	133.9	83.8	60.6	68.2	87.8	60.6	69.5	86.3	60.6	69.0
0960	Flooring	80.0	97.7	84.9	90.5	173.4	113.5	90.0	189.9	117.7	92.8	63.5	84.6	92.1	63.5	84.1	96.8	63.5	87.6
0970, 0990	Wall Finishes & Painting/Coating	84.8	97.2	92.0	102.2	159.9	135.9	102.2	159.9	135.9	104.5	59.7	78.4	97.0	59.7	75.3	98.8	59.7	76.0
09	FINISHES	86.2	97.0	92.1	91.7	147.5	122.0	95.7	159.3	130.3	90.1	62.7	75.2	90.0	62.4	75.0	89.7	62.7	75.0
COVERS	DIVS. 10 - 14, 25, 28, 41, 43, 44, 46	100.0	100.5	100.1	100.0	119.9	104.4	100.0	129.1	106.5	100.0	85.2	96.7	100.0	84.8	96.6	100.0	85.2	96.7
21, 22, 23	FIRE SUPPRESSION, PLUMBING & HVAC	100.2	91.4	96.5	100.4	140.6	117.6	100.4	140.8	117.7	100.5	62.6	84.3	99.9	63.1	84.1	100.5	62.6	84.3
26, 27, 3370	ELECTRICAL, COMMUNICATIONS & UTIL.	99.3	95.2	97.2	92.4	149.6	122.2	99.1	164.7	133.2	100.5	61.1	80.0	99.7	62.3	80.3	98.0	60.6	78.5
MF2016	WEIGHTED AVERAGE	97.3	100.7	98.8	94.6	145.6	116.9	98.9	150.8	121.6	97.6	68.3	84.8	98.1	68.3	85.0	100.2	68.9	86.5

483

City Cost Indexes

NORTH CAROLINA

DIVISION		ELIZABETH CITY 279			FAYETTEVILLE 283			GASTONIA 280			GREENSBORO 270, 272 - 274			HICKORY 286			KINSTON 285		
		MAT.	INST.	TOTAL	MAT.	INST.	TOTAL	MAT.	INST.	TOTAL	MAT.	INST.	TOTAL	MAT.	INST.	TOTAL	MAT.	INST.	TOTAL
015433	CONTRACTOR EQUIPMENT		111.5	111.5		107.3	107.3		101.9	101.9		107.3	107.3		107.3	107.3		107.3	107.3
0241, 31 - 34	SITE & INFRASTRUCTURE, DEMOLITION	105.8	92.5	96.5	96.8	90.6	92.5	97.3	81.9	86.5	101.3	90.8	94.0	96.4	89.4	91.5	95.2	89.3	91.1
0310	Concrete Forming & Accessories	81.6	63.6	66.0	90.8	62.8	66.7	97.3	63.6	68.2	95.0	63.3	67.7	87.7	63.4	66.7	84.1	62.6	65.6
0320	Concrete Reinforcing	96.2	71.9	84.0	98.6	67.0	82.6	95.3	67.0	81.0	97.1	67.0	81.9	94.9	67.0	80.8	94.4	66.9	80.5
0330	Cast-in-Place Concrete	98.4	73.0	88.8	114.7	70.5	97.9	106.9	71.4	93.4	97.5	71.3	87.6	109.3	71.3	94.9	105.5	70.4	92.2
03	CONCRETE	94.4	70.0	83.2	101.4	67.9	86.1	98.0	68.6	84.5	93.6	68.4	82.1	99.3	68.4	85.2	96.1	67.8	83.2
04	MASONRY	98.8	62.3	76.2	93.2	62.3	74.1	94.5	63.7	75.4	82.5	63.7	70.9	78.9	63.7	69.5	85.8	62.3	71.2
05	METALS	100.0	94.0	98.2	117.8	91.3	109.7	98.3	91.6	96.3	106.2	91.3	101.7	97.8	91.3	95.8	96.6	91.1	94.9
06	WOOD, PLASTICS & COMPOSITES	80.1	62.5	70.3	90.0	61.8	74.3	98.5	61.8	78.1	94.6	61.8	76.4	85.9	61.8	72.5	83.0	61.8	71.2
07	THERMAL & MOISTURE PROTECTION	106.6	64.5	88.8	100.4	64.6	85.3	101.2	65.3	86.0	107.1	65.3	89.4	101.3	65.3	86.1	101.2	64.6	85.7
08	OPENINGS	97.6	64.1	89.9	93.8	62.7	86.7	97.5	62.7	89.5	100.8	62.7	92.0	93.8	62.7	86.6	93.9	62.7	86.7
0920	Plaster & Gypsum Board	92.3	60.6	71.0	110.8	60.6	77.1	112.7	60.6	77.7	100.2	60.6	73.6	106.6	60.6	75.7	106.4	60.6	75.7
0950, 0980	Ceilings & Acoustic Treatment	86.3	60.6	69.0	85.5	60.6	68.8	87.3	60.6	69.3	86.3	60.6	69.0	83.8	60.6	68.2	87.3	60.6	69.3
0960	Flooring	89.2	81.6	87.1	93.0	63.5	84.8	96.1	81.6	92.1	96.8	63.5	87.6	92.7	81.6	89.6	90.0	81.6	87.7
0970, 0990	Wall Finishes & Painting/Coating	98.8	59.7	76.0	104.5	59.7	78.4	104.5	59.7	78.4	98.8	59.7	76.0	104.5	59.7	78.4	104.5	59.7	78.4
09	FINISHES	86.9	66.5	75.8	91.1	62.4	75.5	92.6	66.4	78.3	90.0	62.7	75.1	90.3	66.4	77.3	89.9	66.0	76.9
COVERS	DIVS. 10 - 14, 25, 28, 41, 43, 44, 46	100.0	82.7	96.1	100.0	84.7	96.6	100.0	85.2	96.7	100.0	82.4	96.1	100.0	85.2	96.7	100.0	84.7	96.6
21, 22, 23	FIRE SUPPRESSION, PLUMBING & HVAC	97.3	60.5	81.6	100.2	61.9	83.9	100.5	61.5	83.8	100.4	62.6	84.2	97.4	61.5	82.0	97.4	60.3	81.5
26, 27, 3370	ELECTRICAL, COMMUNICATIONS & UTIL.	97.7	68.2	82.4	100.3	60.6	79.6	100.0	62.3	80.4	97.1	61.1	78.4	98.4	62.3	79.6	98.2	58.9	77.8
MF2016	WEIGHTED AVERAGE	97.2	70.4	85.5	101.3	68.4	86.9	98.4	68.7	85.4	98.6	68.9	85.6	96.1	69.3	84.4	95.8	68.2	83.7

NORTH CAROLINA / NORTH DAKOTA

DIVISION		MURPHY 289			RALEIGH 275 - 276			ROCKY MOUNT 278			WILMINGTON 284			WINSTON-SALEM 271			BISMARCK 585		
		MAT.	INST.	TOTAL	MAT.	INST.	TOTAL	MAT.	INST.	TOTAL	MAT.	INST.	TOTAL	MAT.	INST.	TOTAL	MAT.	INST.	TOTAL
015433	CONTRACTOR EQUIPMENT		101.9	101.9		107.3	107.3		107.3	107.3		101.9	101.9		107.3	107.3		100.3	100.3
0241, 31 - 34	SITE & INFRASTRUCTURE, DEMOLITION	98.7	80.1	85.6	101.2	90.7	93.8	103.9	90.7	94.7	98.5	81.5	86.6	101.7	90.8	94.1	102.1	98.6	99.6
0310	Concrete Forming & Accessories	97.9	62.7	67.5	95.5	62.8	67.3	87.5	62.9	66.3	92.5	62.8	66.9	96.8	63.4	68.0	102.8	74.9	78.7
0320	Concrete Reinforcing	94.4	66.3	80.2	99.2	67.0	82.9	96.2	67.0	81.5	95.6	67.0	81.2	97.1	67.0	81.9	93.8	94.8	94.3
0330	Cast-in-Place Concrete	113.1	70.5	96.9	101.1	70.5	89.5	96.3	70.6	86.5	108.9	70.5	94.3	99.9	71.3	89.1	102.9	85.8	96.4
03	CONCRETE	102.4	67.7	86.6	92.5	67.9	81.3	95.1	68.0	82.7	99.4	67.9	85.0	94.9	68.4	82.8	92.5	82.8	88.1
04	MASONRY	82.0	62.3	69.8	80.9	62.3	69.4	76.1	62.3	67.6	79.4	62.3	68.8	82.8	63.7	71.0	103.6	83.3	91.0
05	METALS	95.6	91.3	94.2	98.7	91.3	96.5	99.2	91.4	96.8	97.3	91.3	95.5	103.4	91.3	99.7	103.2	93.7	100.3
06	WOOD, PLASTICS & COMPOSITES	99.1	61.7	78.3	92.7	61.8	75.5	86.6	61.8	72.8	92.5	61.8	75.5	94.6	61.8	76.4	97.2	70.7	82.5
07	THERMAL & MOISTURE PROTECTION	101.2	64.6	85.7	101.8	64.6	86.1	107.1	64.6	89.1	101.0	64.6	85.6	107.1	65.3	89.4	105.0	84.7	96.4
08	OPENINGS	93.7	62.4	86.5	99.1	62.7	90.7	96.8	62.7	89.0	93.9	62.7	86.7	100.8	62.7	92.0	106.5	81.0	100.7
0920	Plaster & Gypsum Board	111.9	60.5	77.4	92.6	60.6	71.1	94.2	60.6	71.7	108.7	60.6	76.4	100.2	60.6	73.6	102.8	70.3	81.0
0950, 0980	Ceilings & Acoustic Treatment	83.8	60.5	68.1	83.3	60.6	68.0	84.6	60.6	68.4	85.5	60.6	68.8	86.3	60.6	69.0	110.2	70.3	83.3
0960	Flooring	96.4	81.6	92.3	90.4	63.5	82.9	92.6	81.6	89.6	93.5	63.5	85.2	96.8	63.5	87.6	86.0	52.6	76.7
0970, 0990	Wall Finishes & Painting/Coating	104.5	59.7	78.4	93.8	59.7	73.9	98.8	59.7	76.0	104.5	59.7	78.4	98.8	59.7	76.0	91.2	60.1	73.1
09	FINISHES	92.1	65.9	77.9	88.6	62.4	74.2	88.0	66.0	76.0	91.0	62.4	75.4	90.0	62.7	75.1	96.0	69.6	81.7
COVERS	DIVS. 10 - 14, 25, 28, 41, 43, 44, 46	100.0	84.7	96.6	100.0	84.7	96.6	100.0	84.7	96.6	100.0	84.7	96.6	100.0	85.2	96.7	100.0	90.9	98.0
21, 22, 23	FIRE SUPPRESSION, PLUMBING & HVAC	97.4	60.7	81.7	99.9	61.9	83.7	97.3	60.7	81.6	100.5	61.9	84.0	100.4	62.6	84.2	100.1	76.9	90.2
26, 27, 3370	ELECTRICAL, COMMUNICATIONS & UTIL.	101.4	58.9	79.3	100.5	59.5	79.1	99.5	60.6	79.3	100.8	58.9	79.0	97.1	58.9	77.3	99.5	76.7	87.6
MF2016	WEIGHTED AVERAGE	96.9	67.5	84.0	96.9	68.3	84.4	96.3	68.6	84.2	97.2	67.5	84.2	98.4	68.7	85.4	100.3	81.4	92.0

NORTH DAKOTA

DIVISION		DEVILS LAKE 583			DICKINSON 586			FARGO 580 - 581			GRAND FORKS 582			JAMESTOWN 584			MINOT 587		
		MAT.	INST.	TOTAL	MAT.	INST.	TOTAL	MAT.	INST.	TOTAL	MAT.	INST.	TOTAL	MAT.	INST.	TOTAL	MAT.	INST.	TOTAL
015433	CONTRACTOR EQUIPMENT		100.3	100.3		100.3	100.3		100.3	100.3		100.3	100.3		100.3	100.3		100.3	100.3
0241, 31 - 34	SITE & INFRASTRUCTURE, DEMOLITION	106.9	98.6	101.1	114.4	98.6	103.3	97.6	98.6	98.3	110.4	98.6	102.1	105.9	98.6	100.8	108.0	98.6	101.4
0310	Concrete Forming & Accessories	99.3	74.8	78.1	89.1	74.8	76.8	95.4	75.0	78.0	92.8	74.8	77.3	90.7	74.7	76.9	88.8	74.8	76.8
0320	Concrete Reinforcing	95.3	94.7	95.0	96.2	94.8	95.5	95.4	95.1	95.3	93.9	94.7	94.3	95.9	95.1	95.5	97.2	94.8	96.0
0330	Cast-in-Place Concrete	123.1	85.8	108.9	111.4	85.8	101.6	100.8	85.8	95.1	111.3	85.8	101.6	121.5	85.7	107.9	111.3	85.8	101.6
03	CONCRETE	101.6	82.7	93.0	100.3	82.8	92.3	93.4	82.9	88.6	97.9	82.8	91.0	100.2	82.8	92.2	96.6	82.8	90.3
04	MASONRY	120.5	82.6	97.0	122.1	83.3	98.0	107.1	89.0	95.9	114.1	82.6	94.6	133.8	89.0	106.0	113.2	83.3	94.7
05	METALS	98.9	93.5	97.3	98.8	93.6	97.2	101.2	94.2	99.1	98.9	93.5	97.2	98.9	93.9	97.4	99.2	93.7	97.5
06	WOOD, PLASTICS & COMPOSITES	92.5	70.7	80.4	80.7	70.7	75.1	92.5	70.7	80.4	84.7	70.7	76.9	82.4	70.7	75.9	80.4	70.7	75.0
07	THERMAL & MOISTURE PROTECTION	105.7	84.5	96.7	106.3	84.7	97.1	105.9	86.7	97.8	105.9	84.5	96.9	105.5	86.7	97.6	105.7	84.7	96.8
08	OPENINGS	100.2	81.0	95.8	100.1	81.0	95.7	101.4	81.0	96.7	98.7	81.0	94.7	100.1	81.0	95.7	98.9	81.0	94.8
0920	Plaster & Gypsum Board	121.8	70.3	87.2	112.6	70.3	84.2	101.0	70.3	80.4	113.9	70.3	84.6	113.6	70.3	84.5	112.6	70.3	84.2
0950, 0980	Ceilings & Acoustic Treatment	108.4	70.3	82.7	108.4	70.3	82.7	99.9	70.3	79.9	108.4	70.3	82.7	108.4	70.3	82.7	108.4	70.3	82.7
0960	Flooring	92.6	52.6	81.5	86.1	52.6	76.8	96.1	52.6	84.1	88.0	52.6	78.2	86.8	52.6	77.3	85.8	52.6	76.6
0970, 0990	Wall Finishes & Painting/Coating	89.6	58.9	71.7	89.6	58.9	71.7	90.8	70.4	78.9	89.6	69.0	77.6	89.6	58.9	71.7	89.6	60.1	72.4
09	FINISHES	96.2	69.4	81.6	93.8	69.4	80.5	96.9	70.6	82.6	94.0	70.5	81.2	93.2	69.4	80.2	93.0	69.5	80.2
COVERS	DIVS. 10 - 14, 25, 28, 41, 43, 44, 46	100.0	90.8	98.0	100.0	90.9	98.0	100.0	90.9	98.0	100.0	90.9	98.0	100.0	90.8	98.0	100.0	90.9	98.0
21, 22, 23	FIRE SUPPRESSION, PLUMBING & HVAC	97.2	81.5	90.5	97.2	75.2	87.8	100.1	77.0	90.2	100.3	74.4	89.2	100.0	72.8	86.8	100.3	75.0	89.5
26, 27, 3370	ELECTRICAL, COMMUNICATIONS & UTIL.	97.4	48.0	71.7	105.8	71.7	88.0	103.5	73.3	87.8	100.8	63.0	81.1	97.4	48.0	71.7	103.8	76.7	89.7
MF2016	WEIGHTED AVERAGE	100.1	78.2	90.5	100.8	80.3	91.8	100.1	81.8	92.1	100.1	79.0	90.8	100.2	77.1	90.1	100.0	81.0	91.7

City Cost Indexes

DIVISION		NORTH DAKOTA WILLISTON 588 MAT.	INST.	TOTAL	OHIO AKRON 442-443 MAT.	INST.	TOTAL	ATHENS 457 MAT.	INST.	TOTAL	CANTON 446-447 MAT.	INST.	TOTAL	CHILLICOTHE 456 MAT.	INST.	TOTAL	CINCINNATI 451-452 MAT.	INST.	TOTAL
015433	CONTRACTOR EQUIPMENT		100.3	100.3		91.6	91.6		87.4	87.4		91.6	91.6		98.5	98.5		96.0	96.0
0241, 31 - 34	SITE & INFRASTRUCTURE, DEMOLITION	108.4	96.3	99.9	97.4	99.2	98.7	115.8	88.9	97.0	97.6	99.0	98.6	101.6	99.8	100.4	96.9	99.1	98.4
0310	Concrete Forming & Accessories	94.5	74.5	77.3	100.5	86.0	88.0	92.6	87.6	88.3	100.5	76.9	80.2	95.0	80.2	82.2	98.6	82.5	84.7
0320	Concrete Reinforcing	98.1	94.7	96.4	103.4	90.2	96.8	89.1	83.5	86.3	103.4	78.6	90.9	86.0	78.3	82.1	91.2	79.4	85.2
0330	Cast-in-Place Concrete	111.3	85.7	101.6	98.9	90.3	95.6	109.4	86.2	100.6	99.8	88.5	95.5	99.3	83.4	93.3	94.8	76.6	87.9
03	CONCRETE	97.8	82.6	90.9	98.3	87.6	93.4	101.1	85.9	94.1	98.7	80.9	90.6	95.5	81.4	89.1	94.6	80.1	88.0
04	MASONRY	107.4	83.3	92.5	93.5	91.6	92.3	80.1	81.2	80.8	94.1	79.1	84.8	87.3	91.2	89.7	90.5	78.0	82.7
05	METALS	99.0	93.3	97.3	96.8	80.1	91.7	103.2	77.5	95.3	96.8	74.8	90.0	95.2	85.7	92.3	97.5	83.8	93.3
06	WOOD, PLASTICS & COMPOSITES	86.2	70.7	77.6	107.2	85.0	94.8	86.4	90.6	88.8	107.5	75.2	89.6	99.7	77.0	87.1	99.4	83.9	90.7
07	THERMAL & MOISTURE PROTECTION	105.9	84.7	96.9	103.3	92.7	98.8	98.5	87.5	93.9	104.4	87.6	97.3	100.4	85.8	94.3	98.6	81.5	91.4
08	OPENINGS	100.2	81.0	95.8	109.6	85.3	104.0	97.1	84.9	94.3	103.3	73.2	96.4	88.7	74.4	85.4	96.6	80.1	92.8
0920	Plaster & Gypsum Board	113.9	70.3	84.6	103.3	84.5	90.7	95.6	90.2	92.0	104.3	74.4	84.2	98.3	76.7	83.8	97.8	83.8	88.4
0950, 0980	Ceilings & Acoustic Treatment	108.4	70.3	82.7	93.4	84.5	87.4	108.9	90.2	96.3	93.4	74.4	80.6	102.5	76.7	85.1	96.2	83.8	87.8
0960	Flooring	88.9	52.6	78.8	95.1	86.2	92.6	120.1	78.2	108.5	95.2	73.1	89.1	98.1	78.2	92.6	99.4	80.8	94.3
0970, 0990	Wall Finishes & Painting/Coating	89.6	58.9	71.7	98.2	95.0	96.3	100.7	88.8	93.7	98.2	72.2	83.0	97.9	80.1	87.5	97.5	74.6	84.1
09	FINISHES	94.2	69.4	80.7	97.4	86.6	91.5	101.5	86.5	93.3	97.6	75.0	85.3	98.4	79.3	88.0	97.7	81.6	88.9
COVERS	DIVS. 10 - 14, 25, 28, 41, 43, 44, 46	100.0	90.9	98.0	100.0	93.6	98.6	100.0	88.0	97.3	100.0	91.6	98.1	100.0	87.9	97.3	100.0	88.9	97.5
21, 22, 23	FIRE SUPPRESSION, PLUMBING & HVAC	97.2	75.2	87.8	100.0	89.0	95.3	96.9	76.3	88.1	100.0	78.0	90.6	97.4	94.6	96.2	99.9	77.1	90.2
26, 27, 3370	ELECTRICAL, COMMUNICATIONS & UTIL.	101.1	72.6	86.3	98.3	85.0	91.4	100.8	90.6	95.5	97.6	85.6	91.4	100.1	76.5	87.8	99.1	74.8	86.5
MF2016	WEIGHTED AVERAGE	99.3	80.2	90.9	99.7	88.2	94.7	99.1	83.7	92.4	99.1	81.0	91.1	96.2	86.1	91.7	97.7	80.9	90.3

DIVISION		OHIO CLEVELAND 441 MAT.	INST.	TOTAL	COLUMBUS 430-432 MAT.	INST.	TOTAL	DAYTON 453-454 MAT.	INST.	TOTAL	HAMILTON 450 MAT.	INST.	TOTAL	LIMA 458 MAT.	INST.	TOTAL	LORAIN 440 MAT.	INST.	TOTAL
015433	CONTRACTOR EQUIPMENT		92.7	92.7		91.4	91.4		91.5	91.5		98.5	98.5		90.8	90.8		91.6	91.6
0241, 31 - 34	SITE & INFRASTRUCTURE, DEMOLITION	96.0	97.5	97.1	101.7	91.9	94.8	97.1	99.2	98.5	97.0	99.5	98.8	109.1	89.0	95.0	96.8	99.5	98.7
0310	Concrete Forming & Accessories	100.1	90.7	92.0	97.7	77.4	80.1	96.8	73.2	76.5	96.8	71.9	75.3	92.6	79.2	81.1	100.6	77.7	80.8
0320	Concrete Reinforcing	103.9	92.0	97.9	96.2	80.3	88.2	91.2	81.5	86.3	91.2	79.4	85.2	89.1	81.6	85.3	103.4	90.5	96.9
0330	Cast-in-Place Concrete	95.8	99.3	97.1	96.9	82.2	91.3	85.1	78.8	82.7	91.2	77.2	85.9	100.5	88.0	95.8	94.1	93.7	94.0
03	CONCRETE	98.5	93.4	96.2	96.2	79.6	88.6	86.9	76.6	82.2	89.8	75.7	83.4	94.0	82.7	88.8	96.0	85.2	91.1
04	MASONRY	100.0	99.2	99.5	91.9	86.5	88.5	86.3	77.2	80.6	86.7	79.4	82.2	108.7	78.6	90.0	90.2	94.6	92.9
05	METALS	98.4	84.9	94.3	97.5	80.8	92.4	96.7	77.8	90.9	96.8	86.9	93.7	103.2	80.7	96.3	97.4	81.5	92.5
06	WOOD, PLASTICS & COMPOSITES	101.0	88.3	93.9	99.4	76.1	86.4	103.5	71.7	85.8	102.1	69.0	83.7	86.4	78.7	82.1	107.2	73.4	88.4
07	THERMAL & MOISTURE PROTECTION	100.2	98.4	99.5	100.4	85.8	94.2	104.8	79.1	93.9	100.5	80.5	92.1	98.0	85.0	92.5	104.3	94.2	100.0
08	OPENINGS	97.9	87.5	95.5	99.7	74.4	93.9	95.8	72.8	90.5	93.5	71.5	88.4	97.1	75.9	92.2	103.3	78.9	97.7
0920	Plaster & Gypsum Board	103.2	87.7	92.8	97.2	75.5	82.6	100.1	71.3	80.8	100.1	68.5	78.9	95.6	78.0	83.8	103.3	72.6	82.7
0950, 0980	Ceilings & Acoustic Treatment	89.0	87.7	88.1	90.9	75.5	80.5	104.3	71.3	82.0	103.3	68.5	79.8	108.0	78.0	87.7	93.4	72.6	79.4
0960	Flooring	96.5	92.6	95.4	92.8	78.2	88.8	101.8	71.9	93.5	99.2	80.8	94.1	119.0	77.9	107.6	95.2	90.8	94.0
0970, 0990	Wall Finishes & Painting/Coating	101.1	95.0	97.5	100.4	80.1	88.5	97.9	71.6	82.6	97.9	71.0	82.2	100.7	71.9	83.9	98.2	95.0	96.3
09	FINISHES	97.8	91.2	94.2	93.9	77.3	84.8	99.9	72.3	84.8	98.9	72.8	84.7	100.5	78.0	88.3	97.4	81.0	88.5
COVERS	DIVS. 10 - 14, 25, 28, 41, 43, 44, 46	100.0	98.0	99.6	100.0	89.0	97.6	100.0	87.2	97.1	100.0	87.4	97.2	100.0	87.1	97.1	100.0	94.5	98.8
21, 22, 23	FIRE SUPPRESSION, PLUMBING & HVAC	100.0	93.0	97.0	99.9	85.7	93.9	100.8	75.7	90.1	100.5	77.5	90.7	96.9	83.1	91.0	100.0	90.0	95.7
26, 27, 3370	ELECTRICAL, COMMUNICATIONS & UTIL.	98.0	95.7	96.8	99.0	84.7	91.6	97.8	76.4	86.6	98.0	76.7	86.9	101.1	76.4	88.3	97.7	80.8	89.0
MF2016	WEIGHTED AVERAGE	98.9	93.4	96.5	98.1	83.3	91.6	96.7	77.9	88.5	96.6	79.4	89.1	99.4	81.1	91.4	98.6	86.9	93.5

DIVISION		OHIO MANSFIELD 448-449 MAT.	INST.	TOTAL	MARION 433 MAT.	INST.	TOTAL	SPRINGFIELD 455 MAT.	INST.	TOTAL	STEUBENVILLE 439 MAT.	INST.	TOTAL	TOLEDO 434-436 MAT.	INST.	TOTAL	YOUNGSTOWN 444-445 MAT.	INST.	TOTAL
015433	CONTRACTOR EQUIPMENT		91.6	91.6		91.2	91.2		91.5	91.5		95.1	95.1		95.1	95.1		91.6	91.6
0241, 31 - 34	SITE & INFRASTRUCTURE, DEMOLITION	93.4	99.1	97.4	96.3	95.0	95.4	97.4	99.1	98.6	141.4	103.5	114.8	99.9	95.5	96.8	97.3	99.0	98.5
0310	Concrete Forming & Accessories	89.8	76.3	78.2	95.6	77.0	79.5	96.8	73.3	76.5	96.8	82.3	84.3	99.2	88.1	89.6	100.5	79.3	82.2
0320	Concrete Reinforcing	94.1	79.3	86.7	88.6	80.5	84.5	91.2	81.5	86.3	86.2	96.8	91.5	96.2	84.5	90.3	103.4	86.4	94.8
0330	Cast-in-Place Concrete	91.6	83.0	88.3	84.0	81.1	82.9	87.4	78.7	84.1	91.2	88.6	90.2	92.0	91.7	91.9	97.9	88.6	94.4
03	CONCRETE	90.6	78.9	85.2	83.4	78.9	81.4	88.0	76.6	82.8	87.2	86.5	86.9	91.0	88.7	89.9	97.8	83.4	91.2
04	MASONRY	92.6	91.7	92.0	93.5	89.2	90.8	86.5	76.9	80.5	80.8	91.3	87.3	99.9	90.7	94.2	93.8	87.3	89.7
05	METALS	97.6	76.0	91.0	96.5	78.9	91.1	96.7	77.9	90.9	93.1	82.2	89.7	97.3	85.9	93.8	96.8	78.2	91.1
06	WOOD, PLASTICS & COMPOSITES	94.9	73.4	83.0	96.6	76.1	85.2	105.0	71.7	86.5	92.1	80.0	85.4	100.5	88.0	93.5	107.2	78.2	91.1
07	THERMAL & MOISTURE PROTECTION	102.5	90.4	97.4	96.9	89.1	93.6	104.6	78.9	93.8	108.7	89.1	100.4	97.0	91.9	94.9	104.5	85.8	96.6
08	OPENINGS	103.7	73.2	96.7	93.4	71.5	88.4	94.0	72.8	89.1	93.7	82.0	91.0	96.2	85.1	93.6	103.3	78.6	97.6
0920	Plaster & Gypsum Board	96.9	72.6	80.6	98.5	75.5	83.1	100.1	71.3	80.8	97.6	79.1	85.1	100.5	87.7	91.9	103.3	77.5	86.0
0950, 0980	Ceilings & Acoustic Treatment	94.3	72.6	79.7	97.1	75.5	82.5	104.3	71.3	82.0	94.2	79.1	84.0	97.1	87.7	90.8	93.4	77.5	82.7
0960	Flooring	89.8	92.2	90.4	92.2	92.2	92.2	101.8	71.9	93.5	119.4	92.8	112.0	92.5	88.8	91.5	95.2	83.4	91.9
0970, 0990	Wall Finishes & Painting/Coating	98.2	76.5	85.5	104.9	76.5	88.3	97.9	71.6	82.6	118.5	88.8	101.2	104.9	87.3	94.6	98.2	82.0	88.7
09	FINISHES	94.8	78.6	86.0	95.3	79.5	86.7	99.9	72.2	84.8	112.9	84.3	97.4	96.0	88.0	91.6	97.5	79.9	87.9
COVERS	DIVS. 10 - 14, 25, 28, 41, 43, 44, 46	100.0	91.7	98.2	100.0	86.1	96.9	100.0	87.1	97.1	100.0	89.0	97.5	100.0	94.8	98.8	100.0	91.8	98.2
21, 22, 23	FIRE SUPPRESSION, PLUMBING & HVAC	96.9	89.0	93.5	96.9	85.1	91.9	100.8	81.1	92.4	97.3	93.3	95.6	100.0	93.5	97.2	100.0	83.8	93.1
26, 27, 3370	ELECTRICAL, COMMUNICATIONS & UTIL.	95.6	70.6	82.6	93.5	70.6	81.6	97.8	84.7	91.0	88.3	107.1	98.1	99.1	109.2	104.4	97.7	77.1	87.0
MF2016	WEIGHTED AVERAGE	96.8	82.8	90.7	94.4	81.6	88.8	96.7	80.2	89.5	96.2	91.8	94.3	97.5	93.1	95.6	98.9	83.3	92.1

485

City Cost Indexes

DIVISION		OHIO ZANESVILLE 437-438			OKLAHOMA ARDMORE 734			CLINTON 736			DURANT 747			ENID 737			GUYMON 739		
		MAT.	INST.	TOTAL	MAT.	INST.	TOTAL	MAT.	INST.	TOTAL	MAT.	INST.	TOTAL	MAT.	INST.	TOTAL	MAT.	INST.	TOTAL
015433	CONTRACTOR EQUIPMENT		91.2	91.2		82.8	82.8		81.8	81.8		81.8	81.8		81.8	81.8		81.8	81.8
0241, 31 - 34	SITE & INFRASTRUCTURE, DEMOLITION	99.4	95.0	96.3	101.6	97.4	98.6	103.1	95.8	98.0	95.5	93.4	94.0	104.7	95.8	98.5	107.6	95.5	99.1
0310	Concrete Forming & Accessories	92.7	76.9	79.1	91.6	57.8	62.4	90.2	57.8	62.2	84.2	57.4	61.1	93.7	57.9	62.8	96.9	57.6	63.0
0320	Concrete Reinforcing	88.1	93.0	90.6	81.1	66.5	73.7	81.6	66.5	74.0	92.1	65.6	78.7	81.0	66.5	73.7	81.6	62.7	72.0
0330	Cast-in-Place Concrete	88.5	80.9	85.6	103.5	73.9	92.2	100.0	73.9	90.1	92.0	73.8	85.1	100.0	74.0	90.1	100.0	73.6	90.0
03	CONCRETE	87.0	81.1	84.3	89.8	64.7	78.3	89.1	64.7	78.0	85.7	64.3	75.9	89.6	64.8	78.3	92.1	63.9	79.2
04	MASONRY	91.2	77.7	82.8	95.8	57.9	72.3	119.7	57.9	81.4	88.7	64.8	73.8	101.5	57.9	74.5	98.0	56.9	72.4
05	METALS	98.0	83.6	93.6	102.0	61.3	89.5	102.1	61.3	89.6	91.3	60.9	82.0	103.6	61.4	90.7	102.6	59.1	89.3
06	WOOD, PLASTICS & COMPOSITES	92.4	76.1	83.3	104.1	57.0	77.9	103.1	57.0	77.5	91.5	57.0	72.3	106.5	57.0	79.0	110.0	57.0	80.5
07	THERMAL & MOISTURE PROTECTION	97.0	82.8	91.0	105.3	65.2	88.3	105.4	65.2	88.4	99.3	66.2	85.2	105.5	65.2	88.5	105.9	64.8	88.5
08	OPENINGS	93.4	78.1	89.9	103.2	57.0	92.6	103.2	57.0	92.6	96.9	56.7	87.7	104.4	57.3	93.6	103.3	56.1	92.5
0920	Plaster & Gypsum Board	95.2	75.5	82.0	88.9	56.4	67.0	88.5	56.4	66.9	77.9	56.4	63.4	89.2	56.4	67.1	89.2	56.4	67.1
0950, 0980	Ceilings & Acoustic Treatment	97.1	75.5	82.5	86.0	56.4	66.0	86.0	56.4	66.0	82.3	56.4	64.8	86.0	56.4	66.0	86.0	56.4	66.0
0960	Flooring	90.3	78.2	87.0	88.5	60.6	80.7	87.4	60.6	79.9	90.8	54.6	80.8	89.1	74.8	85.1	90.6	60.6	82.3
0970, 0990	Wall Finishes & Painting/Coating	104.9	80.1	90.4	84.0	45.1	61.3	84.0	45.1	61.3	90.9	45.1	64.2	84.0	45.1	61.3	84.0	44.2	60.8
09	FINISHES	94.5	77.0	85.0	81.8	55.9	67.7	81.6	55.9	67.6	82.5	54.8	67.4	82.2	58.8	69.5	83.1	57.2	69.0
COVERS	DIVS. 10 - 14, 25, 28, 41, 43, 44, 46	100.0	82.1	96.0	100.0	79.1	95.3	100.0	79.1	95.3	100.0	79.0	95.3	100.0	79.1	95.3	100.0	79.0	95.3
21, 22, 23	FIRE SUPPRESSION, PLUMBING & HVAC	96.9	90.9	94.3	97.2	67.8	84.7	97.2	67.8	84.7	97.2	67.8	84.6	100.3	67.9	86.4	97.2	65.6	83.7
26, 27, 3370	ELECTRICAL, COMMUNICATIONS & UTIL.	93.6	74.0	83.4	93.9	71.2	82.1	94.8	71.2	82.5	96.2	62.1	78.4	94.8	71.2	82.5	96.4	57.5	76.2
MF2016	WEIGHTED AVERAGE	95.0	82.5	89.5	96.7	66.7	83.6	97.9	66.6	84.2	93.2	65.6	81.1	98.3	67.0	84.6	97.8	63.8	82.9

DIVISION		OKLAHOMA LAWTON 735			MCALESTER 745			MIAMI 743			MUSKOGEE 744			OKLAHOMA CITY 730-731			PONCA CITY 746		
		MAT.	INST.	TOTAL	MAT.	INST.	TOTAL	MAT.	INST.	TOTAL	MAT.	INST.	TOTAL	MAT.	INST.	TOTAL	MAT.	INST.	TOTAL
015433	CONTRACTOR EQUIPMENT		82.8	82.8		81.8	81.8		93.5	93.5		93.5	93.5		83.1	83.1		81.8	81.8
0241, 31 - 34	SITE & INFRASTRUCTURE, DEMOLITION	100.6	97.4	98.3	88.7	95.5	93.5	90.0	92.8	91.9	90.3	92.7	92.0	99.0	97.9	98.2	96.0	95.8	95.9
0310	Concrete Forming & Accessories	96.9	57.9	63.3	82.3	43.2	48.6	95.1	57.6	62.7	99.5	57.4	63.2	94.3	57.9	62.9	90.6	57.7	62.3
0320	Concrete Reinforcing	81.2	66.5	73.8	91.8	65.2	78.4	90.3	66.5	78.3	91.2	64.9	77.9	89.7	66.5	78.0	91.2	66.5	78.7
0330	Cast-in-Place Concrete	96.7	74.0	88.1	80.7	73.5	78.0	84.6	74.9	80.9	85.6	74.8	81.5	96.7	74.0	88.1	94.5	73.9	86.7
03	CONCRETE	86.0	64.8	76.3	76.8	57.7	68.1	81.1	66.0	74.2	82.7	65.6	74.9	88.8	64.8	77.9	87.8	64.7	77.2
04	MASONRY	97.8	57.9	73.1	106.4	57.8	76.3	91.6	58.0	70.8	108.3	51.3	73.0	100.3	57.9	74.0	84.4	57.9	68.0
05	METALS	107.5	61.4	93.3	91.2	60.0	81.6	91.2	76.7	86.7	92.7	75.3	87.4	100.4	61.4	88.4	91.2	61.2	82.0
06	WOOD, PLASTICS & COMPOSITES	109.0	57.0	80.1	89.1	37.9	60.6	103.7	57.1	77.8	107.9	57.1	79.7	94.9	57.0	73.8	99.4	57.0	75.8
07	THERMAL & MOISTURE PROTECTION	105.3	65.2	88.3	98.9	62.1	83.3	99.3	65.2	84.8	99.6	62.9	84.1	96.2	65.5	83.2	99.4	65.5	85.1
08	OPENINGS	106.2	57.3	95.0	96.9	46.1	85.2	96.9	57.1	87.7	98.1	56.8	88.6	101.5	57.3	91.4	96.9	57.0	87.7
0920	Plaster & Gypsum Board	90.7	56.4	67.7	76.9	36.7	49.9	83.8	56.4	65.4	85.8	56.4	66.0	96.0	56.4	69.4	82.8	56.4	65.1
0950, 0980	Ceilings & Acoustic Treatment	92.8	56.4	68.2	82.3	36.7	51.6	82.3	56.4	64.8	90.9	56.4	67.6	92.6	56.4	68.2	82.3	56.4	64.8
0960	Flooring	90.9	74.8	86.5	89.7	60.6	81.6	97.0	54.6	85.2	99.4	35.1	81.6	88.2	74.8	84.5	93.9	60.6	84.7
0970, 0990	Wall Finishes & Painting/Coating	84.0	45.1	61.3	90.9	44.2	63.7	90.9	44.2	63.7	90.9	44.2	63.7	87.1	45.1	62.6	90.9	45.1	64.2
09	FINISHES	83.9	58.8	70.3	81.5	44.5	61.4	84.6	54.8	68.3	87.3	51.3	67.7	86.5	58.8	71.4	84.2	56.9	69.4
COVERS	DIVS. 10 - 14, 25, 28, 41, 43, 44, 46	100.0	79.1	95.3	100.0	77.0	94.9	100.0	79.5	95.4	100.0	79.5	95.4	100.0	79.1	95.3	100.0	79.1	95.3
21, 22, 23	FIRE SUPPRESSION, PLUMBING & HVAC	100.3	67.9	86.4	97.2	62.4	82.3	97.2	62.5	82.4	100.3	62.4	84.1	100.1	67.9	86.3	97.2	62.5	82.4
26, 27, 3370	ELECTRICAL, COMMUNICATIONS & UTIL.	96.4	69.4	82.4	94.7	64.5	79.0	96.0	64.6	79.7	94.3	70.9	82.1	101.7	71.2	85.8	94.3	67.6	80.4
MF2016	WEIGHTED AVERAGE	98.7	66.9	84.8	92.6	61.1	78.8	92.9	65.8	81.0	95.1	65.3	82.1	97.7	67.2	84.4	93.3	65.1	81.0

DIVISION		OKLAHOMA POTEAU 749			SHAWNEE 748			TULSA 740-741			WOODWARD 738			OREGON BEND 977			EUGENE 974		
		MAT.	INST.	TOTAL	MAT.	INST.	TOTAL	MAT.	INST.	TOTAL	MAT.	INST.	TOTAL	MAT.	INST.	TOTAL	MAT.	INST.	TOTAL
015433	CONTRACTOR EQUIPMENT		92.2	92.2		81.8	81.8		93.5	93.5		81.8	81.8		98.9	98.9		98.9	98.9
0241, 31 - 34	SITE & INFRASTRUCTURE, DEMOLITION	77.2	88.1	84.9	99.1	95.8	96.8	96.7	94.8	95.3	103.5	95.8	98.1	109.4	102.5	104.6	99.4	102.6	101.6
0310	Concrete Forming & Accessories	88.6	57.3	61.6	84.1	57.7	61.3	99.6	57.6	63.4	90.3	45.5	51.6	108.8	96.2	97.9	105.3	96.3	97.5
0320	Concrete Reinforcing	92.2	66.5	79.2	91.2	62.8	76.8	91.4	66.5	78.9	81.0	66.5	73.7	100.0	109.8	104.9	104.4	109.8	107.1
0330	Cast-in-Place Concrete	84.6	74.8	80.9	97.6	73.9	88.6	93.2	75.0	86.3	100.0	73.9	90.1	105.4	101.3	103.9	102.1	101.4	101.8
03	CONCRETE	83.2	65.8	75.3	89.4	64.0	77.8	87.9	66.1	77.9	89.4	59.2	75.6	103.8	99.9	102.0	95.6	99.9	97.6
04	MASONRY	91.9	58.0	70.9	107.8	57.9	76.8	92.5	58.0	71.1	91.0	57.9	70.5	104.0	100.8	102.0	101.0	100.8	100.9
05	METALS	91.2	76.4	86.7	91.1	59.9	81.5	95.8	76.8	89.9	102.2	61.2	89.6	96.3	94.5	95.7	97.0	94.6	96.3
06	WOOD, PLASTICS & COMPOSITES	96.1	57.1	74.4	91.3	57.0	72.2	107.1	57.1	79.3	103.3	40.5	68.3	101.8	95.1	98.1	97.8	95.1	96.3
07	THERMAL & MOISTURE PROTECTION	99.4	65.2	84.9	99.4	64.9	84.8	99.6	66.1	85.4	105.5	63.6	87.8	115.4	99.4	108.6	114.5	102.5	109.4
08	OPENINGS	96.9	57.1	87.7	96.9	56.1	87.5	99.8	57.1	90.0	103.2	47.9	90.5	101.2	98.9	100.6	101.4	98.9	100.9
0920	Plaster & Gypsum Board	80.9	56.4	64.4	77.9	56.4	63.4	85.8	56.4	66.0	88.5	39.4	55.5	115.2	94.8	101.5	113.2	94.8	100.8
0950, 0980	Ceilings & Acoustic Treatment	82.3	56.4	64.8	82.3	56.4	64.8	90.9	56.4	67.6	86.0	39.4	54.6	90.8	94.8	93.5	91.7	94.8	93.8
0960	Flooring	93.3	54.6	82.6	90.8	60.6	82.4	98.3	62.5	88.4	87.4	57.7	79.1	98.4	105.4	100.3	96.6	105.4	99.1
0970, 0990	Wall Finishes & Painting/Coating	90.9	45.1	64.2	90.9	44.2	63.7	90.9	44.2	63.7	84.0	45.1	61.3	90.9	72.8	80.3	90.9	72.8	80.3
09	FINISHES	82.3	54.9	67.4	82.7	55.8	68.1	87.1	56.3	70.4	81.6	45.6	62.0	96.1	95.1	95.6	94.5	95.1	94.8
COVERS	DIVS. 10 - 14, 25, 28, 41, 43, 44, 46	100.0	79.3	95.4	100.0	79.1	95.3	100.0	79.5	95.4	100.0	77.3	94.9	100.0	99.7	99.9	100.0	99.7	99.9
21, 22, 23	FIRE SUPPRESSION, PLUMBING & HVAC	97.2	62.4	82.4	97.2	67.8	84.6	100.3	64.3	84.9	97.2	67.8	84.7	97.0	102.2	99.2	100.1	102.2	101.0
26, 27, 3370	ELECTRICAL, COMMUNICATIONS & UTIL.	94.4	64.6	78.9	96.2	71.2	83.2	96.2	64.6	79.8	96.3	71.2	83.2	101.0	94.5	97.6	99.6	94.5	97.0
MF2016	WEIGHTED AVERAGE	92.5	65.4	80.6	94.7	66.3	82.3	96.0	66.4	83.0	96.7	63.8	82.3	100.0	98.7	99.4	99.1	98.8	99.0

City Cost Indexes

OREGON

DIVISION		KLAMATH FALLS 976			MEDFORD 975			PENDLETON 978			PORTLAND 970 - 972			SALEM 973			VALE 979		
		MAT.	INST.	TOTAL	MAT.	INST.	TOTAL	MAT.	INST.	TOTAL	MAT.	INST.	TOTAL	MAT.	INST.	TOTAL	MAT.	INST.	TOTAL
015433	CONTRACTOR EQUIPMENT		98.9	98.9		98.9	98.9		96.4	96.4		98.9	98.9		98.9	98.9		96.4	96.4
0241, 31 - 34	SITE & INFRASTRUCTURE, DEMOLITION	113.4	102.5	105.8	107.1	102.5	103.9	106.8	95.5	98.9	102.1	102.6	102.4	93.9	102.5	99.9	94.0	95.4	95.0
0310	Concrete Forming & Accessories	101.7	95.9	96.7	100.8	95.9	96.5	102.2	96.2	97.1	106.4	96.3	97.7	105.9	96.2	97.5	108.7	95.1	97.0
0320	Concrete Reinforcing	100.0	109.7	104.9	101.7	109.7	105.8	99.2	109.8	104.5	105.2	109.8	107.5	113.1	109.8	111.4	96.7	109.6	103.2
0330	Cast-in-Place Concrete	105.4	101.2	103.8	105.4	101.2	103.8	106.2	100.2	103.9	104.9	101.4	103.6	96.4	101.3	98.3	83.6	102.2	90.6
03	CONCRETE	106.4	99.7	103.4	101.4	99.7	100.6	88.6	99.5	93.6	97.1	99.9	98.4	93.3	99.9	96.3	74.1	99.6	85.8
04	MASONRY	118.1	100.8	107.4	98.0	100.8	99.7	108.5	100.9	103.8	102.7	100.8	101.5	107.2	100.8	103.2	106.6	100.9	103.1
05	METALS	96.3	94.3	95.7	96.6	94.2	95.8	103.0	95.0	100.5	98.1	94.6	97.0	103.7	94.5	100.9	102.9	93.9	100.1
06	WOOD, PLASTICS & COMPOSITES	92.9	95.1	94.1	91.8	95.1	93.6	94.6	95.2	94.9	98.7	95.1	96.7	92.5	95.1	93.9	102.9	95.2	98.6
07	THERMAL & MOISTURE PROTECTION	115.6	95.2	107.0	115.2	95.2	106.8	108.0	95.8	102.9	114.4	99.4	108.1	110.5	99.4	105.8	107.4	93.4	101.5
08	OPENINGS	101.2	98.9	100.7	104.3	98.9	103.0	97.7	99.0	98.0	99.1	98.9	99.1	102.7	98.9	101.8	97.7	89.1	95.7
0920	Plaster & Gypsum Board	110.0	94.8	99.8	109.4	94.8	99.6	96.7	94.8	95.4	113.1	94.8	100.8	110.9	94.8	100.1	102.9	94.8	97.5
0950, 0980	Ceilings & Acoustic Treatment	98.4	94.8	96.0	105.1	94.8	98.2	65.0	94.8	85.1	93.6	94.8	94.4	99.6	94.8	96.4	65.0	94.8	85.1
0960	Flooring	95.2	105.4	98.1	94.6	105.4	97.6	66.1	105.4	77.0	94.5	105.4	97.5	98.0	105.4	100.0	68.2	105.4	78.5
0970, 0990	Wall Finishes & Painting/Coating	90.9	68.2	77.7	90.9	68.2	77.7	83.5	75.0	78.6	90.7	75.0	81.6	90.6	75.0	81.5	83.5	72.8	77.2
09	FINISHES	96.4	94.6	95.4	96.7	94.6	95.5	68.1	95.4	83.0	94.2	95.3	94.8	96.1	95.3	95.6	68.7	95.1	83.1
COVERS	DIVS. 10 - 14, 25, 28, 41, 43, 44, 46	100.0	99.6	99.9	100.0	99.6	99.9	100.0	99.5	99.9	100.0	99.7	99.9	100.0	99.7	99.9	100.0	99.9	100.0
21, 22, 23	FIRE SUPPRESSION, PLUMBING & HVAC	97.0	106.1	100.9	100.1	102.2	101.0	98.9	108.7	103.1	100.1	106.2	102.7	100.0	102.2	101.0	98.9	73.5	88.1
26, 27, 3370	ELECTRICAL, COMMUNICATIONS & UTIL.	99.7	77.5	88.2	103.1	77.5	89.8	92.2	96.3	94.3	99.8	103.5	101.7	107.2	94.5	100.6	92.2	67.7	79.4
MF2016	WEIGHTED AVERAGE	101.0	96.9	99.2	100.6	96.1	98.6	96.0	99.7	97.6	99.4	100.8	100.0	100.9	98.7	100.0	93.8	87.7	91.1

PENNSYLVANIA

DIVISION		ALLENTOWN 181			ALTOONA 166			BEDFORD 155			BRADFORD 167			BUTLER 160			CHAMBERSBURG 172		
		MAT.	INST.	TOTAL	MAT.	INST.	TOTAL	MAT.	INST.	TOTAL	MAT.	INST.	TOTAL	MAT.	INST.	TOTAL	MAT.	INST.	TOTAL
015433	CONTRACTOR EQUIPMENT		115.8	115.8		115.8	115.8		114.1	114.1		115.8	115.8		115.8	115.8		115.0	115.0
0241, 31 - 34	SITE & INFRASTRUCTURE, DEMOLITION	93.5	102.2	99.6	96.3	102.1	100.3	105.9	99.9	101.7	92.5	101.1	98.4	87.6	102.8	98.3	91.3	99.4	97.0
0310	Concrete Forming & Accessories	99.1	109.4	108.0	84.2	83.3	83.3	82.6	79.9	80.3	86.3	101.1	99.0	85.6	88.9	88.4	86.9	80.0	81.0
0320	Concrete Reinforcing	101.4	117.0	109.3	98.3	104.2	101.2	96.4	102.0	99.2	100.4	104.0	102.2	99.0	120.4	109.8	99.0	111.9	105.5
0330	Cast-in-Place Concrete	88.5	105.2	94.8	98.6	91.3	95.8	111.9	86.3	102.2	94.1	95.3	94.6	87.1	99.6	91.8	91.3	97.7	93.7
03	CONCRETE	90.8	110.1	99.6	86.8	91.2	88.8	103.3	87.6	96.1	92.7	100.6	96.3	78.9	99.5	88.3	94.5	93.3	93.9
04	MASONRY	94.3	97.1	96.0	97.8	87.0	91.1	105.7	83.7	92.0	95.2	82.1	87.1	100.0	96.7	97.9	100.0	82.3	89.0
05	METALS	98.0	123.2	105.7	92.0	115.6	99.3	97.2	114.0	102.3	95.8	115.4	101.8	91.7	123.4	101.5	95.5	117.8	102.4
06	WOOD, PLASTICS & COMPOSITES	101.3	111.6	107.0	80.5	81.3	80.9	84.0	79.1	81.3	86.9	106.1	97.6	81.9	85.6	84.0	88.2	79.2	83.2
07	THERMAL & MOISTURE PROTECTION	101.7	112.1	106.1	100.7	92.8	97.4	99.6	89.0	95.1	101.5	91.5	97.3	100.2	96.3	98.5	95.7	86.1	91.6
08	OPENINGS	94.2	109.9	97.8	87.9	85.6	87.4	96.3	84.5	93.6	94.1	99.4	95.3	87.9	96.1	89.8	91.4	84.7	89.9
0920	Plaster & Gypsum Board	96.8	111.8	106.9	88.5	80.7	83.2	100.5	78.7	85.8	89.6	106.2	100.7	88.5	85.2	86.3	104.3	78.5	87.0
0950, 0980	Ceilings & Acoustic Treatment	86.4	111.8	103.5	89.0	80.7	83.4	98.8	78.5	85.2	89.1	106.2	100.6	89.9	85.2	86.7	88.5	78.5	81.8
0960	Flooring	88.9	100.5	92.1	82.8	104.6	88.9	94.7	82.4	91.3	83.2	104.6	89.1	83.7	111.3	91.4	87.3	82.4	85.9
0970, 0990	Wall Finishes & Painting/Coating	91.2	106.5	100.1	86.3	111.0	100.9	96.7	111.0	105.1	91.2	105.3	99.4	86.8	111.0	100.9	88.6	105.3	98.3
09	FINISHES	88.8	108.0	99.2	86.5	89.2	88.0	99.4	83.3	90.6	86.6	102.9	95.5	86.5	94.4	90.8	86.5	82.7	84.5
COVERS	DIVS. 10 - 14, 25, 28, 41, 43, 44, 46	100.0	103.2	100.7	100.0	97.9	99.5	100.0	96.4	99.2	100.0	101.1	100.0	100.0	100.0	100.0	100.0	95.6	99.0
21, 22, 23	FIRE SUPPRESSION, PLUMBING & HVAC	100.2	112.0	105.3	99.7	85.6	93.7	96.9	82.3	90.6	97.2	94.4	96.0	96.7	97.1	96.8	97.2	88.1	93.3
26, 27, 3370	ELECTRICAL, COMMUNICATIONS & UTIL.	98.7	98.0	98.3	89.5	110.6	100.5	95.6	110.6	103.4	92.8	110.6	102.1	90.1	109.1	100.0	89.2	86.3	87.7
MF2016	WEIGHTED AVERAGE	96.5	107.7	101.4	93.2	95.1	94.0	98.7	92.2	95.8	94.8	100.2	97.2	91.4	101.5	95.8	94.4	90.8	92.8

PENNSYLVANIA

DIVISION		DOYLESTOWN 189			DUBOIS 158			ERIE 164 - 165			GREENSBURG 156			HARRISBURG 170 - 171			HAZLETON 182		
		MAT.	INST.	TOTAL	MAT.	INST.	TOTAL	MAT.	INST.	TOTAL	MAT.	INST.	TOTAL	MAT.	INST.	TOTAL	MAT.	INST.	TOTAL
015433	CONTRACTOR EQUIPMENT		93.5	93.5		114.1	114.1		115.8	115.8		114.1	114.1		115.0	115.0		115.8	115.8
0241, 31 - 34	SITE & INFRASTRUCTURE, DEMOLITION	107.5	89.2	94.7	110.8	100.0	103.2	93.2	102.4	99.6	101.8	101.9	101.9	91.4	100.3	97.6	86.9	101.5	97.1
0310	Concrete Forming & Accessories	83.3	126.4	120.5	82.1	80.7	80.9	98.4	87.0	88.5	88.8	92.8	92.2	98.6	87.5	89.0	80.9	86.7	85.9
0320	Concrete Reinforcing	98.1	124.0	111.2	95.7	104.1	99.9	100.4	105.2	102.8	95.7	120.1	108.0	108.4	114.5	111.5	98.4	113.0	105.8
0330	Cast-in-Place Concrete	83.6	133.8	102.6	107.9	94.7	102.9	96.9	93.3	95.5	103.8	99.2	102.0	89.8	100.9	94.0	83.6	99.1	89.5
03	CONCRETE	86.5	127.8	105.4	105.1	91.1	98.7	85.8	93.8	89.4	98.2	101.0	99.5	89.9	98.3	93.7	83.7	97.0	89.8
04	MASONRY	97.7	126.7	115.7	106.2	84.1	92.5	86.9	90.6	89.2	116.1	92.9	101.7	94.2	87.4	90.0	107.4	91.5	97.6
05	METALS	95.5	114.2	101.3	97.7	114.2	102.4	92.2	116.2	99.6	97.1	121.7	104.6	102.0	121.2	107.9	97.7	119.9	104.5
06	WOOD, PLASTICS & COMPOSITES	82.6	126.6	107.1	83.1	79.1	80.9	97.4	84.5	90.2	90.1	91.3	90.7	99.8	86.4	92.3	81.3	83.8	82.7
07	THERMAL & MOISTURE PROTECTION	99.2	127.8	111.3	99.9	91.2	96.2	101.2	92.1	97.4	99.5	95.8	97.9	98.6	103.9	100.8	101.0	100.8	100.9
08	OPENINGS	96.5	129.8	104.2	96.3	84.5	93.6	88.1	89.0	88.3	96.3	99.2	97.0	97.8	89.3	95.8	94.7	93.1	94.4
0920	Plaster & Gypsum Board	87.5	127.3	114.2	99.5	78.7	85.4	96.8	83.9	88.2	101.6	91.0	94.5	108.2	86.0	93.3	87.9	83.3	84.8
0950, 0980	Ceilings & Acoustic Treatment	85.6	127.3	113.7	98.8	78.5	85.2	86.4	83.9	84.7	98.0	91.0	93.3	97.0	86.0	89.6	87.4	83.3	84.6
0960	Flooring	73.8	147.3	94.2	94.5	104.6	97.3	89.6	104.6	93.7	98.8	82.4	94.2	89.4	95.6	91.4	80.4	94.4	84.3
0970, 0990	Wall Finishes & Painting/Coating	90.8	145.9	122.9	96.7	111.0	105.1	96.3	91.8	93.7	96.7	111.0	105.1	90.6	88.6	89.4	91.2	108.8	101.5
09	FINISHES	80.4	132.4	108.7	99.6	87.5	93.0	89.8	90.0	89.9	100.3	92.5	96.0	92.0	88.3	90.0	84.8	90.0	87.6
COVERS	DIVS. 10 - 14, 25, 28, 41, 43, 44, 46	100.0	113.0	102.9	100.0	96.9	99.3	100.0	99.5	99.9	100.0	100.4	100.1	100.0	97.7	99.5	100.0	96.8	99.3
21, 22, 23	FIRE SUPPRESSION, PLUMBING & HVAC	96.7	127.8	110.0	96.9	83.0	91.0	99.7	100.5	100.1	96.9	90.9	94.3	100.2	92.0	96.7	97.2	95.7	96.5
26, 27, 3370	ELECTRICAL, COMMUNICATIONS & UTIL.	92.3	127.0	110.3	96.9	110.6	103.7	99.1	92.4	95.6	96.2	110.6	103.7	95.9	88.7	92.2	93.6	91.7	92.6
MF2016	WEIGHTED AVERAGE	94.0	123.5	106.9	99.1	93.5	96.7	93.1	96.8	94.7	98.6	99.9	99.2	97.3	95.2	96.3	94.4	96.8	95.4

City Cost Indexes

PENNSYLVANIA

DIVISION		INDIANA 157			JOHNSTOWN 159			KITTANNING 162			LANCASTER 175 - 176			LEHIGH VALLEY 180			MONTROSE 188		
		MAT.	INST.	TOTAL	MAT.	INST.	TOTAL	MAT.	INST.	TOTAL	MAT.	INST.	TOTAL	MAT.	INST.	TOTAL	MAT.	INST.	TOTAL
015433	CONTRACTOR EQUIPMENT		114.1	114.1		114.1	114.1		115.8	115.8		115.0	115.0		115.8	115.8		115.8	115.8
0241, 31 - 34	SITE & INFRASTRUCTURE, DEMOLITION	99.9	100.9	100.6	106.4	101.1	102.7	90.2	102.4	98.8	83.1	100.4	95.2	90.8	103.0	99.4	89.5	102.2	98.4
0310	Concrete Forming & Accessories	83.2	89.9	89.0	82.1	83.1	83.0	85.6	93.9	92.7	89.0	87.7	87.9	92.5	127.5	122.7	81.8	90.6	89.4
0320	Concrete Reinforcing	95.0	120.1	107.7	96.4	119.9	108.2	99.0	120.2	109.7	98.6	114.6	106.7	98.4	111.3	104.9	103.1	119.9	111.6
0330	Cast-in-Place Concrete	101.8	97.7	100.2	112.9	91.2	104.6	90.5	98.9	93.3	77.6	100.9	86.5	90.5	109.4	97.7	88.7	97.8	92.2
03	CONCRETE	95.7	99.1	97.3	104.3	93.7	99.5	81.4	101.1	90.4	83.1	98.4	90.1	89.9	118.8	103.1	88.6	99.6	93.6
04	MASONRY	102.2	92.4	96.1	103.1	87.3	93.3	102.6	92.3	96.2	106.1	88.9	95.4	94.4	109.9	104.0	94.3	95.5	95.0
05	METALS	97.2	121.2	104.6	97.2	119.8	104.1	91.8	122.4	101.2	95.5	121.4	103.4	97.6	120.9	104.8	95.9	123.0	104.2
06	WOOD, PLASTICS & COMPOSITES	84.7	88.8	87.0	83.1	81.2	82.0	81.9	93.6	88.4	90.9	86.4	88.4	93.2	130.3	113.8	82.0	87.3	85.0
07	THERMAL & MOISTURE PROTECTION	99.4	95.4	97.7	99.6	91.4	96.2	100.3	96.0	98.5	95.2	104.4	99.1	101.4	113.3	106.7	101.1	90.6	96.6
08	OPENINGS	96.3	93.5	95.7	96.3	89.3	94.7	87.9	100.5	90.8	91.4	89.3	90.9	94.7	118.9	100.3	91.4	94.4	92.1
0920	Plaster & Gypsum Board	100.8	88.4	92.5	99.3	80.7	86.8	88.5	93.4	91.8	106.2	86.0	92.6	90.5	131.0	117.7	88.3	86.9	87.4
0950, 0980	Ceilings & Acoustic Treatment	98.8	88.4	91.8	98.0	80.7	86.3	89.9	93.4	92.2	88.5	86.0	86.8	87.4	131.0	116.8	89.1	86.9	87.6
0960	Flooring	95.5	104.6	98.0	94.5	82.4	91.1	83.7	104.6	89.5	88.3	101.1	91.8	85.8	99.5	89.6	81.1	104.6	87.6
0970, 0990	Wall Finishes & Painting/Coating	96.7	111.0	105.1	96.7	111.0	105.1	86.8	111.0	100.9	88.6	88.6	88.6	91.2	62.5	74.4	91.2	108.9	101.5
09	FINISHES	99.2	94.3	96.5	99.0	85.5	91.6	86.6	97.2	92.4	86.5	89.4	88.1	87.0	116.8	103.2	85.6	94.2	90.3
COVERS	DIVS. 10 - 14, 25, 28, 41, 43, 44, 46	100.0	99.5	99.9	100.0	97.9	99.5	100.0	100.2	100.0	100.0	97.9	99.5	100.0	102.9	100.7	100.0	98.4	99.7
21, 22, 23	FIRE SUPPRESSION, PLUMBING & HVAC	96.9	83.3	91.1	96.9	82.1	90.6	96.7	93.3	95.2	97.2	92.3	95.1	97.2	113.0	103.9	97.2	98.6	97.8
26, 27, 3370	ELECTRICAL, COMMUNICATIONS & UTIL.	96.2	110.6	103.7	96.2	110.6	103.7	89.5	110.6	100.5	90.4	94.7	92.6	93.6	136.6	116.0	92.8	96.2	94.6
MF2016	WEIGHTED AVERAGE	97.4	97.8	97.6	98.7	94.7	96.9	91.9	101.2	95.9	93.2	96.4	94.6	94.9	117.4	104.7	93.8	99.5	96.3

PENNSYLVANIA

DIVISION		NEW CASTLE 161			NORRISTOWN 194			OIL CITY 163			PHILADELPHIA 190 - 191			PITTSBURGH 150 - 152			POTTSVILLE 179		
		MAT.	INST.	TOTAL	MAT.	INST.	TOTAL	MAT.	INST.	TOTAL	MAT.	INST.	TOTAL	MAT.	INST.	TOTAL	MAT.	INST.	TOTAL
015433	CONTRACTOR EQUIPMENT		115.8	115.8		100.1	100.1		115.8	115.8		100.3	100.3		102.6	102.6		115.0	115.0
0241, 31 - 34	SITE & INFRASTRUCTURE, DEMOLITION	88.0	102.7	98.3	97.0	100.2	99.2	86.6	101.2	96.8	98.8	100.6	100.1	106.0	100.4	102.1	86.1	100.6	96.3
0310	Concrete Forming & Accessories	85.6	94.6	93.4	84.1	126.7	120.8	85.6	93.4	92.3	101.5	141.9	136.4	99.0	98.8	99.0	80.6	88.9	87.8
0320	Concrete Reinforcing	97.8	101.9	99.8	99.5	126.6	113.2	99.0	97.7	98.3	103.3	126.2	115.1	96.9	120.6	108.8	97.8	114.5	106.2
0330	Cast-in-Place Concrete	87.9	99.2	92.2	83.4	134.1	102.6	85.3	97.6	90.0	91.2	137.7	108.9	111.3	99.9	107.0	82.7	101.3	89.8
03	CONCRETE	79.3	98.7	88.2	85.9	128.5	105.4	77.8	96.9	86.5	98.9	136.6	116.2	104.8	103.0	104.0	86.5	99.1	92.2
04	MASONRY	99.6	96.6	97.7	110.2	127.3	120.8	98.9	88.4	92.4	95.7	130.8	117.5	99.0	101.0	100.2	99.4	91.3	94.4
05	METALS	91.8	116.3	99.4	99.2	114.8	104.0	91.8	114.7	98.8	101.9	115.1	106.0	98.6	107.9	101.5	95.7	121.4	103.6
06	WOOD, PLASTICS & COMPOSITES	81.9	94.0	88.6	82.0	126.8	106.8	81.9	93.6	88.4	96.3	144.5	123.1	102.6	99.0	100.6	81.0	85.6	83.6
07	THERMAL & MOISTURE PROTECTION	100.2	95.7	98.3	104.6	128.2	114.6	100.1	93.2	97.2	101.5	136.9	116.5	99.8	99.1	99.5	95.3	103.1	98.6
08	OPENINGS	87.9	93.0	89.1	86.9	129.8	96.7	87.9	95.5	89.7	97.1	140.3	107.0	98.7	103.5	99.8	91.5	95.0	92.3
0920	Plaster & Gypsum Board	88.5	93.7	92.0	86.5	127.3	113.9	88.5	93.4	91.8	98.0	145.5	129.9	98.0	98.8	98.5	101.0	85.2	90.4
0950, 0980	Ceilings & Acoustic Treatment	89.9	93.7	92.5	91.0	127.3	115.4	89.9	93.4	92.2	101.3	145.5	131.1	92.6	98.8	96.8	88.5	85.2	86.3
0960	Flooring	83.7	111.3	91.4	81.8	147.3	99.9	83.7	106.1	89.9	96.7	147.3	110.8	104.0	107.7	105.0	84.3	101.1	89.0
0970, 0990	Wall Finishes & Painting/Coating	86.8	111.0	100.9	86.8	147.3	121.7	86.8	111.0	100.9	94.6	150.2	127.0	99.8	111.0	106.3	88.6	108.8	100.4
09	FINISHES	86.5	99.1	93.3	84.4	132.5	110.6	86.4	97.4	92.4	100.4	144.5	124.4	101.1	101.5	101.3	84.8	92.3	88.9
COVERS	DIVS. 10 - 14, 25, 28, 41, 43, 44, 46	100.0	100.8	100.2	100.0	113.2	102.9	100.0	100.1	100.0	100.0	120.0	104.4	100.0	101.8	100.4	100.0	95.2	98.9
21, 22, 23	FIRE SUPPRESSION, PLUMBING & HVAC	96.7	100.9	98.5	96.9	126.8	109.7	96.7	96.4	96.6	100.1	136.7	115.7	99.9	98.9	99.5	97.2	97.6	97.4
26, 27, 3370	ELECTRICAL, COMMUNICATIONS & UTIL.	90.1	100.7	95.6	93.7	150.0	123.0	91.7	109.1	100.8	100.1	155.2	128.7	98.5	111.6	105.3	88.8	91.0	89.9
MF2016	WEIGHTED AVERAGE	91.5	100.9	95.6	94.5	127.6	109.0	91.3	99.6	95.0	99.7	134.6	115.0	100.3	103.0	101.5	93.0	97.9	95.1

PENNSYLVANIA

DIVISION		READING 195 - 196			SCRANTON 184 - 185			STATE COLLEGE 168			STROUDSBURG 183			SUNBURY 178			UNIONTOWN 154		
		MAT.	INST.	TOTAL	MAT.	INST.	TOTAL	MAT.	INST.	TOTAL	MAT.	INST.	TOTAL	MAT.	INST.	TOTAL	MAT.	INST.	TOTAL
015433	CONTRACTOR EQUIPMENT		122.9	122.9		115.8	115.8		115.0	115.0		115.8	115.8		115.8	115.8		114.1	114.1
0241, 31 - 34	SITE & INFRASTRUCTURE, DEMOLITION	101.2	113.7	110.0	94.0	102.2	99.8	84.4	100.6	95.8	88.5	103.0	98.7	98.7	101.6	100.7	100.4	101.7	101.3
0310	Concrete Forming & Accessories	100.1	90.2	91.6	99.2	90.8	92.0	84.8	83.4	83.6	87.2	95.5	94.3	92.2	86.1	86.9	76.5	92.6	90.4
0320	Concrete Reinforcing	100.8	143.2	122.2	101.4	120.1	110.8	99.6	104.2	102.0	101.7	120.2	111.0	100.6	114.4	107.6	95.7	120.1	108.0
0330	Cast-in-Place Concrete	74.7	102.2	85.1	92.4	98.1	94.5	89.1	91.4	90.0	87.0	104.3	93.8	90.4	99.7	94.0	101.8	98.9	100.7
03	CONCRETE	84.8	105.0	94.0	92.6	99.8	95.9	92.8	91.3	92.1	87.4	104.2	95.1	89.9	97.2	93.3	95.3	100.7	97.8
04	MASONRY	99.2	95.4	96.8	94.6	97.9	96.6	100.3	87.5	92.3	92.4	109.7	103.1	99.9	84.4	90.3	117.8	92.8	102.3
05	METALS	99.5	132.9	109.7	100.0	123.3	107.1	95.6	115.8	101.8	97.7	123.6	105.7	95.4	121.1	103.3	96.9	121.2	104.4
06	WOOD, PLASTICS & COMPOSITES	99.4	86.4	92.2	101.3	87.3	93.5	88.7	81.3	84.5	87.7	87.3	87.5	88.9	85.6	87.1	77.6	91.2	85.2
07	THERMAL & MOISTURE PROTECTION	104.9	107.9	106.2	101.6	95.1	98.8	100.8	101.5	101.1	101.2	99.0	100.3	96.2	96.3	96.2	99.3	95.8	97.8
08	OPENINGS	91.2	102.0	93.8	94.2	94.4	94.2	91.2	85.6	89.9	94.7	97.3	95.3	91.6	92.2	91.7	96.3	98.7	96.8
0920	Plaster & Gypsum Board	96.3	86.0	89.4	98.5	86.9	90.7	90.4	80.7	83.9	89.2	86.9	87.6	100.2	85.2	90.1	97.7	91.0	93.2
0950, 0980	Ceilings & Acoustic Treatment	84.0	86.0	85.3	94.1	86.9	89.2	86.5	80.7	82.6	85.6	86.9	86.5	85.1	85.2	85.1	98.0	91.0	93.3
0960	Flooring	86.5	103.5	91.2	88.9	98.2	91.5	86.3	103.5	91.1	83.8	99.5	88.1	85.1	104.6	90.5	91.3	82.4	88.8
0970, 0990	Wall Finishes & Painting/Coating	86.7	106.5	98.2	91.2	113.2	104.0	91.2	111.0	102.8	91.2	108.8	101.5	88.6	108.8	100.4	96.7	108.9	103.8
09	FINISHES	86.1	92.9	89.8	90.5	93.8	92.3	86.2	89.1	87.8	85.7	96.5	91.6	85.7	91.2	88.7	97.3	92.2	94.6
COVERS	DIVS. 10 - 14, 25, 28, 41, 43, 44, 46	100.0	99.8	99.9	100.0	98.6	99.7	100.0	97.1	99.3	100.0	102.6	100.6	100.0	95.2	98.9	100.0	100.4	100.1
21, 22, 23	FIRE SUPPRESSION, PLUMBING & HVAC	100.2	111.1	104.8	100.2	98.5	99.6	97.2	91.6	94.8	97.2	104.8	100.4	97.2	89.6	93.9	96.9	85.6	92.1
26, 27, 3370	ELECTRICAL, COMMUNICATIONS & UTIL.	99.8	94.7	97.1	98.7	96.2	97.4	92.0	110.6	101.7	93.6	142.9	119.2	89.1	93.2	91.2	93.3	110.6	102.3
MF2016	WEIGHTED AVERAGE	96.1	105.2	100.1	97.2	100.0	98.4	94.4	96.5	95.3	94.3	110.4	101.3	93.9	95.1	94.4	97.6	98.6	98.1

City Cost Indexes

PENNSYLVANIA

DIVISION		WASHINGTON 153			WELLSBORO 169			WESTCHESTER 193			WILKES-BARRE 186 - 187			WILLIAMSPORT 177			YORK 173 - 174		
		MAT.	INST.	TOTAL	MAT.	INST.	TOTAL	MAT.	INST.	TOTAL	MAT.	INST.	TOTAL	MAT.	INST.	TOTAL	MAT.	INST.	TOTAL
015433	CONTRACTOR EQUIPMENT		114.1	114.1		115.8	115.8		100.1	100.1		115.8	115.8		115.8	115.8		115.0	115.0
0241, 31 - 34	SITE & INFRASTRUCTURE, DEMOLITION	100.5	102.0	101.6	96.0	101.6	99.9	102.9	101.1	101.6	86.5	102.2	97.5	89.3	101.7	98.0	86.9	100.4	96.3
0310	Concrete Forming & Accessories	83.3	94.6	93.1	85.8	85.9	85.9	90.8	127.3	122.3	89.8	89.4	89.4	88.8	86.8	87.1	84.0	87.7	87.1
0320	Concrete Reinforcing	95.7	120.4	108.2	99.6	119.9	109.8	98.5	143.9	121.4	100.4	120.1	110.3	99.8	114.5	107.2	100.6	114.6	107.6
0330	Cast-in-Place Concrete	101.8	99.3	100.8	93.3	92.7	93.1	92.3	135.2	108.6	83.6	97.9	89.0	76.5	93.6	83.0	83.1	100.9	89.9
03	CONCRETE	95.8	101.9	98.6	95.0	95.7	95.3	93.4	132.2	111.1	84.5	99.0	91.1	78.5	95.5	86.2	87.6	98.4	92.5
04	MASONRY	102.2	97.4	99.2	101.4	84.9	91.2	104.9	129.4	120.1	107.7	97.5	101.4	91.4	88.0	89.3	101.0	88.9	93.5
05	METALS	96.9	122.2	104.7	95.7	122.2	103.8	99.2	121.5	106.1	95.8	123.2	104.2	95.5	120.8	103.3	97.1	121.3	104.6
06	WOOD, PLASTICS & COMPOSITES	84.8	93.6	89.7	86.3	85.6	85.9	88.6	126.6	109.7	90.0	85.6	87.6	85.5	86.4	86.0	84.3	86.4	85.5
07	THERMAL & MOISTURE PROTECTION	99.4	97.7	98.6	101.8	88.8	96.3	105.0	124.7	113.3	101.0	94.7	98.4	95.6	90.8	93.6	95.3	104.4	99.2
08	OPENINGS	96.2	100.5	97.2	94.1	93.1	93.9	86.9	134.5	97.8	91.4	93.5	91.9	91.6	92.7	91.8	91.4	89.3	90.9
0920	Plaster & Gypsum Board	100.6	93.4	95.7	89.0	85.2	86.4	87.1	127.3	114.1	89.9	85.2	86.7	101.0	86.0	90.9	101.3	86.0	91.0
0950, 0980	Ceilings & Acoustic Treatment	98.0	93.4	94.9	86.5	85.2	85.6	91.0	127.3	115.4	89.1	85.2	86.4	88.5	86.0	86.8	87.6	86.0	86.5
0960	Flooring	95.6	82.4	91.9	82.8	101.1	87.9	84.6	147.3	102.0	84.6	98.2	88.4	84.0	91.7	86.2	85.6	101.1	89.9
0970, 0990	Wall Finishes & Painting/Coating	96.7	108.9	103.8	91.2	108.8	101.5	87.9	142.1	119.5	91.2	106.5	100.1	88.6	106.5	99.0	88.6	88.6	88.6
09	FINISHES	99.1	93.6	96.1	86.2	91.0	88.8	85.9	132.7	111.3	86.7	92.0	89.5	85.4	88.9	87.3	85.1	89.4	87.5
COVERS	DIVS. 10 - 14, 25, 28, 41, 43, 44, 46	100.0	100.7	100.2	100.0	92.9	98.4	100.0	111.2	102.5	100.0	98.2	99.6	100.0	97.5	99.5	100.0	97.8	99.5
21, 22, 23	FIRE SUPPRESSION, PLUMBING & HVAC	96.9	97.0	97.0	97.2	89.0	93.7	96.9	128.1	110.2	97.2	98.6	97.8	97.2	91.5	94.7	100.2	92.3	96.8
26, 27, 3370	ELECTRICAL, COMMUNICATIONS & UTIL.	95.6	110.6	103.4	92.8	93.6	93.2	93.6	109.4	101.9	93.6	91.7	92.6	89.6	75.9	82.4	90.4	81.2	85.6
MF2016	WEIGHTED AVERAGE	97.3	102.2	99.4	95.5	94.7	95.1	95.5	123.7	107.8	94.1	98.9	96.2	91.9	92.8	92.3	94.4	94.5	94.4

DIVISION		PUERTO RICO SAN JUAN 009			RHODE ISLAND NEWPORT 028			RHODE ISLAND PROVIDENCE 029			SOUTH CAROLINA AIKEN 298			SOUTH CAROLINA BEAUFORT 299			SOUTH CAROLINA CHARLESTON 294		
		MAT.	INST.	TOTAL	MAT.	INST.	TOTAL	MAT.	INST.	TOTAL	MAT.	INST.	TOTAL	MAT.	INST.	TOTAL	MAT.	INST.	TOTAL
015433	CONTRACTOR EQUIPMENT		87.1	87.1		101.1	101.1		101.1	101.1		106.8	106.8		106.8	106.8		106.8	106.8
0241, 31 - 34	SITE & INFRASTRUCTURE, DEMOLITION	131.9	89.9	102.5	88.7	102.8	98.6	90.6	102.8	99.1	128.2	89.6	101.2	123.3	89.0	99.3	108.2	89.3	95.0
0310	Concrete Forming & Accessories	91.0	21.7	31.3	98.6	119.9	117.0	99.6	119.9	117.1	95.7	65.0	69.3	94.7	39.6	47.4	93.9	65.0	69.0
0320	Concrete Reinforcing	189.9	18.4	103.4	102.0	114.6	108.4	104.8	114.6	109.7	95.8	62.6	79.0	94.8	26.2	60.4	94.6	66.1	80.2
0330	Cast-in-Place Concrete	95.0	32.8	71.4	72.7	118.7	90.2	93.2	118.7	102.9	90.9	67.6	82.1	90.9	67.2	81.9	106.7	67.6	91.8
03	CONCRETE	96.0	26.0	64.0	84.3	118.1	99.8	90.6	118.1	103.2	104.7	67.2	87.6	102.0	49.6	78.0	97.6	67.8	84.0
04	MASONRY	88.8	20.8	46.6	97.3	123.6	113.6	99.3	123.6	114.4	78.0	66.7	71.0	92.2	66.7	76.4	93.6	66.7	76.9
05	METALS	116.6	38.7	92.7	97.0	111.8	101.5	101.2	111.8	104.4	97.0	91.0	95.1	97.0	81.0	92.1	98.9	92.1	96.8
06	WOOD, PLASTICS & COMPOSITES	102.4	21.0	57.1	101.3	119.0	111.2	101.1	119.0	111.1	95.0	66.0	79.3	93.7	33.9	60.4	92.6	66.8	78.2
07	THERMAL & MOISTURE PROTECTION	130.6	25.9	86.3	99.6	117.7	107.2	103.1	117.7	109.3	99.1	66.3	85.2	98.8	58.1	81.5	97.9	65.9	84.3
08	OPENINGS	154.0	19.4	123.1	98.8	118.8	103.4	98.7	118.8	103.3	95.3	63.9	88.1	95.4	39.6	82.6	99.2	64.8	91.3
0920	Plaster & Gypsum Board	168.8	18.9	68.2	91.4	119.2	110.0	103.3	119.2	113.9	99.3	65.8	76.8	102.6	32.0	55.2	104.1	65.8	78.4
0950, 0980	Ceilings & Acoustic Treatment	250.5	18.9	94.4	96.7	119.2	111.8	101.6	119.2	113.4	86.4	65.8	72.5	89.0	32.0	50.5	89.0	65.8	73.3
0960	Flooring	203.1	21.3	152.6	89.9	127.6	100.3	87.3	127.6	98.5	95.9	94.9	95.6	97.3	80.1	92.6	97.0	81.6	92.7
0970, 0990	Wall Finishes & Painting/Coating	188.0	22.6	91.5	90.5	116.3	105.6	87.0	116.3	104.1	94.9	60.9	79.8	94.9	59.5	74.2	94.9	60.9	79.8
09	FINISHES	196.9	21.8	101.7	90.1	121.5	107.2	91.0	121.5	107.6	91.7	71.1	80.5	92.6	48.1	68.4	90.8	68.9	78.8
COVERS	DIVS. 10 - 14, 25, 28, 41, 43, 44, 46	100.0	19.8	82.1	100.0	107.5	101.7	100.0	107.5	101.7	100.0	72.1	93.8	100.0	76.9	94.9	100.0	72.0	93.8
21, 22, 23	FIRE SUPPRESSION, PLUMBING & HVAC	103.9	18.2	67.2	100.3	108.7	103.9	100.1	108.7	103.8	97.4	57.1	80.2	97.4	57.0	80.1	100.5	59.4	82.9
26, 27, 3370	ELECTRICAL, COMMUNICATIONS & UTIL.	124.8	17.5	69.0	100.9	96.6	98.6	101.1	96.6	98.7	100.9	65.3	82.4	104.6	32.6	67.2	103.0	60.1	80.7
MF2016	WEIGHTED AVERAGE	120.7	27.7	79.9	96.3	112.0	103.2	98.1	112.0	104.2	98.0	69.2	85.4	98.7	56.8	80.3	98.9	68.8	85.7

DIVISION		SOUTH CAROLINA COLUMBIA 290 - 292			SOUTH CAROLINA FLORENCE 295			SOUTH CAROLINA GREENVILLE 296			SOUTH CAROLINA ROCK HILL 297			SOUTH CAROLINA SPARTANBURG 293			SOUTH DAKOTA ABERDEEN 574		
		MAT.	INST.	TOTAL	MAT.	INST.	TOTAL	MAT.	INST.	TOTAL	MAT.	INST.	TOTAL	MAT.	INST.	TOTAL	MAT.	INST.	TOTAL
015433	CONTRACTOR EQUIPMENT		106.8	106.8		106.8	106.8		106.8	106.8		106.8	106.8		106.8	106.8		100.3	100.3
0241, 31 - 34	SITE & INFRASTRUCTURE, DEMOLITION	106.9	89.3	94.6	117.4	89.1	97.6	112.4	89.4	96.3	110.2	88.7	95.1	112.2	89.4	96.3	102.0	98.2	99.3
0310	Concrete Forming & Accessories	95.3	65.0	69.2	82.1	64.9	67.3	93.4	65.0	68.9	91.5	64.8	68.5	96.2	65.0	69.3	94.1	46.1	52.7
0320	Concrete Reinforcing	99.9	66.1	82.8	94.2	66.1	80.0	94.1	66.1	80.0	95.0	66.1	80.4	94.1	66.1	80.0	96.7	72.5	84.5
0330	Cast-in-Place Concrete	107.9	67.6	92.6	90.9	67.4	82.0	90.8	67.6	82.0	90.8	67.5	82.0	90.8	67.6	82.0	112.5	78.9	99.8
03	CONCRETE	95.8	67.8	83.0	96.5	67.6	83.3	95.1	67.8	82.6	93.0	67.6	81.4	95.3	67.8	82.7	99.3	63.6	83.0
04	MASONRY	87.3	66.7	74.5	78.0	66.7	71.0	75.6	66.7	70.1	99.6	66.7	79.2	78.0	66.7	71.0	113.6	73.4	88.7
05	METALS	96.1	92.1	94.9	97.8	91.5	95.9	97.8	92.1	96.0	97.0	91.8	95.4	97.8	92.1	96.0	100.9	83.0	95.4
06	WOOD, PLASTICS & COMPOSITES	93.1	66.8	78.5	79.9	66.8	72.7	92.2	66.8	78.1	90.9	66.8	77.5	96.1	66.8	79.8	92.4	34.7	60.3
07	THERMAL & MOISTURE PROTECTION	94.2	65.8	82.2	98.2	65.9	84.5	98.1	65.9	84.5	98.0	61.4	82.5	98.1	65.9	84.5	99.8	74.9	89.3
08	OPENINGS	95.4	64.8	88.4	95.4	64.8	88.4	95.3	64.8	88.3	95.4	64.8	88.3	95.4	64.8	88.3	95.7	41.4	83.2
0920	Plaster & Gypsum Board	94.8	65.8	75.3	93.6	65.8	74.9	98.4	65.8	76.5	98.0	65.8	76.4	101.0	65.8	77.4	112.0	33.3	59.1
0950, 0980	Ceilings & Acoustic Treatment	89.7	65.8	73.6	87.3	65.8	72.8	86.4	65.8	72.5	86.4	65.8	72.5	86.4	65.8	72.5	94.2	33.3	53.1
0960	Flooring	87.1	80.2	85.2	88.4	80.1	86.1	94.7	80.1	90.6	93.6	80.1	89.9	96.1	80.1	91.6	92.3	46.3	79.6
0970, 0990	Wall Finishes & Painting/Coating	89.0	69.0	77.3	94.9	69.0	79.8	94.9	69.0	79.8	94.9	69.0	79.8	94.9	69.0	79.8	90.4	34.9	58.0
09	FINISHES	86.8	68.6	76.9	87.6	68.6	77.3	89.6	68.6	78.2	88.9	68.6	77.9	90.3	68.6	78.5	91.4	43.0	65.1
COVERS	DIVS. 10 - 14, 25, 28, 41, 43, 44, 46	100.0	72.1	93.8	100.0	72.1	93.8	100.0	72.1	93.8	100.0	72.0	93.8	100.0	72.1	93.8	100.0	79.6	95.5
21, 22, 23	FIRE SUPPRESSION, PLUMBING & HVAC	100.1	58.7	82.4	100.5	58.7	82.7	100.5	58.7	82.7	97.4	57.1	80.2	100.5	58.7	82.7	100.2	54.8	80.8
26, 27, 3370	ELECTRICAL, COMMUNICATIONS & UTIL.	103.1	63.0	82.3	100.8	63.0	81.1	103.0	61.8	81.6	103.0	61.8	81.6	103.0	61.8	81.6	101.4	65.9	82.9
MF2016	WEIGHTED AVERAGE	96.9	69.1	84.7	97.0	69.0	84.8	97.1	68.9	84.8	97.1	68.3	84.5	97.3	68.9	84.9	99.7	64.5	84.3

City Cost Indexes

DIVISION		SOUTH DAKOTA																	
		MITCHELL 573			MOBRIDGE 576			PIERRE 575			RAPID CITY 577			SIOUX FALLS 570 - 571			WATERTOWN 572		
		MAT.	INST.	TOTAL	MAT.	INST.	TOTAL	MAT.	INST.	TOTAL	MAT.	INST.	TOTAL	MAT.	INST.	TOTAL	MAT.	INST.	TOTAL
015433	CONTRACTOR EQUIPMENT		100.3	100.3		100.3	100.3		100.3	100.3		100.3	100.3		101.3	101.3		100.3	100.3
0241, 31 - 34	SITE & INFRASTRUCTURE, DEMOLITION	98.8	98.1	98.3	98.8	98.2	98.3	100.4	97.6	98.4	100.3	97.6	98.4	93.4	100.0	98.0	98.7	98.1	98.3
0310	Concrete Forming & Accessories	93.3	46.2	52.7	84.4	46.6	51.8	96.5	47.5	54.2	101.5	59.1	64.9	100.7	64.5	69.5	81.2	44.9	49.9
0320	Concrete Reinforcing	96.2	72.7	84.3	98.6	72.7	85.6	98.6	97.0	97.8	90.4	97.2	93.8	96.8	97.3	97.0	93.5	41.1	67.1
0330	Cast-in-Place Concrete	109.4	54.8	88.6	109.4	79.0	97.8	104.2	79.8	94.9	108.5	80.1	97.7	92.5	80.8	88.1	109.4	57.9	89.8
03	CONCRETE	97.0	55.3	77.9	96.7	63.9	81.7	93.4	68.6	82.0	96.3	74.0	86.1	87.8	76.8	82.8	95.9	50.4	75.1
04	MASONRY	101.4	77.9	86.8	110.1	75.9	88.9	112.1	75.7	89.6	110.2	77.2	89.7	92.5	77.9	83.4	137.5	76.9	99.9
05	METALS	99.9	83.0	94.7	100.0	83.5	94.9	103.2	90.0	99.1	102.7	90.8	99.1	102.9	92.9	99.8	99.9	72.0	91.4
06	WOOD, PLASTICS & COMPOSITES	91.3	35.2	60.1	81.0	34.9	55.4	99.4	35.5	63.8	96.0	50.2	70.5	98.2	57.2	75.4	77.5	34.7	53.7
07	THERMAL & MOISTURE PROTECTION	99.6	76.2	89.7	99.7	78.8	90.8	101.9	75.7	90.8	100.3	80.4	91.9	98.4	81.9	91.4	99.4	75.7	89.4
08	OPENINGS	94.8	41.6	82.6	97.3	41.0	84.4	100.5	59.3	91.0	99.4	67.5	92.1	102.0	71.3	95.0	94.8	34.0	80.8
0920	Plaster & Gypsum Board	110.4	33.8	58.9	105.1	33.5	57.0	102.2	34.0	56.4	111.4	49.2	69.6	104.1	56.4	72.1	102.8	33.3	56.1
0950, 0980	Ceilings & Acoustic Treatment	89.9	33.8	52.1	94.2	33.5	53.3	94.2	34.0	53.6	95.9	49.2	64.4	89.7	56.4	67.2	89.9	33.3	51.7
0960	Flooring	91.9	46.3	79.3	87.5	49.1	76.9	93.3	33.0	76.6	91.7	76.8	87.6	95.8	77.8	90.8	86.1	46.3	75.1
0970, 0990	Wall Finishes & Painting/Coating	90.4	38.2	60.0	90.4	39.2	60.5	95.1	98.0	96.8	98.0	94.8	97.4	98.0	97.7	90.4	34.9	58.0
09	FINISHES	90.7	43.1	64.5	88.8	43.6	64.2	94.6	47.1	68.8	91.4	64.7	76.9	95.0	69.0	80.9	87.2	42.5	62.9
COVERS	DIVS. 10 - 14, 25, 28, 41, 43, 44, 46	100.0	79.6	95.5	100.0	79.5	95.4	100.0	81.4	95.9	100.0	83.0	96.2	100.0	83.8	96.4	100.0	44.8	87.7
21, 22, 23	FIRE SUPPRESSION, PLUMBING & HVAC	97.1	51.0	77.4	97.1	70.8	85.8	100.1	79.9	91.5	100.2	80.0	91.5	100.1	71.1	87.7	97.1	53.8	78.6
26, 27, 3370	ELECTRICAL, COMMUNICATIONS & UTIL.	99.7	65.9	82.1	101.4	42.0	70.5	104.1	50.4	76.1	97.9	50.4	73.2	102.5	65.9	83.5	98.9	46.1	71.4
MF2016	WEIGHTED AVERAGE	97.5	63.1	82.4	98.2	65.0	83.7	100.4	70.5	87.3	99.5	74.4	88.5	98.5	76.4	88.8	98.7	57.6	80.7

DIVISION		TENNESSEE																	
		CHATTANOOGA 373 - 374			COLUMBIA 384			COOKEVILLE 385			JACKSON 383			JOHNSON CITY 376			KNOXVILLE 377 - 379		
		MAT.	INST.	TOTAL	MAT.	INST.	TOTAL	MAT.	INST.	TOTAL	MAT.	INST.	TOTAL	MAT.	INST.	TOTAL	MAT.	INST.	TOTAL
015433	CONTRACTOR EQUIPMENT		107.3	107.3		101.9	101.9		101.9	101.9		108.2	108.2		101.0	101.0		101.0	101.0
0241, 31 - 34	SITE & INFRASTRUCTURE, DEMOLITION	102.4	98.4	99.6	88.0	88.5	88.4	93.5	85.3	87.7	96.6	98.7	98.1	108.8	84.7	91.9	88.9	87.6	88.0
0310	Concrete Forming & Accessories	96.0	59.9	64.9	81.9	64.7	67.0	82.0	32.9	39.7	88.8	42.5	49.0	82.5	60.0	63.1	94.2	64.5	68.6
0320	Concrete Reinforcing	96.9	67.1	81.9	88.5	64.7	76.5	88.5	64.2	76.2	88.4	66.0	77.1	97.5	63.6	80.4	96.9	63.7	80.2
0330	Cast-in-Place Concrete	94.9	64.4	83.4	91.1	62.3	80.2	103.3	40.9	79.6	100.8	69.2	88.8	76.4	59.6	70.0	89.2	65.9	80.4
03	CONCRETE	93.2	64.5	80.1	92.1	65.6	80.0	102.2	43.7	75.4	93.0	58.2	77.1	103.2	62.2	84.5	90.8	66.5	79.7
04	MASONRY	99.5	58.7	74.2	116.4	56.4	79.2	111.3	39.8	67.0	116.7	42.7	70.8	113.5	42.1	69.2	77.9	52.8	62.4
05	METALS	96.9	88.9	94.5	90.3	89.6	90.0	90.3	87.6	89.5	92.6	89.6	91.7	94.1	86.7	91.9	97.4	87.2	94.3
06	WOOD, PLASTICS & COMPOSITES	104.1	58.9	78.9	72.3	66.4	69.0	72.5	30.8	49.3	88.5	41.5	62.3	77.4	65.6	70.8	90.4	65.6	76.6
07	THERMAL & MOISTURE PROTECTION	99.4	64.1	84.4	93.8	62.5	80.5	94.3	50.8	75.9	96.2	56.2	79.3	95.1	54.8	78.1	92.8	63.2	80.2
08	OPENINGS	101.2	60.4	91.8	92.4	55.5	83.9	92.4	36.7	79.6	99.6	45.8	87.2	97.5	62.6	89.5	94.7	58.0	86.3
0920	Plaster & Gypsum Board	78.9	58.3	65.1	85.4	66.0	72.3	85.4	29.4	47.8	87.3	40.4	55.8	99.1	65.2	76.3	105.9	65.2	78.5
0950, 0980	Ceilings & Acoustic Treatment	108.2	58.3	74.6	79.6	66.0	70.4	79.6	29.4	45.7	89.0	40.4	56.2	104.5	65.2	78.0	105.4	65.2	78.3
0960	Flooring	100.0	58.4	88.5	79.9	57.0	73.6	80.0	52.9	72.5	79.5	57.3	73.3	94.0	46.4	80.8	99.5	52.5	86.5
0970, 0990	Wall Finishes & Painting/Coating	96.9	62.2	76.7	83.0	59.0	69.0	83.0	59.0	69.0	84.6	59.0	69.7	93.7	61.4	74.9	93.7	60.2	74.2
09	FINISHES	96.6	59.4	76.3	88.6	62.7	74.5	88.5	37.9	59.4	84.9	45.5	63.5	100.0	58.0	77.2	93.6	61.8	76.3
COVERS	DIVS. 10 - 14, 25, 28, 41, 43, 44, 46	100.0	70.5	93.4	100.0	69.5	93.2	100.0	37.2	86.0	100.0	63.7	91.9	100.0	78.8	95.3	100.0	82.6	96.1
21, 22, 23	FIRE SUPPRESSION, PLUMBING & HVAC	100.2	59.7	82.9	98.0	75.9	88.6	98.0	69.8	86.0	100.1	61.1	83.4	99.9	57.3	81.7	99.9	63.0	84.1
26, 27, 3370	ELECTRICAL, COMMUNICATIONS & UTIL.	100.1	87.5	93.6	92.9	53.4	72.3	94.4	63.2	78.2	99.0	54.4	75.8	91.1	43.1	66.1	96.3	58.0	76.4
MF2016	WEIGHTED AVERAGE	98.6	70.3	86.2	94.2	68.4	82.9	95.6	57.7	79.0	97.1	60.6	81.1	98.8	60.3	82.0	95.3	66.2	82.5

DIVISION		TENNESSEE									TEXAS								
		MCKENZIE 382			MEMPHIS 375, 380 - 381			NASHVILLE 370 - 372			ABILENE 795 - 796			AMARILLO 790 - 791			AUSTIN 786 - 787		
		MAT.	INST.	TOTAL	MAT.	INST.	TOTAL	MAT.	INST.	TOTAL	MAT.	INST.	TOTAL	MAT.	INST.	TOTAL	MAT.	INST.	TOTAL
015433	CONTRACTOR EQUIPMENT		101.9	101.9		100.8	100.8		105.2	105.2		93.5	93.5		93.5	93.5		92.5	92.5
0241, 31 - 34	SITE & INFRASTRUCTURE, DEMOLITION	93.2	85.6	87.8	89.6	94.3	92.9	96.7	97.6	97.3	98.2	92.2	94.0	98.4	91.4	93.5	96.7	90.8	92.6
0310	Concrete Forming & Accessories	89.7	35.4	42.9	96.0	64.8	69.2	94.5	63.9	69.8	98.9	61.9	67.0	97.6	54.0	60.0	94.4	53.6	59.2
0320	Concrete Reinforcing	88.6	66.1	77.2	104.1	68.1	85.9	103.4	64.9	84.0	90.4	51.2	70.6	96.8	51.1	73.8	101.1	48.7	74.6
0330	Cast-in-Place Concrete	101.1	54.1	83.2	92.7	77.6	86.9	87.3	65.7	79.1	87.4	68.2	80.1	80.8	68.1	76.0	93.6	68.2	84.0
03	CONCRETE	100.7	49.7	77.4	95.6	70.9	84.3	94.0	67.0	81.6	82.8	63.0	73.7	82.3	59.4	71.8	88.6	58.7	74.9
04	MASONRY	115.4	47.0	73.0	98.0	57.8	73.1	84.6	57.8	68.0	95.1	63.2	75.3	94.5	62.7	74.8	97.3	63.2	76.1
05	METALS	90.3	88.9	89.9	99.8	84.4	95.1	96.9	85.9	93.5	107.8	70.7	96.4	102.7	70.5	92.8	97.2	69.0	88.5
06	WOOD, PLASTICS & COMPOSITES	80.9	33.1	54.3	98.0	65.1	79.7	91.2	66.7	77.6	104.6	63.7	81.8	103.2	53.3	75.4	93.1	52.4	70.5
07	THERMAL & MOISTURE PROTECTION	94.2	53.6	77.0	94.3	67.2	82.8	95.6	64.3	82.4	99.6	66.2	85.5	97.8	64.4	83.7	96.6	66.0	83.7
08	OPENINGS	92.4	38.7	80.1	97.7	61.8	89.4	96.7	63.4	89.1	102.2	59.1	92.3	103.4	53.3	91.9	102.8	50.6	90.8
0920	Plaster & Gypsum Board	88.3	31.8	50.4	90.4	64.4	72.9	91.6	66.0	74.4	84.9	63.1	70.2	94.1	52.4	66.1	88.6	51.6	63.7
0950, 0980	Ceilings & Acoustic Treatment	79.6	31.8	47.4	98.1	64.4	75.4	102.6	66.0	77.9	91.7	63.1	72.4	95.1	52.4	66.3	94.3	51.6	65.5
0960	Flooring	82.8	57.0	75.7	102.7	58.4	90.4	95.1	58.4	84.9	92.9	71.5	87.0	93.9	67.4	86.6	87.7	67.4	82.1
0970, 0990	Wall Finishes & Painting/Coating	83.0	46.2	61.5	91.3	59.6	72.8	100.7	70.3	83.0	91.0	54.0	69.4	86.6	54.0	67.6	92.4	46.2	65.5
09	FINISHES	86.2	39.3	60.7	98.1	62.5	78.8	98.0	64.6	79.8	83.7	63.1	72.5	90.6	56.1	71.8	89.6	54.7	70.6
COVERS	DIVS. 10 - 14, 25, 28, 41, 43, 44, 46	100.0	24.7	83.3	100.0	82.8	96.2	100.0	83.2	96.3	100.0	80.6	95.7	100.0	75.4	94.5	100.0	79.1	95.3
21, 22, 23	FIRE SUPPRESSION, PLUMBING & HVAC	98.0	61.0	82.2	100.0	71.3	87.7	100.0	76.0	90.0	100.3	49.3	78.5	99.9	53.2	79.9	100.0	59.1	82.5
26, 27, 3370	ELECTRICAL, COMMUNICATIONS & UTIL.	94.2	58.5	75.6	99.1	65.7	81.7	96.1	63.2	79.0	98.5	56.1	76.5	101.5	62.2	81.1	95.2	59.4	76.6
MF2016	WEIGHTED AVERAGE	95.8	56.8	78.7	98.4	70.7	86.3	96.7	71.7	85.8	97.7	62.6	82.3	97.6	62.2	82.1	96.7	62.7	81.8

490

City Cost Indexes

TEXAS

DIVISION		BEAUMONT 776-777			BROWNWOOD 768			BRYAN 778			CHILDRESS 792			CORPUS CHRISTI 783-784			DALLAS 752-753		
		MAT.	INST.	TOTAL	MAT.	INST.	TOTAL	MAT.	INST.	TOTAL	MAT.	INST.	TOTAL	MAT.	INST.	TOTAL	MAT.	INST.	TOTAL
015433	CONTRACTOR EQUIPMENT		97.5	97.5		93.5	93.5		97.5	97.5		93.5	93.5		103.8	103.8		107.7	107.7
0241, 31-34	SITE & INFRASTRUCTURE, DEMOLITION	87.6	96.3	93.7	106.2	92.0	96.3	79.0	96.5	91.2	109.4	90.4	96.1	142.0	87.1	103.6	108.7	97.1	100.6
0310	Concrete Forming & Accessories	103.2	57.2	63.5	98.2	61.5	66.5	82.1	60.9	63.8	97.3	61.4	66.3	98.6	54.5	60.6	94.7	62.6	67.0
0320	Concrete Reinforcing	96.9	64.0	80.3	81.3	51.1	66.1	99.3	52.8	75.9	90.6	51.1	70.7	89.2	48.6	68.7	84.7	51.3	67.8
0330	Cast-in-Place Concrete	88.0	68.3	80.5	107.7	61.5	90.1	70.5	62.3	67.4	89.7	61.5	79.0	114.2	70.4	97.6	108.7	70.4	94.1
03	CONCRETE	90.9	63.2	78.3	94.5	60.5	78.9	76.0	60.9	69.1	90.5	60.4	76.7	96.5	61.0	80.3	99.7	64.9	83.8
04	MASONRY	102.5	64.3	78.8	128.3	63.2	87.9	142.8	63.2	93.4	99.2	62.7	76.6	85.5	63.3	71.7	100.0	61.8	76.3
05	METALS	93.5	77.2	88.5	95.5	70.3	87.8	93.3	72.9	87.0	105.2	70.2	94.5	93.5	84.7	90.8	97.6	83.5	93.3
06	WOOD, PLASTICS & COMPOSITES	114.0	56.6	82.0	104.2	63.7	81.8	79.1	62.1	69.7	104.0	63.7	81.6	122.5	53.9	84.3	95.3	64.0	77.9
07	THERMAL & MOISTURE PROTECTION	102.0	66.8	87.1	94.7	64.7	82.0	93.9	66.3	82.2	100.3	63.1	84.6	102.4	65.2	86.6	92.6	67.6	82.0
08	OPENINGS	94.9	57.8	86.4	98.0	59.1	89.1	95.3	58.2	86.8	97.4	59.1	88.6	103.9	51.6	91.9	101.2	59.3	91.6
0920	Plaster & Gypsum Board	97.1	55.9	69.4	85.3	63.1	70.4	85.0	61.5	69.3	84.5	63.1	70.1	96.1	52.9	67.1	93.8	63.1	73.2
0950, 0980	Ceilings & Acoustic Treatment	98.5	55.9	69.8	78.6	63.1	68.1	90.5	61.5	71.0	90.0	63.1	71.8	95.6	52.9	66.8	97.3	63.1	74.2
0960	Flooring	121.1	78.9	109.4	77.9	57.7	72.3	90.5	70.8	85.0	91.4	57.7	82.0	104.4	71.6	95.3	97.3	69.1	89.5
0970, 0990	Wall Finishes & Painting/Coating	88.7	56.3	69.8	89.7	54.0	68.9	86.8	60.0	71.2	91.0	54.0	69.4	104.9	46.2	70.7	102.2	54.0	74.1
09	FINISHES	94.7	60.6	76.2	76.5	60.3	67.7	81.8	62.3	71.2	84.1	60.3	71.1	98.2	56.5	75.5	97.4	62.8	78.6
COVERS	DIVS. 10-14, 25, 28, 41, 43, 44, 46	100.0	80.9	95.8	100.0	76.4	94.8	100.0	80.1	95.6	100.0	76.5	94.8	100.0	81.0	95.8	100.0	81.5	95.9
21, 22, 23	FIRE SUPPRESSION, PLUMBING & HVAC	100.2	64.3	84.8	97.1	47.3	75.8	97.1	63.8	82.8	97.2	53.2	78.4	100.2	50.7	79.0	99.9	60.6	83.1
26, 27, 3370	ELECTRICAL, COMMUNICATIONS & UTIL.	97.0	66.9	81.4	96.5	48.7	71.6	95.2	66.9	80.5	98.5	58.9	77.9	92.8	57.0	74.2	97.8	61.9	79.2
MF2016	WEIGHTED AVERAGE	96.5	68.0	84.0	96.9	60.2	80.8	94.0	67.3	82.3	97.6	62.7	82.3	98.7	62.4	82.8	99.2	67.6	85.4

TEXAS

DIVISION		DEL RIO 788			DENTON 762			EASTLAND 764			EL PASO 798-799, 885			FORT WORTH 760-761			GALVESTON 775		
		MAT.	INST.	TOTAL	MAT.	INST.	TOTAL	MAT.	INST.	TOTAL	MAT.	INST.	TOTAL	MAT.	INST.	TOTAL	MAT.	INST.	TOTAL
015433	CONTRACTOR EQUIPMENT		92.5	92.5		103.4	103.4		93.5	93.5		93.6	93.6		93.5	93.5		110.9	110.9
0241, 31-34	SITE & INFRASTRUCTURE, DEMOLITION	122.7	90.1	99.9	105.2	83.9	90.3	109.2	90.1	95.8	95.7	92.6	93.5	101.6	92.9	95.5	103.0	95.1	97.4
0310	Concrete Forming & Accessories	95.3	53.5	59.2	105.4	61.6	67.6	98.9	61.3	66.4	97.9	58.1	63.7	95.2	62.1	66.7	91.7	58.4	63.0
0320	Concrete Reinforcing	89.8	48.5	69.0	82.6	51.1	66.7	81.5	51.1	66.2	96.7	51.3	73.8	87.5	51.2	69.2	98.8	61.6	80.0
0330	Cast-in-Place Concrete	123.0	61.3	99.6	83.3	62.6	75.4	113.8	61.4	93.9	81.6	68.0	76.4	99.1	68.3	87.4	93.6	63.4	82.1
03	CONCRETE	116.3	56.3	88.8	74.2	62.0	68.6	99.1	60.3	81.4	82.7	61.2	72.9	89.6	63.1	77.5	92.1	62.8	78.7
04	MASONRY	100.5	63.1	77.3	137.5	61.8	90.6	96.9	63.3	76.0	85.9	64.4	72.6	95.9	61.8	74.7	98.6	63.3	76.7
05	METALS	93.3	68.2	85.6	95.2	86.0	92.3	95.3	70.1	87.6	102.7	70.1	92.7	97.1	70.9	89.1	94.9	92.9	94.3
06	WOOD, PLASTICS & COMPOSITES	100.9	52.8	74.1	116.1	63.8	87.0	111.8	63.7	85.0	88.7	58.5	71.9	95.1	63.7	77.6	96.5	58.5	75.3
07	THERMAL & MOISTURE PROTECTION	98.9	65.1	84.6	92.7	65.2	81.1	95.1	64.7	82.2	95.6	65.6	82.9	91.2	66.6	80.8	93.1	66.9	82.0
08	OPENINGS	99.2	50.1	87.9	115.6	58.7	102.5	70.6	59.1	67.9	98.6	54.0	88.3	99.7	59.1	90.4	99.4	58.3	90.0
0920	Plaster & Gypsum Board	92.4	51.9	65.2	89.9	63.1	71.9	85.3	63.1	70.4	92.3	57.7	69.1	95.5	63.1	73.7	91.6	57.7	68.8
0950, 0980	Ceilings & Acoustic Treatment	92.0	51.9	65.0	84.6	63.1	70.1	78.6	63.1	68.1	93.4	57.7	69.4	87.8	63.1	71.1	94.8	57.7	69.8
0960	Flooring	89.9	57.7	81.0	73.7	57.7	69.3	98.6	57.7	87.3	91.1	73.7	86.3	94.8	68.1	87.4	106.4	70.8	96.5
0970, 0990	Wall Finishes & Painting/Coating	92.7	44.5	64.6	99.7	51.1	71.4	91.1	54.0	69.5	95.5	49.9	68.9	92.0	54.1	69.9	97.5	56.1	73.4
09	FINISHES	90.8	52.8	70.1	75.7	60.1	67.2	83.3	60.3	70.8	89.3	60.0	73.4	89.0	62.4	74.6	91.6	59.7	74.3
COVERS	DIVS. 10-14, 25, 28, 41, 43, 44, 46	100.0	76.7	94.8	100.0	75.9	94.6	100.0	74.7	94.4	100.0	75.9	94.6	100.0	80.6	95.7	100.0	81.4	95.9
21, 22, 23	FIRE SUPPRESSION, PLUMBING & HVAC	97.0	61.2	81.7	97.1	58.1	80.4	97.1	47.2	75.8	99.9	66.3	85.5	100.0	57.7	81.9	97.0	63.9	82.8
26, 27, 3370	ELECTRICAL, COMMUNICATIONS & UTIL.	94.8	63.2	78.3	98.8	61.9	79.6	96.4	61.9	78.4	97.5	52.3	74.0	97.8	61.9	79.1	96.7	67.0	81.3
MF2016	WEIGHTED AVERAGE	99.5	62.9	83.4	96.8	65.3	83.0	93.6	61.8	79.7	96.0	64.7	82.3	96.6	65.1	82.8	96.2	69.0	84.3

TEXAS

DIVISION		GIDDINGS 789			GREENVILLE 754			HOUSTON 770-772			HUNTSVILLE 773			LAREDO 780			LONGVIEW 756		
		MAT.	INST.	TOTAL	MAT.	INST.	TOTAL	MAT.	INST.	TOTAL	MAT.	INST.	TOTAL	MAT.	INST.	TOTAL	MAT.	INST.	TOTAL
015433	CONTRACTOR EQUIPMENT		92.5	92.5		104.3	104.3		102.5	102.5		97.5	97.5		92.5	92.5		95.1	95.1
0241, 31-34	SITE & INFRASTRUCTURE, DEMOLITION	107.8	90.3	95.6	99.6	87.1	90.9	101.9	94.7	96.8	94.2	96.2	95.6	101.3	90.8	93.9	99.4	93.8	95.5
0310	Concrete Forming & Accessories	92.7	53.5	58.9	86.6	59.8	63.5	97.1	58.6	63.9	89.3	56.6	61.1	95.3	54.6	60.2	83.1	61.5	64.5
0320	Concrete Reinforcing	90.3	48.6	69.3	85.2	51.1	68.0	98.6	52.9	75.5	99.6	52.7	75.9	89.8	48.6	69.0	84.1	51.1	67.4
0330	Cast-in-Place Concrete	104.2	61.5	88.0	108.1	62.7	90.9	86.9	64.5	78.4	96.9	62.2	83.7	87.9	68.2	80.4	125.8	61.5	101.4
03	CONCRETE	93.6	56.4	76.6	93.4	61.1	78.6	91.3	61.0	77.4	98.4	58.9	80.3	88.0	59.2	74.8	110.5	60.4	87.6
04	MASONRY	107.9	63.2	80.2	155.5	61.8	97.4	97.7	63.3	76.4	141.0	63.2	92.8	93.8	63.2	74.8	151.7	61.7	95.9
05	METALS	92.7	68.7	85.4	95.1	84.6	91.9	97.6	78.4	91.7	93.2	72.6	86.9	95.8	69.1	87.6	88.3	69.3	82.5
06	WOOD, PLASTICS & COMPOSITES	100.0	52.8	73.7	85.5	61.3	72.0	101.9	58.7	77.9	87.9	56.6	70.5	100.9	53.8	74.7	80.3	63.8	71.1
07	THERMAL & MOISTURE PROTECTION	99.4	65.2	84.9	92.6	64.3	80.6	95.1	61.8	83.7	95.1	65.7	82.6	98.2	66.1	84.6	94.2	63.7	81.3
08	OPENINGS	98.3	50.8	87.4	97.8	57.8	88.6	102.5	56.3	91.9	95.3	55.1	86.1	99.2	51.4	88.2	88.4	58.7	81.6
0920	Plaster & Gypsum Board	91.4	51.9	64.9	85.2	60.3	68.5	90.8	57.7	68.6	89.0	55.9	66.7	93.2	52.9	66.2	84.2	63.1	70.0
0950, 0980	Ceilings & Acoustic Treatment	92.0	51.9	65.0	92.8	60.3	70.9	91.7	57.7	68.8	90.5	55.9	67.2	95.4	52.9	66.8	88.5	63.1	71.4
0960	Flooring	89.2	57.7	80.4	91.1	57.7	81.8	107.5	71.6	97.5	95.0	57.7	84.7	89.8	67.4	83.6	96.4	57.7	85.7
0970, 0990	Wall Finishes & Painting/Coating	92.7	46.2	65.6	96.3	54.0	71.6	95.4	58.3	73.8	86.8	58.3	70.1	92.7	46.2	65.6	87.0	51.1	66.0
09	FINISHES	89.4	53.0	69.6	91.9	58.9	74.0	97.3	60.6	77.3	84.6	56.6	69.4	89.9	55.5	71.2	97.3	60.0	77.0
COVERS	DIVS. 10-14, 25, 28, 41, 43, 44, 46	100.0	73.2	94.0	100.0	76.3	94.8	100.0	81.9	96.0	100.0	72.6	93.9	100.0	78.9	95.3	100.0	76.7	94.8
21, 22, 23	FIRE SUPPRESSION, PLUMBING & HVAC	97.1	62.6	82.3	96.9	58.9	80.7	100.1	65.2	85.2	97.1	63.7	82.8	100.1	61.3	83.5	96.9	57.5	80.0
26, 27, 3370	ELECTRICAL, COMMUNICATIONS & UTIL.	92.0	58.7	74.7	94.7	61.9	77.7	98.7	68.5	83.0	95.2	62.4	78.2	94.9	60.3	76.9	95.1	52.8	73.1
MF2016	WEIGHTED AVERAGE	96.1	62.6	81.4	98.6	65.2	84.0	98.3	68.0	85.0	97.4	65.1	83.3	96.1	63.5	81.8	98.9	62.8	83.1

491

City Cost Indexes

TEXAS

DIVISION		LUBBOCK 793-794			LUFKIN 759			MCALLEN 785			MCKINNEY 750			MIDLAND 797			ODESSA 797		
		MAT.	INST.	TOTAL	MAT.	INST.	TOTAL	MAT.	INST.	TOTAL	MAT.	INST.	TOTAL	MAT.	INST.	TOTAL	MAT.	INST.	TOTAL
015433	CONTRACTOR EQUIPMENT		106.2	106.2		95.1	95.1		103.9	103.9		104.3	104.3		106.2	106.2		93.5	93.5
0241, 31-34	SITE & INFRASTRUCTURE, DEMOLITION	123.4	91.3	100.9	94.0	95.4	95.0	146.7	87.2	105.0	95.9	87.1	89.8	126.6	90.4	101.2	98.5	92.9	94.6
0310	Concrete Forming & Accessories	97.7	54.4	60.3	86.0	56.7	60.7	99.5	53.6	59.9	85.8	59.8	63.3	101.5	61.9	67.4	98.9	62.0	67.1
0320	Concrete Reinforcing	91.7	51.2	71.3	85.6	61.5	73.4	89.3	48.6	68.8	85.2	51.1	68.0	92.8	51.2	71.8	90.4	51.2	70.6
0330	Cast-in-Place Concrete	87.6	69.3	80.6	112.5	61.4	93.1	124.1	62.7	100.8	101.4	62.7	86.7	93.1	69.3	84.0	87.4	68.2	80.1
03	CONCRETE	81.7	61.1	72.2	101.8	59.9	82.7	104.2	57.9	83.0	88.4	61.1	75.9	85.7	64.4	76.0	82.8	63.1	73.8
04	MASONRY	94.5	62.8	74.8	116.7	63.1	83.4	100.1	63.3	77.3	166.9	61.8	101.7	111.1	62.8	81.1	95.1	62.7	75.0
05	METALS	111.7	86.5	104.0	95.2	72.4	88.2	93.2	84.5	90.5	95.0	84.6	91.8	109.9	86.4	102.7	107.2	70.8	96.0
06	WOOD, PLASTICS & COMPOSITES	103.8	53.4	75.8	87.6	56.8	70.4	121.2	52.9	83.2	84.6	61.3	71.6	108.5	63.8	83.6	104.6	63.7	81.8
07	THERMAL & MOISTURE PROTECTION	88.9	65.3	78.9	94.0	62.8	80.8	102.1	66.0	86.8	92.4	64.3	80.5	89.2	66.4	79.6	99.6	65.5	85.2
08	OPENINGS	109.8	53.4	96.9	67.2	57.7	65.0	103.1	50.1	90.9	97.8	57.7	88.6	111.3	59.2	99.3	102.2	57.9	92.3
0920	Plaster & Gypsum Board	85.1	52.4	63.1	83.2	55.9	64.8	96.8	51.9	66.7	85.2	60.3	68.5	87.0	63.1	70.9	84.9	63.1	70.2
0950, 0980	Ceilings & Acoustic Treatment	92.6	52.4	65.5	84.2	55.9	65.1	95.4	51.9	66.1	92.8	60.3	70.9	90.9	63.1	72.1	91.7	63.1	72.4
0960	Flooring	86.9	70.7	82.4	129.3	57.7	109.4	103.9	76.9	96.4	90.7	57.7	81.5	88.1	67.4	82.4	92.9	67.4	85.9
0970, 0990	Wall Finishes & Painting/Coating	101.4	54.0	73.8	87.0	54.0	67.7	104.9	44.5	69.7	96.3	54.0	71.6	101.4	54.0	73.8	91.0	54.0	69.4
09	FINISHES	86.1	56.9	70.2	106.1	56.6	79.2	98.5	56.6	75.8	91.6	58.9	73.8	86.8	62.3	73.5	83.7	62.2	72.0
COVERS	DIVS. 10-14, 25, 28, 41, 43, 44, 46	100.0	79.8	95.5	100.0	73.0	94.0	100.0	79.0	95.3	100.0	76.7	94.8	100.0	76.8	94.8	100.0	76.5	94.8
21, 22, 23	FIRE SUPPRESSION, PLUMBING & HVAC	99.7	49.3	78.2	96.9	60.4	81.3	97.1	50.7	77.2	96.9	58.9	80.7	96.6	49.4	76.4	100.3	55.3	81.0
26, 27, 3370	ELECTRICAL, COMMUNICATIONS & UTIL.	97.2	62.2	79.0	96.3	64.8	79.9	92.6	33.4	61.8	94.8	61.9	77.7	97.2	62.2	79.0	98.6	62.2	79.6
MF2016	WEIGHTED AVERAGE	99.3	63.4	83.6	95.7	64.9	82.2	99.6	58.6	81.7	98.4	65.2	83.9	100.0	64.8	84.6	97.6	64.5	83.1

TEXAS

DIVISION		PALESTINE 758			SAN ANGELO 769			SAN ANTONIO 781-782			TEMPLE 765			TEXARKANA 755			TYLER 757		
		MAT.	INST.	TOTAL	MAT.	INST.	TOTAL	MAT.	INST.	TOTAL	MAT.	INST.	TOTAL	MAT.	INST.	TOTAL	MAT.	INST.	TOTAL
015433	CONTRACTOR EQUIPMENT		95.1	95.1		93.5	93.5		93.3	93.3		93.5	93.5		95.1	95.1		95.1	95.1
0241, 31-34	SITE & INFRASTRUCTURE, DEMOLITION	99.5	94.1	95.7	102.4	92.5	95.4	101.1	93.5	95.8	90.3	92.3	91.7	88.3	96.6	94.1	98.6	93.9	95.3
0310	Concrete Forming & Accessories	77.6	61.6	63.8	98.5	53.8	59.9	93.6	54.2	59.6	101.9	53.5	60.2	92.7	62.2	66.4	87.6	61.7	65.3
0320	Concrete Reinforcing	83.5	51.1	67.1	81.2	51.2	66.1	96.0	48.6	72.1	81.4	48.6	64.8	83.3	51.2	67.1	84.1	51.1	67.5
0330	Cast-in-Place Concrete	102.8	61.5	87.1	101.6	68.2	88.9	86.2	69.6	79.9	83.2	61.4	74.9	103.6	68.3	90.2	123.5	61.6	100.0
03	CONCRETE	102.6	60.5	83.4	90.1	59.3	76.0	90.4	59.3	76.2	76.6	56.4	67.4	94.1	63.1	79.9	109.8	60.5	87.3
04	MASONRY	110.8	61.7	80.4	124.7	63.2	86.6	93.5	63.3	74.8	136.5	63.2	91.0	171.1	61.7	103.3	161.3	61.7	99.6
05	METALS	95.0	69.4	87.1	95.7	70.6	88.0	97.6	66.7	88.1	95.4	68.9	87.2	88.2	70.0	82.6	94.9	69.5	87.1
06	WOOD, PLASTICS & COMPOSITES	79.3	63.8	70.7	104.9	52.8	75.9	97.6	53.0	72.8	114.5	52.8	80.2	90.6	63.8	75.7	89.0	63.8	75.0
07	THERMAL & MOISTURE PROTECTION	94.6	64.8	82.0	94.5	65.7	82.3	93.0	67.5	82.2	94.1	64.7	81.7	93.7	66.1	82.0	94.4	64.8	81.9
08	OPENINGS	67.2	59.1	65.3	98.0	53.1	87.7	101.6	50.9	90.0	67.2	52.5	63.8	88.3	59.1	81.6	67.1	59.1	65.3
0920	Plaster & Gypsum Board	80.9	63.1	68.9	85.3	51.9	62.9	91.3	51.9	64.9	85.3	51.9	62.9	87.8	63.1	71.2	83.2	63.1	69.7
0950, 0980	Ceilings & Acoustic Treatment	84.2	63.1	70.0	78.6	51.9	60.6	94.5	51.9	65.8	78.6	51.9	60.6	88.5	63.1	71.4	84.2	63.1	70.0
0960	Flooring	120.2	57.7	102.8	78.0	57.7	72.3	101.6	71.6	93.3	100.2	57.7	88.4	104.8	67.4	94.4	131.5	57.7	111.0
0970, 0990	Wall Finishes & Painting/Coating	87.0	54.0	67.7	89.7	54.0	68.9	91.5	46.2	65.1	91.1	46.2	64.9	87.0	54.0	67.7	87.0	54.0	67.7
09	FINISHES	103.6	60.3	80.1	76.3	53.9	64.1	99.3	55.9	75.7	82.5	53.0	66.5	99.7	62.3	79.4	107.1	60.3	81.7
COVERS	DIVS. 10-14, 25, 28, 41, 43, 44, 46	100.0	76.7	94.8	100.0	79.2	95.4	100.0	79.2	95.4	100.0	75.3	94.5	100.0	80.9	95.7	100.0	80.8	95.7
21, 22, 23	FIRE SUPPRESSION, PLUMBING & HVAC	96.9	57.6	80.1	97.1	49.3	76.7	100.1	64.0	84.6	97.1	53.6	78.5	96.9	56.7	79.7	96.9	60.5	81.3
26, 27, 3370	ELECTRICAL, COMMUNICATIONS & UTIL.	92.6	51.1	71.0	100.4	57.6	78.2	97.3	62.0	79.0	97.6	54.9	75.4	96.2	57.6	76.1	95.1	56.7	75.1
MF2016	WEIGHTED AVERAGE	95.0	62.7	80.9	96.4	60.7	80.8	97.8	64.4	83.2	91.9	60.4	78.1	97.9	64.4	83.2	98.9	64.2	83.7

TEXAS / UTAH

DIVISION		VICTORIA 779			WACO 766-767			WAXAHACHIE 751			WHARTON 774			WICHITA FALLS 763			LOGAN 843		
		MAT.	INST.	TOTAL	MAT.	INST.	TOTAL	MAT.	INST.	TOTAL	MAT.	INST.	TOTAL	MAT.	INST.	TOTAL	MAT.	INST.	TOTAL
015433	CONTRACTOR EQUIPMENT		109.5	109.5		93.5	93.5		104.3	104.3		110.9	110.9		93.5	93.5		96.6	96.6
0241, 31-34	SITE & INFRASTRUCTURE, DEMOLITION	107.8	92.2	96.9	99.1	92.7	94.6	97.7	87.4	90.5	112.8	94.5	100.0	99.9	92.9	95.0	101.4	93.9	96.1
0310	Concrete Forming & Accessories	91.0	53.6	58.8	100.4	62.0	67.3	85.8	61.6	65.0	86.3	55.5	59.7	100.4	62.0	67.3	102.2	67.1	71.9
0320	Concrete Reinforcing	94.9	48.6	71.5	81.1	48.7	64.7	85.2	51.1	68.0	98.7	52.2	75.2	81.1	51.2	66.0	102.1	86.6	94.3
0330	Cast-in-Place Concrete	105.1	63.3	89.2	90.1	68.2	81.8	107.0	62.9	90.2	107.9	62.3	90.6	96.2	68.3	85.6	86.3	75.2	82.1
03	CONCRETE	99.4	58.3	80.6	83.0	62.6	73.7	92.4	62.0	78.5	103.5	59.4	83.3	85.9	63.1	75.5	103.3	73.8	89.8
04	MASONRY	116.5	63.3	83.5	94.9	63.2	75.2	156.0	61.9	97.6	99.8	63.2	77.1	95.4	62.7	75.1	108.4	67.9	83.3
05	METALS	93.4	87.8	91.7	97.7	69.4	89.0	95.1	84.9	92.0	94.9	88.8	93.0	97.6	70.8	89.4	107.9	84.0	100.6
06	WOOD, PLASTICS & COMPOSITES	99.9	52.9	73.7	112.8	63.7	85.4	84.6	63.9	73.1	90.0	55.2	70.6	112.8	63.7	85.4	84.2	67.1	74.6
07	THERMAL & MOISTURE PROTECTION	96.9	64.1	83.0	95.0	66.9	83.1	92.5	64.5	80.6	93.5	66.2	81.9	95.0	65.5	82.5	96.5	71.6	85.9
08	OPENINGS	99.3	52.1	88.4	78.7	58.5	74.1	97.8	59.2	89.0	99.4	54.2	89.0	78.7	59.1	74.2	92.4	66.9	86.5
0920	Plaster & Gypsum Board	88.5	51.9	63.9	85.9	63.1	70.5	85.5	63.1	70.4	87.3	54.3	65.1	85.9	63.1	70.5	77.8	66.2	70.0
0950, 0980	Ceilings & Acoustic Treatment	95.6	51.9	66.2	81.2	63.1	69.0	94.5	63.1	73.3	94.8	54.3	67.5	81.2	63.1	69.0	103.2	66.2	78.2
0960	Flooring	104.9	57.7	91.8	99.5	67.4	90.6	90.7	57.7	81.5	103.4	70.4	94.2	100.3	76.0	93.6	98.5	59.3	87.6
0970, 0990	Wall Finishes & Painting/Coating	97.7	58.3	74.7	91.1	54.0	69.5	96.3	54.0	71.6	97.5	58.3	74.6	93.5	54.0	70.4	93.6	56.7	72.1
09	FINISHES	89.3	54.4	70.3	83.3	62.2	71.9	92.2	60.5	74.9	90.8	57.9	72.9	83.8	64.0	73.0	93.4	64.0	77.4
COVERS	DIVS. 10-14, 25, 28, 41, 43, 44, 46	100.0	72.5	93.9	100.0	80.6	95.7	100.0	77.0	94.9	100.0	72.8	93.9	100.0	76.5	94.8	100.0	85.0	96.7
21, 22, 23	FIRE SUPPRESSION, PLUMBING & HVAC	97.1	63.6	82.8	100.2	59.1	82.6	96.9	52.5	77.9	97.0	61.0	81.6	100.2	52.7	79.8	99.9	70.0	87.1
26, 27, 3370	ELECTRICAL, COMMUNICATIONS & UTIL.	101.4	57.0	78.3	100.5	55.6	77.2	94.8	61.9	77.7	100.4	62.5	80.7	102.3	56.1	78.3	96.4	69.2	82.3
MF2016	WEIGHTED AVERAGE	98.3	64.9	83.7	93.6	64.4	80.8	98.5	64.3	83.5	98.2	66.2	84.2	94.2	63.3	80.7	100.2	72.9	88.3

492

City Cost Indexes

DIVISION		UTAH OGDEN 842, 844 MAT.	INST.	TOTAL	PRICE 845 MAT.	INST.	TOTAL	PROVO 846-847 MAT.	INST.	TOTAL	SALT LAKE CITY 840-841 MAT.	INST.	TOTAL	VERMONT BELLOWS FALLS 051 MAT.	INST.	TOTAL	BENNINGTON 052 MAT.	INST.	TOTAL
015433	CONTRACTOR EQUIPMENT		96.6	96.6		95.6	95.6		95.6	95.6		96.6	96.6		98.8	98.8		98.8	98.8
0241, 31-34	SITE & INFRASTRUCTURE, DEMOLITION	88.8	93.9	92.4	98.8	92.1	94.1	97.5	92.2	93.8	88.5	93.8	92.2	92.2	101.5	98.7	91.5	101.5	98.5
0310	Concrete Forming & Accessories	102.2	67.1	71.9	104.6	66.9	72.1	103.9	67.1	72.1	104.5	67.1	72.2	93.8	106.3	104.6	91.6	106.2	104.1
0320	Concrete Reinforcing	101.7	86.6	94.1	109.4	86.6	97.9	110.4	86.6	98.4	103.9	86.6	95.2	80.9	81.4	81.1	80.9	81.4	81.1
0330	Cast-in-Place Concrete	87.6	75.2	82.9	86.4	75.2	82.1	86.4	75.2	82.2	95.7	75.2	88.0	90.7	115.5	100.1	90.7	115.5	100.1
03	CONCRETE	92.9	73.8	84.2	104.4	73.7	90.4	102.9	73.8	89.6	112.0	73.8	94.5	85.2	104.7	94.2	85.1	104.6	94.0
04	MASONRY	102.9	67.9	81.2	114.4	67.9	85.6	114.5	67.9	85.6	116.9	67.9	86.5	104.2	89.8	95.3	115.7	89.8	99.7
05	METALS	108.4	84.0	100.9	105.0	83.8	98.5	106.0	84.0	99.3	112.1	84.0	103.4	93.4	89.7	92.3	93.4	89.6	92.2
06	WOOD, PLASTICS & COMPOSITES	84.2	67.1	74.6	87.2	67.1	76.0	85.5	67.1	75.2	85.9	67.1	75.4	108.3	111.9	110.3	105.6	111.9	109.1
07	THERMAL & MOISTURE PROTECTION	95.3	71.6	85.3	98.3	71.6	87.0	98.4	71.6	87.0	102.8	71.6	89.6	98.0	92.6	95.7	98.0	92.6	95.7
08	OPENINGS	92.4	66.9	86.5	96.3	63.1	88.7	96.4	66.9	89.6	94.3	66.9	88.0	100.4	100.8	100.5	100.4	100.8	100.5
0920	Plaster & Gypsum Board	77.8	66.2	70.0	80.5	66.2	70.9	78.1	66.2	70.1	90.8	66.2	74.3	105.6	111.9	109.8	103.9	111.9	109.3
0950, 0980	Ceilings & Acoustic Treatment	103.2	66.2	78.2	103.2	66.2	78.2	103.2	66.2	78.2	95.5	66.2	75.8	93.8	111.9	106.0	93.8	111.9	106.0
0960	Flooring	96.4	59.3	86.1	99.7	59.3	88.5	99.4	59.3	88.2	100.4	59.3	89.0	91.1	104.5	94.8	90.4	104.5	94.3
0970, 0990	Wall Finishes & Painting/Coating	93.6	56.7	72.1	93.6	56.7	72.1	93.6	56.7	72.1	96.7	56.7	73.3	86.2	106.1	97.8	86.2	106.1	97.8
09	FINISHES	91.5	64.0	76.6	94.6	64.0	78.0	94.0	64.0	77.7	93.7	64.0	77.6	88.1	107.0	98.4	87.6	107.0	98.2
COVERS	DIVS. 10-14, 25, 28, 41, 43, 44, 46	100.0	85.0	96.7	100.0	85.0	96.7	100.0	85.0	96.7	100.0	85.0	96.7	100.0	95.7	99.0	100.0	95.6	99.0
21, 22, 23	FIRE SUPPRESSION, PLUMBING & HVAC	99.9	70.0	87.1	98.3	65.7	84.4	99.9	70.0	87.1	100.1	70.0	87.2	97.2	90.8	94.5	97.2	90.8	94.5
26, 27, 3370	ELECTRICAL, COMMUNICATIONS & UTIL.	96.7	69.2	82.4	101.6	69.2	84.7	97.0	69.2	82.5	99.3	69.2	83.6	105.2	84.0	94.1	105.1	57.5	80.4
MF2016	WEIGHTED AVERAGE	98.2	72.9	87.2	100.8	71.7	88.1	100.6	72.8	88.5	102.8	72.9	89.7	96.0	95.3	95.7	96.5	91.6	94.3

DIVISION		VERMONT BRATTLEBORO 053 MAT.	INST.	TOTAL	BURLINGTON 054 MAT.	INST.	TOTAL	GUILDHALL 059 MAT.	INST.	TOTAL	MONTPELIER 056 MAT.	INST.	TOTAL	RUTLAND 057 MAT.	INST.	TOTAL	ST. JOHNSBURY 058 MAT.	INST.	TOTAL
015433	CONTRACTOR EQUIPMENT		98.8	98.8		98.8	98.8		98.8	98.8		98.8	98.8		98.8	98.8		98.8	98.8
0241, 31-34	SITE & INFRASTRUCTURE, DEMOLITION	93.1	101.5	99.0	96.9	101.4	100.0	91.1	96.9	95.2	95.4	101.4	99.6	95.6	101.4	99.7	91.2	100.5	97.7
0310	Concrete Forming & Accessories	94.0	106.3	104.6	97.3	82.6	84.6	92.0	99.4	98.4	97.3	105.3	104.2	94.3	82.6	84.2	90.7	99.8	98.6
0320	Concrete Reinforcing	80.0	81.4	80.7	99.4	81.2	90.2	81.6	81.2	81.4	99.4	81.3	90.2	101.1	81.2	91.1	80.0	81.3	80.7
0330	Cast-in-Place Concrete	93.5	115.5	101.9	108.2	114.7	110.7	87.9	106.3	94.9	108.1	114.7	110.6	88.8	114.7	98.6	87.9	106.5	94.9
03	CONCRETE	87.2	104.7	95.2	96.9	93.7	95.4	82.9	98.4	90.0	96.8	104.0	100.1	87.7	93.7	90.4	82.6	98.7	90.0
04	MASONRY	115.2	89.8	99.5	113.8	89.0	98.4	115.6	74.5	90.1	110.1	89.0	97.0	94.8	89.0	91.2	144.6	74.5	101.2
05	METALS	93.4	89.8	92.3	101.1	88.8	97.4	93.4	88.6	91.9	99.1	89.0	96.0	99.2	88.8	96.0	93.4	89.0	92.1
06	WOOD, PLASTICS & COMPOSITES	108.7	111.9	110.5	100.6	81.5	89.9	105.1	111.9	108.9	97.3	111.9	105.5	108.8	81.5	93.6	100.5	111.9	106.9
07	THERMAL & MOISTURE PROTECTION	98.1	92.6	95.8	105.1	88.9	98.2	97.9	85.6	92.7	105.0	92.2	99.6	98.2	88.9	94.3	97.8	85.6	92.6
08	OPENINGS	100.4	101.0	100.5	102.9	80.2	97.7	100.4	97.1	99.6	103.7	97.1	102.2	103.6	80.2	98.2	100.4	97.1	99.6
0920	Plaster & Gypsum Board	105.6	111.9	109.8	105.9	80.6	88.9	111.5	111.9	111.8	105.5	111.9	109.8	106.0	80.6	88.9	112.8	111.9	112.2
0950, 0980	Ceilings & Acoustic Treatment	93.8	111.9	106.0	100.8	80.6	87.1	93.8	111.9	106.0	101.0	111.9	108.3	98.4	80.6	86.4	93.8	111.9	106.0
0960	Flooring	91.2	104.5	94.9	97.3	104.5	99.3	94.0	104.5	96.9	98.4	104.5	100.1	91.1	104.5	94.8	97.1	104.5	99.2
0970, 0990	Wall Finishes & Painting/Coating	86.2	106.1	97.8	95.8	92.4	93.8	86.2	92.4	89.8	92.2	92.4	92.3	86.2	92.4	89.8	86.2	92.4	89.8
09	FINISHES	88.2	107.0	98.4	95.8	87.2	91.1	89.7	101.6	96.2	95.7	105.3	100.9	89.2	87.2	88.1	90.8	101.6	96.7
COVERS	DIVS. 10-14, 25, 28, 41, 43, 44, 46	100.0	95.7	99.0	100.0	92.0	98.2	100.0	90.4	97.9	100.0	95.3	99.0	100.0	92.0	98.2	100.0	90.4	97.9
21, 22, 23	FIRE SUPPRESSION, PLUMBING & HVAC	97.2	90.8	94.5	100.0	68.2	86.4	97.2	60.7	81.6	96.9	68.2	84.7	100.3	68.2	86.6	97.2	60.7	81.6
26, 27, 3370	ELECTRICAL, COMMUNICATIONS & UTIL.	105.1	84.0	94.1	105.0	55.6	79.3	105.2	57.5	80.4	104.3	55.6	79.0	105.2	55.6	79.4	105.2	57.5	80.4
MF2016	WEIGHTED AVERAGE	96.9	95.3	96.2	101.0	80.9	92.2	96.4	81.1	89.7	99.8	85.9	93.7	98.1	80.9	90.6	97.8	81.5	90.7

DIVISION		VERMONT WHITE RIVER JCT. 050 MAT.	INST.	TOTAL	VIRGINIA ALEXANDRIA 223 MAT.	INST.	TOTAL	ARLINGTON 222 MAT.	INST.	TOTAL	BRISTOL 242 MAT.	INST.	TOTAL	CHARLOTTESVILLE 229 MAT.	INST.	TOTAL	CULPEPER 227 MAT.	INST.	TOTAL
015433	CONTRACTOR EQUIPMENT		98.8	98.8		108.6	108.6		107.3	107.3		107.3	107.3		111.5	111.5		107.3	107.3
0241, 31-34	SITE & INFRASTRUCTURE, DEMOLITION	95.7	100.6	99.1	115.4	92.9	99.6	125.6	90.6	101.1	109.8	89.9	95.9	114.2	92.4	99.0	113.1	90.5	97.3
0310	Concrete Forming & Accessories	88.9	100.3	98.8	90.8	71.5	74.1	89.8	71.4	73.9	86.0	66.7	69.5	84.5	48.5	53.5	81.7	71.0	72.5
0320	Concrete Reinforcing	80.9	81.3	81.1	85.2	82.8	84.0	96.2	80.7	88.3	96.2	70.0	83.0	95.5	70.3	82.8	96.2	80.5	88.3
0330	Cast-in-Place Concrete	93.5	107.3	98.8	107.7	78.3	96.5	104.8	78.3	94.7	104.3	46.4	82.3	108.5	78.8	97.2	107.3	78.1	96.2
03	CONCRETE	88.7	99.2	93.5	100.0	77.3	89.6	104.5	76.9	91.9	100.8	62.1	83.1	101.5	65.0	84.8	98.5	76.6	88.5
04	MASONRY	129.7	76.0	96.4	91.2	73.7	80.3	106.3	73.7	86.1	95.3	47.3	65.5	120.2	56.9	80.9	107.2	73.7	86.4
05	METALS	93.4	89.0	92.1	103.4	100.5	102.5	102.0	99.6	101.3	100.8	93.8	98.7	101.1	95.8	99.5	101.2	98.8	100.4
06	WOOD, PLASTICS & COMPOSITES	102.6	111.9	107.8	94.6	69.7	80.7	91.3	69.7	79.2	84.5	73.2	78.2	83.1	41.6	60.0	81.9	69.7	75.1
07	THERMAL & MOISTURE PROTECTION	98.2	86.2	93.1	102.6	81.4	93.6	104.7	80.7	94.5	104.1	60.7	85.7	103.6	69.4	89.1	103.8	80.7	94.0
08	OPENINGS	100.4	97.1	99.6	98.5	74.1	92.9	96.6	73.6	91.3	99.6	67.1	92.2	97.8	55.8	88.2	98.1	73.6	92.5
0920	Plaster & Gypsum Board	102.6	111.9	108.8	103.9	68.7	80.3	100.6	68.7	79.2	97.1	72.3	80.4	97.1	39.1	58.2	97.3	68.7	78.1
0950, 0980	Ceilings & Acoustic Treatment	93.8	111.9	106.0	94.5	68.7	77.1	92.8	68.7	76.5	91.9	72.3	78.7	91.9	39.1	56.3	92.8	68.7	76.5
0960	Flooring	89.3	104.5	93.5	96.3	78.7	91.4	94.7	78.7	90.3	91.2	58.9	82.3	89.7	58.9	81.2	89.7	78.7	86.7
0970, 0990	Wall Finishes & Painting/Coating	86.2	92.4	89.8	114.7	75.0	91.5	114.7	75.0	91.5	101.5	56.6	75.3	101.5	60.0	77.3	114.7	60.0	82.8
09	FINISHES	87.5	102.0	95.4	94.4	72.4	82.4	94.3	72.4	82.4	91.0	65.3	77.1	90.6	49.5	68.3	91.3	70.7	80.1
COVERS	DIVS. 10-14, 25, 28, 41, 43, 44, 46	100.0	90.9	98.0	100.0	89.2	97.6	100.0	86.7	97.0	100.0	77.6	95.0	100.0	82.1	96.0	100.0	86.7	97.0
21, 22, 23	FIRE SUPPRESSION, PLUMBING & HVAC	97.2	61.4	81.9	100.4	85.3	93.9	100.4	85.2	93.9	97.3	47.7	76.1	97.3	70.4	85.8	97.3	70.6	85.9
26, 27, 3370	ELECTRICAL, COMMUNICATIONS & UTIL.	105.2	55.6	79.4	98.0	99.6	98.8	95.7	101.2	98.6	97.6	38.4	66.8	97.6	72.2	84.4	99.9	96.9	98.4
MF2016	WEIGHTED AVERAGE	97.7	81.6	90.7	99.8	84.7	93.2	100.7	84.5	93.7	98.6	60.5	82.0	99.8	69.3	86.5	99.1	80.5	91.0

493

City Cost Indexes

VIRGINIA

DIVISION		FAIRFAX 220-221 MAT.	INST.	TOTAL	FARMVILLE 239 MAT.	INST.	TOTAL	FREDERICKSBURG 224-225 MAT.	INST.	TOTAL	GRUNDY 246 MAT.	INST.	TOTAL	HARRISONBURG 228 MAT.	INST.	TOTAL	LYNCHBURG 245 MAT.	INST.	TOTAL
015433	CONTRACTOR EQUIPMENT		107.3	107.3		111.5	111.5		107.3	107.3		107.3	107.3		107.3	107.3		107.3	107.3
0241, 31-34	SITE & INFRASTRUCTURE, DEMOLITION	124.3	90.6	100.7	108.4	91.4	96.5	112.7	90.4	97.1	107.6	89.2	94.7	121.3	89.0	98.6	108.5	90.6	96.0
0310	Concrete Forming & Accessories	84.5	71.3	73.1	95.5	45.6	52.5	84.5	68.5	70.7	89.1	38.7	45.6	80.7	39.4	45.1	86.1	73.0	74.8
0320	Concrete Reinforcing	96.2	80.6	88.3	94.9	69.9	82.3	96.9	82.7	89.8	94.9	45.4	69.9	96.2	59.1	77.5	95.5	70.8	83.1
0330	Cast-in-Place Concrete	104.8	78.2	94.7	106.5	88.0	99.5	106.4	78.1	95.6	104.3	52.0	84.5	104.7	55.0	85.8	104.3	77.6	94.2
03	CONCRETE	104.2	76.8	91.7	97.2	66.6	83.2	98.3	75.9	88.0	99.4	46.6	75.3	102.0	50.6	78.5	99.3	75.7	88.5
04	MASONRY	106.2	73.7	86.0	104.3	52.1	71.9	106.3	69.6	83.6	96.1	55.7	71.1	104.2	60.3	77.0	111.7	65.8	83.2
05	METALS	101.3	99.5	100.7	98.0	91.8	96.1	101.2	100.3	100.9	100.8	76.1	93.2	101.1	88.8	97.3	101.4	95.9	99.5
06	WOOD, PLASTICS & COMPOSITES	84.5	69.7	76.2	93.8	40.2	64.0	84.5	67.7	75.1	87.1	31.9	56.4	81.0	35.5	55.7	84.5	74.6	79.0
07	THERMAL & MOISTURE PROTECTION	104.4	76.4	92.6	104.2	56.0	83.8	103.8	78.7	93.1	103.9	48.3	80.4	104.2	64.2	87.3	103.8	72.6	90.6
08	OPENINGS	96.6	63.6	91.3	97.6	45.3	85.5	97.8	72.0	91.9	99.6	31.6	84.0	98.1	45.3	86.0	98.1	67.9	91.2
0920	Plaster & Gypsum Board	97.3	68.7	78.1	106.4	37.7	60.3	97.3	66.7	76.7	97.1	29.9	52.0	97.1	33.6	54.5	97.1	73.7	81.4
0950, 0980	Ceilings & Acoustic Treatment	92.8	68.7	76.5	87.6	37.7	53.9	92.8	66.7	75.2	91.9	29.9	50.1	91.9	33.6	52.6	91.9	73.7	79.7
0960	Flooring	91.5	78.7	88.0	92.0	53.4	81.3	91.5	76.6	87.4	92.5	29.8	75.1	89.5	78.7	86.5	91.2	69.1	85.1
0970, 0990	Wall Finishes & Painting/Coating	114.7	75.0	91.5	99.7	59.8	76.4	114.7	59.6	82.6	101.5	32.7	61.3	114.7	50.5	77.3	101.5	56.6	75.3
09	FINISHES	92.9	72.4	81.7	90.5	47.3	67.0	91.8	68.3	79.0	91.2	35.0	60.7	91.7	46.2	67.0	90.8	70.6	79.9
COVERS	DIVS. 10-14, 25, 28, 41, 43, 44, 46	100.0	86.7	97.0	100.0	77.7	95.0	100.0	81.5	95.9	100.0	75.8	94.6	100.0	62.5	91.6	100.0	81.2	95.8
21, 22, 23	FIRE SUPPRESSION, PLUMBING & HVAC	97.3	85.2	92.1	97.4	46.9	75.8	97.3	83.2	91.3	97.3	67.4	84.5	97.3	68.1	84.8	97.3	70.7	85.9
26, 27, 3370	ELECTRICAL, COMMUNICATIONS & UTIL.	98.7	96.9	97.8	92.2	45.1	67.7	95.9	96.9	96.4	97.6	41.7	68.5	97.8	91.2	94.4	98.6	71.6	84.6
MF2016	WEIGHTED AVERAGE	100.0	83.8	92.9	97.4	58.6	80.4	98.7	82.2	91.5	98.5	56.0	79.9	99.5	67.3	85.4	99.2	75.2	88.7

VIRGINIA

DIVISION		NEWPORT NEWS 236 MAT.	INST.	TOTAL	NORFOLK 233-235 MAT.	INST.	TOTAL	PETERSBURG 238 MAT.	INST.	TOTAL	PORTSMOUTH 237 MAT.	INST.	TOTAL	PULASKI 243 MAT.	INST.	TOTAL	RICHMOND 230-232 MAT.	INST.	TOTAL
015433	CONTRACTOR EQUIPMENT		111.6	111.6		112.2	112.2		111.5	111.5		111.5	111.5		107.3	107.3		111.5	111.5
0241, 31-34	SITE & INFRASTRUCTURE, DEMOLITION	107.3	92.4	96.9	105.7	93.5	97.1	111.0	92.4	97.9	105.9	91.7	95.9	106.9	89.7	94.8	102.2	92.4	95.3
0310	Concrete Forming & Accessories	94.8	62.5	67.0	100.4	62.6	67.8	88.8	63.7	67.2	85.0	49.0	53.9	89.1	41.4	48.0	95.2	82.3	84.1
0320	Concrete Reinforcing	94.7	67.5	81.0	102.5	67.5	84.8	94.3	70.9	82.5	94.3	66.8	80.5	94.9	58.2	76.4	105.2	70.9	87.9
0330	Cast-in-Place Concrete	103.5	78.0	93.8	107.5	79.1	96.7	109.9	79.3	98.3	102.5	62.6	87.3	104.3	86.4	97.5	98.4	79.3	91.1
03	CONCRETE	94.5	70.5	83.6	96.5	71.0	84.8	99.7	72.1	87.1	93.4	59.0	77.7	99.4	62.2	82.4	92.2	80.6	86.9
04	MASONRY	98.6	64.5	77.4	96.6	64.5	76.7	112.9	64.5	82.9	104.6	49.4	70.4	90.8	56.6	69.6	97.3	64.5	77.0
05	METALS	100.3	95.1	98.7	102.0	95.2	99.9	98.0	96.8	97.7	99.3	93.6	97.5	100.9	87.4	96.7	102.0	97.0	100.5
06	WOOD, PLASTICS & COMPOSITES	92.8	61.4	75.3	96.1	61.4	76.8	85.2	62.4	72.5	82.0	46.9	62.5	87.1	33.5	57.3	95.9	87.4	91.2
07	THERMAL & MOISTURE PROTECTION	104.1	71.6	90.4	101.4	71.8	88.9	104.1	73.6	91.2	104.2	62.1	86.4	103.9	59.0	84.9	102.5	76.4	91.4
08	OPENINGS	98.0	60.7	89.3	96.2	61.6	88.2	97.3	67.3	90.4	98.0	49.9	87.0	99.7	38.3	85.6	100.2	81.1	95.8
0920	Plaster & Gypsum Board	107.4	59.5	75.2	100.3	59.5	72.9	100.7	60.5	73.7	101.2	44.6	63.2	97.1	31.5	53.1	101.4	86.2	91.2
0950, 0980	Ceilings & Acoustic Treatment	91.8	59.5	70.0	95.4	59.5	71.2	88.4	60.5	69.6	91.8	44.6	60.0	91.9	31.5	51.2	91.4	86.2	87.9
0960	Flooring	92.0	60.2	85.7	87.6	69.1	82.5	88.0	74.3	84.2	85.0	58.9	77.8	92.5	58.9	83.2	87.3	74.3	83.7
0970, 0990	Wall Finishes & Painting/Coating	99.7	60.0	76.5	97.4	60.0	75.6	99.7	60.0	76.5	99.7	60.0	76.5	101.5	50.5	71.8	92.7	60.0	73.6
09	FINISHES	91.3	63.0	75.9	90.7	63.0	75.6	88.9	64.6	75.7	88.4	50.5	67.8	91.2	42.9	64.9	91.0	79.4	84.7
COVERS	DIVS. 10-14, 25, 28, 41, 43, 44, 46	100.0	80.5	95.7	100.0	80.5	95.7	100.0	83.9	96.4	100.0	66.5	92.6	100.0	76.0	94.7	100.0	86.7	97.0
21, 22, 23	FIRE SUPPRESSION, PLUMBING & HVAC	100.5	64.0	84.9	100.1	67.3	86.1	97.4	69.8	85.6	100.5	64.3	85.1	97.3	66.2	84.0	100.1	69.8	87.1
26, 27, 3370	ELECTRICAL, COMMUNICATIONS & UTIL.	94.7	63.7	78.6	97.9	63.8	80.2	94.8	72.2	83.1	93.1	63.8	77.9	97.6	56.7	76.3	98.3	72.2	84.7
MF2016	WEIGHTED AVERAGE	98.2	70.4	86.0	98.5	71.3	86.6	98.3	73.9	87.6	97.7	64.3	83.1	98.2	62.7	82.7	98.5	77.9	89.5

VIRGINIA / WASHINGTON

DIVISION		ROANOKE 240-241 MAT.	INST.	TOTAL	STAUNTON 244 MAT.	INST.	TOTAL	WINCHESTER 226 MAT.	INST.	TOTAL	CLARKSTON 994 MAT.	INST.	TOTAL	EVERETT 982 MAT.	INST.	TOTAL	OLYMPIA 985 MAT.	INST.	TOTAL
015433	CONTRACTOR EQUIPMENT		107.2	107.2		111.5	111.5		107.3	107.3		91.5	91.5		102.2	102.2		102.2	102.2
0241, 31-34	SITE & INFRASTRUCTURE, DEMOLITION	107.5	90.6	95.7	110.7	91.3	97.1	119.9	90.5	99.3	107.5	89.6	94.9	92.9	110.9	105.5	93.0	110.9	105.5
0310	Concrete Forming & Accessories	95.2	73.1	76.1	88.8	50.2	55.5	82.9	69.5	71.4	111.4	67.0	73.1	116.2	102.6	104.5	105.3	102.4	102.8
0320	Concrete Reinforcing	95.9	70.8	83.2	95.5	70.0	82.7	95.6	82.8	89.1	112.0	98.3	105.1	108.9	111.8	110.4	113.8	111.8	112.8
0330	Cast-in-Place Concrete	118.5	87.8	106.8	108.5	88.6	100.9	104.7	67.1	90.5	87.8	84.1	86.4	98.6	109.1	102.6	90.8	109.0	97.7
03	CONCRETE	103.9	79.3	92.6	100.8	68.9	86.2	101.5	72.6	88.3	95.4	78.7	87.8	90.1	105.9	97.3	86.8	105.8	95.5
04	MASONRY	97.4	65.8	77.8	107.0	55.6	75.1	101.6	72.2	83.7	100.8	84.8	90.9	112.7	103.6	107.1	107.1	103.6	104.9
05	METALS	103.2	96.0	101.0	101.1	91.6	98.2	101.2	100.1	100.9	91.3	87.6	90.1	103.3	96.7	101.3	103.0	96.3	101.0
06	WOOD, PLASTICS & COMPOSITES	95.4	74.6	83.8	87.1	45.5	64.0	83.1	67.9	74.6	107.4	61.2	81.7	112.0	101.6	106.2	97.0	101.6	99.6
07	THERMAL & MOISTURE PROTECTION	103.7	76.1	92.0	103.5	57.5	84.1	104.3	78.3	93.3	158.3	81.7	125.8	111.9	105.8	109.3	111.6	105.8	109.2
08	OPENINGS	98.5	67.9	91.5	98.1	48.1	86.6	99.7	71.8	93.3	118.1	68.3	106.7	106.1	104.0	105.6	110.5	104.3	109.0
0920	Plaster & Gypsum Board	103.9	73.7	83.6	97.1	43.2	60.9	97.3	66.9	76.9	149.2	60.1	89.3	112.7	101.8	105.4	107.0	101.8	103.5
0950, 0980	Ceilings & Acoustic Treatment	94.5	73.7	80.5	91.9	43.2	59.1	92.8	66.9	75.3	108.8	60.1	75.9	105.7	101.8	103.1	105.7	101.8	103.1
0960	Flooring	96.3	69.1	88.8	92.1	35.0	76.2	91.0	78.7	87.6	86.7	81.9	85.3	105.2	101.5	104.2	93.1	101.5	95.4
0970, 0990	Wall Finishes & Painting/Coating	101.5	56.6	75.3	101.5	32.1	61.0	114.7	81.1	95.1	78.6	75.4	76.7	91.5	95.7	93.9	87.1	95.7	92.1
09	FINISHES	93.4	70.6	81.0	91.1	44.5	65.8	92.3	71.8	81.1	105.8	69.0	85.8	103.3	101.3	102.2	94.0	101.3	98.0
COVERS	DIVS. 10-14, 25, 28, 41, 43, 44, 46	100.0	81.1	95.8	100.0	78.8	95.3	100.0	86.1	96.9	100.0	92.9	98.4	100.0	100.0	100.0	100.0	102.5	100.6
21, 22, 23	FIRE SUPPRESSION, PLUMBING & HVAC	100.4	66.2	85.8	100.1	60.1	81.4	97.3	84.7	91.9	97.7	83.9	91.8	100.2	101.8	100.9	100.1	101.8	100.8
26, 27, 3370	ELECTRICAL, COMMUNICATIONS & UTIL.	97.6	57.8	76.9	96.6	72.2	83.9	96.3	76.9	86.2	86.6	98.0	92.6	108.2	98.4	103.1	106.5	98.3	102.2
MF2016	WEIGHTED AVERAGE	100.3	73.0	88.3	99.0	65.8	84.5	99.3	82.9	92.2	100.6	83.4	93.1	102.0	102.4	102.2	100.7	102.3	101.4

City Cost Indexes

DIVISION		RICHLAND 993 MAT.	INST.	TOTAL	SEATTLE 980-981, 987 MAT.	INST.	TOTAL	SPOKANE 990-992 MAT.	INST.	TOTAL	TACOMA 983-984 MAT.	INST.	TOTAL	VANCOUVER 986 MAT.	INST.	TOTAL	WENATCHEE 988 MAT.	INST.	TOTAL
							WASHINGTON												
015433	CONTRACTOR EQUIPMENT		91.5	91.5		103.7	103.7		91.5	91.5		102.2	102.2		98.4	98.4		102.2	102.2
0241, 31-34	SITE & INFRASTRUCTURE, DEMOLITION	109.4	89.7	95.6	99.3	110.1	106.9	108.8	89.7	95.4	96.1	110.9	106.5	106.0	97.8	100.3	105.3	108.3	107.4
0310	Concrete Forming & Accessories	111.5	80.0	84.4	112.3	102.9	104.2	116.8	79.6	84.7	106.5	102.5	103.0	107.1	94.7	96.4	108.4	78.9	82.9
0320	Concrete Reinforcing	107.4	98.4	102.9	114.0	111.9	112.9	108.1	98.3	103.2	107.4	111.8	109.6	108.5	110.9	109.7	108.5	98.4	103.4
0330	Cast-in-Place Concrete	88.0	85.5	87.0	102.5	108.8	104.9	91.4	85.3	89.1	101.3	109.0	104.3	113.2	100.7	108.4	103.5	93.8	99.8
03	CONCRETE	95.0	85.1	90.5	98.2	106.2	101.9	97.1	84.8	91.5	91.7	105.8	98.2	101.1	99.4	100.3	98.8	87.4	93.6
04	MASONRY	101.5	86.8	92.4	119.1	103.6	109.5	102.0	86.8	92.6	112.2	103.6	106.9	111.7	87.8	96.9	115.6	84.4	96.3
05	METALS	91.7	88.2	90.6	103.7	99.9	102.5	94.0	87.8	92.1	105.1	96.3	102.4	102.7	96.4	100.8	102.5	87.9	98.0
06	WOOD, PLASTICS & COMPOSITES	107.6	77.0	90.6	107.3	101.6	104.1	116.2	77.0	94.4	101.5	101.6	101.6	93.0	93.9	93.5	103.2	76.8	88.5
07	THERMAL & MOISTURE PROTECTION	159.4	85.7	128.2	107.1	105.2	106.3	155.6	87.1	126.6	111.6	102.0	107.6	112.0	97.3	105.8	111.1	87.9	101.3
08	OPENINGS	116.1	75.9	106.9	106.5	104.9	106.1	116.7	79.5	108.2	106.9	104.3	106.3	103.2	98.7	102.2	106.4	76.7	99.5
0920	Plaster & Gypsum Board	149.2	76.3	100.2	108.6	101.8	104.0	139.6	76.3	97.1	108.8	101.8	104.1	106.9	94.1	98.3	111.7	76.3	87.9
0950, 0980	Ceilings & Acoustic Treatment	115.5	76.3	89.1	112.0	101.8	105.1	110.7	76.3	87.5	109.1	101.8	104.2	104.2	94.1	97.4	101.3	76.3	84.4
0960	Flooring	87.0	81.9	85.6	103.6	101.5	103.0	86.0	81.9	84.9	97.9	101.5	98.9	103.6	83.6	98.1	100.9	81.9	95.6
0970, 0990	Wall Finishes & Painting/Coating	78.6	79.9	79.3	105.4	95.7	99.7	78.7	79.9	79.4	91.5	95.7	93.9	94.0	75.2	83.0	91.5	74.1	81.4
09	FINISHES	107.4	79.3	92.1	106.9	101.3	103.9	105.0	79.3	91.0	101.4	101.3	101.3	99.2	90.1	94.2	102.1	77.9	88.9
COVERS	DIVS. 10-14, 25, 28, 41, 43, 44, 46	100.0	95.3	99.0	100.0	102.6	100.6	100.0	95.2	98.9	100.0	102.5	100.6	100.0	98.0	99.6	100.0	94.0	98.7
21, 22, 23	FIRE SUPPRESSION, PLUMBING & HVAC	100.8	112.6	105.9	100.0	113.5	105.8	100.8	86.6	94.7	100.2	101.8	100.9	100.3	101.5	100.8	97.1	94.2	95.8
26, 27, 3370	ELECTRICAL, COMMUNICATIONS & UTIL.	84.6	98.0	91.6	107.4	113.1	110.4	83.0	81.4	82.1	108.0	98.3	103.0	113.8	101.6	107.5	108.8	93.3	100.7
MF2016	WEIGHTED AVERAGE	101.1	92.7	97.4	103.6	107.3	105.2	101.4	85.0	94.2	102.4	102.3	102.3	103.3	97.2	100.6	102.6	89.5	96.9

DIVISION		WASHINGTON YAKIMA 989 MAT.	INST.	TOTAL	BECKLEY 258-259 MAT.	INST.	TOTAL	BLUEFIELD 247-248 MAT.	INST.	TOTAL	BUCKHANNON 262 MAT.	INST.	TOTAL	CHARLESTON 250-253 MAT.	INST.	TOTAL	CLARKSBURG 263-264 MAT.	INST.	TOTAL
								WEST VIRGINIA												
015433	CONTRACTOR EQUIPMENT		102.2	102.2		107.3	107.3		107.3	107.3		107.3	107.3		107.3	107.3		107.3	107.3
0241, 31-34	SITE & INFRASTRUCTURE, DEMOLITION	98.6	109.4	106.2	101.5	91.8	94.7	101.5	91.8	94.7	107.7	91.7	96.5	100.7	92.8	95.2	108.5	91.7	96.7
0310	Concrete Forming & Accessories	107.0	98.0	99.2	86.9	90.2	89.7	86.0	89.9	89.3	85.5	86.4	86.3	97.7	91.3	92.2	83.0	86.4	85.9
0320	Concrete Reinforcing	108.0	98.5	103.2	91.8	89.4	90.6	94.5	70.8	82.6	95.1	94.3	94.7	99.3	89.7	94.4	95.1	97.3	96.2
0330	Cast-in-Place Concrete	108.2	84.6	99.3	104.4	93.1	100.1	102.0	92.9	98.6	101.7	93.4	98.5	101.0	94.5	98.5	111.5	91.6	103.9
03	CONCRETE	96.2	92.9	94.7	95.9	92.0	94.1	95.4	88.7	92.3	98.3	91.3	95.1	94.5	93.1	93.8	102.4	91.2	97.3
04	MASONRY	105.1	84.5	92.3	93.0	88.8	90.4	92.5	88.8	90.2	104.5	86.5	93.3	88.7	94.2	92.1	108.4	86.5	94.8
05	METALS	103.2	88.7	98.7	102.8	104.5	103.3	101.1	97.9	100.1	101.3	106.1	102.8	101.4	104.9	102.5	101.3	107.1	103.1
06	WOOD, PLASTICS & COMPOSITES	101.9	101.6	101.8	85.1	90.5	88.1	86.3	90.5	88.6	85.6	85.9	85.8	92.3	90.5	91.3	82.3	85.9	84.3
07	THERMAL & MOISTURE PROTECTION	111.7	88.9	102.1	106.5	88.6	98.9	103.7	88.6	97.3	104.0	87.6	97.1	103.1	90.6	97.8	103.9	87.3	96.9
08	OPENINGS	106.3	101.3	105.2	96.3	85.6	93.8	100.1	81.3	95.7	100.1	84.1	96.4	94.4	85.6	92.4	100.1	84.8	96.6
0920	Plaster & Gypsum Board	108.4	101.8	103.9	98.9	90.1	93.0	96.4	90.1	92.1	96.8	85.4	89.1	99.9	90.1	93.3	94.1	85.4	88.3
0950, 0980	Ceilings & Acoustic Treatment	103.2	101.8	102.2	84.1	90.1	88.1	90.2	90.1	90.1	91.9	85.4	87.5	95.2	90.1	91.7	91.9	85.4	87.5
0960	Flooring	98.8	81.9	94.1	91.6	100.6	94.1	88.9	100.6	92.2	88.7	96.5	90.8	94.0	100.6	95.8	87.6	96.5	90.1
0970, 0990	Wall Finishes & Painting/Coating	91.5	79.9	84.7	92.6	91.7	92.1	101.5	91.7	95.8	101.5	87.9	93.6	88.2	91.7	90.3	101.5	87.9	93.6
09	FINISHES	100.6	93.2	96.6	88.2	92.6	90.6	89.3	92.6	91.1	90.1	88.3	89.1	93.4	93.2	93.3	89.4	88.3	88.8
COVERS	DIVS. 10-14, 25, 28, 41, 43, 44, 46	100.0	99.3	99.8	100.0	93.8	98.6	100.0	93.8	98.6	100.0	92.4	98.3	100.0	94.1	98.7	100.0	92.4	98.3
21, 22, 23	FIRE SUPPRESSION, PLUMBING & HVAC	100.2	111.8	105.1	97.5	91.4	94.9	97.3	87.1	92.9	97.3	91.2	94.7	100.1	92.8	97.0	97.3	91.1	94.7
26, 27, 3370	ELECTRICAL, COMMUNICATIONS & UTIL.	111.0	98.1	104.3	94.6	87.0	90.7	96.6	87.0	91.6	98.0	91.9	94.8	99.7	88.8	94.0	98.0	91.9	94.8
MF2016	WEIGHTED AVERAGE	102.5	98.2	100.6	97.3	91.8	94.8	97.5	89.6	94.0	98.8	91.5	95.6	97.9	93.3	95.9	99.4	91.6	96.0

DIVISION		GASSAWAY 266 MAT.	INST.	TOTAL	HUNTINGTON 255-257 MAT.	INST.	TOTAL	LEWISBURG 249 MAT.	INST.	TOTAL	MARTINSBURG 254 MAT.	INST.	TOTAL	MORGANTOWN 265 MAT.	INST.	TOTAL	PARKERSBURG 261 MAT.	INST.	TOTAL
								WEST VIRGINIA												
015433	CONTRACTOR EQUIPMENT		107.3	107.3		107.3	107.3		107.3	107.3		107.3	107.3		107.3	107.3		107.3	107.3
0241, 31-34	SITE & INFRASTRUCTURE, DEMOLITION	105.2	91.7	95.7	106.2	92.8	96.8	117.2	91.8	99.4	105.5	92.5	96.4	102.5	92.6	95.5	110.7	92.7	98.1
0310	Concrete Forming & Accessories	84.9	86.3	86.1	98.6	91.0	92.1	83.3	89.5	88.6	87.0	77.7	79.0	83.3	86.5	86.1	87.6	86.8	86.9
0320	Concrete Reinforcing	95.1	94.1	94.6	93.1	93.6	93.3	95.1	70.6	82.7	91.8	94.2	93.0	95.1	97.3	96.2	94.5	94.3	94.4
0330	Cast-in-Place Concrete	106.5	92.4	101.1	113.9	98.4	108.0	102.1	92.8	98.6	109.4	86.9	100.8	101.7	93.4	98.5	104.0	93.5	100.0
03	CONCRETE	98.7	90.9	95.1	101.2	95.0	98.3	105.0	88.4	97.4	99.6	84.8	92.8	95.1	91.9	93.6	100.4	91.5	96.3
04	MASONRY	109.4	84.8	94.1	91.9	96.7	94.9	95.5	85.9	89.6	94.6	87.6	90.2	126.6	86.5	101.7	82.0	88.8	86.2
05	METALS	101.2	105.8	102.6	105.3	106.6	105.7	101.2	97.7	100.0	103.2	99.5	102.1	101.3	107.2	103.1	102.0	106.1	103.2
06	WOOD, PLASTICS & COMPOSITES	84.9	85.9	85.4	95.8	90.0	92.6	82.6	90.5	87.0	85.1	75.3	79.6	82.6	85.9	84.4	85.7	85.4	85.5
07	THERMAL & MOISTURE PROTECTION	103.7	87.0	96.6	106.6	91.7	100.3	104.6	87.8	97.5	106.7	83.0	96.7	103.8	87.6	96.9	103.8	88.4	97.3
08	OPENINGS	98.2	84.1	95.0	95.6	86.2	93.4	100.1	81.3	95.8	98.2	68.9	91.4	101.4	84.8	97.6	99.0	83.9	95.5
0920	Plaster & Gypsum Board	96.1	85.4	88.9	106.2	89.6	95.1	94.1	90.1	91.4	99.3	74.4	82.6	94.1	85.4	88.3	97.1	84.9	88.9
0950, 0980	Ceilings & Acoustic Treatment	91.9	85.4	87.5	85.9	89.6	88.4	91.9	90.1	90.7	85.9	74.4	78.2	91.9	85.4	87.5	91.9	84.9	87.2
0960	Flooring	88.4	100.6	91.8	99.0	109.2	101.8	87.7	100.6	91.3	91.6	96.6	93.0	87.7	96.5	90.2	91.6	97.2	93.2
0970, 0990	Wall Finishes & Painting/Coating	101.5	91.7	95.8	92.6	91.7	92.1	101.5	67.4	81.6	92.6	87.5	89.7	101.5	87.9	93.6	101.5	87.5	93.3
09	FINISHES	89.7	89.6	89.6	91.8	94.6	93.3	90.4	89.9	90.2	88.8	81.6	84.9	89.0	88.3	88.6	91.1	88.6	89.8
COVERS	DIVS. 10-14, 25, 28, 41, 43, 44, 46	100.0	92.4	98.3	100.0	93.9	98.6	100.0	67.7	92.8	100.0	84.0	96.4	100.0	86.7	97.0	100.0	93.0	98.4
21, 22, 23	FIRE SUPPRESSION, PLUMBING & HVAC	97.3	86.5	92.7	100.6	89.8	96.0	97.3	91.2	94.7	97.5	84.0	91.7	97.3	91.2	94.7	100.3	89.2	95.6
26, 27, 3370	ELECTRICAL, COMMUNICATIONS & UTIL.	98.0	88.8	93.2	98.2	91.0	94.4	94.2	87.0	90.5	100.2	76.0	87.6	98.1	91.9	94.9	98.1	78.3	87.8
MF2016	WEIGHTED AVERAGE	98.8	89.9	94.9	99.7	93.8	97.1	99.1	88.9	94.6	98.8	84.4	92.5	99.4	91.6	96.0	98.8	89.5	94.7

495

City Cost Indexes

		WEST VIRGINIA									WISCONSIN								
	DIVISION	PETERSBURG			ROMNEY			WHEELING			BELOIT			EAU CLAIRE			GREEN BAY		
		268			267			260			535			547			541 - 543		
		MAT.	INST.	TOTAL	MAT.	INST.	TOTAL	MAT.	INST.	TOTAL	MAT.	INST.	TOTAL	MAT.	INST.	TOTAL	MAT.	INST.	TOTAL
015433	CONTRACTOR EQUIPMENT		107.3	107.3		107.3	107.3		107.3	107.3		101.9	101.9		102.7	102.7		100.3	100.3
0241, 31 - 34	SITE & INFRASTRUCTURE, DEMOLITION	101.7	92.5	95.3	104.6	92.6	96.2	111.4	92.6	98.2	95.8	106.6	103.4	97.0	104.3	102.1	100.3	99.8	99.9
0310	Concrete Forming & Accessories	86.4	77.8	79.0	82.5	78.2	78.8	89.1	86.8	87.1	96.4	92.3	92.9	95.0	105.8	104.4	103.6	105.6	105.3
0320	Concrete Reinforcing	94.5	94.1	94.3	95.1	94.3	94.7	93.9	97.3	95.6	95.5	131.6	113.7	91.4	110.6	101.1	89.4	106.3	97.9
0330	Cast-in-Place Concrete	101.7	87.0	96.1	106.5	87.1	99.1	104.0	96.6	101.2	106.4	99.1	103.6	100.2	99.8	100.0	103.6	103.8	103.7
03	CONCRETE	95.2	85.2	90.6	98.6	85.4	92.6	100.4	93.1	97.1	96.1	101.7	98.7	91.8	104.5	97.6	94.7	105.1	99.5
04	MASONRY	99.5	86.5	91.4	95.8	87.6	90.7	107.6	87.0	94.8	100.3	102.3	101.6	92.0	98.7	96.1	123.3	99.7	108.6
05	METALS	101.4	105.4	102.6	101.4	105.9	102.8	102.1	107.3	103.7	96.5	110.6	100.8	96.3	104.5	98.8	98.9	103.9	100.4
06	WOOD, PLASTICS & COMPOSITES	86.5	75.3	80.3	81.8	75.3	78.2	87.1	85.9	86.4	93.5	88.8	90.9	98.3	107.8	103.6	103.0	107.8	105.7
07	THERMAL & MOISTURE PROTECTION	103.8	82.9	94.9	103.9	83.9	95.4	104.2	88.8	97.7	100.7	94.0	97.9	103.5	98.9	101.6	105.8	100.8	103.7
08	OPENINGS	101.4	78.2	96.1	101.3	78.2	96.0	99.8	84.8	96.4	96.3	106.1	98.5	101.8	107.2	103.1	98.2	107.0	100.2
0920	Plaster & Gypsum Board	96.8	74.4	81.8	93.8	74.4	80.8	97.1	85.4	89.2	97.3	88.9	91.7	110.1	108.4	109.0	106.9	108.4	107.9
0950, 0980	Ceilings & Acoustic Treatment	91.9	74.4	80.1	91.9	74.4	80.1	91.9	85.4	87.5	86.3	88.9	88.1	90.3	108.4	102.5	84.6	108.4	100.7
0960	Flooring	89.5	96.5	91.4	87.5	98.5	90.6	92.5	96.5	93.6	91.3	125.2	100.7	80.8	112.6	89.6	96.5	121.4	103.4
0970, 0990	Wall Finishes & Painting/Coating	101.5	87.9	93.6	101.5	87.9	93.6	101.5	87.9	93.6	96.8	104.5	101.3	84.9	79.9	82.0	94.0	83.6	88.0
09	FINISHES	89.8	82.0	85.6	89.1	82.4	85.5	91.4	88.5	89.9	92.0	99.0	95.8	87.5	105.0	97.0	91.9	107.0	100.1
COVERS	DIVS. 10 - 14, 25, 28, 41, 43, 44, 46	100.0	55.1	90.0	100.0	91.2	98.0	100.0	87.8	97.3	100.0	94.1	98.7	100.0	96.4	99.2	100.0	96.3	99.2
21, 22, 23	FIRE SUPPRESSION, PLUMBING & HVAC	97.3	86.7	92.8	97.3	86.6	92.7	100.4	91.4	96.6	100.1	95.8	98.3	100.1	87.3	94.7	100.4	85.6	94.1
26, 27, 3370	ELECTRICAL, COMMUNICATIONS & UTIL.	101.1	76.0	88.0	100.4	76.0	87.7	95.4	91.9	93.6	99.3	85.2	91.9	104.0	84.8	94.0	98.6	81.3	89.6
MF2016	WEIGHTED AVERAGE	98.5	85.0	92.6	98.6	86.4	93.3	100.0	91.9	96.5	97.7	98.6	98.1	97.6	97.3	97.5	99.6	96.5	98.2

		WISCONSIN																
	DIVISION	KENOSHA			LA CROSSE			LANCASTER			MADISON			MILWAUKEE			NEW RICHMOND		
		531			546			538			537			530, 532			540		
		MAT.	INST.	TOTAL	MAT.	INST.	TOTAL	MAT.	INST.	TOTAL	MAT.	INST.	TOTAL	MAT.	INST.	TOTAL	MAT.	INST.	TOTAL
015433	CONTRACTOR EQUIPMENT		99.8	99.8		102.7	102.7		101.9	101.9		101.9	101.9		89.4	89.4		103.0	103.0
0241, 31 - 34	SITE & INFRASTRUCTURE, DEMOLITION	101.3	104.1	103.3	90.7	104.3	100.2	94.9	106.4	103.0	93.9	107.3	103.3	93.2	95.3	94.6	95.9	104.4	101.9
0310	Concrete Forming & Accessories	104.3	111.2	110.3	82.6	105.7	102.5	95.8	96.3	96.2	100.5	95.7	96.3	100.8	112.4	110.8	90.5	93.1	92.8
0320	Concrete Reinforcing	95.3	113.9	104.7	91.1	103.0	97.1	97.0	102.8	99.9	95.7	103.2	99.5	102.9	114.2	108.6	88.4	110.2	99.4
0330	Cast-in-Place Concrete	115.7	108.3	112.9	90.1	101.6	94.5	105.8	98.7	103.1	102.4	104.8	103.3	93.6	110.9	100.4	104.3	79.8	95.0
03	CONCRETE	101.0	110.4	105.3	83.4	103.8	92.7	95.9	98.4	97.0	93.7	100.3	96.7	95.7	111.2	102.8	89.8	91.9	90.7
04	MASONRY	97.8	110.7	105.8	91.1	107.8	101.5	100.3	95.9	97.6	95.6	99.9	98.1	105.8	114.7	111.3	118.1	95.7	104.2
05	METALS	97.4	105.5	99.9	96.2	102.5	98.1	93.9	99.3	95.5	98.3	100.6	99.0	97.9	97.4	97.8	96.6	103.5	98.7
06	WOOD, PLASTICS & COMPOSITES	97.3	110.8	104.8	84.3	107.8	97.4	92.8	95.7	94.4	93.9	93.4	93.6	98.8	111.3	105.7	87.8	91.7	90.0
07	THERMAL & MOISTURE PROTECTION	100.9	107.2	103.6	103.0	98.7	101.1	100.5	93.2	97.4	98.3	101.2	99.5	102.8	109.9	105.8	104.6	88.3	97.7
08	OPENINGS	90.9	110.8	95.5	101.8	100.2	101.4	92.3	93.5	92.5	102.3	98.3	101.3	101.0	111.1	103.3	87.9	91.8	88.8
0920	Plaster & Gypsum Board	87.3	111.6	103.6	105.0	108.4	107.3	96.5	96.1	96.2	104.3	93.6	97.1	100.3	111.6	107.9	95.6	92.0	93.2
0950, 0980	Ceilings & Acoustic Treatment	86.3	111.6	103.4	89.5	108.4	102.2	82.9	96.1	91.8	89.6	93.6	92.3	96.5	111.6	106.7	57.0	92.0	80.6
0960	Flooring	108.3	121.4	112.0	74.8	118.0	86.8	90.8	105.3	94.8	89.5	113.7	96.2	96.6	117.4	102.3	89.6	109.8	95.2
0970, 0990	Wall Finishes & Painting/Coating	108.0	118.8	114.3	84.9	81.2	82.8	96.8	102.1	99.9	90.1	104.5	98.5	106.8	123.4	116.5	96.2	85.4	89.9
09	FINISHES	96.8	114.3	106.3	84.3	106.3	96.3	91.1	99.0	95.4	91.7	99.6	96.0	100.5	114.7	108.2	82.4	95.7	89.7
COVERS	DIVS. 10 - 14, 25, 28, 41, 43, 44, 46	100.0	101.5	100.3	100.0	96.4	99.2	100.0	86.7	97.0	100.0	99.7	99.9	100.0	102.9	100.6	100.0	88.9	97.5
21, 22, 23	FIRE SUPPRESSION, PLUMBING & HVAC	100.3	97.0	98.9	100.1	87.3	94.6	97.0	87.1	92.8	100.0	96.7	98.6	99.9	105.5	102.3	96.5	87.4	92.6
26, 27, 3370	ELECTRICAL, COMMUNICATIONS & UTIL.	99.6	97.3	98.4	104.3	84.8	94.2	99.0	84.8	91.6	100.0	94.1	96.9	99.1	101.5	100.4	102.1	84.8	93.1
MF2016	WEIGHTED AVERAGE	98.4	105.0	101.3	95.9	96.9	96.4	96.0	93.9	95.1	98.0	98.9	98.4	99.3	106.6	102.5	95.6	92.7	94.3

		WISCONSIN																
	DIVISION	OSHKOSH			PORTAGE			RACINE			RHINELANDER			SUPERIOR			WAUSAU		
		549			539			534			545			548			544		
		MAT.	INST.	TOTAL	MAT.	INST.	TOTAL	MAT.	INST.	TOTAL	MAT.	INST.	TOTAL	MAT.	INST.	TOTAL	MAT.	INST.	TOTAL
015433	CONTRACTOR EQUIPMENT		100.3	100.3		101.9	101.9		101.9	101.9		100.3	100.3		103.0	103.0		100.3	100.3
0241, 31 - 34	SITE & INFRASTRUCTURE, DEMOLITION	92.1	99.4	97.2	85.8	106.2	100.1	95.6	108.1	104.3	104.1	99.5	100.9	92.6	104.1	100.7	87.9	100.7	96.9
0310	Concrete Forming & Accessories	87.1	89.6	89.3	88.5	91.5	91.1	96.8	111.3	109.3	84.9	90.3	89.6	88.6	89.6	89.5	86.6	105.0	102.4
0320	Concrete Reinforcing	89.6	98.5	94.1	97.1	102.9	100.0	95.5	114.0	104.8	89.7	96.8	93.3	88.4	106.9	97.8	89.7	102.8	96.3
0330	Cast-in-Place Concrete	96.1	94.2	95.4	90.8	99.3	94.0	104.3	108.1	105.8	108.9	96.9	104.4	98.3	101.9	99.6	89.6	95.8	91.9
03	CONCRETE	85.1	93.2	88.8	83.9	96.4	89.6	95.2	110.4	102.1	96.6	94.2	95.5	84.6	97.3	90.4	80.3	101.4	90.0
04	MASONRY	105.5	97.3	100.4	99.1	97.0	97.8	100.2	110.7	106.7	123.9	94.7	105.8	117.4	100.8	107.1	105.0	94.8	98.7
05	METALS	96.8	99.4	97.6	94.6	99.7	96.2	98.2	105.5	100.4	96.6	99.1	97.4	97.6	103.8	99.5	96.5	101.8	98.1
06	WOOD, PLASTICS & COMPOSITES	83.9	88.9	86.7	83.7	88.8	86.5	93.7	110.8	103.2	81.6	88.9	85.7	86.3	87.5	87.0	83.4	107.8	97.0
07	THERMAL & MOISTURE PROTECTION	104.8	82.2	95.2	99.9	88.9	95.3	100.8	106.8	103.3	105.7	82.7	96.0	104.2	89.4	98.0	104.6	84.2	96.0
08	OPENINGS	94.6	89.4	93.4	92.4	95.4	93.1	96.3	110.8	99.6	94.6	88.2	93.2	87.4	93.4	88.8	94.8	100.6	96.2
0920	Plaster & Gypsum Board	94.4	88.9	90.7	89.2	88.9	89.1	97.3	111.6	106.9	94.4	88.9	90.7	95.4	87.7	90.2	94.4	108.4	103.8
0950, 0980	Ceilings & Acoustic Treatment	84.6	88.9	87.5	85.4	88.9	87.8	86.3	111.6	103.4	84.6	88.9	87.5	57.8	87.7	78.0	84.6	108.4	100.7
0960	Flooring	87.6	121.4	97.0	87.2	114.8	94.9	91.3	121.4	99.6	87.0	111.7	93.9	90.7	127.2	100.8	87.5	111.7	94.2
0970, 0990	Wall Finishes & Painting/Coating	90.9	83.6	86.6	96.8	102.1	99.9	96.8	121.2	111.0	90.9	83.6	86.6	85.3	110.6	100.1	90.9	83.6	86.6
09	FINISHES	86.7	95.2	91.3	89.0	96.6	93.1	92.0	114.6	104.3	87.5	92.7	90.3	81.8	98.6	90.9	86.4	105.1	96.5
COVERS	DIVS. 10 - 14, 25, 28, 41, 43, 44, 46	100.0	86.4	97.0	100.0	87.4	97.2	100.0	101.5	100.3	100.0	87.6	97.2	100.0	87.2	97.2	100.0	96.3	99.2
21, 22, 23	FIRE SUPPRESSION, PLUMBING & HVAC	97.3	80.9	90.3	97.0	96.5	96.8	100.1	97.1	98.8	97.3	86.4	92.6	96.5	91.5	94.4	97.3	86.8	92.8
26, 27, 3370	ELECTRICAL, COMMUNICATIONS & UTIL.	102.6	76.3	88.9	102.7	94.1	98.2	99.1	103.5	101.4	102.0	77.6	89.3	106.9	98.7	102.6	103.8	80.2	91.5
MF2016	WEIGHTED AVERAGE	95.7	89.2	92.9	94.4	96.6	95.4	97.8	106.2	101.5	98.3	90.1	94.7	95.4	97.1	96.1	95.0	94.5	94.8

City Cost Indexes

WYOMING

DIVISION		CASPER 826			CHEYENNE 820			NEWCASTLE 827			RAWLINS 823			RIVERTON 825			ROCK SPRINGS 829 - 831		
		MAT.	INST.	TOTAL	MAT.	INST.	TOTAL	MAT.	INST.	TOTAL	MAT.	INST.	TOTAL	MAT.	INST.	TOTAL	MAT.	INST.	TOTAL
015433	CONTRACTOR EQUIPMENT		97.4	97.4		97.4	97.4		97.4	97.4		97.4	97.4		97.4	97.4		97.4	97.4
0241, 31 - 34	SITE & INFRASTRUCTURE, DEMOLITION	100.6	94.7	96.5	96.1	94.7	95.1	88.0	94.2	92.4	102.6	94.2	96.7	95.8	94.1	94.6	92.2	94.2	93.6
0310	Concrete Forming & Accessories	100.5	55.2	61.4	101.0	68.4	72.9	92.2	73.8	76.4	96.3	74.1	77.1	91.3	62.9	66.8	98.3	63.9	68.6
0320	Concrete Reinforcing	111.9	85.2	98.4	107.4	85.3	96.2	115.3	85.0	100.0	115.0	85.0	99.9	116.1	85.0	100.4	116.1	83.2	99.5
0330	Cast-in-Place Concrete	104.4	77.5	94.2	98.6	77.6	90.6	99.6	76.5	90.8	99.6	76.7	90.9	99.6	76.5	90.8	99.6	76.5	90.8
03	CONCRETE	100.5	68.9	86.1	98.0	74.9	87.5	98.3	77.0	88.6	111.3	77.1	95.7	106.2	72.0	90.6	98.8	72.2	86.6
04	MASONRY	103.9	66.1	80.5	107.4	67.3	82.5	103.9	61.8	77.8	103.9	61.8	77.8	103.9	61.8	77.8	168.0	57.5	99.5
05	METALS	103.6	81.5	96.8	106.1	81.8	98.6	102.3	81.2	95.8	102.3	81.4	95.9	102.4	81.1	95.9	103.2	80.3	96.1
06	WOOD, PLASTICS & COMPOSITES	94.7	49.8	69.7	91.0	67.7	78.0	82.2	76.2	78.8	85.8	76.2	80.4	81.2	61.5	70.3	90.5	62.8	75.1
07	THERMAL & MOISTURE PROTECTION	102.5	67.1	87.5	97.1	69.4	85.4	98.7	66.3	85.0	100.3	77.9	90.8	99.7	64.8	84.9	98.8	67.9	85.7
08	OPENINGS	103.1	61.3	93.5	104.0	71.2	96.5	108.1	75.9	100.7	107.7	75.9	100.4	107.9	67.8	98.7	108.4	68.1	99.2
0920	Plaster & Gypsum Board	103.4	48.5	66.5	91.7	66.8	75.0	88.5	75.5	79.8	88.9	75.5	79.9	88.5	60.5	69.7	100.6	61.8	74.4
0950, 0980	Ceilings & Acoustic Treatment	103.1	48.5	66.3	98.7	66.8	77.2	100.6	75.5	83.7	100.6	75.5	83.7	100.6	60.5	73.6	100.6	61.8	74.5
0960	Flooring	105.8	73.6	96.9	105.0	73.6	96.3	98.7	47.1	84.4	101.6	47.1	86.5	98.2	63.7	88.7	103.9	47.1	88.1
0970, 0990	Wall Finishes & Painting/Coating	91.5	61.0	73.7	97.4	61.0	76.2	94.1	61.0	74.8	94.1	61.0	74.8	94.1	61.0	74.8	94.1	61.0	74.8
09	FINISHES	99.0	57.8	76.6	95.8	68.3	80.8	91.0	67.6	78.3	93.3	67.6	79.3	91.7	62.3	75.7	94.2	59.7	75.4
COVERS	DIVS. 10 - 14, 25, 28, 41, 43, 44, 46	100.0	84.5	96.6	100.0	86.5	97.0	100.0	94.5	98.8	100.0	94.5	98.8	100.0	80.5	95.7	100.0	84.7	96.6
21, 22, 23	FIRE SUPPRESSION, PLUMBING & HVAC	100.1	72.6	88.3	100.0	72.6	88.3	98.3	71.8	87.0	98.3	71.8	87.0	98.3	71.7	87.0	99.9	71.7	87.9
26, 27, 3370	ELECTRICAL, COMMUNICATIONS & UTIL.	101.9	63.7	82.0	104.0	64.6	83.5	102.7	63.3	82.2	102.7	63.3	82.2	102.7	62.4	81.8	100.8	80.9	90.5
MF2016	WEIGHTED AVERAGE	101.4	70.3	87.8	101.3	73.5	89.2	99.9	73.1	88.2	102.1	73.5	89.6	101.2	70.7	87.8	103.9	72.7	90.2

WYOMING / CANADA

DIVISION		SHERIDAN 828			WHEATLAND 822			WORLAND 824			YELLOWSTONE NAT'L PA 821			BARRIE, ONTARIO			BATHURST, NEW BRUNSWICK		
		MAT.	INST.	TOTAL	MAT.	INST.	TOTAL	MAT.	INST.	TOTAL	MAT.	INST.	TOTAL	MAT.	INST.	TOTAL	MAT.	INST.	TOTAL
015433	CONTRACTOR EQUIPMENT		97.4	97.4		97.4	97.4		97.4	97.4		97.4	97.4		103.0	103.0		102.8	102.8
0241, 31 - 34	SITE & INFRASTRUCTURE, DEMOLITION	96.2	94.7	95.1	93.0	94.2	93.8	90.2	94.2	93.0	90.3	94.2	93.0	119.2	99.9	105.7	107.0	95.7	99.1
0310	Concrete Forming & Accessories	99.0	63.7	68.6	94.1	50.6	56.6	94.1	63.9	68.0	94.2	63.9	68.1	124.2	86.3	91.5	103.6	60.6	66.5
0320	Concrete Reinforcing	116.1	85.0	100.4	115.3	84.9	99.8	116.1	85.0	100.4	118.1	85.0	101.4	175.3	89.7	132.1	137.7	59.4	98.2
0330	Cast-in-Place Concrete	103.0	77.5	93.3	103.9	76.4	93.5	99.6	76.5	90.8	99.6	76.5	90.8	158.9	86.5	131.4	117.1	59.1	95.4
03	CONCRETE	106.3	72.7	91.0	103.2	66.3	86.3	98.5	72.4	86.6	98.8	72.5	86.8	139.8	87.3	115.8	113.6	60.8	89.5
04	MASONRY	104.2	63.3	78.9	104.3	53.4	72.7	103.9	61.8	77.8	104.0	61.8	77.8	167.9	93.1	121.5	162.5	59.9	98.9
05	METALS	105.9	81.3	98.3	102.2	80.3	95.5	102.4	81.1	95.9	103.0	80.6	96.1	110.3	93.5	105.2	113.7	75.0	101.8
06	WOOD, PLASTICS & COMPOSITES	92.2	61.5	75.1	83.9	45.0	62.2	83.9	62.8	72.2	83.9	62.8	72.2	118.0	84.7	99.5	98.4	60.6	77.4
07	THERMAL & MOISTURE PROTECTION	100.0	67.6	86.3	99.0	60.3	82.6	98.8	66.3	85.0	98.2	66.3	84.7	113.8	90.3	103.9	109.4	61.3	89.0
08	OPENINGS	108.6	67.8	99.2	106.6	58.6	95.6	108.3	68.5	99.1	101.3	68.1	93.7	92.4	85.0	90.7	86.4	53.8	78.9
0920	Plaster & Gypsum Board	112.5	60.5	77.6	88.5	43.5	58.3	88.5	61.8	70.6	88.7	61.8	70.7	151.5	84.2	106.3	126.6	59.5	81.5
0950, 0980	Ceilings & Acoustic Treatment	103.5	60.5	74.5	100.6	43.5	62.1	100.6	61.8	74.5	101.5	61.8	74.7	95.3	84.2	87.9	112.5	59.5	76.7
0960	Flooring	102.5	63.7	91.7	100.3	46.3	85.3	100.3	47.1	85.5	100.3	47.1	85.5	118.1	92.3	110.9	98.6	43.8	83.4
0970, 0990	Wall Finishes & Painting/Coating	96.3	61.0	75.7	94.1	61.0	74.8	94.1	61.0	74.8	94.1	61.0	74.8	104.4	87.6	94.6	109.9	50.1	75.0
09	FINISHES	98.6	63.0	79.2	91.8	49.0	68.5	91.5	59.7	74.2	91.7	59.8	74.4	109.8	87.7	97.8	104.7	56.5	78.5
COVERS	DIVS. 10 - 14, 25, 28, 41, 43, 44, 46	100.0	85.8	96.8	100.0	83.5	96.3	100.0	79.3	95.4	100.0	79.4	95.4	139.2	67.6	123.3	131.1	60.2	115.4
21, 22, 23	FIRE SUPPRESSION, PLUMBING & HVAC	98.3	72.6	87.3	98.3	71.7	86.9	98.3	71.7	87.0	98.3	71.7	87.0	104.5	97.5	101.5	104.6	67.5	88.7
26, 27, 3370	ELECTRICAL, COMMUNICATIONS & UTIL.	105.3	62.4	83.0	102.7	80.9	91.4	102.7	80.9	91.4	101.6	90.9	96.1	116.1	87.6	101.3	112.0	59.0	84.4
MF2016	WEIGHTED AVERAGE	102.8	71.5	89.1	100.6	69.2	86.9	100.1	73.0	88.2	99.4	74.4	88.4	117.0	91.0	105.6	111.3	65.0	91.0

CANADA

DIVISION		BRANDON, MANITOBA			BRANTFORD, ONTARIO			BRIDGEWATER, NOVA SCOTIA			CALGARY, ALBERTA			CAP-DE-LA-MADELEINE, QUEBEC			CHARLESBOURG, QUEBEC		
		MAT.	INST.	TOTAL	MAT.	INST.	TOTAL	MAT.	INST.	TOTAL	MAT.	INST.	TOTAL	MAT.	INST.	TOTAL	MAT.	INST.	TOTAL
015433	CONTRACTOR EQUIPMENT		105.8	105.8		103.1	103.1		102.6	102.6		128.2	128.2		103.3	103.3		103.3	103.3
0241, 31 - 34	SITE & INFRASTRUCTURE, DEMOLITION	134.2	98.8	109.4	119.6	100.3	106.1	103.7	97.5	99.3	123.1	120.8	121.5	99.2	98.9	99.0	99.2	98.9	99.0
0310	Concrete Forming & Accessories	143.5	69.4	79.6	123.5	93.5	97.6	96.6	71.2	74.7	123.0	99.2	102.5	129.2	83.0	89.4	129.2	83.0	89.4
0320	Concrete Reinforcing	192.0	56.3	123.5	169.0	88.3	128.3	144.0	49.2	96.2	135.2	84.5	109.6	144.0	74.8	109.1	144.0	74.8	109.1
0330	Cast-in-Place Concrete	118.3	74.1	101.5	135.8	107.5	125.0	139.5	70.4	113.3	143.2	108.3	129.9	109.6	92.2	103.0	109.6	92.2	103.0
03	CONCRETE	127.0	69.7	100.8	127.0	97.6	113.6	125.3	68.0	99.1	129.2	100.5	116.1	111.7	85.2	99.6	111.7	85.2	99.6
04	MASONRY	221.4	63.3	123.3	168.8	97.4	124.5	164.2	68.4	104.8	200.4	90.6	132.3	164.9	79.6	112.0	164.9	79.6	112.0
05	METALS	133.5	80.4	117.2	112.4	94.3	106.8	111.7	77.6	101.2	129.5	104.8	121.9	110.8	86.9	103.5	110.8	86.9	103.5
06	WOOD, PLASTICS & COMPOSITES	150.9	70.0	105.9	119.8	92.0	104.3	90.7	70.6	79.5	96.4	98.8	97.8	130.5	82.8	103.9	130.5	82.8	103.9
07	THERMAL & MOISTURE PROTECTION	131.5	72.1	106.4	118.6	96.0	109.0	113.2	70.9	95.3	129.9	97.8	116.3	111.9	88.3	101.9	111.9	88.3	101.9
08	OPENINGS	102.2	63.0	93.2	90.3	91.1	90.5	84.5	64.4	79.9	83.5	87.8	84.4	91.6	76.0	88.0	91.6	76.0	88.0
0920	Plaster & Gypsum Board	113.1	68.8	83.3	116.6	91.7	99.9	122.4	69.8	87.1	121.5	97.7	105.6	144.8	82.2	102.8	144.8	82.2	102.8
0950, 0980	Ceilings & Acoustic Treatment	119.2	68.8	85.2	103.2	91.7	95.5	103.2	69.8	80.6	142.1	97.9	112.3	103.2	82.2	89.0	103.2	82.2	89.0
0960	Flooring	130.3	65.4	112.3	112.1	92.3	106.6	94.7	62.3	85.7	117.9	88.6	109.8	112.1	90.9	106.2	112.1	90.9	106.2
0970, 0990	Wall Finishes & Painting/Coating	117.0	56.5	81.8	109.0	96.2	101.5	109.0	62.0	81.6	117.1	111.2	113.7	109.0	87.4	96.4	109.0	87.4	96.4
09	FINISHES	118.4	67.6	90.8	106.3	93.8	99.5	101.1	68.8	83.6	122.2	99.1	109.6	109.4	85.2	96.3	109.4	85.2	96.3
COVERS	DIVS. 10 - 14, 25, 28, 41, 43, 44, 46	131.1	62.7	115.9	131.1	69.2	117.5	131.1	63.3	116.0	131.1	95.5	123.2	131.1	78.8	119.5	131.1	78.8	119.5
21, 22, 23	FIRE SUPPRESSION, PLUMBING & HVAC	104.7	82.2	95.1	104.6	100.4	102.8	104.6	82.8	95.3	105.5	93.3	100.3	105.1	87.7	97.6	105.1	87.7	97.6
26, 27, 3370	ELECTRICAL, COMMUNICATIONS & UTIL.	111.1	66.6	88.0	111.4	87.1	98.7	116.0	62.0	87.9	107.3	99.1	103.1	110.4	68.9	88.8	110.4	68.9	88.8
MF2016	WEIGHTED AVERAGE	123.6	73.8	101.8	114.3	94.9	105.8	112.3	73.4	95.3	119.5	98.8	110.4	111.7	83.6	99.4	111.7	83.6	99.4

497

City Cost Indexes

CANADA

DIVISION		CHARLOTTETOWN, PRINCE EDWARD ISLAND			CHICOUTIMI, QUEBEC			CORNER BROOK, NEWFOUNDLAND			CORNWALL, ONTARIO			DALHOUSIE, NEW BRUNSWICK			DARTMOUTH, NOVA SCOTIA		
		MAT.	INST.	TOTAL	MAT.	INST.	TOTAL	MAT.	INST.	TOTAL	MAT.	INST.	TOTAL	MAT.	INST.	TOTAL	MAT.	INST.	TOTAL
015433	CONTRACTOR EQUIPMENT		120.7	120.7		103.4	103.4		104.0	104.0		103.1	103.1		102.6	102.6		102.9	102.9
0241, 31 - 34	SITE & INFRASTRUCTURE, DEMOLITION	133.6	108.5	116.0	103.9	98.6	100.2	138.7	96.1	108.8	117.7	99.7	105.1	102.8	95.5	97.7	124.9	97.7	105.9
0310	Concrete Forming & Accessories	118.4	55.4	64.1	131.9	91.0	96.7	120.7	79.3	85.0	121.3	86.5	91.3	102.4	60.8	66.5	110.5	71.2	76.6
0320	Concrete Reinforcing	152.2	48.0	99.6	103.9	94.2	99.0	176.3	50.4	112.8	169.0	88.0	128.2	147.3	59.4	102.9	184.1	49.2	116.0
0330	Cast-in-Place Concrete	149.0	59.1	114.9	110.8	97.0	105.6	137.7	67.0	110.8	122.1	97.9	112.9	115.9	59.1	94.3	132.9	70.4	109.2
03	CONCRETE	134.7	57.3	99.3	104.6	93.8	99.7	159.1	70.7	118.7	120.4	91.1	107.0	118.1	60.9	91.9	141.6	68.1	108.0
04	MASONRY	177.7	57.2	103.0	164.8	90.3	118.6	217.1	77.5	130.5	167.6	89.3	119.0	164.5	59.9	99.6	232.1	68.4	130.6
05	METALS	137.2	81.7	120.2	113.4	92.4	107.0	133.9	77.1	116.5	112.2	93.0	106.3	106.9	75.1	97.2	134.6	77.8	117.1
06	WOOD, PLASTICS & COMPOSITES	99.9	54.8	74.8	131.2	91.4	109.0	129.3	85.4	104.9	118.1	85.5	100.0	97.5	60.6	77.0	117.5	70.6	91.4
07	THERMAL & MOISTURE PROTECTION	128.5	59.1	99.1	109.8	98.0	104.8	136.2	69.2	107.9	118.4	90.5	106.6	116.2	61.3	92.9	133.2	71.0	106.9
08	OPENINGS	85.1	48.0	76.6	90.5	77.8	87.5	108.7	70.0	99.8	91.6	84.7	90.0	87.3	53.8	79.6	92.6	64.4	86.1
0920	Plaster & Gypsum Board	119.5	53.0	74.9	144.8	91.0	108.7	147.0	84.8	105.3	173.2	85.1	114.1	130.5	59.5	82.8	142.6	69.8	93.7
0950, 0980	Ceilings & Acoustic Treatment	128.0	53.0	77.4	111.7	91.0	97.8	120.0	84.8	96.3	105.7	85.1	91.8	106.5	59.5	74.8	126.9	69.8	88.4
0960	Flooring	106.3	58.4	93.0	114.3	90.9	107.8	112.4	52.4	95.7	112.1	90.9	106.2	100.6	67.1	91.3	107.3	62.3	94.8
0970, 0990	Wall Finishes & Painting/Coating	117.5	41.7	73.3	109.9	105.2	107.1	116.9	59.0	83.1	109.0	89.6	97.7	112.5	50.1	76.1	116.9	62.0	84.9
09	FINISHES	116.7	54.8	83.0	111.5	93.4	101.7	118.1	73.7	94.0	114.4	87.8	99.9	105.9	61.1	81.6	116.0	68.8	90.3
COVERS	DIVS. 10 - 14, 25, 28, 41, 43, 44, 46	131.1	60.4	115.4	131.1	82.5	120.3	131.1	63.1	116.0	131.1	67.3	116.9	131.1	60.1	115.3	131.1	63.3	116.1
21, 22, 23	FIRE SUPPRESSION, PLUMBING & HVAC	104.9	61.4	86.3	104.6	81.5	94.7	104.7	68.2	89.3	105.1	98.3	102.2	104.7	67.5	88.8	104.7	82.8	95.4
26, 27, 3370	ELECTRICAL, COMMUNICATIONS & UTIL.	114.3	50.1	80.9	108.7	85.6	96.7	108.8	54.4	80.5	111.7	88.0	99.4	113.9	55.8	83.6	113.0	62.0	86.5
MF2016	WEIGHTED AVERAGE	120.9	62.8	95.5	111.1	88.9	101.4	128.0	71.5	103.3	114.2	91.3	104.2	111.3	65.2	91.1	124.6	73.5	102.2

CANADA

DIVISION		EDMONTON, ALBERTA			FORT MCMURRAY, ALBERTA			FREDERICTON, NEW BRUNSWICK			GATINEAU, QUEBEC			GRANBY, QUEBEC			HALIFAX, NOVA SCOTIA		
		MAT.	INST.	TOTAL	MAT.	INST.	TOTAL	MAT.	INST.	TOTAL	MAT.	INST.	TOTAL	MAT.	INST.	TOTAL	MAT.	INST.	TOTAL
015433	CONTRACTOR EQUIPMENT		128.5	128.5		105.5	105.5		120.7	120.7		103.3	103.3		103.3	103.3		118.3	118.3
0241, 31 - 34	SITE & INFRASTRUCTURE, DEMOLITION	129.3	121.0	123.5	124.8	101.1	108.1	113.6	110.3	111.3	99.0	98.9	99.0	99.5	98.9	99.1	107.8	109.8	109.2
0310	Concrete Forming & Accessories	119.7	99.2	102.0	121.4	91.7	95.7	120.2	61.4	69.5	129.2	82.9	89.3	129.2	82.9	89.3	117.4	85.0	89.4
0320	Concrete Reinforcing	135.7	84.5	109.9	156.5	84.3	120.1	151.1	59.6	105.0	152.2	74.8	113.1	152.2	74.7	113.1	152.2	72.3	111.9
0330	Cast-in-Place Concrete	147.7	108.4	132.7	180.3	103.5	151.1	116.8	59.5	95.0	108.1	92.2	102.1	111.7	92.2	104.3	106.9	86.0	98.9
03	CONCRETE	131.2	100.6	117.2	146.3	94.7	122.7	119.4	62.1	93.2	112.1	85.2	99.8	113.8	85.1	100.7	114.0	84.3	100.4
04	MASONRY	196.0	90.6	130.7	209.5	87.3	133.7	182.5	61.2	107.3	164.8	79.6	112.0	165.1	79.6	112.1	180.1	87.1	122.4
05	METALS	136.2	105.0	126.6	139.9	92.8	125.4	134.2	87.1	119.7	110.8	86.8	103.4	111.0	86.7	103.6	138.4	98.1	126.0
06	WOOD, PLASTICS & COMPOSITES	96.8	98.8	97.9	114.2	90.9	101.2	109.4	60.0	82.4	130.5	82.8	103.9	130.5	82.8	103.9	100.5	84.0	91.3
07	THERMAL & MOISTURE PROTECTION	129.7	97.8	116.2	127.1	93.9	113.0	123.7	61.3	97.3	111.9	88.3	101.9	111.9	86.7	101.2	129.0	86.1	110.8
08	OPENINGS	81.8	87.8	83.2	91.6	83.4	89.7	86.1	52.8	78.5	91.6	71.4	87.0	91.6	71.4	87.0	88.6	76.8	85.9
0920	Plaster & Gypsum Board	116.7	97.9	104.1	117.4	90.3	99.2	123.5	59.5	80.5	114.5	82.2	92.8	114.5	82.2	92.8	118.1	83.3	94.7
0950, 0980	Ceilings & Acoustic Treatment	137.2	97.9	110.7	110.8	90.3	97.0	133.9	59.5	83.7	103.2	82.2	89.0	103.2	82.2	89.0	128.5	83.3	98.0
0960	Flooring	114.0	88.6	107.0	112.1	88.6	105.6	109.5	70.0	98.6	112.1	90.9	106.2	112.1	90.9	106.2	99.6	83.8	95.2
0970, 0990	Wall Finishes & Painting/Coating	108.3	111.2	110.0	109.1	92.3	99.3	114.8	63.8	85.1	109.0	87.4	96.4	109.0	87.4	96.4	112.8	91.7	100.5
09	FINISHES	115.6	99.1	106.6	109.2	91.4	99.5	118.5	63.4	88.5	105.3	85.2	94.4	105.3	85.2	94.4	110.4	85.9	97.1
COVERS	DIVS. 10 - 14, 25, 28, 41, 43, 44, 46	131.1	95.5	123.2	131.1	92.3	122.5	131.1	60.7	115.5	131.1	78.8	119.5	131.1	78.8	119.5	131.1	68.7	117.2
21, 22, 23	FIRE SUPPRESSION, PLUMBING & HVAC	105.5	93.3	100.3	105.1	97.1	101.7	105.0	76.7	92.9	105.1	87.7	97.6	104.6	87.7	97.4	105.3	82.4	95.5
26, 27, 3370	ELECTRICAL, COMMUNICATIONS & UTIL.	110.3	99.1	104.5	105.6	81.8	93.3	111.9	73.6	92.0	110.4	68.9	88.8	111.0	68.9	89.1	109.4	87.0	97.7
MF2016	WEIGHTED AVERAGE	120.4	98.8	110.9	123.4	91.9	109.7	118.2	72.5	98.2	111.4	83.4	99.1	111.6	83.3	99.2	117.4	87.2	104.2

CANADA

DIVISION		HAMILTON, ONTARIO			HULL, QUEBEC			JOLIETTE, QUEBEC			KAMLOOPS, BRITISH COLUMBIA			KINGSTON, ONTARIO			KITCHENER, ONTARIO		
		MAT.	INST.	TOTAL	MAT.	INST.	TOTAL	MAT.	INST.	TOTAL	MAT.	INST.	TOTAL	MAT.	INST.	TOTAL	MAT.	INST.	TOTAL
015433	CONTRACTOR EQUIPMENT		118.4	118.4		103.3	103.3		103.3	103.3		106.7	106.7		105.4	105.4		105.3	105.3
0241, 31 - 34	SITE & INFRASTRUCTURE, DEMOLITION	112.1	113.0	112.7	99.0	98.9	99.0	99.7	98.9	99.2	122.5	102.7	108.6	117.7	103.7	107.9	97.2	105.0	102.7
0310	Concrete Forming & Accessories	122.8	95.7	99.5	129.2	82.9	89.3	129.2	83.0	89.4	121.4	86.3	91.1	121.4	86.5	91.3	113.1	88.6	92.0
0320	Concrete Reinforcing	150.1	98.8	124.2	152.2	74.8	113.1	144.0	74.8	109.1	112.8	78.3	95.4	169.0	88.0	128.2	104.2	98.7	101.4
0330	Cast-in-Place Concrete	118.5	103.5	112.8	108.1	92.2	102.1	112.6	92.2	104.9	97.5	96.8	97.2	122.1	97.9	112.9	113.4	99.5	108.1
03	CONCRETE	116.3	99.6	108.7	112.1	85.2	99.8	113.2	85.2	100.4	121.2	88.9	106.4	122.3	91.1	108.0	100.5	94.4	97.7
04	MASONRY	170.9	101.7	128.0	164.8	79.6	112.0	165.2	79.6	112.1	172.2	87.6	119.7	174.7	89.3	121.8	145.6	99.0	116.7
05	METALS	131.7	106.4	123.9	111.0	86.8	103.6	111.0	86.9	103.6	112.8	89.2	105.6	113.5	92.9	107.2	121.0	97.5	113.8
06	WOOD, PLASTICS & COMPOSITES	99.9	94.7	97.0	130.5	82.8	103.9	130.5	82.8	103.9	102.5	84.5	92.5	118.1	85.6	100.0	107.6	86.4	95.8
07	THERMAL & MOISTURE PROTECTION	122.0	101.6	113.4	111.9	88.3	101.9	111.9	88.3	101.9	128.2	85.8	110.3	118.4	91.6	107.1	115.0	98.8	108.2
08	OPENINGS	85.6	93.8	87.5	91.6	71.4	87.0	91.6	76.0	88.0	88.4	82.5	87.1	91.6	84.4	90.0	83.1	87.4	84.1
0920	Plaster & Gypsum Board	121.1	94.1	103.0	114.5	82.2	92.8	144.8	82.2	102.8	102.2	83.7	89.8	176.2	85.2	115.1	105.6	86.0	92.4
0950, 0980	Ceilings & Acoustic Treatment	130.0	94.1	105.8	103.2	82.2	89.0	103.2	82.2	89.0	103.2	83.7	90.0	118.5	85.2	96.1	105.1	86.0	92.2
0960	Flooring	109.7	97.8	106.4	112.1	90.9	106.2	112.1	90.9	106.2	111.0	52.0	94.6	112.1	90.9	106.2	100.1	97.8	99.4
0970, 0990	Wall Finishes & Painting/Coating	102.9	105.4	104.3	109.0	87.4	96.4	109.0	87.4	96.4	109.0	79.9	92.0	109.0	82.8	93.7	103.1	95.1	98.4
09	FINISHES	113.5	97.1	104.6	105.3	85.2	94.4	109.4	85.2	96.3	105.8	79.6	91.5	117.3	87.1	100.9	99.1	90.5	94.4
COVERS	DIVS. 10 - 14, 25, 28, 41, 43, 44, 46	131.1	93.3	122.7	131.1	78.8	119.5	131.1	78.8	119.5	131.1	87.9	121.5	131.1	67.3	116.9	131.1	90.7	122.2
21, 22, 23	FIRE SUPPRESSION, PLUMBING & HVAC	105.5	92.2	99.8	104.6	87.7	97.4	104.6	87.7	97.4	104.6	91.2	98.9	105.1	98.4	102.2	104.8	90.9	98.8
26, 27, 3370	ELECTRICAL, COMMUNICATIONS & UTIL.	108.4	102.7	105.4	112.3	68.9	89.7	111.0	68.9	89.1	114.3	78.3	95.6	111.7	86.8	98.7	110.8	100.1	105.2
MF2016	WEIGHTED AVERAGE	116.0	99.6	108.8	111.5	83.4	99.2	111.9	83.6	99.5	114.1	87.2	102.3	115.3	91.4	104.8	109.1	95.1	103.0

For customer support on your Green Building Costs with RSMeans data, call 800.448.8182.

City Cost Indexes

CANADA

DIVISION		LAVAL, QUEBEC			LETHBRIDGE, ALBERTA			LLOYDMINSTER, ALBERTA			LONDON, ONTARIO			MEDICINE HAT, ALBERTA			MONCTON, NEW BRUNSWICK		
		MAT.	INST.	TOTAL	MAT.	INST.	TOTAL	MAT.	INST.	TOTAL	MAT.	INST.	TOTAL	MAT.	INST.	TOTAL	MAT.	INST.	TOTAL
015433	CONTRACTOR EQUIPMENT		103.3	103.3		105.5	105.5		105.5	105.5		119.8	119.8		105.5	105.5		102.8	102.8
0241, 31 - 34	SITE & INFRASTRUCTURE, DEMOLITION	99.5	98.9	99.1	117.2	101.6	106.3	117.1	101.0	105.8	104.6	112.2	109.9	115.8	101.0	105.5	106.4	96.0	99.1
0310	Concrete Forming & Accessories	129.5	82.9	89.3	122.8	91.7	96.0	120.9	82.0	87.3	121.9	90.0	94.4	122.7	81.9	87.5	103.6	63.2	68.8
0320	Concrete Reinforcing	152.2	74.8	113.1	156.5	84.3	120.1	156.5	84.3	120.1	150.1	97.6	123.6	156.5	84.3	120.1	137.7	71.0	104.1
0330	Cast-in-Place Concrete	111.7	92.2	104.3	135.2	103.5	123.2	125.5	99.8	115.7	117.1	101.6	111.2	125.5	99.8	115.7	113.3	69.7	96.7
03	CONCRETE	113.8	85.2	100.7	125.1	94.8	111.2	120.3	89.1	106.0	115.6	96.2	106.7	124.0	89.0	106.1	111.5	68.0	91.6
04	MASONRY	165.1	79.6	112.1	183.2	87.3	123.7	164.1	80.9	112.5	179.6	99.9	130.2	164.1	80.9	112.5	162.1	61.4	99.7
05	METALS	110.9	86.8	103.5	134.6	92.8	121.8	112.8	92.7	106.6	131.7	107.7	124.3	113.0	92.6	106.7	113.7	85.9	105.2
06	WOOD, PLASTICS & COMPOSITES	130.6	82.8	104.0	117.6	90.9	102.7	114.2	81.2	95.8	106.2	87.7	95.9	117.6	81.2	97.3	98.4	62.6	78.4
07	THERMAL & MOISTURE PROTECTION	112.4	88.3	102.2	124.2	93.9	111.4	120.7	89.3	107.4	124.0	99.5	113.6	127.4	89.3	111.3	113.9	65.5	93.4
08	OPENINGS	91.6	71.4	87.0	91.6	83.4	89.7	91.6	78.0	88.5	80.4	88.8	82.4	91.6	78.0	88.5	86.4	61.5	80.7
0920	Plaster & Gypsum Board	114.8	82.2	92.9	106.7	90.3	95.7	102.7	80.3	87.6	123.0	86.9	98.8	105.0	80.3	88.4	126.6	61.5	82.8
0950, 0980	Ceilings & Acoustic Treatment	103.2	82.2	89.0	110.8	90.3	97.0	103.2	80.3	87.8	138.5	86.9	103.7	103.2	80.3	87.8	112.5	61.5	78.1
0960	Flooring	112.1	90.9	106.2	112.1	88.6	105.6	112.1	88.6	105.6	106.2	97.8	103.9	112.1	88.6	105.6	98.6	68.7	90.3
0970, 0990	Wall Finishes & Painting/Coating	109.0	87.4	96.4	108.9	100.8	104.2	109.1	78.5	91.3	109.3	102.0	105.0	108.9	78.5	91.2	109.7	51.4	75.8
09	FINISHES	105.3	85.2	94.4	106.8	92.4	99.0	104.9	82.6	92.7	116.2	92.3	103.2	105.0	82.6	92.8	104.7	62.9	82.0
COVERS	DIVS. 10 - 14, 25, 28, 41, 43, 44, 46	131.1	78.8	119.5	131.1	92.3	122.5	131.1	89.0	121.8	131.1	92.1	122.5	131.1	89.0	121.8	131.1	61.8	115.7
21, 22, 23	FIRE SUPPRESSION, PLUMBING & HVAC	104.8	87.7	97.5	104.9	93.8	100.2	105.1	93.7	100.2	105.5	89.4	98.6	104.6	90.5	98.6	104.6	69.9	89.8
26, 27, 3370	ELECTRICAL, COMMUNICATIONS & UTIL.	109.3	68.9	88.3	107.1	81.8	94.0	104.8	81.8	92.9	105.3	100.1	102.6	104.8	81.8	92.9	115.8	60.8	87.2
MF2016	WEIGHTED AVERAGE	111.5	83.4	99.2	118.3	91.4	106.5	112.7	88.1	101.9	115.6	97.0	107.5	112.9	87.4	101.7	111.5	69.3	93.0

CANADA

DIVISION		MONTREAL, QUEBEC			MOOSE JAW, SASKATCHEWAN			NEW GLASGOW, NOVA SCOTIA			NEWCASTLE, NEW BRUNSWICK			NORTH BAY, ONTARIO			OSHAWA, ONTARIO		
		MAT.	INST.	TOTAL	MAT.	INST.	TOTAL	MAT.	INST.	TOTAL	MAT.	INST.	TOTAL	MAT.	INST.	TOTAL	MAT.	INST.	TOTAL
015433	CONTRACTOR EQUIPMENT		123.5	123.5		101.7	101.7		102.9	102.9		102.8	102.8		103.5	103.5		105.3	105.3
0241, 31 - 34	SITE & INFRASTRUCTURE, DEMOLITION	114.0	113.5	113.6	117.1	95.1	101.7	119.1	97.7	104.1	107.0	95.7	99.1	134.5	99.6	110.0	108.3	103.9	105.2
0310	Concrete Forming & Accessories	124.4	91.6	96.1	106.3	57.2	64.0	110.5	71.2	76.6	103.6	60.8	66.7	144.3	84.0	92.3	118.5	88.7	92.8
0320	Concrete Reinforcing	126.8	94.3	110.4	110.4	63.4	86.7	176.3	49.2	112.2	137.7	59.4	98.2	207.8	87.6	147.1	165.2	93.6	129.1
0330	Cast-in-Place Concrete	130.9	99.1	118.8	121.7	67.0	100.9	132.9	70.4	109.2	117.7	59.1	95.4	128.0	84.7	111.5	131.1	87.2	114.4
03	CONCRETE	119.3	95.5	108.4	105.8	62.7	86.1	140.6	68.1	107.4	113.6	61.0	89.5	142.4	85.3	116.3	122.7	89.4	107.5
04	MASONRY	176.1	90.3	122.9	162.8	58.8	98.3	216.7	68.4	124.7	162.5	59.9	98.9	223.0	85.4	137.7	148.6	91.9	113.4
05	METALS	139.5	104.4	128.7	109.8	76.7	99.6	131.8	77.8	115.2	113.7	75.2	101.9	132.7	92.8	120.4	111.5	96.2	106.8
06	WOOD, PLASTICS & COMPOSITES	105.6	91.9	98.0	100.1	55.7	75.4	117.5	70.6	91.4	98.4	60.6	77.4	153.9	84.2	115.1	114.1	87.4	99.3
07	THERMAL & MOISTURE PROTECTION	119.2	98.2	110.3	111.3	63.0	90.9	133.2	71.0	106.9	113.9	61.3	91.6	139.8	86.8	117.4	116.0	91.1	105.4
08	OPENINGS	84.8	79.9	83.7	87.6	54.0	79.9	92.6	64.4	86.1	86.4	53.8	78.9	100.6	82.3	96.4	88.5	88.9	88.6
0920	Plaster & Gypsum Board	125.4	91.0	102.3	99.6	54.5	69.3	140.9	69.8	93.1	126.6	59.5	81.5	134.7	83.7	100.4	108.8	87.1	94.2
0950, 0980	Ceilings & Acoustic Treatment	140.4	91.0	107.1	103.2	54.5	70.3	119.2	69.8	85.9	112.5	59.5	76.7	119.2	83.7	95.3	101.7	87.1	91.8
0960	Flooring	110.0	93.1	105.3	102.4	56.7	89.7	107.3	62.3	94.8	98.6	67.1	89.9	130.3	90.9	119.4	102.9	100.3	102.2
0970, 0990	Wall Finishes & Painting/Coating	104.5	105.2	104.9	109.0	63.8	82.6	116.9	62.0	84.9	109.9	50.1	75.0	116.9	88.9	100.6	103.1	109.5	106.9
09	FINISHES	116.1	94.2	104.2	101.3	57.5	77.5	114.2	68.8	89.5	104.7	61.1	81.0	121.1	86.1	102.1	100.3	92.9	96.3
COVERS	DIVS. 10 - 14, 25, 28, 41, 43, 44, 46	131.1	83.7	120.6	131.1	59.8	115.3	131.1	63.3	116.1	131.1	60.2	115.4	131.1	66.1	116.7	131.1	90.4	122.1
21, 22, 23	FIRE SUPPRESSION, PLUMBING & HVAC	105.6	81.6	95.4	105.1	73.3	91.5	104.7	82.8	95.4	104.6	67.5	88.7	104.7	96.3	101.1	104.8	101.9	103.5
26, 27, 3370	ELECTRICAL, COMMUNICATIONS & UTIL.	108.4	85.7	96.6	113.3	59.5	85.3	109.1	62.0	84.6	111.4	59.0	84.1	109.4	87.9	98.2	111.9	90.3	100.7
MF2016	WEIGHTED AVERAGE	118.0	91.7	106.5	110.1	66.7	91.1	122.6	73.5	101.1	111.3	65.7	91.3	125.6	89.2	109.7	111.6	94.7	104.2

CANADA

DIVISION		OTTAWA, ONTARIO			OWEN SOUND, ONTARIO			PETERBOROUGH, ONTARIO			PORTAGE LA PRAIRIE, MANITOBA			PRINCE ALBERT, SASKATCHEWAN			PRINCE GEORGE, BRITISH COLUMBIA		
		MAT.	INST.	TOTAL	MAT.	INST.	TOTAL	MAT.	INST.	TOTAL	MAT.	INST.	TOTAL	MAT.	INST.	TOTAL	MAT.	INST.	TOTAL
015433	CONTRACTOR EQUIPMENT		121.6	121.6		103.0	103.0		103.1	103.1		105.4	105.4		101.7	101.7		106.7	106.7
0241, 31 - 34	SITE & INFRASTRUCTURE, DEMOLITION	108.4	114.4	112.6	119.2	99.7	105.6	119.6	99.7	105.7	118.3	98.5	104.5	112.6	95.3	100.5	126.0	102.7	109.7
0310	Concrete Forming & Accessories	122.2	90.0	94.4	124.2	82.5	88.2	123.5	85.0	90.3	122.9	68.9	76.3	106.3	57.0	63.8	111.6	81.3	85.4
0320	Concrete Reinforcing	130.3	97.6	113.8	175.3	89.7	132.1	169.0	88.1	128.2	156.5	56.3	105.9	115.3	63.3	89.1	112.8	78.3	95.4
0330	Cast-in-Place Concrete	126.9	104.4	118.4	158.9	80.6	129.2	135.8	86.2	116.9	125.5	73.4	105.7	110.3	66.9	93.8	122.2	96.8	112.5
03	CONCRETE	117.8	97.3	108.4	139.8	83.6	114.1	127.0	86.4	108.4	114.2	69.3	93.7	101.0	62.6	83.4	132.3	86.7	111.4
04	MASONRY	172.3	102.5	129.0	167.9	90.8	120.1	168.8	91.8	121.0	167.3	62.3	102.2	161.9	58.8	98.0	174.2	87.6	120.5
05	METALS	132.4	109.0	125.2	110.3	93.3	105.1	112.4	93.1	106.4	113.0	80.2	102.9	109.8	76.5	99.6	112.8	89.2	105.6
06	WOOD, PLASTICS & COMPOSITES	106.4	86.5	95.4	118.0	80.9	97.4	119.8	82.8	99.2	117.5	70.0	91.1	100.1	55.7	75.4	102.5	77.7	88.7
07	THERMAL & MOISTURE PROTECTION	130.7	100.6	118.0	113.8	87.6	102.7	118.6	92.4	107.5	111.8	71.6	94.8	111.2	61.9	90.3	122.0	85.0	106.4
08	OPENINGS	89.1	88.1	88.9	92.4	81.6	89.9	90.3	84.0	88.9	91.6	63.0	85.1	86.5	54.0	79.1	88.4	78.7	86.2
0920	Plaster & Gypsum Board	129.7	85.7	100.2	151.5	80.4	103.8	116.6	82.4	93.6	104.6	68.8	80.6	99.6	54.5	69.3	102.2	76.6	85.0
0950, 0980	Ceilings & Acoustic Treatment	134.2	85.7	101.5	95.3	80.4	85.3	103.2	82.4	89.1	103.2	68.8	80.0	103.2	54.5	70.3	103.2	76.6	85.3
0960	Flooring	102.3	93.2	99.8	118.1	92.3	110.9	112.1	90.9	106.2	112.1	65.4	99.2	102.4	56.7	89.7	107.7	71.2	97.6
0970, 0990	Wall Finishes & Painting/Coating	110.0	96.7	102.2	104.4	87.6	94.6	109.1	90.1	98.6	109.1	56.5	78.4	109.1	50.4	77.1	109.0	79.9	92.0
09	FINISHES	116.1	90.8	102.4	109.8	84.9	96.3	106.3	86.7	95.6	105.0	67.3	84.5	101.3	56.5	76.9	104.8	78.8	90.7
COVERS	DIVS. 10 - 14, 25, 28, 41, 43, 44, 46	131.1	90.7	122.1	139.2	66.4	123.0	131.1	67.5	117.0	131.1	62.3	115.8	131.1	59.8	115.3	131.1	87.2	121.4
21, 22, 23	FIRE SUPPRESSION, PLUMBING & HVAC	105.6	91.1	99.4	104.5	96.2	101.0	104.6	99.8	102.6	104.6	81.7	94.8	105.1	66.0	88.4	104.6	91.2	98.9
26, 27, 3370	ELECTRICAL, COMMUNICATIONS & UTIL.	108.5	100.9	104.5	117.6	86.7	101.5	111.4	87.5	99.0	113.0	57.0	84.1	113.3	59.5	85.3	111.4	78.3	94.2
MF2016	WEIGHTED AVERAGE	117.2	98.0	108.8	117.1	89.2	104.9	114.3	91.1	104.1	112.7	72.2	94.9	109.2	65.0	89.8	115.1	86.6	102.6

For customer support on your Green Building Costs with RSMeans data, call 800.448.8182.

City Cost Indexes

CANADA

DIVISION		QUEBEC CITY, QUEBEC			RED DEER, ALBERTA			REGINA, SASKATCHEWAN			RIMOUSKI, QUEBEC			ROUYN-NORANDA, QUEBEC			SAINT HYACINTHE, QUEBEC		
		MAT.	INST.	TOTAL	MAT.	INST.	TOTAL	MAT.	INST.	TOTAL	MAT.	INST.	TOTAL	MAT.	INST.	TOTAL	MAT.	INST.	TOTAL
015433	CONTRACTOR EQUIPMENT		124.2	124.2		105.5	105.5		124.2	124.2		103.3	103.3		103.3	103.3		103.3	103.3
0241, 31 - 34	SITE & INFRASTRUCTURE, DEMOLITION	115.4	113.3	113.9	115.8	101.0	105.5	127.4	115.0	118.7	99.3	98.5	98.8	99.0	98.9	99.0	99.5	98.9	99.1
0310	Concrete Forming & Accessories	122.5	91.7	95.9	136.9	81.9	89.5	124.8	95.6	99.6	129.2	91.0	96.3	129.2	82.9	89.3	129.2	82.9	89.3
0320	Concrete Reinforcing	129.3	94.3	111.7	156.5	84.3	120.1	147.1	91.7	119.1	108.6	94.2	101.3	152.2	74.8	113.1	152.2	74.8	113.1
0330	Cast-in-Place Concrete	132.7	98.9	119.9	125.5	99.8	115.7	144.3	100.7	127.7	113.7	97.0	107.4	108.1	92.2	102.1	111.7	92.2	104.3
03	CONCRETE	120.4	95.6	109.0	121.3	89.0	106.6	129.7	97.4	114.9	109.2	93.7	102.1	112.1	85.2	99.8	113.8	85.2	100.7
04	MASONRY	170.9	90.3	120.9	164.1	80.9	112.5	194.2	91.1	130.3	164.5	90.3	118.5	164.8	79.6	112.0	165.0	79.6	112.1
05	METALS	139.5	106.1	129.3	113.0	92.6	106.7	143.2	103.9	131.1	110.5	92.3	105.0	111.0	86.8	103.6	111.0	86.8	103.6
06	WOOD, PLASTICS & COMPOSITES	111.7	91.8	100.6	117.6	81.2	97.3	109.2	96.2	102.0	130.5	91.4	108.7	130.5	82.8	103.9	130.5	82.8	103.9
07	THERMAL & MOISTURE PROTECTION	115.8	98.4	108.4	137.7	89.3	117.2	132.7	90.0	114.7	111.9	98.0	106.0	111.9	88.3	101.9	112.2	88.3	102.1
08	OPENINGS	88.5	87.4	88.2	91.6	78.0	88.5	86.9	83.4	86.1	91.2	77.8	88.1	91.6	71.4	87.0	91.6	71.4	87.0
0920	Plaster & Gypsum Board	128.6	91.0	103.4	105.0	80.3	88.4	134.8	95.6	108.5	144.6	91.0	108.6	114.3	82.2	92.8	114.3	82.2	92.8
0950, 0980	Ceilings & Acoustic Treatment	137.2	91.0	106.1	103.2	80.3	87.8	141.5	95.6	110.6	102.3	91.0	94.7	102.3	82.2	88.8	102.3	82.2	88.8
0960	Flooring	110.8	93.1	105.9	114.5	88.6	107.3	113.4	97.8	109.1	113.4	90.9	107.2	112.1	90.9	106.2	112.1	90.9	106.2
0970, 0990	Wall Finishes & Painting/Coating	122.1	105.2	112.2	108.9	78.5	91.2	115.1	93.1	102.2	112.1	105.2	108.1	109.0	87.4	96.4	109.0	87.4	96.4
09	FINISHES	117.5	94.1	104.8	105.8	82.6	93.2	125.2	96.7	109.7	109.9	93.4	100.9	105.1	85.2	94.3	105.1	85.2	94.3
COVERS	DIVS. 10 - 14, 25, 28, 41, 43, 44, 46	131.1	83.4	120.5	131.1	89.0	121.8	131.1	71.8	117.9	131.1	82.5	120.3	131.1	78.8	119.5	131.1	78.8	119.5
21, 22, 23	FIRE SUPPRESSION, PLUMBING & HVAC	105.5	81.6	95.3	104.6	90.5	98.6	105.2	90.5	98.9	104.6	81.5	94.7	104.6	87.7	97.4	100.8	87.7	95.2
26, 27, 3370	ELECTRICAL, COMMUNICATIONS & UTIL.	109.6	85.7	97.2	104.8	81.8	92.9	111.4	96.6	103.7	111.0	85.6	97.8	111.0	68.9	89.1	111.6	68.9	89.4
MF2016	WEIGHTED AVERAGE	118.5	92.2	107.0	113.3	87.4	102.0	122.8	95.4	110.8	111.3	88.9	101.5	111.4	83.4	99.1	110.8	83.4	98.8

CANADA

DIVISION		SAINT JOHN, NEW BRUNSWICK			SARNIA, ONTARIO			SASKATOON, SASKATCHEWAN			SAULT STE MARIE, ONTARIO			SHERBROOKE, QUEBEC			SOREL, QUEBEC		
		MAT.	INST.	TOTAL	MAT.	INST.	TOTAL	MAT.	INST.	TOTAL	MAT.	INST.	TOTAL	MAT.	INST.	TOTAL	MAT.	INST.	TOTAL
015433	CONTRACTOR EQUIPMENT		102.8	102.8		103.1	103.1		101.5	101.5		103.1	103.1		103.3	103.3		103.3	103.3
0241, 31 - 34	SITE & INFRASTRUCTURE, DEMOLITION	107.1	97.4	100.3	118.2	99.8	105.3	114.1	97.9	102.7	107.9	99.4	101.9	99.5	98.9	99.1	99.7	98.9	99.2
0310	Concrete Forming & Accessories	123.5	66.3	74.1	122.2	91.9	96.1	106.0	95.1	96.6	111.8	87.9	91.2	129.2	82.9	89.3	129.2	83.0	89.4
0320	Concrete Reinforcing	137.7	71.6	104.4	120.7	89.5	104.9	117.9	91.6	104.6	108.4	88.2	98.2	152.2	74.8	113.1	144.0	74.8	109.1
0330	Cast-in-Place Concrete	115.9	71.4	99.0	125.3	99.4	115.5	119.1	98.1	111.1	112.6	84.8	102.0	111.7	92.2	104.3	112.6	92.2	104.9
03	CONCRETE	114.1	70.1	94.0	115.8	94.3	105.9	106.2	95.5	101.3	101.5	87.3	95.0	113.8	85.2	100.7	113.2	85.2	100.4
04	MASONRY	183.9	71.5	114.2	180.5	94.4	127.1	173.5	91.1	122.4	165.5	93.9	121.1	165.1	79.6	112.2	165.2	79.6	112.1
05	METALS	113.6	87.3	105.5	112.3	93.5	106.5	107.8	90.6	102.5	111.5	95.2	106.5	110.8	86.8	103.4	111.0	86.9	103.6
06	WOOD, PLASTICS & COMPOSITES	120.4	64.3	89.2	118.7	90.9	103.3	97.6	95.7	96.6	106.6	88.7	96.7	130.5	82.8	103.9	130.5	82.8	103.9
07	THERMAL & MOISTURE PROTECTION	114.2	72.4	96.5	118.7	96.0	109.1	112.3	89.2	102.5	117.4	91.2	106.3	111.9	88.3	101.9	111.9	88.3	101.9
08	OPENINGS	86.3	61.3	80.6	92.9	87.8	91.7	87.1	83.2	86.2	84.7	87.1	85.2	91.6	71.4	87.0	91.6	76.0	88.0
0920	Plaster & Gypsum Board	139.3	63.3	88.2	139.9	90.7	106.8	115.6	95.5	102.2	107.8	88.4	94.8	114.3	82.2	92.8	144.6	82.2	102.7
0950, 0980	Ceilings & Acoustic Treatment	117.6	63.3	81.0	107.4	90.7	96.1	123.5	95.5	104.7	103.2	88.4	93.2	102.3	82.2	88.8	102.3	82.2	88.8
0960	Flooring	110.1	68.7	98.6	112.1	99.5	108.6	105.0	97.8	103.0	105.2	96.4	102.7	112.1	90.9	106.2	112.1	90.9	106.2
0970, 0990	Wall Finishes & Painting/Coating	109.9	84.2	94.9	109.0	103.0	105.5	112.5	93.1	101.2	109.0	95.4	101.1	109.0	87.4	96.4	109.0	87.4	96.4
09	FINISHES	111.0	68.1	87.7	110.3	94.8	101.9	109.3	96.3	102.3	102.3	90.5	95.9	105.1	85.2	94.3	109.2	85.2	96.2
COVERS	DIVS. 10 - 14, 25, 28, 41, 43, 44, 46	131.1	63.0	116.0	131.1	68.8	117.3	131.1	71.0	117.8	131.1	89.5	121.9	131.1	78.8	119.5	131.1	78.8	119.5
21, 22, 23	FIRE SUPPRESSION, PLUMBING & HVAC	104.6	77.9	93.2	104.6	105.8	105.1	105.0	90.3	98.7	104.6	94.0	100.1	105.1	87.7	97.6	104.6	87.7	97.4
26, 27, 3370	ELECTRICAL, COMMUNICATIONS & UTIL.	118.5	86.3	101.7	114.3	89.7	101.5	112.6	96.6	104.3	113.0	87.9	100.0	111.0	68.9	89.1	111.0	68.9	89.1
MF2016	WEIGHTED AVERAGE	113.8	77.0	97.7	114.3	95.5	106.0	110.8	92.5	102.7	109.6	91.7	101.8	111.7	83.4	99.3	111.9	83.6	99.5

CANADA

DIVISION		ST CATHARINES, ONTARIO			ST JEROME, QUEBEC			ST JOHNS, NEWFOUNDLAND			SUDBURY, ONTARIO			SUMMERSIDE, PRINCE EDWARD ISLAND			SYDNEY, NOVA SCOTIA		
		MAT.	INST.	TOTAL	MAT.	INST.	TOTAL	MAT.	INST.	TOTAL	MAT.	INST.	TOTAL	MAT.	INST.	TOTAL	MAT.	INST.	TOTAL
015433	CONTRACTOR EQUIPMENT		103.1	103.1		103.3	103.3		121.7	121.7		103.1	103.1		102.9	102.9		102.9	102.9
0241, 31 - 34	SITE & INFRASTRUCTURE, DEMOLITION	97.4	101.4	100.2	99.0	98.9	99.0	121.6	111.7	114.7	97.5	101.0	99.9	129.3	95.0	105.3	114.8	97.7	102.9
0310	Concrete Forming & Accessories	111.1	94.9	97.1	129.2	82.9	89.3	122.8	88.0	92.8	107.1	89.9	92.3	110.8	55.0	62.7	110.5	71.2	76.6
0320	Concrete Reinforcing	105.1	98.7	101.9	152.2	74.8	113.1	161.2	85.0	122.8	106.0	102.5	104.3	173.8	48.0	110.3	176.3	49.2	112.2
0330	Cast-in-Place Concrete	108.3	101.4	105.6	108.1	92.2	102.1	140.6	101.1	125.6	109.1	98.0	104.9	126.2	57.7	100.1	102.5	70.4	90.4
03	CONCRETE	98.1	97.9	98.0	112.1	85.2	99.8	132.7	93.0	114.5	98.4	95.0	96.8	148.5	55.9	106.2	126.2	68.1	99.6
04	MASONRY	145.2	101.3	118.0	164.8	79.6	112.0	184.6	93.7	128.2	145.3	97.6	115.7	215.9	57.2	117.5	214.2	68.4	123.8
05	METALS	111.4	97.4	107.1	111.0	86.8	103.6	135.7	101.0	125.1	110.8	97.0	106.6	131.8	71.0	113.1	131.8	77.8	115.2
06	WOOD, PLASTICS & COMPOSITES	105.3	94.2	99.1	130.5	82.8	103.9	102.1	85.8	93.0	101.8	88.7	94.4	117.9	54.3	82.5	117.5	70.6	91.4
07	THERMAL & MOISTURE PROTECTION	115.0	103.0	109.9	111.9	88.3	101.9	139.2	98.0	121.8	114.5	97.5	107.3	132.6	60.1	101.9	133.2	71.0	106.9
08	OPENINGS	82.6	92.1	84.8	91.6	71.4	87.0	85.7	77.0	83.7	83.3	87.6	84.3	104.6	47.8	91.5	92.6	64.4	86.1
0920	Plaster & Gypsum Board	97.0	94.0	95.0	114.3	82.2	92.8	139.6	84.9	102.8	98.8	88.4	91.8	141.5	53.0	82.1	140.9	69.8	93.1
0950, 0980	Ceilings & Acoustic Treatment	101.7	94.0	96.5	102.3	82.2	88.8	129.6	84.9	99.4	96.6	88.4	91.1	119.2	53.0	74.6	119.2	69.8	85.9
0960	Flooring	98.9	94.5	97.7	112.1	90.9	106.2	111.1	54.2	95.3	97.1	96.4	96.9	107.4	58.4	93.8	107.3	62.3	94.8
0970, 0990	Wall Finishes & Painting/Coating	103.1	105.4	104.4	109.0	87.4	96.4	112.5	103.1	107.0	103.1	96.1	99.0	116.9	41.7	73.0	116.9	62.0	84.9
09	FINISHES	96.9	96.0	96.4	105.1	85.2	94.3	119.6	83.3	99.8	95.5	91.5	93.4	115.3	54.5	82.2	114.2	68.8	89.5
COVERS	DIVS. 10 - 14, 25, 28, 41, 43, 44, 46	131.1	70.5	117.7	131.1	78.8	119.5	131.1	69.7	117.5	131.1	90.8	122.2	131.1	59.4	115.2	131.1	63.3	116.1
21, 22, 23	FIRE SUPPRESSION, PLUMBING & HVAC	104.8	90.8	98.8	104.6	87.7	97.4	105.3	86.3	97.2	104.5	90.2	98.4	104.7	61.3	86.2	104.7	82.8	95.4
26, 27, 3370	ELECTRICAL, COMMUNICATIONS & UTIL.	112.4	100.9	106.4	111.7	68.9	89.4	109.3	85.9	97.1	112.5	101.3	106.7	108.2	50.0	78.0	109.1	62.0	84.6
MF2016	WEIGHTED AVERAGE	107.1	96.1	102.3	111.4	83.4	99.1	120.7	90.3	107.4	106.9	94.9	101.6	125.1	60.5	96.8	120.6	73.5	100.0

500

For customer support on your Green Building Costs with RSMeans data, call 800.448.8182.

City Cost Indexes

CANADA

DIVISION		THUNDER BAY, ONTARIO MAT.	INST.	TOTAL	TIMMINS, ONTARIO MAT.	INST.	TOTAL	TORONTO, ONTARIO MAT.	INST.	TOTAL	TROIS RIVIERES, QUEBEC MAT.	INST.	TOTAL	TRURO, NOVA SCOTIA MAT.	INST.	TOTAL	VANCOUVER, BRITISH COLUMBIA MAT.	INST.	TOTAL
015433	CONTRACTOR EQUIPMENT		103.1	103.1		103.1	103.1		121.8	121.8		103.7	103.7		102.6	102.6		137.0	137.0
0241, 31 - 34	SITE & INFRASTRUCTURE, DEMOLITION	102.2	101.3	101.6	119.6	99.3	105.4	119.5	115.3	116.6	115.2	99.2	104.0	103.9	97.5	99.4	114.7	124.5	121.6
0310	Concrete Forming & Accessories	118.4	93.2	96.6	123.5	84.0	89.4	122.8	101.0	104.0	151.9	83.1	92.5	96.8	71.2	74.7	122.6	88.8	93.5
0320	Concrete Reinforcing	94.0	98.2	96.1	169.0	87.6	127.9	150.1	100.6	125.1	176.3	74.8	125.1	144.0	49.2	96.2	123.7	93.7	108.6
0330	Cast-in-Place Concrete	119.2	100.6	112.1	135.8	84.6	116.3	116.9	113.6	115.6	106.2	92.3	100.9	141.0	70.4	114.2	125.3	93.5	113.2
03	CONCRETE	105.4	96.7	101.4	127.0	85.3	107.9	115.6	105.9	111.1	128.5	85.3	108.7	126.0	68.0	99.5	118.7	92.7	106.8
04	MASONRY	145.8	101.5	118.3	168.8	85.4	117.1	170.9	108.4	132.1	218.4	79.6	132.3	164.3	68.4	104.8	170.9	88.0	119.5
05	METALS	111.4	96.4	106.8	112.4	92.7	106.3	132.3	109.7	125.3	131.0	87.1	117.5	111.7	77.6	101.2	139.8	111.4	131.1
06	WOOD, PLASTICS & COMPOSITES	114.1	91.5	101.6	119.8	84.1	99.9	105.5	98.5	101.6	168.1	82.8	120.7	90.7	70.6	79.5	100.9	86.8	93.1
07	THERMAL & MOISTURE PROTECTION	115.3	100.2	108.9	118.6	86.8	105.1	133.0	108.0	122.4	131.7	88.3	113.3	113.2	70.9	95.3	133.0	88.3	114.1
08	OPENINGS	81.9	90.0	83.8	90.3	82.3	88.5	84.1	98.0	87.3	102.2	76.0	96.2	84.5	64.4	79.9	83.0	87.2	84.0
0920	Plaster & Gypsum Board	124.9	91.3	102.3	116.6	83.7	94.5	119.4	98.1	105.1	169.3	82.2	110.8	122.4	69.8	87.1	114.2	85.4	94.8
0950, 0980	Ceilings & Acoustic Treatment	96.6	91.3	93.0	103.2	83.7	90.0	128.1	98.1	107.9	118.3	82.2	94.0	103.2	69.8	80.6	135.5	85.4	101.7
0960	Flooring	102.9	101.2	102.4	112.1	90.9	106.2	104.5	103.7	104.3	130.3	90.4	119.4	94.7	62.3	85.7	119.7	91.9	112.0
0970, 0990	Wall Finishes & Painting/Coating	103.1	97.1	99.6	109.0	88.9	97.3	100.8	109.5	105.9	116.9	87.4	99.7	109.0	62.0	81.6	110.8	89.2	98.2
09	FINISHES	101.2	95.0	97.9	106.3	86.1	95.3	110.6	102.3	106.1	124.8	85.2	103.3	101.1	68.8	83.6	119.1	89.3	102.9
COVERS	DIVS. 10 - 14, 25, 28, 41, 43, 44, 46	131.1	70.7	117.7	131.1	66.0	116.7	131.1	95.5	123.2	131.1	78.8	119.5	131.1	63.3	116.0	131.1	92.0	122.4
21, 22, 23	FIRE SUPPRESSION, PLUMBING & HVAC	104.8	91.0	98.9	104.6	96.3	101.1	105.4	99.0	102.7	104.7	87.7	97.5	104.6	82.8	95.3	105.5	78.6	94.0
26, 27, 3370	ELECTRICAL, COMMUNICATIONS & UTIL.	110.8	99.5	104.9	113.0	87.9	100.0	106.2	103.1	104.6	109.4	68.9	88.3	110.7	62.0	85.4	107.1	83.0	94.6
MF2016	WEIGHTED AVERAGE	108.3	95.4	102.7	114.4	89.2	103.4	115.9	104.2	110.8	123.3	83.6	105.9	111.9	73.4	95.1	118.0	91.2	106.3

CANADA

DIVISION		VICTORIA, BRITISH COLUMBIA MAT.	INST.	TOTAL	WHITEHORSE, YUKON MAT.	INST.	TOTAL	WINDSOR, ONTARIO MAT.	INST.	TOTAL	WINNIPEG, MANITOBA MAT.	INST.	TOTAL	YARMOUTH, NOVA SCOTIA MAT.	INST.	TOTAL	YELLOWKNIFE, NWT MAT.	INST.	TOTAL
015433	CONTRACTOR EQUIPMENT		109.7	109.7		130.0	130.0		103.1	103.1		123.9	123.9		102.9	102.9		129.9	129.9
0241, 31 - 34	SITE & INFRASTRUCTURE, DEMOLITION	125.5	106.8	112.4	146.2	116.0	125.0	93.8	101.3	99.0	117.4	111.2	113.1	118.9	97.7	104.1	154.5	122.1	131.8
0310	Concrete Forming & Accessories	110.8	87.6	90.8	133.6	59.2	69.5	118.4	91.4	95.1	125.4	66.2	74.8	110.5	71.2	76.6	135.9	79.3	87.1
0320	Concrete Reinforcing	115.3	93.5	104.3	159.8	65.3	112.1	103.0	97.5	100.2	142.1	61.3	101.3	176.3	49.2	112.2	156.6	67.9	111.9
0330	Cast-in-Place Concrete	123.4	90.8	111.0	179.5	73.1	139.1	110.9	102.1	107.6	144.8	73.4	117.6	131.5	70.4	108.3	177.1	90.8	144.3
03	CONCRETE	134.7	90.0	114.2	155.6	67.0	115.1	99.5	96.4	98.1	129.3	69.6	102.0	139.9	68.1	107.1	154.2	82.6	121.5
04	MASONRY	176.5	88.0	121.6	250.8	60.4	132.8	145.4	100.5	117.5	185.3	66.2	111.4	216.6	68.4	124.7	244.4	71.8	137.4
05	METALS	109.0	92.3	103.9	148.5	92.5	131.3	111.4	96.9	106.9	143.2	90.0	126.8	131.8	77.8	115.2	147.4	96.0	131.6
06	WOOD, PLASTICS & COMPOSITES	101.3	86.2	92.9	123.4	57.7	86.8	114.1	89.8	100.6	107.8	67.3	85.2	117.5	70.6	91.4	129.7	80.6	102.4
07	THERMAL & MOISTURE PROTECTION	122.2	89.3	108.3	142.8	64.9	109.9	115.1	99.6	108.5	125.3	71.0	102.3	133.2	71.0	106.9	144.1	81.4	117.5
08	OPENINGS	88.6	82.6	87.2	104.4	55.6	93.2	81.7	89.5	83.5	83.9	61.0	78.7	92.6	64.4	86.1	96.5	68.8	90.1
0920	Plaster & Gypsum Board	108.8	85.4	93.1	167.4	55.6	92.3	109.8	89.5	96.2	121.9	65.4	84.0	140.9	69.8	93.1	172.4	79.2	109.8
0950, 0980	Ceilings & Acoustic Treatment	105.6	85.4	92.0	161.4	55.6	90.1	96.6	89.5	91.8	143.8	65.4	91.0	119.2	69.8	85.9	155.1	79.2	103.9
0960	Flooring	110.4	71.2	99.5	125.4	58.3	106.8	102.9	98.5	101.7	109.0	70.4	98.3	107.3	62.3	94.8	123.4	87.6	113.5
0970, 0990	Wall Finishes & Painting/Coating	112.5	89.2	98.9	119.7	56.6	82.3	103.1	98.1	100.2	107.7	54.4	76.6	116.9	62.0	84.9	118.9	79.3	95.8
09	FINISHES	108.0	85.3	95.6	142.3	58.4	96.6	98.8	93.4	95.9	119.8	66.4	90.8	114.2	68.8	89.5	138.6	80.3	106.9
COVERS	DIVS. 10 - 14, 25, 28, 41, 43, 44, 46	131.1	67.4	116.9	131.1	62.6	115.9	131.1	70.1	117.6	131.1	64.7	116.4	131.1	63.3	116.1	131.1	66.1	116.7
21, 22, 23	FIRE SUPPRESSION, PLUMBING & HVAC	104.7	76.6	92.7	105.3	74.6	92.1	104.8	90.9	98.8	105.5	65.5	88.4	104.7	82.8	95.4	105.4	92.1	99.7
26, 27, 3370	ELECTRICAL, COMMUNICATIONS & UTIL.	112.8	82.4	97.0	132.0	60.3	94.7	115.6	101.0	108.0	112.8	65.1	88.0	109.1	62.0	84.6	121.5	81.8	100.8
MF2016	WEIGHTED AVERAGE	115.3	85.7	102.3	135.9	71.3	107.6	107.6	95.2	102.2	121.3	72.0	99.7	122.5	73.5	101.1	133.4	86.2	112.7

Location Factors - Commercial

Costs shown in RSMeans cost data publications are based on national averages for materials and installation. To adjust these costs to a specific location, simply multiply the base cost by the factor and divide by 100 for that city. The data is arranged alphabetically by state and postal zip code numbers. For a city not listed, use the factor for a nearby city with similar economic characteristics.

STATE/ZIP	CITY	MAT.	INST.	TOTAL
ALABAMA				
350-352	Birmingham	95.9	71.4	85.2
354	Tuscaloosa	96.0	72.3	85.6
355	Jasper	96.5	71.2	85.5
356	Decatur	96.0	71.3	85.2
357-358	Huntsville	96.0	70.7	84.9
359	Gadsden	96.1	71.0	85.1
360-361	Montgomery	94.8	72.3	85.0
362	Anniston	94.5	68.5	83.1
363	Dothan	94.9	72.9	85.3
364	Evergreen	94.5	72.6	84.9
365-366	Mobile	95.4	70.2	84.4
367	Selma	94.6	73.6	85.4
368	Phenix City	95.4	72.7	85.4
369	Butler	94.8	72.8	85.2
ALASKA				
995-996	Anchorage	118.9	114.8	117.1
997	Fairbanks	120.1	115.3	118.0
998	Juneau	118.8	114.8	117.0
999	Ketchikan	130.8	114.8	123.8
ARIZONA				
850,853	Phoenix	99.5	74.1	88.4
851,852	Mesa/Tempe	98.2	72.5	87.0
855	Globe	99.2	72.4	87.4
856-857	Tucson	97.1	71.8	86.0
859	Show Low	99.4	72.5	87.6
860	Flagstaff	101.7	72.1	88.8
863	Prescott	99.3	72.2	87.5
864	Kingman	97.9	72.5	86.8
865	Chambers	97.9	75.0	87.9
ARKANSAS				
716	Pine Bluff	96.9	65.0	82.9
717	Camden	95.0	60.5	79.9
718	Texarkana	95.7	60.7	80.3
719	Hot Springs	94.3	62.0	80.1
720-722	Little Rock	95.3	66.6	82.7
723	West Memphis	94.2	66.6	82.1
724	Jonesboro	94.5	63.7	81.0
725	Batesville	92.6	60.8	78.7
726	Harrison	93.9	58.9	78.6
727	Fayetteville	91.5	61.6	78.5
728	Russellville	92.7	59.4	78.1
729	Fort Smith	95.0	63.1	81.0
CALIFORNIA				
900-902	Los Angeles	99.9	129.3	112.8
903-905	Inglewood	95.5	125.5	108.6
906-908	Long Beach	97.1	126.1	109.8
910-912	Pasadena	96.0	125.3	108.8
913-916	Van Nuys	99.1	125.3	110.6
917-918	Alhambra	98.0	125.9	110.2
919-921	San Diego	101.0	119.5	109.1
922	Palm Springs	97.2	123.9	108.9
923-924	San Bernardino	94.8	125.7	108.4
925	Riverside	99.0	125.6	110.7
926-927	Santa Ana	96.8	122.9	108.3
928	Anaheim	99.1	125.9	110.8
930	Oxnard	97.6	126.5	110.2
931	Santa Barbara	96.9	126.3	109.8
932-933	Bakersfield	98.3	121.3	108.3
934	San Luis Obispo	98.1	124.4	109.6
935	Mojave	95.2	121.4	106.7
936-938	Fresno	98.2	128.2	111.3
939	Salinas	98.8	134.8	114.6
940-941	San Francisco	106.3	158.5	129.1
942,956-958	Sacramento	100.0	131.6	113.8
943	Palo Alto	98.5	148.0	120.2
944	San Mateo	100.8	147.7	121.3
945	Vallejo	99.5	139.6	117.0
946	Oakland	102.5	148.9	122.8
947	Berkeley	102.5	148.9	122.8
948	Richmond	101.7	143.0	119.8
949	San Rafael	103.8	148.4	123.3
950	Santa Cruz	104.3	135.1	117.8

STATE/ZIP	CITY	MAT.	INST.	TOTAL
CALIFORNIA (CONT'D)				
951	San Jose	102.4	150.4	123.4
952	Stockton	100.5	127.7	112.4
953	Modesto	100.4	126.9	112.0
954	Santa Rosa	101.1	147.3	121.3
955	Eureka	102.4	130.0	114.4
959	Marysville	101.6	128.8	113.5
960	Redding	109.1	128.8	117.7
961	Susanville	108.8	127.0	116.8
COLORADO				
800-802	Denver	102.8	74.6	90.5
803	Boulder	98.8	75.9	88.8
804	Golden	101.0	72.6	88.6
805	Fort Collins	102.1	74.3	89.9
806	Greeley	99.3	75.1	88.7
807	Fort Morgan	99.4	71.2	87.0
808-809	Colorado Springs	101.0	73.2	88.8
810	Pueblo	101.3	68.8	87.1
811	Alamosa	103.3	69.0	88.3
812	Salida	103.0	65.8	86.7
813	Durango	103.7	65.5	87.0
814	Montrose	102.4	67.8	87.3
815	Grand Junction	105.5	73.0	91.3
816	Glenwood Springs	103.5	65.9	87.0
CONNECTICUT				
060	New Britain	97.4	117.9	106.3
061	Hartford	98.4	118.6	107.3
062	Willimantic	97.9	118.5	106.9
063	New London	94.7	118.5	105.1
064	Meriden	96.6	117.8	105.9
065	New Haven	98.9	118.9	107.6
066	Bridgeport	98.5	118.4	107.2
067	Waterbury	98.1	118.7	107.1
068	Norwalk	98.0	118.6	107.0
069	Stamford	98.1	125.5	110.1
D.C.				
200-205	Washington	101.1	87.6	95.2
DELAWARE				
197	Newark	97.9	112.4	104.3
198	Wilmington	97.6	112.5	104.1
199	Dover	98.0	112.4	104.3
FLORIDA				
320,322	Jacksonville	94.7	65.3	81.8
321	Daytona Beach	94.9	71.0	84.4
323	Tallahassee	95.6	66.2	82.7
324	Panama City	96.2	65.1	82.5
325	Pensacola	98.8	67.1	84.9
326,344	Gainesville	96.4	65.0	82.7
327-328,347	Orlando	96.8	67.0	83.8
329	Melbourne	97.6	71.2	86.0
330-332,340	Miami	95.6	64.6	82.0
333	Fort Lauderdale	95.1	66.0	82.4
334,349	West Palm Beach	94.2	64.0	81.0
335-336,346	Tampa	96.6	67.6	83.9
337	St. Petersburg	99.0	65.9	84.5
338	Lakeland	96.2	67.8	83.7
339,341	Fort Myers	95.4	65.4	82.3
342	Sarasota	98.1	67.9	84.9
GEORGIA				
300-303,399	Atlanta	98.7	75.0	88.3
304	Statesboro	98.7	66.3	84.5
305	Gainesville	97.2	67.6	84.2
306	Athens	96.6	69.1	84.5
307	Dalton	98.3	72.2	86.9
308-309	Augusta	96.8	74.2	86.9
310-312	Macon	93.8	75.1	85.6
313-314	Savannah	95.4	74.4	86.2
315	Waycross	95.3	69.5	84.0
316	Valdosta	95.1	67.3	82.9
317,398	Albany	95.0	73.4	85.5
318-319	Columbus	94.9	73.8	85.7

Location Factors - Commercial

STATE/ZIP	CITY	MAT.	INST.	TOTAL
HAWAII				
967	Hilo	116.9	116.0	116.5
968	Honolulu	121.1	116.0	118.9
STATES & POSS.				
969	Guam	139.1	53.4	101.6
IDAHO				
832	Pocatello	101.5	79.5	91.9
833	Twin Falls	102.8	77.8	91.8
834	Idaho Falls	100.0	78.5	90.6
835	Lewiston	108.2	86.3	98.6
836-837	Boise	100.5	79.8	91.4
838	Coeur d'Alene	108.1	84.7	97.8
ILLINOIS				
600-603	North Suburban	98.9	140.6	117.1
604	Joliet	98.8	142.0	117.7
605	South Suburban	98.9	140.6	117.1
606-608	Chicago	100.8	145.8	120.5
609	Kankakee	95.6	133.5	112.2
610-611	Rockford	98.2	128.3	111.4
612	Rock Island	96.4	101.9	98.8
613	La Salle	97.6	126.5	110.3
614	Galesburg	97.4	108.9	102.5
615-616	Peoria	99.3	112.2	104.9
617	Bloomington	96.8	113.0	103.9
618-619	Champaign	100.3	110.6	104.8
620-622	East St. Louis	94.4	109.4	100.9
623	Quincy	96.7	103.9	99.8
624	Effingham	95.8	108.7	101.5
625	Decatur	97.3	109.0	102.4
626-627	Springfield	97.8	108.8	102.6
628	Centralia	93.4	108.8	100.1
629	Carbondale	93.2	108.8	100.0
INDIANA				
460	Anderson	95.1	83.3	89.9
461-462	Indianapolis	98.3	83.2	91.7
463-464	Gary	96.5	110.4	102.6
465-466	South Bend	96.3	85.0	91.4
467-468	Fort Wayne	95.7	77.7	87.8
469	Kokomo	93.5	81.7	88.3
470	Lawrenceburg	92.8	79.6	87.0
471	New Albany	94.0	78.0	87.0
472	Columbus	96.3	80.8	89.5
473	Muncie	96.3	81.7	89.9
474	Bloomington	97.9	81.3	90.6
475	Washington	94.8	86.5	91.1
476-477	Evansville	95.5	85.5	91.1
478	Terre Haute	96.3	85.4	91.5
479	Lafayette	96.0	81.6	89.7
IOWA				
500-503,509	Des Moines	97.2	88.6	93.5
504	Mason City	95.8	76.0	87.1
505	Fort Dodge	95.9	73.0	85.9
506-507	Waterloo	97.2	80.2	89.7
508	Creston	96.2	82.1	90.0
510-511	Sioux City	97.9	79.2	89.7
512	Sibley	97.1	61.0	81.3
513	Spencer	98.7	62.1	82.7
514	Carroll	95.8	79.9	88.8
515	Council Bluffs	99.0	81.1	91.2
516	Shenandoah	96.4	76.5	87.7
520	Dubuque	97.3	82.8	91.0
521	Decorah	96.8	74.0	86.8
522-524	Cedar Rapids	98.2	86.5	93.1
525	Ottumwa	96.7	76.2	87.7
526	Burlington	96.0	82.3	90.0
527-528	Davenport	97.3	98.6	97.9
KANSAS				
660-662	Kansas City	98.4	99.3	98.8
664-666	Topeka	99.1	78.1	89.9
667	Fort Scott	97.3	79.1	89.3
668	Emporia	97.4	75.8	87.9
669	Belleville	99.1	69.9	86.3
670-672	Wichita	99.2	72.1	87.3
673	Independence	99.6	75.6	89.1
674	Salina	99.6	70.8	87.0
675	Hutchinson	95.0	70.5	84.3
676	Hays	99.1	71.3	86.9
677	Colby	99.8	73.5	88.3

STATE/ZIP	CITY	MAT.	INST.	TOTAL
KANSAS (CONT'D)				
678	Dodge City	100.9	72.9	88.7
679	Liberal	99.0	70.6	86.6
KENTUCKY				
400-402	Louisville	95.1	79.1	88.1
403-405	Lexington	94.8	80.3	88.5
406	Frankfort	96.0	78.5	88.3
407-409	Corbin	92.7	77.7	86.2
410	Covington	94.7	80.5	88.5
411-412	Ashland	93.5	93.4	93.5
413-414	Campton	94.7	80.2	88.3
415-416	Pikeville	95.9	81.4	89.6
417-418	Hazard	94.1	78.7	87.4
420	Paducah	92.6	84.5	89.1
421-422	Bowling Green	94.6	79.9	88.2
423	Owensboro	94.7	84.3	90.2
424	Henderson	92.4	83.0	88.3
425-426	Somerset	91.9	79.2	86.4
427	Elizabethtown	91.5	77.2	85.3
LOUISIANA				
700-701	New Orleans	98.7	68.4	85.5
703	Thibodaux	95.6	67.4	83.3
704	Hammond	93.2	65.1	80.9
705	Lafayette	94.9	70.1	84.0
706	Lake Charles	95.1	70.9	84.5
707-708	Baton Rouge	96.3	70.1	84.8
710-711	Shreveport	97.9	66.7	84.2
712	Monroe	96.7	66.9	83.7
713-714	Alexandria	96.9	68.2	84.3
MAINE				
039	Kittery	93.0	84.9	89.5
040-041	Portland	98.7	85.6	93.0
042	Lewiston	96.3	85.6	91.6
043	Augusta	98.4	79.8	90.3
044	Bangor	95.8	85.0	91.1
045	Bath	94.8	82.2	89.3
046	Machias	94.2	79.2	87.7
047	Houlton	94.4	79.2	87.8
048	Rockland	93.5	79.2	87.2
049	Waterville	94.7	79.8	88.2
MARYLAND				
206	Waldorf	97.9	85.2	92.3
207-208	College Park	97.9	86.8	93.0
209	Silver Spring	97.2	85.8	92.2
210-212	Baltimore	101.4	84.7	94.1
214	Annapolis	98.9	84.2	92.4
215	Cumberland	96.9	86.3	92.3
216	Easton	98.6	76.6	88.9
217	Hagerstown	97.2	87.7	93.0
218	Salisbury	99.0	69.8	86.2
219	Elkton	95.8	87.4	92.1
MASSACHUSETTS				
010-011	Springfield	97.8	109.0	102.7
012	Pittsfield	97.3	106.5	101.3
013	Greenfield	95.7	109.0	101.5
014	Fitchburg	94.4	120.8	105.9
015-016	Worcester	97.7	120.8	107.8
017	Framingham	93.7	127.9	108.7
018	Lowell	97.1	127.1	110.3
019	Lawrence	98.0	128.5	111.4
020-022, 024	Boston	101.2	133.1	115.2
023	Brockton	97.9	121.8	108.4
025	Buzzards Bay	92.8	119.5	104.5
026	Hyannis	95.1	119.5	105.8
027	New Bedford	97.0	119.8	107.0
MICHIGAN				
480,483	Royal Oak	94.3	100.5	97.0
481	Ann Arbor	96.2	102.4	98.9
482	Detroit	99.2	103.0	100.9
484-485	Flint	95.9	92.3	94.4
486	Saginaw	95.6	88.7	92.6
487	Bay City	95.7	88.3	92.5
488-489	Lansing	97.0	90.1	94.0
490	Battle Creek	94.8	83.7	89.9
491	Kalamazoo	95.1	82.1	89.4
492	Jackson	93.4	91.8	92.7
493,495	Grand Rapids	96.4	82.9	90.5
494	Muskegon	93.6	81.2	88.2

For customer support on your Green Building Costs with RSMeans data, call 800.448.8182.

Location Factors - Commercial

STATE/ZIP	CITY	MAT.	INST.	TOTAL
MICHIGAN (CONT'D)				
496	Traverse City	92.9	78.4	86.6
497	Gaylord	94.1	80.7	88.2
498-499	Iron Mountain	96.0	82.4	90.0
MINNESOTA				
550-551	Saint Paul	98.9	114.1	105.6
553-555	Minneapolis	100.4	113.0	105.9
556-558	Duluth	99.8	102.7	101.1
559	Rochester	98.8	100.9	99.7
560	Mankato	96.0	98.0	96.9
561	Windom	94.6	92.3	93.6
562	Willmar	94.3	97.4	95.6
563	St. Cloud	95.2	111.3	102.3
564	Brainerd	95.9	97.5	96.6
565	Detroit Lakes	97.8	92.0	95.3
566	Bemidji	97.0	96.0	96.6
567	Thief River Falls	96.6	89.2	93.4
MISSISSIPPI				
386	Clarksdale	94.7	55.2	77.4
387	Greenville	98.3	65.6	83.9
388	Tupelo	96.2	55.9	78.6
389	Greenwood	96.0	53.2	77.3
390-392	Jackson	97.3	65.3	83.3
393	Meridian	95.1	65.9	82.3
394	Laurel	96.7	56.3	79.0
395	Biloxi	96.7	65.5	83.1
396	McComb	95.0	53.7	76.9
397	Columbus	96.6	55.8	78.7
MISSOURI				
630-631	St. Louis	100.5	106.2	103.0
633	Bowling Green	98.7	95.0	97.1
634	Hannibal	97.6	93.6	95.9
635	Kirksville	101.1	88.5	95.6
636	Flat River	99.6	95.7	97.9
637	Cape Girardeau	99.1	91.5	95.8
638	Sikeston	98.0	89.1	94.1
639	Poplar Bluff	97.5	89.7	94.1
640-641	Kansas City	100.3	102.7	101.4
644-645	St. Joseph	98.9	92.8	96.2
646	Chillicothe	96.5	95.1	95.9
647	Harrisonville	95.9	102.8	98.9
648	Joplin	97.8	79.6	89.8
650-651	Jefferson City	97.8	92.5	95.5
652	Columbia	98.1	92.5	95.7
653	Sedalia	98.6	93.2	96.2
654-655	Rolla	96.2	96.9	96.5
656-658	Springfield	99.6	81.7	91.7
MONTANA				
590-591	Billings	100.0	76.4	89.6
592	Wolf Point	99.9	76.5	89.7
593	Miles City	97.8	76.7	88.6
594	Great Falls	101.3	75.3	89.9
595	Havre	98.9	75.2	88.5
596	Helena	99.6	75.3	88.9
597	Butte	99.8	75.3	89.1
598	Missoula	97.4	74.5	87.4
599	Kalispell	96.8	75.0	87.2
NEBRASKA				
680-681	Omaha	98.4	80.8	90.7
683-685	Lincoln	98.3	80.2	90.4
686	Columbus	97.3	81.4	90.3
687	Norfolk	98.8	78.6	90.0
688	Grand Island	98.5	78.4	89.7
689	Hastings	98.5	79.0	89.9
690	McCook	98.0	71.5	86.4
691	North Platte	97.8	75.2	87.9
692	Valentine	100.5	70.5	87.4
693	Alliance	100.4	71.9	87.9
NEVADA				
889-891	Las Vegas	103.1	105.2	104.0
893	Ely	101.9	94.1	98.5
894-895	Reno	101.8	85.3	94.6
897	Carson City	101.0	84.9	93.9
898	Elko	100.6	81.2	92.1
NEW HAMPSHIRE				
030	Nashua	97.7	92.6	95.5
031	Manchester	98.3	92.7	95.9

STATE/ZIP	CITY	MAT.	INST.	TOTAL
NEW HAMPSHIRE (CONT'D)				
032-033	Concord	97.9	92.4	95.5
034	Keene	94.8	79.6	88.1
035	Littleton	94.9	79.8	88.3
036	Charleston	94.3	76.3	86.4
037	Claremont	93.5	76.3	86.0
038	Portsmouth	95.1	92.4	93.9
NEW JERSEY				
070-071	Newark	99.1	137.9	116.1
072	Elizabeth	96.8	138.2	114.9
073	Jersey City	95.9	137.9	114.1
074-075	Paterson	97.4	138.2	115.3
076	Hackensack	95.5	137.9	114.0
077	Long Branch	95.0	136.2	113.1
078	Dover	95.7	138.2	114.3
079	Summit	95.8	138.2	114.3
080,083	Vineland	95.0	134.4	112.2
081	Camden	97.0	133.3	112.9
082,084	Atlantic City	95.7	134.7	112.8
085-086	Trenton	98.5	133.9	114.0
087	Point Pleasant	96.8	135.8	113.9
088-089	New Brunswick	97.4	137.8	115.1
NEW MEXICO				
870-872	Albuquerque	98.5	75.1	88.3
873	Gallup	98.9	75.1	88.5
874	Farmington	99.1	75.1	88.6
875	Santa Fe	99.1	75.1	88.6
877	Las Vegas	97.2	75.1	87.5
878	Socorro	96.8	75.1	87.3
879	Truth/Consequences	96.6	71.8	85.7
880	Las Cruces	96.4	71.7	85.6
881	Clovis	98.9	75.0	88.4
882	Roswell	100.3	75.1	89.3
883	Carrizozo	101.1	75.1	89.7
884	Tucumcari	99.5	75.0	88.8
NEW YORK				
100-102	New York	100.6	178.2	134.6
103	Staten Island	96.4	172.2	129.6
104	Bronx	94.7	173.4	129.2
105	Mount Vernon	95.1	145.6	117.2
106	White Plains	94.6	145.6	116.9
107	Yonkers	98.9	150.8	121.6
108	New Rochelle	95.5	145.5	117.4
109	Suffern	95.1	136.0	113.0
110	Queens	99.6	174.8	132.6
111	Long Island City	101.2	174.8	133.5
112	Brooklyn	101.6	172.5	132.7
113	Flushing	101.9	174.8	133.8
114	Jamaica	100.2	174.8	132.9
115,117,118	Hicksville	99.6	158.9	125.6
116	Far Rockaway	102.0	174.8	133.9
119	Riverhead	100.4	159.0	126.1
120-122	Albany	95.8	111.2	102.5
123	Schenectady	96.1	111.2	102.7
124	Kingston	100.0	131.6	113.8
125-126	Poughkeepsie	99.2	142.4	118.1
127	Monticello	98.5	130.8	112.7
128	Glens Falls	91.4	106.4	98.0
129	Plattsburgh	96.6	100.9	98.5
130-132	Syracuse	97.6	102.0	99.5
133-135	Utica	95.7	100.8	97.9
136	Watertown	97.3	100.7	98.8
137-139	Binghamton	97.2	101.7	99.2
140-142	Buffalo	101.2	111.6	105.8
143	Niagara Falls	97.6	111.9	103.9
144-146	Rochester	99.5	102.7	100.9
147	Jamestown	96.6	93.9	95.4
148-149	Elmira	96.5	103.0	99.3
NORTH CAROLINA				
270,272-274	Greensboro	98.6	68.9	85.6
271	Winston-Salem	98.4	68.7	85.4
275-276	Raleigh	96.9	68.3	84.4
277	Durham	100.2	68.9	86.5
278	Rocky Mount	96.3	68.6	84.2
279	Elizabeth City	97.2	70.4	85.5
280	Gastonia	98.4	68.7	85.4
281-282	Charlotte	98.1	68.3	85.0
283	Fayetteville	101.3	68.4	86.9
284	Wilmington	97.2	67.5	84.2
285	Kinston	95.8	68.2	83.7

504

For customer support on your Green Building Costs with RSMeans data, call 800.448.8182.

Location Factors - Commercial

STATE/ZIP	CITY	MAT.	INST.	TOTAL
NORTH CAROLINA (CONT'D)				
286	Hickory	96.1	69.3	84.4
287-288	Asheville	97.6	68.3	84.8
289	Murphy	96.9	67.5	84.0
NORTH DAKOTA				
580-581	Fargo	100.1	81.8	92.1
582	Grand Forks	100.1	79.0	90.8
583	Devils Lake	100.1	78.2	90.5
584	Jamestown	100.2	77.1	90.1
585	Bismarck	100.3	81.4	92.0
586	Dickinson	100.8	80.3	91.8
587	Minot	100.0	81.0	91.7
588	Williston	99.3	80.2	90.9
OHIO				
430-432	Columbus	98.1	83.3	91.6
433	Marion	94.4	81.6	88.8
434-436	Toledo	97.5	93.1	95.6
437-438	Zanesville	95.0	82.5	89.5
439	Steubenville	96.2	91.8	94.3
440	Lorain	98.6	86.9	93.5
441	Cleveland	98.9	93.4	96.5
442-443	Akron	99.7	88.2	94.7
444-445	Youngstown	98.9	83.3	92.1
446-447	Canton	99.1	81.0	91.1
448-449	Mansfield	96.8	82.8	90.7
450	Hamilton	96.6	79.4	89.1
451-452	Cincinnati	97.7	80.9	90.3
453-454	Dayton	96.7	77.9	88.5
455	Springfield	96.7	80.2	89.5
456	Chillicothe	96.2	86.1	91.7
457	Athens	99.1	83.7	92.4
458	Lima	99.4	81.1	91.4
OKLAHOMA				
730-731	Oklahoma City	97.7	67.2	84.4
734	Ardmore	96.7	66.7	83.6
735	Lawton	98.7	66.9	84.8
736	Clinton	97.9	66.6	84.2
737	Enid	98.3	67.0	84.6
738	Woodward	96.7	63.8	82.3
739	Guymon	97.8	63.8	82.9
740-741	Tulsa	96.0	66.4	83.0
743	Miami	92.9	65.8	81.0
744	Muskogee	95.1	65.3	82.1
745	McAlester	92.6	61.1	78.8
746	Ponca City	93.3	65.1	81.0
747	Durant	93.2	65.6	81.1
748	Shawnee	94.7	66.3	82.3
749	Poteau	92.5	65.4	80.6
OREGON				
970-972	Portland	99.4	100.8	100.0
973	Salem	100.9	98.7	100.0
974	Eugene	99.1	98.8	99.0
975	Medford	100.6	96.1	98.6
976	Klamath Falls	101.0	96.9	99.2
977	Bend	100.0	98.7	99.4
978	Pendleton	96.0	99.7	97.6
979	Vale	93.8	87.7	91.1
PENNSYLVANIA				
150-152	Pittsburgh	100.3	103.0	101.5
153	Washington	97.3	102.2	99.4
154	Uniontown	97.6	98.6	98.1
155	Bedford	98.7	92.2	95.8
156	Greensburg	98.6	99.9	99.2
157	Indiana	97.4	97.8	97.6
158	Dubois	99.1	93.5	96.7
159	Johnstown	98.7	94.7	96.9
160	Butler	91.4	101.5	95.8
161	New Castle	91.5	100.9	95.6
162	Kittanning	91.9	101.2	95.9
163	Oil City	91.3	99.6	95.0
164-165	Erie	93.1	96.8	94.7
166	Altoona	93.2	95.1	94.0
167	Bradford	94.8	100.2	97.2
168	State College	94.4	96.5	95.3
169	Wellsboro	95.5	94.7	95.1
170-171	Harrisburg	97.3	95.2	96.3
172	Chambersburg	94.4	90.8	92.8
173-174	York	94.4	94.5	94.4
175-176	Lancaster	93.2	96.4	94.6

STATE/ZIP	CITY	MAT.	INST.	TOTAL
PENNSYLVANIA (CONT'D)				
177	Williamsport	91.9	92.8	92.3
178	Sunbury	93.9	95.1	94.4
179	Pottsville	93.0	97.9	95.1
180	Lehigh Valley	94.9	117.4	104.7
181	Allentown	96.5	107.7	101.4
182	Hazleton	94.4	96.8	95.4
183	Stroudsburg	94.3	110.4	101.3
184-185	Scranton	97.2	100.0	98.4
186-187	Wilkes-Barre	94.1	98.9	96.2
188	Montrose	93.8	99.5	96.3
189	Doylestown	94.0	123.5	106.9
190-191	Philadelphia	99.7	134.6	115.0
193	Westchester	95.5	123.7	107.8
194	Norristown	94.5	127.6	109.0
195-196	Reading	96.1	105.2	100.1
PUERTO RICO				
009	San Juan	120.7	27.7	79.9
RHODE ISLAND				
028	Newport	96.3	112.0	103.2
029	Providence	98.1	112.0	104.2
SOUTH CAROLINA				
290-292	Columbia	96.9	69.1	84.7
293	Spartanburg	97.3	68.9	84.9
294	Charleston	98.9	68.8	85.7
295	Florence	97.0	69.0	84.8
296	Greenville	97.1	68.9	84.8
297	Rock Hill	97.1	68.3	84.5
298	Aiken	98.0	69.2	85.4
299	Beaufort	98.7	56.8	80.3
SOUTH DAKOTA				
570-571	Sioux Falls	98.5	76.4	88.8
572	Watertown	98.7	57.6	80.7
573	Mitchell	97.5	63.1	82.4
574	Aberdeen	99.7	64.5	84.3
575	Pierre	100.4	70.5	87.3
576	Mobridge	98.2	65.0	83.7
577	Rapid City	99.5	74.4	88.5
TENNESSEE				
370-372	Nashville	96.7	71.7	85.8
373-374	Chattanooga	98.6	70.3	86.2
375,380-381	Memphis	98.4	70.7	86.3
376	Johnson City	98.8	60.3	82.0
377-379	Knoxville	95.3	66.2	82.5
382	McKenzie	95.8	56.8	78.7
383	Jackson	97.1	60.6	81.1
384	Columbia	94.2	68.4	82.9
385	Cookeville	95.6	57.7	79.0
TEXAS				
750	McKinney	98.4	65.2	83.9
751	Waxahachie	98.5	64.3	83.5
752-753	Dallas	99.2	67.6	85.4
754	Greenville	98.6	65.2	84.0
755	Texarkana	97.9	64.4	83.2
756	Longview	98.9	62.8	83.1
757	Tyler	98.9	64.2	83.7
758	Palestine	95.0	62.7	80.9
759	Lufkin	95.7	64.9	82.2
760-761	Fort Worth	96.6	65.1	82.8
762	Denton	96.8	65.3	83.0
763	Wichita Falls	94.2	63.3	80.7
764	Eastland	93.6	61.8	79.7
765	Temple	91.9	60.4	78.1
766-767	Waco	93.6	64.4	80.8
768	Brownwood	96.9	60.2	80.8
769	San Angelo	96.4	60.7	80.8
770-772	Houston	98.3	68.0	85.0
773	Huntsville	97.4	65.1	83.3
774	Wharton	98.2	66.2	84.2
775	Galveston	96.2	69.0	84.3
776-777	Beaumont	96.5	68.0	84.0
778	Bryan	94.0	67.3	82.3
779	Victoria	98.3	64.9	83.7
780	Laredo	96.1	63.5	81.8
781-782	San Antonio	97.8	64.4	83.2
783-784	Corpus Christi	98.7	62.4	82.8
785	McAllen	99.6	58.6	81.7
786-787	Austin	96.7	62.7	81.8

For customer support on your Green Building Costs with RSMeans data, call 800.448.8182.

Location Factors - Commercial

STATE/ZIP	CITY	MAT.	INST.	TOTAL
TEXAS (CONT'D)				
788	Del Rio	99.5	62.9	83.4
789	Giddings	96.1	62.6	81.4
790-791	Amarillo	97.6	62.2	82.1
792	Childress	97.6	62.7	82.3
793-794	Lubbock	99.3	63.4	83.6
795-796	Abilene	97.7	62.6	82.3
797	Midland	100.0	64.8	84.6
798-799,885	El Paso	96.0	64.7	82.3
UTAH				
840-841	Salt Lake City	102.8	72.9	89.7
842,844	Ogden	98.2	72.9	87.2
843	Logan	100.2	72.9	88.3
845	Price	100.8	71.7	88.1
846-847	Provo	100.6	72.8	88.5
VERMONT				
050	White River Jct.	97.7	81.6	90.7
051	Bellows Falls	96.0	95.3	95.7
052	Bennington	96.5	91.6	94.3
053	Brattleboro	96.9	95.3	96.2
054	Burlington	101.0	80.9	92.2
056	Montpelier	99.8	85.9	93.7
057	Rutland	98.1	80.9	90.6
058	St. Johnsbury	97.8	81.5	90.7
059	Guildhall	96.4	81.1	89.7
VIRGINIA				
220-221	Fairfax	100.0	83.8	92.9
222	Arlington	100.7	84.5	93.7
223	Alexandria	99.8	84.7	93.2
224-225	Fredericksburg	98.7	82.2	91.5
226	Winchester	99.3	82.9	92.2
227	Culpeper	99.1	80.5	91.0
228	Harrisonburg	99.5	67.3	85.4
229	Charlottesville	99.8	69.3	86.5
230-232	Richmond	98.5	77.9	89.5
233-235	Norfolk	98.5	71.3	86.6
236	Newport News	98.2	70.4	86.0
237	Portsmouth	97.7	64.3	83.1
238	Petersburg	98.3	73.9	87.6
239	Farmville	97.4	58.6	80.4
240-241	Roanoke	100.3	73.0	88.3
242	Bristol	98.6	60.5	82.0
243	Pulaski	98.2	62.7	82.7
244	Staunton	99.0	65.8	84.5
245	Lynchburg	99.2	75.2	88.7
246	Grundy	98.5	56.0	79.9
WASHINGTON				
980-981,987	Seattle	103.6	107.3	105.2
982	Everett	102.0	102.4	102.2
983-984	Tacoma	102.4	102.3	102.3
985	Olympia	100.7	102.3	101.4
986	Vancouver	103.3	97.2	100.6
988	Wenatchee	102.6	89.5	96.9
989	Yakima	102.5	98.2	100.6
990-992	Spokane	101.4	85.0	94.2
993	Richland	101.1	92.7	97.4
994	Clarkston	100.6	83.4	93.1
WEST VIRGINIA				
247-248	Bluefield	97.5	89.6	94.0
249	Lewisburg	99.1	88.9	94.6
250-253	Charleston	97.9	93.3	95.9
254	Martinsburg	98.8	84.4	92.5
255-257	Huntington	99.7	93.8	97.1
258-259	Beckley	97.3	91.8	94.8
260	Wheeling	100.0	91.9	96.5
261	Parkersburg	98.8	89.5	94.8
262	Buckhannon	98.8	91.5	95.6
263-264	Clarksburg	99.4	91.6	96.0
265	Morgantown	99.4	91.6	96.0
266	Gassaway	98.8	89.9	94.9
267	Romney	98.6	86.4	93.3
268	Petersburg	98.5	85.0	92.6
WISCONSIN				
530,532	Milwaukee	99.3	106.6	102.5
531	Kenosha	98.4	105.0	101.3
534	Racine	97.8	106.2	101.5
535	Beloit	97.7	98.6	98.1
537	Madison	98.0	98.9	98.4

STATE/ZIP	CITY	MAT.	INST.	TOTAL
WISCONSIN (CONT'D)				
538	Lancaster	96.0	93.9	95.1
539	Portage	94.4	96.6	95.4
540	New Richmond	95.6	92.7	94.3
541-543	Green Bay	99.6	96.5	98.2
544	Wausau	95.0	94.5	94.8
545	Rhinelander	98.3	90.1	94.7
546	La Crosse	95.9	96.9	96.4
547	Eau Claire	97.6	97.3	97.5
548	Superior	95.4	97.1	96.1
549	Oshkosh	95.7	89.2	92.9
WYOMING				
820	Cheyenne	101.3	73.5	89.2
821	Yellowstone Nat'l Park	99.4	74.4	88.4
822	Wheatland	100.6	69.2	86.9
823	Rawlins	102.1	73.5	89.6
824	Worland	100.1	73.0	88.2
825	Riverton	101.2	70.7	87.8
826	Casper	101.4	70.3	87.8
827	Newcastle	99.9	73.1	88.2
828	Sheridan	102.8	71.5	89.1
829-831	Rock Springs	103.9	72.7	90.2
CANADIAN FACTORS (reflect Canadian currency)				
ALBERTA				
	Calgary	119.5	98.8	110.4
	Edmonton	120.4	98.8	110.9
	Fort McMurray	123.4	91.9	109.7
	Lethbridge	118.3	91.4	106.5
	Lloydminster	112.7	88.1	101.9
	Medicine Hat	112.9	87.4	101.7
	Red Deer	113.3	87.4	102.0
BRITISH COLUMBIA				
	Kamloops	114.1	87.2	102.3
	Prince George	115.1	86.6	102.6
	Vancouver	118.0	91.2	106.3
	Victoria	115.3	85.7	102.3
MANITOBA				
	Brandon	123.6	73.8	101.8
	Portage la Prairie	112.7	72.2	94.9
	Winnipeg	121.3	72.0	99.7
NEW BRUNSWICK				
	Bathurst	111.3	65.0	91.0
	Dalhousie	111.3	65.2	91.1
	Fredericton	118.2	72.5	98.2
	Moncton	111.5	69.3	93.0
	Newcastle	111.3	65.7	91.3
	St. John	113.8	77.0	97.7
NEWFOUNDLAND				
	Corner Brook	128.0	71.5	103.3
	St. Johns	120.7	90.3	107.4
NORTHWEST TERRITORIES				
	Yellowknife	133.4	86.2	112.7
NOVA SCOTIA				
	Bridgewater	112.3	73.4	95.3
	Dartmouth	124.6	73.5	102.2
	Halifax	117.4	87.2	104.2
	New Glasgow	122.6	73.5	101.1
	Sydney	120.6	73.5	100.0
	Truro	111.9	73.4	95.1
	Yarmouth	122.5	73.5	101.1
ONTARIO				
	Barrie	117.0	91.0	105.6
	Brantford	114.3	94.9	105.8
	Cornwall	114.2	91.3	104.2
	Hamilton	116.0	99.6	108.8
	Kingston	115.3	91.4	104.8
	Kitchener	109.1	95.1	103.0
	London	115.6	97.0	107.5
	North Bay	125.6	89.2	109.7
	Oshawa	111.6	94.7	104.2
	Ottawa	117.2	98.0	108.8
	Owen Sound	117.1	89.2	104.9
	Peterborough	114.3	91.1	104.1
	Sarnia	114.3	95.5	106.0
ONTARIO (CONT'D)				

For customer support on your Green Building Costs with RSMeans data, call 800.448.8182.

Location Factors - Commercial

STATE/ZIP	CITY	MAT.	INST.	TOTAL
	Sault Ste. Marie	109.6	91.7	101.8
	St. Catharines	107.1	96.1	102.3
	Sudbury	106.9	94.9	101.6
	Thunder Bay	108.3	95.4	102.7
	Timmins	114.4	89.2	103.4
	Toronto	115.9	104.2	110.8
	Windsor	107.6	95.2	102.2
PRINCE EDWARD ISLAND				
	Charlottetown	120.9	62.8	95.5
	Summerside	125.1	60.5	96.8
QUEBEC				
	Cap-de-la-Madeleine	111.7	83.6	99.4
	Charlesbourg	111.7	83.6	99.4
	Chicoutimi	111.1	88.9	101.4
	Gatineau	111.4	83.4	99.1
	Granby	111.6	83.3	99.2
	Hull	111.5	83.4	99.2
	Joliette	111.9	83.6	99.5
	Laval	111.5	83.4	99.2
	Montreal	118.0	91.7	106.5
	Quebec City	118.5	92.2	107.0
	Rimouski	111.3	88.9	101.5
	Rouyn-Noranda	111.4	83.4	99.1
	Saint-Hyacinthe	110.8	83.4	98.8
	Sherbrooke	111.7	83.4	99.3
	Sorel	111.9	83.6	99.5
	Saint-Jerome	111.4	83.4	99.1
	Trois-Rivieres	123.3	83.6	105.9
SASKATCHEWAN				
	Moose Jaw	110.1	66.7	91.1
	Prince Albert	109.2	65.0	89.8
	Regina	122.8	95.4	110.8
	Saskatoon	110.8	92.5	102.7
YUKON				
	Whitehorse	135.9	71.3	107.6

General Requirements   R0111 Summary of Work

R011105-05 Tips for Accurate Estimating

1. Use pre-printed or columnar forms for orderly sequence of dimensions and locations and for recording telephone quotations.
2. Use only the front side of each paper or form except for certain pre-printed summary forms.
3. Be consistent in listing dimensions: For example, length x width x height. This helps in rechecking to ensure that, the total length of partitions is appropriate for the building area.
4. Use printed (rather than measured) dimensions where given.
5. Add up multiple printed dimensions for a single entry where possible.
6. Measure all other dimensions carefully.
7. Use each set of dimensions to calculate multiple related quantities.
8. Convert foot and inch measurements to decimal feet when listing. Memorize decimal equivalents to .01 parts of a foot (1/8″ equals approximately .01′).
9. Do not "round off" quantities until the final summary.
10. Mark drawings with different colors as items are taken off.
11. Keep similar items together, different items separate.
12. Identify location and drawing numbers to aid in future checking for completeness.
13. Measure or list everything on the drawings or mentioned in the specifications.
14. It may be necessary to list items not called for to make the job complete.
15. Be alert for: Notes on plans such as N.T.S. (not to scale); changes in scale throughout the drawings; reduced size drawings; discrepancies between the specifications and the drawings.
16. Develop a consistent pattern of performing an estimate. For example:
    a. Start the quantity takeoff at the lower floor and move to the next higher floor.
    b. Proceed from the main section of the building to the wings.
    c. Proceed from south to north or vice versa, clockwise or counterclockwise.
    d. Take off floor plan quantities first, elevations next, then detail drawings.
17. List all gross dimensions that can be either used again for different quantities, or used as a rough check of other quantities for verification (exterior perimeter, gross floor area, individual floor areas, etc.).
18. Utilize design symmetry or repetition (repetitive floors, repetitive wings, symmetrical design around a center line, similar room layouts, etc.). Note: Extreme caution is needed here so as not to omit or duplicate an area.
19. Do not convert units until the final total is obtained. For instance, when estimating concrete work, keep all units to the nearest cubic foot, then summarize and convert to cubic yards.
20. When figuring alternatives, it is best to total all items involved in the basic system, then total all items involved in the alternates. Therefore you work with positive numbers in all cases. When adds and deducts are used, it is often confusing whether to add or subtract a portion of an item; especially on a complicated or involved alternate.

R011110-10 Architectural Fees

Tabulated below are typical percentage fees by project size, for good professional architectural service. Fees may vary from those listed depending upon degree of design difficulty and economic conditions in any particular area.

Rates can be interpolated horizontally and vertically. Various portions of the same project requiring different rates should be adjusted proportionately. For alterations, add 50% to the fee for the first $500,000 of project cost and add 25% to the fee for project cost over $500,000.

Architectural fees tabulated below include Structural, Mechanical and Electrical Engineering Fees. They do not include the fees for special consultants such as kitchen planning, security, acoustical, interior design, etc.

Civil Engineering fees are included in the Architectural fee for project sites requiring minimal design such as city sites. However, separate Civil Engineering fees must be added when utility connections require design, drainage calculations are needed, stepped foundations are required, or provisions are required to protect adjacent wetlands.

Building Types	100	250	500	1,000	5,000	10,000	50,000
Factories, garages, warehouses, repetitive housing	9.0%	8.0%	7.0%	6.2%	5.3%	4.9%	4.5%
Apartments, banks, schools, libraries, offices, municipal buildings	12.2	12.3	9.2	8.0	7.0	6.6	6.2
Churches, hospitals, homes, laboratories, museums, research	15.0	13.6	12.7	11.9	9.5	8.8	8.0
Memorials, monumental work, decorative furnishings	—	16.0	14.5	13.1	10.0	9.0	8.3

Total Project Size in Thousands of Dollars

General Requirements — R0111 Summary of Work

R011110-30   Engineering Fees

Typical **Structural Engineering Fees** based on type of construction and total project size. These fees are included in Architectural Fees.

Type of Construction	Total Project Size (in thousands of dollars)			
	$500	$500-$1,000	$1,000-$5,000	Over $5000
Industrial buildings, factories & warehouses	Technical payroll times 2.0 to 2.5	1.60%	1.25%	1.00%
Hotels, apartments, offices, dormitories, hospitals, public buildings, food stores		2.00%	1.70%	1.20%
Museums, banks, churches and cathedrals		2.00%	1.75%	1.25%
Thin shells, prestressed concrete, earthquake resistive		2.00%	1.75%	1.50%
Parking ramps, auditoriums, stadiums, convention halls, hangars & boiler houses		2.50%	2.00%	1.75%
Special buildings, major alterations, underpinning & future expansion	↓	Add to above 0.5%	Add to above 0.5%	Add to above 0.5%

For complex reinforced concrete or unusually complicated structures, add 20% to 50%.

Typical **Mechanical and Electrical Engineering Fees** are based on the size of the subcontract. The fee structure for both is shown below. These fees are included in Architectural Fees.

Type of Construction	Subcontract Size							
	$25,000	$50,000	$100,000	$225,000	$350,000	$500,000	$750,000	$1,000,000
Simple structures	6.4%	5.7%	4.8%	4.5%	4.4%	4.3%	4.2%	4.1%
Intermediate structures	8.0	7.3	6.5	5.6	5.1	5.0	4.9	4.8
Complex structures	10.1	9.0	9.0	8.0	7.5	7.5	7.0	7.0

For renovations, add 15% to 25% to applicable fee.

R011110-80   Green Globes New Construction Checklist

Points Score	Areas and Sub-Areas of Assessment
50	1 – Project Management Policies and Practices
115	2 – Site
390	3 – Energy
110	4 – Water
125	5 – Resources, Building Materials and Solid Waste
50	6 – Emissions, Effluents and Other Impact
160	7 – Indoor Environment
1000 Total Points Available	

"Green Globes New Construction Criteria and Point Allocation." *Green Building Initiative.* Green Building Initiative, n.d. Web. 31 Dec. 2013.

General Requirements — R0111 Summary of Work

R011110-90 Green Globes Continual Improvement of Existing Buildings Checklist

Points Score	Areas and Sub-Areas of Assessment
350	**1 – Energy**
80	1.1 – Energy consumption
130	1.2 – Energy efficiency features *(lighting, boilers, controls, hot water, envelope, green energy)*
80	1.3 – Energy management *(energy policy, audits, monitoring and targets, energy training, financial resources, sub-metering, operating manual, maintenance schedules)*
60	1.4 – Transportation *(public transportation, cycling facilities, car-pooling)*
80	**2 – Water**
80	2.1 – Water efficiency *(water consumption, water saving features, landscaping and irrigation, management)*
110	**3 – Resources**
55	3.1 – Waste reduction and recycling *(facilities, waste reduction workplan)*
55	3.2 – Site *(environmental site assessments, remediation and ecological enhancement)*
175	**4 – Emissions, Effluents and Pollution Control**
30	4.1 – Air emissions *(low emission burners, management)*
45	4.2 – Ozone depletion *(refrigerants, management of refrigerants, halons)*
20	4.3 – Water effluents *(floor drains, roof drains, management)*
47	4.4 – Hazardous materials *(asbestos, radon, PCBs, storage tanks, drinking water)*
33	4.5 – Hazardous products and HCS *(HCS, health and safety, management, pesticides)*
185	**5 – Indoor Environment**
143	5.1 – Indoor air quality *(ventilation, filtration, humidification, cooling towers, parking and receiving, pollution at source, IAQ management)*
32	5.2 – Lighting *(features, management)*
10	5.3 – Noise *(volume, acoustic privacy)*
100	**6 – Environmental Management System**
30	6.1 – Environmental Management System (EMS) documentation *(policy, goals, targets, action plans)*
25	6.2 – Environmental purchasing *(including energy efficient products)*
20	6.3 – Emergency response *(procedures, legislation, contingency plan)*
25	6.4 – Tenant awareness *(communication strategies, tenant satisfaction)*

1000 Total Points Available

"Green Globes CIEB Criteria and Point Allocation." *Green Building Initiative.* Green Building Initiative, n.d. Web. 31 Dec. 2013.

General Requirements — R0121 Allowances

R012153-60 Security Factors

Contractors entering, working in, and exiting secure facilities often lose productive time during a normal workday. The recommended allowances in this section are intended to provide for the loss of productivity by increasing labor costs. Note that different costs are associated with searches upon entry only and searches upon entry and exit. Time spent in a queue is unpredictable and not part of these allowances. Contractors should plan ahead for this situation.

Security checkpoints are designed to reflect the level of security required to gain access or egress. An extreme example is when contractors, along with any materials, tools, equipment, and vehicles, must be physically searched and have all materials, tools, equipment, and vehicles inventoried and documented prior to both entry and exit.

Physical searches without going through the documentation process represent the next level and take up less time.

Electronic searches—passing through a detector or x-ray machine with no documentation of materials, tools, equipment, and vehicles—take less time than physical searches.

Visual searches of materials, tools, equipment, and vehicles represent the next level of security.

Finally, access by means of an ID card or displayed sticker takes the least amount of time.

Another consideration is if the searches described above are performed each and every day, or if they are performed only on the first day with access granted by ID card or displayed sticker for the remainder of the project. The figures for this situation have been calculated to represent the initial check-in as described and subsequent entry by ID card or displayed sticker for up to 20 days on site. For the situation described above, where the time period is beyond 20 days, the impact on labor cost is negligible.

There are situations where tradespeople must be accompanied by an escort and observed during the work day. The loss of freedom of movement will slow down productivity for the tradesperson. Costs for the observer have not been included. Those costs are normally born by the owner.

General Requirements — R0129 Payment Procedures

R012909-80 Sales Tax by State

State sales tax on materials is tabulated below (5 states have no sales tax). Many states allow local jurisdictions, such as a county or city, to levy additional sales tax.

Some projects may be sales tax exempt, particularly those constructed with public funds.

State	Tax (%)	State	Tax (%)	State	Tax (%)	State	Tax (%)
Alabama	4	Illinois	6.25	Montana	0	Rhode Island	7
Alaska	0	Indiana	7	Nebraska	5.5	South Carolina	6
Arizona	5.6	Iowa	6	Nevada	6.85	South Dakota	5
Arkansas	6.5	Kansas	6.5	New Hampshire	0	Tennessee	7
California	7.25	Kentucky	6	New Jersey	7	Texas	6.25
Colorado	2.9	Louisiana	4	New Mexico	5.125	Utah	5.95
Connecticut	6.35	Maine	5.5	New York	4	Vermont	6
Delaware	0	Maryland	6	North Carolina	4.75	Virginia	5.3
District of Columbia	5.75	Massachusetts	6.25	North Dakota	5	Washington	6.5
Florida	6	Michigan	6	Ohio	5.75	West Virginia	6
Georgia	4	Minnesota	6.875	Oklahoma	4.5	Wisconsin	5
Hawaii	4	Mississippi	7	Oregon	0	Wyoming	4
Idaho	6	Missouri	4.225	Pennsylvania	6	Average	5.11 %

Sales Tax by Province (Canada)

GST - a value-added tax, which the government imposes on most goods and services provided in or imported into Canada. PST - a retail sales tax, which five of the provinces impose on the prices of most goods and some services. QST - a value-added tax, similar to the federal GST, which Quebec imposes. HST - Three provinces have combined their retail sales taxes with the federal GST into one harmonized tax.

Province	PST (%)	QST (%)	GST (%)	HST (%)
Alberta	0	0	5	0
British Columbia	7	0	5	0
Manitoba	8	0	5	0
New Brunswick	0	0	0	15
Newfoundland	0	0	0	15
Northwest Territories	0	0	5	0
Nova Scotia	0	0	0	15
Ontario	0	0	0	13
Prince Edward Island	0	0	0	15
Quebec	0	9.975	5	0
Saskatchewan	6	0	5	0
Yukon	0	0	5	0

General Requirements — R0129 Payment Procedures

R012909-85 Unemployment Taxes and Social Security Taxes

State unemployment tax rates vary not only from state to state, but also with the experience rating of the contractor. The federal unemployment tax rate is 6.0% of the first $7,000 of wages. This is reduced by a credit of up to 5.4% for timely payment to the state. The minimum federal unemployment tax is 0.6% after all credits.

Social security (FICA) for 2018 is estimated at time of publication to be 7.65% of wages up to $127,200.

R012909-86 Unemployment Tax by State

Information is from the U.S. Department of Labor, state unemployment tax rates.

State	Tax (%)	State	Tax (%)	State	Tax (%)	State	Tax (%)
Alabama	6.74	Illinois	7.75	Montana	6.12	Rhode Island	9.79
Alaska	5.4	Indiana	7.474	Nebraska	5.4	South Carolina	5.46
Arizona	8.91	Iowa	8	Nevada	5.4	South Dakota	9.5
Arkansas	6.0	Kansas	7.6	New Hampshire	7.5	Tennessee	10.0
California	6.2	Kentucky	10.0	New Jersey	5.8	Texas	7.5
Colorado	8.9	Louisiana	6.2	New Mexico	5.4	Utah	7.2
Connecticut	6.8	Maine	5.4	New York	8.5	Vermont	8.4
Delaware	8.0	Maryland	7.50	North Carolina	5.76	Virginia	6.27
District of Columbia	7	Massachusetts	11.13	North Dakota	10.72	Washington	5.7
Florida	5.4	Michigan	10.3	Ohio	8.7	West Virginia	7.5
Georgia	5.4	Minnesota	9.0	Oklahoma	5.5	Wisconsin	12.0
Hawaii	5.6	Mississippi	5.4	Oregon	5.4	Wyoming	8.8
Idaho	5.4	Missouri	9.75	Pennsylvania	10.89	Median	7.47%

R012909-90 Overtime

One way to improve the completion date of a project or eliminate negative float from a schedule is to compress activity duration times. This can be achieved by increasing the crew size or working overtime with the proposed crew.

To determine the costs of working overtime to compress activity duration times, consider the following examples. Below is an overtime efficiency and cost chart based on a five, six, or seven day week with an eight through twelve hour day. Payroll percentage increases for time and one half and double times are shown for the various working days.

Days per Week	Hours per Day	1st Week	2nd Week	3rd Week	4th Week	Average 4 Weeks	@ 1-1/2 Times	@ 2 Times
5	8	100%	100%	100%	100%	100%	1.000	1.000
5	9	100	100	95	90	96	1.056	1.111
5	10	100	95	90	85	93	1.100	1.200
5	11	95	90	75	65	81	1.136	1.273
5	12	90	85	70	60	76	1.167	1.333
6	8	100	100	95	90	96	1.083	1.167
6	9	100	95	90	85	93	1.130	1.259
6	10	95	90	85	80	88	1.167	1.333
6	11	95	85	70	65	79	1.197	1.394
6	12	90	80	65	60	74	1.222	1.444
7	8	100	95	85	75	89	1.143	1.286
7	9	95	90	80	70	84	1.183	1.365
7	10	90	85	75	65	79	1.214	1.429
7	11	85	80	65	60	73	1.240	1.481
7	12	85	75	60	55	69	1.262	1.524

General Requirements — R0131 Project Management & Coordination

R013113-40 Builder's Risk Insurance

Builder's risk insurance is insurance on a building during construction. Premiums are paid by the owner or the contractor. Blasting, collapse and underground insurance would raise total insurance costs.

General Requirements — R0131 Project Management & Coordination

R013113-50 General Contractor's Overhead

There are two distinct types of overhead on a construction project: Project Overhead and Main Office Overhead. Project Overhead includes those costs at a construction site not directly associated with the installation of construction materials. Examples of Project Overhead costs include the following:
1. Superintendent
2. Construction office and storage trailers
3. Temporary sanitary facilities
4. Temporary utilities
5. Security fencing
6. Photographs
7. Clean up
8. Performance and payment bonds

The above Project Overhead items are also referred to as General Requirements and therefore are estimated in Division 1. Division 1 is the first division listed in the CSI MasterFormat but it is usually the last division estimated. The sum of the costs in Divisions 1 through 49 is referred to as the sum of the direct costs.

All construction projects also include indirect costs. The primary components of indirect costs are the contractor's Main Office Overhead and profit. The amount of the Main Office Overhead expense varies depending on the following:
1. Owner's compensation
2. Project managers and estimator's wages
3. Clerical support wages
4. Office rent and utilities
5. Corporate legal and accounting costs
6. Advertising
7. Automobile expenses
8. Association dues
9. Travel and entertainment expenses

These costs are usually calculated as a percentage of annual sales volume. This percentage can range from 35% for a small contractor doing less than $500,000 to 5% for a large contractor with sales in excess of $100 million.

R013113-55 Installing Contractor's Overhead

Installing contractors (subcontractors) also incur costs for general requirements and main office overhead.

Included within the total incl. overhead and profit costs is a percent mark-up for overhead that includes:
1. Compensation and benefits for office staff and project managers
2. Office rent, utilities, business equipment, and maintenance
3. Corporate legal and accounting costs
4. Advertising
5. Vehicle expenses (for office staff and project managers)
6. Association dues
7. Travel, entertainment
8. Insurance
9. Small tools and equipment

General Requirements — R0131 Project Management & Coordination

R013113-60 Workers' Compensation Insurance Rates by Trade

The table below tabulates the national averages for workers' compensation insurance rates by trade and type of building. The average "Insurance Rate" is multiplied by the "% of Building Cost" for each trade. This produces the "Workers' Compensation" cost by % of total labor cost, to be added for each trade by building type to determine the weighted average workers' compensation rate for the building types analyzed.

Trade	Insurance Rate (% Labor Cost) Range	Insurance Rate Average	% Building Cost Office Bldgs.	% Building Cost Schools & Apts.	% Building Cost Mfg.	Workers' Comp Office Bldgs.	Workers' Comp Schools & Apts.	Workers' Comp Mfg.
Excavation, Grading, etc.	2.7% to 20.1%	8.5%	4.8%	4.9%	4.5%	0.41%	0.42%	0.38%
Piles & Foundations	5.3 to 29.8	13.4	7.1	5.2	8.7	0.95	0.70	1.17
Concrete	4.1 to 28.0	11.8	5.0	14.8	3.7	0.59	1.75	0.44
Masonry	3.9 to 49.3	13.8	6.9	7.5	1.9	0.95	1.04	0.26
Structural Steel	5.3 to 59.1	21.2	10.7	3.9	17.6	2.27	0.83	3.73
Miscellaneous & Ornamental Metals	3.3 to 24.4	10.6	2.8	4.0	3.6	0.30	0.42	0.38
Carpentry & Millwork	4.4 to 32.4	13.0	3.7	4.0	0.5	0.48	0.52	0.07
Metal or Composition Siding	5.5 to 107.2	19.0	2.3	0.3	4.3	0.44	0.06	0.82
Roofing	5.5 to 120.3	29.0	2.3	2.6	3.1	0.67	0.75	0.90
Doors & Hardware	3.2 to 32.4	11.0	0.9	1.4	0.4	0.10	0.15	0.04
Sash & Glazing	4.7 to 25.5	12.1	3.5	4.0	1.0	0.42	0.48	0.12
Lath & Plaster	3.0 to 31.6	10.7	3.3	6.9	0.8	0.35	0.74	0.09
Tile, Marble & Floors	2.7 to 18.3	8.7	2.6	3.0	0.5	0.23	0.26	0.04
Acoustical Ceilings	2.4 to 46.3	8.5	2.4	0.2	0.3	0.20	0.02	0.03
Painting	3.3 to 38.8	11.2	1.5	1.6	1.6	0.17	0.18	0.18
Interior Partitions	4.4 to 32.4	13.0	3.9	4.3	4.4	0.51	0.56	0.57
Miscellaneous Items	2.3 to 97.7	11.2	5.2	3.7	9.7	0.58	0.42	1.09
Elevators	1.3 to 13.7	4.7	2.1	1.1	2.2	0.10	0.05	0.10
Sprinklers	2.0 to 15.5	6.7	0.5	—	2.0	0.03	—	0.13
Plumbing	1.7 to 14.0	6.3	4.9	7.2	5.2	0.31	0.45	0.33
Heat., Vent., Air Conditioning	3.3 to 17.8	8.3	13.5	11.0	12.9	1.12	0.91	1.07
Electrical	1.9 to 11.6	5.2	10.1	8.4	11.1	0.53	0.44	0.58
Total	1.3% to 120.3%	—	100.0%	100.0%	100.0%	11.71%	11.15%	12.52%

Overall Weighted Average 11.79%

Workers' Compensation Insurance Rates by States

The table below lists the weighted average Workers' Compensation base rate for each state with a factor comparing this with the national average of 11.8%.

State	Weighted Average	Factor	State	Weighted Average	Factor	State	Weighted Average	Factor
Alabama	15.0%	127	Kentucky	10.4%	88	North Dakota	6.2%	53
Alaska	10.4	88	Louisiana	18.7	158	Ohio	7.2	61
Arizona	9.6	81	Maine	10.4	88	Oklahoma	8.9	75
Arkansas	7.0	59	Maryland	11.3	96	Oregon	9.3	79
California	22.2	188	Massachusetts	11.2	95	Pennsylvania	21.1	179
Colorado	7.5	64	Michigan	8.2	69	Rhode Island	13.7	116
Connecticut	17.5	148	Minnesota	16.9	143	South Carolina	16.5	140
Delaware	13.9	118	Mississippi	11.8	100	South Dakota	11.8	100
District of Columbia	9.1	77	Missouri	12.4	105	Tennessee	8.6	73
Florida	11.1	94	Montana	8.8	75	Texas	6.6	56
Georgia	31.9	270	Nebraska	13.5	114	Utah	7.4	63
Hawaii	8.5	72	Nevada	7.5	64	Vermont	10.9	92
Idaho	9.4	80	New Hampshire	12.0	102	Virginia	6.9	58
Illinois	21.1	179	New Jersey	14.8	125	Washington	9.1	77
Indiana	4.1	35	New Mexico	13.3	113	West Virginia	4.5	38
Iowa	13.7	116	New York	19.2	163	Wisconsin	12.2	103
Kansas	6.5	55	North Carolina	15.8	134	Wyoming	5.6	47

Weighted Average for U.S. is 11.8% of payroll = 100%

The weighted average skilled worker rate for 35 trades is 11.8%. For bidding purposes, apply the full value of Workers' Compensation directly to total labor costs, or if labor is 38%, materials 42% and overhead and profit 20% of total cost, carry 38/80 x 11.8% = 6.0% of cost (before overhead and profit) into overhead. Rates vary not only from state to state but also with the experience rating of the contractor.

Rates are the most current available at the time of publication.

General Requirements — R0131 Project Management & Coordination

R013113-80 Performance Bond

This table shows the cost of a Performance Bond for a construction job scheduled to be completed in 12 months. Add 1% of the premium cost per month for jobs requiring more than 12 months to complete. The rates are "standard" rates offered to contractors that the bonding company considers financially sound and capable of doing the work. Preferred rates are offered by some bonding companies based upon financial strength of the contractor. Actual rates vary from contractor to contractor and from bonding company to bonding company. Contractors should prequalify through a bonding agency before submitting a bid on a contract that requires a bond.

Contract Amount	Building Construction — Class B Projects	Highways & Bridges — Class A New Construction	Class A-1 Highway Resurfacing
First $ 100,000 bid	$25.00 per M	$15.00 per M	$9.40 per M
Next 400,000 bid	$ 2,500 plus $15.00 per M	$ 1,500 plus $10.00 per M	$ 940 plus $7.20 per M
Next 2,000,000 bid	8,500 plus 10.00 per M	5,500 plus 7.00 per M	3,820 plus 5.00 per M
Next 2,500,000 bid	28,500 plus 7.50 per M	19,500 plus 5.50 per M	15,820 plus 4.50 per M
Next 2,500,000 bid	47,250 plus 7.00 per M	33,250 plus 5.00 per M	28,320 plus 4.50 per M
Over 7,500,000 bid	64,750 plus 6.00 per M	45,750 plus 4.50 per M	39,570 plus 4.00 per M

Existing Conditions — R0241 Demolition

R024119-10 Demolition Defined

Whole Building Demolition - Demolition of the whole building with no concern for any particular building element, component, or material type being demolished. This type of demolition is accomplished with large pieces of construction equipment that break up the structure, load it into trucks and haul it to a disposal site, but disposal or dump fees are not included. Demolition of below-grade foundation elements, such as footings, foundation walls, grade beams, slabs on grade, etc., is not included. Certain mechanical equipment containing flammable liquids or ozone-depleting refrigerants, electric lighting elements, communication equipment components, and other building elements may contain hazardous waste, and must be removed, either selectively or carefully, as hazardous waste before the building can be demolished.

Foundation Demolition - Demolition of below-grade foundation footings, foundation walls, grade beams, and slabs on grade. This type of demolition is accomplished by hand or pneumatic hand tools, and does not include saw cutting, or handling, loading, hauling, or disposal of the debris.

Gutting - Removal of building interior finishes and electrical/mechanical systems down to the load-bearing and sub-floor elements of the rough building frame, with no concern for any particular building element, component, or material type being demolished. This type of demolition is accomplished by hand or pneumatic hand tools, and includes loading into trucks, but not hauling, disposal or dump fees, scaffolding, or shoring. Certain mechanical equipment containing flammable liquids or ozone-depleting refrigerants, electric lighting elements, communication equipment components, and other building elements may contain hazardous waste, and must be removed, either selectively or carefully, as hazardous waste, before the building is gutted.

Selective Demolition - Demolition of a selected building element, component, or finish, with some concern for surrounding or adjacent elements, components, or finishes (see the first Subdivision (s) at the beginning of appropriate Divisions). This type of demolition is accomplished by hand or pneumatic hand tools, and does not include handling, loading, storing, hauling, or disposal of the debris, scaffolding, or shoring. "Gutting" methods may be used in order to save time, but damage that is caused to surrounding or adjacent elements, components, or finishes may have to be repaired at a later time.

Careful Removal - Removal of a piece of service equipment, building element or component, or material type, with great concern for both the removed item and surrounding or adjacent elements, components or finishes. The purpose of careful removal may be to protect the removed item for later re-use, preserve a higher salvage value of the removed item, or replace an item while taking care to protect surrounding or adjacent elements, components, connections, or finishes from cosmetic and/or structural damage. An approximation of the time required to perform this type of removal is 1/3 to 1/2 the time it would take to install a new item of like kind. This type of removal is accomplished by hand or pneumatic hand tools, and does not include loading, hauling, or storing the removed item, scaffolding, shoring, or lifting equipment.

Cutout Demolition - Demolition of a small quantity of floor, wall, roof, or other assembly, with concern for the appearance and structural integrity of the surrounding materials. This type of demolition is accomplished by hand or pneumatic hand tools, and does not include saw cutting, handling, loading, hauling, or disposal of debris, scaffolding, or shoring.

Rubbish Handling - Work activities that involve handling, loading or hauling of debris. Generally, the cost of rubbish handling must be added to the cost of all types of demolition, with the exception of whole building demolition.

Minor Site Demolition - Demolition of site elements outside the footprint of a building. This type of demolition is accomplished by hand or pneumatic hand tools, or with larger pieces of construction equipment, and may include loading a removed item onto a truck (check the Crew for equipment used). It does not include saw cutting, hauling or disposal of debris, and, sometimes, handling or loading.

Existing Conditions — R0265 Underground Storage Tank Removal

R026510-20 Underground Storage Tank Removal

Underground Storage Tank Removal can be divided into two categories: Non-Leaking and Leaking. Prior to removing an underground storage tank, tests should be made, with the proper authorities present, to determine whether a tank has been leaking or the surrounding soil has been contaminated.

To safely remove Liquid Underground Storage Tanks:
1. Excavate to the top of the tank.
2. Disconnect all piping.
3. Open all tank vents and access ports.
4. Remove all liquids and/or sludge.
5. Purge the tank with an inert gas.
6. Provide access to the inside of the tank and clean out the interior using proper personal protective equipment (PPE).
7. Excavate soil surrounding the tank using proper PPE for on-site personnel.
8. Pull and properly dispose of the tank.
9. Clean up the site of all contaminated material.
10. Install new tanks or close the excavation.

Concrete   R0311 Concrete Forming

R031113-10   Wall Form Materials

Aluminum Forms
Approximate weight is 3 lbs. per S.F.C.A. Standard widths are available from 4" to 36" with 36" most common. Standard lengths of 2', 4', 6' to 8' are available. Forms are lightweight and fewer ties are needed with the wider widths. The form face is either smooth or textured.

Metal Framed Plywood Forms
Manufacturers claim over 75 reuses of plywood and over 300 reuses of steel frames. Many specials such as corners, fillers, pilasters, etc. are available. Monthly rental is generally about 15% of purchase price for first month and 9% per month thereafter with 90% of rental applied to purchase for the first month and decreasing percentages thereafter. Aluminum framed forms cost 25% to 30% more than steel framed.

After the first month, extra days may be prorated from the monthly charge. Rental rates do not include ties, accessories, cleaning, loss of hardware or freight in and out. Approximate weight is 5 lbs. per S.F. for steel; 3 lbs. per S.F. for aluminum.

Forms can be rented with option to buy.

Plywood Forms, Job Fabricated
There are two types of plywood used for concrete forms.
1. Exterior plyform is completely waterproof. This is face oiled to facilitate stripping. Ten reuses can be expected with this type with 25 reuses possible.
2. An overlaid type consists of a resin fiber fused to exterior plyform. No oiling is required except to facilitate cleaning. This is available in both high density (HDO) and medium density overlaid (MDO). Using HDO, 50 reuses can be expected with 200 possible.

Plyform is available in 5/8" and 3/4" thickness. High density overlaid is available in 3/8", 1/2", 5/8" and 3/4" thickness.

5/8" thick is sufficient for most building forms, while 3/4" is best on heavy construction.

Plywood Forms, Modular, Prefabricated
There are many plywood forming systems without frames. Most of these are manufactured from 1-1/8" (HDO) plywood and have some hardware attached. These are used principally for foundation walls 8' or less high. With care and maintenance, 100 reuses can be attained with decreasing quality of surface finish.

Steel Forms
Approximate weight is 6-1/2 lbs. per S.F.C.A. including accessories. Standard widths are available from 2" to 24", with 24" the most common. Standard lengths are from 2' to 8', with 4' the most common. Forms are easily ganged into modular units.

Forms are usually leased for 15% of the purchase price per month prorated daily over 30 days.

Rental may be applied to sale price, and usually rental forms are bought. With careful handling and cleaning 200 to 400 reuses are possible.

Straight wall gang forms up to 12' x 20' or 8' x 30' can be fabricated. These crane handled forms usually lease for approx. 9% per month.

Individual job analysis is available from the manufacturer at no charge.

R031113-40   Forms for Reinforced Concrete

Design Economy
Avoid many sizes in proportioning beams and columns.

From story to story avoid changing column dimensions. Gain strength by adding steel or using a richer mix. If a change in size of column is necessary, vary one dimension only to minimize form alterations. Keep beams and columns the same width.

From floor to floor in a multi-story building vary beam depth, not width, as that will leave the slab panel form unchanged. It is cheaper to vary the strength of a beam from floor to floor by means of a steel area than by 2" changes in either width or depth.

Cost Factors
Material includes the cost of lumber, cost of rent for metal pans or forms if used, nails, form ties, form oil, bolts and accessories.

Labor includes the cost of carpenters to make up, erect, remove and repair, plus common labor to clean and move. Having carpenters remove forms minimizes repairs.

Improper alignment and condition of forms will increase finishing cost. When forms are heavily oiled, concrete surfaces must be neutralized before finishing. Special curing compounds will cause spillages to spall off in first frost. Gang forming methods will reduce costs on large projects.

Materials Used
Boards are seldom used unless their architectural finish is required. Generally, steel, fiberglass and plywood are used for contact surfaces. Labor on plywood is 10% less than with boards. The plywood is backed up with 2 x 4's at 12" to 32" O.C. Walers are generally 2 - 2 x 4's. Column forms are held together with steel yokes or bands. Shoring is with adjustable shoring or scaffolding for high ceilings.

Reuse
Floor and column forms can be reused four or possibly five times without excessive repair. Remember to allow for 10% waste on each reuse.

When modular sized wall forms are made, up to twenty uses can be expected with exterior plyform.

When forms are reused, the cost to erect, strip, clean and move will not be affected. 10% replacement of lumber should be included and about one hour of carpenter time for repairs on each reuse per 100 S.F.

The reuse cost for certain accessory items normally rented on a monthly basis will be lower than the cost for the first use.

After the fifth use, new material required plus time needed for repair prevent the form cost from dropping further; it may go up. Much depends on care in stripping, the number of special bays, changes in beam or column sizes and other factors.

Costs for multiple use of formwork may be developed as follows:

2 Uses	3 Uses	4 Uses
$\dfrac{\text{(1st Use + Reuse)}}{2} = \text{avg. cost/2 uses}$	$\dfrac{\text{(1st Use + 2 Reuses)}}{3} = \text{avg. cost/3 uses}$	$\dfrac{\text{(1st use + 3 Reuses)}}{4} = \text{avg. cost/4 uses}$

Concrete

R0311 Concrete Forming

R031113-60 Formwork Labor-Hours

Item	Unit	Hours Required - Fabricate	Hours Required - Erect & Strip	Hours Required - Clean & Move	Total Hours 1 Use	Multiple Use 2 Use	Multiple Use 3 Use	Multiple Use 4 Use
Beam and Girder, interior beams, 12" wide	100 S.F.	6.4	8.3	1.3	16.0	13.3	12.4	12.0
Hung from steel beams		5.8	7.7	1.3	14.8	12.4	11.6	11.2
Beam sides only, 36" high		5.8	7.2	1.3	14.3	11.9	11.1	10.7
Beam bottoms only, 24" wide		6.6	13.0	1.3	20.9	18.1	17.2	16.7
Box out for openings		9.9	10.0	1.1	21.0	16.6	15.1	14.3
Buttress forms, to 8' high		6.0	6.5	1.2	13.7	11.2	10.4	10.0
Centering, steel, 3/4" rib lath	▼		1.0		1.0			
3/8" rib lath or slab form			0.9		0.9			
Chamfer strip or keyway	100 L.F.		1.5		1.5	1.5	1.5	1.5
Columns, fiber tube 8" diameter			20.6		20.6			
12"			21.3		21.3			
16"			22.9		22.9			
20"			23.7		23.7			
24"			24.6		24.6			
30"	▼		25.6		25.6			
Columns, round steel, 12" diameter			22.0		22.0	22.0	22.0	22.0
16"			25.6		25.6	25.6	25.6	25.6
20"			30.5		30.5	30.5	30.5	30.5
24"	▼		37.7		37.7	37.7	37.7	37.7
Columns, plywood 8" x 8"	100 S.F.	7.0	11.0	1.2	19.2	16.2	15.2	14.7
12" x 12"		6.0	10.5	1.2	17.7	15.2	14.4	14.0
16" x 16"		5.9	10.0	1.2	17.1	14.7	13.8	13.4
24" x 24"		5.8	9.8	1.2	16.8	14.4	13.6	13.2
Columns, steel framed plywood 8" x 8"			10.0	1.0	11.0	11.0	11.0	11.0
12" x 12"			9.3	1.0	10.3	10.3	10.3	10.3
16" x 16"			8.5	1.0	9.5	9.5	9.5	9.5
24" x 24"			7.8	1.0	8.8	8.8	8.8	8.8
Drop head forms, plywood		9.0	12.5	1.5	23.0	19.0	17.7	17.0
Coping forms		8.5	15.0	1.5	25.0	21.3	20.0	19.4
Culvert, box			14.5	4.3	18.8	18.8	18.8	18.8
Curb forms, 6" to 12" high, on grade		5.0	8.5	1.2	14.7	12.7	12.1	11.7
On elevated slabs		6.0	10.8	1.2	18.0	15.5	14.7	14.3
Edge forms to 6" high, on grade	100 L.F.	2.0	3.5	0.6	6.1	5.6	5.4	5.3
7" to 12" high	100 S.F.	2.5	5.0	1.0	8.5	7.8	7.5	7.4
Equipment foundations		10.0	18.0	2.0	30.0	25.5	24.0	23.3
Flat slabs, including drops		3.5	6.0	1.2	10.7	9.5	9.0	8.8
Hung from steel		3.0	5.5	1.2	9.7	8.7	8.4	8.2
Closed deck for domes		3.0	5.8	1.2	10.0	9.0	8.7	8.5
Open deck for pans		2.2	5.3	1.0	8.5	7.9	7.7	7.6
Footings, continuous, 12" high		3.5	3.5	1.5	8.5	7.3	6.8	6.6
Spread, 12" high		4.7	4.2	1.6	10.5	8.7	8.0	7.7
Pile caps, square or rectangular		4.5	5.0	1.5	11.0	9.3	8.7	8.4
Grade beams, 24" deep		2.5	5.3	1.2	9.0	8.3	8.0	7.9
Lintel or Sill forms		8.0	17.0	2.0	27.0	23.5	22.3	21.8
Spandrel beams, 12" wide		9.0	11.2	1.3	21.5	17.5	16.2	15.5
Stairs			25.0	4.0	29.0	29.0	29.0	29.0
Trench forms in floor		4.5	14.0	1.5	20.0	18.3	17.7	17.4
Walls, Plywood, at grade, to 8' high		5.0	6.5	1.5	13.0	11.0	9.7	9.5
8' to 16'		7.5	8.0	1.5	17.0	13.8	12.7	12.1
16' to 20'		9.0	10.0	1.5	20.5	16.5	15.2	14.5
Foundation walls, to 8' high		4.5	6.5	1.0	12.0	10.3	9.7	9.4
8' to 16' high		5.5	7.5	1.0	14.0	11.8	11.0	10.6
Retaining wall to 12' high, battered		6.0	8.5	1.5	16.0	13.5	12.7	12.3
Radial walls to 12' high, smooth		8.0	9.5	2.0	19.5	16.0	14.8	14.3
2' chords		7.0	8.0	1.5	16.5	13.5	12.5	12.0
Prefabricated modular, to 8' high		—	4.3	1.0	5.3	5.3	5.3	5.3
Steel, to 8' high		—	6.8	1.2	8.0	8.0	8.0	8.0
8' to 16' high		—	9.1	1.5	10.6	10.3	10.2	10.2
Steel framed plywood to 8' high		—	6.8	1.2	8.0	7.5	7.3	7.2
8' to 16' high	▼	—	9.3	1.2	10.5	9.5	9.2	9.0

For customer support on your Green Building Costs with RSMeans data, call 800.448.8182.

Concrete — R0321 Reinforcing Steel

R032110-10 Reinforcing Steel Weights and Measures

Bar Designation No.**	Nominal Weight Lb./Ft.	U.S. Customary Units Nominal Dimensions* Diameter in.	Cross Sectional Area, in.²	Perimeter in.	SI Units Nominal Dimensions* Nominal Weight kg/m	Diameter mm	Cross Sectional Area, cm²	Perimeter mm
3	.376	.375	.11	1.178	.560	9.52	.71	29.9
4	.668	.500	.20	1.571	.994	12.70	1.29	39.9
5	1.043	.625	.31	1.963	1.552	15.88	2.00	49.9
6	1.502	.750	.44	2.356	2.235	19.05	2.84	59.8
7	2.044	.875	.60	2.749	3.042	22.22	3.87	69.8
8	2.670	1.000	.79	3.142	3.973	25.40	5.10	79.8
9	3.400	1.128	1.00	3.544	5.059	28.65	6.45	90.0
10	4.303	1.270	1.27	3.990	6.403	32.26	8.19	101.4
11	5.313	1.410	1.56	4.430	7.906	35.81	10.06	112.5
14	7.650	1.693	2.25	5.320	11.384	43.00	14.52	135.1
18	13.600	2.257	4.00	7.090	20.238	57.33	25.81	180.1

* The nominal dimensions of a deformed bar are equivalent to those of a plain round bar having the same weight per foot as the deformed bar.
** Bar numbers are based on the number of eighths of an inch included in the nominal diameter of the bars.

R032110-20 Metric Rebar Specification - ASTM A615-81

Grade 300 (300 MPa* = 43,560 psi; +8.7% vs. Grade 40)
Grade 400 (400 MPa* = 58,000 psi; −3.4% vs. Grade 60)

Bar No.	Diameter mm	Area mm²	Equivalent in.²	Comparison with U.S. Customary Bars
10M	11.3	100	.16	Between #3 & #4
15M	16.0	200	.31	#5 (.31 in.²)
20M	19.5	300	.47	#6 (.44 in.²)
25M	25.2	500	.78	#8 (.79 in.²)
30M	29.9	700	1.09	#9 (1.00 in.²)
35M	35.7	1000	1.55	#11 (1.56 in.²)
45M	43.7	1500	2.33	#14 (2.25 in.²)
55M	56.4	2500	3.88	#18 (4.00 in.²)

* MPa = megapascals

Concrete

R0321 Reinforcing Steel

R032110-50 Minimum Wall Reinforcement Weight (PSF)

This table lists the approximate minimum wall reinforcement weights per S.F. according to the specification of .12% of gross area for vertical bars and .20% of gross area for horizontal bars.

Location	Wall Thickness	Bar Size	Horizontal Steel Spacing C/C	Sq. In. Req'd per S.F.	Total Wt. per S.F.	Bar Size	Vertical Steel Spacing C/C	Sq. In. Req'd per S.F.	Total Wt. per S.F.	Horizontal & Vertical Steel Total Weight per S.F.
Both Faces	10"	#4	18"	.24	.89#	#3	18"	.14	.50#	1.39#
	12"	#4	16"	.29	1.00	#3	16"	.17	.60	1.60
	14"	#4	14"	.34	1.14	#3	13"	.20	.69	1.84
	16"	#4	12"	.38	1.34	#3	11"	.23	.82	2.16
	18"	#5	17"	.43	1.47	#4	18"	.26	.89	2.36
One Face	6"	#3	9"	.15	.50	#3	18"	.09	.25	.75
	8"	#4	12"	.19	.67	#3	11"	.12	.41	1.08
	10"	#5	15"	.24	.83	#4	16"	.14	.50	1.34

Concrete | R0321 Reinforcing Steel

R032110-70 Bend, Place and Tie Reinforcing

Placing and tying by rodmen for footings and slabs run from nine hrs. per ton for heavy bars to fifteen hrs. per ton for light bars. For beams, columns, and walls, production runs from eight hrs. per ton for heavy bars to twenty hrs. per ton for light bars. The overall average for typical reinforced concrete buildings is about fourteen hrs. per ton. These production figures include the time for placing accessories and usual inserts, but not their material cost (allow 15% of the cost of delivered bent rods). Equipment handling is necessary for the larger-sized bars so that installation costs for the very heavy bars will not decrease proportionately.

Installation costs for splicing reinforcing bars include allowance for equipment to hold the bars in place while splicing as well as necessary scaffolding for iron workers.

R032110-80 Shop-Fabricated Reinforcing Steel

The material prices for reinforcing, shown in the unit cost sections of the data set, are for 50 tons or more of shop-fabricated reinforcing steel and include:

1. Mill base price of reinforcing steel
2. Mill grade/size/length extras
3. Mill delivery to the fabrication shop
4. Shop storage and handling
5. Shop drafting/detailing
6. Shop shearing and bending
7. Shop listing
8. Shop delivery to the job site

Both material and installation costs can be considerably higher for small jobs consisting primarily of smaller bars, while material costs may be slightly lower for larger jobs.

Concrete   R0331 Structural Concrete

R033105-10   Proportionate Quantities

The tables below show both quantities per S.F. of floor areas as well as form and reinforcing quantities per C.Y. Unusual structural requirements would increase the ratios below. High strength reinforcing would reduce the steel weights. Figures are for 3000 psi concrete and 60,000 psi reinforcing unless specified otherwise.

Type of Construction	Live Load	Span	Per S.F. of Floor Area — Concrete	Forms	Reinf.	Pans	Per C.Y. of Concrete — Forms	Reinf.	Pans
Flat Plate	50 psf	15 Ft.	.46 C.F.	1.06 S.F.	1.71 lb.		62 S.F.	101 lb.	
		20	.63	1.02	2.40		44	104	
		25	.79	1.02	3.03		35	104	
	100	15	.46	1.04	2.14		61	126	
		20	.71	1.02	2.72		39	104	
		25	.83	1.01	3.47		33	113	
Flat Plate (waffle construction) 20" domes	50	20	.43	1.00	2.10	.84 S.F.	63	135	53 S.F.
		25	.52	1.00	2.90	.89	52	150	46
		30	.64	1.00	3.70	.87	42	155	37
	100	20	.51	1.00	2.30	.84	53	125	45
		25	.64	1.00	3.20	.83	42	135	35
		30	.76	1.00	4.40	.81	36	160	29
Waffle Construction 30" domes	50	25	.69	1.06	1.83	.68	42	72	40
		30	.74	1.06	2.39	.69	39	87	39
		35	.86	1.05	2.71	.69	33	85	39
		40	.78	1.00	4.80	.68	35	165	40
Flat Slab (two way with drop panels)	50	20	.62	1.03	2.34		45	102	
		25	.77	1.03	2.99		36	105	
		30	.95	1.03	4.09		29	116	
	100	20	.64	1.03	2.83		43	119	
		25	.79	1.03	3.88		35	133	
		30	.96	1.03	4.66		29	131	
	200	20	.73	1.03	3.03		38	112	
		25	.86	1.03	4.23		32	133	
		30	1.06	1.03	5.30		26	135	
One Way Joists 20" Pans	50	15	.36	1.04	1.40	.93	78	105	70
		20	.42	1.05	1.80	.94	67	120	60
		25	.47	1.05	2.60	.94	60	150	54
	100	15	.38	1.07	1.90	.93	77	140	66
		20	.44	1.08	2.40	.94	67	150	58
		25	.52	1.07	3.50	.94	55	185	49
One Way Joists 8" x 16" filler blocks	50	15	.34	1.06	1.80	.81 Ea.	84	145	64 Ea.
		20	.40	1.08	2.20	.82	73	145	55
		25	.46	1.07	3.20	.83	63	190	49
	100	15	.39	1.07	1.90	.81	74	130	56
		20	.46	1.09	2.80	.82	64	160	48
		25	.53	1.10	3.60	.83	56	190	42
One Way Beam & Slab	50	15	.42	1.30	1.73		84	111	
		20	.51	1.28	2.61		68	138	
		25	.64	1.25	2.78		53	117	
	100	15	.42	1.30	1.90		84	122	
		20	.54	1.35	2.69		68	154	
		25	.69	1.37	3.93		54	145	
	200	15	.44	1.31	2.24		80	137	
		20	.58	1.40	3.30		65	163	
		25	.69	1.42	4.89		53	183	
Two Way Beam & Slab	100	15	.47	1.20	2.26		69	130	
		20	.63	1.29	3.06		55	131	
		25	.83	1.33	3.79		43	123	
	200	15	.49	1.25	2.70		41	149	
		20	.66	1.32	4.04		54	165	
		25	.88	1.32	6.08		41	187	

Concrete R0331 Structural Concrete

R033105-10 Proportionate Quantities (cont.)

| \multicolumn{6}{c}{4000 psi Concrete and 60,000 psi Reinforcing—Form and Reinforcing Quantities per C.Y.} |
Item	Size	Forms	Reinforcing	Minimum	Maximum
Columns (square tied)	10" x 10"	130 S.F.C.A.	#5 to #11	220 lbs.	875 lbs.
	12" x 12"	108	#6 to #14	200	955
	14" x 14"	92	#7 to #14	190	900
	16" x 16"	81	#6 to #14	187	1082
	18" x 18"	72	#6 to #14	170	906
	20" x 20"	65	#7 to #18	150	1080
	22" x 22"	59	#8 to #18	153	902
	24" x 24"	54	#8 to #18	164	884
	26" x 26"	50	#9 to #18	169	994
	28" x 28"	46	#9 to #18	147	864
	30" x 30"	43	#10 to #18	146	983
	32" x 32"	40	#10 to #18	175	866
	34" x 34"	38	#10 to #18	157	772
	36" x 36"	36	#10 to #18	175	852
	38" x 38"	34	#10 to #18	158	765
	40" x 40"	32	#10 to #18	143	692

Item	Size	Form	Spiral	Reinforcing	Minimum	Maximum
Columns (spirally reinforced)	12" diameter	34.5 L.F.	190 lbs.	#4 to #11	165 lbs.	1505 lb.
		34.5	190	#14 & #18	—	1100
	14"	25	170	#4 to #11	150	970
		25	170	#14 & #18	800	1000
	16"	19	160	#4 to #11	160	950
		19	160	#14 & #18	605	1080
	18"	15	150	#4 to #11	160	915
		15	150	#14 & #18	480	1075
	20"	12	130	#4 to #11	155	865
		12	130	#14 & #18	385	1020
	22"	10	125	#4 to #11	165	775
		10	125	#14 & #18	320	995
	24"	9	120	#4 to #11	195	800
		9	120	#14 & #18	290	1150
	26"	7.3	100	#4 to #11	200	729
		7.3	100	#14 & #18	235	1035
	28"	6.3	95	#4 to #11	175	700
		6.3	95	#14 & #18	200	1075
	30"	5.5	90	#4 to #11	180	670
		5.5	90	#14 & #18	175	1015
	32"	4.8	85	#4 to #11	185	615
		4.8	85	#14 & #18	155	955
	34"	4.3	80	#4 to #11	180	600
		4.3	80	#14 & #18	170	855
	36"	3.8	75	#4 to #11	165	570
		3.8	75	#14 & #18	155	865
	40"	3.0	70	#4 to #11	165	500
		3.0	70	#14 & #18	145	765

For customer support on your Green Building Costs with RSMeans data, call 800.448.8182.

Concrete

R0331 Structural Concrete

R033105-10 Proportionate Quantities (cont.)

3000 psi Concrete and 60,000 psi Reinforcing—Form and Reinforcing Quantities per C.Y.

Item	Type	Loading	Height	C.Y./L.F.	Forms/C.Y.	Reinf./C.Y.
Retaining Walls	Cantilever	Level Backfill	4 Ft.	0.2 C.Y.	49 S.F.	35 lbs.
			8	0.5	42	45
			12	0.8	35	70
			16	1.1	32	85
			20	1.6	28	105
		Highway Surcharge	4	0.3	41	35
			8	0.5	36	55
			12	0.8	33	90
			16	1.2	30	120
			20	1.7	27	155
		Railroad Surcharge	4	0.4	28	45
			8	0.8	25	65
			12	1.3	22	90
			16	1.9	20	100
			20	2.6	18	120
	Gravity, with Vertical Face	Level Backfill	4	0.4	37	None
			7	0.6	27	
			10	1.2	20	
		Sloping Backfill	4	0.3	31	
			7	0.8	21	
			10	1.6	15	

Live Load in Kips per Linear Foot

	Span	Under 1 Kip		2 to 3 Kips		4 to 5 Kips		6 to 7 Kips	
		Forms	Reinf.	Forms	Reinf.	Forms	Reinf.	Forms	Reinf.
Beams	10 Ft.	—	—	90 S.F.	170 #	85 S.F.	175 #	75 S.F.	185 #
	16	130 S.F.	165 #	85	180	75	180	65	225
	20	110	170	75	185	62	200	51	200
	26	90	170	65	215	62	215	—	—
	30	85	175	60	200	—	—	—	—

Item	Size	Type	Forms per C.Y.	Reinforcing per C.Y.
Spread Footings	Under 1 C.Y.	1,000 psf soil	24 S.F.	44 lbs.
		5,000	24	42
		10,000	24	52
	1 C.Y. to 5 C.Y.	1,000	14	49
		5,000	14	50
		10,000	14	50
	Over 5 C.Y.	1,000	9	54
		5,000	9	52
		10,000	9	56
Pile Caps (30 Ton Concrete Piles)	Under 5 C.Y.	shallow caps	20	65
		medium	20	50
		deep	20	40
	5 C.Y. to 10 C.Y.	shallow	14	55
		medium	15	45
		deep	15	40
	10 C.Y. to 20 C.Y.	shallow	11	60
		medium	11	45
		deep	12	35
	Over 20 C.Y.	shallow	9	60
		medium	9	45
		deep	10	40

Concrete   R0331 Structural Concrete

R033105-10 Proportionate Quantities (cont.)

		3000 psi Concrete and 60,000 psi Reinforcing — Form and Reinforcing Quantities per C.Y.					
Item	Size	Pile Spacing	50 T Pile	100 T Pile	50 T Pile	100 T Pile	
Pile Caps (Steel H Piles)	Under 5 C.Y.	24" O.C.	24 S.F.	24 S.F.	75 lbs.	90 lbs.	
		30"	25	25	80	100	
		36"	24	24	80	110	
	5 C.Y. to 10 C.Y.	24"	15	15	80	110	
		30"	15	15	85	110	
		36"	15	15	75	90	
	Over 10 C.Y.	24"	13	13	85	90	
		30"	11	11	85	95	
		36"	10	10	85	90	

		8" Thick		10" Thick		12" Thick		15" Thick	
	Height	Forms	Reinf.	Forms	Reinf.	Forms	Reinf.	Forms	Reinf.
Basement Walls	7 Ft.	81 S.F.	44 lbs.	65 S.F.	45 lbs.	54 S.F.	44 lbs.	41 S.F.	43 lbs.
	8		44		45		44		43
	9		46		45		44		43
	10		57		45		44		43
	12		83		50		52		43
	14		116		65		64		51
	16				86		90		65
	18						106		70

R033105-20 Materials for One C.Y. of Concrete

This is an approximate method of figuring quantities of cement, sand and coarse aggregate for a field mix with waste allowance included.

With crushed gravel as coarse aggregate, to determine barrels of cement required, divide 10 by total mix; that is, for 1:2:4 mix, 10 divided by 7 = 1-3/7 barrels.

If the coarse aggregate is crushed stone, use 10-1/2 instead of 10 as given for gravel.

To determine tons of sand required, multiply barrels of cement by parts of sand and then by 0.2; that is, for the 1:2:4 mix, as above, 1-3/7 x 2 x .2 = .57 tons.

Tons of crushed gravel are in the same ratio to tons of sand as parts in the mix, or 4/2 x .57 = 1.14 tons.

1 bag cement = 94#   1 C.Y. sand or crushed gravel = 2700#   1 C.Y. crushed stone = 2575#
4 bags = 1 barrel   1 ton sand or crushed gravel = 20 C.F.   1 ton crushed stone = 21 C.F.

Average carload of cement is 692 bags; of sand or gravel is 56 tons.

Do not stack stored cement over 10 bags high.

Concrete

R0331 Structural Concrete

R033105-40 Metric Equivalents of Common Concrete Strengths
(to convert other psi values to megapascals, multiply by 0.006895)

U.S. Values psi	SI Values Megapascals	Non-SI Metric Values kgf/cm^2*
2000	14	140
2500	17	175
3000	21	210
3500	24	245
4000	28	280
4500	31	315
5000	34	350
6000	41	420
7000	48	490
8000	55	560
9000	62	630
10,000	69	705

* kilograms force per square centimeter

R033105-50 Quantities of Cement, Sand and Stone for One C.Y. of Concrete per Various Mixes

This table can be used to determine the quantities of the ingredients for smaller quantities of site mixed concrete.

Concrete (C.Y.)	Mix = 1:1:1-3/4 Cement (sacks)	Sand (C.Y.)	Stone (C.Y.)	Mix = 1:2:2.25 Cement (sacks)	Sand (C.Y.)	Stone (C.Y.)	Mix = 1:2.25:3 Cement (sacks)	Sand (C.Y.)	Stone (C.Y.)	Mix = 1:3:4 Cement (sacks)	Sand (C.Y.)	Stone (C.Y.)
1	10	.37	.63	7.75	.56	.65	6.25	.52	.70	5	.56	.74
2	20	.74	1.26	15.50	1.12	1.30	12.50	1.04	1.40	10	1.12	1.48
3	30	1.11	1.89	23.25	1.68	1.95	18.75	1.56	2.10	15	1.68	2.22
4	40	1.48	2.52	31.00	2.24	2.60	25.00	2.08	2.80	20	2.24	2.96
5	50	1.85	3.15	38.75	2.80	3.25	31.25	2.60	3.50	25	2.80	3.70
6	60	2.22	3.78	46.50	3.36	3.90	37.50	3.12	4.20	30	3.36	4.44
7	70	2.59	4.41	54.25	3.92	4.55	43.75	3.64	4.90	35	3.92	5.18
8	80	2.96	5.04	62.00	4.48	5.20	50.00	4.16	5.60	40	4.48	5.92
9	90	3.33	5.67	69.75	5.04	5.85	56.25	4.68	6.30	45	5.04	6.66
10	100	3.70	6.30	77.50	5.60	6.50	62.50	5.20	7.00	50	5.60	7.40
11	110	4.07	6.93	85.25	6.16	7.15	68.75	5.72	7.70	55	6.16	8.14
12	120	4.44	7.56	93.00	6.72	7.80	75.00	6.24	8.40	60	6.72	8.88
13	130	4.82	8.20	100.76	7.28	8.46	81.26	6.76	9.10	65	7.28	9.62
14	140	5.18	8.82	108.50	7.84	9.10	87.50	7.28	9.80	70	7.84	10.36
15	150	5.56	9.46	116.26	8.40	9.76	93.76	7.80	10.50	75	8.40	11.10
16	160	5.92	10.08	124.00	8.96	10.40	100.00	8.32	11.20	80	8.96	11.84
17	170	6.30	10.72	131.76	9.52	11.06	106.26	8.84	11.90	85	9.52	12.58
18	180	6.66	11.34	139.50	10.08	11.70	112.50	9.36	12.60	90	10.08	13.32
19	190	7.04	11.98	147.26	10.64	12.36	118.76	9.84	13.30	95	10.64	14.06
20	200	7.40	12.60	155.00	11.20	13.00	125.00	10.40	14.00	100	11.20	14.80
21	210	7.77	13.23	162.75	11.76	13.65	131.25	10.92	14.70	105	11.76	15.54
22	220	8.14	13.86	170.05	12.32	14.30	137.50	11.44	15.40	110	12.32	16.28
23	230	8.51	14.49	178.25	12.88	14.95	143.75	11.96	16.10	115	12.88	17.02
24	240	8.88	15.12	186.00	13.44	15.60	150.00	12.48	16.80	120	13.44	17.76
25	250	9.25	15.75	193.75	14.00	16.25	156.25	13.00	17.50	125	14.00	18.50
26	260	9.64	16.40	201.52	14.56	16.92	162.52	13.52	18.20	130	14.56	19.24
27	270	10.00	17.00	209.26	15.12	17.56	168.76	14.04	18.90	135	15.02	20.00
28	280	10.36	17.64	217.00	15.68	18.20	175.00	14.56	19.60	140	15.68	20.72
29	290	10.74	18.28	224.76	16.24	18.86	181.26	15.08	20.30	145	16.24	21.46

Concrete — R0331 Structural Concrete

R033105-70 Placing Ready-Mixed Concrete

For ground pours allow for 5% waste when figuring quantities.

Prices in the front of the data set assume normal deliveries. If deliveries are made before 8 A.M. or after 5 P.M. or on Saturday afternoons add 30%. Negotiated discounts for large volumes are not included in prices in front of the data set.

For the lower floors without truck access, concrete may be wheeled in rubber-tired buggies, conveyer handled, crane handled or pumped. Pumping is economical if there is top steel. Conveyers are more efficient for thick slabs.

At higher floors the rubber-tired buggies may be hoisted by a hoisting tower and wheeled to the location. Placement by a conveyer is limited to three floors and is best for high-volume pours. Pumped concrete is best when the building has no crane access. Concrete may be pumped directly as high as thirty-six stories using special pumping techniques. Normal maximum height is about fifteen stories.

The best pumping aggregate is screened and graded bank gravel rather than crushed stone.

Pumping downward is more difficult than pumping upward. The horizontal distance from pump to pour may increase preparation time prior to pour. Placing by cranes, either mobile, climbing or tower types, continues as the most efficient method for high-rise concrete buildings.

Concrete   R0331 Structural Concrete

R033105-80   Slab on Grade

General: Ground slabs are classified on the basis of use. Thickness is generally controlled by the heaviest concentrated load supported. If load area is greater than 80 sq. in., soil bearing may be important. The base granular fill must be a uniformly compacted material of limited capillarity, such as gravel or crushed rock. Concrete is placed on this surface of the vapor barrier on top of the base.

Ground slabs are either single or two course floors. Single course floors are widely used. Two course floors have a subsequent wear resistant topping.

Reinforcement is provided to maintain tightly closed cracks.

Control joints limit crack locations and provide for differential horizontal movement only. Isolation joints allow both horizontal and vertical differential movement.

Use of Table: Determine the appropriate type of slab (A, B, C, or D) by considering the type of use or amount of abrasive wear of traffic type.

Determine thickness by maximum allowable wheel load or uniform load, opposite 1st column, thickness. Increase the controlling thickness if details require, and select either plain or reinforced slab thickness and type.

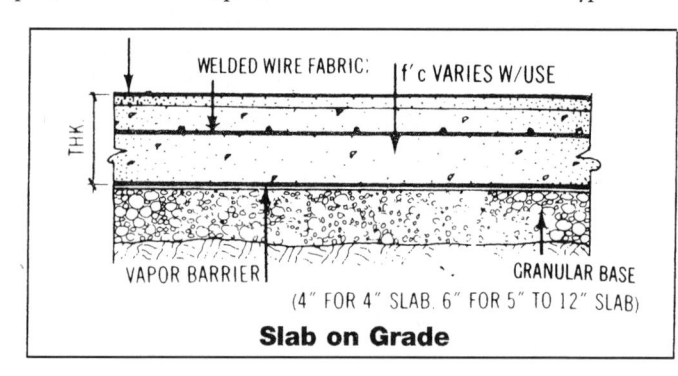

Slab on Grade

Thickness and Loading Assumptions by Type of Use

SLAB THICKNESS (IN.)	TYPE	A Non Little Foot Only Load* (K)	B Light Light Pneumatic Wheels Load* (K)	C Normal Moderate Solid Rubber Wheels Load* (K)	D Heavy Severe Steel Tires Load* (K)	◄ Slab I.D. ◄ Industrial ◄ Abrasion ◄ Type of Traffic Max. Uniform Load to Slab ▼ (PSF)
4"	Reinf. Plain	4K				100
5"	Reinf. Plain	6K	4K			200
6"	Reinf. Plain		8K	6K	6K	500 to 800
7"	Reinf. Plain			9K	8K	1,500
8"	Reinf. Plain				11K	* Max. Wheel Load in Kips (incl. impact)
10"	Reinf. Plain				14K	
12"	Reinf. Plain					
DESIGN ASSUMPTIONS	Concrete, Chuted	f'c = 3.5 KSI	4 KSI	4.5 KSI	Slab @ 3.5 KSI	ASSUMPTIONS BY SLAB TYPE
	Toppings			1" Integral	1" Bonded	
	Finish	Steel Trowel	Steel Trowel	Steel Trowel	Screed & Steel Trowel	
	Compacted Granular Base	4" deep for 4" slab thickness 6" deep for 5" slab thickness & greater				ASSUMPTIONS FOR ALL SLAB TYPES
	Vapor Barrier	6 mil polyethylene				
	Forms & Joints	Allowances included				
	Reinforcement	WWF as required ≥ 60,000 psi				

Concrete — R0331 Structural Concrete

R033105-85 Lift Slabs

The cost advantage of the lift slab method is due to placing all concrete, reinforcing steel, inserts and electrical conduit at ground level and in reduction of formwork. The minimum economical project size is about 30,000 S.F. Slabs may be tilted for parking garage ramps.

It is now used in all types of buildings and has gone up to 22 stories high in apartment buildings. The current trend is to use post-tensioned flat plate slabs with spans from 22′ to 35′. Cylindrical void forms are used when deep slabs are required. One pound of prestressing steel is about equal to seven pounds of conventional reinforcing.

To be considered cured for stressing and lifting, a slab must have attained 75% of design strength. Seven days are usually sufficient with four to five days possible if high early strength cement is used. Slabs can be stacked using two coats of a non-bonding agent to insure that slabs do not stick to each other. Lifting is done by companies specializing in this work. Lift rate is 5′ to 15′ per hour with an average of 10′ per hour. Total areas up to 33,000 S.F. have been lifted at one time. 24 to 36 jacking columns are common. Most economical bay sizes are 24′ to 28′ with four to fourteen stories most efficient. Continuous design reduces reinforcing steel cost. Use of post-tensioned slabs allows larger bay sizes.

Concrete — R0341 Precast Structural Concrete

R034136-90 Prestressed Concrete, Post-Tensioned

In post-tensioned concrete the steel tendons are tensioned after the concrete has reached about 3/4 of its ultimate strength. The cableways are grouted after tensioning to provide bond between the steel and concrete. If bond is to be prevented, the tendons are coated with a corrosion-preventative grease and wrapped with waterproofed paper or plastic. Bonded tendons are usually used when ultimate strength (beams & girders) are controlling factors.

High strength concrete is used to fully utilize the steel, thereby reducing the size and weight of the member. A plasticizing agent may be added to reduce water content. Maximum size aggregate ranges from 1/2″ to 1-1/2″ depending on the spacing of the tendons.

The types of steel commonly used are bars and strands. Job conditions determine which is best suited. Bars are best for vertical prestresses since they are easy to support. The trend is for steel manufacturers to supply a finished package, cut to length, which reduces field preparation to a minimum.

Bars vary from 3/4″ to 1-3/8″ diameter. The table below gives time in labor-hours per tendon for placing, tensioning and grouting (if required) a 75′ beam. Tendons used in buildings are not usually grouted; tendons for bridges usually are grouted. For strands the table indicates the labor-hours per pound for typical prestressed units 100′ long. Simple span beams usually require one-end stressing regardless of lengths. Continuous beams are usually stressed from two ends. Long slabs are poured from the center outward and stressed in 75′ increments after the initial 150′ center pour.

Labor Hours per Tendon and per Pound of Prestressed Steel					
Length	100′ Beam		75′ Beam		100′ Slab	
Type Steel	Strand		Bars		Strand	
Diameter	0.5″		3/4″	1-3/8″	0.5″	0.6″
Number	4	12	1	1	1	1
Force in Kips	100	300	42	143	25	35
Preparation & Placing Cables	3.6	7.4	0.9	2.9	0.9	1.1
Stressing Cables	2.0	2.4	0.8	1.6	0.5	0.5
Grouting, if required	2.5	3.0	0.6	1.3		
Total Labor Hours	8.1	12.8	2.3	5.8	1.4	1.6
Prestressing Steel Weights (Lbs.)	215	640	115	380	53	74
Labor-hours per Lb. Bonded	0.038	0.020	0.020	0.015		
Non-bonded					0.026	0.022

Flat Slab construction — 4000 psi concrete with span-to-depth ratio between 36 and 44. Two way post-tensioned steel averages 1.0 lb. per S.F. for 24′ to 28′ bays (usually strand) and additional reinforcing steel averages .5 lb. per S.F.

Pan and Joist construction — 4000 psi concrete with span-to-depth ratio between 28 to 30. Post-tensioned steel averages .8 lb. per S.F. and reinforcing steel about 1.0 lb. per S.F. Placing and stressing average 40 hours per ton of total material.

Beam construction — 4000 to 5000 psi concrete. Steel weights vary greatly.

Labor cost per pound goes down as the size and length of the tendon increase. The primary economic consideration is the cost per kip for the member.

Post-tensioning becomes feasible for beams and girders over 30′ long; for continuous two-way slabs over 20′ clear; and for transferring upper building loads over longer spans at lower levels. Post-tension suppliers will provide engineering services at no cost to the user. Substantial economies are possible by using post-tensioned Lift Slabs.

Concrete — R0345 Precast Architectural Concrete

R034513-10   Precast Concrete Wall Panels

Panels are either solid or insulated with plain, colored or textured finishes. Transportation is an important cost factor. Prices shown in the unit cost section of the data set are based on delivery within 50 miles of a plant including fabricators' overhead and profit. Engineering data is available from fabricators to assist with construction details. Usual minimum job size for economical use of panels is about 5000 S.F. Small jobs can double the prices shown. For large, highly repetitive jobs, deduct up to 15% from the prices shown.

2" thick panels cost about the same as 3" thick panels, and maximum panel size is less. For building panels faced with granite, marble or stone, add the material prices from those unit cost sections to the plain panel price shown. There is a growing trend toward aggregate facings and broken rib finishes rather than plain gray concrete panels.

No allowance has been made in the unit cost section for supporting steel framework. On one story buildings, panels may rest on grade beams and require only wind bracing and fasteners. On multi-story buildings panels can span from column to column and floor to floor. Plastic-designed steel-framed structures may have large deflections which slow down erection and raise costs.

Large panels are more economical than small panels on a S.F. basis. When figuring areas include all protrusions, returns, etc. Overhangs can triple erection costs. Panels over 45' have been produced. Larger flat units should be prestressed. Vacuum lifting of smooth finish panels eliminates inserts and can speed erection.

Concrete — R0352 Lightweight Concrete Roof Insulation

R035216-10   Lightweight Concrete

Lightweight aggregate concrete is usually purchased ready mixed, but it can also be field mixed.

Vermiculite or Perlite comes in bags of 4 C.F. under various trade names. The weight is about 8 lbs. per C.F. For insulating roof fill use 1:6 mix. For a structural deck use 1:4 mix over gypsum boards, steeltex, steel centering, etc., supported by closely spaced joists or bulb trees. For structural slabs use 1:3:2 vermiculite sand concrete over steeltex, metal lath, steel centering, etc., on joists spaced 2'-0" O.C. for maximum L.L. of 80 P.S.F. Use same mix for slab base fill over steel flooring or regular reinforced concrete slab when tile, terrazzo or other finish is to be laid over.

For slabs on grade use 1:3:2 mix when tile, etc., finish is to be laid over. If radiant heating units are installed use a 1:6 mix for a base. After coils are in place, cover with a regular granolithic finish (mix 1:3:2) to a minimum depth of 1-1/2" over top of units.

Reinforce all slabs with 6 x 6 or 10 x 10 welded wire mesh.

Masonry — R0421 Clay Unit Masonry

R042110-50 Brick, Block & Mortar Quantities

	Running Bond			C.F. of Mortar per M Bricks, Waste Included		For Other Bonds Standard Size Add to S.F. Quantities in Table to Left		
Type Brick	Nominal Size (incl. mortar) L H W	Modular Coursing	Number of Brick per S.F.	3/8" Joint	1/2" Joint	Bond Type	Description	Factor
Standard	8 x 2-2/3 x 4	3C=8"	6.75	10.3	12.9	Common	full header every fifth course	+20%
Economy	8 x 4 x 4	1C=4"	4.50	11.4	14.6		full header every sixth course	+16.7%
Engineer	8 x 3-1/5 x 4	5C=16"	5.63	10.6	13.6	English	full header every second course	+50%
Fire	9 x 2-1/2 x 4-1/2	2C=5"	6.40	550 # Fireclay	—	Flemish	alternate headers every course	+33.3%
Jumbo	12 x 4 x 6 or 8	1C=4"	3.00	23.8	30.8		every sixth course	+5.6%
Norman	12 x 2-2/3 x 4	3C=8"	4.50	14.0	17.9	Header = W x H exposed		+100%
Norwegian	12 x 3-1/5 x 4	5C=16"	3.75	14.6	18.6	Rowlock = H x W exposed		+100%
Roman	12 x 2 x 4	2C=4"	6.00	13.4	17.0	Rowlock stretcher = L x W exposed		+33.3%
SCR	12 x 2-2/3 x 6	3C=8"	4.50	21.8	28.0	Soldier = H x L exposed		—
Utility	12 x 4 x 4	1C=4"	3.00	15.4	19.6	Sailor = W x L exposed		-33.3%

Concrete Blocks Nominal Size		Approximate Weight per S.F.		Blocks per 100 S.F.	Mortar per M block, waste included	
		Standard	Lightweight		Partitions	Back up
2" x 8" x 16"		20 PSF	15 PSF	113	27 C.F.	36 C.F.
4"		30	20		41	51
6"		42	30		56	66
8"		55	38		72	82
10"		70	47		87	97
12"		85	55			102	112

Brick & Mortar Quantities
©Brick Industry Association. 2009 Feb. Technical Notes on Brick Construction 10:
  Dimensioning and Estimating Brick Masonry. Reston (VA): BIA. Table 1 Modular Brick Sizes and Table 4 Quantity Estimates for Brick Masonry.

Masonry — R0422 Concrete Unit Masonry

R042210-20 Concrete Block

The material cost of special block such as corner, jamb and head block can be figured at the same price as ordinary block of equal size. Labor on specials is about the same as equal-sized regular block.

Bond beams and 16" high lintel blocks are more expensive than regular units of equal size. Lintel blocks are 8" long and either 8" or 16" high.

Use of a motorized mortar spreader box will speed construction of continuous walls.

Hollow non-load-bearing units are made according to ASTM C129 and hollow load-bearing units according to ASTM C90.

Metals — R0505 Common Work Results for Metals

R050521-20 Welded Structural Steel

Usual weight reductions with welded design run 10% to 20% compared with bolted or riveted connections. This amounts to about the same total cost compared with bolted structures since field welding is more expensive than bolts. For normal spans of 18' to 24' figure 6 to 7 connections per ton.

Trusses — For welded trusses add 4% to weight of main members for connections. Up to 15% less steel can be expected in a welded truss compared to one that is shop bolted. Cost of erection is the same whether shop bolted or welded.

General — Typical electrodes for structural steel welding are E6010, E6011, E60T and E70T. Typical buildings vary between 2# to 8# of weld rod per ton of steel. Buildings utilizing continuous design require about three times as much welding as conventional welded structures. In estimating field erection by welding, it is best to use the average linear feet of weld per ton to arrive at the welding cost per ton. The type, size and position of the weld will have a direct bearing on the cost per linear foot. A typical field welder will deposit 1.8# to 2# of weld rod per hour manually. Using semiautomatic methods can increase production by as much as 50% to 75%.

R050523-10 High Strength Bolts

Common bolts (A307) are usually used in secondary connections (see Division 05 05 23.10).

High strength bolts (A325 and A490) are usually specified for primary connections such as column splices, beam and girder connections to columns, column bracing, connections for supports of operating equipment or of other live loads which produce impact or reversal of stress, and in structures carrying cranes of over 5-ton capacity.

Allow 20 field bolts per ton of steel for a 6 story office building, apartment house or light industrial building. For 6 to 12 stories allow 25 bolts per ton, and above 12 stories, 30 bolts per ton. On power stations, 20 to 25 bolts per ton are needed.

Metals R0512 Structural Steel Framing

R051223-10 Structural Steel

The bare material prices for structural steel, shown in the unit cost sections of the data set, are for 100 tons of shop-fabricated structural steel and include:
1. Mill base price of structural steel
2. Mill scrap/grade/size/length extras
3. Mill delivery to a metals service center (warehouse)
4. Service center storage and handling
5. Service center delivery to a fabrication shop
6. Shop storage and handling
7. Shop drafting/detailing
8. Shop fabrication
9. Shop coat of primer paint
10. Shop listing
11. Shop delivery to the job site

In unit cost sections of the data set that contain items for field fabrication of steel components, the bare material cost of steel includes:
1. Mill base price of structural steel
2. Mill scrap/grade/size/length extras
3. Mill delivery to a metals service center (warehouse)
4. Service center storage and handling
5. Service center delivery to the job site

R051223-20 Steel Estimating Quantities

One estimate on erection is that a crane can handle 35 to 60 pieces per day. Say the average is 45. With usual sizes of beams, girders, and columns, this would amount to about 20 tons per day. The type of connection greatly affects the speed of erection. Moment connections for continuous design slow down production and increase erection costs.

Short open web bar joists can be set at the rate of 75 to 80 per day, with 50 per day being the average for setting long span joists.

After main members are calculated, add the following for usual allowances: base plates 2% to 3%; column splices 4% to 5%; and miscellaneous details 4% to 5%, for a total of 10% to 13% in addition to main members.

The ratio of column to beam tonnage varies depending on type of steels used, typical spans, story heights and live loads.

It is more economical to keep the column size constant and to vary the strength of the column by using high strength steels. This also saves floor space. Buildings have recently gone as high as ten stories with 8" high strength columns. For light columns under W8X31 lb. sections, concrete filled steel columns are economical.

High strength steels may be used in columns and beams to save floor space and to meet head room requirements. High strength steels in some sizes sometimes require long lead times.

Round, square and rectangular columns, both plain and concrete filled, are readily available and save floor area, but are higher in cost per pound than rolled columns. For high unbraced columns, tube columns may be less expensive.

Below are average minimum figures for the weights of the structural steel frame for different types of buildings using A36 steel, rolled shapes and simple joints. For economy in domes, rise to span ratio = .13. Open web joist framing systems will reduce weights by 10% to 40%. Composite design can reduce steel weight by up to 25% but additional concrete floor slab thickness may be required. Continuous design can reduce the weights up to 20%. There are many building codes with different live load requirements and different structural requirements, such as hurricane and earthquake loadings, which can alter the figures.

Structural Steel Weights per S.F. of Floor Area

Type of Building	No. of Stories	Avg. Spans	L.L. #/S.F.	Lbs. Per S.F.	Type of Building	No. of Stories	Avg. Spans	L.L. #/S.F.	Lbs. Per S.F.
Steel Frame Mfg.	1	20'x20'	40	8	Apartments	2-8	20'x20'	40	8
		30'x30'		13		9-25			14
		40'x40'		18	Office	to 10	Various	80	10
Parking garage	4	Various	80	8.5		20			18
Domes (Schwedler)*	1	200'	30	10		30			26
		300'		15		over 50			35

R051223-30 High Strength Steels

The mill price of high strength steels may be higher than A992 carbon steel, but their proper use can achieve overall savings thru total reduced weights. For columns with L/r over 100, A992 steel is best; under 100, high strength steels are economical. For heavy columns, high strength steels are economical when cover plates are eliminated. There is no economy using high strength steels for clip angles or supports or for beams where deflection governs. Thinner members are more economical than thick.

The per ton erection and fabricating costs of the high strength steels will be higher than for A992 since the same number of pieces, but less weight, will be installed.

Metals — R0512 Structural Steel Framing

R051223-35 Common Steel Sections

The upper portion of this table shows the name, shape, common designation and basic characteristics of commonly used steel sections. The lower portion explains how to read the designations used for the above illustrated common sections.

Shape & Designation	Name & Characteristics	Shape & Designation	Name & Characteristics
W	W Shape — Parallel flange surfaces	MC	Miscellaneous Channel — Infrequently rolled by some producers
S	American Standard Beam (I Beam) — Sloped inner flange	L	Angle — Equal or unequal legs, constant thickness
M	Miscellaneous Beams — Cannot be classified as W, HP or S; infrequently rolled by some producers	T	Structural Tee — Cut from W, M or S on center of web
C	American Standard Channel — Sloped inner flange	HP	Bearing Pile — Parallel flanges and equal flange and web thickness

Common drawing designations follow:

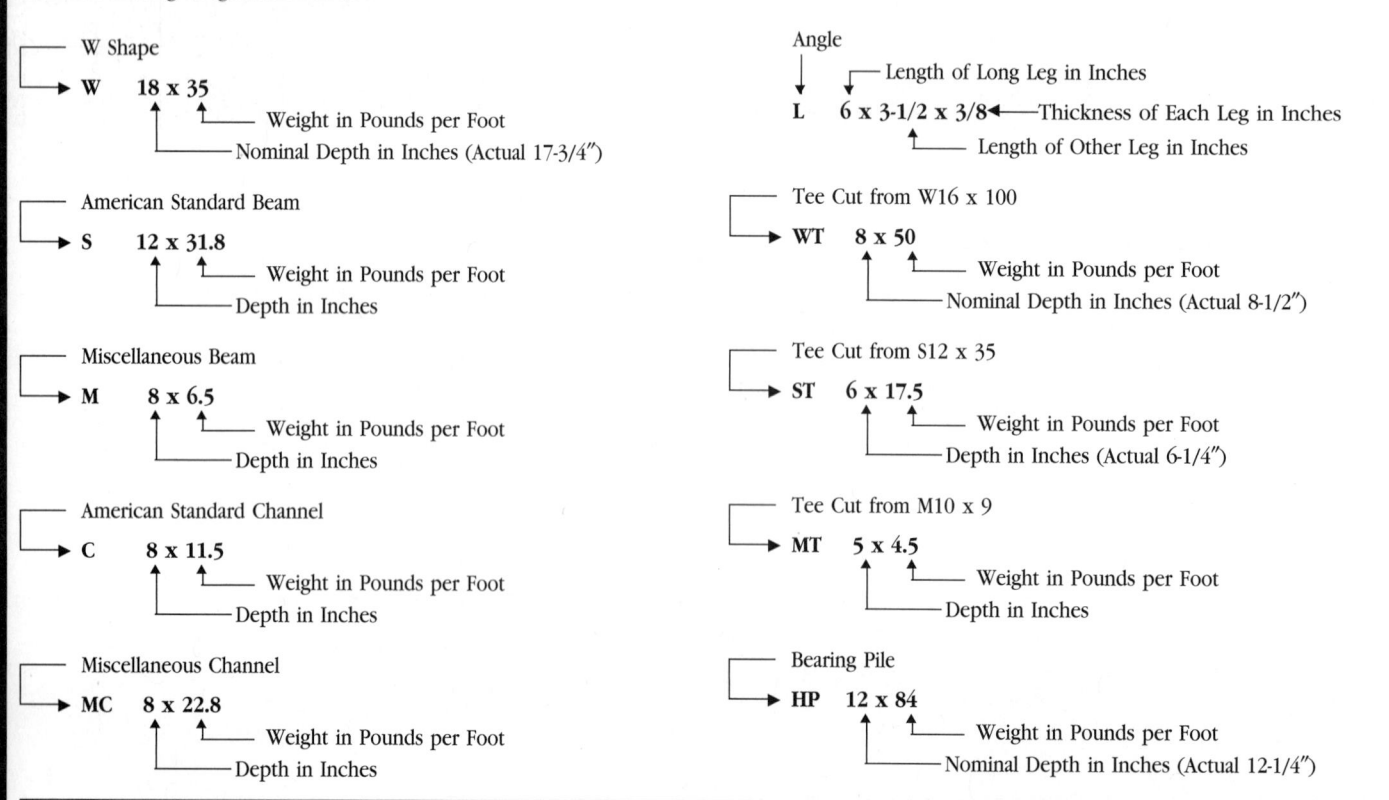

W Shape
- **W 18 x 35**
  - Weight in Pounds per Foot
  - Nominal Depth in Inches (Actual 17-3/4")

American Standard Beam
- **S 12 x 31.8**
  - Weight in Pounds per Foot
  - Depth in Inches

Miscellaneous Beam
- **M 8 x 6.5**
  - Weight in Pounds per Foot
  - Depth in Inches

American Standard Channel
- **C 8 x 11.5**
  - Weight in Pounds per Foot
  - Depth in Inches

Miscellaneous Channel
- **MC 8 x 22.8**
  - Weight in Pounds per Foot
  - Depth in Inches

Angle
- **L 6 x 3-1/2 x 3/8**
  - Length of Long Leg in Inches
  - Length of Other Leg in Inches
  - Thickness of Each Leg in Inches

Tee Cut from W16 x 100
- **WT 8 x 50**
  - Weight in Pounds per Foot
  - Nominal Depth in Inches (Actual 8-1/2")

Tee Cut from S12 x 35
- **ST 6 x 17.5**
  - Weight in Pounds per Foot
  - Depth in Inches (Actual 6-1/4")

Tee Cut from M10 x 9
- **MT 5 x 4.5**
  - Weight in Pounds per Foot
  - Depth in Inches

Bearing Pile
- **HP 12 x 84**
  - Weight in Pounds per Foot
  - Nominal Depth in Inches (Actual 12-1/4")

Metals   R0512 Structural Steel Framing

R051223-45   Installation Time for Structural Steel Building Components

The following tables show the expected average installation times for various structural steel shapes. Table A presents installation times for columns, Table B for beams, Table C for light framing and bolts, and Table D for structural steel for various project types.

Table A

Description	Labor-Hours	Unit
Columns		
Steel, Concrete Filled		
3-1/2" Diameter	.933	Ea.
6-5/8" Diameter	1.120	Ea.
Steel Pipe		
3" Diameter	.933	Ea.
8" Diameter	1.120	Ea.
12" Diameter	1.244	Ea.
Structural Tubing		
4" x 4"	.966	Ea.
8" x 8"	1.120	Ea.
12" x 8"	1.167	Ea.
W Shape 2 Tier		
W8 x 31	.052	L.F.
W8 x 67	.057	L.F.
W10 x 45	.054	L.F.
W10 x 112	.058	L.F.
W12 x 50	.054	L.F.
W12 x 190	.061	L.F.
W14 x 74	.057	L.F.
W14 x 176	.061	L.F.

Table B

Description	Labor-Hours	Unit	Labor-Hours	Unit
Beams, W Shape				
W6 x 9	.949	Ea.	.093	L.F.
W10 x 22	1.037	Ea.	.085	L.F.
W12 x 26	1.037	Ea.	.064	L.F.
W14 x 34	1.333	Ea.	.069	L.F.
W16 x 31	1.333	Ea.	.062	L.F.
W18 x 50	2.162	Ea.	.088	L.F.
W21 x 62	2.222	Ea.	.077	L.F.
W24 x 76	2.353	Ea.	.072	L.F.
W27 x 94	2.581	Ea.	.067	L.F.
W30 x 108	2.857	Ea.	.067	L.F.
W33 x 130	3.200	Ea.	.071	L.F.
W36 x 300	3.810	Ea.	.077	L.F.

Table C

Description	Labor-Hours	Unit
Light Framing		
Angles 4" and Larger	.055	lbs.
Less than 4"	.091	lbs.
Channels 8" and Larger	.048	lbs.
Less than 8"	.072	lbs.
Cross Bracing Angles	.055	lbs.
Rods	.034	lbs.
Hanging Lintels	.069	lbs.
High Strength Bolts in Place		
3/4" Bolts	.070	Ea.
7/8" Bolts	.076	Ea.

Table D

Description	Labor-Hours	Unit	Labor-Hours	Unit
Apartments, Nursing Homes, etc.				
1-2 Stories	4.211	Piece	7.767	Ton
3-6 Stories	4.444	Piece	7.921	Ton
7-15 Stories	4.923	Piece	9.014	Ton
Over 15 Stories	5.333	Piece	9.209	Ton
Offices, Hospitals, etc.				
1-2 Stories	4.211	Piece	7.767	Ton
3-6 Stories	4.741	Piece	8.889	Ton
7-15 Stories	4.923	Piece	9.014	Ton
Over 15 Stories	5.120	Piece	9.209	Ton
Industrial Buildings				
1 Story	3.478	Piece	6.202	Ton

R051223-50   Subpurlins

Bulb tee subpurlins are structural members designed to support and reinforce a variety of roof deck systems such as precast cement fiber roof deck tiles, monolithic roof deck systems, and gypsum or lightweight concrete over formboard. Other uses include interstitial service ceiling systems, wall panel systems, and joist anchoring in bond beams. See the Unit Price section for pricing on a square foot basis at 32-5/8" O.C. Maximum span is based on a 3-span condition with a total allowable vertical load of 40 psf.

Metals

R0512 Structural Steel Framing

R051223-80 Dimensions and Weights of Sheet Steel

Gauge No.	Inches (in fractions) Wrought Iron	Inches (in decimal parts) Wrought Iron	Steel	Millimeters Steel	Weight per S.F. in Ounces	per S.F. in Lbs.	per Square Meter in Kg.
0000000	1/2"	.5	.4782	12.146	320	20.000	97.650
000000	15/32"	.46875	.4484	11.389	300	18.750	91.550
00000	7/16"	.4375	.4185	10.630	280	17.500	85.440
0000	13/32"	.40625	.3886	9.870	260	16.250	79.330
000	3/8"	.375	.3587	9.111	240	15.000	73.240
00	11/32"	.34375	.3288	8.352	220	13.750	67.130
0	5/16"	.3125	.2989	7.592	200	12.500	61.030
1	9/32"	.28125	.2690	6.833	180	11.250	54.930
2	17/64"	.265625	.2541	6.454	170	10.625	51.880
3	1/4"	.25	.2391	6.073	160	10.000	48.820
4	15/64"	.234375	.2242	5.695	150	9.375	45.770
5	7/32"	.21875	.2092	5.314	140	8.750	42.720
6	13/64"	.203125	.1943	4.935	130	8.125	39.670
7	3/16"	.1875	.1793	4.554	120	7.500	36.320
8	11/64"	.171875	.1644	4.176	110	6.875	33.570
9	5/32"	.15625	.1495	3.797	100	6.250	30.520
10	9/64"	.140625	.1345	3.416	90	5.625	27.460
11	1/8"	.125	.1196	3.038	80	5.000	24.410
12	7/64"	.109375	.1046	2.657	70	4.375	21.360
13	3/32"	.09375	.0897	2.278	60	3.750	18.310
14	5/64"	.078125	.0747	1.897	50	3.125	15.260
15	9/128"	.0713125	.0673	1.709	45	2.813	13.730
16	1/16"	.0625	.0598	1.519	40	2.500	12.210
17	9/160"	.05625	.0538	1.367	36	2.250	10.990
18	1/20"	.05	.0478	1.214	32	2.000	9.765
19	7/160"	.04375	.0418	1.062	28	1.750	8.544
20	3/80"	.0375	.0359	.912	24	1.500	7.324
21	11/320"	.034375	.0329	.836	22	1.375	6.713
22	1/32"	.03125	.0299	.759	20	1.250	6.103
23	9/320"	.028125	.0269	.683	18	1.125	5.490
24	1/40"	.025	.0239	.607	16	1.000	4.882
25	7/320"	.021875	.0209	.531	14	.875	4.272
26	3/160"	.01875	.0179	.455	12	.750	3.662
27	11/640"	.0171875	.0164	.417	11	.688	3.357
28	1/64"	.015625	.0149	.378	10	.625	3.052

Metals — R0531 Steel Decking

R053100-10 Decking Descriptions

General - All Deck Products

A steel deck is made by cold forming structural grade sheet steel into a repeating pattern of parallel ribs. The strength and stiffness of the panels are the result of the ribs and the material properties of the steel. The deck lengths can be varied to suit job conditions, but because of shipping considerations, are usually less than 40 feet. Standard deck width varies with the product used but full sheets are usually 12", 18", 24", 30", or 36". The deck is typically furnished in a standard width with the ends cut square. Any cutting for width, such as at openings or for angular fit, is done at the job site.

The deck is typically attached to the building frame with arc puddle welds, self-drilling screws, or powder or pneumatically driven pins. Sheet to sheet fastening is done with screws, button punching (crimping), or welds.

Composite Floor Deck

After installation and adequate fastening, a floor deck serves several purposes. It (a) acts as a working platform, (b) stabilizes the frame, (c) serves as a concrete form for the slab, and (d) reinforces the slab to carry the design loads applied during the life of the building. Composite decks are distinguished by the presence of shear connector devices as part of the deck. These devices are designed to mechanically lock the concrete and deck together so that the concrete and the deck work together to carry subsequent floor loads. These shear connector devices can be rolled-in embossments, lugs, holes, or wires welded to the panels. The deck profile can also be used to interlock concrete and steel.

Composite deck finishes are either galvanized (zinc coated) or phosphatized/painted. Galvanized deck has a zinc coating on both the top and bottom surfaces. The phosphatized/painted deck has a bare (phosphatized) top surface that will come into contact with the concrete. This bare top surface can be expected to develop rust before the concrete is placed. The bottom side of the deck has a primer coat of paint.

A composite floor deck is normally installed so the panel ends do not overlap on the supporting beams. Shear lugs or panel profile shapes often prevent a tight metal to metal fit if the panel ends overlap; the air gap caused by overlapping will prevent proper fusion with the structural steel supports when the panel end laps are shear stud welded.

Adequate end bearing of the deck must be obtained as shown on the drawings. If bearing is actually less in the field than shown on the drawings, further investigation is required.

Roof Deck

A roof deck is not designed to act compositely with other materials. A roof deck acts alone in transferring horizontal and vertical loads into the building frame. Roof deck rib openings are usually narrower than floor deck rib openings. This provides adequate support of the rigid thermal insulation board.

A roof deck is typically installed to endlap approximately 2" over supports. However, it can be butted (or lapped more than 2") to solve field fit problems. Since designers frequently use the installed deck system as part of the horizontal bracing system (the deck as a diaphragm), any fastening substitution or change should be approved by the designer. Continuous perimeter support of the deck is necessary to limit edge deflection in the finished roof and may be required for diaphragm shear transfer.

Standard roof deck finishes are galvanized or primer painted. The standard factory applied paint for roof decks is a primer paint and is not intended to weather for extended periods of time. Field painting or touching up of abrasions and deterioration of the primer coat or other protective finishes is the responsibility of the contractor.

Cellular Deck

A cellular deck is made by attaching a bottom steel sheet to a roof deck or composite floor deck panel. A cellular deck can be used in the same manner as a floor deck. Electrical, telephone, and data wires are easily run through the chase created between the deck panel and the bottom sheet.

When used as part of the electrical distribution system, the cellular deck must be installed so that the ribs line up and create a smooth cell transition at abutting ends. The joint that occurs at butting cell ends must be taped or otherwise sealed to prevent wet concrete from seeping into the cell. Cell interiors must be free of welding burrs, or other sharp intrusions, to prevent damage to wires.

When used as a roof deck, the bottom flat plate is usually left exposed to view. Care must be maintained during erection to keep good alignment and prevent damage.

A cellular deck is sometimes used with the flat plate on the top side to provide a flat working surface. Installation of the deck for this purpose requires special methods for attachment to the frame because the flat plate, now on the top, can prevent direct access to the deck material that is bearing on the structural steel. It may be advisable to treat the flat top surface to prevent slipping.

A cellular deck is always furnished galvanized or painted over galvanized.

Form Deck

A form deck can be any floor or roof deck product used as a concrete form. Connections to the frame are by the same methods used to anchor floor and roof decks. Welding washers are recommended when welding a deck that is less than 20 gauge thickness.

A form deck is furnished galvanized, prime painted, or uncoated. A galvanized deck must be used for those roof deck systems where a form deck is used to carry a lightweight insulating concrete fill.

Wood, Plastics & Comp. — R0611 Wood Framing

R061110-30 Lumber Product Material Prices

The price of forest products fluctuates widely from location to location and from season to season depending upon economic conditions. The bare material prices in the unit cost sections of the data set show the National Average material prices in effect Jan. 1 of this data year. It must be noted that lumber prices in general may change significantly during the year.

Availability of certain items depends upon geographic location and must be checked prior to firm-price bidding.

Wood, Plastics & Comp. — R0616 Sheathing

R061636-20 Plywood

There are two types of plywood used in construction: interior, which is moisture-resistant but not waterproofed, and exterior, which is waterproofed.

The grade of the exterior surface of the plywood sheets is designated by the first letter: A, for smooth surface with patches allowed; B, for solid surface with patches and plugs allowed; C, which may be surface plugged or may have knot holes up to 1" wide; and D, which is used only for interior type plywood and may have knot holes up to 2-1/2" wide. "Structural Grade" is specifically designed for engineered applications such as box beams. All CC & DD grades have roof and floor spans marked on them.

Underlayment-grade plywood runs from 1/4" to 1-1/4" thick. Thicknesses 5/8" and over have optional tongue and groove joints which eliminate the need for blocking the edges. Underlayment 19/32" and over may be referred to as Sturd-i-Floor.

The price of plywood can fluctuate widely due to geographic and economic conditions.

Typical uses for various plywood grades are as follows:

AA-AD Interior — cupboards, shelving, paneling, furniture
BB Plyform — concrete form plywood
CDX — wall and roof sheathing
Structural — box beams, girders, stressed skin panels
AA-AC Exterior — fences, signs, siding, soffits, etc.
Underlayment — base for resilient floor coverings
Overlaid HDO — high density for concrete forms & highway signs
Overlaid MDO — medium density for painting, siding, soffits & signs
303 Siding — exterior siding, textured, striated, embossed, etc.

Thermal & Moist. Protec. — R0731 Shingles & Shakes

R073126-20 Roof Slate

16", 18" and 20" are standard lengths, and slate usually comes in random widths. For standard 3/16" thickness use 1-1/2" copper nails. Allow for 3% breakage.

Thermal & Moist. Protec. — R0751 Built-Up Bituminous Roofing

R075113-20 Built-Up Roofing

Asphalt is available in kegs of 100 lbs. each; coal tar pitch in 560 lb. kegs. Prepared roofing felts are available in a wide range of sizes, weights and characteristics. However, the most commonly used are #15 (432 S.F. per roll, 13 lbs. per square) and #30 (216 S.F. per roll, 27 lbs. per square).

Inter-ply bitumen varies from 24 lbs. per sq. (asphalt) to 30 lbs. per sq. (coal tar) per ply, MF4@ 25%. Flood coat bitumen also varies from 60 lbs. per sq. (asphalt) to 75 lbs. per sq. (coal tar), MF4@ 25%. Expendable equipment (mops, brooms, screeds, etc.) runs about 16% of the bitumen cost. For new, inexperienced crews this factor may be much higher.

A rigid insulation board is typically applied in two layers. The first is mechanically attached to nailable decks or spot or solid mopped to non-nailable decks; the second layer is then spot or solid mopped to the first layer. Membrane application follows the insulation, except in protected membrane roofs, where the membrane goes down first and the insulation on top, followed with ballast (stone or concrete pavers). Insulation and related labor costs are NOT included in prices for built-up roofing.

Openings — R0813 Metal Doors

R081313-20 Steel Door Selection Guide

Standard steel doors are classified into four levels, as recommended by the Steel Door Institute in the chart below. Each of the four levels offers a range of construction models and designs to meet architectural requirements for preference and appearance, including full flush, seamless, and stile & rail. Recommended minimum gauge requirements are also included.

For complete standard steel door construction specifications and available sizes, refer to the Steel Door Institute Technical Data Series, ANSI A250.8-98 (SDI-100), and ANSI A250.4-94 Test Procedure and Acceptance Criteria for Physical Endurance of Steel Door and Hardware Reinforcements.

Level	Model		Construction	For Full Flush or Seamless		
				Min. Gauge	Thickness (in)	Thickness (mm)
I	Standard Duty	1	Full Flush	20	0.032	0.8
		2	Seamless			
II	Heavy Duty	1	Full Flush	18	0.042	1.0
		2	Seamless			
III	Extra Heavy Duty	1	Full Flush	16	0.053	1.3
		2	Seamless			
		3	*Stile & Rail			
IV	Maximum Duty	1	Full Flush	14	0.067	1.6
		2	Seamless			

*Stiles & rails are 16 gauge; flush panels, when specified, are 18 gauge

Openings — R0852 Wood Windows

R085216-10 Window Estimates

To ensure a complete window estimate, be sure to include the material and labor costs for each window, as well as the material and labor costs for an interior wood trim set.

Openings — R0853 Plastic Windows

R085313-20 Replacement Windows

Replacement windows are typically measured per United Inch.

United Inches are calculated by rounding the width and height of the window opening up to the nearest inch, then adding the two figures.

The labor cost for replacement windows includes removal of sash, existing sash balance or weights, parting bead where necessary and installation of new window.

Debris hauling and dump fees are not included.

Openings — R0881 Glass Glazing

R088110-10 Glazing Productivity

Some glass sizes are estimated by the "united inch" (height + width). The table below shows the number of lights glazed in an eight-hour period by the crew size indicated, for glass up to 1/4" thick. Square or nearly square lights are more economical on a S.F. basis. Long slender lights will have a high S.F. installation cost. For insulated glass reduce production by 33%. For 1/2" float glass reduce production by 50%. Production time for glazing with two glaziers per day averages: 1/4" float glass 120 S.F.; 1/2" float glass 55 S.F.; 1/2" insulated glass 95 S.F.; 3/4" insulated glass 75 S.F.

Glazing Method	\multicolumn{8}{c}{United Inches per Light}
	40"	60"	80"	100"	135"	165"	200"	240"
Number of Men in Crew	1	1	1	1	2	3	3	4
Industrial sash, putty	60	45	24	15	18	—	—	—
With stops, putty bed	50	36	21	12	16	8	4	3
Wood stops, rubber	40	27	15	9	11	6	3	2
Metal stops, rubber	30	24	14	9	9	6	3	2
Structural glass	10	7	4	3	—	—	—	—
Corrugated glass	12	9	7	4	4	4	3	—
Storefronts	16	15	13	11	7	6	4	4
Skylights, putty glass	60	36	21	12	16	—	—	—
Thiokol set	15	15	11	9	9	6	3	2
Vinyl set, snap on	18	18	13	12	12	7	5	4
Maximum area per light	2.8 S.F.	6.3 S.F.	11.1 S.F.	17.4 S.F.	31.6 S.F.	47 S.F.	69 S.F.	100 S.F.

Finishes — R0972 Wall Coverings

R097223-10 Wall Covering

The table below lists the quantities required for 100 S.F. of wall covering.

Description	Medium-Priced Paper	Expensive Paper
Paper	1.6 dbl. rolls	1.6 dbl. rolls
Wall sizing	0.25 gallon	0.25 gallon
Vinyl wall paste	0.6 gallon	0.6 gallon
Apply sizing	0.3 hour	0.3 hour
Apply paper	1.2 hours	1.5 hours

Most wallpapers now come in double rolls only.
To remove old paper, allow 1.3 hours per 100 S.F.

Finishes — R0991 Painting

R099100-10 Painting Estimating Techniques

Proper estimating methodology is needed to obtain an accurate painting estimate. There is no known reliable shortcut or square foot method. The following steps should be followed:

- List all surfaces to be painted, with an accurate quantity (area) of each. Items having similar surface condition, finish, application method and accessibility may be grouped together.
- List all the tasks required for each surface to be painted, including surface preparation, masking, and protection of adjacent surfaces. Surface preparation may include minor repairs, washing, sanding and puttying.
- Select the proper Means line for each task. Review and consider all adjustments to labor and materials for type of paint and location of work. Apply the height adjustment carefully. For instance, when applying the adjustment for work over 8' high to a wall that is 12' high, apply the adjustment only to the area between 8' and 12' high, and not to the entire wall.

When applying more than one percent (%) adjustment, apply each to the base cost of the data, rather than applying one percentage adjustment on top of the other.

When estimating the cost of painting walls and ceilings remember to add the brushwork for all cut-ins at inside corners and around windows and doors as a LF measure. One linear foot of cut-in with a brush equals one square foot of painting.

All items for spray painting include the labor for roll-back.

Deduct for openings greater than 100 SF or openings that extend from floor to ceiling and are greater than 5' wide. Do not deduct small openings.

The cost of brushes, rollers, ladders and spray equipment are considered part of a painting contractor's overhead, and should not be added to the estimate. The cost of rented equipment such as scaffolding and swing staging should be added to the estimate.

Finishes — R0991 Painting

R099100-20 Painting

Item	Coat	One Gallon Covers Brush	One Gallon Covers Roller	One Gallon Covers Spray	In 8 Hours a Laborer Covers Brush	In 8 Hours a Laborer Covers Roller	In 8 Hours a Laborer Covers Spray	Labor-Hours per 100 S.F. Brush	Labor-Hours per 100 S.F. Roller	Labor-Hours per 100 S.F. Spray
Paint wood siding	prime	250 S.F.	225 S.F.	290 S.F.	1150 S.F.	1300 S.F.	2275 S.F.	.695	.615	.351
	others	270	250	290	1300	1625	2600	.615	.492	.307
Paint exterior trim	prime	400	—	—	650	—	—	1.230	—	—
	1st	475	—	—	800	—	—	1.000	—	—
	2nd	520	—	—	975	—	—	.820	—	—
Paint shingle siding	prime	270	255	300	650	975	1950	1.230	.820	.410
	others	360	340	380	800	1150	2275	1.000	.695	.351
Stain shingle siding	1st	180	170	200	750	1125	2250	1.068	.711	.355
	2nd	270	250	290	900	1325	2600	.888	.603	.307
Paint brick masonry	prime	180	135	160	750	800	1800	1.066	1.000	.444
	1st	270	225	290	815	975	2275	.981	.820	.351
	2nd	340	305	360	815	1150	2925	.981	.695	.273
Paint interior plaster or drywall	prime	400	380	495	1150	2000	3250	.695	.400	.246
	others	450	425	495	1300	2300	4000	.615	.347	.200
Paint interior doors and windows	prime	400	—	—	650	—	—	1.230	—	—
	1st	425	—	—	800	—	—	1.000	—	—
	2nd	450	—	—	975	—	—	.820	—	—

Special Construction — R1331 Fabric Structures

R133113-10 Air Supported Structures

Air supported structures are made from fabrics that can be classified into two groups: temporary and permanent. Temporary fabrics include nylon, woven polyethylene, vinyl film, and vinyl coated dacron. These have lifespans that range from five to fifteen plus years. The cost per square foot includes a fabric shell, tension cables, primary and back-up inflation systems and doors. The lower cost structures are used for construction shelters, bulk storage and pond covers. The more expensive are used for recreational structures and warehouses.

Permanent fabrics are teflon coated fiberglass. The life of this structure is twenty plus years. The high cost limits its application to architectural designed structures which call for a clear span covered area, such as stadiums and convention centers. Both temporary and permanent structures are available in translucent fabrics which eliminate the need for daytime lighting.

Areas to be covered vary from 10,000 S.F. to any area up to 1000 feet wide by any length. Height restrictions range from a maximum of 1/2 of the width to a minimum of 1/6 of the width. Erection of even the largest of the temporary structures requires no more than a week.

Centrifugal fans provide the inflation necessary to support the structure during application of live loads. Airlocks are usually used at large entrances to prevent loss of static pressure. Some manufacturers employ propeller fans which generate sufficient airflow (30,000 CFM) to eliminate the need for airlocks. These fans may also be automatically controlled to resist high wind conditions, regulate humidity (air changes), and provide cooling and heat.

Insulation can be provided with the addition of a second or even third interior liner, creating a dead air space with an "R" value of four to nine. Some structures allow for the liner to be collapsed into the outer shell to enable the internal heat to melt accumulated snow. For cooling or air conditioning, the exterior face of the liner can be aluminized to reflect the sun's heat.

Special Construction — R1334 Fabricated Engineered Structures

R133423-30 Dome Structures

Steel — The four types are Lamella, Schwedler, Arch and Geodesic. For maximum economy, the rise should be about 15 to 20% of the diameter. Most common diameters are in the 200' to 300' range. Lamella domes weigh about 5 P.S.F. of floor area less than Schwedler domes. The Schwedler dome weight in lbs. per S.F. approaches .046 times the diameter. Domes below 125' in diameter weigh .07 times the diameter and the cost per ton of steel is higher. See R051223-20 for estimating weight.

Wood — Small domes are of sawn lumber. Larger ones are laminated. In larger sizes, triaxial and triangular cost about the same; radial domes cost more. Radial domes are economical in the 60' to 70' diameter range. The most economical range of all types is 80' to 200' diameters. Diameters can run over 400'. All costs are quoted above the foundation. Prices include 2" decking and a tension tie ring in place.

Plywood — Stock prefab geodesic domes are available with diameters from 24' to 60'.

Fiberglass — Aluminum framed translucent sandwich panels with spans from 5' to 45' are commercially available.

Aluminum — Stressed skin aluminum panels form geodesic domes with spans ranging from 82' to 232'. An aluminum space truss, triangulated or nontriangulated, with aluminum or clear acrylic closure panels can be used for clear spans of 40' to 415'.

Plumbing — R2211 Facility Water Distribution

R221113-50 Pipe Material Considerations

1. Malleable fittings should be used for gas service.
2. Malleable fittings are used where there are stresses/strains due to expansion and vibration.
3. Cast fittings may be broken as an aid to disassembling heating lines frozen by long use, temperature and minerals.
4. A cast iron pipe is extensively used for underground and submerged service.
5. Type M (light wall) copper tubing is available in hard temper only and is used for nonpressure and less severe applications than K and L.
6. Type L (medium wall) copper tubing, available hard or soft for interior service.
7. Type K (heavy wall) copper tubing, available in hard or soft temper for use where conditions are severe. For underground and interior service.
8. Hard drawn tubing requires fewer hangers or supports but should not be bent. Silver brazed fittings are recommended, but soft solder is normally used.
9. Type DMV (very light wall) copper tubing designed for drainage, waste and vent plus other non-critical pressure services.

Domestic/Imported Pipe and Fittings Costs

The prices shown in this publication for steel/cast iron pipe and steel, cast iron, and malleable iron fittings are based on domestic production sold at the normal trade discounts. The above listed items of foreign manufacture may be available at prices 1/3 to 1/2 of those shown. Some imported items after minor machining or finishing operations are being sold as domestic to further complicate the system.

Caution: Most pipe prices in this data set also include a coupling and pipe hangers which for the larger sizes can add significantly to the per foot cost and should be taken into account when comparing "book cost" with the quoted supplier's cost.

Plumbing — R2240 Plumbing Fixtures

R224000-40 Plumbing Fixture Installation Time

Item	Rough-In	Set	Total Hours	Item	Rough-In	Set	Total Hours
Bathtub	5	5	10	Shower head only	2	1	3
Bathtub and shower, cast iron	6	6	12	Shower drain	3	1	4
Fire hose reel and cabinet	4	2	6	Shower stall, slate		15	15
Floor drain to 4 inch diameter	3	1	4	Slop sink	5	3	8
Grease trap, single, cast iron	5	3	8	Test 6 fixtures			14
Kitchen gas range		4	4	Urinal, wall	6	2	8
Kitchen sink, single	4	4	8	Urinal, pedestal or floor	6	4	10
Kitchen sink, double	6	6	12	Water closet and tank	4	3	7
Laundry tubs	4	2	6	Water closet and tank, wall hung	5	3	8
Lavatory wall hung	5	3	8	Water heater, 45 gals. gas, automatic	5	2	7
Lavatory pedestal	5	3	8	Water heaters, 65 gals. gas, automatic	5	2	7
Shower and stall	6	4	10	Water heaters, electric, plumbing only	4	2	6

Fixture prices in front of the data set are based on the cost per fixture set in place. The rough-in cost, which must be added for each fixture, includes carrier, if required, some supply, waste and vent pipe connecting fittings and stops. The lengths of rough-in pipe are nominal runs which would connect to the larger runs and stacks. The supply runs and DWV runs and stacks must be accounted for in separate entries. In the eastern half of the United States it is common for the plumber to carry these to a point 5' outside the building.

Heating, Ventilating & A.C. — R2305 Common Work Results for HVAC

R230500-10 Subcontractors

On the unit cost pages of the RSMeans Cost Data sets, the last column is entitled "Total Incl. O&P". This is normally the cost of the installing contractor. In the HVAC Division, this is the cost of the mechanical contractor. If the particular work being estimated is to be performed by a sub to the mechanical contractor, the mechanical's profit and handling charge (usually 10%) is added to the total of the last column.

Heating, Ventilating & A.C. R2350 Central Heating Equipment

R235000-10 Heating Systems

Heating Systems

The basic function of a heating system is to bring an enclosed volume up to a desired temperature and then maintain that temperature within a reasonable range. To accomplish this, the selected system must have sufficient capacity to offset transmission losses resulting from the temperature difference on the interior and exterior of the enclosing walls in addition to losses due to cold air infiltration through cracks, crevices and around doors and windows. The amount of heat to be furnished is dependent upon the building size, construction, temperature difference, air leakage, use, shape, orientation and exposure. Air circulation is also an important consideration. Circulation will prevent stratification which could result in heat losses through uneven temperatures at various levels. For example, the most efficient use of unit heaters can usually be achieved by circulating the space volume through the total number of units once every 20 minutes or 3 times an hour. This general rule must, of course, be adapted for special cases such as large buildings with low ratios of heat transmitting surface to cubical volume. The type of occupancy of a building will have considerable bearing on the number of heat transmitting units and the location selected. It is axiomatic, however, that the basis of any successful heating system is to provide the maximum amount of heat at the points of maximum heat loss such as exposed walls, windows, and doors. Large roof areas, wind direction, and wide doorways create problems of excessive heat loss and require special consideration and treatment.

Heat Transmission

Heat transfer is an important parameter to consider during selection of the exterior wall style, material and window area. A high rate of transfer will permit greater heat loss during the wintertime with the resultant increase in heating energy costs and a greater rate of heat gain in the summer with proportionally greater cooling cost. Several terms are used to describe various aspects of heat transfer. However, for general estimating purposes this data set lists U values for systems of construction materials. U is the "overall heat transfer coefficient." It is defined as the heat flow per hour through one square foot when the temperature difference in the air on either side of the structure wall, roof, ceiling or floor is one degree Fahrenheit. The structural segment may be a single homogeneous material or a composite.

Total heat transfer is found using the following equation:

$Q = AU(T_2 - T_1)$ where
- Q = Heat flow, BTU per hour
- A = Area, square feet
- U = Overall heat transfer coefficient
- $(T_2 - T_1)$ = Difference in temperature of air on each side of the construction component. (Also abbreviated TD)

Note that heat can flow through all surfaces of any building and this flow is in addition to heat gain or loss due to ventilation, infiltration and generation (appliances, machinery, people).

Heating, Ventilating & A.C. R2356 Solar Energy Heating Equipment

R235616-60 Solar Heating (Space and Hot Water)

Collectors should face as close to due South as possible, but variations of up to 20 degrees on either side of true South are acceptable. Local climate and collector type may influence the choice between east or west deviations. Obviously they should be located so they are not shaded from the sun's rays. Incline collectors at a slope of latitude minus 5 degrees for domestic hot water and latitude plus 15 degrees for space heating.

Flat plate collectors consist of a number of components as follows: Insulation to reduce heat loss through the bottom and sides of the collector. The enclosure which contains all the components in this assembly is usually weatherproof and prevents dust, wind and water from coming in contact with the absorber plate. The cover plate usually consists of one or more layers of a variety of glass or plastic and reduces the reradiation by creating an air space which traps the heat between the cover and the absorber plates.

The absorber plate must have a good thermal bond with the fluid passages. The absorber plate is usually metallic and treated with a surface coating which improves absorptivity. Black or dark paints or selective coatings are used for this purpose, and the design of this passage and plate combination helps determine a solar system's effectiveness.

Heat transfer fluid passage tubes are attached above and below or integral with an absorber plate for the purpose of transferring thermal energy from the absorber plate to a heat transfer medium. The heat exchanger is a device for transferring thermal energy from one fluid to another.

Piping and storage tanks should be well insulated to minimize heat losses.

Size domestic water heating storage tanks to hold 20 gallons of water per user, minimum, plus 10 gallons per dishwasher or washing machine. For domestic water heating an optimum collector size is approximately 3/4 square foot of area per gallon of water storage. For space heating of residences and small commercial applications the collector is commonly sized between 30% and 50% of the internal floor area. For space heating of large commercial applications, collector areas less than 30% of the internal floor area can still provide significant heat reductions.

A supplementary heat source is recommended for Northern states for December through February.

The solar energy transmission per square foot of collector surface varies greatly with the material used. Initial cost, heat transmittance and useful life are obviously interrelated.

Heating, Ventilating & A.C. R2360 Central Cooling Equipment

R236000-30 Psychrometric Table

Dewpoint or Saturation Temperature (F)

Relative humidity (%)														
100	32	35	40	45	50	55	60	65	70	75	80	85	90	95	100
90	30	33	37	42	47	52	57	62	67	72	77	82	87	92	97
80	27	30	34	39	44	49	54	58	64	68	73	78	83	88	93
70	24	27	31	36	40	45	50	55	60	64	69	74	79	84	88
60	20	24	28	32	36	41	46	51	55	60	65	69	74	79	83
50	16	20	24	28	33	36	41	46	50	55	60	64	69	73	78
40	12	15	18	23	27	31	35	40	45	49	53	58	62	67	71
30	8	10	14	18	21	25	29	33	37	42	46	50	54	59	62
20	6	7	8	9	13	16	20	24	28	31	35	40	43	48	52
10	4	4	5	5	6	8	9	10	13	17	20	24	27	30	34
	32	35	40	45	50	55	60	65	70	75	80	85	90	95	100

Dry bulb temperature (F)

This table shows the relationship between RELATIVE HUMIDITY, DRY BULB TEMPERATURE AND DEWPOINT.

As an example, assume that the thermometer in a room reads 75° F, and we know that the relative humidity is 50%. The chart shows the dewpoint temperature to be 55° F. That is, any surface colder than 55° F will "sweat" or collect condensing moisture. This surface could be the outside of an uninsulated chilled water pipe in the summertime, or the inside surface of a wall or deck in the wintertime. After determining the extreme ambient parameters, the table at the left is useful in determining which surfaces need insulation or vapor barrier protection.

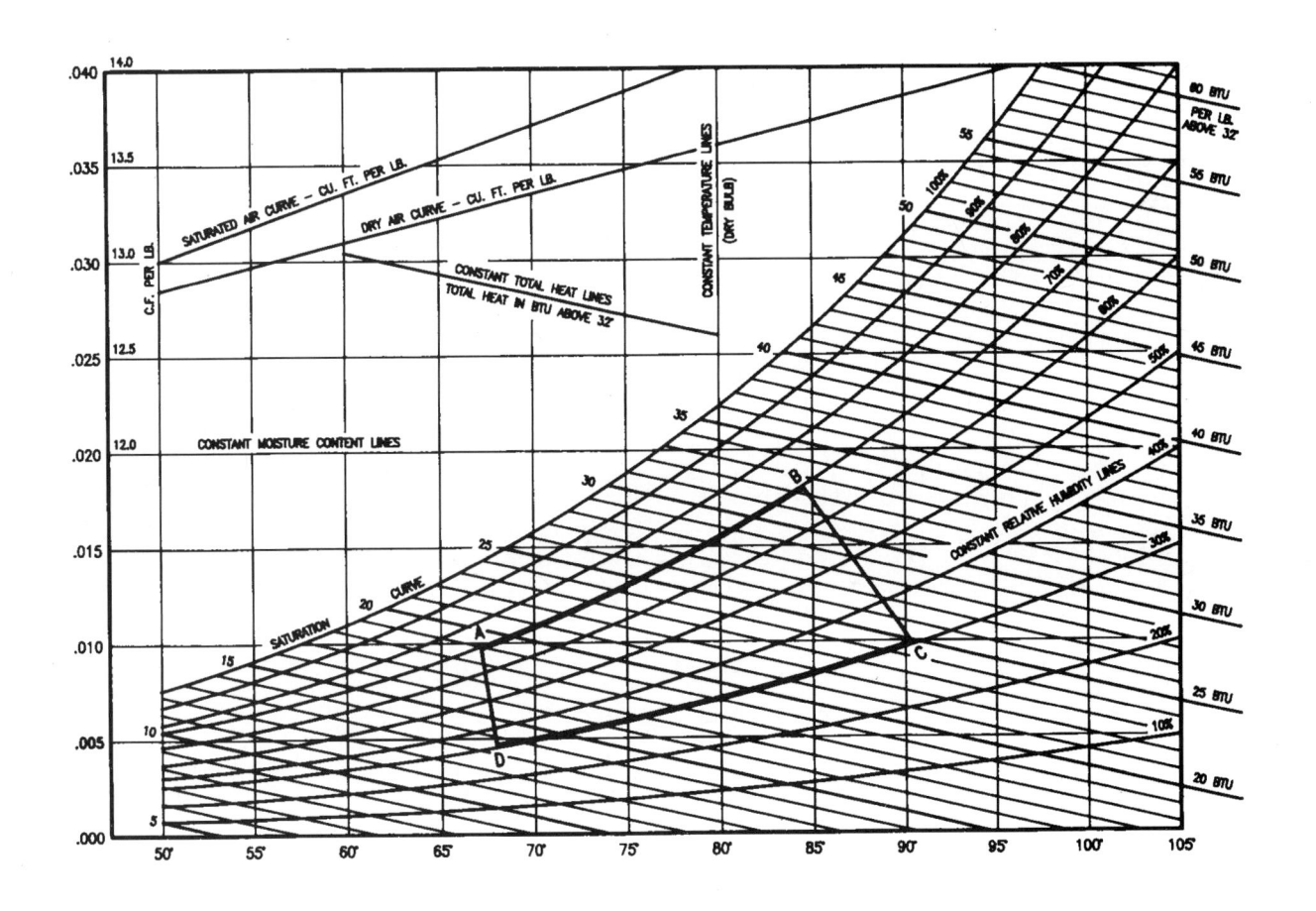

TEMPERATURE DEGREES FAHRENHEIT
TOTAL PRESSURE = 14.696 LB. PER SQ. IN. ABS.

Psychrometric chart showing different variables based on one pound of dry air. Space marked A B C D is temperature-humidity range which is most comfortable for most people.

Electrical | R2627 Low Voltage Distribution Equipment

R262726-90 Wiring Devices

Wiring devices should be priced on a separate takeoff form which includes boxes, covers, conduit and wire.

Labor-hours for devices include:
1. Stripping of wire
2. Attaching wire to device using terminators on the device itself, lugs, set screws etc.
3. Mounting of device in box

Labor-hours do not include:
1. Conduit
2. Wire
3. Boxes
4. Plates

Economy of Scale – for large concentrations of devices in the same area deduct the following percentages from labor-hours:

1	to	10	0%
11	to	25	20%
26	to	50	25%
51	to	100	30%
	over	100	35%

Electrical — R2651 Interior Lighting

R265113-40 Interior Lighting Fixtures

When taking off interior lighting fixtures, it is advisable to set up your quantity worksheet to conform to the lighting schedule as it appears on the print. Include the alpha-numeric code plus the symbol on your work sheet.

Take off a particular section or floor of the building and count each type of fixture before going on to another type. It would also be advantageous to include on the same worksheet the pipe, wire, fittings and circuit number associated with each type of lighting fixture. This will help you identify the costs associated with any particular lighting system and in turn make material purchases more specific as to when and how much to order under the classification of lighting.

By taking off lighting first you can get a complete "walk-through" of the job. This will become helpful when doing other phases of the project.

Materials for a recessed fixture include:
1. Fixture
2. Lamps
3. 6' of jack chain
4. (2) S hooks
5. (2) Wire nuts

Labor for interior recessed fixtures include:
1. Unloading by hand
2. Hauling by hand to an area up to 200' from loading dock
3. Uncrating
4. Layout
5. Installing fixture
6. Attaching jack chain & S hooks
7. Connecting circuit power
8. Reassembling fixture
9. Installing lamps
10. Testing

Material for surface mounted fixtures includes:
1. Fixture
2. Lamps
3. Either (4) lead type anchors, (4) toggle bolts, or (4) ceiling grid clips
4. (2) Wire nuts

Material for pendent mounted fixtures includes:
1. Fixture
2. Lamps
3. (2) Wire nuts

4. Rigid pendents as required by type of fixtures
5. Canopies as required by type of fixture

Labor hours include the following for both surface and pendent fixtures:
1. Unloading by hand
2. Hauling by hand to an area up to 200' from loading dock
3. Uncrating
4. Layout and marking
5. Drilling (4) holes for either lead anchors or toggle bolts using a hammer drill
6. Installing fixture
7. Leveling fixture
8. Connecting circuit power
9. Installing lamps
10. Testing

Labor for surface or pendent fixtures does not include:
1. Conduit
2. Boxes or covers
3. Connectors
4. Fixture whips
5. Special support
6. Switching
7. Wire

Economy of Scale: For large concentrations of lighting fixtures in the same area deduct the following percentages from labor:

25	to	50	fixtures	15%
51	to	75	fixtures	20%
76	to	100	fixtures	25%
101 and over				30%

Job Conditions: Productivity is based on new construction in an unobstructed first floor location, using rolling staging to 15' high.

Material staging is assumed to be within 100' of work being performed.

Add the following percentages to labor for elevated installations:

15'	to	20'	high	10%
21'	to	25'	high	20%
26'	to	30'	high	30%
31'	to	35'	high	40%
36'	to	40'	high	50%
41' and over				60%

Electrical — R2657 Lamps

R265723-10 For Other than Regular Cool White (CW) Lamps

Multiply Material Costs as Follows:					
Regular Lamps	Cool white deluxe (CWX)	x 1.35	Energy Saving Lamps	Cool white (CW/ES)	x 1.35
	Warm white deluxe (WWX)	x 1.35		Cool white deluxe (CWX/ES)	x 1.65
	Warm white (WW)	x 1.30		Warm white (WW/ES)	x 1.55
	Natural (N)	x 2.05		Warm white deluxe (WWX/ES)	x 1.65

Change Orders

Change Order Considerations

A change order is a written document usually prepared by the design professional and signed by the owner, the architect/engineer, and the contractor. A change order states the agreement of the parties to: an addition, deletion, or revision in the work; an adjustment in the contract sum, if any; or an adjustment in the contract time, if any. Change orders, or "extras", in the construction process occur after execution of the construction contract and impact architects/engineers, contractors, and owners.

Change orders that are properly recognized and managed can ensure orderly, professional, and profitable progress for everyone involved in the project. There are many causes for change orders and change order requests. In all cases, change orders or change order requests should be addressed promptly and in a precise and prescribed manner. The following paragraphs include information regarding change order pricing and procedures.

The Causes of Change Orders

Reasons for issuing change orders include:

- Unforeseen field conditions that require a change in the work
- Correction of design discrepancies, errors, or omissions in the contract documents
- Owner-requested changes, either by design criteria, scope of work, or project objectives
- Completion date changes for reasons unrelated to the construction process
- Changes in building code interpretations, or other public authority requirements that require a change in the work
- Changes in availability of existing or new materials and products

Procedures

Properly written contract documents must include the correct change order procedures for all parties—owners, design professionals, and contractors—to follow in order to avoid costly delays and litigation.

Being "in the right" is not always a sufficient or acceptable defense. The contract provisions requiring notification and documentation must be adhered to within a defined or reasonable time frame.

The appropriate method of handling change orders is by a written proposal and acceptance by all parties involved. Prior to starting work on a project, all parties should identify their authorized agents who may sign and accept change orders, as well as any limits placed on their authority.

Time may be a critical factor when the need for a change arises. For such cases, the contractor might be directed to proceed on a "time and materials" basis, rather than wait for all paperwork to be processed—a delay that could impede progress. In this situation, the contractor must still follow the prescribed change order procedures including, but not limited to, notification and documentation.

Lack of documentation can be very costly, especially if legal judgments are to be made, and if certain field personnel are no longer available. For time and material change orders, the contractor should keep accurate daily records of all labor and material allocated to the change.

Owners or awarding authorities who do considerable and continual building construction (such as the federal government) realize the inevitability of change orders for numerous reasons, both predictable and unpredictable. As a result, the federal government, the American Institute of Architects (AIA), the Engineers Joint Contract Documents Committee (EJCDC), and other contractor, legal, and technical organizations have developed standards and procedures to be followed by all parties to achieve contract continuance and timely completion, while being financially fair to all concerned.

Pricing Change Orders

When pricing change orders, regardless of their cause, the most significant factor is when the change occurs. The need for a change may be perceived in the field or requested by the architect/engineer *before* any of the actual installation has begun, or may evolve or appear *during* construction when the item of work in question is partially installed. In the latter cases, the original sequence of construction is disrupted, along with all contiguous and supporting systems. Change orders cause the greatest impact when they occur *after* the installation has been completed and must be uncovered, or even replaced. Post-completion changes may be caused by necessary design changes, product failure, or changes in the owner's requirements that are not discovered until the building or the systems begin to function.

Specified procedures of notification and record keeping must be adhered to and enforced regardless of the stage of construction: *before*, *during*, or *after* installation. Some bidding documents anticipate change orders by requiring that unit prices including overhead and profit percentages—for additional as well as deductible changes—be listed. Generally these unit prices do not fully take into account the ripple effect, or impact on other trades, and should be used for general guidance only.

When pricing change orders, it is important to classify the time frame in which the change occurs. There are two basic time frames for change orders: *pre-installation change orders*, which occur before the start of construction, and *post-installation change orders*, which involve reworking after the original installation. Change orders that occur between these stages may be priced according to the extent of work completed using a combination of techniques developed for pricing *pre-* and *post-installation* changes.

Factors To Consider When Pricing Change Orders

As an estimator begins to prepare a change order, the following questions should be reviewed to determine their impact on the final price.

General

- *Is the change order work* pre-installation *or* post-installation?

  Change order work costs vary according to how much of the installation has been completed. Once workers have the project scoped in their minds, even though they have not started, it can be difficult to refocus. Consequently they may spend more than the normal amount of time understanding the change. Also, modifications to work in place, such as trimming or refitting, usually take more time than was initially estimated. The greater the amount of work in place, the more reluctant workers are to change it. Psychologically they may resent the change and as a result the rework takes longer than normal. Post-installation change order estimates must include demolition of existing work as required to accomplish the change. If the work is performed at a later time, additional obstacles, such as building finishes, may be present which must be protected. Regardless of whether the change occurs pre-installation or post-installation, attempt to isolate the identifiable factors and price them separately. For example, add shipping costs that may be required pre-installation or any demolition required post-installation. Then analyze the potential impact on productivity of psychological and/or learning curve factors and adjust the output rates accordingly. One approach is to break down the typical workday into segments and quantify the impact on each segment.

Change Order Installation Efficiency

The labor-hours expressed (for new construction) are based on average installation time, using an efficiency level. For change order situations, adjustments to this efficiency level should reflect the daily labor-hour allocation for that particular occurrence.

- *Will the change substantially delay the original completion date?*

A significant change in the project may cause the original completion date to be extended. The extended schedule may subject the contractor to new wage rates dictated by relevant labor contracts. Project supervision and other project overhead must also be extended beyond the original completion date. The schedule extension may also put installation into a new weather season. For example, underground piping scheduled for October installation was delayed until January. As a result, frost penetrated the trench area, thereby changing the degree of difficulty of the task. Changes and delays may have a ripple effect throughout the project. This effect must be analyzed and negotiated with the owner.

- *What is the net effect of a deduct change order?*

In most cases, change orders resulting in a deduction or credit reflect only bare costs. The contractor may retain the overhead and profit based on the original bid.

Materials

- *Will you have to pay more or less for the new material, required by the change order, than you paid for the original purchase?*

The same material prices or discounts will usually apply to materials purchased for change orders as new construction. In some instances, however, the contractor may forfeit the advantages of competitive pricing for change orders. Consider the following example:

A contractor purchased over $20,000 worth of fan coil units for an installation and obtained the maximum discount. Some time later it was determined the project required an additional matching unit. The contractor has to purchase this unit from the original supplier to ensure a match. The supplier at this time may not discount the unit because of the small quantity, and he is no longer in a competitive situation. The impact of quantity on purchase can add between 0% and 25% to material prices and/or subcontractor quotes.

- *If materials have been ordered or delivered to the job site, will they be subject to a cancellation charge or restocking fee?*

Check with the supplier to determine if ordered materials are subject to a cancellation charge. Delivered materials not used as a result of a change order may be subject to a restocking fee if returned to the supplier. Common restocking charges run between 20% and 40%. Also, delivery charges to return the goods to the supplier must be added.

Labor

- *How efficient is the existing crew at the actual installation?*

Is the same crew that performed the initial work going to do the change order? Possibly the change consists of the installation of a unit identical to one already installed; therefore, the change should take less time. Be sure to consider this potential productivity increase and modify the productivity rates accordingly.

- *If the crew size is increased, what impact will that have on supervision requirements?*

Under most bargaining agreements or management practices, there is a point at which a working foreman is replaced by a nonworking foreman. This replacement increases project overhead by adding a nonproductive worker. If additional workers are added to accelerate the project or to perform changes while maintaining the schedule, be sure to add additional supervision time if warranted. Calculate the hours involved and the additional cost directly if possible.

- *What are the other impacts of increased crew size?*

The larger the crew, the greater the potential for productivity to decrease. Some of the factors that cause this productivity loss are: overcrowding (producing restrictive conditions in the working space) and possibly a shortage of any special tools and equipment required. Such factors affect not only the crew working on the elements directly involved in the change order, but other crews whose movements may also be hampered. As the crew increases, check its basic composition for changes by the addition or deletion of apprentices or nonworking foreman, and quantify the potential effects of equipment shortages or other logistical factors.

- *As new crews, unfamiliar with the project, are brought onto the site, how long will it take them to become oriented to the project requirements?*

The orientation time for a new crew to become 100% effective varies with the site and type of project. Orientation is easiest at a new construction site and most difficult at existing, very restrictive renovation sites. The type of work also affects orientation time. When all elements of the work are exposed, such as concrete or masonry work, orientation is decreased. When the work is concealed or less visible, such as existing electrical systems, orientation takes longer. Usually orientation can be accomplished in one day or less. Costs for added orientation should be itemized and added to the total estimated cost.

- *How much actual production can be gained by working overtime?*

Short term overtime can be used effectively to accomplish more work in a day. However, as overtime is scheduled to run beyond several weeks, studies have shown marked decreases in output. The following chart shows the effect of long term overtime on worker efficiency. If the anticipated change requires extended overtime to keep the job on schedule, these factors can be used as a guide to predict the impact on time and cost. Add project overhead, particularly supervision, that may also be incurred.

| Days per Week | Hours per Day | Production Efficiency ||||| Payroll Cost Factors ||
		1st Week	2nd Week	3rd Week	4th Week	Average 4 Weeks	@ 1-1/2 Times	@ 2 Times
5	8	100%	100%	100%	100%	100%	100%	100%
	9	100	100	95	90	96.25	105.6	111.1
	10	100	95	90	85	92.50	110.0	120.0
	11	95	90	75	65	81.25	113.6	127.3
	12	90	85	70	60	76.25	116.7	133.3
6	8	100	100	95	90	96.25	108.3	116.7
	9	100	95	90	85	92.50	113.0	125.9
	10	95	90	85	80	87.50	116.7	133.3
	11	95	85	70	65	78.75	119.7	139.4
	12	90	80	65	60	73.75	122.2	144.4
7	8	100	95	85	75	88.75	114.3	128.6
	9	95	90	80	70	83.75	118.3	136.5
	10	90	85	75	65	78.75	121.4	142.9
	11	85	80	65	60	72.50	124.0	148.1
	12	85	75	60	55	68.75	126.2	152.4

Effects of Overtime

Caution: Under many labor agreements, Sundays and holidays are paid at a higher premium than the normal overtime rate.

The use of long-term overtime is counterproductive on almost any construction job; that is, the longer the period of overtime, the lower the actual production rate. Numerous studies have been conducted, and while they have resulted in slightly different numbers, all reach the same conclusion. The figure above tabulates the effects of overtime work on efficiency.

As illustrated, there can be a difference between the *actual* payroll cost per hour and the *effective* cost per hour for overtime work. This is due to the reduced production efficiency with the increase in weekly hours beyond 40. This difference between actual and effective cost results from overtime work over a prolonged period. Short-term overtime work does not result in as great a reduction in efficiency and, in such cases, effective cost may not vary significantly from the actual payroll cost. As the total hours per week are increased on a regular basis, more time is lost due to fatigue, lowered morale, and an increased accident rate.

As an example, assume a project where workers are working 6 days a week, 10 hours per day. From the figure above (based on productivity studies), the average effective productive hours over a 4-week period are:

$$0.875 \times 60 = 52.5$$

Depending upon the locale and day of week, overtime hours may be paid at time and a half or double time. For time and a half, the overall (average) *actual* payroll cost (including regular and overtime hours) is determined as follows:

$$\frac{40 \text{ reg. hrs.} + (20 \text{ overtime hrs.} \times 1.5)}{60 \text{ hrs.}} = 1.167$$

Based on 60 hours, the payroll cost per hour will be 116.7% of the normal rate at 40 hours per week. However, because the effective production (efficiency) for 60 hours is reduced to the equivalent of 52.5 hours, the effective cost of overtime is calculated as follows:

For time and a half:

$$\frac{40 \text{ reg. hrs.} + (20 \text{ overtime hrs.} \times 1.5)}{52.5 \text{ hrs.}} = 1.33$$

The installed cost will be 133% of the normal rate (for labor).

Thus, when figuring overtime, the actual cost per unit of work will be higher than the apparent overtime payroll dollar increase, due to the reduced productivity of the longer work week. These efficiency calculations are true only for those cost factors determined by hours worked. Costs that are applied weekly or monthly, such as equipment rentals, will not be similarly affected.

Equipment

- *What equipment is required to complete the change order?*

Change orders may require extending the rental period of equipment already on the job site, or the addition of special equipment brought in to accomplish the change work. In either case, the additional rental charges and operator labor charges must be added.

Summary

The preceding considerations and others you deem appropriate should be analyzed and applied to a change order estimate. The impact of each should be quantified and listed on the estimate to form an audit trail.

Change orders that are properly identified, documented, and managed help to ensure the orderly, professional, and profitable progress of the work. They also minimize potential claims or disputes at the end of the project.

Project Costs

Back by customer demand!

You asked and we listened. For customer convenience and estimating ease, we have made the 2018 Project Costs available for download at www.RSMeans.com/2018books. You will also find sample estimates, an RSMeans data overview video and book registration form to receive quarterly data updates throughout 2018.

Estimating Tips

- The cost figures available in the download were derived from hundreds of projects contained in the RSMeans database of completed construction projects. They include the contractor's overhead and profit. The figures have been adjusted to January of the current year.

- These projects were located throughout the U.S. and reflect a tremendous variation in square foot (S.F.) costs. This is due to differences, not only in labor and material costs, but also in individual owners' requirements. For instance, a bank in a large city would have different features than one in a rural area. This is true of all the different types of buildings analyzed. Therefore, caution should be exercised when using these Project Costs. For example, for courthouses, costs in the database are local courthouse costs and will not apply to the larger, more elaborate federal courthouses.

- None of the figures "go with" any others. All individual cost items were computed and tabulated separately. Thus, the sum of the median figures for plumbing, HVAC, and electrical will not normally total up to the total mechanical and electrical costs arrived at by separate analysis and tabulation of the projects.

- Each building was analyzed as to total and component costs and percentages. The figures were arranged in ascending order with the results tabulated as shown. The 1/4 column shows that 25% of the projects had lower costs and 75% had higher. The 3/4 column shows that 75% of the projects had lower costs and 25% had higher. The median column shows that 50% of the projects had lower costs and 50% had higher.

- Project Costs are useful in the conceptual stage when no details are available. As soon as details become available in the project design, the square foot approach should be discontinued and the project priced as to its particular components. When more precision is required, or for estimating the replacement cost of specific buildings, the current edition of *RSMeans Square Foot Costs* should be used.

- In using the figures in this section, it is recommended that the median column be used for preliminary figures if no additional information is available. The median figures, when multiplied by the total city construction cost index figures (see City Cost Indexes) and then multiplied by the project size modifier at the end of this section, should present a fairly accurate base figure, which would then have to be adjusted in view of the estimator's experience, local economic conditions, code requirements, and the owner's particular requirements. There is no need to factor the percentage figures, as these should remain constant from city to city.

- The editors of this data would greatly appreciate receiving cost figures on one or more of your recent projects, which would then be included in the averages for next year. All cost figures received will be kept confidential, except that they will be averaged with other similar projects to arrive at square foot cost figures for next year.

See the website above for details and the discount available for submitting one or more of your projects.

Did you know?

RSMeans data is available through our online application with 24/7 access:

- Search for unit prices by keyword
- Leverage the most up-to-date data
- Build and export estimates

Try it free for 30 days!
www.rsmeans.com/2018freetrial

No part of this cost data may be reproduced, stored in a retrieval system, or transmitted in any form or by any means without prior written permission of Gordian.

50 17 | Project Costs

50 17 00 | Project Costs

				UNIT COSTS			% OF TOTAL		
			UNIT	1/4	MEDIAN	3/4	1/4	MEDIAN	3/4
01	0000	**Auto Sales with Repair**	S.F.						
	0100	Architectural		98.50	110	119	58%	64%	67%
	0200	Plumbing		8.25	8.65	11.55	4.84%	5.20%	6.80%
	0300	Mechanical		11.05	14.80	16.35	6.40%	8.70%	10.15%
	0400	Electrical		17	21	26.50	9.05%	11.70%	15.90%
	0500	Total Project Costs		165	173	177			
02	0000	**Banking Institutions**	S.F.						
	0100	Architectural		149	183	222	59%	65%	69%
	0200	Plumbing		6	8.35	11.60	2.12%	3.39%	4.19%
	0300	Mechanical		11.90	16.45	19.40	4.41%	5.10%	10.75%
	0400	Electrical		29	35	54	10.45%	13.05%	15.90%
	0500	Total Project Costs		247	278	340			
03	0000	**Court House**	S.F.						
	0100	Architectural		78.50	78.50	78.50	54.50%	54.50%	54.50%
	0200	Plumbing		2.96	2.96	2.96	2.07%	2.07%	2.07%
	0300	Mechanical		18.55	18.55	18.55	12.95%	12.95%	12.95%
	0400	Electrical		24	24	24	16.60%	16.60%	16.60%
	0500	Total Project Costs		143	143	143			
04	0000	**Data Centers**	S.F.						
	0100	Architectural		177	177	177	68%	68%	68%
	0200	Plumbing		9.70	9.70	9.70	3.71%	3.71%	3.71%
	0300	Mechanical		24.50	24.50	24.50	9.45%	9.45%	9.45%
	0400	Electrical		23.50	23.50	23.50	9%	9%	9%
	0500	Total Project Costs		261	261	261			
05	0000	**Detention Centers**	S.F.						
	0100	Architectural		164	174	184	52%	53%	60.50%
	0200	Plumbing		17.35	21	25.50	5.15%	7.10%	7.25%
	0300	Mechanical		22	31.50	37.50	7.55%	9.50%	13.80%
	0400	Electrical		36	42.50	55.50	10.90%	14.85%	17.95%
	0500	Total Project Costs		278	293	345			
06	0000	**Fire Stations**	S.F.						
	0100	Architectural		97	120	174	49%	55.50%	63%
	0200	Plumbing		9.45	13.30	15.75	4.86%	5.80%	6.30%
	0300	Mechanical		12.80	18.65	24	5.45%	8.25%	9.70%
	0400	Electrical		21.50	27.50	32.50	8.35%	12.80%	14.70%
	0500	Total Project Costs		195	222	294			
07	0000	**Gymnasium**	S.F.						
	0100	Architectural		82	108	108	57%	64.50%	64.50%
	0200	Plumbing		2.01	6.60	6.60	1.58%	3.48%	3.48%
	0300	Mechanical		3.09	28	28	2.42%	14.65%	14.65%
	0400	Electrical		10.10	19.60	19.60	7.95%	10.35%	10.35%
	0500	Total Project Costs		128	189	189			
08	0000	**Hospitals**	S.F.						
	0100	Architectural		99.50	164	178	43%	47.50%	48%
	0200	Plumbing		7.30	13.95	30	6%	7.45%	7.65%
	0300	Mechanical		48.50	54.50	71	14.20%	17.95%	23.50%
	0400	Electrical		22	44	57.50	10.95%	13.75%	16.85%
	0500	Total Project Costs		233	345	375			
09	0000	**Industrial Buildings**	S.F.						
	0100	Architectural		42	66.50	216	46%	54%	56.50%
	0200	Plumbing		1.62	6.10	12.30	2%	3.06%	6.30%
	0300	Mechanical		4.47	8.50	40.50	4.77%	5.55%	14.80%
	0400	Electrical		6.80	7.80	65	7.85%	13.55%	16.20%
	0500	Total Project Costs		74.50	97	400			
10	0000	**Medical Clinics & Offices**	S.F.						
	0100	Architectural		79.50	118	152	48.50%	55.50%	62.50%
	0200	Plumbing		8.10	12.20	19.65	4.44%	6.40%	8.05%
	0300	Mechanical		13.70	25	42.50	8.30%	11.05%	17.25%
	0400	Electrical		18.60	25	36	8.55%	12.10%	14.65%
	0500	Total Project Costs		156	208	272			

For customer support on your Green Building Costs with RSMeans data, call 800.448.8182.

50 17 | Project Costs

50 17 00 | Project Costs

			UNIT	UNIT COSTS 1/4	MEDIAN	3/4	% OF TOTAL 1/4	MEDIAN	3/4
11	0000	**Mixed Use**	S.F.						
	0100	Architectural		85	120	182	45.50%	52.50%	70%
	0200	Plumbing		5.70	8.70	11	2.84%	3.44%	4.18%
	0300	Mechanical		14.05	36.50	65	8.05%	13.75%	20%
	0400	Electrical		14.85	36.50	49	8.30%	12.95%	15.80%
	0500	Total Project Costs		179	201	320			
12	0000	**Multi-Family Housing**	S.F.						
	0100	Architectural		70.50	106	158	56.50%	61.50%	66.50%
	0200	Plumbing		5.90	10.20	13.90	4.81%	6.30%	7.40%
	0300	Mechanical		6.60	8.80	35.50	4.92%	6.90%	11.20%
	0400	Electrical		9.20	14.35	17.40	6.20%	8.45%	10.25%
	0500	Total Project Costs		104	194	233			
13	0000	**Nursing Home & Assisted Living**	S.F.						
	0100	Architectural		66.50	87	116	51.50%	56.50%	69%
	0200	Plumbing		6.75	10.45	11.70	6.05%	7.40%	8.80%
	0300	Mechanical		5.90	7.55	17.05	4.04%	6.70%	9.55%
	0400	Electrical		9.75	12.80	21.50	7%	10.05%	12.20%
	0500	Total Project Costs		114	135	179			
14	0000	**Office Buildings**	S.F.						
	0100	Architectural		90.50	120	168	56.50%	62%	71.50%
	0200	Plumbing		4.73	7.05	11.45	2.62%	3.48%	5.85%
	0300	Mechanical		10.25	15.80	23.50	5.50%	8.20%	11.10%
	0400	Electrical		11.85	20	31.50	7.75%	10%	12.70%
	0500	Total Project Costs		150	186	262			
15	0000	**Parking Garage**	S.F.						
	0100	Architectural		29.50	36	37.50	70%	79%	88%
	0200	Plumbing		.97	1.01	1.90	2.05%	2.70%	2.83%
	0300	Mechanical		.75	1.16	4.39	2.11%	3.62%	3.81%
	0400	Electrical		2.58	2.83	5.90	5.30%	6.35%	7.95%
	0500	Total Project Costs		36	43.50	47			
16	0000	**Parking Garage/Mixed Use**	S.F.						
	0100	Architectural		95.50	104	106	61%	62%	65.50%
	0200	Plumbing		3.06	4.01	6.15	2.47%	2.72%	3.66%
	0300	Mechanical		13.10	14.75	21	7.80%	13.10%	13.60%
	0400	Electrical		13.70	19.70	20.50	8.20%	12.65%	18.15%
	0500	Total Project Costs		156	162	168			
17	0000	**Police Stations**	S.F.						
	0100	Architectural		108	121	152	49%	56.50%	61%
	0200	Plumbing		14.25	17.10	17.20	5.05%	5.55%	9.05%
	0300	Mechanical		32.50	45	46.50	13%	14.55%	16.55%
	0400	Electrical		24.50	26.50	28	9.15%	12.10%	14%
	0500	Total Project Costs		202	248	282			
18	0000	**Police/Fire**	S.F.						
	0100	Architectural		105	105	320	55.50%	66%	68%
	0200	Plumbing		8.40	8.70	32	5.45%	5.50%	5.55%
	0300	Mechanical		12.85	20.50	73.50	8.35%	12.70%	12.80%
	0400	Electrical		14.65	18.70	84	9.50%	11.75%	14.55%
	0500	Total Project Costs		154	159	580			
19	0000	**Public Assembly Buildings**	S.F.						
	0100	Architectural		119	148	200	58%	61.50%	64%
	0200	Plumbing		5.65	7.40	11.45	2.60%	3.32%	4.01%
	0300	Mechanical		14.95	23	33	6.90%	9.15%	12.75%
	0400	Electrical		19.70	24.50	38.50	8.65%	10.75%	13%
	0500	Total Project Costs		188	242	335			
20	0000	**Recreational**	S.F.						
	0100	Architectural		103	162	219	53.50%	59%	66%
	0200	Plumbing		8.40	15.30	20	3.12%	4.76%	7.40%
	0300	Mechanical		12.65	19.25	30.50	5.35%	7.90%	12.75%
	0400	Electrical		14.15	24.50	33	7.35%	8.50%	10.65%
	0500	Total Project Costs		183	272	375			

For customer support on your Green Building Costs with RSMeans data, call 800.448.8182.

50 17 | Project Costs

50 17 00 | Project Costs

			UNIT	UNIT COSTS 1/4	UNIT COSTS MEDIAN	UNIT COSTS 3/4	% OF TOTAL 1/4	% OF TOTAL MEDIAN	% OF TOTAL 3/4	
21	0000	**Restaurants**	S.F.							21
	0100	Architectural		50.50	179	231	57.50%	60.50%	78%	
	0200	Plumbing		9.45	29.50	37	7.35%	7.75%	8.95%	
	0300	Mechanical		7.25	18.30	44.50	6.50%	10.80%	18.30%	
	0400	Electrical		11.65	21.50	48.50	6.75%	8.45%	12.45%	
	0500	Total Project Costs		65	283	400				
22	0000	**Retail**	S.F.							22
	0100	Architectural		52	57.50	104	60%	60%	64.50%	
	0200	Plumbing		5.35	8.05	10.15	5.05%	6.70%	9%	
	0300	Mechanical		4.88	7	8.60	5.05%	6.15%	6.60%	
	0400	Electrical		6.85	10.95	17.60	7.90%	10.15%	12.25%	
	0500	Total Project Costs		87	106	173				
23	0000	**Schools**	S.F.							23
	0100	Architectural		88.50	114	152	52.50%	57%	61.50%	
	0200	Plumbing		7.10	9.85	14.40	3.75%	4.82%	7%	
	0300	Mechanical		16.85	23	35.50	9.50%	12.25%	14.55%	
	0400	Electrical		16.65	23	29	9.45%	11.40%	13.05%	
	0500	Total Project Costs		151	206	272				
24	0000	**University, College & Private School Classroom & Admin Buildings**	S.F.							24
	0100	Architectural		115	142	179	50.50%	55%	59.50%	
	0200	Plumbing		6.55	10.15	14.35	2.74%	4.30%	6.35%	
	0300	Mechanical		24.50	35.50	43	10.10%	12.15%	14.70%	
	0400	Electrical		18.55	26	31.50	7.65%	9.50%	11.55%	
	0500	Total Project Costs		191	264	350				
25	0000	**University, College & Private School Dormitories**	S.F.							25
	0100	Architectural		75	132	140	54.50%	65%	68.50%	
	0200	Plumbing		9.95	14.05	21	6.45%	7.30%	9.15%	
	0300	Mechanical		4.46	18.95	30	4.13%	9%	12.05%	
	0400	Electrical		5.30	18.40	28	4.75%	7.35%	12.30%	
	0500	Total Project Costs		111	211	249				
26	0000	**University, College & Private School Science, Eng. & Lab Buildings**	S.F.							26
	0100	Architectural		129	137	178	50.50%	56.50%	58%	
	0200	Plumbing		8.90	9.30	24.50	3.29%	3.95%	8.40%	
	0300	Mechanical		40.50	64	64	13.20%	21.50%	23.50%	
	0400	Electrical		26	30	35.50	8.95%	9.70%	12.85%	
	0500	Total Project Costs		265	271	295				
27	0000	**University, College & Private School Student Union Buildings**	S.F.							27
	0100	Architectural		69.50	102	102	51%	59.50%	59.50%	
	0200	Plumbing		5	23	23	4.27%	11.45%	11.45%	
	0300	Mechanical		11.25	29.50	29.50	9.60%	14.55%	14.55%	
	0400	Electrical		15.40	25.50	25.50	12.80%	13.15%	13.15%	
	0500	Total Project Costs		117	201	201				
28	0000	**Warehouses**	S.F.							28
	0100	Architectural		44	68.50	162	61.50%	67.50%	72%	
	0200	Plumbing		2.28	4.88	9.40	2.82%	3.72%	5%	
	0300	Mechanical		2.70	15.40	24	4.56%	8.20%	10.70%	
	0400	Electrical		4.91	18.45	30.50	7.50%	10.10%	18.30%	
	0500	Total Project Costs		65.50	116	226				

Square Foot Project Size Modifier

One factor that affects the S.F. cost of a particular building is the size. In general, for buildings built to the same specifications in the same locality, the larger building will have the lower S.F. cost. This is due mainly to the decreasing contribution of the exterior walls plus the economy of scale usually achievable in larger buildings. The Area Conversion Scale shown below will give a factor to convert costs for the typical size building to an adjusted cost for the particular project.

The Square Foot Base Size lists the median costs, most typical project size in our accumulated data, and the range in size of the projects.

The Size Factor for your project is determined by dividing your project area in S.F. by the typical project size for the particular Building Type. With this factor, enter the Area Conversion Scale at the appropriate Size Factor and determine the appropriate cost multiplier for your building size.

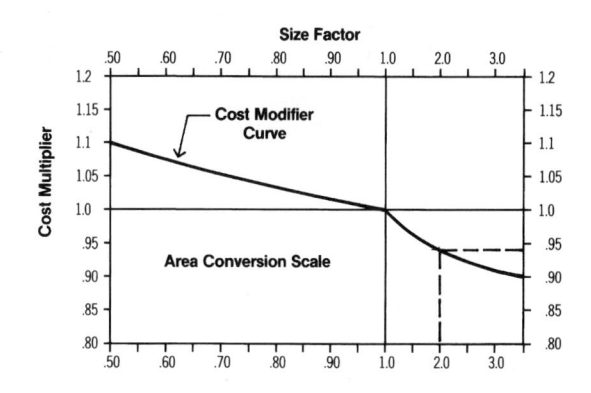

Example: Determine the cost per S.F. for a 152,600 S.F. Multi-family housing.

$$\frac{\text{Proposed building area} = 152,600 \text{ S.F.}}{\text{Typical size from below} = 76,300 \text{ S.F.}} = 2.00$$

Enter Area Conversion scale at 2.0, intersect curve, read horizontally the appropriate cost multiplier of .94. Size adjusted cost becomes .94 x $194.00 = $182.36 based on national average costs.

Note: For Size Factors less than .50, the Cost Multiplier is 1.1
For Size Factors greater than 3.5, the Cost Multiplier is .90

System	Median Cost (Total Project Costs)	Typical Size Gross S.F. (Median of Projects)	Typical Range (Low – High) (Projects)
Auto Sales with Repair	$173.00	25,300	8,200 – 28,700
Banking Institutions	278.00	26,300	3,300 – 28,700
Detention Centers	293.00	42,000	12,300 – 183,300
Fire Stations	222.00	14,600	6,300 – 29,600
Hospitals	345.00	137,500	54,700 – 410,300
Industrial Buildings	$97.00	16,900	5,100 – 200,600
Medical Clinics & Offices	208.00	5,500	2,600 – 327,000
Mixed Use	201.00	49,900	14,400 – 49,900
Multi-Family Housing	194.00	76,300	12,500 – 1,161,500
Nursing Home & Assisted Living	135.00	16,200	1,500 – 242,600
Office Buildings	186.00	10,000	1,100 – 930,000
Parking Garage	43.50	174,600	99,900 – 287,000
Parking Garage/Mixed Use	162.00	5,300	5,300 – 318,000
Police Stations	248.00	15,400	15,400 – 31,600
Public Assembly Buildings	242.00	30,500	2,200 – 235,300
Recreational	272.00	2,300	1,500 – 223,800
Restaurants	283.00	6,100	5,500 – 42,000
Retail	106.00	28,700	5,800 – 61,000
Schools	206.00	30,000	5,500 – 410,800
University, College & Private School Classroom & Admin Buildings	264.00	89,200	9,400 – 196,200
University, College & Private School Dormitories	211.00	50,800	1,500 – 126,900
University, College & Private School Science, Eng. & Lab Buildings	271.00	39,800	36,000 – 117,600
Warehouses	116.00	2,100	600 – 303,800

Abbreviations

A	Area Square Feet; Ampere	Brk., brk	Brick	Csc	Cosecant
AAFES	Army and Air Force Exchange Service	brkt	Bracket	C.S.F.	Hundred Square Feet
ABS	Acrylonitrile Butadiene Stryrene; Asbestos Bonded Steel	Brs.	Brass	CSI	Construction Specifications Institute
A.C., AC	Alternating Current; Air-Conditioning; Asbestos Cement; Plywood Grade A & C	Brz.	Bronze	CT	Current Transformer
		Bsn.	Basin	CTS	Copper Tube Size
		Btr.	Better	Cu	Copper, Cubic
		BTU	British Thermal Unit	Cu. Ft.	Cubic Foot
		BTUH	BTU per Hour	cw	Continuous Wave
ACI	American Concrete Institute	Bu.	Bushels	C.W.	Cool White; Cold Water
ACR	Air Conditioning Refrigeration	BUR	Built-up Roofing	Cwt.	100 Pounds
ADA	Americans with Disabilities Act	BX	Interlocked Armored Cable	C.W.X.	Cool White Deluxe
AD	Plywood, Grade A & D	°C	Degree Centigrade	C.Y.	Cubic Yard (27 cubic feet)
Addit.	Additional	c	Conductivity, Copper Sweat	C.Y./Hr.	Cubic Yard per Hour
Adh.	Adhesive	C	Hundred; Centigrade	Cyl.	Cylinder
Adj.	Adjustable	C/C	Center to Center, Cedar on Cedar	d	Penny (nail size)
af	Audio-frequency	C-C	Center to Center	D	Deep; Depth; Discharge
AFFF	Aqueous Film Forming Foam	Cab	Cabinet	Dis., Disch.	Discharge
AFUE	Annual Fuel Utilization Efficiency	Cair.	Air Tool Laborer	Db	Decibel
AGA	American Gas Association	Cal.	Caliper	Dbl.	Double
Agg.	Aggregate	Calc	Calculated	DC	Direct Current
A.H., Ah	Ampere Hours	Cap.	Capacity	DDC	Direct Digital Control
A hr	Ampere-hour	Carp.	Carpenter	Demob.	Demobilization
A.H.U., AHU	Air Handling Unit	C.B.	Circuit Breaker	d.f.t.	Dry Film Thickness
A.I.A.	American Institute of Architects	C.C.A.	Chromate Copper Arsenate	d.f.u.	Drainage Fixture Units
AIC	Ampere Interrupting Capacity	C.C.F.	Hundred Cubic Feet	D.H.	Double Hung
Allow.	Allowance	cd	Candela	DHW	Domestic Hot Water
alt., alt	Alternate	cd/sf	Candela per Square Foot	DI	Ductile Iron
Alum.	Aluminum	CD	Grade of Plywood Face & Back	Diag.	Diagonal
a.m.	Ante Meridiem	CDX	Plywood, Grade C & D, exterior glue	Diam., Dia	Diameter
Amp.	Ampere	Cefi.	Cement Finisher	Distrib.	Distribution
Anod.	Anodized	Cem.	Cement	Div.	Division
ANSI	American National Standards Institute	CF	Hundred Feet	Dk.	Deck
		C.F.	Cubic Feet	D.L.	Dead Load; Diesel
APA	American Plywood Association	CFM	Cubic Feet per Minute	DLH	Deep Long Span Bar Joist
Approx.	Approximate	CFRP	Carbon Fiber Reinforced Plastic	dlx	Deluxe
Apt.	Apartment	c.g.	Center of Gravity	Do.	Ditto
Asb.	Asbestos	CHW	Chilled Water; Commercial Hot Water	DOP	Dioctyl Phthalate Penetration Test (Air Filters)
A.S.B.C.	American Standard Building Code				
Asbe.	Asbestos Worker	C.I., CI	Cast Iron	Dp., dp	Depth
ASCE	American Society of Civil Engineers	C.I.P., CIP	Cast in Place	D.P.S.T.	Double Pole, Single Throw
A.S.H.R.A.E.	American Society of Heating, Refrig. & AC Engineers	Circ.	Circuit	Dr.	Drive
		C.L.	Carload Lot	DR	Dimension Ratio
ASME	American Society of Mechanical Engineers	CL	Chain Link	Drink.	Drinking
		Clab.	Common Laborer	D.S.	Double Strength
ASTM	American Society for Testing and Materials	Clam	Common Maintenance Laborer	D.S.A.	Double Strength A Grade
		C.L.F.	Hundred Linear Feet	D.S.B.	Double Strength B Grade
Attchmt.	Attachment	CLF	Current Limiting Fuse	Dty.	Duty
Avg., Ave.	Average	CLP	Cross Linked Polyethylene	DWV	Drain Waste Vent
AWG	American Wire Gauge	cm	Centimeter	DX	Deluxe White, Direct Expansion
AWWA	American Water Works Assoc.	CMP	Corr. Metal Pipe	dyn	Dyne
Bbl.	Barrel	CMU	Concrete Masonry Unit	e	Eccentricity
B&B, BB	Grade B and Better; Balled & Burlapped	CN	Change Notice	E	Equipment Only; East; Emissivity
		Col.	Column	Ea.	Each
B&S	Bell and Spigot	CO₂	Carbon Dioxide	EB	Encased Burial
B.&W.	Black and White	Comb.	Combination	Econ.	Economy
b.c.c.	Body-centered Cubic	comm.	Commercial, Communication	E.C.Y	Embankment Cubic Yards
B.C.Y.	Bank Cubic Yards	Compr.	Compressor	EDP	Electronic Data Processing
BE	Bevel End	Conc.	Concrete	EIFS	Exterior Insulation Finish System
B.F.	Board Feet	Cont., cont	Continuous; Continued, Container	E.D.R.	Equiv. Direct Radiation
Bg. cem.	Bag of Cement	Corkbd.	Cork Board	Eq.	Equation
BHP	Boiler Horsepower; Brake Horsepower	Corr.	Corrugated	EL	Elevation
		Cos	Cosine	Elec.	Electrician; Electrical
B.I.	Black Iron	Cot	Cotangent	Elev.	Elevator; Elevating
bidir.	bidirectional	Cov.	Cover	EMT	Electrical Metallic Conduit; Thin Wall Conduit
Bit., Bitum.	Bituminous	C/P	Cedar on Paneling		
Bit., Conc.	Bituminous Concrete	CPA	Control Point Adjustment	Eng.	Engine, Engineered
Bk.	Backed	Cplg.	Coupling	EPDM	Ethylene Propylene Diene Monomer
Bkrs.	Breakers	CPM	Critical Path Method		
Bldg., bldg	Building	CPVC	Chlorinated Polyvinyl Chloride	EPS	Expanded Polystyrene
Blk.	Block	C.Pr.	Hundred Pair	Eqhv.	Equip. Oper., Heavy
Bm.	Beam	CRC	Cold Rolled Channel	Eqlt.	Equip. Oper., Light
Boil.	Boilermaker	Creos.	Creosote	Eqmd.	Equip. Oper., Medium
bpm	Blows per Minute	Crpt.	Carpet & Linoleum Layer	Eqmm.	Equip. Oper., Master Mechanic
BR	Bedroom	CRT	Cathode-ray Tube	Eqol.	Equip. Oper., Oilers
Brg., brng.	Bearing	CS	Carbon Steel, Constant Shear Bar Joist	Equip.	Equipment
Brhe.	Bricklayer Helper			ERW	Electric Resistance Welded
Bric.	Bricklayer				

556

For customer support on your Green Building Costs with RSMeans data, call 800.448.8182.

Abbreviations

E.S.	Energy Saver	H	High Henry	Lath.	Lather
Est.	Estimated	HC	High Capacity	Lav.	Lavatory
esu	Electrostatic Units	H.D., HD	Heavy Duty; High Density	lb.; #	Pound
E.W.	Each Way	H.D.O.	High Density Overlaid	L.B., LB	Load Bearing; L Conduit Body
EWT	Entering Water Temperature	HDPE	High Density Polyethylene Plastic	L. & E.	Labor & Equipment
Excav.	Excavation	Hdr.	Header	lb./hr.	Pounds per Hour
excl	Excluding	Hdwe.	Hardware	lb./L.F.	Pounds per Linear Foot
Exp., exp	Expansion, Exposure	H.I.D., HID	High Intensity Discharge	lbf/sq.in.	Pound-force per Square Inch
Ext., ext	Exterior; Extension	Help.	Helper Average	L.C.L.	Less than Carload Lot
Extru.	Extrusion	HEPA	High Efficiency Particulate Air Filter	L.C.Y.	Loose Cubic Yard
f.	Fiber Stress			Ld.	Load
F	Fahrenheit; Female; Fill	Hg	Mercury	LE	Lead Equivalent
Fab., fab	Fabricated; Fabric	HIC	High Interrupting Capacity	LED	Light Emitting Diode
FBGS	Fiberglass	HM	Hollow Metal	L.F.	Linear Foot
F.C.	Footcandles	HMWPE	High Molecular Weight Polyethylene	L.F. Hdr	Linear Feet of Header
f.c.c.	Face-centered Cubic			L.F. Nose	Linear Foot of Stair Nosing
f'c.	Compressive Stress in Concrete; Extreme Compressive Stress	HO	High Output	L.F. Rsr	Linear Foot of Stair Riser
		Horiz.	Horizontal	Lg.	Long; Length; Large
F.E.	Front End	H.P., HP	Horsepower; High Pressure	L & H	Light and Heat
FEP	Fluorinated Ethylene Propylene (Teflon)	H.P.F.	High Power Factor	LH	Long Span Bar Joist
		Hr.	Hour	L.H.	Labor Hours
F.G.	Flat Grain	Hrs./Day	Hours per Day	L.L., LL	Live Load
F.H.A.	Federal Housing Administration	HSC	High Short Circuit	L.L.D.	Lamp Lumen Depreciation
Fig.	Figure	Ht.	Height	lm	Lumen
Fin.	Finished	Htg.	Heating	lm/sf	Lumen per Square Foot
FIPS	Female Iron Pipe Size	Htrs.	Heaters	lm/W	Lumen per Watt
Fixt.	Fixture	HVAC	Heating, Ventilation & Air-Conditioning	LOA	Length Over All
FJP	Finger jointed and primed			log	Logarithm
Fl. Oz.	Fluid Ounces	Hvy.	Heavy	L-O-L	Lateralolet
Flr.	Floor	HW	Hot Water	long.	Longitude
Flrs.	Floors	Hyd.; Hydr.	Hydraulic	L.P., LP	Liquefied Petroleum; Low Pressure
FM	Frequency Modulation; Factory Mutual	Hz	Hertz (cycles)	L.P.F.	Low Power Factor
		I.	Moment of Inertia	LR	Long Radius
Fmg.	Framing	IBC	International Building Code	L.S.	Lump Sum
FM/UL	Factory Mutual/Underwriters Labs	I.C.	Interrupting Capacity	Lt.	Light
Fdn.	Foundation	ID	Inside Diameter	Lt. Ga.	Light Gauge
FNPT	Female National Pipe Thread	I.D.	Inside Dimension; Identification	L.T.L.	Less than Truckload Lot
Fori.	Foreman, Inside	I.F.	Inside Frosted	Lt. Wt.	Lightweight
Foro.	Foreman, Outside	I.M.C.	Intermediate Metal Conduit	L.V.	Low Voltage
Fount.	Fountain	In.	Inch	M	Thousand; Material; Male; Light Wall Copper Tubing
fpm	Feet per Minute	Incan.	Incandescent		
FPT	Female Pipe Thread	Incl.	Included; Including	M²CA	Meters Squared Contact Area
Fr	Frame	Int.	Interior	m/hr.; M.H.	Man-hour
F.R.	Fire Rating	Inst.	Installation	mA	Milliampere
FRK	Foil Reinforced Kraft	Insul., insul	Insulation/Insulated	Mach.	Machine
FSK	Foil/Scrim/Kraft	I.P.	Iron Pipe	Mag. Str.	Magnetic Starter
FRP	Fiberglass Reinforced Plastic	I.P.S., IPS	Iron Pipe Size	Maint.	Maintenance
FS	Forged Steel	IPT	Iron Pipe Threaded	Marb.	Marble Setter
FSC	Cast Body; Cast Switch Box	I.W.	Indirect Waste	Mat; Mat'l.	Material
Ft., ft	Foot; Feet	J	Joule	Max.	Maximum
Ftng.	Fitting	J.I.C.	Joint Industrial Council	MBF	Thousand Board Feet
Ftg.	Footing	K	Thousand; Thousand Pounds; Heavy Wall Copper Tubing, Kelvin	MBH	Thousand BTU's per hr.
Ft lb.	Foot Pound			MC	Metal Clad Cable
Furn.	Furniture	K.A.H.	Thousand Amp. Hours	MCC	Motor Control Center
FVNR	Full Voltage Non-Reversing	kcmil	Thousand Circular Mils	M.C.F.	Thousand Cubic Feet
FVR	Full Voltage Reversing	KD	Knock Down	MCFM	Thousand Cubic Feet per Minute
FXM	Female by Male	K.D.A.T.	Kiln Dried After Treatment	M.C.M.	Thousand Circular Mils
Fy.	Minimum Yield Stress of Steel	kg	Kilogram	MCP	Motor Circuit Protector
g	Gram	kG	Kilogauss	MD	Medium Duty
G	Gauss	kgf	Kilogram Force	MDF	Medium-density fibreboard
Ga.	Gauge	kHz	Kilohertz	M.D.O.	Medium Density Overlaid
Gal., gal.	Gallon	Kip	1000 Pounds	Med.	Medium
Galv., galv	Galvanized	KJ	Kilojoule	MF	Thousand Feet
GC/MS	Gas Chromatograph/Mass Spectrometer	K.L.	Effective Length Factor	M.F.B.M.	Thousand Feet Board Measure
		K.L.F.	Kips per Linear Foot	Mfg.	Manufacturing
Gen.	General	Km	Kilometer	Mfrs.	Manufacturers
GFI	Ground Fault Interrupter	KO	Knock Out	mg	Milligram
GFRC	Glass Fiber Reinforced Concrete	K.S.F.	Kips per Square Foot	MGD	Million Gallons per Day
Glaz.	Glazier	K.S.I.	Kips per Square Inch	MGPH	Million Gallons per Hour
GPD	Gallons per Day	kV	Kilovolt	MH, M.H.	Manhole; Metal Halide; Man-Hour
gpf	Gallon per Flush	kVA	Kilovolt Ampere	MHz	Megahertz
GPH	Gallons per Hour	kVAR	Kilovar (Reactance)	Mi.	Mile
gpm, GPM	Gallons per Minute	KW	Kilowatt	MI	Malleable Iron; Mineral Insulated
GR	Grade	KWh	Kilowatt-hour	MIPS	Male Iron Pipe Size
Gran.	Granular	L	Labor Only; Length; Long; Medium Wall Copper Tubing	mj	Mechanical Joint
Grnd.	Ground			m	Meter
GVW	Gross Vehicle Weight	Lab.	Labor	mm	Millimeter
GWB	Gypsum Wall Board	lat	Latitude	Mill.	Millwright
				Min., min.	Minimum, Minute

For customer support on your Green Building Costs with RSMeans data, call 800.448.8182.

Abbreviations

Misc.	Miscellaneous	PCM	Phase Contrast Microscopy	SBS	Styrene Butadiere Styrene
ml	Milliliter, Mainline	PDCA	Painting and Decorating	SC	Screw Cover
M.L.F.	Thousand Linear Feet		Contractors of America	SCFM	Standard Cubic Feet per Minute
Mo.	Month	P.E., PE	Professional Engineer;	Scaf.	Scaffold
Mobil.	Mobilization		Porcelain Enamel;	Sch., Sched.	Schedule
Mog.	Mogul Base		Polyethylene; Plain End	S.C.R.	Modular Brick
MPH	Miles per Hour	P.E.C.I.	Porcelain Enamel on Cast Iron	S.D.	Sound Deadening
MPT	Male Pipe Thread	Perf.	Perforated	SDR	Standard Dimension Ratio
MRGWB	Moisture Resistant Gypsum Wallboard	PEX	Cross Linked Polyethylene	S.E.	Surfaced Edge
MRT	Mile Round Trip	Ph.	Phase	Sel.	Select
ms	Millisecond	P.I.	Pressure Injected	SER, SEU	Service Entrance Cable
M.S.F.	Thousand Square Feet	Pile.	Pile Driver	S.F.	Square Foot
Mstz.	Mosaic & Terrazzo Worker	Pkg.	Package	S.F.C.A.	Square Foot Contact Area
M.S.Y.	Thousand Square Yards	Pl.	Plate	S.F. Flr.	Square Foot of Floor
Mtd., mtd., mtd	Mounted	Plah.	Plasterer Helper	S.F.G.	Square Foot of Ground
Mthe.	Mosaic & Terrazzo Helper	Plas.	Plasterer	S.F. Hor.	Square Foot Horizontal
Mtng.	Mounting	plf	Pounds Per Linear Foot	SFR	Square Feet of Radiation
Mult.	Multi; Multiply	Pluh.	Plumber Helper	S.F. Shlf.	Square Foot of Shelf
MUTCD	Manual on Uniform Traffic Control Devices	Plum.	Plumber	S4S	Surface 4 Sides
		Ply.	Plywood	Shee.	Sheet Metal Worker
		p.m.	Post Meridiem	Sin.	Sine
M.V.A.	Million Volt Amperes	Pntd.	Painted	Skwk.	Skilled Worker
M.V.A.R.	Million Volt Amperes Reactance	Pord.	Painter, Ordinary	SL	Saran Lined
MV	Megavolt	pp	Pages	S.L.	Slimline
MW	Megawatt	PP, PPL	Polypropylene	Sldr.	Solder
MXM	Male by Male	P.P.M.	Parts per Million	SLH	Super Long Span Bar Joist
MYD	Thousand Yards	Pr.	Pair	S.N.	Solid Neutral
N	Natural; North	P.E.S.B.	Pre-engineered Steel Building	SO	Stranded with oil resistant inside insulation
nA	Nanoampere	Prefab.	Prefabricated		
NA	Not Available; Not Applicable	Prefin.	Prefinished	S-O-L	Socketolet
N.B.C.	National Building Code	Prop.	Propelled	sp	Standpipe
NC	Normally Closed	PSF, psf	Pounds per Square Foot	S.P.	Static Pressure; Single Pole; Self-Propelled
NEMA	National Electrical Manufacturers Assoc.	PSI, psi	Pounds per Square Inch		
		PSIG	Pounds per Square Inch Gauge	Spri.	Sprinkler Installer
NEHB	Bolted Circuit Breaker to 600V.	PSP	Plastic Sewer Pipe	spwg	Static Pressure Water Gauge
NFPA	National Fire Protection Association	Pspr.	Painter, Spray	S.P.D.T.	Single Pole, Double Throw
NLB	Non-Load-Bearing	Psst.	Painter, Structural Steel	SPF	Spruce Pine Fir; Sprayed Polyurethane Foam
NM	Non-Metallic Cable	P.T.	Potential Transformer		
nm	Nanometer	P. & T.	Pressure & Temperature	S.P.S.T.	Single Pole, Single Throw
No.	Number	Ptd.	Painted	SPT	Standard Pipe Thread
NO	Normally Open	Ptns.	Partitions	Sq.	Square; 100 Square Feet
N.O.C.	Not Otherwise Classified	Pu	Ultimate Load	Sq. Hd.	Square Head
Nose.	Nosing	PVC	Polyvinyl Chloride	Sq. In.	Square Inch
NPT	National Pipe Thread	Pvmt.	Pavement	S.S.	Single Strength; Stainless Steel
NQOD	Combination Plug-on/Bolt on Circuit Breaker to 240V.	PRV	Pressure Relief Valve	S.S.B.	Single Strength B Grade
		Pwr.	Power	sst, ss	Stainless Steel
N.R.C., NRC	Noise Reduction Coefficient/ Nuclear Regulator Commission	Q	Quantity Heat Flow	Sswk.	Structural Steel Worker
		Qt.	Quart	Sswl.	Structural Steel Welder
N.R.S.	Non Rising Stem	Quan., Qty.	Quantity	St.; Stl.	Steel
ns	Nanosecond	Q.C.	Quick Coupling	STC	Sound Transmission Coefficient
NTP	Notice to Proceed	r	Radius of Gyration	Std.	Standard
nW	Nanowatt	R	Resistance	Stg.	Staging
OB	Opposing Blade	R.C.P.	Reinforced Concrete Pipe	STK	Select Tight Knot
OC	On Center	Rect.	Rectangle	STP	Standard Temperature & Pressure
OD	Outside Diameter	recpt.	Receptacle	Stpi.	Steamfitter, Pipefitter
O.D.	Outside Dimension	Reg.	Regular	Str.	Strength; Starter; Straight
ODS	Overhead Distribution System	Reinf.	Reinforced	Strd.	Stranded
O.G.	Ogee	Req'd.	Required	Struct.	Structural
O.H.	Overhead	Res.	Resistant	Sty.	Story
O&P	Overhead and Profit	Resi.	Residential	Subj.	Subject
Oper.	Operator	RF	Radio Frequency	Subs.	Subcontractors
Opng.	Opening	RFID	Radio-frequency Identification	Surf.	Surface
Orna.	Ornamental	Rgh.	Rough	Sw.	Switch
OSB	Oriented Strand Board	RGS	Rigid Galvanized Steel	Swbd.	Switchboard
OS&Y	Outside Screw and Yoke	RHW	Rubber, Heat & Water Resistant; Residential Hot Water	S.Y.	Square Yard
OSHA	Occupational Safety and Health Act			Syn.	Synthetic
		rms	Root Mean Square	S.Y.P.	Southern Yellow Pine
Ovhd.	Overhead	Rnd.	Round	Sys.	System
OWG	Oil, Water or Gas	Rodm.	Rodman	t.	Thickness
Oz.	Ounce	Rofc.	Roofer, Composition	T	Temperature; Ton
P.	Pole; Applied Load; Projection	Rofp.	Roofer, Precast	Tan	Tangent
p.	Page	Rohe.	Roofer Helpers (Composition)	T.C.	Terra Cotta
Pape.	Paperhanger	Rots.	Roofer, Tile & Slate	T & C	Threaded and Coupled
P.A.P.R.	Powered Air Purifying Respirator	R.O.W.	Right of Way	T.D.	Temperature Difference
PAR	Parabolic Reflector	RPM	Revolutions per Minute	TDD	Telecommunications Device for the Deaf
P.B., PB	Push Button	R.S.	Rapid Start		
Pc., Pcs.	Piece, Pieces	Rsr	Riser	T.E.M.	Transmission Electron Microscopy
P.C.	Portland Cement; Power Connector	RT	Round Trip	temp	Temperature, Tempered, Temporary
P.C.F.	Pounds per Cubic Foot	S.	Suction; Single Entrance; South	TFFN	Nylon Jacketed Wire

Abbreviations

TFE	Tetrafluoroethylene (Teflon)	U.L., UL	Underwriters Laboratory	w/	With
T. & G.	Tongue & Groove; Tar & Gravel	Uld.	Unloading	W.C., WC	Water Column; Water Closet
Th., Thk.	Thick	Unfin.	Unfinished	W.F.	Wide Flange
Thn.	Thin	UPS	Uninterruptible Power Supply	W.G.	Water Gauge
Thrded	Threaded	URD	Underground Residential Distribution	Wldg.	Welding
Tilf.	Tile Layer, Floor			W. Mile	Wire Mile
Tilh.	Tile Layer, Helper	US	United States	W-O-L	Weldolet
THHN	Nylon Jacketed Wire	USGBC	U.S. Green Building Council	W.R.	Water Resistant
THW.	Insulated Strand Wire	USP	United States Primed	Wrck.	Wrecker
THWN	Nylon Jacketed Wire	UTMCD	Uniform Traffic Manual For Control Devices	WSFU	Water Supply Fixture Unit
T.L., TL	Truckload			W.S.P.	Water, Steam, Petroleum
T.M.	Track Mounted	UTP	Unshielded Twisted Pair	WT., Wt.	Weight
Tot.	Total	V	Volt	WWF	Welded Wire Fabric
T-O-L	Threadolet	VA	Volt Amperes	XFER	Transfer
tmpd	Tempered	VAT	Vinyl Asbestos Tile	XFMR	Transformer
TPO	Thermoplastic Polyolefin	V.C.T.	Vinyl Composition Tile	XHD	Extra Heavy Duty
T.S.	Trigger Start	VAV	Variable Air Volume	XHHW	Cross-Linked Polyethylene Wire
Tr.	Trade	VC	Veneer Core	XLPE	Insulation
Transf.	Transformer	VDC	Volts Direct Current	XLP	Cross-linked Polyethylene
Trhv.	Truck Driver, Heavy	Vent.	Ventilation	Xport	Transport
Trlr	Trailer	Vert.	Vertical	Y	Wye
Trlt.	Truck Driver, Light	V.F.	Vinyl Faced	yd	Yard
TTY	Teletypewriter	V.G.	Vertical Grain	yr	Year
TV	Television	VHF	Very High Frequency	Δ	Delta
T.W.	Thermoplastic Water Resistant Wire	VHO	Very High Output	%	Percent
		Vib.	Vibrating	~	Approximately
		VLF	Vertical Linear Foot	∅	Phase; diameter
UCI	Uniform Construction Index	VOC	Volatile Organic Compound	@	At
UF	Underground Feeder	Vol.	Volume	#	Pound; Number
UGND	Underground Feeder	VRP	Vinyl Reinforced Polyester	<	Less Than
UHF	Ultra High Frequency	W	Wire; Watt; Wide; West	>	Greater Than
U.I.	United Inch			Z	Zone

Index

A

Absorption testing 12
Accent light 258
light connector 259
light transformer 259
Accessory rebar 39
reinforcing 39
steel wire rope 72
Accordion door 144
Acid proof floor 169
Acoustic ceiling board 168
Acoustical aluminum duct 231
ceiling 168
enclosure 195
metal deck 79
sealant 167
treatment 172
Acrylic plexiglass 160
wood block 170
Activated sludge treatment cell . . 300
Adhesive removal floor 47
Adjustable frequency drive 253
jack post 64
Admixture concrete 26
Adobe brick 54
Aeration sewage 296
Aggregate lightweight 26
spreader 410, 417
testing 12
AHU ceiling concealed 245
ceiling mounted 245
floor standing unit 246
floor standing unit concealed . 246
wall mounted 246
Air circulator HVLS 233
circulator large diameter 233
cleaner electronic 235
compressor 413
compressor control system . . . 227
compressor portable 413
conditioner direct expansion . . 245
conditioner fan coil 245
conditioner fan coil VRV . 243, 245, 246
conditioner gas heat 242
conditioner maintenance 15
conditioner rooftop 242
conditioning ventilating 227
diffuser system 297, 299
entraining agent 26
filter 233, 235
filter disposable media 233
filter mechanical media 234
filter permanent washable 234
filter roll type 233
filter washable 234
filtration charcoal type 235
handling troffer 256
hose 414
lock 194
process piping 298
spade 414
supply pneumatic control 227
supported building 193
supported storage tank cover . 193
supported structure demo 192
supported structures 541
Air-conditioner direct expansion . 332, 335
single zone 332
Aircraft cable 74
Air-handling unit 245
Air-source heat pump 243
All service jacket insulation . 198, 203
Alloy steel chain 98
Alteration fee 10
Alternating tread ladder 91
Alternative fastening 121
Aluminum column 100
column base 98, 100
column cap 100
dome 194
duct acoustical 231
duct silencer 231
duct silencer flexible 231
extrusion 72
foil 119, 122
form 27
framing 72
grating 93
insulation jacketing 212
joist shoring 31
mesh grating 95
plank grating 94
rivet 62
roof 127
roof panel 127
security driveway gate 147
shape structural 72
sliding door 146
structural 72
trench cover 95
Anchor bolt 35
bolt screw 40
bolt template 35
bumper 182
dovetail 37
expansion 58
hollow wall 58
lead screw 59
machinery 39
metal nailing 59
nailing 59
nylon nailing 59
plastic screw 59
rock 34
screw 40, 59
toggle bolt 58
wedge 59
Angle curb edging 65
Arch laminated 110
radial 110
Architectural fee 10, 508
Articulating boom lift 413
Asbestos remediation plans and methods 23
Asphalt base sheet 131
concrete 272
distributor 414
flood coat 131
paver 415
paving 281
paving hot reused 280
plant portable 417
primer 116
roof shingle 123
sheathing 109
shingle 123
Asphaltic concrete paving 281
cover board 120
emulsion 285
Attachment ripper 417
Attachments skidsteer 413
Audio masking 195
Auger earth 410
Autoclave aerated concrete block . 54
Automatic flush 221
timed thermostat 229
wall switch 252
washing machine 182
Autoscrub machine 414
Awning window 148
window metal-clad 153
window vinyl-clad 153

B

Backflow preventer 216
preventer solar 241
Backhoe 411
bucket 412
extension 417
Baked enamel door 139
enamel frame 138
Balcony fire escape 91
Bale hay 272
Ball wrecking 417
Ballast high intensity discharge . . 260
lighting 260
replacement 260
Bamboo flooring 169
Band joist framing 84
Bar chair reinforcing 40
grating tread 96
grouted 44
joist painting 77
tie reinforcing 39
ungrouted 44
Bare floor conduit 259
Barge construction 420
Bark mulch 284
mulch redwood 285
Barrels flasher 414
reflectorized 414
Barricade flasher 414
Barrier and enclosure 14
dust 14
parking 282
slipform paver 418
weed 285
Base course 280, 281
course drainage layer 280
gravel 280
plate column 70
road 281
screed 40
sheet 131
sheet asphalt 131
stabilizer 418
stone 280
transformer 262
Bathroom fixture 220
Batt insulation 117
Battery charger 260
Beacon warning 261
Bead blast demo 164
Beam & girder framing 102
and girder formwork 27
castellated 70
concrete placement 46
drywall 166
laminated 110
load-bearing stud wall box 81
reinforcing 42
reinforcing bolster 39
steel 71
wood 102
Bench 283
greenhouse 195
Bicycle rack 184, 189
Bi-fold door 143
Bi-passing closet door 143
Birch hollow core door 144
paneling 112
solid core door 142
Bituminous concrete plant mixed recycled 272
Bituminous paver 415
Blanket insulation 224
insulation wall 117
sound attenuation 172
Blast demo bead 164
floor shot 164
Blaster shot 416
Blind structural bolt 62
Block autoclave concrete 54
Block, brick and mortar 531
Block concrete 53, 531
floor 170
Blower control panel 298
control single phase duplex . . 299
control single phase simplex . . 298
control three phase duplex . . . 299
control three phase simplex . . 299
coupling 297
insulation 415
prepackaged 297
pressure relief valve 298
rotary lobe 297
Blown-in cellulose 119
fiberglass 119
insulation 119
Board ceiling 168
insulation 116, 224
insulation foam 117
mineral wool 224
sheathing 108
siding wood 129
Boat work 420
Boiler 235
condensing 235
control system 227
gas fired 235
gas pulse 235
insulation 225
Bollard 64
light 264
Bolster beam reinforcing 39
slab reinforcing 39
Bolt & hex nut steel 60
anchor 35
blind structural 62
high strength 61
remove 58
Bond performance 515
Boom lift articulating 413
lift telescoping 413
Borer horizontal 417
Boring machine horizontal 410
Bowstring truss 110
Box beam load-bearing stud wall . 81
trench 417
Boxed header/beam 85
header/beam framing 85
Brace cross 66
Bracing framing 87
load-bearing stud wall 80
metal joist 83
roof rafter 87
Breaker pavement 414
Breeching insulation 225
Brick adobe 54
Brick, block and mortar 531
Brick cart 414
demolition 52, 164
floor 169
flooring miscellaneous 169
paving 282
simulated 55
veneer demolition 53
Bridging framing 87

Index

joist 76
  load-bearing stud wall 80
  metal joist 84
  roof rafter 87
Broom finish concrete 47
  sidewalk 416
Brush chipper 411
  cutter 411, 412
Bucket backhoe 412
  clamshell 411
  concrete 410
  dragline 411
  excavator 417
  pavement 417
Buggy concrete 410
Builder's risk insurance 512
Building air supported 193
  air-conditioning 331, 332, 334
  certification green 10
  component deconstruction 19
  deconstruction 18, 19
  greenhouse 194
  insulation 119
  moving 21
  paper 122
  prefabricated 194
  relocation 21
Built-up roof 131
  roofing 538
  roofing system 131
Bulb incandescent 267
  tee subpurlin 49
Bulb tee subpurlin 71
Bulldozer 412
Bullfloat concrete 410
Bumper car 282
  dock 182
  parking 282
Buncher feller 411
Burner gas conversion 236
  gas/oil 236
  gun type 236
  industrial 236
  oil 236
  residential 236
Butt fusion machine 414
Butterfly valve gear operated ... 298
  valve lever operated 298

C

Cable aircraft 74
  jack 420
  pulling 416
  railing 99
  safety railing 74
  tensioning 416
  trailer 416
Cable/wire puller 416
Calcium silicate insulation 225
  silicate pipe covering 201
Canopy framing 63
Capillary water barrier 281
Car bumper 282
  tram 417
Carbon monoxide detector 270
Carpet and padding recycled ... 171
  lighting 258
  pad 171
  removal 164
  sheet 171
  tile removal 164
Cart brick 414
  concrete 410
Cartridge style water filter 219

Casement window 148
  window metal-clad 153
  window vinyl 158
Cast in place concrete 45, 46
  iron grate cover 95
Castellated beam 70
Casting construction 98
Cast-iron column base 98
Catch basin cleaner 417
  basin vacuum 417
Cavity wall insulation 119
Cedar closet 113
  paneling 112
  shingle 124
Ceiling 168
  acoustical 168
  board 168
  board acoustic 168
  concealed AHU 245
  drywall 166
  insulation 117, 119
  mounted AHU 245
  painting 175
  support 63
Cell activated sludge treatment .. 300
  fuel 304
Cellular decking 79
  glass insulation 199
Cellulose blown-in 119
  insulation 118
Cement flashing 116
Cementitious wood fiber plank .. 49
Centrifugal pump 416
Ceramic disc air diffuser system ... 299
  mulch 285
  tile 168
  tile demolition 164
  tiling 168
Certification leed 10
  welding 12
Chain fall hoist 419
  link fence 14
  saw 416
  steel 98
  trencher 413
Chamber silencer 297
Chandelier 258
Channel curb edging 65
  frame 138
  grating tread 97
  metal frame 138
  window 153
Charcoal type air filter 235
Charge powder 62
Charger battery 260
Check valve flanged steel 298
  valve wafer style 298
Checkered plate 95
  plate cover 95, 96
  plate platform 95
Chemical spreader 417
  termite control 273
  toilet 416
  water closet 296
Chimney demolition 52
  foundation 45
Chip wood 285
Chipper brush 411
  log 412
  stump 412
Chipping hammer 414
Chloride accelerator concrete ... 46
Circular saw 416
Circulating pump 230
Clamshell bucket 411
Clay tile 125

Clean ductwork 15
  tank 22
Cleaner catch basin 417
  crack 417
  steam 416
Cleaning & disposal equipment .. 183
  duct 15
  internal pipe 292
Clevis hook 98
Climbing crane 418
  hydraulic jack 419
Clip wire rope 72
Closet cedar 113
  door 144
  water 220
CMU 53
Coal tar pitch 116, 132
Coating roof 116
  structural steel 532
Coil bolt formwork 33
  tie formwork 33
Cold mix paver 418
  recycling 280
Collector solar energy system .. 239, 240
Colonial door 142
Column accessory formwork 30
  aluminum 100
  base aluminum 98, 100
  base cast-iron 98
  base plate 70
  cap aluminum 100
  concrete placement 46
  demolition 52
  drywall 166
  formwork 27
  lally 64
  laminated wood 111
  lightweight 64
  ornamental 100
  plywood formwork 27
  reinforcing 42
  removal 52
  round fiber tube formwork ... 27
  round steel formwork 27
  steel 71
  steel framed formwork 27
  structural 64
  structural shape 64
Combination storm door 142
Commercial air-conditioning ... 332, 334
  dishwasher 183
  greenhouse 195
  greywater 217
  half glass door 139
  refrigeration 183
Commissioning 15
Compaction test Proctor 12
Compactor earth 411
  landfill 412
Compartment toilet 178
Component control 226, 228
Component/DDC sys. control .. 225
Composite decking 103
  door 139, 146
  insulation 121
  metal deck 78
Composition flooring removal .. 164
Compound dustproofing 26
Compressive strength 12
Compressor air 413
  tank mounted 227
Concrete 522-526
  admixture 26
  asphalt 272

block 53, 531
block autoclave 54
block insulation 119
broom finish 47
bucket 410
buggy 410
bullfloat 410
cart 410
cast in place 45, 46
chloride accelerator 46
conversion 526
conveyer 410
crane and bucket 46
cylinder 12
demolition 26
equipment rental 410
fiber reinforcing 46
fill lightweight 49
float finish 47
floor edger 410
floor grinder 410
form buy or rent 26
forms 517
grinding 47
hand trowel finish 47
lance 415
lift slab 529
lightweight 47, 530
lightweight insulating 49
machine trowel finish 47
materials 525
mixer 410
mixes 526
non-chloride accelerator 46
paver 415
placement beam 46
placement column 46
placement footing 46
placement slab 46
placement wall 47
placing 46, 527
plant mixed recycled bitum ... 272
plantable paver precast 282
polishing 47
prestressed 529
processing 47
pump 410
pumped 46
ready mix 46
reinforcing 42
retarder 46
saw 410
scarify 164
shingle 126
short load 46
slab cutting 49
slab X-ray 13
spreader 415
stair 45
strengths 526
testing 12
tile 126
trowel 410
truck 410
truck holding 46
vertical shoring 31
vibrator 410
water reducer 46
winter 46
Condensate removal pump 230
Condensing boiler 235
  furnace 237
Conditioner maintenance air ... 15
Conduit bare floor 259
Connector accent light 259
Construction aid 13

561

Index

barge	420
casting	98
management fee	10
time	10, 511
Contaminated soil	22
Contingency	11
Control component	226, 228
component relay	228
component sensor	228
component transmitter	229
component/DDC system	225
DDC	225
DDC system	226
erosion	272
panel blower	298
system	225
system air compressor	227
system boiler	227
system cooling	227
system electronic	227
system pneumatic	227
system split system	227
system VAV box	228
system ventilator	227
valve heating	229
Control component	229
Controller room	253
Cooler evaporative	243
swamp	243
Cooling control system	227
Coping removal	52
Copper rivet	62
roof	134
Core drill	12, 410
testing	12
Coreboard	167
Cork floor	169
tile	169
tile flooring	169
Corrugated roof tile	125
siding	127
Countertop	186
Coupling blower	297
Course drainage layer base	280
Court air supported	193
Cover aluminum trench	95
board asphaltic	120
board gypsum	120
cast iron grate	95
checkered plate	95, 96
ground	285
stadium	193
tank	193
trench	95
Covering calcium silicate pipe	200
wall	540
Crack cleaner	417
filler	418
Crane and bucket concrete	46
climbing	418
crawler	418
crew daily	13
hydraulic	419
tower	418
truck mounted	419
Crawler crane	418
drill rotary	414
shovel	412
Crew daily crane	13
survey	15
Cross brace	66
CSPE roof	132
Cultured stone	55
Curb builder	410
edging	65
edging angle	65

edging channel	65
extruder	411
slipform paver	418
Cutter brush	411, 412
Cutting concrete floor saw	49
concrete slab	49
concrete wall saw	50
steel	60
torch	60, 416
Cylinder concrete	12

D

Daily crane crew	13
Daylight control	253
dimming control system	340
dimming system	340
on/off control system	341
Daylighting sensor	252
DDC control	225
Deciduous shrub	287
tree	288
Deck edge form	79
framing	114
metal floor	79
roof	109
slab form	79
Decking	537
cellular	79
composite	103
floor	78, 79
form	79
roof	78
Deconstruction building	18, 19
building component	19
material handling	21
Deep longspan joist	74
Dehumidifier	414
self contained	249
Delivery charge	14
Demo air supported structure	192
roof window	137
skylight	137
storage tank	192
Demolition	515
brick	52, 164
brick veneer	53
ceramic tile	164
chimney	52
column	52
concrete	26
drywall	164
fireplace	53
flooring	164
granite	53
hammer	411
masonry	52, 164
metal	58
metal stud	165
movable wall	165
partition	164
plaster	165
plenum	165
plywood	165
steel	58
stucco	164
subfloor	164
terra cotta	165
terrazzo	164
wall	164
wall and partition	164
window	137
window & door	137
Derrick crane guyed	419
crane stiffleg	419

Detection leak	270
probe leak	270
Detector carbon monoxide	270
smoke	270
Device wiring	253
Dewatering equipment	420
Diamond plate tread	96
Diaphragm pump	416
Diesel hammer	412
tugboat	420
Diffuser system air	297, 299
Dimensions and weights of sheet steel	536
Dimmer switch	253
Dimming control modular	253
Directional drill horizontal	417
Disc harrow	411
Discharge hose	415
Dishwasher commercial	183
residential	182
Disposal or salvage value	19
Distributor asphalt	414
Dock bumper	182
Dome geodesic	194
structures	541
Domed skylight	159
Door & window interior paint	174
accordion	144
air lock	194
and window material	137
bi-fold	143
bi-passing closet	143
birch hollow core	144
birch solid core	142
closet	144
colonial	142
combination storm	142
commercial half glass	139
composite	139, 146
double	140
dutch	142
entrance	142
exterior	146
fiberglass	146
flush	141, 142
flush wood	140
folding accordion	144
frame	137, 138
french exterior	146
glass	147
hardboard	143
hollow metal	138
louvered	145
molded	142
panel	142
paneled	140
passage	144
patio	147
plastic laminate	141
porch	143
prefinished	140
pre-hung	146
residential	140, 142
residential steel	140
revolving	194
sidelight	146
sliding aluminum	146
sliding glass	146, 147
sliding glass vinyl clad	147
sliding vinyl clad	147
steel	138, 539
torrified	145
wood	140
wood panel	142
Double hung window	154
hung wood window	153

Dovetail anchor	37
Dowel reinforcing	43
Dozer	412
Dragline bucket	411
Drain geotextile	292
trap seal floor	217
Drainage mat	292
Draindown valve	241
Drainwater heat recovery	220
Drill core	12, 410
quarry	414
steel	414
track	414
wood	283
Drilling rig	410
Drip irrigation	284
irrigation subsurface	284
Driver post	418
sheeting	414
Driveway gate security	147
security gate	147
security gate opener	147
security gate solar panel	148
Drywall column	166
demolition	164
frame	137
gypsum	166
painting	175
prefinished	166
removal	164
Dual flush flushometer	220, 221
flush valve toilet	221
Duct acoustical aluminum	231
cleaning	15
fire rated blanket	224
flexible	230
flexible insulated	230
humidifier	248
insulation	224
liner	232
liner non-fibrous	232
thermal insulation	224
Ducted evaporative cooler	243
Ductwork	231
clean	15
fabric coated flexible	230
flexible	230
Dump truck	413
Dumpster	18
Dump truck off highway	413
Dust barrier	14
Dustproofing compound	26
Dutch door	142

E

Earth auger	410
compactor	411
scraper	412
Earthquake shutoff gas	236
valve gas	236
Earthwork equipment rental	410
Economizer shower head water	220
Edger concrete floor	410
Edging	289
curb	65
Efficiency flush valve high	221
EIFS	122
Electric ballast	258
fixture	255, 264, 266
fixture exterior	263
generator	415
heating	248
lamp	266
vehicle charging	255

562

Index

Electrical fee 10
   metering smart 252
Electronic air cleaner 235
   control system 227
Elevated slab formwork 28
   slab reinforcing 42
Elevator fee 10
Embossed print door 142
Emergency lighting 260
   lighting unit 260
Emulsion asphaltic 285
   sprayer 414
Enclosure acoustical 195
Energy circulator air solar 239
   modeling fee 10
   monitoring system 345
   recovery wheel 242
   saving lighting device 252
   system air purger solar 241
   system air vent solar 241
   system balancing valve solar . . . 241
   system control valve solar 241
   system controller solar 240
   system expansion tank solar . . . 241
   system gauge pressure solar . . . 241
   system heat exchanger solar . . 240
   system storage tank solar 240
   system vacuum relief solar 241
Engineering fee 10
   fees 509
Enthalpy control 228
   recovery wheel 242
Entrance door 142
   door fibrous glass 146
   floor mat 186
EPDM roofing 132
Epoxy welded wire 44
Equipment 410
   cleaning & disposal 183
   insulation 225
   loading dock 182
   pad 45
   playfield 184
   playground 184
   refrigerated storage 183
   rental 410
   rental concrete 410
   rental earthwork 410
   rental general 413
   rental highway 417
   rental lifting 418
   rental marine 420
   rental wellpoint 420
Erosion control 272
   control synthetic 272
Escape fire 91
Estimates window 539
Estimating 508
Evaporative cooler 243
   cooler ducted 243
Evergreen shrub 286
   tree 286
Excavator bucket 417
   hydraulic 410
Exit light 260
   lighting 260
Expansion anchor 58
   joint 35
   joint assembly 134
   joint floor 134
   shield 58
Expense office 11
Explosion proof fixture 261
   fixture incandescent 261
   lighting 261
Extension backhoe 417

ladder 415
Exterior door 146
   fixture LED 263
   fixture lighting 263
   floodlamp 265
   insulation 122
   insulation finish system 122
   LED fixture 263
   lighting fixture 263
   residential door 142
   surface preparation 172
Extruder curb 411
Extrusion aluminum 72
Eye bolt screw 40

F

Fabric filter 292
   polypropylene 292
   stabilization 281
   structure 193
   welded wire 43
Fan coil air conditioning 245
Fastening alternative 121
Faucet & fitting 220
   lavatory 220
Fee architectural 10
   energy modeling 10
   engineering 10
Feller buncher 411
Fence chain link 14
   plywood 14
   recycled plastic 282
   temporary 14
   wire 14
Fiber reinforcing concrete 46
   steel 44
Fiberboard insulation 120
Fiberglass blown-in 119
   door 146
   formboard 30
   insulation 116, 117, 119
   light pole 262
   panel 129
   pipe covering 203
   rainwater storage tank 218
   single hung window 158
   underground storage tank 217
   window 158
   wool 119
Field personnel 11
Fieldstone 55
Fill by borrow & utility bedding . 272
   flowable 46
Filler crack 418
Fillet welding 60
Film polyethylene 285
   safety 161
Filter air 235
   fabric 292
   HEPA 234
   iron removal 219
   mechanical media 233
   rainwater 296
   water 219
Finish floor 170
   wall 172
Finishing floor concrete 47
Fir floor 170
Fire door frame 138
   escape 91
   escape balcony 91
   escape stair 91
   rated blanket duct 224
   resistant drywall 166

Fireplace demolition 53
Fixture bathroom 220
   electric 255
   explosion proof 261
   high intensity 339
   incandescent 257
   incandescent vaportight 257
   interior light 255, 261
   landscape 264
   LED exterior 263
   lighting 263
   metal halide 256
   metal halide explosion proof . . 261
   mirror light 258
   plumbing 219, 220
   sodium high pressure 261, 265
   vandalproof 258
   wet location 256
Flagging 169
Flasher barrels 414
   barricade 414
Flashing cement 116
Flatbed truck 413, 417
   truck crane 418
Flexible aluminum duct silencer . 231
   duct 230
   ductwork 230
   ductwork fabric coated 230
   insulated duct 230
Float finish concrete 47
Floating floor 168
Floodlamp exterior 265
Floodlight LED 265
   pole mounted 265
   trailer 414
   tripod 414
Floor 169
   acid proof 169
   adhesive removal 47
   athletic resilient 171
   brick 169
   concrete finishing 47
   cork 169
   decking 78, 79
   drain trap seal 217
   expansion joint 134
   grating aluminum 93
   grating steel 94
   grinding 47
   heating radiant 246
   honing 48
   insulation 117
   mat 186
   mat entrance 186
   oak 170
   paint removal 47
   parquet 170
   plate stair 90
   rubber and vinyl sheet 171
   sander 416
   standing unit AHU 246
   standing unit concealed AHU . 246
   underlayment 108
   wood 170
   wood composition 170
Flooring bamboo 169
   demolition 164
   masonry 169
   miscellaneous brick 169
   wood strip 170
Flowable fill 46
Fluid applied membrane
   air barrier 123
   heat transfer 240
Fluorescent fixture high bay 339
Flush automatic 221

door 141, 142
flushometer dual 220, 221
high efficiency toilet (HET) . . . 221
wood door 140
Flying truss shoring 31
Foam board insulation 117
   insulation 119
   pipe covering 206
   rubber pipe covering 206
   spray rig 414
Foamed in place insulation 118
Fog seal 280
Foil aluminum 119, 122
   metallic 119
Folding accordion door 144
Footing concrete placement 46
   formwork continuous 28
   formwork spread 28
   reinforcing 43
   spread 45
Forest stewardship council 102
Forklift 414
Form aluminum 27
   buy or rent concrete 26
   deck edge 79
   decking 79
   material 517
Formboard fiberglass 30
   roof deck 30
   wood fiber 30
Forms 517
   concrete 517
Formwork beam and girder 27
   coil bolt 33
   coil tie 33
   column 27
   column accessory 30
   column plywood 27
   column round fiber tube 27
   column round steel 27
   column steel framed 27
   continuous footing 28
   elevated slab 28
   gas station 28
   gas station island 28
   girder 27
   grade beam 28
   hanger accessory 30
   insert concrete 38
   insulating concrete 29
   interior beam 27
   labor hours 518
   light base 28
   mat foundation 28
   pencil rod 34
   plywood 27
   she-bolt 34
   shoring concrete 31
   sign base 28
   slab bulkhead 29
   slab edge 29
   slab flat plate 28
   slab on grade 29
   slab void 28, 29
   slab with drop panel 28
   sleeve 32
   snap-tie 32
   spandrel beam 27
   spread footing 28
   stair 30
   stake 34
   steel framed plywood 29
   taper tie 34
   tie cone 33
   waler holder 33
   wall 29

Index

wall accessory 33
wall plywood 29
wall prefab plywood 29
wall steel framed 29
Foundation chimney 45
   mat 45
Fountain 192
   indoor 192
   outdoor 192
   yard 192
Frame baked enamel 138
   door 137, 138
   drywall 137
   fire door 138
   grating 95
   labeled 138
   metal 137
   metal butt 138
   shoring 31
   steel 137
   trench grating 95
   welded 138
Framing aluminum 72
   band joist 84
   beam & girder 102
   boxed header/beam 85
   bracing 87
   bridging 87
   canopy 63
   deck 114
   laminated 110
   lightweight 65
   lightweight angle 65
   lightweight channel 65
   lightweight junior beam ... 66
   lightweight tee 66
   lightweight zee 66
   load-bearing stud partition .. 81
   load-bearing stud wall 81
   metal joist 85
   metal roof parapet 87
   pipe support 67
   porch 103
   roof metal rafter 88
   roof metal truss 89
   roof soffit 88
   slotted channel 66
   steel 69
   steel tee 66
   steel zee 66
   wall 103
   web stiffener 86
   wood 102
Freezer 183
French exterior door 146
Frequency drive adjustable .. 253
   drive variable 253
Fryer 183
Fuel cell 304
   furnace solid 237
Full spectrum fixture 266
Furnace condensing 237
   type humidifier 248
   wood 237
Furnishing site 189
Fusion machine butt 414

G

Galvanized plank grating 95
   roof 128
   welded wire 44
Galvanizing lintel 66
Garden pond 192
Gas conversion burner 236

earthquake valve 236
fired boiler 235
fired infrared heater 238
furnace wood 237
pulse combustion 235
safety valve 236
station formwork 28
station island formwork 28
water heater instantaneous .. 220
water heater tankless 220
Gasket toilet 220
Gas/oil burner 236
Gate opener driveway security .. 147
   security driveway 147
Gauge pressure 228
   pressure/vacuum 228
   vacuum 228
General contractor's overhead .. 513
   equipment rental 413
   maintenance 15
Generator electric 415
Geodesic dome 194
   hemisphere greenhouse 195
Geotextile drain 292
   soil stabilization 273
   stabilization 273
   subsurface drainage 292
Geothermal heat pump system .. 337, 338
Girder formwork 27
   reinforcing 42
   wood 102
Girt steel 70
Glass door 147
   door sliding 147
   heat reflective 160
   insulating 160
   insulation cellular 199
   reduce heat transfer 160
   reflective 160
   safety 160
   solar film 161
Glazing 160
   plastic 160
   productivity 540
   solar direct gain ... 326, 327
   solar indirect gain . 328, 329
Globe certification green 10
Glued laminated 110
Gradall 411
Grade beam formwork 28
Grader motorized 411
Granite chip 285
   demolition 53
Grass cloth wallpaper 172
Grating aluminum 93
   aluminum floor 93
   aluminum mesh 95
   aluminum plank 94
   frame 95
   galvanized plank 95
   plank 95
   stainless bar 95
   stainless plank 95
   stair 91
   steel 94
   steel floor 94
   steel mesh 95
Gravel base 280
   pea 285
Green building certification .. 10
   globe certification 10
   globes continual improvement
   of existing building checklist .. 510
   roof 312
   roof membrane 127

roof soil mixture 127
roof system 127
Greenhouse 194
   air supported 193
   commercial 195
   cooling 195
   geodesic hemisphere 195
   residential 194
Greywater commercial 217
   lift station 218
   recovery system resi 217
   residential 217
   system component 218
Grinder concrete floor 410
Grinding concrete 47
   floor 47
Grit removal and handling
   equipment 296
Ground cover 285
   water monitoring 13
Grout pump 416
Grouted bar 44
   strand 44
Guard tree 289
   window 98
Gun type burner 236
Guyed derrick crane 419
Gypsum board removal 165
   board synthetic 166
   cover board 120
   drywall 166
   sheathing 110
   weatherproof 110

H

Hammer chipping 414
   demolition 411
   diesel 412
   drill rotary 414
   hydraulic 411, 415
   pile 411
   vibratory 412
Hammermill 417
Hand split shake 125
   trowel finish concrete 47
Handicap ramp 45
Handling material 15
Hanger accessory formwork ... 30
Hanging lintel 66
Hardboard door 143
   molding 111
   paneling 111
   tempered 111
   underlayment 108
Hardwood floor 170
Harrow disc 411
Harvesting rainwater 218
Hatch roof 314
Hay 284
   bale 272
Hazardous waste cleanup 23
   waste disposal 23
Header load-bearing stud wall .. 81
   pipe wellpoint 420
   wood 104
Header/beam boxed 85
Heat greenhouse 195
   pump 243
   pump air-source 243
   pump gas driven 243
   pump water heater 244
   pump water source 244
   recovery air to air 242
   recovery drainwater 220

recovery package 242
recovery wheel 242
reflective film 160
reflective glass 160
transfer fluid 240
Heater gas fired infrared ... 238
   infrared 238
   infrared quartz 248
   quartz 248
   space 415
   swimming pool solar 325
   terminal 238
   tubular infrared 238
Heating electric 248
   hot water solar 319
   insulation 198, 202, 203, 225
   kettle 418
   passive solar 326, 327
   solar 240
   solar passive 329, 330
   solar energy 325
   systems 543
Heating/cooling system 331
Helicopter 419
HEPA filter 234
Hex bolt steel 60
High bay fluorescent fixture .. 339
   chair reinforcing 39
   efficiency flush valve ... 221
   efficiency toilet (HET) flush .. 221
   efficiency urinal 221
   intensity discharge ballast .. 260
   intensity discharge lamp .. 266
   intensity discharge lamps .. 547
   intensity discharge lighting .. 261
   pressure fixture sodium .. 257
   pressure sodium lighting .. 257
   strength bolt 61
   strength bolts 532
   strength steel 70
   strength steels 533
Highway equipment rental 417
Hoist chain fall 419
   personnel 419
   tower 419
Holder screed 40
Holding tank 296
Hollow core door 140, 145
   metal door 138
   metal frame 137
   wall anchor 58
Honing floor 48
Hook clevis 98
Hook-up electric service 345
   mechanical service 345
Horizontal borer 417
   boring machine 410
   directional drill 417
Hose air 414
   discharge 415
   suction 415
   water 415
Hot water solar drain down .. 320
Hot water solar energy .. 317, 319, 321, 323
Humidification equipment 195
Humidifier 248
   duct 248
   furnace type 248
   room 248
Humus peat 284
HVAC equipment insulation ... 225
   power circulator & ventilator .. 233
HVLS air circulator 233
Hydraulic crane 419
   excavator 410

Index

hammer . . . 411, 415
jack . . . 419
jack climbing . . . 419
Hydromulcher . . . 417

I

Impact wrench . . . 414
Impact resistant replacement window . . . 136
Incandescent bulb . . . 267
explosion proof fixture . . . 261
exterior lamp . . . 267
fixture . . . 257
interior lamp . . . 267
Indirect gain solar wall . . . 328
Indoor AHU VRV . . . 245
fountain . . . 192
Induction lighting . . . 263
Industrial burner . . . 236
lighting . . . 256
railing . . . 93
Inert gas . . . 22
Infrared heater . . . 238
heater gas fired . . . 238
heater tubular . . . 238
quartz heater . . . 248
Insert concrete formwork . . . 38
slab lifting . . . 40
Inspection internal pipe . . . 292
technician . . . 12
Instantaneous gas water heater . . 220
Insulated panel . . . 122
precast wall panel . . . 48
protector ADA . . . 198
Insulating concrete formwork . . . 29
glass . . . 160
sheathing . . . 108
Insulation . . . 116, 119, 203
all service jacket . . . 198, 203
batt . . . 117
blanket . . . 224
blower . . . 415
blown-in . . . 119
board . . . 116, 224
boiler . . . 225
breeching . . . 225
building . . . 119
calcium silicate . . . 225
cavity wall . . . 119
ceiling . . . 117, 119
cellulose . . . 118
composite . . . 121
duct . . . 224
duct thermal . . . 224
equipment . . . 225
exterior . . . 122
fiberglass . . . 116, 117, 119
finish system exterior . . . 122
floor . . . 117
foam . . . 119
foamed in place . . . 118
heating . . . 198, 202, 203, 225
HVAC equipment . . . 225
isocyanurate . . . 116
jacketing . . . 208
jacketing aluminum . . . 212
jacketing protective . . . 208
loose fill . . . 118
masonry . . . 119
mineral fiber . . . 118
pipe . . . 198
polyethylene . . . 205, 224
polyolefin . . . 207
polystyrene . . . 116, 117, 119
reflective . . . 119
rigid . . . 116, 117
roof . . . 120
roof deck . . . 120
spray . . . 120
sprayed-on . . . 120
vapor barrier . . . 122
vapor proof . . . 199, 207
vermiculite . . . 119
wall . . . 116
wall blanket . . . 117
water heater . . . 198
Insurance . . . 512
Interior beam formwork . . . 27
LED fixture . . . 259
light fixture . . . 255, 261
lighting . . . 257
paint wall & ceiling . . . 175
planter . . . 187
residential door . . . 143
Internal cleaning pipe . . . 292
Iron removal filter . . . 219
Ironspot brick . . . 169
Irrigation drip . . . 284
Isocyanurate insulation . . . 116

J

Jack cable . . . 420
hydraulic . . . 419
post adjustable . . . 64
Jacketing insulation . . . 208
Jackhammer . . . 414
Joint assembly expansion . . . 134
expansion . . . 35
Joist bridging . . . 76
deep longspan . . . 74
longspan . . . 75
metal framing . . . 85
open web bar . . . 76
truss . . . 77
web stiffener . . . 86
Jute mesh . . . 272

K

Ketone ethylene ester roofing . . . 133
Kettle heating . . . 418
tar . . . 416, 418
Kitchen equipment . . . 183
equipment fee . . . 10
Knotty pine paneling . . . 112
Kraft paper . . . 122

L

Labeled frame . . . 138
Labor formwork . . . 518
Ladder alternating tread . . . 91
extension . . . 415
inclined metal . . . 91
ship . . . 91
vertical metal . . . 91
Lag screw . . . 62
screw shield . . . 59
Lally column . . . 64
Laminated beam . . . 110
framing . . . 110
glued . . . 110
veneer member . . . 111
wood . . . 110
Lamp electric . . . 266
high intensity discharge . . . 266
incandescent exterior . . . 267
incandescent interior . . . 267
mercury vapor . . . 266
metal halide . . . 266
post . . . 98, 262
quartz line . . . 267
slimline . . . 266
sodium high pressure . . . 266
sodium low pressure . . . 266
tungsten halogen . . . 267
Lamps . . . 547
high intensity discharge . . . 547
Lance concrete . . . 415
Landfill compactor . . . 412
Landing metal pan . . . 90
Landscape fee . . . 10
fixture . . . 264
LED fixture . . . 264
light . . . 264
Laser level . . . 415
Lauan door . . . 144
Lava stone . . . 55
Lavatory faucet . . . 220
Lawn mower . . . 415
Lead paint remediation . . . 23
screw anchor . . . 59
testing . . . 23
Leads pile . . . 411
Leak detection . . . 270
detection probe . . . 270
detection tank . . . 270
Lean-to type greenhouse . . . 194
LED fixture exterior . . . 263
fixture interior . . . 259
floodlight . . . 265
lighting parking . . . 263
luminaire roadway . . . 263
luminaire walkway . . . 265
Leed certification . . . 10
Level laser . . . 415
Liability insurance . . . 513
Lift scissor . . . 413
slab . . . 529
station greywater . . . 218
Lifting equipment rental . . . 418
Light accent . . . 258
base formwork . . . 28
bollard . . . 264
exit . . . 260
fixture interior . . . 261
fixture troffer . . . 256
landscape . . . 264
pole aluminum . . . 262
pole fiberglass . . . 262
pole steel . . . 262
pole wood . . . 262
safety . . . 258
support . . . 64
tower . . . 415
Lighting . . . 266
ballast . . . 260
carpet . . . 258
control panelboard . . . 252
emergency . . . 260
exit . . . 260
explosion proof . . . 261
exterior fixture . . . 263
fixture . . . 263
fixture exterior . . . 263
high intensity discharge . . . 261
high pressure sodium . . . 257
incandescent . . . 257
induction . . . 263
industrial . . . 256
interior . . . 257
metal halide . . . 256
on/off control system . . . 341
picture . . . 258
pole . . . 262
stair . . . 259
unit emergency . . . 260
Lightweight aggregate . . . 26
angle framing . . . 65
channel framing . . . 65
column . . . 64
concrete . . . 47, 530
concrete fill . . . 49
framing . . . 65
insulating concrete . . . 49
junior beam framing . . . 66
natural stone . . . 55
tee framing . . . 66
zee framing . . . 66
Line remover traffic . . . 418
Liner duct . . . 232
non-fibrous duct . . . 232
Lintel galvanizing . . . 66
hanging . . . 66
precast concrete . . . 48
steel . . . 66
Load-bearing stud partition framing . . . 81
stud wall bracing . . . 80
stud wall bridging . . . 80
stud wall framing . . . 81
stud wall header . . . 81
Loader skidsteer . . . 413
tractor . . . 412
wheeled . . . 412
windrow . . . 418
Loading dock equipment . . . 182
Locker plastic . . . 178
Locomotive tunnel . . . 418
Log chipper . . . 412
skidder . . . 412
Longspan joist . . . 75
Loose fill insulation . . . 118
Louvered door . . . 145
Lowbed trailer . . . 418
Lumber core paneling . . . 113
plastic . . . 114
product prices . . . 510, 538
recycled plastic . . . 113
structural plastic . . . 114
Luminaire roadway . . . 263
walkway . . . 264, 265

M

Machine autoscrub . . . 414
screw . . . 62
trowel finish concrete . . . 47
welding . . . 417
Machinery anchor . . . 39
Magnetic particle test . . . 12
Main office expense . . . 11
Maintenance general . . . 15
mechanical . . . 15
Management fee construction . . . 10
Man-made soil mix . . . 127
Marble chip . . . 285
Marine equipment rental . . . 420
recycled plastic/steel pile . . . 273
Masonry demolition . . . 52, 164
flooring . . . 169
insulation . . . 119
removal . . . 52
saw . . . 416
selective demolition . . . 52
Mat drainage . . . 292
floor . . . 186

For customer support on your Green Building Costs with RSMeans data, call 800.448.8182.

Index

foundation ... 45
foundation formwork ... 28
Material door and window ... 137
handling ... 15
handling deconstruction ... 21
removal/salvage ... 19
Materials concrete ... 525
Mechanical fee ... 10
maintenance ... 15
media filter ... 233
Membrane roofing ... 131
Mercury vapor lamp ... 266
Metal butt frame ... 138
deck ... 78
deck acoustical ... 79
deck composite ... 78
deck ventilated ... 79
demolition ... 58
facing panel ... 129
floor deck ... 79
frame ... 137
frame channel ... 138
framing parapet ... 87
halide explosion proof fixture . 261
halide fixture ... 256
halide lamp ... 266
halide lighting ... 256
joist bracing ... 83
joist bridging ... 84
joist framing ... 85
ladder inclined ... 91
nailing anchor ... 59
pan landing ... 90
pan stair ... 90
plate stair ... 90
rafter framing ... 88
roof ... 127, 128
roof parapet framing ... 87
roof truss ... 69
siding ... 127
stud demolition ... 165
truss framing ... 89
Metal-clad double hung window ... 153
Metallic foil ... 119
Metric conversion ... 526
rebar specs ... 519
Mill base price reinforcing ... 42
extra steel ... 70
Mineral fiber insulation ... 118
wool board ... 224
wool pipe covering ... 198
Mirror light fixture ... 258
plexiglass ... 161
wall ... 161
Miscellaneous painting ... 174
Mix asphaltic base course plant . 281
Mixed bituminous conc. plant ... 272
Mixer concrete ... 410
mortar ... 410, 415
plaster ... 415
road ... 418
Mixes concrete ... 526
Mobilization or demobilization ... 14
Modified bituminous barrier sheet ... 123
Modular dimming control ... 253
Moil point ... 414
Moisture content test ... 12
Molding hardboard ... 111
wood transition ... 170
Monitor support ... 63
Mortar, brick and block ... 531
Mortar mixer ... 410, 415
Moss peat ... 285
Motor actuated valve ... 229
controlled valve ... 229
support ... 63
Motorized grader ... 411
zone valve ... 229
Molded door ... 142
Mounting board plywood ... 109
Movable wall demolition ... 165
Moving building ... 21
structure ... 21
Mower lawn ... 415
Muck car tunnel ... 418
Mud pump ... 410
trailer ... 417
Mulch bark ... 284
ceramic ... 285
stone ... 285
Mulcher power ... 412
Mulching ... 284
Multizone air conditioner rooftop ... 242

N

Nail recycled steel ... 102
stake ... 34
Nailer pneumatic ... 414, 415
Nailing anchor ... 59
Net safety ... 13
Non-chloride accelerator conc. ... 46
Non-destructive testing ... 12
Nut remove ... 58
Nylon nailing anchor ... 59

O

Oak floor ... 170
paneling ... 112
Occupancy sensor ... 252
Off highway dump truck ... 413
Office expense ... 11
Oil burner ... 236
furnace wood ... 237
Oil/water separator ... 296
Open web bar joist ... 76
Opener driveway security gate .. 147
Opening roof frame ... 66
Ornamental aluminum rail ... 99
column ... 100
glass rail ... 99
railing ... 99
steel rail ... 99
wrought iron rail ... 99
OSB faced panel ... 107
Outdoor fountain ... 192
unit VRV ... 243
Outlet box plastic ... 252
Overhead contractor ... 513
Overlay face door ... 140
Overtime ... 512

P

Pad carpet ... 171
equipment ... 45
Padding and carpet recycled ... 171
Paddle blade air circulator ... 233
Paint & coating ... 172
door & window interior ... 174
remediation lead ... 23
removal floor ... 47
sprayer ... 415
striper ... 418
wall & ceiling interior ... 175
Painting ... 540, 541
bar joist ... 77
ceiling ... 175
drywall ... 175
miscellaneous ... 174
plaster ... 175
wall ... 175
Pan stair metal ... 90
Panel door ... 142
fiberglass ... 129
insulated ... 122
metal facing ... 129
OSB faced ... 107
prefabricated ... 122
relay ... 252
solar indirect gain ... 329
steel roofing ... 128
structural ... 107
structural insulated ... 107
wall ... 55
Panelboard lighting control ... 252
Paneled door ... 140
pine door ... 145
Paneling ... 111
birch ... 112
cedar ... 112
hardboard ... 111
knotty pine ... 112
particle board ... 112
plywood ... 112
wood ... 111
Panelized shingle ... 125
Paper building ... 122
sheathing ... 122
Parapet metal framing ... 87
Parking barrier ... 282
bumper ... 282
bumper wood ... 282
LED lighting ... 263
lot paving ... 281
Parquet floor ... 170
wood ... 170
Particle board paneling ... 112
board underlayment ... 108
core door ... 141
Partition demolition ... 164
framing load bearing stud ... 81
support ... 63
toilet ... 178
Passage door ... 144
Passive solar indirect gain panel . 329
solar indirect gain wall ... 328
solar sunspace ... 330
Patch core hole ... 12
roof ... 116
Patio door ... 147
Pavement ... 282
breaker ... 414
bucket ... 417
marking ... 282
planer ... 418
profiler ... 418
recycled ... 272
widener ... 418
Paver asphalt ... 415
bituminous ... 415
cold mix ... 418
concrete ... 415
floor ... 169
shoulder ... 418
tile exposed aggregate ... 282
Paving asphalt ... 281
asphaltic concrete ... 281
brick ... 282
hot reused asphalt ... 280
parking lot ... 281
Pea gravel ... 285
Peat humus ... 284
moss ... 285
Pegboard ... 111
Pencil rod formwork ... 34
Performance bond ... 515
Perlite insulation ... 116
Personnel field ... 11
hoist ... 419
protection ... 13
Pex tubing ... 246
tubing fitting ... 247
Photoelectric control ... 252
Photovoltaic ... 254
power ... 342, 344
rack system ... 255
system grid connected ... 344
PIB roof ... 133
Picket railing ... 93
Pickup truck ... 417
Pick-up vacuum ... 410
Picture lighting ... 258
Pile hammer ... 411
leads ... 411
recycled plastic and steel ... 273
Pin powder ... 62
Pine door ... 142
floor ... 170
straw ... 285
Pipe & fitting backflow preventer ... 216
and fittings ... 542
cleaning internal ... 292
covering ... 198
covering calcium silicate ... 200
covering fiberglass ... 203
covering foam ... 206
covering mineral wool ... 198
inspection internal ... 292
insulation ... 198
internal cleaning ... 292
rail aluminum ... 92
rail galvanized ... 92
rail stainless ... 92
rail steel ... 92
rail wall ... 92
railing ... 92
rodding ... 292
sleeve plastic ... 32
sleeve sheet metal ... 32
sleeve steel ... 32
support framing ... 67
Piping air process ... 298
Pitch coal tar ... 132
emulsion tar ... 280
Placing concrete ... 46, 527
reinforcment ... 521
Plan remediation ... 23
Planer pavement ... 418
Plank grating ... 95
Plant and planter ... 187
mix asphaltic base course ... 281
mixed bitum conc. recycled .. 272
mixed bituminous concrete ... 272
screening ... 412
Planter ... 187, 283
interior ... 187
Plant-mix asphalt paving ... 281
Plaster demolition ... 165
mixer ... 415
painting ... 175
venetian ... 165
Plasterboard synthetic ... 166
Plastic and steel pile recycled ... 273
faced hardboard ... 111
fence recycled ... 282

Index

glazing	160
laminate door	141
locker	178
lumber	114
lumber structural	114
outlet box	252
screw anchor	59
shelving	178
skylight	159
window	156
Plate checkered	95
roadway	418
steel	67
stiffener	67
Platform checkered plate	95
trailer	416
Playfield equipment	184
Playground equipment	184
Plenum demolition	165
Plexiglass	160
acrylic	160
mirror	161
Plow vibrator	413
Plumbing	216
fixture	219, 220, 542
Plywood	538
demolition	165
fence	14
formwork	27
formwork steel framed	29
mounting board	109
paneling	112
sheathing roof & wall	109
underlayment	108
Pneumatic air operated valve	229
control system	227
nailer	414, 415
Point moil	414
Pole aluminum light	262
fiberglass light	262
lighting	262
steel light	262
utility	262
wood light	262
Polishing concrete	47
Polyethylene film	285
insulation	205, 224
Polyolefin insulation	207
roofing thermoplastic	133
Polypropylene fabric	292
siding	131
Polystyrene insulation	116, 117, 119
Pond garden	192
Porch door	143
framing	103
Portable air compressor	413
asphalt plant	417
Post driver	418
lamp	98, 262
shore	31
Post-tensioned concrete	529
Potable-water storage tank	217
Powder actuated tool	62
charge	62
pin	62
Power mulcher	412
trowel	410
Precast concrete lintel	48
concrete plantable paver	282
concrete wall	48
concrete window sill	48
conrete	530
wall	530
wall panel	48
wall panel insulated	48
Prefabricated building	194

panel	122
Prefinished door	140
drywall	166
floor	170
hardboard paneling	111
Preformed roof panel	127
roofing & siding	127
Pre-hung door	146
Prepackaged blower	297
Preparation exterior surface	172
interior surface	173
Pressure gauge	228
relief valve adjustable	298
relief valve preset	298
relief valve weight loaded	298
wash	173
washer	416
Pressure/vacuum gauge	228
Prestressed concrete	529
Prestressing steel	44
Preventer backflow	216
Prices lumber products	538
Primer asphalt	116
Processing concrete	47
Proctor compaction test	12
Productivity glazing	540
Profiler pavement	418
Protection slope	272
Protective insulation jacketing	208
Protector ADA insulated	198
Psychrometric table	545
Pulse boiler gas	235
combustion gas	235
Pump centrifugal	416
circulating	230
concrete	410
condensate removal	230
diaphragm	416
gas driven heat	243
grout	416
heat	243
mud	410
shotcrete	410
submersible	416
trash	416
water	416
wellpoint	420
Pumped concrete	46
Purlin steel	70

Q

Quarry drill	414
Quartz	285
heater	248
line lamp	267

R

Rack bicycle	184, 189
system photovoltaic	255
Radial arch	110
Radiant floor heating	246
Radiator thermostat control sys.	227
Radiography test	12
Rafter framing metal	88
metal bracing	87
metal bridging	87
Rail aluminum pipe	92
galvanized pipe	92
ornamental aluminum	99
ornamental glass	99
ornamental steel	99
ornamental wrought iron	99

stainless pipe	92
steel pipe	92
wall pipe	92
Railing cable	99
industrial	93
ornamental	99
picket	93
pipe	92
Rainwater	218
filter	296
harvesting	218
harvesting system	293
storage tank fiberglass	218
Rake tractor	412
Rammer/tamper	411
Ramp handicap	45
Ranch plank floor	170
Reach-in refrigeration	183
Ready mix concrete	46, 527
Rebar accessory	39
Receptacle trash	189
Recirculating chemical toilet	296
Recovery package heat	242
system resi greywater	217
wheel energy	242
wheel enthalpy	242
Recycled carpet and padding	171
padding and carpet	171
pavement	272
plant mixed bitum concrete	272
plastic and steel pile	273
plastic lumber	113
plastic shim	102
plastic/steel pile marine	273
rubber tire tile	186
steel nail	102
Recycling cold	280
Reduce heat transfer glass	160
Redwood bark mulch	285
Refinish floor	170
Reflective film heat	160
glass	160
insulation	119
Reflectorized barrels	414
Refrigerated storage equipment	183
Refrigeration commercial	183
reach-in	183
Reinforcement	520
Reinforcing	521
accessory	39
bar chair	40
bar splicing	41
bar tie	39
beam	42
chair subgrade	41
column	42
concrete	42
dowel	43
elevated slab	42
footing	43
girder	42
high chair	39
metric	519
mill base price	42
shop extra	42
slab	43
sorting	43
spiral	42
stainless steel	43
steel	519-521
steel fiber	44
tie wire	41
wall	43
Relay control component	228
panel	252
Remediation plan	23

plan/method asbestos	23
Remote power pack	252
Removal masonry	52
tank	22
Removal/salvage material	19
Remove bolt	58
nut	58
Renovation tread cover	97
Rental equipment	410
Repair slate	124
Replacement window	136
window impact-resistant	136
windows	539
Restaurant roof	116
Residential burner	236
dishwasher	182
door	140, 142
greenhouse	194
greywater	217
storage	218
Resilient floor athletic	171
Resquared shingle	124
Retaining wall timber	283
Retarder concrete	46
vapor	122
Revolving door	194
Ridge cap	128
roll	129
shingle	125
shingle slate	124
Rigid insulation	116, 117
Ripper attachment	417
Riser pipe wellpoint	420
Rivet	62
aluminum	62
copper	62
stainless	62
steel	62
tool	62
Road base	281
mixer	418
sweeper	418
Roadway LED luminaire	263
luminaire	263
plate	418
Rock anchor	34
trencher	413
Rod tie	66
Roll ridge	129
Roller sheepsfoot	412
tandem	412
vibratory	412
Roof aluminum	127
beam	110
built-up	131
clay tile	125
coating	116
copper	134
CSPE	132
deck formboard	30
deck insulation	120
decking	78
fiberglass	129
fill	530
frame opening	66
insulation	120
membrane green	127
metal	127, 128
metal rafter framing	88
metal tile	126
metal truss framing	89
panel aluminum	127
panel preformed	127
patch	116
PIB	133
rafter bracing	87

567

For customer support on your Green Building Costs with RSMeans data, call 800.448.8182.

Index

rafter bridging . . . 87
resaturant . . . 116
sheathing . . . 109
shingle asphalt . . . 123
slate . . . 124, 538
soffit framing . . . 88
soil mixture green . . . 127
steel . . . 128
stressed skin . . . 67
system green . . . 127
thermoplastic polyolefin . . . 133
tile . . . 126
TPO . . . 133
truss . . . 110
window demo . . . 137
Roofing & siding preformed . . . 127
built-up . . . 538
EPDM . . . 132
ketone ethylene ester . . . 133
membrane . . . 131
single-ply . . . 132
system built-up . . . 131
Rooftop air conditioner . . . 242
air-conditioner . . . 332, 334, 335
multizone . . . 334
multizone air conditioner . . . 242
multizone unit SEER 14 . . 334, 335
single zone unit SEER 14 . 332, 333
Room controller . . . 253
humidifier . . . 248
Rope steel wire . . . 73
Rotary crawler drill . . . 414
hammer drill . . . 414
lobe blower . . . 297
Rototiller . . . 412
Rough stone wall . . . 55
Rubber and vinyl sheet floor . . . 171
floor tile . . . 171
pipe insulation . . . 206
Rubbish handling . . . 18

S

Safety film . . . 161
glass . . . 160
light . . . 258
net . . . 13
railing cable . . . 74
valve gas . . . 236
Salamander . . . 416
Sales tax . . . 511, 512
Salvage or disposal value . . . 19
Sandblasting equipment . . . 416
Sander floor . . . 416
Sanding floor . . . 170
Saw chain . . . 416
circular . . . 416
concrete . . . 410
cutting concrete floor . . . 49
cutting concrete wall . . . 50
cutting slab . . . 49
masonry . . . 416
Scarify concrete . . . 164
Scissor lift . . . 413
Scraper earth . . . 412
Screed base . . . 40
Screed, gas engine, 8 HP vibrating . . . 410
Screed holder . . . 40
Screen security . . . 98
sun . . . 179
Screening plant . . . 412
Screw anchor . . . 40, 59
anchor bolt . . . 40
eye bolt . . . 40
lag . . . 62
machine . . . 62
Seal floor drain trap . . . 217
fog . . . 280
Sealant acoustical . . . 167
Sealcoat . . . 280
Secondary treatment plant . . . 296
Security driveway gate . . . 147
driveway gate aluminum . . . 147
driveway gate steel . . . 147
driveway gate wood . . . 147
gate driveway . . . 147
gate opener driveway . . . 147
screen . . . 98
Selective demolition masonry . . . 52
Self contained dehumidifier . . . 249
Sensor control component . . . 228
Separator oil/water . . . 296
Sewage aeration . . . 296
municipal waste water . . . 296
treatment plant . . . 296
Shade . . . 186
Shake wood . . . 125
Shape structural aluminum . . . 72
Shear connector welded . . . 63
test . . . 12
wall . . . 109
Sheathing . . . 109
asphalt . . . 109
board . . . 108
gypsum . . . 110
insulating . . . 108
paper . . . 122
roof . . . 109
roof & wall plywood . . . 109
wall . . . 109
She-bolt formwork . . . 34
Sheepsfoot roller . . . 412
Sheet carpet . . . 171
metal membrane air barrier . . . 123
modified bituminous barrier . . 123
Sheeting driver . . . 414
Shelving plastic . . . 178
storage . . . 178
Shield expansion . . . 58
lag screw . . . 59
Shim recycled plastic . . . 102
Shingle . . . 123
asphalt . . . 123
cedar . . . 124
concrete . . . 126
panelized . . . 125
ridge . . . 125
slate . . . 124
strip . . . 123
wood . . . 124
Ship ladder . . . 91
Shop extra reinforcing . . . 42
Shore post . . . 31
Shoring aluminum joist . . . 31
concrete formwork . . . 31
concrete vertical . . . 31
flying truss . . . 31
frame . . . 31
steel beam . . . 31
Short load concrete . . . 46
Shot blast floor . . . 164
blaster . . . 416
Shotcrete pump . . . 410
Shoulder paver . . . 418
Shovel crawler . . . 412
Shower head water economizer . 220
Shrub and tree . . . 286
broadleaf evergreen . . . 286
deciduous . . . 287
evergreen . . . 286
Shutoff gas earthquake . . . 236
Sidelight door . . . 146
Sidewalk . . . 169
broom . . . 416
Siding metal . . . 127
polypropylene . . . 131
vinyl . . . 130
wood board . . . 129
Sign base formwork . . . 28
Silencer . . . 297
aluminum duct . . . 231
chamber . . . 297
with paper filter . . . 297
with polyester filter . . . 297
Sill precast concrete window . . . 48
Silt fence . . . 272
Simulated brick . . . 55
stone . . . 55, 56
Single-ply roofing . . . 132
Site furnishing . . . 189
improvement . . . 284
Skidder log . . . 412
Skidsteer attachments . . . 413
loader . . . 413
Skylight . . . 314
demo . . . 137
domed . . . 159
plastic . . . 159
Skyroof . . . 148
Slab bulkhead formwork . . . 29
concrete placement . . . 46
edge form . . . 79
edge formwork . . . 29
flat plate formwork . . . 28
lift . . . 529
lifting insert . . . 40
on grade formwork . . . 29
on ground . . . 528
reinforcing . . . 43
reinforcing bolster . . . 39
saw cutting . . . 49
textured . . . 45
void formwork . . . 28, 29
with drop panel formwork . . . 28
Slate repair . . . 124
roof . . . 124, 538
shingle . . . 124
Sleeve formwork . . . 32
plastic pipe . . . 32
sheet metal pipe . . . 32
steel pipe . . . 32
Sliding aluminum door . . . 146
glass door . . . 146
glass vinyl clad door . . . 147
vinyl clad door . . . 147
window . . . 153
Slipform paver barrier . . . 418
paver curb . . . 418
Slope protection . . . 272
Slotted channel framing . . . 66
Sludge treatment cell . . . 300
treatment cell activated . . . 300
Smart electrical metering . . . 252
Smoke detector . . . 270
Snap tie formwork . . . 32
Socket wire rope . . . 72
Sodium high pressure fixture . . . 257, 261, 265
high pressure lamp . . . 266
low pressure fixture . . . 263
low pressure lamp . . . 266
Soffit drywall . . . 166
Soil decontamination . . . 22
mix man-made . . . 127
stabilization . . . 273
stabilization geotextile . . . 273
test . . . 12
treatment . . . 273
Solar backflow preventer . . . 241
closed loop add-on hot water . 317
closed loop hot water system . 323
collector component . . . 239
direct gain glazing . . . 326, 327
direct gain glazing door . . . 326
direct gain glazing window . . . 327
direct gain sunspace . . . 330
drain back hot water . . . 318
draindown hot water . . . 321
energy . . . 240
energy circulator air . . . 239
energy photovoltaic . . . 254
energy system . . . 317, 323
energy system air purger . . . 241
energy system air vent . . . 241
energy sys. balancing valve . . . 241
energy system collector . . 239, 240
energy system control valve . . . 241
energy system controller . . . 240
energy system expansion tank . 241
energy sys. gauge pressure . . . 241
energy sys. heat exchanger . . . 240
energy system storage tank . . . 240
energy system thermometer . . 241
energy system vacuum relief . . 241
film glass . . . 161
heating . . . 240, 544
heating system . . . 239
indirect gain panel . . . 329
panel driveway security gate . . 148
passive heating . . . 326-329
swimming pool heater . . . 325
system solenoid valve . . . 241
Solar energy pool heater . . . 325
Solid fuel furnace . . . 237
wood door . . . 142
Sorting reinforcing . . . 43
Sound attenuation blanket . . . 172
Source heat pump water . . . 244
Space heater . . . 415
Spade air . . . 414
tree . . . 413
Spandrel beam formwork . . . 27
Spanish roof tile . . . 125
Spiral reinforcing . . . 42
stair . . . 99
Splicing reinforcing bar . . . 41
Split system control system . . . 227
Spray insulation . . . 120
rig foam . . . 414
Sprayed-on insulation . . . 120
Sprayer emulsion . . . 414
paint . . . 415
Spread footing . . . 45
footing formwork . . . 28
Spreader aggregate . . . 410, 417
chemical . . . 417
concrete . . . 415
Stabilization fabric . . . 281
geotextile . . . 273
soil . . . 273
Stabilizer base . . . 418
Stadium cover . . . 193
Stain lumber . . . 111
Stainless bar grating . . . 95
plank grating . . . 95
rivet . . . 62
steel reinforcing . . . 43
Stair concrete . . . 45
fire escape . . . 91
floor plate . . . 90
formwork . . . 30
grating . . . 91

Index

lighting	259
metal pan	90
metal plate	90
spiral	99
tread	96
tread insert	32
Stake formwork	34
nail	34
subgrade	41
Stall urinal	221
Steam cleaner	416
humidifier	248
Steel beam	71
beam shoring	31
beam W-shape	67
bolt & hex nut	60
building components	535
chain	98
column	71
cutting	60
demolition	58
door	138, 539
door residential	140
drill	414
estimating	533
fiber	44
fiber reinforcing	44
frame	137
framing	69
girt	70
grating	94
hex bolt	60
high strength	70
lintel	66
member structural	67, 71
mesh grating	95
mill extra	70
plate	67
prestressing	44
project structural	69
purlin	70
reinforcing	519, 521
rivet	62
roof	128
roofing panel	128
sections	534
security driveway gate	147
structural	533
testing	12
wire rope	73
wire rope accessory	72
Stiffener joist web	86
plate	67
Stiffleg derrick crane	419
Stone base	280
cast	55
cultured	55
mulch	285
simulated	55, 56
wall	55
Storage residential	218
shelving	178
tank cover	193
tank demo	192
tank fiberglass rainwater	218
tank fiberglass underground	217
tank potable-water	217
Storm window	156
window aluminum residential	156
Stove	178
Strand grouted	44
ungrouted	44
Straw	285
bale construction	195
pine	285
Streetlight	263

Strength compressive	12
Stressed skin roof	67
Strip floor	170
footing	45
shingle	123
Striper paint	418
Structural aluminum	72
column	64
fabrication cost	70
fee	10
insulated panel	107
panel	107
shape column	64
steel	533
steel member	67, 71
steel project	69
welding	60, 69
Structure fabric	193
moving	21
Stucco demolition	164
Stud partition framing	
load bearing	81
wall blocking load-bearing	80
wall box beam load-bearing	81
wall bracing load-bearing	80
wall framing load-bearing	81
wall header load-bearing	81
welded	63
Stump chipper	412
Subcontractors	542
Subfloor demolition	164
Subgrade reinforcing chair	41
stake	41
Submersible pump	416
Subpurlin bulb tee	49
bulbtee	71
Subpurlins	535
Subsurface drip irrigation	284
Suction hose	415
Sun screen	179
Sunshade louver	179
Sunspace solar direct gain	330
Support ceiling	63
framing pipe	67
light	64
monitor	63
motor	63
partition	63
X-ray	64
Surface preparation exterior	172
preparation interior	173
Surfacing	280
Survey crew	15
Swamp cooler	243
Sweeper road	418
Switch dimmer	253
Synthetic erosion control	272
gypsum board	166
System component greywater	218
control	225, 227
solar energy	325
solenoid valve solar	241
VAV box control	228

T

Tamper	414
Tandem roller	412
Tank clean	22
cover	193
disposal	22
fiberglass rainwater storage	218
fiberglass undergrnd storage	217
holding	296
leak detection	270

potable-water storage	217
removal	22
testing	12
water	417
water storage solar	241
Tankless gas water heater	220
Taper tie formwork	34
Tar kettle	416, 418
paper	285
pitch emulsion	280
roof	116
Taxes	512
Teak floor	170
paneling	112
Technician inspection	12
Tee framing steel	66
Telescoping boom lift	413
Tempered glass greenhouse	195
hardboard	111
Template anchor bolt	35
Temporary fence	14
toilet	416
Tennis court air supported	193
Terminal heater	238
Termite control chemical	273
Terra cotta demolition	165
Terrazzo demolition	164
Test moisture content	12
soil	12
ultrasonic	12
Testing	12
lead	23
tank	12
Textile wall covering	172
Textured slab	45
Thermal solar wall	328
Thermometer	228
solar energy system	241
Thermoplastic polyolefin roof	133
polyolefin roofing	133
Thermostat	228
automatic timed	229
control system radiator	227
Thermosyphon solar panel	329
Thimble wire rope	72
Thin-set tile	168
Tie cone formwork	33
rod	66
wire reinforcing	41
Tile ceramic	168
clay	125
concrete	126
cork	169
exposed aggregate paver	282
flooring cork	169
recycled rubber tire	186
roof	126
roof metal	126
Tiling ceramic	168
Timber laminated	110
retaining wall	283
Toggle bolt anchor	58
Toilet	296
chemical	416
compartment	178
dual flush valve	221
gasket	220
partition	178
partition removal	165
temporary	416
Tool powder actuated	62
rivet	62
Torch cutting	60, 416
Torrified door	145
Tower crane	418
hoist	419

light	415
TPO roof	133
Track drill	414
Tractor loader	412
rake	412
truck	417
Traffic line remover	418
Trailer floodlight	414
lowbed	418
mud	417
platform	416
truck	416
water	416
Tram car	417
Transformer accent light	259
base	262
Transition molding wood	170
Transmitter control component	229
Transom lite frame	138
Trap seal floor drain	217
Trash pump	416
receptacle	189
Tread bar grating	96
channel grating	97
cover renovation	97
diamond plate	96
insert stair	32
stair	96
Treatment acoustical	172
cell activated sludge	300
cell sludge	300
plant secondary	296
plant sewage	296
Tree deciduous	288
evergreen	286
guard	289
guying system	289
spade	413
Trench box	417
cover	95
grating frame	95
Trencher chain	413
rock	413
wheel	413
Tripod floodlight	414
Troffer air handling	256
direct/indirect	256
light fixture	256
Trowel concrete	410
power	410
Truck concrete	410
crane flatbed	418
dump	413
flatbed	413, 417
holding concrete	46
mounted crane	419
pickup	417
tractor	417
trailer	416
vacuum	417
winch	417
Truss bowstring	110
framing metal	89
joist	77
metal roof	69
roof	110
Tubing fitting PEX	247
PEX	246
Tugboat diesel	420
Tungsten halogen lamp	267
Tunnel locomotive	418
muck car	418
ventilator	418
Turbine wind	304
Turnbuckle wire rope	73
TV inspection sewer pipeline	292

569

Index

Tying wire 31

U

Ultrasonic test 12
Underground storage tank
  fiberglass 217
    storage tank removal 516
Underlayment hardboard 108
Ungrouted bar 44
    strand 44
Unit air-handling 245
Urinal 221
  high efficiency 221
  stall 221
  waterless 221
  watersaving 221
U.S. customary units and SI units for reinforcing bars 519
Utility pole 262

V

Vacuum catch basin 417
  gauge 228
  pick-up 410
  truck 417
  wet/dry 417
Valve blower pressure relief .. 298
  control solar energy system ... 241
  draindown 241
  motor actuated 229
  motor controlled 229
  motorized zone 229
  pneumatic air operated 229
Vandalproof fixture 258
Vapor barrier 122
  barrier sheathing 109
  proof insulation 199
  retarder 122
Vaporproof insulation 207
Vaportight fixture incandescent . 257
Variable frequency drive 253
VCT removal 164
Vehicle charging electric 255
Veneer core paneling 113
  member laminated 111
  removal 53
Venetian plaster 165
Ventilated metal deck 79
Ventilating air conditioning .. 227
Ventilator control system 227
  tunnel 418
Vermiculite insulation 119
Vertical metal ladder 91
Vibrating screed, gas engine,
  8 HP 410
Vibrator concrete 410
  plow 413
Vibratory hammer 412
  roller 412
Vine 285
Vinyl casement window 158
  clad premium window 155
  faced wallboard 166
  replacement window 136
  siding 130
  window 157

window double hung 157
window single hung 156
VRV indoor AHU 245
  outdoor unit 243

W

Waler holder formwork 33
Walkway LED luminaire 265
  luminaire 264, 265
Wall accessory formwork 33
  and partition demolition ... 164
  blocking load-bearing stud .. 80
  box beam load-bearing stud .. 81
  bracing load-bearing stud ... 80
  concrete placement 47
  covering 540
  covering textile 172
  demolition 164
  drywall 166
  finish 172
  forms 517
  formwork 29
  framing 103
  framing load-bearing stud .. 81
  header load-bearing stud ... 81
  indirect gain solar 328
  insulation 116
  mirror 161
  mounted AHU 246
  painting 175
  panel 55
  panel precast 48
  paneling 112
  plywood formwork 29
  precast concrete 48, 530
  prefab plywood formwork 29
  reinforcing 43, 520
  shear 109
  sheathing 109
  steel framed formwork 29
  stone 55
Wallpaper 540
  grass cloth 172
Walnut floor 170
Warehouse 193
Warning beacon 261
Wash pressure 173
Washable air filter 234
  air filter permanent 234
Washer pressure 416
Washing machine automatic 182
Waste cleanup hazardous 23
  disposal hazardous 23
Water barrier capillary 281
  closet 220
  closet chemical 296
  filter 219
  filter dirt and rust 219
  heater heat pump 244
  heater insulation 198
  heater wrap kit 198
  hose 415
  pump 416
  purification 219
  reducer concrete 46
  retainage reservoir 293
  source heat pump 244
  storage solar tank 241

tank 417
trailer 416
treatment potable 219
Water heater solar energy .. 319, 321, 323
Waterless urinal 221
Watersaving urinal 221
Water-source heat pump 244
Web stiffener framing 86
Wedge anchor 59
Weed barrier 285
Welded frame 138
  shear connector 63
  structural steel 532
  stud 63
  wire epoxy 44
  wire fabric 43
  wire galvanized 44
Welding certification 12
  fillet 60
  machine 417
  structural 60, 69
Well & accessory 292
Wellpoint discharge pipe 420
  equipment rental 420
  header pipe 420
  pump 420
  riser pipe 420
Wet/dry vacuum 417
Wheel trencher 413
Wheelbarrow 417
Wheeled loader 412
Widener pavement 418
Winch truck 417
Wind turbine 304
Window 159
  & door demolition 137
  aluminum residential storm . 156
  awning 148
  casement 148
  casement wood 148
  channel 153
  demolition 137
  double hung 154
  double hung vinyl 157
  double hung wood 153
  estimates 539
  fiberglass 158
  fiberglass single hung 158
  guard 98
  impact-resistant replacement . 136
  metal-clad awning 153
  metal-clad casement 153
  metal-clad double hung 153
  plastic 156
  precast concrete sill 48
  replacement 136
  single hung vinyl 156
  sliding 153
  sliding wood 153
  storm 156
  vinyl 157
  vinyl casement 158
  vinyl clad awning 153
  vinyl clad premium 155
  vinyl replacement 136
  wood 148
  wood awning 148
  wood double hung 153

Windrow loader 418
Winter concrete 46
Wire fabric welded 43
  fence 14
  rope clip 72
  rope socket 72
  rope thimble 72
  rope turnbuckle 73
  tying 31
Wiring device 253
  devices 546
Wood awning window 148
  beam 102
  block floor demolition 164
  chip 285
  composition floor 170
  door 140
  door residential 142
  double hung window 153
  fiber formboard 30
  fiber plank cementitious .. 49
  fiber sheathing 109
  fiber underlayment 108
  floor 170
  floor demolition 164
  framing 102
  furnace 237
  gas furnace 237
  girder 102
  laminated 110
  oil furnace 237
  panel door 142
  paneling 111
  parking bumper 282
  parquet 170
  security driveway gate 147
  shake 125
  shingle 124
  strip flooring 170
  window 148
  window casement 148
  window sliding 153
Wool fiberglass 119
Work boat 420
Workers compensation 514
Wrecking ball 417
Wrench impact 414

X

X-ray concrete slab 13
  support 64

Y

Yard fountain 192
Yellow pine floor 170

Z

Zee framing steel 66

Notes

Notes

Other Data & Services
A tradition of excellence in construction cost information and services since 1942

For more information visit our website at www.RSMeans.com

Table of Contents
Annual Cost Guides
Online Estimating Solution
Seminars and Professional Development

Unit prices according to the latest MasterFormat®

Cost Data Selection Guide

The following table provides definitive information on the content of each cost data publication. The number of lines of data provided in each unit price or assemblies division, as well as the number of crews, is listed for each data set. The presence of other elements such as reference tables, square foot models, equipment rental costs, historical cost indexes, and city cost indexes, is also indicated. You can use the table to help select the RSMeans data set that has the quantity and type of information you most need in your work.

Unit Cost Divisions	Building Construction	Mechanical	Electrical	Commercial Renovation	Square Foot	Site Work Landsc.	Green Building	Interior	Concrete Masonry	Open Shop	Heavy Construction	Light Commercial	Facilities Construction	Plumbing	Residential
1	590	411	428	530	0	524	200	331	473	589	527	273	1065	421	178
2	777	280	86	733	0	991	207	399	214	776	733	481	1220	287	274
3	1688	340	230	1081	0	1480	986	354	2034	1688	1690	482	1788	316	389
4	960	21	0	920	0	725	180	615	1158	928	615	533	1175	0	447
5	1901	158	155	1093	0	852	1799	1106	729	1901	1037	979	1918	204	746
6	2453	18	18	2111	0	110	589	1528	281	2449	123	2141	2125	22	2661
7	1596	215	128	1634	0	580	763	532	523	1593	26	1329	1697	227	1049
8	2140	80	3	2733	0	255	1140	1813	105	2142	0	2328	2966	0	1552
9	2107	86	45	1931	0	309	455	2193	412	2050	15	1756	2356	54	1521
10	1090	17	10	685	0	234	32	899	136	1090	34	589	1181	237	224
11	1097	201	166	541	0	135	56	925	29	1064	0	231	1117	164	110
12	548	0	2	299	0	219	147	1551	14	515	0	273	1574	23	217
13	744	149	158	253	0	366	125	254	78	720	267	109	760	115	104
14	273	36	0	223	0	0	0	257	0	273	0	12	293	16	6
21	130	0	41	37	0	0	0	296	0	130	0	121	668	688	259
22	1165	7557	160	1226	0	1572	1063	849	20	1154	1681	875	7505	9414	719
23	1194	6995	581	938	0	157	898	787	38	1177	110	886	5235	1917	480
25	0	0	14	14	0	0	0	0	0	0	0	0	0	0	0
26	1512	491	10456	1293	0	811	644	1159	55	1438	600	1360	10237	399	636
27	94	0	447	101	0	0	0	71	0	94	39	67	388	0	56
28	143	79	223	124	0	0	28	97	0	127	0	70	209	57	41
31	1510	733	610	806	0	3265	288	7	1217	1455	3276	604	1569	660	613
32	836	49	8	905	0	4472	353	405	314	808	1889	440	1751	142	487
33	1246	1076	534	252	0	3021	38	0	237	523	3058	128	1698	2085	154
34	107	0	47	4	0	190	0	0	31	62	212	0	136	0	0
35	18	0	0	0	0	327	0	0	0	18	442	0	84	0	0
41	62	0	0	33	0	8	0	22	0	61	31	0	68	14	0
44	75	79	0	0	0	0	0	0	0	0	0	0	75	75	0
46	23	16	0	0	0	274	261	0	0	23	264	0	33	33	0
48	10	0	38	2	0	0	23	0	0	10	17	10	23	0	10
Totals	26089	19087	14588	20502	0	20877	10275	16450	8098	24858	16686	16077	50914	17570	12933

Assem Div	Building Construction	Mechanical	Electrical	Commercial Renovation	Square Foot	Site Work Landscape	Assemblies	Green Building	Interior	Concrete Masonry	Heavy Construction	Light Commercial	Facilities Construction	Plumbing	Asm Div	Residential
A		15	0	188	164	577	598	0	0	536	571	154	24	0	1	378
B		0	0	848	2554	0	5661	56	329	1976	368	2094	174	0	2	211
C		0	0	647	954	0	1334	0	1642	146	0	844	255	0	3	588
D		1057	941	712	1859	72	2538	330	825	0	0	1345	1105	1088	4	851
E		0	0	86	261	0	301	0	5	0	0	258	5	0	5	391
F		0	0	0	114	0	143	0	0	0	0	114	0	0	6	357
G		527	447	318	312	3377	792	0	0	534	1349	205	293	677	7	307
															8	760
															9	80
															10	0
															11	0
															12	0
Totals		1599	1388	2799	6218	4026	11367	386	2801	3192	2288	5014	1856	1765		3923

Reference Section	Building Construction Costs	Mechanical	Electrical	Commercial Renovation	Square Foot	Site Work Landscape	Assem.	Green Building	Interior	Concrete Masonry	Open Shop	Heavy Construction	Light Commercial	Facilities Construction	Plumbing	Resi.
Reference Tables	yes	yes	yes	yes	no	yes	yes	yes	yes	yes	yes	yes	yes	yes	yes	yes
Models					111			25					50			28
Crews	578	578	578	556		578		578	578	578	555	578	555	556	578	555
Equipment Rental Costs	yes	yes	yes	yes		yes		yes	yes	yes	yes	yes	yes	yes	yes	yes
Historical Cost Indexes	yes	yes	yes	yes	yes	yes	yes	yes	yes	yes	yes	yes	yes	yes	yes	no
City Cost Indexes	yes	yes	yes	yes	yes	yes	yes	yes	yes	yes	yes	yes	yes	yes	yes	yes

Visit RSMeans.com/Online for more details on data titles in online format.

For more information visit our website at www.RSMeans.com

Our Online Estimating Solution

Competitive Cost Estimates Made Easy

Our online estimating solution is a web-based service that provides accurate and up-to-date cost information to help you build competitive estimates or budgets in less time.

Quick, intuitive, easy to use and automatically updated, you'll gain instant access to hundreds of thousands of material, labor, and equipment costs from RSMeans' comprehensive database, delivering the information you need to build budgets and competitive estimates every time.

With our online estimating solutions, you can perform quick searches to locate specific costs and adjust costs to reflect prices in your geographic area. Tag and store your favorites for fast access to your frequently used line items and assemblies and clone estimates to save time. System notifications will alert you as updated data becomes available. This data is automatically updated throughout the year.

Our visual, interactive estimating features help you create, manage, save and share estimates with ease! You'll enjoy increased flexibility with customizable advanced reports. Easily edit custom report templates and import your company logo onto your estimates.

	Core	Advanced	Complete
Unit Prices	✓	✓	✓
Assemblies	⊘	✓	✓
Sq Foot Models	⊘	⊘	✓
Editable Sq Foot Models	⊘	⊘	✓
Editable Assembly Components	⊘	✓	✓
Custom Cost Data	⊘	✓	✓
User Defined Components	⊘	✓	✓
Advanced Reporting & Customization	⊘	✓	✓
Union Labor Type	✓	✓	✓

Continue to check our website at www.RSMeans.com for more product offerings.

Estimate with Precision
Find everything you need to develop complete, accurate estimates.
- Verified costs for construction materials
- Equipment rental costs
- Crew sizing, labor hours and labor rates
- Localized costs for U.S. and Canada

Save Time & Increase Efficiency
Make cost estimating and calculating faster and easier than ever with secure, online estimating tools.
- Quickly locate costs in the searchable database
- Create estimates in minutes with RSMeans cost lines
- Tag and store favorites for fast access to frequently used items

Improve Planning & Decision-Making
Back your estimates with complete, accurate and up-to-date cost data for informed business decisions.
- Verify construction costs from third parties
- Check validity of subcontractor proposals
- Evaluate material and assembly alternatives

Increase Profits
Use our online estimating solution to estimate projects quickly and accurately, so you can gain an edge over your competition.
- Create accurate and competitive bids
- Minimize the risk of cost overruns
- Reduce variability

Visit RSMeans.com/Online for more details on data titles in online format.

For more information visit our website at www.RSMeans.com

Access the data online

Search for unit prices by keyword   Leverage the most up-to-date data   Build and export estimates

Try it free for 30 days   www.rsmeans.com/2018freetrial

2018 Seminar Schedule   ☎ 877-620-6245

Note: call for exact dates, locations, and details as some cities are subject to change.

Location	Dates	Location	Dates
Seattle, WA	January and August	San Francisco, CA	June
Dallas/Ft. Worth, TX	January	Bethesda, MD	June
Austin, TX	February	El Segundo, CA	August
Anchorage, AK	March and September	Dallas, TX	September
Las Vegas, NV	March	Raleigh, NC	October
New Orleans, LA	March	Salt Lake City, UT	October
Washington, DC	April and September	Baltimore, MD	November
Phoenix, AZ	April	Orlando, FL	November
Toronto	May	San Diego, CA	December
Denver, CO	May	San Antonio, TX	December

Gordian also offers a suite of online RSMeans data self-paced offerings. Check our website www.RSMeans.com for more information.

Self-Paced Professional Development Courses

Training on how to use RSMeans data and estimating tools, as well as Professional Development courses on industry topics are now offered in a convenient self-paced format. These courses are on-demand and allow more flexibility to learn around your busy schedule, while saving the cost of travel and time.

Current course offerings include:

Facilities Construction Estimating—our best-selling live class now available as an on-demand training course! Let the subject matter experts of construction estimating—the RSMeans Engineering Staff—walk you through the basics and much more of estimating for renovation and facilities construction.

RSMeansOnline.com Training—learn the ins and outs of the flagship delivery method of RSMeans data!

The Construction Process—how much do you and your team really know about the ins and outs of the "contract-side" of a construction project? This self-paced course will clarify best practices for items such as schedules, change orders, and project closeout.

These self-paced training courses can be completed over the course of 45 days and are comprised of multiple lessons with documentation, video presentation, software simulation, assessment quizzes and certificate of completion.

Site Work Estimating with RSMeans data

This new one-day program focuses directly on site work costs, a unique portion of most construction projects that often is the wild card in determining whether you have developed a good estimate or not. Accurately scoping, quantifying, and pricing site preparation, underground utility work, and improvements to exterior site elements are often the most difficult estimating tasks on any project. The program takes the participant from preparing a never-developed site through underground utility installation, pad preparation, paving and sidewalks, and landscaping. Attendees will use the full array of site work cost data through the RSMeans online program and participate in exercises to strengthen their estimating skills.

Some of what you'll learn:
- Evaluation of site work and understanding site scope of work.
- Site work estimating topics including: site clearing, grading, excavation, disposal and trucking of materials, erosion control devices, backfill and compaction, underground utilities, paving, sidewalks, fences & gates, and seeding & planting.
- Unit price site work estimates—Correct use of RSMeans site work cost data to develop a cost estimate.
- Using and modifying assemblies—Save valuable time when estimating site work activities using custom assemblies.

Who should attend: Engineers, contractors, estimators, project managers, owner's representatives, and others who are concerned with the proper preparation and/or evaluation of site work estimates.

Please bring a laptop with ability to access the internet.

Visit RSMeans.com/Online for more details on data titles in online format.

For more information visit our website at www.RSMeans.com

Professional Development

Training for our Online Estimating Solution

Construction estimating is vital to the decision-making process at each state of every project. Our online solution works the way you do. It's systematic, flexible and intuitive. In this one-day class you will see how you can estimate any phase of any project faster and better.

Some of what you'll learn:
- Customizing our online estimating solution
- Making the most of RSMeans "Circle Reference" numbers
- How to integrate your cost data
- Generating reports, exporting estimates to MS Excel, sharing, collaborating and more

Also offered as a self-paced or on-site training program!

Maintenance & Repair Estimating for Facilities

This two-day course teaches attendees how to plan, budget, and estimate the cost of ongoing and preventive maintenance and repair for existing buildings and grounds.

Some of what you'll learn:
- The most financially favorable maintenance, repair, and replacement scheduling and estimating
- Auditing and value engineering facilities
- Preventive planning and facilities upgrading
- Determining both in-house and contract-out service costs
- Annual, asset-protecting M&R plan

Who should attend: facility managers, maintenance supervisors, buildings and grounds superintendents, plant managers, planners, estimators, and others involved in facilities planning and budgeting.

Facilities Construction Estimating

In this two-day course, professionals working in facilities management can get help with their daily challenges to establish budgets for all phases of a project.

Some of what you'll learn:
- Determining the full scope of a project
- Identifying the scope of risks and opportunities
- Creative solutions to estimating issues
- Organizing estimates for presentation and discussion
- Special techniques for repair/remodel and maintenance projects
- Negotiating project change orders

Who should attend: facility managers, engineers, contractors, facility tradespeople, planners, and project managers.

Practical Project Management for Construction Professionals

In this two-day course, acquire the essential knowledge and develop the skills to effectively and efficiently execute the day-to-day responsibilities of the construction project manager.

Some of what you'll learn:
- General conditions of the construction contract
- Contract modifications: change orders and construction change directives
- Negotiations with subcontractors and vendors
- Effective writing: notification and communications
- Dispute resolution: claims and liens

Who should attend: architects, engineers, owners' representatives, and project managers.

Construction Cost Estimating: Concepts and Practice

This one-day introductory course to improve estimating skills and effectiveness starts with the details of interpreting bid documents and ends with the summary of the estimate and bid submission.

Some of what you'll learn:
- Using the plans and specifications to create estimates
- The takeoff process—deriving all tasks with correct quantities
- Developing pricing using various sources; how subcontractor pricing fits in
- Summarizing the estimate to arrive at the final number
- Formulas for area and cubic measure, adding waste and adjusting productivity to specific projects
- Evaluating subcontractors' proposals and prices
- Adding insurance and bonds
- Understanding how labor costs are calculated
- Submitting bids and proposals

Who should attend: project managers, architects, engineers, owners' representatives, contractors, and anyone who's responsible for budgeting or estimating construction projects.

Mechanical & Electrical Estimating

This two-day course teaches attendees how to prepare more accurate and complete mechanical/electrical estimates, avoid the pitfalls of omission and double-counting, and understand the composition and rationale within the RSMeans mechanical/electrical database.

Some of what you'll learn:
- The unique way mechanical and electrical systems are interrelated
- M&E estimates—conceptual, planning, budgeting, and bidding stages
- Order of magnitude, square foot, assemblies, and unit price estimating
- Comparative cost analysis of equipment and design alternatives

Who should attend: architects, engineers, facilities managers, mechanical and electrical contractors, and others who need a highly reliable method for developing, understanding, and evaluating mechanical and electrical contracts.

Unit Price Estimating

This interactive two-day seminar teaches attendees how to interpret project information and process it into final, detailed estimates with the greatest accuracy level.

The most important credential an estimator can take to the job is the ability to visualize construction and estimate accurately.

Some of what you'll learn:
- Interpreting the design in terms of cost
- The most detailed, time-tested methodology for accurate pricing
- Key cost drivers—material, labor, equipment, staging, and subcontracts
- Understanding direct and indirect costs for accurate job cost accounting and change order management

Who should attend: corporate and government estimators and purchasers, architects, engineers, and others who need to produce accurate project estimates.

Training for our CD Estimating Solution

This one-day course helps users become more familiar with the functionality of the CD. Each menu, icon, screen, and function found in the program is explained in depth. Time is devoted to hands-on estimating exercises.

Some of what you'll learn:
- Searching the database using all navigation methods
- Exporting RSMeans data to your preferred spreadsheet format
- Viewing crews, assembly components, and much more
- Automatically regionalizing the database

This training session requires you to bring a laptop computer to class.

When you register for this course you will receive an outline for your laptop requirements.

Also offered as a self-paced or on-site training program!

Facilities Estimating Using the CD

This two-day class combines hands-on skill-building with best estimating practices and real-life problems. You will learn key concepts, tips, pointers, and guidelines to save time and avoid cost oversights and errors.

Some of what you'll learn:
- Estimating process concepts
- Customizing and adapting RSMeans cost data
- Establishing scope of work to account for all known variables
- Budget estimating: when, why, and how
- Site visits: what to look for and what you can't afford to overlook
- How to estimate repair and remodeling variables

This training session requires you to bring a laptop computer to class.

Who should attend: facility managers, architects, engineers, contractors, facility tradespeople, planners, project managers, and anyone involved with JOC, SABRE, or IDIQ.

Life Cycle Cost Estimating for Facility Asset Managers

Life Cycle Cost Estimating will take the attendee through choosing the correct RSMeans database to use and then correctly applying RSMeans data to their specific life cycle application. Conceptual estimating through RSMeans new building models, conceptual estimating of major existing building projects through RSMeans renovation models, pricing specific renovation elements, estimating repair, replacement and preventive maintenance costs today and forward up to 30 years will be covered.

Some of what you'll learn:
- Cost implications of managing assets
- Planning projects and initial & life cycle costs
- How to use RSMeans data online

Who should attend: facilities owners and managers and anyone involved in the financial side of the decision making process in the planning, design, procurement, and operation of facility real assets.

Please bring a laptop with ability to access the internet.

Assessing Scope of Work for Facilities Construction Estimating

This two-day practical training program addresses the vital importance of understanding the scope of projects in order to produce accurate cost estimates for facility repair and remodeling.

Some of what you'll learn:
- Discussions of site visits, plans/specs, record drawings of facilities, and site-specific lists
- Review of CSI divisions, including means, methods, materials, and the challenges of scoping each topic
- Exercises in scope identification and scope writing for accurate estimating of projects
- Hands-on exercises that require scope, take-off, and pricing

Who should attend: corporate and government estimators, planners, facility managers, and others who need to produce accurate project estimates.

Building Systems and the Construction Process

This one-day course was written to assist novices and those outside the industry in obtaining a solid understanding of the construction process - from both a building systems and construction administration approach.

Some of what you'll learn:
- Various systems used and how components come together to create a building
- Start with foundation and end with the physical systems of the structure such as HVAC and Electrical
- Focus on the process from start of design through project closeout

This training session requires you to bring a laptop computer to class.

Who should attend: building professionals or novices to help make the crossover to the construction industry; suited for anyone responsible for providing high level oversight on construction projects.

Visit RSMeans.com/Online for more details on data titles in online format.

For more information visit our website at www.RSMeans.com

Registration Information

Register early and save up to $100!
Register 30 days before the start date of a seminar and save $100 off your total fee. Note: This discount can be applied only once per order. It cannot be applied to team discount registrations or any other special offer.

How to register
By Phone
Register by phone at 877-620-6245

Online
Register online at www.RSMeans.com/products/seminars.aspx

Note: Purchase Orders or Credits Cards are required to register.

Two-day seminar registration fee - $1,045.

One-Day Construction Cost Estimating or Building Systems and the Construction Process - $630.

Government pricing
All federal government employees save off the regular seminar price. Other promotional discounts cannot be combined with the government discount.

Team discount program
For over five attendee registrations. Call for pricing: 781-422-5115

Refund policy
Cancellations will be accepted up to ten business days prior to the seminar start. There are no refunds for cancellations received later than ten working days prior to the first day of the seminar. A $150 processing fee will be applied for all cancellations. Written notice of the cancellation is required. Substitutions can be made at any time before the session starts. No-shows are subject to the full seminar fee.

Note: Pricing subject to change.

AACE approved courses
Many seminars described and offered here have been approved for 14 hours (1.4 recertification credits) of credit by the AACE International Certification Board toward meeting the continuing education requirements for recertification as a Certified Cost Engineer/Certified Cost Consultant.

AIA Continuing Education
We are registered with the AIA Continuing Education System (AIA/CES) and are committed to developing quality learning activities in accordance with the CES criteria. Many seminars meet the AIA/CES criteria for Quality Level 2. AIA members may receive 14 learning units (LUs) for each two-day RSMeans course.

Daily course schedule
The first day of each seminar session begins at 8:30 a.m. and ends at 4:30 p.m. The second day begins at 8:00 a.m. and ends at 4:00 p.m. Participants are urged to bring a hand-held calculator since many actual problems will be worked out in each session.

Continental breakfast
Your registration includes the cost of a continental breakfast and a morning and afternoon refreshment break. These informal segments allow you to discuss topics of mutual interest with other seminar attendees. (You are free to make your own lunch and dinner arrangements.)

Hotel/transportation arrangements
We arrange to hold a block of rooms at most host hotels. To take advantage of special group rates when making your reservation, be sure to mention that you are attending the RSMeans Institute data seminar. You are, of course, free to stay at the lodging place of your choice. (Hotel reservations and transportation arrangements should be made directly by seminar attendees.)

Important
Class sizes are limited, so please register as soon as possible.